Applied Statistics for Engineers and Scientists

Joseph D. Petruccelli
Balgobin Nandram
Minghui Chen

Worcester Polytechnic Institute

PRENTICE HALL, Upper Saddle River, New Jersey 07458

Library of Congress Cataloging-in-Publication Data

Petruccelli, J. D. (Joseph D.)
   Applied statistics for engineers and scientists / J. D.
Petruccelli, B. Nandram, M. Chen. – 1 st ed.
      p.   cm.
   Includes index.
   ISBN: 0-13-565953-1
   1. Engineering—Statistical methods.   2. Mathematical statistics.
I. Nandram, B. (Balgobin)   II. Chen, M. (Minghui)   III. Title.
1942-   . II. Title.
   TA340.P48   1999
   519.5′024′62—dc 21
                                                        94-44438
                                                           CIP

Executive Editor: Ann Heath
Editorial Assistant: Joanne Wendelken
Editorial Director: Tim Bozik
Editor-in-Chief: Jerome Grant
Assistant Vice President of Production and Manufacturing: David W. Riccardi
Editorial/Production Supervision: Richard DeLorenzo
Managing Editor: Linda Mihatov Behrens
Executive Managing Editor: Kathleen Schiaparelli
Manufacturing Buyer: Alan Fischer
Manufacturing Manager: Trudy Pisciotti
Marketing Manager: Melody Marcus
Marketing Assistant: Amy Lysik
Creative Director: Paula Maylahn
Art Director: Jayne Conte
Cover Designer: Bruce Kenselaar

*For Sherry, Jon, Dave, and Chris
and for all 1804 students
who "beta tested" this book.*

ⓒ 1999 by Prentice-Hall, Inc.
Simon & Schuster / A Viacom Company
Upper Saddle River, New Jersey 07458

Printed in the United States of America

10   9   8   7   6   5   4   3   2   1

ISBN   0-13-565953-1

Prentice-Hall International (UK) Limited, London
Prentice-Hall of Australia Pty. Limited, Sydney
Prentice-Hall Canada Inc., Toronto
Prentice-Hall Hispanoamericana, S.A., Mexico
Prentice-Hall of India Private Limited, New Delhi
Prentice-Hall of Japan, Inc., Tokyo
Simon & Schuster Asia Pte. Ltd., Singapore
Editora Prentice-Hall do Brasil, Ltda., Rio de Janeiro

Contents

3 DESIGNING STUDIES AND OBTAINING DATA   83

4 AN INTRODUCTION TO STATISTICAL MODELING   130

5 INTRODUCTION TO INFERENCE: ESTIMATION AND PREDICTION   227

6 HYPOTHESIS TESTS   287

Preface

Beginning in January, 1993, with funding from the National Science Foundation, we began developing new versions of WPI's introductory statistics courses. At WPI, our students are predominantly science and engineering majors who bring a knowledge of elementary differential and integral calculus to the course.

In developing the new versions of these courses, we attempted to change the courses in three ways.

1. First, we changed the course content in order to emphasize the kind of technologically advanced statistical techniques that will be needed for the twenty-first century. This meant an emphasis on computer graphics and computer-intensive statistical techniques.
2. Second, we changed the course structure. Each of the new courses consisted of a number of modules. Each module was tied to one or more labs and to a group project.
3. Third, we changed the methods of presenting the material. In these courses more emphasis was placed on active and interactive learning and on cooperative group learning.

It became evident early in the development stages of these courses that in order to make these changes, new written materials and computer software would have to be developed. The written materials evolved into class notes that have been used at WPI for a number of years.

The results in our courses showed enough promise to interest Prentice Hall in making these materials available to a wider audience. The result is the text before you.

ix

FEATURES

Innovative Coverage

The text features a number of curricular innovations. Among these are:

- Beginning in chapter 1, emphasis is placed on the processes that generate data. Particular attention is paid to checking the stationarity of the data generating process as a standard part of the analysis of data taken over time.
- The importance of data collection and the design of studies is stressed beginning in chapter 3.
- Chapter 11 on distribution-free methods introduces not only the standard rank-based procedures, but also permutation and randomization tests, and bootstrap estimation and prediction. In addition, software support is supplied to make these methods practical.

Chapter Contents

Each chapter of the text incorporates the innovative features and approaches we have developed and tested for the introductory statistics courses at WPI. Each chapter contains:

- **Narrative sections.** These sections introduce and explain the material in narrative fashion and through examples. In keeping with the philosophy of the curriculum project from which they were born, the narrative sections emphasize modern statistical computing, particularly statistical graphics, as a tool for data analysis. SAS computer output is featured prominently in examples throughout the text.
- **Discussion questions.** These questions provide a framework for review at the end of each chapter.
- **Exercises.** The numerous exercises include conceptual problems to challenge students to think critically about statistical concepts, and real data problems to develop data analysis skills.
- **Miniproject.** Miniprojects are small projects designed to be done by student teams. All have several features in common:
  - These projects emphasize material from the chapter in which they appear.
  - In order to inspire student interest and creativity, miniproject instructions set general goals only; students are expected to come up with the specific means for achieving those goals.
  - Miniprojects present statistics as an integrated part of scientific inquiry, in that they require students to design a data collection scheme, collect the data, analyze the data, draw conclusions based on the data and write a report summarizing their methodology and findings.

- **Labs.** Each chapter contains one or more labs. Labs are more structured than miniprojects, with specific tasks and instructions. They are designed to be conducted in a supervised setting. There are several types of labs:
  - ○ **Hands-on.** Hands-on labs involve students in producing data through some physical activity.
  - ○ **Computer simulation.** In computer simulation labs, students use the computer to simulate data that demonstrate statistical concepts or to explore the behavior of statistical procedures applied under different conditions.
  - ○ **Computer data analysis.** Computer data analysis labs introduce students to data analysis strategies and practice using the computer.

Capstone Projects

In addition to the miniprojects, a number of larger-scale projects, which we call capstone projects, are included at appropriate points in the text. Capstone projects serve to integrate the material in several chapters. They are designed to be conducted over a substantial period of time, such as a semester or half semester, and consist of a number of sub-tasks.

Software Support

Statistics today cannot be practiced or taught without the use of computer software. While statistics courses are taught using calculators or spreadsheet programs to do the calculations, these computational tools have neither the power nor the adaptability of a specialized statistical computer software package.

SAS

At WPI, we use SAS statistical software in all our statistics courses. In our introductory courses, we make extensive use of a graphically-oriented component of SAS called SAS/INSIGHT. [1] In order to further customize SAS to our needs, and also to make it easier for beginning student use, we have written over fifty macro programs in the SAS language. To help users of this text to learn to use SAS, we have written a computer supplement, entitled **Doing It with SAS**. This supplement details how to use SAS, the set of SAS macros we have written, and SAS/INSIGHT, to conduct many of the analyses in the text. The disk accompanying the supplement contains the SAS macros as well as all data sets used in the text in both ASCII (that is, text) and SAS transport formats.

MINITAB

For MINITAB[2] users, we have produced a collection of MINITAB macros. To help students learn to use MINITAB, we have written a computer supplement, entitled

---

[1] SAS and SAS/INSIGHT are registered trademarks of SAS Institute, Inc.
[2] MINITAB is a registered trademark of MINITAB, Inc.

Doing It with MINITAB. This supplement details how to use MINITAB and the set of MINITAB macros we have written, to conduct many of the analyses in the text. The disk accompanying the supplement contains the MINITAB macros as well as all data sets used in the text in both the ASCII and portable MINITAB worksheet data formats.

SUPPLEMENTS

Instructor's Solutions Manual (ISBN 0-13-080437-1) Written by the text authors, this manual includes full solutions to all of the exercises, and suggested solutions and tips for facilitating the miniprojects and labs.

Doing It with SAS (ISBN 0-13-084107-2) A brief introduction to using SAS and SAS/INSIGHT and the SAS macro collection for conducting many of the analyses covered in the text and labs.

Text and Doing It with SAS package (ISBN 0-13-084687-2)

Doing It with MINITAB (ISBN 0-13-084108-0) A brief introduction to using MINITAB and the MINITAB macro collection for conducting many of the analyses covered in the text and Labs.

Text and Doing It with MINITAB package (ISBN 0-13-084686-4)

Text and MINITAB Student Version Release 12.0 package (includes the Textbook, Doing It with MINITAB, and a CD containing MINITAB Student Version Release 12.0 and the MINITAB files for the text)(ISBN 0-13-085449-2).

Companion Web Site http://www.prenhall.com/petruccelli.

ACKNOWLEDGMENTS

We are grateful to the National Science Foundation's Division of Undergraduate Education for its support[3] in the development of the curriculum and early versions of these materials. Without their support, this project would not have been attempted.

We acknowledge the software support provided by Minitab, Inc.[4]

To Bert Gunter, WPI graduate, statistical consultant, teacher, writer, editor, and gadfly, we owe a great debt. He provided inspiration and well-deserved criticism throughout the development process. Much that is creative in the present work is due to Bert.

[3]NSF grant DUE 9254087.

[4]Minitab, Inc., 3081 Enterprise Drive, State College, PA 16801-3008, Tel: 814-238-3280, Fax: 814-238-4383.

Bob Hogg generously gave of his time and apparently unbounded energy in order to impart to us whatever of his wisdom we were wise enough to accept. We thank him for his contribution.

Reviewers whose comments contributed to the improvement of this book include Richard Burke of Renssaelaer Polytechnic Institute, Nasrollah Etemadi of the University of Illinois-Chicago, Chris Franklin of the University of Georgia, S. Rao Jammalamadaka of the University of California-Santa Barbara, Kun-Liang Lu of the University of Nebraska, Rhonda Magel of North Dakota State University, Colm O'Cinneide of Purdue University, and Jay Rajgopal of the University of Pittsburgh. Donald S. Burdick of Duke University, Linda C. Malone of the University of Central Florida, and Major John J. Tomick of the United States Air Force Academy deserve special thanks for reviewing several drafts of the manuscript and helping shape the final volume.

Our thanks also go to the folks at Prentice Hall who guided three rookie authors through the publication process. We want to particularly thank Ann Heath and Rick DeLorenzo.

IN CLOSING

We have worked hard to try to make this text relevant, current and interesting. We intend to continually improve on it. In order to do this, we need your help. We welcome your comments and suggestions on any aspect of the text: typographical errors, content, exposition, or anything else. We may be reached via e-mail at jdp@wpi.edu, balnan@wpi.edu or mhchen@wpi.edu.

Joseph D. Petruccelli
Balgobin Nandram
Minghui Chen

Preface – To the Student

So you're about to take statistics! We congratulate you. You are obviously a knowledgeable and discerning individual. Could we be **biased** about this? Possibly. But then, the topic of bias is covered in Chapter 3. Before you get to Chapter 3, though, we have a few tips on what you'll find in the book and how to use what you find effectively.

HOW TO USE THIS BOOK

- The first thing is very basic: read whatever sections you're assigned before coming to the class in which they'll be discussed. Things will make a lot more sense that way.
- Each chapter begins with a short introduction which lays out the topic being studied. The basic knowledge and skills you are expected to acquire are listed immediately after.
- The narrative sections follow. These describe the concepts in the chapter. The narrative sections can be read by themselves, but sometimes, especially when computerized data analysis techniques are described, it might be useful for you to be at a computer terminal in order to perform the techniques being described. If you are a SAS or MINITAB user, consult the **Doing It with SAS** or **Doing It with MINITAB** supplement for information on how to conduct analyses in the text using your software package.
- Next is a section with discussion questions. If you can answer these questions, you have a good grasp of the concepts discussed in the narrative. Use these questions as a check on your knowledge, and as a guide to what you need to study more.
- Exercises follow. You may use these for your own benefit, or your instructor may assign them to you. Answers to nearly all odd-numbered exercises are found at the back of the book.

- A description of the miniproject for the chapter is next. Your instructor will let you know how this is to be used.
- The final section(s) of a chapter are instructions for each lab in the chapter. These describe exactly what you are to do for the lab. If the lab involves computer use, and if you are a SAS or MINITAB user, consult the **Doing It with SAS** or **Doing It with MINITAB** supplement for specific information on conducting the lab using your software package.
- Appendix A at the end of the book contains statistical tables.

We wish you the best in your study of statistics.

1

Introduction to Data Analysis

To learn truly what each thing is, is a matter of uncertainty.

—Democritus

INTRODUCTION

In this introductory chapter, you will learn about variation in a process and some tools for analyzing that variation.

KNOWLEDGE AND SKILLS

By successfully completing this chapter, you will acquire the following knowledge and skills:

KNOWLEDGE	SKILLS
1. What data are.	1. Use of plots versus time to assess process stationarity.
2. The nature of variation.	2. Use of stratified plots to identify causes of variation in a stationary process.
3. What a stationary process is.	3. Use of statistics as a tool in scientific inquiry and quality improvement.
4. Causes of process variation, including common and special causes.	4. Brainstorming, process flow diagrams, and Ishikawa diagrams and their use in the identification of possible causes of variation in a stationary process.

STATISTICS IN REAL LIFE

We know a famous statistician who carries a notebook in his pocket. In this notebook, he records his "defects." By a defect he means substandard performance in any of a number of activities on which he is trying to improve. Recently, we noticed him giving himself a defect for such things as making an unkind remark, eating too much rich food, and taking an elevator when he could have walked one flight of stairs. His goal is self-improvement, or, as he phrases it, "zero defects."

Perhaps he sounds eccentric, but if you stop and think about it, he has one very real advantage over the rest of us: He knows where he is in his efforts at self-improvement and he knows how successful his efforts have been up to now. He has the recorded information to show him. Not opinions or guesses or feelings, but the information he recorded.

During the last two decades, U.S. companies in many manufacturing sectors have been driven to or near extinction by overseas competition. U.S. consumer electronics (TVs, VCRs, camcorders, etc.) is an extinct industry. U.S. auto manufacturers are making a sustained comeback after years of falling sales and mounting losses. Curiously, the story of these industries has a lot to do with the famous statistician and his "defects."

The decline of these American industries came about for a number of reasons, but one important reason was the ability of overseas competitors to make superior products at lower cost. One reason for their success was that they kept track of their defects, as did our statistician, and constantly strove to obtain zero defects. In the 1980s, this quality improvement strategy was adopted by U.S. auto manufacturers and has largely succeeded, as shown by the resurgence of the U.S. auto industry.

What the statistician and the manufacturers have in common is the collection of information and its use in improving quality. There is a name given to such information: **data.**

> **DEFINITION**
>
> **Data** are facts (numerical or otherwise) that convey information from which conclusions can be drawn.

In the absence of any further information, the following are not data:

- {Homer, Marge, Bart, Lisa, Maggie}
- {4, 5, 6, 7}
- {17.99, 18.06, 17.94}

However, if we add the information

- the human members of the Simpsons cartoon family are {Homer, Marge, Bart, Lisa, Maggie}
- the possible numbers of games in a World Series are {4, 5, 6, 7}

- the measured diameters in centimeters of three ball bearings chosen from a production lot are {17.99, 18.06, 17.94},

then, since they convey information from which we can draw conclusions, the sets of numbers or names become data.

Data are of little use by themselves. To be useful, the information they contain must be extracted, analyzed, and interpreted. For the information contained in the data to be appropriate to its use, and for conclusions based on that information to be reliable, the data must be properly obtained. This is where **statistics** comes in.

> **DEFINITION**
>
> **Statistics** is the science (some would call it an art) of data: obtaining data, analyzing data, and interpreting data.

Statistics plays a vital role in many fields, such as engineering, science, medicine, government, business, and industry. In this text, we hope to help you experience statistics as something you can and will use in your career, in your civic life, and in your personal life.

The world is now making a transition from an industrial age to an information age. As a worker in the information age, you will be asked to obtain data, process data, and make decisions based on data. A knowledge of statistics is vital for these tasks. Remember, information is conveyed by data, and statistics is the science of data.

As a citizen in a democratic republic, you will be asked to make choices based on candidates' or policymakers' competing claims. It will be up to you to judge the validity of those claims based on data. To do so, you may have to obtain and process the data necessary to make intelligent decisions. It is here that statistics can help you be a better citizen.

Finally, statistics can help you in your personal life. The famous statistician's quest for self-improvement is one example. Other examples are found in the next section and in the exercises at the end of the chapter. Perhaps you can think of a way to collect and use data to help improve the quality of your life.

1.2

VARIATION IN DATA

In the fall of 1993, Professor P. began monitoring his household's electric usage in order to detect an in-ground water-pipe failure before it could do costly damage. Professor P. lives in a neighborhood of single-family homes, each of which has its water supplied by its own well. An in-ground pump moves the water from the well to a holding tank in the basement of each home. What had happened to several of Professor P.'s neighbors was that a crack developed underground in the plastic water pipe leading from the submerged pump. This crack resulted in the water pump running continuously in an

TABLE 1.1　The First Five Observations in Professor P.'s KWH Data

Date	KWH
18OCT93	24
19OCT93	21
20OCT93	23
21OCT93	24
22OCT93	19

effort to maintain water pressure. Unfortunately, there were no symptoms of the water-pipe cracks, so the neighbors to whom this happened were alerted to the problem by a sixfold jump in their monthly electric bills. In the hope of quickly detecting a water-pipe crack, and thereby avoiding a $600 monthly electric bill, Professor P. records the reading on his electric meter each morning.

One hundred seventy-four of the observations are stored in the data set ELECE on the data disk that accompanies this text. The daily electric usage, in kilowatt-hours (KWH) is stored under the variable name KWH and the date of the reading is stored under the name DATE. The first five observations in the data set are shown in Table 1.1.

From these first five observations, it is clear that electric usage in Professor P.'s household is not exactly the same from day to day. Why might that be the case? Think of your own experience: Do you watch television or play your stereo exactly the same amount each day? These differences in the KWH values are called **variation.** The variation in the KWH readings may be due to different patterns of use of electric appliances, to the wear or condition of the appliances, to different operating conditions, such as temperature or humidity, and so on. But even careful, repeated measurements on the same quantity, such as repeated weighings of a test weight on an extremely accurate scale, show variation.

The variation in a set of data is quantified in a **data distribution.**

> **DEFINITION**
>
> A **data distribution** is a summary of the variation in a set of data. The data distribution is a list of each data value and its frequency (i.e., how often it occurs).

The data distribution of Professor P.'s KWH data is given by Table 1.2.

Though the 174 observations in this data set consist of only 34 different values, it is difficult to get a feel for the information in the data by looking at Table 1.2. For larger data sets, in which the data might take hundreds or even thousands of values, it is impossible to make sense of the data using a table of the distribution. Instead, we turn to data summary measures, such as the mean (or average) or the median, and especially to graphical displays to help. We will postpone the introduction of data

TABLE 1.2   The Data Distribution of Professor P.'s KWH Data

KWH	Frequency	KWH	Frequency	KWH	Frequency
10	1	24	11	36	7
12	1	25	9	37	6
14	1	26	16	38	2
15	2	27	9	39	2
16	1	28	9	40	5
17	2	29	7	41	2
18	2	30	10	42	1
19	6	31	5	43	1
20	6	32	3	44	4
21	12	33	3	51	3
22	9	34	4		
23	9	35	3		

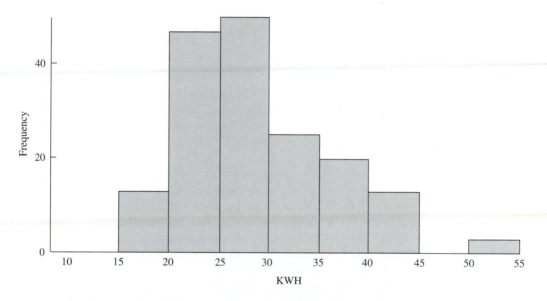

Figure 1.1   Histogram of kilowatt-hours (KWH) used daily by Professor P.'s household.

summary measures until the next chapter, but we will now introduce a standard tool for displaying the variation in numerical data: the **histogram.** Figure 1.1 displays a histogram for the daily KWH values.

Construction of a histogram begins by breaking the range of data values into a number of intervals and counting the frequencies of observations in each interval. For the intervals used to construct the histogram in Figure 1.1, Table 1.3 summarizes the frequencies. These may be obtained from the full data distribution in Table 1.2. Note

TABLE 1.3   Summary Counts of Professor P.'s KWH Data Used in Construction of the Histogram in Figure 1.1

Interval	10–15	15–20	20–25	25–30	30–35	35–40	40–45	45–50	50–55
Frequency	3	13	47	50	25	20	13	0	3

that in this construction, we count data values equal to the left endpoint of the interval but not those equal to the right endpoint.

In the histogram shown in Figure 1.1, the intervals are displayed on a horizontal axis. Above each interval is drawn a vertical bar with height proportional to the frequency of observations in that interval. Sometimes a histogram will be rotated so that the intervals are displayed on a vertical axis and the bars are horizontal. Figure 1.2 contains examples of such histograms.

From Figure 1.1, we observe that the histogram of the daily KWH values has a definite pattern: there is a small number of observations in the leftmost interval, then a modest jump followed by a large jump in the interval 20–25. A small further jump ensures that the greatest number of observations in any interval occurs in the interval 25–30. The frequency declines by half to the 30–35 interval and then falls off slowly in the next three intervals. There are no observations in the interval 45–50, and only three in the rightmost interval. The values in the data range from around 10 to around 55 KWH. The histogram is much more effective at summarizing the pattern of variation in the data than is the actual distribution displayed in Table 1.2.

Simple graphical displays and simple summary measures can tell us a great deal about a data set. Professor P. wants to do more with these data, however. Specifically, he wants to know when something has gone wrong with his well. Professor P. can use the information contained in the histogram to predict tomorrow's KWH reading. From the histogram in Figure 1.1, he would predict tomorrow's KWH reading to be between 25 and 30, since the 25–30 interval contains the greatest number of daily KWH readings. Or, since both the 20–25 and 25–30 intervals contain nearly the same numbers of readings, he might want to predict that tomorrow's reading will be in the 20–30 range, if he is satisfied with a larger prediction range.

Professor P. can also use the information in the histogram to help judge whether tomorrow's KWH reading shows evidence of a water-pipe crack. Clearly, if tomorrow's reading is 26, Professor P. will not be concerned. A reading of 52 KWH may give him some concern, but a glance at the histogram will reassure him that values like this have occurred in the past. What about a reading of 58? 75? 100? When should he call the well company to come look at the well?

This question cannot be answered by looking at the histogram. It cannot be answered by calculating some summary measures. We must find a way of quantifying how extreme an observation has to be before it gives us concern. We must find a way to quantify how likely such readings are when the well is operating normally. The solution will rely on two concepts: the concept of a statistical model, which is introduced in Chapter 4, and the concept of statistical inference, which is introduced in Chapters 5 and 6.

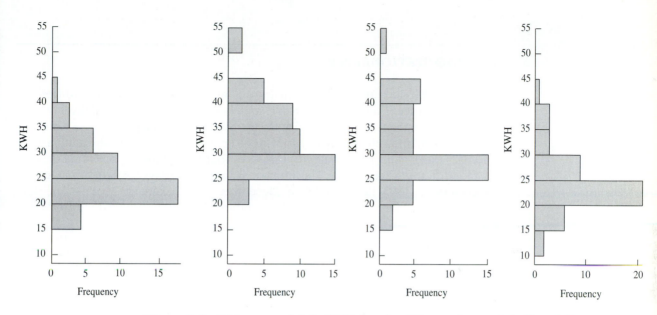

Figure 1.2 Histograms of daily KWH data for different time periods. From left to right, the data are for the periods October 17–December 5, 1993; December 6, 1993–January 24, 1994; January 25–March 15, 1994; and March 16–May 6, 1994.

1.3

STATIONARY PROCESSES

For data such as the KWH data, which are taken over time, there is more to be considered. To make consistently good predictions of future observations based on past and present data, those future observations must have the same pattern of variation as the the past and present data. In other words, the pattern of variation must not change as more measurements are taken. For example, Professor P. will not be able to use past and present KWH data to make accurate predictions of tomorrow's KWH usage if tomorrow is the hottest day of the year and he just had a central air conditioning system installed today. And he will not be able to make accurate predictions if the water pipe in his well fails. This brings us to the notion of a **stationary process.**

DEFINITION

A **stationary process** is a data-generating mechanism for which the distribution of the resulting data does not change appreciably as more data are generated.

Are the KWH data the result of a stationary process? To see, we must consider how to assess process stationarity.

1.4

ASSESSING STATIONARITY

How can we tell if the pattern of KWH measurements is changing? Change is a difference over time, so to see if the pattern of KWH values is changing, we should display them over time. We might make one such display by dividing the time period over which the data were taken into subperiods and drawing a separate histogram for the data in each. Figure 1.2 is such a display. The figure consists of four histograms representing the data from four different time periods. The leftmost histogram displays the data from October 17–December 5, 1993, the second from December 6, 1993–January 24, 1994, the third from January 25–March 15, 1994, and the rightmost histogram from March 16–May 6, 1994.

If the process is stationary, these histograms should display roughly the same pattern of variation. Although the shapes of the four histograms differ modestly, the most noticeable differences among the histograms concern where they are located on the KWH axis. The second and third histograms, representing December 6, 1993–January 24, 1994, and January 25–March 15, 1994, are clearly shifted toward larger KWH values compared with the first histogram. This shift indicates a generally higher electric use during these time periods. The pattern of variation shown in the rightmost histogram is very similar to that found in the leftmost histogram, which indicates a return to generally lower electric use during this time period. These differences make the stationarity of the process questionable.

What does this mean in a practical sense? Suppose on December 5, 1993, Professor P. wanted to to predict KWH use for data beginning December 6, 1993, using the data from October 17–December 5, 1993. Then, based on the leftmost histogram in Figure 1.2, if he had to predict to within 5 KWH, he would predict daily usage to be between 20 and 25 KWH. The second histogram shows, however, that only a few such values occurred between December 6, 1993, and January 24, 1994, and that those few values were the very smallest in that time period. So if Professor P. used the data from October 17–December 5, 1993, to predict KWH values in the next time period, he would greatly underpredict. In fact, some of the values in the 50–55-KWH range would look uncomfortably like the results of a water-pipe crack. Of course, we know now that the water pipe did not crack, as shown by the return to low KWH values in the rightmost histogram. What happened is that the pattern of variation changed as time passed, rendering conclusions based on the earlier data questionable at best.

Displaying histograms for different time periods makes the point about stationarity effectively, but it can be a difficult display to create. For instance, someone must decide which subintervals to use. Figure 1.3 is a different display of the daily KWH values versus time. In fact, it is two displays in one. On the left is a **scatterplot,** showing the KWH values on the vertical axis and the date they were observed on the horizontal axis. On the right is a histogram[1] showing the distribution of all KWH values

---

[1]This histogram is just the histogram in Figure 1.1 with a different orientation.

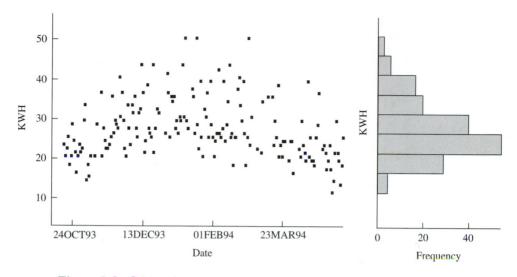

Figure 1.3   Scatterplot of daily kilowatt-hour usage versus date and the histogram of daily kilowatt-hour usage.

regardless of when they were observed. Its vertical axis is on the same scale as the vertical axis of the scatterplot. The scatterplot shows how the KWH values vary with time.

This example illustrates two key points.

DETECTING STATIONARITY: TWO KEY POINTS

- **Some displays, such as a single histogram, cannot detect process stationarity or nonstationarity.** In fact, the histogram is designed to display the unchanging pattern of a stationary process, for which it is well suited.
- **In order to assess stationarity, data must be plotted versus time.** A plot such as the scatterplot in Figure 1.3 or the series of histograms in Figure 1.2 can show change over time.

However, it is still difficult to judge the stationarity of the process from the scatterplot. Connecting the points at consecutive times with a line can make it easier to recognize patterns evolving over time. The resulting plot is called a time-series plot. Figure 1.4 is a time-series plot of the daily KWH data. This time-series plot reveals that although there is a good deal of variation in the series as evidenced in the vertical oscillations, there seems to be a curved pattern to the data, with a general level that rises from October to January and then declines from January to April.

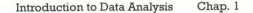

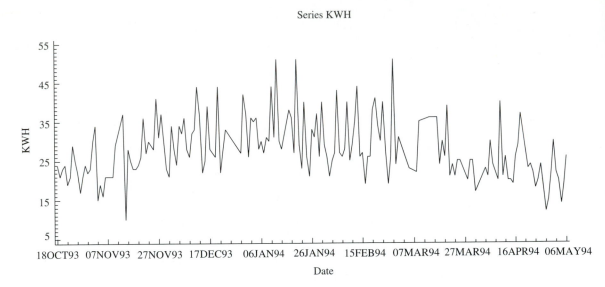

Figure 1.4   Time-series plot of daily kilowatt-hours. When data are taken over time, a time-series plot, which connects successive observations with lines, makes it easier to recognize patterns evolving over time.

The time-series plot in Figure 1.4 still exhibits a lot of the high-frequency oscillations, which appear as jagged up and down lines.

These high-frequency oscillations, known as **noise,** make it difficult to see the underlying patterns in the data. They also make it difficult to obtain effective predictions of future observations, a fact that frustrates Professor P. in his efforts at early detection of a crack in his well pipe. By reducing noise, we can improve detection of the underlying pattern in the data, called the **signal,** and also improve prediction of future observations. Statistical methods called **filtering methods** are often used to suppress high-frequency oscillations.[2] There are many filtering methods that are used to reduce noise, but we will use the simplest, called a **moving average.**

> DEFINITION
>
> A **moving average** filter replaces each data value by the average of itself and observations occurring immediately before it in time.

For example, a 3-term **moving-average** replaces each observation by the average of itself and the two terms immediately preceding it. A 5-term moving average replaces each observation by the average of itself and the four terms immediately preceding it. If l is any positive integer, the general formula for an l-term moving average is

---

[2]Filtering methods are well known to electrical engineers. They are used extensively in signal processing, where they perform in applications ranging from satellite telemetry to the audio controls on your home stereo system.

FORMULA FOR CALCULATING A MOVING AVERAGE

If the observation at time t is denoted Y_t, and l is any positive integer, an l-term moving average replaces Y_t with

$$A_{l,t} = \frac{1}{l}(Y_t + Y_{t-1} + Y_{t-2} + \ldots + Y_{t-l+1})$$

Thus, for example, a 3-term moving average has the formula $A_{3,t} = (Y_t + Y_{t-1} + Y_{t-2})/3$. Try writing out the formula for a 5- or a 9-term moving average.

EXAMPLE 1.1   MOVING AVERAGE CALCULATION

Let's return to our study of the daily KWH data. The first ten observations are

Date	KWH
18OCT93	24
19OCT93	21
20OCT93	23
21OCT93	24
22OCT93	19
23OCT93	21
24OCT93	29
25OCT93	25
26OCT93	22
27OCT93	17

We will now calculate a 4-term moving average for $t = $ 19OCT93 and 22OCT93.

To compute the 4-term moving average $A_{4,t}$ for $t = $ 22OCT93, we average the KWH values for 22OCT93, 21OCT93, 20OCT93, and 19OCT93 to obtain $(19 + 24 + 23 + 21)/4 = 21.75$. To compute the 4-term moving average for $t = $ 19OCT93, we would like to average the KWH hour values for 19OCT93, 18OCT93, 17OCT93, and 16OCT93, but we do not have the last two observations. So, instead, we will just average those values; we have $(21 + 24)/2 = 22.5$. Try computing $A_{4,t}$ for $t = $ 26OCT93 (the answer is 24.25).   ◆

Figure 1.5 shows a 7-term moving average as a dotted line superimposed on the time-series plot of daily KWH. Notice that the moving average has greatly reduced the noise, enabling us to better see the signal in the data. The reduction of the noise corresponds to an overall reduction in variation, which is characteristic of averages.

A KEY POINT ABOUT AVERAGES

Averages are less variable than raw data.

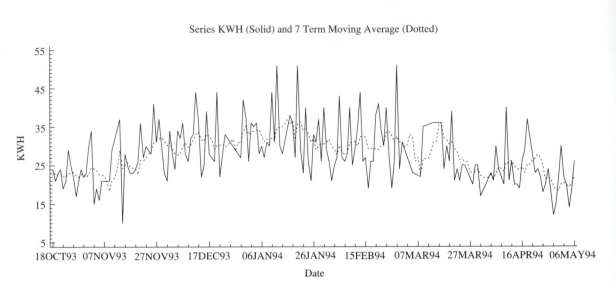

Figure 1.5   Time-series plot of daily kilowatt-hours with 7-term moving average (dotted line). The moving average reduces high-frequency variation and allows us to more clearly see underlying trends over time.

Why did we choose a 7-term moving average for the daily KWH data? Our society runs on a number of cycles, and one of the most basic is the weekly cycle (doesn't everyone look forward to the weekend?). It's the same with Professor P.'s household. During the week, his kids are in school, he is at work, and his wife is either working or running errands. On the weekend, everyone is home using lights, TV, computer and video games, doing laundry and vacuuming, and so on. So it makes sense that electric usage would follow a 7-day cycle. As a result of this reasoning, we decided to use a 7-term moving average to filter the daily KWH data.

Figure 1.6 is a time-series plot of the daily KWH data with a 28-term moving average, the dotted line, superimposed. The 28-term moving average was selected because it is multiple of the 7-day weekly cycle and because it represents roughly a monthly cycle. Notice how it is even smoother than the 7-term moving average, which brings up a second key point about averages.

ANOTHER KEY POINT ABOUT AVERAGES

Averages with more terms are less variable than averages with fewer terms.

Both the 7- and 28-term moving averages show that stationarity of the process producing the KWH data is questionable: Both filters show that the signal is increasing and then decreasing, as we first observed in Figure 1.4. Whereas the 7-term moving

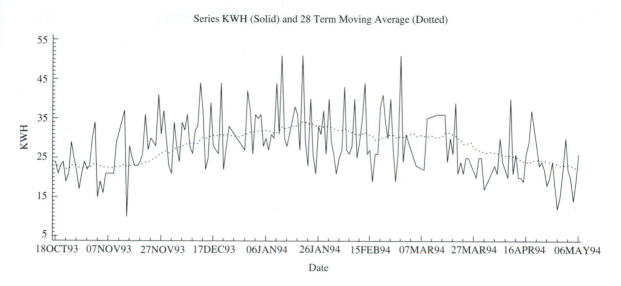

Figure 1.6   Time-series plot of daily kilowatt-hours with a 28-term moving average (dotted line). The more terms in the moving average, the smoother the result, as comparison with the 7-term moving average in Figure 1.5 shows.

average summarizes the signal reasonably well from beginning to end, the 28-term moving average does not. Until March 1994, the 28-term moving average tracks the signal well, but after that, it is consistently too high. Here, for example, the moving average is still using many of the large KWH values from several weeks past, and the present KWH usage has declined steeply. This poor performance of the 28-term moving average is due to the nonstationarity of the data. In general, the larger the number of terms in a moving average, the more difficulty it will have tracking a nonstationary process.

Once we agree that the data are from a nonstationary process, the next task of a data analyst would be to explain the observed pattern of nonstationarity. For the electric data, we will leave that to you in the exercises.

An example of a plot of a stationary process is found in Figure 1.7. This plot shows the measured thicknesses in millimeters of 100 washers plotted versus the order in which they were taken from the production line. A 5-term moving average is superimposed on the plot. In contrast to the nonstationary KWH data, the variation of the washer thicknesses has no systematic pattern over time.

1.5

CAUSES OF VARIATION

It is common for measurements from the same process to vary. This variation is found in physicists' measurements of the speed of light. It is found in repeated measurements of the same object with a very accurate scale. And it is found in virtually all industrial

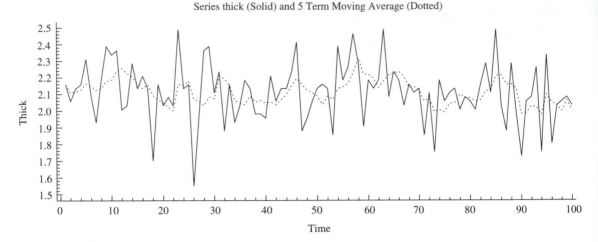

Figure 1.7 Time-series plot of thicknesses of 100 washers with a 5-term moving average (dotted line). This graph demonstrates data from a stationary process.

processes. Often, in order to understand the workings of a process, it is essential to understand the **causes of variation** in process measurements.

DEFINITION

A **cause of variation** is a mechanism responsible for some of the observed variation in a process. It is useful to distinguish between two different kinds of causes of variation, **common causes of variation** and **special causes of variation.**

- The variation in the process is due entirely to **common causes of variation** if the process, as presently constituted, is running as well as it can. Common causes make up the "noise" inherent in the process. Removal of common causes requires a change in the process itself and in an industrial setting can only be done by management. Examples of common causes are poor supervision, inadequate training, or substandard maintenance.

- A **special cause of variation** is a problem that arises periodically and unpredictably. In an industrial setting, special causes can usually be handled where and when they occur by production personnel. Examples of special causes are broken tools, a jammed machine, or improper machine settings.

Appropriate plots of data can help identify causes of variation as the following example shows.

EXAMPLE 1.2   A STATIONARY PROCESS THAT WASN'T

Consider the washer thicknesses plotted in Figure 1.7. The plot provides no evidence that the washer thicknesses were produced by an nonstationary process.

If management were happy with the output of the process, perhaps there would be no reason to look further into it. But management was displeased that their competitors were producing washers that had thicknesses nearer on average to the specified thickness of 2.16 mm. To make matters worse, the competition's washer thicknesses were also more consistent; that is, there was less variation in the thicknesses.

What was wrong? It turned out that the company's managers and engineers violated an important rule of competitiveness: **Understand the process.**

They confused the process of producing the washers with the product, which was the washers themselves. Therefore, to monitor the process, they looked only at the end product, which suggested, as you have seen in Figure 1.7, a stationary process. Only by looking at the process, that is, how the product is created, can understanding be obtained. And only with understanding can steps be taken to improve the process and ultimately the product.

When they looked at the process, management realized that the washers were produced by three different machines. Figure 1.8 shows three plots of the same data plotted in Figure 1.7, but the data produced by each machine are plotted separately.

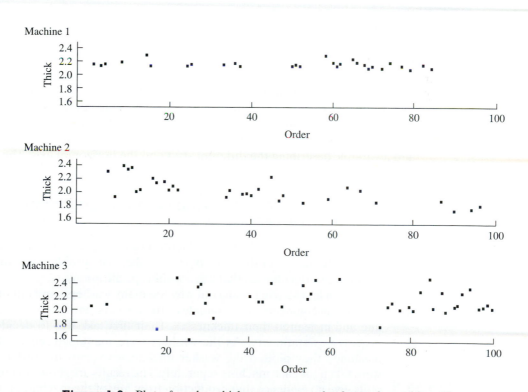

Figure 1.8 Plot of washer thickness versus order for each machine. The first machine is operating normally and so the observed variation is due to common causes only. The second and third machines display abnormal patterns of variation due to special causes.

These plots make the source of the problem immediately clear. Only machine 1 is producing washers of acceptable thicknesses. The output of machine 2 is not stationary, with a declining trend in washer thicknesses evident. Machine 3 is producing washers of widely varying thicknesses. By looking at each machine separately, management took the first step in isolating the causes responsible for the unsatisfactory product.

Looking at each machine more closely, inspectors found that machine 1 was behaving normally, so that only common causes were responsible for the observed variation. To reduce the variation in the washer thicknesses from machine 1, the process itself would have to be changed. Upon investigation, inspectors found a worn cam responsible for the excessive variation in washers produced by machine 3. An overstretched spring on machine 2 was allowing a key control setting to drift, resulting in the trend in the thicknesses. The worn cam and overstretched spring were special causes of variation. The cam and spring were both replaced, eliminating the special causes and restoring those machines to normal operation. ✦

1.6

STRATIFIED PLOTS

A graphical tool we will use in identifying causes of variation in a stationary process is the **stratified plot.** Process stationarity simplifies things, because we do not need to look at the development of the process over time. In a stratified plot, data are broken up into smaller groups or strata with the goal of looking at the distributions of the data within each stratum and at how these distributions differ from stratum to stratum. The simplest stratified plot is just an *X–Y* plot with the measured variable on the vertical axis and a variable describing the different strata on the horizontal axis. The next example illustrates the use of stratified plots.

EXAMPLE 1.3   USING STRATIFIED PLOTS TO IDENTIFY CAUSES OF VARIATION

A competitor to the washer manufacturer of Example 1.2 was having trouble with its own production of the same type of washer. The problem was that not enough washers had thicknesses that were within specifications.

As a first step in finding out why too many washers were out of specification, production engineers took a sample of 100 washers at random from the production line and measured their thicknesses. Their first task was to decide whether the process was stationary. As the washers were manufactured by three different machines, they plotted the washer thicknesses versus the order in which they were taken for each machine separately. The results are shown in Figure 1.9. These plots give no evidence that production from any of the machines is nonstationary. However, the plotted patterns for the different machines do not all look the same, suggesting that at least some of the excessive variation the company is experiencing may be due to differences between machines.

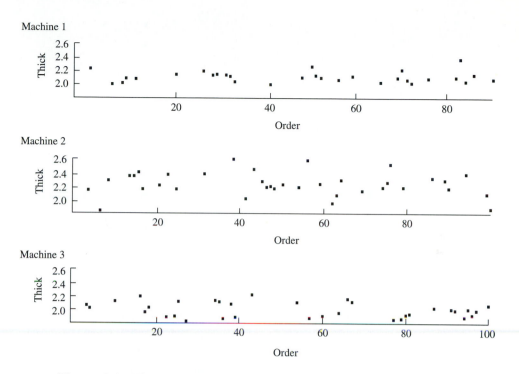

Figure 1.9 Plot of washer thicknesses versus order for each of three machines.

A stratified plot that stratifies these data by machine may help in visualizing these differences between machines. Such a stratified plot is displayed in Figure 1.10.

The stratified plot stratifies the data by machine and allows us to compare the pattern of variation of the washer thicknesses produced by the different machines. Two things to look for in the stratified plot are the vertical spread of washer thicknesses from each machine, and the center about which the thicknesses seem to be spread for each machine. Do they differ greatly or are they nearly the same? Is the difference **between** the centers of the thicknesses for the individual machines, also called the **between variation,** large compared with the spread of the thicknesses **within** each machine, also called the **within variation?** Answering this last question does two important things.

- It helps us identify the primary cause of variation in the thicknesses and therefore tells us something about how the process that produced the data operates.
- It tells us where to focus our efforts if our goal is to reduce process variation.

On the stratified plot, we notice that not all machines show equal variation in washer thickness. The within variation of machine 1 is about the same as that of machine 3, but the within variation of machine 2 is considerably larger. In terms of between variation, machine 1 values seem to be centered around the 2.16-mm

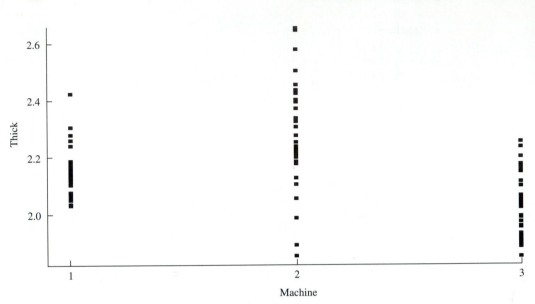

Figure 1.10 Stratified plot of thickness versus machine.

specification, the center of machine 2 thicknesses is closer to 2.30 mm and that of machine 3 thicknesses is around 2.05 mm. A large part of the overall variation seems to be accounted for by the within variation, particularly within machine 2. The variation between machines 2 and 3 also seems to account for a substantial part of the total variation in the data.

Based on this analysis of the variation in the thicknesses:

- The operation of machine 2 was looked at carefully to identify causes for excessive variation and higher than desired thicknesses. It turned out that the first problem was due to a poorly trained operator, and the second was caused by a faulty gage used in setting the machine parameters. Proper training of the operator and replacement of the gage remedied the problems.
- The operation of machine 3 was looked at carefully to identify causes for the low thicknesses. It turned out that a miscalibrated control was responsible. The control was recalibrated and output returned to the acceptable range. ✦

1.7

IDENTIFYING POSSIBLE CAUSES OF VARIATION

Often identifying causes of variation in a process is of critical importance. So that input is obtained from as many different perspectives as possible, and so that critical factors are not overlooked, it is essential that the identification of causes of variation be a **team effort,** involving everyone with knowledge of the process.

Brainstorming

An excellent way for the team to obtain a list of possible causes of variation is through **brainstorming.** In order to be successful in an organizational setting, a brainstorming session will bring different people, departments, groups, and so forth, together. It will use devices such as flowcharts and diagrams to document and encourage ideas on causes of variation in the process. In order for brainstorming to succeed, all participants must abide by the **cardinal rule of brainstorming:**

THE CARDINAL RULE OF BRAINSTORMING: ABSOLUTELY NO CRITICISM

This cardinal rule is essential to ensure that each team member feels free to contribute openly to the discussion. The idea of brainstorming is to get as many ideas as possible from the team, no matter how silly or impractical they may seem at the time. Though brainstorming sessions often result in many outlandish ideas being put forth, there are two things to remember: First, many revolutionary ideas at first sounded outlandish (how do you think relativity theory sounded at first?); second, even an outlandish idea by one member of the team may inspire others to come up with new insights.

Brainstorming should result in the identification of a large number of possible causes of variation. Using data, knowledge, and experience, the team should try to reach consensus on what are the major causes of variation. Only by understanding these causes of variation can the process be truly understood and improved.

Graphical Tools for Identifying Possible Causes of Variation

During and immediately following brainstorming sessions, graphical tools are often used to organize and summarize ideas about process function and causes of variation. Two such tools are the process flow diagram and the Ishikawa diagram.

The Process Flow Diagram

A process flow diagram is a schematic diagram showing process steps and the flow of material and information linking them during the process. It illustrates how the process is supposed to work.

The Ishikawa Diagram

An Ishikawa diagram, sometimes called a fishbone diagram or a cause-and-effect diagram, is a visual aid for initially identifying possible causes of observed phenomena.

The following example illustrates the nature and use of these diagrams in identifying possible causes of variation in a process.

EXAMPLE 1.4   PROCESS FLOW AND ISHIKAWA DIAGRAMS

A company makes a kind of fine-mesh netting used for filtering purposes in various industries. There is always a demand to make the mesh finer, but the finer the mesh is made, the weaker it becomes, and the more it tends to rip in manufacturing, shipping, and use. A team was assigned the task of determining whether changes could be made in manufacturing the mesh so as to improve strength without adding major new equipment or processing procedures that would increase cost greatly.

The first thing the team did was to assemble all interested parties in the company at a brainstorming session. They began by making a process flow diagram of the mesh-making process in order to have in detail before them what was (supposed to be, at least) the way the process worked. This diagram is shown in Figure 1.11.

At the same session, they developed the Ishikawa diagram shown in Figure 1.12, giving a complete list of the possible causes of variation the team came up with. In developing the Ishikawa diagram, the team used the **5Ms + E** as categories: man, machine, methods, materials, measurement, and environment.

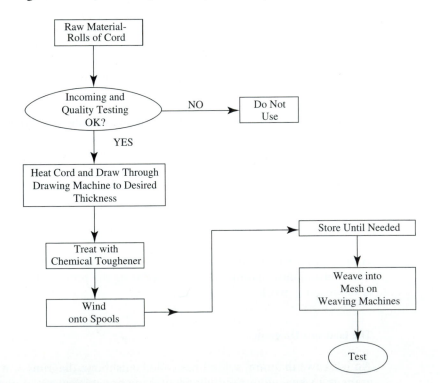

Figure 1.11   Process flow diagram for mesh netting problem.

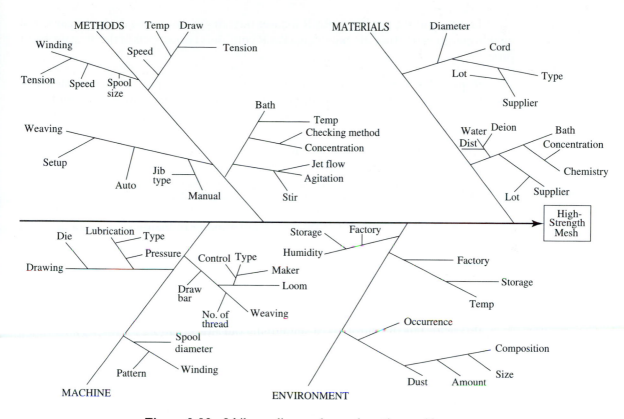

Figure 1.12   Ishikawa diagram for mesh netting problem.

In the diagram, the main arrow or trunk points to the phenomenon being studied: high-strength mesh. The branches pointing directly to the trunk are the relevant causes of variation among the 5Ms + E. The smaller branches list possible causes of variation identified as affecting the major causes of variation, and so forth.

These two diagrams focused the team's thinking on possible causes of variation in the process, and served as a starting point for finding ways to improve the manufacturing process. ✦

1.8

AN APPLICATION: GAGE R&R

Much of the data used in science and industry results from taking measurements of such quantities as length, weight, area, or volume. Conclusions drawn from such data are only as good as the quality of the measurements. **Gage Repeatability and Reproducibility (Gage R&R)** is a statistical procedure used to assess the quality of a measurement process.

In its simplest form, Gage R&R focuses on a single measuring device or gage, and on the operators who use the gage. Gage R&R considers two aspects of the measurement process:

- **Repeatability** measures the consistency of the gage in repeated measurements by the same operator on the same part. If the repeatability of measurement is low, the problem could be a faulty gage, flawed measurement methodology, or poor operator training.
- **Reproducibility** measures the variation between different operators. Low reproducibility means measurements vary greatly from operator to operator. Problems of reproducibility may be due to poor operator training.

In order to evaluate Gage R&R for a single gage, typically a number of different operators will use that one gage to make a fixed number of identical measurements on each of several identical parts.

EXAMPLE 1.5   GAGE R&R

A manufacturer of roller bearings uses a special gage to measure the play in an assembled bearing. It is desired to evaluate repeatability and reproducibility for this gage. For the purposes of simplifying our presentation, we will assume that a single bearing and three operators are used in the study and that each operator makes 10 measurements on the bearing. The first thing to check in such a study is the stationarity of the processes that produced the data. In the present case, the question is whether the measurements taken by any operator show a systematic trend or pattern as more measurements are taken. Figure 1.13 shows three time-series plots of the measurements in the order taken: one plot for each operator. From these plots, we can see three things:

1. None of the time-series plots shows evidence of nonstationarity in the measuring process.
2. Operators 1 and 2 are making measurements that are close to each other, but operator 3 is making measurements that are consistently higher than those of the other two operators.
3. The measurements made by operator 3 vary more than those made by the other two operators.

Since we have concluded that the measurement process is stationary, a stratified plot is an appropriate tool for displaying the measurements for the three operators. Figure 1.14 shows the data stratified by operator. The stratified plot reinforces points 2 and 3 that we made about the time-series plots: The observations for operator 3 are both higher in general than those of the other two operators, and they also vary more. Thus, we can conclude the following from this study:

- There is a reproducibility problem in the measuring process, since the measurements made by operator 3 differ substantially from the others. The measuring method used by operator 3 should be looked at closely to see why this

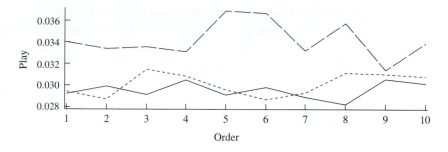

Figure 1.13 Data from the Gage R&R study of Example 1.5. Presented are three time-series plots, each consisting of ten measurements of the play in a roller bearing, in the order in which they were taken. Each time-series plot corresponds to measurements from one of the three operators used in the study. The solid line marks the measurements from operator 1, the line with short dashes marks the measurements from operator 2 and the line with long dashes marks the measurements from operator 3.

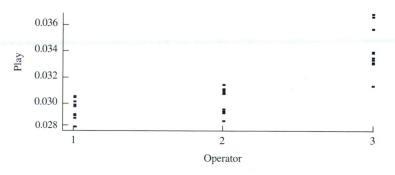

Figure 1.14 Data from the Gage R&R study of Example 1.5 stratified by operator.

is so. When a reason has been found for the aberrant measurements from operator 3, the operator training procedures should be examined for ways to improve the consistency of measurement between operators.

- There may or may not be a repeatability problem. If the variation in the measurements of operators 1 and 2 is acceptably small, then there is no problem. If that variation is too large, then the gage and process of taking measurements should be looked at. ◆

DISCUSSION QUESTIONS

1. What is a stationary process? Can a single histogram be used to check for stationarity? Why or why not? If not, how would you graphically check for stationarity?
2. Explain what a moving average is and what it is used for.

3. What is a stratified plot? What is it used for?

4. Name two graphical tools used for identifying possible causes of process variation.

5. What is brainstorming? How can it help in identifying possible causes of process variation?

6. What six categories might form the main branches of an Ishikawa diagram?

E XERCISES

1.1. A certain news organization takes two kinds of polls of voter preference:

    (a) A different group of prospective voters is polled on each of the 14 days leading up to the election.

    (b) On election day, voters who have just voted are interviewed. This is known as an **exit poll.**

    One of these polling methods definitely results from a stationary process; the other may be nonstationary. In two sentences, tell which is which and why. Use this example to explain why it is important to determine if a process is stationary.

1.2. In a metal stamping process, there are three identical machines making identical parts. Each machine is run by a different operator. A study of the waste produced by the process reveals that most of the process variation is between operators rather than within operators. Sketch what a stratified plot of the data from this process might look like.

1.3. A large supermarket receives complaints about the quality of its baked bread. Suppose you are in charge of the bakery. Develop an Ishikawa diagram that could help you locate the causes of the poor quality.

1.4. Are data (i.e., measurements) needed to construct an effective Ishikawa diagram? If so, why? If not, what is needed?

1.5. Figure 1.15 displays ozone readings taken at Stamford, Connecticut, over a 120-day period. A statistics student claims that the graph shows the ozone levels to be from a stationary process. How would you answer her?

1.6. The file UNEMGNP contains (among other variables), the quarterly unemployment rate for the United States (variable URATE) from the first quarter of 1946 through the second quarter of 1991 (variable DATE). Is the process that generated these data stationary? Provide an appropriate plot and justify your answer.

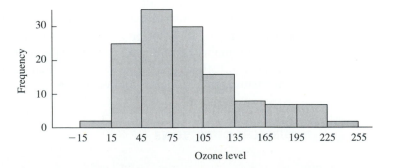

Figure 1.15   Stamford ozone readings.

1.7. A bakery finds that there is too much variation in the weights of its 1-pound loaves of white bread. Production specifications call for a weight of 1.06 pounds. The weight of the dough going into a loaf of bread is controlled by a scale. There are two potential problems with the scale: worn gears or miscalibration. The first problem results in excessive variation in the weights, and the second results in the weights being too heavy or too light, on average. The data set BREAD contains the weights of eight randomly selected loaves from each of the bakery's 10 scales.

    (a) Produce one appropriate plot showing the variation for each of the scales.

    (b) Tell which kind(s) of problem(s), if any, is (are) associated with each scale by putting a check in each box corresponding to a scale with the designated problem (leave empty any box for which a given scale does not have that particular problem):

Scale	1	2	3	4	5	6	7	8	9	10
Worn Gears										
Miscalibration										

1.8. Three machines are designed to produce washers that are 2-mm thick. Each machine is run by a different operator. A random sample of 20 washers is taken from the day's production of each machine. The data are displayed in Figure 1.16.

    (a) Describe the variation in the data.

    (b) Explain how the following causes of variation might be reflected in Figure 1.16:

        i. Miscalibration of machine settings.

        ii. Worn machine parts.

      iii. Poor operator training.

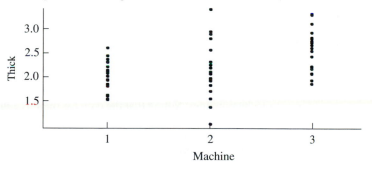

Figure 1.16   Thickness versus machine for washer production.

1.9. The SAS data file DERBY contains the winning time, owner name, and horse name of all Kentucky Derby winners from 1875 through 1980.

    (a) Do the winning times appear to be the result of a stationary process? Why or why not? Supply one appropriate plot to support your claim.

    (b) Summarize one other aspect of the data.

1.10. In a certain factory workers come in three shifts: 7:00 A.M. to 3:00 P.M., 3:00 P.M. to 11:00 P.M., and 11:00 P.M. to 7:00 A.M.. The data set, FACTORY, contains the percentage of nondefective items produced for each shift during a 10-day period.

    (a) Draw an appropriate plot to compare performance during the three shifts.

    (b) How might you explain the variation in the data?

1.11. Look at Figure 1.6. Describe the trend summarized by the moving average. What events do you think are responsible for some of the features you describe?

1.12. Look at Figure 1.5. Describe the trend summarized by the moving average. There are two places where the moving average jumps substantially. What events do you think are responsible for the jumps?

1.13. Professor P. is at it again! The data set COMMUTE contains the times (in seconds) it took him to commute from his house to WPI on a number of recent occasions. Is the process that generated the data stationary? Make an appropriate plot to decide.

1.14. Come up with two ways you can make use of data to improve the quality of your life. Tell how you would collect and display the data.

1.15. Universities depend on the "quality" of their instruction. Develop an Ishikawa diagram that lists the factors that affect quality.

1.16. The ratings of a product over the past 6 months, starting with the first month, are 5, 7, 8, 6, 9, and 12. Smooth the data by using a 2-term moving average.

1.17. A quality engineer has been monitoring a production process. Once each month he takes a sample of 200 items and computes the percentage of defective items. In time order, his readings for the past year are 1, 2, 2.5, 2.5, 3, 4, 4.5, 5, 5, 5.5, 6, and 6. Draw an appropriate plot to decide the stationarity of the process. What do you conclude?

1.18. In computer chip manufacture, the end-use product is an integrated circuit called a die. A number of die are processed from a single silicon wafer. Not all die manufactured from a wafer are usable. The yield (the proportion of good die per wafer) is extremely important to computer manufacturers. A certain computer chip manufacturer uses two processes to produce integrated circuits. In evaluating the performance of the processes, 30 wafers are sampled from each process. The yield for each wafer is to be evaluated. The data are displayed in Figure 1.17.
   (a) What is the name of the type of plot in Figure 1.17?
   (b) Describe the variation in the data.
   (c) If you were the manufacturer, which process would you prefer? Why?

1.19. Engineers are investigating a process that produces drill bits having a nominal diameter of 5 mm. Figure 1.18 is a stratified plot of the diameters of 25 drill bits sampled from each of three production lines. Noting that the data for the three lines show nearly identical center and spread, the foreman declares the production process to be stationary with respect to drill bit diameters. Sketch three hypothetical plots, one for each production line, illustrating how a nonstationary process could still give the stratified plot shown in Figure 1.18.

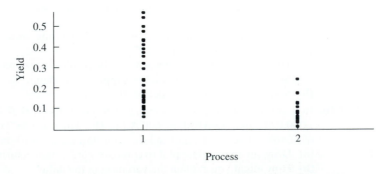

Figure 1.17   Yield versus process for computer chip data.

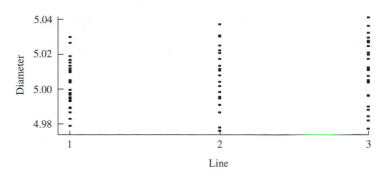

Figure 1.18   Stratified plot of drill-bit diameters.

1.20. Each time I fill my car with gas, I keep track of the mileage since the last fill-up and the number of gallons used. Then I use this information to compute the miles per gallon (MPG) I obtained. No two MPG values are the same! Create an Ishikawa diagram to identify possible causes for the variation in the MPG values.

1.21. In order to ensure a more uniform color, a paint producer performs the following procedure. For any given color, one large batch is made fresh each day. The batch is then divided into thirds. One-third is mixed with one-third of the previous day's batch of the same color, and one-third of the batch of the same color produced two days previously. The other two-thirds are set aside for future mixing. What statistical technique is the manufacturer using? Give a specific formula for what is happening.

1.22. Consider a person measuring his weight daily, in anticipation of a special event for which he wishes to stay slim and svelte! He wishes to predict his weight at some point in the future, in particular the date of this event, from the data he has kept by tracking his daily weight over the last few months. In order to do so accurately, what property must the data possess? How might he verify that the data have this property?

1.23. There are eight campfire locations at a camp, and two counselors will each start four fires in preparation for the evening activities. The (eight) times recorded for getting each of the fires started showed substantial variation. Name the two types of variation that might be exhibited in this setting. What sort of plot would you use to identify the causes of variation?

1.24. Twelve meals were ordered from a restaurant and the preparation time (time elapsed between when the order was placed and when the meal was served) was recorded for each meal. An appropriate analysis showed that the process was stationary. However, there was substantial variation in the preparation times. The meals were created by three different chefs, and the times (in minutes) are as follows: Martin: 8.9, 14.2, 9.7, and 10.1; François: 18.6, 20.1, 17.9, and 19.7; and Julia: 18.2, 9.6, 11.7, and 12.5. Construct a plot appropriate to display the pattern of variation. Briefly describe what you see. What do you think are the possible causes of the variation?

1.25. At one step in the manufacture of an aluminum-silicon-magnesium alloy, strontium is added to control the growth of silicon particles. As the amount of strontium must be precisely controlled, the scales used to weigh it are tested eight times per day by weighing a known calibration weight. Figure 1.19 displays a histogram of last week's weighings. After seeing this, a process engineer stated: "This histogram shows that the measurement process was stationary last week." What is your response?

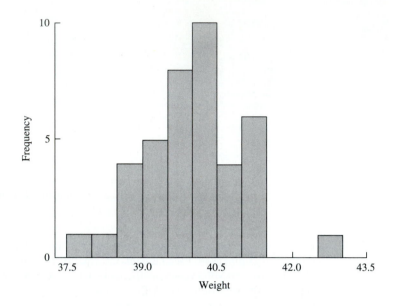

Figure 1.19   Forty consecutive measurements of a 40-gram weight.

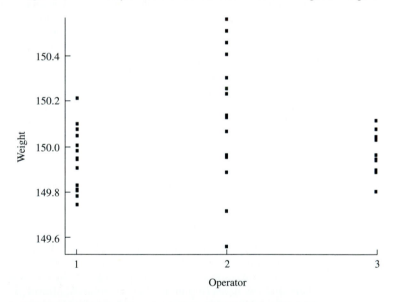

Figure 1.20   Weights for R&R study described in Exercise 1.26.

1.26. In order to analyze a weighing process, a Gage R&R study is conducted with one part
having a nominal weight of 150 gram, one scale, and three operators. The part is weighed
15 times by each operator.
(a) Explain what is meant by "R&R" in terms of this study.
(b) Figure 1.20 is a stratified plot of the resulting weights. Before conclusions can be drawn
from this plot, what aspect of the data should be checked? How can it be checked?

(c) Assuming a satisfactory outcome to the checking you described in (b), what do you conclude about the R&R of this process from Figure 1.20?

MINIPROJECT

Purpose

The purpose of this mini-project is to give you experience with the collection and analysis of data. In particular, the mini-project will give you an opportunity to assess the stationarity of the process you choose.

Process

Each group is to design and take measurements from some stationary process. The group is to demonstrate that the process is stationary using the tools developed in this chapter. Before taking the measurements, the group is to submit a short (less than one-page) proposal stating what it intends to measure, how it intends to measure it, and why it thinks the measurements will represent a stationary process. After receiving approval, the group is to take the measurements as described in the proposal.

Tools

In its project report, the group should demonstrate the stationarity or nonstationarity of the process. In the latter case, the report should tell why the process failed to be stationary as predicted. If appropriate, the causes of variation in the process should also be analyzed.

LAB 1.1: All Thumbs

Introduction

Think you're fast? Let's collect some data to find out! In this lab, you and your group will compete to see who's got the fastest reactions. Along the way, you'll hopefully learn something about how stationary your reaction times are under repeated use, and about how variable the times are both within and between individuals.

Objectives

To give you a practical understanding of stationarity and between and within sources of variation.

Lab Materials

Stopwatch

Experimental Procedure

Data Collection

1. Each group should have one stopwatch. Choose the first group member to test his or her reactions. That group member will obtain 20 reaction measurements quickly in succession.

2. To obtain one measurement:
   (a) Set the stopwatch to 0.
   (b) Click the start/stop button to start the time running.
   (c) Click the start/stop button as quickly as possible to stop the watch.
   (d) Record the elapsed time. (This should be done by another group member.)
   (e) Quickly zero out the watch and begin again.

3. Continue until 20 measurements have been taken.

4. Pass the watch to the next group member and continue until 20 measurements have been obtained for all group members.

5. As it is being taken, enter the data into a data-recording sheet. The sheet should have places for the sequence number, the time, and comments. You should make comments about any unusual occurrences, such as "Thumb slipped," that would help explain unusual times.[3]

6. When all data have been collected, enter them into the computer.

7. Your instructor will combine the data from all groups into a single data set and make it available to all students.

Analysis

Now comes the analysis. The analysis should proceed as follows.

1. First, clean up the data. By this we mean, decide what to do about any observations that don't belong. For instance, if an observation is larger than any other by a factor of 10, check to see if it has been recorded incorrectly (perhaps the decimal place is wrong?). If so, correct it. On the other hand, if a thumb slip results in a time that is larger than any other by a factor of 10, you have to decide what to do. Do you want to include thumb slips as real observations that occur in practice? Do you want to regard them as mistakes and treat them separately? Whatever you decide for your data, give your reasons.

2. Next, use an appropriate plot or plots to decide if the process that produced the data is stationary.

3. Use an appropriate plot or plots to decide if the principal source of variation is within the times for the various individuals or between different individuals.

4. Investigate anything else of interest.

5. Give your conclusions in your lab report.

LAB 1.2: Helicopter Drop

Introduction

In this, lab your group will obtain data by running experiments in which a helicopter is dropped.[4] The measurement you will record is how long it takes the helicopter to hit the floor.

---

[3] A sample data-recording sheet is displayed on page 31.

[4] We got the idea for this helicopter experiment from the 1993 paper "Quality Improvement—The New Industrial Revolution," by George Box, *International Statistical Review*, 61 (1993): 3–19. Box, in turn, credits Kip Rogers of Digital Equipment Corporation with giving him the idea.

Lab 1.2 Data Sheet

Student	Trial	Time	Comments
	1		
	2		
	3		
	4		
	5		
	6		
	7		
	8		
	9		
	10		
	11		
	12		
	13		
	14		
	15		
	16		
	17		
	18		
	19		
	20		

Objectives

To give you experience with

- gathering data
- analyzing data
- identifying causes of variation
- writing a lab report

Lab Materials

- Sheets of paper
- Ruler
- Scissors
- Stopwatch
- Paper clips (to weight the helicopter)

Experimental Procedure

After you have been assigned to a lab group, each member of your group will create a helicopter by cutting a sheet of paper in the pattern given in Figure 1.21.

One trial run of today's activity will consist of one group member dropping the helicopter from a specified height, a second group member timing its fall and a third group member recording the time and anything unusual that might have happened. Do a few trial runs, with each group member taking turns at each task until all group members are familiar with the process.

For each trial, one group member will release the helicopter and another will time its drop with a stopwatch, and a third will record the result on paper. Your group will perform one set of three trials with each possible combination of group members performing the different tasks. (So, if there are four in your group, you will do 12 sets of 3 trials each).

For each trial, you should record the set number, the name of the releaser and timer, the order of the trial in the set (1 to 3), and the time.[5]

When you have finished collecting the data, use the methods described in the chapter to analyze it. Specifically:

- Check the process for stationarity.
- Look for patterns of variation.

Finally, use brainstorming methods to create an Ishikawa diagram to help in identifying possible causes of variation in the helicopter manufacturing and dropping process. Write a short report detailing your results.

---

[5]A sample data-recording sheet is displayed on page 34.

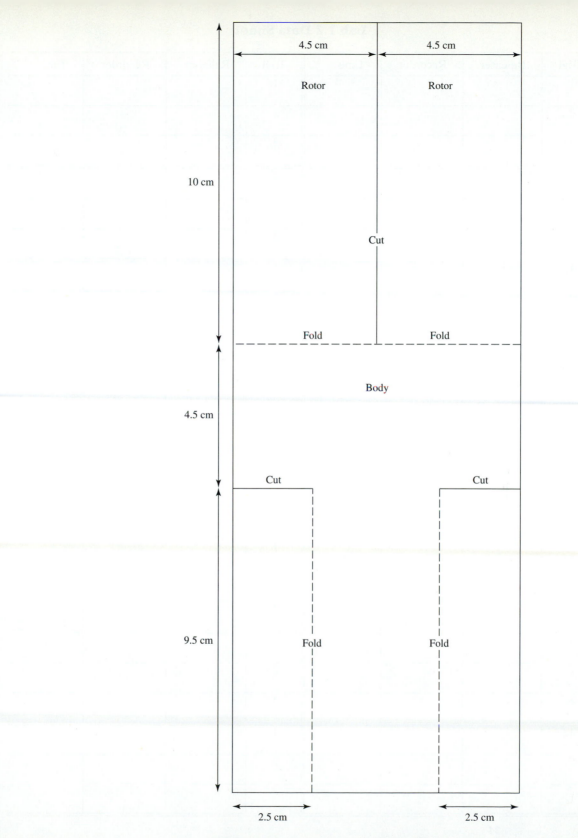

Figure 1.21 One pattern for making the helicopter.

Lab 1.2 Data Sheet

Trial	Releaser	Recorder	Time	Trial	Releaser	Recorder	Time
1.				1.			
2.				2.			
3.				3.			
1.				1.			
2.				2.			
3.				3.			
1.				1.			
2.				2.			
3.				3.			
1.				1.			
2.				2.			
3.				3.			
1.				1.			
2.				2.			
3.				3.			
1.				1.			
2.				2.			
3.				3.			
1.				1.			
2.				2.			
3.				3.			
1.				1.			
2.				2.			
3.				3.			

2

Summarizing Data

We look forward to the day when everyone will receive more than the average wage.

—Attributed to the Australian Minister of Labour, 1973

Lake Woebegone . . . where all the women are strong, all the men are good-looking, and all the children are above average.

—*Garrison Keillor,* A Prairie Home Companion

INTRODUCTION

Recall from Chapter 1 that data are facts that convey information. In order to enable us to extract the information from data, we need effective graphical and numerical tools to summarize that information, particularly when there are many data values. In this chapter, you will be introduced to a number of such tools. You will learn how to use them and how to interpret the results they give.

Knowledge and Skills

By successfully completing this chapter, you will acquire the following knowledge and skills:

KNOWLEDGE	SKILLS
1. Bar charts and histograms.	1. The ability to select and create appropriate graphical displays and numerical measures for summarizing a set of data.
	(continued)

35

KNOWLEDGE	SKILLS
2. Several common distributional shapes and what circumstances might generate data having each of those shapes. **3.** Summary measures of location: mean, median, mode, quantiles, and percentiles. **4.** Summary measures of spread: mean absolute deviation, standard deviation, and interquartile range. **5.** Resistant measures.	**2.** Identification and disposition of outliers.

KEY POINT

For data taken over time, it is imperative that you check the stationarity of the process that produced the data before using the techniques discussed in this chapter. The reason is that the methods you will learn here seek to summarize a single, constant pattern of variation. Although the methods studied here can be used with nonstationary data, if the pattern of variation is changing as more data are taken, these methods may give misleading results.

The best and fastest check of stationarity is **a plot of the data versus time order.** For data taken over time, such a plot should always be done before using the measures discussed in this chapter.

2.1

VARIABLES AND DATA

By its nature, the science of statistics deals with data, which are facts that convey information. These facts result from measuring, counting, or observing. **Variable** is the name we give to *what* is being measured, counted, or observed.

> **DEFINITION**
>
> **Variable** is the name given to what is being measured, counted, or observed when data are collected.

For example, height, weight, gender, and religious preference are all variables.

TABLE 2.1   Age, Gender, Height, and Armspan of 10 High School Students

Student	Age	Gender	Height	Armspan
Bill H.	17	M	178.5	183.5
Ron Y.	18	M	177.0	171.0
Jayson W.	18	M	185.5	194.0
Brian C.	18	M	179.0	181.0
Rich C.	17	M	172.0	181.0
Rachel V.	15	F	167.5	171.5
Barbara A.	17	F	174.5	174.5
Sherry C.	17	F	161.0	155.0
Chris P.	17	F	165.0	164.5
Alicia Z.	16	F	166.0	161.0

In conducting any study, we need to decide exactly how measurements, counts, or observations for each variable are to be taken, and we need to actually take those measurements, counts, or observations. How to best do so is a question of great importance, which we will address in Chapter 3. In the present chapter, we will assume that the data have already been obtained in an appropriate manner.

EXAMPLE 2.1   VARIABLES, OBSERVATIONS, AND DATA

Table 2.1 displays a data set consisting of the age in years, gender, height and armspan in centimeters of 10 students at a Massachusetts high school.

The variables in this data set are Age, Gender, Height, and Armspan. The data values are the numbers, such as 17 for Age, 178.5 for Height, and 161.0 for Armspan, or the letters M and F for Gender. The student names serve as an identifier.

Each row in Table 2.1 is one observation and consists of all data for one student. Thus, we see that Sherry C. is a 17-year-old female who is 161.0 cm tall and who has an armspan of 155.0 cm.   ✦

Variable Types

Two different ways of classifying variables are of interest to us. The first distinguishes between **quantitative** and **categorical** variables.

> DEFINITION
>
> - A variable is **quantitative** if it results from a physical measurement or a count.
> - A variable is **categorical** if it defines categories.

EXAMPLE 2.1   CONTINUED

The variables age, height and armspan in Table 2.1 are quantative. The variable Gender is categorical. ✦

Sometimes, as for the variable Gender in Table 2.1, the categories associated with a categorical variable occur naturally. Sometimes they are derived from a quantitative variable. As an example, consider again the data displayed in Table 2.1. Define a new categorical variable, Tallness, that takes the value "short" if Height is less than 152.4, the value "average" if Height is less than 182.9 and greater than or equal to 152.4, and the value "tall" if Height is greater than or equal to 182.9. The categorical variable Tallness is derived from the quantitative variable Height.

Another way of classifying variables distinguishes between discrete and continuous variables. To understand the distinction, we must first define the notion of a **discrete set.**

> **DEFINITION**
>
> A set is **discrete** if each of the elements in the set can be assigned a unique counting number; that is, one of the integers $1, 2, 3, \ldots$.

What the definition says is that, at least in principle, a discrete set is one whose elements we can list as the first, second, third, and so on, elements.

We will most often use two kinds of discrete sets:

- Any set with a finite number of elements.
- The integers $\{0, \pm 1, \pm 2, \ldots, \}$, or any subset of them, such as the positive integers.

Any interval of real numbers, such as all real numbers between 0 and 1, is not a discrete set.

> **DEFINITION**
>
> - A **discrete variable** is one that can take values only in a discrete set.
> - A **continuous variable** is one that can take any value in an interval.

EXAMPLE 2.1   CONTINUED

The variable Gender in Table 2.1 is discrete, because it takes values in the finite set $\{M, F\}$. The variable Age might be considered continuous, since, at least in principle, time varies continuously. However, the usual meaning of someone's age, and the meaning it has here, is a count of the number of whole years completed on this earth. In this context, it is discrete, as are all counts, which by definition take values among the counting numbers. The variables Height and Armspan in Table 2.1 are considered continuous, the idea being that, at least in theory, they can take any values in some interval, say, from 137 to 214 cm. ✦

Of course, in reality, the notion of a continuous variable is only an abstraction, since we can only measure with finite accuracy. Even if we can measure to a billion decimal places, the number of possible values a variable can take is finite. However, the abstraction is one that is very useful in simplifying how we view the world. Consider how complicated a variable like Height would be if we regarded it as a discrete variable that we could measure to an accuracy of 0.001 cm. Then to measure human heights ranging from 137 to 214 cm would require us to keep track of 77,000 distinct values. How much simpler it is to assume that Height can take any value between 137 and 214!

2.2

DISPLAYING DATA DISTRIBUTIONS

It has often been said that a picture is worth a thousand words, and nowhere is the truth of this saying more evident than in data analysis. A graph is the fastest and most effective way of grasping the features of a data distribution.[1] Two of the graphs most widely used in displaying data distributions are the bar chart and its close relative, the frequency histogram.

Displaying Categorical Data

A **bar chart** forms a visual summary of the data distribution of data obtained from a categorical variable. Bar charts are constructed as follows.

CONSTRUCTING A BAR CHART

1. Count the frequency of data in each category.
2. List the categories equally spaced on the horizontal axis.
3. Draw a bar above each category. The height of the bar is equal to the frequency of data in the category.

EXAMPLE 2.2   BAR CHART

Figure 2.1 is a bar chart of the numbers of students enrolled in the various engineering majors at a private engineering college in the fall of 1994.

The majors are the categories. The height of a bar for a given major is proportional to the number of students enrolled in that major. The actual bar frequencies are, from left to right, 244, 360, 462, 18, 35, and 736. ✦

---

[1] Recall from Chapter 1 that a data distribution is a list of each data value and its frequency.

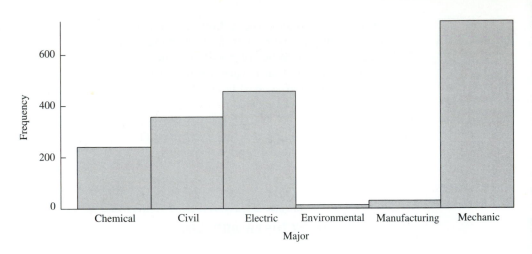

Figure 2.1 Bar chart of numbers of students enrolled in the various engineering majors at a private engineering college in the fall of 1994.

Displaying Quantitative Data

A close relative of the bar chart, called a **frequency histogram,** can be used to summarize quantitative data. In order to generate a frequency histogram, some initial decisions must be made. If the variable to be plotted is discrete, and if it has a small number of possible values, then steps 1 and 3 in the method for generating a bar chart may be followed, with the distinct data values serving as categories. Step 2 should be changed, however, so that each bar is located on a number line over the value it represents. An example of a frequency histogram that results from discrete quantitative data taking few values is found in Figure 2.2, which shows the numbers of children of the 22 faculty in a Mathematical Sciences Department at a private engineering college in the spring of 1996. From this frequency histogram, we can see that the numbers of faculty having 0, 1, 2, 3, 4, 5, and 6 children are 5, 4, 8, 1, 3, 0, and 1, respectively.

    If the variable to be plotted is continuous, or if it is discrete with a large number of possible values, the data have to be grouped before a frequency histogram can be constructed. The following are the steps involved:

CONSTRUCTING A FREQUENCY HISTOGRAM

1. Determine b, the number of bars to be plotted.
2. Find the smallest data value, y_{low} and the largest data value y_{high}.
3. Divide the interval (y_{low}, y_{high}) into b subintervals, each of length $(y_{high} - y_{low})/b$.
4. Determine whether data values at subinterval boundaries go into the lower or upper subinterval. This can be done either way, as long as you are consistent.
5. Count the frequency of data in each subinterval.
6. On a number line, draw a bar above each subinterval. The height of the bar is equal to the frequency of data in the subinterval.

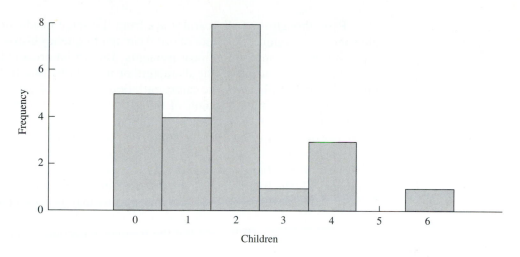

Figure 2.2   Frequency histogram of numbers of children of faculty in a Mathematical Sciences Department at a private engineering college in the spring of 1996.

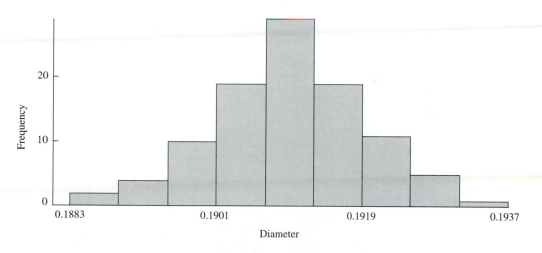

Figure 2.3   Frequency histogram of the diameters (in cm) of 100 ball bearings.

The form of the data distribution displayed by a frequency histogram— its shape, where it is located on a number line, how far it is spread out—can tell a great deal about the process that generated the data.

EXAMPLE 2.3   FREQUENCY HISTOGRAM

The diameters of 100 ball bearings sampled from the same production process are summarized in the frequency histogram in Figure 2.3.

Prior to deciding on using a histogram to display the data, the diameters were plotted versus the order in which they were obtained. The resulting plot revealed no evidence that the process was nonstationary, so the histogram is a good summary of the data distribution.

Even though the ball bearings are from the same production process and have the same nominal diameter of 0.190 cm, the frequency histogram shows that there is variation among the measurements. This variation could be due to the procedure used to measure the diameters or it could be due to the production process itself, but whatever the cause, variation is typical of data.

In Figure 2.3, the endpoints of the subintervals are 0.1883, 0.1889, 0.1895, . . . , 0.1931, and 0.1937. The height of the bar over a subinterval represents the frequency of observations in that subinterval. Thus, two of the 100 diameter measurements lie between 0.1883 and 0.1889, four lie between 0.1889 and 0.1895, and so on. The subinterval (0.1907, 0.1913) contains the highest frequency of diameters, 29. The frequencies in the other subintervals decline as we move away from (0.1907, 0.1913), and they do so at approximately an equal rate in either direction. It is clear that the subinterval (0.1907, 0.1913) represents the center of the data distribution. The spread of the frequency histogram can be represented by the extremes of the subintervals, which range from 0.1883 to 0.1937, a spread of 0.0054. However, approximately 70 of the 100 data values lie in the center three subintervals, spanning values 0.1901 to 0.1919. ◆

Analyzing Data Distributions Using Frequency Histograms

As experience is the best way to learn to analyze data distributions, we present a number of examples.

EXAMPLE 2.4   ANALYZING A FREQUENCY HISTOGRAM

Figure 2.4 is a frequency histogram consisting of yearly salaries of 250 technical support workers employed full time by a large software manufacturer. Its appearance is very different from the frequency histogram in Figure 2.3. What are the main features of the data represented by this frequency histogram?

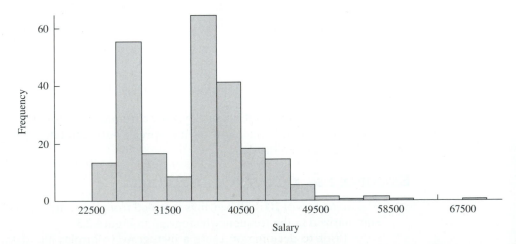

Figure 2.4   Frequency histogram of the salaries of 250 technical support workers.

The most striking feature is the presence of two "peaks" separated by a "valley." The peaks occur over the subintervals (25500, 28500), where 56 of the 250 salaries lie, and (34500, 37500), where 65 of the 250 salaries lie. The valley is over the subinterval (31500, 34500), where 9 salaries lie.

Because of the two peaks, it makes no sense to look for a single center of the distribution, such as we found for the ball bearing measurements. Rather, there are two centers here. Similarly, each peak has its own spread of data, so looking for a single measure of spread is not reasonable for these data. ✦

We'll need some additional terminology for dealing with data distributions displayed in frequency histograms.

> **DEFINITION**
>
> - A **modal bar** on a frequency histogram is a bar with height greater than or equal to the bar(s) adjacent to it.
> - A frequency histogram with a single modal bar is called **unimodal.**
> - A frequency histogram with more than one modal bar is called **multimodal.** A multimodal frequency histogram with exactly two modal bars is called **bimodal.**

EXAMPLES 2.3 AND 2.4   CONTINUED

The frequency histogram for the ball bearing data in Figure 2.3 is unimodal.

Technically, according to the preceding definition, the histogram for the salary data in Figure 2.4 has four modal bars: at the intervals (25500, 28500), (34500, 37500), (55500, 58500), and (67500, 70500). However, the latter two modal bars are inconsequential, and therefore this frequency histogram is considered bimodal. ✦

At this point, you are probably asking yourself how we know those two small modal bars in the frequency histogram in Figure 2.4 are inconsequential, and, more importantly, how you are supposed to know it. Knowing such things is really part of what's called the art, as opposed to the science, of data analysis, and there are two answers we can give to the question. First, it's a judgment call that is based on common sense. For the Figure 2.4 frequency histogram, ask yourself if these two small modal bars represent main features of the data. We think you'll agree that they don't. Second, with experience, you'll get better at making judgment calls like this. To help you along, we'll give you a number of examples and a set of guidelines to help you develop your data analysis skills. In fact, here's one of those examples now.

EXAMPLE 2.4   CONTINUED

Figure 2.5 displays two frequency histograms. We think you'll agree that they show quite different patterns. The interesting thing is that both are histograms of the same data set: the technical support worker salaries of Example 2.4.

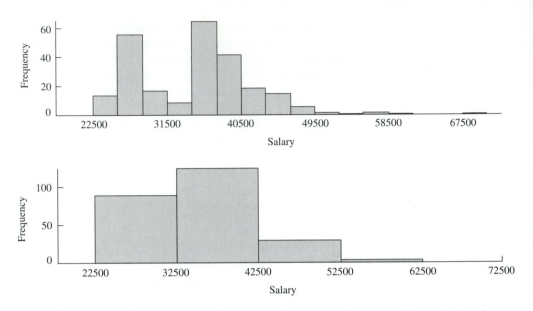

Figure 2.5 Two frequency histograms of the same data set of the salaries of 250 technical support workers.

The top frequency histogram is the same one shown in Figure 2.4. The bottom frequency histogram was created from the same set of data by using a different set of subintervals. Looking at the bottom frequency histogram, you would never know that it was created from the same set of data. The bimodality that is the main feature of the top frequency histogram is gone in the bottom frequency histogram. ✦

What are we to make of this? We can think of two points that should be considered.

• **Don't believe everything you see.** *"In God we trust; all others must bring their data,"* is an old saying of statisticians. It should be a saying of yours, too. Data summaries can mislead. Sometimes misleading data summaries result from well-meaning analysts with too little skill or experience. Too often, the unscrupulous use data analysis methods to deliberately mislead. In either case, you should be wary of any data summaries unless you have examined the data yourself.

• **How can we know which display is the right one?** Most often you can't know just by looking at the display. You have to obtain some familiarity with the data, and particularly with the process that generated them. It is difficult to have that familiarity if you are using the display to help you ask the right questions about a poorly understood process. However, you can try several different displays to give you insight into the process.

The frequency histograms displayed in Figure 2.5 were generated using SAS/INSIGHT. This program is one of a number of statistical programs that allow

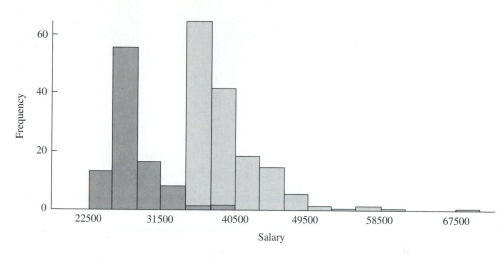

Figure 2.6   Frequency histogram of the salaries of 250 technical support workers. The darkened part of a bar indicates the frequency of female workers in the corresponding interval.

users to change the widths and locations of subintervals in a frequency histogram at the computer screen by moving the mouse. By doing so, we got an idea of what kinds of features different frequency histograms for this data set would have. The top frequency histogram in Figure 2.5 is the default frequency histogram displayed by SAS/INSIGHT, and most frequency histograms we created for these data showed the same bimodal structure. The bottom histogram is not typical of the frequency histograms we produced.

Users who don't have a statistics program with on-screen graph-modification capabilities can, and should, produce several different frequency histograms with different sets of subintervals in order to get an idea of possible features in the data.

Having identified a set of possible features from a set of data, the analyst can return to the investigation of the process that produced the data with the aim of finding out what process features produced the observed data features.

EXAMPLE 2.4   CONTINUED

We have identified possible bimodality in the salary data. Bimodality indicates the presence of two subgroups in the data, which differ with respect to the variable being summarized. After further investigation, we find large gender differences in salary. Figure 2.6 is a reproduction of Figure 2.4 in which the darkened part of a bar indicates the frequency of female workers in the corresponding interval.

From this frequency histogram, we see that data around the lower modal bar are largely composed of females, whereas the data around the upper modal bar are largely composed of males.   ✦

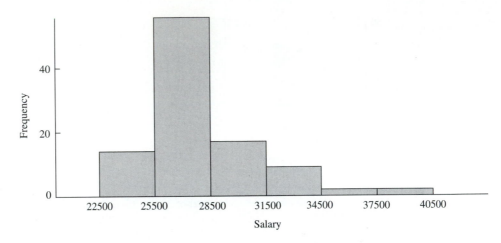

Figure 2.7 Frequency histogram of salaries of female technical support workers.

What we have found from the salary data are typical of multimodal data: The data around the different modal bars represent different subgroups. If the observations belonging to each subgroup can be identified, as they can for the salary data, the features of the data distributions can be summarized for each subgroup separately, and they can then be compared with each other. If the observations belonging to each subgroup cannot be identified, the features of the data around the different modal bars, such as where they are centered and how spread out they are, should be described to the extent possible.

EXAMPLES 2.3 AND 2.4   CONTINUED

Let's look more closely at the salary data for females. Figure 2.7 is a frequency histogram of these data. The frequency histogram in Figure 2.7 is unimodal. Apart from the unimodality, the most noticeable feature of the frequency histogram is that the bars extend farther to the right than to the left of the modal bar. Compare the shape of this frequency histogram with the shape of the frequency histogram of ball bearing diameters in Figure 2.3. The frequency histogram in Figure 2.3 is also unimodal, but the bars extend equally to the left and right of the modal bar. In addition, the shape of the histogram looks nearly like a mirror image about the modal bar.   ✦

DEFINITION

A frequency histogram is

- **Symmetric** if the bars to the left of some point are mirror images of those to the right of the same point.
- **Skewed** if it is not symmetric.

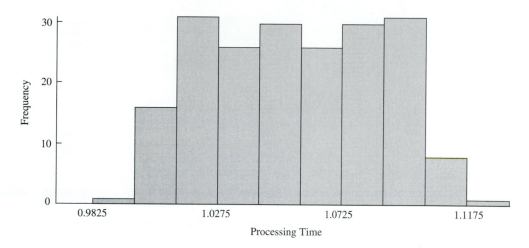

Figure 2.8   Frequency histogram of processing times for 20 computer chip clones from each of 10 manufacturers.

A unimodal frequency histogram is **skewed right** if the bars of positive height extend farther to the right of the modal bar than to the left. It is **skewed left** if the reverse is true.

EXAMPLES 2.3 AND 2.4   CONTINUED

Look again at Figure 2.3. Since there is approximate mirror symmetry about the center of the modal bar, this frequency histogram is approximately symmetric. Because data are so variable, it is rare to find a frequency histogram that is exactly symmetric.

Figure 2.7 shows a much different pattern. The four bars to the right of the modal bar extend four times as far as the single bar to its left. This frequency histogram is very clearly skewed right.   ◆

Not all approximately symmetric frequency histograms look like the one shown in Figure 2.3. The next example considers an approximately symmetric frequency histogram pattern that occurs commonly and is known as a **short-tailed frequency histogram.**

EXAMPLE 2.5   A SHORT-TAILED FREQUENCY HISTOGRAM

In an effort to evaluate the performance of computer chip clones, testers ran an identical test program on chips from 10 manufacturers. The chips were tested on the same apparatus in random order. Twenty chips of the same type from each manufacturer were tested, yielding 200 times in all. Figure 2.8 is a frequency histogram of the resulting times, in seconds. The frequency histogram of the processing times is approximately symmetric about the value 1.0575 seconds, but the frequencies in the intervals do not fall off until near the upper

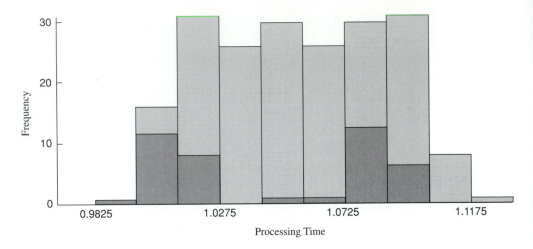

Figure 2.9 Frequency histogram of processing times for 20 computer chip clones from each of 10 manufacturers, with data for two manufacturers highlighted.

and lower intervals. The frequencies are, in fact, fairly constant over the range 1.0125 to 1.1025 seconds. This rapid drop-off at the extremes is what is meant by "short-tailed."   ✦

The frequency histogram pattern displayed in Figure 2.8 is characterized by bars of near-constant height over the central part of the distribution and a quick drop-off at the ends. This pattern is typical of data obtained from several process streams. In the computer chip data, the process streams are the 10 manufacturers. Figure 2.9 gives an idea of what is happening here. The frequency histogram is the same as that in Figure 2.8, but the shaded-in portion on the left corresponds to the 20 times from one manufacturer's chips and the shaded-in portion on the right corresponds to the 20 times from a different manufacturer's chips. When data from 10 of these smaller frequency histograms are combined, the result is the characteristic shape of the large frequency histogram.

Each data distribution displayed in a frequency histogram is unique and will present the perceptive analyst with new features to interpret. There are, however, features of frequency histograms that occur frequently and that have proven important for analyzing frequency histograms. Here are some guidelines to use in analyzing any frequency histogram.

GUIDELINES FOR ANALYZING FREQUENCY HISTOGRAMS

You will want to summarize what you see in a frequency histogram. To do this, begin with the overall shape of the frequency histogram. Among the questions you will want to ask are

- Does the frequency histogram have a single modal bar or more than one modal bar? If there are modal bars, where are they located?
- Is the frequency histogram symmetric? If it is not symmetric, in what way is it skewed?
- Does it make sense to speak of a center of the histogram? If so, where is that center? If not, how can you describe where the data are located?
- How would you describe the spread of the frequency histogram? That is, how widely scattered are the data values?
- Are there deviations from the overall pattern of the frequency histogram, such as gaps in the range of values or values lying well away from the rest of the data?

Finally, here is one technique we have found useful in describing any statistical graph. Pretend you are the representative of a company competing for a large contract. Whether you land the contract depends on how accurately you can describe the graph to the president of the company awarding the contract. The catch is that you are doing this in a long-distance phone call and the president is a busy person who cannot see the graph. The accuracy and conciseness required in this scenario are exactly what you want in all your descriptions of statistical graphs.

What Kinds of Data Might Have These Distributional Shapes?

In the preceding examples of frequency histograms, we have seen a number of shapes associated with data from different sources. Based on experience, we can make some generalizations about what kinds of data might produce certain kinds of histogram shapes.

SOURCES OF COMMON FREQUENCY HISTOGRAM SHAPES

- Symmetric unimodal histograms are often the result of measurements in which there are a number of small measurement errors introduced. An example is repeated measurements on the same weight using a very sensitive scale. The measurement errors could result from differences in temperature, humidity, and so forth. Measurements taken on large homogeneous populations also often show this kind of distribution. Examples are test scores (IQ, SAT, etc.), weights and heights of men (or women), and so forth.
- Right skewness often results from data that have a definite lower bound but no upper bound. Salaries, house prices, failure times of manufactured parts are some examples. Another source of such data are measurements of the physical limits, such as the breaking strength, of a material.

There are also data that are skewed left. These often result from looking at the reverse measure of data that are skewed right. For example, instead of looking at the ages of living adults, we might look at the ages at death.

Either right or left skewness can be the result of the mixture of several process streams.

- Short-tailed histograms occur commonly in industry as a result of inspection or mixing together several different process streams. Example 2.5 illustrates this type of data.

- Data that are multimodal result from taking measurements from nonhomogeneous subgroups. Examples might be diameters of washers produced by two machines, one of which is set incorrectly; or heights of a mixed group of males and females.

2.3

SUMMARY MEASURES FOR QUANTITATIVE DATA

Although an appropriate graph conveys a great deal of information about the data distribution of a quantitative variable, there are times when numerical summaries of the data are desirable as well. Numerical summaries characterize the distribution by quantifying some of its main features. Two of the features talked about in the last section, for example, are the center and spread of the distribution.

In the following discussion of summary measures, assume the data consist of the n observations $y_1, y_2, \ldots, y_n$.

Measures of Location

Measures of location attempt to describe the "center" of a distribution. You may think of this as a "typical" value for the data. The most common of these are the mean, the median, and the mode.

The Mean

The mean of a set of numbers is perhaps better known to you as the average of that set of numbers.

> **DEFINITION**
>
> The **mean** is the sum of the observations divided by the number of observations.

FORMULA FOR THE MEAN

The mean is denoted $\bar{y}$ and is computed as follows

$$\bar{y} = \frac{1}{n}(y_1 + y_2 + \ldots + y_n) = \frac{1}{n}\sum_{i=1}^{n} y_i$$

There is an interesting physical interpretation of the mean. Picture a frequency histogram of the data and imagine that the bars are made of a uniform material and that their bases are resting on a see-saw so that the leftmost point of the histogram rests at one end of the see-saw and the rightmost point of the histogram at the other. Then $\bar{y}$ is the unique location for the fulcrum of the see-saw if the see-saw is to be exactly balanced.

The Median

DEFINITION

A **median** Q_2 is a "halfway point" of the distribution in the sense that the same number of observations is greater than or equal to Q_2 as is less than or equal to it.

The definition does not uniquely define Q_2, however. To see why, consider the data set consisting of the four observations 1.1, 1.5, 6.2, and 7.3. The value 5 is a median of these data, since the same number of observations (2) is less than or equal to 5 as is greater than or equal to 5. But the same is true of 2, 3.7, or 6. In fact, any number between 1.5 and 6.2 is a median of these data.

In order to avoid this kind of confusion, we will use the following formula for computing a median uniquely. This formula uniquely selects one from among all possible medians for a data set.

FORMULA FOR THE MEDIAN

How the median is computed depends on whether n is even or odd.

- Suppose n is odd so that $n = 2m + 1$ for some integer m. Now sort the data from smallest to largest and call $y_{(1)}$ the smallest value, $y_{(2)}$ the second smallest, and so on. Then $Q_2 = y_{(m+1)}$, the $(m + 1)^{st}$ smallest or "middle" observation.
- If n is even, there is no middle number, so Q_2 is taken to be the average of the middle two numbers. Mathematically, $n = 2m$ for some integer m, and the middle two data values are $y_{(m)}$ and $y_{(m+1)}$. So $Q_2 = (y_{(m)} + y_{(m+1)})/2$.

The median has its own physical interpretation. Consider a frequency histogram, and suppose you are to cut the histogram in half with a vertical line. The median is the place you cut so that the area of the left half equals the area of the right half.

The Mode

The concept of the mode is embodied in the definition of the modal bar in a frequency histogram. We will expand on this definition in order to identify a single value that we will call the mode of the data distribution. Our definition depends on the data analyst producing a frequency histogram that he or she feels accurately summarizes the data distribution.[2]

> **DEFINITION**
>
> Given a frequency histogram that accurately summarizes the distribution of a set of data,
>
> - If the frequency histogram is unimodal, the **mode** is the center point of the interval over which the modal bar lies.
> - If the frequency histogram is multimodal, the **modes** are the center points of the intervals over which the modal bars lie.

Some examples will illustrate the computation of these measures.

EXAMPLE 2.3   CONTINUED

Consider again the ball bearing data displayed in the frequency histogram in Figure 2.3. As we are satisfied that this frequency histogram accurately summarizes the data, we will use the modal bar to compute the mode. The modal bar is over the interval $(0.1907, 0.1913)$, so the mode is the center point of this interval, $(0.1907 + 0.1913)/2 = 0.1910$. The mean and median are 0.1910 and 0.1911, respectively. This close agreement among different measures of location is typical of data distributions represented by symmetric unimodal frequency histograms, and it indicates as well our certainty about what constitutes the "center" of such a distribution.   ✦

EXAMPLE 2.4   CONTINUED

Consider again the salary data exhibited in the frequency histogram in Figure 2.4. As we are satisfied that this frequency histogram accurately summarizes the data, we will use the two large modal bars to compute modes. The lower mode is computed as the center of the interval $(25500, 28500)$, which lies under the modal bar. This value is $(25500 + 28500)/2 = 27000$. A similar computation gives the second mode as 36000. The interpretation of these modes is that the most likely salaries in any of the salary intervals are around \$27000 and \$36000. Of course,

---

[2]In many texts and computer programs, the mode is defined as the value or values of the data that occur with greatest frequency. We find this definition to be of little use, and Exercise 2.29 tells why.

**TABLE 2.2   Measures of
Location for the Technical
Support Salary Data**

Measure	Females	Males
Mean	28058	39811
Median	27013	37882
Mode	27000	36000

since we know the lower mode refers to women's salaries and the upper to men's salaries, we can say that women's salaries are most likely to occur around $27000 and men's salaries are most likely to occur around $36000. The mode is also the value we would use for prediction. By this we mean that if a new female technical support worker joins the company, we would predict her salary to be $27000, and if a new male technical support worker joins the company, our prediction would be $36000.

The mean and median are not appropriate summaries for the entire set of data, because they do not take the bimodality into account. We can use them to summarize the men's and women's salaries separately, however. As we have seen, the frequency histograms for both the men's and women's salary data are unimodal and skewed right, which is typical of salary data. For such data, the mean tends to be pulled upward by the very large observations, and therefore is not an appropriate measure of location. The mode, as the value near which salaries are most likely to occur, and the median, as the value separating the lower from the upper half of the salaries, are better measures. For the female and male salary data, the values of all three measures are given in Table 2.2.

Notice how the relatively few large salaries draw the mean upward away from the median and the mode, which are affected very little by the large salaries. These differences indicate our uncertainty about what constitutes the center of such a distribution.   ✦

Generalized Measures of Location: Percentiles and Quantiles

The measures of location we have studied so far attempt to describe the center of a distribution. In particular, the median Q_2 attempts to find a midpoint of the data in the sense that the same number of observations is greater than or equal to Q_2 as is less than or equal to it. A good way to think of the median is the value at or below which lies half the data. The generalized measures of location considered next attempt to find values at or below which lie 1/3, 1/4, or any proportion p of the data.

Quartiles

The first quartile, Q_1, can be thought of as a point at or below which lies one-quarter of the observations. The third quartile, Q_3, is a point at or below which lies three-quarters of the data. The formal definition is a little more precise:

> **DEFINITION**
>
> - A **first quartile,** Q_1, is a number having the property that at least one-quarter of the observations are less than or equal to Q_1 and at least three-quarters of the observations are greater than or equal to Q_1.
> - A **third quartile,** Q_3, is a number having the property that at least three-quarters of the observations are less than or equal to Q_3 and at least one-quarter of the observations are greater than or equal to Q_3.

As was the case with the median, quartiles are not necessarily uniquely defined. In Section 2.7, we will give a computational formula that explicitly and uniquely calculates Q_1 and Q_3.

Percentiles and Quantiles

The idea of quartiles can be extended to include any proportion of the data, not just multiples of 0.25. For any number q between 0 and 1, the qth quantile of the data is a value at or below which lies a proportion q of the data. This same value is also known as the $100q$th percentile. So, for example, Q_1 is the 25th percentile and the 0.25th quantile.

> **DEFINITION**
>
> The **qth quantile** of a data distribution is a value at or below which a proportion at least q of the data lies and at or above which a proportion at least $1 - q$ of the data lies.
>
> The qth quantile is also known as the **100 qth percentile.**

As with quartiles, the preceding definition does not necessarily uniquely define the qth quantile. In Section 2.7, we will give a computational formula that explicitly and uniquely calculates the qth quantile.

Unlike the mean, quantiles are appropriate summaries for almost any data distribution. They can also be used to check the symmetry of a data distribution, as the following two examples illustrate.

EXAMPLE 2.3   CONTINUED

Table 2.3 shows selected quantiles for the ball bearing data. The values in the table tell us several things. First, we see that 50% of the data lies between 0.1905 and 0.1916 and 80% lies between 0.1897 and 0.1921. Also, the fact that the distance from Q_2 to Q_3, 0.0005, is nearly equal to the 0.0006 unit separating Q_1 and Q_2 indicates symmetry in the middle part of the distribution. The fact that the distance from the 0.10 quantile to Q_2, 0.0014, is considerably larger than the 0.0010 unit separating Q_2 and the 0.90 quantile shows evidence of some asymmetry in the more extreme regions of the data.   ◆

TABLE 2.3   Selected Quantiles for the Ball Bearing Data

q	qth Quantile
0.10	0.1897
0.25 (Q_1)	0.1905
0.50 (Q_2)	0.1911
0.75 (Q_3)	0.1916
0.90	0.1921

TABLE 2.4   Selected Quantiles for the Technical Support Salary Data

q	qth Quantile (Females)	qth Quantile (Males)
0.10	25410	35690
0.25 (Q_1)	25924	36292
0.50 (Q_2)	27013	37882
0.75 (Q_3)	29642	42019
0.90	32271	46016

EXAMPLE 2.4   CONTINUED

Table 2.4 shows selected quantiles for the technical support salary data. The table reveals a number of interesting features of these data. For example, the 0.90 quantile of female salaries is less than the 0.10 quantile of male salaries. This means that there is very little overlap in the salaries of the two groups. The right skewness of the distribution of female salaries is indicated by the value of $Q_3 - Q_2 = 2629$ being considerably larger than $Q_2 - Q_1 = 1089$, and especially by the value of the 0.90 quantile minus the median, 5258, being much greater than that of the median minus the 0.10 quantile, 1603.   ◆

A CAUTION ABOUT QUANTILES

It is an unfortunate fact that there is no general agreement among statisticians about the proper definition for quantiles. Further, different statistical computer packages use different definitions. A recent paper on the topic[a] compiled nine different definitions of quantiles and showed a wide disparity in the definitions used by a number of the most popular statistical computer packages.

Although for large data sets, the quantiles produced by all these definitions will be nearly the same, for small data sets, there could be substantial differences. All we can suggest is for you, the user, to be aware of the definition or definitions used by your software package.

[a] Rob J. Hyndman, and Yunan Fan, "Sample Quantiles in Statistical Packages," *The American Statistician*, 50 (4) (1996): 361–365.

Measures of Spread

As the terminology implies, measures of spread summarize how spread out a data distribution is. Some common measures of spread are the mean absolute deviation, the standard deviation, and the interquartile range.

The Mean Absolute Deviation

If you consider $\bar{y}$ to be the center of the distribution, and if you define "mean" appropriately, the MAD tells the mean distance of the observations, y_i, from the center of the distribution, $\bar{y}$. Here is its formula:

FORMULA FOR THE MEAN ABSOLUTE DEVIATION

The mean absolute deviation is computed as follows:

$$\text{MAD} = \frac{1}{n-1} \sum_{i=1}^{n} |y_i - \bar{y}|$$

The appropriate definition of "mean" for this interpretation is to divide by $n-1$ rather than by n. The rationale for using the divisor $n-1$ is that only $n-1$ of the n summands are free to vary. It is true that there are n observations, y_i, but we're not averaging the y_i. Rather, the data going into the MAD consist of the deviations $y_i - \bar{y}$, and, since $\sum_{i=1}^{n}(y_i - \bar{y}) = 0$, the values of any $n-1$ of the $y_i - \bar{y}$ determine the value of the nth one. We express this idea by saying that the n deviations $y_i - \bar{y}$ have $n-1$ **degrees of freedom.** You will encounter this concept repeatedly in statistics: that a mean is computed by dividing by its degrees of freedom, rather than the number of terms summed.

Because it is based on mean distance from $\bar{y}$, the mean absolute deviation is most appropriately used as a measure of spread when the mean is used as the measure of location.

The Standard Deviation and the Variance

Everyone who has taken the SAT, the ACT, or other aptitude or achievement tests has heard of the standard deviation. Here is its formula.

FORMULA FOR THE STANDARD DEVIATION AND VARIANCE

- The formula for the **variance** is

$$s^2 = \frac{1}{n-1} \sum_{i=1}^{n}(y_i - \bar{y})^2$$

- The formula for the **standard deviation** is

$$s = +\sqrt{s^2}$$

The variance is like the MAD except that the variance gives the mean **squared** distance of the data values, y_i, from the mean, $\bar{y}$. The variance has the disadvantage that its units are the squares of the original data units, making it difficult for use with the original data. The usual, though not entirely satisfactory, solution is to use the standard deviation, which is in the same units as the original data.[3]

As an aside to engineering students, what the formula for the standard deviation computes is the **root mean square** of the deviations $y_i - \bar{y}$: (**square** the deviations, then take the **mean,** then take the **root**).

Because it is based on mean squared distance from $\bar{y}$, the standard deviation is most appropriately used as a measure of spread when the mean is used as the measure of location.

The Interquartile Range (IQR)

The IQR is the difference between the third and first quartiles. That is,
$$\text{IQR} = Q_3 - Q_1$$
The IQR is the range or spread of the "middle" 50% of the data. Because it is based on quartiles, the IQR is the natural measure of spread when the median is used as the measure of location.

EXAMPLE 2.3   CONTINUED

Consider the ball bearing diameters displayed in the frequency histogram in Figure 2.3. Since the histogram is nearly symmetric, the location and meaning of the center of the distribution is clear and we use the mean to measure the location of that center. Because of the symmetry of the distribution, it also makes sense to talk about how far from the center the data values lie, on average. This argues for using the mean absolute deviation as a measure of spread. For historical reasons, however, and because the mean absolute deviation is not generally available in statistical computer programs, the measure that is generally used is the standard deviation. For the ball bearing data, the mean absolute deviation is 0.0008, which means that the average distance of a data value from the mean is 0.0008 cm. The standard deviation, which doesn't have such a nice interpretation, is 0.0009. ✦

EXAMPLE 2.4   CONTINUED

Consider the distribution of technical support workers' salaries displayed in Figure 2.6. Because of the bimodality of the distribution, no single measure of spread

---

[3] Why would anyone want to take the mean of the squared distance? We can't provide a really satisfactory response until you study statistical models in Chapter 4. However, it suffices to say that for data generated by a certain theoretical statistical model called the normal distribution model, taking the mean of the squared distance turns out to be the optimal method for measuring spread. For this reason, R. A. Fisher, the most renowned statistician of the first half of the twentieth century, was an advocate of the standard deviation as a measure of spread. Arthur Eddington, a British astronomer, was a vocal advocate of the MAD. The issue seemed settled when Fisher showed the optimality of the standard deviation for data from the normal distribution model. However, in recent years, interest has shifted toward measures that perform well both when the data are from the normal model and also when they are not. Since the MAD is often better than the standard deviation when the data are not from the normal model, Eddington's view may eventually prevail.

is adequate to summarize the spread of these data. Rather, it is best to analyze the spread of the male and female salaries separately. We will analyze the salaries of female workers illustrated in Figure 2.7. As these data are skewed right, it is not entirely clear what constitutes the "center" of these data. Even if we could agree on what the "center" means for these data, the skewness ensures that the data vary differently above and below that center. Thus, any measure of how far on average the data values lie from the "center" is of questionable value. As a result, the mean absolute deviation and the standard deviation are inappropriate measures of spread. A better measure is the interquartile range, which measures the spread of the middle half of the data. For these data, the first quartile, Q_1, is 25924 and the third quartile, Q_3, is 29642, so the interquartile range is IQR $= Q_3 - Q_1 = 29642 - 25924 = 3718$.   ✦

2.4

OUTLIERS

It may happen in analyzing data that a particular value is clearly different from the pattern of the rest of the data. Such a value is called an **outlier.**

> ### DEFINITION
>
> An **outlier** is an extremely unrepresentative data point.

The word "outlier" comes from the adjective "outlying," which our dictionary defines as "lying at a distance from a center or main body." In order to be an outlier, a data point must lie well away from the main body of the data, and it must be one of only a small number of such data points.

Outliers can result from such mundane causes as typing errors or machine malfunction. Or they can be just unusual, but real, data values. Great scientific discoveries tend to be outliers—if not always in data, then in scientific thought. Why? Because they're always what nobody expects! So it stands to reason, and it has been borne out by experience, that outliers can be a signal for a great scientific truth waiting to be discovered. This notion is captured perfectly in the following comment by an industrial statistician of our acquaintance: *"Whenever I find an outlier, I'm never sure whether to throw it away or patent it."*

For this reason outliers should not be discarded lightly. In fact, every effort should be made to identify the cause of each outlier. Once a cause has been found, an outlier may be discarded or replaced if appropriate: for example, a data value resulting from a typing error may be corrected if possible or omitted if not.

If a cause for an outlier cannot be found, a good strategy is to analyze the data both with and without the outlier. If the results are similar, then the outlier is having little effect. If the results are substantially different, then the presence of the outlier should be reported, and both analyses presented. Further, in order to decide which is the appropriate analysis, it may be necessary to make extra efforts to identify a cause for the outlier, or to obtain more data.

EXAMPLE 2.6   OUTLIERS

A weir box is a device used to measure water flow. Engineers at a paper mill were developing a protocol for calibrating an ultrasound device for measuring the water depth in a weir box. The ultrasound device measures depth by bouncing high-frequency sound waves off the surface of the water in the box. By timing the echo, a computer can measure the distance to the water surface, and, knowing the height of the ultrasound source, determine the depth of the water. In the calibration procedure, the level of water in the box was deliberately varied at set depths, and compared with the resulting depth as calculated by the ultrasound device. The data are in the data set ULTRACAL. Figure 2.10 is a histogram of the difference between depth measured by ultrasound and the actual depth for each of the 32 different depth measurements. Although most of the data values range between 0 and 0.04 feet, there are four observations in the 0.15-to-0.21-foot range, which are clear outliers.

Puzzled, the engineers searched for a cause for the outliers. The first thing they noticed was that the outliers corresponded to the four lowest actual water depths. This led them to investigate the calibration apparatus. As they performed more test runs over the range of water depths, one of the engineers noticed that at depths below 0.3 feet, the radiation pattern of the ultrasound device intersected

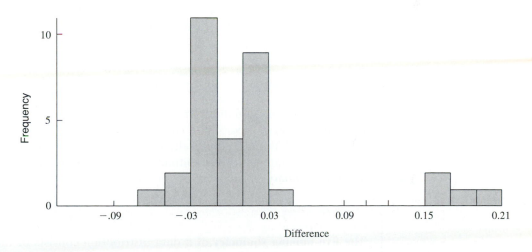

Figure 2.10 Frequency histogram of differences between water-depth measurements taken by an ultrasound measuring device and the actual water depth.

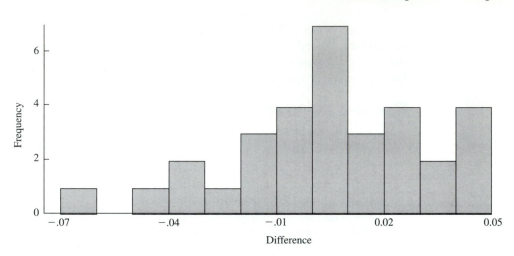

Figure 2.11 Frequency histogram of differences between water-depth measurements taken by an ultrasound measuring device and the actual water depth: second run, after repositioning ultrasound device.

the side wall of the weir. She reasoned that this disturbance of the radiation pattern produced spurious echoes that interfered with the returning signals, resulting in the observed outliers. To test her theory, the ultrasound device was repositioned so that its radiation pattern fell completely within the weir at all water depths, and a new set of data was obtained. Figure 2.11 is a histogram of the difference between depth measured by ultrasound and the actual depth for each of the 32 different depth measurements in the new data set. The histogram shows that the changed placement of the ultrasound device was successful in eliminating the faulty readings. ✦

Box-and-Whisker Plots

Outliers may be identified visually from frequency histograms, as we have just seen. However, there is a special type of plot called a **box-and-whisker plot,** or just **boxplot** for short, which, in addition to graphically displaying some of the main features of a data distribution, also automatically identifies possible outliers. The boxplot is based on the **five-number summary** of the data distribution.

> **DEFINITION**
>
> The **five-number summary** of a data distribution consists of the median, the first quartile, the third quartile, and two other numbers called **adjacent values.** The **lower adjacent value,** which we will denote A_-, is the smallest data value greater than $Q_1 - 1.5 \times \text{IQR}$. The **upper adjacent value,** which we will denote A_+, is the largest data value smaller than $Q_3 + 1.5 \times \text{IQR}$.

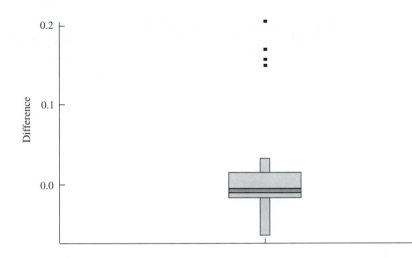

Figure 2.12   Boxplot of the differences between depth measured by ultrasound and the actual depth for each of the 32 different depth measurements in the first experiment in Example 2.6.

EXAMPLE 2.6   CONTINUED

Figure 2.12 shows a box-and-whisker plot of the differences between depth measured by ultrasound and the actual depth for each of the 32 different depth measurements in the first experiment in Example 2.6. We will use the five-number summary to construct this boxplot as follows.

- The five-number summary of the data is first obtained. The quartiles are $Q_1 = -0.0163$, $Q_2 = -0.0072$, and $Q_3 = 0.0159$. The interquartile range is IQR $= Q_3 - Q_1 = 0.0159 - (-0.0163) = 0.0322$. The lower adjacent value, A_- is the smallest data value greater than

$$Q_1 - 1.5 \times \text{IQR} = -0.0163 - 1.5 \times 0.0322 = -0.0646$$

It turns out that the smallest difference is -0.0630, which, since it is greater than -0.0646, equals A_-. The upper adjacent value A_+ is the largest data value smaller than

$$Q_3 + 1.5 \times \text{IQR} = 0.0159 + 1.5 \times 0.0322 = 0.0642$$

The five largest differences in the data set are 0.0339, 0.1508, 0.1577, 0.1712, and 0.2066, therefore, $A_+ = 0.0339$.

- The box is drawn next. The box is a rectangle, two sides of which are parallel to a number line and range from Q_1 to Q_3. In Figure 2.12, the number line and these sides of the box are vertical. A line perpendicular to and connecting these two sides is drawn at the median. In Figure 2.12, the median line is the dark horizontal line inside the box.

- Next, whiskers are constructed. The lower whisker is drawn parallel to the number line from A_- to the center of the lower side of the box. The upper whisker is drawn parallel to the number line from the center of the upper side of the box to A_+. In Figure 2.12, the lower whisker is the long thin rectangle below the box and the upper whisker is the small rectangle above the box.
- Finally, each data value outside the whiskers is drawn as a point along the axis defined by the whiskers. In the ultrasound data, the smallest difference is -0.0630, which is greater than A_-, so the lower whisker is drawn exactly to -0.0630 and no values lie below. There are four values above A_+, however: 0.1508, 0.1577, 0.1712, and 0.2066. These are plotted as single points above the upper whisker in Figure 2.12. Graphing data outside the adjacent values as individual points identifies them as possible outliers. ◆

Here is a summary of how to construct a box-and-whisker plot.

CONSTRUCTING A BOX-AND-WHISKER PLOT

- Obtain the five-number summary of the data: Q_1, Q_2, Q_3, the lower adjacent value A_-: the smallest data value greater than $Q_1 - 1.5 \times$ IQR, and the upper adjacent value A_+: the largest data value smaller than $Q_3 + 1.5 \times$ IQR.
- Draw the box, a rectangle with two sides parallel to a number line and ranging from Q_1 to Q_3. Draw a line at the median perpendicular to and connecting the two sides of the box that are parallel to the number line.
- Construct the whiskers. The lower whisker is drawn parallel to the number line from A_- to the center of the lower side of the box. The upper whisker is drawn parallel to the number line from the center of the upper side of the box to A_+.
- Draw in each data value outside the whiskers as a point along the axis defined by the whiskers.

The five-number summary is designed so that values representative of the data distribution lie within the adjacent values. In terms of the box-and-whisker plot, these values will lie between the ends of the whiskers. Observations beyond the whiskers in a box-and-whisker plot may be considered outliers, and should be checked.

EXAMPLE 2.6   CONTINUED

The observations represented by the dots above the upper whisker in Figure 2.12 are the outliers identified by the box-and-whisker plot. ◆

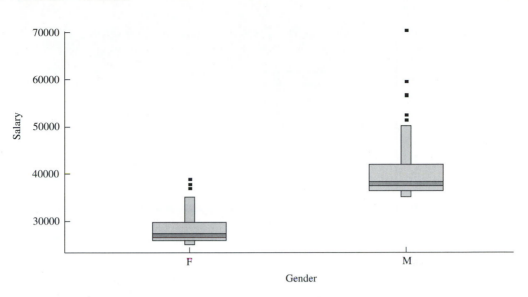

Figure 2.13   Side-by-side boxplots of the salaries of the technical support workers from Example 2.4, broken down by gender.

Side-by-Side Boxplots

Figure 2.13 displays a pair of box-and-whiskers plots of the salaries of the technical support workers from Example 2.4 broken down by gender. Such plots are called **side-by-side boxplots.** Side-by-side boxplots are valuable in comparing different sets of data. For the salary data, both boxplots show that the distributions of the salaries are skewed to the right, and reveal the disparity in the salary ranges for males and females. The greater length of the box for the male salaries indicates greater spread in the central values than is found in the female salaries.

Boxplots Can Hide Features, Too

Based as they are on only a five-number summary, boxplots can hide important data features. For example, consider Figure 2.14, which is a boxplot of the combined male and female technical support salary data.[4] The boxplot gives no indication of the bimodality that is the central feature of these data. In general, a boxplot cannot show multimodality, and so should always be used in conjunction with a display, such as a frequency histogram, that can show multimodality.

---

[4] Boxplots can be displayed either vertically, as in Figures 2.12 and 2.13, or horizontally, as in Figure 2.14.

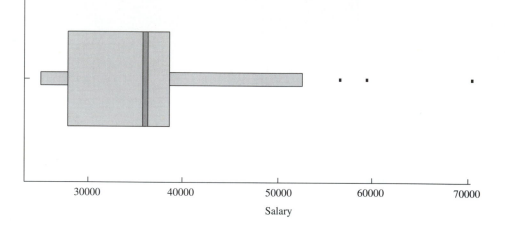

Figure 2.14   Boxplot of the salaries of the technical support workers from Example 2.4. A boxplot cannot show the bimodality of the distribution.

2.5

RESISTANCE OF SUMMARY MEASURES

The presence of outliers in many data sets raises a natural question: Can outliers alter the values of summary measures so that they no longer accurately reflect features of the main part of the data? If the answer is "yes," how do outliers affect the measures used to summarize a data distribution, and which measures will and which will not be greatly altered if one or more outliers are added to a data set?

> **DEFINITION**
>
> Summary measures that are not greatly changed by one or more outliers are said to be **resistant.** Summary measures that are greatly changed by one or more outliers are said to be **nonresistant.**

Let's examine some of the measures we've looked at so far in terms of their resistance.

EXAMPLE 2.7   RESISTANCE OF SUMMARY MEASURES

Ken Griffey Jr. is a very, very talented baseball player. He also earns a very, very nice salary, something in excess of $7,000,000 per year. Suppose Ken takes an off-season job as a technical support worker with the computer firm discussed in Example 2.4, and suppose his total income, including that from baseball, is included in that data set. By any measure, Ken's salary is an outlier in the resulting data set. How will his large salary alter the measures of location and spread we have discussed?

Table 2.5 compares several measures of location and spread for the salary data for males with and without Ken's $7,000,000 salary. For the computation

TABLE 2.5   Measures of Location and Spread Compared for the Male Technical Support Salary Data with and without Ken Griffey Jr.'s $7,000,000 Salary

Measure	Without Ken's salary	With Ken's salary
Mean	39773	84678
Median	38246	38249
Mode	36000	36000
Mean Absolute Deviation	3940	89809
Standard Deviation	5199	559083
Interquartile Range	6139	6089

of the mode, it is assumed that the frequency histogram summarizing the data without Ken's salary will be unaltered for all but the very extreme bar of height 1 representing Ken's salary.

From these results, we can see that the mean, mean absolute deviation, and standard deviation are not resistant and that the other measures are.   ✦

The results illustrated in Example 2.7 give a true picture of the resistance of these measures in general: The mean and standard deviation are nonresistant, whereas the median, mode, and interquartile range are.

To see why the mean is nonresistant, recall the discussion on page 51 of how the mean can be interpreted as the place where the frequency histogram balances. Putting a new data value far above the largest observation will move the balance point drastically upward. In Example 2.7, Ken's salary is so extreme that it moves the balance point from $39773 to $84678. If Ken made $70,000,000, the mean would move even more. The situation is much the same with the mean absolute deviation, which is a mean of a number of relatively small deviations and the one very large deviation belonging to Griffey. The standard deviation is even worse, because it is computed from the variance, which averages squares of the deviations. The square of the deviation associated with Ken Griffey Jr. is really large, much larger in relation to the squares of the other workers' salaries than his unsquared salary is to their unsquared salaries. Even taking the square root of the variance to obtain the standard deviation does not eliminate the effect of that large squared deviation.

On the other hand, the median is very resistant because it measures a value that separates the upper and lower halves of the data values. Adding a large value may move the median up slightly, but not beyond the data point immediately above it. In addition, it doesn't matter how large a value is added. If Ken makes $70,000,000 instead of $7,000,000, the median will change by the same amount. Since the median separates the lower and upper halves of the data, we would have to add as many large observations as there are original data values before the median would move upward beyond the original data. The quartiles are also resistant, but are less resistant than the median. For instance, if we had n original observations, we would have to add at least $n/3$ large observations before the third quartile would move upward beyond the original data.

TRIMMED AND WINSORIZED MEANS

As we have just seen, the median is one resistant measure of location. However, because the mean has better theoretical properties in certain common circumstances,[5] many people prefer to have a resistant location measure that acts like the mean when there are no outliers. Several such measures have been developed. Two of these are the **k-times trimmed mean** and **k-times Winsorized mean.**

The k-Times Trimmed Mean

The idea behind the k-times trimmed mean is simple: It is the central data values that really define the location of the data distribution, and the extreme values that cause trouble as outliers. To solve this problem, the trimmed mean omits the most extreme low or high values in the computation of the mean. Specifically, the k-times trimmed mean $\bar{y}_{tk}$ omits the k largest and k smallest observations and computes the mean of the rest.

FORMULA FOR THE k-TIMES TRIMMED MEAN

If $y_{(i)}$ denotes the ith smallest of the n observations, the k-times trimmed mean is computed by the formula

$$\bar{y}_{tk} = \frac{1}{n-2k} \sum_{i=k+1}^{n-k} y_{(i)}$$

Actually, you are probably already familiar with the concept of the trimmed mean. It is used in evaluating judges' scores in certain Olympic sporting events. Can you think which? Why do you think trimmed means are used in these sporting events? Can you think of other places you've seen the trimmed mean?

The k-Times Winsorized Mean

The k-times Winsorized mean, named after statistician Charles Winsor, is similar to the k-times trimmed mean. Recall that for the k-times trimmed mean, the k smallest data values $y_{(1)}, y_{(2)}, \ldots, y_{(k)}$, and the k largest data values $y_{(n-k+1)}, y_{(n-k+2)}, \ldots, y_{(n)}$, are omitted from the calculations. In computing the k-times Winsorized mean, the k smallest data values are all changed to the value $y_{(k+1)}$, the value of the $(k+1)$st smallest

---

[5]Recall from the discussion in an earlier footnote that the standard deviation is the optimal measure of spread when the data are generated by the normal distribution model. For this theoretical model, which you will study in Chapter 4, the mean is the optimal measure of location.

TABLE 2.6   Measures of Location Compared for the Male Technical Support Salary Data with and without Ken Griffey Jr.'s $7,000,000 Salary

Measure	Without Ken's salary	With Ken's salary
Mean	39773	84678
Median	38246	38249
Mode	36000	36000
1-Time Trimmed Mean	39728	39841
1-Time Winsorized Mean	39780	39892

observation, and the k largest data values are all changed to the value $y_{(n-k)}$, the value of $(k+1)$st largest observation. The remaining $n-2k$ data values are unaltered. The k-times Winsorized mean is computed by taking the average of the n resulting values, $2k$ of which were altered, and $n-2k$ of which were not.

FORMULA FOR THE k-TIMES WINSORIZED MEAN

In terms of the original ordered observations, the k-times Winsorized mean is given by the formula

$$\bar{y}_{wk} = \frac{1}{n}\left[(k+1)y_{(k+1)} + \sum_{i=k+2}^{n-k-1} y_{(i)} + (k+1)y_{(n-k)}\right]$$

EXAMPLE 2.7   CONTINUED

Table 2.6 compares the performance of the 1-time trimmed and Winsorized means with other measures of location for the salary data for males with and without Ken Griffey Jr.'s $7,000,000 salary. From the table, we can see that both the trimmed and Winsorized means take values close to the mean when Griffey's salary is not included in the data, and are quite resistant to the addition of Griffey's salary. ✦

2.7

THE CALCULATION AND USE OF SUMMARY MEASURES: AN EXTENDED ILLUSTRATION

Although computers have largely taken over the task of calculating summary measures in modern data analysis, seeing detailed computations for a small data set can help clarify what the computer is doing. In this section, we show the calculations for a small data set in detail, and then use those measures to analyze the data.

Calculation of Measures

Consider the following data:

Planet	Equatorial Diameter (km)
Mercury	4,880
Venus	12,100
Earth	12,756
Mars	6,794
Jupiter	142,800
Saturn	120,660
Uranus	51,810
Neptune	49,528
Pluto	2,290

Calculating the Mean

The mean of the planetary diameters is

$$\bar{y} = (4{,}880 + 12{,}100 + \cdots + 49{,}528 + 2{,}290)/9 = 44{,}846 \text{ km}$$

Calculating the Median and Quartiles

Sorting the diameters from smallest to largest, we have

$y_{(1)}$	2,290
$y_{(2)}$	4,880
$y_{(3)}$	6,794
$y_{(4)}$	12,100
$y_{(5)}$	12,756
$y_{(6)}$	49,528
$y_{(7)}$	51,810
$y_{(8)}$	120,660
$y_{(9)}$	142,800

In the terminology used on page 51 to describe the calculation of the median, $n = 9 = 2m + 1$, where $m = 4$. Since n is odd, the median is

$$Q_2 = y_{(m+1)} = y_{(5)} = 12{,}756$$

To illustrate the computation of the median for even n, consider only the four gaseous planets, Jupiter, Saturn, Uranus, and Neptune. Their sorted values are

$y_{(1)}$	49,528
$y_{(2)}$	51,810
$y_{(3)}$	120,660
$y_{(4)}$	142,800

Here $n = 4 = 2m$, where $m = 2$. Since n is even, the median is

$$Q_2 = (y_{(m)} + y_{(m+1)})/2 = (y_{(2)} + y_{(3)})/2 = (51,810 + 120,660)/2 = 86,235$$

We have already seen how to calculate $\bar{y}$ and Q_2. We'll now illustrate the calculation of Q_1, Q_3, IQR, MAD, and s^2 using the planetary data.

Calculating Measures of Spread

The following are the quantities needed for mean absolute deviation and the standard deviation.

Planet	Diameter	$\lvert y_i - \bar{y} \rvert$	$(y_i - \bar{y})^2$
Mercury	4,880	39,966	1.60×10^9
Venus	12,100	32,746	1.07×10^9
Earth	12,756	32,090	1.03×10^9
Mars	6,794	38,052	1.45×10^9
Jupiter	142,800	94,954	9.59×10^9
Saturn	120,660	75,814	5.75×10^9
Uranus	51,810	6,964	4.85×10^7
Neptune	49,528	4,682	2.19×10^7
Pluto	2,290	42,556	1.81×10^9
Sum		367,824	22.37×10^9

Based on these numbers,

$$\text{MAD} = 367,824/8 = 45,978$$

$$s^2 = (22.37 \times 10^9)/8 = 2.80 \times 10^9$$

and

$$s = \sqrt{s^2} = \sqrt{2.80 \times 10^9} = 52,881$$

To compute the quartiles, recall that Q_1 is the median of the observations smaller than or equal to $Q_2 = 12,756$. That is, Q_1 is the median of the values 2,290; 4,880; 6,794; 12,100; and 12,756. Thus, $Q_1 = 6,794$. Similarly, Q_3 is the median of the observations greater than or equal to Q_2. It is left to you to show that $Q_3 = 51,810$. From this, it follows that

$$\text{IQR} = Q_3 - Q_1 = 51,810 - 6,794 = 45,016$$

Calculating Quantiles

To calculate the qth quantile, proceed as follows:

1. Order the observations $y_{(1)} \leq y_{(2)} \leq \cdots \leq y_{(n)}$.
2. There are four possible cases:
   (a) $q = 1$. In this case, the qth quantile is $y_{(n)}$, the largest observation.
   (b) $q = 0$. In this case, the qth quantile is $y_{(1)}$, the smallest observation.

(c) $q = k/n$ for some integer $1 \leq k < n$. In this case, the qth quantile is $(y_{(k)} + y_{(k+1)})/2$.

(d) There is an integer m for which $m/n < q < (m+1)/n$. In this case, the qth quantile is $y_{(m+1)}$.

For the planetary data, we will calculate the 0.5 quantile (which is Q_2), the 0.25 quantile (which is Q_1), and the $1/3 (= 0.\overline{333})$ quantile (or, if you prefer, the 50th, 25th, and 33.$\overline{3}$rd percentiles) using the preceding rule.

In step 1, we order the planet diameters:

$$2{,}290 < 4{,}880 < 6{,}794 < 12{,}100 < 12{,}756 < 49{,}528 < 51{,}810 < 120{,}660 < 142{,}800$$

- Since $4/9 < 0.5 < 5/9$, we use step 2(d) to compute the 0.5 quantile as $y_{(5)} = 12{,}756$, which is the answer we obtained previously for Q_2.
- Since $2/9 < 0.25 < 3/9$, we use step 2(d) to compute the 0.25 quantile as $y_{(3)} = 6{,}794$ which is the value we obtained for Q_1.
- Since $1/3 = 3/9$, we use step 2(c) to compute the 1/3 quantile as $(y_{(3)} + y_{(4)})/2 = (6{,}794 + 12{,}100)/2 = 9{,}447$.

Recall that earlier in this chapter, we mentioned that quantiles are not necessarily unique. To see this, notice that for the planet data, any value between $y_{(3)} = 6{,}794$ and $y_{(4)} = 12{,}100$ satisfies the definition of a 1/3 quantile, as given on page 54.

Analyzing the Planet Data

How can we best summarize the planet data?

The first thing to do, as always, is to plot them. The frequency histogram and boxplot in Figure 2.15 serve to summarize the data distribution.

We can see immediately from both plots that the distribution is skewed to the right with two extreme outliers, Saturn and Jupiter. The large discrepancy between the mean and median (44846 versus 12756) verifies this. There are a number of options for handling these outliers. Let's consider a few.

- We could remove these two from the data set and analyze the remaining seven. However, there is something unsatisfying about ignoring nearly 30% of the data. In addition, if we remove Saturn and Jupiter, we will have the same problem with Neptune and Uranus (believe us, we tried it).
- There are in fact two different kinds of planets: five small rocky ones and four large gaseous ones. This is reason enough to analyze the two different kinds of planets separately. Figure 2.16 displays a stratified plot of the diameters for the two groups of planets. There is a great difference in the central value of the two distributions however measured (mean or median). There is also a great difference in the spreads whether IQR or standard deviation is used.
- Another alternative, if we want to analyze all the planet diameters together, is to transform the observations to another scale, as was done to the KWH data in

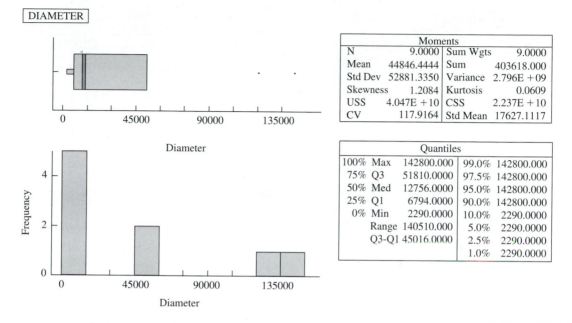

DIAMETER

Moments			
N	9.0000	Sum Wgts	9.0000
Mean	44846.4444	Sum	403618.000
Std Dev	52881.3350	Variance	2.796E +09
Skewness	1.2084	Kurtosis	0.0609
USS	4.047E +10	CSS	2.237E +10
CV	117.9164	Std Mean	17627.1117

Quantiles				
100%	Max	142800.000	99.0%	142800.000
75%	Q3	51810.0000	97.5%	142800.000
50%	Med	12756.0000	95.0%	142800.000
25%	Q1	6794.0000	90.0%	142800.000
0%	Min	2290.0000	10.0%	2290.0000
	Range	140510.000	5.0%	2290.0000
	Q3-Q1	45016.0000	2.5%	2290.0000
			1.0%	2290.0000

Figure 2.15 Summary measures, frequency histogram, and boxplot of planet diameters.

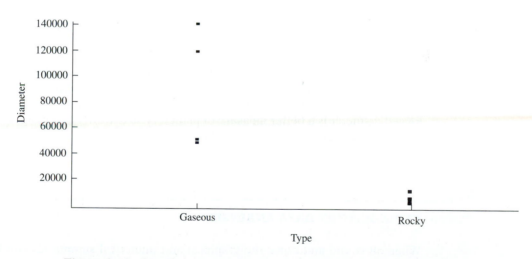

Figure 2.16 Stratified plot of planet diameters: Rocky versus gaseous planets.

Chapter 1. By taking the log of the diameters, we obtain the distribution pictured in Figure 2.17. The log transformation has removed the outliers and most of the skewness: Notice that the mean is now much closer to the median. Either the mean and standard deviation or the median and IQR are appropriate measures for location and spread.

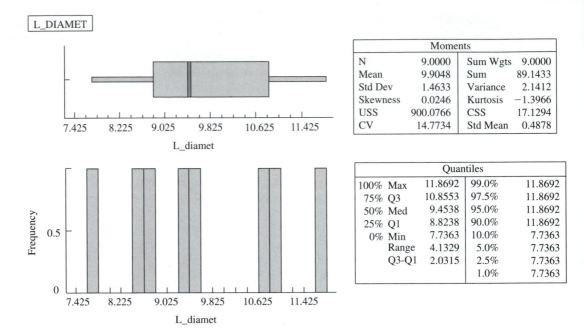

Figure 2.17 Summary measures, frequency histogram, and boxplot of logged planet diameters.

Which is the appropriate way to analyze the data? Analyzing the rocky and the gaseous planets separately has the advantage of emphasizing the differences in planet structure, and of being in the original, most easily understood units of measurement. On the other hand, analysis of the logged data is much simpler, involving only one set of summaries. Perhaps also, the regularity of the logged diameters indicates that the logged diameter is a better measure of planetary size. Both analyses offer insights into the data, and there is no reason we cannot learn from both.

2.8

EXPLORATORY DATA ANALYSIS

When all is said and done, the graphical and numerical summaries you have studied in this chapter are tools to help make sense of data. But what "sense" these tools can make depends critically on how the data were obtained.

Often, at the beginning stages of study of some phenomenon, researchers have little to guide them. At this stage, they may be looking at **available data:** data collected for some other purpose. For example, the U.S. government, through agencies such as the Census Bureau and the Bureau of Labor Statistics, collects vast amounts of data in order to assess where the nation stands socially, economically, and technologically. These data are collected for various purposes, such as to monitor the effectiveness of current government programs, or to identify future trends and needs for government planners. Often, these data are also made available to researchers outside the government, who may use them for different purposes. When used in this way, these government data constitute available data.

Available data are appropriately analyzed by a collection of methods called **exploratory data analysis,** or **EDA.**

> ### DEFINITION
>
> **Exploratory data analysis** is the name given to the process of looking at data in many different ways in order to get an initial understanding of the phenomenon under study.

Exploratory data analysis relies heavily on computer graphics, such as frequency histograms and boxplots, and simple summary measures, such as means, medians, standard deviations, and interquartile ranges, to display patterns in the data and to suggest interesting questions to be studied later in more formal designed studies. Exploratory data analysis is not meant to establish conclusive evidence to answer specific questions, nor is it meant to generalize beyond the set of data being analyzed. In order to establish such evidence and to make such generalizations, a methodology known as statistical inference is used. Statistical inference can be properly conducted only with data obtained from designed studies. The design of such studies is the topic of Chapter 3.

D ISCUSSION QUESTIONS

1. What is a variable?
2. Distinguish between quantitative and categorical variables.
3. Distinguish between discrete and continuous variables.
4. Describe a good strategy for graphically summarizing a data distribution.
5. Discuss the four distribution shapes shown in Figures 2.3, 2.4, 2.7, and 2.8. Can you come up with other examples of data that might have these shapes?
6. Tell what each of the following summary measures is used for, how to compute it, and how to interpret it: mean, median, mode, MAD, standard deviation, variance, IQR, percentiles, and quantiles. Which of these summary measures are appropriate for each of the distribution shapes shown in Figures 2.3, 2.4, 2.7, and 2.8? Which are inappropriate? Give reasons for your answers.
7. What are outliers? How should they be handled?
8. What is a boxplot and how is it constructed? How is a boxplot used to help identify outliers?
9. What is a resistant measure? Why and when would you want to use a resistant measure? Why and when might you use a nonresistant measure?

10. Which of the measures mentioned in Discussion Question 6 are resistant? Which are not?

11. Would IQR or s be a more resistant measure of spread? Why?

12. What is a k-times trimmed mean? Where have you seen it used? What is a k-times Winsorized mean?

E XERCISES

2.1. A data distribution has $Q_1 = 1$ and $Q_3 = 2$. Where will a data value of 3.6 appear on a boxplot? A data value of 3.4? Would either be considered a possible outlier?

2.2. Refer to the planet data given in Section 2.7. The Sun's equatorial diameter is 1,393,559 km. Compare the mean, median, and 1-time trimmed mean for the diameters of the nine planets plus the Sun. Which is most resistant in this case?

2.3. In a certain city, two judges sit on the criminal court bench: "Lockemup" Logan and "Letemgo" Leland. The sentences, in years, given to the past 10 armed robbery cases decided by this court are

$$3, \ 15, \ 4, \ 2, \ 12, \ 13, \ 20, \ 5, \ 18, \ 15$$

Use appropriate summary measures to describe the distribution, and interpret the meaning of those measures. What explanation can you give for the pattern in these data?

2.4. Seven young adults weigh (lb) 100, 120, 200, 90, 110, 105, and 112.
  (a) Use the data to explain why the interquartile range is a resistant measure of spread but the standard deviation is not. (*Hint:* You can change a value in the data set.)
  (b) Compute a numerical measure of the center of the data. Why is this measure appropriate?
  (c) Draw a boxplot summary of the data.

2.5. In computer chip manufacture, the end-use product is an integrated circuit called a die. A number of die are processed from a single silicon wafer. Not all die manufactured from a wafer are usable. The yield (the proportion of good die per wafer) is extremely important to computer manufacturers. A certain computer chip manufacturer uses two processes to produce integrated circuits. In evaluating the performance of the processes, 100 wafers are sampled from each process. Figure 2.18 shows side-by-side boxplots of the yields from these 100 wafers from each process. Use appropriate summary measures to describe the distribution of yields for each process (approximate these from the graph). What do you conclude about the processes from this graph?

2.6. The following paragraph is from an article on income trends in the United States. There is something very wrong in what it says. Explain what is wrong.

> *The low earnings of the bottom fifth of U.S. households—those with an income of $12,500 or less in 1990—pull the median income down so far that it misleadingly reflects the income trend among the middle class.*

2.7. The tensile strengths (psi) of 10 bars of metal are

$$78 \ 102 \ 101 \ 81 \ 82 \ 99 \ 100 \ 80 \ 79 \ 98$$

What summary statistics will you use for these data? (No calculation is required.) How can you explain the variation?

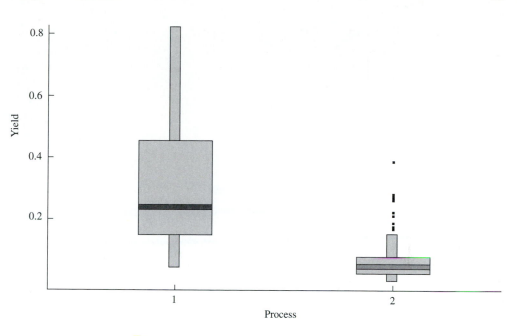

Figure 2.18   Boxplots of computer chip data.

2.8. The article "Americans' Median Age Climbs Slowly, Steadily" in *The Boston Globe* of March 11, 1994, reported that according to the Census Bureau, the median age of Americans increased from 32.8 at the time of the last census in 1990 to 33.7 as of July 1, 1993.

(a) Describe in ordinary language what the numbers 32.8 and 33.7 represent.

(b) What demographic trends do you think are responsible for an increase in the median age?

(c) Why do you think the median age increased only about 1 year in a 3-year span?

(d) Based on these figures, do you think the age of the population represents a stationary process over time?

2.9. A civil engineer wishes to compare the strength properties of three different types of beams, one made of steel and two made of different and more expensive alloys. The engineer determines the strength of a beam by setting it in a horizontal position, supported only on each end, applying a force of 3000 pounds at the center and measuring the deflection (in units of 0.001 inch). The data set BEAM contains strength measurements for eight beams of one alloy (labeled A), six beams of the second alloy (labeled B), and six steel beams (labeled C).

(a) Use boxplots to summarize the data. Are there outliers?

(b) Describe the variation in the data. Draw a graph that shows all the data.

(c) Is one beam weaker than the others? What might be a possible problem with your comparisons?

2.10. What percent of the observations lies at or below the 0.8 quantile? What proportion of the observations lies at or below the 15th percentile?

2.11. The age distributions of tenants of two apartment complexes are summarized in Figure 2.19.

(a) Give three summary statistics (to the nearest year) for each distribution.

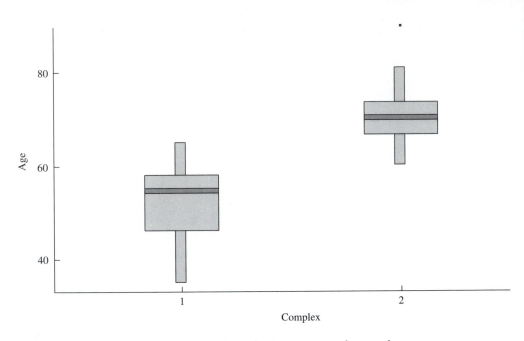

Figure 2.19   Boxplots of apartment complex age data.

   (b) Is there an outlier? If so, what is it?
   (c) Present one useful piece of information a sales manager could use before deciding to send a sales person to complex 1 or complex 2.
2.12. The data set FSALARY contains the 1993–1994 salaries (in $1000's) of full-time WPI faculty members, along with their academic rank (assistant, associate, or full professor).
   (a) Draw a stratified plot and a side-by-side boxplot for this data set. Which graphical display is more effective for presenting this data set? Why?
   (b) Are there any outliers? If yes, explain them.
   (c) Compare the salaries of assistant professors, associate professors, and full professors.
   (d) How might you explain the variation in the data?
2.13. The data set SALARY contains the weekly salaries of production workers in Anaheim, California. It is desired to compare men's salaries with women's salaries.
   (a) How might you summarize the data graphically? Are there outliers? What are they?
   (b) Is there evidence in these data of a wage differential between men and women? Explain.
2.14. A certain company uses raw materials from two suppliers, A and B. The company considers the materials from supplier B somewhat better. The data set BATCH contains the yields of 30 consecutive batches of products from the company in the order in which they were made.
   (a) By drawing a histogram and a plot of YIELD versus ORDER, identify which batches were made with material from supplier A.
   (b) Summarize the data.
2.15. For your data from Lab 1.1, obtain a printout of the frequency histogram. On the printout, display the mean and the median in a way that shows the physical interpretation of each, as described on pages 51 and 52. Also display the IQR in a way that shows its physical interpretation, as described on page 57.
2.16. What percentile is Q_3? What quantile is Q_2?

2.17. Write a one-page report (not including graphs) reanalyzing your data from Lab 1.1, using the outlier detection techniques discussed in this chapter. If you find outliers, take appropriate action and discuss the reasons for your action. Have your conclusions changed from those you found in Chapter 1?

2.18. Look at the quote of the Australian Minister of Labour displayed at the beginning of this chapter. Explain, in terms of the "see-saw" interpretation of the mean, why he was spouting nonsense.

2.19. Consider the planet diameter data discussed in Section 2.7. The median of the untransformed diameter values is 12,756, the value of Earth's diameter. Relate this fact to the median of the logged data. If using the definition on page 51, will a median of logs always be the log of a median? If using the formula on pages 69–70?

2.20. Seven pumpkins weigh (lb) 10, 12, 20, 9, 11, 8, and 13. Draw a boxplot summary of the data. Are there outliers? If so, what are they?

2.21. Provide a data set of your own to illustrate why the median is a resistant measure of center and the mean is not.

2.22. The hours of successful operation of a computer before each of its last seven crashes were

$$20, \quad 9, \quad 71, \quad 30, \quad 85, \quad 40, \quad 12.$$

Compute the 2-times trimmed and Winsorized means for these data.

2.23. A data set of 263 data points has the values 100, 190, 425, 750, and 1050 for its 10th, 25th, 50th, 75th, and 90th percentiles. Is this distribution approximately symmetric? Support your conclusion.

2.24. Figure 2.20 contains graphical and numerical summaries of the distribution of minimum list prices for ninety-three 1993 cars. Summarize the distribution.

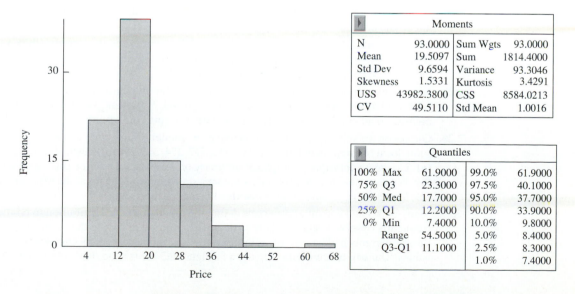

Figure 2.20   Minimum list prices for ninety-three 1993 cars.

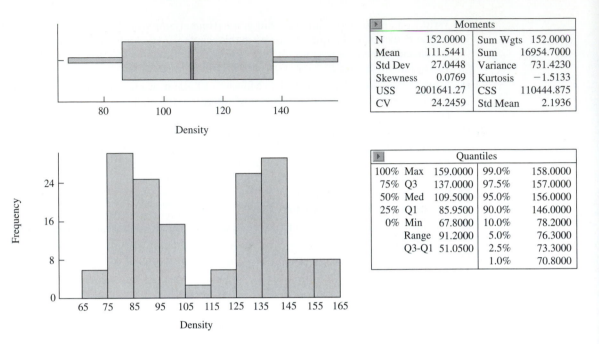

Figure 2.21   Concrete density.

2.25. The following are the measured thicknesses of nine sheets of paper (in one-hundredths of a millimeter):

$$6.55, \ 7.70, \ 7.55, \ 7.78, \ 7.61, \ 7.69, \ 7.88, \ 7.92, \ 7.59$$

Draw a boxplot summary of these data. Label the values of the ends of the box, the middle line in the box, and the ends of the whiskers. Specifically label as "outlier" any outliers.

2.26. The SAS/INSIGHT output shown in Figure 2.21 summarizes the density (lb/ft^3) of 152 concrete batches. Summarize the data descriptively and through appropriate summary measures. What might explain the pattern you see?

2.27. Nine randomly selected student car owners gave the numbers of miles on their cars as 6,000; 170,000; 93,000; 152,000; 88,000; 57,000; 70,000; 71,000; and 146,000. Use appropriate measures and graphs to summarize these data. Interpret the results.

2.28. Quotes on the selling price of a certain make and model 20-inch color stereo television from some local retailers, in dollars, are 234, 342, 377, 334, 347, 327, 318, 299, 300, and 360.
(a) Create an appropriate graphical summary of these data. Describe this summary.
(b) What are the most appropriate summary statistics for these data? Justify your choice.
(c) Compute $\bar{y}_{w2}$, the 2-times Winsorized mean for these data.

2.29. Many books and computer programs define the mode of a data distribution to be the most frequently observed value. If there is more than one value having the greatest frequency, these programs have a rule for selecting only one mode (e.g., SAS chooses the smallest value). The ball bearing data displayed in Figure 2.3 contain no duplicate values: No two

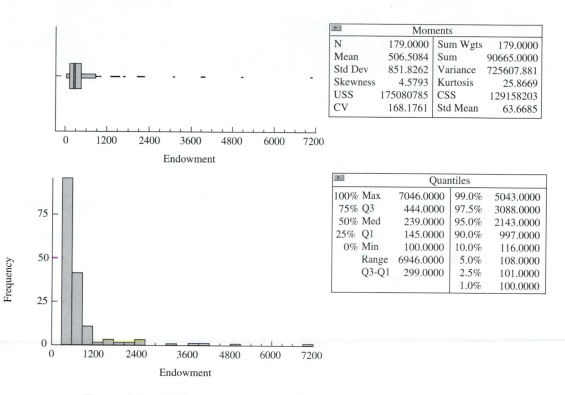

Figure 2.22   1995 endowments of the 179 U.S. and Canadian colleges and universities valued at $100 million or more.

of the 100 ball bearing diameters are the same. If the largest bearing diameter is 0.1932, the smallest bearing diameter is 0.1884, and the mean bearing diameter is 0.1910, what will SAS compute as the mode for the ball bearing diameters? Do you think this value does a good job of summarizing the "center" of the data? Justify your answer.

2.30. Explain how the quantiles in Table 2.4 show the male technical support salary data to be skewed.

2.31. Show that in order to move the median upward beyond the original data, we would have to add as many large observations as there are original data values.

2.32. Figure 2.22 shows a boxplot, a frequency histogram, and summary measures for the endowments of the 179 U.S. and Canadian colleges and universities with 1995 endowments valued at $100 million or more.[6]

(a) Choose one measure of location and one measure of spread to summarize these data.

(b) Tell why the measures you chose are appropriate for these data.

(c) What does each of the measures you chose tell you about the data (i.e., what does it mean)?

---

[6] An endowment is to a college what a savings account is to an individual. These data are found in the data set ENDOW95.

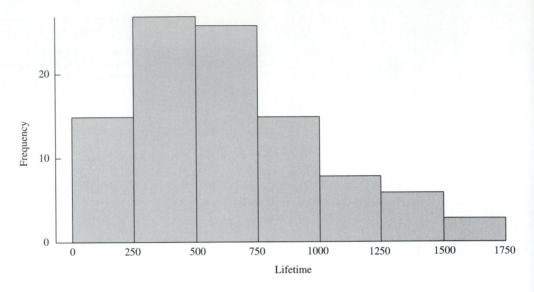

Figure 2.23   Impeller blade lifetimes.

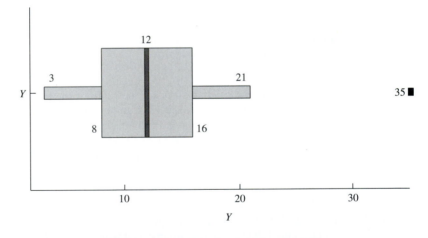

Figure 2.24   Boxplot for Exercise 2.35.

2.33. Figure 2.23 is a frequency histogram of the lifetimes, in hours, of 100 water-pump impeller blades, produced by a stationary process. For these data, we note that $Q_1 = 358.5$,
$Q_2 = 565.5$, and $Q_3 = 837.5$.

(a) On the graph, note the approximate location of the mean.

(b) Give the value of one meaningful measure of location and one of spread for these data.
Tell what each measures.

(c) Obtain the 5-number summary of the data. If the 10 largest impeller lifetimes are 1605, 1573, 1547, 1474, 1471, 1395, 1352, 1285, 1272, and 1237, and if the smallest observation is 48, construct a box-and-whisker plot of the data. Are any outliers suggested by this plot? If so, what are their values?

(d) A new water pump of the same type has just been put into service. If you had to supply one number as an estimate of the lifetime of its impeller blade, what number would you use? Tell how you obtained this number and why you chose it.

2.34. For the planet data, show that any value between $y_{(3)} = 6{,}794$ and $y_{(4)} = 12{,}100$ satisfies the definition of a 1/3 quantile as given on page 54.

2.35. Figure 2.24 shows a boxplot of a data set with 10 observations. In the plot, the values defining the box and whiskers and the value of an outlier are displayed.

(a) Construct a data set of 10 observations that will give this boxplot. Verify your result by reproducing the boxplot shown.

(b) Is this the only possible data set of 10 observations that can give this boxplot? If so, explain why. If not, construct another.

MINIPROJECT

Purpose

The purposes of this miniproject are

- To make you think about how various distributional patterns of data might arise.
- To give you experience in using graphs and summary measures to analyze data having various distributional patterns.
- To give you experience in generating data.

Process

Your group must choose three distinct distributional shapes. For each shape, the group must propose a method to obtain data having that shape. For example, you may get the data from a physical experiment or from simulation, or collect it from some secondary source. Evaluation of the project will be in two stages.

1. First, prior to collecting the data, the group must submit a proposal of no more than one typed page. In the proposal, for each distributional shape chosen, the group must explain why it feels the distribution of the data will have the claimed shape.

2. Second, the group must obtain the data as outlined in the proposal and then analyze them. In the project report, the group must evaluate the extent to which the distribution of the data generated by each proposed method matched the group's predictions. The report should also explain the observed distributional patterns, even if they don't match the predictions. Appropriate measures should be used to summarize the observed distributions.

LAB 2.1: Resistance of Summary Measures

Introduction

In this chapter, you have been told the meaning of "resistant" when referring to a summary measure for data. You have **read** that certain measures are resistant and that certain measures are not, but have you **learned** it? In this lab, you will explore in detail the resistance of the summary measures you have studied.

Objectives

To give you a practical understanding of the notion of resistance of summary measures, and to demonstrate the resistance of the measures you have studied in the chapter.

Lab Materials

None needed.

Experimental Procedure

In this lab, you will look at how the summary measures $\bar{y}$, Q_2, s, IQR, and $\bar{y}_{tk}$ (the k-times trimmed mean) respond to the presence of outliers in a data set. You may use your favorite statistical software or calculator to compute the necessary statistical measures and graphs. The **Doing It with SAS** and **Doing It with MINITAB** supplements give explicit, time-saving instructions for users of those packages.

1. Open the data set CRIME. This data set contains crime statistics for the 50 states. We will concentrate on the variable AUTO, which is the automobile crime rate.
2. For AUTO, compute the values of $\bar{y}$, Q_2, s, and IQR. Also compute the 3-time trimmed mean. Record your results.
3. Create a histogram and a boxplot for these data. Print out and summarize these graphs.
4. On the boxplot, you will notice an outlier representing a state with an auto crime rate much higher than the rest of the nation. Mark the outlier on the printouts of the graphs. By using your software, or otherwise scanning the data, identify the state.
5. Let's see what would happen to the summary statistics if the auto crime rate for Massachusetts were still higher. To do this, change the current value of 1140.1 to a value of, say, 2140.1, and recompute the measures and the plots. Record the new values of the measures.
6. Finally, to demonstrate the effect of removing an outlier, remove Massachusetts from the data and recompute the measures and the plots. Record the changes in the summary measures.

Write a short (one-page) report detailing what you found about the resistance of the summary measures $\bar{y}$, Q_2, s, IQR, and $\bar{y}_{tk}$ from this exercise.

3

Designing Studies and Obtaining Data

To call in the statistician after the experiment is done may be no more than asking him to perform a post-mortem examination: he may be able to say what the experiment died of.

—*R. A. Fisher*

I am monarch of all I survey.

—*William Cowper*

INTRODUCTION

In the information age, we find ourselves inundated with data. A substantial amount of these data are obtained in a haphazard manner, or for purposes other than that for which they are being used. In order to give scientifically valid results, data must result from designed studies. This chapter introduces some basic issues involved in the design and analysis of designed studies.

Knowledge and Skills

By successfully completing this chapter, you will acquire the following knowledge and skills:

KNOWLEDGE	SKILLS
1. Designed studies, and their role in producing data.	**1.** You will be able to identify a designed study as a controlled experiment or an observational study.
	(continued)

KNOWLEDGE	SKILLS
2. Basic sampling designs, including simple random samples and stratified random samples.	**2.** You will be able to design a sampling plan for simple random sampling or stratified random sampling.
3. Controlled experiments and the principles of experimental design.	**3.** You will be able to assign treatments to sampling units in completely randomized and randomized complete block experimental designs.
4. Observational studies.	**4.** You will be able to identify an observational study as a prospective study, a retrospective study, or a sample survey.
	5. You will be able to identify some basic deficiencies of designed studies, such as confounding or possible sources of bias.

3.1

THE ROLE OF STATISTICS IN PRODUCING AND ANALYZING DATA

As was mentioned in Chapter 2, in exploratory studies of poorly understood phenomena, exploratory data analysis is used to gain initial understanding and to suggest interesting questions for further study. Exploratory data analysis is most often conducted on available data: data collected for some other purpose.

Designed studies, which are the topic of this chapter, are appropriate when enough is understood about the phenomenon under study to ask specific questions and to know how to collect data to answer those questions. In contrast to the open-ended approach of exploratory data analysis, designed studies must be carefully planned and conducted to ensure that statistically valid results are obtained.

> **DEFINITION**
>
> A **designed study** is one that employs a systematic arrangement or pattern for collecting data.

We will study two types of designed studies in this chapter: **controlled experiments** and **observational studies.** We will describe each type of study in detail later in the chapter, but first we want to consider a characteristic shared by both types of studies: the **sampling unit.**

> **DEFINITION**
>
> A **sampling unit** is an entity on which measurements or observations can be made.

For both types of designed studies, the first task is to decide how to select the sampling units to be used in the study.

3.2   SELECTING SAMPLING UNITS

We begin by defining some terms.

> **DEFINITIONS**
>
> - The **target population** is the collection of sampling units about which we want to draw conclusions.
> - A **frame** is a list of all sampling units in the target population.
> - A **sample** is a subset of the target population from which observations are actually obtained, and from which conclusions about the target population will be drawn. We will assume that a sample is always smaller than the target population.
> - A **sampling design** is a pattern, arrangement or method used for selecting a sample of sampling units from the target population.
> - A **sampling plan** is the operational plan, including the sampling design, for actually obtaining or accessing the sampling units for the study.

EXAMPLE 3.1   SAMPLING CONCEPTS

The following illustrates the concepts of sampling unit, target population, frame, and sample.

(a) A cable television company wants to measure the satisfaction of its customers. To do so, it mails a questionnaire to 800 selected households. Assume that all 800 households return the questionnaire. For this example, we will focus on the question, "Overall, are you satisfied with the cable service we provide?"

The sampling unit is the household, and the observation is the answer to the question, "Overall, are you satisfied with the cable service we provide?" The target population is all subscribing households, and the sample consists of the 800 households returning the questionnaires. The frame is the list of all subscribing households maintained by the cable company. The sampling design is the method used to obtain the 800 households. The sampling plan is the operational plan, which includes the sampling design as well as the method of contacting the households in the sample.

(b) Quality engineers at an industrial fastener company have the responsibility for assessing the quality of outgoing products. One product of interest is a certain type of bolt produced and sold to auto manufacturers and other manufacturing firms in shipments of tens of thousands of items. To assess the quality of the current shipment of 15,000 bolts, inspectors obtain 100 bolts from the shipment and subject them to various quality tests and measurements. For this example, we will focus on thread pitch measured on the 100 bolts.

The sampling unit is an individual bolt, and the observation is the measured thread pitch of the bolt. The target population is the shipment and the sample is the 100 bolts whose thread pitch is being measured. As the bolts are probably not numbered, it is doubtful if a frame exists for this shipment. The sampling design is the method used to obtain the 100 bolts. The sampling plan is the operational plan, which includes the sampling design as well as the method of physically obtaining the bolts in the sample.

(c) Ecologists frequently measure wildlife populations and epidemiologists frequently measure incidence of disease. One recent study of the relation between the size of the deer population and the incidence of Lyme disease combined both disciplines.[1] In the study, researchers divided a county into 1000 smaller "tracts," and 50 tracts were chosen for observation. Within each of the selected tracts, ecologists tried to obtain a complete enumeration of the deer population, while epidemiologists obtained data on the human population and the number of cases of Lyme disease.

The sampling unit is a tract, and the observations are the count of deer, the human population, and the number of Lyme disease cases in a tract. The target population is all tracts in the county and the sample consists of the 50 chosen tracts. The frame is the list of all 1000 tracts. The sampling design is the method used to obtain the 50 tracts. The sampling plan is the operational plan, which includes the sampling design as well as the method of accessing the tracts in the sample.

(d) To assess the effectiveness of a new training program on employee productivity, 50 workers are selected from all hourly workers for participation in a study. Twenty-five of the workers are given the training program and the remainder are not. After completion of the program, the productivity of each of the 50 workers is assessed over a 3-week period.

The sampling unit is a worker and the observation is the worker's productivity. The target population is all hourly workers and the sample consists of the 50 chosen workers. The frame is the list of all hourly workers. The sampling design is the method used to obtain the 50 workers. The sampling plan is the operational plan, which includes the sampling design as well as the method of accessing the worker productivity records.   ✦

---

[1] The deer tick, which is carried by deer, has been identified as one of the primary agents in the spread of Lyme disease.

Why Sample At All?

One alternative to sampling is to obtain observations from every sampling unit in the population. This is referred to as a **census.** The Constitution of the United States requires an enumeration of the population every 10 years in order to determine how many seats each state should have among the 435-member House of Representatives. From 1790 through 1990, this requirement was met by a census. Yet even the U.S. decennial census only tries to ask very basic questions of every American. Most information obtained by the Census Bureau during the decennial census, or on other occasions, comes from samples of the population.[2] There are at least four good reasons why a sample is preferred to a census:

1. **Cost:** Because of the enormous expense involved, sufficient funds are not usually available to carry out a census. The 1980 census of 86 million households required 7 years of planning and about 280,000 workers. The questionnaires filled so many boxes that, if stacked up, they would have been 30 miles high.

2. **Time:** Even if a census is financially feasible, it may take too long to complete, seriously reducing the value of the results.

3. **Precision:** Modern sampling techniques can provide results to a great degree of precision. Usually, in a census, it is difficult to get accurate information from each individual in the population. It is preferable to take a small sample and ensure that accurate information is obtained from each individual in the sample.

4. **Feasibility:** Sometimes a census is not feasible. An example of this occurs in destructive testing. If, for example, we are measuring the time to failure of an electronic component, testing all components produced would leave none to sell!

In most situations, the considerations of cost, time, precision, and feasibility make sampling a more sensible choice than taking a census.

Some Commonly Used Sampling Designs

If a census is conducted, analysis will consist of simple summaries of the observations, such as those described in Chapter 2, or of more sophisticated summaries that might, for example, relate observations from two or more variables, or compare two or more subgroups in the population. If there is no larger target population to which we want to extend our conclusions, then we need only summarize those observations found in the sample.

When sampling, however, we will want to obtain conclusions from the sample that can be extended to the target population. To ensure that such conclusions are valid, we want to select a sample that is representative of the target population. Although there

---

[2]Interestingly, the Census Bureau is proposing to use sampling, instead of attempting a complete count, for the first time in the year 2000 census. Opinions differ over whether this proposal violates the constitutional requirement to obtain an enumeration.

are many ways to select samples from the target population,[3] selection mechanisms based on chance help assure that we obtain a representative sample. Such methods are called **probability sampling** methods.

> **DEFINITION**
>
> **Probability sampling** is a method of choosing a sample using a prespecified chance mechanism.

In addition to helping assure the representativeness of the sample, only mechanisms based on chance allow us to statistically characterize the accuracy and precision of the results. For these reasons, probability sampling methods are the only methods of obtaining samples that allow the results of the study to be extended to the population in a scientifically valid way. In the next three sections, we describe some commonly used probability sampling methods.

Simple Random Sampling

The most basic probability sampling method is simple random sampling.

> **DEFINITION**
>
> **Simple random sampling** is a probability sampling method in which each potential sample has the same chance of being chosen.

Conceptually, you can think of drawing a simple random sample as follows:

- Assign to each sampling unit in the target population a different number.
- Put each number on an individual slip of paper and place all of the slips in a hat.
- Draw out one slip at a time until you have drawn as many slips as you want there to be observations in your sample.

The simple random sample consists of those units in the population corresponding to the drawn numbers. Observations are then taken on these units.

In practice, samples are rarely selected using slips of paper and a hat. Most often, a table of random digits or a computer is used. Table A.7, in Appendix A, page 911, is a table of random digits. Accompanying the table is a detailed description of its use. Here is a method for using a computer to select a simple random sample of size n from a target population of size N:

1. Assign each sampling unit in the target population a number from 1 to N.
2. Generate N random numbers using a random-number generator. Assign the first random number to sampling unit number 1, the second to sampling unit number 2, and so on.

---

[3]Two such methods are to obtain a **convenience sample,** which consists of sampling units that are easy to obtain, or to obtain a **judgment sample,** which consists of sampling units selected by the researchers as being "typical."

3. Sort the random numbers from smallest to largest (or vice versa).

4. Take as the sample the sampling units associated with the first *n* sorted random numbers.

Detailed directions for doing this in SAS or in MINITAB are found in the **Doing It with SAS** or **Doing It with MINITAB** computer supplement that accompanies this text.

Stratified Random Sampling

Sometimes there are homogeneous subgroups of the population. These are subgroups in which the sampling units are similar in one or more ways. Such groups are called **strata.**

EXAMPLE 3.2   STRATA

During the much-publicized O. J. Simpson murder trial in 1995, several opinion surveys revealed that black Americans held very different opinions about Simpson's guilt than did white Americans. By a substantial margin, blacks reported that they believed Simpson not guilty, whereas by an even greater margin, whites reported that they believed Simpson guilty. If we consider the population to be divided into two strata, blacks and whites, then in terms of their opinion of O. J. Simpson's guilt, these strata are much more homogeneous than is the population as a whole. ✦

> **DEFINITION**
>
> Suppose a population is divided into a number of strata. **Stratified random sampling** is a sampling method in which a separate simple random sample is taken from each stratum.

There are two reasons for taking a stratified random sample rather than a simple random sample:

- When the sampling units within each stratum are more homogeneous than those between different strata, stratified random sampling will provide gains in the precision of quantitative measures used to describe the population.
- When we want to separately analyze the different strata, stratified random sampling can ensure adequate sample size for each.

EXAMPLE 3.3   STRATIFIED RANDOM SAMPLING

The administration of a certain college wants to study the opinions of undergraduate students on a number of issues. To do so, they intend to interview a sample of students. They decide to conduct a stratified random sampling rather than a simple random sampling for two reasons:

1. The opinions of all majors are of interest and some majors have few students: for example, only 1% of the students are classics majors. Unless a simple random sample was very large, it would contain few, if any, classics majors, so little could be said about their opinions. However, by taking majors as strata, the administration can structure a stratified random sample so that reasonable numbers of all majors, including classics majors, are obtained, resulting in opinions of all majors being represented in the study.

2. The administration suspects that different majors have widely different opinions on a number of issues. If true, a simple random sample would be a poor choice because the results would display large variation. Assuming the opinions of students in the same major are relatively homogeneous, it is, therefore, sensible to take a simple random sample from each major. This procedure constitutes stratified random sampling, with the majors as the strata.   ✦

For stratified random sampling, there are various criteria for determining the sizes of the samples to be taken in the different strata. One commonly used criterion is **proportional allocation:** choosing the sample size from a stratum proportional to the number of sampling units in the stratum.

Other Sampling Designs

Government surveys, especially in the United States, are very large and, therefore, use very complex sample designs. They use simple random sampling and stratified sampling as building blocks.

During the years between the decennial census, the U.S. government needs information about its citizens. In order to plan government programs, elected representatives must have a reasonably accurate estimate of how many people are unemployed, poor, and sick. The government has used sampling since the early 1940s for this purpose, and approximately 250 studies involving sampling are conducted by the Census Bureau each year. The best known of these is the **Current Population Survey,** which is conducted monthly. The Current Population Survey estimates unemployment, income, schooling, and other measures by questioning about 100,000 people in 60,000 households obtained from a nationwide probability sample.

The Current Population Survey uses a multistage sampling design and cluster sampling.

DEFINITION

- **Cluster sampling** is a sampling design in which sampling units are grouped into clusters and the clusters are sampled.
- **Multistage sampling** is a sampling design in which a sample is taken in stages.

In multistage cluster sampling, there is a hierarchy of clusters, with smaller ones contained in larger ones. For example, in most national sampling designs, the United States is divided up into counties, the counties are divided up into townships, the townships are divided up into blocks, and the blocks are divided up into households. Beginning with the largest clusters, a sample is taken at each stage. Thus, a national multistage sample might be obtained as follows:

Stage 1: A sample of 3000 counties in the United States is chosen.

Stage 2: A sample of townships within each of the selected counties is chosen.

Stage 3: A sample of city blocks within each of the selected townships is chosen.

Stage 4: A sample of households within each of the selected blocks is chosen. The required information is then obtained from these households.

Multistage cluster sampling has several advantages over simple or stratified random sampling.

• First, for large studies, it may not be practical to obtain a frame of the sampling units. For the Current Population Survey, for example, a list of all U.S. households is not available, and, therefore, it is not feasible to obtain a simple random sample from the entire U.S. population of households. However, lists of counties and townships are easily available, making the multistage cluster sampling design possible.

• Second, if interviewers have to travel across the country, the traveling costs associated with a simple random sample could be very high.[4] For sampling plans using door-to-door interviews, multistage sampling will save traveling costs because the sample households occur in clusters in the same block.

Errors in Sampling

The main objective of sampling designs is to obtain a sample of sampling units from which we can draw conclusions about the target population. As the sample is not an exact image of the population, conclusions obtained from the sample won't exactly match the true state of the population. For instance, an election exit poll may find that 55 out of a sample of 100 voters interviewed voted in favor of Clinton for President. It is unlikely that when the votes are counted, exactly 55% will favor Clinton for President, although if the sample of 100 voters is representative of the target population of all voters in this election, the actual percent favoring Clinton for President should be close to 55%.

> **DEFINITION**
>
> **Sampling error** is the error obtained when, due to chance, a sample quantity gives results different than the analogous population quantity.

When probability samples are taken, statistical theory allows us to characterize the nature of the sampling error and to make well-defined statements about the population.

---

[4]We note, however, that for national sampling designs like the Current Population Survey, observations are either obtained by questionnaires or by telephone, making traveling cost unimportant.

The ability to precisely quantify sampling errors is an important reason to use probability sampling methods.

Sampling error is an unfortunate term, because it seems to imply that a mistake has been made. In reality, sampling error is not the result of a mistake, but rather of the natural variability in the sampling process. In other words, sampling error will occur even if everything in the sampling plan has been done correctly.

However, there are other sources of error that really do result from mistakes, whether those mistakes can be avoided or not. These are referred to as nonsampling errors.

DEFINITION

Nonsampling errors are errors that result from an inability to carry out the sampling plan correctly.

DEFINITION

Bias is any systematic error in data collection or measurement.

Nonsampling errors introduce biases into the conclusions from designed studies due to one of two reasons: either the sample is unrepresentative of the population for reasons other than the randomness of sampling,[5] or measurements have been obtained in a biased manner. An example of a nonsampling error that results in unrepresentative samples is **selection bias.**

DEFINITION

Selection bias is a systematic tendency on the part of a sampling procedure to underrepresent or exclude one or more kinds of sampling units from the sample.

EXAMPLE 3.4   SELECTION BIAS

If the target population is all Americans, a sampling plan that samples only households will miss the homeless, prison inmates, and students in dormitories. A sampling plan that contacts interviewees by telephone will miss that part of the American population without telephones. Both sampling plans will result in selection bias. ✦

There are no simple fixes for selection bias. Investigators must be careful in identifying the target population and clever and thorough in designing methods for selecting sampling units from that population.

---

[5]Of course, it can happen that the sample is unrepresentative of the population simply because of the "luck of the draw." This cannot be avoided and is a part of sampling error.

Steps in Designing Sampling Plans

It is useful to think about designing a sampling plan in four steps:

1. Identify the target population. Care must be taken that the frame truly represents the target population. If that cannot be done, it is essential to ascertain exactly what population is being sampled. For instance, many magazines solicit the opinions of their readers about various issues. If the target population is the readers of the magazine, then all is well. However, the target population may initially have been the general public. Then, since the sampled population (the readers of the magazine) may differ in important ways from the target population (the general public), it would be incorrect to generalize the responses beyond the population of readers of that magazine. Sometimes it is too difficult to get a frame that is identical to the target population. For example a telephone directory generally lists households, rather than individuals, and omits those who have unlisted telephones or no telephone at all. In addition, households with more than one telephone number are overrepresented.

2. Decide what mechanism(s) is to be used for sample selection. There is no unique mechanism for selecting a sample from a frame. The appropriate choice will depend on the problem under consideration and on the budget. However, there is one rule that should always be observed: Probability sampling methods, such as simple or stratified random sampling or more complex procedures, should always be used.

3. Establish procedures to reduce nonsampling errors. For example, efforts should be made to reduce selection bias by identifying sources of selection bias and putting extra resources into obtaining data from undercovered groups. The sampling units in the sample should be analyzed with respect to possibly undercovered subgroups: This will identify the extent of selection bias and help to define the population being sampled.

4. Do a pilot study. It is essential that a pilot study be conducted, especially when sampling human populations. Among the uses of a pilot study are

- To obtain information about the target population necessary to design the main study properly. Such information can help select an appropriate sample size or suggest new or modified directions of inquiry.
- To identify and correct any problems with the sampling plan.

3.3

TYPES OF DESIGNED STUDIES

Design of the sampling plan and selection of the sampling units are only the first steps in conducting a designed study. The next steps depend on and, in fact, define, the kind of study being conducted. We will divide designed studies into two classes: **controlled experiments** and **observational studies.** We will consider each in turn.

3.4

CONTROLLED EXPERIMENTS

Before we can define what a controlled experiment is, we will need to define some terms.

> **DEFINITIONS**
>
> - An **experimental unit** is the name given to any sampling unit that has been selected for use in a controlled experiment.
> - A **response** is a measurement or observation of interest that is made on an experimental unit.
> - A **factor** is a quantity that is thought to influence the response.
>   - –An **experimental factor** is a factor that is purposely varied by the experimenter.
>   - –A **nuisance factor** is a factor that cannot be controlled by the experimenter. Nuisance factors may or may not be known to the experimenter.
> - Each value assumed by a factor in an experiment is called a **level.**
> - The combinations of levels of factors for which the response will be observed are called **treatments.**
> - An **effect** is the change in the average response between two factor levels or between two combinations of factor levels.

Now that we have the necessary definitions, we are ready to say what a controlled experiment is.

> **DEFINITION**
>
> Any study in which treatments are imposed on experimental units in order to observe responses is a **controlled experiment.**

The key idea behind a controlled experiment is the idea of control: that the experimenter can decide which experimental units receive which treatments. It is control that gives controlled experiments the unique ability to establish cause-and-effect relationships and that makes them the most powerful of all scientific tools.

EXAMPLE 3.5   A CONTROLLED EXPERIMENT

Researchers are studying the effect of exercise on cholesterol levels in men. To do so, they obtain a sample of 500 men who are nonexercisers and who are willing to participate in their study. Half the men are assigned an exercise regimen and are monitored at monthly intervals over a 6-month period to ascertain their compliance with the exercise regimen and their general health, including their cholesterol levels. The other half are given no exercise regimen, but are monitored in the same way. After 6 months, cholesterol levels for the two groups of men are measured and compared.

In this study, the 500 men are the experimental units. The response is the cholesterol level after 6 months. There is a single experimental factor, exercise, which has two levels: level 1 is the absence of the exercise regimen and level 2 is the presence of the exercise regimen. This factor is also the treatment. This is a controlled experiment since the treatment (presence or absence of exercise regimen) is assigned to the experimental units (the men) and a response (cholesterol level after 6 months) observed. There are many possible nuisance factors for this experiment: how much an individual smokes or drinks or takes other drugs; weight; personality; and so on.   ✦

EXAMPLE 3.6   ANOTHER CONTROLLED EXPERIMENT

Consider a controlled experiment conducted to characterize the hardness of a new type of plastic, measured in Brinell units, as a function of the pressure and temperature at the time of molding. In the experiment, pressure is set to one of 200, 300, or 400 pounds per square inch (psi), and temperature to one of 200 or 300 degrees Fahrenheit (°F), so that there are six pressure–temperature combinations: (200 psi, 200°F), (300 psi, 200°F), (400 psi, 200°F), (200 psi, 300°F), (300 psi, 300°F), and (400 psi, 300°F). Two pieces of plastic are molded at each of the six pressure–temperature combinations and their hardnesses measured. Table 3.1 shows the resulting data.

In this example, the experimental units are the plastic pieces. The response is the hardness of the molded plastic. The experimental factors are pressure and temperature. The pressure is at three levels, 200, 300, and 400 psi, and temperature is at two levels, 200 and 300°F. The six pressure–temperature combinations are the treatments. This is a controlled experiment because the treatments are imposed on the experimental units and the resulting plastic hardness measured.

Nuisance factors for this experiment might include environmental factors, such as ambient temperature, barometric pressure, and humidity.

TABLE 3.1   Data from Plastic Hardness Experiment

Temperature (°F)	Pressure (psi) 200	300	400	Row Mean
200	196.00	207.00	213.00	
	188.00	201.00	219.00	
Mean	192.00	204.00	216.00	204.00
300	211.00	226.00	237.00	
	215.00	231.00	239.00	
Mean	213.00	228.50	238.00	226.50
Column Mean	202.50	216.25	227.00	215.25

The mean of the four responses taken at 300 psi is 216.25, and that of the four responses taken at 200 psi is 202.5, so the effect of pressure of 300 psi over that of 200 psi is $216.25 - 202.5 = 13.75$. Similarly, since the mean of the two observations taken at pressure–temperature (400 psi, 300°F) is 238, whereas that of the two observations taken at pressure–temperature (200 psi, 200°F) is 192, the effect of pressure–temperature of (400 psi, 300°F) over that of (200 psi, 200°F) is $238 - 192 = 46$. ✦

Measurement Bias

Recall that bias is the name given to any systematic error in data collection or measurement. One kind of data-collection bias is selection bias, which you have already encountered.

Measurement bias can arise in different ways. A simple example of measurement bias results from using a magnetic compass to identify true north. Since the compass points to magnetic north, the readings at a given location will systematically deviate from true north. Fortunately, this bias is known and correctable. Another example of measurement bias results from measurements taken with a miscalibrated measuring device. For instance, suppose a cloth merchant uses a stretched measuring tape to measure the cloth she sells. The measurements obtained from such a stretched tape will be consistently smaller than the true length of what is being measured. We would say the measurements are biased downward. If a 2-meter measuring tape were stretched 1 centimeter, then a merchant who used it to measure an order of 100 meters of cloth would be giving the customer half a meter of cloth for free.

Although known biases can be corrected, unsuspected biases can lead to incorrect conclusions. As a result, experimenters should make themselves aware of potential sources of measurement bias, such as miscalibrated instruments, which may affect the results of an experiment.

Experimental Error

When two or more observations are taken at the same treatment, the responses will usually be different.

> **DEFINITION**
>
> In an experiment, the difference in responses taken in exactly the same manner at the same treatment is called **experimental error.**

Experimental error consists of measurement errors, variation in experimental units, and errors due to nuisance factors.

EXAMPLE 3.6   CONTINUED

In Table 3.1, the differences in the two measurements taken at each pressure–temperature combination are experimental errors. Sources of these differences might be

- **Measurement errors:** The inability to determine plastic hardness perfectly. If the hardness of the same plastic piece were measured twice, differences in the measurements would be due to measurement errors.
- **Variation in experimental units:** Such variation might be due to different suppliers of the plastic pieces, different batches from the same supplier, or variation within a batch from which the pieces are produced.
- **Nuisance factors:** Environmental factors such as ambient temperature, barometric pressure, or humidity might be one set of nuisance factors contributing to experimental error. ✦

Confounded Factors

> **DEFINITION**
>
> Two or more factors are **confounded** if it is impossible to separate their individual effects.

In general, if two groups are compared with respect to some factor, and this is the only factor in which these groups differ, any difference between the two groups is due to the difference in the levels of the factor (e.g., one group is treated at a low level and the other at a high level). However, if one group differs from the other with respect to other factors as well, the observed difference may be due, at least in part, to those factors. Confounded factors are a major source of uncertainty and error when analyzing experimental results, as the following illustrates.

EXAMPLE 3.6   CONTINUED

Because the experimenters in the plastic hardness experiment were using a single oven that required 72 hours to change temperatures, all results at 200°F were obtained first. Due to an oversight, the plastic pieces originally intended for molding at 400°F were unavailable at the time the experiment was to be run. The experimenters had no choice but to obtain plastic pieces from a different supplier. This means that supplier and temperature are confounded, since all experimental units at 200°F are from one supplier and all experimental units at 400°F are from another supplier. As a result, the experimenters cannot know if the apparent effect of temperature, $22.5 = 226.5 - 204$, is due to temperature or plastic supplier or both. ✦

Principles of Experimental Design

The study of experimental design originated in England. In the early years, it was associated solely with agricultural experimentation. The need for experimental design in agriculture was very clear: It took a full year to obtain a single observation on the yield of a new variety of wheat. Consequently, the need to save time and money led to the study of ways to obtain more information using less data. Similar motivations led to its subsequent acceptance and wide use in all fields of scientific experimentation.

Over the years, experimenters have developed a number of principles to ensure efficient and scientifically valid experimentation. Some of these follow.

Principle 1: Make Sure the Process is Stationary

In addition to the variation attributable to experimental factors, experimental data from a nonstationary process have extraneous variation due to process nonstationarity. This additional variation makes it more difficult to identify the effects of experimental factors. Consequently, experimenters should try to stabilize a process before conducting experiments on it.

EXAMPLE 3.6   CONTINUED

In the plastic hardness experiment, the experimenters found that the fans in the oven were not working properly, resulting in an uneven heat distribution in the oven. As the actual temperatures drifted over time, the molding process was nonstationary. Differences in plastic hardness due to this nonstationarity might prove larger than the differences the experimenters could hope to observe due to changes in factor levels. If so, variation due to process nonstationarity could mask any real effects that might otherwise be detected, or it might make small effects look large. Either way, it could result in misleading conclusions.   ◆

Principle 2: Block What You Can

> **DEFINITION**
>
> A **blocking factor** is a nuisance factor whose levels can be selected for each experimental unit. These levels define groups of experimental units, called **blocks,** that are treated similarly during the experiment.

Blocking is a useful tool in minimizing variation due to nuisance factors. It can also be used to help minimize the effects of nonstationarity when data are taken from a nonstationary process, as the following example shows.

EXAMPLE 3.7   BLOCKING

It is well known that the durability of house paint is related to the environmental conditions, such as temperature and humidity, under which it is applied. A paint manufacturer wanted to compare the durability of three new paint formulations with each other and with the old formulation. The experimenters had at their disposal a large number of test panels, the experimental units, that they could paint with any of the formulations. The experimenters reasoned that environmental conditions might vary considerably from day to day, but would be more nearly constant on any one day. That is, the durability of paint might be nonstationary over time, but the durability of paint applications made on the same day should have much less variation. Day of application is a nuisance factor, whose levels, being the days themselves, could be assigned to the experimental units. Thus, the experimenters decided to make day of application a blocking factor. Each different day on which the panels were painted is a block, and a number of panels with each paint formulation were painted on each of several days. This design brought two benefits:

1. Since all formulations were applied each day, a direct comparison among the four formulations was available on each day. The environmental conditions each day were the same for all four paint types, so differences on any given day were due solely to differences in paint formulations under that day's environmental conditions.

2. Since comparisons among the formulations were obtained on a number of days, these comparisons were made under a range of environmental conditions. Having results that hold over a range of conditions made the experimental conclusions more generally applicable. ✦

There are two types of blocking factors:

1. **Characteristics associated with an experimental unit.** For instance, when people are experimental units, blocking is frequently done by gender, age, income, education, job experience, and so on.

2. **Characteristics associated with the experimental setting.** Examples of such blocking factors are observer, time of processing, machine, batch of material, measuring instrument, and so on.

The use of time as a blocking factor often captures a number of different sources of variability such as learning by an observer, changes in equipment, and drifts in environmental conditions, all of which are also sources of process nonstationarity. Blocking by observers frequently eliminates a substantial amount of interobserver variability. Blocking by batches of materials can be very effective in reducing batch-to-batch variation.

In experiments using living subjects as experimental units, the blocking factors can be the subjects themselves. With the subject as a block, some or all treatments are given to every subject. As an example, consider an experiment with experimental units being students taking an advanced typing course to increase their speed. At the beginning of the course, the students are given a speed test, and after a 6-week course, they are given another test. Each student is a block and is observed at two time points. The design is called a **matched pairs** design. If the students are tested at more than two points in time, the design is an example of a **repeated measures design.**

Good blocking factors can be selected based on past experiments or on expert advice in the particular field of study.

Principle 3: Randomize What You Cannot Block

> **DEFINITION**
>
> **Randomization** is the chance assignment of treatments to experimental units in order to nullify the effects of unsuspected nuisance factors.

The following example illustrates randomization.

EXAMPLE 3.8   RANDOMIZATION AND BLOCKING

At a certain industrial site, there are two shifts, one in the morning and the other in the afternoon. A study was conducted to decide which of two incentive programs has a better effect on worker productivity. All the workers on the first shift were given the first incentive program and those on the second shift were given the second incentive program. The results showed that the first incentive program was far superior. That program was instituted companywide, but after 6 months, the results were disappointing. A statistician was called in to look at the original experiment.

The statistician found that the morning workers in the study were full-time workers, and the afternoon workers were part-time workers. A management consultant called in to assist explained that whereas full-time workers in that industry generally respond to incentive programs, part-time workers seldom do. Since all full-time workers were assigned to one incentive program and all part-time workers to the other, the effect of the incentive program was confounded with the type of worker.

The experimenter didn't think about or didn't know about the difference between full- and part-time workers in their response to incentives, but that is exactly the kind of situation in which randomization is valuable! By assigning the workers randomly to the first or second incentive plan, he would have been very likely to have obtained a mix of full- and part-time workers in each incentive plan. Then any differences in output that he found would have been a more accurate reflection of the differences due to incentive plans.

Management decided to rerun the experiment with a different set of workers in order to see if the incentive plan that had not been chosen was, in fact, effective. One way the new study could avoid the confounding problem that beset the first study was to assign workers randomly to the two incentive programs, but the experimenter did something even better.

Since the experimenter now knew about the different responses of full- and part-time workers to incentive programs, he used that knowledge to make the type of worker a blocking factor. Basically, he made two blocks: one with full-time workers only and one with part-time workers only. Then, within each block, he randomly assigned one incentive program to half the workers and the other incentive program to the rest. Remember, randomization is used to guard against the effects of unsuspected nuisance factors, and blocking is used to minimize variation due to known nuisance factors. Once the experimenter learned about the difference in the response of full- and part-time workers to incentive programs, blocking was the more effective way to deal with the nuisance factor, worker type. ◆

Example 3.8 illustrates the difference in approach and use of randomization and blocking. We block to eliminate variation due to nuisance factors we know. We randomize to eliminate bias due to nuisance factors we don't know.

Example 3.9 shows the benefits that can result from blocking.

EXAMPLE 3.9   BENEFITS FROM BLOCKING

A watch manufacturer wants to design an experiment to compare the length of time required to assemble a digital watch using three different methods of assembly. Assembly method is the factor of interest. Because it is well known that assembly times differ greatly from worker to worker, and because these worker-to-worker differences are not of primary interest, it is decided to use five assemblers, and to assign all three assembly methods to each worker in random order. In this design, each assembler is a block and all three assembly methods are applied in each block. The results are shown in Figure 3.1, where assembly time versus worker is graphed. The response for method 1 is marked by an "**x**," that for method 2 is marked by a circle and that for method 3 by a triangle.

From Figure 3.1, we see two things:

1. There is wider variability in the assembly times from worker to worker than in the different methods for a given worker.
2. Method 1 gives the best time—sometimes by far—for each worker.

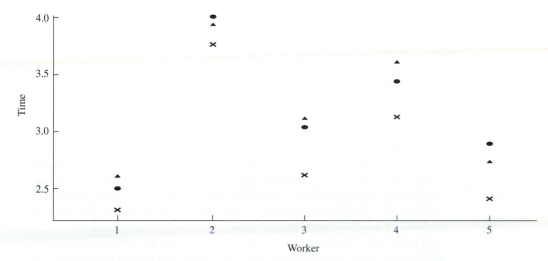

Figure 3.1   Watch assembly problem; plot of time versus worker (plotting symbol denotes method).

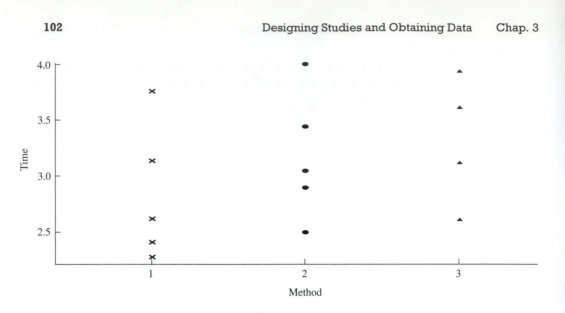

Figure 3.2   Watch assembly problem; plot of time versus method.

Figure 3.2 shows the same data plotted versus the assembly method. The blocking in the experiment is ignored in this plot. The wide variation of times for each method makes it much more difficult to see what Figure 3.1 plainly shows: that method 1 is superior to the other methods. The difference between Figures 3.1 and 3.2 shows the benefit of blocking.   ✦

Principle 4: Replicate as Time and Budget Permit

> **DEFINITION**
>
> **Replication** is the repetition of each treatment in an experiment.

It is generally true that more data result in greater precision of conclusions.[6] The greater the number of replications, the better able we are to identify small differences in response due to different treatments. Replication also helps to provide reliable estimates of the likely size of experimental error. In general, the number of replicates will be decided by the requirements of precision in the study and by time and budget constraints.

It is important to distinguish between true replicates and **duplicates.** To understand the difference, suppose an experiment is being planned to compare two different machining methods to see which produces less runout (out-of-roundness) in a hole-boring procedure. The experiment will consist of setting up the apparatus and boring holes with each method. To test the results over different conditions, 5 different setups will be used for each method, and for each setup, 10 different holes ("replicates") will be drilled. Thus, there will be 100 holes drilled in all: 50 for each method (5 setups ×

---

[6]In Chapter 4, you will see this demonstrated mathematically.

10 holes each). If all 100 runs are conducted in random order, with the setup redone for each run (even with two consecutive replicates from the same setup), then we have a true replication and the standard deviation of the means is reduced by a factor of $\sqrt{10}$ over that produced by a single replicate.[7] If, however, only the setups are randomized, and once a setup has been made all 10 "replicates" are run consecutively on that setup, we have duplication, not true replication. The result will be a smaller standard deviation in the responses than would result from true replication.

The key idea here is that with replication, the entire experiment is repeated; with duplication, it is not. In this example, the difference between duplication and replication is that a new setup must be done to obtain a new replicate, whereas all 10 duplicates are done on a single setup.

Treating duplication as replication can seriously alter the conclusions drawn from experimental data.

Principle 5: Confirm the Results

After experimentation is done, results obtained, and conclusions drawn, a wise experimenter will confirm the results by running additional trials. A relatively small amount of effort spent on such confirmatory experiments will be repaid handsomely in information gained about the replicability and persistence of the original conclusions.

RECAP: PRINCIPLES OF EXPERIMENTAL DESIGN

- Principle 1: Make sure the process is stationary.
- Principle 2: Block what you can.
- Principle 3: Randomize what you cannot block.
- Principle 4: Replicate as time and budget permit.
- Principle 5: Confirm the results.

Assigning Treatments to Experimental Units

We have seen that it is important to use an appropriate sampling method when obtaining experimental units, and that there are a number of different sampling methods designed for specific needs. The problem of how to assign treatments to experimental units in a controlled experiment is similar in many respects to the problem of how to sample sampling units. We will present two commonly used methods for assigning treatments to experimental units: **completely randomized** assignment, which is similar in concept to simple random sampling, and **randomized complete block** assignment, which is similar in concept to stratified random sampling.

---

[7]In Chapter 4, this, too, will be demonstrated.

Completely Randomized Design

The simplest statistical design[8] for a controlled experiment is the completely randomized design.

> **DEFINITION**
>
> A **completely randomized design** is a design in which treatments are assigned to experimental units completely at random: that is, every unit has an equal chance to receive any one of the treatments.

The Idea behind Completely Randomized Assignment.   Assume there are k treatments and $n\ (\geq k)$ experimental units. Then, conceptually, you can think of completely randomized assignment as follows:

- For each $i = 1, 2, \ldots, k$, decide how many experimental units are to be assigned the ith treatment. Call this number n_i.
- Put each of the numbers $1, 2, \ldots, n$ on an individual slip of paper and place all n of the papers in a hat.
- Draw out the slips from the hat one at a time.
- The experimental units whose numbers are on the first n_1 slips drawn are assigned treatment 1, the experimental units whose numbers are on the next n_2 slips drawn are assigned treatment 2, and so on.

EXAMPLE 3.10   COMPLETELY RANDOMIZED ASSIGNMENT

Researchers want to compare the effectiveness of three kinds of water repellent used on furniture fabric. Fifteen identical test samples of fabric are prepared for the experiment. Each of the three kinds of repellent is to be applied to five of the test samples. The kinds of water repellent are the three treatments and the fabric samples are the experimental units. The test is conducted by pouring a fixed amount of water on each treated sample and recording the time until the water drips through.

 To conduct the experiment as a completely randomized design, the experimenters would randomly assign each treatment to five fabric samples and record the drip-through times for each of the 15 fabric samples included in the experiment. In terms of the steps outlined before, $k = 3$, $n = 15$, and $n_1 = n_2 = n_3 = 5$. To do the random assignment, slips numbered 1 through 15 are placed in a hat and the fabric samples whose numbers are the first five drawn are assigned treatment 1, the fabric samples whose numbers are the second five drawn are assigned treatment 2, and the remaining fabric samples are assigned treatment 3. ◆

---

[8]In a controlled experiment, the pattern or plan for assigning treatments to experimental units is called a design.

Randomizing in Practice.   In practice, experimenters do not assign treatments to experimental units using slips of paper drawn from a hat.

If the experiment is small, one can use a **random-number table,** such as Table A.7, in Appendix A, page 911. Details of how to use this table to assign treatments to experimental units in a completely randomized design accompany the table. Another method for conducting random assignment is to use the computer or a calculator to generate "pseudo-random" numbers. Basic directions for assigning treatments to experimental units are similar to those given previously for choosing a simple random sample:

1. Assign each experimental unit a unique number from 1 to n.
2. Generate n random numbers using a random-number generator. Assign the first random number to experimental unit number 1, the second to experimental unit number 2, and so on.
3. Sort the random numbers from smallest to largest.
4. Assign treatment 1 to the experimental units with the n_1 smallest random numbers, treatment 2 to the experimental units with the next n_2 smallest random numbers, and so on.

Detailed directions for doing this in SAS or MINITAB are found in the corresponding computer supplement that accompanies this text.

Advantages and Disadvantages of the Completely Randomized Design.   When experimental units are similar, they are said to be **homogeneous.** When they are dissimilar, they are said to be **heterogeneous.** Mice from the same litter might be considered homogeneous, and those from different litters might be considered heterogeneous.

A completely randomized design is useful when the experimental units are homogeneous. The completely randomized design has at least two important advantages:

1. It is flexible and can accommodate any number of treatments and any numbers of observations per treatment.
2. Missing observations, such as might result from the death of a subject or loss of a data sheet, create no problems in the analysis of single-factor studies.

The main disadvantage of the completely randomized design is its inefficiency when the experimental units are heterogeneous. That is why, when the experimental units are heterogeneous, a design involving blocking can be preferable.

Randomized Complete Block Designs

We have seen that known sources of data variation can be reduced or eliminated by blocking. That is, the experimenter can observe all treatments within relatively homogeneous blocks. In this way, some prior knowledge about the units can be incorporated into the experiment. The **randomized complete block design** is the simplest design that uses blocking.

> **DEFINITION**
>
> A **randomized complete block design** is a design in which the experimental units are divided into blocks, and, separately within each block, all the treatments are assigned at random to the experimental units within that block.

The paint experiment described in Example 3.7 and the watch assembly experiment described in Example 3.9 are both randomized complete block designs. In the paint experiment, each day is a block, and within a day, the four paint formulations are randomly assigned to the experimental units. In the watch assembly experiment, each worker is a block, and all three assembly methods are assigned in a random order to each worker.

Randomized complete block designs are useful because they can provide substantially more precision than a completely randomized design of comparable size, particularly when the experimental units are heterogeneous. However, missing observations are more difficult to handle than is the case with completely randomized designs.

The randomized complete block design is conceptually similar to stratified random sampling. The blocks play the role that the strata play in stratified random sampling. The completely randomized designs run in each block of the randomized complete block design are analogous to the simple random samples taken within each stratum of the stratified random sampling.

The Choice of Experimental Units

We have stressed that a controlled experiment involves the assignment of treatments to experimental units, but we have said little about how these experimental units are chosen. In fact, the method of choosing the experimental units determines the kinds of conclusions we can draw from the experiment.

If we want the results of the experiment to apply to all sampling units in a given target population, then we must use a valid probability sampling method to obtain those experimental units from the target population. Sampling methods such as those described earlier in this chapter are appropriate for choosing the experimental units.

If we do not use a valid probability sampling method to choose the experimental units, then we may not be able to say to what population of sampling units the experimental results apply. In fact, the results may not apply beyond the set of experimental units used in the experiment!

EXAMPLE 3.10   CONTINUED

The experimental units in the water-repellent experiment are test samples of fabric. There are different ways these test samples could be chosen, depending on the target population to which the experimenters want the results to apply. For example:

- They could be pieces of fabric lying around the factory when the experimenters were ready to perform the experiment. Since the experimental units were not chosen using a probability sampling design, generalizing the results beyond these fabric samples is risky. For example, perhaps all pieces lying around the factory at that time were defective in some way that is related to the performance of the water repellent on them. If so, their observed water-repellent properties would not be representative of nondefective fabric.

- If the experimenters want the results to apply to one particular batch of one particular type of fabric, the samples should be selected from that batch.
- If the experimenters want the results to apply to all batches of one particular type of fabric, the samples should be selected from the target population of all batches. There are different ways to do this, but one approach might be to use stratified random sampling to obtain the experimental units, with batches as strata. Treatments could then be assigned to the experimental units in a randomized complete block design with the units from the different batches treated as blocks.
- If the experimenters want the results to apply to all batches of a number of different types of fabric, the samples should be selected from the target population of all batches of those different fabric types.

In all cases, an appropriate probability sampling design should be used to select the experimental units. If a probability sampling design is not used to select the experimental units from the desired target population, we can say the experimental results hold for the fabric samples in the experiment, but we cannot be confident that the results apply more generally.   ✦

Cause and Effect in Controlled Experiments

The goal of every controlled experiment is to establish a cause-and-effect relationship between treatments and outcomes specified by the response variable. In fact, of all studies, **only a properly designed and conducted controlled experiment can establish a cause-and-effect relationship.** This is because only in a controlled experiment can the experimenter ensure, through the assignment of treatments to experimental units, that the only possible differences in observed responses are due to differences in treatments. We will have more to say about cause and effect when we discuss observational studies later in this chapter.

Experimenting with Human Subjects

There are some special considerations involved when the experimental units are human subjects. Many of these involve ethical issues, which we will not discuss. Some design issues are of interest to us, however.

Often it is desired to compare one or more treatments with each other and also with nontreatment. In the simplest application, called the **method of comparison,** a treatment is assigned to a group of human subjects, called the **treatment group,** and no treatment is given to a second group of human subjects, called the **control group.** Though such an experiment could be run on the treatment group alone, a proper evaluation of the effect of the treatment cannot be obtained without a control group for comparison.[9] The control group enables experimenters to establish a baseline for evaluating the effect of the treatment.

Whenever possible, the control group should be given a **placebo,** which is neutral but resembles the treatment. The placebo ensures that the response is to the treatment rather than the idea of the treatment.[10] Whenever possible, a well-designed experiment should be run **double-blind.** This means that the subjects do not know whether they are in the treatment or in the control group, and that those who administer the treatments or placebos, or (in some instances) who evaluate the responses are unaware of this also. Double-blinding protects the experimental results against bias arising from both the subjects and those who conduct the experiment.

EXAMPLE 3.11   A DOUBLE-BLIND RANDOMIZED CONTROLLED EXPERIMENT

More than 40 years after it was concluded, the **Salk Vaccine Field Trial** remains the largest experiment ever conducted. The first polio epidemic hit the United States in 1916. By the 1950s, Jonas Salk had developed a vaccine that had proven safe in laboratory trials. To test whether the vaccine was effective in protecting children against polio outside the laboratory, it had to be tested in a large-scale field trial. The National Foundation for Infantile Paralysis (NFIP) wanted to vaccinate all grade-2 children whose parents would consent, leaving the children in grades 1 and 3 as controls. However, this NFIP design had two flaws:

1. Polio is a contagious disease, spreading through contact. On the one hand, the incidence of polio could have been much higher in grade 2 than in grades 1 and 3, thus creating a bias against the vaccine. On the other hand, the incidence could have been much lower in grade 2, thus biasing the study in favor of the vaccine.

2. Children in the treatment group could be vaccinated only with their parents' permission. It was known that higher-income parents would consent to treatment much more readily than lower-income parents. Unfortunately, children from higher-income parents were more vulnerable to polio than children from lower-income parents. (Lower-income children lived in less hygienic conditions and were more often exposed to the polio virus. Hence, they developed a natural immunity.) Thus, the group with parental consent was substantially different from the group without parental consent in that its members were naturally more likely to get polio.

When these flaws in the NFIP design were pointed out, many school districts decided to adopt a different design. The alternative design was a double-blind ran-

---

[9]In more complex experiments, other valid comparisons may be obtained among a number of competing treatments without a control group, as long as a baseline is not needed. In such cases, it is essential to have more than one treatment for comparison purposes.

[10]In a number of experiments to evaluate the psychological aspects of pain, 30% or more of hospital patients given a placebo instead of pain killer reported relief!

domized controlled design. Both the control and the treatment groups were chosen from children whose parents consented to vaccination. Children were assigned to the treatment or control group by randomization (essentially tossing a fair coin). The children were not told which group they belonged to, so the experiment was run blind.

As a placebo, the children in the control group were given an injection of salt dissolved in water. To make the experiment double-blind, two sets of people had to be kept ignorant of which subjects received the treatment and which received the placebo:

1. Those who administered the vaccine might communicate the information to the subjects, if only subconsciously. Or they might be tempted to change the random assignment for subjects that they considered high-risk cases.

2. The doctors who were later to diagnose cases of polio among the subjects might let information about the vaccination influence their diagnoses of borderline cases. ✦

Steps for Planning an Experiment

In a recent article, Coleman and Montgomery[11] list twelve steps that should be considered in designing an experiment:

STEPS FOR PLANNING AN EXPERIMENT

1. Decide the objectives of the experiment. These should be unbiased, measurable, and of practical consequence.

2. Obtain relevant background on responses and factors. Where does this experiment fit into the study of the process or system?

3. Decide each response variable that will be measured.

4. Select the factors that are to be systematically varied.

5. Decide each factor to be "held constant" in the experiment.

6. Determine which nuisance factor(s) might affect the response.

7. List and label known or suspected interactions among factors.

8. List restrictions on the experiment.

9. Give current design preferences, if any.

10. If possible, propose analysis and presentation techniques.

11. Determine who will be responsible for the coordination of the experiment.

12. Decide whether trial runs will be conducted.

[11]David E. Coleman and Douglas C. Montgomery, "A Systematic Approach to Planning for a Designed Industrial Experiment (with Discussion)," *Technometrics*, **35**(1) (1993) : 1–27.

This is a long list, and you do not yet know many of the terms on it. It is presented here to give you an idea of the level of planning that may be required for successful experimentation.

3.5　OBSERVATIONAL STUDIES

Broadly speaking, an observational study is any designed study that is not a controlled experiment. Observational studies take their name from the fact that once the sampling units are selected, all data are obtained by observing characteristics of those units, rather than as the result of imposing treatments on those units. We will consider three classes of observational studies: **prospective studies, retrospective studies,** and **sample surveys.**

Prospective Studies

Prospective studies are the observational studies closest in design to a controlled experiment, which is why they are sometimes called **quasi-experiments.** As with a controlled experiment, the goal of a prospective study is to show cause and effect. Hence, the data obtained from each sampling unit consist of hypothesized causal factors and responses. As we will see, however, observational studies cannot show cause and effect.

EXAMPLE 3.12　PROSPECTIVE STUDIES

The most famous examples of prospective studies are those designed to show that smoking causes lung cancer. Sampling units are persons. The hypothesized causal factor is smoking behavior, such as the amount smoked. The individuals are followed over time and the response is occurrence (or not) of lung cancer in that time.

What makes this an observational study is that both the hypothesized causal factor, smoking behavior, and the response, occurrence of lung cancer, are observed characteristics of the sampling units, which cannot be controlled by the researchers.

This lack of control is the major weakness of all observational studies. Suppose, as has consistently happened, that an observational study shows a higher incidence of lung cancer among individuals who smoke than among nonsmokers. This observed difference could be the result of smoking, but it could also be the result of some other cause. For example, there could a genetic defect in a significant fraction of the population that causes both a craving for tobacco and lung cancer. If so, then it may be that smoking does not cause lung cancer, but rather that there is a genetic cause for both smoking and lung cancer.

Examples such as this demonstrate that an observational study cannot show cause and effect. Rather, the most it can establish is an **association.** In the present case, the study might show that an increased incidence of lung cancer is associated with smoking.

It may be useful to consider how we would design an experiment to show that smoking causes lung cancer, if we could. We would first obtain a random sample of nonsmokers from the population of interest. Then, we would assign these nonsmokers at random to treatment and control groups. Those in the treatment group would be forced to smoke according to an assigned regimen; the controls would not be allowed to smoke at all. All individuals would be followed over time and the incidence of lung cancer for the two groups compared. Notice that since the only difference between the two groups is smoking behavior, we can state that an observed difference in lung cancer rates is caused by the difference in smoking behavior.   ◆

Though observational studies do not have the control of assigning treatments to experimental units, there is a sense in which control can be used to make these studies more effective: Observational studies can be controlled for nuisance factors. By this we mean that comparisons can be made only between sampling units having the same or similar values of nuisance factors, or adjusted for values of the nuisance factors. The following example illustrates.

EXAMPLE 3.13   CONTROL IN OBSERVATIONAL STUDIES

Cochran[12] reports the results of several studies relating death rates to smoking behavior. In these studies, information about smoking habits, including type of smoking and amount smoked per day, was first obtained by a mail questionnaire from a large sample of men. For those men who returned the questionnaire, the investigators kept track of deaths over time. Each study found that cigar/pipe smokers[13] had substantially higher death rates than either cigarette smokers or nonsmokers. Does this mean that cigar/pipe smoking carries greater risks than cigarette smoking or non-smoking? Not necessarily. It turns out that cigar/pipe smokers are older on average than men in the other two groups. Therefore, type of smoker and age are confounded, and the increased death rate for cigar/pipe smokers probably reflects the naturally greater death rate for older men. Two options available to investigators to correct this age-induced bias, are:

- Stratify test subjects by age and compare death rates for the three types of smoking behavior within each stratum.
- Use statistical methods to adjust the death rates for the effect of age.   ◆

Retrospective Studies

Retrospective studies are particularly applicable in studying conditions, such as chronic diseases, for which the time between the hypothesized cause and the observed effect

---

[12]William G. Cochran, *Planning and Analysis of Observational Studies*. New York: Wiley, 1983.

[13]Cigar and pipe smokers were combined for analysis because of small sample sizes.

can be substantial. These studies are also useful when the effect occurs rarely. In the first case, a prospective study would be long and costly, and in the second, a prospective study would have to follow a very large number of individuals, at a very large cost, in order to observe enough cases of the effect.

In a retrospective study, the end result is observed, and differences in the hypothesized causes are sought, as the following example illustrates.

EXAMPLE 3.14   RETROSPECTIVE STUDIES

A retrospective study of the relation between smoking and lung cancer would begin by identifying one group consisting of individuals with lung cancer (the end result) and a control group of individuals without lung cancer. Then, investigators would explore how the two groups differ with respect to smoking behavior (the hypothesized cause).

Note that this kind of study lends itself to exploratory analysis. For instance, investigators unsure of the causes of lung cancer could look for differences in the cancer and control groups with respect to a whole range of potential causes.   ◆

Sample Surveys

Sample surveys use a sample of sampling units obtained from a population to obtain information about the whole population. Unlike prospective and retrospective studies, whose primary goal is to establish cause and effect between hypothesized causal factors and responses, sample surveys have as their primary goals description of various aspects of the population from which the sample is obtained, or comparison of subgroups from that population.

EXAMPLE 3.15   A SAMPLE SURVEY

Quality engineers are charged with measuring the defect rate in shipments of paper clips. The shipments consist of cases of 24 boxes each having 100 paper clips. A code on each case indicates which of seven production lines manufactured the clips. Technicians take a simple random sample of cases from each production line (this is a stratified random sample with production lines as strata) and from each case randomly select one paper clip box. Each paper clip in the box is examined for a number of quality characteristics. The results are to be used to describe the numbers of defective paper clips in the shipment, and to compare the proportions of defective paper clips from the different production lines.   ◆

EXAMPLE 3.16   ANOTHER SAMPLE SURVEY

A recently reported sample survey[14] examined attitudes of American adults toward air travel. The poll, conducted by Marist College's Institute for Public Opinion, surveyed 935 adults by telephone. Of those surveyed, 24% said they were

---

[14] Associated Press, "In Poll of Adults, One-Fourth Fear Flying," *The Boston Globe,* November 25, 1997.

afraid to fly. The pollsters used this result to conclude that more than 45 million American adults, the target population, fear flying. ✦

Nonsampling Errors in Studies of Human Populations

You have already been introduced to one kind of nonsampling error: selection bias. Two other kinds of nonsampling errors commonly occur in studies of human populations, such as the study described in Example 3.16, in which individuals are asked to respond to questions, verbally or in writing:

> **DEFINITION**
>
> - **Nonresponse bias** occurs in studies of human populations when a selected individual cannot be contacted or refuses to cooperate. Nonresponse introduces two distinct errors:
>   - The achieved sample size will be smaller than the planned sample size.
>   - The population that is sampled is not the target population but rather a population of those willing to respond.
> - **Response bias** occurs in studies of human populations when questions are phrased in a manner that is difficult to understand or in a fashion that makes a particular answer seem more desirable to the respondent.

Although these nonsampling errors can occur in controlled experiments, they are most prevalent in observational studies, and particularly in sample surveys.

EXAMPLE 3.17   NONSAMPLING ERRORS

Here are some examples of nonresponse bias and response bias.

- **Nonresponse Bias:** A telephone survey firm that calls only during evening hours will fail to contact individuals who live alone and who work at night. A government survey using uniformed police as interviewers will get low response in neighborhoods with a high percentage of illegal alien residents.
- **Response Bias:** It is well known that in order to avoid payroll taxes, some employers pay some workers "under the table." An interviewer from the U.S. Bureau of Labor Statistics will be unlikely to get an accurate answer when asking such an employer about his payroll, even after giving assurances of confidentiality.

    Another way to obtain response bias is to word the questions in a slanted way. "Are you in favor of using tax money to help the needy?" will elicit more positive responses than "Given the welfare mess in this country, are you in favor of spending more tax money on welfare?" ✦

There are no simple fixes for nonresponse and response bias. The investigator must be cautious in designing questionnaires and in dealing with nonresponse so as to minimize the effects of these nonsampling errors.

EXAMPLE 3.18   HOW NOT TO DO A SURVEY

Franklin D. Roosevelt ran for reelection against Alfred Landon in the 1936 presidential election. In all presidential races since 1916, the *Literary Digest,* a popular magazine, had correctly predicted the winner. However, it was wrong in 1936 when the largest sample survey in history was conducted. The magazine predicted that Landon would win, 57% to 43%. In reality, Roosevelt won, 62% to 38%. What went wrong?

There were two major problems with this study.

- **How the *Literary Digest* Picked Its Sample.** The *Literary Digest* mailed questionnaires to 10 million people, but got only 2.4 million replies. The names and addresses that made up the frame came from sources such as telephone books, lists of automobile owners, club membership lists, and the *Digest*'s own subscription lists. This sample, in effect, screened out the poor, who were unlikely to have telephones or belong to clubs.[15] In the *Digest* surveys conducted prior to 1936, the rich and poor voted along similar lines, but this was not the case in 1936. Therefore, the *Digest* did very badly at the first step in choosing the sample; selection bias created a tremendous error.
- **How Nonrespondents Affected the Sample Survey.** The 2.4 million respondents did not even represent the 10 million people who were sampled, and, even worse, they did not represent the population of all voters in the United States at that time. It is known that the lower-class and upper-class tend not to respond to questionnaires. Thus, in the *Digest* poll, the middle class was overrepresented among respondents.

In summary, the *Digest* poll was spoiled by both **selection bias** and **nonresponse bias.** The sample was not representative of the population of U.S. voters.

In 1936, a young man named George Gallup was just setting up a survey sampling organization. By taking a random sample of 3,000 voters from the *Digest*'s list of voters, and mailing all of them a postcard asking them how they would vote, he was able to predict the *Digest*'s predictions within 1% error. Using another better-designed and better-conducted sample of 50,000, he correctly forecast the Roosevelt victory. ✦

Steps in Designing an Observational Study

It is useful to think about designing an observational study in five steps:

1. Determine What Information Is Required. First, we must decide what information is to be collected. Though cost is always a consideration, often, with little additional cost, we can investigate other issues of interest. When data are to be obtained by questioning human subjects, it is important for the investigator to strike a balance in the number of questions that are asked. On the one hand, the omission of an important

---

[15]There were 11 million residential telephones and 9 million unemployed in 1936.

question may require the investigator to repeat the entire study, which might prove too costly. On the other hand, too many questions may convert potential respondents to nonrespondents.

In addition to the questions of direct interest, it is often of interest to collect demographic data such as gender, age, or race. Such information can be used to characterize the sample and to compare it with the target population. Samples whose demographic composition differs greatly from that of the target population might prove unrepresentative in the responses of interest as well.

2. Design the Sampling Plan. The steps involved in designing the sampling plan are given on page 93.

3. Decide How the Data Are to Be Obtained. If objects, such as ball bearings or patient records, are the sampled units, the questions to be answered are exactly how the samples are to be physically collected from the target population. If humans are the sampled units and are to be questioned directly, choices might include mailings, phone calls, or face-to-face interviews.

4. Establish Procedures to Reduce Nonsampling Errors.

(a) **Nonresponse Bias.** Nonresponse tends to be a major problem with studies in which human subjects are questioned directly. If nonresponse is high, we cannot be confident that the results will reflect the true nature of the population. Therefore, it is important to design a study to keep the nonresponse rate (the proportion of the chosen sample not responding) as low as possible. For studies with high nonresponse, we must ensure that the respondents are representative of the target population.

The number of questions asked and the manner in which sample members are contacted are important. The major mechanisms for eliciting information from sample members are by mailed questionnaires, telephone interviews, and in-person interviews. Telephone and in-person sample surveys have higher response rates, but they can be expensive.

It is cheaper to use questionnaires mailed to those selected for the sample, but it is not unusual to have a large number of unreturned questionnaires. It is good design practice to include a covering letter explaining the purposes of the study and politely asking for help. The respondents can be assured that their responses will remain anonymous. A stamped pre-addressed envelope can be included for returning the completed questionnaires. Sometimes it is a good strategy to include a modest monetary inducement or a small gift. However, no matter what strategy is used, there will always be nonresponse.

To try to reduce the rate of nonresponse, nonrespondents should be followed up. Often, it will take several follow-ups to get the nonresponse rate down to a reasonable level. One follow-up strategy is to use telephone or in-person interviews on the nonrespondents to a mailed questionnaire as these are likely to produce higher response rates.

After the data are collected, a comparison can be made to see if non-respondents and respondents differ in crucial ways. Some characteristics that can be considered are age, gender, race, and occupation. These must be obtained from some of the nonrespondents. If the two groups do not differ significantly, nonresponse is less likely to seriously affect the results of the study.

  (b) **Response Bias.** To avoid response bias, questions should be carefully worded and tested and the order in which they are asked randomized. If interviewers are involved, they should be carefully trained to be neutral in their presentation.

5. Do a Pilot Study. It is essential that a pilot study be conducted. Among the uses of a pilot study are

  (a) To obtain information about the target population necessary to design the main study properly.

  (b) To test the operational procedures for conducting the study.

Cause and Effect in Observational Studies

Despite the fact that some observational studies, particularly prospective and retrospective studies, seek to establish a cause-and-effect relationship between hypothesized causal factors and outcomes specified by the response variable, by their very nature, they cannot do so. Because of the lack of controlled experimental conditions, including randomization, we cannot be sure that the observed hypothesized causal factors are not confounded with other factors that are the causes of the observed responses.[16] As a result, the most that observational studies can establish is an **association** between hypothesized causal factors and outcomes. Such association may be strongly suggestive of cause and effect, but by itself does not establish cause and effect.

Nevertheless, when a large number and variety of observational studies establish a strong and consistent association, and when these studies are supplemented indirectly by experimentation and a scientific explanation of the mechanism behind the hypothesized cause and effect, we may consider cause and effect to have been established. This is the story behind our certainty that smoking causes lung cancer. Many observational studies done over the last 50 years show a strong association between smoking and lung cancer. That association holds consistently for various population subgroups. Animal experiments demonstrate that cause and effect conclusively holds for a variety of mammals closely related to humans. In addition, scientists have identified mechanisms at the molecular level that explain a cause-and-effect relationship. Thus, even though no controlled experiments on human populations have been done, the overwhelming weight of evidence establishes cause and effect in this instance.

Coming Attractions

Properly designed studies enable researchers to use the results from a sample of sampling units to make statements about the population from which those sampling units are

---

[16]See Example 3.13.

drawn. Using statistical methods and data from a sample to make statements about the population from which it is drawn is called **statistical inference.** But there is more: something that is of crucial importance for scientific investigation. With a properly designed study and an appropriate **statistical model,** the precision of those statistical inference statements can be mathematically quantified. This offers a rational, quantifiable basis for making decisions based on data.

In the next chapter, we introduce statistical models. Chapters 5 and 6 show how to use the simplest of these models to do inference. The ideas and methods of modeling and inference are extended in later chapters.

D ISCUSSION QUESTIONS

1. Give an overview of the role of statistics, specifically exploratory data analysis and designed studies, in understanding the world.
2. Explain the following: sampling unit, target population, sample, frame, census, sampling design, and sampling plan.
3. What is probability sampling?
4. What is a simple random sample? A stratified random sample? Under what circumstances would each be preferred?
5. What is cluster sampling? Multistage sampling?
6. Explain the following: sampling error, nonsampling error, and selection bias. Give an example of each.
7. What is a controlled experiment?
8. Explain the following terms: experimental unit, factor, treatment, effect, measurement bias, and experimental error.
9. What is a completely randomized design?
10. What is blocking, and why is it done?
11. Explain the difference between a randomized complete block design and a completely randomized design. When would each be used?
12. List the five principles of experimental design. Explain what each means.
13. Explain the terms: method of comparison, treatment group, control group, placebo, and double-blind. How do they relate to experimentation?
14. What is the difference between a true replicate and a duplicate? Give an example of each.
15. How does the way experimental units are chosen affect the kinds of conclusions that can be drawn from an experiment?
16. What is an observational study? Name three classes of observational studies. Give an example of each.
17. What are response bias and nonresponse bias? Give an example of each.
18. Comment on cause and effect with special attention to controlled experiments and observational studies.

E XERCISES

3.1. A biologist wants to investigate the difference among three drugs using a controlled experiment. He has five people on whom he can do this experiment, and these people can behave differently when a drug is administered. What is the most appropriate design? Describe how randomization is used in this design.

3.2. Taste testing is usually done on a 5-point hedonic scale on which 1 means "very poor," 2 means "poor," 3 means "average," 4 means "good," and 5 means "very good." In a taste-testing experiment on Pepsi and Coke among 9 people assigned one of the brands at random, 5 people rated Pepsi 4, 3, 5, 4, and 2, and 4 people rated Coke 3, 2, 1, and 3. What is the effect of Pepsi over Coke?

3.3. Give an original example (i.e., an example not found in the chapter) of a study conducted in a way that results in selection bias. Now show how the same study might be conducted so that it suffers from nonresponse bias. Be clear about the source(s) of bias in each case.

3.4. Suppose that the administration of your college or university has approached the faculty with a controversial proposal on educational policy. It is suspected that faculty opinions on the proposal differ greatly from department to department. You work for the campus newspaper, and your editor has assigned you the task of sampling faculty opinion on the proposal. Specifically, you are to summarize faculty opinion in four departments whose faculty sizes are 30, 40, 20, and 10. Your deadline gives you only enough time to interview 20 faculty in all. What sampling design would you use, and how many members would you take from each department? Give your reasons.

3.5. The following is an example of one or more of selection bias, nonresponse bias, or response bias. Which one(s) is it an example of? Defend your choice(s).

> *In a study to ascertain the incidence of IV drug use, interviewers at several shopping malls in a certain city select every tenth shopper and ask them if they are an IV drug user.*

3.6. In a clinical trial to evaluate the effectiveness of a new DNA-based treatment for major blood clots, patients are randomly assigned to two groups: one to receive the traditional treatment and one to receive the new treatment. Eight weeks after the treatment, the patients are evaluated to see whether the blood clots have been removed. Is this a controlled experiment? Why? If it is, identify the experimental units, the treatment, and the response.

3.7. In a study to compare the durability of two brands of marine paint, six private boats from different areas of the country were painted with brand A and another six with brand B. After 1 year of normal use, the paint condition was measured. In no more than two short sentences, discuss how and why blocking might provide a better design.

3.8. The following is an excerpt from an article that appeared in *The Boston Globe* of June 6, 1994:

> *The number of heart-attack victims fell dramatically among coronary patients who were taking the cholesterol-lowering drug Pravastatin, according to researchers. Scientists at the Bowman Gray School of Medicine reported in the* American Journal of Cardiology *that in addition to the unexpectedly sharp drop in heart attacks, there was also a slide in other diseases. The study was aimed at evaluating the effect of the drug on the growth of atherosclerosis.*

The team found that 5 percent of the 75 patients taking the drug experienced fatal or non-fatal coronary episodes during the three-year study period, compared to 13 percent of the 76 patients who got an inert placebo.

(a) Was this study a controlled experiment? Why? If not an experiment, what kind of study was it?

(b) What is the response variable here? What are the factors?

(c) What further information about the design would you need to evaluate the statistical validity of the results obtained?

3.9. There are potential biases associated with each of the sampling plans described in what follows. Describe what they are and how you expect them to affect the results. What, if anything, can be done to obtain better results?

(a) In an interview of heads of families with both husband and wife present, the interviewer asks how many sex partners each had in the past year.

(b) The U.S. Census Bureau tries to estimate the number of illegal aliens in the country by sending out interviewers to go door to door.

(c) To gage public sentiment on gun control, a TV news show has viewers call a 900 number during the 11 o'clock newscast. The question to be answered is, "Should the government infringe on our constitutional right to bear arms?"

3.10. In one study, it was necessary to draw a representative sample of Japanese-American residents in San Francisco. The procedure was as follows. After consultation with representative figures in the Japanese-American community, the four most representative blocks in the Japanese area of the city were chosen; all Japanese-Americans resident in those four blocks were taken for the sample. However, a comparison with census data shows that the sample did not include a high-enough proportion of Japanese-Americans with college degrees. How can this be explained?

3.11. A study is carried out by the Social Service Department to determine the distribution of household size in a city. A random sample of 500 households was taken. After several visits, the interviewers found people at home in only 270 of the sample households. Based on these households, the average household size was three persons per family. Is this estimate likely to be too low, too high, or just right? Justify your answer.

3.12. What is your major? Imagine you have graduated with a degree in your major, and that you have obtained a job in your major field. Give an example of how a simple random sample and a stratified random sample might arise in your work.

3.13. Give an original example (i.e., an example not found in the chapter) of a controlled experiment in which two factors are confounded.

3.14. A new alloy is believed to be more durable than the one in current use for making front disk brakes in cars. A car company wanted to test these brakes on cars. The company selected 12 new cars that were divided at random into two groups of six each with one group having the old alloy and the other the new alloy. To test drive the cars, they randomly select 12 drivers from a group of volunteers. The selected drivers were assigned at random to the cars and were asked to drive the cars in 5000 miles of normal day-to-day driving. Come up with a better design and explain why it is better.

3.15. For each of the following, tell whether it is a designed study or not. If it is a designed study, tell what kind it is. Be as specific as you can.

(a) In a study on the effect of aspirin in preventing heart attacks, 50,000 physicians were randomly assigned to a treatment group, which took aspirin every day, and a control group, which took a placebo (a sugar capsule) every day.

(b) Fifteen hundred randomly selected male voters were asked their preference for President. Their answers were compared with those of fifteen hundred randomly selected female voters.

(c) A company marketing team looks at all customer orders for the past 3 years to see if any demographic patterns stand out.

3.16. A *Boston Globe* article of September 21, 1994, reported:

> *Regular exercise beginning in adolescence and continuing into adulthood can significantly reduce the risk of breast cancer in younger women, an intriguing new study has found. . . . The exercise study . . . looked at 1,090 women aged 40 or under—545 of them newly diagnosed breast cancer patients and 545 "controls" without cancer who were similar in age and other characteristics. All were interviewed on physical activity since puberty . . . menstrual periods, family history of breast cancer and pregnancy history.*

(a) Was this study a controlled experiment? Why? If not, what kind of study was it? Be as specific as you can.

(b) Based on what you know of this study, do you think it is valid to conclude that increased exercise causes a reduction in breast cancer rates? Why or why not?

(c) What alternative explanation can you offer for the observed association between exercise and breast cancer?

3.17. Give an example of a poor design of a controlled experiment of your choice. Point out its problems. Explain how you might correct these problems.

3.18. Dr. Josephine Lo and her associates treated 31 patients suffering from severe headaches as a result of spinal punctures. Conventional treatment did not help. She found that 30 out of 31 patients experienced "complete and permanent relief" after one to five acupuncture treatments. Is this good evidence for the effectiveness of acupuncture? Why or why not?

3.19. You've run into them: waiters or waitresses who draw happy faces on your restaurant check. A psychologist wants to determine whether drawing such a face will affect the tips that a server gets. How would you design the study?[17]

3.20. In Example 3.8, suppose that the experimenter had known prior to running the experiment about the different response of full- and part-time workers to incentive programs. Explain how he could have used blocking to design a more effective experiment.

3.21. Which of the following are true replicates, and which are duplicates? In each case, how many replicates or duplicates are there? If a duplicate, how can the experiment be changed to give a true replicate? Give reasons for your answers.

(a) In order to test the corrosiveness of different fluxes used in soldering computer circuit boards, a specimen of copper is immersed in one of the fluxes and the resulting electrical potential measured three times in succession. The same is done for each flux in succession in a randomly chosen order.

(b) Bleach is used in the paper industry to whiten the product. In order to determine the effect of bleach concentration on the tear strength of letter paper, a process engineer divided a batch of paper pulp into three equal portions, and added a different level of bleach concentration to each of these three portions. She then randomly selected eight

---

[17]An actual study of this phenomenon was conducted by two Temple University psychologists. They found that drawing happy faces resulted in a 19% increase in tips, on average, for waitresses, but a slight decrease for waiters.

paper sheets from the finished product of each batch portion and measured their tear strengths.

3.22. The following article appeared in *The Boston Globe* of February 20, 1992.

Heavy Use of Asthma Drug Raises Risk of Death, Study Finds

People who overuse a common kind of inhaled drug to relieve asthma attacks face a greatly increased risk of death, a study concludes.

The researchers don't know whether the drugs, called beta agonists, are themselves to blame. But they said asthmatics nearly triple their chance of death with each canister of the spray they use per month.

The risk varies, depending on the specific kind of beta agonist taken, the researchers reported in today's issue of The New England Journal of Medicine. *Beta agonists have long been the primary drug used to treat asthma, but some doctors are now recommending that other drugs be used first and beta agonists reserved as a backup to relieve acute attacks.*

"If a patient is using more than one canister of beta agonist a month, they are using too much, and their asthma ... needs to be evaluated," said Dr. A. Sonia Buist of the Oregon Health Sciences University, coauthor of the study.

The findings were based on insurance records from Saskatchewan, Canada. The study was financed by Boihringer-Ingelheim Pharmaceuticals, a German drug company. The researchers reviewed the records of 129 people who had fatal or nearly fatal asthma attacks and compared them with 655 asthmatics who had never had life-threatening attacks.

The risk of death increased fivefold with each canister of fenoterol, a double-strength variety of beta agonist made by Boihringer-Ingelheim. It is not available in the United States.

The risk of death about doubled with each canister per month of another variety of beta agonist, called albuterol, which is widely used in the United States and sold under such brands as Preventil and Ventolin.

Researchers suspect that beta agonists might somehow make the air passages in the lungs grow more irritable over time, so they overreact to irritants that trigger attacks.

Answer the following questions about the article:
(a) Was this study a controlled experiment? Why? If not a controlled experiment, what kind of study was it? Be as specific as you can.
(b) What is the response variable here? What are the factors?
(c) What in the article suggests a causal link between increased use of beta agonists and increased death rates?
(d) What alternative explanation can you offer for the observed association between increased use of beta agonists and increased death rates?

3.23. In a paper published in the journal *Epidemiology*, Dr. James E. Enstrom and colleagues at UCLA recently reported on a study they conducted to assess the effects of taking multivitamin supplements containing vitamin C. In their study, the authors reviewed health data from a national sample of 11,348 people questioned in 1971–1974 and followed up in 1984 to see if they were still alive. The study purported to show significantly lower death rates in men, and slightly lower death rates in women, among the group who took multivitamin pills containing vitamin C compared with those who didn't.

(a) Was this study a controlled experiment? Why? If not a controlled experiment, what kind of study was it? Be as specific as possible.

(b) What is the response variable here? What are the factors?

(c) Is it valid to conclude that taking vitamin C causes lower death rates? Why or why not?

(d) What alternative explanation can you offer for the observed association between taking multivitamins with vitamin C and lower death rates?

3.24. Scientists have long wondered what role, if any, fever plays in defending the body against infection. In order to determine whether fever is a beneficial response to infection, researchers assigned laboratory mice at random to two groups. Both groups were infected with a fever-causing virus. Fevers in the first group were brought within normal limits with carefully monitored doses of aspirin. The second group was given nothing. The researchers found that the death rate for the first group was significantly higher than that of the second group.

(a) Was this study a controlled experiment? Justify your answer. If not a controlled experiment, what kind of study was it? Be as specific as possible.

(b) Can the researchers conclude that the increased death rate in the treatment group is due to the absence of fever? Justify your answer.

3.25. A local TV station recently took a poll of the public's views on the governor's performance in office. The question: "How do you rate the governor's performance: excellent, good, average, poor or terrible?" was displayed at the beginning of the newscast. A 900 number was also displayed for viewers to register their views on this question. The results were announced at the end of the newscast. Name three reasons not to trust the results of this poll.

3.26. *The New York Times* of May 16, 1994, reported on a sample survey question that produced unexpected results. A Roper Poll asked adult Americans and high school students the following question:

> *Does it seem possible or does it seem impossible to you that the Nazi extermination of the Jews never happened?*

The published results said that 22% of the adults and 20% of the high school students surveyed said that they thought it was possible that the Nazi extermination of the Jews never happened and that an additional 12% of adults said that they did not know if it was possible or impossible.

The Gallup organization later conducted its own sample survey to test the validity of the Roper sample survey. Responding to a differently worded question, less than 0.5% responded that the Holocaust "definitely" did not happen, and 2% said it "probably" did not happen.

Why do you think the results differ so dramatically? Do you think the Roper results accurately reflect the thinking of the populations surveyed? Give your reasons.

3.27. Use a small population to explain the term "frame" in sampling. Then use a sample from this population to explain selection bias.

3.28. A company has four departments with 20, 30, 30, and 20 employees. You suspect that employees in different departments might have quite different opinions about the statement, "The company is heading in the wrong direction." If a sample of opinions is required from 10 employees, what sampling design would you use, and how many members would you take from each department? Justify your choices.

3.29. A food technologist wants to investigate the effect of storage temperature on the quality of three entree items: pork sausage, ham–chicken loaf, and beef patty. The three entrees are to be stored at temperatures 4°C and 30°C, respectively. He has 60 taste-testing panelists available for this experiment, and these panelists are similar. What is the most appropriate design for this experiment? What are the factors?

3.30. The following sample survey design might result in one or more of selection bias, nonresponse bias, or response bias. Which one(s) might it result in? Predict how these biases might affect the results. Defend your choice(s).

> *A manufacturer of laundry soaps wants to know what fraction of Boston households do more than six loads of wash per week. A simple random sample of 300 residential addresses is drawn from a telephone book and interviewers are sent to these addresses. The interviewers are employed during regular working hours on weekdays and they interview only during those hours.*

3.31. A *Boston Globe* article of September 14, 1995, reports on a study published in the *New England Journal of Medicine*. In the study, researchers followed 115,195 nurses aged 30 to 55 over a 16-year period. They found that obese women—who weighed more than 30 to 40 pounds above optimal weight—had three times the risk of dying from cardiovascular disease of the leanest women in the study, and double the risk of overall mortality. Death rates from cancer among obese women were also double those of the leanest women.

  (a) Was this study a controlled experiment? Why? If not a controlled experiment, what kind of study was it? Be as specific as you can.

  (b) What is the response variable here? What are the factors you can identify?

  (c) Based on what you know of this study, do you think it is valid to conclude that obesity causes early death? Why or why not?

  (d) What alternative explanation can you offer for the observed association between obesity and early death?

3.32. Consider the studies described in Example 3.1. Tell what kind of study each is. Be as specific as you can.

3.33. Explain how you would use blocking, randomization, and replication in a controlled experiment to determine whether most people prefer Pepsi or Coke.

3.34. The following sample survey design might result in one or more of selection bias, nonresponse bias, or response bias. Which one(s) might it result in? Defend your choice(s).

> *To assess public support for balancing the budget by the year 2002, a simple random sample is taken from a list of magazine subscribers supplied by a publisher. The persons in the sample are interviewed by telephone and asked the following question: "Don't you feel that cutbacks in government spending are necessary to restore fiscal stability to our country?"*

3.35. Consider a post-Thanksgiving controlled experiment in which one piece of apple pie is placed in the refrigerator and one piece is left on the counter, and the time it takes for each to develop mold is recorded. What is the *treatment* and what is the *response?*

3.36. A study on the quality of the rustproofing of 1978 Honda Accords is being done. One hundred original owners of Accords that had the factory rustproofing, and who still own the cars, are contacted. In addition, 100 original owners of Accords that did not have factory rustproofing, and who still own the cars, are contacted. Information about the sample survey is sent to all 200 of these owners, who live in various cities and towns all across the United States. The sample survey questionnaire asks about the amount and location of rust on the cars. Briefly, discuss how and why stratification might provide a better design.

3.37. Recall the sample survey on factory rustproofing discussed in the previous question. Factory rustproofing for 1978 Accords was an option that had to be specially ordered. With this knowledge, do you think the effectiveness of rustproofing found in the sample survey might be confounded with other factors? Discuss.

3.38. As an avid gardener, I want to use the most effective fertilizer on my plants. This year I am planning to try a new fertilizer for my tomatoes. I grow tomatoes at three different locations in my yard. How should I design a controlled experiment to test this new fertilizer against the one I use now?

3.39. I have recently purchased a very old home and I am planning to refinish the old wide pine floors in my kitchen, which are in very bad shape. To refinish them, I plan to experiment with four grades of sandpaper. I split the room into 16 equal-size sections, use sandpaper number 1 on the first four sections, sandpaper number 2 on the next four sections, and so on, and in this way have four replicates using each type of sandpaper. Or do I? Are these true replicates? If not, what are they? Propose a better design.

3.40. A sports psychologist is conducting a study on the eating habits of students on campus, and how they differ between "ordinary" students and those involved with athletic programs. Her hypothesis is that many students on athletic teams have eating disorders as a result of pressure (self-imposed or otherwise) to attain or maintain certain physical properties (weight, strength, etc.). However, on the questionnaire that she distributes to students, she is careful not to ask the question: "Do you think you have an eating disorder?" outright, figuring that students sensitive to this issue in their own lives might be troubled by the question and so refuse to complete the questionnaire. What sort of bias is the psychologist trying to avoid by asking more subtle questions? Explain your answer.

3.41. In order to determine if the well-off get more aggressive medical treatment than the poor, two trained actors were given identical fictitious medical histories and symptoms. The first actor was sent to tell his story to 12 physicians randomly selected from the medical directory of a large U.S. city, and the second actor did likewise with another set of 12 randomly selected physicians. In their meetings with the doctors, one actor played a wealthy CEO and the other a blue-collar worker. Among other data, the number of diagnostic tests ordered by the physicians was recorded.

(a) Tell why this is a controlled experiment.

(b) Identify the response variable(s), treatments, and experimental units.

(c) Use blocking to improve the design of this experiment. Explain why your design is an improvement.

3.42. The June 26, 1996, edition of *The New York Times* reports on a study published in the journal *Pediatrics*. The researchers randomly selected 716 children from two counties in upstate New York. These children were followed from adolescence/preadolescence until adulthood. They were evaluated for depression, separation anxiety, and overanxious disorder. Among the findings were that girls who were overly anxious grew up to be 1 to 2 inches shorter, on average, than girls who were not overly anxious.

(a) What kind of study is this? Be as specific as possible.

(b) Identify the target population and the sample.

MINIPROJECT

Purpose

The purpose of this miniproject is to give you experience in the design, conduct, and analysis of a controlled experiment.

Process

Your group is to design, conduct, and analyze a controlled experiment comparing the taste preferences of people for two different sodas, Pepsi and Coke, for example.

You are required to submit a short (no more than one-page) proposal for your instructor's approval before conducting the experiment. Your proposal must state at the outset the question or questions you propose to investigate. You must describe in detail both the sampling plan and the experimental design. In particular, you should say what factors you are going to consider, how you are going to measure the responses, who your subjects are and what characteristics your subjects might have that can help in assessing any difference between the two sodas, and in ensuring that the results can be generalized to the target population. Tell why the proposed experiment will answer the question(s) you are asking.

After you have collected the data, analyze them and draw conclusions. You can, and should, use knowledge and techniques obtained from other chapters. In particular, use graphical and numerical summaries of the data to back up your conclusions.

LAB 3.1: The Election of '36

Introduction

You have read about the Presidential election of 1936, and the *Literary Digest* poll. In this lab, you will relive those fateful days of yesteryear! The frame or list of "voters" that is attached contains demographic data and the votes of 60 "voters" that make up the population you'll be sampling from. This population is meant to simulate that of the United States in 1936. The variables are

VOTER	An identification number.
CLASS	L = lower; U = upper and middle.
CAR	N = doesn't own one. Y = owns one.
PHONE	N = doesn't have one. Y = has one.
VOTE	R = Roosevelt. L = Landon.

In this lab, you are to take three different samples from this population: a simple random sample of size 12, a stratified random sample of size 12, and a sample of size 12 done to mimic the *Literary Digest* sample survey.

Objectives

To give you a practical understanding of simple random sampling and stratified random sampling. To demonstrate the advantages of stratified random sampling. To show where and how the *Literary Digest* went wrong in 1936.

Lab Materials

A 10-sided die.

Experimental Procedure

Data Collection

1. Begin by drawing the simple random sample. Use two rolls of your die to obtain a two-digit number. Use the "0" or the "10" (whichever your die has) as 0. If the two-digit number belongs to one of the so far unselected "voters," include that "voter" in the sample. Keep going until you have a sample of 12 "voters." Your estimate of the proportion of "voters" voting for Roosevelt is the sample proportion of "voters" voting for Roosevelt. Record its value. (Note that we're assuming that the "voters" will tell the truth about their votes, and that all will vote.)

2. Next, draw a stratified random sample. Since we suspect that lower-class "voters" will vote differently than upper- and middle-class, we'll stratify according to class with lower-class "voters" forming one stratum and upper- and middle-class "voters" a second stratum. We'll also use sample sizes in the strata proportional to the size of each stratum in the population: 8 from the lower-class stratum and 4 from the upper- and middle-class stratum. Use your die to obtain a simple random sample from each stratum. The correct estimate of the population proportion of votes for Roosevelt is computed by the following formula: let $\hat{p}_l$ and $\hat{p}_u$ denote the sample proportion of lower- and upper-class votes for Roosevelt, respectively. Then the overall estimate of the votes for Roosevelt weights these proportions by the relative frequencies of the population strata. Here, since 2/3 of the "voters" are lower-class, the formula is

$$\hat{p} = \frac{2}{3}\hat{p}_l + \frac{1}{3}\hat{p}_u$$

Compute this estimate and record its value.

3. Finally, pretend you're the *Literary Digest*. You'll take a simple random sample from those who own either telephones or cars or both. Since you think you're taking a simple random sample of the entire population, you'll use the sample proportion of Roosevelt votes to estimate the true proportion. Calculate this value and record it.

Analysis

Your instructor will now collect the data from all of you and combine it into one data set. The variable SRS will contain the proportions each of you computed for the first simple random sample. The variable STRAT will contain the proportions each of you computed for the stratified random sample. The variable LD will contain the proportions each of you computed for the *Literary Digest* sample survey. You are to analyze these three variables in terms of how they perform on these data. You should especially consider the following:

1. Whether they are **unbiased.** That is, is the mean value very close to the true proportion of Roosevelt votes? (By the way, what was the true proportion of "votes" for Roosevelt?)
2. How precise are they? Do they vary a lot, or a little?

"Voter" Population Data

VOTER	CLASS	CAR	PHONE	VOTE	VOTER	CLASS	CAR	PHONE	VOTE
1	L	N	N	R	31	L	Y	Y	R
2	L	N	Y	L	32	L	N	N	L
3	L	N	N	R	33	L	N	N	R
4	L	N	N	R	34	L	N	N	R
5	L	N	N	R	35	L	N	Y	L
6	L	N	N	R	36	L	N	N	R
7	L	N	N	R	37	L	N	Y	R
8	L	N	N	R	38	L	N	N	R
9	L	Y	Y	R	39	L	N	N	R
10	L	N	N	R	40	L	N	N	R
11	L	N	N	R	41	U	Y	Y	L
12	L	N	N	R	42	U	Y	Y	L
13	L	Y	Y	L	43	U	Y	Y	R
14	L	N	N	R	44	U	Y	Y	R
15	L	N	Y	L	45	U	Y	Y	L
16	L	N	N	R	46	U	Y	Y	L
17	L	N	N	R	47	U	Y	Y	L
18	L	N	N	R	48	U	Y	Y	L
19	L	N	N	R	49	U	Y	Y	L
20	L	N	N	R	50	U	Y	Y	L
21	L	N	Y	L	51	U	N	Y	R
22	L	N	N	R	52	U	Y	Y	L
23	L	N	N	R	53	U	Y	Y	L
24	L	N	N	R	54	U	Y	Y	L
25	L	N	Y	L	55	U	N	Y	R
26	L	N	N	R	56	U	Y	Y	L
27	L	N	N	R	57	U	Y	Y	L
28	L	N	Y	L	58	U	N	Y	R
29	L	N	N	R	59	U	Y	Y	L
30	L	N	N	R	60	U	Y	Y	L

LAB 3.2: Working for Scale

Introduction

In Chapter 3, the basic motivations for blocking in experimental design were discussed. In particular, the **completely randomized design** was contrasted with the **randomized complete block**

design. Pairing is the simplest form of blocking. In fact, it is the special case of the randomized complete block design in which there are two treatments.

In this lab, you will conduct a controlled experiment. The experimental design will be what is called a paired comparison design. A paired comparison design is the simplest version of a randomized complete block design. To demonstrate the effect of blocking (or, in this case, pairing), the data will be analyzed in two different ways: first, as paired comparisons (i.e., making use of the blocking), and then as if the data resulted from a completely randomized design (i.e., ignoring the blocking). The results should show you that "block what you can, randomize the rest," is good advice.

Objectives

To give you a practical understanding of the advantages of blocking.

Lab Materials

A bathroom scale.

Experimental Procedure

Data Collection

1. Come up to the "weigh station" when the instructor calls your name.
2. Before beginning, zero out the scale.
3. The instructor will flip a coin (randomization). If the coin comes up heads, hold the scale in your right hand so that it doesn't touch anything except your hand (the instructor will show you how). Squeeze as hard as you can while watching the dial on the scale. Tell the instructor the maximum pressure registered, to the nearest pound. When you have finished with the right hand, repeat with your left hand (be sure to zero out the scale again). You may now return to your seat.
4. If the coin comes up tails, do the steps explained in 3 with the left hand first, then the right hand.

Your instructor will now collect the data from all of you and combine it into a data set, which will contain the following variables:

STUDENT	The student's name.
HAND	Right or left hand.
PRESS	Pressure exerted on the scale.

For example, if there are three students, the data might look like this:

STUDENT	HAND	PRESS
Chico	l	50
Groucho	l	54
Harpo	l	33
Chico	r	61
Groucho	r	49
Harpo	r	36

Analysis

Now analyze the data as follows:

1. Plot PRESS versus STUDENT on a scatterplot. There will be two values for each student. On the plot, indicate next to each point whether it was done with the left or right hand.[18]
   (a) Describe the pattern of variation in the PRESS values. Is a substantial amount of the total spread of these values accounted for by the different students (student-to-student variation)? Or is the student-to-student variation small compared with the within-student variation (the spread of the left- and right-hand pressures for each student)? If the first is true, then blocking may be useful, and paired data analysis might help. Which do you think is the case here?
   (b) How many of the students have a stronger right hand? How many have a stronger left hand?

2. Now plot PRESS versus HAND. This plot compares overall left-handed versus right-handed scores, but does not distinguish which score belongs to which student. This is equivalent to ignoring the blocking in the data. Just by viewing the graph, can you tell whether the left hand or right hand is stronger? How does this compare with what you saw in part 1?

Because the data were paired, the proper analysis for this study is the paired analysis. However, we might have designed the study as two unpaired samples by measuring the right-hand strength of one sample of subjects and the left-hand strength of a different sample of subjects. For such a study, the results might have looked similar to the data we obtained, and the proper graph would be the plot of PRESS versus HAND.

---

[18]SAS and MINITAB users can find directions for doing this in the accompanying **Doing It with SAS** or **Doing It with MINITAB** computer supplement.

An Introduction
to Statistical Modeling

All models are wrong, but some are useful.

—G. E. P. Box

Models are to be used but not to be believed.

—H. Theil

INTRODUCTION

Webster's dictionary defines a **model** as "a generalized hypothetical description used in analyzing or explaining something." Models are the essence of science. Science proceeds by forming a tentative model, collecting or producing data to test that model, and then using the data to criticize and refine that model. Then the cycle begins again and the latest model will eventually be replaced by a new and better model. The evolution of cosmology illustrates the point well. At the dawn of modern science, the accepted model of the universe was one of geocentric crystalline spheres on which the sun and the seven known planets danced in an elaborate series of cycles and epicycles. The Copernican model of planets revolving about the sun simplified the universe and made better predictions of planetary motions. Over the succeeding years, the accepted model of the universe was iteratively improved, tested, and criticized as it grew to explain the presence first of neighboring stars, then of our galaxy, of other galaxies, of clusters of galaxies, and of the expansion of the universe (the Big Bang). Should we take the current Big Bang theory as "truth"? The answer is no. It, like all models, is flawed and tentative. For example, there is not enough observable matter in the universe to account for the Big Bang. Eventually, the present cosmological model will be superseded by an improved theory.

What have models to do with statistics? Over the years, statisticians and scientists have noticed that certain data-distribution patterns occur repeatedly in nature. From these patterns has arisen the idea of theoretical distributions: mathematical curves that serve as **models** for these observed data-distribution patterns. One of the great advantages of mathematics is that the essential features of quite different phenomena can be described by the same mathematical model. However, it is useful to note at the outset that a model is only an approximation to reality, a point made in the Box and Theil quotes at the beginning of the chapter.

In this chapter, you will learn about some of the most widely used distribution models. You will learn the types of data for which these models are appropriate, and the assumptions on which they are based, by performing physical and computer experiments. In particular, you will learn

- Why these distribution models explain patterns that occur so often in nature.
- What kinds of data these models might represent.
- How some of these models are related to each other.

Knowledge and Skills

By successfully completing this chapter, you will acquire the following knowledge and skills:

KNOWLEDGE	SKILLS
1. What a density histogram is.	1. You will learn how to define and interpret probabilities for random phenomena.
2. The basic ideas of probability.	2. You will learn basic rules for calculating probabilities.
3. An understanding of the power, uses, and limitations of statistical models.	3. You will be able to work with the distributions of discrete and continuous random variables: finding means, variances, and standard deviations, and relevant probabilities.
4. An understanding of discrete and continuous random variables and their distribution models as models for many random phenomena.	4. You will be able to model phenomena using binomial, Poisson, uniform, or normal distribution models.
5. An understanding of the underlying principles defining the binomial, Poisson, uniform, and normal distributions, and an acquaintance with several other distribution models.	5. You will be able to apply the Central Limit Theorem. *(continued)*

KNOWLEDGE	SKILLS
6. The Central Limit Theorem, and its use as an approximation tool.	**6.** You will be able to identify an appropriate distribution for a given data set by use of Q–Q plots.
7. Transformations to normality.	**7.** You will be able to use transformations (e.g., transformations to normality) to obtain a simpler model.

4.1

DENSITY HISTOGRAMS

Beginning in Chapter 1, we have been using frequency histograms to display data. To construct a frequency histogram, data are first divided into subgroups and the number, or frequency, of data values in each subgroup is computed. Then one bar is drawn for each subgroup. The height of the bar is equal to the frequency of the subgroup. The frequency histogram of the salaries of technical support workers displayed in Figure 2.4 in Chapter 2 groups salaries into those falling between $22,500 and $25,500, those falling between $25,500 and $28,500, those falling between $28,500 and $31,500, and so on.

Another graph for quantitative data that is similar to the frequency histogram is the **density histogram.** As with the frequency histogram, construction of a density histogram begins with the division of the data into subgroups. The subgroups are formed by dividing the range of data values into subintervals, just as was done with the salary data. Then a bar is drawn above each interval. The density histogram differs from the frequency histogram in the height of its bars. In a density histogram, bar height is not equal to the frequency of data in the subinterval. Rather, the bar height is chosen so that the area of the bar is equal to the proportion of data in the subinterval. This is a better way to display data when the intervals are not of equal width, since in any two-dimensional graph, the human eye equates area with "how much." This is why it is poor practice to use bars of unequal width in a frequency histogram.

In a density histogram, the height of a bar is the **density** of data in the subinterval. The density of data in a subinterval is computed as the frequency of data in the subinterval divided by the product of the total number of observations and the width of the subinterval. Thus, if f_i is the frequency of data in the ith subinterval, if w_i is the width of the subinterval, and if n is the total number of data values in the data set, then the density of data in the subinterval is $f_i/(w_i \times n)$. As a result:

- The area of the bar over the subinterval is its width times its height, or

$$\text{Area} = w_i \times \frac{f_i}{w_i \times n} = \frac{f_i}{n}$$

which equals the proportion of the data that lies in the subinterval.

- The total area of any density histogram, being the sum of the areas of all the bars, equals the sum of the proportions of data in all subintervals. This sum is 1.

When the subintervals are of equal width, as they should be for all frequency histograms, the frequency histogram and the density histogram look exactly the same: only the units on the vertical axis change.

CONSTRUCTING A DENSITY HISTOGRAM

- Determine the subintervals for grouping the data. These need not be of equal width.
- Determine whether data values at subinterval boundaries go into the lower or upper subinterval. This can be done either way, as long as you are consistent.
- Count the frequency of data in each subinterval.
- Compute the density of data in each subinterval. The density is the frequency divided by the product of the total number of observations and the subinterval width.
- On a number line, draw a bar above each subinterval. The height of the bar is equal to the density of data in the subinterval.

EXAMPLE 4.1   A DENSITY HISTOGRAM

Figure 4.1 is a density histogram of the technical support salary data in which the subintervals are of unequal width. This density histogram is constructed as follows. First, the subintervals are determined. They are shown in the leftmost column

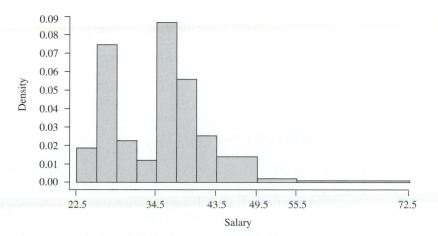

Figure 4.1 Density histogram of technical support salary data; units are $1000s.

TABLE 4.1   Subintervals, Subinterval Widths, Frequencies, and Densities Used in Constructing the Density Histogram in Figure 4.1. The Last Column Shows the Areas of the Bars, Which Measure the Proportion of All Observations That Lie in the Different Subintervals

Subinterval ($1000s)	Subinterval width	Frequency	Density	Area of bar
22.5–25.5	3	14	0.0186̄	0.056
25.5–28.5	3	56	0.0753̄	0.224
28.5–31.5	3	17	0.0226̄	0.068
31.5–34.5	3	9	0.0120	0.036
34.5–37.5	3	65	0.0866̄	0.260
37.5–40.5	3	42	0.0560	0.168
40.5–43.5	3	19	0.0253̄	0.076
43.5–49.5	6	21	0.0140	0.084
49.5–55.5	6	3	0.0020	0.012
55.5–72.5	17	4	0.0009	0.016
Totals:		250		1.00

of Table 4.1, and their widths are in the next column. Next, the frequencies of observations in the subintervals are found. These are listed in the third column. Finally, the densities for each interval are computed by dividing the frequencies by the product of the interval widths and 250, the total number of observations. The heights of the bars are the densities. The last column of the table shows the area of each bar, which is the proportion of all observations contained in the corresponding subinterval. For example, the table shows that the width of the subinterval (43.5, 49.5) (units are thousands of dollars) in Figure 4.1 is 6, that the frequency of observations in the subinterval is 21, and that the density of data in the subinterval is $21/(6 \times 250) = 0.0140$, which is the height of the bar in the density histogram. Consequently, the area of the bar over the subinterval equals $6 \times 0.0140 = 0.084$, which implies that 8.4% of the 250 technical support workers have salaries in the $43,500–$49,500 range.   ◆

4.2

THE NOTION OF PROBABILITY

There is a well-known saying that in life only two things are certain: death and taxes. Although we might find a few additional items to add to that list, we all know that many things are uncertain. If we roll a die or flip a coin, we cannot say with certainty, before the roll or flip, exactly what will happen. If we invest in the stock market, we cannot say with certainty what will happen to our investment tomorrow. Fortunately for us, it often happens that uncertainty follows a pattern. For example, if a coin is fair, then if it is tossed repeatedly, about half the time it will land heads. If a six-sided die is fair, then about 1/6 of the time, a 3 will come up.

Probability is the mathematical quantification of uncertainty. In order to formulate and use statistical models, it is essential that we understand the basic notion of probability. We begin our investigation of probability with the definition of a **Bernoulli trial.**[1]

> **DEFINITION**
>
> A **Bernoulli trial** is an occurrence in which exactly one of two possible outcomes can occur.

Depending on the application, these outcomes can be denoted as 1/0, on/off, yes/no, and so on. For our purposes, they will be denoted "success" and "failure."

EXAMPLE 4.2   BERNOULLI TRIALS

1. Suppose you have a coin that you are going to toss once. Tossing the coin can be regarded as a Bernoulli trial, with the two possible outcomes of "head" and "tail." For the purposes of describing the Bernoulli trial, we can either call getting a head a "success" or we can call getting a tail a "success," as long as we are consistent and clear about which we choose.

2. Before an electronics firm will accept an incoming lot of controller chips for compact disc players, the quality of the chips is tested by selecting one at random and running it through a series of tests. This procedure constitutes a Bernoulli trial with two possible outcomes: "pass" or "fail." For the purposes of describing the trial, we can call either "pass" or "fail" a "success."[2]   ◆

The only other thing to know about a Bernoulli trial is how likely success is to occur. The measure of how likely a success is to occur is called the **probability** of success, and will be denoted p. The interpretation most often given to the probability of success in a single Bernoulli trial is that it is equal to the relative frequency of success in infinitely many identical repeated Bernoulli trials. Actually, it is the limit of the relative frequencies of success in n trials as n approaches infinity. To see what this means, consider again the Bernoulli trials described in Example 4.2.

EXAMPLE 4.2   CONTINUED

1. Consider the Bernoulli trial consisting of tossing a coin. For definiteness, call the result a success if the coin lands heads up. Suppose you begin tossing the coin repeatedly, in exactly the same way each time. After n tosses, count the number of times the coin landed heads up. Denote this number N_n. Let $p_n = N_n/n$ denote the relative frequency of heads in the first n tosses. For example, if the coin has been tossed 11 times and heads occurred 6 times, $N_{11} = 6$ and $p_{11} = 6/11$. Now as n becomes very large (approaching infinity: we're assuming you have lots

---

[1]Named after the Swiss mathematician Jacob Bernoulli, 1654–1705.

[2]Though, in regular English, it makes more sense to call "pass" a "success."

of time on your hands), p_n converges to p. If the probability of heads is $p = 0.5$, the coin is considered fair.

2. For the controller chip example, the Bernoulli trial consists of drawing a chip from the shipment at random and testing it. You can think of random drawing as putting all the chips in a bin, mixing them well, and then reaching in and pulling one out. If the chip is nondefective, we will call the result a success. After testing the chip, we put it back into the shipment and perform the trial again. Let N_n denote the number of nondefective chips drawn, and let $p_n = N_n/n$ denote the relative frequency of nondefective chips drawn in the first n such trials. As n goes to infinity, p_n converges to p, the probability of drawing a nondefective chip.   ◆

Some of you are objecting right now that the interpretation of p in the controller chip example makes little sense if testing destroys the chip. How can we replace the chip with the possibility of drawing and testing it again, if it has been destroyed? The answer is, we can't. The idea of the probability of a success as a limiting relative frequency is **conceptual:** it is a way of thinking that gives a meaning to the probability of a success in a Bernoulli trial. Even if we cannot physically repeat the trial, we can still think of doing identical repetitions. In addition, even with nondestructive testing of the chip, the idea is conceptual, since we couldn't really perform an infinite number of repeated trials.

When a Bernoulli trial consists of selecting and testing one item from a finite set of items, there is another way of thinking about the probability of success, p. In this case, p is the relative frequency of the number of items that result in a success among all items in the set. In the controller chip example, suppose there are 1000 controller chips in the production lot, consisting of 96 defective ones that won't pass the test and 904 nondefective ones that will pass. Since the controller chip to be tested is selected at random, p is equal to $904/1000 = 0.904$, the proportion of good controller chips in the lot.

In what follows, we will continue to interpret the probability of success in a Bernoulli trial as the limiting relative frequency of successes in infinitely many identical repeated Bernoulli trials.

Since it is a relative frequency, or a limit of relative frequencies, all of which are nonnegative and at most 1, the probability of success in a Bernoulli trial is always nonnegative and at most 1. Further, since the Bernoulli trial can have only two outcomes, success or failure, the relative frequency of success plus the relative frequency of failure must equal 1. This means the probability of a failure is $1 - p$.

The idea of the probability of success in a Bernoulli trial as a limit of the relative frequencies of successes in repeated Bernoulli trials is the foundation of the study of randomness known as **probability theory.** Underlying probability theory is the idea of a **random phenomenon.**

> **DEFINITION**
>
> A **random phenomenon** is an occurrence that results in one of a known set of definite, identifiable outcomes, but whose actual outcome cannot be predicted with certainty in advance.

EXAMPLE 4.2   CONTINUED

1. Tossing a coin is a random phenomenon because we can say that there are two possible outcomes: "heads" and "tails," but before the coin is tossed, we cannot be certain which will occur.

2. Similarly, selecting a controller chip at random from the production lot and testing it is a random phenomenon, because we can tell that the outcome will be either "pass" or "fail," but we cannot predict with certainty which will occur until the testing is done.   ✦

We can use what we now know about the notion of probability as a limit of relative frequencies of success in Bernoulli trials, to give a more general meaning of probability. But first, we need some terminology.

> **DEFINITION**
>
> - A **trial** is a single occurrence of a random phenomenon.
> - An **event** is any set of possible outcomes of a random phenomenon.

EXAMPLE 4.3   RANDOM PHENOMENA, TRIALS, AND EVENTS

1. Consider a random phenomenon that consists of tossing a coin three times. A trial consists of one set of three tosses. There are eight possible outcomes: HHH, HHT, HTH, THH, HTT, THT, TTH, and TTT.

   (a) If we define A to be the event that two or more heads occur in a row, then A consists of the outcomes HHH, HHT, and THH.

   (b) Denote by B the event that two or more heads occur. B consists of the four outcomes HHH, HHT, HTH, and THH.

   (c) Denote by C the event that the three tosses are all the same: either all heads or all tails. C consists of the two outcomes HHH and TTT.

2. Consider a random phenomenon that consists of counting the number of particles emitted from a certain amount of a radioactive material over a 7.5-second time period. The possible outcomes are the integers $0, 1, 2, \ldots,$ N, where N is the total number of particles in the radioactive material. If G represents the event that at least one particle is emitted, G consists of the outcomes $1, 2, \ldots, N$.   ✦

The Probability of an Event

Suppose for a given random phenomenon, and an event E, we want to quantify the probability that E occurs, where by the statement "E occurs" we mean that one of the outcomes in E occurs. Call this probability $P(E)$. We may consider a trial of the random phenomenon to be a Bernoulli trial in which a "success" occurs if one of the outcomes in event E occurs, and a "failure" occurs otherwise. The probability that E occurs, $P(E)$, is the probability of "success" in the Bernoulli trial. As such, it can be defined as the limit of the relative frequency with which E occurs in repeated trials of the random phenomenon.

To put this a bit more mathematically, suppose that in n trials of the random phenomenon, we let $N_n(E)$ denote the number of trials in which event E occurs. Then $P_n(E) = N_n(E)/n$ is the relative frequency with which E occurs in those n trials. As n approaches infinity, $P_n(E)$ approaches $P(E)$, the probability of E.

EXAMPLE 4.3   CONTINUED

1. Consider again the random phenomenon that consists of tossing a coin three times. A is the event that at least two heads occur in a row. Here is one way to compute the probability of A:
   (a) Conduct repeated trials of the random phenomenon. Each trial consists of tossing the coin three times.
   (b) After n trials, compute the number of trials that resulted in at least two heads in a row. Call this $N_n(A)$.
   (c) Compute the proportion of the n trials that resulted in at least two heads in a row. We will call this quantity $P_n(A)$. It equals $N_n(A)/n$.
   (d) As $n \to \infty$, $P_n(A) \to P(A)$.
   The same method can be used to obtain the probabilities of events B and C.

2. Consider again the random phenomenon that consists of counting the number of particles emitted from a certain amount of a radioactive material over a 7.5-second time period. G is the event that at least one particle is emitted. The probability of G can be computed by going through preceding steps (a) to (d). In step (a), the researchers must be careful that the same amount of material is used for each trial, so the trials are identical.

   Clearly, we cannot perform an infinite number of trials of any random phenomenon, so we cannot use the relative frequency method to compute probabilities exactly. In situations where repeated trials are feasible, relative frequencies of repeated trials can be used to approximate the true probabilities. For example, in 1920, Rutherford, Chadwick, and Ellis conducted 2608 trials of the radioactive particle random phenomenon we have described. They reported that 2551 of the 2608 trials had resulted in the emission of at least one radioactive particle. In this case, $n = 2608$, $N_n(G) = 2551$, and $P_n(G) = 2551/2608 = 0.978$. Since n is large, 0.978 is likely a good approximation to $P(G)$. ✦

In any case, the relative frequency method of computing probability provides a way of thinking about and interpreting probability. In some cases, we can use other methods to compute exact probabilities, as the following shows.

EXAMPLE 4.3   CONTINUED

Consider again the random phenomenon that consists of tossing a coin three times. As we have seen, there are eight possible outcomes. If the coin is fair, then heads will come up with the same relative frequency as tails in repeated trials, so each of the eight outcomes will have equal probability. If $P_n(\{HHH\})$ is the proportion of the first n trials that result in HHH, $P_n(\{HHT\})$ is the proportion of the first n trials that result in HHT, and so on, then for each n, the sum

$$P_n(\{HHH\}) + P_n(\{HHT\}) + P_n(\{HTH\}) + P_n(\{THH\}) + P_n(\{HTT\})$$
$$+ \ P_n(\{THT\}) + P_n(\{TTH\}) + P_n(\{TTT\}) = 1$$

As a result, the sum of the probabilities of the eight outcomes, being the limit of these relative frequencies, also equals 1. Therefore, for a fair coin, the probability of each of the eight outcomes is $1/8$. ✦

The Addition Rule of Probability

A very useful tool for computing probabilities is provided by the **addition rule of probability.** The rule has to do with **disjoint events, unions of events,** and **intersections of events.**

> **DEFINITION**
>
> Suppose A and B are two events consisting of outcomes from the same random phenomenon.
>
> - The **intersection** of A and B is the event consisting of all outcomes common to both A and B. It is denoted $A \cap B$.
> - The **union** of A and B is the event consisting of all outcomes in A or in B or in both A and B. It is denoted $A \cup B$.
> - Two events, A and B, are said to be **disjoint** if they have no outcomes in common. This is the same as saying that $A \cap B = \emptyset$, where $\emptyset$ is the **null event**: the event containing no outcomes.

EXAMPLE 4.3   CONTINUED

1. Consider again the random phenomenon that consists of tossing a coin three times. If A is the event that at least two heads occur in a row, then A consists of the outcomes HHH, HHT, and THH. If D is the event that a tail occurs on the second toss, then D consists of the outcomes HTH, HTT, TTH, and TTT. A and D are disjoint since they have no outcomes in common. If C is the event that the three tosses are all the same, then C consists of the outcomes HHH and TTT. Then $A \cap C = \{HHH\}$, so A and C are not disjoint. $A \cup C = \{HHH, HHT, THH, TTT\}$.

2. Consider again the random phenomenon that consists of counting the number of particles emitted from a certain amount of a radioactive material over a 7.5-second time period. If G is the event that at least one particle is emitted, then G consists of the outcomes $1, 2, \ldots, N$. If H is the event that no particle is emitted, then G and H are disjoint. If V is the event that an odd number of particles is emitted, $V \cap G = \{1, 3, 5, \ldots, N\}$, if N is odd and $\{1, 3, 5, \ldots, N-1\}$ if N is even. Therefore, G and V are not disjoint. $H \cup V = \{0, 1, 3, 5, \ldots, N\}$, if N is odd and $\{0, 1, 3, 5, \ldots, N-1\}$ if N is even.   ✦

The addition rule of probability states that if two events A and B are disjoint, then the probability of their union is the sum of their individual probabilities. We can give an argument for this result as follows.

Suppose A and B are two disjoint events consisting of outcomes from the same random phenomenon. Suppose repeated trials of the random phenomenon are conducted. Since A and B have no outcomes in common, to count the number of times $A \cup B$ occurs in the first n trials, we need only count the number of times any of the outcomes in A occurs and add to it the number of times any of the outcomes in B occurs. Using the terminology that $N_n(C)$ is the number of the first n trials in which event C occurs,

$$N_n(A \cup B) = N_n(A) + N_n(B) \tag{4.1}$$

Dividing both sides of (4.1) by n, gives

$$P_n(A \cup B) = P_n(A) + P_n(B), \tag{4.2}$$

and, taking limits of both sides of Equation (4.2) as $n \to \infty$ gives the addition rule of probability.

THE ADDITION RULE OF PROBABILITY

If A and B are two disjoint events, then

$$P(A \cup B) = P(A) + P(B)$$

A similar argument will show that if A, B, and C are events, each pair of which are disjoint, then

$$P(A \cup B \cup C) = P(A) + P(B) + P(C)$$

In fact, the argument may be extended to any number of events, each pair of which are disjoint.

EXAMPLE 4.3   CONTINUED

Consider again the random phenomenon that consists of tossing a fair coin three times. If A is the event that at least two heads occur in a row, then A consists of the outcomes HHH, HHT, and THH. A can be considered the union of the three events {HHH}, {HHT}, and {THH}, each of which is a single outcome. As each pair of these three events is disjoint, the addition rule says that

$$P(A) = P(\{HHH\}) + P(\{HHT\}) + P(\{THH\}) = 1/8 + 1/8 + 1/8 = 3/8$$

In fact, because each outcome in this example has probability $1/8$, any event consisting of k out of the eight possible outcomes will have probability $k/8$.

If C is the event that the three tosses are all the same, then C consists of the outcomes HHH and TTT. Therefore, $P(C) = 2/8 = 1/4$.

On the other hand, $A \cup C = \{HHH, HHT, THH, TTT\}$, so

$$P(A \cup C) = 4/8 = 1/2 \neq 3/8 + 1/4 = P(A) + P(C)$$

which shows that the addition rule does not hold if the events are not disjoint.   ◆

Implicit in the last example is one immediate consequence of the addition rule: the probability rule for equally likely outcomes. If a random phenomenon has m equally likely outcomes, $O_1, O_2, \ldots, O_m$, then each outcome has probability $1/m$. Suppose E is an event consisting of k of the outcomes, say, $O_{i_1}, O_{i_2}, \ldots, O_{i_k}$. Since outcomes are by definition disjoint, and since each outcome has equal probability,

$$P(E) = P(O_{i_1} \cup O_{i_2} \cup \cdots \cup O_{i_k}) = P(O_{i_1}) + P(O_{i_2}) + \cdots + P(O_{i_k}) = k/m$$

Note that this computation does not depend on which k outcomes comprise the event. We summarize this useful rule as follows:

THE EQUALLY LIKELY OUTCOMES RULE

If a random phenomenon has m outcomes, each with probability $1/m$, and if E is any event consisting of k of those outcomes, then $P(E) = k/m$.

Independence

The notion of independence is fundamental to our understanding of probability. We will give a somewhat informal definition of the independence of events, and then a rule, called the multiplication rule for independent events, that may be used to define independence.

> **DEFINITION**
>
> Two events are **independent** if knowing whether one occurs does not change the probability that the other occurs.

Not all events are independent. Consider the random phenomenon consisting of tossing a fair coin three times, and let E be the event that three heads occur, and F the event that a tail occurs on the first toss. It is easy to show that $P(E) = 1/8$ and $P(F) = 1/2$. However, if we know that F occurs, then three heads cannot occur, and so the probability that E occurs changes from $1/8$ to 0. Therefore, E and F are not independent. On the other hand, some events are independent. If G is the event a tail occurs on the second toss, then, since the two tosses are not related, the probability of G must equal $1/2$ whether or not we know that F occurs. Therefore, F and G are independent.

Consider the random phenomenon that consists of tossing a fair coin followed by rolling a fair die. Let A denote the event that a head occurs on the coin toss, and let B denote the event that six dots turn up on the die. We know from the equally likely outcomes rule that $P(A) = 1/2$ and $P(B) = 1/6$. Can we use this information to compute the probability of getting both a head and a 6: that is, $P(A \cap B)$?

The answer is yes, if A and B are independent, as we will demonstrate. But, first, we must answer the question: Is it reasonable to assume that A and B are independent? The answer is again yes, since the die should have the same probability of coming up 6 no matter how the coin lands.

Now, how can we compute $P(A \cap B)$? Suppose we conduct repeated trials of the random phenomenon consisting of a coin toss followed by a die roll. Using our usual notation, after the first n trials, there will be $N_n(A)$ heads on the coin toss. Let's consider only the outcomes for those $N_n(A)$ trials that had a head on the coin toss. Since rolling the die is independent of tossing the coin, the results of those $N_n(A)$ die rolls are just as if we had done $N_n(A)$ die rolls without tossing a coin at all. Therefore, approximately $1/6$ of those $N_n(A)$ trials should also have a 6 on the die roll.[3] So the number of the n trials that result in both a head on the coin toss and a 6 on the die roll will approximately equal $N_n(A)/6$, which equals $N_n(A)P(B)$. Another name for the number of the n trials that result in both a head on the coin toss and a 6 on the die roll is $N_n(A \cap B)$. So we have the following relation:

$$N_n(A \cap B) \approx N_n(A)P(B)$$

If we divide by n, and take the limit as $n \to \infty$, the approximation becomes exact, and we get

$$P(A \cap B) = P(A)P(B)$$

This last relation, which can be used to define the independence of any two events, A and B, is known as the **multiplication rule for two independent events.**

---

[3]For those who are more mathematically inclined, here is an argument without approximations. There are $N_n(A)$ trials that result in a head on the coin toss. Let $N_{N_n(A)}(B)$ denote the number of those $N_n(A)$ trials that have a 6 on the die roll. Note that $N_{N_n(A)}(B) = N_n(A \cap B)$. Then

$$P(A \cap B) = \lim_n \frac{N_n(A \cap B)}{n} = \lim_n \frac{N_{N_n(A)}(B)}{n} = \lim_n \frac{N_n(A)}{n} \frac{N_{N_n(A)}(B)}{N_n(A)} = P(A)P(B)$$

THE MULTIPLICATION RULE FOR TWO INDEPENDENT EVENTS

Two events, A and B, are independent if and only if

$$P(A \cap B) = P(A)P(B)$$

We can use the definition of the independence of events to define the independence of two trials of a random phenomenon.

> **DEFINITION**
>
> Two **trials** of a random phenomenon are **independent** if any event from the first trial is independent of any event from the second trial.

We can define the independence of more than two events or of more than two trials as well.

> **DEFINITION**
>
> - The events $E_1, E_2, \ldots, E_k$ are **mutually independent** if for each subset $\{i_1, i_2, \ldots, i_m\}$, of $\{1, 2, \ldots, k\}$,
>
> $$P(E_{i_1} \cap E_{i_2} \cap \cdots \cap E_{i_m}) = P(E_{i_1})P(E_{i_2}) \cdots P(E_{i_m})$$
>
> - A sequence of k trials is independent if any events $E_1, E_2, \ldots, E_k$, from trials $1, 2, \ldots, k$, respectively, are mutually independent.

EXAMPLE 4.3   CONTINUED

Consider again the random phenomenon that consists of tossing a fair coin three times.

1. If A is the event that at least two heads occur in a row, then we saw previously that A consists of the outcomes HHH, HHT, and THH, and that $P(A) = 3/8$. We also saw that if C is the event that the three tosses are all the same, then C consists of the outcomes HHH and TTT, and $P(C) = 1/4$. It follows that
   - $A \cap B$ consists of the outcome HHH, so that $P(A \cap B) = 1/8$.
   - $P(A)P(B) = (3/8)(1/4) = 3/32$.
   - Since $P(A \cap B) \neq P(A)P(B)$, A and B are not independent events.
2. If D is the event that a head occurs on the first toss, and if E is the event that a head occurs on the second toss, then

$$D = \{\text{HHH, HHT, HTH, HTT}\} \quad \text{and} \quad E = \{\text{HHH, HHT, THT, THH}\}$$

**TABLE 4.2   Probabilities of Each Outcome in
Three Tosses of a Coin with Probability p of Heads**

$P(\{HHH\}) = p^3$	$P(\{HTT\}) = p(1 - p)^2$
$P(\{HHT\}) = p^2(1 - p)$	$P(\{THT\}) = p(1 - p)^2$
$P(\{HTH\}) = p^2(1 - p)$	$P(\{TTH\}) = p(1 - p)^2$
$P(\{THH\}) = p^2(1 - p)$	$P(\{TTT\}) = (1 - p)^3$

Therefore,

- $P(D) = P(E) = 1/2$, so that $P(D)P(E) = 1/4$.
- $D \cap E$ consists of the outcomes HHH and HHT, so $P(D \cap E) = 2/8 = 1/4$.
- Since $P(D \cap E) = P(D)P(E)$, D and E are independent events.

3. Independence gives us an alternative way of computing probabilities. Previously, to compute probabilities when tossing a fair coin three times, we used an argument based on equal probabilities of all eight possible outcomes to conclude that the probability of each outcome is $1/8$. We can obtain the same result using the idea of independent trials.

   Suppose that we want to find the probability of the outcome HHT. If we are willing to assume that the tosses are independent trials, then, if H_1 is the event of getting a head on the first trial, H_2 the event of getting a head on the second trial, and T_3 the event of getting a tail on the third trial, the outcome HHT equals the event $H_1 \cap H_2 \cap T_3$. By independence, we have

$$P(H_1 \cap H_2 \cap T_3) = P(H_1)P(H_2)P(T_3)$$

If the coin is fair, each of $P(H_1)$, $P(H_2)$, and $P(T_3)$ equals $1/2$, so the probability of the outcome HHT is $1/8$. The same argument shows that each outcome has probability $1/8$.

   This kind of argument can give us probabilities of outcomes even when the coin is not fair. Suppose that the three coin tosses are still independent trials, but that the probability of a head is p. If $p = 1/2$, the coin is fair, but if $p \neq 1/2$, the coin is unfair. Since the probability of a head on any toss is p, the probability of a tail on any toss is $1 - p$. By the above argument, the probability of outcome HHT is

$$P(H_1 \cap H_2 \cap T_3) = P(H_1)P(H_2)P(T_3) = p \times p \times (1 - p) = p^2(1 - p)$$

We will leave it to you to show that the eight possible outcomes have the probabilities given in Table 4.2.   ✦

4.3

DISCRETE RANDOM VARIABLES AND THEIR DISTRIBUTION MODELS

For many applications, it is preferable to work with numerical outcomes from a random phenomenon. In a Bernoulli trial, for example, investigators often prefer to consider the number of "successes," rather than whether there was a "success" or "failure." Suppose

**TABLE 4.3   How the Random
Variable Y, Which Is the Number
of Heads in Three Tosses of a Coin,
Assigns Numbers to All Possible
Outcomes**

$Y(\{HHH\}) = 3$	$Y(\{HTT\}) = 1$
$Y(\{HHT\}) = 2$	$Y(\{THT\}) = 1$
$Y(\{HTH\}) = 2$	$Y(\{TTH\}) = 1$
$Y(\{THH\}) = 2$	$Y(\{TTT\}) = 0$

the variable Y denotes the number of successes from a Bernoulli trial. Then Y can take on the values 0 or 1, and we refer to the possible outcomes of the Bernoulli trial as $\{Y = 0\}$ or $\{Y = 1\}$. In this context, Y is an example of a **random variable.**

> **DEFINITION**
>
> A **random variable** is a function that assigns a real number to each outcome of a random phenomenon.

By this definition, Y is a random variable since it is a function that assigns the number 0 to the outcome "failure" and the number 1 to the outcome "success" from the Bernoulli trial.

A random variable whose possible values form a discrete set[4] is called a **discrete random variable.** Since the set of possible values of Y, the number of successes in a Bernoulli trial, is the discrete set $\{0, 1\}$, Y is a discrete random variable.

EXAMPLE 4.3   CONTINUED

Consider once again the random phenomenon of tossing a coin three times. Define Y to be the number of heads in the three tosses. Then Y is a function that assigns a number to each outcome of the random phenomenon. Table 4.3 shows exactly how the random variable Y assigns a number to each possible outcome. From this table, we see that Y is a discrete random variable that can take on the values in the set $\{0, 1, 2, 3\}$.   ✦

EXAMPLE 4.4   DISCRETE RANDOM VARIABLES

1. Die Tossing. Consider a trial in which a fair six-sided die is rolled once and the number of dots showing on the top face is recorded. Let Y denote the number of dots observed. Then Y is a discrete random variable taking values in the set $\{1, 2, 3, 4, 5, 6\}$.

2. Radioactive Particle Emission. In 1920, Rutherford, Chadwick, and Ellis reported on a famous series of trials. Each trial consisted of counting the number

---

[4]See Chapter 2.

of α particles emitted by a certain amount of radioactive material in a 7.5-second time interval. Let Y denote the number of α particles emitted in the 7.5-second period. Then Y is a discrete random variable that can take on nonnegative integer values $\{0, 1, 2, \ldots, N\}$, where N is the total number of α particles that can be emitted from the radioactive material.   ✦

One of the central ideas in statistical modeling is the idea of a **distribution model** for a random variable. A distribution model precisely quantifies the pattern of variation of a random variable. One of the simplest distribution models is the Bernoulli distribution model, which arises from the Bernoulli trial.

The Bernoulli Distribution Model

The distribution model of a Bernoulli random variable is called a Bernoulli distribution model. If the Bernoulli random variable Y results from a Bernoulli trial with probability of success p, the two possible values of Y are 0 and 1, and the probabilities of obtaining those values are $1 - p$ and p, respectively. If for each possible value y that the random variable Y can assume, we denote the probability that $Y = y$ by $p_Y(y) = P(Y = y)$, the Bernoulli distribution model can be expressed as

$$p_Y(0) = P(Y = 0) = 1 - p \qquad \text{and} \qquad p_Y(1) = P(Y = 1) = p$$

or in mathematical shorthand,

$$p_Y(y) = p^y(1 - p)^{1-y}, \qquad y = 0, 1$$

The probability of success, p, is called a **model parameter** of the Bernoulli distribution model.

> ### DEFINITION
>
> A **model parameter** is a quantity describing the model that may take on more than one value, and that must be specified to determine the model as completely as possible.

The quantity p is a model parameter for the Bernoulli distribution model since we must specify p to determine the model as completely as possible. To signify that the random variable Y follows the Bernoulli distribution model with parameter p, we write $Y \sim \text{Bernoulli}(p)$.

Discrete Distribution Models

In general, if Y is a discrete random variable that can take values y in some discrete set, then the distribution model for Y can be expressed as $p_Y(y) = P(Y = y)$, for each y in that discrete set. The function $p_Y(y)$ is called the **probability mass function** of Y.

> **DEFINITION**
>
> A **discrete distribution model** is a distribution model for a discrete random variable. It consists of a list of the possible values the random variable can assume along with the probability of assuming each possible value. The function describing these probabilities is called the **probability mass function.**

EXAMPLE 4.4   CONTINUED

1. Die Tossing. Since the die is fair, each face should come up about one-sixth of the time in repeated tosses. This means the relative frequency of each face in repeated tosses will converge to 1/6 as the number of tosses approaches infinity. So the distribution model for Y is

$$p_Y(y) = 1/6, \qquad y = 1, 2, 3, 4, 5, 6$$

This distribution model is called a **discrete uniform distribution model** since the probabilities for obtaining the different outcomes are uniform, meaning they are all the same.

2. Radioactive Particle Emission. In reporting the results of their trials, Rutherford, Chadwick, and Ellis showed that a distribution model called the **Poisson distribution model,**[5] successfully models their data on radioactive decay.

If the random variable Y is the number of α particles emitted in the 7.5-second time interval, the probability mass function they used for their model is

$$p_Y(y) = \frac{(3.87)^y}{y!} e^{-3.87}, \qquad y = 0, 1, 2, \ldots \qquad (4.3)$$

where for $y \geq 1$, $y! = 1 \times 2 \times 3 \times \cdots \times (y-1) \times y$, and 0! is defined to equal 1.[6]

Table 4.4 shows the relative frequencies, $r(y)$, of the occurrence of y particles, observed by Rutherford, Chadwick, and Ellis in 2608 trials, and the corresponding values predicted by the Poisson distribution model, $p_Y(y)$. The agreement between model and data is generally good. For instance, since $p_Y(0) = 0.02086$, the model states that the probability a trial results in no emission is 0.02086. Translated into the frequency interpretation, we can say that the model predicts that the proportion of trials in which no emission occurs should be 0.02086. The table shows that the actual proportion of the 2608 trials that resulted in no emission was $r(0) = 57/2608 = 0.02186$. Agreement is not as good for trials with exactly eight emissions: $p_Y(8) = 0.02603$, and $r(8) = 0.01725$.

Notice that the Poisson probability mass function (4.3), is defined for an infinite set of possible values, y: all nonnegative integers. Of course, in any given application, there will be a finite upper bound on the values of y actually observed.

---

[5]Named for the French mathematician Siméon Denis Poisson, 1781–1840.

[6]The "!" denotes the factorial function, and $y!$ is pronounced "y factorial."

TABLE 4.4   Counts and Relative Frequencies, r(y) in 2608 Trials of Rutherford, Chadwick, and Ellis, Compared with Those Predicted by a Poisson Distribution Model, $p_Y(y)$

y	Count	$r(y)$	$p_Y(y)$
0	57	0.02186	0.02086
1	203	0.07784	0.08072
2	383	0.14686	0.15620
3	525	0.20130	0.20149
4	532	0.20399	0.19495
5	408	0.15644	0.15089
6	273	0.10468	0.09732
7	139	0.05330	0.05381
8	45	0.01725	0.02603
9	27	0.01035	0.01119
10	10	0.00383	0.00433
11	4	0.00153	0.00152
12	2	0.00077	0.00049
Total:	2608	1.00000	0.99980

TABLE 4.5   Computation of the Probability Mass Function for Three Tosses of a Fair Coin

$$p_Y(0) = P(Y = 0) = P(\{TTT\}) \qquad\qquad = 1/8$$
$$p_Y(1) = P(Y = 1) = P(\{HTT, THT, TTH\}) = 3/8$$
$$p_Y(2) = P(Y = 2) = P(\{HHT, HTH, THH\}) = 3/8$$
$$p_Y(3) = P(Y = 3) = P(\{HHH\}) \qquad\qquad = 1/8$$

In the Rutherford, Chadwick, and Ellis trials, for example, the greatest number of α-particle counts observed was 12, and that was observed on only 2 of 2608 occasions. However, in many random phenomena of this type, scientists do not know what that upper bound will be. The Poisson distribution model allows us to model such random phenomena without the difficulty of having to know the maximum that the random variable will take. In the present example, the price we pay for this generality is small, indeed: The probability the model assigns to all possible counts greater than 12 is only $1 - 0.99980 = 0.00020$.

The Poisson distribution model is widely used in applications, and we will consider it in more detail a bit later in the chapter.   ✦

EXAMPLE 4.3   CONTINUED

Consider again the random phenomenon of tossing a fair coin three times. We have seen that any of the eight outcomes occurs with probability 1/8. Therefore, if Y is the number of heads in the three tosses, we may compute the probability mass function of Y as shown in Table 4.5   ✦

What Is Random about a Random Variable?

Though we have formally defined a random variable as a function that assigns a number to every outcome from a random phenomenon, it is often easier to think of it as a numerical measurement we take on the outcome.

You may have noticed that we have been using uppercase letters, like Y, to represent random variables and lowercase letters, like y, to represent the values they take on. This is the result of a very important distinction you must be aware of if you are to understand random variables. The basic distinction is this: A random variable Y is a random quantity; the value it takes, y, isn't random. Or, to put it another way, Y refers to the action of taking measurements from a random phenomenon; y refers to the actual measurement taken. Some examples may help clarify the distinction.

EXAMPLE 4.5   RANDOM VARIABLES AND THEIR VALUES

1. An automotive supplier manufactures gaskets. A shipment of 7500 gaskets is to be checked for maximum thickness. The random phenomenon is that a gasket is selected at random from the shipment and its maximum thickness measured. The random variable, Y, is the maximum thickness of the selected gasket. Now what is the source of the randomness in the random variable Y? Assume for the moment that we can measure maximum gasket thickness exactly. The source of the randomness in the random variable Y is in the selection of the gasket. In other words, the random variable is random not because it describes the measurement, but because it describes the process of obtaining the measurement. Until the gasket is selected, we cannot be certain which gasket will be chosen, and if the gaskets are not all exactly the same thickness, the final measurement is random. Once the gasket is selected, there is nothing random left: Its maximum thickness will be measured exactly. The actual measured maximum thickness, y, is just a number, say, it is 1.5 mm. There is nothing random about 1.5 mm, and nothing random about y.

The randomness just described is due solely to sampling from a finite population: the process of selecting a gasket from the shipment. There can also be, and often is, randomness in taking the measurement. If so, this randomness is also part of the measuring process described by Y. For example, once the gasket is selected, we may get a measurement of 1.4 mm instead of the true value of 1.5 mm, simply because of imperfections in the measuring process. In this case, the randomness in Y is due to both the sampling and the measurement process. Once the measurement is taken, however, the observed value y is nonrandom.

2. A physicist is measuring the speed of light. With instruments sensitive enough to make meaningful measurements, no two measurements of the speed of light will be the same. In other words, there is randomness involved in obtaining the observations. If Y is the random variable denoting one observation of the speed of light, where does the randomness in Y originate? As in the previous example, random variable Y does not describe the measurement alone, but the process of measurement. As such, the randomness arises from all the uncontrollable factors that influence the measurement process. These may include environmental factors such as temperature and humidity, deficiencies in instrumentation, human error, and so on.

Another way to view the source of randomness in measuring the speed of light is to think of all possible measurements that could ever be taken as an infinite population. This population consists of measurements taken under all sorts of environmental conditions, with the instruments performing over the range of their capabilities, good and bad, with good and bad human operators, and so on. The measurement Y can be thought of as selecting one measurement at random from this population of all possible measurements.

Of course, whichever way you like to think of it, the actual number obtained, y, is not random.   ✦

Displaying Discrete Distribution Models

The Probability Histogram

A distribution model may be represented graphically by a **probability histogram,** which has a bar of area $p_Y(y)$ centered over $Y = y$ for each possible value y that the random variable Y can take.

EXAMPLE 4.4   CONTINUED

1. Figure 4.2 is the probability histogram for Y, the number of dots obtained from one roll of a fair die. Since the die is fair with $p_Y(y) = 1/6$, for $y = 1, 2, 3, 4, 5$, and 6, each bar has area $1/6$.
2. Figure 4.3 is an abbreviated version of the probability histogram for the Poisson distribution model with probability mass function given by Equation (4.3).

   The true probability histogram has an infinite number of bars, one for each of $y = 0, 1, 2, 3, \ldots$, but Figure 4.3 shows only the first 10 bars. The areas of the bars are the values $p_Y(y)$ given in Table 4.4.   ✦

Probability Histograms as Limits of Density Histograms

The definition of the probability of an event as the limit of the relative frequency of that event in repeated trials of a random phenomenon means that there is an analogous limiting relation between density histograms and the probability histogram. Specifically, suppose that we have constructed a probability histogram, and that we begin conducting a sequence of repeated trials of the random phenomenon. After the nth trial, we construct the density histogram of the data from the first n trials, so that the intervals under the bars are the same as those for the probability histogram. In the probability histogram, the area of the bar over the value y is $P(Y = y)$, and in the density histogram for the first n trials, the area of the bar over the value y is $P_n(Y = y)$, the proportion

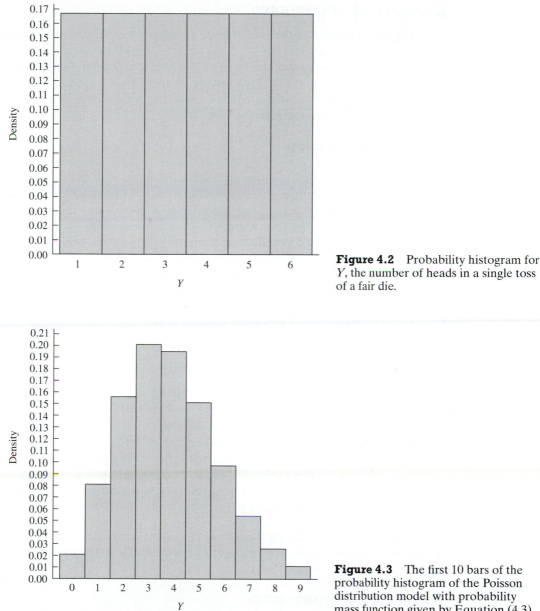

Figure 4.2 Probability histogram for Y, the number of heads in a single toss of a fair die.

Figure 4.3 The first 10 bars of the probability histogram of the Poisson distribution model with probability mass function given by Equation (4.3).

of the first n trials for which $Y = y$. By the definition of probability as the limit of relative frequencies, we know that $P_n(Y = y)$ converges to $P(Y = y)$ as $n \to \infty$. Since the intervals under the bars of each density histogram are the same as those of the probability histogram, the bars themselves must converge to the bars of the probability histogram.

EXAMPLE 4.4 CONTINUED

Figure 4.4 illustrates the convergence of density histograms to a probability histogram.

The top histogram results from 100 rolls of a fair die, the second histogram from 1000 rolls, and the third histogram from 10,000 rolls.[7] Notice how these density histograms get closer and closer to the probability histogram, which is the bottom histogram in Figure 4.4. ✦

Samples and Populations

In Chapter 3, you learned about populations and samples in the context of designed studies. Samples of sampling units are selected from a population of units. Observations are taken on the selected sampling units. These observations are taken directly, in an observational study, or after the imposition of treatments on the sampling (now experimental) units, in a controlled experiment.

Although not all random phenomena are designed studies, the concepts of population and sample may also be related to observations taken on repeated trials of a random phenomenon. In this setting, the population consists of the observations that would be observed from all possible trials of the random phenomenon, if all possible trials could be conducted. The sample consists of the observations actually obtained in the repeated trials of the random phenomenon.

EXAMPLE 4.2 CONTINUED

1. For the coin-tossing trial, the population is the result of all possible tosses. This is an infinite population! If we actually toss the coin 10 times, the sample consists of the results of those 10 tosses.

2. For the trial in which a controller chip is selected at random from the production lot and tested, the population is the status (pass or fail) of all controller chips in the production lot, and the sample is the status of the controller chip selected for testing. If more than one controller chip is selected and tested, the sample is the status of those controller chips selected. ✦

In the sample/population framework, the distribution model describes the population. The value of the probability mass function, $p_Y(y)$ is interpreted as the proportion of the population for which $Y = y$.

EXAMPLE 4.4 CONTINUED

1. Consider the random phenomenon consisting of a roll of a fair die, and let the random variable Y denote the number of dots that come up. Then the population consists of the results of all possible rolls. If we actually roll the die once, the sample is the number of dots that comes up. If we actually roll the

---

[7]In case you were wondering, no, we didn't roll a die 10,000 times. The data for these histograms were produced by computer simulation, as were the data in Labs 4.1 and 4.2.

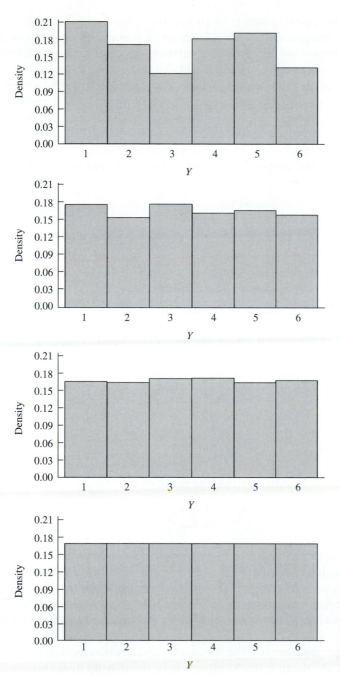

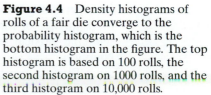

Figure 4.4 Density histograms of rolls of a fair die converge to the probability histogram, which is the bottom histogram in the figure. The top histogram is based on 100 rolls, the second histogram on 1000 rolls, and the third histogram on 10,000 rolls.

die 10 times, the sample consists of 10 numbers: the results of the ten rolls. We have seen that the probability mass function of Y is $p_Y(y) = 1/6$, $y = 1, \ldots, 6$. Therefore, a proportion 1/6 of the population, that is, of all possible rolls, will result in 1 dot, a proportion 1/6 will result in 2 dots, and so on.

2. Consider the radioactive particle emission random phenomenon. The population consists of the counts of α particles in all possible trials. Rutherford, Chadwick, and Ellis reported the results of 2608 trials, so their sample consists of the 2608 counts that resulted. If we are willing to assume that the Poisson distribution model having probability mass function (4.3) is the actual model for the population,[8] then the proportion of all possible trials that result in no emissions is $p_Y(0) \approx 0.02086$. ◆

Graphically, sample data are summarized by displays such as the density histogram, and the population is summarized by the probability histogram. Numerically, sample data are summarized by the measures introduced in Chapter 2, such as the mean and standard deviation. We now turn to population analogues of these numerical measures.

The Mean, Variance, and Standard Deviation

Recall that for a set of quantitative data, the mean is defined as the average: the sum of all data values divided by the number of data values. We can also define the mean of a distribution model. Suppose Y is a discrete random variable that denotes the measurement we are taking from a random phenomenon. Assume that the probability mass function of Y satisfies

$$\sum_y |y| p_Y(y) < \infty \tag{4.4}$$

Suppose we perform repeated trials of the random phenomenon, and at trial i, we obtain the measurement Y_i. After n trials, the mean of the measurements is

$$\bar{Y}_n = \frac{1}{n} \sum_{i=1}^n Y_i$$

Under a suitable condition, as $n \to \infty$, $\bar{Y}_n$ will approach a real number, called the **mean of the distribution model,** which we will denote by μ_Y. The quantity μ_Y is a **phenomenon average:** a long-term average of data from the underlying random phenomenon. That the sequence of random quantities $\bar{Y}_n$ converges to a nonrandom number, μ_Y, may seem paradoxical, but it is nevertheless true. This result is known as the **Law of Large Numbers.**

There is another way to view the mean of a distribution model. Recall that for a density histogram, the mean is the location where the density histogram "balances." Recall also that in repeated trials of the underlying random phenomenon, the resulting

---

[8]It isn't the true model, but it may be close enough for us to pretend that it is. See the quotes at the beginning of this chapter.

density histograms converge to the probability histogram. So it would seem sensible that as the number of repeated trials of the random phenomenon becomes larger, the places where the corresponding density histograms balance would converge to a single value: namely, the place where the probability histogram balances. This is exactly what happens. Therefore, we can think of μ_Y as the place where the probability histogram of Y balances.

Another name for μ_Y is the **expected value** or **expectation.** Using this terminology, we call μ_Y the expected value (or the expectation) of Y. The expected value of Y is most often written as $E(Y)$.

Whether it is called the mean or the expected value, the following is a simple formula for computing $\mu_Y = E(Y)$ for a discrete random variable:

$$\mu_Y = E(Y) = \sum_y y p_Y(y) \tag{4.5}$$

where the sum is taken over all values that Y can assume. Equation (4.5) shows μ_Y to be an average of the values Y can assume, with each value y weighted by its probability $p_Y(y)$.

Note that the condition (4.4) ensures that a unique finite value for μ_Y exists. In terms of expectations, it says that

$$E(|Y|) = \sum_y |y| p_Y(y) < \infty$$

If this condition is not satisfied, we will say that μ_Y is not defined.

We have seen that the notion of a mean for a data distribution translates into the mean of a distribution model. Other measures for data distributions also have distribution-model analogues. One of these is the standard deviation. Once again, suppose Y is a discrete random variable that denotes the measurement we are taking from a random phenomenon. Suppose we perform repeated trials of the random phenomenon, and at trial i, we obtain the measurement Y_i. Then after n trials, we can compute the variance of the observed measurements:

$$S_n^2 = \frac{1}{n-1} \sum_{i=1}^{n} (Y_i - \bar{Y}_n)^2$$

As n approaches infinity, S_n^2 will approach the variance of the distribution model, which is denoted by σ_Y^2, provided the variance is defined for the distribution model. The variance is defined for a discrete distribution model with probability mass function $p_Y(y)$ if and only if

$$\sum_y y^2 p_Y(y) < \infty \tag{4.6}$$

The variance of a distribution model measures how much spread about μ_Y there is in the probability histogram. The variance of a discrete distribution model can be computed as

$$\sigma_Y^2 = \sum_y (y - \mu_Y)^2 p_Y(y)$$

where the sum is taken over all values that Y can assume. The standard deviation of a distribution model, σ_Y, is defined as the positive square root of the variance: $\sigma_Y = \sqrt{\sigma_Y^2}$. The standard deviation is often preferred to the variance as a measure of spread, since it is in the same units as the quantity being measured.

MEAN, VARIANCE, AND STANDARD DEVIATION FORMULAS FOR A DISCRETE RANDOM VARIABLE

The mean, μ_Y, also known as the expected value, $E(Y)$, of a discrete random variable Y, is computed as

$$\mu_Y = E(Y) = \sum_y y p_Y(y)$$

The variance of Y is computed as

$$\sigma_Y^2 = \sum_y (y - \mu_Y)^2 p_Y(y)$$

The standard deviation of Y is the positive square root of its variance:

$$\sigma_Y = \sqrt{\sigma_Y^2}$$

Some examples will help to illustrate the computation and interpretation of the mean, variance, and standard deviation.

EXAMPLE 4.4   CONTINUED

1. For the fair die, the mean is the place where the probability histogram in Figure 4.3 "balances." It is easy to see that the balance point is at 3.5, so $\mu_Y = 3.5$. The mean can also be computed as the sum

$$1 \times p_Y(1) + 2 \times p_Y(2) + 3 \times p_Y(3) + 4 \times p_Y(4) + 5 \times p_Y(5) + 6 \times p_Y(6)$$

$$= \frac{1}{6}\{1 + 2 + 3 + 4 + 5 + 6\} = 3.5$$

The mean can be interpreted as the long-run average of the number of dots obtained in repeated rolls of the die. The mean can also be interpreted as the "fair" amount to wager in the following game of chance. The game is that you roll a fair die and are paid i dollars if i spots turn up. Then the mean μ_Y is the amount you should be required to wager to keep the game fair, in the sense that in the long run, you will neither win nor lose, on average. For this game, the fair wager is $3.50.

One other interesting thing to notice about the fact that $\mu_Y = 3.5$ is that just as the mean of a set of data need not equal any of the data values, the mean of a random variable need not be a value that the random variable can attain: You will never see 3.5 spots on a die roll.

The variance is computed as follows:

$$\sigma_Y^2 = (1-3.5)^2 \times p_Y(1) + (2-3.5)^2 \times p_Y(2) + \cdots + (6-3.5)^2 \times p_Y(6) = 2.92$$

so that the standard deviation is $\sqrt{2.92} = 1.71$.

Finally, we note that for a discrete uniform distribution model in which the possible values of the random variable Y are $1, 2, \ldots, k$, and $p_Y(y) = 1/k$, $y = 1, 2, \ldots, k$, $\mu_Y = (k+1)/2$ and $\sigma_Y^2 = (k^2 - 1)/12$. Plugging in $k = 6$, which is the value for a fair die, we obtain $\mu_Y = 3.5$ and $\sigma_Y^2 = 2.92$.

2. The mean of the Poisson distribution model defined by probability mass function (4.3) is computed as

$$\mu_Y = \sum_{y=0}^{\infty} y p_Y(y) = \sum_{y=0}^{\infty} y \frac{(3.87)^y}{y!} e^{-3.87}$$

As we will show when we consider the Poisson distribution model in greater detail, this value equals 3.87.

This mean can be interpreted as the long-run average of the number of particles emitted in a 7.5-second interval obtained in repeated trials.

The variance is computed as follows:

$$\sigma_Y^2 = \sum_{y=0}^{\infty} (y - 3.87)^2 \frac{(3.87)^y}{y!} e^{-3.87}$$

As you will see, it turns out that the variance also equals 3.87, so the standard deviation is $\sqrt{3.87} = 1.97$. ✦

EXAMPLE 4.6   THE MEAN OF A RANDOM VARIABLE AS A LONG-TERM AVERAGE

This example shows how the formula for the mean, Equation (4.5), relates to the idea of μ_Y as a long-term average.

Consider the first random phenomenon in Example 4.3: tossing a coin three times. Let the random variable Y denote the number of heads in the three tosses, and consider the distribution model for Y. To compute the mean of this distribution model, we know we can conduct a large number of trials, each consisting of tossing the coin three times. If Y_i is the number of heads on trial i, we can compute the total number of heads in the n trials, $T_n = \sum_{i=1}^{n} Y_i$, and as n goes to infinity, $\bar{Y}_n = T_n/n$ will converge to μ_Y.

A key connection between μ_Y and Equation (4.5) is that T_n can be written a different way. Specifically, the total number of heads in the n trials is equal to 0 times the number of trials in which no heads occur, plus 1 times the number of trials in which one head occurs, plus 2 times the number of trials in which two heads occur, plus 3 times the number of trials in which three heads occur. Mathematically, we can write this as follows: If $N_n(\{Y = 0\})$ is the total number of the n trials in which 0 heads turn up, $N_n(\{Y = 1\})$ is the total number of the n trials in which 1 head turns up, and so on, then

$$T_n = 0 \times N_n(\{Y = 0\}) + 1 \times N_n(\{Y = 1\}) + 2 \times N_n(\{Y = 2\}) + 3 \times N_n(\{Y = 3\})$$

Therefore, the average number of heads in the n trials is given by

$$\bar{Y}_n = \frac{1}{n} \sum_{i=1}^{n} Y_i = \frac{1}{n} T_n = 0 \times \frac{1}{n} N_n(\{Y = 0\}) + 1 \times \frac{1}{n} N_n(\{Y = 1\})$$

$$+ 2 \times \frac{1}{n} N_n(\{Y = 2\}) + 3 \times \frac{1}{n} N_n(\{Y = 3\}) \qquad (4.7)$$

Recall the interpretation of probability as a limit of relative frequencies. In that discussion, we denoted the number of times event E occurred in n repeated trials of a random phenomenon as $N_n(E)$, and the relative frequency of the occurrence of event E as $P_n(E) = N_n(E)/n$. With this in mind, we rewrite Equation (4.7) as

$$\bar{Y}_n = 0 \times P_n(Y = 0) + 1 \times P_n(Y = 1) + 2 \times P_n(Y = 2) + 3 \times P_n(Y = 3) \qquad (4.8)$$

Now recall that as $n \rightarrow \infty$, $P_n(E)$ converges to $P(E)$, the probability of E, and $\bar{Y}_n$ converges to μ_Y, the mean, or expected value of Y. Therefore, as $n \rightarrow \infty$ in Equation (4.8), we get

$$\mu_Y = 0 \times P(Y = 0) + 1 \times P(Y = 1) + 2 \times P(Y = 2) + 3 \times P(Y = 3)$$

$$= 0 \times p_Y(0) + 1 \times p_Y(1) + 2 \times p_Y(2) + 3 \times p_Y(3)$$

But this last equation is just Equation (4.5) for the example we are considering here. ✦

Linear Transformations

Recall that a random variable is a function that assigns a number to each outcome of a random phenomenon. Sometimes, it is of interest to transform a random variable by taking a function of it. Since a function of a random variable still assigns a number (though possibly a different number) to each outcome of the random phenomenon, transforming a random variable results in a new random variable. In general, it is difficult to tell exactly how such a transformation changes the mean, variance, and standard deviation. However, when the transformation is of a particularly simple form, called linear, the result is easy to obtain.

> **DEFINITION**
>
> Suppose Y is a random variable. A **linear transformation** of Y is a new random variable X that results from the formula
>
> $$X = aY + b$$
>
> where a and b are constants.

EXAMPLE 4.7   A LINEAR TRANSFORMATION OF A RANDOM VARIABLE

Pedro has just signed a lucrative contract to pitch for a major league baseball team. The base salary of the contract for next year is $10 million. The contract also has a number of incentives that provide opportunities for increasing Pedro's pay. One incentive is that Pedro gets $100,000 per start after he has started 25 games. If Y is the number of starts above 25 that Pedro makes next year, Pedro's total income from base salary and this incentive is, in millions of dollars,

$$X = 0.1Y + 10.0$$

Thus, X is a linear transformation of Y, where $a = 0.1$ and $b = 10.0$.   ◆

We want to find the relation between μ_Y and μ_X, where $X = aY + b$. Think about it this way: The mean of a random variable is the long-run average of the values obtained by the random variable in repeated trials of the random phenomenon. Suppose we perform n trials of the random phenomenon, and obtain the values $Y_1, Y_2, \ldots, Y_n$ for Y. Then the corresponding values of X are $X_1 = aY_1 + b$, $X_2 = aY_2 + b$, $\ldots$, $X_n = aY_n + b$. The mean of the values of Y is

$$\bar{Y}_n = \frac{1}{n}(Y_1 + Y_2 + \cdots + Y_n)$$

and the mean of the values of X is

$$
\begin{aligned}
\bar{X}_n &= \frac{1}{n}(X_1 + X_2 + \cdots + X_n) \\
&= \frac{1}{n}[(aY_1 + b) + (aY_2 + b) + \cdots + a(Y_n + b)] \\
&= \frac{1}{n}[a(Y_1 + Y_2 + \cdots + Y_n) + nb] \\
&= a\bar{Y}_n + b
\end{aligned}
$$

Taking the limit as $n \to \infty$, we get

$$\mu_X = \lim_{n\to\infty} \bar{X}_n = \lim_{n\to\infty} (a\bar{Y}_n + b) = a\mu_Y + b$$

A similar kind of argument will show that

$$\sigma_X^2 = a^2\sigma_Y^2 = |a|^2\sigma_Y^2$$

and, therefore, that

$$\sigma_X = |a|\sigma_Y^2$$

To summarize:

MEAN, VARIANCE, AND STANDARD DEVIATION FORMULAS FOR A LINEAR TRANSFORMATION

If the random variable X is obtained from the random variable Y by the linear transformation $X = aY + b$, then

$$\mu_X = a\mu_Y + b \tag{4.9}$$

$$\sigma_X^2 = a^2\sigma_Y^2 \tag{4.10}$$

$$\sigma_X = |a|\sigma_Y \tag{4.11}$$

EXAMPLE 4.7   CONTINUED

Suppose from Pedro's past history, we are willing to assume that the random variable Y, the number of starts above 25 that Pedro makes next year, has the following distribution:

y	0	1	2	3	4	5	6
$p_Y(y)$	0.35	0.25	0.20	0.10	0.05	0.04	0.01

Then

$$\mu_Y = 0 \times 0.35 + 1 \times 0.25 + 2 \times 0.20 + 3 \times 0.10 + 4 \times 0.05$$
$$+ 5 \times 0.04 + 6 \times 0.01 = 1.41$$

$$\sigma_Y^2 = (0 - 1.41)^2 \times 0.35 + (1 - 1.41)^2 \times 0.25 + (2 - 1.41)^2 \times 0.20$$
$$+ (3 - 1.41)^2 \times 0.10 + (4 - 1.41)^2 \times 0.05 + (5 - 1.41)^2 \times 0.04$$
$$+ (6 - 1.41)^2 \times 0.01 = 2.81$$

and

$$\sigma_Y = \sqrt{2.81} = 1.68$$

Pedro's compensation from salary and the start incentive is $X = 0.1Y + 10.0$, so we find that

$$\mu_X = 0.1\mu_Y + 10.0 = (0.1)(1.41) + 10.0 = 10.141$$

so we expect Pedro to make around \$141,000 from the incentive. We can also compute

$$\sigma_X^2 = (0.1)^2\sigma_Y^2 = (0.1)^2(2.81) = 2.81 \times 10^{-4}$$

and

$$\sigma_X = |0.01|\sigma_Y = (0.01)(1.68) = 0.0168 \quad \blacklozenge$$

More Than One Random Variable

There are many instances when we are interested in two or more random variables. Here is one example.

EXAMPLE 4.8   TWO RANDOM VARIABLES

The quality division of a computer manufacturer keeps track of all defects on new computers reported by customers. To know where to target improvement efforts, quality personnel classify all noncosmetic defects as electrical or mechanical. If E and M are the number of electrical or mechanical defects on a randomly chosen computer, then E and M are two random variables defined on the random phenomenon of selecting a new computer at random and checking for defects. Suppose that these two random variables have means μ_E and μ_M, and variances σ_E^2 and σ_M^2.

If N is the number of noncosmetic defects on a randomly selected computer, then N is another random variable, and $N = E + M$. Knowing the means and variances of E and M, can we say anything about the mean N?

If we think about the mean of a random variable as a long-run average, then it is clear that in n repeated trials of the random phenomenon (i.e., after looking at n randomly selected computers), the average number of noncosmetic defects per computer is equal to the average number of electrical defects per computer plus the average number of mechanical defects per computer. Taking limits as $n \to \infty$, we obtain $\mu_N = \mu_E + \mu_M$. A nice way to remember this is that the mean of the sum equals the sum of the means.

It turns out that this result holds for any number of random variables, as will be summarized in what follows.   ◆

MEANS OF SUMS OF RANDOM VARIABLES

If $Y_1, Y_2, \ldots, Y_n$ are random variables for which a mean is defined, and if $X = Y_1 + Y_2 + \cdots + Y_n$, then

$$\mu_X = \mu_{Y_1} + \mu_{Y_2} + \cdots + \mu_{Y_n} \tag{4.12}$$

If the random variables $Y_1, Y_2, \ldots, Y_n$ all have the same mean, μ, then

$$\mu_X = n\mu \tag{4.13}$$

The result for variances is not so simple. To see why, consider the random phenomenon consisting of tossing a coin three times. Let Y_1 equal the number of heads and Y_2 the number of tails. Both Y_1 and Y_2 are random variables, and so is their sum, T. It is easy to show that $\sigma_{Y_1}^2 > 0$ and $\sigma_{Y_2}^2 > 0$. But, since T always equals 3, $\sigma_T^2 = 0$. So we know that the variance of a sum does not equal the sum of the variances.

There is one setting in which the variance of a sum does equal the sum of the variances, but, first, we need to introduce the notion of independence of random variables.

DEFINITION

The discrete random variables $Y_1, Y_2, \ldots, Y_n$ are **independent** if for all values $y_1, y_2, \ldots, y_n$ for which

$$P(Y_1 = y_1) > 0, \, P(Y_2 = y_2) > 0, \ldots, \text{ and } P(Y_n = y_n) > 0$$

$$P(\{Y_1 = y_1\} \cap \{Y_2 = y_2\} \cap \cdots \cap \{Y_n = y_n\})$$
$$= P(Y_1 = y_1) P(Y_2 = y_2) \cdots P(Y_n = y_n)$$

If two random variables Y_1 and Y_2 are independent, then the variance of their sum equals the sum of their variances:

$$\sigma^2_{Y_1 + Y_2} = \sigma^2_{Y_1} + \sigma^2_{Y_2}$$

In fact, since $Y_1 - Y_2 = Y_1 + (-Y_2)$, and the variance of $-Y_2$ is the same as the variance of Y_2, we also obtain

$$\sigma^2_{Y_1 - Y_2} = \sigma^2_{Y_1} + \sigma^2_{Y_2}$$

VARIANCES OF SUMS AND DIFFERENCES OF RANDOM VARIABLES

- If Y_1 and Y_2 are independent random variables for which variances are defined,

  ○ If $Z = Y_1 + Y_2$, then $\sigma^2_Z = \sigma^2_{Y_1} + \sigma^2_{Y_2}$.
  ○ If $W = Y_1 - Y_2$, then $\sigma^2_W = \sigma^2_{Y_1} + \sigma^2_{Y_2}$.

- If $Y_1, Y_2, \ldots, Y_n$ are independent random variables for which variances are defined, and if $X = Y_1 + Y_2 + \cdots + Y_n$, then

$$\sigma^2_X = \sigma^2_{Y_1} + \sigma^2_{Y_2} + \cdots + \sigma^2_{Y_n} \tag{4.14}$$

If the random variables $Y_1, Y_2, \ldots, Y_n$ all have the same variance, σ^2, then

$$\sigma^2_X = n\sigma^2 \tag{4.15}$$

EXAMPLE 4.8   CONTINUED

If E and M are the number of electrical or mechanical defects on a randomly chosen computer, and if $N = E + M$, then $\sigma^2_N = \sigma^2_E + \sigma^2_M$ only if the number of electrical defects is independent of the number of mechanical defects. Before relying on this formula, we would have to have evidence of their independence, either through experience or other knowledge of the process.   ✦

Suppose we perform n trials of a random phenomenon and at each trial observe the value of a random variable, Y. Denote the observations $Y_1, Y_2, \ldots, Y_n$. The Y_i are independent random variables having the same distribution. Suppose their common mean is μ and their common variance is σ^2. In statistical applications, we are often interested in the mean of the Y_i:

$$\bar{Y}_n = \frac{1}{n}(Y_1 + Y_2 + \cdots + Y_n)$$

which is called the **sample mean.** In those statistical applications, the random variables $Y_1, Y_2, \ldots, Y_n$, model n data values obtained as a random sample of measurements from a population. The distribution model of the random variables describes the population measurements.

The sample mean, $\bar{Y}_n$, may be written as

$$\bar{Y}_n = aW + b$$

where $W = Y_1 + Y_2 + \cdots + Y_n$, $a = 1/n$ and $b = 0$. Since, from Equation (4.13), $\mu_W = n\mu$, we can apply Equation (4.9) to give us the result

$$\mu_{\bar{Y}_n} = \mu$$

Exercise 4.65 asks you to use Equations (4.10), (4.11), and (4.15) to show that

$$\sigma_{\bar{Y}_n}^2 = \frac{\sigma^2}{n}, \qquad \text{and} \qquad \sigma_{\bar{Y}_n} = \frac{\sigma}{\sqrt{n}}$$

We summarize these results as follows.

MEAN, VARIANCE, AND STANDARD DEVIATION OF THE SAMPLE MEAN

If $\bar{Y}_n$ is the sample mean, defined by

$$\bar{Y}_n = \frac{1}{n}(Y_1 + Y_2 + \cdots + Y_n)$$

where $Y_1, Y_2, \ldots, Y_n$ are independent random variables having the same distribution with mean μ and variance σ^2, then

$$\mu_{\bar{Y}_n} = \mu \tag{4.16}$$

$$\sigma_{\bar{Y}_n}^2 = \frac{\sigma^2}{n} \tag{4.17}$$

and

$$\sigma_{\bar{Y}_n} = \frac{\sigma}{\sqrt{n}} \tag{4.18}$$

The Binomial Distribution Model

A distribution model that is related to the Bernoulli is the **binomial distribution model.** Just as the Bernoulli distribution model is defined in terms of a Bernoulli trial, the binomial distribution model is defined in terms of the **binomial trial.** As the following definition shows, a binomial trial is made up of one or more Bernoulli trials.

> **DEFINITION**
>
> A **binomial trial** satisfies the following conditions:
>
> 1. It consists of n independent Bernoulli trials.
> 2. The probability of success is the same value, p, for each of the n Bernoulli trials.

The quantity of most interest in a binomial trial is the random variable Y, the total number of successes in the n Bernoulli trials. The distribution model of Y is called a **binomial distribution model.** Recall that to describe a Bernoulli distribution model, we needed to specify one parameter: p, the probability of a success. To describe the binomial distribution model, we need to specify two parameters: n, the number of Bernoulli trials in the binomial trial, and p, the probability of success at each Bernoulli trial. In what follows, we will abbreviate "binomial distribution model with parameters n and p" as $b(n, p)$. If Y represents an observation from a $b(n, p)$, we'll write $Y \sim b(n, p)$.

EXAMPLE 4.9 BINOMIAL TRIALS

The following are examples of binomial trials. For each example, we describe the corresponding binomial random variable and its distribution model.

1. Recall that tossing a coin with probability p of heads is a Bernoulli trial. Tossing the same coin n times is a binomial trial. If we call "heads" a success, then a random variable of interest is Y, the number of heads in the n tosses, and $Y \sim b(n, p)$. For example, if the coin is fair and is tossed 100 times, then $Y \sim b(100, 0.5)$.

2. Television networks often predict election winners minutes after the polls close, and their predictions are usually correct. Such quick and accurate predictions result from exit polling: asking randomly selected voters leaving polling places which candidate they voted for. Suppose that, to predict the outcome of a two-candidate election, a polling firm interviews 100 voters in an exit poll. The population here is all those who voted. The sample is the set of 100 voters included in the exit poll.

Asking each voter whom he or she voted for is a Bernoulli trial because there are only two possible outcomes.[9] Since 100 voters are interviewed, there are 100 of these Bernoulli trials. Does this mean that the 100 Bernoulli trials constitute

---

[9]We'll ignore the reality that some may have voted for neither candidate, and we'll assume that each voter interviewed answers the question and tells the truth.

a binomial trial? Technically, no. The difficulty is that the Bernoulli trials are not independent and the probability of success is not the same from trial to trial. To see why, suppose that there are 200 voters in the election. If 100 actually voted for candidate 1, then the probability the first voter interviewed voted for candidate 1 is $p = 100/200 = 0.500$. Suppose the first voter interviewed voted for candidate 1. Then, on the second interview, the probability of finding a voter who voted for candidate 1 is $p = 99/199 = 0.497$. If the first voter interviewed voted for candidate 2, then the probability of the second interviewee voting for candidate 1 is $p = 100/199 = 0.503$. So p is changing and its value on a given interview depends on what happened in previous interviews. This means the sequence of Bernoulli trials does not constitute a binomial trial.

However, if the turnout was large, instead of only 200, then p would not change very much even after 99 interviews, so the 100 interviews would be very well approximated as independent Bernoulli trials with constant probability p of success. In a practical sense, if the population of voters is large, the binomial distribution model $b(100, p)$ can be assumed for Y, the number of candidate 1 voters in the sample, where p is the proportion of candidate 1 voters in the population. So if, for example, there are 10,000 voters and if the true proportion of votes for candidate 1 is 0.51, then each individual response can be considered a Bernoulli measurement with $p = 0.51$. If we interview 100 voters, the number of the 100 who vote for candidate 1 can be modeled as a measurement from a binomial distribution model with $n = 100$ trials and $p = 0.51$; that is, a $b(100, 0.51)$.   ◆

Before we present the probability mass function for the $b(n, p)$ distribution model, we return to an earlier example.

EXAMPLE 4.3   CONTINUED

Consider again the random phenomenon of tossing a fair coin three times. If we consider a head a success, one trial of this random phenomenon consists of three independent Bernoulli trials with the same probability of success at each. That is, it is a binomial trial.

Let's assume that the probability of a head at each toss is p. If Y is the number of heads obtained in the three tosses, then $Y \sim b(3, p)$.

We can find the probability mass function of Y as follows. First, note that Y can take on only four values: 0, 1, 2, or 3. For these values of y, the probability mass function is $p_Y(y) = P(Y = y)$. Let's consider the case $y = 1$. That is, we want to compute $p_Y(1) = P(Y = 1)$. The event $\{Y = 1\}$ consists of the outcomes HTT, THT, and TTH, so

$$P(Y = 1) = P(\{\text{HTT, THT, TTH}\})$$

By the addition rule of probability,

$$P(\{\text{HTT, THT, TTH}\}) = P(\{\text{HTT}\}) + P(\{\text{THT}\}) + P(\{\text{TTH}\})$$

A glance at Table 4.2 shows that

$$P(\{\text{HTT}\}) = P(\{\text{THT}\}) = P(\{\text{TTH}\}) = p(1 - p)^2$$

TABLE 4.6   Computation of the Probability Mass Function for Three Tosses of a Coin

$p_Y(0) = P(Y = 0) = P(\{TTT\})$		$= (1 - p)^3$
$p_Y(1) = P(Y = 1) = P(\{HTT, THT, TTH\})$	$= 3p(1 - p)^2$
$p_Y(2) = P(Y = 2) = P(\{HHT, HTH, THH\})$	$= 3p^2(1 - p)$
$p_Y(3) = P(Y = 3) = P(\{HHH\})$		$= p^3$

so, putting this all together, we see that

$$p_Y(1) = 3p(1 - p)^2$$

Table 4.6 shows the results of similar computations for the other three values of y.

Observe that the probability of each of the eight outcomes of the random phenomenon relies only on the number of successes (i.e., heads), and not on the order in which they occurred. For example, all outcomes with exactly two successes have probability $p^2(1 - p)$, and all with exactly one success have probability $p(1 - p)^2$. Any one outcome consisting of y successes and $3 - y$ failures has probability $p^y(1 - p)^{3-y}$, for $y = 0, 1, 2,$ and 3. For $y = 0$ and $y = 3$, there is only one such outcome. For $y = 1$ and $y = 2$, there are three.

There is one more interesting characteristic of the probabilities in Table 4.6. For any two numbers, a and b, we may write

$$(a + b)^3 = a^3 + 3a^2b + 3ab^2 + b^3 \tag{4.19}$$

If we choose $a = p$ and $b = 1 - p$, Equation (4.19) becomes

$$[p + (1 - p)]^3 = p^3 + 3p^2(1 - p) + 3p(1 - p)^2 + (1 - p)^3 \tag{4.20}$$

Equation (4.20) tells us two things. First, the probabilities $p_Y(y)$, $y = 0, 1, 2,$ and 3, can be found by expanding $[p + (1 - p)]^3$ as a polynomial. Second, since $[p + (1 - p)]^3 = 1^3 = 1$, the $p_Y(y)$ sum to 1.   ✦

We can build on the derivation of the probability mass function in the last example to obtain the probability mass function for the general binomial distribution model. Suppose $Y \sim b(n, p)$. We want to compute $p_Y(y) = P(Y = y)$, for any $y = 0, 1, \ldots, n$. Now, $Y = y$ if and only if there are exactly y successes in the n trials. Any sequence of y successes and $n - y$ failures occurs with probability $p^y(1 - p)^{n-y}$, no matter what order the successes and failures are in. How many different sequences with y successes and $n - y$ failures are there? The answer is[10]

$$\binom{n}{y} = \frac{n!}{y!(n - y)!}$$

---

[10]The quantity $\binom{n}{y}$ is called the binomial coefficient. Since it counts the number of ways of choosing y items from a set of n items, it also answers to the name "n choose y."

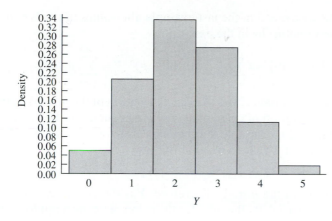

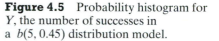

Figure 4.5 Probability histogram for Y, the number of successes in a $b(5, 0.45)$ distribution model.

Therefore, the probability mass function of the $b(n, p)$ distribution model is

$$p_Y(y) = \binom{n}{y} p^y (1 - p)^{n-y} = \frac{n!}{y!(n - y)!} p^y (1 - p)^{n-y}, \qquad y = 0, 1, \ldots, n$$

Graphically, the $b(n, p)$ model is represented by a probability histogram that has $n + 1$ bars. The yth bar is centered at y and has area $p_Y(y)$.

EXAMPLE 4.10   EVALUATING THE PROBABILITY MASS FUNCTION OF A BINOMIAL DISTRIBUTION MODEL

For a $b(5, 0.45)$ distribution, the values of $p_Y(y)$ are computed as

$$p_Y(0) = \binom{5}{0} 0.45^0 (1 - 0.45)^{5-0} = \frac{5!}{0!(5 - 0)!}(1 - 0.45)^5 \qquad = 0.0503$$

$$p_Y(1) = \binom{5}{1} 0.45^1 (1 - 0.45)^{5-1} = \frac{5!}{1!(5 - 1)!}0.45(1 - 0.45)^4 \quad = 0.2059$$

$$p_Y(2) = \binom{5}{2} 0.45^2 (1 - 0.45)^{5-2} = \frac{5!}{2!(5 - 2)!}0.45^2(1 - 0.45)^3 = 0.3369$$

$$p_Y(3) = \binom{5}{3} 0.45^3 (1 - 0.45)^{5-3} = \frac{5!}{3!(5 - 3)!}0.45^3(1 - 0.45)^2 = 0.2757$$

$$p_Y(4) = \binom{5}{4} 0.45^4 (1 - 0.45)^{5-4} = \frac{5!}{4!(5 - 4)!}0.45^4(1 - 0.45) \quad = 0.1127$$

$$p_Y(5) = \binom{5}{5} 0.45^5 (1 - 0.45)^{5-5} = \frac{5!}{5!(5 - 5)!}0.45^5 \qquad = 0.0185$$

Figure 4.5 shows the population histogram of the $b(5, 0.45)$ distribution model. ◆

As we saw for the case $n = 3$ in the last example, the values of the $b(n, p)$ probability mass function occur naturally in the expansion

$$1 = [p + (1 - p)]^n = \sum_{y=0}^{n} \binom{n}{y} p^y (1 - p)^{n-y} = \sum_{y=0}^{n} p_Y(y)$$

To compute the mean, variance, and standard deviation of the $b(n, p)$ distribution model, we return to the definition of a binomial trial as a sequence of Bernoulli trials. If we let Y_i be a Bernoulli random variable that equals 1 if there is a success at Bernoulli trial i and 0 otherwise, then it is easy to see that the sum

$$Y = Y_1 + Y_2 + \cdots + Y_n$$

is the number of successes in the n trials. Therefore, Y is the $b(n, p)$ random variable associated with the binomial trial. By the rules for the mean of a sum of random variables, we have

$$\mu_Y = \mu_{Y_1} + \mu_{Y_2} + \cdots + \mu_{Y_n}$$

Also, since the Y_i are independent, the rules for the variance of a sum of random variables give us

$$\sigma_Y^2 = \sigma_{Y_1}^2 + \sigma_{Y_2}^2 + \cdots + \sigma_{Y_n}^2$$

Now,

$$\mu_{Y_i} = 0 \times p_{Y_i}(0) + 1 \times p_{Y_i}(1) = 0 \times (1 - p) + 1 \times p = p$$

and

$$\sigma_{Y_i}^2 = (0 - p)^2 p_{Y_i}(0) + (1 - p)^2 p_{Y_i}(1) = p(1 - p)$$

Therefore,

$$\mu_Y = np \qquad \text{and} \qquad \sigma_Y^2 = np(1 - p)$$

To summarize:

THE BINOMIAL DISTRIBUTION MODEL

A random variable Y that counts the number of successes in n independent Bernoulli trials, each with probability p of success, follows the binomial distribution model with parameters n and p, $b(n, p)$. The $b(n, p)$ distribution model has probability mass function

$$p_Y(y) = \binom{n}{y} p^y (1 - p)^{n-y}, \qquad y = 0, 1, \ldots, n$$

mean $\mu_Y = np$, variance $\sigma_Y^2 = np(1 - p)$, and standard deviation $\sigma_Y = \sqrt{np(1 - p)}$.

The binomial distribution model is used extensively in statistical applications. The following is an example of statistical decision making using the binomial distribution model.

EXAMPLE 4.11   DECISION MAKING USING THE BINOMIAL DISTRIBUTION MODEL

In a certain state, the State Gaming Commission supervises the gambling casinos. The recent performance of a particular roulette wheel raised suspicions that the wheel wasn't fair. Roulette wheels have 38 slots: 18 red, 18 black, and 2 neutral ones. It was suspected that for the wheel in question, red came up too often. To test the wheel's fairness, the wheel was spun 100 times, and each result recorded. Red came up in 58 of the 100 spins. Does this result constitute good evidence that the wheel is unfair?

The 100 spins of the wheel can be viewed as 100 Bernoulli trials, in which a result of "red" constitutes a success and "not red" a failure. The true parameter p is unknown, but if the wheel is fair it is $18/38 = 0.47$. We are concerned with Y, the number of times red occurred in the 100 spins. If the wheel is fair, $Y \sim b(100, 0.47)$. In this case, the mean number of reds that should be observed is $100 \times 0.47 = 47$.

Now the question the State Gaming Commission must answer is whether the 58 reds is too large to have occurred by chance in the $b(100, 0.47)$ distribution model. One way to measure this is to compute the proportion of values Y from a $b(100, 0.47)$ population that are greater than or equal to 58. Using a computer package or a table, we can show that this value, $P(Y \geq 58)$, equals 0.0177. This means that only a proportion 0.0177 of all such trials would result in 58 or more successes. This result leaves the State Gaming Commission two choices:

1. Stick with the assumption that the wheel is fair and conclude that they have just observed a rare event: one that has a smaller than 1.8% chance of occurring.

2. Conclude that the wheel is not fair.

Most people, statisticians included, would look at the 1.8% chance of seeing 58 or more reds in 100 spins of a fair wheel, and conclude that there is a reason to question the fairness of the wheel. ✦

The Cumulative Distribution Function

Thus far, we have used the probability mass function to summarize discrete distribution models. A different, but equivalent, way of summarizing a distribution model is the **cumulative distribution function.**

> **DEFINITION**
>
> The **cumulative distribution function** of a random variable, Y, is a function, $F_Y(y)$, defined for all real numbers, y, as
>
> $$F_Y(y) = P(Y \leq y)$$

The cumulative distribution function of a $b(n, p)$ random variable, Y, is defined at the points $y = 0, 1, \ldots, n$ by

$$F_Y(y) = \sum_{x=0}^{y} p_Y(x) = \sum_{x=0}^{y} \binom{n}{x} p^x (1-p)^{n-x}$$

where $p_Y(x)$ is the probability mass function. This means that if we know the cumulative distribution function of a $b(n, p)$ random variable, we may obtain its probability mass function by using the relation

$$p_Y(y) = F_Y(0), \qquad y = 0$$
$$= F_Y(y) - F_Y(y - 1), \qquad 0 < y \le n$$

This relation is of particular interest when using Table A.1 in Appendix A, which contains values of the cumulative distribution function for $b(n, p)$ distributions.

EXAMPLE 4.10   CONTINUED

We previously computed the values of the probability mass function, $p_Y(y)$, for a $b(5, 0.45)$ distribution directly. We will now use Table A.1. From the table, we see that

$$p_Y(0) = F_Y(0) \qquad\qquad\qquad\qquad = 0.0503$$
$$p_Y(1) = F_Y(1) - F_Y(0) = 0.2562 - 0.0503 = 0.2059$$
$$p_Y(2) = F_Y(2) - F_Y(1) = 0.5931 - 0.2562 = 0.3369$$
$$p_Y(3) = F_Y(3) - F_Y(2) = 0.8688 - 0.5931 = 0.2757$$
$$p_Y(4) = F_Y(4) - F_Y(3) = 0.9815 - 0.8688 = 0.1127$$
$$p_Y(5) = F_Y(5) - F_Y(4) = 1.0000 - 0.9815 = 0.0185. \qquad \blacklozenge$$

The Poisson Distribution Model

We have already had a brief encounter with the Poisson distribution model as a model for the number of particles emitted by a mass of radioactive material in a 7.5-second interval. The model can arise as an approximation to the binomial distribution or from a separate set of assumptions.

The Poisson as Approximation to the Binomial

Consider a sequence of binomial models, where the nth model is a $b(n, p_n)$ model. We will assume that the parameters p_n converge to 0 in such a way that $\lim_{n \to \infty} np_n = \lambda$, where λ is some positive constant. For any integer $0 \le y \le n$, the probability a $b(n, p_n)$ random variable equals y is

$$\binom{n}{y} p_n^y (1 - p_n)^{n-y} \tag{4.21}$$

It can be shown that as $n \to \infty$, the probability given by Equation (4.21) converges to

$$\frac{\lambda^y e^{-\lambda}}{y!}$$

The function

$$p_Y(y) = \frac{\lambda^y e^{-\lambda}}{y!}, \qquad y = 0, 1, 2, \ldots \tag{4.22}$$

is the probability mass function of a **Poisson distribution model** with parameter λ.

When n is large and p is small, the Poisson distribution model with parameter $\lambda = np$ can be used to approximate probabilities associated with a $b(n, p)$ distribution. As a rule of thumb, the approximation will be good if $n \geq 100$, $p \leq 0.01$, and $np \leq 20$. In this sense, the Poisson distribution models the total number of occurrences in a large number of independent trials, when the probability of an occurrence on any one trial is small.

The mean and variance of a $b(n, p_n)$ distribution model are np_n and $np_n(1 - p_n)$, respectively. Under the assumption that $\lim_{n \to \infty} np_n = \lambda$, both the mean and variance converge to λ, so it seems reasonable to suppose that the mean and variance of the Poisson distribution equal λ. In fact, this can be shown directly from the definitions of mean and variance.

EXAMPLE 4.12   THE POISSON APPROXIMATION TO THE BINOMIAL DISTRIBUTION MODEL

To compete in today's market, computer chips have to be very reliable. It is known that the probability of a defective chip of a particular type is 0.0001. What is the probability of finding more than two defective chips in a production lot of 25,000?

Assuming that the number of defectives in the lot is modeled adequately by a $b(25000, 0.0001)$ distribution, we want to find $P(Y > 2)$, where $Y \sim b(25000, 0.0001)$. Since $n = 25000 > 100$, $p = 0.0001 < 0.01$, and $np = 2.5 < 20$, we can approximate this probability by finding $P(X > 2)$, where X is a Poisson random variable with parameter $\lambda = (25000)(0.0001) = 2.5$. The computation is

$$P(X > 2) = 1 - P(X \leq 2)$$

$$= 1 - \sum_{x=0}^{2} \frac{2.5^x}{x!} e^{-2.5}$$

$$= 1 - \left(\frac{2.5^0}{0!} e^{-2.5} + \frac{2.5^1}{1!} e^{-2.5} + \frac{2.5^2}{2!} e^{-2.5} \right)$$

$$= 1 - (0.082 + 0.205 + 0.257)$$

$$= 0.456 \quad \blacklozenge$$

Defining Criteria for the Poisson Distribution Model

Apart from its usefulness as an approximation to the binomial distribution, the Poisson distribution is a versatile model for counts of the occurrences of various phenomena over time, area, or space. In addition to the emission of particles from a mass of radioactive material over a given time period, examples of such phenomena might include telephone calls coming into a switchboard over a given time period, eagle nests located over a given area of wilderness, or galaxies located in a given volume of space.

The Poisson distribution will model such counts effectively if the phenomenon being counted satisfies three criteria. To state the criteria, we first assume that λ equals the mean number of counts over the entire interval, area, or volume that we are modeling. We next assume that the entire length, area, or volume equals M units, units^2, or units^3. Finally, we assume that the entire interval, area, or volume can be partitioned into subunits of smaller and smaller length, area, or volume. We denote as $U(\delta)$ any subunit of size (length, area, or volume) δ. Then the criteria are,

P.1 Counts in disjoint subunits are independent.

P.2 $\dfrac{1}{\delta} P(\text{There is exactly 1 count in } U(\delta)) \rightarrow \dfrac{\lambda}{M}, \text{ as } \delta \rightarrow 0.$

P.3 $\dfrac{1}{\delta} P(\text{There is more than 1 count in } U(\delta)) \rightarrow 0, \text{ as } \delta \rightarrow 0.$

If these criteria are satisfied, then it can be shown mathematically that the counts in the entire interval, area, or volume follow a Poisson distribution with parameter λ.

The idea behind these criteria is similar to that behind the Poisson approximation to the binomial. The small subunits are like independent (criterion P.1) Bernoulli trials (criterion P.3 ensures there is little chance of anything other than 0 or 1 occurrence in any subunit). Criterion P.2 says that the probability of an occurrence (success) in each is approximately $\delta\lambda/M$. Since there are approximately M/δ subunits of size δ, the number of subunits times the probability of a success in each is approximately λ (this is the role played by np_n in the binomial approximation).

EXAMPLE 4.4 CONTINUED

For the Rutherford, Chadwick, and Ellis radioactivity trials, the entire time interval is 7.5 seconds and the mean number of counts per 7.5-second interval is 3.87. Thus, the mean number of counts per second is $3.87/7.5 = 0.516$. We assume that the entire 7.5-second time interval can be partitioned into subunits of smaller and smaller length. We denote as $U(\delta)$ any subunit of δ seconds. Then, the criteria are

P.1 Counts in disjoint time intervals are independent.

P.2 $\dfrac{1}{\delta} P(\text{There is exactly 1 count in } U(\delta)) \rightarrow \dfrac{3.87}{7.5} = 0.516, \text{ as } \delta \rightarrow 0.$

P.3 $\dfrac{1}{\delta} P(\text{There is more than 1 count in } U(\delta)) \rightarrow 0, \text{ as } \delta \rightarrow 0.$

The Poisson distribution model allows Y to be arbitrarily large. Of course, Y can never be arbitrarily large, since there is a finite number of particles in any piece of matter. We can still use the Poisson distribution model, however, because of the following:

1. Although there is a finite number of particles, there is a very large number, and we have no way of knowing how many. Setting an upper bound of infinity greatly simplifies things.

2. We must always remember that models are simplified approximations to help us better understand phenomena. The approximation we obtain does not have to be perfect, only good enough for our needs. In fact, as we have seen, the Poisson model predicted the observed results quite well.   ◆

EXAMPLE 4.13   AN APPLICATION OF THE POISSON DISTRIBUTION MODEL

In an oil pipeline, the number of leaks serious enough to require a special repair crew is assumed to follow a Poisson distribution with mean of one leak every 10 miles. In a 100-mile section of pipe, what is the probability there are at least five such leaks?

Since the mean number of leaks is one per 10 miles, the mean number along the 100-mile section is $\lambda = 10$ leaks. Thus, if Y is the number of leaks along the 100 miles of pipeline, Y has a Poisson distribution with parameter $\lambda = 10$. The probability there are fewer than five serious leaks is

$$P(Y \leq 4) = \sum_{y=0}^{4} p_Y(y) = \sum_{y=0}^{4} \frac{10^y e^{-10}}{y!} = 0.029$$

Therefore, the probability there are at least five serious leaks is

$$P(Y > 4) = 1 - P(Y \leq 4) = 1 - 0.029 = 0.971$$

The value $P(Y \leq 4) = 0.029$ may also be obtained from the table of the Poisson cumulative distribution function found in Table A.2 in Appendix A, page 899, where the cumulative distribution function of the Poisson distribution model is tabulated.   ◆

THE POISSON DISTRIBUTION MODEL

The Poisson distribution model with parameter λ has probability mass function

$$p_Y(y) = \frac{\lambda^y e^{-\lambda}}{y!}, \qquad y = 0, 1, 2, \ldots$$

mean $\mu_Y = \lambda$, variance $\sigma_Y^2 = \lambda$, and standard deviation $\sigma_Y = \sqrt{\lambda}$.

In applications, the Poisson distribution model is used in one of two settings:

• As an approximation to the $b(n, p)$ model when n is large and p is small. Then the Poisson parameter λ is chosen to equal np.

• In its own right, as a result of random phenomena satisfying criteria P.1–P.3 defined earlier.

4.4

THE POWER OF MODELS

So far, you have learned something about three basic distribution models: the Bernoulli, the binomial, and the Poisson. Particularly, if this is your first exposure to statistical modeling, you may be wondering what the use of distribution models is. The short answer is that models are powerful and widely used tools in many fields. Models enable engineers and scientists to understand and draw conclusions about the phenomena they study. Models provide the basis for policymakers and managers to make rational and informed decisions. Thinking about Example 4.11 will reveal two particular reasons for the power of models:

- **Models are the quantifiers of data that make strong scientific conclusions possible.** The roulette wheel example illustrates the power of models. To think about why this is, imagine the State Gaming Commission went before a judge to try to stop the wheel's owner from using the wheel. Without the binomial model, the lawyer for the Commission would point out that 58 of 100 red spins was too many for a fair wheel, and the lawyer for the wheel owner would say that this kind of result happened all the time with fair wheels. Since there would be no quantification of these claims, it would be one lawyer's word against the other's.

  But with the model and the analysis it provided, the results of the 100 spins of this particular roulette wheel could be compared to all possible spins of a fair wheel. The chance of observing 58 or more red spins from a fair wheel could be quantified and a judgment rendered based on that chance.

- **Models extend the range of what we can legitimately conclude from data.** Without a model, conclusions based on a set of data can be drawn only for that set of data. With a model, the conclusions can be extended to the population defined by the model. Thus, in the roulette example, without the model, we can only base conclusions on the 58 red spins in the 100 spins of that wheel. With the model, we know how any fair wheel (or unfair wheel with a specific chance of coming up red), should behave, and we can evaluate data from any wheel with that knowledge.

4.5

CONTINUOUS DISTRIBUTION MODELS

We have learned what a discrete random variable and a discrete distribution model are, and we have made the acquaintance of several discrete distribution models: the Bernoulli, the binomial, the Poisson, and the uniform. A second widely used type of distribution model is the **continuous distribution model,** which is a distribution model for a **continuous random variable.** A random variable is continuous if it can take any value in an interval (a, b) of real numbers or on the entire real line $(-\infty, \infty)$. Continuous random variables are measurements such as weight, height, temperature, or pressure, which occur on a continuous scale.[11]

A continuous distribution model precisely quantifies the pattern of variation of a continuous random variable. Recall that a discrete distribution model consists of all values the random variable can assume along with the probability of assuming each possible value. Unfortunately, we can't present a continuous distribution model in the same way, because we can't make a list of all the values in an interval: there are just too many. This means we need another approach to defining a continuous distribution model: an approach based on continuous analogues of probability histograms, called **probability density functions.**

> ### DEFINITION
>
> A **continuous distribution model** is a distribution model for a continuous random variable. It is most often characterized by a probability density function describing the pattern of variation of the random variable.

The Probability Density Function

We have seen that a probability histogram displays distribution of a discrete distribution model. The analogous graph for a continuous distribution model is the graph of a function called a **probability density function.**

> ### DEFINITION
>
> A **probability density function** for a continuous random variable, Y, is a non-negative function $p_Y(y)$, $-\infty < y < \infty$, which has that property that for any real numbers a and b, with $a < b$, the probability Y takes a value between a and b, $P(a < Y \leq b)$, equals the area below the probability density function and above the interval (a, b).

The area described in the definition is illustrated by the shaded region in Figure 4.6.

Two further points follow from this definition. First, unlike a probability mass function, which is defined only on a discrete set, a probability density function is always defined for all real numbers. Second, since $P(-\infty < Y < \infty) = 1$, and since this probability is the total area under the probability density function, we see that the total area under the probability density function must always equal 1.

Interpreting the Probability Density Function

Since we originally defined probability as a limiting relative frequency, it makes sense to look at the idea of a probability density function from a limiting perspective. Suppose

---

[11] In reality, we can only measure to a finite number of decimal places, so all measurements are discrete. But a random variable is an abstraction and the concept of a continuous random variable is a useful one. The discussion on page 38 is relevant here.

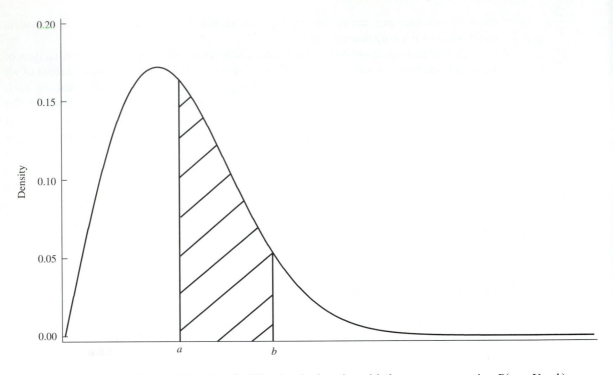

Figure 4.6   A probability density function with the area representing $P(a < Y \leq b)$ shaded.

the continuous random variable Y results from a certain random phenomenon, and suppose we conduct repeated trials of this random phenomenon, with trial i resulting in the value y_i of Y. Suppose after the first n trials, we draw a density histogram of the data values $y_1, y_2, \ldots, y_n$. As n grows larger, we can take the bars to be narrower and narrower to get a better graph. Finally, as $n \to \infty$, the graph of the density histograms will converge so that they fill in the area beneath a curve. This curve is the graph of the probability density function.

Figure 4.7 shows the density histograms produced by (from top to bottom) 100, 1000, and 10,000 observations as they converge toward the plotted probability density function. In this sense, the probability density function represents the population distribution of all possible observations from the distribution model. This leads directly to the following interpretation of the probability density function.

The area under the probability density function between a and b corresponds to the proportion of the population values, or of all possible data values, that lie between a and b. Let $p_Y(y)$ denote the height of the probability density function at the data value y, and let δ be a very small positive number. Then, if the probability density function is continuous, the proportion of population values in the tiny interval $(y - \delta/2, y + \delta/2)$ is approximately $p_Y(y) \times \delta$, since the continuous probability density function is close to $p_Y(y)$ on the entire small interval. The average density of population values

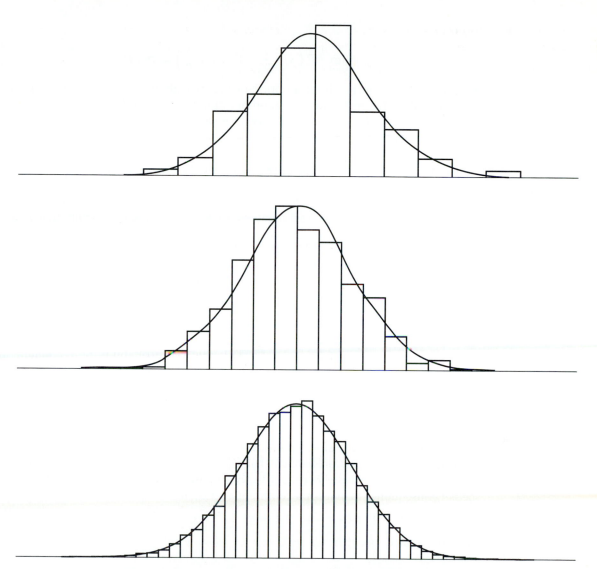

Figure 4.7 Convergence of density histograms to a probability density function. The top histogram is based on 100 data values, the middle histogram on 1000 data values, and the bottom histogram on 10,000 data values.

in this interval is the area under the probability density function over the interval $(y-\delta/2,\ y+\delta/2)$, divided by the length of the interval, which, by the preceding argument, is approximately $[p_Y(y) \times \delta]/\delta$ or $p_Y(y)$. This is why the curve describing a continuous distribution model is called a probability density function.

   In the limit, as the length of an interval about y goes to 0, the ratio of the probability of obtaining an observation in that interval to the length of the interval converges to $p_Y(y)$:

$$\lim_{\delta \to 0} \frac{1}{\delta} P\left(y - \frac{\delta}{2} < Y < y + \frac{\delta}{2}\right) = p_Y(y)$$

All this leads to another interpretation of the probability density function: $p_Y(y)$ is proportional to the probability of an observation occurring near y. So if $p_Y(x) = 2 \times p_Y(y)$, it is twice as likely that an observation will occur very near x as it is that it will occur very near y.

Computing Probabilities using the Probability Density Function

Suppose Y is a continuous random variable with probability density function $p_Y(y)$. Then if A is any subset of the real numbers, we know that the probability that Y lies in A is the area under $p_Y(y)$ over the set A. Since the area beneath a function is computed by an integral, we obtain the formula

$$P(Y \in A) = \int_A p_Y(y)dy \qquad (4.23)$$

Note that by regarding the probability density function as summarizing the distribution of measurement Y in a population, $P(Y \in A)$ can also be interpreted as the proportion of the population that has values of Y in the set A.

One consequence of Equation (4.23) is that the probability of Y equaling any single value is 0. To see this, take A to be the set $\{y_0\}$, consisting of the single real number y_0. From Equation (4.23), we get

$$P(Y = y_0) = \int_{\{y_0\}} p_Y(y)dy = 0$$

since the integral over a single point is 0. It may seem strange that Y must take on some value, but that the probability that Y equals *any* single value is 0. This seeming paradox happens because there is a very large number of points in an interval.[12] A second consequence is that for a continuous random variable Y with density $P_Y(y)$,

$$P(a < Y < b) = P(a \le Y < b) = P(a < Y \le b) = P(a \le Y \le b)$$

since all equal $\int_a^b p_Y(y)dy$.

The Cumulative Distribution Function

Recall that in our study of discrete random variables, we defined $F_Y(y)$, the cumulative distribution function of the random variable Y, as

$$F_Y(y) = P(Y \le y), \quad -\infty < y < \infty$$

The same definition holds if Y is a continuous random variable. If Y has probability density function $p_Y(y)$, then

$$F_Y(y) = P(Y \le y) = \int_{-\infty}^{y} p_Y(x)dx$$

---

[12] In contrast, at least one value of a discrete random variable must have positive probability.

By the Fundamental Theorem of Calculus, differentiation is the opposite of integration, and so we have

$$p_Y(y) = \frac{d}{dy} \int_{-\infty}^{y} p_Y(x)dx = \frac{d}{dy} F_Y(y)$$

Therefore, knowing the cumulative distribution function is equivalent to knowing the probability density function, and vice versa.

The Mean, Variance, and Standard Deviation

Just as we did for a discrete distribution model, we can also define a mean, a variance, and a standard deviation for a continuous distribution model. We can think of these quantities as analogous to their discrete distribution counterparts. For example, the mean for a continuous distribution model can be thought of as the point where the probability density function "balances." It can also be thought of as the population "average" as well as the limit of the average of repeated measurements from the underlying random phenomenon.

The mean of Y is defined only if a condition analogous to condition (4.4) for discrete random variables is satisfied. The condition, which replaces the sum in condition (4.4) with an integral, is $\int_{-\infty}^{\infty} |y| p_Y(y)dy < \infty$. In computing the mean or expected value, we must replace the sum in Equation (4.5) with an integral, which is the analogue of the sum for continuous variables. The resulting formula is

$$\mu_Y = E(Y) = \int_{-\infty}^{\infty} y p_Y(y)dy$$

The variance of Y is defined if and only if a condition analogous to condition (4.6) for discrete random variables is satisfied. The condition, which replaces the sum in condition (4.6) with an integral, is $\int_{-\infty}^{\infty} y^2 p_Y(y)dy < \infty$.

If it is defined, the formula for the variance becomes

$$\sigma_Y^2 = \int_{-\infty}^{\infty} (y - \mu_Y)^2 p_Y(y)dy$$

and the standard deviation is $\sigma_Y = \sqrt{\sigma_Y^2}$.

SOME KEY FACTS ABOUT PROBABILITY DENSITY FUNCTIONS

- A function $p_Y(y)$, defined for all real numbers y, is a probability density function for a continuous random variable Y, if it satisfies three conditions:

    1. $p_Y(y) \geq 0$.
    2. $\int_{-\infty}^{\infty} p_y(y)dy = 1$.
    3. For any real numbers $a < b$, $P(a < Y \leq b) = \int_{a}^{b} p_Y(y)dy$.

- The cumulative distribution function of Y is defined, for all real numbers y, to be $F_Y(y) = \int_{-\infty}^{y} p_Y(x)dx$.
- The mean of Y is defined if and only if $\int_{-\infty}^{\infty} |y| p_Y(y)dy < \infty$, in which case it equals

$$\mu_Y = E(Y) = \int_{-\infty}^{\infty} y p_Y(y)dy$$

- The variance of Y is defined if and only if $\int_{-\infty}^{\infty} y^2 p_Y(y)dy < \infty$, in which case it equals

$$\sigma_Y^2 = \int_{-\infty}^{\infty} (y - \mu_Y)^2 p_Y(y)dy$$

More Than One Continuous Random Variable

Recall that the discrete random variables $Y_1, Y_2, \ldots, Y_n$ are independent if for all values $y_1, y_2, \ldots, y_n$ for which

$$P(Y_1 = y_1) > 0, \, P(Y_2 = y_2) > 0, \ldots, \, P(Y_n = y_n) > 0$$

$$P(\{Y_1 = y_1\} \cap \{Y_2 = y_2\} \cap \cdots \cap \{Y_n = y_n\}) = P(Y_1 = y_1)P(Y_2 = y_2)\cdots P(Y_n = y_n)$$

It can be shown that an equivalent formulation of this criterion is that

$$P(\{Y_1 \le y_1\} \cap \{Y_2 \le y_2\} \cap \cdots \cap \{Y_n \le y_n\}) = P(Y_1 \le y_1)P(Y_2 \le y_2)\cdots P(Y_n \le y_n)$$

for all real numbers $y_1, y_2, \ldots, y_n$. This last criterion also defines the independence of continuous random variables.

DEFINITION

The continuous random variables $Y_1, Y_2, \ldots, Y_n$ are **independent** if

$$P(\{Y_1 \le y_1\} \cap \{Y_2 \le y_2\} \cap \cdots \cap \{Y_n \le y_n\})$$
$$= P(Y_1 \le y_1)P(Y_2 \le y_2)\cdots P(Y_n \le y_n)$$

for all real numbers $y_1, y_2, \ldots, y_n$.

We note that Equations (4.12) to (4.15) for discrete random variables are also valid for sums of continuous random variables, as are Equations (4.16) to (4.18) for the sample mean.

Some Useful Continuous Probability Distribution Models

Probability density functions come in many different shapes, just as did the data distributions you studied in Chapter 2: skewed, symmetric, and so on. This is not surprising since these curves are used to model data, taking advantage of the fact that often the overall pattern of a data distribution can be expressed, at least approximately, by a mathematical equation.

Four commonly used continuous distribution models are the **uniform,** the **normal,** the **Weibull,** and the **exponential.**

The Continuous Uniform Distribution Model

We have already studied the discrete uniform distribution model on $\{1, 2, \ldots, k\}$, which modeled the random phenomenon of choosing one of the first k positive integers at random. In a similar way, we can think of randomly selecting a real number from the interval (a, b). One way to visualize such a model is to think of a fair spinner that turns freely on its axis and slowly comes to a stop. The pointer can come to rest anywhere on a circle that is marked with all real numbers from a to b, and its chance of stopping in any small interval between a and b is the same as its chance of stopping in any other interval of equal length. If Y is the number selected, the distribution model for Y is the continuous uniform distribution model on (a, b), and we say $Y \sim U(a, b)$. The probability density function for Y is

$$p_Y(y) = \frac{1}{b - a}, \qquad \text{if } a < y < b$$
$$= 0, \qquad\qquad \text{otherwise}$$

Figure 4.8 is a graph of the $U(0, 1)$ probability density function.

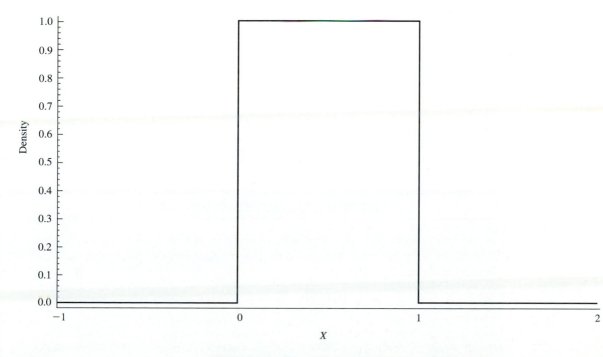

Figure 4.8   The $U(0, 1)$ probability density function.

The cumulative distribution function of Y is given by

$$F_Y(y) = \int_{-\infty}^{y} 0 \, dx \qquad\qquad\qquad\qquad = 0, \qquad\qquad \text{if } y \leq a$$

$$= \int_{-\infty}^{a} 0 \, dx + \int_{a}^{y} \frac{1}{b-a} \, dx \qquad = \frac{y-a}{b-a}, \qquad \text{if } a < y \leq b$$

$$= \int_{-\infty}^{a} 0 \, dx + \int_{a}^{b} \frac{1}{b-a} \, dx + \int_{b}^{y} 0 \, dx = 1, \qquad \text{if } y > b$$

Computing Probabilities. If $Y \sim U(a, b)$, and if (c, d) is a subinterval of (a, b), then it seems obvious that the probability Y takes a value in (c, d) is just the ratio of the length of (c, d) to that of (a, b). This is borne out by the computation

$$P(c < Y \leq d) = \int_{c}^{d} \frac{1}{b-a} \, dy = \frac{d-c}{b-a}$$

For any c and d, we may obtain $P(c < Y \leq d)$ from the cumulative distribution function using the formula

$$P(c < Y \leq d) = P(Y \leq d) - P(Y \leq c) = F_Y(d) - F_Y(c)$$

Mean, Variance, and Standard Deviation. For the $U(a, b)$ distribution model, the place where the probability density function balances is clearly the midpoint of the interval (a, b): $(a + b)/2$. This can also be computed as

$$\mu_Y = \int_{-\infty}^{\infty} y p_Y(y) \, dy = \int_{a}^{b} y \frac{1}{b-a} \, dy = \frac{a+b}{2}$$

The variance is computed as

$$\sigma_Y^2 = \int_{a}^{b} (y - \mu_Y)^2 \frac{1}{b-a} \, dy = \frac{(b-a)^2}{12}$$

and the standard deviation is

$$\sigma_Y = \frac{b-a}{\sqrt{12}}$$

THE UNIFORM DISTRIBUTION MODEL

A random variable $Y \sim U(a, b)$ can be thought of as a number selected completely at random from the interval (a, b). The $U(a, b)$ distribution model has probability density function

$$p_Y(y) = \frac{1}{b-a}, \qquad a < y < b$$
$$= 0, \qquad\qquad \text{otherwise}$$

mean $\mu_Y = (b + a)/2$, variance $\sigma_Y^2 = (b - a)^2/12$, and standard deviation $\sigma_Y = (b - a)/\sqrt{12}$.

Here are two examples involving the uniform distribution model.

EXAMPLE 4.14   COMPUTING PROBABILITIES USING THE UNIFORM DISTRIBUTION MODEL

Consider the random phenomenon of choosing one real number at random from the interval (0, 1), and let Y be the number chosen. Then, Y has a $U(0, 1)$ distribution.

(a) What is the probability that the first digit to the right of the decimal point in the decimal expansion of Y is 3? To solve this problem, note that the first digit to the right of the decimal point in the decimal expansion of Y is 3 if and only if $0.3 \leq Y < 0.4$. So the desired probability is

$$P(0.3 \leq Y < 0.4) = \int_{0.3}^{0.4} dy = 0.1$$

(b) What is the probability that the second digit to the right of the decimal point in the decimal expansion of Y is 3? To solve this problem, note that the event

$$D = \{\text{The second digit to the right of the decimal point}$$
$$\text{in the decimal expansion of } Y \text{ is 3.}\}$$

is the union of the 10 disjoint events

$$\{0.03 \leq Y < 0.04\} \cup \{0.13 \leq Y < 0.14\} \cup \cdots \cup \{0.93 \leq Y < 0.94\}$$

Each of these disjoint events has probability 0.01. For instance,

$$P(0.63 \leq Y < 0.64) = \int_{0.63}^{0.64} dy = 0.01$$

Therefore,

$$P(D) = P(0.03 \leq Y < 0.04) + P(0.13 \leq Y < 0.14) + \cdots$$
$$+ P(0.93 \leq Y < 0.94)$$
$$= 0.01 + 0.01 + \cdots + 0.01$$
$$= 0.1 \quad \blacklozenge$$

EXAMPLE 4.15   COMPUTING ANOTHER PROBABILITY USING THE UNIFORM DISTRIBUTION MODEL

The real numbers can be divided into two kinds: the rational numbers,[13] which consist of all the integers and quotients of integers, such as $1/3$, $-7/8$, and $17/5$, and the irrational numbers, which consist of all the rest. Virtually all the numbers we talk about or use every day are rational. Based on our admittedly nonscientific

---

[13] Rational, here, means ratio.

experience, most people have trouble naming even one irrational number.[14] So if you ask someone to think of a number, the chances are it will be rational.

If we could choose a number from the interval (a, b) completely at random, what is the probability that we would choose a rational number? The answer may surprise you.

If Q is the set of rational numbers in (a, b) then the probability is

$$P(Y \in Q) = \int_Q \frac{1}{b-a} dy$$

What is this integral? The answer is 0. This means the probability of selecting a rational number at random is 0.

Why is the integral 0? Consider a subinterval (c, d) of (a, b). This subinterval has length $d - c$. We can also define the concept of length for other kinds of subsets of (a, b) that are not subintervals. One such subset is Q, the set of rational numbers in (a, b). Even though there are an infinite number of rational numbers in (a, b), it turns out that the rational numbers have total length 0. As a result, the integral, and therefore, $P(Y \in Q)$, equals 0. ✦

The Normal Distribution Model

Scientists have known for over 100 years that many data distributions can be closely approximated by symmetric, bell-shaped curves. In fact, the distribution model defined by the bell-shaped curve, the normal distribution model, is prominent in statistical applications. The Central Limit Theorem, to be discussed in the next section, explains why the normal model is so prevalent in nature and even provides a method for approximating other distributions, such as the binomial, by the normal curve. Data that have been successfully modeled by normal distribution models include repeated careful measurements of the same quantity, characteristics of homogeneous biological populations such as the weights and heights of male students, and sums and averages of random quantities.

Sometimes known as the Gaussian[15] distribution model, the normal distribution model is really a family of distribution models, all of whose densities are symmetric, unimodal, bell-shaped curves. The exact mathematical form of the normal distribution is governed by two parameters: μ and σ^2, and we write $Y \sim N(\mu, \sigma^2)$ to signify that the random variable Y follows a normal distribution model with parameters μ and σ^2. We call μ a **location parameter** since changing μ changes only where the curve is centered. We call σ^2 a **scale parameter** since changing σ^2 only changes the scale or spread of the curve, as the three normal probability density functions in Figure 4.9 demonstrate.

Each $N(\mu, \sigma^2)$ probability density function is centered at μ and is symmetric about μ. The $N(\mu, \sigma^2)$ probability density function is

$$p_Y(y) = \frac{1}{\sigma\sqrt{2\pi}} e^{-(1/2)[(y-\mu)/\sigma]^2}, \qquad -\infty < y < \infty$$

---

[14] In case you're one of those people, here are two: π and $\sqrt{2}$.

[15] After the German mathematician Carl Friedrich Gauss, 1777–1855.

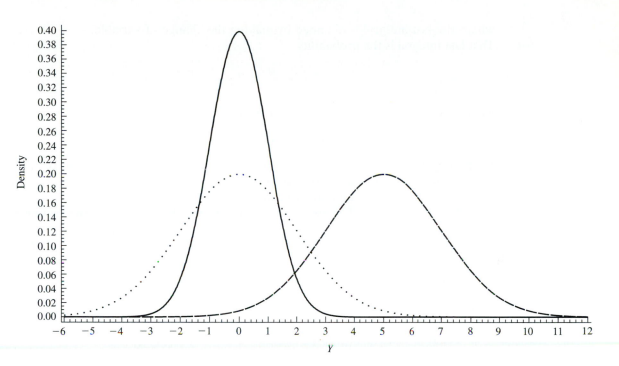

Figure 4.9   Three normal probability density functions: $N(0, 1)$ (tall curve at left), $N(0, 4)$ (short curve at left), and $N(5, 4)$.

The cumulative distribution function

$$F_Y(y) = \int_{-\infty}^{y} \frac{1}{\sigma\sqrt{2\pi}} e^{-(1/2)[(x-\mu)/\sigma]^2} dx, \qquad -\infty < y < \infty$$

has no closed form, and must be evaluated numerically.

Computing Probabilities.   Because the normal probability density function does not have an antiderivative, it is not possible to obtain probabilities involving the normal distribution using a simple formula. The solution is to either have a computer always available or to have tables of the normal cumulative distribution function or its equivalent. At first, this might seem an impossible task, since it would require a different table for each value of μ and σ^2. Fortunately, there is one feature of the normal distribution that makes only a single table necessary.

Suppose $Y \sim N(\mu, \sigma^2)$, and that we want to find $P(c < Y \le d)$, for some real numbers $c < d$. We can use the formula

$$P(c < Y \le d) = \int_{c}^{d} \frac{1}{\sigma\sqrt{2\pi}} e^{-(1/2)[(y-\mu)/\sigma]^2} dy.$$

$$= \int_{(c-\mu)/\sigma}^{(d-\mu)/\sigma} \frac{1}{\sqrt{2\pi}} e^{-z^2/2} dz,$$

where the last integral is obtained by making the change of variable $z = (y - \mu)/\sigma$. That last integral is the probability

$$P\left(\frac{c - \mu}{\sigma} < Z \le \frac{d - \mu}{\sigma}\right)$$

where Z is a $N(0, 1)$ random variable. This shows:

$$\text{If } Y \sim N(\mu, \sigma^2), \text{ then } Z = \frac{Y - \mu}{\sigma} \sim N(0, 1) \tag{4.24}$$

In a practical sense, the result of Equation (4.24) means that we can reduce all probability computations involving any normal distribution to a probability computation involving the $N(0, 1)$ distribution, by **standardizing.**

Standardizing involves two steps: centering the distribution by subtracting the mean and rescaling the distribution by dividing by the standard deviation. Standardizing any random variable ensures that the resulting distribution has mean 0 and variance 1. Standardizing a normal random variable also ensures the resulting distribution is normal. For this reason, $N(0, 1)$ is called the **standard normal distribution.**

A good way to proceed when translating probabilities about any normal distribution into probabilities about the standard normal distribution is the following:

1. Begin with the probability you want to find: $P(c < Y \le d)$. (Note that c can be $-\infty$ and d can be ∞.)
2. Now, standardize Y, remembering that to keep the inequality valid, you have to also standardize c and d:

$$P(c < Y \le d) = P\left(\frac{c - \mu}{\sigma} < \frac{Y - \mu}{\sigma} \le \frac{d - \mu}{\sigma}\right)$$

3. Finally, remember that the standardized Y, $Z = (Y - \mu)/\sigma$, has a standard normal distribution.

The cumulative distribution function of the standard normal distribution is used so often in applications that we will denote it with the special notation as $\Phi(z)$. Since, if $Z \sim N(0, 1)$,

$$P\left(\frac{c - \mu}{\sigma} < Z \le \frac{d - \mu}{\sigma}\right) = \Phi\left(\frac{d - \mu}{\sigma}\right) - \Phi\left(\frac{c - \mu}{\sigma}\right)$$

we have the following simple formula for computing probabilities involving the normal distribution:

COMPUTING NORMAL PROBABILITIES

If $Y \sim N(\mu, \sigma^2)$, and if $\Phi(z)$ is the cumulative distribution function of a $N(0, 1)$ distribution,

$$P(c < Y \le d) = \Phi\left(\frac{d - \mu}{\sigma}\right) - \Phi\left(\frac{c - \mu}{\sigma}\right) \tag{4.25}$$

Although more and more probability computations are being done with computers, there are still many occasions when it easier to use tabled values of the standard normal distribution. Table A.3, in Appendix A, page 901, contains values of $\Phi(z)$ for a large range of z. The following examples demonstrate how to use this table to compute normal probabilities.

EXAMPLE 4.16   COMPUTING PROBABILITIES USING THE NORMAL DISTRIBUTION MODEL

1. Suppose the lengths in inches of steel rivets produced by the River Riveting Company follow a $N(0.126, 0.0004)$ distribution model. Production personnel want to find the proportion of all rivets that fall within the specification limits of 0.120 and 0.130. In terms of the distribution model, this proportion is the probability that the length, Y, of a randomly chosen rivet is between 0.120 and 0.130 inch: $P(0.120 < Y < 0.130)$, where $Y \sim N(0.126, 0.0004)$.

   The desired probability can be obtained from many statistical computer packages, but here we will concentrate on how to obtain it from the table of the standard normal cumulative distribution function, $\Phi(z)$, Table A.3, page 901. Using formula (4.25), we get

$$P(0.120 < Y < 0.130) = \Phi\left(\frac{0.130 - 0.126}{\sqrt{0.0004}}\right) - \Phi\left(\frac{0.120 - 0.126}{\sqrt{0.0004}}\right)$$

$$= \Phi(0.2) - \Phi(-0.3)$$

$$= 0.5793 - 0.3821 = 0.1972$$

So the proportion of all rivets that fall in spec is 0.1972: not a very high proportion!

2. A student receives a 570 on the verbal SAT test. Nationally, these SAT scores follow a $N(435, 10000)$ distribution model. What is the student's percentile score among all scores nationally?

   What is wanted is the proportion of all SAT verbal scores that are less than 570. That is, if Y represents a randomly chosen SAT verbal score, we want $P(Y \le 570)$. As stated in the previous example, we may use the computer to compute this probability, or we may use the Table A.3, page 901. To use the table,

$$P(Y \le 570) = \Phi\left(\frac{570 - 435}{\sqrt{10000}}\right) = \Phi(1.35) = 0.9115$$

where 0.9115 is obtained from the table as the proportion of the $N(0, 1)$ population at or below 1.35. This means that 91.15% of the population scores are at or below 570. Thus, the student's percentile score is 91.15.

   If we had wanted the proportion of the population who scored better than the student, we would compute

$$P(Y > 570) = 1 - \Phi(1.35) = 1 - 0.9115 = 0.0885 \quad \blacklozenge$$

We will find the following result useful later in the chapter:

If a and b are constants, and if $Z \sim N(0, 1)$, then $Y = aZ + b \sim N(b, a^2)$.   (4.26)

Result (4.26) is a converse to (4.24). It may be shown by reversing the argument that gave us (4.24). Its derivation is left as an exercise.

Mean, Variance, and Standard Deviation.   If $Y \sim N(\mu, \sigma^2)$, its mean μ_Y is obtained by evaluating

$$\mu_Y = \int_{-\infty}^{\infty} y p_Y(y) dy$$

$$= \int_{-\infty}^{\infty} y \frac{1}{\sigma \sqrt{2\pi}} e^{-(1/2)[(y-\mu)/\sigma]^2} dy$$

$$= \int_{-\infty}^{\infty} (\mu + \sigma z) \frac{1}{\sqrt{2\pi}} e^{-z^2/2} dz \qquad \left(\text{substitution: } z = \frac{y - \mu}{\sigma} \right)$$

$$= \mu \int_{-\infty}^{\infty} \frac{1}{\sqrt{2\pi}} e^{-z^2/2} dz + \sigma \int_{-\infty}^{\infty} z \frac{1}{\sqrt{2\pi}} e^{-z^2/2} dz$$

$$= \mu + \sigma \left[-\frac{e^{-z^2/2}}{\sqrt{2\pi}} \right]_{-\infty}^{\infty} \qquad \text{(The first is the integral of the density, which equals 1.)}$$

$$= \mu$$

The result is that the population mean μ_Y is really equal to the parameter μ in the definition of the normal distribution model. This is why the parameter was called μ. This result is apparent by looking at the graph of the probability density function, since any probability density function symmetric about a value must have that value as its balance point.

The variance is computed as

$$\sigma_Y^2 = \int_{-\infty}^{\infty} (y - \mu)^2 \frac{1}{\sigma \sqrt{2\pi}} e^{-(1/2)[(y-\mu)/\sigma]^2} dy$$

Using integration by parts, it can be shown that $\sigma_Y^2 = \sigma^2$. Therefore, the standard deviation σ_Y equals σ.

THE NORMAL DISTRIBUTION MODEL

The $N(\mu, \sigma^2)$ distribution model has the probability density function

$$p_Y(y) = \frac{1}{\sigma \sqrt{2\pi}} e^{-(1/2)[(y-\mu)/\sigma]^2}, \qquad -\infty < y < \infty$$

mean $\mu_Y = \mu$, variance $\sigma_Y^2 = \sigma^2$, and standard deviation $\sigma_Y = \sigma$.

The Weibull and Exponential Distribution Models

It is well known that a chain is only as strong as its weakest link. Suppose a chain is made of n links. If the links in a chain are considered identical components, and the breaking strength of the ith link is the random variable Y_i, then the strength of the chain is the random variable $Y = \min\{Y_1, Y_2, \ldots, Y_n\}$. The Weibull distribution model is often used as a model for random variables, such as the strength of a chain, that are the minimum of measurements from systems of identical components. Named after the Swedish physicist Waloddi Weibull, who in 1939 first used it to model the breaking strengths of materials, the Weibull distribution has since become a standard modeling tool for such applications. The Weibull distribution with parameters α and β, which we will denote $W(\alpha, \beta)$, has probability density function

$$p_Y(y) = \frac{\alpha}{\beta^{\alpha}} y^{\alpha-1} e^{-(y/\beta)^{\alpha}}, \qquad y > 0$$

$$= 0, \qquad\qquad\qquad y \leq 0$$

The Weibull distribution is also used to model waiting times or lifetimes. For example, it is used to model human longevity after age 20 or so.

When $\alpha = 1$, the Weibull distribution model is called an **exponential distribution model.** If $Y \sim W(1, \beta)$, then Y has probability density function

$$p_Y(y) = \frac{1}{\beta} e^{-y/\beta}, \qquad y > 0$$

$$= 0, \qquad\qquad y \leq 0$$

and we will write $Y \sim$ exponential(β), to signify that Y has an exponential distribution with parameter β. The exponential distribution model is often used to model waiting times, such as the time until an electrical component fails.

Figure 4.10 shows Weibull densities for $\beta = 5$ and $\alpha = 1, 2,$ and 5. The $W(1, 5)$ density is the same as the exponential(5) density.

Computing Probabilities.   If $Y \sim W(\alpha, \beta)$, then the cumulative distribution function of Y is

$$F_Y(y) = 0, \qquad y \leq 0$$

$$= \int_0^y \frac{\alpha}{\beta^{\alpha}} x^{\alpha-1} e^{-(x/\beta)^{\alpha}} dx$$

$$= \int_0^{(y/\beta)^{\alpha}} e^{-u} du \qquad \text{(substitution: } u = (x/\beta)^{\alpha})$$

$$= 1 - e^{-(y/\beta)^{\alpha}}, \qquad y > 0$$

In particular, the cumulative distribution function of the exponential(β) distribution is

$$F_Y(y) = 0, \qquad\qquad y \leq 0$$

$$= 1 - e^{-y/\beta}, \qquad y > 0$$

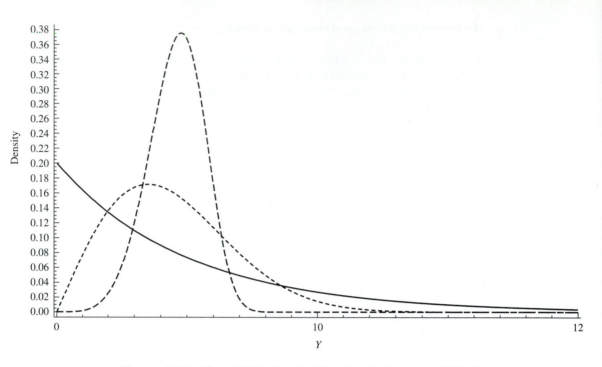

Figure 4.10 Three Weibull probability density functions: $W(1,5)$ or exponential(5) (curve with mode at 0), $W(2,5)$ (shortest curve), and $W(5,5)$.

EXAMPLE 4.17   COMPUTING PROBABILITIES USING THE WEIBULL DISTRIBUTION MODEL

The lifetime, in hours, of an electronic relay is thought to follow a Weibull distribution with parameters $\beta = 750$ and $\alpha = 0.5$. What can the producer tell a customer who requests a 1000-hour lifetime for this particular relay?

The proportion of all relays that will last more than 1000 hours is

$$P(Y > 1000) = 1 - F_Y(1000) = 1 - (1 - e^{-(1000/750)^{0.5}}) = e^{-1.1547} = 0.3152$$

So about 31.5% of all relays will last the requested 1000-hour lifetime.   ◆

Mean, Variance, and Standard Deviation.   The mean and variance of the Weibull distribution model are messy to compute, so we'll consider only the much neater special case of the exponential distribution model. The mean is computed, using integration by parts, as

$$\mu_Y = \int_{-\infty}^{\infty} y p_Y(y)\,dy = \int_0^{\infty} \frac{1}{\beta} y e^{-y/\beta}\,dy = \beta$$

The variance is

$$\sigma_Y^2 = \int_0^{\infty} \frac{1}{\beta}(y - \mu_Y)^2 e^{-y/\beta}\,dy = \beta^2$$

and the standard deviation is $\sigma_Y = \sqrt{\beta^2} = \beta$.

EXAMPLE 4.18   COMPUTING PROBABILITIES USING THE EXPONENTIAL DISTRIBUTION MODEL

The up times between crashes on a computer network are found to approximately follow an exponential distribution. If approximately 50% of all up times are less than 12 hours, what is the mean time between crashes?

If Y, the time between crashes has an exponential distribution with parameter β, then, since 50% of all up times are less than 12 hours, we know that

$$0.5 = F_Y(12) = 1 - e^{-12/\beta}$$

which implies

$$\beta = -12/\ln(0.5) = 17.3$$

Therefore, the mean time between crashes is 17.3 hours.   ◆

THE WEIBULL DISTRIBUTION MODEL

The $W(\alpha, \beta)$ distribution model has probability density function

$$p_Y(y) = \frac{\alpha}{\beta^\alpha} y^{\alpha-1} e^{-(y/\beta)^\alpha}, \qquad y > 0$$

$$= 0, \qquad\qquad\qquad y \le 0$$

THE EXPONENTIAL DISTRIBUTION MODEL

The exponential distribution model with parameter β is a special case of the Weibull distribution model: It is the $W(1, \beta)$ distribution model. It has probability density function

$$p_Y(y) = \frac{1}{\beta} e^{-(y/\beta)}, \qquad y > 0$$

$$= 0, \qquad\qquad y \le 0$$

mean β, variance β^2, and standard deviation β.

4.6

THE CENTRAL LIMIT THEOREM

On April 9, 1810, the French mathematician Laplace[16] presented before the French Academy his major result in probability: that any sum or mean will, if the number of terms is large, be approximately normally distributed. This result, called the **Central**

---

[16]Pierre Simon Laplace, 1749–1827.

Limit Theorem, played a vital role in the growth of statistics, and has been refined and generalized in many ways since 1810.

The Statement of the Central Limit Theorem

A precise statement of the Central Limit Theorem begins with n independent random variables, $Y_1, Y_2, \ldots, Y_n$, drawn from the same distribution, either continuous or discrete, having mean μ and variance σ^2. From these, we construct the sample mean

$$\bar{Y}_n = \frac{1}{n}(Y_1 + Y_2 + \cdots + Y_n)$$

We know from Equations (4.16) and (4.17) that the mean and variance of $\bar{Y}_n$ are μ and σ^2/n, respectively. With this information, we can standardize $\bar{Y}_n$ by subtracting its mean and dividing by its standard deviation. If we let Z_n denote the resulting standardized $\bar{Y}_n$, we have

$$Z_n = \frac{\bar{Y}_n - \mu}{\sigma/\sqrt{n}}$$

The Central Limit Theorem states that in the limit as $n \to \infty$, the distribution of Z_n approaches a $N(0, 1)$. Stating this formally, we have the following.

Theorem (Central Limit Theorem).   If $Y_1, Y_2, \ldots$ are independent random variables from the same distribution with mean μ and variance σ^2, if

$$\bar{Y}_n = \frac{1}{n}(Y_1 + Y_2 + \cdots + Y_n)$$

and if

$$Z_n = \frac{\bar{Y}_n - \mu}{\sigma/\sqrt{n}} \tag{4.27}$$

then for any real number z,

$$\lim_{n \to \infty} P(Z_n \le z) = \frac{1}{\sqrt{2\pi}} \int_{-\infty}^{z} e^{-y^2/2} dy \tag{4.28}$$

Equation (4.28) literally says that the cumulative distribution function of the standardized sample mean, Z_n, converges to the cumulative distribution function of the standard normal distribution. That is, if n is large enough, the standardized mean Z_n will have approximately an $N(0, 1)$ distribution, regardless of the distribution of the random variables Y_i. The practical implication is that for large n, we can use probabilities computed from the normal distribution to approximate probabilities involving Z_n.

Figure 4.11 shows the density histograms produced by (from top to bottom) 200 standardized observations from a $U(0, 1)$ distribution, 200 standardized means of 10 observations each from a $U(0, 1)$ distribution, and 200 standardized means of 100 observations each from a $U(0, 1)$ distribution. An $N(0, 1)$ density curve is superimposed

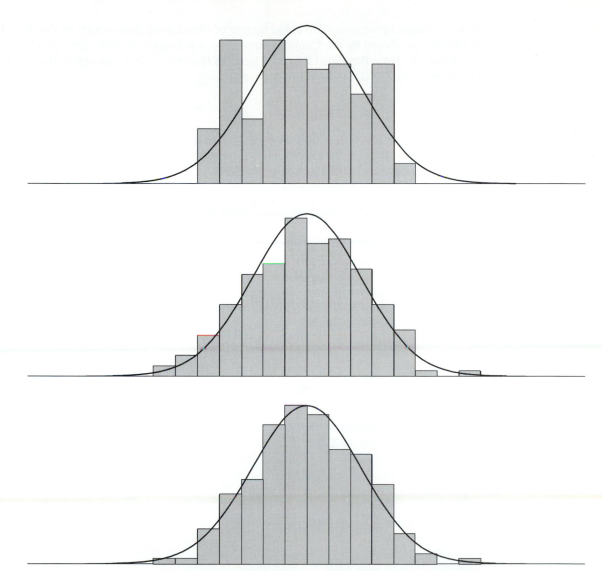

Figure 4.11 Convergence of density histograms of standardized means to the $N(0, 1)$ density curve, illustrates the Central Limit Theorem. From top to bottom, the graphs show the density histograms produced by 200 standardized observations from a $U(0, 1)$ distribution, 200 standardized means of 10 observations each from a $U(0, 1)$ distribution, and 200 standardized means of 100 observation each from a $U(0, 1)$ distribution. An $N(0, 1)$ density curve is superimposed on each density histogram.

on each density histogram. The convergence of the density histograms to the $N(0, 1)$ distribution predicted by the Central Limit Theorem is evident from these graphs.

It follows from the Central Limit Theorem that if n is large enough so that Z_n has approximately an $N(0, 1)$ distribution, then

$$\bar{Y}_n = \frac{\sigma}{\sqrt{n}} Z_n + \mu$$

has approximately an $N(\mu, \sigma^2/n)$ distribution. This follows from the earlier result (4.26).

It also follows from the Central limit Theorem that if n is large enough so that Z_n has approximately an $N(0, 1)$ distribution, then

$$\sum_{i=1}^{n} Y_i = n\bar{Y}_n$$

has approximately an $N(n\mu, n\sigma^2)$ distribution.

Thus, for practical purposes, the Central Limit Theorem may be used with unstandardized sample means and sums as well as with standardized sample means.

For some applications, it is more convenient to rewrite the standardization used to give Z_n in Equation (4.27) in terms of the sum $\sum_{i=1}^{n} Y_i$ rather than the sample mean $\bar{Y}_n$. Some basic algebra shows that the appropriate standardization for the sum is

$$Z_n = \frac{\bar{Y}_n - \mu}{\sigma/\sqrt{n}} = \frac{\sum_{i=1}^{n} Y_i - n\mu}{\sigma\sqrt{n}} \tag{4.29}$$

We summarize the meaning of the Central Limit Theorem as follows:

SUMMARY OF THE CENTRAL LIMIT THEOREM

If $Y_1, Y_2, \ldots$ are independent random variables from the same distribution with mean μ and variance σ^2 and if

$$\bar{Y}_n = \frac{1}{n}(Y_1 + Y_2 + \cdots + Y_n)$$

then for large n,

- $\dfrac{\bar{Y}_n - \mu}{\sigma/\sqrt{n}} = \dfrac{\sum_{i=1}^{n} Y_i - n\mu}{\sigma\sqrt{n}}$ has approximately an $N(0, 1)$ distribution.
- $\bar{Y}_n$ has approximately an $N(\mu, \sigma^2/n)$ distribution.
- $\sum_{i=1}^{n} Y_i$ has approximately an $N(n\mu, n\sigma^2)$ distribution.

Where Do Data Come In?

The Central Limit Theorem is a mathematical statement about distribution models, but it is also extremely useful in the analysis of data. In applications, the independent random variables, $Y_1, Y_2, \ldots, Y_n$, that make up the sample mean $\bar{Y}_n$, or the sum $\sum_{i=1}^{n} Y_i$, represent observations drawn at random from an infinite, or at least large, population. In the parlance of Chapter 3, they are a simple random sample of all possible observations from the population. In recognition of this interpretation, when speaking of independent random variables from the same distribution, statisticians use the term **random sample.**[17]

The Central Limit Theorem is a celebrated fact in probability theory and statistics. It is, indeed, a powerful result that the limiting distribution of the standardized means does not depend on the population distribution of the original data values Y_i. In other words, the population distribution can be discrete or continuous, symmetric or asymmetric, unimodal or multimodal, or have any other characteristics at all; if the variance is defined for the population, and if n is large enough, the sum and sample mean will both have approximately a normal distribution.

If the random sample is from a normal distribution, then the sum and sample mean are exactly normally distributed no matter what the sample size: No Central Limit Theorem is needed. If the population is nearly normal, small sample sizes are enough to ensure approximate normality of the sum and sample mean. If the population distribution is extremely nonnormal, a large sample size may be needed for the Central Limit Theorem to give approximate normality. Since in any application the quality of the normal approximation will depend on the population distribution and the requirements of the application, it is difficult to specify the sample size required for approximate normality. In most cases, a sample size of 30 or more gives an adequate approximation. A sample size of 100 or more will assure normality when the data are taken from virtually any distribution you are likely to see in practice.

Here is an example of the use of the Central Limit Theorem.

EXAMPLE 4.19   AN APPLICATION OF THE CENTRAL LIMIT THEOREM

A lumber and building materials outlet sells "odd-size" 1 inch × 10 inch scrap piece boards. The milling process that generates these boards is known to operate in such a manner that the lengths of boards come from a distribution model with mean 22 inches and standard deviation 6 inches. You buy a package of 36 randomly selected scrap boards. Which are you more likely to get: pieces whose average length exceeds 20 inches or whose average length is less than 23 inches? Suppose that for this problem, we are satisfied that use of the Central Limit Theorem is appropriate. Then by Equation (4.7), we may assume that

$$Z_{36} = \frac{\bar{Y}_{36} - 22}{6/\sqrt{36}}$$

has approximately an $N(0, 1)$ distribution.

How likely is it that the average length of the pieces exceeds 20 inches? This is the event $\{\bar{Y}_{36} > 20\}$, which is the same as $\{(\bar{Y}_{36} - 22)/(6/\sqrt{36}) > -2\}$. From the table of the areas under the standard normal density, the proportion of the $N(0, 1)$

---

[17]The "simple" in simple random sample seems to have been lost somewhere along the way.

population exceeding -2 is 0.9772. As an exercise, you can compute the proportion of the packages whose average length is less than 23 inches. (*Answer:* 0.8413). So you are more likely to get pieces whose average length exceeds 20 inches than whose average length is less than 23 inches.

Before using the Central Limit Theorem for a problem such as this, we should make sure its use is appropriate. If the population distribution of board lengths is not badly nonnormal, then a sample of size 36 should be large enough to ensure the adequacy of the normal approximation to the distribution of the sample mean. If we are not familiar with the population distribution from past data, then we should, whenever possible, obtain data from the population and examine it for evidence of serious nonnormality using tools for displaying data distributions, such as histograms. Later in this chapter, we will discuss some other tools for using data to evaluate the normality of the population distribution. ◆

The Normal Approximation to the Binomial Distribution

We have already seen that when n is large and p is small, the Poisson distribution can be used to approximate the binomial distribution, $b(n, p)$. When n is large, and p is not small, the Central Limit Theorem allows us to use the normal distribution to approximate the $b(n, p)$ distribution. The reason is that a random variable $Y \sim b(n, p)$ can be regarded as a sum of n independent Bernoullis, $Y_1, Y_2, \ldots, Y_n$, each with success probability p. Each Y_i has mean $\mu = p$ and standard deviation $\sigma = \sqrt{p(1 - p)}$. In this setting, if we standardize $Y = \sum_{i=1}^{n} Y_i$ as in Equation (4.29), we get

$$Z_n = \frac{Y - np}{\sqrt{np(1 - p)}} \tag{4.30}$$

which, by the Central Limit Theorem, has approximately an $N(0, 1)$ distribution.

The approximation of the $b(n, p)$ distribution by a normal distribution is reasonable for almost all applications if values of n and p satisfy $np \geq 10$ and $n(1 - p) \geq 10$. If the values of p are between 0.3 and 0.7, $np \geq 5$ and $n(1 - p) \geq 5$, will give an adequate approximation, and for the symmetric binomial distribution model $b(n, 0.5)$, n as small as 5 can provide a reasonable approximation.

EXAMPLE 4.20   THE NORMAL APPROXIMATION TO THE BINOMIAL

Recall Example 4.11 concerning the State Gaming Commission's investigation of a roulette wheel. Let's use the Central Limit Theorem to approximate the proportion of $b(100, 0.47)$ population outcomes having 58 or more successes. That is, we want to compute the probability a $b(100, 0.47)$ random variable Y is greater than or equal to 58. The Central Limit Theorem should give a good approximation to the $b(100, 0.47)$ distribution, since both 100×0.47 and $100 \times (1 - 0.47)$ greatly exceed 10. Using Equation (4.30) with $p = 0.47$, we have

$$\frac{Y - np}{\sqrt{np(1 - p)}} = \frac{58 - (100)(0.47)}{\sqrt{(100)(0.47)(1 - 0.47)}} = 2.20$$

The probability that Y is greater than or equal to 58 is approximately the same as the probability that an $N(0, 1)$ random variable exceeds 2.20.

We may use either a computer package or the table of the standard normal cumulative distribution function found in Table A.3 in Appendix A, page 901, to compute this probability. From the normal table, we find that

$$\Phi(2.20) = P(Z \leq 2.20) = 0.9861$$

Therefore, the probability that a standard normal random variable is greater than or equal to 2.20 is

$$1 - \Phi(2.20) = 1 - 0.9861 = 0.0139$$

From the solution given in Example 4.11, you know that the probability Y is greater than or equal to 58 is exactly 0.0177, so the normal approximation is pretty close. As before, this indicates that so many as 58 reds out of 100 spins of a fair wheel is unlikely to have happened by chance, and therefore this seems good evidence that the wheel is not fair.

Incidentally, why would anyone want to use the Central Limit Theorem approximation when they could get the exact result based on the binomial distribution model? The answer is that there are times a computer is not available, that tabled values of the binomial distribution do not go as high as $n = 100$, and that tabled values of the $N(0, 1)$ distribution are available in every statistics text. ◆

The Continuity Correction

When we use the normal distribution model to approximate the binomial distribution model, we are using a continuous distribution model to approximate probabilities from a discrete distribution model. If we are not careful, this type of approximation can give poor results, as the following example illustrates.

EXAMPLE 4.21   THE CONTINUITY CORRECTION

Suppose $Y \sim b(50, 0.4)$. Using a computer, we can calculate $P(Y = 21) = 0.1091$. Suppose we want to use the Central Limit Theorem to approximate $P(Y = 21)$. Since $np = 50 \times 0.4 = 20$ and $n(1 - p) = 50 \times 0.6 = 30$, we are confident that the approximation will be a good one. Equation (4.30) states that the distribution of

$$\frac{Y - (50)(0.4)}{\sqrt{(50)(0.4)(1 - 0.4)}} = \frac{Y - 20}{3.464}$$

can be approximated by an $N(0, 1)$ distribution. Therefore, we have the approximation

$$P(Y = 21) = P\left(\frac{Y - 20}{3.464} = \frac{21 - 20}{3.464}\right) \approx P(Z = 0.289) = 0 \tag{4.31}$$

where $Z \sim N(0, 1)$. This is a poor approximation to the true value, 0.1091. The difficulty in Equation (4.31) is that Z is a continuous random variable, and therefore the probability that Z equals any one number, such as 0.289, is always 0. One solution to this difficulty is the **continuity correction.**

For the problem at hand, the continuity correction arises from noticing that

$$P(Y = 21) = P(20.5 \leq Y \leq 21.5)$$

Using this simple observation, we obtain

$$P(Y = 21) = P(20.5 \leq Y \leq 21.5)$$

$$= P\left(\frac{20.5 - 20}{3.464} \leq \frac{Y - 20}{3.464} \leq \frac{21.5 - 20}{3.464}\right) \tag{4.32}$$

$$\approx P(0.145 \leq Z \leq 0.435) = 0.1106$$

which is a much better approximation to the true value. ✦

In general, the continuity correction for the normal approximation to the binomial works as follows:

THE NORMAL APPROXIMATION TO THE BINOMIAL USING THE CONTINUITY CORRECTION

If $Y \sim b(n, p)$ represents the number of successes from a binomial distribution model with parameters n and p, and if $0 \leq k \leq m \leq n$ are integers,

$$P(k \leq Y \leq m) = P(k - 0.5 \leq Y \leq m + 0.5)$$

$$= P\left(\frac{k - 0.5 - np}{\sqrt{np(1-p)}} \leq \frac{Y - np}{\sqrt{np(1-p)}} \leq \frac{m + 0.5 - np}{\sqrt{np(1-p)}}\right) \tag{4.33}$$

$$\approx P\left(\frac{k - 0.5 - np}{\sqrt{np(1-p)}} \leq Z \leq \frac{m + 0.5 - np}{\sqrt{np(1-p)}}\right)$$

where $Z \sim N(0, 1)$.

EXAMPLE 4.20   CONTINUED

We illustrate the use of the continuity correction by applying it to the roulette wheel example. We want to approximate $P(58 \leq Y)$. We will use Equation (4.33), but since this is a one-sided inequality, we only need to use a one-sided approximation.

$$P(58 \leq Y) = P(58 - 0.5 \leq Y)$$

$$= P\left(\frac{57.5 - 47}{\sqrt{(100)(0.47)(0.53)}} \leq \frac{Y - 47}{\sqrt{(100)(0.47)(0.53)}}\right)$$

$$\approx P(2.10 \leq Z)$$

$$= 0.0179$$

This result obtained using the continuity correction is a much closer approximation to the true value 0.0177. ✦

Why the Normal Distribution?

Over the years, scientists and engineers have noticed that measurements, even of the same quantity, vary. To explain the variation in measurements, a simple model has proven useful. This model says that the measurement is the sum of a central value—what we would measure if we could—and the variation in measurement from whatever source. We can write this as

$$\text{DATA} = \text{CENTER} + \text{ERROR}$$

For unimodal symmetric probability density functions, we can think of the center as the mean or median value of all possible observations that can arise from this distribution. All other numbers are larger or smaller than the center by quantities that we call **errors.** Observe that the error at the center is 0. We can think of the center as a number that is fixed but unknown to us, and the error as being generated by a random mechanism. This way of thinking about data is often useful in practice.

Over the centuries, scientists have noticed that when they consider data in this way, quite often the errors have a nearly normal distribution. Why should this be? The Central Limit Theorem provides a reason. Often, the errors consist of the sum of a number of small independent disturbances caused by random fluctuations in variables such as temperature, humidity, or the composition of raw material inputs to a process. But, as we have just learned, sums of independent random terms tend toward normality. Hence, once the variables that affect the response in a major way have been accounted for, the remaining errors tend to be normally distributed.

4.7

IDENTIFYING COMMON DISTRIBUTIONS

If we are going to use data to choose a distribution model to successfully approximate the underlying population distribution, we need to know how closely the distribution model and the data agree.

Plots are a useful first step in deciding which distribution model(s) to try in approximating the population distribution of the data under study. Histograms, for example, can reveal the main features of the data distribution. Once a candidate distribution model has been decided on, a **quantile–quantile plot,** often called a **Q–Q plot** for short, can be used to evaluate how well that model agrees with the data.

Recall the definition of quantile for a set of data from Chapter 2: For any number q between 0 and 1, a qth **quantile** of the data is a value at or below which lies a proportion q of the data. We can also define a qth quantile of a distribution model in a very similar way: For any number q between 0 and 1, a qth **quantile** of the distribution model is a value at or below which lies an area q beneath the probability density function, if the distribution is continuous, or the probability histogram, if the distribution is discrete.

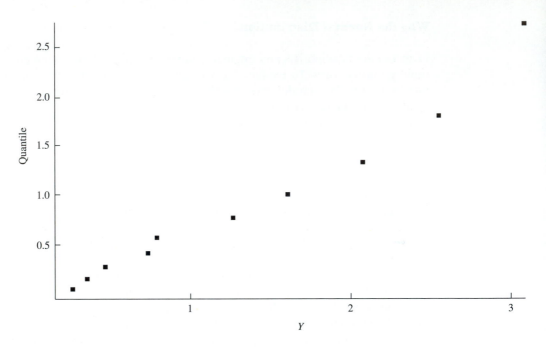

Figure 4.12   Exponential Q–Q plot of 10 pseudo-random exponential(1) observations.

We may also express the idea of a quantile of a distribution model in terms of the cumulative distribution function, and this is how we define it:

> **DEFINITION**
>
> Suppose q is a number between 0 and 1. Then the number y_q is a qth **quantile** for a distribution model if
>
> $$F_Y(y_q) = P(Y \leq y_q) = q$$
>
> where Y is a random variable from the distribution model.

Q–Q plots are designed to show graphically how well the data distribution matches a known distribution model by plotting the quantiles of the data against the corresponding quantiles of the known distribution. If the data match the distribution well, the plot should roughly follow a straight line. Figure 4.12 shows a Q–Q plot of a set of 10 **pseudo-random observations** from an exponential distribution model with parameter $\beta = 1$.[18]

---

[18]"Pseudo-random" means that these observations were generated by a computer algorithm to mimic independent measurements from a user-specified random phenomenon. Were these data really taken as independent measurements from a user-specified random phenomenon, they would be called **random observations.** Pseudo-random data generated by modern computer algorithms can fool virtually all statistical tests designed to detect nonrandomness. Pseudo-random data are a widely used part of modern statistical methodology.

The data values in this Q–Q plot are displayed on the horizontal axis, and for each data value, the vertical axis displays the corresponding quantile of an exponential(1) distribution model.[19] The kind of pattern seen in this Q–Q plot, roughly linear but not exactly a straight line, is typical of real data that are reasonably well approximated by the distribution model being considered. This plot gives us little reason to reject the exponential as a distribution model for these data.

Constructing a Q–Q Plot

Recall the discussion in Chapter 2[20] on the computation of quantiles for a set of data. In order to construct a Q–Q plot to compare data to a specified distribution, we must compute quantiles for the data values based on that specified distribution. Assume that we have chosen a distribution model, which we will call the candidate distribution model, with which to compare the data, and that Y is a random variable from that distribution model.

To construct a Q–Q plot, a **quantile rank,** based on the candidate distribution, is associated with each data value. The idea is that if the candidate distribution is correct, the probability that Y is less than or equal to the smallest data value should be approximately $1/n$, the probability that Y is less than or equal to the second smallest data value should be approximately $2/n$, and so on. We say approximately, since there is not a unique agreed-upon way to do this: Different statistical computer packages use different formulas. However, since all give similar results, we give the formula used by SAS and MINITAB. The following tells how to construct a Q–Q plot using this formula.

CONSTRUCTING A Q–Q PLOT

1. Order the observations $y_{(1)} \le y_{(2)} \le \cdots \le y_{(n)}$.
2. For each observation, compute a **quantile rank** with respect to the candidate distribution model. For the kth smallest observation, $y_{(k)}$, the quantile rank is the value $q_{(k)}$ satisfying

$$P(Y \le q_{(k)}) = \frac{k - 0.375}{n + 0.250}$$

where Y is a random variable from the candidate distribution model.
3. Plot the pairs $(y_{(k)}, q_{(k)})$, $k = 1, \ldots, n$.

Example 4.22 illustrates the calculations involved in constructing the Q–Q plot in Figure 4.12.

---

[19]The choice of which axis of a Q–Q plot displays the data and which displays the distribution quantiles is largely a matter of taste.

[20]Page 69.

TABLE 4.7   **Ordered Pseudo-Random Exponential(1) Observations and the Corresponding Exponential(1) Quantiles**

k	$y_{(k)}$	$q_{(k)}$
1	0.262	0.063
2	0.352	0.173
3	0.467	0.296
4	0.732	0.436
5	0.790	0.600
6	1.268	0.796
7	1.609	1.039
8	2.079	1.362
9	2.554	1.842
10	3.094	2.797

EXAMPLE 4.22   CONSTRUCTING A Q–Q PLOT

We will show the calculations involved in constructing the Q–Q plot in Figure 4.12.

The ordered pseudo-random observations used in Figure 4.12 are given in the left column of Table 4.7.

The candidate distribution model is the exponential(1), which has density

$$p_Y(y) = e^{-y}, \qquad y > 0$$
$$= 0, \qquad y \le 0$$

Therefore, $q_{(k)}$ satisfies

$$\frac{k - 0.375}{n + 0.250} = P(Y \le q_{(k)}) = \int_0^{q_{(k)}} e^{-y}dy = 1 - e^{-q_{(k)}}$$

Solving, we get

$$q_{(k)} = -\ln\left(1 - \frac{k - 0.375}{n + 0.250}\right) \quad \blacklozenge$$

Assessing Normality

As the normal distribution model plays the most important role of any distribution model in statistical applications, it is often important to decide if a set of data can be appropriately modeled by a normal distribution.

How can we judge whether data are approximately normal? To begin with, it is important to decide which normal population we think it most likely the data come from. Or, to put it another way, which normal distribution model best fits the data. This means identifying the two parameters, μ, the mean, and σ^2, the variance, of the $N(\mu, \sigma^2)$ model. One simple and often effective way to do this is to assume that the population mean, μ, is the mean of the data, $\bar{y}$, and that the population variance, σ^2, is the variance of the data, s^2. That is, we guess that the data come from an $N(\bar{y}, s^2)$ population. Using the data to tell us which model to use is called **fitting** a model to data. In this case, we fit the model by using the data to estimate the model parameters (here μ and σ^2). Statistical theory tells us that if the data are really from a normal population, then the preceding method of fitting a normal model is the optimal method to use.

One simple and rough method to assess normality is to use the **68–95–99.7 rule.** This rule arises from the fact that 68% of an $N(\mu, \sigma^2)$ population lies between $\mu - \sigma$ and $\mu + \sigma$, 95% lies between $\mu - 2\sigma$ and $\mu + 2\sigma$, and 99.7% lies between $\mu - 3\sigma$ and $\mu + 3\sigma$. To use the 68–95–99.7 rule on a set of data, compute the sample mean, $\bar{y}$, and sample standard deviation, s. Then count how many observations lie between $\bar{y} - s$ and $\bar{y} + s$, how many lie between $\bar{y} - 2s$ and $\bar{y} + 2s$, how many lie between $\bar{y} - 3s$ and $\bar{y} + 3s$. If the data follow a normal curve, then by the 68–95–99.7 rule, roughly 68, 95, and 99.7% of the data should fall within 1, 2, and 3 standard deviations of the mean, respectively.

A more sensitive and informative tool for assessing normality is the Q–Q plot, which for the normal distribution is also called a **normal quantile plot.** To give you an idea of what normal quantile plots of normal data look like, Figure 4.13 displays normal quantile plots for four different sets of 20 computer-generated pseudo-random $N(0, 1)$

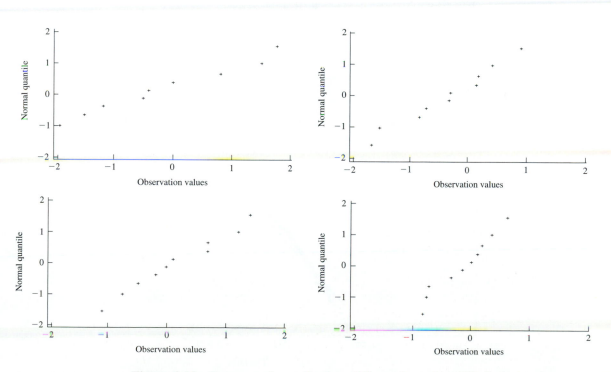

Figure 4.13   Four normal quantile plots of 20 pseudo-random $N(0, 1)$ observations each.

numbers each. You can see that while each plot shows a rough linear pattern, there is a fair amount of variation from plot to plot.

EXAMPLE 4.23   ASSESSING NORMALITY

Figure 4.14 displays a boxplot, a density histogram, and a normal quantile plot for the maximum thicknesses of 75 automotive gaskets, having nominal thickness of 1.5 mm, sampled from a large shipment of gaskets.

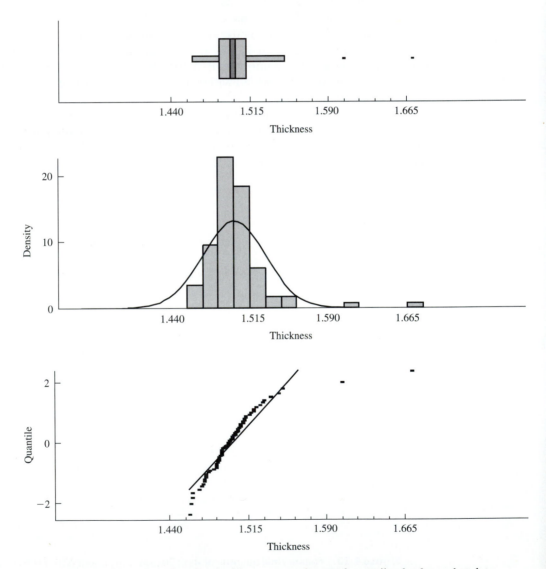

Figure 4.14   Boxplot, density histogram, and normal quantile plot for gasket data.

The density histogram has a normal probability density function superimposed. The probability density function was fit to the data by choosing its mean to be $\bar{y}$, the sample mean, and its variance to be s^2, the sample variance (in other words, it is a $N(\bar{y}, s^2)$ density). The normal quantile plot has a reference line superimposed. The line has intercept $\bar{y}$ and slope s. If the data quantiles exactly equalled the quantiles of $N(\bar{y}, s^2)$ distribution model, all points in the normal quantile plot would lie exactly on this line. Of course, because of the random nature of data, even data from a $N(\bar{y}, s^2)$ distribution model will not lie exactly on the line. Rather, the line should be used as a guide to give an indication of extreme departures from the assumed distribution model.

There are clearly two outliers in the data. Looking at the normal quantile plot and comparing the normal probability density function with the density histogram, we see that the normal probability density function does not fit these data well: The histogram is too tall and bunched in the center of the density curve, and the two outliers lie too far along the upper tail of the density curve.

The 68–95–99.7 rule applied to these data backs up the story told by the graphs. The percentages of observations lying within 1, 2, and 3 standard deviations of the mean are 86.7, 97.3, and 97.3, respectively, which do not closely match the 68, 95, and 99.7 values for the normal distribution.

Figure 4.15 displays the same graphs as Figure 4.14 for the data with the two outliers removed. The normal curve now appears to fit better and the normal quantile plot more closely follows a straight line. With the outliers removed, the percentages of observations lying within 1, 2, and 3 standard deviations of the mean are 69.4, 94.7, and 97.3, which more closely match the values expected for a normal distribution.

The big question is: What should be done about the outliers? First of all, these outliers represent gaskets whose maximum thicknesses greatly exceed the thicknesses of the other 73 as well as the nominal 1.5 mm. Even though they represent only two of 75 observations, these outliers may be an indication of problems with the production process. As such, management might want to investigate the process that produced these gaskets to see what caused such large thicknesses. Causes such as defective machinery, inferior raw materials, or poorly trained operators should be considered.

Setting aside the outliers to fit a model to the rest of the data is acceptable, as long as their existence is reported, so that causes for them may be sought. In the present case, quality personnel were puzzled by the outliers until they plotted the thicknesses versus the order in which the gaskets were produced. The two gaskets with abnormally large thicknesses were the first two of the 75 to be produced. Investigation of the production process revealed startup problems in producing the present shipment. The existence of these outliers led to the identification of a number of boxes of faulty gaskets before they could be shipped.

One last thought on this: Often observations that don't fit a model are the source of great discoveries: This is how penicillin and the planet Pluto were discovered. So a scientist should always investigate unexplained outliers carefully. ✦

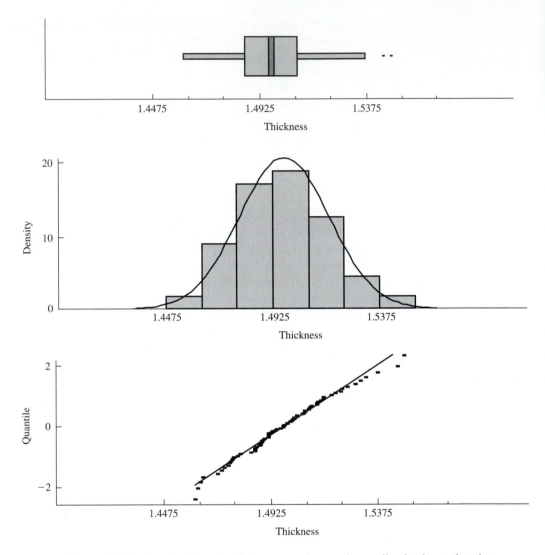

Figure 4.15   Boxplot, density histogram, and normal quantile plot for gasket data with two outliers removed.

TRANSFORMATIONS TO NORMALITY

In practice, none of the common models we have encountered might fit a set of data well. However, in many cases, we can **transform** the data values so that one of our simple models is appropriate for the transformed data. By a transformation we mean a function, for example, a square root, of the raw data values.

Since the normal distribution has played a central role in data analysis and modeling for over 100 years, it is the best understood distribution model. In addition, many, if not most, statistical methods have been designed with the normal distribution in mind. Therefore, when considering how to analyze nonnormal data, it is appropriate that we consider transformations that help make the data look more normal.

Transformations are chosen and implemented in various ways. Engineers and scientists routinely plot variables on semi-log or log-log paper, which is equivalent to choosing a log transformation. Subject matter knowledge can help provide a theoretical basis for choosing a transformation.

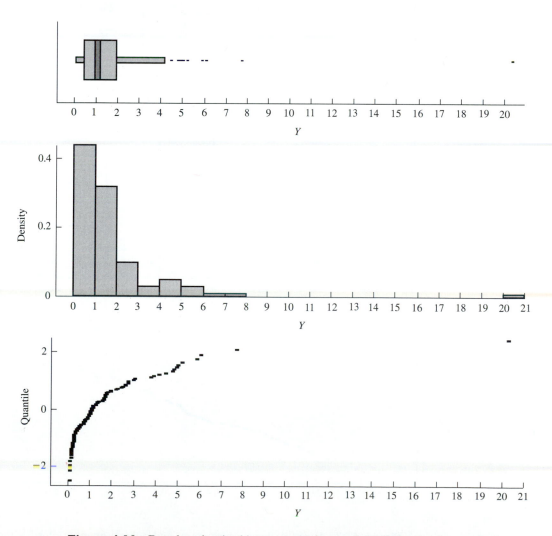

Figure 4.16   Boxplot, density histogram, and normal quantile plot for a set of highly skewed data.

Suppose Y denotes an observation in the original units. Some common situations and suggested transformations are as follows:

- If the data are positive and skewed to the right, $\ln(Y)$ or $\sqrt{Y}$ should look more normal.
- If the data vary by more than 1 or 2 orders of magnitude, try analyzing $\ln(Y)$, for positive data, or $-1/Y$.
- If the data consist of counts, try analyzing $\sqrt{Y}$.
- If the data are proportions and the ratio of the largest to smallest proportion exceeds 2, try the logit transformation: $\ln[Y/(1-Y)]$.

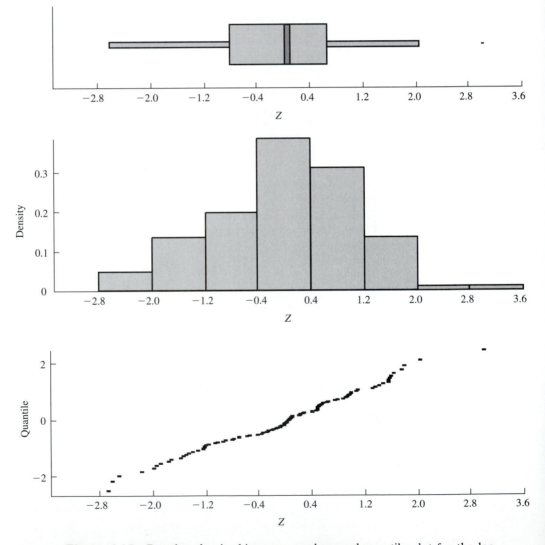

Figure 4.17 Boxplot, density histogram, and normal quantile plot for the log-transformed data from Figure 4.16. The log transformation has made the data more nearly normal.

Combinations of transformations are also used: Recall that we applied the logarithm twice to the KWH values from Professor P.'s electric data in Chapter 1. Of course, if nothing else seems to help, you can always try a selection of transformations and see what happens.

Figures 4.16 and 4.17 illustrate the effect of a natural log transformation on a highly skewed data set. Figure 4.16 displays a boxplot, density histogram, and normal quantile plot for the highly skewed original data. Figure 4.17 shows the same graphs for the natural logs of the original data values. The transformation has made the data more nearly normal.

D ISCUSSION QUESTIONS

1. What is a density histogram?
2. What is a Bernoulli trial?
3. What is a random phenomenon? What is an event from a random phenomenon? How is the probability of an event defined?
4. Tell what each of the following is and give an example of an application of each:
   (a) The addition rule of probability.
   (b) The equally likely outcomes rule.
   (c) The multiplication rule for independent events.
   (d) Mutual independence of a collection of events.
5. What is a random variable? What is the source of randomness for a random variable? What is a discrete random variable? Of what does a distribution model for a discrete random variable consist?
6. Tell in your own words what the mean, variance, and standard deviation of a distribution measure. Give the formula of each for a discrete distribution model.
7. Give the formulas that relate the mean, variance, and standard deviation of a linear transformation to those of the original random variable.
8. State the formulas for the mean of a sum or difference of random variables.
9. What is the Bernoulli distribution model? What parameter defines this model? Answer these questions for the binomial distribution model.
10. What is the Poisson distribution model? What parameters define this model? Explain how the Poisson can be used to approximate the binomial. Explain the three criteria for the Poisson distribution model.
11. Explain the difference between a population and a sample. Give an example of each.
12. What is the difference between a discrete and a continuous distribution model?
13. Suppose a density curve is given by the equation $z = p_Y(y)$. How can you interpret this curve? How can it be used to interpret data?
14. Name two continuous distribution models and sketch their density functions. What kind of data could they serve as models for?
15. State the Central Limit Theorem in your own words. How can it be used to help model data?
16. Why and how is the continuity correction used?
17. What is a Q–Q plot? A normal quantile plot?

18. Give one reason that transformations are used on data. What are some common transformations, and on what kinds of data are they used?

E XERCISES

4.1. Which of the following is a Bernoulli trial? If the described trial is a Bernoulli trial, tell why and give its parameter, p. If not, tell why not.

(a) A bottle of cola is selected from a production line and the weight of its contents is measured. The average weight of cola is 0.35 kg.

(b) Five bottles of cola are selected from a production line and the weight of their contents is measured. The average weight is 0.35 kg.

(c) The number of in-specification parts from a sample of size 100 is computed. The proportion of in-specification parts in the population is 0.95.

(d) An incoming shipment of steel ingots is inspected and given a "pass" or "no pass" sticker by the inspector. The proportion of all incoming shipments given a "pass" is 0.85.

4.2. Repeated Bernoulli trials are run. The same parameter p is used for each Bernoulli trial. The Bernoulli trials are run until a total of two "successes" occurs. Suppose that Y is the total number of Bernoulli trials conducted. Does Y follow a binomial distribution model? Give your reasons.

4.3. Using a coin of your choice, perform the random phenomenon of tossing a coin three times a total of 25 times. Use your results to assign probabilities to each possible outcome. In addition, assign probabilities to the following events:

(a) At least two heads occur and at least one tail occurs.

(b) No more than two heads occur.

(c) All of one side of the coin comes up.

4.4. Under what condition can two events be independent and disjoint? Prove your answer.

4.5. Consider tossing a coin three times. Which of the following pairs of events are independent? Justify your answer.

(a) $A = \{$H on first toss$\}$, $B = \{$H on second toss$\}$.

(b) $A = \{$exactly two heads$\}$, $B = \{$at least two heads$\}$.

4.6. Consider tossing a coin three times. Are the events $A = \{$exactly two heads$\}$ and $B = \{$exactly one tail$\}$ independent?

4.7. A particular model of jet engine is used in a two-engine plane and a four-engine plane. The probability that one of these engines fails in flight is p. The two-engine plane will crash only if both engines fail and the four-engine plane will crash only if three or more engines fail. Assume engine failure is the only cause of plane crashes and that the engines operate independently.

(a) What is the probability that the two-engine plane crashes?

(b) What is the probability that the four-engine plane crashes?

(c) For which values of p is the two-engine plane safer?

4.8. Suppose A and B are two events such that $P(A) = 0.60$ and $P(B) = 0.80$. Are A and B disjoint? Explain.

4.9. One of four batteries in a laboratory is defective. The batteries are to be tested one at a time in random order until the defective one is found. Let X represent the number of batteries tested. What is probability mass function of X?

4.10. True or false: If A and B are events, then $P(A \cup B) \geq P(A) + P(B)$. Justify your answer.

4.11. In a game of chance, you win \$1 for each head and lose \$1 for each tail in three tosses of a coin, which has probability p of turning up heads on each toss.
  (a) Let the random variable Y be your winnings in this game. Write out the distribution of Y.
  (b) How much do you expect to win on one play of the game? What is the variance of the winnings?
  (c) For which value(s) of p is the game fair?

4.12. Ming's Seafood Shop stocks live lobsters. Ming pays \$6.00 for each lobster and sells each one for \$12.00. The **demand** X for these lobsters in a given day has the following probability mass function:

x	0	1	2	3	4	5
$p_X(x)$	0.05	0.15	0.30	0.20	0.20	0.10

  (a) What is the expected demand?
  (b) What is the expected profit on a given day if Ming has a stock of exactly three lobsters that day?

4.13. A fair coin is independently tossed three times or until a head appears, whichever comes first. Let the random variable X denote the number of **heads** and let the random variable Y denote the number of **tails** obtained.
  (a) Find the probability mass function of X.
  (b) Find the probability mass function of Y.
  (c) What is the expected number of heads?
  (d) What is the expected number of tails?
  (e) What is the probability that at least two tails are observed?
  (f) What is the probability that exactly one head is observed?

4.14. An unfair die looks exactly like an ordinary six-sided die. The probability of a face landing up on this die is proportional to the number of dots on the face. Let Y denote the number of dots on the "up" face.
  (a) Give the probability mass function of Y.
  (b) Compute the mean and variance of Y.

4.15. Two electrical connections link an electrical component to a circuit board. Experience shows that Y, the number of faulty connections on a randomly chosen component, has the following probability mass function:

$$p_Y(y) = 0.80, \qquad y = 0$$
$$= 0.19, \qquad y = 1$$
$$= 0.01, \qquad y = 2$$

  (a) Draw the probability histogram of Y. Be sure to label the axes appropriately.
  (b) Of the next 100 components produced, how many do you estimate will have 0, 1, and 2 faulty connections? Show how you arrived at your estimates.
  (c) On average, how many faulty connections per component occur?

4.16. It may seem counterintuitive, but the distribution of the first significant (i.e., nonzero) digit in many collections of numbers is not uniform on the integers 1 through 9, but rather follows

Benford's distribution,[21] which has probability mass function

$$p_X(x) = \log_{10}\left(1 + \frac{1}{x}\right), \qquad x = 1, \ldots, 9$$

Thus, for example, according to Benford's distribution, the probability that the first significant digit of a randomly chosen number is an 8 is

$$p_X(8) = \log_{10}\left(1 + \frac{1}{8}\right)$$

$$= \log_{10}\left(\frac{9}{8}\right) = 0.051$$

One use of this distribution is in auditing financial records. The idea is that if the books have been artificially altered, the distribution of the first significant digit will differ markedly from what is predicted by Benford's distribution. Suppose the IRS is auditing the financial records of a large company.

(a) If the numbers in the company's records follow Benford's distribution, what is the probability that a randomly chosen number from the company's records has a first significant digit equal to 1?

(b) If the IRS randomly samples 1000 numbers from the company's records, and if these numbers follow Benford's distribution, what is the distribution of Y, the number of the 1000 numbers having a first significant digit equal to 1?

(c) Suppose 258 of the 1000 numbers in the IRS sample have a first significant digit equal to 1. Is this convincing evidence that the company's financial records do not follow Benford's law? Show your reasoning.

4.17. You have two scales for measuring weight in a chemistry lab. Both scales give answers that vary a bit in repeated weighings of the same item. If the true weight of a compound is 2 grams (g), the first scale produces readings Z that have mean 2.000 g and standard deviation 0.002 g. The second scale's readings Y have mean 2.001 g and standard deviation 0.001 g. Assume that the readings Z and Y are independent.

(a) What are the mean and standard deviation of the difference, $X = Z - Y$, between the readings?

(b) You measure once with each scale and average the readings. Your result is $W = (Z + Y)/2$. What are μ_W and σ_W? Is the average W more or less variable than the reading Y of the less variable scale?

4.18. Consider the random variable Z describing your winnings if you win $\$p$ for each head and lose $\$(1 - p)$ for each tail in three tosses of a coin with probability p of a head.

(a) Find the distribution of Z. Using this distribution, calculate the mean of Z.

(b) Write Z as a function of Y, the number of heads. Use your knowledge of the mean and variance of a binomial distribution and the rules for computing means and variances to compute the mean and variance of Z from those of Y. Notice how much easier it is to compute the mean of Z this way.

4.19. One of the numbers 1 to 4 is randomly chosen. You are to try to guess the number chosen by asking questions with "yes/no" answers. Suppose your ith question is: "Is it i?" ($i =$

---

[21] As so often happens, this distribution was not discovered by the person for whom it is named. The American scientist Simon Newcomb knew about it as early as 1881. Benford, a physicist, rediscovered it in 1936.

1, 2, 3, or 4). Let the random variable Y denote the number of questions required to guess the chosen number. Find the following:

(a) The probability mass function of Y.

(b) The cumulative distribution function of Y.

(c) The mean and variance of Y.

4.20. The following are weights reported by 100 female students, along with the number of students reporting each weight:

Weight	Number	Weight	Number
98	1	125	4
100	1	127	4
102	4	128	5
105	2	130	5
108	4	132	4
110	3	133	4
112	4	134	5
113	4	135	5
115	3	136	4
117	4	137	3
119	4	138	3
120	4	140	4
121	4	141	4
122	3	150	1

Do these data constitute evidence that students round their reported weights? (*Hint:* Assume there is no rounding and call a weight ending in a 0 or a 5 a "success".)

4.21. Which of the following is a binomial trial? If the described trial is a binomial trial, tell why and give its parameters, n and p. If not, tell why not.

(a) A bottle of cola is selected from a production line and the weight of its contents is measured. The average weight of cola is 0.35 kg.

(b) Five bottles of cola are selected from a production line and the weight of each bottle's contents is measured. The average weight is 0.35 kg.

(c) The number of in-specification parts from a sample of size 100 is computed. The proportion of in-specification parts in the population is 0.95.

(d) An incoming shipment of steel ingots is inspected and given a "pass" or "no pass" sticker by the inspector. The proportion of all incoming lots given a "pass" is 0.85.

4.22. What is your birth month? What is the mean number of successes in the 10,000 binomial trials you simulated in Lab 4.2? What is the mean for the distribution model?

4.23. Is it reasonable to use a binomial distribution model to model the following trial? If so, tell why and tell what the parameters of the binomial distribution model are. If not, tell why not.

> *One hundred fifty blood samples, randomly chosen from all donors nationwide, are tested for the presence of HIV infection. The number testing positive is recorded.*

4.24. A large supermarket chain reports that 40% of all beer purchases are "light." Consider the next 20 beer purchases made.

(a) Suppose Y is the number of those 20 beer purchases that are "light." What distribution model does Y follow? What are you assuming about the 20 beer purchases in naming this distribution?

(b) What is the chance that between six and eight (inclusive) of these 20 purchases are "light."

4.25. Suppose that the proportion of beer drinkers nationwide who prefer "Too Heavy" over "Too Light" beer is 0.75. Ten beer drinkers are randomly selected.

(a) Approximately what distribution model does the number beer drinkers out of 10 who prefer "Too Heavy" follow, and what are the parameters of the distribution model?

(b) Suppose 100 samples of 10 beer drinkers are taken. In approximately how many of the samples will 5 or 6 out of the 10 prefer "Too Heavy"?

4.26. The cost of rotating tires once on Bal's Ford Tempo is $12.00. The probability that Bal rotates tires once in a given month is 0.1. Whether he rotates the tires in any one month is independent of whether he rotates the tires in any other month.

(a) What is the probability that Bal rotates tires at least once this year?

(b) What should Bal expect to pay for rotating tires this year? Give the standard deviation as well.

4.27. A medical test for the presence of a disease gives a false positive if it identifies the disease as being present when in fact it is not. A false negative occurs when the test fails to detect the presence of the disease when it is indeed present. The probability of a certain test providing a false result, either positive or negative, is 0.0015. In a given month, a laboratory performs 10,000 tests.

(a) Explain why the binomial distribution model is a reasonable choice to model Y, the number of the 10,000 tests that give a false result. What are the parameters of this model?

(b) Can the Poisson distribution model be used to approximate probabilities from the binomial model? Justify your answer.

(c) Find the probability that there are no more than 20 false results in the 10,000 tests.
   i. Exactly, using a computer.
   ii. Approximately, using the Poisson approximation.
   Compare the results.

4.28. Serious paint blemishes on a flat automotive body panel occur at a rate of one blemish for every 10 body panels. The blemishes occur uniformly over the area of the panel.

(a) Argue that the three criteria for a Poisson distrubution model are reasonably satisfied by counts of blemishes on these body panels.

(b) What Poisson distribution model describes Y, the number of blemishes on a randomly chosen body panel? Justify your choice.

(c) Based on this model, find the probability of more than one serious blemish on a randomly chosen body panel.

4.29. What is the variance of a Poisson random variable X for which $P(X = 1) = P(X = 2)$?

4.30. Determine whether each of the following statements is true. If true, explain your reasoning, and if false, give a simple example to show it.

(a) Let X be a random variable. No matter what the distribution of X is, the probability $P(X = a)$ is always zero for all a.

(b) For an $N(\mu, \sigma^2)$ distribution model:
   i. the probability density curve tends to be flatter as μ increases.
   ii. the probability density curve tends to be narrower as σ^2 increases.

(c) A coin is independently tossed 10,000 times. Let $p = P(\{head\})$ and assume $0.001 < p < 0.999$. If Y denotes the number of heads obtained in 10,000 tosses, then, whether the coin is fair or biased, the probability

$$P\left[10{,}000p - \sqrt{10{,}000p(1-p)} \le Y \le 10{,}000p + \sqrt{10{,}000p(1-p)}\right]$$

is approximately 0.68.

4.31. A probability density function for a continuous distribution model has the following form:

$$\begin{aligned}
p_Y(y) &= c, & 0 < y \le 1 \\
&= 0.3, & 1 < y \le 2 \\
&= 0.1, & 2 < y \le 4 \\
&= 0, & \text{otherwise}
\end{aligned}$$

(a) What is the value of c?
(b) What proportion of the population modeled by this probability density function takes values above 1.5?

4.32. A population is modeled by the density

$$\begin{aligned}
p_Y(y) &= 0, & y \le 1 \\
&= 1/y^2, & y > 1
\end{aligned}$$

Based on this model, how much more likely is it that a randomly selected value from the population lies in the immediate vicinity of 2 than in the immediate vicinity of 3?

4.33. The random variable Y has density

$$\begin{aligned}
p_Y(y) &= c/y^4, & y > 1 \\
&= 0, & \text{otherwise}
\end{aligned}$$

(a) Find the mean and variance of Y.
(b) How relatively likely (e.g., twice as likely) is it that Y occurs in an interval about $y = 2$ of width dy compared with occurring in an interval about $y = 3$ of width dy, where dy is infinitesimally small?

4.34. Experience has shown that the width, in mm, of the flange on a plastic connector has the following distribution:

$$\begin{aligned}
p_Y(y) &= 50y, & 0.48 < y < 0.52 \\
&= 0, & \text{otherwise}
\end{aligned}$$

(a) Of the next 1000 connectors produced, how many do you estimate will have widths between 0.50 and 0.51 mm? Show how you arrived at your estimates.
(b) How many times as likely is it to produce connectors with a flange width close to 0.51 mm as it is to produce connectors with a flange width close to 0.49 mm? Justify your answer.

4.35. Suppose you pick 10,000 points completely at random in the interval $(0, 1)$. What distribution model describes this situation? What proportion of the points should fall in the interval $(1/4, 3/4)$?

4.36. A bus can arrive at any time between 7:00 A.M. and 7:15 A.M. Assume that it is no more likely to arrive at one instant than at any other instant.
(a) What is the name of the distribution model that describes the population of possible arrival times of the bus? Draw its probability histogram. How likely is it for the bus to arrive later than 7:05 A.M.?

(b) If a large number of arrival times is available, what can you say about the distribution model of the mean of those arrival times?

4.37. The pointer of a spinner will stop at random on the circle: that is, anywhere between $0°$ and $360°$ from its initial position.

    (a) What is the appropriate distribution model for the angle between its resting and its starting position? What assumption(s) are you making? Draw its probability histogram.

    (b) How likely it is for the pointer to settle down between $90°$ and $180°$?

    (c) If a **large** number of spins is performed, what can you say about the distribution model of the **mean** resting position?

4.38. Suppose the random variable U has a uniform probability density function in the interval $(0, 1)$. What is the probability density function of $1 - U$? Show your arguments.

4.39. Suppose a set of data approximately follows a normal distribution, and that the mean of the data is 5.1 and the standard deviation is 2.2. If we are willing to model the population from which the data were drawn using the normal distribution, which normal probability density function would you use? What would be your estimate of the proportion of population values that lie between 0 and 10?

4.40. There were two exams in an introductory statistics course. The scores on Exam 1 followed a normal curve with mean 60 and standard deviation 10, and on Exam 2, the scores followed a normal curve with mean 80 and standard deviation 5. Jon scored 80 on each exam. Find Jon's percentile scores on each. Comment.

4.41. Derive result (4.26).

4.42. The weight of anodized reciprocating pistons produced by Brown Company follows a normal distribution with mean 10 lb and standard deviation 0.2 lb.

    (a) The heaviest 2.5% of the pistons produced are rejected as overweight. What weight, in pounds, determines the overweight classification? Give your arguments.

    (b) Suppose Brown Company can sell only those pistons weighing between 9.8 and 10.4 lb. What proportion of the pistons is lost?

    (c) If a sample of pistons is available, how might you answer (a) and (b) without the normal population model?

4.43. Let Y represent the number of years that a randomly chosen Ph.D. on the faculty spent obtaining his or her doctorate. Assume that Y is normally distributed with a mean of 5.8 years, and a variance of 6.25 years squared. What proportion of the faculty members spent more than 9 years obtaining their doctorate?

4.44. A paint company knows from experience that the area in square feet, that 1 gallon of its premium paint will cover follows an $N(250, 25)$ distribution model. The company wishes to advertize that if a gallon of this paint fails to cover t square feet, it will refund the purchase price plus 10%. What is the largest value of t that will ensure that on average no more than 0.5% of all purchases will be given the refund?

4.45. Suppose the random variable X has a normal distribution with mean 3 and variance 9. Let $Y = \frac{1}{3} X - 1$.

    (a) What are the mean and variance of Y?

    (b) What is the probability that Y is at least 1?

4.46. It has been found that the effective lifetime of a subway train brake assembly, in hundreds of hours of operation, follows a Weibull distribution with parameters $\alpha = 4.6$ and $\beta = 3.8$. What percentage of these assemblies last more than 500 hours?

4.47. The breaking strength of a steel cable, in thousands of pounds, is found to follow a Weibull distribution with parameters $\alpha = 3.5$ and $\beta = 2.1$.

   (a) A cable is considered defective if it fails to hold a 1200-pound weight. What is the probability that a randomly selected cable is defective?

   (b) Each production lot consists of 1000 cables. Two cables are randomly selected from each production lot and tested with a 1200-pound weight. If both cables fail, the lot is pulled and extensive testing is done. Approximately, what is the probability that both cables fail the test?

4.48. The waiting time, in minutes, to see a teller at a large bank follows an exponential distribution. If the proportion of all customers who wait more than 15 minutes is 0.01, what is the mean waiting time for all customers?

4.49. By using a change of variable in the integral defining the $W(\alpha, \beta)$ cumulative distribution function, show that if $Y \sim W(\alpha, \beta)$, then the random variable $V = (Y/\beta)^{\alpha} \sim$ exponential(1).

4.50. In 1000 flips of a supposedly fair coin, heads came up 560 times and tails 440 times. Are these results consistent with a fair coin?

4.51. A roulette wheel has 18 red slots among its 38 slots.

   (a) Assume the wheel is fair. What distribution model describes the number of times red comes up in 100 spins of the wheel?

   (b) It is suspected that red comes up too seldom for this particular wheel. In 100 test spins of the roulette wheel, red came up 35 times. Do the 35 reds constitute good evidence that the wheel is unfair? Justify your answer.

4.52. Of 1000 four-child families chosen at random in Massachusetts, 600 families have 2 boys and 2 girls. Is this consistent with the notion that boys and girls are equally likely in families with four children? Explain your reasoning.

4.53. What is the chance of team A winning exactly 2 of 3 games from team B when the teams are evenly matched?

   (a) Find the result exactly.

   (b) Shirley decided to approximate the true chance by using the Central Limit Theorem and Equation (4.30) in the text. Do you think this will give her a good result? Why or why not?

4.54. A six-sided die is tossed 500 times and 105 fours are observed. Is the die fair? Explain.

4.55. According to government data, 22% of American children under the age of 6 live in households with income less than the official poverty level. A random sample of 300 children under the age of 6 is selected for a study of learning in early childhood. Approximately how likely it is that at least 80 of the children in the sample live in poverty?

4.56. A six-sided die is tossed 200 times.

   (a) Suppose the number of 1's, 2's, 3's observed is 125. Is the die fair? Give your reasons.

   (b) Suppose the die is actually fair. Which is more likely:

      i. The number of 1's, 2's, and 3's is between 93 and 107.

      ii. The number of 1's, 2's, and 3's is at least 100?

   (c) How might you determine experimentally whether the die is fair?

4.57. After I explained the Central Limit Theorem last week, one of my students said, "The theorem guarantees that the n observations in a random sample will be approximately normally distributed if n is sufficiently large." Does the student understand the Central Limit Theorem? Explain.

4.58. A coin is tossed 400 times.

   (a) It is suspected that tails are too likely. Suppose 170 heads are observed. Is the coin fair? Give your reasoning.

(b) Suppose the coin is actually fair. Which is more likely: (i) between 190 and 200 heads or (ii) at least 210 heads?

(c) How might you determine experimentally whether or not the coin is fair?

4.59. Of 1500 single-child families chosen at random in Massachusetts, 900 families have girls. Is this consistent with the notion that boys and girls are equally likely in single-child families?

4.60. For a single trial of an experiment, Dr. Ming simultaneously tossed four coins. As he had nothing else to do that day, he did a total of 500 trials. The number of the 500 trials that resulted in three heads and one tail was 170.

(a) Do you think these coins are fair? Give your reasons.

(b) Suppose the coins are fair. Which is more likely:

  i. The number of trials that result in three heads and one tail is between 115 and 135.

  ii. The number of trials that result in three heads and one tail is at least 125. Support your answer.

(c) How might you determine experimentally whether these coins are fair?

4.61. Guido does a quick estimate of the total dollar amount of checks he has written by adding up only the whole dollar amounts and then adding to this total a correction of $0.50 per check. Assume he does this with 48 checks. Approximately how likely is it that the total he obtains is more than $6 off from the true total. (*Hint:* If Y_i is the amount that the estimate for the ith check differs from its actual value, assume that the Y_i are independent observations from a $U(-0.50, 0.50)$ distribution model.)

4.62. In a particular communications network, messages are coded into bits (0's or 1's) for transmission. Performance is seriously degraded if more than 0.001% of the bits are incorrectly transmitted or received. The probability of a single bit (0 or 1) being incorrectly transmitted or received is 0.00002, independent of what happens to any other bits. Approximately, what is the probability that communication of a message of 100,000 bits is seriously degraded?

4.63. In a particular communications network, messages are coded into bits (0's or 1's) for transmission. Performance is seriously degraded if more than 0.12% of the bits are incorrectly transmitted or received. The probability of a single bit (0 or 1) being incorrectly transmitted or received is 0.001, independent of what happens to any other bits. Approximately, what is the probability that communication of a message of 100,000 bits is seriously degraded?

4.64. Look at Figure 2.18 in Chapter 2. Do you think the data follow normal distributions? If not, suggest a transformation to make them more normal.

4.65. Find transformations that will make the data in data sets SET4_1 and SET4_2 nearly normal.

4.66. The data values 4.12, 1.29, 0.01, 9.65, and 0.91 are thought to follow a Weibull distribution model with parameters $\alpha = 0.5$ and $\beta = 3.0$. Construct a Q–Q plot to decide if these observations are at all consistent with this Weibull distribution model.

4.67. Use Equations (4.10), (4.11), and (4.15) to show that

$$\sigma_{\bar{Y}_n}^2 = \frac{\sigma^2}{n}, \quad \text{and} \quad \sigma_{\bar{Y}_n} = \frac{\sigma}{\sqrt{n}}$$

MINIPROJECT

Purpose

The purpose of this miniproject is to give you experience in obtaining and modeling data using one of the distribution models from the chapter.

Process

The miniproject for this chapter requires student teams to design a data-collection mechanism to obtain data that can be modeled by one of the following distribution models: Poisson, normal, or Weibull. The data may be transformed, for example, by a log transformation, before using the proposed distribution to model it.

Your group is to submit a one-page proposal detailing how you plan to collect the data and what distribution you intend to try as the model. After receiving your instructor's approval, you may begin to collect the data.

In your report you must

- Give the theoretical justification for your choice of distribution and data-collection method by relating the properties of the distribution to the method you used to generate the data.
- Explain how you used your observations to construct the model.
- Interpret the model you constructed.

LAB 4.1: The Bernoulli Distribution Model

Introduction

Recall that a **Bernoulli trial** is a trial in which one of two outcomes can occur. Depending on the application, these outcomes can be denoted as 1/0, on/off, yes/no, and so on. For our purposes, they will be denoted "success" or "failure." The only other thing to know about a Bernoulli trial is how likely success or failure is to occur. Once this is quantified, we have a **Bernoulli distribution model.** This lab is designed to teach you about this model.

Objectives

To give you an understanding of the Bernoulli distribution model. To see how data from such a model can be generated. To see the relationship between such data and the model. To see probability as a limiting relative frequency.

Lab Materials

A 10-sided die.

TABLE 4.8 Summary Table for Simulation of 10 Bernoulli Trials and the Resulting Values of the Bernoulli Random Variable, Y

Trial	Die Roll	Outcome	y	Cumulative Proportion of $Y = 1$
1	3	{success}	1	$1/1 = 1.00$
2	6	{success}	1	$2/2 = 1.00$
3	2	{success}	1	$3/3 = 1.00$
4	8	{failure}	0	$3/4 = 0.75$
5	7	{success}	1	$4/5 = 0.80$
6	10	{failure}	0	$4/6 = 0.\overline{66}$
7	3	{success}	1	$5/7 = 0.71$
8	5	{success}	1	$6/8 = 0.75$
9	6	{success}	1	$7/9 = 0.78$
10	4	{success}	1	$8/10 = 0.80$

Experimental Procedure

Data Generation and Display

By Hand.   You will begin the lab by generating 10 observations from a Bernoulli distribution model.

1. If you were born in the months January through September, let N be the number of your birth month. Otherwise, let it be the number of your birth month modulo 9 (i.e., January $= 1$, February $= 2, \ldots$, September $= 9$, October $= 1$, November $= 2$, and December $= 3$). You will be using the die to simulate a random phenomenon whose two possible outcomes are {success} and {failure}, and for which the probabilities are

$$P(\{\text{success}\}) = p = N/10 \quad \text{and} \quad P(\{\text{failure}\}) = 1 - p$$

   From these simulated results of the random phenomenon, you will generate observations from a Bernoulli distribution model with parameter p.

2. Roll the die. Record the outcome of the roll as {success} if the number showing is less than or equal to N (on a die with "0" through "9" on the faces, take "0" to be "10." Otherwise, record it as {failure}. You have now completed the **simulation** of one Bernoulli trial.

3. Now create the measurement, Y, from the Bernoulli distribution model. Y is the number of successes on the trial. If the outcome of the die roll was {success}, $Y = 1$. Otherwise, $Y = 0$. You have now completed the simulation of one measurement from the Bernoulli distribution model, based on the Bernoulli trial you simulated in step 2.

4. Simulate another nine Bernoulli trials as in step 2, then for each, simulate a measurement from the Bernoulli distribution model as in step 3.

5. Table 4.8 gives the results of one set of simulations done by a student born in July, so that $p = 7/10$. Create a table such as Table 4.8 to summarize your results.

6. Sketch two plots based on Table 4.8:
   (a) A density histogram of the values of Y. There will be two bars: one $Y = 0$ and one for $Y = 1$. Make the height of the bar for $Y = 0$ equal to the relative frequency of

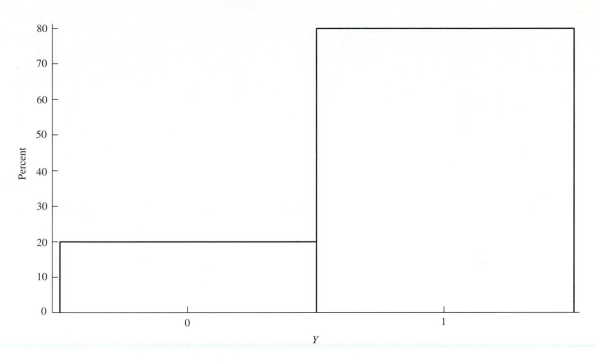

Figure 4.18   Density histogram for the values of Y from Table 4.8.

the 10 measurements that resulted in $Y = 0$, and the height of the bar for $Y = 1$ equal to the relative frequency of the 10 measurements that resulted in $Y = 1$. For the data in Table 4.8, the heights of the bars are 0.2 and 0.8 (or 20% and 80%), respectively.

(b) A plot of the cumulative proportion of values $Y = 1$ (vertical axis) versus trial (horizontal axis). The cumulative proportion of values $Y = 1$ at trial t is the number of trials that resulted in $Y = 1$ in the first t trials divided by t. The rightmost column of Table 4.8 contains the computation of the cumulative proportion of values $Y = 1$.

Figures 4.18 and 4.19 show these two plots for the data in Table 4.8.

By Computer.   Now repeat the preceding 10,000 more times using your computer. You should generate and store 10,000 data values from a Bernoulli distribution model with parameter $p = N/10$. Each data value will be either a 0 (call this a failure) or 1 (a success). From these 10,000 values, produce both a histogram of the values of Y and a plot of the cumulative proportion of values $Y = 1$ versus trial. The Doing It with SAS and Doing It with MINITAB supplements give explicit instructions for users of those packages.

Analysis

In your analysis, you should address two questions:

1. How do the histograms you produced relate to the probability histogram that describes the Bernoulli distribution model with parameter $p = N/10$?

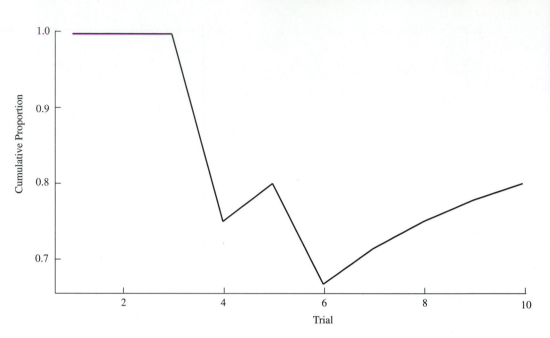

Figure 4.19   Plot of the cumulative proportion of values $Y = 1$ versus trial for the data from Table 4.8.

2. What do the plots of the cumulative proportion of values $Y = 1$ versus trial that you produced have to do with the meaning and interpretation of probability? How do they relate the model to data produced by that model?

LAB 4.2: The Binomial Distribution

Introduction

You have learned in Chapter 4 that a binomial trial consists of n repeats of a Bernoulli trial. Just as Lab 4.1 did for the Bernoulli trial, this lab will provide you with some hands-on experience with the binomial trial.

Objectives

To give you an understanding of the binomial distribution model. To see how data from such a model can be generated. To see the relationship between such data and the model.

Lab Materials

A 10-sided die.

Experimental Procedure

Data Generation and Display

By Hand.   You will begin the lab by generating 10 observations from a $b(5, p)$ distribution model, where p is the same value determined by your birth month that was used in Lab 4.1.

1. Let N be the number of your birth month computed as in Lab 4.1. What did this make p equal to in the Bernoulli trial?
2. Recall that a $b(5, p)$ random variable Y is the sum of five Bernoulli trials, each with probability p of a success. Now you will run a single binomial trial with $n = 5$ and the value p that you obtain from step 1 as follows:
   (a) Roll the die. Record the roll as a "success" if the number showing is less than or equal to N. Otherwise, record it as a "failure."
   (b) Repeat step (a) four more times.
   (c) Record the total number of successes in the five rolls.
3. Repeat step 2 for a total of ten binomial trials.
4. Sketch a density histogram of the results. Make the height of each bar equal to the relative frequency of the number of successes corresponding to that bar in the ten measurements: that is, the total number of times in the ten binomial trials that you got that number of successes, divided by 10. So, for example, the bar corresponding to 3 should record the relative frequency of exactly 3 successes in the 10 binomial trials. You should have six bars: one bar for each of $y = 0, 1, 2, 3, 4,$ and 5 successes.

By Computer.   Now repeat step 2 10,000 more times using your computer. You should generate and store 10,000 data values from a $b(5, p)$ distribution model. Each data value will be one of the integers 0, 1, 2, 3, 4, or 5. From these 10,000 values, produce a density histogram of the values of Y. The Doing It with SAS and Doing It with MINITAB supplements give explicit instructions for users of those packages.

Analysis

In your analysis, you should tell how the histograms you produced relate to the probability histogram that describes the binomial distribution model with parameters $n = 5$ and $p = N/10$.

LAB 4.3: The Central Limit Theorem

Introduction

In this lab, you will use computer simulation to demonstrate the Central Limit Theorem, one of the most important theorems in statistics. As you know from the text, the Central Limit Theorem states that regardless from which population we take our data, the sample mean of a random sample will have approximately a normal distribution if the number of observations in that sample is large enough and if the population obeys certain conditions. In the following, you can explore the practical implications of this theorem through computer simulation.

Objectives

To investigate how the Central Limit Theorem works on simulated data.

Lab Materials

None needed.

Experimental Procedure

We are going to describe the steps to be done using a computer. The Doing It with SAS and Doing It with MINITAB supplements give explicit instructions for users of those packages.

The Central Limit Theorem for Rolls of a Die

1. Generate random data from the discrete uniform distribution having an equal probability of producing any of the integers $1, 2, 3, 4, 5$, or 6, just like a fair die. The random phenomenon being modeled consists of rolling a fair die 50 times. There will be 250 replications of this phenomenon, giving in all 12,500 simulated die rolls. The data should be stored in a 250 (rows) by 50 (columns) data array. Each row consists of one replication and the 50 values in each row can be viewed as the results of 50 die rolls. We will assume that the columns (variables) are called $c1, c2, \ldots, c50$. From these data, compute the means of the first 2, 10, 30, and 50 rolls from each replicate, calling them MEAN2, MEAN10, MEAN30, and MEAN50, respectively.

2. To get an idea of what data from the discrete uniform distribution looks like, make a density histogram of $c1$ using your statistical software. The display should roughly resemble a rectangle, the shape of the probability histogram for rolling a fair die.

It will be instructive for you to compare the density histograms of $c1$, MEAN2, MEAN10, and MEAN50, all plotted on the same horizontal scale. Generate and print a plot of these. You should notice two things as the number of data in the mean increases. First, the shape of the plots becomes more like a normal curve, and, second, the plots cluster closer about their center (i.e., their variance decreases).

3. Make normal quantile plots of $c1$, MEAN2, MEAN10, and MEAN50. Print these graphs now.

4. You know from the Chapter 4 discussion that the sample mean of n observations, $\bar{Y}_n$, has mean value equal to the population mean μ and standard deviation equal to $\sigma/\sqrt{n}$. For the die roll example, the population mean and standard deviation are 3.5 and 1.71, respectively. Use your statistical software on $c1$, MEAN2, MEAN10, and MEAN50 to check that the sample means roughly follow these formulas.

5. Standardize the data in $c1$ and the sample means in MEAN2, MEAN10, and MEAN50 by subtracting $\mu = 3.5$ and dividing by $\sigma/\sqrt{n} = 1.71/\sqrt{n}$. The theory says that these standardized means should get closer and closer to the $N(0, 1)$ distribution as n becomes large. Use your statistical software to check that the means of each of these variables are nearly 0 and the standard deviations are nearly 1. Generate density histograms and normal quantile plots of the standardized means. What are your conclusions?

An Example in Which the Central Limit Theorem Fails

As was stated in the introduction, the Central Limit Theorem holds if the population the data comes from obeys certain conditions. One such condition is that the variance must be defined for the population. An example of a continuous distribution model for which the variance is not defined is the Cauchy distribution model. In fact, although the Cauchy distribution model is symmetric about 0, it is so widely spread out that a mean is not defined for it, either.

1. The probability density function of the Cauchy distribution model is

$$p_Y(y) = \frac{1}{\pi(1 + y^2)}, \qquad -\infty < y < \infty$$

   (a) Recall that a mean is defined for a continuous distribution with probability density function $p_Y(y)$ if and only if $\int_{-\infty}^{\infty} |y| p_Y(y) dy < \infty$. Use this fact to show that a mean is not defined for the Cauchy distribution model.
   (b) Recall that a variance is defined for a continuous distribution with probability density function $p_Y(y)$ if and only if $\int_{-\infty}^{\infty} y^2 p_Y(y) \, dy < \infty$. Use this fact to show that a variance is not defined for the Cauchy distribution model.

2. Repeat steps 1 to 3 of the last section with the following difference: In step 1, generate 250 replicates of samples of size 50 from the Cauchy distribution, in place of the simulated die rolling data. Now repeat the steps you performed with the die rolling data. What happens? How is this different than what happened with the dice rolls? Did you expect this?

Analysis

In your analysis, you should tell how the graphs you produced for the simulated die rolling data demonstrate the Central Limit Theorem. Tell how the graphs you produced for the Cauchy data demonstrate the failure of the Central Limit Theorem.

One further interesting fact may help you in your analysis. You know that if $Y_1, Y_2, \ldots, Y_n$ is a random sample from a distribution with mean μ and variance σ^2, then the sample mean, $\bar{Y}_n$, has mean (i.e., expected value) μ and variance σ^2/n. This means that the variance of the sample mean decreases as the sample size increases. It also means that the sample mean will be closer and closer, on average, to the population mean μ. So taking the sample mean of more data gives us more precise information about the population mean.

When the random sample is taken from the Cauchy distribution, the sample mean has the same distribution as the original data, no matter how many observations are in the random sample! Therefore, taking the sample mean of more data does nothing to improve our information about a Cauchy population.

LAB 4.4: Means Versus Ends

Introduction

Consider two normal distribution models, which differ only in their means. Suppose model 1 is an $N(\mu_1, \sigma^2)$ and model 2 is an $N(\mu_2, \sigma^2)$. It is natural to think that if μ_1 and μ_2 are nearly the same, and if A is any set of real numbers, then the probability an observation from model 1 is in A is nearly the same as the probability an observation from model 2 is in A. In this lab, you will see that if A consists of very large or very small numbers, then there can be relatively large differences in these probabilities.

Objectives

To show that closeness in means does not imply closeness in probabilities of extremes. To explore the effect of different variances on the probabilities of extremes.

Lab Materials

None needed.

Experimental Procedure

Small Differences in Means Can Yield Large Differences in Extremes

We begin with a story. Suppose that there are 7,500,000 male high school students in the United States, and that the distribution of their heights is normal with mean 178 cm and variance 100 cm^2. Suppose also that there is another country, which we'll call Randomnesia, that also has 7,500,000 male high school students, but that on average these students are 2 cm shorter than the American students: that is, we'll assume that the distribution of their heights is normal with mean 176 cm and variance 100 cm^2. Now, 2 cm isn't very much[22] and we'd expect the numbers of male students in different height ranges to be similar for the two countries.

1. First, consider people of average heights, say, those with heights between 170 and 180 cm.
    (a) Calculate the proportion of American male high school students with heights between 170 and 180 cm. Calculate the proportion of Randomnesian male high school students with heights between 170 and 180 cm. Are these two proportions close?
    (b) In all, according to the distribution models, how many American and Randomnesian male high school students are between 170 and 180 cm tall? What proportion of these students are American?

2. Now consider tall students, let's say those with heights over 214 cm. Using the distribution models:
    (a) Find the number of Randomnesian male high-schoolers taller than 214 cm.
    (b) Find the number of Americans male high-schoolers taller than 214 cm.
    (c) Of all male high school students in both countries whose heights are greater than 214 cm, what proportion are American?

3. Based on your results, explain what is meant by the expression: "Small differences in means can yield large differences in extremes."

What about Differences in Variances?

We have seen how a small difference in means can result in a large difference in extremes. How does a small difference in variances affect the extremes? Suppose that there are 7,500,000 male high school students in the country of Stochastica and that their heights follow a normal distribution model with mean 178 and variance 90.

1. Compare with their American counterparts the numbers of Stochastican male high school students whose heights are
    (a) between 170 and 180 cm.
    (b) greater than 214 cm.

2. In each of these two categories, what proportion of all students is American?

3. Repeat your exploration with some other values of σ^2 until you see a pattern. Tell what you conclude about the effect of differences in variances on normal probabilities.

---

[22] One inch $\approx$ 2.54 cm.

5

Introduction to Inference: Estimation and Prediction

*The
normal
law of error
stands out in the
experience of mankind
as one of the broadest
generalizations of natural
philosophy ◇ It serves as the
guiding instrument in researches
in the physical and social sciences and
in medicine agriculture and engineering ◇
It is an indispensable tool for the analysis and the
interpretation of the basic data obtained by observation and experiment.*

—*W. J. Youden*

INTRODUCTION

Statistical inference is the use of a subset of a population, called a **sample,** to draw conclusions about the entire population from which it was taken. So, for example, a poll of 1500 voters (the sample) might be used to estimate the preferences of all voters (the population), or 32 sets of five ball bearings each (the sample) are taken from a production line every 15 minutes during an 8-hour shift in order to monitor the entire production of bearings turned out during that shift (the population).

The statistical inference methods we will study in this chapter and in Chapter 6 can be called **classical inference methods.** These are methods developed in the first half of the twentieth century that rely on assumptions about the underlying distribution model for the data, and that place particular emphasis on the normal distribution model.

In this chapter, we will study the basics of estimation and prediction, two kinds of statistical inference. In Chapter 6, we will study the basics of hypothesis testing, another kind of statistical inference. Chapter 11 will present some more recently developed alternatives to these classical inference methods.

Knowledge and Skills

By successfully completing this chapter, you will acquire the following knowledge and skills:

KNOWLEDGE	SKILLS
1. The Center+Error (C+E) model.	**1.** The construction, use, and interpretation of classical confidence intervals for one and two sample means and proportions.
2. Sampling distributions.	**2.** The construction, use, and interpretation of classical prediction intervals in the one sample setting.
3. The concepts behind • Point and interval estimation for the C+E and binomial models. • Prediction for the C+E model. • Classical tolerance intervals.	**3.** The construction, use, and interpretation of normal theory tolerance intervals.

5.1

INFERENCE: SOME PRELIMINARY CONSIDERATIONS

In order to use statistical inference properly, it is essential to understand its relation to two topics you have already studied: sampling and stationarity.

Inference and How Data Are Obtained

The validity of statistical inference depends on the method used to obtain the sample of sampling units or experimental units upon which measurements are made. In an experiment, it also depends on how treatments are assigned to experimental units.

There are many schemes for drawing samples from a population. In order to be suitable for inference, a sample must be drawn by some sort of prespecified random mechanism. Recall from Chapter 3 that such a sample is called a **probability sample.**

Only a probability sample will

- give the best protection available against unknowingly selecting a sample that is unrepresentative of the population.
- enable us to assess the precision of estimation.

From a statistical perspective, the validity of conclusions based on a nonprobability sample may be open to question.

Several commonly used probability sampling schemes are discussed in Chapter 3. The only kind of probability sampling considered in this chapter is simple random sampling, which was introduced in Chapter 3. Recall that simple random sampling means not only that all units in a population have equal chance of appearing in the sample, but also that given the sample size n, all possible samples of size n have an equal chance of being selected. A sample obtained from a simple random sampling is called a **simple random sample.**

Conceptually, you can think of drawing a simple random sample (SRS) as follows:

- Assign to each unit in the population a different number.
- Put each number on an individual slip of paper and place all of the slips into a hat.
- Draw out one slip at a time until you have drawn as many slips as you want there to be observations in your sample.

The simple random sample consists of those sampling units in the population corresponding to the drawn numbers. Observations are then taken on these units. Of course, in practice, you would be unlikely to use paper slips and a hat to choose a SRS. A table of random numbers[1] or the computer would more likely be used.

The SRS is the "most random" type of sampling. There are many other kinds of probability samples, all of them restricting the randomness of the draw either out of necessity or in order to obtain better precision in estimation. You were introduced to other sampling schemes in Chapter 3.

If the study is a controlled experiment, then the treatments must be assigned to the experimental units using a suitable random mechanism as well.

In Chapter 3, observational studies were distinguished from controlled experiments as designed methods of obtaining data. Based on this distinction, you might think that statistical inference cannot be done using data obtained from a controlled experiment. This is not the case, however. When considering inference using experimental data, the population to which inference is made is the population consisting of results from all possible replications of the experiment. All possible replications consist of all possible choices of experimental units from the population of sampling units and all possible assignments of treatments to those experimental units selected. The data obtained from the experiment that is actually run are then considered a sample obtained from that population. The following is a good way to think of it: Suppose you had a machine that could run the experiment an infinite number of times and output the data obtained from each on its own sheet of paper. Imagine that the sheets of paper belonging to this infinite number of experiments are placed in an infinitely large jar. When you perform your experiment, it is like reaching into the jar and selecting one sheet of paper at random. The data on the sheet you select are the data you obtain from your experiment.

---

[1] See Table A.7, in Appendix A, page 911.

Inference and Stationarity

One further point is worth noting. All the statistical inference procedures you will learn in this chapter depend on the idea that the distribution of the observations does not change as more data are taken; in other words, that the process producing the data is stationary. Consequently, when doing statistical inference, you should always do diagnostic checks for process stability, such as plots of the observed responses versus time or order.

In fact, something stronger than stationarity is needed. For the inference procedures considered here, the data are assumed to result from independent draws from an unchanging population. To put it more mathematically, we assume there are n data values that result from observing the random variables $Y_1, Y_2, \ldots, Y_n$, which are independent and have the same distribution. It is difficult to check the independence of these random variables, and at this stage of our statistical knowledge, the best we can reasonably do is to check for stationarity.

5.2

THE MODELS

Behind any kind of statistical inference, whether it is stated explicitly or not, there is a model that is supposed to provide a satisfactory description of the population in question. Throughout our treatment of inference, we will explicitly state the models used in each application.

In this chapter, we consider two basic models, both of which you have encountered in Chapter 4.

The C+E Model

The first model is what we will call the **C+E model.** Although we did not use that name in Chapter 4, perhaps you will remember the word equation that was used there to describe it:

$$\textbf{DATA} = \textbf{CENTER} + \textbf{ERROR}$$

From this equation, it is clear that C+E stands for Center+Error. The C+E model can be expressed in mathematical symbols as

$$Y = \mu + \epsilon \tag{5.1}$$

Equation (5.1) says that, ideally, the response, Y, would equal an unknown constant μ (the center of the population), but that we cannot observe this value μ exactly. We can only observe it with some added error. As an example of a process that might follow the C+E model, consider a physicist using very precise instruments to measure the speed of light in a vacuum. The assumption is that there is a unique value for the true speed

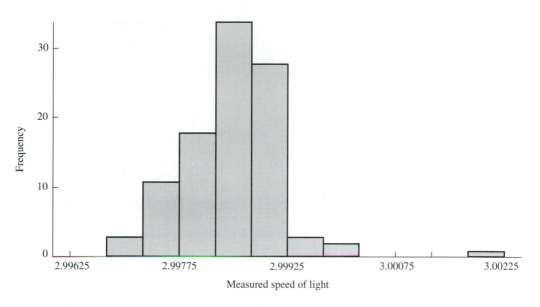

Figure 5.1 Frequency histogram of 100 measurements of the speed of light in units of 10^{10} cm/sec.

of light, so that the physicist is taking repeated measurements of the same quantity. It is a fact, however, that repeated measurements of the speed of light made each time with the same sensitive apparatus, will display variation. Since the physicist is taking repeated measurements of the same quantity, the variation in the observed data is due to errors in measurement. For this example, μ is the true speed of light, ϵ is the error of measurement due to whatever source: atmospheric conditions, inconsistencies in the timing or recording mechanism, human error, and so on, and Y is the observed value. Figure 5.1 displays a frequency histogram of a set of 100 measurements of the speed of light, in units of 10^{10} cm/sec.

Another type of process that is appropriately modeled by the C+E model is represented by the diameters in centimeters of 100 ball bearings recorded by a very accurate measuring device: accurate to one millionth of a centimeter. A histogram of these data is shown in Figure 5.2.

Since we are measuring the ball bearings with such precision, we can be sure the diameters are accurate to the four decimal places recorded. Therefore, the variation in these data is due to the differences in the diameters of the ball bearings rather than the process of measurement, as it was for the measurements of the speed of light. In the C+E model for these data, μ is the true mean diameter of all ball bearings produced, ϵ is the discrepency between the measured bearing's diameter and μ, and Y is the diameter that was observed.

Whatever the source of the variation, we will assume that the data consist of n observations $Y_i, i = 1, \ldots, n$, and that these are generated by the formula

$$Y_i = \mu + \epsilon_i$$

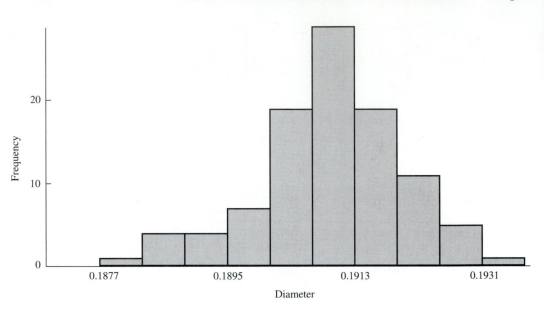

Figure 5.2   Frequency histogram of diameters (in centimeters) of 100 ball bearings.

We assume that the ϵ_i are independent random variables having the same distribution, and their distribution is assumed to be centered about 0, where "center" might denote the mean or median or mode or some other location on the distribution. With these assumptions, we can conclude that μ is the "center" of the population, and that the observations Y_i are independent random variables from that population.

If the distribution of the error term, ϵ, is known, then the C+E model will be completely specified by specifying the value of μ. This means that μ is an example of a **model parameter.**

> **DEFINITION**
>
> A **model parameter** is a quantity describing the model that may take on more than one value, and that must be specified to determine the model as completely as possible.

A model may depend on more than one parameter. For instance, we might describe the C+E model by Equation (5.1), where μ is some real number, and $\epsilon \sim N(0, \sigma^2)$, for some positive number σ^2. Then μ and σ^2 are parameters for the model, since both have to be specified to determine the model as completely as possible.

As we have seen, models are used as simplified descriptions of populations. It is natural, therefore, that model parameters are associated with measures of the population. For example, in the C+E model, we have seen that the parameter μ is associated with the "center" of the population. For this reason, the model parameters are sometimes called **population parameters.**

The Binomial Model

The second model we'll consider in this chapter is the binomial model $b(n, p)$. Recall from Chapter 4 that a random variable, Y, follows a $b(n, p)$ distribution model if Y is the total number of successes in n independent Bernoulli trials, each of which has a probability p of yielding a success.

We are going to be interested in applying the binomial distribution model in the population/sample framework of statistical inference. For the binomial distribution model to apply exactly, the population must be infinite, or, if it is finite, we must sample from it with replacement.

Example 4.11 in Chapter 4 provides an instance of an infinite population. There, a State Gaming Commission, in order to judge the fairness of a roulette wheel, spun the wheel 100 times and observed the number of times the wheel came up red. The spins are assumed to constitute 100 independent Bernoulli trials with the same probability, p, of red coming up at each trial. Then Y, the total number of times red occurs, follows a $b(100, p)$ distribution. Since, in principle at least, they may continue spinning the wheel as many times as desired, the population of all possible spins is infinite.

Example 5.1 shows how the binomial model applies exactly to a finite population in which sampling is done with replacement.

EXAMPLE 5.1   SAMPLING WITH REPLACEMENT

Suppose that there are 10,000 ball bearings in a production lot. Quality personnel wish to use a simple random sample of 100 bearings to estimate the true proportion of defective bearings in the lot. Here, the population is the 10,000 bearings in the production lot. The procedure using sampling with replacement consists of the following:

1. Drawing a bearing at random.
2. Determining whether the bearing is defective.
3. Replacing the bearing into the production lot in such a way that all 10,000 bearings have the same probability of being drawn on the next draw.
4. If fewer than 100 draws have been made, returning to step 1. Otherwise, stopping.

It is easy to see that this procedure generates 100 independent Bernoulli trials, each of whose possible outcomes is "defective" or "not defective." The probability of obtaining a defective bearing at each trial is p, the proportion of defective bearings in the production lot. This means that Y, the total number of defectives in the 100 sampled bearings, has a $b(100, p)$ distribution. If, for example, there are 10 defective bearings in the lot, then $Y \sim b(100, 0.001)$.   ◆

If sampling from a finite population is done without replacement, the binomial distribution model no longer holds exactly. If the population is large, however, the binomial will provide a good approximation. A continuation of Example 5.1 will illustrate.

EXAMPLE 5.1   CONTINUED

Suppose that the sample of 100 bearings is selected without replacement. The procedure is the same as that described for sampling with replacement, except that once a bearing has been selected, it is removed from the production lot for subsequent draws. Thus, a bearing may appear in the sample only once, if it appears at all. When the bearings are sampled without replacement, the number of defectives in the sample, Y, no longer has a binomial distribution. This is because the draws no longer have the same probability of drawing a defective.

For this problem, the first ball bearing sampled has a probability $p = 10/10000 = 0.001$ of being defective. If a defective bearing is the first item sampled, then for the second draw, the population proportion of defectives changes to $9/9999 \approx 0.0009$. If a good bearing is the first sampled, the population proportion of defectives changes to $10/9999 \approx 0.0010001$ for the second draw.

Note, however, that due to the large population size, these proportions are very close to the original value 0.001. The number of bearings in this lot is so large relative to the 100 in the sample that we may consider the population size infinite for all practical purposes. This means that the $b(n, p)$ model is a good approximation to the actual distribution of the sample.   ✦

If sampling with replacement from a finite population can always be modeled exactly by the binomial distribution, why don't we always sample with replacement? There are basically two reasons:

1. Sampling with replacement introduces greater variation into the response, Y. If we sample with replacement, we have just shown that $Y \sim b(n, p)$, and we know from Chapter 4 that the variance of Y is $np(1 - p)$. If we sample without replacement, Y follows a discrete distribution model called a **hypergeometric distribution model.** It can be shown that the variance of Y is

$$\left(1 - \frac{n - 1}{N - 1}\right) np(1 - p)$$

where N is the population size. If the sample size, n, is a substantial fraction of the population size, the variance obtained by sampling without replacement will be substantially smaller than that obtained by sampling with replacement. This problem becomes negligible if the population is large and the sample is not a substantial fraction of the population.

The practical result of the increased variation in Y when sampling with replacement is that there is less precision in any conclusions we can make using the information in Y. For this reason, sampling is usually done without replacement.

2. It may be very difficult, or even impossible, to sample with replacement. An example of the latter is destructive testing: If the unit being tested is destroyed, it cannot be used in the sample again.

In the rest of the chapter, we will assume that when the binomial distribution model is used, it is either exact or an adequate approximation. We will not cover the case in which the hypergeometric is the appropriate distribution model: taking a sample of size n from a population of size N without replacement, where n is a substantial proportion of N.

5.3

TYPES OF INFERENCE

We have seen that if the distribution of the error terms, ϵ, in the C+E model is known, then in order to completely specify the C+E model, we need to know one model parameter, μ. If we are willing to accept the model as an adequate description of the population, specifying this parameter is equivalent to knowing everything we can about the population that produced the data. Since in real-life situations we won't know this parameter, we must use the data to tell us about it. That is, we must use the data (i.e., the sample) to tell us about the true parameter (i.e., the population). Using data to draw conclusions about the population is statistical inference.

For the $b(n, p)$ model we will usually know n, and so the only model parameter we need to make inference about is p. Throughout this chapter, unless we state otherwise, it will be assumed that n is known in any problem involving the $b(n, p)$ model.

In addition to estimating model parameters, we will study two other kinds of inference: prediction of a new observation and tolerance intervals. Here is a brief summary of each.

- **Estimation of model parameters** uses the data to estimate model parameters and to tell us how much uncertainty is contained in the estimates we make.
- **Prediction of a new observation** uses presently available data to predict the value of a new observation from a population.
- A **tolerance interval** is a range of values that has a user-specified probability of containing a user-specified proportion of the population.

5.4

ESTIMATION FOR THE C+E MODEL

> **DEFINITION**
>
> **Fitting a model** consists of using the data to estimate the unknown model parameters.
>
> Any value computed from the data that we use to estimate a model parameter is called a **point estimate** of that parameter.

We begin our study of estimation by considering how to fit the C+E model, and, in particular, how to estimate the center of the population model, μ. Since we'll want to fit the best model we can, we need some criterion so that we can decide which estimate of μ is best. One such criterion would be some measure of how far from the data points a given estimate is. Suppose we guess μ to be 3.5. How far is this value (i.e., 3.5) from the data? That depends on how we measure distance.

Least Absolute Errors

The usual measure of the distance from 3.5 to the data point y_i is $|y_i - 3.5|$. Using this as our distance measure for the ith data point, one measure of how far our guess of 3.5 is from all the data is the sum of all these individual distances:

$$\text{SAE} = \sum_{i=1}^{n} |y_i - 3.5|$$

Here SAE stands for sum of absolute errors.

Now for a given set of data, the SAE will depend on the specific guess made for μ. So the SAE previously computed can be denoted SAE(3.5). To generalize this a bit, suppose we let m stand for a guess of μ. Then we can write

$$\text{SAE}(m) = \sum_{i=1}^{n} |y_i - m|$$

The best estimate of μ, using SAE as the criterion, is the value of m that minimizes SAE(m). Call this value $\tilde{\mu}$. It turns out that $\tilde{\mu}$ is any median of the $\{y_i\}$.

Least Squares

Sum of squared errors, or SSE, is a second measure of how far from the data points a given guess, m, of μ is. It is defined as

$$\text{SSE}(m) = \sum_{i=1}^{n} (y_i - m)^2$$

SSE sums the squares of the distances from each data value to m rather than the distances themselves.

SSE is easily minimized by setting its derivative with respect to m equal to 0:

$$\frac{d\text{SSE}}{dm}(m) = -2 \sum_{i=1}^{n} (y_i - m) = 0 \tag{5.2}$$

Solving Equation (5.2) for m gives the least squares estimate, $\hat{\mu} = \bar{y}$, the sample mean.

EXAMPLE 5.2   ESTIMATING μ

A quality engineer wants to evaluate the quality of a large production lot of ball bearings. To do this, he takes a simple random sample of three bearings from the lot. One of the quality characteristics he measures from this sample is ball-bearing

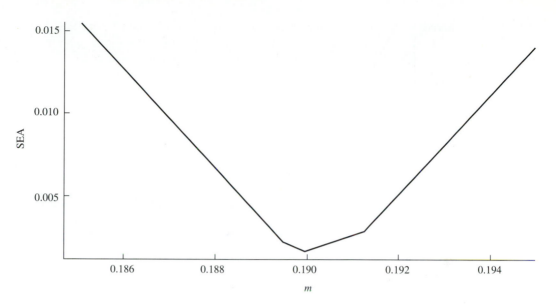

Figure 5.3   Graph of SAE(m) versus m for Example 5.2. SAE(m) is minimized at $m = 0.1900$, the median of the data values.

diameter. The diameters he obtains are 0.1896, 0.1913, and 0.1900. Using these three values, we can calculate SAE(m) for a range of values of m using the equation

$$SAE(m) = |0.1896 - m| + |0.1913 - m| + |0.1900 - m|$$

Figure 5.3 plots the resulting values, SAE(m) versus m. Notice that SAE is minimized at 0.1900, the median of the three diameters.

Similarly, we can compute SSE(m) as

$$SSE(m) = (0.1896 - m)^2 + (0.1913 - m)^2 + (0.1900 - m)^2$$

Figure 5.4 plots the resulting values, SSE(m) versus m. Notice that SSE is minimized at 0.1903, the mean of the three diameters. ✦

SAE and SSE are not the only possible criteria for obtaining an estimator of μ in the C+E model, but they are two criteria that make sense, and that give sensible results. It turns out that SSE is a natural criterion to use if the data are from a normal distribution (equivalently, if the error terms, ϵ, in the C+E model are normally distributed). SAE may perform better with certain nonnormal distributions and in the presence of outliers. Historically, SSE is the criterion that has been used, and it is the one we will use in this chapter.

When using SSE as the criterion for choosing an estimator of μ, it is natural to interpret μ as the population mean. This is the interpretation when we assume, as is usually done, that the errors in the C+E model, ϵ, have mean 0. Unless otherwise stated, we will assume throughout the rest of this chapter that the ϵ have mean 0 and that μ is the population mean.

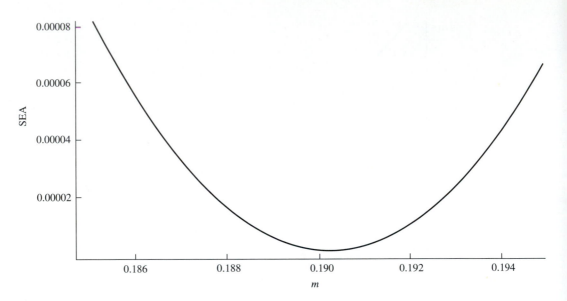

Figure 5.4 Graph of SSE(m) versus m for Example 5.2. SSE(m) is minimized at $m = 0.1903$, the mean of the data values.

Estimator or Estimate?

In order to proceed to the important idea of a sampling distribution, we need to define the difference between an **estimator** and an **estimate.** But before we can make the required definitions, we need to think about what randomness means and how we can describe it.

   To fix our ideas, consider again the quality engineer from Example 5.2 who wants to take a sample of three ball bearings from a large production lot. In a memo written to his boss describing what he intends to do, the engineer denotes the diameters of the three ball bearings he intends to sample as Y_1, Y_2, and Y_3. The use of capital letters to describe the as-yet-untaken measurements is a convention that means "these quantities are random." Indeed, before the data are taken, the diameters are random variables, and you know from Chapter 4 that random variables are denoted by capital letters.

   With any statistical problem, it is very important to understand the sources of the randomness. In the present problem, there are several possible sources. First, there may be error in the measuring process. In some problems, the measurement error is a large, if not the largest, source of randomness. However, that is unlikely to be the case when measuring the diameters of ball bearings: the measuring devices can measure to many decimal places' greater precision than mean bearing diameter or the variation in diameter from bearing to bearing. In fact, it is reasonable to suppose that the measurements are so precise that we can assume the measured diameters of the bearings to be the true diameters.

What, then, is the source of the randomness? For the ball bearings, the randomness resides primarily in the sampling. To see what this means, consider what can happen when the sample is taken. Suppose we can write down all possible samples of three ball bearings from the production lot and number them 1, 2, 3, 4, ... Then if we have enough paper, we can make a list of the diameters we would measure from each sample:

Sample	Y_1	Y_2	Y_3
1	0.1911	0.1899	0.1893
2	0.1901	0.1905	0.1909
3	0.1896	0.1913	0.1900
.	.	.	.
.	.	.	.
.	.	.	.

The simple random sampling the engineer proposes will have an equal chance of selecting any one of the samples on our list. That is what makes for the randomness.

Now what happens when the engineer actually takes his sample? Suppose he does and that he ends up with sample 3 from the list. That is, he ends up with the diameters 0.1896, 0.1913, and 0.1900. Are these values random? The answer is a resounding **NO!** This is just a set of numbers. There is no chance involved here because the sampling is over.

For data obtained from a controlled experiment, if measurement error can be ignored, the randomness results from two sources: the sampling procedure used to obtain the experimental units and the randomization scheme used to assign treatments to experimental units. Even this can be regarded as a two-stage sampling scheme: first, sample the experimental units from a larger population of such units, then select a smaller sample of this first sample to receive treatment 1, another smaller sample to receive treatment 2, and so on. The upshot is that we can use the same basic idea about sampling as the source of randomness in an experiment as well.[2]

The key point we want to make here is that the randomness is in the production of the data: measuring, sampling, treatment assignment; and not in the data themselves. We repeat the key point:

KEY POINT

The randomness in a set of data from a designed study is in the production of the data: measuring, sampling, treatment assignment, and so on.

---

[2]What happens if the experimental units are not randomly sampled from a larger population? Then the randomness in the experimental data lies exclusively in the assignment of treatments to experimental units. Permutation and randomization inference methods, which we consider in Chapter 11, can be used in such a situation.

However, we are left with a small notational problem. We would like to discuss in general terms the results obtained from the sample: We can't always go around talking about numbers like 0.1896, 0.1913, and 0.1900. So the convention is to use lowercase letters to denote the actual values that are obtained from the sample. Our quality engineer would use the notation y_1, y_2, and y_3 to represent the values obtained from the sampling scheme described by Y_1, Y_2, and Y_3. So, for example, in the memo to his boss, the engineer might say, "I intend to take a sample Y_1, Y_2, Y_3 of ball-bearing diameters. Once the data have been obtained, I will use the values y_1, y_2, y_3 to estimate the population mean diameter."

Now that we understand the difference between the randomness inherent in producing the data and the nonrandomness of the resulting data, we are ready to discuss the difference between an **estimate** and an **estimator.** Recall that we have already defined one type of estimate, a point estimate, as any value computed from the data that we use to estimate a model parameter. Later, we will discuss another kind of estimate called an interval estimate.

> **DEFINITION**
>
> An **estimator** is a **rule** for computing a quantity **from a sample** that is to be used to estimate a model parameter.
>
> An **estimate** is the **value** that rule gives **when the data are taken.**

Or, to put it another way, an estimator is the rule that tells what to do with the data once they are taken; an estimate is what results when the actual data values obtained from the sample are plugged into the rule.

For example, suppose our engineer proposes to compute the sample mean diameter to estimate the population mean diameter. Then the **estimator** is[3]

$$\bar{Y} = \frac{1}{3} \sum_{i=1}^{3} Y_i$$

If we don't know the data values obtained from the sample, but we want to talk about the **estimate,** we denote it as

$$\bar{y} = \frac{1}{3} \sum_{i=1}^{3} y_i$$

If the sample has the diameters 0.1896, 0.1913, and 0.1900, then the estimate is $(0.1896 + 0.1913 + 0.1900)/3 = 0.1903$. Notice that an estimator is random; an estimate is not.

We conclude with one important note. An estimator is a rule or formula. That rule or formula cannot involve the model parameter being estimated. This makes sense, since having to know the value of the parameter in order to compute the estimate would not produce a very workable procedure!

---

[3]Back in Chapter 4, we used notation for the sample mean that emphasized its dependence on the sample size, n: $\bar{Y}_n$. The reason is that we were taking limits as $n \to \infty$. Now that we are not so concerned with the sample size, we will drop the subscript whenever the meaning remains clear.

Sampling Distributions

Once we decide on a point estimator of μ, we would like to know how much faith we can put in the estimate that is produced. One way to approach the problem is to find the distribution of the estimator. Such a distribution is called a **sampling distribution.**

EXAMPLE 5.3   SAMPLING DISTRIBUTIONS

Consider the C+E model $Y = \mu + \epsilon$, where $\epsilon \sim N(0, \sigma^2)$. Suppose the data are a random sample $Y_1, Y_2, \ldots, Y_n$. The least squares estimator of μ is the sample mean:

$$\hat{\mu} = \bar{Y} = \frac{1}{n} \sum_{i=1}^{n} Y_i$$

We know from Chapter 4 that the sample mean has a normal distribution with parameters μ and σ^2/n, so the sampling distribution of $\hat{\mu}$ is $N(\mu, \sigma^2/n)$.

Now, suppose that ϵ does not have a normal distribution, but that its mean and variance are still 0 and σ^2, respectively. The least squares estimator of μ is still the sample mean: $\hat{\mu} = \bar{Y}$. If n is large, the Central Limit Theorem tells us that the sampling distribution of $\hat{\mu}$ is approximately $N(\mu, \sigma^2/n)$. ◆

EXAMPLE 5.4   A NONNORMAL SAMPLING DISTRIBUTION

Consider the C+E model $Y = \mu + \epsilon$, where $\mu = 5$, $\epsilon = X - 1$, and X has an exponential(1) distribution.[4] Five independent observations, $Y_1, \ldots, Y_5$, are taken from this model and the least squares estimator of μ,

$$\hat{\mu} = \bar{Y} = \frac{1}{5} \sum_{i=1}^{5} Y_i$$

is computed. Figure 5.5 is a graph of the probability density function that characterizes the sampling distribution of $\bar{Y}$.[5]

This sampling distribution tells us how we can expect the estimator to behave. For instance, Table 5.1 gives selected quantiles for the sampling distribution of $\hat{\mu}$ whose density is pictured in Figure 5.5. From this table, we see that half of all estimates lie between 4.67 and 5.26 and that 98% lie between 4.26 and 6.32. These quantiles give some idea of the variation in the estimates.

For instance, suppose we have to estimate $\mu = 5$ to an accuracy of 0.01. This means that we need the estimate to be between 4.99 and 5.01. Calculation using the sampling density of $\hat{\mu}$ shows that only 1.8% of all estimates lie in this range, indicating that this requirement is unlikely to be satisfied. On the other hand, if we need an accuracy of only ± 0.4, we are in better shape as 64.2% of all estimates lie in this range. ◆

---

[4]Subtracting 1 from X ensures that the expected value of ϵ is 0.

[5]The skewness of this density shows that $n = 5$ is not large enough to make the normal approximation reasonable.

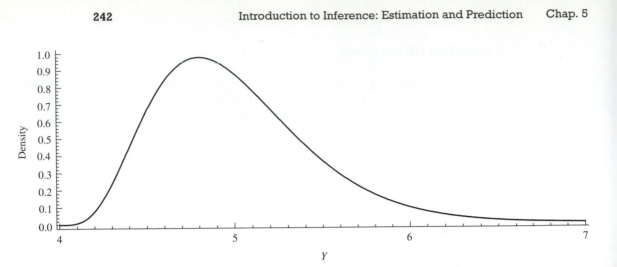

Figure 5.5   Probability density of the least squares estimator $\hat{\mu} = \bar{Y}$ from a sample of size 5 from the C+E model $Y = 5 + \epsilon$. Here, $\epsilon = X - 1$, where X has an exponential(1) distribution.

TABLE 5.1   Quantiles of the Sampling Distribution of $\hat{\mu}$ in Example 5.4

q	0.01	0.05	0.10	0.25	0.50	0.75	0.90	0.95	0.99
Quantile: $\hat{\mu}_q$	4.26	4.39	4.49	4.67	4.93	5.26	5.60	5.83	6.32

A Confidence Interval for μ in the C+E Model

If we know the sampling distribution of an estimator, we can use this knowledge to compute a likely range of values for the parameter being estimated. Such a range of values is called an **interval estimate** or a **confidence interval.** The concept of "likely" is quantified as a **confidence level,** which we'll call L.

> **DEFINITION**
>
> A level L confidence interval for a parameter θ is an interval $(\hat{\theta}_1, \hat{\theta}_2)$, where $\hat{\theta}_1$ and $\hat{\theta}_2$ are estimators having the property that
>
> $$P(\hat{\theta}_1 < \theta < \hat{\theta}_2) = L$$

For estimation of the parameter μ in the C+E model:

- We will assume that the mean of the error term, ϵ, in the C+E model is 0. This means that the expected value, or population mean, of the observed value Y is μ.
- We will use the least squares estimator, $\bar{Y}$, to estimate the population mean, μ.

In this section, we will assume that the variance, σ^2, of the error term, ϵ, in the C+E model is known. Finally, we will assume that n data values are observed.

In classical estimation, the sampling distribution of the estimator is assumed to be either exactly or approximately known. For large n, the Central Limit Theorem assures us that the sample mean $\bar{Y}$ has approximately an $N(\mu, \sigma^2/n)$ distribution, where σ^2 is the population variance.[6] For small n, this approximation will be good if the data are from a normal or nearly normal population.

If $\hat{\mu} = \bar{Y}$ can be assumed have approximately an $N(\mu, \sigma^2/n)$ distribution, then the quantity

$$\frac{\sqrt{n}(\bar{Y} - \mu)}{\sigma} \tag{5.3}$$

has approximately an $N(0, 1)$ distribution. If we denote the $(1 + L)/2$ and $(1 - L)/2$ quantiles of the $N(0, 1)$ distribution by $z_{(1+L)/2}$ and $z_{(1-L)/2}$, respectively,[7] then

$$L = P\left(z_{(1-L)/2} < \frac{\sqrt{n}(\bar{Y} - \mu)}{\sigma} < z_{(1+L)/2}\right)$$

$$= P\left(\bar{Y} - \frac{\sigma}{\sqrt{n}}z_{(1+L)/2} < \mu < \bar{Y} - \frac{\sigma}{\sqrt{n}}z_{(1-L)/2}\right)$$

where the last inequalities follow from the first inequalities through some algebraic manipulation. Now we've got exactly what we want: an interval for μ that holds true for a proportion L of all samples. The interval is

$$\left(\bar{Y} - \frac{\sigma}{\sqrt{n}}z_{(1+L)/2}, \bar{Y} - \frac{\sigma}{\sqrt{n}}z_{(1-L)/2}\right) \tag{5.4}$$

We can simplify Equation (5.4) by noting that by the symmetry of the $N(0, 1)$ distribution,

$$z_{(1-L)/2} = -z_{(1+L)/2}$$

This gives the formula for a level L confidence interval for μ:

$$\left(\bar{Y} - \frac{\sigma}{\sqrt{n}}z_{(1+L)/2}, \bar{Y} + \frac{\sigma}{\sqrt{n}}z_{(1+L)/2}\right) \tag{5.5}$$

A closer look at Equation (5.5) is enlightening. The standard deviation of the sampling distribution of an estimator is called the **standard error** of the estimator. The standard error of the estimator $\bar{Y}$, which we denote $\sigma(\bar{Y})$, equals $\sigma/\sqrt{n}$. So Equation (5.5)

---

[6]Recall from Chapter 4, that unless the data are heavily skewed or have extreme outliers, $n = 30$ should suffice to give an adequate approximation to normality.

[7]Recall from Chapter 4 that the qth quantile, z_q, of the $N(0, 1)$ distribution is the value at or below which lies a proportion q of the $N(0, 1)$ population.

may be described in words as

ESTIMATOR $\pm$ (STANDARD ERROR OF ESTIMATOR) ($N(0, 1)$ QUANTILE)

and written as follows.

**CLASSICAL CONFIDENCE INTERVAL FORMULA
FOR A POPULATION MEAN: KNOWN VARIANCE**

- **Model:** C+E model, $Y = \mu + \epsilon$.
- **Data:** $Y_i = \mu + \epsilon_i$, $i = 1, \ldots, n$.
- **Assumptions:**
  - The $\{Y_i\}$ are independent.
  - n is large, or the ϵ_i are independent $N(0, \sigma^2)$ random variables (so the Y_i are independent $N(\mu, \sigma^2)$ random variables).
  - σ^2 is known.
- **The Interval:** A level L classical confidence interval for the mean, μ, is

$$\left(\bar{Y} - \sigma(\bar{Y})z_{(1+L)/2}, \ \bar{Y} + \sigma(\bar{Y})z_{(1+L)/2}\right) \tag{5.6}$$

where $\sigma(\bar{Y}) = \sigma/\sqrt{n}$.

In this chapter you will encounter many different formulas, like Equation (5.6) for classical intervals. The summary in Appendix 5.1, beginning on page 281, can help you keep track of these intervals, and of the underlying assumptions.

Before moving on to an example using the confidence interval (5.6), we would like to point out something about its derivation. The quantity (5.3), which made the derivation of the confidence interval possible, is called a **pivotal quantity** for μ. A pivotal quantity for a parameter is a function of the data, which depends on no unknown model parameters except the parameter being estimated, and whose distribution is completely known. The quantity (5.3) is a pivotal quantity for μ because of the following:

- It is a function of the data (through $\bar{Y}$).
- The only unknown parameter it depends on is μ. (Remember, we're assuming σ is known.)
- Its distribution, $N(0, 1)$, is completely known.

Notice how the three criteria defining the pivotal quantity made the derivation of the confidence interval (5.6) possible:

- Because it is a function of the data, we can use data to calculate the interval.
- Because the only unknown parameter it depends on is μ, we can isolate μ and bound it above and below by functions that can be computed from the data (here, $\bar{Y}$) and known parameters (here, $\sigma/\sqrt{n}$) only.

- Because its distribution, $N(0, 1)$, is completely known, we can obtain the needed value $z_{(1+L)/2}$.

Pivotal quantities are useful tools that are widely used in the construction of confidence intervals in statistics.

EXAMPLE 5.5   CONSTRUCTING A CONFIDENCE INTERVAL FOR μ

A researcher at a biotechnology company is testing an artificial pancreas on laboratory rats. She gives diabetic rats, who have had this pancreas implanted, an initial dose of glucose in solution and then measures their blood-sugar levels (serum/plasma glucose, mg/100 ml) after 1 hour. The data are

$$266 \quad 149 \quad 161 \quad 220$$

The population is all possible diabetic rats of this type with this kind of artificial pancreas, and the sample is the four diabetic rats on which the researcher has data. We assume that the rats were randomly selected from the population.

The researcher wants to estimate μ, the mean population blood-sugar level after 1 hour. In addition, she wants to know whether the artificial pancreas is effective in lowering blood-sugar levels. As a benchmark, she cites numerous studies that point to a mean blood-sugar level of 275 in untreated diabetic rats 1 hour after ingestion of glucose.

From experience with other studies, the researcher is willing to assume that the population variance is $\sigma^2 = 2958$, which implies that $\sigma = 54.4$. Because she will be using interval (5.6) and because n is small, the researcher will be assuming that the data are from a population having a normal distribution.

Prior to doing any inference, the data should be checked for violations of model assumptions that might lead to erroneous results. There are too few data here to really check for normality, but the data can still be checked for any kind of unusual pattern, such as a very extreme outlier. Three of the four data values closely clustered together, with the fourth a large distance away would constitute such a pattern, for example. The researcher checked and found no unusual pattern to these data. Similarly, there are too few data to check for stationarity, though a plot versus the order in which the data were obtained revealed no pattern.

For the point estimate of μ, the researcher uses the least squares estimate of μ, $\hat{\mu} = \bar{y} = 199$.

The researcher wants to compute a level 0.95 (also known as a 95%) confidence interval for μ. Since $(1 + L)/2 = (1 + 0.95)/2 = 0.975$, and since $z_{0.975} = 1.96$, a 95% confidence interval for μ is computed from (5.6) as

$$\left(199 - \frac{54.4}{\sqrt{4}}1.96, \; 199 + \frac{54.4}{\sqrt{4}}1.96\right) = (145.7, 252.3)$$

"Great!" says the researcher. "But what does it mean?" This is where learning how to properly interpret these intervals is important. ✦

The Meaning and Interpretation of Confidence Intervals

We continue Example 5.5 to demonstrate what the confidence level means and how to interpret the resulting confidence interval.

EXAMPLE 5.5   CONTINUED

Here is how to think about the interval we just constructed.

Imagine that we take 999 more samples of four rats each from the same population, and that for each sample, we run the same experiment and calculate $\bar{y}$ and the resulting 95% confidence interval. So now we have 1000 confidence intervals. The first few might look like

$$(145.7, 252.3)$$

$$(129.5, 236.1)$$

$$(187.7, 294.3)$$

$$\cdot$$
$$\cdot$$
$$\cdot$$

The interpretation rests on the fact that approximately 950, or 95%, of the 1000 intervals will contain the true value of μ. Does this mean that μ is between 145.7 and 252.3? Or between 129.5 and 236.1? We don't know (and never will). We only know that about 95% of all intervals constructed by the method we used will actually contain μ.

So here's what the researcher can say:

I am 95% confident that the true mean blood-sugar level in rats with this artificial pancreas 1 hour after the ingestion of glucose solution is between 145.7 and 252.3. My confidence rests in my use of a method to compute this interval that will produce an interval containing the true mean blood-sugar level in 95% of all possible identically run experiments.

In addition, since this interval lies entirely below 275, I am at least 95% confident that the artificial pancreas is effective in lowering blood-sugar levels. ◆

Let's state the interpretation of a confidence interval more formally:

THE INTERPRETATION OF CONFIDENCE INTERVALS

A level L confidence interval for a parameter θ is interpreted as follows: Consider all possible samples that can be taken from the population described by θ, and for each sample, imagine constructing a level L confidence interval for θ. Then a proportion L of all the constructed intervals will really contain θ.

With regard to confidence intervals, there are some additional issues to think about.

- The interpretation of confidence intervals in terms of **repeatedly sampling from the same distribution** shows why it makes no sense to construct a confidence interval if the process producing the data is not stationary. What would happen if, as before, the researcher constructed the interval and decided to recommend that the company market the pancreas for humans, but before delivery, a key supplier changed the manufacturing process? The pancreas that was produced might give different results than the one she based her decision on! The results could be catastrophic for her employer and her career.
- Even if all assumptions are satisfied, there is no guarantee the right decision has been made. After all, when using a 95% confidence interval, 5% of all possible intervals will not contain μ even if everything has been done correctly! Of course, we can go to a 99% or 99.9% interval, but this will result in wider intervals, which are less useful for decision making. When you live in the real (i.e., uncertain) world, you have to give up on guarantees and learn to make decisions based on the odds.

Classical Estimation for the C+E Model: Unknown Variance

Often, the population variance σ^2 is unknown. In this case, we estimate it from the data, using the sample variance

$$S^2 = \frac{\sum_{i=1}^{n}(Y_i - \bar{Y})^2}{n - 1}$$

in place of σ^2. This substitution results in the standard error of $\bar{Y}$, $\sigma(\bar{Y})$, being replaced by the **estimated standard error** of $\bar{Y}$:

$$\hat{\sigma}(\bar{Y}) = \frac{S}{\sqrt{n}}$$

Recall that Equation (5.6) for the confidence interval for μ when σ is known depends on the pivotal quantity $(\bar{Y}-\mu)/\sigma(\bar{Y})$, having, at least approximately, an $N(0, 1)$ distribution. If we replace $\sigma(\bar{Y})$ with $\hat{\sigma}(\bar{Y})$, we obtain the quantity

$$\frac{\bar{Y} - \mu}{\hat{\sigma}(\bar{Y})} \tag{5.7}$$

for estimating μ when σ is unknown. The question is: In what sense can we use Equation (5.7) to construct a confidence interval for μ?

The Large-Sample Case

To come up with a partial answer, we ask you to recall the law of large numbers from Chapter 4. The law of large numbers states that if $Y_1, Y_2, \ldots$ is a sequence of independent random variables from the same distribution with mean μ, then[8]

$$\bar{Y}_n = \frac{1}{n} \sum_{i=1}^{n} Y_i \to \mu, \qquad \text{as } n \to \infty$$

That is, the sample mean converges to the population mean. A similar result tells us that the sample variance converges to the population variance, σ^2:

$$S_n = \frac{1}{n-1} \sum_{i=1}^{n} (Y_i - \bar{Y}_n)^2 \to \sigma^2, \qquad \text{as } n \to \infty$$

The practical implication is that if n is large, then even if the population is not normal, S will likely be close to σ, and the confidence interval can still be constructed using Equation (5.6), with $\hat{\sigma}(\bar{Y})$ taking the place of $\sigma(\bar{Y})$. How large is large? That will depend on the population distribution. For a normal or near-normal distribution, sample sizes as small as 30 may be acceptable. The more nonnormal the distribution, the larger the sample size necessary for the Central Limit Theorem and the law of large numbers to work their magic.

The Small-Sample Case

What if n is not large? Note that Equation (5.7) satisfies the first two criteria to be a pivotal quantity for μ:

- It is a function of the data (through $\bar{Y}$ and S).
- The only unknown parameter it depends on is μ (σ is unknown, but Equation (5.7) doesn't depend on σ.)

The gratifying and useful result, discovered by the statistician W. S. Gosset,[9] is that if n is small and the population distribution is normal, then the quantity (5.7) does not have a $N(0, 1)$ distribution. Rather, it has what is called a **t distribution.** Of course, this means that (5.7) satisfies the third, and final, criterion to be a pivotal quantity: Its distribution is completely known. Therefore, (5.7) is a pivotal quantity for μ, which enables us to use it to construct a confidence interval for μ when the population variance is unknown. Before we proceed to do so, however, let us learn about the t distribution.

The t Distribution

Actually, the t distribution is a family of distributions indexed by an integer parameter called **degrees of freedom.** For example, we talk about a t_1 or a t_5 or a t_{10} distribution

---

[8]Here we revert to the notation $\bar{Y}_n$ and S_n used in Chapter 4, instead of the simpler notation $\bar{Y}$ and S used so far in this chapter, in order to emphasize the convergence of the sample mean and standard deviation as the sample size, n, goes to ∞.

[9]W. S. Gosset, 1876–1936, worked at the Guinness Brewery. He published his statistical results under the pseudonym "Student," because his employers would not let him use his real name or otherwise reveal his affiliation with Guinness. In honor of its discoverer, the t distribution is often called Student's t distribution.

$\mu \pm 1\sigma - 68.3\%$

$\mu \pm 2\sigma - 95.5\%$

$\mu \pm 3\sigma - 99.7\%$

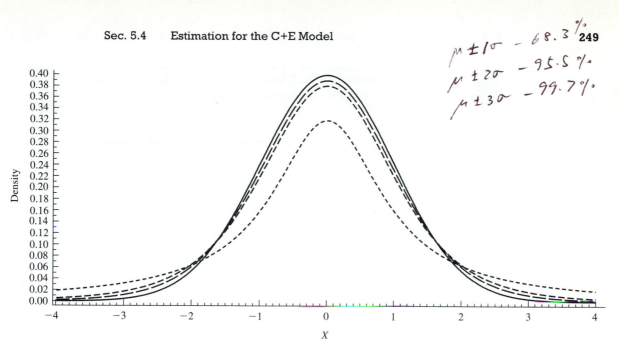

Figure 5.6 Four density curves. In order of decreasing center height: $N(0, 1)$, t_{10}, t_5, and t_1.

(i.e., t distributions with 1, 5, or 10 degrees of freedom, respectively), each of which has a different density curve (see Figure 5.6). All t distributions are unimodal and symmetric about 0. They are like an $N(0, 1)$ curve that has been squashed down in the middle and raised up in the tails. As the number of degrees of freedom rises, the t curves come closer to the $N(0, 1)$ curve; for 100 degrees of freedom, the two curves are virtually identical.

Recall that we let z_q denote quantile q of a $N(0, 1)$ population (i.e., the value below which lies proportion q of a $N(0, 1)$ population). In a similar way, we will let $t_{k,q}$ denote quantile q of a t_k population: that is, the value below which lies a proportion q of a t_k population. These values are also called **critical values** in statistical terminology.

Values of $t_{k,q}$ for selected k and q are found in Table A.4, in Appendix A, page 904.

Confidence Intervals for μ Based on the t Distribution

If the n observations $\{Y_i\}$ are from a normal population, the pivotal quantity $(\bar{Y} - \mu)/\hat{\sigma}(\bar{Y})$ has a t distribution with $n - 1$ degrees of freedom. By an argument identical to that given for the known σ case, a level L confidence interval for μ is

$$(\bar{Y} - \hat{\sigma}(\bar{Y})t_{n-1,(1+L)/2}, \ \bar{Y} + \hat{\sigma}(\bar{Y})t_{n-1,(1+L)/2})$$

where $t_{n-1,(1+L)/2}$ denotes the $(1 + L)/2$ quantile of a t_{n-1} population.

CLASSICAL CONFIDENCE INTERVAL FORMULA FOR A POPULATION MEAN: UNKNOWN VARIANCE

- **Model:** C+E model, $Y = \mu + \epsilon$.
- **Data:** $Y_i = \mu + \epsilon_i$, $i = 1, \ldots, n$.
- **Assumptions:**
  - The $\{Y_i\}$ are independent.
  - n is large (in which case the interval (5.6) can also be used with $\hat{\sigma}(\bar{Y})$ substituted for $\sigma(\bar{Y})$), or the ϵ_i are independent $N(0, \sigma^2)$ random variables (so the Y_i are independent $N(\mu, \sigma^2)$ random variables).
  - σ^2 is unknown.
- **The Interval:** A level L classical confidence interval for the mean, μ, is

$$(\bar{Y} - \hat{\sigma}(\bar{Y})t_{n-1,(1+L)/2}, \; \bar{Y} + \hat{\sigma}(\bar{Y})t_{n-1,(1+L)/2}) \tag{5.8}$$

where $\hat{\sigma}(\bar{Y}) = S/\sqrt{n}$.

The interpretation of the confidence level L is that in repeated samples from the same normal population, a proportion L of all intervals will contain μ.

One final point about the $n - 1$ degrees of freedom in the t distribution. These are the degrees of freedom associated with $S^2 = \sum_{i=1}^{n}(Y_i - \bar{Y})^2/(n-1)$. At first glance, the formula for S^2 seems to require the n quantities, $Y_i - \bar{Y}$, $i = 1, \ldots, n$. However, a closer look reveals that the sum of the $Y_i - \bar{Y}$ equals 0. This means that knowing any $n - 1$ of the $Y_i - \bar{Y}$ is the same as knowing all n of them: for any j between 1 and n, $Y_j - \bar{Y}$ is the negative of the sum of the rest of the $Y_i - \bar{Y}$. The degrees of freedom counts the minimum number of the quantities $Y_i - \bar{Y}$ that are needed to compute S^2.

EXAMPLE 5.5   CONTINUED

Suppose that the researcher at the biotechnology company really doesn't know σ^2. To obtain a 95% confidence interval for μ, the researcher would use Equation (5.8). As the sample standard deviation of the measurements on the four rats is 54.4,[10] she obtains

$$\left(199 - \frac{54.4}{\sqrt{4}}t_{3,0.975}, \; 199 + \frac{54.4}{\sqrt{4}}t_{3,0.975}\right) = \left(199 - \frac{54.4}{\sqrt{4}}3.18, \; 199 + \frac{54.4}{\sqrt{4}}3.18\right)$$

$$= (112.4, 285.6)$$

Notice how the much larger value of $t_{3,0.975} = 3.18$ (compared with $z_{0.975} = 1.96$) results in a much wider interval. The greater width of this interval represents

---

[10]Although these data are from an actual experiment, in initially introducing Example 5.5, we pre-
that the sample standard deviation, S, was actually the population standard deviation, σ, and that
known to the experimenter. Neither was true, but this little white lie helped introduce confidence
ls in the simplest possible way.

the greater uncertainty about the value of μ due to having to estimate σ^2 from only four pieces of data.   ✦

If n is small and the population distribution is badly nonnormal, then we cannot say what the sampling distribution of $(\bar{Y} - \mu)/\hat{\sigma}(\bar{Y})$ will be. In this case, a transformation of the data, such as one of those suggested in Chapter 4, may help make the data more normal. However, the assumption is that the transformed data follows the C+E model and the resulting confidence interval will be for the population mean of that model.

5.5

PREDICTING A NEW OBSERVATION FROM THE C+E MODEL

We have seen how to estimate μ in the C+E model and how to quantify the uncertainty in that estimate by use of a confidence interval. Often, it is desired to predict a new observation from the C+E model that generated the data. Prediction is an extensive topic in its own right, and the selection of a predictor requires knowledge and skill. In this introduction to the topic, we will assume that the errors, ϵ, and hence the observed values, Y, in the C+E model, have a normal distribution. We will also assume that if we know μ in the C+E model, we will use μ to predict a future observation, and that if we don't know μ, we will use our chosen estimator of μ, $\hat{\mu}$.

Suppose to begin with that we know μ in the C+E model and that we use μ to predict a new observation. Call this new observation Y_{new}. When it is observed, Y_{new} will be generated from the C+E model as $Y_{\text{new}} = \mu + \epsilon_{\text{new}}$, where ϵ_{new} is a random-error term. The error in using μ to predict Y_{new} will be $Y_{\text{new}} - \mu = \epsilon_{\text{new}}$. There are two points to be made about predicting Y_{new} using the known value of μ:

- There is still going to be prediction error, even though we know μ.
- The prediction error, ϵ_{new}, is just the random error term associated with Y_{new}. This means that the variance of the prediction of a new observation is going to be the variance of the prediction error, ϵ_{new}, which is σ^2.

Of course, in reality we don't know μ, so we estimate it using $\hat{\mu} = \bar{Y}$. When using $\hat{\mu}$ to predict a new observation, we'll call it $\hat{Y}_{\text{new}}$. When using $\hat{Y}_{\text{new}}$ to predict a new observation, the prediction error is

$$Y_{\text{new}} - \hat{Y}_{\text{new}} = (\mu + \epsilon_{\text{new}}) - \hat{Y}_{\text{new}} = (\mu - \hat{Y}_{\text{new}}) + \epsilon_{\text{new}} \tag{5.9}$$

The term $(\mu - \hat{Y}_{\text{new}})$ in the rightmost expression of Equation (5.9) equals $(\mu - \hat{\mu})$ and is the error due to using $\hat{\mu}$ to estimate μ. Its variance is the variance of $\hat{\mu} = \bar{Y}$, which, as we know, is σ^2/n. The second term, ϵ_{new}, is the random error inherent in Y_{new}. Its variance, as we saw before, is σ^2. Since $\hat{Y}_{\text{new}}$, being computed from the current data, is independent of the new observation Y_{new}, the variance of $Y_{\text{new}} - \hat{Y}_{\text{new}}$ is the sum of the variances of $(\mu - \hat{Y}_{new})$ and ϵ_{new}. That is,

$$\sigma^2(Y_{new} - \hat{Y}_{new}) = \sigma^2(\mu - \hat{Y}_{new}) + \sigma^2(\epsilon_{new}) = \frac{\sigma^2}{n} + \sigma^2 = \sigma^2\left(1 + \frac{1}{n}\right) \qquad (5.10)$$

Now, of course, we rarely know σ^2, so we use the sample variance, S^2, to estimate it, which gives the estimated standard error of prediction

$$\hat{\sigma}(Y_{new} - \hat{Y}_{new}) = \sqrt{S^2\left[1 + \frac{1}{n}\right]} = S\sqrt{1 + \frac{1}{n}}$$

It turns out that

$$T = \frac{Y_{new} - \hat{Y}_{new}}{\hat{\sigma}(Y_{new} - \hat{Y}_{new})}$$

has a t_{n-1} distribution. Therefore,

$$L = P(-t_{n-1,(1+L)/2} < T < t_{n-1,(1+L)/2})$$
$$= P(\hat{Y}_{new} - \hat{\sigma}(Y_{new} - \hat{Y}_{new})t_{n-1,(1+L)/2} < Y_{new} < \hat{Y}_{new} + \hat{\sigma}(Y_{new} - \hat{Y}_{new})t_{n-1,(1+L)/2})$$

It follows that a level L prediction interval for a new observation is

$$(\hat{Y}_{new} - \hat{\sigma}(Y_{new} - \hat{Y}_{new})t_{n-1,(1+L)/2}, \ \hat{Y}_{new} + \hat{\sigma}(Y_{new} - \hat{Y}_{new})t_{n-1,(1+L)/2})$$

CLASSICAL PREDICTION INTERVAL FORMULA

- **Model:** C+E model, $Y = \mu + \epsilon$.
- **Data:** $Y_i = \mu + \epsilon_i$, $i = 1, \ldots, n$.
- **Assumptions:** The $\{\epsilon_i\}$ are independent $N(0, \sigma^2)$ random variables (so the $\{Y_i\}$ are independent $N(\mu, \sigma^2)$ random variables).
- **The Interval:** A level L classical prediction interval for a new observation is

$$(\hat{Y}_{new} - \hat{\sigma}(Y_{new} - \hat{Y}_{new})t_{n-1,(1+L)/2}, \ \hat{Y}_{new} + \hat{\sigma}(Y_{new} - \hat{Y}_{new})t_{n-1,(1+L)/2}) \qquad (5.11)$$

As with confidence intervals for a model parameter, the interpretation of a prediction is based on repeated samples from the given population. Suppose for each sample, a level L prediction interval is computed and that a new observation is then taken from the population. A proportion L of all constructed intervals will contain the new observation.

EXAMPLE 5.5   CONTINUED

We will use the artificial pancreas data to construct a 95% prediction interval for a new observation. We already know that $t_{3,0.975} = 3.18$. We compute

$$\hat{\sigma}(y_{new} - \hat{y}_{new}) = \sqrt{2958\left(1 + \frac{1}{4}\right)} = \sqrt{3697.5} = 60.8$$

So the desired interval is

$$(199 - (60.8)(3.18), 199 + (60.8)(3.18)) = (5.6, 392.4)$$

Notice that this 95% prediction interval for a new observation is much wider than the classical 95% confidence interval for μ. The extra width reflects the extra uncertainty involved in obtaining a completely new observation from the C+E model.

In interpreting this interval, the researcher can say:

Suppose I obtain another rat (i.e., a rat not in the sample of four rats) with the artificial pancreas. Suppose that I measure the blood-sugar level of this rat 1 hour after the ingestion of the glucose solution. I am 95% confident that the blood-sugar level of this new rat will fall between 5.6 and 392.4. My confidence rests in my use of a method to compute this interval that will produce an interval containing the blood-sugar level of a new rat in 95% of all possible identically run experiments. ◆

5.6

ESTIMATION OF A POPULATION PROPORTION

Consider a large population of which a proportion p has a certain characteristic. A random sample of size n is taken from the population and the presence or absence of the characteristic is measured. We will assume that Y, the total number of sample items having the characteristic, has, approximately or exactly, a $b(n, p)$ distribution. It is desired to estimate p.

A point estimator of p is the sample proportion having the characteristic, $\hat{p} = Y/n$. Since we know the distribution of Y and the value of n, we can find the distribution of $\hat{p}$. Using this, we can generate an exact confidence interval for p.

Exact Confidence Intervals

It is possible to compute exact confidence intervals for p, where by "exact" we mean that the probability a level L interval contains the true population proportion p is exactly L. These intervals are suitable for any n. However, these have traditionally been difficult to compute and so are usually introduced only in more advanced statistics courses. With modern computers, exact intervals can be computed easily, provided n is not too large. Whenever they can be used, exact intervals are the preferred choice.[11]

EXACT CONFIDENCE INTERVALS FOR A POPULATION PROPORTION

- **Data, Model:** $Y \sim b(n, p)$.
- **The Interval:** An exact level L confidence interval for p is (p_D, p_U), where
  - if $Y > 0$, p_D is the unique solution of

$$\sum_{y=Y}^{n} \frac{n!}{y!(n-y)!} p_D^y (1 - p_D)^{n-y} = \frac{1-L}{2} \tag{5.12}$$

  - if $Y = 0$,

$$p_D = 0 \tag{5.13}$$

and

  - if $Y < n$, p_U is the unique solution of

$$\sum_{y=0}^{Y} \frac{n!}{y!(n-y)!} p_U^y (1 - p_U)^{n-y} = \frac{1-L}{2} \tag{5.14}$$

  - if $Y = n$,

$$p_U = 1 \tag{5.15}$$

EXAMPLE 5.6   EXACT CONFIDENCE INTERVAL FOR A POPULATION PROPORTION

A quality inspector for a wire manufacturer must decide whether each outgoing shipment of wire spools meets quality standards. One quality measure involves taking a number of spools from the shipment at random and measuring the wire diameter at three places on each spool. The spool is acceptable if and only if all three measurements are in specification. The company is interested in the proportion of unacceptable wire spools in the shipment. In this instance, the population is the outgoing shipment of wire spools. To estimate the proportion of unacceptable wire spools in the shipment of 50,000 spools, the inspector takes a sample of 200 wire spools from the shipment, and finds that 11 are out of specification. The inspector decides to obtain an exact level 0.95 confidence interval for the true proportion of unacceptable wire spools in the shipment.

The size of the shipment is very large relative to the size of the sample, so the number of unacceptable spools in the sample should approximately follow

---

[11] The **Doing It with SAS** and **Doing It with MINITAB** supplements to this text give explicit instructions for generating exact confidence intervals for p in a $b(n, p)$ distribution using those packages.

a $b(200, p)$ distribution, where p is the true proportion of unacceptable wire spools in the shipment. The point estimate of p is $\hat{p} = 11/200 = 0.055$. As $0 < Y = 11 < 200$, we can find the endpoints of the exact level 0.95 confidence interval, p_D and p_U, by solving

$$p_D = \text{ the unique solution of } \sum_{y=11}^{200} \frac{200!}{y!(200-y)!} p_D^y (1 - p_D)^{200-y} = 0.025$$

$$p_U = \text{ the unique solution of } \sum_{y=0}^{11} \frac{200!}{y!(200-y)!} p_U^y (1 - p_U)^{200-y} = 0.025$$

The interval that results is $(0.028, 0.096)$. ✦

When n is very large, exact confidence intervals for p can be difficult to compute. In this case, the Central Limit Theorem provides a workable approximate solution.

Classical Estimation for Large Samples

If n is large, then we know from Chapter 4 that Y has approximately an $N(np, np(1-p))$ distribution. Since $\hat{p} = Y/n$, it also follows from the results of Chapter 4 that $\hat{p}$ has approximately an $N(p, p(1-p)/n)$ distribution. [12]

We can use this result to obtain confidence intervals for p. Noting that the standard error of $\hat{p}$ is $\sigma(\hat{p}) = \sqrt{p(1-p)/n}$, we have that (approximately)

$$\frac{\hat{p} - p}{\sigma(\hat{p})} \sim N(0, 1) \tag{5.16}$$

Starting with Equation (5.16) and using the same reasoning as we did in constructing confidence intervals for μ in the C+E model, we can obtain an approximate level L confidence interval for p as

$$(\hat{p} - \sigma(\hat{p})z_{(1+L)/2}, \ \hat{p} + \sigma(\hat{p})z_{(1+L)/2})$$

The only problem is that in order to compute this interval, we need to know $\sigma(\hat{p}) = \sqrt{p(1-p)/n}$, which means that we need to know p, the quantity we're trying to estimate! One solution is to replace $\sigma(\hat{p})$ with its estimate $\hat{\sigma}(\hat{p}) = \sqrt{\hat{p}(1-\hat{p})/n}$ in Equation (5.16), giving the approximate interval

$$(\hat{p} - \hat{\sigma}(\hat{p})z_{(1+L)/2}, \ \hat{p} + \hat{\sigma}(\hat{p})z_{(1+L)/2})$$

---

[12] Recall from Chapter 4 that the approximation of the $b(n, p)$ distribution by a normal distribution is reasonable for almost all applications if values of n and p satisfy $np \geq 10$ and $n(1-p) \geq 10$. If the values of p are between 0.3 and 0.7, $np \geq 5$ and $n(1-p) \geq 5$, will give an adequate approximation, and for the symmetric binomial distribution model $b(n, 0.5)$, n as small as 5 can provide a reasonable approximation. Of course, we won't know p, so we can substitute $n\hat{p} = Y$ for np and $n(1-\hat{p}) = n - Y$ for $n(1-p)$ when checking these rules of thumb.

CLASSICAL LARGE-SAMPLE CONFIDENCE INTERVAL FOR A POPULATION PROPORTION

- **Data, Model:** $Y \sim b(n, p)$.
- **Assumptions:** n is large (see footnote 12).
- **The Interval:** An approximate level L classical large-sample confidence interval for a population proportion, p, is

$$(\hat{p} - \hat{\sigma}(\hat{p})z_{(1+L)/2}, \ \hat{p} + \hat{\sigma}(\hat{p})z_{(1+L)/2}) \tag{5.17}$$

EXAMPLE 5.6　CONTINUED

We obtain an approximate level 0.95 classical large-sample confidence interval for the proportion of defective wire spools in the shipment. Recall that the wire inspector selected a sample of 200 spools and found that 11 are out of specification. He computes the estimate of p as $\hat{p} = 11/200 = 0.055$. He can't compute np and $n(1 - p)$, but he uses $n\hat{p} = 11$ and $n(1 - \hat{p}) = 189$ to estimate them. Since both exceed 10, the inspector is comfortable using the normal approximation. He computes

$$\hat{\sigma}(\hat{p}) = \sqrt{\frac{0.055(1 - 0.055)}{200}} = 0.016$$

Using Equation (5.17) and noting that $z_{(1+0.95)/2} = z_{0.975} = 1.96$, an approximate 95% confidence interval for p based on the normal approximation is

$$(0.055 - (0.016)(1.96), 0.055 + (0.016)(1.96)) = (0.023, 0.087)$$

Compare this approximate interval with the exact interval previously computed: (0.028, 0.096). ◆

5.7

DETERMINING THE SAMPLE SIZE

One consideration in designing a study is the **precision** desired in estimators or predictors. The precision of an estimator is a measure of how variable that estimator is. A useful way of expressing precision of an estimator is the width of a level L confidence interval based on that estimator. For a given population, precision is a function of the size of the sample: the larger the sample, the greater the precision.

　　Usually in designing a study, the desired precision is specified first and the sample size needed to attain that precision computed. As an example, suppose it is desired to estimate a population proportion p to within d units with confidence level L. If we assume a large enough sample size so the normal approximation can be used in computing the confidence interval, the requirement is that one-half the length of the confidence interval equal d, or

$$z_{(1+L)/2}\sqrt{p(1-p)/n} = d \qquad (5.18)$$

Solving Equation (5.18) for n gives the required sample size as

$$n = [p(1-p) \cdot z_{(1+L)/2}^2]/d^2 \qquad (5.19)$$

Of course, all this supposes we know p. If we don't, we can get an estimate from a pilot study. Or, since $p(1-p) \leq 0.25$,[13] we can use 0.25 in place of $p(1-p)$ in Equation (5.19) to get a conservative (i.e., too large) sample-size estimate.

There is an analogous formula when a simple random sample will be used and it is desired to estimate a population mean μ to within d units with confidence level L. If we assume a normal population, or a sample size large enough for the normal approximation to hold, the required sample size is

$$n = (\sigma^2 \cdot z_{(1+L)/2}^2)/d^2 \qquad (5.20)$$

Again, this supposes we know σ^2. If we don't, we can get an estimate from a pilot study. The following example illustrates these sample-size calculations.

EXAMPLE 5.7   CALCULATING SAMPLE SIZE

Consider the sample size necessary to estimate the proportion of Americans who prefer that federal government cutbacks be returned to taxpayers through lower taxes instead of being used to reduce the federal deficit. As a first approximation, assume that there are 200 million adult Americans, which for all intents and purposes is the same as an infinite population, and that we will take a simple random sample, despite the fact that a random sample is not really practical. Suppose we want the estimate to be accurate to within three percentage points with 90% confidence. Finally, assume that we have no idea what the true population proportion, p, is.

Since we have no idea what p is, we will use the upper bound 0.25 in place of $p(1-p)$. Since $z_{0.95} = 1.645$, we use Equation (5.19) to give a conservative estimate:

$$n = (0.25)(1.645)^2/(0.03)^2 = 752$$

rounded upward. So we have to sample 752 people to obtain the desired precision with the specified level of confidence.

If p is of moderate size, say, between 0.3 and 0.7, the n estimated using 0.25 for $p(1-p)$ will be reasonably close to the true n. However, it can overestimate appreciably if p is near 0 or 1. For example, suppose we know that $p = 0.7$. Then Equation (5.19) yields

$$n = (0.7)(0.3)(1.645)^2/(0.03)^2 = 642$$

[13] A demonstration of this fact is left as an exercise.

which is reasonably close to the conservative value of 752 computed previously. However, if $p = 0.92$, we get

$$n = (0.92)(0.08)(1.645)^2/(0.03)^2 = 222$$

a far smaller number than the conservative value of 752 or the value 642 obtained for $p = 0.7$.

As an example of the use of Equation (5.20), suppose we are measuring the diameters of ball bearings in a large shipment, and that we know that the variance of these measurements is always near 0.1 mm. Suppose also that we would like our estimate of mean diameter to be within 0.025 mm with 99% confidence. Since $z_{0.995} = 2.5758$, Equation (5.20) gives the sample size

$$n = (0.1)(2.5758)^2/(0.025)^2 = 1062 \quad \blacklozenge$$

5.8

ESTIMATION FOR TWO-POPULATION C+E DATA

Researchers and analysts are often confronted with the problem of comparing two populations. In particular, for a given measurement, are the two population distributions, or at least some aspects of the distributions, the same?

We will assume that there are n_1 measurements from population 1 generated by the C+E model

$$Y_{1,i} = \mu_1 + \epsilon_{1,i}, \qquad i = 1, \ldots, n_1$$

and n_2 measurements from population 2 generated by the C+E model

$$Y_{2,i} = \mu_2 + \epsilon_{2,i}, \qquad i = 1, \ldots, n_2$$

In this section, we will consider the most important comparisons for C+E data: comparison of μ_1 and μ_2.

Paired Comparisons

The simplest case is when we have **paired comparisons.** These are situations in which the data are paired in some way. Example 5.8 illustrates.

EXAMPLE 5.8   PAIRED COMPARISONS

Consider again the artificial pancreas experiment described previously. In the experiment, the researcher took readings of each rat's blood-sugar level prior to injection, just after injection, and then periodically during the 60 minutes after injection. She would like to compare the mean preinjection readings with the mean of the readings taken 60 minutes after the injection to see how far toward the normal levels the artificial pancreas had reduced blood sugar in 1 hour. The data are found in the first two columns of Table 5.2

**TABLE 5.2   Before and After Blood-Sugar Readings
and After–Before Differences: Rat Data, Example 5.8**

Rat	Initial Reading	Reading after 60 Minutes	Difference
1	170	266	96
2	134	149	15
3	99	161	62
4	84	220	136

The two populations are the preinjection readings and the readings 60 minutes after injection of all possible diabetic rats with this kind of artificial pancreas. The data are naturally paired since there are two blood-sugar readings on each rat. These scores are very likely to be related: Rats with high initial readings will likely have high readings after 60 minutes and rats with low initial readings will likely have low readings after 60 minutes.   ✦

Other examples of paired data are as follows:

- Repeated before-and-after test scores on each of a class of students.
- Measurements of paint reflectance of each of a set of panels just after painting and 6 months later.
- The IQs of identical twins separated at birth and raised in different environments.

As the last example shows, repeated measurements on the same sampling or experimental unit are not the only source of paired data. In some studies, different sampling or experimental units are artificially paired by matching them in terms of various characteristics: for example, patients in a study on medication may be matched for gender, race, age, health history, and other variables.

To obtain a confidence interval for the difference of population means, $\mu_1 - \mu_2$, we reduce the problem from a two-population one to a single-population one by considering the differences $D_i = Y_{1,i} - Y_{2,i}$. These differences follow a C+E model of their own:

$$D_i = (\mu_1 - \mu_2) + (\epsilon_{1,i} - \epsilon_{1,i}) = \mu_D + \epsilon_{D,i}$$

where $\mu_D = \mu_1 - \mu_2$ is the mean of the population of differences, and $\epsilon_{D,i} = \epsilon_{1,i} - \epsilon_{2,i}$ is the random error associated with the difference D_i.

A point estimator of μ_D is the sample mean of the differences:

$$\bar{D} = \frac{1}{n}\sum_{i=1}^{n} D_i$$

where $n = n_1 = n_2$. A confidence interval for μ_D is then obtained using Equation (5.8) for the differences:

$$(\bar{D} - \hat{\sigma}(\bar{D})t_{n-1,(1+L)/2}, \ \bar{D} + \hat{\sigma}(\bar{D})t_{n-1,(1+L)/2})$$

where $\hat{\sigma}(\bar{D}) = S_D/\sqrt{n}$, and

$$S_D = \sqrt{\frac{1}{n-1}\sum_{i=1}^{n}(D_i - \bar{D})^2}$$

Example 5.8 demonstrates estimation for paired data.

EXAMPLE 5.8 CONTINUED

The investigator in the artificial pancreas experiment wanted to calculate a classical level 0.95 confidence interval for mean differences in initial and 60-minute blood-sugar levels of diabetic rats. From Table 5.2, the differences between the readings after 60 minutes and the initial readings are

$$96 \quad 15 \quad 62 \quad 136$$

The mean of the differences is $\bar{d} = 77.25$ and the standard deviation is $s_d = 51.35$. The differenced data exhibit no extreme outliers, so the researcher concludes that a classical confidence interval is appropriate. Since $t_{3,0.975} = 3.18$, a 95% classical confidence interval for μ_d is

$$\left(77.25 - 3.18\frac{51.35}{\sqrt{4}}, \ 77.25 + 3.18\frac{51.35}{\sqrt{4}}\right) = (-4.5, 159.0)$$

Since this interval contains 0, the researcher cannot rule out the possibility that the population mean of the preinjection readings is the same as that of the readings taken 60 minutes after the injection. ◆

Independent Populations

When the two populations of interest are independent, comparisons do not reduce to the one-population case as they do for paired data. Mathematically, independence of the two populations means that the random variables representing the observations from population 1, $Y_{1,1}, Y_{1,2}, \ldots, Y_{1,n_1}$, are independent of those representing the observations from population 2, $Y_{2,1}, Y_{2,2}, \ldots, Y_{2,n_2}$. Practically speaking, independence will result from the way the data are obtained. If the samples from the two populations are selected randomly and independently of each other, and if the populations are not related in any way, then methods for independent populations are appropriate.

Let $\bar{Y}_1$ and $\bar{Y}_2$ denote the sample means from populations 1 and 2, respectively, and let S_1^2 and S_2^2 denote the corresponding sample variances.

The point estimator of the difference of the two population means, $\mu_1 - \mu_2$, is the difference of the sample means, $\bar{Y}_1 - \bar{Y}_2$. If the data are approximately normal, or if the sample sizes are large (the Central Limit Theorem strikes again!), then, at least approximately, $\bar{Y}_1$ and $\bar{Y}_2$ can be considered to have been drawn from an $N(\mu_1, \sigma_1^2/n_1)$

and $N(\mu_2, \sigma_2^2/n_2)$ distribution, respectively. This means that, approximately, at least, $\bar{Y}_1 - \bar{Y}_2$ can be considered to have come from an $N(\mu_1 - \mu_2, \sigma_1^2/n_1 + \sigma_2^2/n_2)$ distribution. Thus, the standard error of $\bar{Y}_1 - \bar{Y}_2$ is

$$\sigma(\bar{Y}_1 - \bar{Y}_2) = \sqrt{\frac{\sigma_1^2}{n_1} + \frac{\sigma_2^2}{n_2}}$$

and

$$Z = \frac{\bar{Y}_1 - \bar{Y}_2 - (\mu_1 - \mu_2)}{\sigma(\bar{Y}_1 - \bar{Y}_2)} \tag{5.21}$$

can be assumed to have been drawn from an $N(0, 1)$ distribution.

The procedure we will follow in constructing a confidence interval for $\mu_1 - \mu_2$ will be broken into four cases based on what we know or are willing to assume about the population.

Case 1: Known variances.   If σ_1^2 and σ_2^2 are known, then Z defined in Equation (5.21) is a pivotal quantity for $\mu_1 - \mu_2$, and we can use the same reasoning as for the one-population case to construct a level L classical confidence interval for $\mu_1 - \mu_2$:

$$(\bar{Y}_1 - \bar{Y}_2 - \sigma(\bar{Y}_1 - \bar{Y}_2)z_{(1+L)/2}, \ \bar{Y}_1 - \bar{Y}_2 + \sigma(\bar{Y}_1 - \bar{Y}_2)z_{(1+L)/2}) \tag{5.22}$$

Now, of course, the population variances are rarely known. So following the development of the one sample case, we substitute the sample variances from populations 1 and 2,

$$S_1^2 = \frac{\sum_{i=1}^{n_1}(Y_{1,i} - \bar{Y}_1)^2}{n_1 - 1}$$

$$S_2^2 = \frac{\sum_{i=1}^{n_2}(Y_{2,i} - \bar{Y}_2)^2}{n_2 - 1}$$

for σ_1^2 and σ_2^2 in the standard error formula, giving the estimated standard error

$$\hat{\sigma}(\bar{Y}_1 - \bar{Y}_2) = \sqrt{\frac{S_1^2}{n_1} + \frac{S_2^2}{n_2}}$$

Using the estimated standard error in Equation (5.21), we obtain

$$T = \frac{\bar{Y}_1 - \bar{Y}_2 - (\mu_1 - \mu_2)}{\hat{\sigma}(\bar{Y}_1 - \bar{Y}_2)} \tag{5.23}$$

At this point, we run into a difficulty, however, since t given by Equation (5.23) is not a pivotal quantity for $\mu_1 - \mu_2$, and there is no simple, general procedure on which to base a confidence interval for $\mu_1 - \mu_2$. To give a workable procedure for computing a confidence interval for $\mu_1 - \mu_2$, when the variances are unknown, we will consider three further cases.

Case 2: Unknown variances and both sample sizes large. If n_1 and n_2 are both large, t defined in Equation (5.23) has approximately a $N(0, 1)$ distribution. The size of n_1 and n_2 required for a good normal approximation depends on the population distribution: the more nearly normal the population is, the smaller the sample size needs be. A rule of thumb is that if the distributions are not terribly non-normal (you will have graphed them, of course!), then sample sizes of 30 or more will be sufficient. In this case, since the sample variances will be close to the population variances, and we get normality by the Central Limit Theorem, just use Equation (5.22) with the sample variances substituted for the population variances.

Case 3: Unknown variances, at least one sample size is small, and we are willing to assume that the two population variances are equal (but we don't know what they are). In this case, we can use a **pooled variance** confidence interval.

The idea is this. The common variance σ^2 of both populations can be estimated from population 1 by S_1^2 and from population 2 by S_2^2. The pooled variance estimator S_p^2 combines these two separate estimators together, weighting each according to its degrees of freedom:

$$S_p^2 = \frac{(n_1 - 1)S_1^2 + (n_2 - 1)S_2^2}{(n_1 - 1) + (n_2 - 1)} = \frac{(n_1 - 1)S_1^2 + (n_2 - 1)S_2^2}{n_1 + n_2 - 2}$$

The standard error of the estimator $\bar{Y}_1 - \bar{Y}_2$ is

$$\sigma_p(\bar{Y}_1 - \bar{Y}_2) = \sqrt{\sigma^2 \left(\frac{1}{n_1} + \frac{1}{n_2}\right)}$$

and we estimate this standard error by

$$\hat{\sigma}_p(\bar{Y}_1 - \bar{Y}_2) = \sqrt{S_p^2 \left(\frac{1}{n_1} + \frac{1}{n_2}\right)}$$

with the end result that

$$T^{(p)} = \frac{\bar{Y}_1 - \bar{Y}_2 - (\mu_1 - \mu_2)}{\hat{\sigma}_p(\bar{Y}_1 - \bar{Y}_2)}$$

is a pivotal quantity for $\mu_1 - \mu_2$, which has a $t_{n_1+n_2-2}$ distribution. This leads to a level L pooled variance confidence interval for $\mu_1 - \mu_2$:

$$(\bar{Y}_1 - \bar{Y}_2 - \hat{\sigma}_p(\bar{Y}_1 - \bar{Y}_2)t_{n_1+n_2-2,(1+L)/2}, \ \bar{Y}_1 - \bar{Y}_2 + \hat{\sigma}_p(\bar{Y}_1 - \bar{Y}_2)t_{n_1+n_2-2,(1+L)/2})$$

Case 4: Unknown variances, at least one sample size is small, and we are unwilling to assume the population variances are equal. In this case, we can use a modified version of Equation (5.22) as an **approximate** confidence interval. The formula is the following:

$$(\bar{Y}_1 - \bar{Y}_2 - \hat{\sigma}(\bar{Y}_1 - \bar{Y}_2)t_{\nu,(1+L)/2}, \ \bar{Y}_1 - \bar{Y}_2 + \hat{\sigma}(\bar{Y}_1 - \bar{Y}_2)t_{\nu,(1+L)/2}) \tag{5.24}$$

The degrees of freedom ν in Equation (5.24) is an approximate value taken as the largest integer less than or equal to

$$\left(\frac{S_1^2}{n_1} + \frac{S_2^2}{n_2}\right)^2 \bigg/ \left[\frac{(S_1^2/n_1)^2}{n_1 - 1} + \frac{(S_2^2/n_2)^2}{n_2 - 1}\right]$$

Most computer packages will compute a classical confidence interval for $\mu_1 - \mu_2$ based on Equation (5.24) or an equivalent formulation. The **Doing It with SAS** and **Doing It with MINITAB** supplements to this text give explicit instructions for users of those packages.

In deciding whether Case 3 or Case 4 applies, we must make a decision about whether the population variances are equal. Because such a decision must be based on the sample variances, the criteria for making such a decision are not clear cut, particularly if the sample sizes are small. One strategy, if we are really uncertain about which procedure to use, is to compute a confidence interval using both methods. If the two intervals are similar, then use the pooled variance interval, since it is based on a pivotal quantity if the population variances are equal, and as such is based on a known distribution. If the two intervals are substantially different, use the approximate, unequal variance interval.

CLASSICAL CONFIDENCE INTERVAL FORMULA FOR MEANS IN THE C+E MODEL: TWO INDEPENDENT POPULATIONS

- **For All Cases:**
    - **Model:** C+E model for population $i = 1, 2$; $Y_i = \mu_i + \epsilon_i$.
    - **Data:**

        $$Y_{1,j} = \mu_1 + \epsilon_{1,j}; \; j = 1, \ldots, n_1 (\text{population } 1)$$

        $$Y_{2,j} = \mu_2 + \epsilon_{2,j}; \; j = 1, \ldots, n_2 (\text{population } 2).$$

    - **Assumptions:** The $\{Y_{1,j}\}$ are independent of each other and of the $\{Y_{2,j}\}$. The $\{Y_{2,j}\}$ are independent of each other and of the $\{Y_{1,j}\}$.

- **Case 1: Known Variances**
    - **Assumptions:**
        1. Either
            (a) n_1 and n_2 are large, or
            (b) The $\epsilon_{1,j}$ are from an $N(0, \sigma_1^2)$ population, and the $\epsilon_{2,j}$ are from an $N(0, \sigma_2^2)$ population.
        2. σ_1^2 and σ_2^2 are known.
    - **The Interval:** A level L classical confidence interval for the difference of means, $\mu_1 - \mu_2$, is

        $$\left(\bar{Y}_1 - \bar{Y}_2 - \sigma(\bar{Y}_1 - \bar{Y}_2)z_{(1+L)/2}, \; \bar{Y}_1 - \bar{Y}_2 + \sigma(\bar{Y}_1 - \bar{Y}_2)z_{(1+L)/2}\right)$$

        (continued)

where

$$\sigma(\bar{Y}_1 - \bar{Y}_2) = \sqrt{\frac{\sigma_1^2}{n_1} + \frac{\sigma_2^2}{n_2}}$$

- **Case 2: Uknown Variances, n_1 and n_2 Large.** This case is treated exactly as Case 1 except that $\sigma(\bar{Y}_1 - \bar{Y}_2)$ is replaced by $\hat{\sigma}(\bar{Y}_1 - \bar{Y}_2) = \sqrt{S_1^2/n_1 + S_2^2/n_2}$, where S_1 and S_2 are the sample standard deviations computed from the data from populations 1 and 2, respectively.

- **Case 3: Variances Unknown, but Assumed to Be Equal, n_1 and n_2 Not Both Large**
  - **Assumptions:**
    1. The $\epsilon_{1,j}$ are from an $N(0, \sigma_1^2)$ population, and the $\epsilon_{2,j}$ are from an $N(0, \sigma_2^2)$ population.
    2. σ_1^2 and σ_2^2 are unknown, but are assumed to be equal.
  - **The Interval:** A level L confidence interval for $\mu_1 - \mu_2$ is

$$\left(\bar{Y}_1 - \bar{Y}_2 - \hat{\sigma}_p(\bar{Y}_1 - \bar{Y}_2)t_{\nu,(1+L)/2}, \ \bar{Y}_1 - \bar{Y}_2 + \hat{\sigma}_p(\bar{Y}_1 - \bar{Y}_2)t_{\nu,(1+L)/2}\right)$$

where

$$\hat{\sigma}_p(\bar{Y}_1 - \bar{Y}_2) = \sqrt{S_p^2\left(\frac{1}{n_1} + \frac{1}{n_2}\right)}, \qquad S_p^2 = \frac{(n_1 - 1)S_1^2 + (n_2 - 1)S_2^2}{n_1 + n_2 - 2}$$

S_1 and S_2 are the sample standard deviations computed from the data from populations 1 and 2, respectively, and $\nu = n_1 + n_2 - 2$.

- **Case 4: Variances Unknown, and Not Assumed to Be Equal, n_1 and n_2 Not Both Large**
  - **Assumptions:**
    1. The $\epsilon_{1,j}$ are from an $N(0, \sigma_1^2)$ population, and the $\epsilon_{2,j}$ are from an $N(0, \sigma_2^2)$ population.
    2. σ_1^2 and σ_2^2 are unknown, and are not assumed to be equal.
  - **The Interval:** A level L confidence interval for $\mu_1 - \mu_2$ is

$$\left(\bar{Y}_1 - \bar{Y}_2 - \hat{\sigma}(\bar{Y}_1 - \bar{Y}_2)t_{\nu,(1+L)/2}, \ \bar{Y}_1 - \bar{Y}_2 + \hat{\sigma}(\bar{Y}_1 - \bar{Y}_2)t_{\nu,(1+L)/2}\right)$$

where

$$\hat{\sigma}(\bar{Y}_1 - \bar{Y}_2) = \sqrt{\frac{S_1^2}{n_1} + \frac{S_2^2}{n_2}}$$

S_1 and S_2 are the sample standard deviations computed from the data from populations 1 and 2, respectively, and the degrees of freedom ν is taken as the largest integer less than or equal to

$$\left(\frac{S_1^2}{n_1} + \frac{S_2^2}{n_2}\right)^2 \bigg/ \left[\frac{(S_1^2/n_1)^2}{n_1 - 1} + \frac{(S_2^2/n_2)^2}{n_2 - 1}\right]$$

Example 5.9 shows how to compute confidence intervals for the differences of means of two independent populations.

EXAMPLE 5.9   CONFIDENCE INTERVALS FOR DIFFERENCES OF MEANS OF TWO INDEPENDENT POPULATIONS

We revisit the artificial pancreas experiment. In order to evaluate the performance of the artificial pancreas, the researcher performed the same experiment on a control group consisting of diabetic rats drawn from the same population as the experimental group of rats. The control group did not receive the artificial pancreas, however. The researcher wished to compare the blood-sugar readings 60 minutes after injection for the experimental group with those for the control group. In particular, she wanted to estimate the difference in population means using a 99% confidence interval. The data are

	Untreated Diabetic	Artificial Pancreas
	402	266
	305	149
	496	161
	421	220
$\bar{y}$	406.0	199.0
s	78.6	54.4

The standard deviations between the two groups are not excessively different, so the pooled variance procedure should give good results. As a check, the researcher decides to also compute a confidence interval based on the approximate t procedure. If both procedures give similar results, she can be confident of her conclusions. If they give very different results, she will have to check the data carefully. Plots of these data reveal no extreme outliers, so neither the pooled nor the approximate t procedure is ruled out on that account.

She first obtains the pooled variance interval.

$$s_p^2 = \frac{(n_1 - 1)s_1^2 + (n_2 - 1)s_2^2}{n_1 + n_2 - 2} = \frac{(4 - 1)78.6^2 + (4 - 1)54.4^2}{4 + 4 - 2} = 4568.7$$

$$\hat{\sigma}_p(\bar{y}_1 - \bar{y}_2) = \sqrt{s_p^2\left(\frac{1}{n_1} + \frac{1}{n_2}\right)} = \sqrt{4568.7\left(\frac{1}{4} + \frac{1}{4}\right)} = 47.9$$

and so, since $t_{6,0.995} = 3.707$, a 99% confidence interval for $\mu_1 - \mu_2$ is

$$(406 - 199 - (47.9)(3.707), 406 - 199 + (47.9)(3.707)) = (29.4, 384.6)$$

The researcher concludes that the mean blood-sugar readings 60 minutes after injection for the population of diabetic rats with the artificial pancreas is between 29.4 and 384.6 units lower than for the population of those without the artificial pancreas. Notice that the entire interval lies above 0, suggesting a real difference in the population means.

The researcher next uses the approximate t procedure. She first computes the degrees of freedom ν for the approximate t procedure.

$$\left(\frac{S_1^2}{n_1} + \frac{S_2^2}{n_2}\right)^2 \Big/ \left[\frac{(S_1^2/n_1)^2}{n_1 - 1} + \frac{(S_2^2/n_2)^2}{n_2 - 1}\right]$$

$$= \left(\frac{78.6^2}{4} + \frac{54.4^2}{4}\right)^2 \Big/ \left[\frac{(78.6^2/4)^2}{4 - 1} + \frac{(54.4^2/4)^2}{4 - 1}\right] = 5.3$$

so she takes $\nu = 5$. The estimated standard error is

$$\hat{\sigma}(\bar{y}_1 - \bar{y}_2) = \sqrt{\frac{78.6^2}{4} + \frac{54.4^2}{4}} = 47.8$$

As the researcher wanted a 99% confidence interval, and as $t_{5,0.995} = 4.032$, the interval is

$$(406 - 199 - (47.8)(4.032), 406 - 199 + (47.8)(4.032)) = (14.3, 399.7)$$

The researcher concludes from the approximate interval that the mean blood-sugar readings 60 minutes after injection for the population of diabetic rats with the artificial pancreas is between 14.3 and 399.7 units lower than for the population of those without the artificial pancreas.

Notice that the two intervals are similar. This should be the case if the sample variances are reasonably close, as they are here. ◆

5.9

COMPARING TWO POPULATION PROPORTIONS

Suppose there are two populations, in the first of which a proportion p_1 has a certain characteristic and in the second of which a proportion p_2 has that same characteristic. We want to compare the two proportions p_1 and p_2. To do so, we take a random sample of size n_1 from population 1 and another random sample of size n_2 from population 2. Suppose that Y_1 of the sample from population 1 and Y_2 of the sample from population 2 have the characteristic. We assume the following:

- $Y_1 \sim b(n_1, p_1)$ and $Y_2 \sim b(n_2, p_2)$.
- Y_1 and Y_2 are independent random variables.
- n_1 and n_2 are large enough for the Central Limit Theorem to hold.[14]

[14]Each of n_1 and n_2 should satisfy the guidelines given in footnote 12 for binomial data from a single population.

Then the sample proportions $\hat{p}_1 = Y_1/n_1$ and $\hat{p}_2 = Y_2/n_2$ are independent, and $\hat{p}_1$ has approximately an $N(p_1, p_1(1 - p_1)/n_1)$ distribution and $\hat{p}_2$ has approximately an $N(p_2, p_2(1 - p_2)/n_2)$ distribution.

The natural point estimator of $p_1 - p_2$ is $\hat{p}_1 - \hat{p}_2$, which has approximately an

$$N\left(p_1 - p_2, \frac{p_1(1 - p_1)}{n_1} + \frac{p_2(1 - p_2)}{n_2}\right)$$

distribution. We may then use the (by now) standard reasoning to come up with an approximate level L confidence interval for $p_1 - p_2$:

$$(\hat{p}_1 - \hat{p}_2 - \hat{\sigma}(\hat{p}_1 - \hat{p}_2)z_{(1+L)/2}, \hat{p}_1 - \hat{p}_2 + \hat{\sigma}(\hat{p}_1 - \hat{p}_2)z_{(1+L)/2}) \qquad (5.25)$$

where

$$\hat{\sigma}(\hat{p}_1 - \hat{p}_2) = \sqrt{\frac{\hat{p}_1(1 - \hat{p}_1)}{n_1} + \frac{\hat{p}_2(1 - \hat{p}_2)}{n_2}}$$

is the estimated standard error of $\hat{p}_1 - \hat{p}_2$.

CLASSICAL LARGE-SAMPLE CONFIDENCE INTERVAL: DIFFERENCE IN POPULATION PROPORTIONS

- **Data, Model:** $Y_1 \sim b(n_1, p_1)$; $Y_2 \sim b(n_2, p_2)$.
- **Assumptions:**
  - n_1 and n_2 are large (see footnote 12).
  - Y_1 and Y_2 are independent.
- **The Interval:** An approximate level L classical large-sample confidence interval for the difference in population proportion, $p_1 - p_2$, is

$$(\hat{p}_1 - \hat{p}_2 - \hat{\sigma}(\hat{p}_1 - \hat{p}_2)z_{(1+L)/2}, \hat{p}_1 - \hat{p}_2 + \hat{\sigma}(\hat{p}_1 - \hat{p}_2)z_{(1+L)/2})$$

where

$$\hat{\sigma}(\hat{p}_1 - \hat{p}_2) = \sqrt{\frac{\hat{p}_1(1 - \hat{p}_1)}{n_1} + \frac{\hat{p}_2(1 - \hat{p}_2)}{n_2}}$$

EXAMPLE 5.10   CONFIDENCE INTERVAL FOR THE DIFFERENCE OF TWO POPULATION PROPORTIONS

The quality inspector from Example 5.6 wants to use a 90% confidence interval to compare the proportions of defectives in two large shipments of wire spools. For data, he takes a random sample of 100 spools from shipment 1 and another random sample of 200 spools from shipment 2. Since the number of spools in each shipment is very large, the inspector feels comfortable in using the binomial distribution to model the numbers of defective spools in the two samples.

Of the 100 spools from shipment 1, 13 are defective, and 34 of the 200 spools from shipment 2 are defective. Therefore, the sample proportions of defectives are $\hat{p}_1 = 0.13$ and $\hat{p}_2 = 0.17$, respectively. Since $n_1\hat{p}_1 = Y_1 = 13$, $n_1(1 - \hat{p}_1) = n_1 - Y_1 = 87$, $n_2\hat{p}_2 = Y_2 = 34$ and $n_2(1 - \hat{p}_2) = n_2 - Y_2 = 166$ all exceed 10, the inspector knows he is justified in using the normal approximation. The estimated standard error of $\hat{p}_1 - \hat{p}_2$ is

$$\hat{\sigma}(\hat{p}_1 - \hat{p}_2) = \sqrt{\frac{0.13(1 - 0.13)}{100} + \frac{0.17(1 - 0.17)}{200}} = 0.043$$

Since $z_{0.95} = 1.645$, an approximate 90% confidence interval for $p_1 - p_2$ is

$$(0.13 - 0.17 - (0.043)(1.645), 0.13 - 0.17 + (0.043)(1.645)) = (-0.11, 0.03)$$

Do the two shipments differ in their proportions of defectives? Since the confidence interval contains 0, these data provide insufficient evidence to conclude that there is a difference. ✦

5.10

CLASSICAL TOLERANCE INTERVALS

Confidence intervals are a tool to quantify the uncertainty about model parameters. Prediction intervals quantify the uncertainty about new observations from a population. **Tolerance intervals** quantify another kind of uncertainty. Tolerance intervals are used to give a range of values that, with a prespecified confidence, will contain at least a prespecified proportion of the measurements in the population.

To define a tolerance interval, we first introduce the following notation. Suppose T_1 and T_2 are estimators with $T_1 \leq T_2$, and that γ is a real number between 0 and 1. Let $A(T_1, T_2, \gamma)$ denote the event {The proportion of measurements in the population between T_1 and T_2 is at least γ}.

> **DEFINITION**
>
> A level L tolerance interval for a proportion γ of a population is an interval (T_1, T_2), where T_1 and T_2 are estimators, having the property that
>
> $$P(A(T_1, T_2, \gamma)) = L$$

Classical tolerance intervals may be used if the population distribution is approximately normal. Therefore, throughout our discussion of tolerance intervals, we will assume that the data $Y_1, Y_2, \ldots, Y_n$ constitute a random sample from an $N(\mu, \sigma^2)$ distribution.

To give an idea of what a tolerance interval measures, suppose we know μ and σ^2. Then the interval

$$(\mu - K\sigma, \mu + K\sigma)$$

will contain a proportion γ of the population if $K = z_{(1+\gamma)/2}$. In this case, we are certain that the interval given by

$$(\mu - z_{(1+\gamma)/2}\sigma, \mu + z_{(1+\gamma)/2}\sigma) \tag{5.26}$$

will contain a proportion γ of the population. Therefore, the interval given by Equation (5.26) is a level $L = 1$ tolerance interval for a proportion γ of the population.

Unfortunately, we don't often know μ and σ, so we use the data to estimate them. We would like to use an interval of the form

$$(\bar{Y} - KS, \bar{Y} + KS) \tag{5.27}$$

as a tolerance interval, where the sample mean $\bar{Y}$ is used to estimate the population mean, μ, and the sample standard deviation S is used to estimate the population standard deviation, σ. The problem is that $\bar{Y}$ and S are computed from the sample data, and therefore are random. No matter what we choose for K, for some samples, the interval (5.27) will contain at least a proportion γ of the population, and for some samples, it won't. Using statistical theory, the best we can do is to choose K to ensure that a proportion L of all possible intervals computed using Equation (5.27) will contain at least a proportion γ of the population. These constants K have been computed for $L = 0.90,\ 0.95,$ and 0.99, and are found in Table A.8, in Appendix A, page 913.

CLASSICAL TOLERANCE INTERVAL FORMULA

- **Model:** C+E model, $Y = \mu + \epsilon$.
- **Data:** $Y_i = \mu + \epsilon_i,\ i = 1, \ldots, n$.
- **Assumptions:** The $\{\epsilon_i\}$ are independent $N(0, \sigma^2)$ random variables (so the $\{Y_i\}$ are independent $N(\mu, \sigma^2)$ random variables).
- **The Interval:** A level L normal theory tolerance interval for a proportion γ of the population of measurements is

$$(\bar{Y} - KS, \bar{Y} + KS)$$

where $\bar{Y}$ and S are the sample mean and standard deviation, and K is a mathematically derived constant depending on L, γ, and the number of observations, n.

Before using the classical tolerance interval, you should check the data to see if the assumption of normality is reasonable.

EXAMPLE 5.11 CLASSICAL TOLERANCE INTERVAL

A manufacturer of ceramic tiles is concerned about the uniformity of thickness in a certain model of tile. To measure the uniformity of thickness, the thickness of each tile is measured at nine prespecified locations, and the standard deviation of the nine measurements is computed. Based on historical data, the manufacturer is willing to assume that the uniformity measurements follow a normal distribution.

For this study, the manufacturer takes a sample of 200 tiles from a single large production lot with the goal of finding a range of values that he is 95% certain will contain at least 99% of all uniformity measurements in the lot. Suppose Y_i denotes the uniformity measure of tile i, and that $\bar{y}$ and s from the sample of 200 tiles are 0.191 and 0.001 mm, respectively. In order to obtain a tolerance interval that he will be 95% certain will contain at least 99% of all uniformity measurements, the manufacturer takes $L = 0.95$ and $\gamma = 0.99$. From the table of constants for normal-theory tolerance intervals, Table A.8 in Appendix A, page 913, the value of K is found to be 2.816, and so the desired tolerance interval is

$$0.191 \pm (2.816)(0.001) = (0.188, 0.194).$$

The interpretation of this interval involves long-run proportions: If the manufacturer repeatedly selects samples from the lot and for each sample computes a level 0.95 tolerance interval for a proportion 0.99 of the population, then approximately 95% of all those intervals will actually contain 99% or more of the lot's uniformity measurements. ✦

5.11

ROBUSTNESS

Recall from Chapter 2 that a measure is **resistant** if it is not greatly altered by outliers in a data set. An analogous concept for estimators and other statistical procedures is **robustness.** An estimator or procedure is **robust** if it performs well even when the assumptions on which it is based are violated. The classical normal-theory t interval defined in this chapter is reasonably robust to nonnormality, especially if the true population has a symmetric distribution. Interestingly, the normal-theory interval (5.6) is less robust to nonnormality than the t interval is.

Some estimators of μ, such as the sample mean, are not robust to outliers. As a result, the performance of the classical intervals for μ can suffer in the presence of outliers. Lab 5.2 shows that for at least some kinds of simulated data, the effect of outliers on the classical t interval (5.8) for μ is to cause

- the proportion of intervals containing μ to be lower than the stated confidence level.
- interval widths to be wider, on average.

This lack of robustness is a good reason to carefully examine the data for outliers when constructing confidence intervals, especially for small sample sizes.

Some robust estimators are described in Chapter 11.

D ISCUSSION QUESTIONS

1. What is statistical inference? What types of inference are considered in this chapter?
2. What is the C+E model? Describe two different applications for which it is appropriate.
3. What is a sampling distribution?
4. What is a point estimator? A confidence interval?
5. Compare and contrast the notions of estimator and estimate.
6. Describe classical confidence intervals for μ when σ^2 is known. Describe their interpretation.
7. Describe the t distribution. How does it differ from an $N(0, 1)$?
8. Describe classical confidence intervals for μ when σ^2 is unknown.
9. Describe classical predictions for future observations from the C+E model. How do prediction intervals differ from confidence intervals?
10. Describe exact and large sample classical confidence intervals for p from a binomial population. Which would you prefer to use?
11. Explain how you would find a classical confidence interval for the difference in means in a paired comparison.
12. Describe how to construct classical confidence intervals for the difference of means in two independent populations.
13. Describe how to construct large-sample classical confidence intervals for the difference of proportions in two independent populations.
14. What are tolerance intervals? How do they differ from confidence and prediction intervals? Give the ideas behind classical tolerance intervals.
15. Explain the idea of robustness of an estimator. Is the classical t interval for a population mean robust to nonnormality? Is it robust to outliers?

E XERCISES

5.1. Explain the meaning of "sampling distribution of an estimator." What is the value of knowing it, either exactly or approximately? Give an example.
5.2. A test for the level of potassium in the blood is not perfectly precise. Moreover, the actual level of potassium in a person's blood varies slightly from day to day. Julie's blood potassium level was measured over the past 16 days, and the mean and standard deviation for these 16 measurements are 3.2 and 0.2, respectively. Past experience indicates that these measurements behave as independent observations from a normal distribution.
    (a) Assuming interest is in inference about Julie's mean blood potassium level, name the kind of interval that should be used. Compute it for a 90% level of confidence.
    (b) If Julie does not want to take her blood potassium level tomorrow, and interest is in

inference about that reading, name the kind of interval that should be used. Compute it for a 90% level of confidence.

(c) Explain the meaning of the intervals in both (a) and (b).

5.3. It is believed that a sample taken in a recent TV survey was representative of the American public. Individuals interviewed in the survey were asked whether they approved of Mr. Clinton's presidency. Of the 10,000 responses, 5,500 people said "yes." Do the responses suggest that President Clinton is doing better than 50–50? Explain your arguments using a confidence interval. Explain why you chose the particular kind of interval you used.

5.4. The percentages of carbon in incoming shipments of steel from two different vendors are to be compared. The means and variances of percent carbon computed from random samples taken from the shipments are shown in Table 5.3. Assuming that all necessary assumptions are satisfied, compute and interpret an appropriate confidence interval.

TABLE 5.3   Summary Statistics for Carbon in Steel, Exercise 5.4

Shipment	n	$\bar{y}$	s^2
1	10	3.62	0.086
2	8	3.18	0.082

5.5. Creators of a new method for forecasting company profits claim that their method will be accurate to within 5% on average for 1 year ahead forecasts. Data from a random sample of companies yielded a 95% confidence interval of (3.2%, 5.9%) for the mean accuracy of their method.

(a) Interpret this interval in terms of long-run frequencies.

(b) Does this interval contradict the claim of forecasting accuracy? Why or why not?

5.6. Suppose we compute two 99% classical confidence intervals for μ when σ is known: one using a sample of 100 observations and one using a sample of 10,000 observations. Which interval will be wider? By what factor will it be wider?

5.7. The breaking strengths of five large metal pins used in building construction randomly chosen from a large production lot are (in psi)

$$42,110, \quad 42,550, \quad 41,895, \quad 42,285, \quad 41,990$$

The head of the quality unit wants a 95% confidence interval for μ, the mean strength of the pins in the lot.

(a) Construct the interval.

(b) Interpret what "95% confidence" means.

(c) Over the years, the company has managed to maintain a mean strength of 42,300 for these pins. Does that seem reasonable in light of these data? Why?

5.8. Noted television personality Stuart Smalley claims: "I'm good enough, I'm smart enough, and gosh darn it, people like me." To ascertain whether the last part of the statement is true, a national polling organization asked 900 individuals randomly sampled from the American public, "Gosh darn it, do you like Stuart?" Of the 900 sampled, 423 said they liked Stuart and the other 477 said they didn't.

(a) To what population can the pollsters make inference?

(b) With 95% confidence, estimate the proportion of the population that likes Stuart.

(c) Tell what is meant by "95% confidence" here.

(d) When asked to clarify his statement, Stuart said he meant that a majority of the American public like him. Does the result in (b) contradict this claim? Why?

5.9. Zeolites are aluminum and silicon crystals that are used as sieves and catalysts in many industries—especially petroleum refining. The relative yields (in percent) of the 16 most recent batches of zeolite produced by a particular manufacturer are, in order of production:

> 39.5 33.3 36.2 33.0 40.4 31.1 40.1 44.4 35.7 33.4 42.6 34.5 35.7 29.5 35.3 37.8

(a) Do these data provide evidence that the process that generated the data is nonstationary? Make an appropriate plot to decide.

(b) If you conclude that the process that generated the data is stationary, analyze the pattern of variation. Include a discussion of possible outliers, and use appropriate graphs and numerical measures to summarize the data.

(c) Is it reasonable to assume that the yields were generated by the C+E model? Why? If your answer is yes, tell what the model components mean for these data.

(d) If appropriate, obtain a point estimate of μ in the C+E model. Obtain a level 0.95 classical confidence interval for the mean yield. Interpret the interval. What does level 0.95 mean here?

(e) For planning purposes, management needs a range of values which they are 95% confident will encompass at least 99% of all batch yields. Construct and interpret an interval that will meet their needs.

(f) Based on these data, predict the yield of the next zeolite batch and construct a level 0.95 prediction interval. The yield of the next zeolite batch is 26.5. Based on the interval you constructed, what do you conclude?

5.10. The following table shows the preferences for two brands of chocolate chip cookies in a recently conducted double-blind taste-testing experiment involving 245 randomly selected college students. Do the data provide evidence that the proportion of female students who prefer cookie A to cookie B is greater than is the proportion of male students who prefer cookie A to cookie B? Use an appropriate confidence interval to decide. Tell why the particular kind of interval you use is the best choice.

	Cookie A	Cookie B	Total
Male Students	94	85	179
Female Students	39	27	66
Total	133	112	245

5.11. Recently, a student group conducted a double-blind taste-testing experiment to study whether the taste of Sprite is preferred to that of 7-Up. An SRS of 185 individuals was obtained from students at a local college and 115 of the 185 said they preferred Sprite over 7-Up.

(a) To what population can the student group make inference?

(b) Obtain a point estimate of the proportion of the population that prefers Sprite. Construct an interval estimate that estimates this proportion with 95% confidence. Justify your choice of interval.

(c) A Sprite drinker claims that a majority of American people prefer Sprite over 7-Up. Can the result in (b) be used to decide whether his claim is accurate? Why or why not?

(d) Based on the result in (b), what kind of conclusion can you draw in order to decide whether the taste of Sprite is preferred to that of 7-up? Give your argument.

5.12. A production engineer wants to determine the effect of machine configuration on the maximum force, in pounds, applied at a joint on an articulated arm of the machine during its normal operation. To do this, she obtains maximum force readings for each of two different machine configurations. Neither historical experience nor investigation of the present data give any reason to suspect that the data are nonnormal. The summary measures for the data are shown in Table 5.4.

TABLE 5.4   Summary Statistics for Machine Force, Exercise 5.12

Configuration	n	$\bar{y}$	s
1	6	543.1	98.7
2	9	593.6	33.2

Compare the population mean force readings for the two configurations at a 0.95 confidence level. What do you conclude?

5.13. WPI undergraduates, for whom three courses in every 7-week term is considered a full load, are supposed to spend an average of 17 hours per week on each course (including class time). A random sample of 49 students in the introductory statistics course was asked to keep track of the time they spent on the course during the term. The mean time was 17.5 hours per week with a standard deviation of 4.2 hours.

(a) Construct a level 0.95 confidence interval for the mean time spent on introductory statistics.

(b) Do these data supply convincing evidence that the mean time spent by introductory statistics students exceeds the school guideline? Justify your answer.

5.14. The fire endurance of a wall is the time required for a fire of a given intensity on one side of the wall to breach the wall, to raise the temperature at any single point on the opposite side of the wall to one prespecified level or to raise the overall temperature on the opposite side of the wall to another prespecified level. In 16 tests of a new type of wall, the mean fire endurance is 126 minutes and the standard deviation is 16 minutes. The data show no evidence of nonnormality.

(a) If the building code requires 99% confidence that the mean fire endurance of walls exceeds 120 minutes, what conclusions can you draw?

(b) Obtain a 99% prediction interval for the fire endurance of the next wall to be tested. Interpret the interval.

(c) The testers want a range of fire endurance values they can be 99% confident will contain at least 95% of the actual fire endurances of all walls of this type. Obtain such an interval.

(d) Another set of 25 fire-endurance tests is done on an alternative type of wall, resulting in a mean fire endurance of 116 minutes and standard deviation of 9 minutes. These data also show no evidence of nonnormality. Obtain a 99% confidence interval for the difference in mean fire endurance of the two wall types. With 99% confidence, can we conclude that there is no difference in the mean fire endurance of the two types of walls? If not, what can we conclude?

5.15. Just before the O. J. Simpson murder case went to the jury, a national poll was done in which 108 of a random sample of 150 whites told interviewers they thought Simpson was guilty and 77 of a random sample of 100 nonwhites told interviewers they thought Simpson was not guilty.

(a) Obtain a point estimate of the difference in the proportion of all whites and nonwhites who thought Simpson was guilty.

(b) Obtain a 99% confidence interval for the difference in proportions. Can we be 99% confident that the true proportions are different? Explain what is meant by 99% confidence in the statistical procedure you use.

5.16. We take a sample of 16 rats and measure the lengths of their tails, and find the standard deviation of the lengths to be 1.1 inches ($s = 1.1$). What is the estimate of the standard error of the prediction of the length of the next rat's tail to be measured?

5.17. Ten measurements of the weight of a "1-kilogram" brick of gold have an average of 1 kg, 245 μg,[15] with a standard deviation of 328 μg.

(a) What characteristics of the process that produced the data do you think are responsible for the observed variation?

(b) Explain why the C+E model is appropriate for these data. What are the parameters of the model and their meanings for these data?

(c) Find a 90% confidence interval for the true weight of the gold brick. What assumptions are necessary for this interval to be valid?

(d) Each day over the next year, 10 weighings of the brick will be taken and a 90% confidence interval computed. How many of those intervals do you expect to contain the true weight of the brick? What are you assuming about the weighing process in making this statement?

5.18. I am selecting students to be on a basketball team. It is hoped that a good percentage of the students whom I select will be fairly tall. To help judge how tall is tall, I wish to use a random sample of students to construct an interval that I am 95% confident will cover the heights of 75% of the students on campus. What is the name of the kind of interval that I wish to construct? Explain briefly why this was your choice, and a bit about the interval.

5.19. One technique for detecting breast cancer is graphic stress telethermometry (GST). Scientists are planning to take a sample of women known to have breast cancer and see how many were accurately diagnosed with breast cancer via GST. How many women must they sample to construct a level 0.90 confidence interval for the true proportion of accurate detections by GST if the interval is to be only 0.05 wide (i.e., they wish to estimate the true proportion to within ± 0.025.)?

5.20. A study is done to see if secondborn children are any more intelligent than firstborn children. A sample of 23 two-child families is taken, and the IQ score of each of the 46 children (at age 10) is recorded. What kind of confidence interval should be constructed to investigate the difference in mean IQ scores between the firstborns and secondborns? Be very specific!

5.21. In order to evaluate the performance of a certain brand of alkaline battery, researchers at a consumer testing organization took a random sample of 152 new AA batteries. The batteries were subjected to the same pattern of discharge designed to simulate typical moderate use. The time for the output of each 1.5-volt battery to drop to 0.9 volt was recorded. The mean lifetime of these 152 batteries was 46.7 hours and the standard deviation was 13.3 hours.

---

[15] one microgram $= 1 \times 10^{-6}$ gram.

    (a) To what population would inferences based on this sample of 152 be made?

    (b) Find a level 0.95 confidence interval for mean lifetime of the population. Interpret this interval.

    (c) Explain exactly what is meant by "level 0.95" for this interval.

5.22. This exercise refers to the study of battery lifetimes described in Exercise 5.21.

    (a) Using the data from Exercise 5.21, construct a level 0.95 interval for the lifetime of a newly purchased battery of the same type as tested in Exercise 5-21. Interpret this interval.

    (b) What must be true about the process that generated the data from Exercise 5-21 and the one that produced the new battery in order for this interval to be valid? Why?

    (c) Explain exactly what is meant by "level 0.95" for this interval.

5.23. This problem refers to the study of battery lifetimes described in the previous two exercises.

    (a) Assuming the population values are normally distributed, construct an interval you can be 90% certain will contain at least 95% of lifetimes for the population in question. Interpret this interval.

    (b) Explain exactly what is meant by "90% certain" for this interval.

5.24. It has been suggested that keeping batteries under refrigeration can maintain their potency. The consumer research organization described in Exercises 5-21 to 5-23 conducted a controlled experiment to evaluate the truth of this suggestion. Organization researchers obtained a random sample of 100 identical AA alkaline batteries. Fifty of these were randomly assigned to a treatment group that was kept under refrigeration at 37°F for 30 months. The other 50 constituted the control group and were kept at room temperature for the same 30 months. At the end of the storage period, all batteries were subjected to the same test described in Exercise 5-21, and the lifetime of each was recorded. The batteries in the treatment group had a mean lifetime of 40.7 hours with a standard deviation of 10.8 hours, and those in the control group had a mean lifetime of 39.0 hours with a standard deviation of 12.2 hours. Inspection of the data revealed no outliers or other large deviations from normality.

        Estimate the difference in mean lifetime for batteries stored under refrigeration and those stored at room temperature. Construct a level 0.99 confidence interval for this difference. Interpret this interval. Do these data suggest that there is a difference in the mean lifetimes?

5.25. Refer to the continuation of Example 5.5, on page 246. Suppose the researcher had obtained the third of the three confidence intervals listed: (187.7, 294.3). What could she conclude? In particular, what could she conclude about the effectiveness of the artificial pancreas?

5.26. The following is an excerpt from an article that appeared in **The Boston Globe** of June 6, 1994:

> *The number of heart-attack victims fell dramatically among coronary patients who were taking the cholesterol-lowering drug Pravastatin, according to researchers. Scientists at the Bowman Gray School of Medicine reported in the* American Journal of Cardiology *that in addition to the unexpectedly sharp drop in heart attacks, there was also a slide in other diseases. The study was aimed at evaluating the effect of the drug on the growth of atherosclerosis.*

> *The team found that 5 percent of the 75 patients taking the drug experienced fatal or nonfatal coronary episodes during the three-year study period, compared to 13 percent of the 76 patients who got an inert placebo.*

(a) There are two populations involved in the study. Can you tell from the article what they are? If so, describe them.

(b) What is the distribution of the number of coronary episodes experienced by the Pravastatin users? By the nonusers?

(c) What kind of confidence interval would you use with these data to check the validity of the statement: "The number of heart-attack victims fell dramatically among coronary patients who were taking the cholesterol-lowering drug Pravastatin." Are the necessary assumptions for this interval satisfied?

(d) Compute and interpret the interval. What do you conclude?

5.27. The data set PENNIES contains the weights of 100 newly minted U.S. pennies as measured by an extremely accurate scale. For these data, find the following:

(a) What is the source of the variation you observe in the data?

(b) What is the population you will be making inference to? Construct a 90% confidence interval for the population mean. Be sure to check all assumptions. Interpret the interval.

(c) Repeat (b) for a prediction interval for the weight of another penny.

(d) Construct a normal-theory tolerance interval with $\gamma = 0.95$ and $L = 0.99$. Interpret the interval.

5.28. For the same set of data, will a 90% or a 95% classical confidence interval for μ be wider? Why?

5.29. Bars of metal are cut and their tensile strengths (psi) are measured using a destructive method. The data set TENSILE contains the strengths of 20 bars chosen at random from the production process in a day's run. An engineer wants to use a bar taken at random from the next day's run.

(a) Use an appropriate level 0.95 interval based on these data to supply the engineer with information about the tensile strength the selected bar might have. How is the interval to be interpreted? What assumptions are necessary for the interval to be valid?

(b) What would you use for a 95% prediction interval for the AVERAGE OF ALL measurements that can possibly be made in the future? Justify your choice.

5.30. It is believed that oil carried in pipelines from Port A to Port B picks up suspended solids along the way. The data set PIPELINE gives the percentage of suspended solids in a fixed volume of the fluid sampled from each end (Port A or Port B) of each of nine pipelines connecting the two ports.

(a) Because of the proximity of the ports, the two measurements in each pipeline might not be independent. How might you advise the investigators to proceed in analyzing these data?

(b) Would you change your advice if the ports were very far apart?

5.31. A manufacturer claims that a certain drug is effective in treating arthritis. In a controlled experiment, a random sample of 250 arthritis sufferers was obtained. Of that sample, 150 were randomly assigned to the treatment group and given a course of treatment with the drug, and the remaining 100 were a given placebo. In order to monitor their condition, the subjects were given checkups 6 months after treatment began. The results are shown in Table 5.5.

(a) Summarize the data in the table using percentages. Relate your summary to the manufacturer's claim.

(b) How can you evaluate the manufacturer's claim using a confidence interval?

(c) Proceed with the analysis you suggested in (b). Present your conclusions.

TABLE 5.5   Experimental Results for 250 People with Arthritis

	Improved	Not improved	Total
Drug	100	50	150
Sugar	60	40	100

5.32. After a lecture on confidence intervals, a student approached the professor and said, "I don't see why all the fuss about selecting a level of 0.95 or 0.99 or whatever. I say select level 1.0 and have it done with. This is a better interval since it is certain to contain the true population parameter." What would you tell this student?

5.33. Powder metallurgy is a process of fabricating metal parts from metal powder. The parts are formed to the desired shape in a special press and then given a heat treatment called sintering to bond the metal particles. Low-frequency impedance (LFI) is a method for testing green-state (i.e., presintering) powder metallurgy parts for microscopic flaws. In LFI, current is injected into a grid of probes on the part surface and the voltage differences between probes are recorded. The voltage differences of flawed parts will have a different distribution than those of good parts. Assume the measured differential voltages between two specific probes for a sample of 16 good parts have a sample mean of 0.75 volt with a sample standard deviation of 0.10 volt. The data appear normally distributed and there are no outliers.

   (a) Use these data to obtain an interval that with 95% confidence will contain the differential voltage reading of a new good part.

   (b) A new part of the same type is now tested and shows a differential voltage reading of 1.30 volts. What do you conclude about this part?

5.34. Show that $p(1 - p) \leq 0.25$. Conclude that the variance of a $b(n, p)$ random variable is no greater than $n/4$.

MINIPROJECT

Purpose

The purpose of this miniproject is to

- Make you think about what processes might generate two of the models in this chapter.
- Teach you how to analyze data from these models using the inference tools you've learned in the chapter.

Process

Your group will be assigned two of the following models:

1. The one-sample C+E model.
2. The one-sample binomial model.

3. Paired C+E data.

4. The two-sample C+E model.

5. The two-sample binomial model.

Your group's task will be to design and conduct a small experiment or observational study to generate data for each type of assigned model. You must show that the data are reasonably modeled by the models you choose.

   Where appropriate, compute and interpret:

1. Classical 95% confidence intervals for the parameter(s) of interest.

2. Classical 95% prediction intervals.

3. Classical 95% tolerance intervals for at least 90% of the population.

Be sure to check all necessary assumptions to help determine what is appropriate.

   A short (one-page or less) proposal of what your group plans to do for this miniproject must be submitted and approved before you begin your work.

LAB 5.1: Sampling Distributions

Introduction

In Chapter 5, you have been introduced to the C+E model and the least squares estimator of the population mean μ. In this lab, you will see how this estimator behaves under repeated sampling from the C+E model.

Objectives

The purpose of this lab is to introduce the idea of a **sampling distribution** through computer simulation of the C+E model.

Lab Materials

None needed.

Experimental Procedure

1. Use your statistical software to generate five data sets each of size 20 from an $N(\mu, \sigma^2)$ distribution, for your choice of μ and σ^2.[16] Give the response variables the names Y1–Y5. Plot the distributions and compute the parameter estimates $\hat{\mu} = \bar{y}$ and $\hat{\sigma}^2 = s^2$ for each of these five data sets. Are these distributions or estimates all the same?

   Create normal quantile plots of all five data sets. This will give you some experience with how normal data looks on a normal quantile plot.

---

[16]The **Doing It with SAS** and **Doing It with MINITAB** supplements to this text have explicit instructions for generating the five data sets here and the 500 data sets in step 3 for users of those packages.

2. Input the values of the parameter estimators into a data set and then form histograms of them. The basic idea here is that for different data sets generated from the same C+E model, the parameter estimates will be different. In fact, they will have a distribution. The distribution of parameter estimates under repeated sampling is called a **sampling distribution.**

3. Now, to get a really good idea of what the sampling distribution of the parameter estimates looks like, you'd need to graph the estimate values from a lot more than five data sets. Generate 500 data sets each of size 20 from the same C+E model that you chose before, compute the parameter estimates $\bar{y}$ and s^2 for each, and then draw histograms of the 500 parameter estimates $\bar{y}$, and the 500 parameter estimates s^2. These will be good approximations to the sampling distributions of the parameter estimates.

4. Use your data analysis skills to summarize the sampling distributions. Write a short (one-page or less) report detailing what you have found in this lab.

LAB 5.2: Classical Confidence Intervals

Introduction

As you have learned in this chapter, the interpretation of confidence intervals relies on the notion of repeated samples taken from the underlying model. In this lab, you will experience this interpretation through computer simulation. In addition, you will see how confidence intervals behave when the errors are not normal.

Objectives

To illustrate the interpretation of classical confidence intervals for the parameter μ in the C+E model. To assess the validity of these intervals under a variety of error distributions.

Lab Materials

None needed.

Experimental Procedure

1. Begin by using your computer software to create 100 samples each of size 20 from the C+E model $Y = \mu + \epsilon$, with $\epsilon \sim N(0, \sigma^2)$, for your choice of μ and σ^2. For each sample, calculate a level 0.95 confidence interval for μ.[17]

   (a) Count the number of intervals that do not contain μ. How does this number compare with what you expect from the confidence level 0.95?

   (b) Record the mean width of the intervals.

---

[17]The **Doing It with SAS** and **Doing It with MINITAB** supplements to this text have explicit instructions for generating these data sets and for generating the contaminated data sets in step 3 for users of those packages.

2. Do the tasks in step 1 for a different sample size and confidence level one or more additional times. Each time, record your results.

3. Now you will perform the tasks in step 1 for a different error distribution. You are going to generate errors that mimic outliers in real data. These distributions are called **contaminated distributions**. In the contaminated distribution you will generate, some of the errors, ϵ, will be taken from a normal distribution and some from a nonnormal distribution. Specifically, a proportion of contamination, c, is chosen, where $0 \le c \le 1$. Then, each random error is chosen from an $N(0, \sigma^2)$ distribution with probability $1 - c$ and from an exponential(σ) distribution, centered to have mean 0, with probability c. The algorithm the computer will use to generate the 100 contaminated observations is as follows:

   i. Start with $i = 1$.

   ii. To generate Y_i, the ith observation, generate a Bernoulli random variable, B, with probability c of taking the value 1 and probability $1 - c$ of taking the value 0.

   iii. If $B = 1$, then $Y_i = \mu + \eta_i$, where η_i is a centered exponential(σ) random variable.

   iv. If $B = 0$, then $Y_i = \mu + \xi_i$, where ξ_i is an $N(0, \sigma^2)$ random variable.

   v. If $i = 100$, finish. Else, set $i = i + 1$ and go to **ii.**

Generate two sets of data using the same parameters, μ and σ^2, as in step 1, the first with a $c = 0.1$ proportion of contamination and the second with a $c = 0.5$ proportion of contamination. For each data set, perform tasks (a) and (b) (counting the number of the 100 intervals that do not contain μ and obtaining the mean width of the 100 intervals) from step 1. Record the results.

4. Write a short (one- to two-page) report describing what you observed and drawing conclusions about the validity of the classical confidence intervals under the various conditions you specified.

APPENDIX 5.1: Classical Interval Guide

Confidence Intervals for Means in the C+E Model: One Population

Case 1: Known Variance

Assumptions

1. The data are $Y_1, Y_2, \ldots, Y_n$, where $Y_j = \mu + \epsilon_j$.
2. Either
   (a) n is large or
   (b) The ϵ_j are from an $N(0, \sigma^2)$ population.
3. σ^2 is known.

Formulas   A level L confidence interval for μ is

$$\left(\bar{Y} - \sigma(\bar{Y})z_{(1+L)/2}, \ \bar{Y} + \sigma(\bar{Y})z_{(1+L)/2} \right),$$

where $\sigma(\bar{Y}) = \sqrt{\dfrac{\sigma^2}{n}}$.

Case 2: Unknown Variance, n Large

This case is treated exactly as Case 1 except that $\sigma(\bar{Y})$ is replaced by $\hat{\sigma}(\bar{Y}) = \sqrt{\dfrac{S^2}{n}}$, where S is the sample standard deviation.

Case 3: Unknown Variance, n Small

Assumptions

1. The data are $Y_1, Y_2, \ldots, Y_n$, where $Y_j = \mu + \epsilon_j$.
2. The ϵ_j are from an $N(0, \sigma^2)$ population.
3. σ^2 is unknown.

Formulas   A level L confidence interval for μ is

$$\left(\bar{Y} - \hat{\sigma}(\bar{Y}) t_{n-1, (1+L)/2}, \; \bar{Y} + \hat{\sigma}(\bar{Y}) t_{n-1, (1+L)/2} \right),$$

where $\hat{\sigma}(\bar{Y})$ is defined as in Case 2.

Prediction Interval for a Future Observation from the C+E Model: One Population

Assumptions

1. The data are $Y_1, Y_2, \ldots, Y_n$, where $Y_j = \mu + \epsilon_j$.
2. The ϵ_j are from an $N(0, \sigma^2)$ population.
3. σ^2 is unknown.

Formulas   A level L prediction interval for a future observation is

$$\left(\hat{Y}_{\text{new}} - \hat{\sigma}(Y_{\text{new}} - \hat{Y}_{\text{new}}) t_{n-1, (1+L)/2}, \; \hat{Y}_{\text{new}} + \hat{\sigma}(Y_{\text{new}} - \hat{Y}_{\text{new}}) t_{n-1, (1+L)/2} \right),$$

where $\hat{\sigma}(Y_{\text{new}} - \hat{Y}_{\text{new}}) = S\sqrt{1 + 1/n}$.

Large-Sample Confidence Intervals for the Proportion in the Binomial Model: One Population

Assumptions

1. The datum is Y from a $b(n, p)$ population.
2. The sample size is large: $Y \geq 10$ and $n - Y \geq 10$ is a good rule of thumb overall. If $0.3 \leq \hat{p} = Y/n \leq 0.7$, then $Y \geq 5$ and $n - Y \geq 5$ is a good rule of thumb.

Formulas   An approximate level L confidence interval for p is

$$\left(\hat{p} - \hat{\sigma}(\hat{p})z_{(1+L)/2},\ \hat{p} + \hat{\sigma}(\hat{p})z_{(1+L)/2}\right),$$

where $\hat{\sigma}(\hat{p}) = \sqrt{\hat{p}(1 - \hat{p})/n}$, and $\hat{p} = Y/n$.

Confidence Intervals for Means in the C+E Model: Two Independent Populations

In all cases, we assume:

1. The data are

$$Y_{1,1},\ Y_{1,2},\ \ldots,\ Y_{1,n_1},\ \text{where } Y_{1,j} = \mu_1 + \epsilon_{1,j}\ \text{(population 1)}$$

$$Y_{2,1},\ Y_{2,2},\ \ldots,\ Y_{2,n_2},\ \text{where } Y_{2,j} = \mu_2 + \epsilon_{2,j}\ \text{(population 2)}.$$

2. The two populations are independent.

Case 1: Known Variances

Assumptions

1. Either
   (a) n_1 and n_2 are large or
   (b) The $\epsilon_{1,j}$ are from an $N(0, \sigma_1^2)$ population, and the $\epsilon_{2,j}$ are from an $N(0, \sigma_2^2)$ population.
2. σ_1^2 and σ_2^2 are known.

Formulas   A level L confidence interval for $\mu_1 - \mu_2$ is

$$\left(\bar{Y}_1 - \bar{Y}_2 - \sigma(\bar{Y}_1 - \bar{Y}_2)z_{(1+L)/2},\ \bar{Y}_1 - \bar{Y}_2 + \sigma(\bar{Y}_1 - \bar{Y}_2)z_{(1+L)/2}\right),$$

where $\sigma(\bar{Y}_1 - \bar{Y}_2) = \sqrt{(\sigma_1^2/n_1) + (\sigma_2^2/n_2)}$.

Case 2: Unknown Variances, n_1 and n_2 Large

This case is treated exactly as Case 1 except that $\sigma(\bar{Y}_1 - \bar{Y}_2)$ is replaced by $\hat{\sigma}(\bar{Y}_1 - \bar{Y}_2) = \sqrt{S_1^2/n_1 + S_2^2/n_2}$, where S_1 and S_2 are the sample standard deviations computed from the data from populations 1 and 2, respectively.

Case 3: Variances Unknown, but Assumed to Be Equal, n_1 and n_2 Not Both Large

Assumptions

1. The $\epsilon_{1,j}$ are from an $N(0, \sigma_1^2)$ population, and the $\epsilon_{2,j}$ are from an $N(0, \sigma_2^2)$ population.
2. σ_1^2 and σ_2^2 are unknown, but are assumed to be equal.

Formulas   A level L confidence interval for $\mu_1 - \mu_2$ is

$$\left(\bar{Y}_1 - \bar{Y}_2 - \hat{\sigma}_p(\bar{Y}_1 - \bar{Y}_2)t_{v,(1+L)/2},\ \bar{Y}_1 - \bar{Y}_2 + \hat{\sigma}_p(\bar{Y}_1 - \bar{Y}_2)t_{v,(1+L)/2} \right)$$

where

$$\hat{\sigma}_p(\bar{Y}_1 - \bar{Y}_2) = \sqrt{S_p^2[(1/n_1) + (1/n_2)]},$$

where

$$S_p^2 = \frac{(n_1 - 1)S_1^2 + (n_2 - 1)S_2^2}{n_1 + n_2 - 2}$$

S_1 and S_2 are the sample standard deviations computed from the data from populations 1 and 2, respectively, and $v = n_1 + n_2 - 2$.

Case 4: Variances Unknown, and Not Assumed to Be Equal, n_1 and n_2 Not Both Large

Assumptions

1. The $\epsilon_{1,j}$ are from an $N(0, \sigma_1^2)$ population, and the $\epsilon_{2,j}$ are from an $N(0, \sigma_2^2)$ population.
2. σ_1^2 and σ_2^2 are unknown, and are not assumed to be equal.

Formulas   A level L confidence interval for $\mu_1 - \mu_2$ is

$$\left(\bar{Y}_1 - \bar{Y}_2 - \hat{\sigma}(\bar{Y}_1 - \bar{Y}_2)t_{v,(1+L)/2},\ \bar{Y}_1 - \bar{Y}_2 + \hat{\sigma}(\bar{Y}_1 - \bar{Y}_2)t_{v,(1+L)/2} \right)$$

where $\hat{\sigma}(\bar{Y}_1 - \bar{Y}_2) = \sqrt{(S_1^2/n_1) + (S_2^2/n_2)}$, S_1 and S_2 are the sample standard deviations computed from the data from populations 1 and 2, respectively, and the degrees of freedom v is taken as the largest integer less than or equal to

$$\left(\frac{S_1^2}{n_1} + \frac{S_2^2}{n_2} \right)^2 \bigg/ \left[\frac{(S_1^2/n_1)^2}{n_1 - 1} + \frac{(S_2^2/n_2)^2}{n_2 - 1} \right]$$

Confidence Intervals for Proportions in the Binomial Model: Two Independent Populations

Assumptions

1. The data are Y_1 from a $b(n_1, p_1)$ population and Y_2 from a $b(n_2, p_2)$ population.
2. Y_1 and Y_2 are independent.
3. n_1 and n_2 are large: $Y_i \geq 10$ and $n_i - Y_i \geq 10$, $i = 1, 2$, is a good rule of thumb overall. If $0.3 \leq \hat{p}_i = Y_i/n_i \leq 0.7$, then $Y_i \geq 5$ and $n_i - Y_i \geq 5$, $i = 1, 2$, is a good rule of thumb.

Formulas   A level L confidence interval for $p_1 - p_2$ is

$$\left(\hat{p}_1 - \hat{p}_2 - \hat{\sigma}(\hat{p}_1 - \hat{p}_2)z_{(1+L)/2},\; \hat{p}_1 - \hat{p}_2 + \hat{\sigma}(\hat{p}_1 - \hat{p}_2)z_{(1+L)/2} \right)$$

where

$$\hat{\sigma}(\hat{p}_1 - \hat{p}_2) = \sqrt{\frac{\hat{p}_1(1 - \hat{p}_1)}{n_1} + \frac{\hat{p}_2(1 - \hat{p}_2)}{n_2}}$$

is the estimated standard error of $\hat{p}_1 - \hat{p}_2$.

CAPSTONE PROJECT: Chapters 1 to 5

The goal of a **Capstone Project** is to give you experience in all phases of a statistical study: planning, data collection, analysis, and conclusions. Each of Chapters 1 to 5 must make a contribution to the project:

- Planning and data collection are covered in Chapter 3.
- Basic data analysis is covered in Chapters 1 and 2.
- The basics of statistical modeling are covered in Chapter 4.
- Basic statistical inference is covered in Chapter 5.

Tasks

Your group must accomplish several tasks in the course of the project.

1. Decide what to study. First, your must have something to study. You study will probably be better and will certainly be more enjoyable if you choose something that interests you. One important requirement to keep in mind when deciding what to study is that **the data you use for this study must be quantitative.** Your instructor will give you a timetable for the project, including a date by which you must decide what to study, but you should begin thinking about and discussing it with your group as soon as possible.

2. Do a Pilot study. A pilot study is done prior to the main study. You may conduct a pilot study for one or more of the following reasons:

- As an exploratory study to familiarize yourself with the subject matter and to identify topics and specific questions to be explored in the main study. A pilot study can also help you decide what data to collect and how to collect them. You do not have to generate the data for the pilot study yourself: The pilot study may rely on available data.
- To obtain valuable information on population parameters. For example, you may obtain estimates of population variances needed to determine sample sizes for the main study.
- To get the bugs out of the whole operation. By conducting a pilot study, you will find out which parts of the operational plan work and which don't. You can then revise the plan as necessary for the main study.

3. Design the main study. The main study must be a designed study: either a controlled experiment or an observational study. The data obtained must be suitable to answering the question(s) you are asking. Data must be obtained in a manner that will allow valid statistical inferences to be drawn. The material of Chapters 1 and 3 will be particularly useful in deciding how to generate the data for the main study.

4. Obtain the data for the main study.

5. Analyze the results. This involves checking model assumptions and drawing inferences. It might also require that more or different data be obtained, after an initial analysis.

6. Draw your conclusions.

7. Write your report.

6

Hypothesis Tests

By a small sample, we may judge of the whole piece.

—*Miguel de Cervantes*, Don Quixote

■ INTRODUCTION

Recall from Chapter 5 that statistical inference is the use of a subset of a population, called a sample, to draw conclusions about the entire population from which it is taken. In Chapter 5, you learned about one type of statistical inference: estimation. In this chapter, you will learn about a second type of statistical inference: **hypothesis testing.**

Knowledge and Skills

By successfully completing this chapter, you will acquire the following knowledge and skills:

KNOWLEDGE	SKILLS
1. What hypothesis tests are, and the philosophical and statistical reasoning behind them. **2.** One- and two-sided tests.	**1.** How to conduct and interpret hypothesis tests about the mean in the C+E model. **2.** How to conduct and interpret hypothesis tests about the difference of means in the two sample C+E model.
3. P-values.	**3.** How to conduct and interpret hypothesis tests about a population proportion.

KNOWLEDGE	SKILLS
4. Fixed significance level tests.	**4.** How to conduct and interpret hypothesis tests about the difference of proportions from two populations.
5. The power of a test.	
6. The relation between hypothesis tests and confidence intervals.	

<table>
<tr><td colspan="2" style="text-align:center">KNOWLEDGE</td></tr>
</table>

6.1

PRELIMINARIES

This chapter builds on the knowledge of statistical inference that you acquired in your study of estimation in Chapter 5. In particular, before beginning your study of hypothesis testing, you should be familiar with the following topics found in Chapter 5:

- Inference and how data are obtained
- Inference and stationarity
- The C+E and binomial models
- Estimators and their sampling distributions, in particular the t distribution

The hypothesis testing methods presented in this chapter are analogues of the classical estimation methods you studied in Chapter 5. As such, we can describe them as classical hypothesis testing methods. Chapter 11 presents some more recently developed alternatives to these classical inference methods.

6.2

THE MACHINERY OF HYPOTHESIS TESTING

To begin your introduction to hypothesis testing, consider the following example, which is also found as Example 5.5 in Chapter 5:

EXAMPLE 6.1   EXAMPLE 5.5 REVISITED

A researcher at a biotechnology company is testing an artificial pancreas on laboratory rats. She gives diabetic rats who have had this pancreas implanted an initial weight-adjusted dose of glucose in solution and then measures their blood-sugar levels (serum/plasma glucose, mg/100 ml) 60 minutes later. The data are

266   149   161   220

The population is all possible diabetic rats with this kind of artificial pancreas, and the sample is the four diabetic rats on which the researcher has data. We assume that the rats are a random selection from the population.

The researcher hypothesizes that the artificial pancreas is effective in lowering blood-sugar levels. The purpose of the experiment is to test this hypothesis. ✦

We will use Example 6.1 to illustrate the concepts of hypothesis testing.

The Components of a Statistical Hypothesis Testing Problem

A statistical hypothesis testing problem consists of five main components:

1. The Scientific Hypothesis
2. The Statistical Model
3. The Statistical Hypotheses
4. The Test Statistic
5. The p-Value

We will consider each in turn.

1. The Scientific Hypothesis. The scientific hypothesis is the hypothesized outcome of the experiment or study. The research is being done to see if there is evidence for the scientific hypothesis. A scientific hypothesis need not be mathematical or statistical in nature. In the artificial pancreas example, the scientific hypothesis is that the artificial pancreas is effective in lowering blood-sugar levels. In a given experiment, there may be more than one measurement made and more than one scientific hypothesis of interest.

2. The Statistical Model. There must be a model that attempts to describe the observed data, and in some cases, the phenomenon under study. The model depends on the design of the experiment or observational study: that is, on how the data are obtained. So, for example, if blocking is used in an experiment or stratification is used in an observational study, the statistical model should account for the blocking or stratification. The model may also depend on scientific knowledge of the phenomenon producing the data. For example, any model for experimental measurements of electromotive force as current and resistance are varied should make use of Ohm's law.

The model will most often be completely specified by a few parameters. In the artificial pancreas example, the model we will use is the C+E model

$$Y = \mu + \epsilon \tag{6.1}$$

where Y is the observed blood-sugar level 60 minutes after administration of glucose, μ is the true population mean of blood-sugar levels 60 minutes after administration of glucose (i.e., the mean of blood-sugar levels from all rats of this type with this kind of artificial pancreas that could be observed under these conditions), and ϵ is random error, assumed to follow an $N(0, \sigma^2)$ distribution. Here the parameters that specify the model are μ and σ^2.

Prior to doing any inference, the data should be checked for violations of model assumptions that might lead to erroneous results. There are too few data in the artificial pancreas example to really check for normality, but the data can still be checked for any kind of unusual pattern, such as a very extreme outlier. Three of the four data values closely clustered together, with the fourth a large distance away would constitute such a pattern, for example. The researcher checked and found no unusual pattern to these data. Similarly, there are too few data to check for stationarity, though a plot versus the order in which the data were obtained revealed no pattern.

3. The Statistical Hypotheses. In order to have an hypothesis test, there must be something to test. Those somethings are statistical hypotheses. A statistical hypothesis is a statement about one or more parameters in the model we are considering. In statistical hypothesis testing, there are two hypotheses: a **null hypothesis** and an **alternative hypothesis.** One of these two statistical hypotheses, most often the alternative hypothesis, corresponds to the scientific hypothesis of interest. The other statistical hypothesis contradicts the scientific hypothesis.

Consider again the artificial pancreas example. As a benchmark, the researcher cites numerous studies that point to a mean blood-sugar level of 275 in untreated diabetic rats 1 hour after ingestion of glucose. This suggests that one way to decide if the artificial pancreas is effective in lowering blood-sugar levels is to compare μ, the population mean blood-sugar level for diabetic rats with the artificial pancreas 1 hour after ingestion of glucose, with 275, the corresponding population mean blood-sugar level for untreated diabetic rats. Therefore, we will take as the null hypothesis that μ equals 275, the mean blood-sugar level measured after 1 hour for the population of diabetic rats without an artificial pancreas. If the experiment has been conducted properly, and the artificial pancreas is the only difference between the two populations of rats, then the null hypothesis asserts that the artificial pancreas has no effect on mean blood-sugar levels. The alternative hypothesis is that μ is lower than 275; that is, that on average, blood-sugar levels 60 minutes after injection are lower in rats with the artificial pancreas.

Usually, the null hypothesis is abbreviated H_0 and the alternative hypothesis H_a. For this example, the two hypotheses together can be concisely written in the form

$$H_0: \quad \mu = 275$$

$$H_a: \quad \mu < 275$$

Notice that the alternative statistical hypothesis is a statement of the scientific hypothesis in terms of parameters of the statistical model. It is not the only possible way to state the scientific hypothesis: We could have adopted a different model that might lead to different statistical hypotheses, for example. But given the model we have postulated, the statistical hypothesis H_a is a reasonable interpretation of the scientific hypothesis that the artificial pancreas is effective in lowering blood-sugar levels.

4. The Test Statistic. To decide between the null and alternative hypotheses, we must have evidence. Such evidence consists of measurements or observations. In Example 6.1, the observations are the four measured blood-sugar levels.

The hypothesis test is based on a **statistic,** which is a function of the observations that does not depend on the value of the parameter being tested in the hypotheses. In Example 6.1, the mean of the four observations, $\bar{Y}$, is a statistic, since it can be computed from the data alone. $\bar{Y} - \mu$ is not a statistic, however, since it cannot be computed without knowing μ, the parameter being tested.

Often a test statistic is based on the estimator used to estimate the parameter. This is true for the artificial pancreas example, where the test statistic is $\bar{Y}$, the least squares estimator of μ (see Chapter 5). For the artificial pancreas example, the observed value of the test statistic is $\bar{y} = (266 + 149 + 161 + 220)/4 = 199$.

5. The p-Value. The test is conducted by assuming at the outset that H_0 is true. Under this assumption, the test statistic follows a known distribution model. The observed value of the test statistic is then examined to see if it is consistent with this distribution model. The **p-value** quantifies how consistent the observed value of the test statistic is with this distribution model, and hence with H_0. The p-value is the proportion of the values from this distribution model that gives as much or more evidence against H_0 and in favor of H_a as does the observed value of the test statistic.

In the artificial pancreas example, we begin by assuming that H_0 is true. That is, we assume that the artificial pancreas does not lower blood-sugar levels, on average. This means that $\mu = 275$ in the C+E model.

Recall from Chapter 5 that if there are n observations, $Y_1, Y_2, \ldots, Y_n$ from the C+E model, if S is the standard deviation of those observations, and if $\hat{\sigma}(\bar{Y}) = S/\sqrt{n}$ is the estimated standard error of $\bar{Y}$, then the sampling distribution of $t = (\bar{Y} - \mu)/\hat{\sigma}(\bar{Y})$ is a t_{n-1} distribution. Applying this result to the artificial pancreas example, we see that $t = (\bar{Y} - 275)/\hat{\sigma}(\bar{Y})$ has a t_3 distribution if H_0 is true.

Now, the observed value of the test statistic $\bar{Y}$ is $\bar{y} = 199$, and the observed value of S is $s = 54.4$, which means that the observed value of $\hat{\sigma}(\bar{Y})$ is $\hat{\sigma}(\bar{y}) = 54.4/\sqrt{4} = 27.2$.[1] Therefore, the observed value of the standardized test statistic $t = (\bar{Y} - 275)/\hat{\sigma}(\bar{Y})$ is [2]

$$t^* = (\bar{y} - 275)/\hat{\sigma}(\bar{y}) = -2.79$$

In Example 6.1, the p-value is the proportion of the values from the t_3 distribution model that give as much or more evidence against H_0 and in favor of H_a as does the observed value of the standardized test statistic, $t^* = -2.79$. H_a determines what "as much or more evidence against H_0 and in favor of H_a" means. In Example 6.1, H_a is the hypothesis that $\mu < 275$, and $\bar{Y}$ is the estimator of μ, so small values of $\bar{Y}$ support H_a over H_0. It follows that small values of $t = (\bar{Y} - 275)/\hat{\sigma}(\bar{Y})$ will be regarded as evidence against H_0 and in favor of H_a. The p-value is then obtained as the proportion of the t_3 population that is as small as or smaller than $t^* = -2.79$. This proportion equals 0.0341. The p-value of 0.0341 is shown graphically as the shaded area under the t_3 density in Figure 6.1.

---

[1] The notation $\hat{\sigma}(\bar{y})$ stands for the value of the estimated standard error of $\bar{Y}$, $\hat{\sigma}(\bar{Y})$, evaluated at the observed sample mean $\bar{y}$. It does not stand for the estimated standard error of $\bar{y}$, a quantity that would have no meaning since $\bar{y}$ is a constant.

[2] Since its distribution is easier to work with, we will use the standardized test statistic $t = (\bar{Y} - 275)/\hat{\sigma}(\bar{Y})$, instead of the unstandardized test statistic $\bar{Y}$.

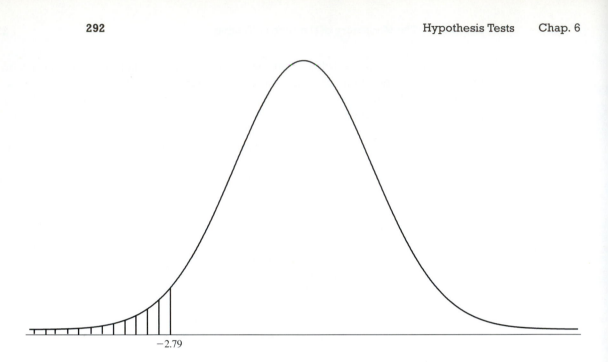

Figure 6.1   Shaded area is p-value for testing H_0 against H_a for the artificial pancreas data. It represents the proportion of a t_3 population that is as small as or smaller than the observed value, $t^* = -2.79$.

TABLE 6.1   Interpreting the Strength of Evidence against H_0 and in Favor of H_a Provided by p-Values

If the p-value is less than:	The evidence against H_0 and in favor of H_a is:
0.100	borderline
0.050	reasonably strong
0.025	strong
0.010	very strong

The interpretation is that if H_0 is true (i.e., the artificial pancreas makes no difference in blood-sugar levels), then a value of -2.79 or smaller for $t = (\bar{Y} - 275)/\hat{\sigma}(\bar{Y})$ (equivalently, a value of 199 or smaller for $\bar{Y}$) would be observed in about 3.41% of all possible experiments.

The p-value quantifies the evidence against H_0 and in favor of H_a. The smaller the p-value, the more inconsistent the data are with H_0 and the more they support H_a. Some generally accepted rules of thumb for interpreting p-values are shown in Table 6.1. Based on these, we see that the p-value of 0.034 provides reasonably strong evidence against H_0 and in favor of H_a. That is, there is reasonably strong evidence that the artificial pancreas is effective.

A good way to remember what the p-value measures is to think of the p-value as an abbreviation for **plausibility-value.** The p-value is a measure, assuming H_0 is true, of how plausible the observed data are. The nice thing about assuming that the p in p-value stands for "plausibility" is that you automatically remember that small p-values mean small plausibility and large p-values mean large plausibility. Small plausibility means the data do not fit very well with the assumption that H_0 is true; large plausibility means the data do fit the assumption well.

We summarize the components of a statistical hypothesis testing problem as follows:

THE COMPONENTS OF A STATISTICAL HYPOTHESIS TESTING PROBLEM

- **The Scientific Hypothesis.** This is the hypothesized outcome of the experiment or study. In fact, the research is being done to see if there is evidence for the scientific hypothesis.

- **The Statistical Model.** The model refers to a family of models indexed by one or more parameters. The data are assumed generated by one of these models. We want to test hypotheses about model parameters.

- **The Statistical Hypotheses.** There will be a null hypothesis, H_0, and an alternative hypothesis, H_a, to decide between. One of the hypotheses, most likely the alternative, is the scientific hypothesis stated in terms of the statistical model. The other hypothesis contradicts the scientific hypothesis.

- **The Test Statistic.** The test statistic is a function of the data whose value doesn't depend on the parameter being tested. The test statistic is used to decide between H_0 and H_a.

- **The p-Value.** The p-value quantifies how consistent, relative to H_a, the data are with the assumption that H_0 is true.

Although a statistical hypothesis testing problem always begins with a scientific hypothesis, the next step is not necessarily to devise the statistical model. Often, the scientific hypothesis is translated directly into the statistical hypothesis and the design of the study and the model decided third. For example, the pancreas researcher might translate the scientific hypothesis into statistical terminology immediately by equating the scientific hypothesis "The artificial pancreas is effective in lowering blood-sugar levels" with the hypothesis: "On average, the blood-sugar level for diabetic rats with the artificial pancreas is lower than that for diabetic rats without the artificial pancreas". The latter can then be put into statistical terms as "$\mu < 275$." The experiment would then be designed so that the data followed the C+E model and so that the appropriate test for the population mean could be obtained.

By now, you may have recognized that you learned about hypothesis tests in Chapter 4: Examples 4.11 and 4.20 presented the ideas of hypothesis testing. We reproduce one of these problems as Example 6.2 to illustrate the components of an hypothesis testing problem using a different model:

EXAMPLE 6.2   EXAMPLE 4.11 REVISITED

A state gaming commission supervises gambling casinos. Recently, after complaints that it was coming up red too often, a roulette wheel was tested for fairness. Roulette wheels have 38 slots: 18 red, 18 black, and 2 neutral ones. The test consisted of spinning the wheel 100 times and recording whether the ball landed in a red slot or not. In the test, the ball landed red in 58 of the 100 spins. Does this result constitute good evidence that the wheel is unfair?

The solution presented in Chapter 4 went as follows. The 100 spins of the wheel can be viewed as 100 Bernoulli trials, in which a result of "red" constitutes a success and "not red" a failure. The true parameter p is unknown, but if the wheel is fair, it is $18/38 = 0.47$. The observation is Y, the number of times red occurs in the 100 spins. If the wheel is fair $Y \sim b(100, 0.47)$. In this case, the mean number of reds that should be observed is $100 \times 0.47 = 47$.

The question the state gaming commission must ask is whether the 58 reds is too large to have occurred by chance in the $b(100, 0.47)$ distribution model. One way to measure this is to compute the proportion of values Y from a $b(100, 0.47)$ population that are greater than or equal to 58. This proportion is approximately 0.0177, which means that only about 1.77% of all such experiments would result in 58 or more reds. As this is unlikely to have happened by chance, the 58 observed red outcomes seem good evidence that the wheel is not fair.

We will now restate this example in terms of the machinery of hypothesis testing we have just introduced.

1. **The Scientific Hypothesis.** The scientific hypothesis is that the wheel is unfair: specifically, that reds come up too often.

2. **The Statistical Model.** In the roulette wheel example, the data consist of the outcomes of 100 spins of the wheel. In particular, we observe the number of the 100 spins that result in the ball landing on red. The model for the number of reds observed in the 100 test spins is $b(100, p)$, and p, the probability of the ball landing on red, is the unknown parameter.

3. **The Statistical Hypotheses.** The null hypothesis is that the probability of red coming up equals that of a fair wheel. In terms of the parameter p, this is the hypothesis that $p = 0.47$. The alternative hypothesis is that red is more likely to occur. In terms of p, this is the hypothesis that $p > 0.47$. We abbreviate these hypotheses as

$$H_0: \quad p = 0.47$$

$$H_a: \quad p > 0.47$$

4. **The Test Statistic.** The test statistic is Y, the number of times red came up in the 100 spins of the wheel.

5. **The p-Value.** We begin by assuming that H_0 is true. That is, we assume that $p = 0.47$. This defines the distribution model for Y, the number of times red came up in the 100 spins of the wheel, as $b(100, 0.47)$. Since H_a contends that p is greater than 0.47, large values of Y (i.e., lots of red spins) constitute evidence against H_0 and in favor of H_a. Thus, the p-value is the proportion of observations from a $b(100, 0.47)$ population that are greater than or equal to the observed number of 58 red spins. That proportion can be computed as[3]

$$\sum_{y=58}^{100} \binom{100}{y} 0.47^y (1 - 0.47)^{100-y} = 0.0177$$

Based on the guidelines in Table 6.1, the 58 times that red came up in 100 spins constitute strong evidence against H_0 and in favor of H_a. That is, there is strong evidence that the probability of red coming up on this wheel is too large.   ✦

Types of Hypotheses

Hypotheses about a single parameter can be either **simple** or **composite**.

• **Simple Hypotheses.** A simple hypothesis specifies that the parameter have a single value. In both the artificial pancreas and the roulette wheel examples the null hypotheses were simple. In the first, the parameter μ was taken to have the single value 275, and in the second, the parameter p was taken to have the single value 0.47.

• **Composite Hypotheses.** Any hypothesis that allows the parameter to take more than one value is a composite hypothesis. The alternative hypotheses in both the artificial pancreas and the roulette wheel examples were composite. In the former, the hypothesis that $\mu < 275$ allowed all values between 0 and 275; in the latter, the hypothesis that $p > 0.47$ allowed all values between 0.47 and 1.

Because they are useful and easy to understand, virtually all the hypotheses we will consider in this chapter will be simple (H_0) versus composite (H_a). However, in practice, this does not have to be the case. For example, in the artificial pancreas example, the experimenter could have taken the null hypothesis to be "On average, the artificial pancreas does no better than no intervention." This would have made the null hypothesis $H_0: \mu \geq 275$.[4]

---

[3]See the formula for the binomial probability mass function in Chapter 4.

[4]Incidentally, had the experimenter chosen $H_0: \mu \geq 275$, more advanced statistical theory shows that the test statistic, the p-value, and the conclusion would have been identical to those obtained for $H_0: \mu = 275$.

One- and Two-Sided Hypotheses

Two types of composite hypotheses about a single parameter are as follows:

- **One-Sided Hypotheses.** A one-sided hypothesis specifies that a parameter be greater than, greater than or equal to, less than, or less than or equal to some value. Examples of one-sided hypotheses are the alternative hypotheses in both the artificial pancreas ($\mu < 275$) and the roulette wheel ($p > 0.47$) examples.
- **Two-Sided Hypotheses.** For our purposes, a two-sided hypothesis specifies that a parameter not equal some value. Examples are $\mu \neq 275$ and $p \neq 0.47$.

The knowledge of the investigator prior to looking at the data determines whether an hypothesis is one- or two-sided. For instance, in the artificial pancreas example, the alternative hypothesis was one-sided ($\mu < 275$) because the investigator knew that the artificial pancreas would not do worse, on average, than no intervention. Had there been a realistic possibility that the artificial pancreas could have either done better or worse than no intervention, or had the researcher been uncertain about the kind of effect the artificial pancreas might have had, the correct alternative hypothesis would have been two-sided ($\mu \neq 275$).

One- and Two-Sided Tests

Suppose in an hypothesis testing problem, the null hypothesis is simple (e.g., $\mu = 275$). As you have seen, to compute the p-value, we assume that the null hypothesis is true. This defines a distribution model. The p-value is the proportion of the values from this distribution model that give as much or more evidence against H_0 and in favor of H_a as does the observed value of the test statistic. As you have also seen, the alternative hypothesis determines what is meant by "as much or more evidence against H_0 and in favor of H_a."

One-Sided Tests

One-sided tests correspond to one-sided alternative hypotheses.

EXAMPLE 6.1   CONTINUED

Consider again the artificial pancreas example. Recall the following:

- The null hypothesis is $\mu = 275$.
- The standardized test statistic, $t = (\bar{Y} - 275)/\hat{\sigma}(\bar{Y})$, has a t_3 distribution when the null hypothesis is true.
- The observed value of the standardized test statistic is $t^* = (\bar{y} - 275)/\hat{\sigma}(\bar{y}) = -2.79$.
- Since the alternative hypothesis is $\mu < 275$, small values of the test statistic, $\bar{Y}$, are taken as evidence against the null and in favor of the alternative

hypothesis. Therefore, the p-value is the proportion of a t_3 population below the value of -2.79.

This is an example of a one-sided test, meaning that the p-value is computed as the proportion of a population below an observed value of the test statistic (or above that value, as would happen in this example if the alternative hypothesis were $\mu > 275$). ✦

Two-Sided Tests

Two-sided tests correspond to two-sided alternative hypotheses.

EXAMPLE 6.1   CONTINUED

Consider the artificial pancreas example with the same null hypothesis, H_0: $\mu = 275$, and suppose that the alternative hypothesis is $\mu \neq 275$. In this case, $\bar{Y}$ values that are too far from 275—either too large or too small—would be evidence against H_0 and in favor of H_a. Values of $\bar{Y}$ that are larger than 275 correspond to values of the standardized test statistic, $t = (\bar{Y} - 275)/\hat{\sigma}(\bar{Y})$ that are larger than 0, and values of $\bar{Y}$ smaller than 275 correspond to values of t that are smaller than 0. Thus, in computing the p-value, we must count the proportion of all values from a t_3 distribution that are as far from 0 as is t^*. Since $t^* = -2.79$, this means all values from a t_3 distribution below -2.79 or above 2.79. We already know that the proportion of values from a t_3 population below -2.79 is 0.034. Since all t distributions are symmetric about 0, the proportion of values from a t_3 population above 2.79 is also 0.034. Thus, the p-value, being the proportion of a t_3 population above 2.79 or below -2.79, equals $0.034 + 0.034$, or 0.068. Notice that this is just twice the one-sided p-value.   ✦

6.3

THE PHILOSOPHY OF HYPOTHESIS TESTING

A Page from the History of Science

In 1915, Albert Einstein published his general theory of relativity, a beautiful and coherent theory of the large-scale mechanics of the universe that was radically different from the prevailing two-century-old Newtonian system. Immediately, scientists looked for experiments to verify or dismiss aspects of the new theory. The most widely publicized of these experiments occurred in 1919.

One of the predictions of Einstein's theory is that the path of light is curved by gravity. Therefore, scientists looked for a way to observe the phenomenon of curved light to test a part of the general theory of relativity. In 1919, their opportunity came during a total solar eclipse. Stars close to the sun's position in the sky are ordinarily obscured by the extreme brightness. However, during a total eclipse, such stars become visible.

If light from these stars is bent by the sun's gravitation, then the apparent positions of these stars will be different than their positions known from previous observations. Measurements taken during the 1919 eclipse showed the discrepancy in position that Einstein's theory predicted, and provided dramatic validation of the theory.[5]

Where Statistics Fits In

You may wonder what philosophy has to do with statistics, and you may be surprised to find that the answer is "quite a bit." It has often been said that mathematics is the language of science, and justifiably so. We can make a similar observation about statistics:

Statistics is the language of the scientific method.

One example of this is the close relation between scientific investigation and statistical experimental design, which was explored in Chapter 3 and which is expanded upon in Chapters 12 to 14. Another example, which we consider here, is the relation between hypothesis tests and scientific investigation.

Hypothesis tests are modeled on the methods of scientific investigation. A scientific investigation of some phenomenon might begin with a scientific hypothesis about that phenomenon. This hypothesis may:

(1a) Offer a new or different view of some aspect of the phenomenon, in contrast with the accepted scientific view. Einstein's theory of general relativity was a new scientific view of mechanics that contrasted with the accepted Newtonian theory. In the light-bending experiment, the hypothesis was that light from distant stars would be bent by the sun's gravity. Newtonian mechanics postulated no bending.

(2a) Predict a change in the phenomenon resulting from some treatment applied to experimental units. An example is predicting a lowering of blood-sugar levels (the change), on average, in diabetic mice (the experimental units) with an artificial pancreas (the treatment).

(3a) Predict a difference between one or more experimental units and a theoretical norm. Testing a roulette wheel (the experimental unit) with the idea that it favors red (the difference) is an example.

The scientific hypothesis must make a **testable prediction** that can then be supported or refuted by experiment. This hypothesis is contrasted with another hypothesis that, in terms of the preceding examples, postulates one of the following:

(1b) The accepted scientific view. In the light-bending experiment, this is the hypothesis that light does not bend (i.e., that Newtonian mechanics explains the phenomenon).

---

[5]Informed of the confirmation of light bending, Einstein seemed unimpressed. He later wrote, "I do not by any means find the chief significance of the general theory of relativity in the fact that it has predicted a few minute observable facts, but rather in the simplicity of its foundation and in its logical consistency."

(2b) That there is no effect. In the artificial pancreas example, this hypothesis might be that the artificial pancreas will have no effect on blood-sugar levels.

(3b) That there is no difference. In the roulette wheel example, this hypothesis might be that the wheel is fair, or at least that red occurs on average as often for the tested wheel as it does for a fair wheel.

Which Hypothesis Is Which?

Notice that in all three of the previous examples, the hypothesis representing change, difference or an aspect of a new theory is what we have called the alternative hypothesis. You may take this as a general rule:

HOW TO TELL THE NULL FROM THE ALTERNATIVE HYPOTHESIS

- The **alternative hypothesis** is the hypothesis that suggests change, difference, or an aspect of a new theory.
- The **null hypothesis** is the hypothesis that represents the accepted scientific view or that, most often, suggests no difference or change.

All Hypotheses Are Not Created Equal

Why does it make a difference which is the null and which the alternative hypothesis? The reason is that an hypothesis test does not treat the two hypotheses equally. Of the two, the null hypothesis is given the favored position. This is easily seen by considering that p-values are computed by **assuming that the null hypothesis is true.** Only by providing convincing evidence against the null hypothesis, in the form of a small p-value, can the alternative hypothesis establish itself.

This asymmetry in the treatment of the two hypotheses is reflected in the language of hypothesis tests. If we feel that the p-value is small enough to conclude that the alternative hypothesis is true, we say that we reject **the null hypothesis in favor of the alternative hypothesis.** But if the p-value is not small enough, we do not say that we accept the null hypothesis: How could we, we are already assuming it to be true! Rather, we say that we do not reject (or that there is insufficient evidence to reject) the null hypothesis.

A good analogy is the trial system in the United States. An individual put on trial is innocent until "proven" guilty. The null hypothesis is that the accused is innocent, the alternative that he is guilty. By initially assuming that the defendant is innocent, we are assuming that H_0 is true. A judge or jury must not convict the accused (i.e., reject the null in favor of the alternative hypothesis) unless there is strong evidence of guilt (i.e., a small p-value). If the accused is found not guilty (i.e., the null hypothesis is not rejected), it does not necessarily mean he is innocent (i.e., that the null hypothesis is true): It just means that there is insufficient evidence to convict.

There is another point that cannot be emphasized too strongly. With small amounts of data, it is very common to have insufficient evidence to reject the null hypothesis, even if the alternative hypothesis is true. Consequently, if there are few data, an hypothesis test will often not reject a false null hypothesis. So beware of concluding that the null is true just because the test you conducted did not reject it.

Similarly, virtually any null hypothesis will be rejected if there are enough data, because with enough data, any difference, no matter how small, will produce a small p-value. To see why, recall the standardized test statistic we considered in the artificial pancreas example. It had the form

$$t = \frac{\bar{Y} - 275}{S/\sqrt{n}} = \sqrt{n}\frac{\bar{Y} - 275}{S}$$

As n becomes large, S will approach the population standard deviation, σ, so that even if $\bar{Y}$ is very close to (and smaller than) 275, the test statistic will take a large negative value, resulting in a small p-value.

6.4

STATISTICAL SIGNIFICANCE

Table 6.1 gives guidance on interpreting p-values in terms of the strength of evidence in the data against the null and in favor of the alternative hypothesis. Often, however, statistics consumers need a stronger basis for decision making. One approach is to determine a prespecified level of evidence against the null and in favor of the alternative hypothesis. We call this level of evidence the **significance level** of the test and denote it by the Greek letter alpha: α. The test is said to give a **statistically significant** result if the p-value is smaller than α. It is also common to use the phrase **significant at the α level** to mean the same thing.

If the result of the test is statistically significant, the null hypothesis is rejected in favor of the alternative hypothesis. Common choices for α are 0.05 (in which case, the result is often called "significant") or 0.01 (in which case, the result is often called "highly significant"). These choices of α are somewhat arbitrary, having been determined to be reasonable guidelines by the famous statistician R. A. Fisher many years ago. We will have more to say on the choice of α in Section 6.5.

As an example of the determination of statistical significance, consider the artificial pancreas example, and recall that for the one-sided test, the p-value is 0.034. Since this p-value is less than 0.05, the result is judged significant at the 0.05 level of significance. However, since 0.034 exceeds 0.01, the result is not significant at the 0.01 level.

Now consider what happens in the artificial pancreas example if the alternative hypothesis is two-sided. In this case, the p-value is 0.068. This result is not significant at the 0.05 level, let alone the 0.01 level. From this, we can see that, even with the same data, the choice of alternative hypothesis can have a strong effect on the resulting decision. As a result, it is very important that the hypotheses and the significance level be chosen before the data are examined.

6.5

PITFALLS OF HYPOTHESIS TESTING

Whether through ignorance, or worse, everyday statistical procedures are misused. From our experiences, none are more often misused than hypothesis tests. In this section, we discuss some of the most common pitfalls confronting users of hypothesis tests.

Statistical Significance Is Not Practical Significance

Statistical significance results when the amount of evidence contained in the data against the null hypothesis and in favor of the alternative hypothesis is deemed sufficient to reject the null in favor of the alternative. It does not measure whether any difference found is of practical importance.

An hypothesis test can detect very small differences if there are enough data. Suppose in an effort to assess the effectiveness of a new drug in lowering blood pressure, medical researchers give the drug to a large treatment group, and also track a large control group who are given a placebo. Suppose that the mean blood diastolic pressure for the treatment group is found to be 1 mm lower than that for the control group, and that because of the large sample sizes, this result is found to be highly significant (i.e., significant at the 0.01 level). Does the statistical significance make a 1-mm difference in the mean blood pressure practically important? The answer is no, for the great majority of people.

Don't Let the Data Suggest the Hypotheses

Exploratory and Confirmatory Studies

Data may be used for a number of purposes. One purpose is to suggest patterns or relationships that might be explored in greater detail in a study specifically designed to look at those patterns or relationships. Any study having the purpose of suggesting patterns or relationships is called **exploratory.** Once enough is known about a phenomenon to enable investigators to formulate a precise set of questions they would like answered, a study can be designed to produce data to answer those questions. Such a study is called **confirmatory.**

Problems arise when investigators try to use the same observations to provide both exploratory and confirmatory analyses. In the exploratory phase, the investigator will choose as interesting hypotheses those in which the data show large differences. When these differences are then tested for statistical significance using the same data, a disproportionate number will be significant, because they were chosen for the large differences they exhibited! The results of the study are thus biased in a self-fulfilling manner.

When used as inferential tools based on the laws of probability, hypothesis tests can only be done on confirmatory data. Such data must be generated according to an appropriate design.[6] In addition, in order for an hypothesis test to be valid, the hypotheses and the significance level must be specified prior to viewing the data. To proceed in a valid way:

- If you know from theory or past studies the hypotheses you want to test, then use an appropriate design to generate a set of data to test those hypotheses.
- If you need data to suggest the hypotheses you want to test, then obtain data to suggest the hypotheses. You may, but need not generate the data especially for this purpose. Once you have settled on the hypotheses you want to test, generate another set of data, using an appropriate design, to test those hypotheses.
- You can sometimes use the same set of data for exploratory and confirmatory purposes. For example, if the data have been properly generated for inference, and if there are enough data, then the data may be split into two sets: an exploratory and a confirmatory set. The exploratory set will be used to suggest hypotheses and the confirmatory set to test those hypotheses.

EXAMPLE 6.3   HUMOR AT WORK

Recently, two management students approached us for help in designing and analyzing a survey about humor in the workplace. The primary focus of the survey was to study the types of humor used by managers and how they relate this humor to subordinates. The students were particularly interested in differences due to gender and age of managers and subordinates. The students came to us knowing what hypotheses they wanted to test. Together, we designed a survey to obtain data to test those hypotheses. The result was a properly designed confirmatory study. ✦

Publication Bias

Back in the 1920s, R. A. Fisher, one of the major figures in statistics, suggested that an observed difference should be declared statistically significant only if it was significant at the $\alpha = 0.05$ level. Since Fisher was very influential, this guideline was widely followed. Over the years, it has become so established that in papers reporting hypothesis test results, failure to attain a 0.05 level of significance means that the paper has little chance of publication in some scientific journals. One consequence of publication policies that favor studies that obtain positive results (i.e., reject the null hypothesis) over those that do not is **publication bias.** Publication bias is the tendency of articles published in scientific journals to overrepresent positive results and underrepresent negative results.[7]

---

[6]An appropriate design means a simple random sample or other properly designed and conducted probability sampling scheme to obtain sampling units, and, if the study is a controlled experiment, appropriate assignment of treatments to experimental units. See Chapter 3 for a detailed discussion of designed studies.

[7]Lab 6.2 looks at publication bias in more detail.

Ethical Dilemmas

A second consequence of publication policies that favor positive results is pressure on scientists to obtain significant hypothesis test results. Since for many scientists, jobs and promotion depend on publications, this pressure can be substantial, and can lead to ethical dilemmas.

Consider the following hypothetical example. Imagine you are a young scientist trying to make a career. In a major paper representing a year's work, you intend to test an hypothesis about a population mean (much as in the artificial pancreas example). The null hypothesis is simple. The alternative hypothesis is two-sided since you only hypothesize a difference but don't know the direction of the difference in advance. You run the test, and obtain a p-value of 0.084. This does not make the 0.05 cutoff, and you fear your paper won't be accepted. However, you notice that the mean of the observations is greater than the value hypothesized under the null hypothesis, and you also know that if the alternative hypothesis were one-sided, the p-value would be 0.042. This value is less than 0.05, and makes your publication problem go away. Mightn't you be tempted to go back and change the alternative hypothesis after the fact?

The problem is that changing hypotheses after the fact biases your results and is therefore unethical. It should **never** be done. This is why we say that the hypotheses and the significance level must always be specified prior to viewing the data.

One final point should be made here. If the young researcher obtains from the experiment information that convinces him that the one-sided alternative hypothesis is appropriate, he is then justified in conducting another experiment in which the one-sided hypothesis test is the preplanned test to be conducted.

If You Do Enough Tests, Something Statistically Significant Will Turn Up

Investigators who perform a large number of tests and observe a few seemingly significant results often make a mistake thinking that these results are statistically meaningful. A return to Example 6.3 will illustrate.

EXAMPLE 6.3   CONTINUED

The students doing the previously mentioned survey about humor in the workplace decided that they wanted to test 28 hypotheses. These hypotheses were set up first, and a 5% level of significance was chosen for each test. Then the survey was designed, the data collected, and the tests performed. Of the 28 p-values obtained, only 2 were less than 0.05. This means that those two p-values represent real differences, and are not due to chance, right? Not necessarily!

Suppose that the null hypothesis is true for each of the 28 hypothesis tests. Then there is a 0.05 probability of the p-value being less than 0.05 for each hypothesis tested. This means that, on average, $28 \times 0.05 = 1.4$ of the 28 p-values will be less than 0.05. So even though they are less than 0.05, those two p-values do not provide much evidence of statistical significance when viewed in the context of all 28 tests. The point is, if you do enough tests, some observed difference will turn up significant even if there are really no differences in the parameters being tested.

In this kind of situation, more sophisticated statistical techniques are needed. We analyzed the 28 hypothesis tests as follows. We first noted that if the null hypothesis was true for each of the 28 tests, then the 28 p-values follow a $U(0, 1)$ distribution. Therefore, we reasoned that any truly extreme p-values would show up as unusual points on a Q–Q plot of the p-values versus quantiles of the $U(0, 1)$ distribution. Of the 28 p-values, the two apparently significant ones were 0.0269 and 0.0014. On the Q–Q plot, only the second of these appeared unusual, so we concluded that only that test gave sufficient evidence to reject the null hypothesis.   ✦

Lack of Significance Does Not Mean the Study Failed

Despite the overemphasis on statistical significance in scientific journals, there are occasions when an hypothesis test provides useful information even though it shows no significant differences. Knowing that a treatment does not cause a difference can be as great a contribution to scientific knowledge as knowing that a treatment does cause a difference.

6.6

HYPOTHESIS TESTS FOR THE MEAN IN THE C+E MODEL

In this and the next three sections, we present hypothesis tests for means and proportions in the one- and two-population setting. For each test, we will state the model, the statistical hypotheses being tested, the test statistic (sometimes normalized), and the formula for computing the p-value. Since the appropriate scientific hypothesis depends on the problem being investigated, we consider the scientific hypotheses only in the examples.

The tests and the examples are the hypothesis test versions of the estimation procedures covered in Chapter 5. An appendix at the end of this chapter summarizes all tests covered in the chapter, and is intended to serve as a quick reference.

The remainder of this section describes hypothesis tests for the parameter μ in the C+E model given by Equation (6.1).

Assumptions

In small samples, it is assumed that the random errors ϵ have an $N(0, \sigma^2)$ distribution, or one close to it. Since the test statistics are based on sample means, the Central Limit Theorem renders this assumption less important for larger samples.

Some Rules of Thumb

In any event, before doing an hypothesis test, the data should be graphed to look at distributional shapes and for outliers, which can, in small and moderate samples, appreciably alter the results. Some rules of thumb on when it is appropriate to use these procedures are as follows:

- For small samples (less than 15 or so), do not use the test procedures presented in this section if there is evidence of nonnormality or if there are outliers.
- For moderate samples (between 15 and 30), do not use these procedures if there are extreme outliers or extreme nonnormality (e.g, extreme skewness).
- For larger samples, these procedures are nearly always appropriate.

Violations of underlying model assumptions raise fundamental issues that should be resolved before doing any analysis. For example, we know from Chapter 2 that if a set of data is severely skewed, then the sample mean is probably not a good measure of the "center" of the distribution. In fact, it is not at all clear what "center" means. This difficulty carries over to inference. Severe skewness of the sample indicates severe skewness of the population. In this case, before performing inference for the population mean, we should ask whether the population mean is an appropriate summary measure for the population.

Remedial Measures

If you want to use one of the tests for the population mean, but you find that violations of model assumptions make use of the test inappropriate for your data, there are remedial measures you can try.

- **Outliers.** As always, try to find a cause for outliers, and remove those whose removal is warranted. Examples of valid causes are data-entry errors or failure of the equipment used to collect the data. Be aware, however, that the sampling distributions on which hypothesis tests are based, and therefore the tests themselves, are no longer valid if outliers are removed without cause. Even worse, because it is dishonest, is to remove outliers in order to make the results come out better (meaning the way the investigator wants).

  If a cause or causes cannot be found, you can conduct the test with and without the outlier(s) and see if the results are substantially different. If they aren't, the outlier(s) didn't matter. If they are, then both sets of results should be reported. In this case, you may need to investigate the cause(s) of the outlier(s) further to settle the matter.

- **Nonnormality.** If the data are nonnormal, a transformation may help induce normality. For example, a square root or log transformation often helps eliminate right-skewness. The tests are then conducted on the transformed data. It is important to note that the population is then the population of transformed values, and the parameters being tested are parameters for that population.

There are also robust methods[8] that can be used for performing tests. Some of these methods are introduced in Chapter 11.

Tests for μ When the Variance Is Known

We begin by assuming that σ^2, the variance of the error terms, is known.

- **The Statistical Model.** The statistical model is the one population C+E model (6.1).
- **The Statistical Hypotheses.** The null hypothesis is, as it will be in all applications in this chapter, simple; that is, that $\mu = \mu_0$, where μ_0 is some value known to the investigator. In a one-sided test, the alternative hypothesis is either that $\mu > \mu_0$ or that $\mu < \mu_0$. Denote the first of these H_{a+} and the second H_{a-}. In a two-sided test, the alternative hypothesis is that $\mu \neq \mu_0$. Denote this $H_{a\pm}$. In summary, the possible sets of hypotheses are:

$$H_0: \quad \mu = \mu_0$$
$$H_{a+}: \quad \mu > \mu_0$$

$$H_0: \quad \mu = \mu_0$$
$$H_{a-}: \quad \mu < \mu_0$$

$$H_0: \quad \mu = \mu_0$$
$$H_{a\pm}: \quad \mu \neq \mu_0$$

- **The Test Statistic.** The data are $Y_1, Y_2, \ldots, Y_n$, a random sample from the population, having mean μ and variance σ^2. The test statistic is the sample mean, $\bar{Y}$. The standardized test statistic is

$$Z = \frac{\bar{Y} - \mu_0}{\sigma(\bar{Y})} \tag{6.2}$$

where

$$\sigma(\bar{Y}) = \frac{\sigma}{\sqrt{n}}$$

is the standard error of $\bar{Y}$ (see Chapter 5).

- **The p-Value.** Let z^* be the observed value of Z (i.e., z^* is obtained by plugging the observed Y values into Equation (6.2)). Under H_0, Z has an $N(0, 1)$ distribution. Therefore, the p-value for testing H_0 against H_{a+} is $p^+ = P(Z \geq z^*)$, and the p-value for testing against H_{a-} is $p_- = P(Z \leq z^*)$. The p-value for testing $H_{a\pm}$ is $p\pm = P(|Z| \geq |z^*|)$. In other words, p^+ is the proportion of an $N(0, 1)$ population greater than or equal to z^*, p_- is the proportion of an $N(0, 1)$ population less than or equal to z^*, and $p\pm$ is

---

[8] Recall that robust methods are methods that perform well in the presence of outliers, nonnormality, or other violations of model assumptions, and that perform nearly as well as standard methods when the assumptions are satisfied.

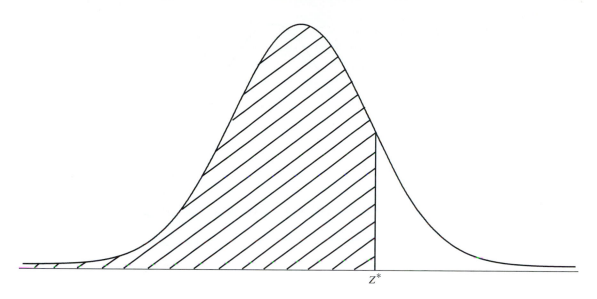

Figure 6.2   Shaded area is the p-value for testing H_0 against H_{a_-}.

the proportion of an $N(0, 1)$ population either greater than or equal to $|z^*|$ or less than or equal to $-|z^*|$. Figures 6.2 to 6.4 display these p-values graphically.

Note that by the symmetry of the $N(0, 1)$ density about 0,

$$p\pm = 2P(Z \geq |z^*|) = 2\min(p_-, p^+)$$

where $\min(p_-, p^+)$ denotes the minimum of p_- and p^+.

EXAMPLE 6.4   HOSPITAL STAYS

Recently, there have been reports that postdelivery stays for women giving birth in hospitals are shorter than they have been in the past. Based on these reports, a hospital administrator hypothesized that the stays at her hospital are shorter than they were 5 years ago.

- **The Scientific Hypothesis.** The scientific hypothesis is that postdelivery stays at the administrator's hospital are shorter than they were 5 years ago.
- **The Statistical Model.** In theory, the administrator could have obtained the lengths of stay for all births at the hospital, but the recent records hadn't been entered into the database yet, and she didn't have the resources to have all of them entered quickly. Therefore, she decided to obtain the length of stay from a random sample of recent postdelivery stays. She felt that the data would follow the C+E model, where each length of stay differs from the true mean length of stay by a random amount.

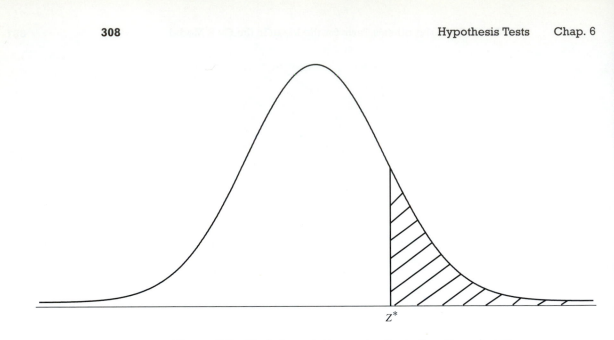

Figure 6.3   Shaded area is the p-value for testing H_0 against H_{a+}.

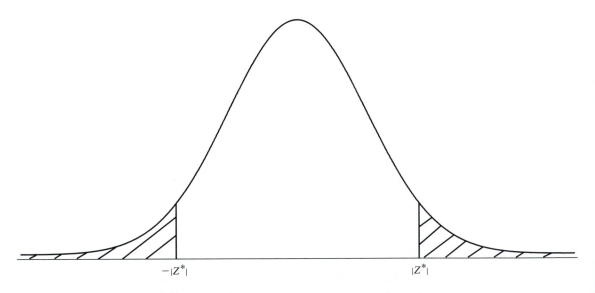

Figure 6.4   Shaded area is the p-value for testing H_0 against $H_{a\pm}$.

• **The Statistical Hypotheses.** The administrator decided that in statistical terms, she would look into whether the mean length of stay is shorter now than it was 5 years ago. From complete hospital records, the administrator knew that 5 years ago the mean postdelivery stay was 79.2 hours with a standard deviation of 60 hours.

As a result, the administrator wanted to test

$$H_0: \quad \mu = 79.2$$

$$H_{a_-}: \quad \mu < 79.2$$

where μ is the current true mean postdelivery stay in her hospital. Note that H_0 asserts that the mean length of stay now is the same as it was 5 years ago, and that H_{a_-} is the scientific hypothesis that the mean length of stay now is shorter than it was 5 years ago.

• **The Test Statistic.** The hospital administrator randomly sampled the lengths of 25 recent postdelivery stays at her hospital, and found them to have a mean of 62.4 hours.

The administrator noticed that data show a slight right skewness, but as there are no outliers, she concluded that the sample mean computed from 25 observations should be nearly normal.

From the data, $\bar{y} = 62.4$. The administrator was willing to assume that the true standard deviation of hospital stays is the same today as it was 5 years ago: that is, she was willing to assume that $\sigma = 60$. Therefore,

$$\sigma(\bar{y}) = \frac{60}{\sqrt{25}} = 12$$

and the standardized value of the test statistic is

$$z^* = \frac{62.4 - 79.2}{12} = -1.4$$

• **The p-Value.** The p-value is

$$p_- = P(Z \leq -1.4) = 0.0808$$

By using the guidelines of Table 6.1, the evidence that mean postdelivery hospital stays at the administrator's hospital are shorter today than 5 years ago is not compelling. ✦

For the record, had the alternative hypothesis in Example 6.4 been $H_{a+}: \mu > 79.2$, the p-value would have been $p^+ = 0.9192$. Had the alternative hypothesis been $H_{a\pm}: \mu \neq 79.2$, the p-value would have been $p\pm = 2\min(0.0808, 0.9192) = 0.1616$.

Tests for μ When the Variance Is Unknown

When σ^2 is not known, it must be estimated from the data. In the tests considered here, the population variance σ^2 is estimated by the sample variance S^2.

• **The Statistical Model.** The statistical model is the C+E model.
• **The Statistical Hypotheses.** H_0, H_{a+}, H_{a-}, and $H_{a\pm}$ are the same as for the known variance case.

- **The Test Statistic.** The test statistic is similar to Z in the known variance case, except that the standard error of $\bar{Y}$ must be estimated as

$$\hat{\sigma}(\bar{Y}) = \frac{S}{\sqrt{n}}$$

where S is the sample standard deviation of the observations. This gives the standardized statistic

$$T = \frac{\bar{Y} - \mu_0}{\hat{\sigma}(\bar{Y})} \tag{6.3}$$

that was introduced in Section 6.2. Under H_0, T has a t_{n-1} distribution.

- **The p-Value.** Suppose t^* is the observed value of T. The p-value for testing H_0 against H_{a^+} is $p^+ = P(T \geq t^*)$, and the p-value for testing H_{a^-} is $p_- = P(T \leq t^*)$. The p-value for testing $H_{a\pm}$ is $p\pm = P(|T| \geq |t^*|)$. In computing the p-values, T is assumed to have a t_{n-1} distribution. If the densities in Figures 6.2 to 6.4 are taken to be t_{n-1} densities, and if we replace z^* by t^*, these figures provide a graphical illustration of these p-values. Note that by the symmetry of the t density about 0,

$$p\pm = 2P(T \geq |t^*|) = 2\min(p_-, p^+)$$

EXAMPLE 6.4   CONTINUED

Consider again the data on postdelivery hospital stays. The standard deviation of the 25 postdelivery hospital stays is 26.4 hours. Suppose that instead of using the historical standard deviation of 60 hours, the administrator chose to use the sample standard deviation.

We test the same hypotheses as previously. The observed value of the estimated standard error of $\bar{Y}$ is

$$\hat{\sigma}(\bar{y}) = \frac{s}{\sqrt{n}} = \frac{26.4}{\sqrt{25}} = 5.28$$

The observed value of the standardized test statistic is then

$$t^* = \frac{62.4 - 79.2}{5.28} = -3.18$$

The p-value, which is the area of the $t_{n-1} = t_{24}$ distribution below -3.18, is 0.002.

This p-value provides strong evidence that the mean of current postdelivery hospital stays is shorter than it was 5 years ago. This result is different than the one obtained by taking the historical standard deviation as the current population standard deviation. What is the reason for this difference and which result should we believe?

The answer lies in the difference between the value of the historical standard deviation, 60, and that of the current sample standard deviation, 26.4. The current value is less than half the historical value, which may indicate that there is less variation in postdelivery hospital stays today. If so, use of the historical value is inappropriate, and we should use the estimate computed from the sample, as is done here. ✦

One good property of the *t*-test is its robustness to moderate departures from normality. In fact, the *t*-test is even more robust than the test based on the Z statistic (6.2).

ONE-SAMPLE HYPOTHESIS TESTS FOR A POPULATION PROPORTION

Assume the data are Y, the number of successes from a $b(n, p)$ distribution, that n is known, and that it is desired to test an hypothesis about p. Two tests will be considered: an exact test based on the binomial distribution, and a large-sample test based on the normal distribution. The exact test requires a table of the binomial distribution, such as that found in Table A.1, in Appendix A, page 894, but whenever feasible, its use is preferable. The large-sample test requires a table of the normal distribution. Of course, a computer can be used instead of tables to compute the *p*-value for either test.

Exact Tests

- **The Statistical Model.** Y, the number of successes from a $b(n, p)$ distribution, is observed.
- **The Statistical Hypotheses.** The null hypothesis is $p = p_0$, where p_0 is some value known to the investigator. We will consider three possible alternative hypotheses:

$$H_{a^+}: \quad p > p_0$$
$$H_{a^-}: \quad p < p_0$$
$$H_{a\pm}: \quad p \neq p_0$$

- **The Test Statistic.** The test statistic is Y, the number of successes.
- **The *p*-Value.** Let y^* be the observed value of Y. Under H_0, Y has a $b(n, p_0)$ distribution. Large values of Y favor H_{a^+} over H_0, small values of Y favor H_{a^-} over H_0, and values of Y that are either large or small favor $H_{a\pm}$ over H_0. Therefore, the *p*-value for testing H_0 against H_{a^+} is $p^+ = P(Y \geq y^*)$, and the *p*-value for testing H_{a^-} is $p_- = P(Y \leq y^*)$, where the probability is computed assuming $Y \sim b(n, p_0)$.

  We must be a little bit careful in defining the *p*-value for testing $H_{a\pm}$. We would like to compute it as was done for the C+E model: that is, $p\pm = 2 \min(p^+, p_-)$. However, this is not correct for the present case. To see what can go wrong, suppose $p_0 = 0.5$, $n = 2$, and $y^* = 1$. Then it is easy to show that $p^+ = p_- = 0.75$. Therefore, defining $p\pm$ as $2 \min(p^+, p_-)$ will result in a value of 1.5! The correct way to compute $p\pm$ is as follows:

  1. Recall that the $b(n, p_0)$ probability mass function is

$$p_Y(y) = \frac{n!}{y!(n-y)!} p_0^y (1 - p_0)^{n-y}, \qquad y = 0, 1, \ldots, n$$

Using this fact, compute $p_Y(y^*)$.

2. To compute $p\pm$, sum the $b(n, p_0)$ probability mass function, $p_Y(y)$, over all values y from 0 to n for which $p_Y(y) \leq p_Y(y^*)$:

$$p\pm = \sum_{y : p_Y(y) \leq p_Y(y^*)} p_Y(y) \tag{6.4}$$

Consider how Equation (6.4) works when $p_0 = 0.5$, $n = 2$, and $y^* = 1$. First, it is easy to show that $p_Y(0) = 0.25$, $p_Y(1) = 0.50$, and $p_Y(2) = 0.25$. We then know that $p_Y(y^*) = 0.50$. Since $p_Y(y) \leq p_Y(y^*)$ for $y = 0, 1, 2$, we have

$$p\pm = p_Y(0) + p_Y(1) + p_Y(2) = 0.25 + 0.50 + 0.25 = 1.0$$

EXAMPLE 6.5   TESTING THE QUALITY OF A WIRE SHIPMENT

A quality inspector for a wire manufacturer must decide whether each outgoing shipment of wire spools meets quality standards. One quality measure involves taking a number of spools from the shipment at random and measuring the wire diameter at three places on each spool. The spool is acceptable if and only if all three measurements are in specification. The company is interested in the proportion of unacceptable wire spools in the shipment. In particular, the company's contract stipulates that this proportion not exceed 0.01. To test whether the proportion in the shipment of 50,000 spools exceeds 0.01, the inspector takes a sample of 200 wire spools from the shipment and finds that 11 are out of specification. What can he conclude?

- **The Scientific Hypothesis.** The scientific hypothesis is that the proportion of defective spools in the shipment exceeds 0.01.
- **The Statistical Model.** To test whether the proportion in the shipment of 50,000 spools exceeds 0.01, the inspector takes a sample of 200 wire spools from the shipment. If p denotes the true proportion of defectives in the shipment and Y denotes the number of defectives in the sample, then since 200 is small relative to 50,000, we have that approximately $Y \sim b(200, p)$.
- **The Statistical Hypotheses.** The inspector wants to test[9]

$$H_0: \quad p = 0.01$$
$$H_{a^+}: \quad p > 0.01$$

- **The Test Statistic.** The test statistic is Y, the number of defective spools in the sample of 200.
- **The p-Value.** The p-value is calculated as the probability that a $b(200, 0.01)$ random variable exceeds the observed value 11. This can be found by computer or table to equal 6.88×10^{-6}. So if the true proportion of defectives

---

[9]Actually, he wants the null hypothesis to be $H_0: p \leq 0.01$. By theory that is above the level of this book, it turns out that the test of this null hypothesis is exactly the same as the one done in Example 6.5, and consequently the results and conclusions are the same.

in the shipment is 0.01, the chance of observing 11 or more unacceptable spools in a random sample of 200 is less than 7 in a million. Such a small p-value is convincing evidence that the true proportion of defectives in the shipment exceeds 0.01. ✦

A Large-Sample Test Using the Normal Approximation

If n is large,[10] a reasonably accurate approximate test may be obtained by appealing to the Central Limit Theorem.

- **The Hypotheses.** All hypotheses, both scientific and statistical, are the same as for the exact test.
- **The Statistical Model.** The statistical model is again a $b(n, p)$.
- **The Test Statistic.** The test statistic is again Y, the number successes. Under H_0, Y has a $b(n, p_0)$ distribution. However, if n is large enough (see the preceding guidelines), the distribution of Y under H_0 is approximately $N(np_0, np_0(1 - p_0))$. Therefore, instead of using the exact binomial distribution to compute the p-values, we may use the approximate normal distribution.

  As we did for the C+E model, we will use a standardized test statistic,

$$Z = \frac{Y - np_0}{\sigma(Y)} \tag{6.5}$$

where $\sigma(Y) = \sqrt{np_0(1 - p_0)}$ is the standard error of Y under H_0.

An alternative formula for Z is given by Equation (6.6) in terms of the point estimator of p, $\hat{p} = Y/n$:

$$Z = \frac{\hat{p} - p_0}{\sigma(\hat{p})} \tag{6.6}$$

where

$$\sigma(\hat{p}) = \sqrt{\frac{p_0(1 - p_0)}{n}}$$

is the standard error of $\hat{p}$ assuming H_0 is true. It is left as an exercise to show that Equations (6.5) and (6.6) define the same quantity Z.

Whichever formula we use, under H_0, Z has approximately an $N(0, 1)$ distribution.

- **The p-Value.** In computing an approximate p-value using the normal approximation, we will make use of the continuity correction.[11] If the alternative hypothesis

---

[10] Recall from Chapter 4 that the approximation of the $b(n, p)$ distribution by a normal distribution is reasonable for almost all applications if values of n and p satisfy $np \geq 10$ and $n(1 - p) \geq 10$. If the values of p are between 0.3 and 0.7, $np \geq 5$ and $n(1 - p) \geq 5$ will give an adequate approximation, and for the symmetric binomial distribution model $b(n, 0.5)$, n as small as 5 can provide a reasonable approximation. Of course, we won't know p, so we can substitute $n\hat{p} = Y$ for np and $n(1 - \hat{p}) = n - Y$ when checking these rules of thumb.

[11] See page 198.

is H_{a^+}, the p-value is

$$p^+ = P(Y \geq y^*)$$
$$= P(Y \geq y^* - 0.5)$$
$$= P\left(\frac{Y - np_0}{\sigma(Y)} \geq \frac{y^* - np_0 - 0.5}{\sigma(Y)}\right)$$
$$\approx P(Z \geq z_u^*)$$

where

$$Z \sim N(0, 1) \quad \text{and} \quad z_u^* = \frac{y^* - np_0 - 0.5}{\sigma(Y)}$$

Similarly, we may approximate p_- by $P(Z \leq z_l^*)$, where

$$z_l^* = \frac{y^* - np_0 + 0.5}{\sigma(Y)}$$

We approximate $p\pm$ by $2\min(P(Z \geq z_u^*), P(Z \leq z_l^*))$.

EXAMPLE 6.5   CONTINUED

To illustrate the large-sample test, we will redo the test of Example 6.5 using a large-sample normal approximation.

Here $p_0 = 0.01$ and $n = 200$, so $np_0 = 2 < 10$, which indicates that the minimum-sample-size guideline is violated in this instance. Despite this, we will proceed in order to demonstrate the computations, and in particular to show how inaccurate the final result will be.

The observed value of Y is $y^* = 11$, so

$$z_u^* = \frac{11 - (200)(0.01) - 0.5}{\sqrt{(200)(0.01)(0.99)}} = 6.041$$

The p-value is then $P(Z \geq 6.041) = 7.6581 \times 10^{-10}$. Note that both this and the p-value from the exact test are extremely small, indicating very strong evidence against H_0 and in favor of H_{a^+}. Note also, however, that this p-value is much smaller than the exact value obtained previously, indicating that too small a sample size can result in a poor approximation to the true p-value.   ◆

6.8

COMPARING TWO-POPULATION MEANS

Researchers and analysts are often confronted with the problem of comparing two populations: In particular, are the two population distributions, or at least some aspects of the distributions, the same? In the next two sections, we will consider the most important comparison for measurement data: comparison of the means of two populations.

Paired Comparisons

We begin with the simplest case, **paired comparisons.** Paired comparisons are made when the two populations consist of measurements that are paired in some way. The most common pairing is when two observations are taken on each sampling or experimental unit. For example, the effect of a heat treatment on the tensile strength of metal might be evaluated by taking a sample of test pieces of the metal, cutting each in half, and randomly choosing one of the halves of each test piece to receive the heat treatment. Here is another example:

EXAMPLE 6.6   MORE ON THE ARTIFICIAL PANCREAS

Consider again the artificial pancreas experiment. In the experiment, the researcher took readings of each rat's blood-sugar level prior to injection, just after injection, and then periodically until 60 minutes after injection. If the artificial pancreas is as effective as a real pancreas, then 60 minutes after the injection the blood-sugar levels should return to their normal, or preinjection, levels, on average. The researcher believes that the artificial pancreas will not be as effective as a real pancreas. Therefore, the scientific hypothesis is that the artificial pancreas will not lower blood-sugar levels to their preinjection levels. The data are

Rat	Initial reading	Reading after 60 minutes
1	170	266
2	134	149
3	99	161
4	84	220
Means	121.7	199.0

The two populations are the preinjection readings and the readings 60 minutes after injection of all possible diabetic rats with this kind of artificial pancreas. The data are naturally paired since there are two readings on each rat. These readings are very likely to be related: rats with high initial readings will likely have high final readings and vice versa.   ◆

Repeated measurements on the same units are not the only source of paired data. In some studies, different units are artificially paired by matching them in terms of various characteristics: for example, patients in a study on medication may be matched for gender, race, age, health history, and other variables. Paired observations are an example of blocking,[12] with each block consisting of one pairing.

[12]See Chapter 3.

- **The Statistical Hypotheses.** Suppose $Y_{1,i}$ and $Y_{2,i}$ are the ith set of paired measures, $i = 1, \ldots, n$. Let μ_1 denote the mean of the $Y_{1,i}$ and μ_2 the mean of the $Y_{2,i}$. The null hypothesis of interest is

$$H_0: \quad \mu_1 - \mu_2 = \delta_0$$

that is, the difference in the means equals some postulated value δ_0. Usually, in applications (but not always), $\delta_0 = 0$, which corresponds to the assumption that $\mu_1 = \mu_2$.

The alternative hypothesis of interest is one of

$$H_{a+}: \quad \mu_1 - \mu_2 > \delta_0$$

$$H_{a-}: \quad \mu_1 - \mu_2 < \delta_0$$

$$H_{a\pm}: \quad \mu_1 - \mu_2 \neq \delta_0$$

To simplify the problem, transform the data by forming the differences $D_i = Y_{1,i} - Y_{2,i}$. D_i is the difference between the two paired measurements for observation i. The D_i are considered data values from a single population with mean $\mu_D = \mu_1 - \mu_2$, where μ_1 is the mean of the first population, and μ_2 is the mean of the second population. In terms of the differences D_i, the hypotheses become

$$H_0: \quad \mu_D = \delta_0$$

$$H_{a+}: \quad \mu_D > \delta_0$$

$$H_{a-}: \quad \mu_D < \delta_0$$

$$H_{a\pm}: \quad \mu_D \neq \delta_0$$

- **The Statistical Model.** These hypotheses may be tested by treating the D_i as observations from the C+E model:

$$D = \mu_D + \epsilon$$

- **The Test Statistic.** The standardized statistic is

$$T = \frac{\bar{D} - \delta_0}{\hat{\sigma}(\bar{D})}$$

- **The p-Value.** Suppose t^* is the observed value of T. The p-value for testing H_0 against H_{a+} is $p^+ = P(T \geq t^*)$, and the p-value for testing H_{a-} is $p_- = P(T \leq t^*)$. The p-value for testing $H_{a\pm}$ is $p\pm = P(|T| \geq |t^*|) = 2\min(p_-, p_+)$.

EXAMPLE 6.6   CONTINUED

We now conduct the appropriate hypothesis test with the paired artificial pancreas data.

- **The Statistical Hypotheses.** We take the first population to be the postinjection readings. The scientific hypothesis that the artificial pancreas will not lower blood-sugar levels to preinjection levels translates into the statistical hypothesis $H_{a+}: \mu_D > 0$. The null hypothesis is that there is no difference between the mean initial reading and the mean reading after 1 hour (i.e., the artificial pancreas is as effective as a real pancreas). In symbols,

$$H_0: \quad \mu_D = 0$$

$$H_{a+}: \quad \mu_D > 0$$

- **The Test Statistic.** The observed differences d_i are

$$266 - 170 = 96, \quad 149 - 134 = 15, \quad 161 - 99 = 62, \quad 220 - 84 = 136$$

The mean of the differences is $\bar{d} = 77.25$ and the standard deviation is $s_d = 51.35$. The estimated standard error of $\bar{D}$ is $\hat{\sigma}(\bar{d}) = s_d/\sqrt{n} = 51.35/\sqrt{4} = 25.68$. After checking the differenced data, the researcher concludes that there is no evidence of strong departures from model assumptions. The observed value of the standardized test statistic is

$$t^* = \frac{\bar{d}}{\hat{\sigma}(\bar{d})} = \frac{77.25}{25.68} = 3.01$$

- **The p-Value.** The p-value is the proportion of a t_3 population greater than 3.01, which is 0.0274. ✦

Independent Populations: Known Variances

When the two populations of interest are independent, comparisons do not reduce to the one-population case as they do for paired data. Mathematically, independence of the two populations means that the random variables representing the observations from population 1, $Y_{1,1}, Y_{1,2}, \ldots, Y_{1,n_1}$, are independent of those representing the observations from population 2, $Y_{2,1}, Y_{2,2}, \ldots, Y_{2,n_2}$. Practically speaking, independence will result from the way the data are obtained. If the samples from the two populations are selected randomly and independently of each other, and if the populations are not related in any way, then methods for independent populations are appropriate.

The Tests

- **The Statistical Model.** Assume that the data are

$$Y_{1,1}, Y_{1,2}, \ldots, Y_{1,n_1} \qquad \text{from population 1, generated}$$

by the C+E model

$$Y_{1,i} = \mu_1 + \epsilon_{1,i}$$

and

$$Y_{2,1}, Y_{2,2}, \ldots, Y_{2,n_2} \qquad \text{from population 2, generated}$$

by the C+E model

$$Y_{2,i} = \mu_2 + \epsilon_{2,i}$$

The $\epsilon_{1,i}$ are assumed from a $N(0, \sigma_1^2)$ distribution, or n_1 is assumed large enough for the Central Limit Theorem to hold. Similarly, the $\epsilon_{2,i}$ are assumed from a $N(0, \sigma_2^2)$ distribution, or n_2 is assumed large enough for the Central Limit Theorem to hold.

The two populations are assumed independent, meaning that $Y_{1,1}, \ldots, Y_{1,n_1}$, are independent of $Y_{2,1}, \ldots, Y_{2,n_2}$.

Notice that the number of data from population 1 can be different than the number from population 2.

- **The Statistical Hypotheses.** The null hypothesis will be that the difference between μ_1 and μ_2 equals some known value δ_0. In most applications, δ_0 is taken to be 0, which corresponds to the assumption that $\mu_1 = \mu_2$. We have the usual one- and two-sided alternative hypotheses. In summary,

$$H_0: \quad \mu_1 - \mu_2 = \delta_0$$

$$H_{a^+}: \quad \mu_1 - \mu_2 > \delta_0$$

$$H_{a^-}: \quad \mu_1 - \mu_2 < \delta_0$$

$$H_{a\pm}: \quad \mu_1 - \mu_2 \neq \delta_0$$

- **Test Statistic.** Let
  - $\bar{Y}_1$ and $\bar{Y}_2$ denote the sample means from populations 1 and 2, respectively
  - S_1^2 and S_2^2 denote the corresponding sample variances

  The point estimator of the difference of the two population means, $\mu_1 - \mu_2$, is the difference of the sample means, $\bar{Y}_1 - \bar{Y}_2$. If the data are approximately normal, or if the sample sizes are large, then, at least approximately, $\bar{Y}_1$ and $\bar{Y}_2$ can be considered to have an $N(\mu_1, \sigma_1^2/n_1)$ and $N(\mu_2, \sigma_2^2/n_2)$ distribution, respectively. Because $\bar{Y}_1$ and $\bar{Y}_2$ are independent, $\bar{Y}_1 - \bar{Y}_2$ can be considered to have come from an $N(\mu_1 - \mu_2, \sigma_1^2/n_1 + \sigma_2^2/n_2)$ distribution. Thus, the standard error of $\bar{Y}_1 - \bar{Y}_2$ is

$$\sigma(\bar{Y}_1 - \bar{Y}_2) = \sqrt{\frac{\sigma_1^2}{n_1} + \frac{\sigma_2^2}{n_2}} \tag{6.7}$$

  and

$$Z = \frac{\bar{Y}_1 - \bar{Y}_2 - (\mu_1 - \mu_2)}{\sigma(\bar{Y}_1 - \bar{Y}_2)}$$

  can be assumed to have been drawn from an $N(0, 1)$ distribution. If the population variances are known, we can use the reasoning from Section 6.7, and the fact that under H_0, $\mu_1 - \mu_2 = \delta_0$ to construct the standardized test statistic

$$Z = \frac{\bar{Y}_1 - \bar{Y}_2 - \delta_0}{\sigma(\bar{Y}_1 - \bar{Y}_2)} \tag{6.8}$$

- **The p-Value.** Let z^* be the observed value of Z. Under H_0, Z has an $N(0, 1)$ distribution. Therefore, the p-value for testing H_0 against H_{a^+} is $p^+ = P(Z \geq z^*)$, and the p-value for testing H_{a^-} is $p_- = P(Z \leq z^*)$. The p-value for testing $H_{a\pm}$ is $p\pm = P(|Z| \geq |z^*|) = 2\min(p_-, p^+)$.

Independent Populations: Unknown Variances

Of course, the population variances are rarely known. So, following the development of the one-sample case, we should be able to substitute the estimated standard error:

$$\hat{\sigma}(\bar{Y}_1 - \bar{Y}_2) = \sqrt{\frac{S_1^2}{n_1} + \frac{S_2^2}{n_2}} \tag{6.9}$$

for $\sigma(\bar{Y}_1 - \bar{Y}_2)$ in Equation (6.8), and compute the p-values using the t rather than the $N(0, 1)$ distribution.

Unfortunately, life isn't so simple. The resulting test statistic does not have a t distribution under H_0. The test statistic used and the p-values obtained depend on which of three situations we find ourselves in:

Both Sample Sizes Are Large

- **The Test Statistic.** The size of n_1 and n_2 required for a good normal approximation depends on the population distributions: The more nonnormal the populations are, the larger the sample sizes need be. A rule of thumb is that if the distributions are not terribly nonnormal (you will have graphed them, of course!), then sample sizes of 30 or more will be sufficient. In this case, the sample variances will likely be close to the population variances, and we get normality by the Central Limit Theorem.

  The standardized test statistic we will use is

  $$\frac{\bar{Y}_1 - \bar{Y}_2 - \delta_0}{\hat{\sigma}(\bar{Y}_1 - \bar{Y}_2)}$$

  where $\hat{\sigma}(\bar{Y}_1 - \bar{Y}_2)$ is given by Equation (6.9).

- **The p-Value.** The p-values are computed using the $N(0, 1)$ distribution as if the variances were known.

At Least One Sample Size Is Small, and We Are Willing to Assume That the Two Population Variances Are Equal (but We Don't Know What They Are)

In this case, we can use a **pooled variance** test.

- **The Test Statistic.** Recall from Chapter 5 that the pooled variance estimator of the common variance of the two populations is

  $$S_p^2 = \frac{(n_1 - 1)S_1^2 + (n_2 - 1)S_2^2}{n_1 + n_2 - 2}$$

giving the estimated standard error of $\bar{Y}_1 - \bar{Y}_2$:

$$\hat{\sigma}_p(\bar{Y}_1 - \bar{Y}_2) = \sqrt{S_p^2 \left(\frac{1}{n_1} + \frac{1}{n_2}\right)} \tag{6.10}$$

As a result

$$T^{(p)} = \frac{\bar{Y}_1 - \bar{Y}_2 - (\mu_1 - \mu_2)}{\hat{\sigma}_p(\bar{Y}_1 - \bar{Y}_2)}$$

has a $t_{n_1+n_2-2}$ distribution. Since $\mu_1 - \mu_2 = \delta_0$ under H_0, this leads to the standardized test statistic

$$T^{(p)} = \frac{\bar{Y}_1 - \bar{Y}_2 - \delta_0}{\hat{\sigma}_p(\bar{Y}_1 - \bar{Y}_2)} \qquad (6.11)$$

- **The p-Value.** Under H_0, $T^{(p)}$ has a $t_{n_1+n_2-2}$ distribution, and this distribution is used to compute p-values.

At Least One Sample Size Is Small, and We Are Unwilling to Assume the Population Variances Are Equal

- **The Test Statistic.** In this case, we can use the standardized test statistic

$$T^{(ap)} = \frac{\bar{Y}_1 - \bar{Y}_2 - \delta_0}{\hat{\sigma}(\bar{Y}_1 - \bar{Y}_2)} \qquad (6.12)$$

- **The p-Value.** Under H_0, the distribution of $T^{(ap)}$ is approximately t_ν, where the degrees of freedom ν is taken as the largest integer less than or equal to

$$\left(\frac{S_1^2}{n_1} + \frac{S_2^2}{n_2}\right)^2 \Big/ \left[\frac{(S_1^2/n_1)^2}{n_1 - 1} + \frac{(S_2^2/n_2)^2}{n_2 - 1}\right]$$

The observed value of $T^{(ap)}$ is compared with the t_ν distribution to obtain the appropriate p-value.

Assumptions.   The basic assumption is that $\bar{Y}_1 - \bar{Y}_2$ has a normal distribution. This is difficult to check, as there is no meaningful transformation of the data, similar to the D_i in the paired data case, that we can look at. So we must rely on checking the data from each population separately for normality and outliers, as discussed in Section 6.6.

EXAMPLE 6.7   ANOTHER ANALYSIS OF THE ARTIFICIAL PANCREAS: THE TWO SAMPLE CASE

We revisit the artificial pancreas experiment. In order to evaluate the performance of the artificial pancreas, the researcher performed the same experiment on a control group consisting of diabetic rats drawn from the same population as the experimental group of rats. The control group did not receive the artificial pancreas, however. The researcher wished to compare the blood-sugar readings 60 minutes after injection for the experimental group with those for the control group. Her scientific hypothesis was that diabetic rats having the artificial pancreas would have lower blood-sugar levels 60 minutes after the injection than would diabetic rats without the artificial pancreas.

Since the treatment and control groups were independently selected and administered, the measurements represent samples from two independent populations:[13] diabetic rats given the artificial pancreas and diabetic rats not given the artificial pancreas.

Let group 1 denote the control group and group 2 the experimental group. The researcher translates the scientific hypothesis into a statistical hypothesis about means: namely, the mean blood-sugar level is lower in the experimental group than in the control group. She chose to test for significance at the 0.01 level.

The hypotheses are

$$H_0: \quad \mu_1 - \mu_2 = 0$$

$$H_{a+}: \quad \mu_1 - \mu_2 > 0$$

Notice that $\delta_0 = 0$, with the implication that under H_0, the population means are equal. Notice also that H_{a+} is the scientific hypothesis.

The data from the experiment are

	Untreated diabetic	Artificial pancreas
	402	266
	305	149
	496	161
	421	220
$\bar{Y}$	406.0	199.0
s	78.6	54.4

Plots of these data reveal no outliers or evidence that model assumptions are violated, so neither the pooled nor approximate t procedures are ruled out. Looking at the standard deviations between the two groups, the researcher concluded that the pooled variance procedure should be used, but we will also illustrate the use of the approximate t procedure.

- **The Pooled Variance Procedure**
  - **The Test Statistic**

$$s_p^2 = \frac{(n_1 - 1)s_1^2 + (n_2 - 1)s_2^2}{n_1 + n_2 - 2} = \frac{(4 - 1)78.6^2 + (4 - 1)54.4^2}{4 + 4 - 2} = 4568.7$$

$$\hat{\sigma}_p(\bar{y}_1 - \bar{y}_2) = \sqrt{s_p^2 \left(\frac{1}{n_1} + \frac{1}{n_2} \right)} = \sqrt{4568.7 \left(\frac{1}{4} + \frac{1}{4} \right)} = 47.8$$

---

[13]Note that these independent populations are not the same as the rat population, although the measurements come from rats originally selected from the same population of diabetic rats. Rather, assigning treatments (artificial pancreas, nothing) to experimental units (the selected rats) creates two populations of rats: those given the artificial pancreas and those not given the artificial pancreas.

and so from Equation (6.11), the observed value of $T^{(p)}$ is

$$t^{(p)*} = \frac{406 - 199}{47.8} = 4.33$$

○ **The p-Value.** As $n_1 + n_2 - 2 = 6$, the p-value is the area under the t_6 density that exceeds 4.32. This value is found to be 0.0025. As 0.0025 is less than 0.01, the researcher concluded that the mean blood-sugar level is lower in the experimental group than in the control group.

- **The Approximate t Procedure**
  ○ **The Test Statistic.** We first compute the degrees of freedom v for the approximate t procedure. Since

$$\left(\frac{S_1^2}{n_1} + \frac{S_2^2}{n_2}\right)^2 \Big/ \left[\frac{(S_1^2/n_1)^2}{n_1 - 1} + \frac{(S_2^2/n_2)^2}{n_2 - 1}\right]$$

$$= \left(\frac{78.6^2}{4} + \frac{54.4^2}{4}\right)^2 \Big/ \left[\frac{(78.6^2/4)^2}{4 - 1} + \frac{(54.4^2/4)^2}{4 - 1}\right] = 5.3$$

we take $v = 5$. The estimated standard error is[14]

$$\hat{\sigma}(\bar{y}_1 - \bar{y}_2) = \sqrt{\frac{78.6^2}{4} + \frac{54.4^2}{4}} = 47.8.$$

From Equation (6.12), the observed value of $T^{(ap)}$ is

$$t^{(ap)*} = \frac{406 - 199}{47.8} = 4.33$$

○ **The p-Value.** The p-value is the area under the t_5 density that exceeds 4.33. This value is found to be 0.0037. As 0.0037 is less than 0.01, the researcher concludes that the mean blood-sugar level is lower in the experimental group than in the control group. ◆

In Example 6.6, the degrees of freedom for the pooled variance test, 6, and for the approximate test, 5, do not differ by much. This reflects the fact that the two sample variances do not differ by much. The fact that the computed value of the latter, 5.3, is rounded down, makes the difference appear larger than it really is. This rounding down results in a **conservative** test. A conservative test is one that generates high p-values. Conservative tests are less likely to reject H_0.

---

[14] You may have noticed that in this example, $\hat{\sigma}(\bar{y}_1 - \bar{y}_2)$ and $\hat{\sigma}_p(\bar{y}_1 - \bar{y}_2)$ have the same value. This will always be the case when $n_1 = n_2$, as Exercise 6.32 asks you to show.

6.9

COMPARING TWO-POPULATION PROPORTIONS

The data are assumed to be the number of successes in two independent binomial populations: $Y_1 \sim b(n_1, p_1)$ and $Y_2 \sim b(n_2, p_2)$. We want to compare the two proportions p_1 and p_2.

- **The Statistical Hypotheses.** We wish to test a null hypothesis that the two population proportions differ by a known amount δ_0,

$$H_0: \quad p_1 - p_2 = \delta_0,$$

against one of three possible alternative hypotheses:

$$H_{a+}: \quad p_1 - p_2 > \delta_0$$
$$H_{a-}: \quad p_1 - p_2 < \delta_0$$
$$H_{a\pm}: \quad p_1 - p_2 \neq \delta_0$$

- **The Test Statistic.** When n_1 and n_2 are large enough, so that the Central Limit Theorem holds,[15] then the sample proportions $\hat{p}_1 = Y_1/n_1$ and $\hat{p}_2 = Y_2/n_2$ are independent, $\hat{p}_1$ has approximately an $N(p_1, p_1(1 - p_1)/n_1)$ distribution and $\hat{p}_2$ has approximately an $N(p_2, p_2(1 - p_2)/n_2)$ distribution.

    The natural point estimator of $p_1 - p_2$ is $\hat{p}_1 - \hat{p}_2$, which has approximately a normal distribution with mean $p_1 - p_2$ and variance $p_1(1 - p_1)/n_1 + p_2(1 - p_2)/n_2$. The standardized test statistic is computed in different ways depending on whether $\delta_0 = 0$ or not.

    o **If $\delta_0 \neq 0$,** the (by now) standard reasoning gives the standardized test statistic

$$Z = \frac{\hat{p}_1 - \hat{p}_2 - \delta_0}{\hat{\sigma}(\hat{p}_1 - \hat{p}_2)} \tag{6.13}$$

    where

$$\hat{\sigma}(\hat{p}_1 - \hat{p}_2) = \sqrt{\frac{\hat{p}_1(1 - \hat{p}_1)}{n_1} + \frac{\hat{p}_2(1 - \hat{p}_2)}{n_2}}$$

    is the estimated standard error of $\hat{p}_1 - \hat{p}_2$.

    o **If $\delta_0 = 0$,** then under H_0, $p_1 = p_2$. Call their common value p. The natural point estimator of p is

$$\hat{p} = \frac{Y_1 + Y_2}{n_1 + n_2}$$

    We now use this estimator and the fact that under H_0, $p_1 = p_2$, to estimate

---

[15]The guidelines given in footnote 9 should apply to each sample.

the standard error of $\hat{p}_1 - \hat{p}_2$ as

$$\hat{\sigma}_0(\hat{p}_1 - \hat{p}_2) = \sqrt{\frac{\hat{p}(1 - \hat{p})}{n_1} + \frac{\hat{p}(1 - \hat{p})}{n_2}} = \sqrt{\hat{p}(1 - \hat{p})\left(\frac{1}{n_1} + \frac{1}{n_2}\right)}$$

The standardized test statistic is then

$$Z_0 = \frac{\hat{p}_1 - \hat{p}_2}{\hat{\sigma}_0(\hat{p}_1 - \hat{p}_2)} \tag{6.14}$$

- **The p-Value.** Under H_0, if $\delta_0 \neq 0$, Z has approximately an $N(0, 1)$ distribution. If z^* is the observed value of Z, p-values are computed exactly as for the large sample test in Section 6.7.

  If $\delta_0 = 0$, then under H_0, Z_0 has approximately an $N(0, 1)$ distribution, and the computation of p-values proceeds as with Z.

EXAMPLE 6.8   COMPARING THE QUALITY OF TWO WIRE SHIPMENTS

The inspector from Example 6.5 wants to compare the quality of two large shipments of wire spools. To do so, he tests a random sample of size 500 from shipment 1 and a random sample of size 400 from shipment 2. He finds that 11 of the spools from shipment 1 and 16 of the spools from shipment 2 are defective. Is this convincing evidence that the proportions of defective spools from the two shipments differ?

- **The Scientific Hypothesis.** The scientific hypothesis is that the proportions of defective spools from the two shipments differ.
- **The Statistical Model.** Let p_1 and p_2 denote the proportions of defective spools for shipments 1 and 2, respectively. Since the shipments are large, we may consider Y_1, the number of defective spools from the shipment 1 sample to have a $b(500, p_1)$ distribution. Similarly, we may consider Y_2, the number of defective spools from the shipment 2 sample to have a $b(400, p_2)$ distribution.
- **The Statistical Hypotheses.** The inspector wants to test the hypotheses

$$H_0: \quad p_1 - p_2 = 0$$
$$H_{a\pm}: \quad p_1 - p_2 \neq 0$$

  $H_{a\pm}$ is the statistical interpretation of the scientific hypothesis.
- **The Test Statistic.** The sample proportions of defectives are $\hat{p}_1 = 11/500 = 0.022$ and $\hat{p}_2 = 16/400 = 0.040$. Since the number of defectives and nondefectives observed in each sample exceeds 10, we are justified in using the normal approximation.

  Since $\delta_0 = 0$, the standardized test statistic Z_0 will be used.

The estimate of p, the common value of p_1 and p_2, is

$$\hat{p} = \frac{11 + 16}{500 + 400} = 0.030$$

which implies that the estimated standard error is

$$\hat{\sigma}_0(\hat{p}_1 - \hat{p}_2) = \sqrt{(0.030)(1 - 0.030)\left(\frac{1}{500} + \frac{1}{400}\right)} = 0.011$$

Thus, the observed value of Z_0 is

$$z_0^* = \frac{0.022 - 0.040}{0.011} = -1.64$$

- **The p-Value.** The p-value is $2P(Z \le -1.64) = 0.1010$. This p-value indicates borderline significance, and even if the inspector chooses to reject H_0, the evidence for doing so cannot be regarded as strong. ✦

6.10

FIXED-SIGNIFICANCE-LEVEL TESTS

In what we have done so far, p-values have played a central role. Even when we performed hypothesis tests at a prespecified significance level α, the tests relied on comparing the p-value with α.

In this section, we will outline a way to perform hypothesis tests at a prespecified significance level that does not use p-values at all. One benefit of this way of testing is that it leads to a measure of the ability of a test to reject H_0 when H_a is true.

We will illustrate this alternative way of testing by considering the test for the mean in the C+E model when the variance is known. The steps involved in conducting such a test are as follows:

- **Specify the hypotheses to be tested.** This step is the same whether using the p-value approach or doing a fixed-significance-level test. For the test for the mean in the C+E model, the null hypothesis is

$$H_0: \quad \mu = \mu_0$$

while the alternative hypotheses are

$$H_{a-}: \quad \mu < \mu_0$$
$$H_{a+}: \quad \mu > \mu_0$$
$$H_{a\pm}: \quad \mu \ne \mu_0$$

- **Set the significance level α.**

- **Specify the (standardized) test statistic and its distribution under H_0.** For our example, the standardized test statistic is

$$Z = \frac{\bar{Y} - \mu_0}{\sigma(\bar{Y})}$$

where

$$\sigma(\bar{Y}) = \frac{\sigma}{\sqrt{n}}$$

is the standard error of $\bar{Y}$. Its distribution under H_0 is $N(0, 1)$.

- **Find the critical region of the test.** The **critical region** of the test consists of the values of the (standardized) test statistic for which H_0 will be rejected in favor of H_a.
  - If the alternative hypothesis is H_{a-}, small values of the test statistic Z will lead to rejection of H_0 in favor of H_{a-}. Therefore, the critical region will be all values at or below a cutoff z_{crit} such that if $Z \leq z_{\text{crit}}$, we will reject H_0 in favor of H_{a-}, and not otherwise. In other words, the critical region is $(-\infty, z_{\text{crit}}]$.

    The cutoff z_{crit} is called a **critical value** of the test. We choose z_{crit} so that if H_0 is true, the probability of rejecting H_0 equals α. Since under H_0, Z has an $N(0, 1)$ distribution, z_{crit} is the value at or below which lies a proportion α of an $N(0, 1)$ population. That is, $z_{\text{crit}} = z_\alpha$, the α quantile of an $N(0, 1)$ population. As a result, the critical region is $(-\infty, z_\alpha]$. Since $z_\alpha = -z_{1-\alpha}$, this critical region is often written as $(-\infty, -z_{1-\alpha}]$.
  - If the alternative hypothesis is H_{a+}, then the critical region is $[z_{\text{crit}}, \infty)$, and the critical value is $z_{\text{crit}} = z_{1-\alpha}$ (the value at or above which lies a proportion α of the $N(0, 1)$ distribution).
  - If the alternative hypothesis is $H_{a\pm}$, there are two critical values: one, $z_{\text{crit}}^+ = z_{1-\alpha/2}$, with a proportion $\alpha/2$ of the $N(0, 1)$ distribution above it and the other, $z_{\text{crit}}^- = z_{\alpha/2} = -z_{1-\alpha/2}$, with a proportion $\alpha/2$ of the $N(0, 1)$ distribution below it. The critical region is the union of the values at or below the lower critical value and at or above the upper critical value: $(-\infty, -z_{1-\alpha/2}] \cup [z_{1-\alpha/2}, \infty)$.

- **Perform the test.** The observed value of Z is z^*. If z^* lies in the critical region, we reject the null in favor of the alternative hypothesis. Otherwise, we do not reject.

EXAMPLE 6.9   CONDUCTING A FIXED-SIGNIFICANCE-LEVEL TEST

To illustrate the steps in conducting a fixed-significance-level test, we will look at the artificial pancreas data from Example 6.1, making the simplifying assumption that the sample standard deviation, 54.4, is the population standard deviation, σ.

- **Specify the hypotheses to be tested.** For the artificial pancreas example, the hypotheses are

$$H_0: \quad \mu = 275$$

$$H_{a-}: \quad \mu < 275$$

- **Set a significance level α.** We will take $\alpha = 0.05$.
- **Specify the (standardized) test statistic and its distribution under H_0.** For our example, the standardized test statistic is

$$Z = \frac{\bar{Y} - 275}{\sigma(\bar{Y})}$$

where

$$\sigma(\bar{Y}) = \frac{\sigma}{\sqrt{n}} = \frac{54.4}{\sqrt{4}} = 27.2$$

Its distributions under H_0 is $N(0, 1)$.

- **Find the critical region of the test.** Since $\alpha = 0.05$, the critical value is $z_{\text{crit}} = z_{0.05} = -1.645$, and the critical region is $(-\infty, -1.645]$.
- **Perform the test.** The observed value of Z for the artificial pancreas example is $z^* = -2.79$. Since this value is less than $z_{\text{crit}} = -1.645$, we reject H_0 in favor of H_{a-} at the 0.05 level of significance.

If the alternative hypothesis were H_{a+}: $\mu > 275$, then the critical value would be $z_{\text{crit}} = z_{1-0.05} = z_{0.95} = 1.645$, and the critical region would be $[1.645, \infty)$.

If the alternative hypothesis were $H_{a\pm}$: $\mu \neq 275$, the critical values would be $z_{\text{crit}}^+ = z_{1-0.05/2} = z_{0.975} = 1.96$ and $z_{\text{crit}}^- = z_{0.05/2} = z_{0.025} = -1.96$. The critical region is the union of $(-\infty, -1.96]$ and $[1.96, \infty)$. Since $z^* = -2.79$ is in the critical region, the conclusion is to reject H_0 in favor of $H_{a\pm}$. ◆

6.11

POWER

Consider a fixed-significance-level α test. This means that the probability of rejecting H_0 when H_0 is true is α. The ability of a test to reject H_0 when H_a is true is called the **power** of the test. The power of a test is a function of the true value of the parameter being tested.

The example considered in Section 6.10 of a test for the mean in the C+E model when the variance is known will serve to illustrate the idea of power of a test. Recall that a level α test of

$$H_0: \quad \mu = \mu_0$$
$$H_a: \quad \mu < \mu_0$$

rejects H_0 in favor of H_{a-} if the standardized test statistic Z is less than or equal to the critical value z_α. The probability of this occurring when H_0 is true is α.

Now suppose that μ is really less than μ_0. The test still rejects H_0 if $Z \leq z_\alpha$. What is the probability of this occurring? Since

$$Z = \frac{\bar{Y} - \mu_0}{\sigma(\bar{Y})}$$

$Z \le z_\alpha$ is equivalent to

$$\bar{Y} \le \mu_0 + \sigma(\bar{Y})z_\alpha \tag{6.15}$$

If μ is the true mean, then $\bar{Y}$ has an $N(\mu, \sigma(\bar{Y}))$ distribution, so

$$Z' = \frac{\bar{Y} - \mu}{\sigma(\bar{Y})}$$

has an $N(0, 1)$ distribution. Rewriting inequality (6.15) in terms of Z', we see that the test rejects H_0 when

$$Z' \le \frac{\mu_0 - \mu}{\sigma(\bar{Y})} + z_\alpha$$

Thus, the probability that the test rejects H_0 when the true mean is μ is

$$\Pi(\mu) = P\left(Z' \le \frac{\mu_0 - \mu}{\sigma(\bar{Y})} + z_\alpha\right) \tag{6.16}$$

the proportion of an $N(0, 1)$ population at or below $(\mu_0 - \mu)/\sigma(\bar{Y}) + z_\alpha$.

EXAMPLE 6.9   CONTINUED

Consider the artificial pancreas example and the test of

$$H_0: \mu = 275$$

$$H_{a_-}: \mu < 275$$

at the 0.05 level of significance. Since $z_\alpha = z_{0.05} = -1.645$ and $\sigma(\bar{y}) = 27.2$, the power of the test when the true mean is μ is computed as

$$\Pi(\mu) = P\left(Z' \le \frac{275 - \mu}{27.2} - 1.645\right) \tag{6.17}$$

Equation (6.17) can be used to calculate the power for any value of μ.

Figure 6.5 is a plot of the power function $\Pi(\mu)$ for $0 < \mu \le 275$, and Table 6.2 lists values of $\Pi(\mu)$ for selected values of μ. These displays illustrate two common characteristics of the power function:

- At μ_0, the value of the power function is α.
- The farther μ is from μ_0, the greater is the power.

Knowledge of the power function can help researchers evaluate the performance of tests and plan studies accordingly. For example, the artificial pancreas researcher knows that if μ is really 270, this test has only a 0.07 probability of rejecting H_0 (i.e., 7 out of every 100 identical experiments will reject H_0). So if she wants to have a good chance of detecting a μ of 270, she must change the experiment. On the other hand, if the largest μ she wants to detect is 200, she knows there is a 0.87 probability of doing so.

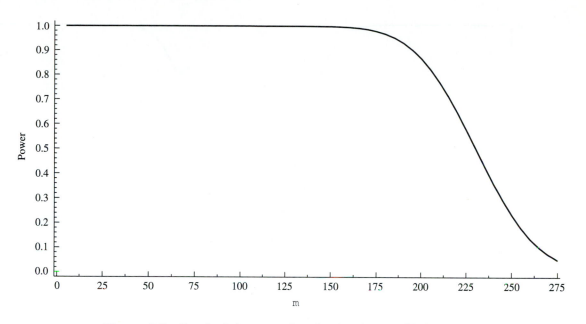

Figure 6.5 Graph of the power function for the one-sided test in the artificial pancreas example.

TABLE 6.2   Values of the Power Function for the One-Sided Test in the Artificial Pancreas Example

μ	110	175	200	225	250	265	270	275
$\Pi(\mu)$	1.00	0.98	0.87	0.57	0.23	0.10	0.07	0.05

Among all possible fixed level α tests, the best test is the one that maximizes power. For the assumed C+E model with normal errors, the one-sided test we are using here is the best level α test in that it has higher power than any other level α test. Best tests do not exist for all testing situations, however. For example, there is no two-sided level α test that has greatest power for all values of μ.

Given that we are using a best level α test and that α is fixed, the only way to increase the power of the test is to increase sample size. To see this, note that in Equation (6.16), the power will increase if

$$\frac{\mu_0 - \mu}{\sigma(\bar{Y})} + z_\alpha = \frac{\sqrt{n}(\mu_0 - \mu)}{\sigma} + z_\alpha \qquad (6.18)$$

increases, since $\sigma(\bar{Y}) = \sigma/\sqrt{n}$. Equation (6.18) can be increased by increasing the sample size, n.

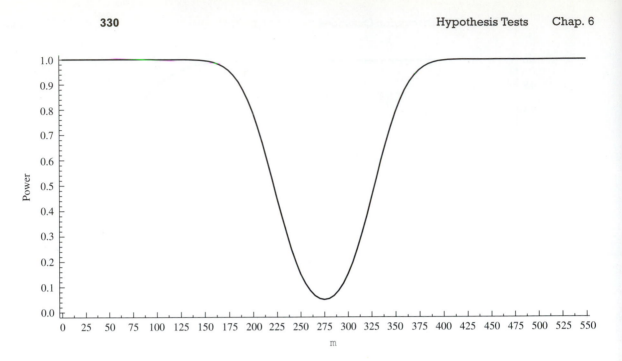

Figure 6.6   Graph of the power function for the two-sided test in the artificial pancreas example.

TABLE 6.3   Values of the Power Function for the Two-Sided Test in the Artificial Pancreas example

μ	110	175	200	225	250	265	275	285	300	325	350	375	450
$\Pi(\mu)$	1.00	0.96	0.79	0.45	0.15	0.07	0.05	0.07	0.15	0.45	0.79	0.96	1.00

If we are unwilling or unable to increase sample size, power can be increased by increasing α, but this increases the chance of rejecting H_0 when it is true.

Figure 6.6 and Table 6.3 show a graph and a table of selected values of the power function of a two-sided level 0.05 test of the hypotheses

$$H_0: \quad \mu = 275$$

$$H_{a_-}: \quad \mu \neq 275$$

for the artificial pancreas data. Computation of these values is left as an exercise. ✦

THE RELATION BETWEEN HYPOTHESIS TESTS AND CONFIDENCE INTERVALS

The two most often used types of statistical inference are estimation (covered in Chapter 5) and hypothesis testing. There is a close relationship between the two: in particular, between fixed-significance-level hypothesis tests and confidence intervals.

Consider the C+E model and two inference procedures based on the same set of data:

- A two-sided level α test of

$$H_0: \quad \mu = \mu_0$$

$$H_a: \quad \mu \neq \mu_0$$

- A level $L = 1 - \alpha$ confidence interval.

If the test rejects H_0 in favor of H_a, then the value μ_0 lies outside the confidence interval and vice versa. Similarly, if the test does not reject H_0 in favor of H_a, then the value μ_0 lies inside the confidence interval and vice versa.

There are such things as one-sided confidence intervals (which we have not studied), which have a similar relation to one-sided hypothesis tests.

D ISCUSSION QUESTIONS

1. What is the C+E model? Describe two types of data for which it is appropriate.
2. List the five components of an hypothesis testing problem, and tell how each fits into the process of testing.
3. What is a simple hypothesis? A composite hypothesis?
4. Describe one- and two-sided hypotheses and tests.
5. Discuss the philosophy of hypothesis testing and its relation to scientific investigation.
6. What is statistical significance?
7. Discuss the following pitfalls of hypothesis testing:
   (a) Statistical significance is not practical significance.
   (b) Don't let the data suggest the hypothesis.
   (c) If you do enough tests, something statistically significant will turn up.
   (d) Lack of significance does not mean the study failed.
8. Describe hypothesis tests for the following situations. In each case, state under what conditions these tests are valid.
   (a) The mean of a C+E model when σ is known and when σ is unknown.
   (b) Exact and large-sample hypothesis tests for a population proportion.
   (c) Differences in means of paired data.

　　(d) Differences in means from independent populations.
　　(e) Differences in proportions from independent populations.
　9. What are fixed-significance-level tests? What steps are involved in constructing them?
　10. What is the power of a test? How can power be increased?
　11. Discuss the relation between hypothesis tests and confidence intervals.

E XERCISES

Note: In all exercises requiring you to conduct hypothesis tests, state the following:
- The scientific hypothesis
- The statistical model
- The statistical hypotheses being tested
- The test statistic being used
- The assumptions made, and why they are, or are not, justified for the data being analyzed
- The p-value and your conclusions

6.1. Show that Equations (6.5) and (6.6) define the same quantity Z.

6.2. It is believed that a sample taken in a recent TV survey is representative of the American public. Individuals interviewed in the survey were asked whether they approved of Mr. Clinton's presidency. Of the 10,000 responses, 5,100 people said "yes." Do the responses suggest that President Clinton is doing significantly better than 50–50? Use an appropriate hypothesis test at the 0.05 level of significance.

6.3. The percentages of carbon in two incoming shipments of steel from different vendors are to be compared. The means and variances of the percentages of carbon computed from random samples taken from the shipments are shown in Table 6.4. Assuming that all necessary assumptions are satisfied, conduct an appropriate hypothesis test.

TABLE 6.4　Summary Statistics for Carbon in Steel

Shipment	n	$\bar{y}$	s^2
1	10	3.62	0.086
2	8	3.18	0.082

6.4. The following is an excerpt from an article that appeared in *The Boston Globe* of June 6, 1994:

> *The number of heart-attack victims fell dramatically among coronary patients who were taking the cholesterol-lowering drug Pravastatin, according to researchers. Scientists at the Bowman Gray School of Medicine reported in the* American Journal of Cardiology *that in addition to the unexpectedly sharp drop in heart attacks, there was also a slide in other diseases. The study was aimed at evaluating the effect of the drug on the growth of atherosclerosis.*

The team found that 5 percent of the 75 patients taking the drug experienced fatal or nonfatal coronary episodes during the three-year study period, compared to 13 percent of the 76 patients who got an inert placebo.

(a) There are two populations involved in the study. Can you tell from the article what they are?

(b) What is the distribution of the number of coronary episodes experienced by the Pravastatin users? By the nonusers?

(c) What kind of hypothesis test would you use with these data to check the statistical significance of the statement that "The number of heart-attack victims fell dramatically among coronary patients who were taking the cholesterol-lowering drug Pravastatin"? Are the necessary assumptions for this test satisfied?

6.5. The data set PENNIES contains the weights of 100 randomly selected newly minted U.S. pennies, in grams, as measured by an extremely accurate scale. For these data:

(a) What is the source of the variation you observe in the data?

(b) What is the population you will be making inference to?

(c) Pennies are supposed to weigh 3.1 grams, on average. Test this using an appropriate hypothesis test. Be sure to check all assumptions.

6.6. The alternative hypothesis in Example 6.2 is one-sided. Why is this appropriate, given the problem statement? Under what circumstances would a two-sided alternative hypothesis be appropriate?

6.7. It is believed that there is an increase in the percentage of suspended solids in pipelines carrying oil from port A to port B. The data set PIPELINE gives the percentage of suspended solids in a fixed volume of the fluid sampled from each end (port A or port B) of each of nine pipelines connecting the two ports.

(a) Because of the proximity of the ports, the two measurements in the each pipeline might not be independent. How might you advise the investigators to proceed in analyzing these data?

(b) Set up and conduct an hypothesis test for this problem.

(c) Would you change the type of analysis if the ports were very far apart? Why?

6.8. The breaking strengths of five large metal pins used in building construction randomly chosen from a large production lot are (in psi)

$$42,110, \quad 42,550, \quad 41,895, \quad 42,285, \quad 41,990$$

The head of the quality unit wants to know if this lot of pins has a mean breaking strength that is significantly less than the historical mean value of 42,300. Conduct an hypothesis test to answer his question.

6.9. A manufacturer claims that a certain drug is effective in treating arthritis. In an experiment, 150 people with arthritis were given a course of treatment with the drug and independently 100 people with arthritis were given sugar pills. The subjects were given checkups 6 months after treatment began. The results are shown in Table 6.5. Conduct an hypothesis test of the manufacturer's claim. Present your conclusions.

6.10. Consider the power function (6.16). Describe how it varies as the significance level α is changed if the values of μ, μ_0, and $\sigma(\bar{Y})$ are kept fixed.

6.11. Zeolites are aluminum and silicon crystals that are used as sieves and catalysts in many industries—especially petroleum refining. The relative yields (in percent) of the 15 most

TABLE 6.5   Classification of 150 People with Arthritis

	Improved	Not Improved	Total
Drug	100	50	150
Sugar	60	40	100

recent batches of zeolite produced by a particular manufacturer are, in order of production:

$$39.5, \ 33.3, \ 36.2, \ 40.4, \ 31.1, \ 40.1, \ 44.4, \ 35.7, \ 33.4, \ 42.6, \ 34.5, \ 35.7,$$

$$29.5, \ 35.3, \ 37.8$$

   (a) Do these data provide evidence that the process that generated the data is nonstationary? Make an appropriate plot to decide.
   (b) If you conclude that the process that generated the data is stationary, analyze the pattern of variation. Include a discussion of possible outliers, and use appropriate graphs and numerical measures to summarize the data.
   (c) Is it reasonable to assume that the yields were generated by the C+E model? Why? If your answer is yes, tell what the model components mean for these data.
   (d) Management wants to know if there is reason to suspect that the mean yield of the production process is currently below the minimum acceptable level of 37.5%. If appropriate, conduct an hypothesis test to help decide. If not appropriate, tell why not.

6.12. Show how to compute the values of the power function in Table 6.3. Compute the value of the power function at $\mu = 255$.

6.13. In order to evaluate the performance of a certain brand of alkaline battery, researchers at a consumer testing organization took a random sample of 152 new 1.5 volt AA batteries. Each of the batteries was subjected to the same pattern of discharge, which was designed to simulate typical moderate use. A battery's lifetime was obtained as the time for the output to drop to 0.9 volt. The mean lifetime of these 152 batteries was 46.7 hours and the standard deviation was 13.3 hours. The industry standard for lifetimes of such batteries is 45 hours. What kind of evidence do these data give that this brand of battery has mean lifetime that exceeds the industry standard?

6.14. It has been suggested that keeping batteries under refrigeration can maintain their potency. The consumer research organization described in Exercise 6.13 conducted a controlled experiment to evaluate the truth of this suggestion. Organization researchers obtained a random sample of 100 identical AA alkaline batteries. Fifty of these were randomly assigned to a treatment group that was kept under refrigeration at 37°F for 30 months. The other 50 constituted the control group and were kept at room temperature for the same 30 months. At the end of the storage period, all batteries were subjected to the same test described in Exercise 6.13, and the lifetime of each was recorded. The batteries in the treatment group had a mean lifetime of 40.7 hours with a standard deviation of 10.8 hours, and those in the control group had a mean lifetime of 39.0 hours with a standard deviation of 12.2 hours. Inspection of the data revealed no outliers or other large deviations from normality. Do these data suggest that there is a difference in the mean lifetimes? Conduct an appropriate hypothesis test to help decide.

6.15. The artificial pancreas researcher wants her level 0.05 test of

$$H_0: \ \mu = 275$$

$$H_a: \ \mu \neq 275$$

to be sensitive enough to detect a mean of 285 or 250. What would you tell her regarding her ability to do so with the data you've seen?

6.16. Consider the artificial pancreas example and the test of

$$H_0: \quad \mu = 275$$

$$H_a: \quad \mu < 275$$

at the 0.05 level of significance.

(a) Draw a graph of the ideal power function for this test.[16]

(b) Do the same for the test of H_0 versus the two-sided alternative hypothesis $\mu \neq 275$.

6.17. Medical researchers want to evaluate the effectiveness of a new drug designed to lower blood-cholesterol levels. It is known that without any drug, the mean cholesterol level of one kind of at-risk patient is 245 milligrams per deciliter of blood serum. A random sample of 1,000 patients from this same at-risk population is given the new drug for 2 months. Their blood-cholesterol levels are then recorded. What is the null hypothesis? The alternative hypothesis? Explain all terms used in describing them. Justify your choices.

6.18. In the cholesterol drug study described in the previous exercise, the mean cholesterol level of the 1,000 patients was 244.3 milligrams per deciliter of blood serum. The p-value was 0.0076. The company that developed the drug proclaimed its effectiveness at a large press conference, and media worldwide carried the story. Comment.

6.19. In another study of the new cholesterol drug, cholesterol levels are measured on 10 patients prior to being given the drug and then again after 2 months on the drug. It is desired to compare the mean level before treatment with the drug with the mean level after treatment. The standard deviation of the before readings is four times that of the after readings. What kind of test should the researchers use?

6.20. A statistics student observes that "a large p-value proves that the null hypothesis is true." Do you agree? Why?

6.21. Consider the problem of testing $H_0: \mu = \mu_0$ against $H_a: \mu \neq \mu_0$ for the C+E model with unknown variance using six observations. A value of -3.75 for the standardized test statistic is obtained. Explain how to compute the p-value for this test (a picture will do). Is this result significant at the 0.05 level?

6.22. In order to compare the proportion of statistics graduates who found employment in their field within 3 months of graduation with the proportion of physics graduates who found employment in their field within 3 months of graduation, a random sample of 100 statistics graduates and a random sample of 200 physics graduates are taken. Of the 100 statistics graduates, 96 were employed as statisticians within 3 months of graduation, whereas 147 of the physics graduates were employed as physicists. Can either Equation (6.13) or (6.14) in the text be used to perform the test? Why or why not?

6.23. Professor P. rides an exercise bike on a regular basis. Each day, he rides the same bike for the same length of time. The bike electronically records the calories he expends at each session. Figure 6.7 displays graphs and summary statistics for the number of calories expended riding the bike during several weeks in the spring of 1995. Figure 6.8 displays the same graphs and summary statistics for data taken in the spring of 1994. Professor P. wants to know if his mean level of energy expenditure on the bike has increased from 1994 to 1995.

(a) Formulate a possible model for these data. Based on this model, formulate hypotheses to find what Professor P. wants to know.

[16]This power function can never be attained by any test, but it is instructive to think about what the ideal would be.

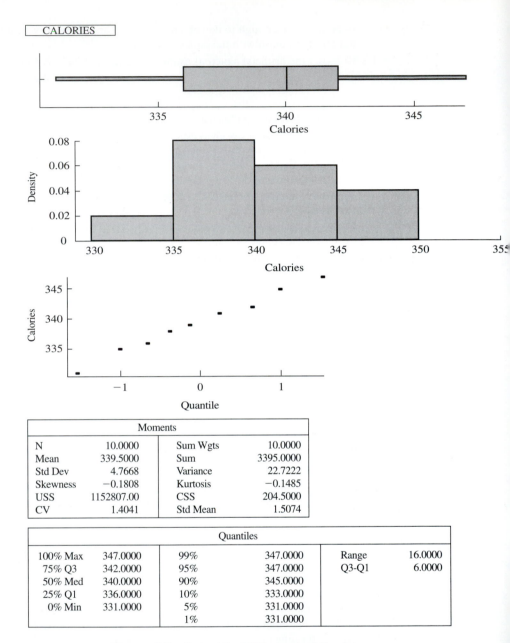

Figure 6.7   Output for 1995 exercise bike data.

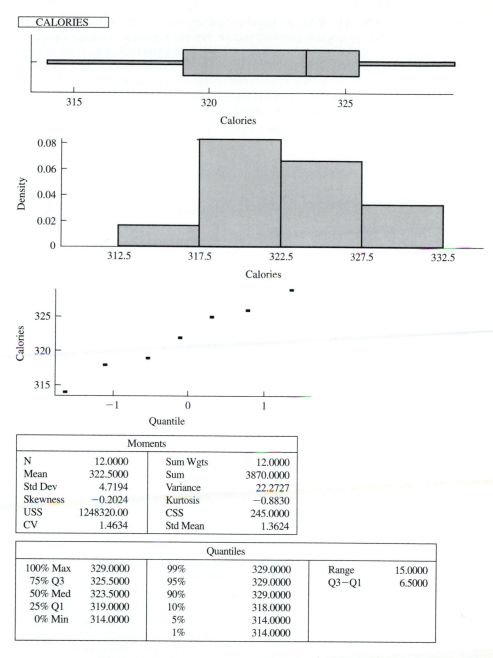

Figure 6.8   Output for 1994 exercise bike data.

(b) What assumptions are necessary for the model to be valid? Look at the distributions in Figures 6.7 and 6.8. Is there evidence that these assumptions are not satisfied? What specific measures or graphs did you look at to make your conclusion?

(c) Conduct an hypothesis test using the given data. Professor P. wants conclusions based on a 0.05-level test. What do you tell him?

(d) Why did you choose the test you did? Justify your choice.

6.24. The following table shows the preferences for two brands of chocolate chip cookie in a recently conducted double-blind taste-testing experiment involving 245 college students. Do the data provide evidence that the proportion of female students who prefer cookie A to cookie B is greater than is the proportion of male students who prefer cookie A to cookie B? Use an appropriate test to decide.

	Cookie A	Cookie B	Total
Male Students	94	85	179
Female Students	39	27	66
Total	133	112	245

6.25. Noted television personality Stuart Smalley claims "I'm good enough, I'm smart enough, and gosh darn it, people like me." To ascertain whether the last part of the statement is true, a national polling organization asked an SRS of 900 individuals randomly sampled from the American public, "Gosh darn it, do you like Stuart?" 423 of the 900 said they liked Stuart and the other 477 said they didn't.

(a) To what population can the pollsters make inference?

(b) When asked to clarify his statement, Stuart said he meant that a majority of the American public like him. Formulate a pair of hypotheses that will test Stuart's claim and then perform the test. What do you conclude?

6.26. A production engineer wants to determine the effect of machine configuration on the maximum force, in pounds, applied at a joint on an articulated arm of the machine during its normal operation. To do this, she obtains maximum-force readings for each of two different machine configurations. There is no reason to suspect that the data are nonnormal. The summary measures for the data are shown in Table 6.6. Compare the population mean force readings for the two configurations at the 0.05 level of significance. What do you conclude?

TABLE 6.6 Summary Statistics for Machine Force

Configuration	n	$\bar{Y}$	s
1	6	543.1	98.7
2	9	593.6	33.2

6.27. Ten measurements of the weight of a "one-kilogram" brick of gold have an average of 1 kg, 245 μg,[17] with a standard deviation of 328 μg.

---

[17] One microgram $= 1 \times 10^{-6}$ gram.

(a) What characteristics of the process that produced the data are responsible for the observed variation?

(b) Explain why the C+E model is appropriate for these data. What are the parameters of the model and their meanings for these data?

(c) At the 0.10 level of significance, test whether the true weight of the brick is 1 kg or not. What assumptions are necessary for this test to be valid?

6.28. A study is done to see if secondborn children are any more intelligent than firstborn children. A sample of 23 two-child families is taken, and the IQ score of each of the 46 children (at age 10) is recorded. What kind of hypothesis test should be conducted to investigate the difference in mean IQ scores between the firstborns and secondborns? Be very specific!

6.29. A researcher reports that a 95% confidence interval for the population mean μ in a C+E model is $(0.11, 0.46)$. This interval was computed in the usual way, given in Chapter 5, using $\bar{Y}$ and its standard error. The researcher also reports that the p-value of an hypothesis test of $H_0: \mu = 0.3$ versus $H_a: \mu \neq 0.3$ is 0.023. This test is the usual t-test for a population mean, using the standardized test statistic (6.3) described on page 310. Its p-value was computed using the same set of data used in computing the confidence interval. Do you believe both results? Give your reasons.

6.30. Software developers could not decide between two different types of help modules used to support a mathematical software package. In order to compare the ease of use of the two modules, they recruited 20 novice users and randomly assigned 10 to each type of help module. A specific set of timed tasks was given to each user and scored for correctness. As the sample variances for the two groups were quite close, and as there was no evidence of nonnormality or outliers, the two-sample, pooled variance t-test was used. The observed value of the standardized test statistic was $t^{(p)*} = 2.011$. Since $t^{(p)*}$ was positive, the experimenters decided to test

$$H_0: \quad \mu_1 - \mu_2 = 0$$

$$H_{a+}: \quad \mu_1 - \mu_2 > 0$$

They obtained the p-value 0.0298 and concluded that module 1 gave a higher mean score than module 2. Do you agree with their analysis?

6.31. Suppose that the software developers in Exercise 6.30 had decided prior to the experiment to test

$$H_0: \quad \mu_1 - \mu_2 = 0$$

$$H_{a\pm}: \quad \mu_1 - \mu_2 \neq 0$$

and to conduct the test at the 0.10 level of significance. Suppose also that they obtained the same data as in Exercise 6.30.

(a) What is the p-value of the test?

(b) Based on this p-value, the software developers rejected H_0 in favor of $H_{a\pm}$. Did they make the correct decision?

(c) Since $t^{(p)*}$ was positive, the software developers concluded that module 1 gave a higher mean score than module 2. Is this conclusion justified? Why or why not?

6.32. Show that if $n_1 = n_2$, then $\hat{\sigma}(\bar{Y}_1 - \bar{Y}_2)$ given by Equation (6.9) and $\hat{\sigma}_p(\bar{Y}_1 - \bar{Y}_2)$ given by Equation (6.10) are the same.

MINIPROJECT

Purpose

The purpose of this project is to

- Make you think about what processes might generate two of the models in this chapter.
- Teach you how to analyze data from these models using the hypothesis testing tools you've learned in the chapter.

Process

Your group will be assigned two of the following models:

1. The C+E model
2. The one-sample binomial model
3. The paired C+E model
4. The two-sample C+E model
5. The two-sample binomial model.

Your group's task will be to design and conduct a small experiment or observational study to generate data for each type of assigned model. You must show that the data are reasonably modeled by the models you choose. Before generating the data, your group must come up with at least one set of hypotheses for each model.

Once the data have been obtained and checked, your group is to conduct the appropriate hypothesis tests and draw conclusions.

A short (one-page or less) proposal of what your group plans to do for this miniproject must be submitted and approved before you begin your work.

LAB 6.1: Exploring Hypothesis Tests

Introduction

Having already studied hypothesis tests in this chapter, you are familiar with their interpretation in terms of a large number of repeated experiments. You are also familiar with the assumptions necessary for the validity of these tests. In this lab, you will use computer simulation to demonstrate the meaning of significance and p-values in hypothesis testing. You will then learn something about the sensitivity of the true significance level to violations of the stated assumptions.

Recall that the p-value of a test is the chance of observing a value of the test statistic that gives as much evidence against the null and in favor of the alternative hypothesis as does the value actually observed, under the assumption that the null hypothesis is true. As such, the

p-value is a measure of the evidence against the null and in favor of the alternative hypothesis. The smaller the p-value, the stronger the evidence the data provide against the null and in favor of the alternative hypothesis.

Recall also that a test is significant at the α level if the evidence in the data against the null and in favor of the alternative hypothesis, as measured by the p-value, is stronger than α. That is, the test is significant at the α level if the p-value is smaller than α.

Recall from Chapter 5 that the "confidence" associated with confidence intervals is interpreted as a long-run proportion. The same is true of p-values. Suppose you conduct an hypothesis test and get a p-value of p^* and a value of the test statistic v^*. Suppose now that you repeat the experiment a large number of times and each time the null hypothesis is true. If the value of the test statistic for the ith experiment is v_i, then about $100p^*\%$ of the v_i will provide as much evidence against the null and in favor of the alternative hypothesis as does v^*. The test is significant at the α level if in the long run no more than $100\alpha\%$ of the v_i provide as much evidence against the null and in favor of the alternative hypothesis as does v^*.

This can be said equivalently in terms of the p-values. The test is significant at the α level if in the long run no more that $100\alpha\%$ of the p-values are smaller than p^*.

Objectives

- To explore the meaning of p-values and statistical significance through simulation.
- To learn about the sensitivity of hypothesis tests to violations of model assumptions.

Lab Materials

None needed.

Experimental Procedure

The Meaning of Statistical Significance and p-values

In this lab, you will illustrate the concepts of statistical significance and p-values using computer simulation.

Proceed as follows:[18]

1. Generate 1 set of 10 observations from an $N(25, 1)$ distribution. Compute the t statistic and the p-value for testing H_0: $\mu = 25$ versus $H_{a\pm}$: $\mu \neq 25$ for this data set. Call the value of the t statistic t^*. Write down the p-value and the value of the test statistic.

2. Suppose you conducted 1000 more experiments exactly like the one that generated t^*. In what proportion of those experiments would you expect the t statistic to provide as much or more evidence against the null and in favor of the alternative hypothesis? In what proportion of those experiments would you expect the p-value to be as small as or smaller than the p-value for t^*? Write down your guesses now for use later in the lab.

3. Generate 1,000 sets of 10 observations each from an $N(25, 1)$ distribution, and compute the t statistic and p-value for testing H_0: $\mu = 25$ versus $H_{a\pm}$: $\mu \neq 25$ for each data set.

---

[18]We have incorporated the needed steps into computer macros for users of SAS and MINITAB. The **Doing It with SAS and Doing It with MINITAB** supplements give explicit instructions on their use.

Save the 1000 values of the t statistic and p-value in a data set. These 1000 pairs of values represent the results of 1000 experiments identical to the original one.

4. Obtain the proportion of the 1000 test statistics that provide as much evidence against the null and in favor of the alternative hypothesis as does t^*. Obtain the proportion of p-values as small as or smaller than the p-value associated with t^*. Did you get the results you expected?

5. What proportion of the tests are significant at the 5% level; the 10% level? Interpret these results.

How Nonnormality Affects the Results

Recall that a stated assumption for small-sample confidence intervals and hypothesis tests for the mean is that the population be normal, or nearly so. What happens if this assumption is violated? That is what you will look at in this part of the lab. You will generate observations from an exponential distribution with mean 25, and conduct hypothesis tests of H_0: $\mu = 25$ versus H_a: $\mu \neq 25$ using the normal theory t statistic. Proceed as follows:

1. To get a feel for the exponential distribution you will be using, generate 1000 observations from it, and from these observations construct a histogram. Describe the distribution.

2. Can you guess what will happen when we conduct hypothesis tests for data from this distribution? Will the computed p-values accurately represent the true chance of rejecting H_0? Let's find out.

3. Generate 1 set of 10 observations from an exponential distribution with mean $\mu = 25$. From these data, compute the t statistic and the p-value for testing H_0: $\mu = 25$ versus $H_{a\pm}$: $\mu \neq 25$. Call the value of the t statistic t^*. Write down the p-value and the value of the test statistic.

4. Suppose you conducted 1000 more experiments exactly like the one that generated t^*. In what proportion of those experiments would you expect the t statistic to provide as much or more evidence against the null and in favor of the alternative hypothesis? In what proportion of those experiments would you expect the p-value to be as small as or smaller than the p-value for t^*? Write down your guesses now for use later in the lab.

5. Generate 1000 sets of 10 observations each from an exponential distribution with mean 25, and compute the t statistic and p-value for testing H_0: $\mu = 25$ versus $H_{a\pm}$: $\mu \neq 25$ for each data set. Save the 1000 values of the t statistic and p-value in a data set. These 1000 pairs of values represent the results of 1000 experiments identical to the original one.

6. Obtain the proportion of the 1000 test statistics that provide as much evidence against the null and in favor of the alternative hypothesis as does t^*. Obtain the proportion of p-values as small as or smaller than the p-value associated with t^*. Did you get the results you expected?

7. What proportion of the tests are significant at the 5% level; the 10% level? Interpret these results.

8. Compare the results you obtained using the exponential distribution with those you obtained using the $N(25, 1)$ distribution. What do you conclude about the effect of using a t test on skewed data?

LAB 6.2: Publication Bias

Introduction

Scientists study how various phenomena work. One of the primary methods of communicating their findings is by publishing scientific research papers in scholarly journals. Often, the scientists substantiate their results by performing hypothesis tests on data. For a given phenomenon under study, publication bias is the tendency of articles published in scientific journals to be unrepresentative of all scientific studies of the phenomenon. Publication bias is primarily due to publication policies that favor studies that obtain positive results (i.e., reject the null hypothesis) over those that do not. In this lab, you will learn about publication bias.

Objectives

To explore the phenomenon of publication bias.

Lab Materials

None needed.

Experimental Procedure

Background

This lab is based on the article by T. D. Sterling, W. L. Rosenbaum, and J. J. Weinkam, "Publication Decisions Revisited: The Effect of the Outcome of Statistical Tests on the Decision to Publish and Vice Versa," *The American Statistician,* 49(1) (1995): 108–112.

Every day we are bombarded with news reports touting astounding new scientific findings published in scientific journals. Often, these are the results of medical research, as exemplified by the titles of two recent newspaper articles: "Heart Study Finds that Intense Exercise Is the Most Beneficial," and "Study Links Saturated Fat to Cancer of Ovaries." Examples abound in engineering, the natural sciences, and the social sciences as well.

Most published studies in scientific journals use statistical inference, and the kind of statistical inference most frequently used is hypothesis testing. In a review of all articles published in a single calendar year in eight journals from four fields of psychology, Sterling, Rosenbaum, and Weinkam found that 94.30% of the 597 articles used hypothesis tests. These authors also found that a lower, but still substantial, percentage of the articles in medical journals use hypothesis tests: 69.25% of all 456 articles published in a single calendar year in three medical journals.

For a statistician, such wide use of statistical methods is good news indeed, as it signals the importance and vitality of the statistics profession. (Not to mention, it keeps us statisticians employed!) However, there is another side to the widespread use of statistical methods. There is evidence that journal publication policies, which favor studies reporting positive results (i.e., rejection of the null hypothesis) over those which do not, result in published studies that constitute a sample that is not representative of all scientific studies. The problem is compounded by the widespread belief that positive results are necessary for publication, which may dissuade researchers from submitting papers that do not report positive results. In what follows, you will look at some evidence for this **publication bias.**

The Evidence for Publication Bias

Sterling, Rosenbaum, and Weinkam found that of the 94.30% of the 597 psychology articles that used hypothesis tests, 95.56% rejected the null hypothesis of the most important test (as determined by Sterling, Rosenbaum, and Weinkam) in the study. This compares with a slightly lower 85.40% rejection rate for the 69.25% of medical articles that used hypothesis tests.

At first glance, this seems like a pretty high rejection rate. The relevant questions are: "Do 94.30% (or something close to it) of all psychology studies, published and unpublished, that use hypothesis tests result in rejection of the null hypothesis of the most important test in the study?" and "Do 85.40% (or something close to it) of all medical studies, published and unpublished, that use hypothesis tests result in rejection of the null hypothesis of the most important test in the study?"

A Model for Publication Bias.   Of course, there is no way of knowing what happens in unpublished studies, but we can make some educated guesses. First, assume that for each study there is a single hypothesis test and that either H_0 or H_a is true. We also set the following notation.

- Let $P(\text{all reject}, \alpha)$ denote the proportion of all studies that reject the null hypothesis at the α level of significance.
- Let $P(\text{reject}, \alpha \mid H_0 \text{ true})$ denote the proportion of studies, for which H_0 is true, that reject the null hypothesis at the α level of significance.
- Let $P(\text{reject}, \alpha \mid H_a \text{ true})$ denote the proportion of studies, for which H_a is true, that reject the null hypothesis at the α level of significance.
- Let $P(H_0 \text{ true})$ denote the proportion of all studies for which H_0 is true.
- Let $P(H_a \text{ true})$ denote the proportion of all studies for which H_a is true. Since we are assuming either H_0 or H_a is true, $P(H_a \text{ true}) = 1 - P(H_0 \text{ true})$.

Then we can write the following relation:

$$P(\text{all reject}, \alpha) = P(\text{reject}, \alpha \mid H_0 \text{ true})P(H_0 \text{ true}) + P(\text{reject}, \alpha \mid H_a \text{ true})P(H_a \text{ true}) \quad (6.19)$$

We will use Equation (6.19) to obtain a range of values for $P(\text{all reject}, \alpha)$. To do so, we need to specify a reasonable set of values for the quantities on the right side of the equals sign. One that we can specify immediately is $P(\text{reject}, \alpha \mid H_0 \text{ true})$, which equals α, by definition of the significance level of a test. $P(\text{reject}, \alpha \mid H_a \text{ true})$ can be interpreted as the average power (see Section 6.11) of all tests for which H_a is true. This value rarely exceeds 0.80 in any study and its average over all studies is certainly much less.

We will do two analyses: a simplified analysis and a more general analysis.

A Simplified Analysis.   We can simplify the analysis by making a few more assumptions. For example, if we assume that $P(\text{all reject}, \alpha) = P(H_a \text{ true})$ (i.e., the proportion of all rejected hypotheses observed equals the proportion of hypotheses for which H_a is true), Equation (6.19) becomes

$$P(\text{all reject}, \alpha) = \alpha(1 - P(\text{all reject}, \alpha)) + P(\text{reject}, \alpha \mid H_a \text{ true})P(\text{all reject}, \alpha)$$

which resolves to

$$P(\text{all reject}, \alpha) = \frac{\alpha}{1 + \alpha - P(\text{reject}, \alpha \mid H_a \text{ true})} \qquad (6.20)$$

Using Equation (6.20), investigate how $P(\text{all reject}, \alpha)$ varies as the average power of the tests, $P(\text{reject}, \alpha \mid H_a \text{ true})$ changes. In your lab report, explain what you find.

A More General Analysis.   For the more general analysis, we will go back to Equation (6.19). For this exercise, assume $\alpha = 0.05$, the usual significance level used in scientific research. This means that we will take $P(\text{reject}, \alpha \mid H_0 \text{ true}) = 0.05$. In addition, specify the following values:

- Take $P(\text{reject}, 0.05 \mid H_a \text{ true})$ to be 0.20, 0.50, and 0.80.
- Take $P(H_0 \text{ true})$ to be 0.00, 0.50, and 1.00.

Now get out your calculator and use Equation (6.19) to obtain a range of values for $P(\text{all reject}, 0.05)$. For example, if $P(\text{reject}, 0.05 \mid H_a \text{ true}) = 0.20$ and $P(H_0 \text{ true}) = 0.50$, we get

$$P(\text{all reject}, 0.05) = (0.05)(0.50) + (0.20)(0.50) = 0.125$$

Calculate the values of $P(\text{all reject}, 0.05)$ for all eight other combinations of values. In your lab report, answer the following:

1. Do any of the results you calculated for $P(\text{all reject}, 0.05)$ come close to the values 0.956 or 0.854 observed by Sterling, Rosenbaum, and Weinkam? If some do, what values for $P(\text{reject}, 0.05 \mid H_a \text{ true})$ and $P(H_0 \text{ true})$ were used?

2. Looking at Equation (6.19), and the values you computed, draw conclusions about how $P(\text{all reject}, 0.05)$ varies with $P(\text{reject}, 0.05 \mid H_a \text{ true})$ and $P(H_0 \text{ true})$.

3. Sterling, Rosenbaum, and Weinkam assert, "If we take this formula at face value, it suggests that only studies with high power are performed and that the investigators formulate only true hypotheses." Does your analysis bear this out?

What Is Wrong with the Publication Process?

Sterling, Rosenbaum, and Weinkam conclude that there is convincing evidence of publication bias. This is a problem for the consumer of scientific research, because the results of published studies do not accurately reflect the results of all scientific studies. Rather, published studies find significance more often than do all studies. Why is this important? What it means is that if H_0 is true and if 100 studies testing it are done at the 0.05 level, what we are likely to see in publications are the five or so that are significant rather than the 95 or so that are not. To put it bluntly, a large proportion of the "statistically significant" results that are published must be in error. They are what is called "false positives."

Sterling, Rosenbaum, and Weinkam fault the emphasis on statistically significant results in journals, and the present peer reviewing process that they believe focuses on those results. To quote them:

> *The influence of the outcome of a statistical test on the decision to publish scientific results is unsatisfactory for the following three reasons:*
>
> *(1) It creates an uncertainty of how to interpret the outcome of a statistical test.*
>
> *(2) It creates a misplaced impression of the relationship of statistical tests to scientific importance.*

(3) *Present conditions fail to inform on true null results. There are many instances where it is just as important to know the experimental conditions that do not produce effects as it is to know those that do.*

In your lab report, tell what Sterling, Rosenbaum, and Weinkam mean by these three points. Do you agree with them?

A Possible Solution?

Under the present peer reviewing process, referees (who are other researchers) read articles submitted for publication and recommend that they be published, that they be resubmitted after more work, or that they be rejected. Their decisions are based on the entire article, including the results of any hypothesis tests.

Sterling, Rosenbaum, and Weinkam suggest changing editorial policy in scientific journals to a blind-to-outcome peer review. Under their suggested scheme, referees would be instructed to ignore the outcomes of hypothesis tests, or might even be kept ignorant of those outcomes.

In your lab report, respond to their suggested solution to publication bias. Do you think it would work? Do you think it will ever be implemented?

APPENDIX 6.1: Hypothesis Test Guide

This appendix provides a guide to the hypothesis tests covered in the chapter.

Hypothesis Tests for Means in the C+E Model: One Population

Case 1: Known Variances

Assumptions

1. The data are $Y_1, Y_2, \ldots, Y_n$, where $Y_j = \mu + \epsilon_j$.
2. Either
   (a) n is large, or
   (b) The ϵ_j are from an $N(0, \sigma^2)$ population.
3. σ^2 is known.

Formulas   Standardized Test Statistic:[1] $Z = (\bar{Y} - \mu_0)/\sigma(\bar{Y})$.

Hypotheses:	H_0: $\mu = \mu_0$	H_0: $\mu = \mu_0$	H_0: $\mu = \mu_0$
	H_{a-}: $\mu < \mu_0$	H_{a+}: $\mu > \mu_0$	$H_{a\pm}$: $\mu \neq \mu_0$
p-value:[2]	$p_- = P(N(0,1) \leq z^*)$	$p_+ = P(N(0,1) \geq z^*)$	$p\pm = 2\min(p_-, p_+)$

[1] $\sigma(\bar{Y}) = \sqrt{\sigma^2/n}$.
[2] z^* is the observed value of Z, $P(N(0,1) \leq z^*)$ is the proportion of an $N(0,1)$ population less than or equal to z^*, and $P(N(0,1) \geq z^*)$ is the proportion of an $N(0,1)$ population greater than or equal to z^*.

Case 2: Unknown Variance, n Large

Assumptions 1 and 2(a) from Case 1 are assumed to hold. This case is treated exactly as Case 1 except that $\sigma(\bar{Y})$ is replaced by $\hat{\sigma}(\bar{Y}) = \sqrt{S^2/n}$ in the computation of the standardized test statistic Z, where S^2 is the sample variance computed from the data.

Case 3: Unknown Variance, n Small

Assumptions

1. The data are $Y_1, Y_2, \ldots, Y_n$, where $Y_j = \mu + \epsilon_j$.
2. The ϵ_j are from an $N(0, \sigma^2)$ population.
3. σ^2 is unknown.

Formulas   Standardized Test Statistic:[1] $T = (\bar{Y} - \mu_0)/\hat{\sigma}(\bar{Y})$.

Hypotheses:	H_0: $\mu = \mu_0$	H_0: $\mu = \mu_0$	H_0: $\mu = \mu_0$
	H_{a-}: $\mu < \mu_0$	H_{a+}: $\mu > \mu_0$	$H_{a\pm}$: $\mu \neq \mu_0$
p-value:[2]	$p_- = P(t_{n-1} \leq t^*)$	$p_+ = P(t_{n-1} \geq t^*)$	$p\pm = 2\min(p_-, p_+)$

[1] $\hat{\sigma}(\bar{Y}) = \sqrt{S^2/n}$.
[2] t^* is the observed value of T, $P(t_{n-1} \leq t^*)$ is the proportion of a t_{n-1} population less than or equal to t^*, and $P(t_{n-1} \geq t^*)$ is the proportion of a t_{n-1} population greater than or equal to t^*.

Hypothesis Tests for the Proportion in the Binomial Model: One Population

Case 1: An Exact Test

Assumption   The datum is Y from a $b(n, p)$ population.

Formulas   Test Statistic: Y.

Hypotheses:	H_0: $p = p_0$	H_0: $p = p_0$	H_0: $p = p_0$
	H_{a-}: $p < p_0$	H_{a+}: $p > p_0$	$H_{a\pm}$: $p \neq p_0$
p-value:[1]	$p_- = P(b(n, p_0) \leq y^*)$	$p_+ = P(b(n, p_0) \geq y^*)$	$p\pm$ is given by Equation (6.4)

[1] y^* is the observed value of Y, $P(b(n, p_0) \leq y^*)$ is the proportion of a $b(n, p_0)$ population less than or equal to y^*, and $P(b(n, p_0) \geq y^*)$ is the proportion of a $b(n, p_0)$ population greater than or equal to y^*.

Case 2: An Approximate Test for n Large

Assumptions

1. The datum is Y from a $b(n, p)$ population.
2. n is large: $Y \geq 10$ and $n - Y \geq 10$ is a good rule of thumb overall. If $0.3 \leq \hat{p} = Y/n \leq 0.7$, then $Y \geq 5$ and $n - Y \geq 5$ is a good rule of thumb.

Formulas   Standardized Test Statistic: $Z = (Y - np_0)/\sigma(Y)$, where $\sigma(Y) = \sqrt{np_0(1 - p_0)}$.

Hypotheses:	H_0: $p = p_0$	H_0: $p = p_0$	H_0: $p = p_0$
	H_{a-}: $p < p_0$	H_{a+}: $p > p_0$	$H_{a\pm}$: $p \neq p_0$
p-value:[1]	$p_- = P(N(0,1) \leq z_l^*)$	$p^+ = P(N(0,1) \geq z_u^*)$	$p\pm = 2\min(p_-, p^+)$

[1]$z_l^* = (y^* - np_0 + 0.5)/\sigma(\bar{Y})$, $z_u^* = (y^* - np_0 - 0.5)/\sigma(\bar{Y})$, where y^* is the observed value of Y, $P(N(0,1) \leq z_l^*)$ is the proportion of a $N(0,1)$ population less than or equal to z_l^*, and $P(N(0,1) \geq z_u^*)$ is the proportion of an $N(0,1)$ population greater than or equal to z_u^*.

Hypothesis Tests for Differences in Means in the C+E Model: Two Independent Populations

Case 1: Known Variances

Assumptions

1. The data are

$$Y_{1,1}, Y_{1,2}, \ldots, Y_{1,n_1}, \text{ where } Y_{1,j} = \mu_1 + \epsilon_{1,j} \quad \text{(population 1)}$$
$$Y_{2,1}, Y_{2,2}, \ldots, Y_{2,n_2}, \text{ where } Y_{2,j} = \mu_2 + \epsilon_{2,j} \quad \text{(population 2)}$$

2. The two populations are independent.
3. Either
   (a) n_1 and n_2 are large, or
   (b) The $\epsilon_{1,j}$ are from an $N(0, \sigma_1^2)$ population, and the $\epsilon_{2,j}$ are from an $N(0, \sigma_2^2)$ population.
4. σ_1^2 and σ_2^2 are known.

Formulas   Standardized Test Statistic:[1] $Z = (\bar{Y}_1 - \bar{Y}_2 - \delta_0)/\sigma(\bar{Y}_1 - \bar{Y}_2)$.

Hypotheses:	H_0: $\mu_1 - \mu_2 = \delta_0$	H_0: $\mu_1 - \mu_2 = \delta_0$	H_0: $\mu_1 - \mu_2 = \delta_0$
	H_{a-}: $\mu_1 - \mu_2 < \delta_0$	H_{a+}: $\mu_1 - \mu_2 > \delta_0$	$H_{a\pm}$: $\mu_1 - \mu_2 \neq \delta_0$
p-value:[2]	$p_- = P(N(0,1) \leq z^*)$	$p^+ = P(N(0,1) \geq z^*)$	$p\pm = 2\min(p_-, p^+)$

[1]$\sigma(\bar{Y}_1 - \bar{Y}_2) = \sqrt{\sigma_1^2/n_1 + \sigma_2^2/n_2}$.
[2]z^* is the observed value of Z, $P(N(0,1) \leq z^*)$ is the proportion of an $N(0,1)$ population less than or equal to z^*, and $P(N(0,1) \geq z^*)$ is the proportion of an $N(0,1)$ population greater than or equal to z^*.

Case 2: Unknown Variances, n_1 and n_2 Large

Assumptions 1, 2, and 3(a) are assumed to hold. This case is treated exactly as Case 1 except that $\sigma(\bar{Y}_1 - \bar{Y}_2)$ is replaced by $\hat{\sigma}(\bar{Y}_1 - \bar{Y}_2) = \sqrt{(S_1^2/n_1) + (S_2^2/n_2)}$ in the computation of the standardized test statistic Z, where S_1^2 and S_2^2 are the sample variances computed from the data from populations 1 and 2, respectively.

Case 3: Variances Unknown, but Assumed to Be Equal, n_1 and n_2 Not Both Large

Assumptions

1. The data are

$$Y_{1,1}, Y_{1,2}, \ldots, Y_{1,n_1}, \text{ where } Y_{1,j} = \mu_1 + \epsilon_{1,j} \quad \text{(population 1)}$$

$$Y_{2,1}, Y_{2,2}, \ldots, Y_{2,n_2}, \text{ where } Y_{2,j} = \mu_2 + \epsilon_{2,j} \quad \text{(population 2)}$$

2. The two populations are independent.
3. The $\epsilon_{1,j}$ are from an $N(0, \sigma_1^2)$ population, and the $\epsilon_{2,j}$ are from an $N(0, \sigma_2^2)$ population.
4. σ_1^2 and σ_2^2 are unknown, but are assumed to be equal.

Formulas   Standardized Test Statistic[1]: $T^{(p)} = (\bar{Y}_1 - \bar{Y}_2 - \delta_0)/\hat{\sigma}_p(\bar{Y}_1 - \bar{Y}_2)$.

Hypotheses:	$H_0: \mu_1 - \mu_2 = \delta_0$ $H_{a-}: \mu_1 - \mu_2 < \delta_0$	$H_0: \mu_1 - \mu_2 = \delta_0$ $H_{a+}: \mu_1 - \mu_2 > \delta_0$	$H_0: \mu_1 - \mu_2 = \delta_0$ $H_{a\pm}: \mu_1 - \mu_2 \neq \delta_0$
p-value:[2]	$p_- = P(t_{n_1+n_2-2} \leq t^{(p)*})$	$p^+ = P(t_{n_1+n_2-2} \geq t^{(p)*})$	$p\pm = 2\min(p_-, p^+)$

[1]$\hat{\sigma}_p(\bar{Y}_1 - \bar{Y}_2) = \sqrt{S_p^2[(1/n_1) + (1/n_2)]}$, where $S_p^2 = [(n_1 - 1)S_1^2 + (n_2 - 1)S_2^2]/(n_1 + n_2 - 2)$, and S_1^2 and S_2^2 are the sample variances computed from the data from populations 1 and 2, respectively.
[2]$t^{(p)*}$ is the observed value of $T^{(p)}$, $P(t_{n_1+n_2-2} \leq t^{(p)*})$ is the proportion of a $t_{n_1+n_2-2}$ population less than or equal to $t^{(p)*}$, and $P(t_{n_1+n_2-2} \geq t^{(p)*})$ is the proportion of a $t_{n_1+n_2-2}$ population greater than or equal to $t^{(p)*}$.

Case 4: Variances Unknown, and Not Assumed to Be Equal, n_1 and n_2 Not Both Large

Assumptions

1. The data are

$$Y_{1,1}, Y_{1,2}, \ldots, Y_{1,n_1}, \text{ where } Y_{1,j} = \mu_1 + \epsilon_{1,j} \quad \text{(population 1)}$$

$$Y_{2,1}, Y_{2,2}, \ldots, Y_{2,n_2}, \text{ where } Y_{2,j} = \mu_2 + \epsilon_{2,j} \quad \text{(population 2)}$$

2. The two populations are independent.
3. The $\epsilon_{1,j}$ are from an $N(0, \sigma_1^2)$ population, and the $\epsilon_{2,j}$ are from an $N(0, \sigma_2^2)$ population.
4. σ_1^2 and σ_2^2 are unknown, and are not assumed to be equal.

Formulas   Standardized Test Statistic:[1] $T^{(ap)} = (\bar{Y}_1 - \bar{Y}_2 - \delta_0)/\hat{\sigma}(\bar{Y}_1 - \bar{Y}_2)$.

Hypotheses:	H_0: $\mu_1 - \mu_2 = \delta_0$ H_{a-}: $\mu_1 - \mu_2 < \delta_0$	H_0: $\mu_1 - \mu_2 = \delta_0$ H_{a+}: $\mu_1 - \mu_2 > \delta_0$	H_0: $\mu_1 - \mu_2 = \delta_0$ $H_{a\pm}$: $\mu_1 - \mu_2 \neq \delta_0$
p-value:[2]	$p_- = P(t_v \leq t^{(ap)*})$	$p^+ = P(t_v \geq t^{(ap)*})$	$p\pm = 2\min(p_-, p^+)$

[1]$\hat{\sigma}(\bar{Y}_1 - \bar{Y}_2) = \sqrt{(S_1^2/n_1) + (S_2^2/n_2)}$, where S_1 and S_2 are the sample standard deviations computed from the data from populations 1 and 2, respectively. Under H_0, the distribution of $t^{(ap)}$ is approximately t_v, where the degrees of freedom v is taken as the largest integer less than or equal to

$$\left(\frac{S_1^2}{n_1} + \frac{S_2^2}{n_2}\right)^2 \bigg/ \left[\frac{\left(S_1^2/n_1\right)^2}{n_1 - 1} + \frac{\left(S_2^2/n_2\right)^2}{n_2 - 1}\right]$$

[2]$t^{(ap)*}$ is the observed value of $T^{(ap)}$, $P(t_v \leq t^{(ap)*})$ is the proportion of a t_v population less than or equal to $t^{(ap)*}$, and $P(t_v \geq t^{(p)*})$ is the proportion of a t_v population greater than or equal to $t^{(ap)*}$.

Hypothesis Tests for Proportions in the Binomial Model: Two Independent Populations

Case 1: A Test of the Equality of Two Proportions

Assumptions

1. The data are Y_1 from a $b(n_1, p_1)$ population and Y_2 from a $b(n_2, p_2)$ population.
2. The two populations are independent.
3. n_1 and n_2 are large: $Y_i \geq 10$ and $n_i - Y_i \geq 10$, $i = 1, 2$, is a good rule of thumb overall. If $0.3 \leq \hat{p}_i = Y_i/n_i \leq 0.7$, then $Y_i \geq 5$ and $n_i - Y_i \geq 5$, $i = 1, 2$, is a good rule of thumb.

Formulas   Standardized Test Statistic:[1] $Z = (\hat{p}_1 - \hat{p}_2)/\hat{\sigma}_0(\hat{p}_1 - \hat{p}_2)$.

Hypotheses:	H_0: $p_1 - p_2 = 0$ H_{a-}: $p_1 - p_2 < 0$	H_0: $p_1 - p_2 = 0$ H_{a+}: $p_1 - p_2 > 0$	H_0: $p_1 - p_2 = 0$ $H_{a\pm}$: $p_1 - p_2 \neq 0$
p-value:[2]	$p_- = P(N(0,1) \leq z^*)$	$p^+ = P(N(0,1) \geq z^*)$	$p\pm = 2\min(p_-, p^+)$

[1]$\hat{\sigma}_0(\hat{p}_1 - \hat{p}_2) = \sqrt{\hat{p}(1 - \hat{p})[(1/n_1) + (1/n_2)]}$, where $\hat{p} = (Y_1 + Y_2)/(n_1 + n_2)$.
[2]z^* is the observed value of Z, $P(N(0,1) \leq z^*)$ is the proportion of an $N(0,1)$ population less than or equal to z^*, and $P(N(0,1) \geq z^*)$ is the proportion of an $N(0,1)$ population greater than or equal to z^*.

Case 2: A Test of the General Difference of Two Proportions

Assumptions

1. The data are Y_1 from a $b(n_1, p_1)$ population and Y_2 from a $b(n_2, p_2)$ population.

2. The two populations are independent.
3. n_1 and n_2 are large: A guideline is given in Case 1.

Formulas   Test Statistic:[1] $Z = (\hat{p}_1 - \hat{p}_2 - \delta_0)/[\hat{\sigma}(\hat{p}_1 - \hat{p}_2)]$.

Hypotheses:[2]	H_0: $p_1 - p_2 = \delta_0$	H_0: $p_1 - p_2 = \delta_0$	H_0: $p_1 - p_2 = \delta_0$
	H_{a-}: $p_1 - p_2 < \delta_0$	H_{a+}: $p_1 - p_2 > \delta_0$	$H_{a\pm}$: $p_1 - p_2 \neq \delta_0$
p-value:[3]	$p_- = P(N(0,1) \leq z^*)$	$p^+ = P(N(0,1) \geq z^*)$	$p\pm = 2\min(p_-, p^+)$

[1] $\hat{\sigma}(\hat{p}_1 - \hat{p}_2) = \sqrt{[\hat{p}_1(1 - \hat{p}_1)/n_1] + [\hat{p}_2(1 - \hat{p}_2)/n_2]}$, where $\hat{p}_1 = Y_1/n_1$ and $\hat{p}_2 = Y_2/n_2$.
[2] $\delta_0 \neq 0$.
[3] z^* is the observed value of Z, $P(N(0,1) \leq z^*)$ is the proportion of an $N(0,1)$ population less than or equal to z^*, and $P(N(0,1) \geq z^*)$ is the proportion of an $N(0,1)$ population greater than or equal to z^*.

CAPSTONE PROJECT: Chapters 1 to 6

The goal of a **Capstone Project** is to give you experience in all phases of a statistical study: planning, data collection, analysis, and conclusions. Each of Chapters 1 to 6 must make a contribution to the project. For a description of this project, see the description of the Capstone Project for Chapter 1 to 5 on page 285. In the Capstone Project for Chapters 1 to 6, the inference must also include hypothesis testing, as covered in Chapter 6.

7

The Relationship Between Two Variables

When Mid-Parents are taller than mediocrity, their Children tend to be shorter than they. When Mid-Parents are shorter than mediocrity, their Children tend to be taller than they.

—*Sir Francis Galton,* explaining his term "regression toward mediocrity"

INTRODUCTION

Often, when collecting or analyzing data, there are two or more variables of interest. In many cases, it is important to know whether two or more variables are related, and if they are, what the nature of that relationship is. For example, doctors and their patients would benefit from knowing which **risk factors** (such as smoking, obesity, diet, or heredity) are related to the incidence of disease. Or economists (and investors!) would like to know which variables (called **leading economic indicators**) are likely to be related to (and might therefore predict) future changes in the economy.

Data sets that consist of more than one variable are called **multivariate;** those that consist of two variables are called **bivariate.** In this chapter, you will learn how to analyze some types of bivariate data.

In Chapter 2, quantitative and categorical variables were introduced. Sections 7.1 to 7.4 of this chapter explain how to analyze the relationship between two quantitative variables. In certain instances, these methods also apply to the relationship between one quantitative and one categorical variable. Methods for analyzing the relationship between two categorical variables are introduced in Section 7.5.

Knowledge and Skills

By successfully completing this chapter, you will acquire the following knowledge and skills:

KNOWLEDGE	**SKILLS**
1. Correlation.	**1.** The ability to summarize the relationship between two quantitative variables using appropriate graphs and descriptive measures.
2. Several methods for summarizing a statistical relationship between two quantitative variables, including nonparametric data smoothing methods and least squares regression.	**2.** The ability to identify, fit, and interpret a model for the statistical relationship between two quantative variables.
3. Residuals, coefficient of determination, mean square error.	**3.** The use of diagnostic tools in regression analysis.
4. The use of transformations to linearize a bivariate plot.	**4.** The ability to describe and analyze two-way tables.
5. Elementary methods for analyzing the relation between two categorical variables.	

7.1

DISPLAYING AND SUMMARIZING ASSOCIATION IN BIVARIATE QUANTITATIVE DATA

We begin by analyzing the relationship between two quantitative variables. As usual, the best way to begin exploration of data is to create a graphical display.

Graphical Display of Bivariate Quantitative Data

The basic plot for showing the relation between two quantitative variables is the **scatterplot,** which is a bivariate (or X–Y) plot that plots one variable against the other.

EXAMPLE 7.1   TOOL WEAR

The data in Table 7.1 are from an experiment to relate wear on a certain kind of carbide-steel cutting tool to the duration of use. In the experiment, 25 identical randomly selected tools were randomly assigned a rotational velocity, VELOCITY (in feet per minute), and a cutting time, TIME (in minutes). Each tool was then used to cut a uniform piece of steel for TIME minutes and the level of tool wear, WEAR (in inches) was recorded. The order in which the tools were used was also randomized (why all this randomization?), and is recorded in the variable

TABLE 7.1   Tool Wear Data

Velocity	Time	Wear	Order	Velocity	Time	Wear	Order
400	130	0.03	4	800	130	0.09	6
400	75	0.02	18	800	120	0.09	12
400	37	0.01	14	800	100	0.07	9
600	200	0.09	25	800	75	0.07	24
600	180	0.08	22	800	70	0.06	20
600	170	0.07	5	800	55	0.05	21
600	150	0.06	10	800	42	0.04	16
600	130	0.05	1	800	30	0.03	8
600	100	0.04	2	800	19	0.02	3
600	70	0.03	13	1000	4.5	0.01	11
600	40	0.02	19	1000	12	0.02	17
600	15	0.01	15	1000	18	0.03	23
				1000	35	0.04	7

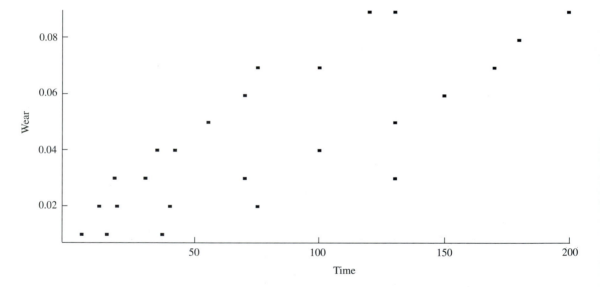

Figure 7.1   Tool wear data; scatterplot of wear versus time.

ORDER. The experimenter wants to investigate the relationship between wear and time. A scatterplot of WEAR versus TIME is displayed in Figure 7.1. ◆

As with the previous data analyses you've conducted, the idea behind analyzing a scatterplot is to first describe the main patterns you see in the plot and then any notable deviations from those patterns.

In a scatterplot, you should first look for the presence of **association.** Association will show up as a definite pattern in the scatterplot. The second thing you should look

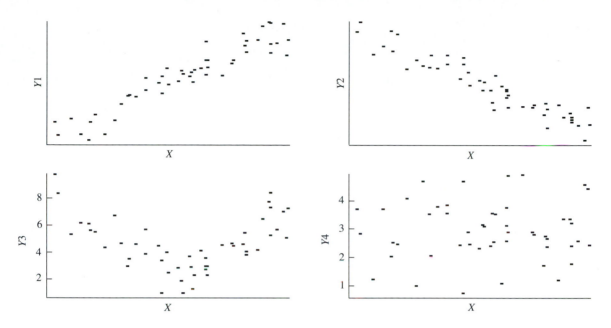

Figure 7.2   Four scatterplots displaying positive linear association (upper left), negative linear association (upper right), nonlinear association (lower left), and no association (lower right). The nonlinear association may be described as decreasing in Y for X values below 2.5 or so, and then increasing in a roughly parabolic curve.

for is the **type of association.** As a first step, you should determine if the association is **linear** (i.e., the pattern follows a line) or **nonlinear.** If the association is linear, you should describe the **direction of association: positive** if large (small) values of the Y variable are associated with large (small) values of the X variable (i.e., the line has a positive slope); **negative** if large (small) values of the Y variable are associated with small (large) values of the X variable (i.e., the line has a negative slope).

Although there are only two possible directions for a linear association, there are many ways for association to be nonlinear. You may still be able to describe a nonlinear association as positive or negative, but be warned that the association may be positive for some values of X and negative for others (think of a parabola), or it may be periodic (think of a sine curve), or it may be even more difficult to describe.

The scatterplots in Figure 7.2 show one example each of positive and negative linear association, nonlinear association, and no association.

After summarizing the type of association, the next step is to summarize the strength of association. For a linear association, the strongest association occurs if all the points lie on a straight line. As points become more scattered and variable, the strength of association weakens. It is as if a strong association shows the pattern in sharp focus, and the weaker the association, the more blurred the pattern. A similar interpretation holds for strength of nonlinear association. The scatterplots in Figure 7.3 show the same kind of linear association in varying strengths.

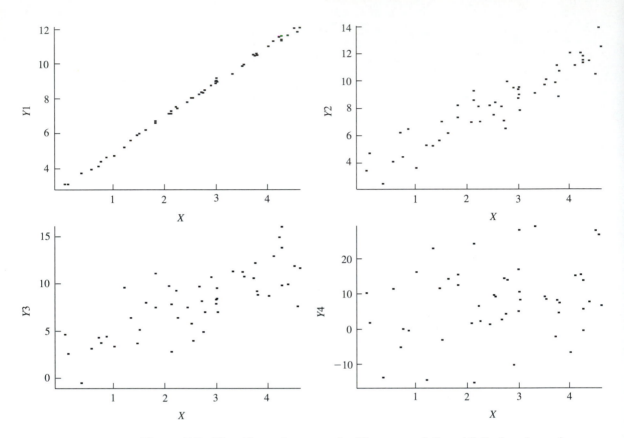

Figure 7.3 Plots illustrating strength of linear association. All displayed associations are positive and linear, but their strengths range from very strong (upper left) to very weak (lower right).

The flowchart in Figure 7.4 summarizes the process of analyzing a scatterplot.

EXAMPLE 7.1 CONTINUED

Let's analyze the scatterplot in Figure 7.1. There are two features that stand out:

- There is an overall positive pattern of association between TIME and WEAR.
- The pattern consists of a number of "spokes" emanating from the origin.

The second feature leads us to investigate what might be causing this pattern. We do not have to look far. There are four "spokes" and four different levels of VELOCITY. Figure 7.5 uses different plotting symbols for the different velocities: +, ×, circle, and square for 400, 600, 800 and 1000 ft/min, respectively.

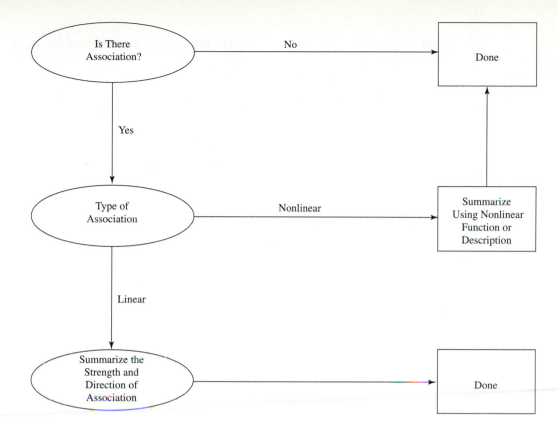

Figure 7.4 Flowchart for analyzing a scatterplot.

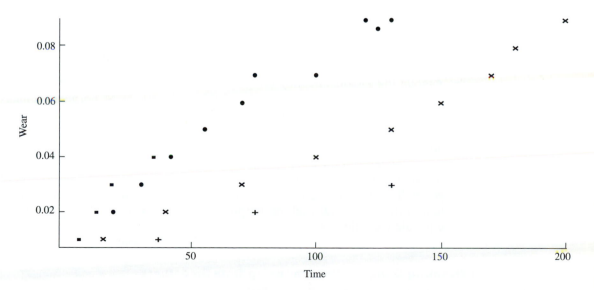

Figure 7.5 Tool wear data; scatterplot of wear versus time with velocity marked: +, ×, circle, and square for 400, 600, 800, and 1000 ft/min, respectively.

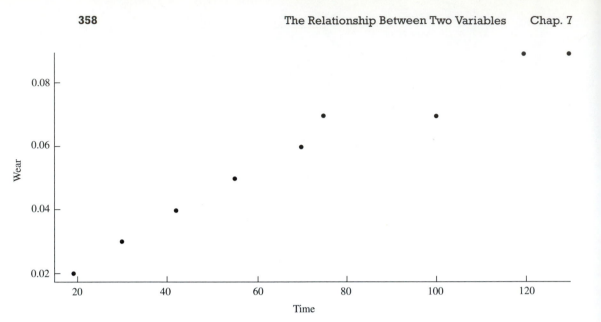

Figure 7.6   Tool wear data; scatterplot of wear versus time for VELOCITY = 800.

From Figure 7.5, we can see that the relationship between WEAR and TIME is different for different values of VELOCITY. Although the relationship is positive at each velocity, the plot shows that the rate that WEAR increases with TIME (this is the slope that the data values follow) is greater for higher velocities.

Figure 7.6 is a plot of WEAR versus time for VELOCITY = 800. We will return to these data later in the chapter.   ✦

EXAMPLE 7.2   AUTOMOBILE ENGINE PERFORMANCE

Among the factors affecting the performance of automobile engines is the air–fuel ratio, the mixture of air and fuel fed into the engine. A normalized measure of this ratio is the equivalence ratio, defined as the quotient (stoichiometric air–fuel ratio)/(actual air–fuel ratio). The higher the equivalence ratio, the richer the air–fuel mixture. Figure 7.7 is a plot of fuel consumption, in μ_g/J, versus the equivalence ratio for a set of experimental data. The plot clearly shows a non-linear association. The association is positive throughout, with fuel consumption generally higher for higher values of the equivalence ratio. However, for equivalence ratios above 1.0, fuel consumption begins to rise more steeply in relation to equivalence ratio.   ✦

Extracting Complex Patterns using Data Smoothers

Although a scatterplot shows all data points in a bivariate data set, it often shows too much detail to allow the eye to grasp subtleties of the overall pattern or sometimes even the overall pattern itself. This is where data smoothers can be helpful. As their name

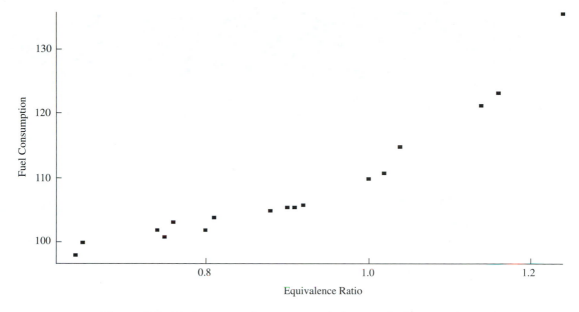

Figure 7.7   Fuel consumption versus equivalence ratio for a set of experimental data.

implies, data smoothers smooth out the jumpiness in a scatterplot to better enable the eye to see overall patterns. In this section, you will explore two data smoothers.

Median Trace

The median trace is a simple but often effective method for smoothing a bivariate plot. In addition, it is easy to understand and resistant to outliers. To make a median trace, divide the range of the X data into vertical slices. Then, for the data in ith slice, find the median of the X values, M_i^X, and of the Y values, M_i^Y. The median trace results from connecting the points (M_i^X, M_i^Y) with straight lines.

EXAMPLE 7.3   THE DRAFT LOTTERY

Let's try a median trace on the data in the data set DRAFTLOT. To explain this data set, a bit of history is helpful. In 1970, the first draft lottery was held. The draft lottery was a system designed to make the selection of individuals for military service fair. Prior to the lottery drawing, 366 identical plastic capsules were obtained and into each was placed one of the 366 possible birth dates. The capsules were loaded into a large drum that rotated to mix them. They were then pulled out one at a time, supposedly at random. The number 1 was assigned to the birth date in the first capsule drawn, the number 2 to the second capsule drawn, and so on. The assigned numbers denoted the order in which eligible 18-year-old men were drafted. For the lottery to have been fair, each birth date should have had an equal chance of being assigned any of the 366 numbers. The

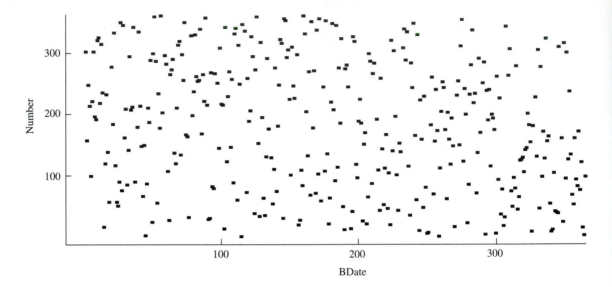

Figure 7.8 Draft lottery data; scatterplot of NUMBER versus BDATE.

data in DRAFTLOT consist of BDATE, the birth date, and NUMBER, the selection number assigned to that birth date. Figure 7.8 is a scatterplot of NUMBER versus BDATE. It is difficult to see any kind of pattern in this plot that would make us doubt the randomness of the selection process.

To construct a median trace for these data, we first have to decide how to slice the X variable, BDATE. A natural way is to make 12 slices, one corresponding to each month. Thus, the first slice will consist of BDATE values 1–31, the second to BDATE values 32–60,[1] and so on. The December slice will consist of BDATES 336–366. The median of the integers 1–31 is 16, the median of the integers 32–60 is 46, and the median of the integers 336–366 is 351, so $M_1^X = 16$, $M_2^X = 46$, and $M_{12}^X = 351$. The median of all the lottery numbers drawn for birth dates 1–31 is 211, the median of all the lottery numbers drawn for birth dates 32–60 is 210, and median of all the lottery numbers drawn for birth dates 336–366 is 100, so $M_1^Y = 211$, $M_2^Y = 210$, and $M_{12}^Y = 100$. We now plot all twelve pairs (M_i^X, M_i^Y), $i = 1, \ldots, 12$, on the scatterplot of NUMBER versus BDATE, and connect adjacent (M_i^X, M_i^Y) with a straight line.

The result is shown in Figure 7.9. Surprisingly, the median trace shows an overall downward trend of selected number with increasing birth date. It has detected a pattern that our eyes were unable to see.

Soon after the lottery was conducted, there were complaints of too many high draft numbers for those born in the first part of the year and too few for those born later in the year. Statistical analysis bore this out. Subsequent investigation revealed that the capsules had been poorly mixed before the drawing. ◆

---

[1]Remember, we have to account for February 29!

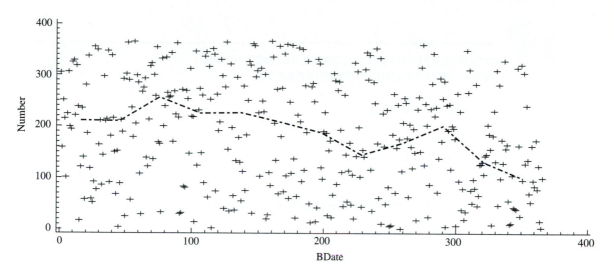

Figure 7.9 Draft lottery data; median trace.

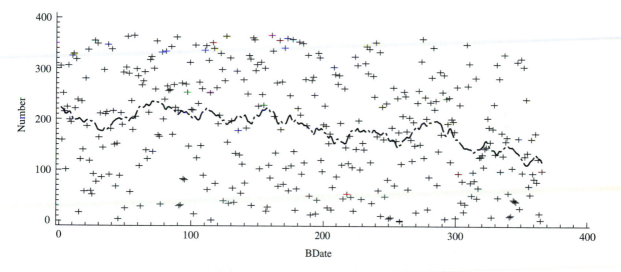

Figure 7.10 Draft lottery data; 30-term moving average.

Moving Averages

You have already learned about moving averages for data taken over time in Chapter 1. We can compute a moving average for any set of bivariate data by treating the X variable as a time variable.[2] Figure 7.10 shows a 30-term (i.e., approximately monthly) moving average for the draft lottery data. It tells roughly the same story as the median trace.

[2] Care must be taken if the X values are not equally spaced.

7.2

CORRELATION: MEASURING ASSOCIATION
IN BIVARIATE QUANTITATIVE DATA

Pearson Correlation

For data that exhibit linear association, it may be of interest to ask how strong that association is. The **Pearson correlation coefficient,** named after Karl Pearson, an early pioneer of statistical inference, is a measure of the strength of **linear association** between two quantitative variables.

To understand what the correlation coefficient measures, we will need some formulas. Suppose there are n pairs of measurements. Denote the ith measurements as X_i, Y_i. So, for example, X_i might be the time for the ith cutting tool and Y_i its wear.

If the correlation is to be a measure only of the strength of linear association between the two variables, then it should not depend on the units used: Whether you measure time in seconds or hours or the wear in inches or centimeters, the strength of association of WEAR with TIME should not change. Further, it should not depend on translations of the data: If you add 1 minute to the time measurement of each tool and call this measurement T-PLUS, then the strength of linear association between WEAR and T-PLUS should be the same as that between WEAR and TIME.

One sensible way to create new data that don't depend on the units of measurement and that don't change under translation is to **standardize** the existing data. To standardize the data for a variable, simply subtract their mean (this is called centering) and divide by their standard deviation.[3] So the standardized values of X_i and Y_i are

$$X_i' = (X_i - \bar{X})/S_X \qquad Y_i' = (Y_i - \bar{Y})/S_Y$$

where $\bar{X}$ is the mean and S_X is the standard deviation of the X observations, and $\bar{Y}$ and S_Y are the same quantities for the Y observations.

Now that we've standardized the data, what do we do with them? One thing we can do is to plot them versus each other. Figure 7.11 shows plots of X_i' versus Y_i' for six concocted data sets. One thing these plots do is show the association on a standard scale centered at the origin. As different scaling of the same data can produce different, even deceptive, visual clues about the strength of association, plots of standardized variables can be a good idea.

---

[3]The general idea of standardization should be familiar: Recall that in Chapter 4, we learned to standardize random variables.

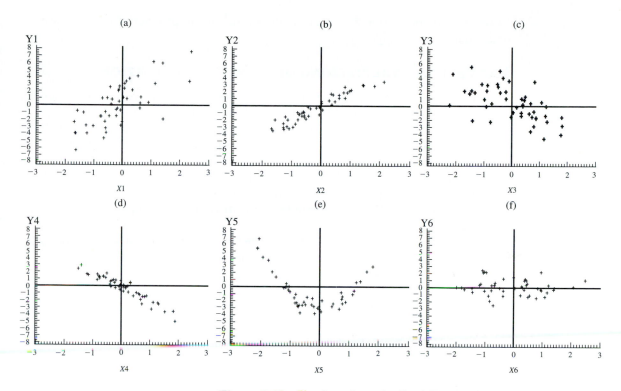

Figure 7.11   Six plots of standardized X and Y data.

We are now ready to give the formula for the Pearson correlation coefficient.

PEARSON CORRELATION COEFFICIENT FORMULA

Suppose n measurements, (X_i, Y_i), $i = 1, \ldots, n$, are taken on the variables X and Y. Then the Pearson correlation between X and Y computed from these data is

$$r = \frac{1}{n-1} \sum_{i=1}^{n} X_i' Y_i'$$

where

$$X_i' = \frac{X_i - \bar{X}}{S_X} \qquad \text{and} \qquad Y_i' = \frac{Y_i - \bar{Y}}{S_Y}$$

are the standardized data.

In words, the correlation coefficient is the mean[4] of the product of the standardized data values.

EXAMPLE 7.4   THE MEANING OF PEARSON CORRELATION

To get a real understanding of what r means, look at Figure 7.11(a), which is a plot of the Y_i' versus the X_i', and think about the four quadrants of the graph. In quadrants 1 and 3, the product $X_i' Y_i'$ will be positive and in the other two quadrants negative. Also, the larger X_i' and Y_i' in absolute value, the larger in absolute value will be their product. In Figure 7.11(a), more points lie in quadrants 1 and 3 than lie in quadrants 2 and 4. In addition, the X_i' and Y_i' values in quadrants 1 and 3 tend to be larger in magnitude than those in quadrants 2 and 4. Therefore, r will be positive. Compared with Figure 7.11(a), the data values in Figure 7.11(b) are even more strongly concentrated in quadrants 1 and 3, and are even larger in magnitude relative to the observations in quadrants 2 and 4. Therefore, r for the data in Figure 7.11(b) will be even larger than r computed from the data in Figure 7.11(a).   ◆

Exercises 7.3 to 7.6 ask you to further analyze the correlations of the plots in Figure 7.11.

Inference Using Pearson Correlation

Recall that statistical inference consists of using a sample to draw conclusions about the population from which it was drawn. Suppose we have drawn a random sample from a large population, and that we have taken two quantitative measurements, X and Y, on each unit in the sample. If we could take these two measurements on every unit in the population, we could compute the Pearson correlation for the entire population as a measure of the strength of linear association between X and Y in the population. This population correlation is often denoted by the Greek letter ρ (pronounced "row").

Even though in most instances we cannot calculate ρ, we can use the sample Pearson correlation r to make inferences about it. Specifically, we use the fact that if the sample size is n, then

$$t = (r - \rho)\sqrt{\frac{n-2}{(1-r^2)(1-\rho^2)}} \tag{7.1}$$

has approximately a t_{n-2} distribution.

Confidence Intervals for ρ

Though it is difficult to use the relation (7.1) to obtain a formula for a level L confidence interval for ρ, we can use it to construct a computer algorithm that will compute such

---

[4]Here, as with the sample standard deviation, we divide by the degrees of freedom, $n-1$, to compute the mean.

an interval.[5] Such an interval will be valid if n is large.[6] If n is small, the interval will be valid provided the two variables X and Y follow a bivariate version of the normal distribution model.

Hypothesis Tests for Correlation

We can also use the fact that (7.1) has a t_{n-2} distribution to test hypotheses about ρ. For a known, user-specified value ρ_0, we will consider tests of $\rho = \rho_0$ versus three common alternatives. In each case, we assume that we have computed the sample Pearson correlation r and we let

$$t^* = (r - \rho_0)\sqrt{\frac{n-2}{(1-r^2)(1-\rho_0^2)}}$$

be the value given by relation (7.1) when H_0 is true.

- The first test we consider is the test versus a one-sided alternative:

$$H_0: \quad \rho = \rho_0$$
$$H_{a+}: \quad \rho > \rho_0$$

  The p-value of this test is $p^+ = P(T \geq t^*)$, where $T \sim t_{n-2}$.
- The second is the test versus the other one-sided alternative:

$$H_0: \quad \rho = \rho_0$$
$$H_{a-}: \quad \rho < \rho_0$$

  The p-value of this test is $p_- = P(T \leq t^*)$, where $T \sim t_{n-2}$.
- The third is the test versus the two-sided alternative:

$$H_0: \quad \rho = \rho_0$$
$$H_{a\pm}: \quad \rho \neq \rho_0$$

  The p-value of this test is $p\pm = 2\min(p_-, p^+)$.

EXAMPLE 7.1   CONTINUED

We consider using the tool wear data to make inferences about the population correlation of WEAR and TIME when VELOCITY $= 800$.

- **Estimation.** The point estimate of the population correlation ρ is $r = 0.9797$. Using a computer algorithm based on relation (7.1), we obtain (0.9027, 0.9957) as a level 0.95 confidence interval for ρ.

---

[5]The macro CORR, which we have written for SAS and MINITAB users, will compute a confidence interval for ρ.

[6]$n \geq 50$ should do in most cases.

- **Hypothesis Tests.** The hypothesis that is usually of interest is whether there is any population correlation between the variables. That is, we take $\rho_0 = 0$, so that we have H_0: $\rho = 0$, and H_a can be either one- or two-sided depending on the situation.

  However, in this case, the experimenters already know that there is a positive population correlation underlying these data. Instead, they are interested in whether the population correlation exceeds 0.9. That is, they want to test

$$H_0: \quad \rho = 0.9$$
$$H_{a^+}: \quad \rho > 0.9$$

To do so, they compute

$$t^* = (r - \rho_0)\sqrt{\frac{n-2}{(1-r^2)(1-\rho_0^2)}}$$

$$= (0.9797 - 0.9)\sqrt{\frac{7}{(1 - 0.9797^2)(1 - 0.9^2)}}$$

$$= 2.413$$

The resulting p-value is $p^+ = P(T \geq 2.413) = 0.0233$, where $T \sim t_7$. That is, if the population correlation is really 0.9, the probability of observing a sample that has a t^* value at least as large as the value observed is 0.0233. ✦

Information about hypothesis tests is summarized in the box.

USING THE SAMPLE PEARSON CORRELATION TO TEST HYPOTHESES ABOUT THE POPULATION CORRELATION

- **The Testing Problem.** It is desired to test hypotheses about the population correlation ρ of bivariate measurements. The null hypothesis is

$$H_0: \quad \rho = \rho_0$$

versus one of the alternative hypotheses

$$H_{a^+}: \quad \rho > \rho_0$$
$$H_{a^-}: \quad \rho < \rho_0$$
$$H_{a^\pm}: \quad \rho \neq \rho_0$$

- **Assumption.** The data $(X_1, Y_1), \ldots, (X_n, Y_n)$ are from a bivariate normal distribution, or the sample size is large.

- **Standardized Test Statistic.**

$$t^* = (r - \rho_0)\sqrt{\frac{n-2}{(1-r^2)(1-\rho_0^2)}}$$

- **The Test.** The p-values for the tests are
  - For the test of H_0 versus H_{a+}, $p^+ = P(T \geq t^*)$, where $T \sim t_{n-2}$.
  - For the test of H_0 versus H_{a-}, $p^- = P(T \leq t^*)$, where $T \sim t_{n-2}$.
  - For the test of H_0 versus $H_{a\pm}$, $p\pm = 2\min(p_-, p_+)$.

More About the Pearson Correlation

1. The correlation between X and Y is the same as the correlation between Y and X. This means that the correlation doesn't regard Y as a function of X or vice versa. The assumption that Y is a function of X (or vice versa) is appropriate for other methodologies, such as regression, which you'll study later in this chapter.

2. Correlation can never by itself adequately summarize a set of bivariate data. Only when used in conjunction with other measures of the distributions of X and Y,[7] **and especially a scatterplot,** can an adequate summary be obtained. In the exercises, you will explore this further.

3. Assuming a scatterplot indicates that there is a linear association between X and Y, how large a correlation is meaningful? There is no single answer for this question.

First, we must determine if the correlation indicates a real linear association between the two variables or whether it is typical of what we can expect from sampling variation. That is, we need to determine if the data give convincing evidence that the population correlation ρ is different from 0. Confidence intervals and hypothesis tests for the population correlation can be used for this task. We must be aware, however, that the results we obtain depend on the size of the sample. For example, a sample correlation as large as 0.5 computed from 100 observations is less likely to have occurred by chance than is a correlation as large as 0.5 computed from 10 observations.

Second, if statistical inference indicates that the population correlation is nonzero, then we still must ask whether the correlation has any practical significance. For example, a sample correlation of 0.01 may provide strong evidence that $\rho \neq 0$ if computed from a large number of observations, but such a small correlation is unlikely to be of any practical significance.

4. It is impossible to use the equations we have given for the Pearson correlation if either or both of S_X and S_Y are 0. It is a fact that a standard deviation equals 0 if and only if all the data values are equal. Though this is unlikely to happen in practice,

---

[7]Such as $\bar{X}$, $\bar{Y}$, S_X, and S_Y, when these are appropriate summaries for the X and Y data considered separately.

we define $r = 0$ if it does. Our reasoning is that if, for example, $S_Y = 0$, there can be no association between X and Y since no matter what the value of X, the value of Y remains the same.

7.3

SIMPLE LINEAR REGRESSION: MODELING BIVARIATE QUANTITATIVE DATA

As in the previous section, we will consider the relationship between two variables, which we will call Z and Y.[8] In contrast to the assumptions for correlation, however, we will regard Y as a quantity to be predicted using the associated value of Z. This is signified by calling Y a **response,** or **dependent** variable, and Z a **predictor,** or **independent** variable. For instance, in Example 7.1 on tool wear, we might be interested in predicting wear (Y) as a function of time (Z). Or in Example 7.2, we might be interested in predicting fuel consumption (Y) as a function of the equivalence ratio (Z).

The Model

We are interested in approximating the relationship between Z and Y with a curve. In seeking a model for doing so, we begin with a simpler model: the C+E model of Chapter 5, which can be expressed in words as

$$\text{RESPONSE} = \text{CENTER} + \text{ERROR}$$

and in symbols as

$$Y = \mu + \epsilon$$

The model we will consider is a direct generalization of the C+E model, in which we let the center be a curve that depends on Z. In words,

$$\text{RESPONSE} = \text{CURVE} + \text{ERROR}$$

or

$$Y = \mu(Z) + \epsilon$$

In fact, we'll parameterize the model further to a form known as a **simple linear regression model,** or **SLR model** for short:

$$Y = \beta_0 + \beta_1 X(Z) + \epsilon \tag{7.2}$$

In model (7.2), the function $X(Z)$ is known, but the model parameters β_0 and β_1 are unknown constants that we'd like to estimate with the help of the data. To distinguish it from the predictor Z, we will call the function $X(Z)$ the **regressor variable,** or just regressor. As with the C+E model, ERROR (or ϵ) is the random-error term, usually due to measurement or experimental error.

---

[8]Previously, we called the variables X and Y, but in this section, we will be using X to denote a slightly different quantity.

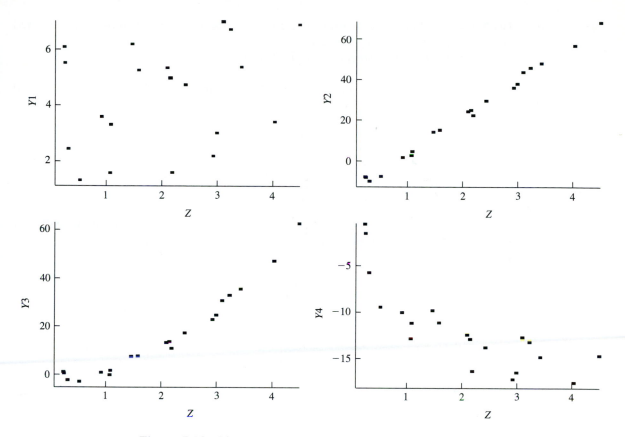

Figure 7.12 Plots of data simulated from models (7.3) (upper left), (7.4) (upper right), (7.5) (lower left), and (7.6) (lower right). In simulating these four data sets, we selected 50 independent Z values from a $U(0, 5)$ distribution and 50 independent ϵ values from an $N(0, 4)$ distribution. The data from model (7.3) were generated by choosing $\mu = 5$.

Here are some examples of SLR models (without peeking at the footnote, see if you can identify the parameters β_0 and β_1, and the regressor $X(Z)$ for each): [9]

$$Y = \mu + \epsilon \qquad \text{(Yes, the C+E model is the simplest SLR model!)} \tag{7.3}$$

$$Y = -12.8 + 17.6Z + \epsilon \tag{7.4}$$

$$Y = 3Z^2 + \epsilon \tag{7.5}$$

$$Y = -9 - 5\ln(Z) + \epsilon \tag{7.6}$$

To give some idea of the range of data that can be modeled by (7.2), we have simulated 50 observations from each of models (7.3) to (7.6). Plots of these data are shown in Figure 7.12. The upper-left scatterplot shows data simulated from model (7.3),

---

[9]Here are the answers. β_0, β_1, and $X(Z)$ are: μ, 0, does not exist; -12.8, 17.6, Z; 0, 3, Z^2; -9, -5, $\ln(Z)$.

with $\mu = 5$. The upper-right, lower-left, and lower-right scatterplots show data simulated from models (7.4) to (7.6), respectively.

The term "simple linear regression" means:

- **Simple.** There is a single regressor variable. A model with more than one is called a **multiple** regression model.
- **Linear.** The model is linear in the regression parameters, β_0 and β_1, and in the regressor, X, but **not** necessarily in the predictor Z!
- **Regression.** This refers to a phenomenon known as the **regression effect.** It's what Galton was talking about in the quote at the beginning of the chapter. We'll have more to say about the regression effect later.

To keep things as simple as possible, from now on, whenever we can, we will omit the explicit dependence of the regressor $X(Z)$ on Z, and just call it X. Thus, we will often write model (7.2) in the form

$$Y = \beta_0 + \beta_1 X + \epsilon \tag{7.7}$$

To summarize:

THE SIMPLE LINEAR REGRESSION MODEL

A **simple linear regression** model is a model for bivariate measurement data (Z, Y) in which Y is viewed as a function of Z, $\beta_0 + \beta_1 X(Z)$, plus random error:

$$Y = \beta_0 + \beta_1 X(Z) + \epsilon$$

where

- Y is the response or dependent variable
- Z is the predictor or independent variable
- $X = X(Z)$ is the regressor variable
- ϵ is a random-error term
- β_0 and β_1 are parameters of the model

Statistical Versus Functional Relationships

One very important point must be made about model (7.7). To understand this point, it will help us to consider a similar model:

$$Y = \beta_0 + \beta_1 X \tag{7.8}$$

Model (7.8) defines a **functional relationship** between X and Y. By this, we mean that if we know the model parameters β_0 and β_1, then for any value X, we know the corresponding value of Y **exactly.** In fact, we can obtain the value of Y simply by evaluating the right side of Equation (7.8).

In contrast, even if we know the model parameters β_0 and β_1, and the value of the regressor X for model (7.7), we won't know the response Y exactly. The problem is that we don't know the value of the random error, ϵ. And because it is random, we can't know its value.

What exactly is this random error that prevents us from evaluating Y? It is the sum total of everything that adds randomness to the process of obtaining the Y value: measurement error, environmental variation (temperature, humidity, etc.), human errors, and so on. Although we may not be able to observe these random errors, we are usually willing to assume that **on average,** their contribution is 0. That is, ϵ is a random variable whose expectation, $E(\epsilon)$, equals 0. This is a reasonable assumption if we believe that all systematic variation in the response is accounted for in the main part of the model: $\beta_0 + \beta_1 X$.

The immediate implication of this assumption is that if we know $X = x$, the expected value of Y is

$$E(Y|X = x) = \beta_0 + \beta_1 x. \tag{7.9}$$

That is, there is a functional relationship between the expected, or average, value of the response and the regressor. The relationship described by model (7.7) and Equation (7.9) is called a **statistical relationship** between X and Y. In a statistical relationship, even if we specify all unknown model parameters and the value of the regressor, we cannot predict the response exactly. However, with that knowledge, we can predict the mean population behavior exactly.

EXAMPLE 7.6   STATISTICAL VERSUS FUNCTIONAL RELATIONSHIP

Figure 7.13 shows a scatterplot of data generated from the functional relationship $E(Y|X = x) = 1 + 2x$ (left) and another of data generated by the statistical relationship $Y = 1 + 2X + \epsilon$, where $\epsilon \sim N(0, 0.04)$ (right). Each data point on the latter graph deviates from the line $Y = 1 + 2X$ by a random amount chosen from the $N(0, 0.04)$ distribution.   ✦

Model Specification

In our discussion of statistical relationships, we saw how a model can be thought of as producing a set of data. In reality, however, when confronted with a set of bivariate data, our first task is often to specify the model we want to use. In some scientific or engineering applications, knowledge about the process that produced the data is sufficient to tell us the form of the model to use. For other applications, we have to look at the data to postulate one or more possible models.

EXAMPLE 7.7   MORE ON AUTOMOBILE ENGINE PERFORMANCE

Recall the fuel-consumption data from Example 7.2 on page 358. The scatterplot in Figure 7.7 shows a definite, but nonlinear, statistical relationship between fuel

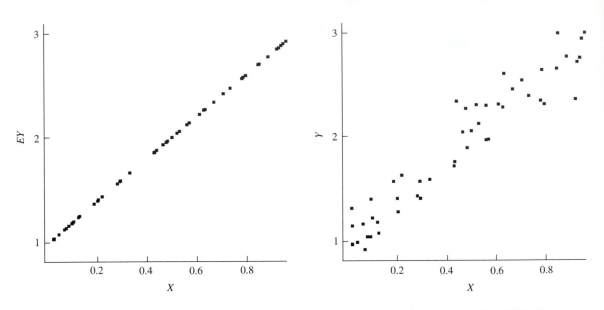

Figure 7.13 Scatterplot of data generated by the functional relationship $E(Y \mid X = x) = 1 + 2x$ (left) and of data generated by the statistical relationship $Y = 1 + 2X + \epsilon$, where $\epsilon \sim N(0, 0.04)$ (right).

consumption and the equivalence ratio. One way to approach the model specification problem is to find out if scientific or engineering theory indicates that the relation between fuel consumption and the equivalence ratio should follow a certain functional relationship. We would then postulate that functional relationship as the nonrandom part of the statistical relationship.

If theory cannot be used to supply the form of the model, then we must build a model empirically. This means looking at the data and selecting one or more candidate models. By exploring the data graphically, we can produce the plot in Figure 7.14, which graphs fuel consumption versus the fifth power of the equivalence ratio.

This relation looks reasonably linear, leading us to try the model

$$Y = \beta_0 + \beta_1 Z^5 + \epsilon$$
$$= \beta_0 + \beta_1 X + \epsilon$$

where Y is the response (fuel consumption), Z is the predictor (equivalence ratio), and $X = X(Z) = Z^5$ is the regressor. Note that this is just model (7.2).[10] Exercise 7.54 asks you to fit this model.   ◆

[10]In fact, whereas the postulated simple linear regression model does a good job of modeling the observed relationship, we can do a little better by specifying the model

$$Y = \beta_0 + \beta_1 Z + \beta_2 Z^2 + \beta_3 Z^3 + \beta_4 Z^5 + \epsilon$$

This more complicated model is an example of a **multiple regression model,** which is the topic of Chapter 8.

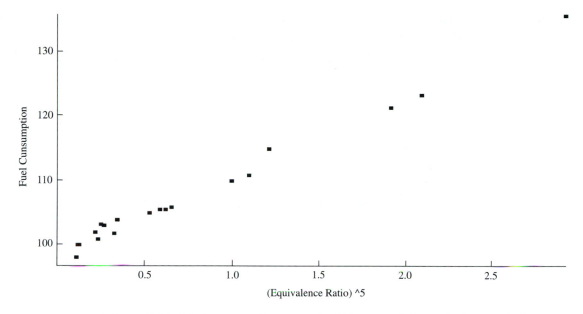

Figure 7.14   Fuel consumption versus the fifth power of the equivalence ratio for the data from Example 7.2.

Fitting the Simple Linear Regression Model

Assume that we have specified a simple linear regression model, and that we have n observations consisting of the regressor-response pairs (X_i, Y_i), $i = 1, \ldots, n$. The next step is to fit the model to the data. Fitting model (7.7) consists of estimating the unknown parameter values β_0, β_1. Fitting a simple linear regression model to data is called **regression.** If Y is the response and X is the regressor, we say that Y is regressed on X. We will discuss the reasons for this terminology later in the chapter.

We can think of fitting model (7.7) to the data as selecting the line $y = \beta_0 + \beta_1 x$ that best matches the data. This means we need some criterion to measure how well any given line matches the data. The two criteria we introduced in Chapter 4 when fitting the C+E model, least absolute errors and least squares, may also be used to fit the simple linear regression model.

Least Absolute Errors

Suppose we are considering the line $y = 5 + 3x$ as a candidate for the best fitting line. How far is this line from the data? Let's take it one point at a time. Because we view the regression problem as one of using the regressors to predict the responses, we measure the distance from the line to the data point (X_i, Y_i) as the absolute value of the difference between the value of the response when $X = X_i$ as predicted by the line, and the true observed value Y_i. When $X = X_i$, the line $y = 5 + 3x$ predicts the response to be $\hat{Y}_i = 5 + 3X_i$. Therefore, the distance from the line to the data point (X_i, Y_i) is $|Y_i - \hat{Y}_i|$. So one measure of how far the line is from all the data is the sum of all these distances for the n data points:

$$\text{SAE} = \sum_{i=1}^{n} |Y_i - \hat{Y}_i|$$

where SAE stands for sum of absolute errors.

      Now for a given set of data, the SAE will depend on the specific line chosen. Since any line can be named by its intercept and slope, here 5 and 3, respectively, the SAE previously computed can be denoted SAE(5, 3). For a line with intercept b_0 and slope b_1, the SAE can be denoted $\text{SAE}(b_0, b_1)$, and computed as

$$\text{SAE}(b_0, b_1) = \sum_{i=1}^{n} |Y_i - \hat{Y}_i| = \sum_{i=1}^{n} |Y_i - (b_0 + b_1 X_i)|$$

The best line, according to the SAE criterion, will have the intercept, b_0, and slope, b_1, that minimizes SAE.

      How do we find that line? To minimize SAE is not an easy task and requires the use of a computer. Since least absolute errors is seldom used in practice, we will not pursue its use further.

Least Squares

It is amazing how much easier it is to find the best line to fit a set of data if we only change our notion a bit about what "best" means! Instead of using the distance $|Y_i - \hat{Y}_i|$ to measure how far a line is from the data, let's try the square of this distance. For the line with intercept b_0 and slope b_1, this measure is:

$$\text{SSE}(b_0, b_1) = \sum_{i=1}^{n} (Y_i - \hat{Y}_i)^2 = \sum_{i=1}^{n} [Y_i - (b_0 + b_1 X_i)]^2 \tag{7.10}$$

where SSE stands for sum of squares error. The best fitting line, according to the SSE measure, will be the line whose intercept and slope, b_0 and b_1, respectively, minimize $\text{SSE}(b_0, b_1)$. These values are called the **least squares estimators** of intercept and slope.

      It is time to brush up on your calculus, because what we have here is a function of two variables, namely, $\text{SSE}(b_0, b_1)$, that we want to minimize. So, calculus skills at the ready? To minimize a differentiable function of two variables, you first find a critical point—that is, a point at which the partial derivatives of the function are zero—and show that the function has a minimum at that point. We'll save you the trouble of the last part by telling you that the only critical point for the SSE function has to be a minimum. So now we take the partial derivatives and set them to zero:

$$\frac{\partial(\text{SSE})}{\partial b_0} = -2\sum_{i=1}^{n}(Y_i - b_0 - b_1 X_i) = 0 \tag{7.11}$$

$$\frac{\partial(\text{SSE})}{\partial b_1} = -2\sum_{i=1}^{n} X_i(Y_i - b_0 - b_1 X_i) = 0 \tag{7.12}$$

Equations (7.11) and (7.12) are known as the **normal equations.** The values of b_0 and b_1 that solve the normal equations are the least squares estimators. Since they are estimators of the unknown slope and intercept, β_0 and β_1, respectively, we will denote the least squares estimators $\hat{\beta}_0$ and $\hat{\beta}_1$, respectively. The formulas for the least squares estimators, obtained by solving the normal equations, are as follows:

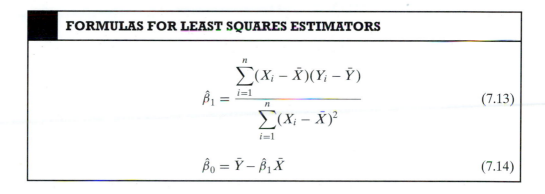

FORMULAS FOR LEAST SQUARES ESTIMATORS

$$\hat{\beta}_1 = \frac{\sum_{i=1}^{n}(X_i - \bar{X})(Y_i - \bar{Y})}{\sum_{i=1}^{n}(X_i - \bar{X})^2} \tag{7.13}$$

$$\hat{\beta}_0 = \bar{Y} - \hat{\beta}_1 \bar{X} \tag{7.14}$$

EXAMPLE 7.1   CONTINUED

Figure 7.15 is some of the SAS/INSIGHT output from the regression of WEAR on TIME when VELOCITY = 800. The top scatterplot shows the least squares line superimposed on the data. The least squares estimates are found in the "Parameter Estimates" table. The estimated intercept is $\hat{\beta}_0 = 0.0133$ and the estimated slope is $\hat{\beta}_1 = 0.0006$, so the fitted model is $\hat{Y} = 0.0133 + 0.0006X$, where X is time, and $\hat{Y}$ is predicted wear.   ◆

EXAMPLE 7.8   LASER TRAP

Biologists use lasers to force bacteria to move in a desired direction in order to trap them for various purposes. As the laser is shined on a bacterium, it moves at a velocity that is a function of the power of the laser beam. The resulting velocity is a measure of the trapping efficiency of the laser. In order to measure the trapping efficiency at various powers, a biologist conducts an experiment with a certain strain of Agrobacterium rhizogenes. In the experiment, laser runs are conducted at various powers, in mW, and the magnitude of the velocity of the bacterium on

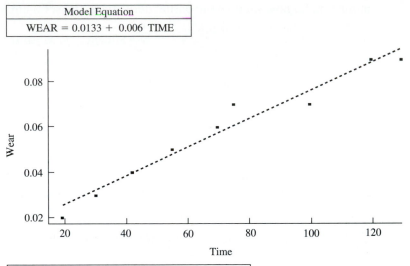

Model Equation
WEAR = 0.0133 + 0.006 TIME

Summary of Fit			
Mean of Response	0.0578	R-Square	0.9598
Root MSE	0.0053	Adj R-Sq	0.9541

Parameter Estimates							
Variable	DF	Estimate	Std Error	T Stat	Prob > |T|	Tolerance	Var Inflation
INTERCEPT	1	0.0133	0.0039	3.4504	0.0107	.	0
TIME	1	0.0006	4.823E-05	12.9341	0.0001	1.0000	1.0000

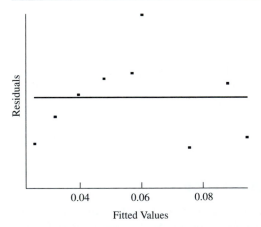

Figure 7.15 SAS/INSIGHT regression output for tool wear data, VELOCITY = 800.

which the laser is focused is measured in mm/s. The data set TRAPDATA contains all 108 data points from this experiment.

Figure 7.16 is some of the SAS/INSIGHT output from the regression of velocity on power. The top scatterplot shows the least squares line superimposed on the data. The least squares estimates are found in the "Parameter Estimates" table. The estimated intercept is $\hat{\beta}_0 = -1.8791$ and the estimated slope is $\hat{\beta}_1 = 0.8991$, so the fitted model is $\hat{Y} = -1.8791 + 0.8991\,X$, where X is the power of the laser, and $\hat{Y}$ is the predicted velocity of the bacterium.   ◆

Predicted Values, Fitted Values, and Residuals

Fitting a regression line to data is only the first step in a successful regression analysis. The next step is to assess the quality of the fit and if necessary look for ways to improve it. Recall that the fitted line has intercept and slope $\hat{\beta}_0$ and $\hat{\beta}_1$, so that the fitted line has equation:

$$\hat{Y} = \hat{\beta}_0 + \hat{\beta}_1 X$$

where $\hat{Y}$ is called the **predicted value** of Y at X. This is because, given the value, X, of the regressor, you would use $\hat{Y}$ to predict the associated response. When the X value is one of the values in the data set used to fit the line, say, X_i, the predicted value $\hat{Y}_i$ is called the **fitted value** at X_i. For the data point (X_i, Y_i), the difference between the actual Y value, Y_i, and the fitted value, $\hat{Y}_i$, is called the ith **residual.** Its formula is

$$e_i = Y_i - \hat{Y}_i$$

To summarize:

PREDICTED VALUES, FITTED VALUES, AND RESIDUALS

If $\hat{\beta}_0$ and $\hat{\beta}_1$ are the fitted intercept and slope in a simple linear regression, then

- The **predicted value** of Y at X is

$$\hat{Y} = \hat{\beta}_0 + \hat{\beta}_1 X$$

- For $X = X_i$, one of the values in the data set, the predicted value is called a **fitted value** and is written

$$\hat{Y}_i = \hat{\beta}_0 + \hat{\beta}_1 X_i$$

- The **residuals,** e_i, $i = 1, \ldots, n$, are the differences between the observed and fitted values for each data value:

$$e_i = Y_i - \hat{Y}_i = Y_i - (\hat{\beta}_0 + \hat{\beta}_1 X_i)$$

Residuals are the main tools used to assess the quality of the fit and to diagnose specific problems with the fit. This is because residuals are our best guess of what the

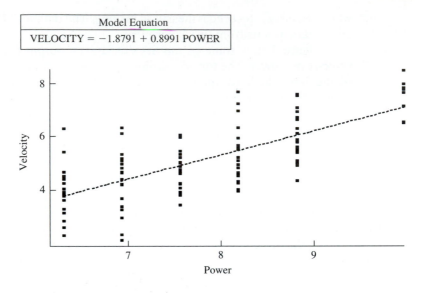

Model Equation
VELOCITY = −1.8791 + 0.8991 POWER

Summary of Fit			
Mean of Response	5.1010	R-Square	0.5022
Root MSE	0.9609	Adj R-Sq	0.4975

Parameter Estimates							
Variable	DF	Estimate	Std Error	T Stat	Prob > |T|	Tolerance	Var Inflation
INTERCEPT	1	−1.8791	0.6813	−2.7583	0.0068	.	0
POWER	1	0.8991	0.0869	10.3417	0.0001	1.0000	1.0000

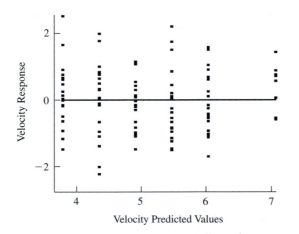

Figure 7.16 SAS/INSIGHT output for regression of velocity on power, bacteria trap data.

unobservable random error is like. Recall that our regression model says that

$$Y_i = \beta_0 + \beta_1 X_i + \epsilon_i \tag{7.15}$$

where ϵ_i is the random error for the ith observation.

But it is also true that

$$Y_i = \hat{\beta}_0 + \hat{\beta}_1 X_i + e_i \tag{7.16}$$

where the least squares estimators, $\hat{\beta}_0$ and $\hat{\beta}_1$, are our guesses for β_0 and β_1, and the residual e_i is our guess for ϵ_i. Therefore, if the residuals don't behave as random errors should, we suspect something is wrong with our model.

And how should random errors behave? Completely randomly. Any patterns that appear in the residuals mean that the data have some structure that the model is not accounting for. And this implies that the model should be revised.

By the way, model fitting is not a one-step procedure. It usually involves several iterations of model specification, model fitting, evaluation of the fit (here's where the residuals come in), model revision and re-specification, then back to model fitting again. This iterative process continues until a satisfactory model has been found.

Some Properties of Residuals and Fitted Values

Since the least squares estimators must satisfy Equations (7.11) and (7.12), we have

$$\sum_{i=1}^{n} e_i = \sum_{i=1}^{n} (Y_i - \hat{\beta}_0 - \hat{\beta}_1 X_i) = 0 \tag{7.17}$$

and

$$\sum_{i=1}^{n} X_i e_i = \sum_{i=1}^{n} X_i (Y_i - \hat{\beta}_0 - \hat{\beta}_1 X_i) = 0 \tag{7.18}$$

Equation (7.17) implies that the mean of the residuals is 0. Equation (7.18) implies that the residuals and the values of the regressor are uncorrelated. This equation can also be used to show that the residuals and the fitted values are uncorrelated.

Estimating the Error Variance

As before, we assume that the data are (X_i, Y_i), $i = 1, \ldots, n$. Because we are fitting model (7.7), we assume, at least tentatively, that the responses Y_i satisfy

$$Y_i = \beta_0 + \beta_1 X_i + \epsilon_i, \qquad i = 1, \ldots, n$$

It is standard practice to assume that the random errors, ϵ_i, are independent random variables having the same distribution with mean 0 and variance σ^2, and we will make this assumption. Often, but not always, it is assumed that the random errors have an $N(0, \sigma^2)$ distribution. We will make this latter assumption only when necessary, and will explicitly state it when we do make it.

In either case, σ^2 is the variance of the random error, and we would like to estimate it. To do so, we resort to an old standby: To estimate a population quantity, use the analogous sample quantity.[11] To estimate the variance of the random error in this way, we need the sample analogue of the random error. Equations (7.15) and (7.16) show that analogue to be the residuals. Thus, we will try to use the variance of the residuals to estimate σ^2. In doing so, we have to be careful about how we compute that variance.

At first glance, it might seem that all we have to do is use the usual sample variance formula:

$$S^2 = \frac{1}{n-1} \sum_{i=1}^{n} (e_i - \bar{e})^2 = \frac{1}{n-1} \sum_{i=1}^{n} e_i^2$$

where the last equality follows because the mean of the residuals is 0. However, $n - 1$ is not the degrees of freedom associated with the sum of the squares of the residuals.

To see this, note that the residuals must satisfy both Equations (7.17) and (7.18). Therefore, if we know $n - 2$ of the residuals (and all the X_i), we can find the other two residuals by solving those two equations. As a result, the degrees of freedom associated with the sum of the squares of the residuals is $n - 2$. Therefore, the appropriate estimator of σ^2 is

$$\text{MSE} = \frac{1}{n-2} \sum_{i=1}^{n} e_i^2.$$

MSE stands for **mean square error,** a term that arises from its computational formula: It takes the "errors" (i.e., residuals) e_i, squares them, and then takes their mean.

Assessing the Quality of Fit

Residual Plots

Plots of the residuals are the main method for assessing the quality of the fit. At a minimum, you should plot the residuals versus the fitted values (i.e., e_i versus $\hat{Y}_i$), since the residuals and the fitted values are uncorrelated. You should also plot the residuals versus anything you can think of that is pertinent. Residuals for data taken in a certain order should always be plotted versus that order. Any pattern over time or order might be a clue that the process that produced the data isn't stationary. Plot residuals versus any natural groupings: For example, if data are from a factory that runs more than one shift, plot versus shift. If more than one machine or operator is involved, plot versus machine or operator. Plot the residuals versus any variable except one: Do not plot residuals versus the responses. Since the residuals and responses are correlated, such a plot will show patterns where none exist in the data.

A normal quantile plot of the residuals is also advisable. However, it is better not to plot the raw residuals on a normal quantile plot. This is because the standard error of the ith residual e_i is the product of the standard deviation of random errors, σ, and a function of the regressors, $f_i = f_i(X_1, X_2, \ldots, X_n)$:

$$\sigma(e_i) = \sigma \cdot f_i, \qquad i = 1, \ldots, n \tag{7.19}$$

---

[11]Recall that in Chapter 5, we used the sample mean to estimate the population mean and the sample proportion to estimate the population proportion.

Plotting all the residuals on the same normal quantile plot assumes that all the residuals have the same normal distribution. However, it is clear that the residuals do not have the same distribution, since each residual has a different standard error.

Studentized Residual Quantile Plots

One solution to the problem of residuals having different standard errors is to **Studentize** them. Studentizing consists of dividing each residual by its estimated standard error. We obtain the estimated standard error of the ith residual by substituting the estimate of σ, $\hat{\sigma} = \sqrt{\text{MSE}}$, into Equation (7.19), giving

$$\hat{\sigma}(e_i) = \hat{\sigma} \cdot f_i, \qquad i = 1, \ldots, n$$

The ith Studentized residual is then computed as

$$r_i = \frac{e_i}{\hat{\sigma}(e_i)}$$

Since r_i is the quotient of the ith residual and its estimated standard error, we would expect it to have a t distribution. It does not, however, since e_i and $\hat{\sigma}(e_i)$ are dependent.

We can remove this dependency by omitting observation i from the calculation of $\hat{\sigma}$ when computing $\hat{\sigma}(e_i)$. The basic idea is,[12] for each $i = 1, 2, \ldots, n$, fit the regression model to all the data except the ith, and let $\hat{\sigma}_{(i)}$ denote the square root of the resulting MSE. Then e_i is independent of the estimated standard error

$$\hat{\sigma}_{(i)}(e_i) = \hat{\sigma}_{(i)} \cdot f_i, \qquad i = 1, \ldots, n$$

As a result, the Studentized residual

$$r_{(i)} = \frac{e_i}{\hat{\sigma}_{(i)}(e_i)} \tag{7.20}$$

has a t_{n-3} distribution. The Studentized residuals (7.20) are called **externally Studentized residuals,** since the estimated standard error $\hat{\sigma}_{(i)}(e_i)$ does not involve the ith observation.[13] In the remainder of this text, when we refer to Studentized residuals, we will be talking about externally Studentized residuals.

Instead of doing a normal quantile plot of the ordinary residuals, we recommend plotting the Studentized residuals versus the quantiles of the t_{n-3} distribution, especially if the number of observations is small.

Outlier Detection with Studentized Residuals

Studentized residuals are better than ordinary residuals at identifying outliers in the data. This is because instead of using MSE to estimate σ^2 in the standard error of the ith residual, the Studentized residual eliminates the ith observation before estimating σ. The reasoning is that if the ith observation is really an outlier, then including

---

[12]Fortunately, neither the user nor the computer package that calculates the $r_{(i)}$ really has to do all these separate regressions; there are clever formulas that provide all necessary results using only quantities from the original least squares fit.

[13]The Studentized residuals r_i are called **internally Studentized residuals.**

it in the estimate of σ will make the estimate artificially large. This will result in the Studentized residual appearing smaller than it should, and thus will hide the fact that the ith observation is an outlier.

Studentized residuals lying in the extreme tails of the t_{n-3} distribution should be investigated as possible outliers. Boxplots of Studentized residuals are also useful in identifying possible outliers.

Residual Plotting Strategies

Though Studentized residuals are often more appropriate than are ordinary residuals in evaluating model fit, ordinary residuals have the advantage that they are in the same units as the response variable. This is valuable information when trying to assess the impact of the model in terms of the response.

Thus, in creating residual plots, we recommend the following:

- For quantile plots, use only Studentized residuals and plot them versus t_{n-3} quantiles.[14] If n is large, or if you cannot easily produce quantiles of the t distribution, a normal quantile plot of the Studentized residuals is acceptable.
- For all other plots, use both ordinary and Studentized residuals whenever possible.
- If you have resources to do only one or the other, opt for Studentized residuals, but to keep your perspective on the true scale of things, do at least one plot of the ordinary residuals as well.

Whichever residuals you use, you should plot them versus the fitted values, versus the regressor variable, versus the predictor variable (if different from the regressor variable), and versus any other variables that might reveal a pattern (e.g., time order).

EXAMPLE 7.1 CONTINUED

The plot of e_i versus $\hat{Y}_i$ for the regression of WEAR on TIME for VELOCITY = 800 is found at the bottom of Figure 7.15. The residuals do not look random: There is an increasing trend in the first six of them (i.e., those belonging to the lowest six time values). In fact, looking back at the top plot, we now see that the first six points and the last three seem to fall on different lines. This is emphasized by Figure 7.17, which shows the least squares fit to only the first six points. By respecifying the model, perhaps we can improve the fit.

Our approach will be to obtain a suitable function of TIME, X(TIME), as a regressor. This function must make TIME small for the last three values relative to the first six values. There are a number of functions we might try: the logarithm X(TIME) = ln(TIME), and the power function X(TIME) = (TIME)^p, for $0 < p < 1$, will all shrink the larger values of TIME by a greater amount than

---

[14]The macro TQPLOT, described in the **Doing It with SAS** and **Doing It with MINITAB** supplements to the text, will generate plots of studentized residuals versus t quantiles.

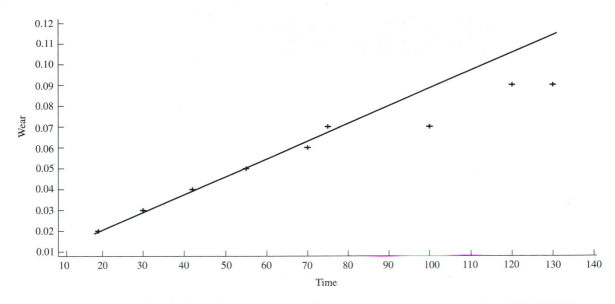

Figure 7.17 Least squares line fit to the first six points, tool wear data, VELOCITY = 800.

smaller values of TIME. One common choice is the power function with $p = 0.5$, also known as the square root.

A plot of WEAR versus $\sqrt{\text{TIME}}$ looks reasonably linear, so we proceed to regress WEAR on $\sqrt{\text{TIME}}$. Some of the SAS/INSIGHT output is displayed in Figure 7.18.

Figure 7.19 displays a plot of the Studentized residuals versus quantiles of the t_6 distribution with the 45° reference line, which is appropriate when using Studentized residuals. The most noticeable feature of this plot is the grouping of the Studentized residuals into six central values, one very small value, and two large values.

Overall, however, the model seems plausible, and we will use it to further illustrate the analysis of simple linear regression models.   ◆

EXAMPLE 7.8   CONTINUED

The residuals of the regression of velocity on power are shown in the bottom scatterplot in Figure 7.16. A plot of the Studentized residuals versus quantiles of the t_{105} distribution is shown in Figure 7.20. Neither of these plots gives evidence of a lack of model adequacy.

A couple of other points are worth making here. First, the data in the scatterplots in Figure 7.16 line up in six vertical columns. This results from the experimenter using only six different power settings. Second, there is a considerable vertical spread in the data values as compared with the tool wear data, for

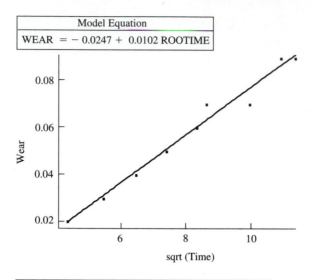

Model Equation
WEAR = − 0.0247 + 0.0102 ROOTIME

Summary of Fit			
Mean of Response	0.0578	R-Square	0.9781
Root MSE	0.0039	Adj R-Sq	0.9750

Parameter Estimates							
Variable	DF	Estimate	Std Error	T Stat	Prob > |T|	Tolerance	Var Inflation
INTERCEPT	1	0.0247	0.0048	−5.1034	0.0014	.	0
POWER	1	0.0102	0.0006	17.6921	0.0001	1.0000	1.0000

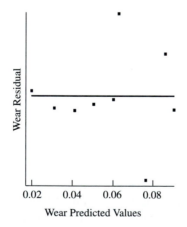

Figure 7.18   SAS/INSIGHT output for regression of WEAR on $\sqrt{\text{TIME}}$.

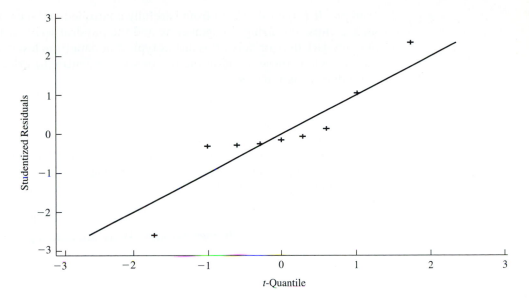

Figure 7.19   Plot of Studentized residuals versus quantiles of the t_6 distribution with 45° reference line, tool wear data, VELOCITY = 800.

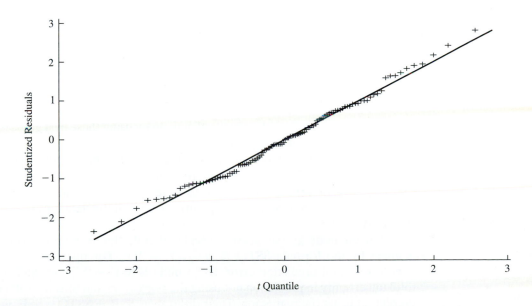

Figure 7.20   Plot of Studentized residuals versus quantiles of the t_{105} distribution with 45° reference line, bacteria trap data.

example. It is typical of data from carefully controlled and measured processes, such as those occurring in engineering and the physical sciences, to exhibit little random variation, or noise. It is just as typical of data from less controllable processes, such as those found in the life or social sciences, to exhibit a good deal of random variation.   ◆

The Coefficient of Determination

A numerical measure of the quality of fit is the **coefficient of determination.** What the coefficient of determination measures is the proportionate reduction in the uncertainty of predicting the response variable in the data set due to using the regression line to predict.

What exactly does this mouthful mean? Suppose you and I play a game called "guess the response variable." It goes like this: There are n data points (X_i, Y_i), $i = 1, \ldots, n$, from the SLR model

$$Y = \beta_0 + \beta_1 X + \epsilon$$

I select a data point (X_i, Y_i) at random and you are to guess Y_i. Suppose also that there are two versions of this game, the regression version and the nonregression version.

- In the regression version, I reveal X_i to you, and the fitted regression equation

$$\hat{Y} = \hat{\beta}_0 + \hat{\beta}_1 X$$

  obtained from regressing the Y_i on the X_i. In this case, the fitted value, $\hat{Y}_i$, is the best predictor of Y_i.
- In the nonregression version, you don't know X_i, but I tell you $\bar{Y}$, which is the best predictor of Y_i when X_i is unknown.

Relatively speaking, how well will you do by using these best guesses? Remember, that I've chosen the data point at random, so that any of the n data points is equally likely. If I choose the ith point (X_i, Y_i), then the "distance" between what I guess and the true Y_i is $(Y_i - \bar{Y})^2$ for the nonregression version of the game and $(Y_i - \hat{Y}_i)^2 = e_i^2$ for the regression version (remember, using least squares means "distance" is really the squared distance). Summing these quantities over all the data tells how far off, in total, the guess will be.

For the nonregression case, let SSTO denote this "total prediction error." SSTO is given by the formula $\text{SSTO} = \sum_{i=1}^{n}(Y_i - \bar{Y})^2$. For the regression case, let SSE denote the total prediction error. Its formula is $\text{SSE} = \sum_{i=1}^{n} e_i^2$. SSTO measures the total uncertainty in prediction not using the regression and SSE the total uncertainty in prediction using the regression. Their difference, $\text{SSR} = \text{SSTO} - \text{SSE}$, is the reduction in uncertainty due to the regression.

Taking the quotient of SSR and SSTO gives the proportionate reduction in the uncertainty of predicting the response variable in the data set due to using the regression line to predict. This is exactly the coefficient of determination we were after. Its formula is

$$r^2 = \frac{\text{SSR}}{\text{SSTO}}$$

The coefficient of determination has a second interpretation as well. This interpretation follows from the fact that SSE is the total variation in the response that is unexplained by the fitted model. As a result, $\text{SSR} = \text{SSTO} - \text{SSE}$ is the total variation in the response explained by the fitted model. Thus, we may interpret the coefficient of determination as the proportion of variation in the response that is explained by the fitted model.

Now we know you've been very alert during this chapter, so you're probably asking yourself why we'd try to confuse you by using the letter r to denote the correlation coefficient and then again in the coefficient of determination. Well, we're not. It turns out that the coefficient of determination is exactly the square of the correlation coefficient!

Sometimes the coefficient of determination is used to compare the quality of fit of different models: The higher r^2, the better the model. But, although r^2 is a valuable measure, it should never be the sole criterion for deciding quality of fit.

There is one final connection of which you should be aware. The quantity SSE defined here is $\text{SSE}(\hat{\beta}_0, \hat{\beta}_1)$, where the formula for the SSE function is given by (7.10), and $\hat{\beta}_0$ and $\hat{\beta}_1$ are the least squares estimators. You have already been told that SSE stands for sum of squares error. The quantities SSR and SSTO stand for **sum of squares regression** and **sum of squares total,** respectively. You will meet these terms again in Chapter 8.

THE COEFFICIENT OF DETERMINATION

The coefficient of determination is computed as

$$r^2 = \frac{\text{SSR}}{\text{SSTO}} = 1 - \frac{\text{SSE}}{\text{SSTO}}$$

where

$$\text{SSTO} = \sum_{i=1}^{n}(Y_i - \bar{Y})^2 \qquad \text{SSE} = \sum_{i=1}^{n} e_i^2 \qquad \text{SSR} = \text{SSTO} - \text{SSE}$$

are the sum of squares total, error, and regression. The coefficient of determination is interpreted as

- The proportion by which the regression reduces the uncertainty in predicting the response, or
- The proportion of variation in the response explained by the regression.

EXAMPLE 7.1   CONTINUED

Consider the regression of WEAR on TIME for VELOCITY = 800. The coefficient of determination is found in Figure 7.15, where it is labeled "R-Square" in the "Summary of Fit" table. Its value is 0.9598. This can be interpreted in two ways:

- Using the fitted simple linear regression model
$$\widehat{\text{WEAR}} = 0.0133 + 0.0006 \cdot \text{TIME}$$
  to predict WEAR causes a 95.98% reduction in uncertainty of prediction over using the prediction $\widehat{\text{WEAR}} = 0.0578$, the mean of the WEAR values in the data set.
- The fitted model explains 95.98% of the variation in WEAR.

Now, of course, we found that we could improve the model fit by regressing WEAR on $\sqrt{\text{TIME}}$. From Figure 7.18, we see that the coefficient of determination for this model is 0.9781. The two interpretations are then as follows:

- Using the fitted simple linear regression model
$$\widehat{\text{WEAR}} = -0.0247 + 0.0102 \cdot \sqrt{\text{TIME}}$$
  to predict WEAR causes a 97.81% reduction in uncertainty of prediction over using the prediction $\widehat{\text{WEAR}} = 0.0578$.
- The fitted model explains 97.81% of the variation in WEAR.

Thus, respecifying the model resulted in a $97.81\% - 95.98\% = 1.83\%$ further reduction in the uncertainty of prediction of WEAR. Or, what amounts to the same thing, the respecified model explains 1.83% more of the variation in WEAR.

In addition to telling us the reduction in uncertainty of prediction, the value of the coefficient of determination can be used to tell us the value of the Pearson correlation. The magnitude of the Pearson correlation is the square root of the coefficient of determination, and its sign is that of the fitted slope, $\hat{\beta}_1$. Thus, we find that the Pearson correlation between WEAR and TIME is $\sqrt{0.9598} = 0.9797$, and the Pearson correlation between WEAR and $\sqrt{\text{TIME}}$ is $\sqrt{0.9781} = 0.9890$.
◆

EXAMPLE 7.8   CONTINUED

Consider the regression of VELOCITY on POWER for the bacteria trap data. The coefficient of determination found in Figure 7.16 is 0.5022. This means

- Using the fitted simple linear regression model
$$\widehat{\text{VELOCITY}} = -1.8791 + 0.8991 \cdot \text{POWER}$$
  to predict VELOCITY causes a 50.22% reduction in uncertainty of pre-

diction over using the prediction $\widehat{\text{VELOCITY}} = 5.1010$, the mean of the VELOCITY values in the data set.

- The fitted model explains 50.22% of the variation in VELOCITY.

This coefficient of determination is much smaller than the values we observed for the tool wear data. The Pearson correlation between VELOCITY and POWER is $\sqrt{0.5022} = 0.7087$.   ✦

Model Interpretation

Once you have fit the model and you are satisfied with the quality of that fit, you will want to interpret the model. Although this may seem straightforward, there are some subtleties to be considered.

The Fitted Slope

The fitted slope may be interpreted as the change in the estimated mean response per unit increase in the regressor. Note that this does not mean that increasing the regressor from x to $x + 1$ units will increase the response $\hat{\beta}_1$ units. It does mean that we estimate that the mean response when the regressor has value $x + 1$ is $\hat{\beta}_1$ units higher than the mean response when the regressor has value x.

If the regressor and the predictor are not the same, and if you want the model interpreted in terms of the predictor, the interpretation of the slope becomes more difficult. Perhaps the best approach when the regressor, $X(Z)$, is a differentiable function of the predictor, Z, is to take the derivative of the fitted model:

$$\frac{d\hat{Y}}{dz} = \hat{\beta}_1 \frac{dX(z)}{dz} \tag{7.21}$$

The interpretation is that the change in the estimated mean response per unit change in the predictor is the fitted slope times the change in the regressor per unit change in the predictor.

The Fitted Intercept

The fitted intercept is the estimate of the response when the regressor equals 0. In some cases, however, it may not even make sense to interpret the intercept. Usually, this occurs when $X = 0$ is outside the sensible range of the data. In addition, care must be taken whenever extrapolation is done beyond the actual range of the data.

EXAMPLE 7.8   CONTINUED

When interpreting a fitted model, it is important to remember that the fitted model is just a summary of a data pattern, not a reflection of the behavior of each data point.

Thus, the fitted slope 0.8991 says, "The overall pattern of the data is that the mean magnitude of the velocity of this type of bacterium subjected to this type of laser at power POWER mW, is about 0.8991 mm/sec less than the mean magnitude of the velocity of this type of bacterium subjected to this type of laser at power POWER + 1 mW." It **does NOT say,** "If you take this bacterium that is being subjected to this type of laser, and turn up the laser by 1 mW, then the magnitude of its velocity will increase by exactly 0.8991 mm/sec."

Does it make sense to interpret the intercept? If it did, the fitted intercept, -1.8791, would be the mean magnitude of velocity when no laser is used. On the face of it, we know this fitted intercept cannot be meaningful, since velocity cannot have a negative magnitude.

But even if the fitted intercept were positive, we would be wise to be cautious in our interpretation of it, since the value POWER = 0 is well below the smallest value of POWER, 6.3 mW, at which the data were taken.

Look at the "Summary of Fit" table in Figure 7.16 to find that the square root of MSE, which is an estimate of σ, the standard deviation of the random error, is 0.9609. ✦

EXAMPLE 7.1   CONTINUED

Consider the regression of WEAR on $\sqrt{\text{TIME}}$. The fitted slope 0.0102 says, "The overall pattern of the data is that the mean wear for this type of tool run at VELOCITY = 800 and a certain unvarying set of environmental conditions for a given value of the regressor $\sqrt{\text{TIME}} = T$ is about 0.0102 inch less than the mean wear for this type of tool run under exactly the same conditions for the value of the regressor $\sqrt{\text{TIME}} = T + 1$."

It may be that we need an interpretation in terms of the predictor TIME. Then we can use Equation (7.21) to give

$$\frac{d(\widehat{\text{WEAR}})}{d(\text{TIME})} = 0.0102 \frac{d\sqrt{\text{TIME}}}{d(\text{TIME})} = 0.0102 \left(\frac{1}{2\sqrt{\text{TIME}}} \right) = \frac{0.0051}{\sqrt{\text{TIME}}}$$

This says that the change in predicted WEAR per unit change in TIME equals $0.0051/\sqrt{\text{TIME}}$.

As in the previous example, the negative estimate of the intercept, in addition to TIME = 0 being outside the range of the data, makes it clear that the intercept has no interpretation of its own.

The estimate of the standard deviation of the random error is $\hat{\sigma} = \sqrt{\text{MSE}} = 0.0039$. ✦

Inference for the Simple Linear Regression Model

Confidence Intervals for Slope and Intercept

For the SLR model with normal errors, the sampling distributions of the least squares estimators of intercept and slope are normal with means β_0 and β_1, respectively. If the errors are not normal, but there are a reasonably large number of observations, then a generalization of the Central Limit Theorem[15] ensures that in most practical applications, the sampling distributions of the least squares estimators of intercept and slope are approximately normal. In either case, the means of $\hat{\beta}_0$ and $\hat{\beta}_1$ are β_0 and β_1, respectively. If we knew σ, the standard deviation of the errors, we could use theory to compute the variance of the sampling distribution of $\hat{\beta}_0$ and $\hat{\beta}_1$, and we could use what we know about the normal distribution to do a complete analysis of these estimators.

To be specific, the standard error[16] of $\hat{\beta}_0$ is

$$\sigma(\hat{\beta}_0) = \sigma \sqrt{\frac{1}{n} + \frac{\bar{X}^2}{\sum_{i=1}^{n}(X_i - \bar{X})^2}} \tag{7.22}$$

and that of $\hat{\beta}_1$ is

$$\sigma(\hat{\beta}_1) = \frac{\sigma}{\sqrt{\sum_{i=1}^{n}(X_i - \bar{X})^2}} \tag{7.23}$$

We would then use the fact that

$$\frac{\hat{\beta}_0 - \beta_0}{\sigma(\hat{\beta}_0)} \quad \text{and} \quad \frac{\hat{\beta}_1 - \beta_1}{\sigma(\hat{\beta}_1)} \tag{7.24}$$

both have $N(0, 1)$ distributions.

Unfortunately, we don't know σ. The best we can do is to replace σ in Equations (7.22) and (7.23) by the estimator $\hat{\sigma} = \sqrt{\text{MSE}}$. The result is the estimated standard errors

$$\hat{\sigma}(\hat{\beta}_0) = \hat{\sigma} \sqrt{\frac{1}{n} + \frac{\bar{X}^2}{\sum_{i=1}^{n}(X_i - \bar{X})^2}} \tag{7.25}$$

and

$$\hat{\sigma}(\hat{\beta}_1) = \frac{\hat{\sigma}}{\sqrt{\sum_{i=1}^{n}(X_i - \bar{X})^2}} \tag{7.26}$$

Replacing the denominators of the two expressions in (7.24) by $\hat{\sigma}(\hat{\beta}_0)$ and $\hat{\sigma}(\hat{\beta}_1)$, gives

$$\frac{\hat{\beta}_0 - \beta_0}{\hat{\sigma}(\hat{\beta}_0)} \quad \text{and} \quad \frac{\hat{\beta}_1 - \beta_1}{\hat{\sigma}(\hat{\beta}_1)}$$

---

[15]To see that this is reasonable, consider, for example, that $\hat{\beta}_1$ is a linear combination of the responses, given by the formula $\hat{\beta}_1 = \sum_{i=1}^{n} c_i Y_i$, where the constant $c_i = (X_i - \bar{X}) / \sum_{i=1}^{n}(X_i - \bar{X})^2$.

[16]Recall that the standard error of an estimator is the standard deviation of its sampling distribution.

both of which have a t_{n-2} distribution. Note that the $n - 2$ degrees of freedom are those associated with MSE, which is used to estimate σ^2.

Following the development of a classical level L confidence interval for μ in Chapter 5, we obtain level L confidence intervals for β_0 and β_1 as

$$(\hat{\beta}_0 - \hat{\sigma}(\hat{\beta}_0)t_{n-2,(1+L)/2}, \ \hat{\beta}_0 + \hat{\sigma}(\hat{\beta}_0)t_{n-2,(1+L)/2})$$

and

$$(\hat{\beta}_1 - \hat{\sigma}(\hat{\beta}_1)t_{n-2,(1+L)/2}, \ \hat{\beta}_1 + \hat{\sigma}(\hat{\beta}_1)t_{n-2,(1+L)/2})$$

respectively.

Hypothesis Tests for Slope and Intercept

To test the hypothesis

$$H_0: \quad \beta_0 = \beta_{00}$$

versus one of the alternative hypotheses

$$H_{a-}: \quad \beta_0 < \beta_{00}$$
$$H_{a+}: \quad \beta_0 > \beta_{00}$$
$$H_{a\pm}: \quad \beta_0 \neq \beta_{00}$$

where β_{00} is a known constant, we make use of the fact that under the distribution theory developed before, if H_0 is true,

$$T = \frac{\hat{\beta}_0 - \beta_{00}}{\hat{\sigma}(\hat{\beta}_0)} \sim t_{n-2}$$

If t^* denotes the observed value of T, the p-value of the tests of H_0 versus H_{a-}, H_{a+}, and $H_{a\pm}$ are $p_- = P(T \leq t^*)$, $p^+ = P(T \geq t^*)$ and $p\pm = P(|T| \geq |t^*|) = 2\min(p_-, p^+)$, respectively.

Similarly, to test the hypothesis

$$H_0: \quad \beta_1 = \beta_{10}$$

versus one of the alternative hypotheses

$$H_{a-}: \quad \beta_1 < \beta_{10}$$
$$H_{a+}: \quad \beta_1 > \beta_{10}$$
$$H_{a\pm}: \quad \beta_1 \neq \beta_{10}$$

we use the fact that under the distribution theory developed before, if H_0 is true,

$$T = \frac{\hat{\beta}_1 - \beta_{10}}{\hat{\sigma}(\hat{\beta}_1)} \sim t_{n-2}$$

If t^* denotes the observed value of T, the p-value of the tests of H_0 versus H_{a-}, H_{a+}, and

$H_{a\pm}$ are $p_- = P(T \leq t^*)$, $p^+ = P(T \geq t^*)$ and $p\pm = P(|T| \geq |t^*|) = 2\min(p_-, p^+)$, respectively.

Most often, but not always, the test of greatest interest is whether, given the SLR model, the response depends on the regressor as specified by the model or not. The appropriate hypothesis test for this purpose is

$$H_0: \quad \beta_1 = 0$$

versus

$$H_{a\pm}: \quad \beta_1 \neq 0$$

EXAMPLE 7.8   CONTINUED

The "Parameter Estimates" table in Figure 7.16 contains the parameter estimates $\hat{\beta}_0 = -1.8791$ and $\hat{\beta}_1 = 0.8991$, and their estimated standard errors $\hat{\sigma}(\hat{\beta}_0) = 0.6813$ and $\hat{\sigma}(\hat{\beta}_1) = 0.0869$. For a test of $H_0: \beta_0 = 0$ versus $H_{a\pm}: \beta_0 \neq 0$, the observed value of the test statistic is

$$t^* = \frac{\hat{\beta}_0}{\hat{\sigma}(\hat{\beta}_0)} = \frac{-1.8791}{0.6813} = -2.7583$$

the value appearing under "T Stat." The p-value is given under "Prob $> |T|$" as 0.0068. The small p-value provides strong evidence against the null hypothesis. For a test of $H_0: \beta_1 = 0$ versus $H_{a\pm}: \beta_1 \neq 0$, the observed value of the test statistic, t^*, is 10.3417 with a p-value no larger than 0.0001.   ◆

INFERENCE FOR SLOPE AND INTERCEPT IN THE SIMPLE LINEAR REGRESSION MODEL

- **The Model.** $Y = \beta_0 + \beta_1 X + \epsilon$
- **The Data.** $(X_1, Y_1), \ldots, (X_n, Y_n)$
- **Estimation.**

  ○ **Estimators.** Least squares estimators, $\hat{\beta}_0, \hat{\beta}_1$, given by (7.13) and (7.14).
  ○ **Estimated Standard Errors.** $\hat{\sigma}(\hat{\beta}_0)$ and $\hat{\sigma}(\hat{\beta}_1)$ given by (7.25) and (7.26).
  ○ **Level L Confidence Intervals**

  $$(\hat{\beta}_0 - \hat{\sigma}(\hat{\beta}_0)t_{n-2,(1+L)/2}, \ \hat{\beta}_0 + \hat{\sigma}(\hat{\beta}_0)t_{n-2,(1+L)/2})$$

  and

  $$(\hat{\beta}_1 - \hat{\sigma}(\hat{\beta}_1)t_{n-2,(1+L)/2}, \ \hat{\beta}_1 + \hat{\sigma}(\hat{\beta}_1)t_{n-2,(1+L)/2})$$

- **Hypothesis Testing**

  - **The Statistical Hypotheses.** For $i = 0$ (intercept) and $i = 1$ (slope):

    $$H_0: \quad \beta_i = \beta_{i0}$$

    versus one of the alternative hypotheses

    $$H_{a+}: \quad \beta_i > \beta_{i0}$$
    $$H_{a-}: \quad \beta_i < \beta_{i0}$$
    $$H_{a\pm}: \quad \beta_i \neq \beta_{i0}$$

  - **Observed Value of Standardized Test Statistic**

    $$t^* = \frac{\hat{\beta}_i - \beta_{i0}}{\hat{\sigma}(\hat{\beta}_i)}$$

  - **The Test.** The p-values for the tests are

    * for the test of H_0 versus H_{a+}, $p^+ = P(T \geq t^*)$,
    * for the test of H_0 versus H_{a-}, $p^- = P(T \leq t^*)$,
    * for the test of H_0 versus $H_{a\pm}$, $p\pm = P(|T| \geq |t^*|) = 2\min(p^-, p^+)$,

    where $T \sim t_{n-2}$.

EXAMPLE 7.1   CONTINUED

Going back to the tool wear data, suppose you are interested in the relation between tool wear and time when VELOCITY = 800. Suppose, actually, that your interest derives because your boss has just dumped the data on your lap, and she wants your decision on whether to buy $10,000,000 worth of these tools from the supplier who provided the sample you tested. And by the way, the estimated increase in mean tool wear per minute of use had better not exceed 0.0025.

Regressing TWEAR on $\sqrt{\text{TIME}}$, you find[17] that $\hat{\beta}_1 = 0.0102$ and $\hat{\sigma}(\hat{\beta}_1) = 0.0006$. From your computer program or a table, you find that $t_{n-2,0.975} = t_{7,0.975} = 2.365$. So the 95% confidence interval for $\hat{\beta}_1$ is

$$(0.0102 - (0.0006)(2.365), 0.0102 + (0.0006)(2.365)) = (0.0088, 0.0116)$$

Thus, we estimate β_1 to be between 0.0088 and 0.0116. To get a confidence interval for the change in mean tool wear per minute of use, we can use Equation (7.21) to give

$$\frac{d(\widehat{\text{WEAR}})}{d(\text{TIME})} = \hat{\beta}_1 \left(\frac{1}{2\sqrt{\text{TIME}}} \right)$$

[17]See Figure 7.18.

which we estimate lies in the interval

$$\left(0.0088 \left(\frac{1}{2\sqrt{\text{TIME}}}\right), 0.0116 \left(\frac{1}{2\sqrt{\text{TIME}}}\right)\right) = \left(\frac{0.0044}{\sqrt{\text{TIME}}}, \frac{0.0058}{\sqrt{\text{TIME}}}\right)$$

In the data, $4.35 \leq \sqrt{\text{TIME}} \leq 11.41$. If this is the range of time values for which inference is desired, we can estimate that the mean tool wear per minute of use will lie between $0.0044/11.41 = 0.0004$ and $0.0058/4.35 = 0.0013$ over that range. You are quite pleased that the upper limit 0.0013 is comfortably below 0.0025.   ◆

One last point. If the interval for β_1 contains 0, there is insufficient evidence that β_1 is different from 0. We would then be justified in concluding that there is insufficient evidence of a relation between the regressor and response variable, at least as far as the model is concerned.

Estimating the Mean Response

The mean response at the value of the regressor $X = x$ is $\mu = \beta_0 + \beta_1 x$. Think of this as the value of the line defining the simple linear regression model at x. Estimation of μ is summarized in the following box:

ESTIMATING THE MEAN RESPONSE

- **Point Estimator.** A point estimator of the mean response at the X value $X = x$ is

$$\hat{Y} = \hat{\beta}_0 + \hat{\beta}_1 x$$

- **Estimated Standard Error.** The estimated standard error of $\hat{Y}$ is

$$\hat{\sigma}(\hat{Y}) = \sqrt{\text{MSE}\left[\frac{1}{n} + \frac{(x - \bar{X})^2}{\sum (X_i - \bar{X})^2}\right]} \tag{7.27}$$

- **Confidence Interval.** If we can assume normality, which will be the case if the errors are normal, or, usually, if the sample size is large, a level L confidence interval for μ is

$$(\hat{Y} - \hat{\sigma}(\hat{Y})t_{n-2,(1+L)/2}, \hat{Y} + \hat{\sigma}(\hat{Y})t_{n-2,(1+L)/2}) \tag{7.28}$$

EXAMPLE 7.1   CONTINUED

Suppose that we want to use the regression of WEAR on $\sqrt{\text{TIME}}$ to compute a 95% confidence interval for the mean wear of tools at 110 minutes. Since

$\sqrt{110} = 10.488$, the point estimate is

$$\hat{y} = -0.0247 + 0.0102 \cdot 10.488 = 0.0823$$

The mean of the nine values of the regressor, $X = \sqrt{\text{TIME}}$, in the data is $\bar{x} = 8.124$, and $\sum(x_i - \bar{x})^2 = 47.004$. Since MSE $= 1.549 \times 10^{-5}$ and $n = 9$,

$$\hat{\sigma}(\hat{y}) = \sqrt{1.549 \times 10^{-5} \left[\frac{1}{9} + \frac{(10.488 - 8.124)^2}{47.004} \right]} = 0.0019$$

Recall that $t_{7,0.975} = 2.365$, so the 95% confidence interval is

$$(0.0823 - [0.0019][2.365], 0.0823 + [0.0019][2.365]) = (0.078, 0.087)$$

Thus, with 95% confidence, we estimate a range of values for $\mu = \beta_0 + \beta_1 \cdot 10.488$ to be $(0.078, 0.087)$.   ✦

EXAMPLE 7.8   CONTINUED

Recall the model fit to the bacteria trap data:

$$\widehat{\text{VELOCITY}} = -1.8791 + 0.8991 \cdot \text{POWER}$$

Suppose the experimenter wants to estimate the mean velocity when the power is set to 7.56 mW. The point estimate is

$$\widehat{\text{VELOCITY}} = -1.8791 + 0.8991 \cdot 7.56 = 4.92$$

Since the mean of the 108 POWER measurements in the data is 7.76, $\sum(x_i - \bar{x})^2 = 122.16$, and MSE $= 0.9233$,

$$\hat{\sigma}(\hat{y}) = \sqrt{0.9233 \left[\frac{1}{108} + \frac{(7.56 - 7.76)^2}{122.16} \right]} = 0.0941.$$

Since $t_{106,0.975} = 1.98$, a 95% confidence interval for the mean response at POWER$= 7.56$ is

$$(4.92 - [0.0941][1.98], 4.92 + [0.0941][1.98]) = (4.73, 5.10).   ✦$$

Using a regression model to estimate the mean response at $X = x$ has a couple of advantages over just using the responses for $X = x$ to do the estimation.

- First, the regression model allows us to estimate the response at values x that are not in the data. There are only six power values in the bacteria trap data, but we can use the regression model to estimate the mean velocity of bacteria at other power levels as well.

- Second, the regression model allows us to bring more data to bear in estimation. This makes for more precise inference. In the bacteria trap data, there are 20 data values at the power level 7.56 mW. We could use only those 20 values to estimate the mean velocity when the power level is 7.56 mW (assuming the 20 observations are from a C+E model). Since the mean of those observations is 4.70 and their standard deviation is 0.73, the standard error of the mean is $0.73/\sqrt{20} = 0.16$. Also, $t_{19,0.975} = 2.093$, so a 95% confidence interval for the mean velocity based on these 20 observations is

$$(4.70 - [0.16][2.093], 4.70 + [0.16][2.093]) = (4.36, 5.05)$$

This interval has width 0.69, almost twice the width of the interval $(4.73, 5.10)$ computed in the last example from the regression.

Predicting a New Response

A problem that looks similar to estimating the mean response at x, but that has one very important difference, is prediction of a new response to be taken at $X = x$.

To understand this difference, it may help to consider the following situation. Suppose you know the true mean response at x, $\mu = \beta_0 + \beta_1 x$. Then the error involved in estimating the mean response at x is 0. What is the error involved in predicting a new response at x? First, since you know μ, that is what you should use to predict the new observation. Since the new observation is

$$Y_{new} = \beta_0 + \beta_1 x + \epsilon_{new} = \mu + \epsilon_{new}$$

the error in prediction will be $Y_{new} - \mu = \epsilon_{new}$. The point is that when estimating the mean response, knowledge of the mean response gives the exact answer, but when predicting a new observation, knowledge of the mean response still leaves prediction error. The variance of the prediction error of a new observation is going to be the variance of $Y_{new} - \mu = \epsilon_{new}$, which is σ^2.

Of course, in reality we don't know μ, so we estimate it using $\hat{Y} = \hat{\beta}_0 + \hat{\beta}_1 x$. When using $\hat{Y}$ to predict a new response, we'll call it $\hat{Y}_{new}$. In this case, the prediction error is $Y_{new} - \hat{Y}_{new}$. Since $Y_{new} = \mu + \epsilon_{new}$, the prediction error equals

$$Y_{new} - \hat{Y}_{new} = (\mu + \epsilon_{new}) - \hat{Y}_{new} = (\mu - \hat{Y}_{new}) + \epsilon_{new} \qquad (7.29)$$

Since $\hat{Y}_{new}$ is computed from the present data and the new observation is independent of the present data, ϵ_{new} and $(\mu - \hat{Y}_{new})$ in Equation (7.29) are independent, which means that the variance of their sum is the sum of their variances, giving

$$\sigma^2(Y_{new} - \hat{Y}_{new}) = \sigma^2(\mu - \hat{Y}_{new}) + \sigma^2(\epsilon_{new}) = \sigma^2(\mu - \hat{Y}_{new}) + \sigma^2$$

Also, $\hat{Y}_{new} = \hat{Y}$, so that

$$\sigma^2(\mu - \hat{Y}_{new}) = \sigma^2(\mu - \hat{Y})$$

Now recall that for a random variable Z, the variance of $aZ + b$ equals a^2 times the variance of Z. This implies that

$$\sigma^2(\mu - \hat{Y}) = \sigma^2(\hat{Y})$$

and hence the variance of prediction is

$$\sigma^2(Y_{\text{new}} - \hat{Y}_{\text{new}}) = \sigma^2(\hat{Y}) + \sigma^2 \qquad (7.30)$$

Of course, evaluating Equation (7.30) requires knowledge of σ^2, which we don't usually have, so we use MSE to estimate it. This, along with Equation (7.27), gives the estimated prediction variance

$$\hat{\sigma}^2(Y_{\text{new}} - \hat{Y}_{\text{new}}) = \text{MSE} + \hat{\sigma}^2(\hat{Y}) = \text{MSE}\left[1 + \frac{1}{n} + \frac{(x - \bar{X})^2}{\sum(X_i - \bar{X})^2}\right]$$

and the standard error of prediction

$$\hat{\sigma}(Y_{\text{new}} - \hat{Y}_{\text{new}}) = \sqrt{\text{MSE}\left[1 + \frac{1}{n} + \frac{(x - \bar{X})^2}{\sum(X_i - \bar{X})^2}\right]} \qquad (7.31)$$

If we can assume normality, the quotient

$$T = \frac{Y_{\text{new}} - \hat{Y}_{\text{new}}}{\hat{\sigma}(Y_{\text{new}} - \hat{Y}_{\text{new}})}$$

has a t_{n-2} distribution, so that

$$L = P(-t_{n-2,(1+L)/2} < T < t_{n-2,(1+L)/2})$$

$$= P(\hat{Y}_{\text{new}} - \hat{\sigma}(Y_{\text{new}} - \hat{Y}_{\text{new}})t_{n-2,(1+L)/2} < Y_{\text{new}} < \hat{Y}_{\text{new}} + \hat{\sigma}(Y_{\text{new}} - \hat{Y}_{\text{new}})t_{n-2,(1+L)/2})$$

Thus, we have

PREDICTING A NEW RESPONSE

- **Predictor.** A predictor of a new response at $X = x$ is

$$\hat{Y}_{\text{new}} = \hat{\beta}_0 + \hat{\beta}_1 x$$

- **Estimated Standard Error.** The estimated standard error of prediction, $\hat{\sigma}(Y_{\text{new}} - Y_{\text{new}})$, is given by Equation (7.31).
- **Prediction Interval.** If we can assume normality, a level L prediction interval for a new response is

$$(\hat{Y}_{\text{new}} - \hat{\sigma}(Y_{\text{new}} - \hat{Y}_{\text{new}})t_{n-2,(1+L)/2}, \ \hat{Y}_{\text{new}} + \hat{\sigma}(Y_{\text{new}} - \hat{Y}_{\text{new}})t_{n-2,(1+L)/2}) \qquad (7.32)$$

EXAMPLE 7.8   CONTINUED

The biologist wants to predict the velocity of the next bacterium subjected to laser power of 7.56 mW. The point predictor is

$$\hat{y}_{new} = -1.8791 + 0.8991 \cdot 7.56 = 4.92$$

The estimated standard error of prediction is

$$\hat{\sigma}(y_{new} - \hat{y}_{new}) = \sqrt{0.9233 \left[1 + \frac{1}{108} + \frac{(7.56 - 7.76)^2}{122.16}\right]} = 0.9654$$

Recall that $t_{106,0.975} = 1.98$, so the 95% prediction interval is

$$(4.92 - [0.9654][1.98], 4.92 + [0.9654][1.98]) = (3.01, 6.83)$$

The biologist is 95% confident that the velocity of the next bacterium subjected to laser power of 7.56 mW will be between 3.01 and 6.83. This interval is about 10 times as wide as the confidence interval for the mean response at POWER = 7.56 mW, which reflects the precision with which 108 observations can estimate the mean response, compared with the imprecision with which we can predict the value of a new observation.

   To understand what 95% confidence means, suppose that the experiment is repeated a large number of times, and each time, a 95% prediction interval for a future response at POWER = 7.56 mW is computed. Let PI(i) denote the prediction interval computed using the data from experiment i. Suppose also that after PI(i) is computed, NR(i), a new response at POWER = 7.56 mW is recorded. Then, approximately 95% of all the PI(i) will contain NR(i).   ◆

EXAMPLE 7.1   CONTINUED

The tool wear experimenters have received a new shipment of cutting tools. They select one at random, and test it at a rotational velocity of 800 ft/min for 110 minutes. The resulting wear is 0.107, which they think excessive based on the previous experiment.

   To statistically evaluate the observed response, they compute a 95% prediction interval for the wear of a new tool at 110 minutes, using their original data. The point predictor is

$$\hat{y}_{new} = -0.0247 + 0.0102 \cdot 10.488 = 0.0823$$

The estimated standard error of prediction is

$$\hat{\sigma}(y_{new} - \hat{y}_{new}) = \sqrt{1.549 \times 10^{-5} \left[1 + \frac{1}{9} + \frac{(10.488 - 8.124)^2}{47.004}\right]} = 0.0044$$

Recall that $t_{7,0.975} = 2.365$, so the 95% prediction interval is

$$(0.0823 - [0.0044][2.365], 0.0823 + [0.0044][2.365]) = (0.072, 0.093)$$

The observed wear of 0.107 on the new tool is above the upper prediction limit of 0.093, which validates the experimenters' suspicion of excessive wear.   ◆

Figure 7.21 shows the tool wear data for VELOCITY $= 800$ and the least squares line (solid). The dashed lines are obtained by computing a level 0.95 confidence interval for the mean response at $X = x$, using Equation (7.28), for many values of x and connecting the upper limits to form the upper curve and the lower limits to form the lower curve. The result is called a **confidence band.** You can view the level 0.95 confidence interval for the mean response at $X = x$ by passing a vertical line at $X = x$ through the band. The endpoints of the interval are the intersections of the line with the confidence band. The confidence band represents the uncertainty in estimating the mean response from this data set.

The dotted lines are obtained by computing a level 0.95 prediction interval for a new observation at $X = x$ (using Equation (7.32)) for many values of x and connecting the upper limits to form the upper curve and the lower limits to form the lower curve. The result is called a **prediction band.** You can view the level 0.95 prediction interval for a new response at $X = x$ by passing a vertical line at $X = x$ through the band. The endpoints of the interval are the intersections of the line with the prediction band.

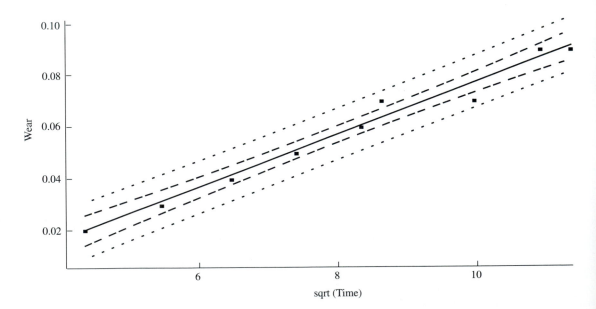

Figure 7.21   Regression of WEAR on $\sqrt{\text{TIME}}$ with the level 0.95 confidence band for the mean response (dashed) and the level 0.95 prediction band for new observation (dotted).

Notice how much wider the prediction band is than the confidence band. This additional width reflects the additional uncertainty inherent in obtaining a new response.

Note also that each band is narrowest when $x = \bar{X}$ and becomes wider the farther x goes from $\bar{X}$. A glance at Equations (7.27), (7.28), (7.31), and (7.32) will show why.

The Relation between the Pearson Correlation and Regression

We saw earlier that the coefficient of determination is the square of the Pearson correlation coefficient. There is an even more fundamental relation between the Pearson correlation and regression.

Suppose that instead of using the original data $\{(X_i, Y_i), i = 1, \ldots, n\}$, we standardize the data by subtracting from each variable its mean and then dividing by its standard deviation. Thus, if $\bar{Y}$ and S_Y are the mean and standard deviation of the responses in the data and if $\bar{X}$ and S_X are the same quantities for the regressors in the data, the standardized responses and regressors are

$$Y_i' = \frac{Y_i - \bar{Y}}{S_Y} \quad \text{and} \quad X_i' = \frac{X_i - \bar{X}}{S_X}$$

Then the regression equation fitted by least squares can be written as

$$\hat{Y}' = r \cdot X' \tag{7.33}$$

where X' is the standardized regressor, and $\hat{Y}' = (\hat{Y} - \bar{Y})/S_Y$.

This equation has an extremely simple interpretation. First, $\hat{Y}'$ is the number of Y standard deviations (S_Y) that $\hat{Y}$ is from $\bar{Y}$, and X' is the number of X standard deviations (S_X) that X is from $\bar{X}$. So Equation (7.33) says that the predictor of the response corresponding to an X value X' standard deviations (S_X) above its mean ($\bar{X}$) is $r \cdot X'$ standard deviations (S_Y) above its mean ($\bar{Y}$).

A couple of examples will illustrate.

EXAMPLE 7.8   CONTINUED

The correlation between VELOCITY and POWER is approximately 0.7087, the positive square root[18] of the coefficient of determination. The mean and standard deviation of VELOCITY are 5.1010 and 1.3566, and of POWER are 7.7633 and 1.0685. Now suppose you want to predict the VELOCITY for POWER $= 10$. Then POWER is approximately 2.09 standard deviations above the mean $[(10 - 7.7633)/1.0685 = 2.09]$. So the predicted standardized VELOCITY will be $(0.7087)(2.09) = 1.48$. That is, we predict the VELOCITY will be about 1.48 standard deviations above the mean VELOCITY, or

$$\widehat{\text{VELOCITY}} = 1.48 \cdot 1.3566 + 5.1010 = 7.11$$

So the predicted VELOCITY is 7.11. ✦

---

[18]Since the association is positive.

EXAMPLE 7.9   PREDICTING GPA FROM SAT SCORES

Suppose that the correlation between combined scores on the SAT and the cumulative GPA for graduating seniors is 0.4. Seamus's combined score is in the 75th percentile on the SAT. What will the SLR model predict the percentile of his GPA to be?

To solve this, we must assume a model for the combined SAT scores in order to obtain a value for the 75th percentile. We will also need to assume a model for the cumulative GPA. As is usually done, we will assume a normal distribution model for both. More specifically, we will assume that the standardized regressor and response both have an $N(0, 1)$ distribution. The 75th percentile of a standard normal distribution is 0.674. We will take this to equal X'. Then the predictor of Y' is $0.4 \times X' = 0.4 \times 0.674 = 0.2696$. Finally, we find that 0.2696 is the 60.6th percentile of the standard normal distribution, and this is the prediction of the percentile of Seamus's GPA.   ✦

Equation (7.33) also explains why the term "regression" is used to describe the least squares fit of a line. "Regression" is short for "regression toward the mean" (or as Galton, one of the originators of regression called it, "regression toward mediocrity"; see his quote at the beginning of this chapter). What is regression toward the mean? Once X and Y are standardized, their means are both 0. So for the standardized variables regression toward the mean is regression toward 0. But what is regression toward 0? It is simply that the predicted value in standard units is closer to 0 than is the regressor value. Furthermore, it is closer by a factor of r. Another name for this phenomenon is the **regression effect.**

In the bacteria trap example, we have seen that if the laser power is set at 2.09 standard units above 0, the predicted VELOCITY value is only 1.48 (0.7087 times 2.09) standard units above 0. The predicted value regresses toward the mean relative to the regressor: 1.48 versus 2.09 standard units. This concept is the same for the regression expressed in the original, unstandardized units; it's just easier to see in terms of standardized units.

Speaking of the relation between regression for standardized and unstandardized variables, we'll finish this section by finding a formula to relate the least squares estimator of slope to the correlation coefficient and the standard deviation of X and Y. From Equation (7.33), we can write

$$\frac{\hat{Y} - \bar{Y}}{S_Y} = r \cdot \frac{X - \bar{X}}{S_X}$$

Using some algebra, we get

$$\hat{Y} = \left(\bar{Y} - r \cdot \bar{X} \cdot \frac{S_Y}{S_X} \right) + \left(r \cdot \frac{S_Y}{S_X} \right) \cdot X$$

The first term in parentheses is the least squares estimator of the intercept, the second is the least squares estimator of the slope, so that

$$\hat{\beta}_1 = r \cdot \frac{S_Y}{S_X}$$

7.4

THE RELATIONSHIP BETWEEN TWO CATEGORICAL VARIABLES

In Chapter 2, you were introduced to categorical variables as variables that define categories. Analysis of categorical data is based on frequencies, proportions or percentages of data that fall into the various categories defined by the variables.

There are several ways of summarizing and displaying data from a single categorical variable. The bar chart, with which you are already familiar, is one type of display. A frequency table, which shows counts and/or percentages in each category, is another.

The Donner Party

The data we'll use to illustrate methods of categorical data analysis are taken from an article on a small but fascinating episode of American history ("Living Through the Donner Party," by Jared Diamond, *Discover* (March 1992): 100–107). The Donner party was a group of 87 settlers who set out in a wagon train from Fort Bridger, Wyoming, for California on July 31, 1846. The party, named after their captain, George Donner, left late in the season and suffered through many mishaps that further slowed their progress. By November 1, however, they reached Truckee Lake (now Donner Lake) at an elevation of 6000 feet on the eastern flank of the Sierra Nevada, just west of the present California–Nevada border. As they tried to cross the 7200-foot pass just west of the lake, the last major obstacle before the descent to California's central valley, they were defeated by a fierce snowstorm. As a result, the party was forced to spend a long winter at the lake with very little food. In the end, nearly half the party died and the remainder survived only by resorting to cannibalism.

The data set DONNER contains information on the members of the Donner party. The variables of interest to us (all categorical) are

- GENDER: M or F
- FATE: lived or died
- FAMILY: member of a family (y) or single individual (n)

Analyzing the Donner Data

The data distribution of a single categorical variable may be displayed using bar charts. For example, the bar chart of FATE in Figure 7.22 shows that 40 of the party died and 47 lived.

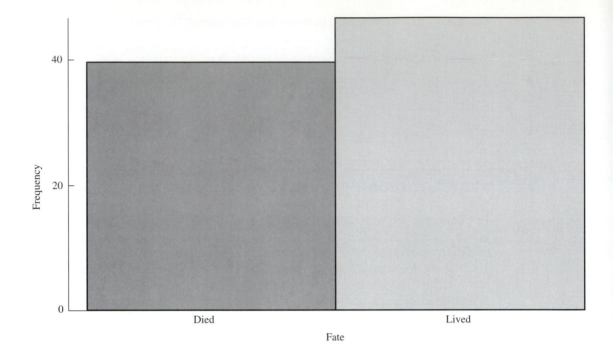

Figure 7.22   Bar chart of the fate of Donner party members.

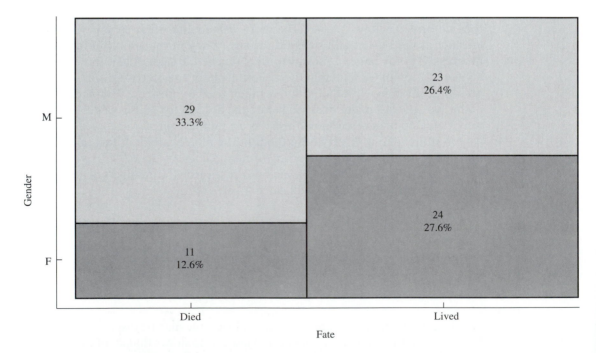

Figure 7.23   Mosaic plot of fates broken down by gender, Donner data.

You can obtain information on the relation between two categorical variables using **mosaic plots.** Figure 7.23 is an example of a mosaic plot comparing gender and fate for the Donner data. This plot shows that the majority of males died: 29 of 52, whereas a minority of females died: 11 of 35. So in this situation your chance of survival was better if you were female. In this mosaic plot, the areas of the individual boxes are proportional to the frequencies represented (for these data, the areas are in the proportions 33.3, 26.4, 12.6, and 27.6). In addition, the widths of the bars, here representing the categories "died" and "lived", are proportional to the proportions in those categories, here, 45.9 and 54.1. The heights of individual boxes in a given vertical bar are proportional to the frequencies within that bar. So, for example, the height of the box representing females who died is 11/40 the height of the entire bar representing those who died.

One-way frequency tables provide the same information as bar charts, and two-way frequency tables provide the same information as mosaic plots, but they do so in tabular form.

One-way tables look at each variable separately. They show totals and percentages for each category of the variable. Table 7.2 is a one-way table that contains the same information as the bar chart in Figure 7.22.

Two-way tables have rows corresponding to the categories of one variable and columns corresponding to the categories of another variable. An example of a two-way table is the GENDER by FATE table shown in Table 7.3.

Each rectangle in the table, which corresponds to one category of the row variable and one of the column variable, is called a **cell.** Table 7.3 has four cells. The numbers in the first cell show that 11 females died, that this represents 12.64% of the 87 settlers in the data set, 31.43% of the 35 females in the data set, and 27.50% of the 40 settlers who died. The percentages in the cells (here the numbers 12.64, 27.59, 33.33, and 26.44) constitute the **joint distribution** of the two variables GENDER and FATE. These percentages show how the two variables vary together.

The numbers on the lower and right margins of the table describe how each variable varies by itself in the data set. For example, in the lower margin, we learn that 40 settlers died and 47 lived, and that this translates into 45.98% dying and 54.02% living. These percentages constitute the **marginal distribution** of FATE. The marginal distribution of GENDER is found in the right margin of the table. Notice that the marginal distributions are computed by summing the cell percentages in the appropriate columns or rows. So the percentage of settlers who died, 45.98%, equals the percentage

TABLE 7.2   One-Way table of Fates of the Donner Party

	Fate		
	Died	Lived	Total
Frequency	40	47	87
Percent	45.98	54.02	100.00

TABLE 7.3   Table of Gender by Fate, Donner Data

Frequency Percent Row % Col %	Fate		
	Died	Lived	Total
M	29 33.33 55.77 72.50	23 26.44 44.23 48.94	52 59.77
F	11 12.64 31.43 27.50	24 27.59 68.57 51.06	35 40.23
Total	40 45.98	47 54.02	87 100.00

(Gender is the row variable label.)

who were women and died, 12.64%, plus the percentage who were men and died, 33.33%.[19]

Two further points about the marginal distributions:

- The marginal distributions and totals are equivalent to the one-way tables for each variable.
- The joint distribution of the two variables contains all the information that the marginal distributions do, and valuable information beyond what the marginal distributions contain. To see this, note that the marginal distributions can be computed from the joint distribution, but the joint distribution cannot be recovered from the marginal distributions (try doing it!).

Within each cell of Table 7.3, the third number down is the row percentage. If we look only at a single row of the table, these percentages constitute the **conditional distribution** of the column variable given the value of the row variable corresponding to the row we're looking at. For example, given that a settler was female, her chance of dying was 31.43% (11/35). Compare that with a 55.77% chance of a settler dying given that he was male. From this, it seems clear that male settlers died at a greater rate than female settlers. This is an indication that there is a relationship between GENDER and FATE among the settlers. Note that if there were no relation, the percentage of males who died would closely match the percentage of females who died.

---

[19] Here (12.64% + 33.33% = 45.97%, not 45.98%), and elsewhere in the discussion, certain sums may not add correctly because of rounding.

Inference for Categorical Data with Two Categories

Inference in a One-Way Table

If the data summarized in a one-way table with two categories consist of a random sample from a population, the inference methods for proportions introduced in Chapters 5 and 6 may be used, as the following example illustrates.

EXAMPLE 7.10   ESTIMATION FOR CATEGORICAL DATA WITH TWO CATEGORIES

In order to assess the quality of a certain make of automobile, the manufacturer surveys a random sample of 200 owners of a model with manual transmission. Among the questions asked is, "Have you had to have the clutch replaced?" Of the 200 responses, 36 answered "yes."

The point estimate of the population proportion p, of all such owners who have had to have the clutch replaced is $\hat{p} = 36/200 = 0.18$. Since both the number who answered "yes" and the number who answered "no" exceed 10, we may obtain a large-sample approximate 95% confidence interval for p as

$$\left(\hat{p} - z_{0.975} \sqrt{\frac{\hat{p}(1-\hat{p})}{200}}, \hat{p} + z_{0.975} \sqrt{\frac{\hat{p}(1-\hat{p})}{200}} \right) = (0.127, 0.233) \quad \blacklozenge$$

Inference in a Two-Way Table

A two-way table with two rows and two columns is called a **two-by-two table.** The inference methods for comparing two proportions, introduced in Chapters 5 and 6, are appropriate when analyzing two-by-two tables whose rows (or columns) consist of random samples from two independent populations. To see how, let's return to Example 7.10:

EXAMPLE 7.10   CONTINUED

The random sample of 200 car owners consisted of 52 who were 25 years old or younger. Of these 52, 17 had had to replace the clutch on their cars. We will estimate the difference in the proportions of younger (i.e., 25 years and under) and older drivers in the population who have had to replace the clutch.

Table 7.4 summarizes the data broken down by age group. Since the data were a random sample from the entire population, we may consider the sample of 52 younger drivers a random sample from those 25 and under and the sample of 148 older drivers a random sample from those over 25. If we let p_{young} denote the proportion of drivers 25 and under in the population who have had the clutch replaced and let p_{old} denote the corresponding population proportion of drivers over 25, then a point estimate for the difference $p_{\text{young}} - p_{\text{old}}$ is $\hat{p}_{\text{young}} - \hat{p}_{\text{old}} = 0.3269 - 0.1284 = 0.1985$. The approximate standard error of the point estimator

TABLE 7.4   Table of Age by Whether the Clutch Was Replaced

		Clutch replaced?		
	Frequency Percent Row % Col %	No	Yes	Total
Age	25 and Under	35 17.50 67.31 21.34	17 8.50 32.69 47.22	52 26.00
	Over 25	129 64.50 87.16 78.66	19 9.50 12.84 52.78	148 74.00
	Total	164 82.00	36 8.00	200 100.00

is

$$\sqrt{\frac{0.1284(1 - 0.1284)}{52} + \frac{0.3269(1 - 0.3269)}{148}} = 0.0706$$

Since the number of owners who have and who have not had the clutch replaced exceeds 10 in both age groups, we may compute a large sample approximate confidence interval for $p_{\text{young}} - p_{\text{old}}$ as

$$(0.1985 - z_{0.975}(0.0706), 0.1985 + z_{0.975}(0.0706)) = (0.0601, 0.3370)$$

It seems that younger drivers are harder on their clutches than older drivers.   ◆

The χ^2 Distribution Model

In order to extend our ability to perform inference on categorical data, we need to learn another distribution model. The χ^2 distribution model[20] is used extensively in the analysis of categorical data. The χ^2 distribution model is the distribution of the sum of squares of n independent values from a standard normal distribution model. Specifically, if $Z_1, Z_2, \ldots, Z_n$ are n independent values from an $N(0, 1)$ distribution model, then $Y = \sum_{i=1}^{n} Z_i^2$ follows a χ^2 distribution with n degrees of freedom, written

$$Y \sim \chi_n^2$$

---

[20] χ^2 is pronounced "ki-square," with a long i sound. It is written in English "chi-square," as chi is the English spelling of the Greek letter χ.

Observe that Y is nonnegative, and that the χ^2 distribution has only one parameter, the degrees of freedom n. The mean of the χ_n^2 distribution model is n, the degrees of freedom, and the variance is $2n$.

Like the normal distribution model, the χ^2 is an example of a continuous distribution model. The height of the density curve of the χ_n^2 distribution model at y is given by $p_Y(y)$, where

$$p_Y(y) = \frac{y^{n/2-1}e^{-y/2}}{2^{n/2}\Gamma(n/2)}, \quad 0 < y < \infty$$

$$= 0, \qquad\qquad \text{otherwise}$$

and $\Gamma(\cdot)$ is the **gamma function,** defined by

$$\Gamma(n/2) = \int_0^\infty t^{n/2-1}e^{-t}\,dt$$

Figure 7.24 shows that the shape of the χ^2 distribution is governed by its degrees of freedom, n. The χ^2 distribution is skewed for all values of n, but as n becomes larger, the distribution becomes more symmetric. In fact, as n becomes larger, the χ^2 distribution can be closely approximated by a normal distribution.

Inference for Categorical Data with More Than Two Categories

The inference procedures introduced for categorical data with two categories will not work if there are more than two categories. In what follows, we introduce inference methods that can be used when categorical data have more than two categories.

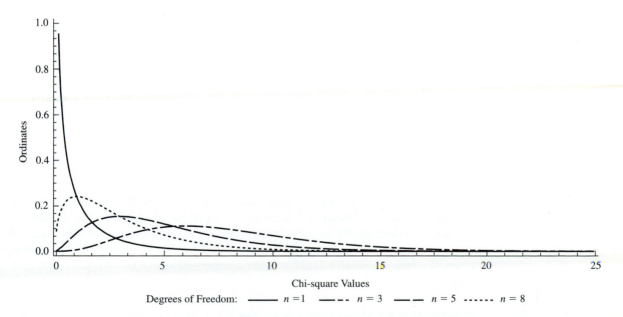

Figure 7.24 Plots of some χ^2 density functions.

Inference in a One-Way Table

Suppose a categorical variable has more than two categories. Suppose also that we have data on this variable that we may summarize in a one-way table. Finally, suppose that we want to use these data to conduct inference on the population proportions in the categories.

As an example, suppose we want to test whether a six-sided die is fair. That is, we test that $p_i = 1/6$, $i = 1, 2, \ldots, 6$, where p_i is the probability the die lands with i spots up. To perform such a test, we would roll the die a number of times and obtain as data the frequencies with which $1, 2, \ldots, 6$ spots occurred.

To construct such a test, suppose the categorical variable has c categories and that the population proportion in category i is p_i. Suppose we want to test the null hypothesis H_0 versus H_a given by

$$H_0: \quad p_i = p_i^{(0)}, \qquad i = 1, 2, \ldots, c$$
$$H_a: \quad p_i \neq p_i^{(0)} \qquad \text{for at least one } i, \ i = 1, 2, \ldots, c$$

for prespecified values $p_i^{(0)}, i = 1, 2, \ldots, c$. For example, the hypotheses for deciding if a die is fair are

$$H_0: \quad p_i = 1/6, \qquad i = 1, 2, \ldots, 6$$
$$H_a: \quad p_i \neq 1/6 \qquad \text{for at least one } i, \ i = 1, 2, \ldots, 6$$

Suppose that the data consist of n observations, of which $Y_1, Y_2, \ldots, Y_c$ are in category $1, 2, \ldots, c$, respectively. If H_0 is true, then of the n observations, we expect to see np_i^0 in category i.[21]

It is sensible to consider a test statistic based on the deviations of the observed category frequencies $Y_1, Y_2, \ldots, Y_c$ from the expected category frequencies under H_0: $np_1^{(0)}, np_2^{(0)}, \ldots, np_c^{(0)}$. Large deviations between the observed and expected category frequencies provide evidence to indicate that the hypothesized population proportions, $p_1^{(0)}, p_2^{(0)}, \ldots, p_c^{(0)}$, are incorrect. The statistic used to test H_0 versus H_a is

$$X^2 = \sum_{i=1}^{c} \frac{(Y_i - np_i^{(0)})^2}{np_i^{(0)}}$$

In short, for each category, we compute **(observed − expected)²/expected** and sum over all categories. The statistic X^2 is called the **Pearson χ^2 statistic.** The division of the squared deviations by the expected values has the effect of expressing the squared deviations as proportions of what was expected and helps us to see which deviations are large and which are small relative to what is expected under H_0. We will expand on this notion shortly.

---

[21] An equivalent way to think of this is to note that Y_i is a random variable with expected value np_i^0, when H_0 is true.

To find the p-value of the test, we use the facts that:

- Under H_0, X^2 has a χ^2_{c-1} distribution provided the number of trials n is large enough: A rule of thumb is that $np_i^{(0)} \geq 5$, for $i = 1, 2, \ldots, c$. The degrees of freedom, $c - 1$, counts the minimum number of the quantities $Y_i - np_i^{(0)}$ that are needed to compute X^2.
- Large values of X^2 indicate a large difference between the expected and observed number in at least one category, and so provide evidence against H_0 and in favor of H_a.

Therefore, if x^{2*} denotes the observed value of the test statistic, the p-value is $P(Y \geq x^{2*})$, where $Y \sim \chi^2_{c-1}$.

**PEARSON'S χ^2 TEST
FOR PROPORTIONS IN A ONE-WAY TABLE**

- **The Statistical Model.** The population is divided into c categories with proportion p_i in category i,
- **The Statistical Hypothesis**

$$H_0: \quad p_i = p_i^{(0)}, \qquad i = 1, 2, \ldots, c$$

$$H_a: \quad p_i \neq p_i^{(0)} \qquad \text{for at least one } i, \ i = 1, 2, \ldots, c$$

for prespecified values $p_i^{(0)}, i = 1, 2, \ldots, c$.

- **The Test Statistic**

$$X^2 = \sum_{i=1}^{c} \frac{(Y_i - np_i^{(0)})^2}{np_i^{(0)}}$$

- **The p-Value.** $P(Y \geq x^{2*})$, where $Y \sim \chi^2_{c-1}$ and x^{2*} is the observed value of the test statistic.

EXAMPLE 7.11   THE χ^2 TEST FOR PROPORTIONS IN A ONE-WAY TABLE

The quality unit of a personal computer manufacturer keeps track of the reasons for rejecting the finished product. They classify these reasons into five categories:

A Mechanical: fans, motors, switches, etc.
B Electrical: power supply, wiring, etc.
C Cosmetic
D Monitor
E Electronic: chips, circuit boards, etc.

TABLE 7.5 Classification of 103 Defective Personal Computers According to Defect Category

Defect category	A	B	C	D	E
Defectives	15	27	31	19	11

A quality engineer would like to test for differences in the proportions of rejections in the five categories. To do so, he takes a random sample of 103 recently rejected computers. Table 7.5 summarizes the distribution of reasons for rejection.

The null hypothesis is that the proportions of all defective computers attributable to the five rejection categories are equal, so that here $c = 5$ and $p_i^{(0)} = 0.2$, $i = 1, 2, \ldots, 5$. The hypotheses are

$$H_0: \quad p_i = 0.2, \quad i = 1, 2, \ldots, 5,$$
$$H_a: \quad p_i \neq 0.2 \quad \text{for at least one } i, \ i = 1, 2, \ldots, 5$$

Under H_0, each cell frequency is expected to be $103 \times 0.2 = 20.6 > 5$, so the χ^2 approximation is valid. We have

$$x^{2*} = \frac{(15 - 20.6)^2}{20.6} + \frac{(27 - 20.6)^2}{20.6} + \frac{(31 - 20.6)^2}{20.6}$$

$$+ \frac{(19 - 20.6)^2}{20.6} + \frac{(11 - 20.6)^2}{20.6} = 13.36$$

Since large values of X^2 provide evidence against H_0 and in favor of H_a, the p-value of the test is approximated by the proportion of a χ_4^2 population that exceeds 13.36. This value is 0.0096. Thus, the data provide convincing evidence that the proportions of all computer rejections attributable to the five categories are not equal. As a follow-up, the engineer wants to know which are the most prevalent and which the least prevalent reasons for rejection.

To answer this question, he considers the contribution of each cell to x^{2*}. Or, more specifically, he considers the residual between what the expected frequency under H_0 and the observed frequency in each cell. There are many versions of residuals, but we use the most common, the **Pearson residual.** Under H_0, the expected frequency in the ith cell of the table is $np_i^{(0)}, i = 1, \ldots, c$. The Pearson residual for cell i, denoted by d_i, is

$$d_i = \frac{Y_i - np_i^{(0)}}{\sqrt{np_i^{(0)}}}$$

which is the difference between the observed and expected (under H_0) frequency in cell i divided by the square root of the expected frequency. It is also the signed square root of the corresponding term in the Pearson χ^2 statistic. In our example, the residuals for cells A, B, C, D, and E are $-1.23, +1.41, +2.29, -0.35,$ and -2.11.

TABLE 7.6   Population Proportions for the General $r \times c$ Table

	Column				
Row	1	2	...	c	Marginals
1	p_{11}	p_{12}	...	p_{1c}	$p_{1\cdot}$
2	p_{21}	p_{22}	...	p_{2c}	$p_{2\cdot}$
.	.	.		.	.
.	.	.		.	.
.	.	.		.	.
r	p_{r1}	p_{r2}	...	p_{rc}	$p_{r\cdot}$
Marginals	$p_{\cdot1}$	$p_{\cdot2}$	...	$p_{\cdot c}$	1

Thus, it appears that cosmetic defects are responsible for a higher proportion of defective computers and electronic defects are responsible for a lower proportion of defective computers than the other kinds of defects.   ✦

Inference for a Two-Way Table

Testing for Independence in a Two-Way Table.   Suppose a population can be classified according to two categorical variables with $r \geq 2$ categories for the first variable and $c \geq 2$ categories for the second variable. Let p_{ij} denote the population proportion in category i of the first variable and category j of the second variable. Table 7.6 summarizes the population proportions. Included in the table are the marginal proportions

$$p_{i\cdot} = \sum_{j=1}^{c} p_{ij} \quad \text{and} \quad p_{\cdot j} = \sum_{i=1}^{r} p_{ij}$$

where $p_{i\cdot}$ is the proportion of the population in category i of the row variable and $p_{\cdot j}$ is the proportion of the population in category j of the column variable.

Recall from Chapter 4 that two events are independent if the probability of their intersection is the product of their individual probabilities. In a similar way, the two categorical variables represented by Table 7.6 are **independent** if

$$p_{ij} = p_{i\cdot} p_{\cdot j}, \quad i = 1, \ldots, r, \, j = 1, \ldots, c$$

If the two variables are independent, then if we select an element at random from category i of the row variable, the probability the element is in category j of the column variable is

$$p_{ij}/p_{i\cdot} = p_{i\cdot} p_{\cdot j}/p_{i\cdot} = p_{\cdot j}$$

This probability is the same regardless of the value of i. Hence, knowing which row the element is from tells us nothing about which column it is from. We can also show that knowing which column the element is from tells us nothing about which row it is from.

In order to determine if the two categorical variables are independent, we select a random sample of size n from a population. The following example will illustrate.

TABLE 7.7   **3 × 4 Table for 1000 Automobiles by Size and Manufacturer**

	Manufacturer				
Size	A	B	C	D	Totals
Small	157	65	181	10	413
Medium	126	82	142	46	396
Large	58	45	60	28	191
Totals	341	45	383	84	1000

EXAMPLE 7.12   ANALYSIS OF A TWO-WAY TABLE

Past energy shortages have made many consumers more aware of the size of the automobiles they purchase. Recently, an automobile manufacturer was interested in determining if there is a relationship between the size and manufacturer of newly purchased automobiles. The manufacturer randomly sampled 1000 recent buyers of American-made cars, and each purchase was classified with respect to the size and the manufacturer of the purchased automobile.

The data are shown in Table 7.7. The question of interest to the manufacturer is, "Are size and manufacturer independent?" This is of interest because if manufacturer D sells a relatively small number of small cars, then perhaps it should have fewer of these cars in its inventory. If the proportions of small cars sold by manufacturers A, B, C, and D are the same for medium and large cars, then this will suggest that the size of cars is irrelevant in manufacturing: that is, the size of the car is independent of the manufacturer.   ◆

In general, if Y_{ij} is the number in the sample falling in the ith category of the first variable and jth category of the second variable, $i = 1, 2, \ldots, r$ and $j = 1, 2, \ldots, c$, then the data may be displayed in an $r \times c$ table, as illustrated by Table 7.8. Included in the table are the marginal totals

$$Y_{i.} = \sum_{j=1}^{c} Y_{ij} \qquad \text{and} \qquad Y_{.j} = \sum_{i=1}^{r} Y_{ij}$$

EXAMPLE 7.12   CONTINUED

In the car data shown in Table 7.7, $r = 3$, $c = 4$, and $n = 1000$. The observed cell frequencies, which we denote with lowercase letters, are $y_{11} = 157$, $y_{12} = 65$, $y_{21} = 126$, and so on. The row (marginal) totals are $y_{1.} = 413$, $y_{2.} = 396$, and $y_{3.} = 191$. The column (marginal) totals are $y_{.1} = 341$, $y_{.2} = 45$, $y_{.3} = 383$, and $y_{.4} = 84$.   ◆

The hypotheses we wish to test are

H_0:   row and column variables are independent
H_a: row and column variables are not independent

TABLE 7.8   The General $r \times c$ Table for a Random Sample of Size n

Row	Column 1	2	...	c	Totals
1	Y_{11}	Y_{12}	...	Y_{1c}	$Y_{1.}$
2	Y_{21}	Y_{22}	...	Y_{2c}	$Y_{2.}$
.	.	.		.	.
.	.	.		.	.
.	.	.		.	.
r	Y_{r1}	Y_{r2}	...	Y_{rc}	$Y_{r.}$
Totals	$Y_{.1}$	$Y_{.2}$	...	$Y_{.c}$	n

Recall that the row and column variables are independent if and only if

$$p_{ij} = p_{i.}p_{.j}, \qquad i = 1, 2, \ldots, r, \quad j = 1, 2, \ldots, c$$

Therefore, when H_0 is true, the expected frequency in cell ij is $np_{ij} = np_{i.}p_{.j}$.

The standard estimators of $p_{i.}$ and $p_{.j}$ are

$$\hat{p}_{i.} = \frac{Y_{i.}}{n} \quad \text{and} \quad \hat{p}_{.j} = \frac{Y_{.j}}{n} \tag{7.34}$$

That is, we simply estimate the population proportion in category i of the row variable by the sample proportion in category i of the row variable. Similarly, we estimate the population proportion in category j of the column variable by the sample proportion in category j of the column variable. Therefore, the expected number in cell ij can be estimated by

$$n\hat{p}_{i.}\hat{p}_{.j} = \frac{Y_{i.}Y_{.j}}{n}, \qquad i = 1, 2, \ldots, r, \quad j = 1, 2, \ldots, c \tag{7.35}$$

In words, under H_0, the expected cell frequencies are given by

$$\text{Expected value} = \frac{\text{row total} \times \text{column total}}{\text{sample size}}$$

To measure the deviations of the observed frequencies from the expected frequencies under the assumption of independence, we construct the Pearson χ^2 statistic

$$X^2 = \sum_{i=1}^{r} \sum_{j=1}^{c} \frac{(Y_{ij} - n\hat{p}_{i.}\hat{p}_{.j})^2}{n\hat{p}_{i.}\hat{p}_{.j}} \tag{7.36}$$

Note that as with the Pearson χ^2 statistic for the one-way table, the individual terms are computed as (observed − expected)^2/expected, for each cell.

Provided that $n\hat{p}_{i.}\hat{p}_{.j} \geq 5$, for all i and j, X^2 has approximately a χ^2 distribution with $(r-1)(c-1)$ degrees of freedom if H_0 is true. The degrees of freedom measures the minimum number of cell frequencies Y_{ij} that must be specified to uniquely determine the $r \times c$ table, Table 7.8, when we know n and the marginal totals $Y_{i.}$ and $Y_{.j}$.

TABLE 7.9   Observed, Estimated Expected Cell Frequencies (First Parentheses), and the Pearson Residuals (Second Parentheses), Automobile Data

Size	Manufacturer			
	A	B	C	D
Small	157	65	181	10
	(140.8)	(79.3)	(158.2)	(34.7)
	(+1.37)	(−1.61)	(+1.81)	(−4.19)
Medium	126	82	142	46
	(135.0)	(76.0)	(151.7)	(33.3)
	(−0.77)	(+0.69)	(−0.79)	(+2.20)
Large	58	45	60	28
	(65.1)	(36.7)	(73.2)	(16.0)
	(−0.88)	(+1.37)	(−1.54)	(+3.00)

To assess the relative contribution of each cell to X^2, we use the Pearson residuals as we did for a single categorical variable. In particular, the Pearson residuals are

$$d_{ij} = \frac{Y_{ij} - n\hat{p}_{i\cdot}\hat{p}_{\cdot j}}{\sqrt{n\hat{p}_{i\cdot}\hat{p}_{\cdot j}}}$$

EXAMPLE 7.12   CONTINUED

Table 7.9 shows the observed and expected (under H_0) cell frequencies and the Pearson residuals for the automobile data.

The observed value of X^2 computed from the data in Table 7.9 is

$$x^{2*} = \frac{(157 - 140.8)^2}{140.8} + \frac{(65 - 79.3)^2}{79.3} + \cdots + \frac{(28 - 16.0)^2}{16.0} = 45.8$$

The p-value of the test is the proportion of the $\chi^2_{(3-1)(4-1)} = \chi^2_6$ population exceeding the observed value $x^{2*} = 45.8$. The p-value ≈ 0. Thus, the data provide strong evidence to suggest that the size of auto sold depends on the manufacturer who sells it.

Large residuals occur for manufacturer D. The number of small cars sold by D is far below what would be expected if size were independent of manufacturer, and the numbers of medium and large cars sold by D are far above expectation. ◆

Testing the Equality of Proportions in Independent Populations. Suppose there are $r \geq 2$ independent populations,[22] each of which can be divided into the same c categories.

---

[22]One way of defining the independence of populations is to let W_i denote a random variable that takes on value j if a randomly selected element from population i falls into category j. If the random variables W_i, $i = 1, \ldots, r$, are independent, the populations are independent.

TABLE 7.10   Population Proportions for an $r \times c$ Table in which the Rows Represent r Independent Populations

	Column				
Row	1	2	...	c	Marginals
1	p_{11}	p_{12}	...	p_{1c}	1
2	p_{21}	p_{22}	...	p_{2c}	1
.	.	.		.	.
.	.	.		.	.
.	.	.		.	.
r	p_{r1}	p_{r2}	...	p_{rc}	1
Marginals	$p_{.1}$	$p_{.2}$	...	$p_{.c}$	

Let $p_{i1}, \ldots, p_{ic}$ denote the proportions of population i that fall into categories $1, \ldots, c$. Then, since all proportions sum to 1, we have $\sum_{j=1}^{c} p_{ij} = 1$. We represent the population proportions in Table 7.10, where row i represents the proportions of population i falling into the c categories. Notice that Table 7.10 differs from Table 7.6 in that the row marginals, $p_{1.}, \ldots, p_{r.}$, all equal 1.

We are interested in testing whether these population proportions falling into the c categories are the same for all populations. That is, we want to test

$$H_0: \quad p_{1j} = p_{2j} = \cdots = p_{rj}, \text{ for each } j = 1, \ldots, c$$
$$H_a: \quad H_0 \text{ is not true}$$

To perform the test, we take a random sample of size $Y_{i.}$ from population i. The data can then be represented in a two-way table just like Table 7.8. It turns out that the same Pearson χ^2 test used for testing for independence in two-way tables will test H_0 versus H_a in this new setting. Example 7.13 illustrates the test for proportions in independent populations.

EXAMPLE 7.13   THE χ^2 TEST FOR PROPORTIONS IN INDEPENDENT POPULATIONS

Researchers are interested in the opinions of students at one local college regarding the problem of sexual harassment, and, in particular, if the student perceptions are related to gender. In order to answer their questions, they take a simple random sample of 50 male students and a separate simple random sample of 50 female students at the college. Each student is asked the question, "How serious a problem do you think sexual harassment is at this college: not serious, moderately serious, or very serious?" The numbers of each gender who gave each response are shown as the top number in each cell in Table 7.11.

The first question the investigators want to consider is whether male and female students have the same opinions about the seriousness of sexual harassment on their campus. This question can be couched in statistical terms as follows.

TABLE 7.11   Contingency Table for the sexual harassment Example

| | Seriousness of Sexual Harassment | | | |
Gender	Not serious	Moderately serious	Very serious	Totals
Male	25	21	4	50
	(14.5)	(23.5)	(12)	
	(+2.76)	(−0.52)	(−2.31)	
Female	4	26	20	50
	(14.5)	(23.5)	(12)	
	(−2.76)	(+0.52)	(+2.31)	
Totals	29	47	24	100

Let p_{1j}, $j = 1, 2, 3$, denote the proportions of male students at the college who think sexual harassment is not serious, moderately serious, and a very serious problem, respectively, and p_{2j}, $j = 1, 2, 3$, be the corresponding proportions of female students. The investigators want to test

$$H_0: \quad p_{11} = p_{21}, \; p_{12} = p_{22}, \; p_{13} = p_{23}$$
$$H_a: \quad \text{At least one of the following holds:}$$
$$p_{11} \neq p_{21}, \; p_{12} \neq p_{22}, \; p_{13} \neq p_{23}$$

H_0 says that for each of the three responses, the proportion of male students who agree is the same as the proportion of female students who agree. How can we test H_0 versus H_a? It turns out that the theory we have just encountered for testing independence in $r \times c$ tables applies. There are two reasons for this:

1. H_0 is just another way of saying that gender and opinion are independent. If H_0 is true, then the proportions of males who would answer "not serious," "moderately serious," or "very serious" are exactly the same as the proportions of females who would answer the same way. Therefore, knowing the gender of an individual is irrelevant to how likely that person is to answer "not serious," "moderately serious," or "very serious." Or, equivalently, knowing which answer a person gave is irrelevant to how likely it is that the person is male or female.

2. When we use the Pearson χ^2 test, we assume that **the totals in the margins are fixed,** so it doesn't matter if we take one simple random sample of students or two independent random samples (one of males and the other of females).

Thus, we can perform the Pearson χ^2 test in exactly the same way it was applied using Equations (7.34) to (7.36). The middle number in each cell in Table 7.11 is the expected frequency in that cell if H_0 is true. The value of the χ^2 statistic is $x^{2*} = 26.41$. Under H_0, this value may be considered to arise from a χ^2 distribution with $(2 − 1)(3 − 1) = 2$ degrees of freedom. The resulting p-value is 1.8×10^{-6}, which suggests there are significant differences in the opinions of male and female students on this subject. The bottom number in each cell is the Pearson residual. From it, we can see that the proportion of females who regard sexual harassment as very serious is a great deal larger than is the proportion of males who regard it as very serious, and that the proportion of females who regard sexual harassment as not serious is a great deal smaller than is the proportion of males who regard sexual harassment as not serious.   ✦

7.5

CAUSE AND EFFECT

In Chapter 3, we discussed the issue of establishing cause and effect in controlled experiments and observational studies. The basic message given there was that a properly designed and conducted controlled experiment could establish a cause-and-effect relationship, whereas at best an observational study could only establish association.

The question of cause and effect is particularly prominent in correlation and regression. There is one very big caution that you must be aware of in interpreting correlation or regression or the association between categorical variables, and it is this:

ASSOCIATION DOES NOT IMPLY CAUSE AND EFFECT

That is, just because there is an association between X and Y, you cannot conclude that changes in X cause changes in Y.

Let's consider what could be occurring between X and Y when there is an association.

1. X could cause Y. Think of the tool wear data for VELOCITY $= 800$ with TIME as the X variable and WEAR as Y. Then it's pretty clear that running tools longer means that the **average WEAR** will increase. Notice this doesn't say that it will necessarily increase by the same amount for the each individual tool. We're talking about the overall trend.

2. Y could cause X. For example, in inner-city schools, where there is a good deal of violent crime, many students come to class carrying weapons. In rural or suburban schools the incidence of both is lower. So we might conclude that the large number of weapons causes higher rates of violent crime. But might not the high rate of violent crime cause students to carry weapons to protect themselves?

3. X and Y could cause each other. As argued before, weapons and violent crime rates might cause each other.

4. X and Y could be caused by a third (lurking) variable Z. Yearly world sales of Bibles and consumption of whiskey plotted over the past 50 years might show a positive relationship. Is religion driving people to drink, or vice versa? Neither explanation is necessarily true. Perhaps both are driven by population increases.

5. X and Y could be related by chance. Check out the U.S. Statistical Abstract (found in any library). There are thousands of tables of data. Lay in some food and drink, camp out in front of a computer, and fire up your favorite statistics computer package. Now plot all possible pairs of variables against each other. We guarantee that you'll find a strong association between two variables that cannot possibly have anything to do with each other. It's an example of the "If you put enough monkeys in front of enough typewriters for long enough, eventually one will produce *Hamlet*" syndrome.

6. Bad (or good) luck. The sample of data you look at could be unrepresentative of the population quantities, so the sample data could show association when in reality there is none.

So, you might ask, can cause and effect ever be established? The answer is yes. The best (and some would contend, the only) way is by careful, controlled, scientific experimentation. In the tool wear experiment, it is clear that running a tool for a longer period of time will increase the wear. In the absence of such experimentation, a good case can be made for cause and effect if

1. the association is found in many valid studies under a variety of conditions among different populations.
2. the association persists when possible lurking variables are accounted for.
3. there is a plausible explanation for cause and effect.

The classic example of a case for cause and effect is the claim that cigarette smoking causes lung cancer. Items 1 and 2 have been repeatedly demonstrated in numerous studies over a period of more than 30 years. Particularly telling are comparisons of nonsmokers who live in a smoking environment with those who live in a nonsmoking environment. Animal experiments and experiments in molecular biology have provided the plausible causal link needed for item 3.

7.6

THE ISSUE OF STATIONARITY

The notion of stationarity of a process was introduced in Chapter 1:

> **DEFINITION**
>
> A **stationary process** is a data-generating mechanism for which the distribution of the resulting data does not change appreciably as more data are generated.

In Chapter 1, appropriate graphical methods for assessing process stationarity were discussed, and in Chapters 5 and 6, the necessity of process stationarity for valid inference about the binomial and C+E models was explained.

The preceding definition of stationarity also holds for bivariate data, but the more sophisticated regression models considered in this chapter require a more sophisticated understanding of process stationarity. For example, when we say the pattern of variation of the measurements does not change, we mean not only the individual patterns of each variable separately, but also the pattern of joint variation of the two variables. Thus, to graphically assess stationarity for bivariate data, it is not enough to plot the values of each variable separately versus time or order. We must also plot the joint relation, as represented, for example, by a scatterplot, versus time or order.

EXAMPLE 7.14   BIVARIATE STATIONARITY

A furniture manufacturer has received a number of customer complaints that corner joints on one of their cabinet models have been coming unglued. In order to find out what is causing the problem, an experiment is done on the part of the process that glues the joints. Engineers suspect the flow rate on the adhesive applicator is the culprit. A single machine operator is selected and a controlled experiment conducted in which flow rate is varied at eight different settings (g/sec). Five replications are done at each flow rate before the flow rate is changed. All other conditions are held constant. Response is the pull-apart force (in.-lb) needed to break the bond after curing.

Engineers first made a plot of pull-apart force versus flow rate, as shown in Figure 7.25. From this plot, we see that variation in the force measurements decreases with increasing flow rate, but that there is little other trend to remark on. Because of this, the engineers' initial thinking was to increase flow rate so as to produce a more consistent product.

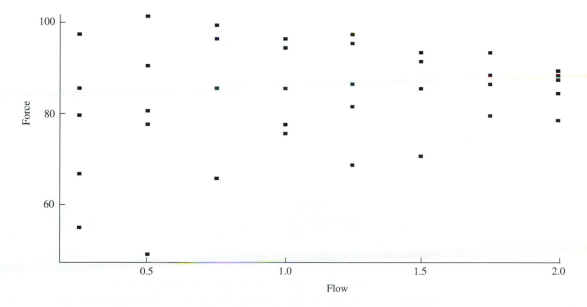

Figure 7.25   Scatterplot of pull-apart force versus adhesive flow rate, Example 7.14.

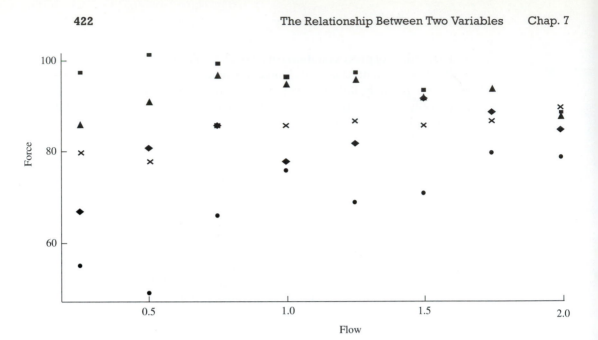

Figure 7.26   Scatterplot of pull-apart force versus adhesive flow rate, Example 7.14. Circles denote replication 1, diamonds replication 2, crosses replication 3, triangles replication 4, and squares replication 5.

However, one engineer suggested that they look at the order in which the replications were run. Figure 7.26 reproduces the scatterplot of Figure 7.25, but uses a different plotting symbol for each replicate. Figure 7.27 shows five scatterplots, one for each replicate. These plots give us valuable information about the process. First, in terms of replication order, the process is not stationary. Variation among pull-apart force values decreases as more replications are done. Also, the pull-apart force values tend to be higher, on average, for the later replications. Finally, the pattern of the relationship between pull-apart force and adhesive flow changes with more replication. For replications 1, 2, and 3, there is a roughly linear positive relationship, so that the strongest bonds result from the highest flow rates. For replication 4, the relationship is nonlinear, with the strongest bonds resulting from intermediate flow rates. For replication 5, the relationship is roughly linear and negative and the strongest bonds result from the lowest flow rates.

Clearly, the process is nonstationary with respect to replication. Is the nonstationarity the result of learning on the part of the operator, or of insufficient warmup of the machine, or perhaps something else altogether? Whatever its cause, the engineers know that in order to understand the process, they needed to understand the sources of nonstationarity.

For data such as these, a rotating three-dimensional plot with X and Y axes to represent the values of the variables and the Z axis to represent time or order can reveal nonstationarity. Figure 7.28 shows such a plot for these data. Unfortunately,

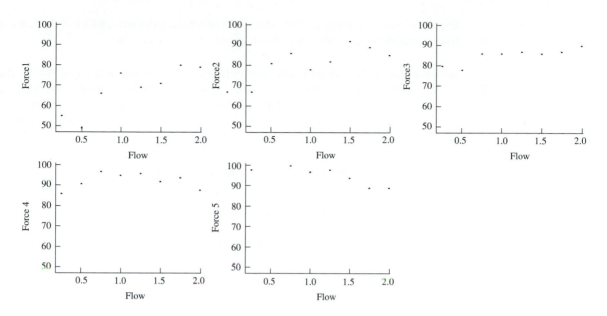

Figure 7.27 Scatterplot of pull-apart force versus adhesive flow rate, broken out by replicate, Example 7.14. Force1 versus flow shows the results for the first replicate, force2 versus flow shows the results for the second replicate, and so on.

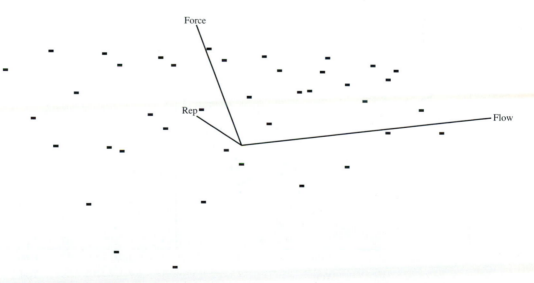

Figure 7.28 Rotating three-dimensional plot of pull-apart force, adhesive flow rate, and replicate, Example 7.14.

this static picture cannot capture the effect of rotating the axes, which is the feature that provides insight into the pattern of nonstationarity. ✦

A somewhat different situation presents itself for bivariate data in which the X variable is time or order. In this case, the response variable viewed alone may be nonstationary over time, but the relation between it and the time variable may be stationary. The latter occurs if, as more data are obtained, the pattern of association between the response and time or order remains the same.

EXAMPLE 7.15   MORE ON BIVARIATE STATIONARITY

Figure 7.29 shows output for the regression of Kentucky Derby winning times on year, for the years 1930 to 1980. Clearly, there is a decreasing trend in the winning times, so the winning times considered by themselves do not constitute a stationary process. However, we observe that the simple linear regression model fits these data well. Because there is no pattern evident in the plot of residuals versus year, we may conclude that **relative to the model,** the winning times are stationary. That is, the times are decreasing on average each year, but the pattern

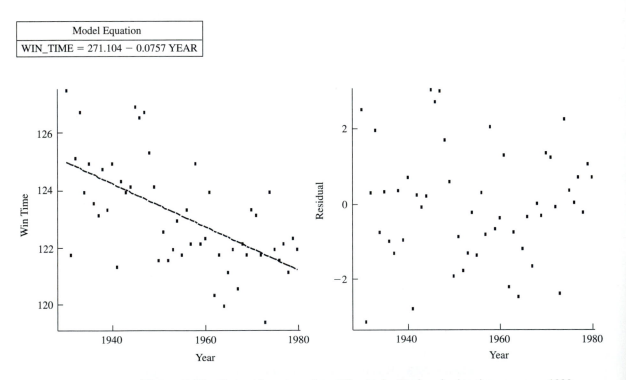

Figure 7.29   Output for regression of Kentucky Derby winning times on year, 1930 to 1980.

of decrease follows the model as more data are taken. Stationarity relative to the model is absolutely necessary if we want to successfully use the fitted model to predict future winning times.   ✦

D ISCUSSION QUESTIONS

1. What are multivariate data? Bivariate data?
2. What things should you look for in analyzing a scatterplot?
3. Describe how the median trace works.
4. In your own words, tell what the Pearson correlation coefficient measures. Draw pictures illustrating your points.
5. Summarize the inference procedures for Pearson correlation you have learned in this chapter.
6. Tell what the following mean in the context of simple linear regression: response variable, predictor variable, regressor variable, random error, and model parameters.
7. What is a statistical relationship? How does it differ from and how does it relate to a functional relationship?
8. Describe the main ideas behind least absolute errors and least squares as methods of fitting lines to bivariate data.
9. Which of least absolute error or least squares would be the more resistant method to use in fitting a line to bivariate data? Why?
10. What is MSE and how is it interpreted?
11. What are fitted values, predicted values, and residuals?
12. What are Studentized residuals? How are residuals and Studentized residuals used in assessing the quality of fit?
13. What is the coefficient of determination? How is it interpreted? What is its relation to the correlation coefficient?
14. How should the slope and intercept of the fitted model be interpreted?
15. Summarize the inference procedures for model parameters, estimation of mean response and prediction of a future response you have learned in this chapter.
16. What is the relation between correlation and regression?
17. Name two ways to display categorical data.
18. In a two-way frequency table, describe what is meant by joint distribution, marginal distribution, and conditional distribution.
19. Describe the inference procedures for one-way and two-way tables discussed in the text, including confidence intervals and Pearsons's χ^2 test. Under what circumstances are these inference procedures used?
20. What is the difference between cause and effect, and association? Does one imply the other? What besides cause and effect could explain an observed association? How can cause and effect be established?
21. What does stationarity mean for bivariate data? How can bivariate data be checked for stationarity?

E XERCISES

7.1. Define T-PLUS as TIME+1 for the tool wear data. How would the graph of WEAR versus TIME differ from that of WEAR versus T-PLUS? If TIME is measured in minutes and HT is in hours, how would the graph of WEAR versus TIME differ from that of WEAR versus HT if the same data were graphed?

7.2. An alternative to using the regressor $\sqrt{\text{TIME}}$ and the response WEAR in the tool wear problem of Example 7.1 is to use the predictor TIME as the regressor and to transform the response. One transformation that will do this is squaring WEAR. Let WEAR2 = WEAR^2. Using plots and the regression of WEAR2 on TIME, evaluate the model with WEAR2 as the response. Compare it with the model using WEAR as the response and the square root of TIME as the regressor. (The data are in TWEAR8.)

7.3. For which of the plots in Figure 7.11 will r be positive? Negative? Near 0?

7.4. Your answer to Exercise 7.3 should lead you to a conclusion about the sign of the slope of the line defining the linear relation between X and Y and the sign of r.

7.5. For those of Figure 7.11 you have identified as having positive r, which will be closest to 1, next closest, etc.?

7.6. For those of Figure 7.11 you have identified as having negative r, which will be closest to -1, next closest, etc.?

7.7. What would the scatterplot of a data set with $r = 1$ look like? What about $r = -1$?

7.8. Does $r = 0$ mean there is no association between X and Y? Explain.

7.9. To see that there is no substitute for a scatterplot to summarize bivariate data, consider **Anscombe's quartet,** four data sets having the same $\bar{x}$, $\bar{y}$, s_x, s_y, and r values,[23] but very different graphs. The data are found in ANSCOMBE, and the variables are named X1 and Y1, X2 and Y2, X3 and Y3, and X4 and Y4. For each data set, compute $\bar{x}$, $\bar{y}$, s_x, s_y, and r, and also produce a scatterplot. Describe what you find. Are you surprised by what you see?

7.10. Regress Y1 on X1, Y2 on X2, Y3 on X3, and Y4 on X4 for Anscombe's quartet (Exercise 7.9). How do the fitted equations compare?

7.11. For the tool wear data with VELOCITY = 600, regress WEAR on TIME. Interpret the fitted model. Assess the quality of the fit. Report your findings. (The data are part of the TWEAR data set.)

7.12. Test scores on the math and verbal part of the SAT are normally distributed and the correlation between the two types of scores is 0.5. Assume that John Q. Student is at the 97.5th percentile of the verbal scores. Use least squares to approximately predict the percentile of his math score.

7.13. Consider the Donner party data. Analyze the relation between FAMILY and FATE. How does it compare with that between GENDER and FATE?

7.14. Recently, scientists claim to have found an association between moderate intake of alcohol and incidence of heart disease. In the study, a large group of volunteers answered a questionnaire about their lifestyles. Their answers were compared with the results of a medical examination and previous medical history. Those who consumed alcohol in moderation (at least three drinks per week, but no more than two per day) were found to have a signifi-

---

[23]To three significant digits.

cantly lower incidence of heart disease than nondrinkers, light drinkers, or heavy drinkers. Is this good evidence that moderate ingestion of alcohol causes improved coronary health? If so, explain why. If not, explain why not and tell what kind of further evidence would be needed to establish cause and effect.

7.15. Suppose a random sample of people of the same height is taken. What is the Pearson correlation coefficient for the relationship of weight versus height for this sample?

7.16. Give an example of a small bivariate data set in which there is a perfect linear relationship between all but one of the points and the Pearson correlation coefficient is zero. What does this teach you?

7.17. If men always marry women who are 5 years younger, what is the Pearson correlation between the ages of married men and women?

7.18. For American men aged 18 to 54, a positive Pearson correlation is observed between blood pressure and income. Does this point to causal connection or can the association be explained another way? If you think there is another explanation, tell what it is.

7.19. In 1971, the draft lottery was again conducted. As you saw in the analysis of the 1970 draft lottery data, there were problems with the randomization of the capsules. In response to this, a new randomization procedure was instituted for the 1971 lottery. The data are found in DRAFT71. Did the changes in randomization work? Justify your answer.

7.20. A study of elementary school children, ages 6 to 11, finds a high positive correlation between shoe size X and score Y on a test of reading comprehension. How can you explain this correlation?

7.21. Some patients were asked by their doctor to measure their blood pressure twice. The correlation between the readings on the two occasions is 0.8, and the standard deviations are virtually the same. Tom, a young man in stable health, was at the 84th percentile on the first occasion.

   (a) Predict the percent of the patients that on the second occasion had blood pressure lower than Tom's.

   (b) What explanation can you give for the difference between Tom's percentile on the first occasion and the prediction of his percentile on the second occasion?

7.22. Medical researchers compared blood flow in stomachs of dogs, measured by using microspheres, with simultaneous measurements obtained using a catheter inserted into a vein. For 10 measurements, average sphere flow is 13.07 ml/min and average catheter flow is 12.82 ml/min, the standard deviations are equal for both, and the correlation coefficient is 0.90. Regress sphere flow on catheter flow and obtain the fitted line.

7.23. In fitting a SLR model, 10 of the residuals for the regression of weight on age for 11 children are:

$$0.02, \quad -0.02, \quad 0.01, \quad -0.01, \quad -0.04, \quad 0.03, \quad 0.01, \quad 0.02, \quad 0.03, \quad 0.05$$

What is the eleventh residual? Are there outliers? Justify your answers.

7.24. A random sample of 200 paired observations (X_i, Y_i), $i = 1, 2, \ldots, 200$, was taken. Of the observations, 150 (X_i, Y_i)'s are $(4, 3.5)$ and 50 (X_i, Y_i)'s are $(1, 9.3)$. What is the correlation coefficient between variables X and Y? No calculation is required, but give a reason for your answer.

7.25. A study of class attendance and grades among freshmen at a state university showed that in general students who attended a higher percent of their classes earned higher grades. The coefficient of determination for the regression of grade index on percent of class attended was 0.64. What is the Pearson correlation between percent of class attended and grade index? Give your reason.

7.26. A random sample of 58 children from age 2 months to 100 months was taken. Their heights were recorded in centimeters. The data set, HEIGHT, contains GENDER, AGE, and HEIGHT for these 58 children.

   (a) Construct an appropriate plot showing the relationship between HEIGHT and AGE for these children. Would you fit a least squares line to these data? Why or why not?

   (b) Regress HEIGHT on AGE. Interpret the fitted model.

   (c) Repeat part (b) for each gender separately. Summarize what you find.

   (d) A female is 240 months old. Based on the regression line, what would you guess for her height? How good is your guess?

7.27. In a study of the effect of age on IQ scores, a large group of individuals was tested once at age 18 and again at age 35. The correlation between the scores at age 18 and those at age 35 is 0.80. The following results were obtained:

Age	Mean score	Standard deviation
18	100	15
35	100	15

Estimate the score at age 35 for an individual who scored 115 at age 18.

7.28. The fat content of the human body can be found by measuring body density, but as this requires doctors to weigh the patient under water, easier predictors of body density have been sought. One such measure is *skinfold thickness,* which is obtained by measuring the thickness of a fold of skin at each of four body locations and adding the measurements. The data set SKINFOLD contains the skinfold measurement (SKIN) and the true body density (ACTUAL) for 24 randomly selected subjects. Look at ACTUAL as a function of SKIN.

   (a) Some researchers prefer to use the log of SKIN as the predictor variable. Create this variable and call it LSKIN. Graph ACTUAL against both SKIN and LSKIN. Describe the plots. Does there seem to be any reason to prefer one over the other?

   (b) Regress ACTUAL on SKIN and do the same for LSKIN. The numerical results of the regression and appropriate plots should indicate a slight preference for one fit over the other. Tell which you prefer and give one measure (numerical or graphical) from your regression to justify your choice.

   (c) For your preferred model, interpret the fitted slope.

   (d) Does the intercept have an interpretation here? Justify your answer. If it does have an interpretation, tell what the interpretation is for the fitted model.

7.29. The data set CARS93 contains information on a sample of 1993 cars. Look at the relation between the midrange price (MIDPRICE) and the EPA estimated city miles per gallon (CITYMPG), with MIDPRICE regarded as a function of CITYMPG.

   (a) Describe the relation between MIDPRICE and CITYMPG. Would you fit a least squares line to these data? Why or why not?

   (b) Consider the relation between the natural logs of MIDPRICE (LPRICE) and of CITYMPG (LMPG). How does it differ from the relation between MIDPRICE and CITYMPG?

   (c) Regress LPRICE on LMPG. What is the fitted model? Interpret the fitted slope.

(d) Recently, a collaboration between Detroit automakers and the government to produce a car getting 80 MPG was announced. Use the fitted model to predict the MIDPRICE of a car with CITYMPG = 80. Do you believe this prediction? Why do you think it gives such a result?

7.30. Explain why it might be more useful to minimize the SAE rather than the SSE.

7.31. Explain why the residuals from a least squares fit add up to zero.

7.32. Explain why a plot of the residuals versus the X_i is sensible for a check on the model.

7.33. Suppose for a given data set, you know that the regression line of Y on X has the same slope as the regression line of X on Y. What can you deduce about s_x, s_y, and/or r?

7.34. An experimenter fits a straight line to a set of X–Y data by eye, and then calculates the SSE by hand, obtaining a value of 36.5. Her assistant uses a regression routine in a statistical package to fit a straight line by least squares to the same data. The resulting SSE is 42.3. The experimenter uses her eyeballed line, noting that it has a smaller SSE than the least squares line. Comment.

7.35. In a multiple-choice exam, there are 10 questions, and for each question there are two options (True/False), exactly one of which is correct. Any question that is not answered is incorrect. What is the correlation coefficient between the number of correct answers and the number of incorrect answers for the 21 students who took the exam? Present your arguments. (*Note:* No calculations are needed.)

7.36. For the period 1960–1990, a study shows that for each year, the cost of an orange is roughly 10 cents more than the cost of an apple. What is the correlation between the costs? Explain.

7.37. A least squares fit of the simple linear regression model $Y = \beta_0 + \beta_1 X + \epsilon$ using a data set with the three X values -1, 0, and 1 gives a zero residual at $X = 0$. What are the other two residuals? Justify your answers.

7.38. Foresters felled a random sample of 31 black cherry trees in the Allegheny National Forest in Pennsylvania, and measured the lumber volume in cubic feet and the tree diameter (in inches) at 4.5 feet above ground level. Figure 7.30 shows part of the SAS/INSIGHT output for the regression of volume on diameter for these data.

(a) What is the fitted regression line? Interpret the fitted slope and intercept, if possible. If not possible, tell why.

(b) Do you feel the model fit is adequate? Why or why not?

(c) The Pearson correlation between tree diameter and volume in this data set is 0.9671. How much does use of this model reduce the uncertainty in predicting tree volume?

7.39. In a recent article that could have an impact on the debate surrounding the safety of silicone breast implants,[24] researchers report the levels of two inflammatory mediators: tumor necrosis factor–alpha (TNF-α) and interleukin-6 (IL-6), obtained from fibrous capsules encasing silicone prostheses removed from the breasts of nine women. Units are pg/ml per 10 g of tissue. The data are in the data set SILICONE. The authors report a Pearson correlation between TNF-α and IL-6 for these data of 0.77, and based on this, they conclude that there is strong statistical relationship between TNF-α and IL-6. Analyze these data yourself. Does your analysis agree with the paper's conclusions? Justify your answers.

7.40. In a study to examine the efficacy of ascorbic acid (vitamin C) in preventing the common cold, 279 French skiers were randomly assigned to one of two groups. Those skiers in the treatment group were given a daily dose of ascorbic acid. Those in the control group were

---

[24]E. A. Mena, N. Kossovsky, C. Chu, and C. Hu, "Inflammatory Intermediates Produced by Tissues Encasing Silicone Breast Prostheses," *Journal of Investigative Surgery,* 8 (1995): 31–42.

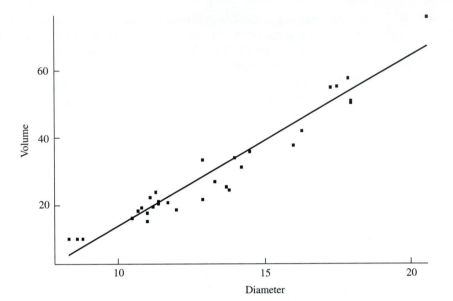

Parameter Estimates						
Variable	DF	Estimate	T Stat	Prob > |T|	Tolerance	Var Inflation
Intercept	1	−36.9435	−10.9783	0.0001	.	0
Diam	1	5.0659	20.4783	0.0001	1.0000	1.0000

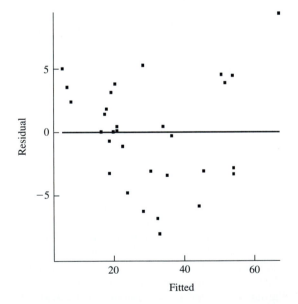

Figure 7.30   SAS/INSIGHT output for regression of tree volume on tree diameter.

TABLE 7.12   Effect of Treatment on the Incidence of Common Colds

Treatment	Cold	No cold	Total
Placebo	31	109	140
Ascorbic acid	25	114	139
Totals	56	223	279

given a placebo. The skiers were then monitored over the ski season to see whether they contracted colds or not. Table 7.12 shows the results.

(a) Do these data suggest that ascorbic acid is effective in preventing common colds? Use joint, marginal, and/or conditional distributions to make your case.

(b) Use an appropriate inference procedure to support the argument you made in (a).

7.41. An engineer, interested in the relation between thickness (cm) and tensile strength (psi) of washers, measured the thickness and tensile strength of 10 washers. He obtained a correlation of 0.80. His experience suggests that the weight and tensile strength of the washers are normally distributed. If a washer is at the 95th percentile in thickness, predict its percentile in tensile strength.

7.42. A biologist measured the weight (lb) and diameter (ft) of five pumpkins. The five bivariate measurements are (5, 0.5), (6, 0.6), (10, 1), (30, 1.5), and (500, 10). Why is the Pearson correlation coefficient inappropriate in this application? Relate its lack of appropriateness to what you know about the relation between diameter and weight.

7.43. A study shows that there is a clear positive Pearson correlation between the size of a hospital measured by the number of beds, X, and the median number of days, Y, that patients remain in the hospital. Are the large hospitals padding their bills by keeping patients longer? Explain.

7.44. A new quality training program is being tested at an auto part manufacturing plant. For one type of part, Table 7.13 gives the numbers of defective and good parts manufactured in the week preceding and the week following the program.

TABLE 7.13   Effect of Training on Auto Part Quality

Quality	Before	After	Total
Good	121	154	275
Defective	46	19	65
Total	167	173	340

(a) Do these data suggest that the program is effective? Use joint, marginal, and/or conditional distributions to make your case.

(b) Use an appropriate inference procedure to support the argument you made in (a).

7.45. For a simple random sample of 600 applicants for a job, a statistician drew up Table 7.14.

(a) Describe the marginal and conditional distributions for this table.

(b) Interpret the conditional distribution of gender for the two nationalities.

(c) Back up your interpretation in (b) with an appropriate statistical inference procedure.

TABLE 7.14   Gender versus Nationality for 600 Job Applicants

	Nationality		
Gender	Indian	Chinese	Total
Male	156	58	214
Female	289	97	386
Total	445	155	600

7.46. Explain why a plot of the residuals e_i versus X_i must show no linear trend if the simple linear regression model holds.

7.47. Suppose in the regression of Y_i on X_i, $\hat{\beta}_0 = 5$ and $\hat{\beta}_1 = 1$, and the standard deviation for the Y_i is twice that for the X_i. What percentage reduction in the uncertainty of prediction is obtained by using the regression to predict?

7.48. A pediatric researcher is studying the relationship between the height and the esophageal length (EL: the distance between the mouth and the lower esophageal sphincter) in children 1 month to 18 years of age. From a random sample of 88 children, she obtained esophageal lengths and the heights in centimeters (1 centimeter $= 0.3937$ inch). Figure 7.31 shows part of the SAS/INSIGHT output for the regression of EL on height for these data.

(a) What is the fitted regression line? Interpret the fitted slope and intercept, if possible. If not possible, tell why.

(b) Do you feel the model fit is adequate? Why or why not?

(c) By what percentage does use of this model reduce the uncertainty in predicting esophageal length?

(d) What is the value of the Pearson correlation coefficient between esophageal length and height?

(e) A child is 93 centimeters tall. Based on the regression line, what would you guess for his esophageal length? Given that $\bar{x} = 88.2$ and that $\sum(x_i - \bar{x})^2 = 3751.5$, how precise is your guess? Support your answer. (*Hint:* You will want to use an appropriate interval to quantify the precision. You can use the information that $\bar{x} = 88.2$ and that $\sum(x_i - \bar{x})^2 = 3751.5$ in computing the interval.)

7.49. The following table shows the preferences for two brands of chocolate chip cookies in a recently conducted double-blind taste-testing experiment involving 245 college students.

	Cookie A	Cookie B	Total
Male students	94	85	179
Female students	39	27	66
Total	133	112	245

(a) Do the data suggest that the proportion of female students who prefer cookie A to cookie B is greater than is the proportion of male students who prefer cookie A to cookie B? Use joint, marginal, and/or conditional distributions to make your case.

(b) Use an appropriate inference procedure to support the argument you made in (a).

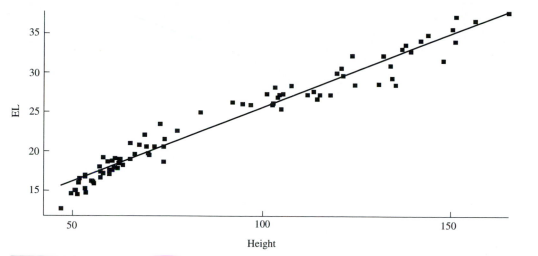

Parameter Estimates							
Variable	DF	Estimate	Std Error	T Stat	Prob > |T|	Tolerance	Var Inflation
INTERCEPT	1	6.7293	0.3966	16.9681	0.0001	.	0
POWER	1	0.1883	0.0042	44.8744	0.0001	1.0000	1.0000

Summary of Fit			
Mean of Response	23.3375	R-Square	0.9590
Root MSE	1.3367	Adj R-Sq	0.9586

Analysis of Variance					
Source	DF	Sum of Square	Mean Square	F Stat	Prob >
Model	1	3597.8790	3597.879	2013.707	19E-62
Error	86	153.6557	1.7867		
C Tot	87	3751.5347			

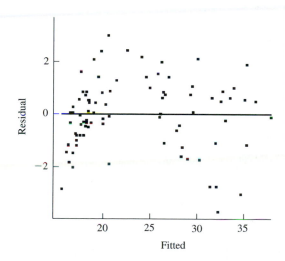

Figure 7.31   Regression output: esophageal data.

7.50. Figure 7.32 contains SAS/INSIGHT output from the regression of height on armspan (both in inches) for a random sample of 51 females. The graphs are a scatterplot of height versus armspan with the fitted regression line superimposed, a plot of the residuals versus the fitted values, and a quantile plot of the Studentized residuals.

(a) Do you feel the model fit is adequate? Why or why not?

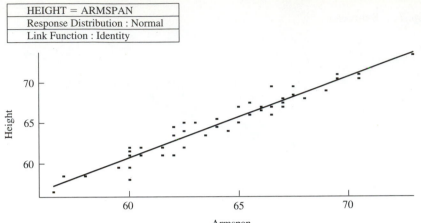

| HEIGHT = ARMSPAN |
| Response Distribution : Normal |
| Link Function : Identity |

Parametric Regression Fit								
	Model		Error					
Type	DF	Mean Square	DF	Mean Square	R-Square	F Stat	Prob > F
Line	1	691.5858	49	1.0025	0.9337	689.8947	0.0001

Summary of Fit			
Mean of Response	65.0294	R-Squre	0.9337
Root MSE	1.0012	Adj R-Sq	0.9323

Analysis of Variance					
Source	DF	Sum of Squares	Mean Square	F Stat	Prob > F
Model	1	691.5858	691.5858	689.8947	0.0001
Error	49	49.1201	1.0025		
C Total	50	740.7059			

Type III Tests					
Source	DF	Sum of Squares	Mean Square	F Stat	Prob > F
ARMSPAN	1	691.5858	691.5858	689.8947	0.0001

Parameter Estimates							
Variable	DF	Estimate	Std Error	T Stat	Prob > |T|	Tolerance	Var Inflation
INTERCEPT	1	0.2533	2.4702	0.1025	0.9188	.	0
ARMSPAN	1	1.0073	0.0384	26.2658	0.0001	1.0000	1.0000

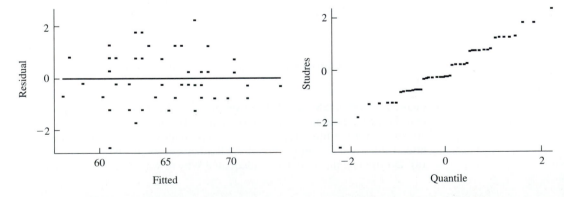

Figure 7.32 SAS/INSIGHT output for regression of height on armspan.

(b) What is the fitted regression line? Interpret the fitted slope and intercept, if possible. If not possible, tell why.

(c) How much does use of this model reduce the uncertainty in predicting height?

(d) What is the value of the Pearson correlation coefficient between height and armspan?

(e) Your sister, who is not in the data set, has an armspan of 67 inches. Predict her height using Figure 7.32 and the additional information that the mean and variance of the 51 armspans in the data set are 65.44 and 22.67, respectively.

7.51. A study of the relationship between burglary and murder rates among the 50 states plus the District of Columbia found a Pearson correlation of 0.0938. When told exactly this, Jedediah concluded that there is little evidence of a relation between burglary and murder rates. Give one reason why this conclusion is unjustified.

7.52. An SLR model is fit to a set of X–Y data. Residual analysis shows a good fit to the data. Level 0.95 confidence intervals for β_0 and β_1 are (6.12, 9.33) and (-1.09, 2.33), respectively. What do you conclude about the relation between X and Y?

7.53. A random sample of 81 children was obtained to study whether handedness is gender-related. The data are shown in Table 7.15.

TABLE 7.15   Gender versus Handedness for 81 Children

	Boys	Girls	Total
Left-handed	9	11	20
Right-handed	29	32	61
Total	38	43	81

(a) Summarize these data using overall, row, and column percentages.

(b) What are the marginal distributions of gender and handedness?

(c) What is the conditional distribution of handedness given the individual is male? Female?

(d) What do you conclude about the relationship between gender and handedness? Why?

7.54. Fit the model described in Example 7.7, page 371, using the data in the FUEL data set. After fitting the model, answer the following. Justify all answers.

(a) Interpret the fitted model.

(b) Evaluate the adequacy of the fit.

(c) By how much does the fitted model reduce the uncertainty of predicting fuel consumption?

(d) Estimate the mean response when the equivalence ratio is 1.1. Predict the fuel consumption obtained from a new measurement when the equivalence ratio is 1.1.

7.55. A six-sided die is tossed 600 times. Table 7.16 shows the outcomes. Is the die fair? You are to use a statistical inference procedure to help you decide. You can proceed in one of two ways.

(a) You can consider each face individually.

(b) You can consider all faces simultaneously.

Which of (a) and (b) is preferable? Explain. Now use your approach to decide if the die is fair.

7.56. Yule (1900) presented data in Table 7.17 on 205 married persons. Are heights of husbands and wives independent? Use an appropriate inference procedure to help you decide.

TABLE 7.16   Outcomes for the Die-Tossing Experiment

Face	1	2	3	4	5	6
Counts	108	102	90	100	105	95

TABLE 7.17   Pairing of Spouses by Height

Husband	Wife			Total
	Tall	Medium	Short	
Tall	18	28	14	60
Medium	20	51	28	99
Short	12	25	9	46
Total	50	104	51	205

MINIPROJECT

How good a shot are you?

Purpose

The purpose of this miniproject is to give you experience with modeling the relation between two variables using the methods in this chapter.

Process

Your task in this project is to use regression methods to investigate the relationship between the distance a person stands from a target placed on the floor, and the accuracy with which a thrown coin lands on the target.

Your group should think of an experiment that will answer the preceding question. In addition, you should design your experiment to answer at least one other question about this relationship. You are free to decide all design issues of the experiment including what will be measured, what the target looks like, and how the experiment will be conducted.

Before conducting the experiment, submit a proposal, no more than one page in length, for your instructor's approval. The proposal should state what data will be collected, exactly how you intend to collect it, and what kind of relationship you expect to find. Your instructor will discuss the proposal with your group, and may suggest modifications.

After your group's proposal has been approved, proceed to collect the data and use any of the techniques discussed in this chapter that are appropriate to analyze the relationship between the two variables.

Write a short report summarizing your findings. Be sure to state whether the data confirmed the kind of relationship you predicted in your initial proposal. Also include two further questions suggested (but not answered) by your data and tell what you could do to get answers to these questions.

LAB 7.1: Fit Your Own Regression Line

Introduction

As you've seen in this chapter, the method of least squares fits a line to a set of (X, Y) data by choosing slope and intercept parameters to minimize SSE, the sum of squared errors. This is the sum of the squares of vertical distances between the data points and the fitted line. It is a testimony to the power of mathematics that simple formulas exist for calculating the least squares parameters. Otherwise, we might have to approach the problem by trial and error. In this laboratory, you will take the trial-and-error approach: you will try to visually fit a line to a set of data.

Objectives

- To develop your ability to "see" what is a good fit in simple linear regression.
- To give you insight into the mechanics of regression.
- To give you insight and experience in interpreting residual plots.

Lab Materials

None needed.

Experimental Procedure

1. Your instructor will tell you how to access or generate a set of bivariate data.[25] Plot the response versus the regressor on a scatterplot.
2. Looking at the scatterplot, come up with an intercept and slope for a line you think best fits the data.
3. Plot the line you guessed on the scatterplot, compute the residuals, and plot the residuals versus the regressor. Compute the SSE for the fit and record the result.
4. Using the feedback from the data plots, you are ready to try to improve your fit. Make another guess, and go to step 3. Keep track of your best fit and keep trying until you think you've done as well as you can.

---

[25]SAS and MINITAB users can access macros that automate the data generation and guessing process. They should consult the **Doing It with SAS** or **Doing It with MINITAB** supplements to the text for explicit directions.

5. When you want to see how close your best guess is to the least squares line, compute the latter. How does your best fit compare?

6. In your report, detail the steps you took, and the results you obtained in coming to your final guess.

LAB 7.2: Transformations to Straighten a Plot

Introduction

Often a plot of a response versus a predictor variable shows the relation to be nonlinear. If we want to fit a regression function to such data, we basically have two choices: fit a nonlinear function, or transform the response to make the relationship linear and then fit a linear function.

Sometimes the nonlinearity can be handled in a simple linear regression by specifying as the regressor an appropriate nonlinear function of the predictor. This was the case in Example 7.7, where fuel consumption seemed to be linearly related to the fifth power of equivalence ratio. Often, however, fitting an appropriate nonlinear function of the predictor can entail serious computational difficulties and is beyond the capabilities of many computer packages.

This lab lets you investigate the second approach: transforming the response variable.

Objectives

To illustrate the method of transforming the response to linearity, fitting a linear function, and transforming back to the original units.

Lab Materials

None needed.

Experimental Procedure

1. A manufacturer of disk drives began marketing a new fault-tolerant storage device in 1990. The number of these devices sold in each of the first eight years after its introduction are the following:

year	1990	1991	1992	1993	1994	1995	1996	1997
sales	84	290	1003	2925	5877	10862	17397	24678

2. Make a plot of sales versus year, and then regress sales on year, and create residual and/or Studentized residual plots. Evaluate the fit.

3. Below you will be asked to apply nonlinear transformations to the response. The reason such transformations can straighten a nonlinear plot is that they shrink (or expand) response values in some regions more than in others. Compare this with a linear transformation which shrinks (or expands) response values by the same amount regardless of where they are. Think of what the square root does to positive real numbers. Which numbers does it

shrink? Which does it expand? Does it shrink or expand some numbers more than others? Which ones? What about the reciprocal transformation? How does taking the reciprocal of a real number affect large numbers relative to small ones?

(a) Apply the square root transformation to sales. Make a plot of the square root of sales versus year, and then regress the square root of sales on year, and create residual and/or Studentized residual plots. Evaluate the fit.

(b) Repeat (a) for the reciprocal transformation.

4. Both the square root and reciprocal transformations are examples of **power transformations.** These are transformations of the form Y^p, where p is some real number. The square root results when $p = 0.5$ and the reciprocal when $p = -1$. It turns out that the transformation corresponding to $p = 0$ is the natural log.

Using the results you obtained from the square root and reciprocal transformations as a starting point, find a power transformation that makes the relation between the transformed sales and year as linear as possible. Justify your selection of transformation by regressing the transformed sales on year and evaluating the fit.

5. Use the fit of the transformed data to predict the sales for 1998.

CAPSTONE PROJECT: Chapters 1 to 4 and 7

The goal of a **Capstone Project** is to give you experience in all phases of a statistical study: planning, data collection, analysis, and conclusions. Each of Chapters 1 to 4 and 7 must make a contribution to the project. For a description of this project, see the description of the Capstone Project for Chapters 1 to 5 on page 285. In addition to the material from Chapters 1 to 4 discussed there, the Capstone Project for Chapters 1 to 4 and 7, must also include modeling and inference for bivariate data using simple linear regression or two-way tables, as covered in Chapter 7.

8

Multiple Regression

A poor relation is the most irrelevant thing in nature.

—*Charles Lamb*

◼ INTRODUCTION

In Chapter 7, you were introduced to the analysis of bivariate measurement data. This chapter extends the topics you studied in that chapter to models with more than one regressor variable. Such models are called **multiple linear regression** models. You will also learn about inference for such models.

Knowledge and Skills

By successfully completing this chapter, you will acquire the following knowledge and skills:

KNOWLEDGE	SKILLS
1. The multiple linear regression model and inference based on it.	**1.** How to build, fit, interpret, and check the aptness of the multiple linear regression model.
2. Multicollinearity and how to identify it.	**2.** The use of diagnostic measures for multicollinearity.
3. Model building strategies.	**3.** Experience in regression model building.

THE MULTIPLE LINEAR REGRESSION MODEL[1]

Like the simple linear regression model you studied in Chapter 7, the multiple linear regression model quantifies a statistical relationship. But whereas the simple linear regression model quantifies the relationship between a response variable and a single regressor, the multiple linear regression model quantifies the relationship between a response variable and more than one regressor. Suppose that Y is the response variable and that there are p predictors, $Z_1, Z_2, \ldots, Z_p$. We will assume that the response is related linearly to q known functions of the predictors: $X_1(Z_1, Z_2, \ldots, Z_p)$, $X_2(Z_1, Z_2, \ldots, Z_p), \ldots, X_q(Z_1, Z_2, \ldots, Z_p)$. That is, the multiple linear regression model we will consider has the form

$$Y = \beta_0 + \beta_1 X_1(Z_1, Z_2, \ldots, Z_p)$$
$$+ \beta_2 X_2(Z_1, Z_2, \ldots, Z_p) + \cdots + \beta_q X_q(Z_1, Z_2, \ldots, Z_p) + \epsilon \tag{8.1}$$

The functions $X_1, X_2, \ldots, X_q$ are called **regressors.** A few points should be made about model (8.1):

- Model (8.1) is a more general version of the simple linear regression model (7.2). Whereas model (7.2) had a single predictor and regressor, model (8.1) allows multiple predictors and regressors.
- Model (8.1) is quite general and can model a great many relationships between the response and predictors.
- The number, q, of regressors $X_1, X_2, \ldots, X_q$, may not equal p, the number of predictors.
- "Multiple" in "multiple linear regression" means that there is more than one regressor. That is, $q > 1$. There may be only one predictor, however.
- "Linear" in "multiple linear regression" means that the model is linear in the parameters $\beta_0, \beta_1, \ldots, \beta_q$, and the regressors $X_1, \ldots, X_q$.
- The ϵ is the random error term, just as in the simple linear regression model you studied in Chapter 7. It will be assumed to have mean 0 and variance σ^2. When necessary, we will also assume it to have a normal distribution.

EXAMPLE 8.1   SOME MULTIPLE LINEAR REGRESSION MODELS

The following are some examples of specific models having the form of the multiple linear regression model (8.1).

---

[1] We will use only scalars to present the multiple linear regression model throughout the body of the text. A more natural way to present the multiple linear regression model is through a vector-matrix formulation. For those students comfortable with vectors and matrices, Appendix 8.1 at the end of this chapter presents the basics of the vector-matrix formulation of the multiple linear regression model.

First, if there is one predictor and one regressor (i.e., $p = q = 1$), then model (8.1) reduces to the simple linear regression model (7.2).

The next two examples show that there can be a single regressor and multiple predictors or multiple regressors and a single predictor.

- **A Simple Linear Regression Model with Two Predictors.** The model given by

$$Y = \beta_0 + \beta_1 Z_1 e^{-5Z_2^2} + \epsilon$$

has two predictors ($p = 2$), Z_1 and Z_2, and the single regressor ($q = 1$), $X_1(Z_1, Z_2) = Z_1 e^{-5Z_2^2}$. Because it has a single regressor, this is a simple linear regression model, and the methods of Chapter 7 can be applied.

- **A Multiple Linear Regression Model with One Predictor.** The simple polynomial model

$$Y = \beta_0 + \beta_1 Z_1 + \beta_2 Z_1^2 + \epsilon$$

has two regressors ($q = 2$), $X_1 = Z_1$ and $X_2 = Z_1^2$, and a single predictor ($p = 1$), Z_1.

The rest of the models we consider here will have two predictors, Z_1 and Z_2, so that $p = 2$.

- **An Additive Model.** The additive model is the simplest multiple linear regression model. It has the form

$$Y = \beta_0 + \beta_1 Z_1 + \beta_2 Z_2 + \epsilon \qquad (8.2)$$

where $q = p = 2$, $X_1(Z_1, Z_2) = Z_1$, and $X_2(Z_1, Z_2) = Z_2$. This model is called additive because the predictors influence the response in an additive way: the contribution from Z_1 adds to the contribution from Z_2. Note that in this model, the regressors are the predictors.

- **A Model with a Product Term.** We can add a term involving the product $Z_1 Z_2$ to the additive model. The resulting model is

$$Y = \beta_0 + \beta_1 Z_1 + \beta_2 Z_2 + \beta_3 Z_1 Z_2 + \epsilon \qquad (8.3)$$

In this model, $q = 3$, $X_1(Z_1, Z_2) = Z_1$, $X_2(Z_1, Z_2) = Z_2$, and $X_3(Z_1, Z_2) = Z_1 Z_2$.

- **A Full Quadratic Model.** A full quadratic model has the form

$$Y = \beta_0 + \beta_1 Z_1 + \beta_2 Z_2 + \beta_3 Z_1^2 + \beta_4 Z_1 Z_2 + \beta_5 Z_2^2 + \epsilon \qquad (8.4)$$

Model (8.4) results from the general multiple linear regression formulation by taking $q = 5$ and $X_1(Z_1, Z_2) = Z_1$, $X_2(Z_1, Z_2) = Z_2$, $X_3(Z_1, Z_2) = Z_1^2$, $X_4(Z_1, Z_2) = Z_1 Z_2$, and $X_5(Z_1, Z_2) = Z_2^2$. Full quadratic models like model (8.4) are often used to approximate responses that are complicated functions of predictor variables, when the approximation is needed over a small region.   ✦

Recall the distinction between a statistical and a functional relationship discussed in Chapter 7. Model (8.1) is an example of a statistical relationship, because the random error ϵ makes it impossible to use knowledge of the model parameters $\beta_0, \beta_1, \ldots, \beta_q$, and of the values of the regressors $X_1, \ldots, X_q$, to give the exact value of Y. On the other hand, since the mean of the random error term, ϵ, is 0, the expected value of Y given that we know $X_1 = x_1, X_2 = x_2, \ldots, X_q = x_q$ is given by the functional relationship

$$E(Y \mid X_1 = x_1, X_2 = x_2, \ldots, X_q = x_q) = \beta_0 + \beta_1 x_1 + \beta_2 x_2 + \cdots + \beta_q x_q$$

8.3

INTERPRETING THE RESPONSE SURFACE

The surface defined by the deterministic part of the multiple linear regression model (8.1),

$$\begin{aligned}
&\beta_0 + \beta_1 X_1(Z_1, Z_2, \ldots, Z_p) \\
&\quad + \beta_2 X_2(Z_1, Z_2, \ldots, Z_p) + \cdots + \beta_q X_q(Z_1, Z_2, \ldots, Z_p)
\end{aligned} \tag{8.5}$$

is called the **response surface** of the model. Depending on what is needed in the interpretation, and on what makes sense, the response surface may be regarded as a function of the predictors or as a function of the regressors.

Interpreting the Response Surface as a Function of the Regressors

When considered a function of the regressors, the response surface is defined by the functional relationship

$$E(Y \mid X_1 = x_1, X_2 = x_2, \ldots, X_q = x_q) = \beta_0 + \beta_1 x_1 + \beta_2 x_2 + \cdots + \beta_q x_q$$

which describes how the expected response varies as a function of the regressors.

If it is possible for the X_i to simultaneously take the value 0, then β_0 is the value of the response surface when all X_i equal 0. Otherwise, β_0 has no interpretation of its own.

For $i = 1, \ldots, q$, β_i is interpreted as the change in the expected response per unit change in the regressor X_i, when all other regressors are held constant. Some care must be taken, however, since such an interpretation may not make sense. Consider, for example, the model with one predictor, Z_1, and regressors $X_1 = Z_1$ and $X_2 = Z_1^3$. It is clearly not possible to change X_1 while holding X_2 fixed.

Interpreting the Response Surface as a Function of the Predictors

It is often desirable to analyze the response surface as a function of the predictors. Unfortunately, this is usually more difficult than analyzing the response surface as a function of the regressors. When considered a function of the predictors, the response surface is defined by the functional relationship

$$E(Y \mid Z_1 = z_1, Z_2 = z_2, \ldots, Z_p = z_p)$$
$$= \beta_0 + \beta_1 X_1(z_1, z_2, \ldots, z_p) + \beta_2 X_2(z_1, z_2, \ldots, z_p) + \cdots + \beta_q X_q(z_1, z_2, \ldots, z_p)$$

which describes how the expected response varies as a function of the predictors.

If it is possible for the X_i to simultaneously take the value 0 for some values of the predictors, then β_0 is the value of the response surface when all X_i equal 0. Otherwise, β_0 has no interpretation of its own.

If the regressors are differentiable functions of the predictors, we can use calculus to help interpret the response surface in terms of the predictors. By using partial derivatives, we can quantify how the surface changes as each predictor varies while the other predictors are held fixed. The instantaneous rate of change of the surface in the direction of predictor Z_i, at the point $z_1, z_2, \ldots, z_p$ is

$$\frac{\partial}{\partial z_i} E(Y \mid Z_1 = z_1, Z_2 = z_2, \ldots, Z_p = z_p)$$

We now illustrate this analysis for some of the models of Example 8.1.

EXAMPLE 8.1   CONTINUED

- **Additive Model.** For the additive model (8.2),

$$E(Y \mid Z_1 = z_1, Z_2 = z_2) = \beta_0 + \beta_1 z_1 + \beta_2 z_2$$

so the change in expected response per unit change in z_i is

$$\frac{\partial}{\partial z_i} E(Y \mid Z_1 = z_1, Z_2 = z_2) = \frac{\partial}{\partial z_i}(\beta_0 + \beta_1 z_1 + \beta_2 z_2) = \beta_i, \quad i = 1, 2 \qquad (8.6)$$

Note that this value is independent of the values z_1 or z_2. This is a characteristic of the additive model: that the surface varies with respect to a predictor in exactly the same way, regardless of the values of the other predictors. Only for an additive model do the regression coefficients β_i have the simple interpretation of rate of change of the response surface (i.e., the expected response) in the Z_i direction.

- **A Model with a Product Term.** For model (8.3),

$$E(Y \mid Z_1 = z_1, Z_2 = z_2) = \beta_0 + \beta_1 z_1 + \beta_2 z_2 + \beta_3 z_1 z_2$$

so that the change in expected response per unit change in z_1 is

$$\frac{\partial}{\partial z_1} E(Y \mid Z_1 = z_1, Z_2 = z_2) = \beta_1 + \beta_3 z_2 \qquad (8.7)$$

and the change in expected response per unit change in z_2 is

$$\frac{\partial}{\partial z_2} E(Y \mid Z_1 = z_1, Z_2 = z_2) = \beta_2 + \beta_3 z_1 \tag{8.8}$$

Notice that the product term causes the change with respect to one predictor to depend on the value of the other predictor. When this happens, we say that there is **interaction** between the predictors. Interaction means that the behavior of the response surface with respect to one predictor depends on the value of one or more other predictors. Interaction cannot occur in an additive model.

- **A Full Quadratic Model.** For the full quadratic model (8.4),

$$E(Y \mid Z_1 = z_1, Z_2 = z_2) = \beta_0 + \beta_1 z_1 + \beta_2 z_2 + \beta_3 z_1^2 + \beta_4 z_2^2 + \beta_5 z_1 z_2$$

so that the change in expected response per unit change in z_1 is

$$\frac{\partial}{\partial z_1} E(Y \mid Z_1 = z_1, Z_2 = z_2) = \beta_1 + 2\beta_3 z_1 + \beta_5 z_2$$

and the change in expected response per unit change in z_2 is

$$\frac{\partial}{\partial z_2} E(Y \mid Z_1 = z_1, Z_2 = z_2) = \beta_2 + 2\beta_4 z_2 + \beta_5 z_1$$

Note that the product term causes the change with respect to one predictor to depend on the value of the other predictor, and the squared terms cause the change with respect to one predictor to depend on its own value.   ◆

If all this sounds confusing, perhaps the following example will help. In this example, we introduce a data set that will be used to illustrate concepts throughout the chapter.

EXAMPLE 8.2   MEASURING TREE VOLUME

The data consist of measurements taken from 31 black cherry trees in the Allegheny National Forest in Pennsylvania.[2] The primary variables and their units of measurement are

- D: tree diameter measured 4.5 feet above ground level (inches)
- H: tree height (feet)
- V: tree volume (cubic feet)

One problem with measuring the volume of a tree is that the tree must be cut down to do it. Data like these are valuable in developing a model that can be used to estimate tree volume with measurements that are relatively easy to make, and that don't require felling the tree. Our goal in the chapter will be to develop

---

[2]The data are found in Barbara F. Ryan, Brian L. Joiner, and Thomas A. Ryan, *Minitab Handbook,* 2nd ed., Boston: Duxbury Press. They are in the data set TREES.

and fit such a model, and to evaluate its fit. Specifically, we will consider models that predict volume as a function of diameter and height.

For the present, we will assume that we are given two multiple linear regression models that express a statistical relationship between tree volume, V and the two predictors diameter, D and height, H. The first is the additive model

$$V = -57.99 + 4.71D + 0.34H + \epsilon \tag{8.9}$$

which is obtained from model (8.2) by taking $Y = V$, $Z_1 = D$, $Z_2 = H$, $\beta_0 = -57.99$, $\beta_1 = 4.71$, and $\beta_2 = 0.34$. The corresponding response surface is

$$E(V \mid D = d, H = h) = -57.99 + 4.71d + 0.34h \tag{8.10}$$

How can we interpret this response surface? Clearly, the intercept has no meaning, since it is negative. Even if it were not negative, the values $D = 0$ and $H = 0$ are well outside the range of possible diameter and height measurements, so it is difficult to see how it could be interpreted.

In terms of Equation (8.6), we see that the change in expected response per unit change in D is $\beta_1 = 4.71$, and the change in expected response per unit change in H is $\beta_2 = 0.34$. So, the model tells us, for example, that the average volume of trees having diameters 10 inches is 4.71 cubic feet more than the average volume of trees having diameters 9 inches. It also tells us that the average volume of trees having height 60 feet is 0.34 cubic foot more than the average volume of trees having height 59 feet.

Let's look a little more closely at the response surface. Suppose we consider trees with diameter 9 inches. Then the response surface is a function only of H, and the expected response when $H = h$ is

$$E(V \mid D = 9, H = h) = -57.99 + 4.71 \cdot 9 + 0.34h = -15.6 + 0.34h \tag{8.11}$$

Similarly, for trees with diameter 12 inches, the expected response when $H = h$ is

$$E(V \mid D = 12, H = h) = -1.47 + 0.34h \tag{8.12}$$

and for trees with diameter 18 inches, the expected response when $H = h$ is

$$E(V \mid D = 18, H = h) = 26.79 + 0.34h \tag{8.13}$$

The lines defined by Equations (8.11) to (8.13) are graphed in the right plot in Figure 8.1. Notice that while the intercepts change as the diameters vary, the slopes remain constant. The graphs of these lines for different diameters are just translates of each other. This is characteristic behavior of the additive model.

The second model we want to consider has a product term as well as linear terms:

$$V = 69.40 - 5.86D - 1.30H + 0.13DH + \epsilon \tag{8.14}$$

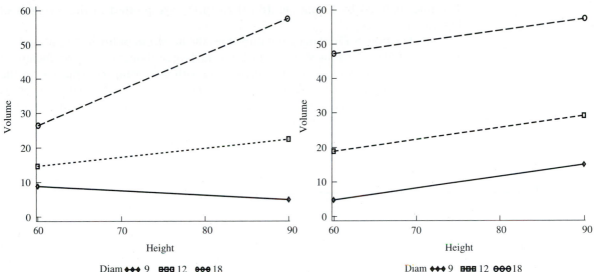

Diam ◆◆◆ 9   ▦▦ 12   ●●● 18   Diam ◆◆◆ 9   ▦▦ 12   ●●● 18

Figure 8.1   The left plot displays the lines defined by Equations (8.16) to (8.18). The differences in both slopes and intercepts indicate interaction between height and diameter. The right plot displays the lines defined by Equations (8.11) to (8.13). The equality of slopes indicate no interaction between height and diameter.

This is model (8.3) with $Y = V$, $Z_1 = D$, $Z_2 = H$, $\beta_0 = 69.40$, $\beta_1 = -5.86$, $\beta_2 = -1.30$, and $\beta_3 = 0.13$. The corresponding response surface is

$$E(V \mid D = d, H = h) = 69.40 - 5.86d - 1.30h + 0.13dh \qquad (8.15)$$

In terms of Equation (8.7), we see that the change in expected response per unit change in d is $-5.86 + 0.13h$, and in terms of Equation (8.8), we see that the change in expected response per unit change in h is $-1.30 + 0.13d$.

If we consider the response surface (8.15) for trees having 9-inch diameters, we obtain

$$\begin{aligned} E(V \mid D = 9, H = h) &= 69.40 - (5.86)(9) - 1.30h + (0.13)(9)h \\ &= 16.66 - 0.13h \end{aligned} \qquad (8.16)$$

Similarly, for trees with diameter 12 inches, the expected response when $H = h$ is

$$E(V \mid D = 12, H = h) = -0.92 + 0.26h \qquad (8.17)$$

and for trees with diameter 18 inches, the expected response when $H = h$ is

$$E(V \mid D = 18, H = h) = -36.08 + 1.04h \qquad (8.18)$$

The lines defined by Equations (8.16) to (8.18) are plotted in the left plot of Figure 8.1.

Notice that as D changes, not only does the intercept of the line relating V to H change, but so does the slope. In fact, for the larger diameters, the coefficient of V is positive, so that expected V is increasing with increasing H, whereas for the smallest diameter, 9 inches, the coefficient of H is negative, implying that expected V decreases with increasing H! This change in the slope of V as a function of H shows the interaction between D and H.   ✦

8.4

THE MODELING PROCESS

In the first two sections of this chapter, we have introduced the multiple linear regression model and shown how its response surface can be interpreted. Ultimately, however, we want to learn how to use these kinds of models to describe or predict some phenomenon. Before we can use such a model, we need to go through a number of steps.

Let's assume that we have a set of data consisting of a response variable and one or more predictor variables, and that we want to use a multiple linear regression model to

- describe the relation between the response and the predictors, or,
- predict the response using known values of the predictors, or,
- both.

Before we can accomplish either or both of these tasks, we must have a suitable multiple linear regression model that we can use. The following steps will produce such a model.

1. **Model Specification.** By model specification, we mean specifying the form of model (8.1). This consists of specifying the number and form of the regressors, $X_1, \ldots, X_q$, and, possibly, of specifying the type of distribution the random error terms have (e.g., a normal distribution).

2. **Model Fitting.** Once a model has been specified, it must be fit to the data, where by fitting, we mean using the data to estimate the model parameters $\beta_0, \beta_1, \ldots, \beta_q$ and σ^2, the variance of the random errors. We will use the method of least squares to estimate the β's.

3. **Model Assessment.** After fitting the model, the adequacy of the fit must be assessed. As in the simple linear regression case, the primary assessment tools are the residuals. If at this stage we conclude that the fit is inadequate, the model-building procedure returns to step 1 by respecifying the model in light of what has been discovered thus far, and continues through steps 2 and 3. Once the fitted model is deemed adequate, we can go to step 4: model validation.

4. **Model Validation.** Fitting a model is a bit like breaking in a pair of shoes. When you first wear the shoes, they may fit well in a generic way, but they fit really well

only after they have have been molded to the contours of your feet. Because they have molded themselves to the unique features of your feet, it will be difficult for them to fit anyone else even as well as a new pair of shoes.

In the same way, a model fit to a set of data will tend to conform to the features of the data. Some of those features will accurately represent the phenomenon under study (just as all size 9D shoes have the same basic shape), and some will be peculiar to the data set used in the fitting (just as your broken-in shoes conform to the peculiarities of your feet). As a result, if the model is used to describe or predict data from a different data set, it will not perform as well as it did on the data to which it was fit. Therefore, before using a model seriously, it is important to test it on a different set of data obtained from the same population or phenomenon it is supposed to model. Such testing is called **model validation,** and it gives a more accurate appraisal of how the model will perform in practice.

Later in the chapter, we will explore model fitting and model assessment, steps 2 and 3, in some detail. For now, we will confine ourselves to step 1: model specification. There are basically two approaches to model specification: **theory-based** and **empirical.**

Model specification is theory-based if the form of the model is deduced from known principles. For example, if we wanted to predict the pressure of a gas in a closed cylinder based on the volume of the gas, Boyle's law[3] might be used to select the reciprocal of volume as the appropriate regressor. When theory is available, theory-based model specification is the preferred method for model specification. Often, however, adequate theory is absent. In that case, we must resort to empirical model specification.

In empirical model specification, data are used to specify the model. In order to do this effectively, the data must be explored visually. If there is a single predictor, a single scatterplot of the response versus the predictor can provide the necessary visual support for model specification. If there are two predictors, a three-dimensional plot can supply the necessary visual support. But what if there are more than two predictors? Can we display more than three-dimensions on a computer screen or a printout? It turns out that we can, and the next section details how.

8.5

THE GRAPHICAL EXPLORATION OF MULTIVARIABLE DATA[4]

The problem confronting us is to find effective ways to graph multivariable data that can be used to empirically specify an appropriate multiple regression model. Throughout this book, we have emphasized the importance of the graphical display of data. Effective

---

[3] Recall that Boyle's law states that for gas at a given temperature, the product of pressure and volume is constant.

[4] This section may be omitted without loss of continuity. The material in this section requires the use of software that can produce scatterplot arrays with brushing, or three-dimensional plots with user-selectable perspective, preferably in real time.

graphical displays are even more important with multivariable data, because of the many ways the variables can be interrelated. Especially important are **interactive displays:** displays in which the user can select observations, variables, and views of the data directly from the graphs.

It is difficult to describe effective visualization techniques theoretically, so we will illustrate some techniques by considering their use with the tree data set.

EXAMPLE 8.2   CONTINUED

Our goal is to empirically specify a model for the tree data, using V as the response and D and H predictors.

First Steps

As always, our first task is to come to an understanding of how the data were collected. We are told that these measurements are from a sample of trees randomly selected from a forest area of uniform composition and measured over a 2-week period. There seems to be nothing unusual about the data-collection method, and the short time span over which the data were collected suggest that the data may be assumed to come from a stationary population. Of course, care must be taken that we do not try to extend the results from these data to forests that consist of a different mix of tree types or which have a different age distribution of trees, such as the sampled forest might have 20 years from now!

Our next task is to look at the data. We begin with graphical and numerical summaries of each variable separately, and of the association between variables. Five graphical summaries are combined in Figure 8.2. Three frequency histograms show the distributions of the three variables, D, H, and V, individually. The histograms are aligned to match the axes on the two scatterplots:[5] V versus H and V versus D. The main features of the histograms are the right skewness of V and D and the left skewness of H.[6] The histogram for V also shows one apparent outlier: a tree with a volume of 77 cubic feet (the second largest value is 58.3).

The two scatterplots show a positive association between V and both D and H. The association with D is the stronger of the two. The association with D seems slightly curved, a perception perhaps heightened by the one tree with large volume and the group of trees having the smallest volumes. The association with H is weaker, with increasing variation in the observed volumes as the heights increase.

Although these plots can summarize the distribution of each variable individually (histograms) and the association between V and H and V and D, they cannot show how V is related to both H and D jointly. To obtain such information, we will have to resort to more sophisticated graphical methods.

---

[5] An upside-down histogram may seem disconcerting at first, but difficulties vanish with a little practice.
[6] Can you think why H might be skewed left?

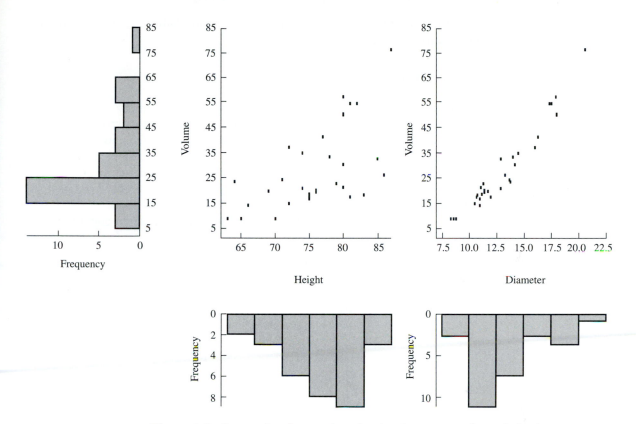

Figure 8.2   Scatterplots for tree data showing the patterns of association between volume and diameter and volume and height, along with frequency histograms showing distributions of volume, height, and diameter.

Multivariable Visualization

The ultimate goal of the analysis is to build a model that describes how mean tree volume varies as a function of tree diameter and height and that can be used to predict the volume of a tree using only diameter and height measurements. In order to intelligently attack the problem of building such a model, we will try to visualize relationships between V and both H and D.

If there were previous scientific evidence or theory to guide us in specifying the form of the model, we would make use of it at this stage. In fact, for the tree data, there is such theory, which we will make use of later in the chapter. For the present, however, we will proceed without the benefit of guidance in model selection. This means we must use empirical model specification.

Empirical model specification is aided greatly if we can visualize the relationships in the data among the variables of interest. Specifically, we will want to look at relationships between the response variable V and both predictor variables H and D.

Two useful graphical tools available for multivariable visualization are **scatterplot arrays** and **3-D plots.**

Scatterplot Arrays

Figure 8.3 shows a **scatterplot array** of the variables D, H, and V.

Displayed in the scatterplot array are all possible scatterplots of pairs of these variables. The main diagonal has no scatterplots (there is no sense plotting a variable against itself), but the smallest and largest values of each variable are displayed there. The arrays below the main diagonal are mirror images of those above the main diagonal. This may seem redundant, but there is a reason for displaying all these scatterplots, as you will shortly see.

We begin our visualization by looking at each scatterplot separately. The scatterplots of primary interest display V versus either D or H, which are the scatterplots shown in Figure 8.2. In the scatterplot array, these are the two plots in the bottom row.

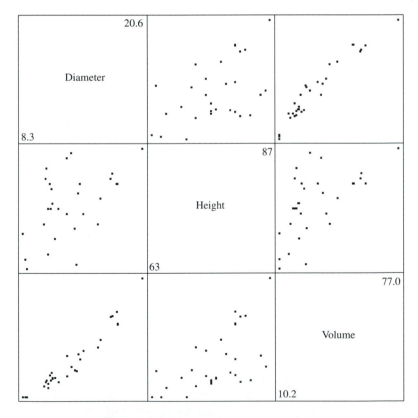

Figure 8.3   Scatterplot array: tree data.

The association between H and D is also of interest. Because of the strong positive association between V and D, we should not be surprised to learn that the scatterplot of D and H resembles that of V and H.

1. Conditioning by Brushing. A **brush** is a rectangle superimposed on a plot, which highlights the data points it encloses on the plot. When looking at multiple plots, we say the plots are **linked** if highlighting data points with a brush in one plot highlights the same data points in the other plots. In a scatterplot array, a brush used on linked plots can show the association between two variables conditional on a range of values of a third variable. Figures 8.4 and 8.5 show the scatterplot array with a brush in the V-versus-D plot.

The brush in Figure 8.4 (which is the small rectangle in the lower-left scatterplot) highlights the data with the smallest values of D, whereas that in Figure 8.5 (also the small rectangle in the lower left scatterplot) highlights data corresponding to larger values of D. You can see that the scatterplots in the scatterplot arrays are linked, since the same data points enclosed, and highlighted, in the brush are also highlighted in each other scatterplot.

These two figures illustrate that the brush can be used to examine how the association between V and H varies for different values of D. To see this, look at the scatterplot of V versus H in both Figure 8.4 and Figure 8.5. (These are the scatterplots in the bottom center position of each scatterplot array.)

Notice how the pattern of the association between V and H changes with changes in D. For the lowest values of D, highlighted in Figure 8.4, there is an increase in V for trees of low height, then a leveling off to a plateau once the tree

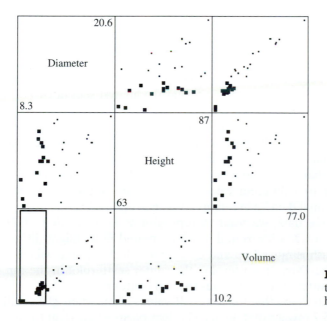

Figure 8.4 Scatterplot array of the tree data with small D values highlighted.

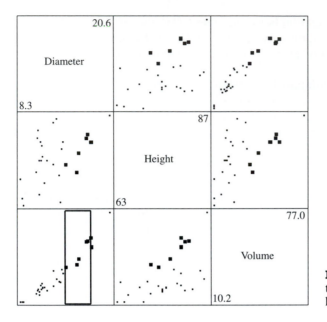

Figure 8.5 Scatterplot array of the tree data with larger D values highlighted.

heights reach 70 or so. For the trees having much larger diameters, highlighted in Figure 8.5, there is a strong positive linear association between V and H.

Using a brush in this manner on linked scatterplots works best if the brush is **dynamic:** that is, if the brush can be moved on the screen by the analyst. This is usually done using the computer mouse. For instance, by moving the brush in Figure 8.4 from left to right in the V-versus-D scatterplot, so that it successively highlights sections of data having higher D values, and simultaneously looking at the points highlighted in the V-versus-H scatterplot, the analyst can get a good idea of how V behaves as a function of both D and H. In terms of a dynamic brush, Figures 8.4 and 8.5 are snapshots of what the analyst sees at two different times as the brush is moved.

2. Level Plots by Brushing. You have all seen contour maps that represent a topographical surface by contours connecting points having the same elevation. Similarly, a function of two variables, $Y = f(X_1, X_2)$, can be represented by a contour plot that plots a number of level contours on the X_1–X_2 plane, each corresponding to a different value of Y. We can explore the surface on which three-dimensional data lie in a similar manner using a brush.

In the tree data, we want to represent V as a function of D and H. In Figures 8.6 and 8.7, a horizontal brush is created to highlight different slices of V. As the brush is moved up and down, the selected points will show different patterns on the D-by-H scatterplot, the center scatterplot in the top row of the array. These patterns are analogous to level contours.

Figure 8.6 shows that the lowest V values occur when D is small regardless of H. Figure 8.7 reveals that higher V values occur when D and H are large.

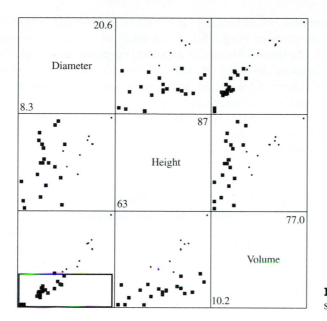

Figure 8.6   Scatterplot array with small *V* values highlighted.

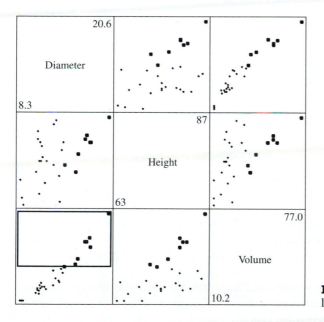

Figure 8.7   Scatterplot array with larger *V* values highlighted.

3. Interactions. When looking for evidence of interaction in data, it is well to remember the plots of Figure 8.1. In an additive model, represented by the right-hand plot, the lines relating the expected response to one predictor (here, H) formed by holding the other predictor (here, D) constant, are parallel as the second predictor (here, D) is varied. In a model with interaction, represented by the left plot, both slope and intercept vary.

The corresponding plots in a scatterplot array are those for which a brush isolates a narrow range of values of one predictor (this is like holding that predictor fixed), while the pattern of the response versus the other predictor is observed (this is like one of the lines in Figure 8.1). As the brush is moved, selecting different values of the one predictor, the changing patterns relating the response to the other predictor are like the set of lines in Figure 8.1: changing intercepts, but parallel slopes indicate an additive model; simultaneously changing intercepts and slopes indicate a model with interaction. Curved patterns of association indicate nonlinear terms in the model.

The changing slope and intercept that you have observed between V and H for different levels of D is an example of an interaction between D and H in their association with the response V. An additive relation between V and both D and H would have been indicated on the scatterplot array if, as the brush was moved isolating different D values, lines with differing intercepts but common slopes summarized the relation between V and H.

The horizontal brush also reveals something about the interaction of D and H. Consider the additive model (8.9). The contour we get when we look at all D and H values giving expected response equal to a constant value C is

$$C = -57.99 + 4.71D + 0.34H$$

which is a line in D and H. In general, if an additive model is appropriate for a set of data, the contours obtained using a horizontal brush should appear linear.

On the other hand, consider the model with interaction (8.14). A contour corresponding to expected response C satisfies

$$C = 69.40 - 5.86D - 1.30H + 0.13DH$$

which is nonlinear in D and H. The contours of a nonadditive model are nonlinear. In general, if a nonadditive model is appropriate for a set of data, the contours obtained using a horizontal brush should appear nonlinear.

One final word about scatterplot arrays. A scatterplot array is more than a collection of scatterplots. Because the axes of the scatterplots are shared, features on the graphs can be **visually linked,** revealing more about the structure of the data. This linking is done by scanning a single row or column of the array. This is the reason for the redundant scatterplots; if only the upper triangle of the array were

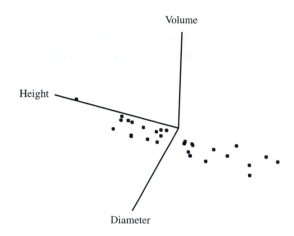

Figure 8.8   3-D plot of tree data.

displayed, your eye would have to make a right turn to visually link all scatterplots for a given variable. Visual linking is particularly effective at finding associations among many variables.

Visual linking is most effective when there are many variables plotted in a scatterplot array. The scatterplot array you are looking at is sufficiently small that visual linking provides minimal benefit above what we have already seen: that D and H are both positively associated with each other and with V, so large values of each go with large values of the other two variables and small values go with small values.

3-D Plots

Three-dimensional plots are another tool that can be used to visualize the relation among three variables at a time. For the tree data, the plot displays one variable on each axis, allowing you to see V as a function of D and H. Effective use of a 3-D plot depends on viewing it from different perspectives. This is best done if the plot can be rotated on the computer screen. If you don't have software that will rotate the plot, another option is to create a number of different static views from different perspectives. Because this kind of plot relies so heavily on what you see when it is viewed from different perspectives, Figure 8.8 can give only an inadequate idea of its power.

What you will see after viewing the 3-D plot of the tree data from different perspectives, is that though there is some curvature apparent, the cluster of data points seems to lie nearly on a plane. If the data lie on a plane, an additive model is suggested. If not, a nonadditive model is appropriate. The question is whether the curvature is severe enough to suggest a nonadditive model.

To answer this question, we need to learn to fit a multiple regression model and to evaluate that fit.   ✦

8.6

FITTING THE MULTIPLE LINEAR REGRESSION MODEL

For specific applications, such as interpreting the response surface, it will often be convenient to write a multiple linear regression model as a function of the predictors $Z_1, \ldots, Z_p$, as we do with models (8.3) and (8.4). When referring to multiple linear regression models in general, however, it will often be necessary to refer to model (8.1). If so, to keep notation simple, we will often drop the explicit dependence of the regressors X_i on the predictors Z_j, so that model (8.1) is written only in terms of the regressors:

$$Y = \beta_0 + \beta_1 X_1 + \beta_2 X_2 + \cdots + \beta_q X_q + \epsilon \qquad (8.19)$$

Assume the data are $\{(Y_i, X_{i1}, X_{i2}, \ldots, X_{iq}), i = 1, \ldots, n\}$. This means that we assume response i is generated by

$$Y_i = \beta_0 + \beta_1 X_{i1} + \beta_2 X_{i2} + \cdots + \beta_q X_{iq} + \epsilon_i$$

We will make the usual assumption that the random error terms ϵ_i are n independent draws from an $N(0, \sigma^2)$ distribution. In order to completely specify multiple linear regression model (8.19) with normal errors, we need to know $q + 2$ **parameters:** $\beta_0, \beta_1, \ldots, \beta_q$, and σ^2. Fitting a regression model consists of estimating these parameters.

Throughout this chapter, we will use least squares as the fitting criterion, although we could just as easily use some other criterion such as the SAE criterion (see Chapter 7). The least squares estimators of $\beta_0, \beta_1, \ldots, \beta_q$ in model (8.19) are those values, of $b_0, b_1, \ldots, b_q$, denoted $\hat{\beta}_0, \hat{\beta}_1, \ldots, \hat{\beta}_q$, which minimize

$$\text{SSE}(b_0, b_1, \ldots, b_q) = \sum_{i=1}^{n} [Y_i - (b_0 + b_1 X_{i1} + b_2 X_{i2} + \cdots + b_q X_{iq})]^2$$

The **fitted values** are

$$\hat{Y}_i = \hat{\beta}_0 + \hat{\beta}_1 X_{i1} + \hat{\beta}_2 X_{i2} + \cdots + \hat{\beta}_q X_{iq} \qquad (8.20)$$

The **residuals** $\{e_i, i = 1, \ldots, n\}$ are

$$e_i = Y_i - \hat{Y}_i = Y_i - (\hat{\beta}_0 + \hat{\beta}_1 X_{i1} + \hat{\beta}_2 X_{i2} + \cdots + \hat{\beta}_q X_{iq}) \qquad (8.21)$$

The error variance σ^2 is estimated (as it was for simple linear regression) by the mean square error

$$\text{MSE} = \frac{\displaystyle\sum_{i=1}^{n} e_i^2}{n - q - 1}$$

The divisor $n - q - 1$ is the **degrees of freedom** associated with the MSE. The degrees of freedom counts the minimum number of residuals that need to be specified to compute MSE (recall the discussion of degrees of freedom in Chapter 7).

EXAMPLE 8.2   CONTINUED

We will fit two models for the tree data. The first is the model with linear and interaction terms:

$$V = \beta_0 + \beta_1 D + \beta_2 H + \beta_3 DH + \epsilon \tag{8.22}$$

The second is the additive model:

$$V = \beta_0 + \beta_1 D + \beta_2 H + \epsilon \tag{8.23}$$

We begin by denoting the 31 data values

$$
\begin{array}{ccc}
V_1 & D_1 & H_1 \\
V_2 & D_2 & H_2 \\
\vdots & \vdots & \vdots \\
V_{31} & D_{31} & H_{31}
\end{array}
$$

Fitting Model (8.22)

The **least squares estimators** of $\beta_0, \beta_1, \beta_2$, and β_3 in model (8.22) are those values $\hat{\beta}_0, \hat{\beta}_1, \hat{\beta}_2$, and $\hat{\beta}_3$ that minimize

$$\text{SSE}(b_0, b_1, b_2, b_3) = \sum_{i=1}^{31}[V_i - (b_0 + b_1 D_i + b_2 H_i + b_3 D_i H_i)]^2$$

The **fitted values** are

$$\hat{V}_i = \hat{\beta}_0 + \hat{\beta}_1 D_i + \hat{\beta}_2 H_i + \hat{\beta}_3 D_i H_i$$

The **residuals** $\{e_i, i = 1, \ldots, 31\}$ are

$$e_i = V_i - \hat{V}_i = V_i - (\hat{\beta}_0 + \hat{\beta}_1 D_i + \hat{\beta}_2 H_i + \hat{\beta}_3 D_i H_i)$$

The error variance σ^2 is estimated by

$$\text{MSE} = \frac{\displaystyle\sum_{i=1}^{31} e_i^2}{27}$$

The MSE has 27 degrees of freedom.

The simplest way to fit model (8.22) using a computer package is to first create a new variable $DH = D \cdot H$, and then fit the model with D, H, and DH.

The least squares estimates for model (8.22) are $\hat{\beta}_0 = 69.40$, $\hat{\beta}_1 = -5.86$, $\hat{\beta}_2 = -1.30$, and $\hat{\beta}_3 = 0.13$, so that the fitted model is[7]

$$\hat{V} = 69.40 - 5.86D - 1.30H + 0.13DH$$

The estimate of σ^2, $\hat{\sigma}^2$ (the MSE), equals 7.34.

Fitting Model (8.23)

Similar results hold for the additive model (8.23). The **least squares estimators** of β_0, β_1, and β_2 in model (8.23) are those values $\hat{\beta}_0$, $\hat{\beta}_1$, and $\hat{\beta}_2$ that minimize

$$\text{SSE}(b_0, b_1, b_2) = \sum_{i=1}^{31} [V_i - (b_0 + b_1 D_i + b_2 H_i)]^2$$

The **fitted values** are

$$\hat{V}_i = \hat{\beta}_0 + \hat{\beta}_1 D_i + \hat{\beta}_2 H_i$$

The **residuals** $\{e_i, i = 1, \ldots, 31\}$ are defined as

$$e_i = V_i - \hat{V}_i = V_i - (\hat{\beta}_0 + \hat{\beta}_1 D_i + \hat{\beta}_2 H_i)$$

The error variance σ^2 is estimated by the mean square error

$$\text{MSE} = \frac{\displaystyle\sum_{i=1}^{31} e_i^2}{28}$$

The MSE has 28 degrees of freedom.

We obtain the least squares estimates $\hat{\beta}_1 = -57.99$, $\hat{\beta}_1 = 4.71$, $\hat{\beta}_2 = 0.34$, so that the fitted model is

$$\hat{V} = -57.99 + 4.71D + 0.34H$$

The estimate of the error variance is $\hat{\sigma}^2 = 15.07$. ✦

Appendix 8.1 at the end of this chapter presents vector-matrix formulas for fitting the multiple linear regression model.

[7]This is model (8.14), which we "borrowed" earlier for illustrative purposes.

8.7

ASSESSING MODEL FIT

Once a model has been fit to a set of data, the next task is to evaluate that fit. If the model is judged a reasonable fit to the data, we may go on to use the model for description of the underlying phenomenon being modeled, or for prediction of the response at specified values of the predictors.

Residual Analysis

As with simple linear regression, residuals are the primary quantities for evaluating the quality of a multiple linear regression fit and plots of residuals are the primary tools that we use.

There are at least two reasons we look at the residuals to tell us how the model fits:

- The residuals are "stand-ins" for the (unobservable) random errors ϵ_i. To see this, suppose we are considering model (8.19). That is, we are assuming that the ith response, Y_i, is generated by the equation

$$Y_i = \beta_0 + \beta_1 X_{i1} + \beta_2 X_{i2} + \cdots + \beta_q X_{iq} + \epsilon_i$$

where the ϵ_i are independent $N(0, \sigma^2)$. Once we fit the model, we have

$$Y_i = \hat{\beta}_0 + \hat{\beta}_1 X_{i1} + \hat{\beta}_2 X_{i2} + \ldots + \hat{\beta}_q X_{iq} + e_i$$

where the e_i are the residuals. Here, the $\hat{\beta}$'s are our best guesses of the unobservable β's and the residuals are our best guesses of the unobservable ϵ_i's. If we want to know what the ϵ_i's are like, we look at the residuals.
- The residuals act like a microscope to focus our attention on the departures of the data from the assumed model. When we look at the residuals, we see only the patterns that have not been explained by the model. If the model fits well, there should be no strong patterns. If there are strong patterns, the form of those patterns can tell us how we have to modify the model. In order to detect these patterns, we should plot the residuals in as many different ways as make sense.

Studentized Residuals

Recall the discussion of Studentized residuals from fits of the simple linear regression model in Chapter 7. Studentized residuals are defined in exactly the same way for the multiple regression model: the ith Studentized residual is the ith ordinary residual divided by its estimated standard error. As in Chapter 7, the quantities we call Studentized residuals are known as externally Studentized residuals because observation i is not used in computing the estimated standard error of residual i.

Quantile Plots for Studentized Residuals.   If the model is correct, the Studentized residuals will have a t_{n-q-2} distribution. For quantile plots, we suggest that you use only Studentized residuals and plot them versus t_{n-q-2} quantiles. If $n - q - 2$ is large, or if it is difficult to produce quantiles of the t distribution, a normal quantile plot of the Studentized residuals is an acceptable alternative.

Detecting Outliers with Studentized Residuals.   Studentized residuals are useful in identifying outliers. As a rule of thumb, Studentized residuals larger than 2 in absolute value should be investigated as possible outliers. Boxplots of Studentized residuals are also useful in identifying possible outliers.

Investigation of Outliers

As you know from previous chapters, it is bad science and bad practice to discard outliers out of hand. A cause should be sought before they are removed. If no cause

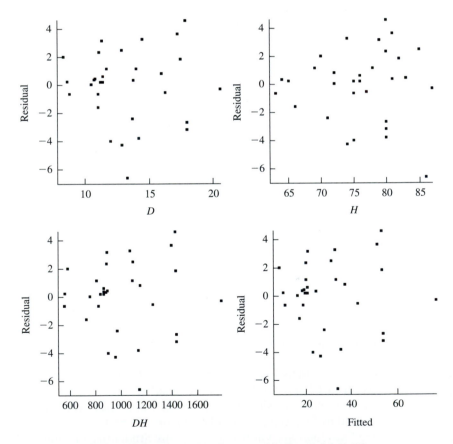

Figure 8.9   Plots of ordinary residuals, model (8.22).

is found, then the analysis should be conducted with and without the outliers and the results compared. If the results are substantially the same, then some confidence can be placed in the model. If the results are substantially different, then a decision must be made as to whether the outlier is a spurious observation or is a legitimate feature of the underlying phenomenon that the model fails to capture. This usually involves one or more of digging deeper into how the data were taken, learning more about the theory behind the phenomenon under investigation, or taking more data.

EXAMPLE 8.2   CONTINUED

We analyze the residuals from the fits of models (8.22) and (8.23).

1. **Model (8.22).** Figures 8.9 and 8.10, respectively, show plots of the ordinary and Studentized residuals versus D, H, DH, and the fitted values. Figure 8.11 is a quantile plot of the Studentized residuals versus t_{26} quantiles.

   The plots versus the predictor variables are essentially the same for both the ordinary and Studentized residual plots. All reveal one potential outlier: observation 18 with a Studentized residual of -2.99. Whether

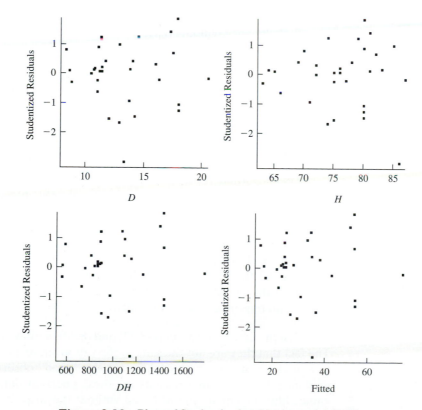

Figure 8.10   Plots of Studentized residuals, model (8.22).

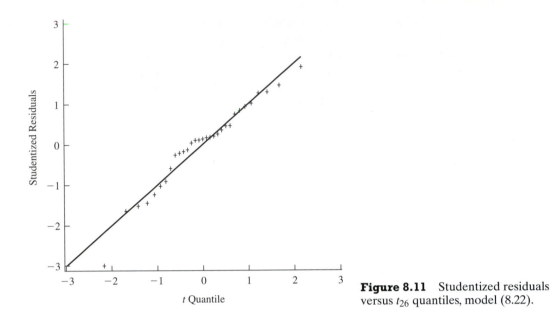

Figure 8.11   Studentized residuals versus t_{26} quantiles, model (8.22).

including or excluding that suspect observation, there are no strong patterns in these residual plots. The same is true of the plots versus the fitted values.

The t quantile plot also shows the potential outlier clearly. The rest of the plot shows no compelling reason to suspect nonnormality.

All in all, except for the potential outlier, the residuals show an adequate fit for model (8.22).

2. **Model (8.23).** For this additive model, the plots of the ordinary and Studentized residuals are similar in all cases, so we display only the latter. The plots are found in Figure 8.12. Note that we have plotted the studentized residuals versus normal, rather than t quantiles. Because the degrees of freedom, 28, is reasonably large, both normal and t quantile plots should look similar.

All plots show one potential outlier: observation 31 with a Studentized residual of 2.77. The plots versus H show no patterns, but the plots versus the fitted values and D show the residuals clumped into four or five isolated clusters. Further, the clusters with the smallest residuals are located near the central fitted and D values while those with the largest residuals are located near the extremes. Except for the suspect observation, the normal plot gives us no reason to doubt normality.

For the fits of both models (8.22) and (8.23), we have found potential outliers. The fact that they are not the same observation shows just how crucial the choice of a model is in determining which are the "good" observations. As we have no guidance in determining reasons for these aberrant data values, we have little choice but to compare fits with and without the suspect observations, and hope that there is little difference.

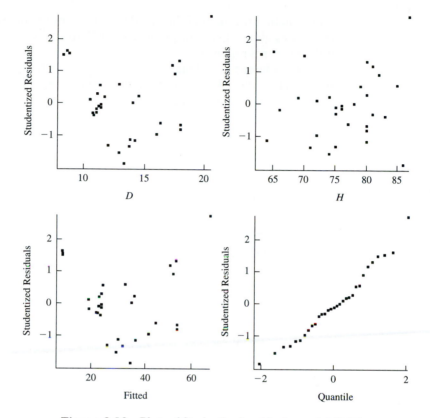

Figure 8.12 Plots of Studentized residuals, model (8.23).

TABLE 8.1   Effect of Outliers on Parameter Estimates

Parameter	Model (8.22)		Model (8.23)	
	With outlier	Without outlier	With outlier	Without outlier
β_0	69.40	65.06	−57.99	−52.24
β_1	−5.86	−6.01	4.71	4.48
β_2	−1.30	−1.22	0.34	0.30
β_3	0.13	0.14	—	—
σ^2	7.34	5.67	15.07	12.18

Table 8.1 compares the parameters fitted with and without the potential outlier for each model.

The outliers do not seem to make much of a difference in the estimates of the β's. However, they have a greater impact on the variance estimates. This implies for both models that although the form of the fitted model is roughly the same whether the outlier is included or not, the precision with which we can make inferences about that fit or predictions of future observations is markedly lower if the outlier is retained.

The clumps of residuals correspond to trees having similar diameters. This suggests that the relationship between volume and diameter may be more complicated than the additive model can capture. ✦

Vector-matrix formulas for fitted values, residuals, standard errors of residuals, and Studentized residuals are presented in Appendix 8.1 at the end of this chapter.

8.8

INTERPRETATION OF THE FITTED MODEL

The fitted model may be written

$$\hat{Y} = \hat{\beta}_0 + \hat{\beta}_1 X_1(Z_1, Z_2, \ldots, Z_p)$$
$$+ \hat{\beta}_2 X_2(Z_1, Z_2, \ldots, Z_p) + \cdots + \hat{\beta}_q X_q(Z_1, Z_2, \ldots, Z_p) \tag{8.24}$$

As it was for the simple linear regression model in Chapter 7, $\hat{Y}$ is called the predicted value of Y. The predicted value serves as our estimator of the response surface. If we wish to regard the response surface as a function of the regressors, then we may write $\hat{Y}$ as a function of the regressors:

$$\hat{Y}(X_1 = x_1, X_2 = x_2, \ldots, X_q = x_q) = \hat{\beta}_0 + \hat{\beta}_1 x_1 + \hat{\beta}_2 x_2 + \cdots + \hat{\beta}_q x_q$$

If we wish to regard the response surface as a function of the predictors, then we may write $\hat{Y}$ as a function of the predictors:

$$\hat{Y}(Z_1 = z_1, Z_2 = z_2, \ldots, Z_q = z_q)$$
$$= \hat{\beta}_0 + \hat{\beta}_1 X_1(z_1, z_2, \ldots, z_p) + \hat{\beta}_2 X_2(z_1, z_2, \ldots, z_p) + \cdots + \hat{\beta}_q X_q(z_1, z_2, \ldots, z_p)$$

In either case, the estimated response surface $\hat{Y}(X_1 = x_1, X_2 = x_2, \ldots, X_q = x_q)$ may be interpreted exactly as the the actual response surface $E(Y \mid X_1 = x_1, X_2 = x_2, \ldots, X_q = x_q)$ was interpreted in Section 8.3, and the estimated response surface $\hat{Y}(Z_1 = z_1, Z_2 = z_2, \ldots, Z_q = z_q)$ may be interpreted exactly as the the actual response surface $E(Y \mid Z_1 = z_1, Z_2 = z_2, \ldots, Z_p = z_p)$ was.

As it is for the SLR model, the fitted intercept, $\hat{\beta}_0$, is interpreted as the expected response when the X_i all take the value 0, *provided*

- it is meaningful for the $X_i, i = 1, \ldots, q$, to all equal 0, and
- the value 0 for all X_i is within the range of the data.

Otherwise, the fitted intercept has no interpretation of its own.

EXAMPLE 8.2   CONTINUED

Including the outliers (we've no reason to omit them), fitted model (8.22) is

$$\hat{V} = 69.40 - 5.86D - 1.30H + 0.13DH \tag{8.25}$$

which is exactly the response surface (8.15) analyzed in Section 8.3. Similarly, fitted model (8.23) is

$$\hat{V} = -57.99 + 4.71D + 0.34H \tag{8.26}$$

which is exactly the response surface (8.10) also analyzed in Section 8.3. In each case, the interpretation of the fitted response surfaces is exactly the same as the interpretation of the response surfaces given in Section 8.3.

We have fit two models and evaluated the fits. If we must choose between these two models, which should we choose? There is little doubt that model (8.25) is the better fit, since

- the residual plots are better for model (8.25).
- the residual variance, MSE, is substantially smaller for model (8.25) (7.34 versus 15.07). This means model (8.25) will give better precision in inference.

But just because model (8.25) is better than model (8.26) doesn't mean that it is as good a model as we can fit. The question now is, can we do better?   ◆

8.9

THEORY-BASED MODELING

We have just specified, fit and analyzed two models for the tree data. In the case of the model (8.25), specification was done empirically, with the assistance of visualization tools such as scatterplot arrays and 3-D plots. Model (8.26) was fit mainly for comparison purposes.

As we know, there is another way to specify a model. Theory-based model specification uses theoretical considerations or knowledge about the relationship between response and predictors to specify the model.

The next example will illustrate how we might use theoretical knowledge to construct another model for the tree data.

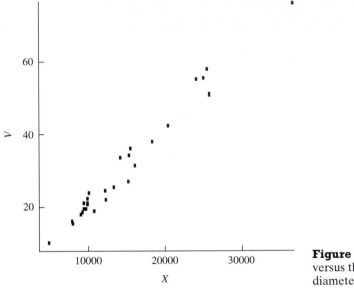

Figure 8.13 Plot of tree volume versus the product of height and diameter squared.

EXAMPLE 8.2   CONTINUED

We know that the volume of a right circular cylinder is proportional to the product of the square of its diameter and its height. It would seem logical that tree volumes follow something like this formula. That is, we would expect tree volume to approximately follow the relation (recall that D is in inches)

$$V = \pi(D/24)^2 H = 0.0055 D^2 H \tag{8.27}$$

Is our intuition reasonable? To find out, we plot V versus $X = D^2 H$. Figure 8.13 shows this plot for the tree data. Clearly, the association is linear, and leads us to propose the model

$$V = \beta_0 + \beta_1 X + \epsilon \tag{8.28}$$

where $X = D^2 H$.

Output for the least squares fit of model (8.28) is shown in Figure 8.14. The fitted model has equation

$$\hat{V} = -0.2977 + 0.0021 X \tag{8.29}$$

which does not look very close to Equation (8.27). The plot of residuals versus the fitted values shows that the residuals are located away from 0 for the larger fitted values, but otherwise reveals no pattern. The plot of the studentized residuals

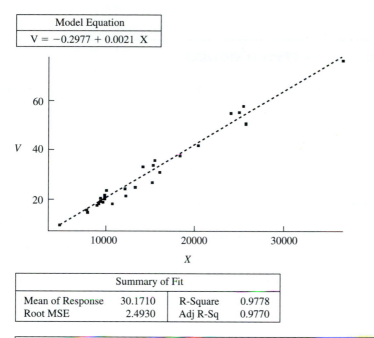

Model Equation
$V = -0.2977 + 0.0021\ X$

Summary of Fit			
Mean of Response	30.1710	R-Square	0.9778
Root MSE	2.4930	Adj R-Sq	0.9770

Parameter Estimates							
Variable	DF	Estimate	Std Error	T Stat	Prob > |T|	Tolerance	Var Inflation
INTERCEPT	1	−0.2977	0.9636	−0.3089	0.7596		0
X	1	0.0021	5.949E-05	35.7109	0.0001	1.0000	1.0000

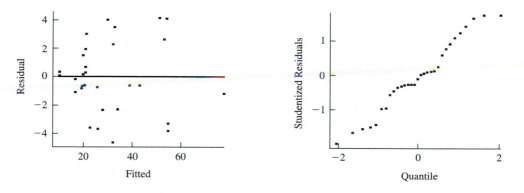

Figure 8.14   Summary of least squares fit of model (8.28).

versus the quantiles of the t_{29} distribution show some interesting, but not extreme, patterns. Neither plot shows evidence of an outlier.

The MSE for model (8.29) is 6.22, which is better than the MSE of 7.34 from model (8.25) and much better than the MSE of 15.07 from model (8.26).

Overall, we conclude that model (8.29) is preferred to the other two.   ✦

8.10

COMPARISON OF FITTED MODELS

Often, when building regression models, we may want to compare one model with another. We did this in Example 8.2 in which we compared models (8.25), (8.26), and (8.29). In that comparison, we concluded that model (8.29) was preferred because its residual plots indicate a satisfactory fit and because the residual variance, MSE, is smaller for model (8.29), which means model (8.29) will give better precision in inference.

Comparisons of models may be based on other considerations as well. Ultimately, any comparison must depend on the use to which the model will be put. If description of the phenomenon is the most important consideration (e.g., if we want some explanation of the biology or geometry of cherry trees), then model simplicity and interpretability may be primary considerations. Additionally, the proportion of data variability the model accounts for may be important. On the other hand, perhaps prediction of future observations is of primary importance. Then accuracy and precision of prediction will be most important.

The Principle of Parsimony

If we are using the model to describe or explain a phenomenon, there is a general principle called the **principle of parsimony,** or **Occam's razor,** which may be stated as follows:

THE PRINCIPLE OF PARSIMONY

Of all explanations for a phenomenon that perform equally well, the simplest is the best.

In statistical modeling, the phenomenon is represented by the data and the explanation is the model. The simplest explanation is most often (but not always) the model having the fewest parameters.

EXAMPLE 8.2   CONTINUED

Since model (8.29) has only two β's to estimate, the principle of parsimony argues that, all other considerations being equal, it will be preferred to models (8.25) and (8.26), which have four and three β's to estimate, respectively.   ◆

The Coefficient of Multiple Determination

Recall that in Chapter 7, you studied the coefficient of determination, r^2, a numerical measure of the quality of fit for a simple linear regression model. For the multiple linear regression model, there is an analogous quantity called the **coefficient of multiple determination,** denoted R^2. R^2 has the same formula as r^2 did in the simple linear regression case:

$$R^2 = \frac{\text{SSR}}{\text{SSTO}} = 1 - \frac{\text{SSE}}{\text{SSTO}}$$

where the total sum of squares, $\text{SSTO} = \sum_{i=1}^{n}(Y_i - \bar{Y})^2$; the error sum of squares, $\text{SSE} = \sum_{i=1}^{n} e_i^2$; and the regression sum of squares, $\text{SSR} = \text{SSTO} - \text{SSE}$.

As with r^2, R^2 can be interpreted in two ways that sound different, but that really amount to the same thing:

- R^2 is the proportionate reduction in the uncertainty of predicting the response in the data set due to using the regression model to predict.
- R^2 is the proportion of the total variation in the response explained by the regression model.

R^2 is a measure of the goodness of model fit in the sense that it measures the proportion of total variation the model explains. As was the case with r^2 for simple linear regression, it takes on values in the interval $[0, 1]$, with higher values indicating a higher proportion of variation explained by the model.

EXAMPLE 8.2   CONTINUED

The R^2 value for model (8.25) is 0.9756. The R^2 value for model (8.29) is 0.9778.

The first interpretation of R^2 then tells us that by using D, H, and their product in model (8.25), we have reduced the uncertainty of predicting V by 97.56%. Can you give a similar interpretation for R^2 for model (8.29)?

The second interpretation tells us that 97.56% of the variation in V is explained by fitted model (8.25). A similar interpretation holds for model (8.29). As both models have similar R^2 values, there is little basis for choosing one over the other based on this measure alone. ✦

R^2 as a Correlation

Recall that for the simple linear regression model, r^2 equals the square of the Pearson correlation between the response and the predictor. In the multiple linear regression model, R^2 has a similar interpretation: It is the square of the Pearson correlation between the response, Y, and the fitted value, $\hat{Y}$.

Comparing Models with Responses in Different Units

Since R^2 measures the goodness of model fit as a proportion of variation, it can be useful in comparing models in which the response is measured in different units. In comparing models (8.25) and (8.29), we compared residual plots and MSEs. These comparisons make sense if responses of the models being compared are in the same units. If the responses are in different units, such comparisons may not be sensible. Comparisons of the MSEs make little sense if the responses are in different units. Comparisons of the residuals might or might not make sense depending on what we are looking for. If we look at residual plots of the different models in order to find general patterns, for example, then comparisons can make sense even for responses in different units. However, it makes little sense to compare sizes of the residuals. Using Studentized residuals instead of ordinary residuals alleviates these difficulties of comparison, but Studentized residuals are not in the original units of either model.

EXAMPLE 8.2   CONTINUED

An alternative to model (8.29) is a model additive in the predictors D and H. Such a model might produce a better fit, and might be easier to interpret in terms of the individual predictors. The natural way to change the product relation (8.27) to an additive relation is to take a logarithm of both sides. The base of the logarithm doesn't matter, but we'll assume the natural logarithm. The result is

$$\ln(V) = \ln(\pi) - 2 \ln(24) + 2 \ln(D) + \ln(H) \tag{8.30}$$

Relation (8.30) is a deterministic relation. That is, it assumes $\ln(V)$ can be computed exactly from D and H using (8.27). More in keeping with what might actually occur is the statistical relation obtained by adding a random error to relation (8.30):

$$\ln(V) = \ln(\pi) - 2 \ln(24) + 2 \ln(D) + \ln(H) + \epsilon \tag{8.31}$$

Relation (8.31) is a multiple linear regression model with $\beta_0 = \ln(\pi) - 2 \ln(24)$, $\beta_1 = 1$, and $\beta_2 = 2$. That is, the β parameters are already specified. Since we know that trees are not exact cylinders, a more flexible approach to modeling the relationship between tree volume and height and diameter is to regress $\ln(V)$ on $\ln(D)$ and $\ln(H)$. That is, instead of choosing $\beta_0 = \ln(\pi) - 2 \ln(24)$, $\beta_1 = 1$, and $\beta_2 = 2$, we will let the data choose the β's through a least squares fit. The model to be fit is

$$LV = \beta_0 + \beta_1 LD + \beta_2 LH + \epsilon \tag{8.32}$$

where we let LV, LD, and LH stand for the natural logarithms of V, D, and H, respectively.

Model Equation
LV $= -6.6316 + 1.9826$ LD $+ 1.1171$ LH

Summary of Fit			
Mean of Response	3.2727	R-Square	0.9777
Root MSE	0.0814	Adj R-Sq	0.9761

Parameter Estimates							
Variable	DF	Estimate	Std Error	T Stat	Prob > |T|	Tolerance	Var Inflation
INTERCEPT	1	-6.6316	0.7998	-8.2917	0.0001		0
LD	1	1.9826	0.0750	26.4316	0.0001	0.7189	1.3910
LH	1	1.1171	0.2044	5.4644	0.0001	0.7189	1.3910

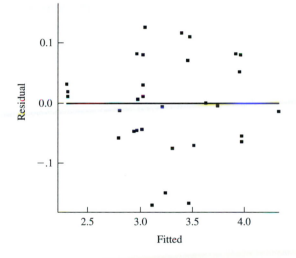

Figure 8.15   Regression of $\ln(V_i)$ on $\ln(D)$ and $\ln(H)$.

Figure 8.15 displays SAS/INSIGHT output from the least squares fit. The fitted model is

$$\widehat{LV} = -6.63 + 1.98LD + 1.12LH \qquad (8.33)$$

Since V is in cubic feet and LV is in log cubic feet, direct comparison of models (8.29) and (8.33) in terms of MSE, for example, is not possible. However, these models may be compared in terms of R^2, which quantifies explanatory power of a model as a proportion of the total variation in the response. The R^2 values of

0.9778 for model (8.29) and 0.9777 for model (8.33) are very close and give little reason to prefer one model to the other. ✦

The Adjusted Coefficient of Multiple Determination

One problem with R^2 is that it can always be increased by adding another regressor. For the tree data, for example, we can raise the R^2 of any of the models we have considered by including the weights of 31 college students as another regressor in the model! In fact, taken to its logical conclusion, if we based model selection only on R^2, we would try to include as many variables as possible in any model!

In response to this undesirable feature of R^2, a modified measure has been developed that adjusts R^2 for the number of variables in the model. Unlike R^2, which always increases as more variables are added, R_a^2, the **adjusted coefficient of multiple determination** can decrease if an additional regressor does not increase R^2 sufficiently. In this respect, R_a^2 can help us implement the principle of parsimony: When considering adding a regressor to a model, we can decide that we will add it only if doing so increases R_a^2; we can decide to remove a regressor already in a model if R_a^2 increases by doing so.

R_a^2 is given by the formula

$$R_a^2 = 1 - \frac{\text{SSE}/(n - q - 1)}{\text{SSTO}/(n - 1)}$$

For a given response and data set, any model that increases R_a^2 decreases MSE and vice versa. To see this, note that $\text{SSTO}/(n - 1)$ is just the sample variance, S^2, of the response, and so is a constant no matter which model is fit. Also, $\text{MSE} = \text{SSE}/(n - q - 1)$. Therefore,

$$R_a^2 = 1 - \frac{\text{MSE}}{S^2}$$

EXAMPLE 8.2 CONTINUED

The R^2 values for the fits of models (8.25) and (8.29) to V and model (8.33) to $\ln(V)$ are 0.9756, 0.9778, and 0.9777, respectively. The corresponding R_a^2 values are 0.9728, 0.9770, and 0.9761, respectively. Although the R^2 values are very close for models (8.29) and (8.33), their R_a^2 values are not quite as close. This is because the fit of model (8.29) required only one regressor to attain virtually the same R^2 that the fit of model (8.33) attained with two regressors. Nevertheless, the R^2 and R_a^2 values are high for all three models, and their differences among the three models are small.

The higher R_a^2 of model (8.29) compared to that of model (8.25) coincides with its lower MSE: 6.215 versus 7.336. Because it is in different units, the MSE for model (8.33) is not comparable to those for models (8.25) and (8.29). ✦

8.11

ANALYSIS OF VARIANCE

Analysis of variance, or **ANOVA,** is a technique for analyzing the total variation in the response in terms of how much of that variation can be attributed to knowledge of the regressors and how much is unexplainable by the model.

Sums of Squares

As we saw in Chapter 7 and in the discussion of R^2 and R_a^2, the total variation in the response is SSTO, the amount of that variation that is explained by the regression is SSR, and the amount left unexplained is SSE. Thus, the total variation is partitioned into variation explained by the regression and variation unexplained by the regression:

$$SSTO = SSR + SSE$$

Degrees of Freedom

Each sum of squares has associated with it an integer called its **degrees of freedom.** You may recall this term from Chapter 7.

Each sum of squares is a sum of squared terms. The degrees of freedom for a sum of squares is the minimum number of those terms needed to compute the sum of squares. The degrees of freedom for SSTO is $n - 1$, because we need to know only $n - 1$ of the quantities $Y_i - \bar{Y}$ in order to compute SSTO.

The degrees of freedom for SSR is q and the degrees of freedom for SSE is $n - q - 1$. Notice that the degrees of freedom for SSR and SSE add up to the degrees of freedom for SSTO.

When taking means (i.e., averages) of a sums of squares, we divide that sum of squares by its degrees of freedom rather than the number of original data. The resulting mean is called a **mean square.** The mean squares for regression and error are denoted MSR and MSE. A total mean square is usually not computed.

The ANOVA Table

The sums of squares, degrees of freedom, and mean squares from a multiple linear regression fit are summarized in an ANOVA table. ANOVA tables constructed in SAS/INSIGHT have the form shown in Table 8.2. Tables constructed using other statistical computer software will be similar.

TABLE 8.2   Analysis of Variance Table, Model (8.19)

			Analysis of variance		
Source	DF	Sum of squares	Mean square	F Stat	Prob > F
Model	q	SSR	MSR	F = MSR/MSE	p-value
Error	$n - q - 1$	SSE	MSE		
C Total	$n - 1$	SSTO			

TABLE 8.3   Analysis of Variance Table, Model (8.25)

			Analysis of variance		
Source	DF	Sum of squares	Mean square	F Stat	Prob > F
Model	3	7908.0053	2636.0018	359.3122	0.0001
Error	27	198.0786	7.3362		
C Total	30	8106.0839			

EXAMPLE 8.2   CONTINUED

For the tree data,

$$\text{SSTO} = \sum_{i=1}^{31}(V_i - \bar{V})^2 = 8106.0839$$

Suppose we have fit the multiple linear regression model (8.25). Then

$$\text{SSR} = 7908.0053 \qquad \text{and} \qquad \text{SSE} = 198.0786$$

Since there are $n = 31$ observations and $q = 3$ regressors, the degrees of freedom for SSTO, SSR, and SSE are $31 - 1 = 30; 3;$ and $31 - 3 - 1 = 27$, respectively. Thus, the mean squares are MSR = SSR/3 = 2636.0018 and MSE = SSE/27 = 198.0786, respectively. These results are shown in Table 8.3.

From this table, we can also obtain R^2 in two ways:

- $R^2 = (\text{SSTO} - \text{SSE})/\text{SSTO} = (8106.08 - 198.08)/8106.08 = 0.9756$
- $R^2 = \text{SSR}/\text{SSTO} = 7908.00/8106.08 = 0.9756$ ◆

8.12

INFERENCE FOR THE REGRESSION MODEL

By analyzing the decomposition of the total variation into SSR and SSE, and by looking at MSR and MSE, we can tell if the regression model is explaining enough of the variation in the responses to justify using the model as a predictor of the response.

We will consider two kinds of hypotheses about the regression model. The first asks whether the regression model explains a significant proportion of the variation in the response. The second is asked only if we conclude that the regression model is worthwhile. If it is, then we want to know if all regressors are making a substantial contribution to the model or if some are making little contribution. And we want to know which regressors are doing which. Similar methods can tell us whether the data supply evidence that the model has a nonzero intercept.

We will also develop confidence intervals for the model coefficients (the β_i) and prediction intervals for both the mean response and a new observation at specified values of the regressors.

The F Test

We begin by asking whether there is evidence of a significant relation between the response and the regressors.

Suppose we are fitting the multiple linear regression model (8.19) to a data set, and suppose that this model is appropriate for the data. Then the hypothesis of no relation between the response and the regressors, of the type specified by the model, is

$$\beta_1 = \beta_2 = \cdots = \beta_q = 0$$

This, then, is H_0, the null hypothesis we wish to investigate. The alternative hypothesis, H_a, is that H_0 is not true: that is, that one or more of the β_i are nonzero:

$$H_0: \quad \beta_1 = \beta_2 = \cdots = \beta_q = 0$$

$$H_a: \quad \text{Not all the } \beta\text{'s are 0}$$

The appropriate test statistic for testing H_0 versus H_a is the ratio of mean square regression to mean square error: F = MSR/MSE. Though we have not explained the statistical theory underlying the choice of F, by considering how MSR and MSE behave, we can see that F will have different behavior under the null and alternative hypotheses. In particular, the more variation in the response the regressors explain, the larger SSR becomes and the smaller SSE becomes. This means that MSR becomes larger and MSE smaller, and therefore the quotient F becomes larger. Thus, small values of F support the null hypothesis and large values of F provide evidence against the null hypothesis and in favor of the alternative hypothesis.

If the null hypothesis is true (i.e., if $\beta_1 = \beta_2 = \cdots = \beta_q = 0$), then it can be shown that the sampling distribution of the ratio F is an **F distribution.** The F distribution is really a family of continuous distributions indexed by two parameters called degrees of freedom. Examples of the probability density functions of different F distributions are shown in Figure 8.16. The sampling distribution for F when the null hypothesis is true is an F distribution with the first parameter equal to the degrees of freedom associated with MSR, and the second parameter equal to the degrees of freedom associated with MSE. For model (8.19), the F ratio has an F distribution with q and $n - q - 1$ degrees of freedom (written $F_{q,n-q-1}$) if the null hypothesis is true.

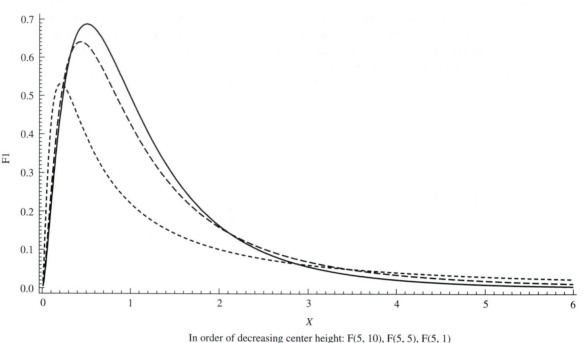

In order of decreasing center height: F(5, 10), F(5, 5), F(5, 1)

Figure 8.16   F distributions.

As in all hypothesis testing, we begin by assuming the null hypothesis is true, and then quantify the evidence in the data against H_0 and in favor of H_a in the form of a p-value. Since large values of the F ratio supply evidence against H_0 and in favor of H_a, the p-value is the proportion of all values from the appropriate F distribution that exceed the observed F ratio (i.e., the F ratio computed from the data). The smaller the p-value, the stronger the evidence against H_0 and in favor of H_a. The value of the F statistic and its p-value are displayed in the ANOVA table as Table 8.2 shows.

EXAMPLE 8.2   CONTINUED

For model (8.25) and the tree data, the F ratio (shown in the ANOVA table, Table 8.3) is 359.31, and the p-value, in the column labeled "Prob>F," is 0.0001.[8] What this means is that if the null hypothesis is true, then the chance of observing an F ratio of 359.31 or larger is no greater than 0.0001 (in fact, as the footnote explains, it is far less in this case). This is a very small chance indeed, and we must conclude that there is some relation between the response and the regressors: that is, not all of β_1, β_2, or β_3 are 0.   ◆

---

[8]Actually, whenever the p-value is less than or equal to 0.0001, the SAS statistical software that constructed this table gives its value as value 0.0001. For this example, the true p-value is considerably smaller than 0.0001.

To summarize:

THE OVERALL F TEST FOR THE REGRESSION MODEL

- **The Model.** Model (8.19).
- **The Hypotheses.**

$$H_0: \quad \beta_1 = \beta_2 = \cdots = \beta_q = 0$$

$$H_a: \quad \text{Not } H_0$$

- **The Test Statistic.** $F = \text{MSR}/\text{MSE}$
- **The p-Value.** $P(F_{q,n-q-1} \geq f^*)$, where $F_{q,n-q-1}$ is a random variable from an $F_{q,n-q-1}$ distribution and f^* is the observed value of the test statistic.

Individual t Tests

Suppose we have conducted the F test for overall significance of the regression model. If the p-value of the test is not small enough, we will conclude that there is insufficient evidence of a relation between the response and predictors postulated by the model being tested. Among our options are then to quit and report the results, to take more data and try again with the same model, or to reformulate the model.

   If, on the other hand, the p-value is small enough to conclude that the model is, as a whole, a statistically significant predictor of the response, we will want to learn more about the nature of the model. In particular, we will next want to know which of the regressors in the model are statistically significant predictors of the response.

   It can be shown that for the multiple linear regression model

$$T = \frac{\hat{\beta}_i - \beta_i}{\hat{\sigma}(\hat{\beta}_i)} \tag{8.34}$$

has a t_{n-q-1} distribution. Here $\hat{\sigma}(\hat{\beta}_i)$ is the estimated standard error of $\hat{\beta}_i$.

   This fact enables us to evaluate the statistical significance of each regressor in the model. In hypothesis-testing terms, we want to test the null hypothesis $H_0: \beta_i = 0$ versus the alternative hypothesis $H_a: \beta_i \neq 0$. By (8.34), we know that if H_0 is true (i.e., $\beta_i = 0$), then

$$T = \frac{\hat{\beta}_i}{\hat{\sigma}(\hat{\beta}_i)} \tag{8.35}$$

has a t_{n-q-1} distribution. If t^* is the observed value of T, the p-value for this test is obtained by computing the area under the t_{n-q-1} curve above $|t^*|$ and below $-|t^*|$. We

TABLE 8.4   Parameter Estimate Table, Model (8.25)

		Parameter estimates					
Variable	DF	Estimate	Std Error	T Stat	Prob > |T|	Tolerance	Var inflation
INTERCEPT	1	69.3963	23.8358	2.9114	0.0071	.	0
D	1	−5.8558	1.9213	−3.0478	0.0051	0.0067	148.6615
H	1	−1.2971	0.3098	−4.1863	0.0003	0.0627	15.9388
DH	1	0.1347	0.0244	5.5238	0.0001	0.0047	210.9730

need to look at both positive and negative values of T that are large in magnitude since the alternative hypothesis is two-sided.

EXAMPLE 8.2   CONTINUED

Consider model (8.25) for the tree data. Previously, using the F test, we found that model (8.25) is, as a whole, a statistically significant predictor of V. We next want to know which of the regressors are statistically significant predictors of V.

Turn your attention now to Table 8.4, which is a copy of a table produced by SAS/INSIGHT in fitting model (8.25) and which summarizes information about the parameter estimates.

In Table 8.4, the column "Estimate" displays $\hat{\beta}$, the column "Std. Error" displays $\hat{\sigma}(\hat{\beta})$, the column "T Stat" displays the t ratio (8.35), and the column labeled "Prob > $|T|$" displays the corresponding p-value for each parameter. Notice that these small p-values indicate statistical significance for all estimates.

One final point that cannot be made too strongly is that unless the regressors in the model are uncorrelated, individual t-tests will depend on which other regressors are in the model. For example, the individual t statistics for D and H in model (8.25) will differ from those for the same regressors for model (8.26). Since the interaction is correlated with both regressors, the inclusion of the interaction term changes the values of the t statistics for those regressors.   ✦

To summarize:

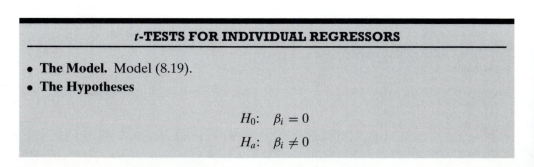

t-TESTS FOR INDIVIDUAL REGRESSORS

- **The Model.** Model (8.19).
- **The Hypotheses**

$$H_0: \quad \beta_i = 0$$

$$H_a: \quad \beta_i \neq 0$$

- **The Test Statistic.** $T = \hat{\beta}_i / \hat{\sigma}(\hat{\beta}_i)$
- **The p-Value.** $P(|t_{n-q-1}| > |t^*|)$, where t_{n-q-1} is a random variable from a t_{n-q-1} distribution and t^* is the observed value of the test statistic.

Confidence Intervals for Model Coefficients

If we wish to consider fixed-significance-level hypothesis tests (e.g., the 0.05 level of significance), the same information about which variables contribute significantly to the model, and more, can be obtained by calculating confidence intervals for the model coefficients.

For example, we can use (8.34) to calculate level L confidence intervals for β_i using the formula

$$(\hat{\beta}_i - \hat{\sigma}(\hat{\beta}_i)t_{n-q-1,(1+L)/2}, \ \hat{\beta}_i + \hat{\sigma}(\hat{\beta}_i)t_{n-q-1,(1+L)/2})$$

Not only do confidence intervals give a reasonable range of values for the parameters, but if a level L confidence interval does not contain 0, we can reject the null hypothesis that the parameter equals 0 at the $1 - L$ level of significance.

EXAMPLE 8.2   CONTINUED

Using the data in Table 8.4 for model (8.25) for the tree data, we calculate 95% confidence intervals for each parameter as (noting that $t_{27,0.975} = 2.052$):

Parameter	Estimate	$\hat{\sigma}(\hat{\beta}_i)$	95% Interval
Intercept	69.40	23.84	(20.48, 118.32)
D	−5.86	1.92	(−9.80, −1.92)
H	−1.30	0.31	(−1.94, −0.66)
DH	0.13	0.02	(0.09, 0.17)

These intervals give a range of values for the individual parameters. In addition, since the intervals for the intercept and all regressors do not contain 0, we conclude at the 0.05 level of significance that these variables contribute significantly to the model.   ✦

Estimating the Mean Response

Just as for the simple linear regression model, the mean response at specified values of the regressor variables

$$E(Y \mid X_1 = x_1, \ldots, X_q = x_q) = \beta_0 + \beta_1 x_1 + \cdots + \beta_q x_q$$

may be estimated and a level L confidence interval computed for it. A level L confidence interval for the mean response at regressor values $x_1, x_2, \ldots, x_q$ is

$$(\hat{Y} - \hat{\sigma}(\hat{Y})t_{n-q-1,(1+L)/2}, \; \hat{Y} + \hat{\sigma}(\hat{Y})t_{n-q-1,(1+L)/2}) \tag{8.36}$$

where

$$\hat{Y} = \hat{\beta}_0 + \hat{\beta}_1 x_1 + \cdots + \hat{\beta}_q x_q$$

and $\hat{\sigma}(\hat{Y})$ is the estimated standard error of the response. The formula for $\hat{\sigma}(\hat{Y})$ is too involved to give here,[9] but can be easily computed using most statistical software packages.

EXAMPLE 8.2   CONTINUED

Consider model (8.25) for the tree data. The predicted volume for the mean response at any user-selected predictor values $D = d$ and $H = h$ is

$$\hat{V}_0 = 69.40 - 5.86d - 1.30h + 0.13 \cdot d \cdot h$$

Suppose the tree foresters are interested in the mean volume of a tree having a diameter $D = 10$ inches and a height $H = 70$ feet. Based on model (8.25), the estimate of mean volume for trees having these diameter and height values is

$$14.30 = 69.40 - (5.86)(10) - (1.30)(70) + (0.13)(10)(70). \tag{8.37}$$

It turns out that the estimated standard error of the mean volume of trees having these diameter and height values is 0.79. As $t_{27,0.975} = 2.052$, a level 0.95 confidence interval for the mean volume of trees having a diameter of 28 inches and a height of 70 feet is $(14.30 - (0.79)(2.052), 14.30 + (0.79)(2.052)) = (12.68, 15.92)$.   ◆

Predicting a New Observation

In predicting a new observation at specified values of the regressor variables, we encounter the same situation as in the simple linear regression case studied in Chapter 7. Namely:

- The predictor of the new observation, $\hat{Y}_{\text{new}}$, is the same as the predictor of the mean response, $\hat{Y}$.
- The standard error of prediction of the new observation includes a term that measures the uncertainty inherent in estimating the model parameters from the data, and a second term that measures the uncertainty inherent in the measurement or observation process itself. The estimate of the former variation is the same as

[9] It is given in vector-matrix notation in Appendix 8.1.

the estimate of the variation involved in predicting the mean response, and the estimate of the latter variation is MSE. Thus, the standard error of prediction of the new observation is

$$\hat{\sigma}(Y_{\text{new}} - \hat{Y}_{\text{new}}) = \sqrt{\text{MSE} + \hat{\sigma}^2(\hat{Y})}$$

A level L prediction interval for a new response at regressor values $x_1, x_2, \ldots, x_q$ is

$$(\hat{Y}_{\text{new}} - \hat{\sigma}(Y_{\text{new}} - \hat{Y}_{\text{new}})t_{n-q-1,(1+L)/2}, \ \hat{Y}_{\text{new}} + \hat{\sigma}(Y_{\text{new}} - \hat{Y}_{\text{new}})t_{n-q-1,(1+L)/2}) \qquad (8.38)$$

where

$$\hat{Y}_{\text{new}} = \hat{\beta}_0 + \hat{\beta}_1 x_1 + \cdots + \hat{\beta}_q x_q$$

EXAMPLE 8.2   CONTINUED

Suppose that the next tree the foresters measure has a diameter of 10 inches and a height of 70 feet. If they use fitted model (8.25) to predict its volume, we know from the last example that $\hat{Y}_{\text{new}} = \hat{Y} = 14.30$ and that $\hat{\sigma}(\hat{Y}) = 0.79$. Since MSE $= 7.3362$, we have $\hat{\sigma}(Y_{\text{new}} - \hat{Y}_{\text{new}}) = \sqrt{7.3362 + 0.79^2} = 2.821$. Since $t_{27,0.975} = 2.052$, a level 0.95 prediction interval for the volume of a new tree of diameter 28 inches and height 70 feet is

$$(14.30 - (2.821)(2.052), 14.30 + (2.821)(2.052)) = (8.51, 20.09) \quad \blacklozenge$$

We summarize these intervals:

SUMMARY OF INTERVALS FOR THE REGRESSION MODEL

- **Confidence Interval for Model Coefficients.** A level L confidence interval for β_i is

$$(\hat{\beta}_i - \hat{\sigma}(\hat{\beta}_i)t_{n-q-1,(1+L)/2}, \ \hat{\beta}_i + \hat{\sigma}(\hat{\beta}_i)t_{n-q-1,(1+L)/2})$$

- **Confidence Interval for Mean Response.** A level L confidence interval for the mean response at regressor values $x_1, x_2, \ldots, x_q$ is

$$(\hat{Y} - \hat{\sigma}(\hat{Y})t_{n-q-1,(1+L)/2}, \ \hat{Y} + \hat{\sigma}(\hat{Y})t_{n-q-1,(1+L)/2})$$

where

$$\hat{Y} = \hat{\beta}_0 + \hat{\beta}_1 x_1 + \cdots + \hat{\beta}_q x_q$$

and $\hat{\sigma}(\hat{Y})$ is its estimated standard error.

- **Prediction Interval for a New Observation.** A level L prediction interval for a new response at regressor values $x_1, x_2, \ldots, x_q$ is

$$(\hat{Y}_{\text{new}} - \hat{\sigma}(Y_{\text{new}} - \hat{Y}_{\text{new}})t_{n-q-1,(1+L)/2}, \ \hat{Y}_{\text{new}} + \hat{\sigma}(Y_{\text{new}} - \hat{Y}_{\text{new}})t_{n-q-1.(1+L)/2})$$

where

$$\hat{Y}_{\text{new}} = \hat{\beta}_0 + \hat{\beta}_1 x_1 + \cdots + \hat{\beta}_q x_q$$

and

$$\hat{\sigma}(Y_{\text{new}} - \hat{Y}_{\text{new}}) = \sqrt{\text{MSE} + \hat{\sigma}^2(\hat{Y})}$$

Prediction performance is of primary importance in deciding among competing models. The only way to determine such performance is to compare model predictions with new observations. However, we can at least use what we know about confidence intervals for mean responses and prediction intervals for new observations to compare models.

EXAMPLE 8.2   CONTINUED

Level 0.95 intervals for mean tree volume and for the prediction of the volume of a new tree having diameter 10 inches and height 70 feet, computed using models (8.25) and (8.29), are shown in Table 8.5.

TABLE 8.5   Comparison of Intervals, Models (8.25) and (8.29)

Model	$\hat{V}_0 = \hat{V}_{\text{new}}$	Level 0.95 CI for mean response	Level 0.95 PI for future observation
(8.25)	14.30	(12.68, 15.92)	(8.51, 20.09)
(8.29)	14.57	(13.29, 15.85)	(9.32, 19.83)

The point estimates and predictions are similar for both models, with the shorter interval widths for model (8.29) giving another reason to favor it over model (8.25).   ◆

Vector-matrix formulas for inference in the multiple linear regression model are presented in Appendix 8.1 at the end of this chapter.

8.13

MULTICOLLINEARITY

When the regressors in a multiple linear regression are highly correlated among themselves, difficulties can occur in inference for individual regressors and in the interpretation of individual regression coefficients. The term used to describe correlation among the regressors is **multicollinearity.**

Consequences of Multicollinearity

Multicollinearity has two potentially serious consequences:

• The estimated regression coefficients $\hat{\beta}_i$ tend to have large sampling variability. This can result in the extreme situation where the overall F test shows a significant overall regression relation, but the t-test for each individual $\hat{\beta}$ is nonsignificant! This anomaly results because the t-tests measure the **additional contribution** of each individual regressor beyond that of all the other regressors in the model. If X_i is highly correlated with the other regressors, then it can make little contribution beyond theirs: if they are in the model, then the regressor is to a large extent redundant.

• The interpretation of $\hat{\beta}_i$ as the change in the predicted response per unit change in X_i **when the other regressors are held constant** becomes questionable, since high correlation among the regressors means that as X_i changes, the other regressors tend to change as well.

On the positive side, multicollinearity does not affect the quality of the fit or inferences about mean response or prediction of a new observation. In addition, while multicollinearity may be unavoidable in some studies, in many controlled experiments the levels of regressors may be selected to eliminate it.

Detecting Multicollinearity

There are several diagnostics used to detect multicollinearity. Two of the simplest and most widely used are the **tolerance** and the **variance inflation factor.**

The idea behind both measures is simple. Recall that the coefficient of multiple determination, R^2, measures the strength of linear relationship between the response and the regressors. Suppose we want to measure the strength of linear relationship between X_i and the rest of the regressors. We can pretend that X_i is a response variable and compute R_i^2, the coefficient of multiple determination from regressing X_i on the other regressors. Large R_i^2 means X_i is highly correlated with the other regressors and indicates large multicollinearity. The tolerance is computed as $\text{TOL}_i = 1 - R_i^2$. Note that TOL_i takes on values between 0 and 1, and that small tolerance is indicative of multicollinearity.

It can be shown that the variance of $\hat{\beta}_i$ is proportional to $1/\text{TOL}_i$. So the variance inflation factor of X_i is defined as $\text{VIF}_i = 1/\text{TOL}_i$. VIF_i can range from 1 to ∞. As a rule of thumb, VIF_i values exceeding 10 (or, equivalently, TOL_i values smaller than 0.1) are considered cause for concern.

Remedial Measures

Two simple steps that can be taken to alleviate multicollinearity are as follows:

- If the regressors are products or powers of the predictors, center the predictors before taking the products or powers.
- Drop one or more regressors from the model. Since variables that are causing the multicollinearity are highly correlated with other regressors, much of their explanatory power is redundant. However, this should be done cautiously, as it results in discarding potentially valuable information, and as the resulting model will still depend on which regressors are discarded.

Other, more sophisticated, methods exist for remedying multicollinearity, but they are beyond the scope of this text. Lab 8.1 explores multicollinearity in greater depth.

EXAMPLE 8.2   CONTINUED

Table 8.4 on page 480 contains information about the parameter estimates for model (8.25). The second-to-last column of the table contains the tolerance values and the last column contains the variance inflation factors. The small tolerance values and large VIF values (tolerance < 0.1, VIF > 10) in Table 8.4 show that there is high multicollinearity among the regressors. Since there is a product term in the model, we will try to reduce the multicollinearity by centering the predictors, D and H. To do so, we first find $\bar{D}$, the mean of the diameters, and $\bar{H}$, the mean of the heights of the trees in the data set. We then compute the centered diameter values by subtracting $\bar{D}$ from each tree's diameter, and the centered height values by subtracting $\bar{H}$ from each tree's height. Table 8.6 shows the calculation for the first three trees; the centered diameters and heights are denoted $\tilde{D}$ and $\tilde{H}$, respectively. After obtaining $\tilde{D}$ and $\tilde{H}$, we fit the model

$$V = \beta_0 + \beta_1 \tilde{D} + \beta_2 \tilde{H} + \beta_3 \tilde{D} \cdot \tilde{H} + \epsilon \tag{8.39}$$

Table 8.7 contains parameter estimation information for the least squares fit of model (8.39) to the tree data. The modest values of both the VIF and the tolerance in the table show how centering the predictors has alleviated the multicollinearity problem. Note that even though they are still highly significant, the p-values for the model with the uncentered predictors are many times larger than those for model with the centered predictors, which is evidence of the effects of the multicollinearity on individual t-tests. ◆

TABLE 8.6   Original and Centered Predictors, Tree Data

Tree	D	H	$\tilde{D}$	$\tilde{H}$
1	8.3	70	−4.948	−6
2	8.6	65	−4.648	−11
3	10.5	63	−4.448	−13
.	.	.	.	.
.	.	.	.	.
.	.	.	.	.

TABLE 8.7   Parameter Estimate Table, Model (8.39)

			Parameter estimates				
Variable	DF	Estimate	Std Error	T Stat	Prob > $\|T\|$	Tolerance	Var Inflation
INTERCEPT	1	28.8179	0.5447	52.9099	0.0001		0
$\tilde{D}$	1	4.3779	0.1938	22.5847	0.0001	0.6609	1.5132
$\tilde{H}$	1	0.4869	0.0947	5.1432	0.0001	0.6721	1.4878
$\tilde{D}\tilde{H}$	1	0.1347	0.0244	5.5238	0.0001	0.8874	1.1268

8.14

MORE ON EMPIRICAL MODEL BUILDING

We have already discussed the notion of an empirically specified model, as compared with a theory-based model.

The steps involved in constructing an empirical model will depend on the data and the use(s) to which the model is to be put. For instance, for description purposes, it is very important to get the form of the model "right," where by "right" we mean that the form of the model helps us better understand the phenomenon being modeled.[10] Getting the form of the model "right" is not as important if the goal is prediction.

Nevertheless, all analyses based on empirically specified models have (or should have) some features in common. The first is laying the foundation for model building by intensive visualization. The second is entertaining several different models. The third is the cycle of fitting, evaluating the fit, modifying the models and fitting, evaluating and modifying again until a satisfactory result is obtained.

The t-tests for the significance of individual regressors described in previous sections can be used as aids in model selection in several different ways. We will describe one of these that is particularly useful if there are many regressors to choose from. The method is called **backward elimination.**

---

[10] Always remember G. E. P. Box's quote: "All models are wrong, but some are useful."

TABLE 8.8 Analysis of Variance Table, Model (8.40)

		Analysis of variance			
Source	DF	Sum of squares	Mean square	F Stat	Prob > F
Model	3	59.1261	19.7087	391.3581	0.0001
Error	27	1.3597	0.0504		
C Total	30	60.4858			

TABLE 8.9 Parameter Estimate Table, Model (8.40)

			Parameter estimates				
Variable	DF	Estimate	Std error	T Stat	Prob > |T|	Tolerance	Var inflation
INTERCEPT	1	5.2826	0.0451	117.0616	0.0001		0
$\tilde{D}$	1	0.3977	0.0161	24.7617	0.0001	0.6609	1.5132
$\tilde{H}$	1	0.0390	0.0078	4.9718	0.0001	0.6721	1.4878
$\tilde{D}\tilde{H}$	1	0.0030	0.0020	1.4617	0.1554	0.8874	1.1268

In backward elimination, we begin with a model containing all potential regressors and eliminate one by one all regressors deemed nonsignificant by the standard t-test. To see exactly how this works, we consider yet another model for the tree data.

EXAMPLE 8.2   CONTINUED

We have seen that a transformation of the response variable can sometimes simplify the form of the model: taking a logarithm of the response can transform products into sums, for example. Transformations of the response variable can also sometimes render product terms nonsignificant, changing a difficult-to-interpret model with a product term into an easy-to-interpret additive model. In an attempt to remove the interaction term from model (8.39), we transform the response by taking its square root. The model we consider for the tree data is identical to model (8.39), except that the response is the square root of volume instead of volume:[11]

$$\sqrt{V} = \beta_0 + \beta_1 \cdot \tilde{D} + \beta_2 \cdot \tilde{H} + \beta_3 \cdot \tilde{D}\tilde{H} + \epsilon \tag{8.40}$$

where $\tilde{D}\tilde{H}$ is the product of $\tilde{D}$ and $\tilde{H}$.

Tables 8.8 and 8.9 provide relevant information about the fit of model (8.40).

---

[11] How do we know to choose the square-root transformation? There are some guidelines based on statistical theory, but sometimes it's just trial and error. Power transformations, that is, transformations of the form Y^p, where Y is the response, and p is a real number, are often tried. The square-root transformation corresponds to $p = 1/2$.

TABLE 8.10   Analysis of Variance Table, Model (8.41)

		Analysis of variance			
Source	DF	Sum of squares	Mean square	F Stat	Prob > F
Model	2	59.0185	29.5092	563.1088	0.0001
Error	28	1.4673	0.0524		
C Total	30	60.4858			

TABLE 8.11   Parameter Estimate Table, Model (8.41)

			Parameter estimates				
Variable	DF	Estimate	Std Error	T Stat	Prob > |T|	Tolerance	Var Inflation
INTERCEPT	1	5.3122	0.0411	119.2037	0.0001	.	0
$\tilde{D}$	1	0.4049	0.0156	25.9828	0.0001	0.7303	1.3692
$\tilde{H}$	1	0.0358	0.0077	4.6589	0.0001	0.7303	1.3692

Also relevant are the fact that $R^2 = 0.9775$ and $R_a^2 = 0.9750$. The p-value of the overall F-test (0.0001) indicates that the relationship between the regressors and $\sqrt{V}$ is significant. The VIFs are all low, indicating that multicollinearity will not be a problem.

Finally, look at the p-values of the significance tests for the individual parameters. Are they all sufficiently small to justify keeping all terms in the model? Because we want to entertain a range of regressors, we'll accept any p-value less than 0.10 as significant, but even with this relatively large benchmark the answer is no. You will see that the variable $\tilde{D}\tilde{H}$ has the largest p-value (i.e., it contributes the least to predicting $\sqrt{V}$ given the other variables in the model), and that its value is about 0.16, which exceeds 0.10. Consequently, we eliminate $\tilde{D}\tilde{H}$ (p-value $= 0.1554$) as a regressor, leaving us with additive model (8.41):

$$\sqrt{V} = \beta_0 + \beta_1 \cdot \tilde{D} + \beta_2 \cdot \tilde{H} + \epsilon \tag{8.41}$$

and refit the model to the remaining two regressors. The resulting $R^2 = 0.9757$ and $R_a^2 = 0.9740$, not as high as before, but close. Tables 8.10 and 8.11 provide other relevant information.

The p-value of the overall F-test is low, R^2, R_a^2, and MSE are comparable to their counterparts in the three-variable model, and the individual t-tests show that both $\tilde{D}$ and $\tilde{H}$ are significant. As we saw earlier, the residual plots show little difference between the two models. Thus, we stop the backward elimination and choose the additive model. This confirms our earlier analysis.

The advantage of variable selection procedures, such as backward elimination, is that they can give guidance in model building when there are large numbers of potential regressors. In that case, there might be a number of iterations in which

1. A model is fit.
2. The individual regressors are checked for significance using a t-test.
3. The least significant regressor is removed, and the reduced model is fit, bringing us back to item 1.

This process is continued until a satisfactory model is obtained.

One final note: These procedures provide guidance only. They do not replace the task of careful visualization and evaluation of model fit.   ◆

EXAMPLE 8.2   CONTINUED

Consider again model (8.29). The estimated intercept is $\hat{\beta}_0 = -0.2977$ with an estimated standard error of 0.9636. The t statistic for testing the null hypothesis that the intercept is 0 is $t^* = -0.2977/0.9636 = -0.3089$ with a p-value of 0.7596. The data hold little evidence that the intercept is nonzero.

As a result, we can try to simplify the model further by assuming the intercept is 0. That is, the model is assumed to be

$$V = \beta_1 X + \epsilon \tag{8.42}$$

where $X = D^2 H$. The fitted model is[12]

$$\hat{V} = 0.0021 X \tag{8.43}$$

The fit of the model is summarized in Figure 8.17. The fit looks very similar to that of model (8.29). The main advantages of the present model are as follows:

- It is simpler, with one fewer parameter to estimate, and therefore, by the principle of parsimony, preferred to model (8.29).
- The MSE is smaller, so that inference will be more precise. For instance, a level 0.95 confidence interval for the mean response when diameter is 10 inches and height 70 feet is (14.37, 15.15), and a level 0.95 prediction interval for a new observation at diameter 10 inches and height 70 feet is (9.73, 19.79), both of which are narrower than their counterparts computed from model (8.29).
- The form of the model makes sense. Although not the volume of a right circular cylinder, it is a multiple of that volume. Further, it makes sense that the relation should have an intercept at the origin: Trees for which HD^2 is near zero should have near-zero volumes.   ◆

---

[12]The least squares fit of a model without an intercept proceeds by minimizing $\text{SSE}(b_1, \ldots, b_q) = \sum_{i=1}^{n} [Y_i - (b_1 X_{1i} + \cdots + b_q X_{qi})]^2$. Almost all statistical computer packages offer a "no intercept" fit as an option.

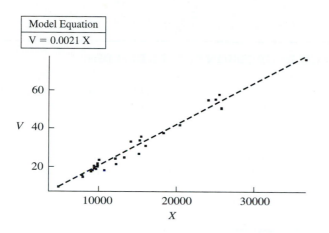

Model Equation
V = 0.0021 X

Summary of Fit			
Mean of Response	30.1710	R-Square	0.9950
Root MSE	2.4551	Adj R-Sq	0.9949

Analysis of Variance					
Source	DF	Sum of Squares	Mean Square	F Stat	Prob > F
Model	1	36144.1609	36144.1609	5996.4062	0.0001
Error	30	180.8291	6.0276		
U Total	31	36324.9900			

Parameter Estimates							
Variable	DF	Estimate	Std Error	T Stat	Prob > |T|	Tolerance	Var Inflation
X	1	0.0021	2.722E-05	77.4365	0.0001	1.0000	1.0000

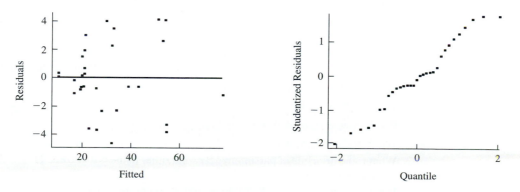

Figure 8.17   Summary of least squares fit of model (8.42).

8.15

A FINAL WORD ON REGRESSION MODEL BUILDING

The idea we would like you to come away with is that in model building, you may consider and compare several models and go through a number of iterations before you are satisfied with the results. Such a process will include model specification, fitting, and checking on one set of data, such as the tree data. The model should then be tested on a different set of data (more tree measurements in the case of the models we developed), modified as needed, and the process of model specification, fitting, and checking continued.

EXAMPLE 8.2   CONTINUED

Which of the models we have presented is the best model for the tree data? We have built a number of models for the tree data in this chapter. Most of them are pretty close in the usual measures of fit we have considered. The best model we have looked at, in terms of measures of model fit, is model (8.43). This model fits well and is parsimonious, having only two parameters, β_1 and σ^2. It is also a satisfying model because we have developed a theoretical justification for it. However, to really test this and the other models, we need to see how it performs on different data. So what we have done here is only a beginning.   ◆

D ISCUSSION QUESTIONS

1. What is a multiple linear regression model?
2. How can a scatterplot array be used in visualizing multivariable data? How can it help in initially specifying a multiple linear regression model?
3. How can a 3-D plot be used in visualizing multivariable data? How can it help in initially specifying a multiple linear regression model?
4. How is the multiple linear regression model usually fit to data?
5. What are two basic quantities used in assessing model fit? How are they used?
6. Interpret the coefficients in the following fitted models:
   (a) $\hat{Y} = \hat{\beta}_0 + \hat{\beta}_1 Z_1 + \hat{\beta}_2 Z_2$
   (b) $\hat{Y} = \hat{\beta}_0 + \hat{\beta}_1 Z_1 + \hat{\beta}_2 Z_2 + \hat{\beta}_3 Z_1 Z_2$
   (c) $\hat{Y} = \hat{\beta}_0 + \hat{\beta}_1 Z_1 + \hat{\beta}_2 Z_2 + \hat{\beta}_3 Z_1^2$
7. What is the principle of parsimony? By what other name is it known? How is it used to build regression models?
8. What does R^2 measure? R_a^2? Why would R_a^2 be preferred to R^2?
9. Relate R^2 to SSTO, SSR, and SSE. Interpret the relation.
10. What is a test of significance? How is it used in ANOVA?

11. Describe the following and how they are used in analyzing the multiple linear regression model:

    (a) F ratio
    (b) t ratio for individual parameters
    (c) p-value
    (d) statistical significance

12. What is multicollinearity? What are its symptoms? How can it be detected? What measures can be taken to remedy it?

13. What is empirical model building?

14. Explain the method of backward elimination and its role in empirical model building.

E XERCISES

8.1. For a sample of 93 cars, the government rating of city miles per gallon (Y) was regressed on engine displacement and car weight. Figure 8.18 displays SAS/INSIGHT output from the regression. Figure 8.19 shows plots of the Studentized residuals (versus displacement, weight, and t quantiles).

    (a) Overall, is the regression relation significant? How do you know?
    (b) Are both predictors contributing significantly to predicting city MPG? How do you know?
    (c) Is multicollinearity a problem here? Why or why not?
    (d) Name two features of the Studentized residuals apparent from the plots.

Model Equation
CITYMPG = 47.1388 + 0.0476 DISPLACE − 0.0081 WEIGHT

Summary of Fit			
Mean of Response	22.3656	R-Square	0.7109
Root MSE	3.0550	Adj R-Sq	0.7045

Analysis of Variance					
Source	DF	Sum of Squares	Mean Square	F Stat	Prob > F
Model	2	2065.5833	1032.7916	110.6580	0.0001
Error	90	839.9866	9.3332		
C Total	92	2905.5699			

Parameter Estimates							
Variable	DF	Estimate	Std Error	T Stat	Prob > |T|	Tolerance	Var Inflation
INTERCEPT	1	47.1388	2.0106	23.4453	0.0001		0
DISPLACE	1	0.0476	0.5743	0.0829	0.9341	0.2858	3.4984
WEIGHT	1	−0.0081	0.0010	−8.0237	0.0001	0.2858	3.4984

Figure 8.18   Output from car data regression.

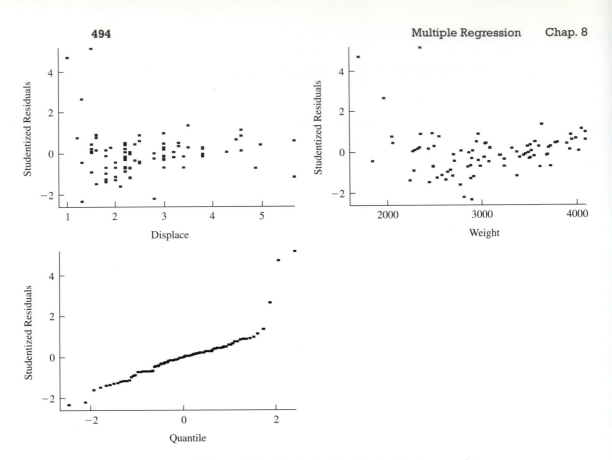

Figure 8.19   Studentized residual plots from car data.

8.2. Interpret the estimated coefficient 0.34 in fitted model (8.26).

8.3. Drinking water in millions of homes is supplied by copper pipes joined with lead-based solder. Lead contamination of the drinking water in these homes is a potentially serious health hazard.

In an effort to understand what variables govern the leaching of lead from solder into drinking water, environmental engineers conducted a controlled experiment. Fifty-six identical lengths of copper pipe were each fitted with a single joint using a type of lead-based solder typical of that found in home drinking supply systems. Water of one of five known acidity levels, as measured by pH, was placed in each pipe, and left there for one of four possible durations. The pipes were randomly assigned to the pH and duration combinations. At the end of the time, the water was measured for lead concentration (in parts per billion).

The data are found in the data set LEAD. For your information:

(a) Lower levels of pH correspond to greater acidity.

(b) The EPA classifies lead concentrations greater than 15 ppb as "unsafe".

Visually explore these data. Write a short (one page or less) report detailing your methodology and conclusions. Be sure to include appropriate supporting graphs.

8.4. Fit at least two models to the lead data from Exercise 8.3. Be sure to center the predictors first. For each model, assess the model fit and interpret the model. Finally, compare the models. Your final product should be an acceptable model for the data. Write a short report detailing your methodology and conclusions. Be sure to include appropriate graphs and other computer output.

8.5. Investigate whether the model you obtained for the lead data in Exercise 8.4 can be improved by transformation. Report your methodology and results.

8.6. Give the two interpretations of R^2 for the fit of your best model for the lead data. For that model, show what R^2 means in terms of SSTO, SSE, and SSR.

8.7. Perform and interpret the analysis of variance for the best model you have obtained for the lead data. If the overall F test is significant, compute confidence intervals and perform individual t-tests for each β. What conclusions do you draw? Report your methodology and results.

8.8. Evaluate the multicollinearity of the regressors in your best model for the lead data. Does your evaluation change any of your previous conclusions about your best fitted model? Make a short final report summarizing your methodology and conclusions.

8.9. In considering Y as a function of X and Z, a data analyst explores a scatterplot array of all three variables. As he moves a brush from small to large X values, a linear relation between Y and Z is revealed at each stage. These different linear relations appear to have a common slope but different intercepts. Write an equation for Y as a function of X and Z that is consistent with the analyst's observations.

8.10. Give two interpretations of R^2 for the fit of model (8.41).

8.11. The fire endurance of a wall is the time required for a fire of a given intensity on one side of the wall to breach the wall, to raise the temperature at any single point on the opposite side of the wall to one prespecified level, or to raise the overall temperature on the opposite side of the wall to another prespecified level.

For a calcareous aggregate concrete wall, fire protection engineers investigated the relationship between fire endurance, in minutes (variable name FIRE_END), and three predictors:

- EQIVTHCK: The equivalent thickness of the wall in inches.
- CONCDENS: The concrete density in lb/ft^3.
- AGG_DENS: The aggregate density in lb/ft^3.

Tests were done on 80 walls. Figure 8.20 displays SAS/INSIGHT output from the regression of FIRE_END on these three predictors, and Figure 8.21 displays a plot of the Studentized residuals versus the fitted values and t quantiles.

(a) Give the equation of the fitted model and interpret it.

(b) The experimenters did a second regression, this one regressing fire endurance (FIRE_END) on equivalent thickness (EQIVTHCK), concrete density (CONCDENS), and their product. Figure 8.22 displays SAS/INSIGHT output from the regression, and Figure 8.23 displays plots of the Studentized residuals versus the fitted values and t quantiles. Compare the fits of these two models. Which do you prefer? Why?

(c) Name one feature of the Studentized residual plots from model 1 that you would like to investigate further.

8.12. Refer to Figure 8.22, which displays SAS/INSIGHT output for the second model for the fire test data (see Exercise 8.11). This model regresses fire endurance (FIRE_END) on equivalent thickness (EQIVTHCK), concrete density (CONCDENS), and their product. Is the overall model significant? How about the individual predictors? Do you see a contradiction here? What is the explanation? What step(s) would you take next to correct it?

8.13. As an analyst moves a horizontal brush from low to high values of a response variable Y in a scatterplot array, the highlighted points in the scatterplot of the predictor variables

Summary of Fit			
Mean of Response	156.1000	R-Square	0.9524
Root MSE	9.5161	Adj R-Sq	0.9505

Analysis of Variance					
Source	DF	Sum of Squares	Mean Square	F Stat	Prob > F
Model	2	137748.930	45916.3102	507.0478	0.0001
Error	76	6882.2695	90.5562		
C Total	79	144631.200			

Parameter Estimates							
Variable	DF	Estimate	Std Error	T Stat	Prob > |T|	Tolerance	Var Inflation
INTERCEPT	1	−5.4017	42.5744	−0.1269	0.8994		0
EQIVTHCK	1	53.3795	1.3754	38.8111	0.0001	0.8160	1.2256
CONCDENS	1	1.8356	0.1377	13.3265	0.0001	0.6166	1.6217
AGG_DENS	1	−2.9610	0.4035	−7.3376	0.0001	0.7226	1.3838

Figure 8.20 Regression output: fire test data, first model.

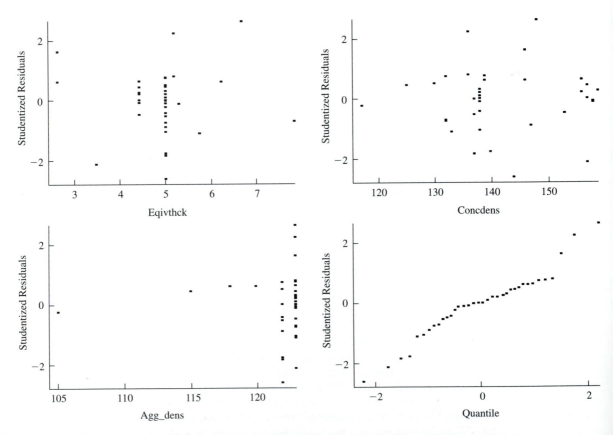

Figure 8.21 Studentized residual plots: fire test data, first model.

Summary of Fit			
Mean of Response	156.1000	R-Square	0.9202
Root MSE	12.3268	Adj R-Sq	0.9170

Analysis of Variance					
Source	DF	Sum of Squares	Mean Square	F Stat	Prob > F
Model	3	133082.953	44360.9842	291.9434	0.0001
Error	76	11548.2474	151.9506		
C Total	79	144631.200			

Parameter Estimates							
Variable	DF	Estimate	Std Error	T Stat	Prob > |T|	Tolerance	Var Inflation
INTERCEPT	1	−107.2774	150.0043	−0.7152	0.4767		0
EQIVTHCK	1	15.1944	30.7698	0.4938	0.6229	0.0027	365.5619
CONCDENS	1	0.0885	1.0456	0.0846	0.9328	0.0180	55.6931
EQIVTHCK*CONCDENS	1	0.2539	0.2162	1.1746	0.2438	0.0032	311.7956

Figure 8.22 Regression output: fire test data, second model.

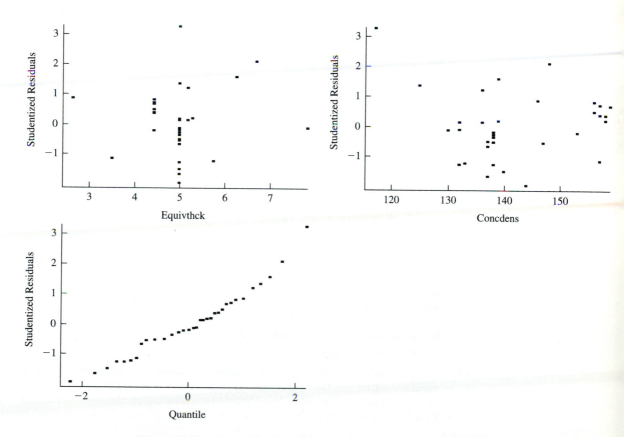

Figure 8.23 Studentized residual plots: fire test data, second model.

Z_1 and Z_2 form smaller and smaller nested ellipses. Draw a 3-D plot of what the surface $Y = f(Z_1, Z_2)$ suggested by these data might look like.

8.14. In an industrial experiment, 30 rubber specimens were rubbed by an abrasive material. Measurements of three variables—abrasion loss, tensile strength, and hardness—were made for each specimen. Abrasion loss is the amount of material abraded from a specimen per unit of energy expended in rubbing; tensile strength is the force per unit of cross-sectional area required to break a specimen; and hardness is the rebound height of a steel indenter dropped onto a specimen. The goal is to determine the dependence of abrasion loss on tensile strength and hardness. The data are found in the data set RUBBER.

  (a) Use visualization techniques to view the nature of the joint dependence of abrasion loss on tensile strength and hardness. What technique(s) did you use? What do you conclude? Include appropriate graphs to support your conclusions.

  (b) Fit a model based on your conclusions from (a). Interpret the fitted model. Specifically:
  - **i.** Write out the fitted model.
  - **ii.** Interpret the fitted coefficients.
  - **iii.** What proportion of the variation in abrasion loss is explained by the fitted model?
  - **iv.** Is the model statistically significant (0.05 level)? Are all regressors in the model statistically significant?

  (c) Is there any indication of multicollinearity among the regressors? Support your answer.

  (d) Perform a residual analysis. Look for outliers and other patterns in the residuals. Is the model fit acceptable? Why?

  (e) If you had more time would you analyze the data further? If not, why not. If so, what would be your next step?

8.15. As a statistics project, a group of college students measured the distance from the arm to the end of the forefinger of 42 of their sorority sisters. They also obtained the height, age, and shoe size of each. These data are found in the file SORORITY.

  (a) Use visualization techniques to view the nature of the joint dependence of height on age, shoe size, and the wrist measurement (called DISTANCE in the data set). What technique(s) did you use? What do you conclude? Include appropriate graphs to support your conclusions.

  (b) Fit a model based on your conclusions from (a). Interpret the fitted model. Specifically:
  - **i.** Write out the fitted model.
  - **ii.** Interpret the fitted coefficients.
  - **iii.** What proportion of the variation in DISTANCE is explained by the fitted model?
  - **iv.** Is the model statistically significant (0.05 level)? Are all regressors in the model statistically significant?

  (c) Is there any indication of multicollinearity among the regressors? Support your answer.

  (d) Perform a residual analysis. Look for outliers and other patterns in the residuals. Is the model fit acceptable? Why?

  (e) If you had more time would you analyze the data further? If not, why not. If so, what would be your next step?

8.16. An alternative to transforming the response variable is to fit a different model in the predictor variables. This is particularly attractive if it is important to have a model in the original response variable. In addition to the centered predictors $\tilde{D}$ and $\tilde{H}$, the data set TREES contains their product $\tilde{D}\tilde{H}$ and their squares $\tilde{D}^2$ and $\tilde{H}^2$ (the centered predictors

Model Equation
V = 27.6109 + 4.2325 CD + 0.3764 CH + 0.2686 CD2

Summary of Fit			
Mean of Response	30.1710	R-Square	0.9771
Root MSE	2.6248	Adj R-Sq	0.9745

Analysis of Variance					
Source	DF	Sum of Squares	Mean Square	F Stat	Prob > F
Model	3	7920.0720	2640.0240	383.2049	0.0001
Error	27	186.0118	6.8893		
C Total	30	8106.0839			

Parameter Estimates							
Variable	DF	Estimate	Std Error	T Stat	Prob > |T|	Tolerance	Var Inflation
Intercept	1	27.6109	0.6431	42.9315	0.0001		0
CD	1	4.2325	0.1963	21.5614	0.0001	0.6051	1.6525
CH	1	0.3764	0.0882	4.2659	0.0002	0.7266	1.3763
CD2	1	0.2686	0.0459	5.8517	0.0001	0.8040	1.2438

Figure 8.24 SAS output: trees quadratic fit.

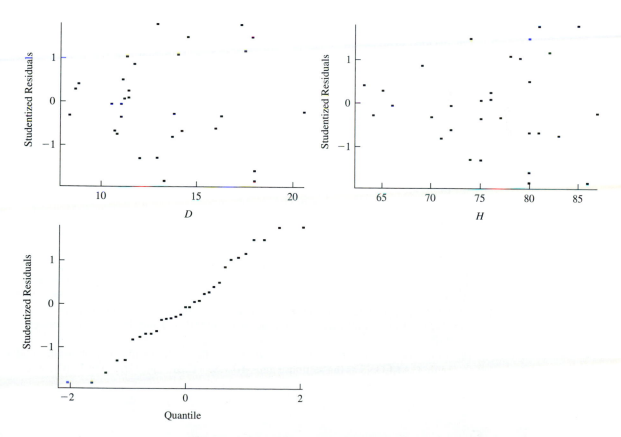

Figure 8.25 Studentized residual plots: trees quadratic fit.

are called CD and CH, their product is $CDCH$ and their squares $CD2$ and $CH2$ in the data set). An analyst obtains the model shown in Figure 8.24.

(a) Is the fitted model significant? Are the individual variables significant?

(b) Studentized residual plots are displayed in Figure 8.25. Use these to assess model fit.

(c) Interpret the fitted model.

(d) Is multicollinearity a problem here?

(e) Compare this model with model (8.25).

8.17. A multiple linear regression model with 6 regressors and an intercept is fit to 25 observations. How many residuals are there? What is the minimum number of residuals we need to know before we can compute SSE?

8.18. A fitted multiple linear regression model yields an R^2 of 0.91. Give two interpretations of this number.

8.19. In considering Y as a function of X and Z, a data analyst explores a scatterplot array of all three variables. As he moves a brush from small to large X values, a linear relation between Y and Z is revealed at each stage. These different linear relations appear to have a common intercept but different slopes. Write an equation for Y as a function of X and Z that is consistent with the analyst's observations.

8.20. In a study of the environmental determinants of ozone concentration, investigators measured solar radiation, temperature, wind speed, and ozone concentration on 111 days at test sites in the New York metropolitan region. Since the ozone readings were skewed, it was decided to work with the cube root of the readings (RT3OZONE) as the response variable. The predictors were first centered and given the names CR, CT, and CW. Then RT3OZONE was regressed on CR, CT, and CW as well as their two- and three-way products and the squares of each. The resulting SAS/INSIGHT output is shown in Figures 8.26 and 8.27. The investigators then used backward elimination to obtain a model with only four variables: CR, CT, CW, and the square of CW. The resulting SAS/INSIGHT output is shown in Figures 8.28 and 8.29.

(a) Compare the two models based on **all relevant measures and/or graphs** found on the output. Which model do you prefer? Why?

(b) Is multicollinearity a problem with either model? Provide evidence to support your position.

(c) Interpret the fitted reduced model.

8.21. Professor P. keeps track of the mileage he gets in his car. At each fill-up, he records the number of miles driven since the last fill-up and the number of gallons used. In the past, he has noticed that he gets poorer mileage when the outside temperature is colder. In an attempt to quantify this, he also records the outside temperature displayed on his home thermometer each morning when he gets up and averages these values over the days between fill-ups to get an average temperature during each period between fill-ups. For each of the 10 fill-ups since the beginning of the year, he therefore has the number of gallons used (the variable GALLONS), the number of miles driven (MILES) and the average temperature (TEMP).

(a) Professor P. uses these data to construct the multiple linear regression model with GALLONS as the response and MILES, TEMP, and MILES*TEMP as the

Summary of Fit			
Mean of Response	3.2478	R-Square	0.7517
Root MSE	0.4654	Adj R-Sq	0.7269

Analysis of Variance					
Source	DF	Sum of Squares	Mean Square	F Stat	Prob > F
Model	10	65.5532	6.5553	30.2709	0.0001
Error	100	21.6555	0.2166		
C Total	110	87.2088			

Parameter Estimates							
Variable	DF	Estimate	Std Error	T Stat	Prob > |T|	Tolerance	Var Inflation
INTERCEPT	1	3.1368	0.0847	37.0136	0.0001		0
CR	1	0.0024	0.0006	3.8733	0.0002	0.6176	1.6191
CT	1	0.0451	0.0063	7.2040	0.0001	0.5528	1.8088
CW	1	−0.0993	0.0177	−5.6050	0.0001	0.4948	2.0209
CR*CR	1	−1.320E-05	6.720E-06	−1.9639	0.0523	0.5951	1.6803
CR*CT	1	6.184E-05	6.594E-05	0.9378	0.3506	0.5333	1.8752
CR*CW	1	−0.0001	0.0002	−0.7118	0.4783	0.5480	1.8247
CT*CT	1	0.0012	0.0006	1.9178	0.0580	0.4617	2.1659
CT*CW	1	0.0039	0.0026	1.5129	0.1335	0.2356	4.2441
CW*CW	1	0.0122	0.0038	3.1742	0.0020	0.3687	2.7120
CR*CT*CW	1	1.209E-05	1.723E-05	0.7021	0.4843	0.3892	2.5694

Figure 8.26 SAS output, ozone fit: full model.

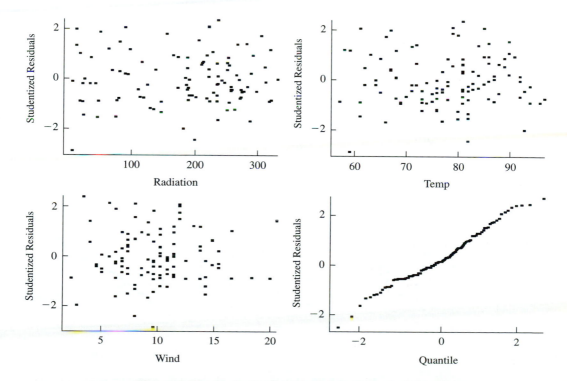

Figure 8.27 Studentized residual plots, ozone fit: full model.

Summary of Fit			
Mean of Response	3.2478	R-Square	0.7220
Root MSE	0.4783	Adj R-Sq	0.7115

Analysis of Variance					
Source	DF	Sum of Squares	Mean Square	F Stat	Prob > F
Model	4	62.9637	15.7409	68.8197	0.0001
Error	106	24.2451	0.2287		
C Total	110	87.2088			

Parameter Estimates							
Variable	DF	Estimate	Std Error	T Stat	Prob > |T|	Tolerance	Var Inflation
INTERCEPT	1	3.1209	0.0555	56.2043	0.0001		0
CR	1	0.0022	0.0005	4.2521	0.0001	0.9130	1.0953
CT	1	0.0462	0.0058	7.9602	0.0001	0.6794	1.4720
CW	1	−0.0973	0.0157	−6.1929	0.0001	0.6648	1.5043
CW*CW	1	0.0101	0.0025	3.9689	0.0001	0.8834	1.1320

Figure 8.28 SAS output, ozone fit: reduced model.

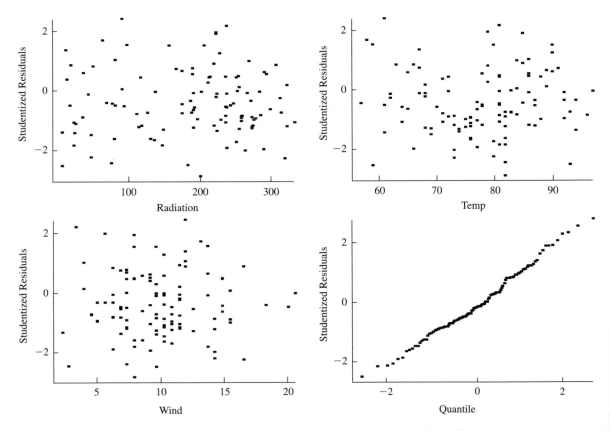

Figure 8.29 Studentized residual plots, ozone fit: reduced model.

Summary of Fit			
Mean of Response	8.0048	R-Square	0.8088
Root MSE	0.2658	Adj R-Sq	0.7903

Analysis of Variance					
Source	DF	Sum of Squares	Mean Square	F Stat	Prob > F
Model	3	9.2694	3.0898	43.7189	0.0001
Error	31	2.1909	0.0707		
C Total	34	11.4603			

Parameter Estimates							
Variable	DF	Estimate	Std Error	T Stat	Prob > |T|	Tolerance	Var Inflation
INTERCEPT	1	2.6175	0.8975	2.9164	0.0065		0
MILES	1	0.0197	0.0030	6.6428	0.0001	0.1911	5.2322
TEMP	1	−0.0344	0.0278	−1.2374	0.2252	0.0096	104.0667
MILES*TEMP	1	1.845E-05	8.403E-05	0.2196	0.8276	0.0076	131.8187

Figure 8.30 Output for first fit: mileage data.

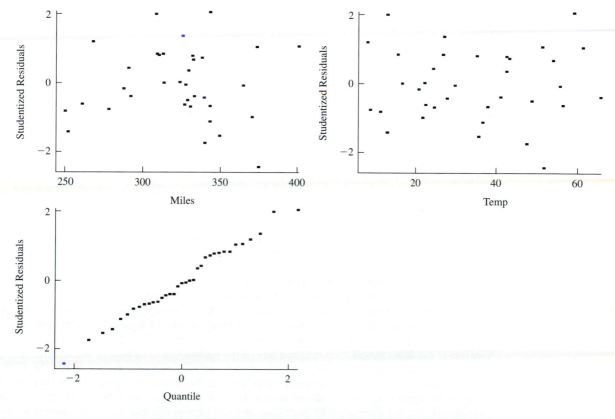

Figure 8.31 Plots of Studentized residuals for first fit: mileage data.

regressor variables. Output from the fit is displayed in Figure 8.30 and Studentized residual plots versus the two regressors, and the t quantiles are displayed in Figure 8.31.

    i. Is the fitted model significant? Why?

    ii. Which individual regressors are significant? Are you happy with this conclusion? Why or why not?

(b) Professor P. considers two other models. Output for the first is displayed in Figures 8.32 and 8.33, and output for the second is displayed in Figures 8.34 and 8.35.

    i. Compare the three models based on all relevant measures and graphs. Which do you think provides the best fit? Why?

    ii. Write out the equation for the best fitting model. Interpret this equation in terms even Professor P. can understand.

    iii. What is the reduction in uncertainty of prediction obtained by using the best fitting model?

MINIPROJECT

Purpose

The purpose of this project is to give you experience with modeling the relation between a response and several predictor variables using the methods in this chapter.

Process

For this project, your group is to collect data on a response variable and at least three predictor variables. You are to build a multiple linear regression model for these data, fit the model, evaluate the fit, interpret the model, and draw conclusions.

    Before collecting the data, submit a proposal, no more than one page in length, for your instructor's approval. The proposal should state what data will be collected, exactly how you intend to collect them, and what kind of relationship you expect to find. Your instructor will discuss the proposal with your group, and may suggest modifications.

    After your group's proposal has been approved, proceed to collect the data. In particular, to guide you in building the model, you must use one or more of the visualization tools discussed in the chapter, perhaps in conjunction with relevant scientific or engineering theory, as a step in building a multiple linear regression model. You must consider at least two models and evaluate them relative to each other. For the best model or models, you must assess the model fit and interpret the fitted model. You may use any of the techniques discussed in this chapter that are appropriate to analyze the relationship between the response and the predictor variables.

    Write a short report summarizing your findings. Be sure to state whether the data confirm the kind of relationship you predicted in your initial proposal. Also include two further questions suggested (but not answered) by your data and tell what you could do to get answers to these questions.

Summary of Fit			
Mean of Response	8.0048	R-Square	0.7994
Root MSE	0.2680	Adj R-Sq	0.7868

Analysis of Variance					
Source	DF	Sum of Squares	Mean Square	F Stat	Prob > F
Model	2	9.1612	4.5806	63.7546	0.0001
Error	32	2.2991	0.0718		
C Total	34	11.4603			

Parameter Estimates							
Variable	DF	Estimate	Std Error	T Stat	Prob > |T|	Tolerance	Var Inflation
INTERCEPT	1	1.7418	0.5566	3.1296	0.0037		0
MILES	1	0.0224	0.0020	11.1865	0.0001	0.4253	2.3513
MILES*TEMP	1	−8.460E-05	1.132E-05	−7.4758	0.0001	0.4253	2.3513

Figure 8.32   Output for second fit: mileage data.

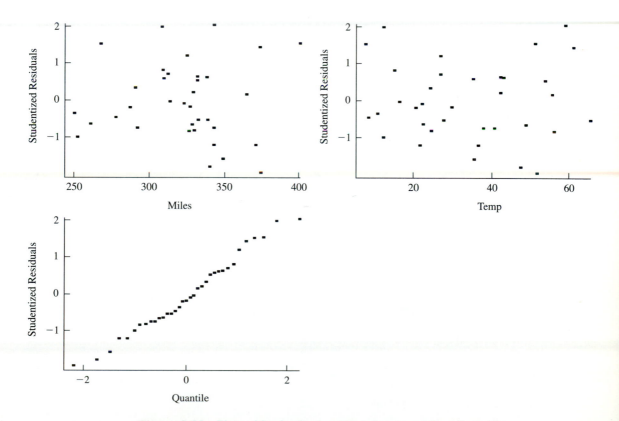

Figure 8.33   Plots of Studentized residuals for second fit: mileage data.

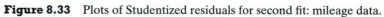

Summary of Fit			
Mean of Response	8.0048	R-Square	0.8085
Root MSE	0.2619	Adj R-Sq	0.7966

Analysis of Variance					
Source	DF	Sum of Squares	Mean Square	F Stat	Prob > F
Model	2	9.2660	4.6330	67.5638	0.0001
Error	32	2.1943	0.0686		
C Total	34	11.4603			

Parameter Estimates							
Variable	DF	Estimate	Std Error	T Stat	Prob > |T|	Tolerance	Var Inflation
INTERCEPT	1	2.4530	0.4870	5.0371	0.0001		0
MILES	1	0.0202	0.0017	11.6228	0.0001	0.5387	1.8563
TEMP	1	−0.0283	0.0037	−7.7515	0.0001	0.5387	1.8563

Figure 8.34   Output for third fit: mileage data.

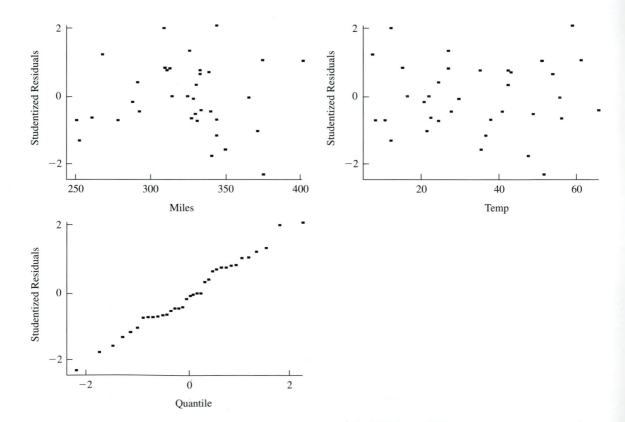

Figure 8.35   Plots of Studentized residuals for third fit: mileage data.

LAB 8.1: Multicollinearity

Introduction

In this chapter, you have learned the meaning of multicollinearity, and you have read about its consequences. In this lab, you will explore in detail the consequences of multicollinearity on data you have simulated.

Objectives

To give you a practical understanding of multicollinearity.

Lab Materials

None needed.

Experimental Procedure

Data Generation

In this part of the lab, you will generate three data sets from the same multiple linear regression model, but with regressors having different degrees of multicollinearity. Each data set will consist of 20 observations from the multiple linear regression model

$$Y = 1 + 2X_1 + 3X_2 + \epsilon$$

where ϵ has an $N(0, 1)$ distribution.

Three data sets will be generated: In the first, the values of the regressors X_1 and X_2 will be chosen so that the population correlation between them is 0.50; in the second, the population correlation between X_1 and X_2 will be 0.90; and in the third, the population correlation between X_1 and X_2 will be 0.99.[13]

To generate the desired set of 20 data values in which the regressor values come from a population having correlation ρ, proceed as follows:[14]

1. Generate 20 pairs of values $Z_{1i}, Z_{2i}, i = 1, \ldots, 20$, where $Z_{1i} \sim N(0, 1)$, $Z_{2i} \sim N(0, 1)$, and the Z_1's are independent of the Z_2's.
2. Take $X_{1i} = Z_{1i}$ and $X_{2i} = \rho Z_{1i} + (1 - \rho)Z_{2i}$. The X_1 and X_2 are the regressors.
3. Compute the response Y_i as $Y_i = 1 + 2X_{1i} + 3X_{2i} + \epsilon_i$, where the ϵ are independent $N(0, 1)$ values.

---

[13]Note that choosing a population correlation equal to a value ρ does not mean that r, the sample Pearson correlation in the data generated, will exactly equal ρ, but r should be smallest in the first data set, intermediate in the second, and largest in the last.

[14]SAS and MINITAB users will find explicit instructions for generating the data using those packages in the **Doing It with SAS** or **Doing It with MINITAB** supplements to the text.

Analysis

Assume the data for correlations 0.50, 0.90, and 0.99 are in data sets called SET50, SET90, and SET99, respectively.

Look for Evidence of the Effects of Multicollinearity.   For each of the data sets, do the following:

1. Plot one regressor versus the other. Do they look highly correlated? Calculate their Pearson correlation.
2. Regress Y on X_1 and X_2. Note the values of R^2, R_a^2, MSE, the overall F statistic and its p-value, the parameter estimates and their standard errors, and the individual t statistics for each parameter and their respective p-values.
3. Note the tolerance and VIF values.

Compare the Results.   Now compare the evidence of multicollinearity for the three data sets. In particular, answer the following:

1. Show and explain how the plots and Pearson correlation reveal multicollinearity in the three data sets.
2. What was the effect of multicollinearity on R^2, R_a^2, MSE, the overall F statistic and its p-value, the parameter estimates and their standard errors, and the individual t statistics for each parameter and their respective p-values?
3. What was the effect of multicollinearity on the VIF and tolerance values?
4. For each data set, how do the parameter estimates compare with the true values in the multiple linear regression model?
5. For SET50, does it make sense to interpret $\hat{\beta}_1$ as the change in predicted response per unit change in X_1 *with X_2 held constant*? For SET90? For SET99? Justify your answers.

LAB 8.2: Outliers

Introduction

In this chapter, you have learned about outliers in the multiple linear regression model. In this lab, you will explore these ideas in detail on data you have simulated.

Objectives

To give you a practical understanding of the effects of outliers on the fitted multiple linear regression model and on regression diagnostics.

Lab Materials

None needed.

Experimental Procedure

Data Generation

Generate a single data set of twenty observations from the multiple linear regression model

$$Y = 1 + 2X_1 + 3X_2 + \epsilon$$

where ϵ has an $N(0, 1)$ distribution, and the population correlation between X_1 and X_2 is 0.50. This is the same multiple linear regression model that generates SET50 in Lab 8.1. See Lab 8.1 for instructions on generating these data.

Analysis

Look at the Original Data.   Look at the original data by following these steps:[15]

1. Plot X_1 versus X_2. Is there anything unusual here?
2. Regress Y on X_1 and X_2 and look at the output.
3. Generate Studentized residuals. Plot these versus the fitted values. A rule of thumb is that Studentized residuals larger than 2 in absolute value should be investigated. Should any of these Studentized residuals be investigated?
4. Generate a t quantile plot of the Studentized residuals, or a normal quantile plot if a t quantile plot cannot be done. Look at the plot. Are any major problems evident?
5. Note the values of R^2, R_a^2, MSE, the overall F statistic and its p-value, the parameter estimates and their standard errors, and the individual t statistics for each parameter and their respective p-values.

Create an Outlier and See What Happens.   Now create an outlier in the data set. If the first response value is positive, add 3 to its value and if it's negative, add -3. So if the original value is 5.1, make it 8.1, and if it is -3.6, make it -6.6.

Create all the previous plots and measures for the revised data. Compare them with the corresponding plots and measures from the original data. Report how the outlier affects them. If you don't see much of an effect, change the value again to be even more extreme.

APPENDIX 8.1: Vector-Matrix Formulation of the Multiple Linear Regression Model

---

This appendix details only that part of the theory of vectors and matrices useful for explaining the material in this chapter.

---

[15]SAS and MINITAB users will find explicit instructions for conducting this lab using those packages in the **Doing It with SAS** or **Doing It with MINITAB** supplements to the text.

Matrices and Vectors

Theory

A **matrix** is a rectangular array of real numbers arranged in rows and columns. An **r × c matrix** has r rows and c columns. A **square matrix** has the same number of rows as columns. Matrices will be denoted by uppercase letters. The general form of an $r \times c$ matrix is

$$A = \begin{bmatrix} a_{11} & a_{12} & a_{13} & \cdots & a_{1c} \\ a_{21} & a_{22} & a_{23} & \cdots & a_{2c} \\ \vdots & \vdots & \vdots & & \vdots \\ a_{r1} & a_{r2} & a_{r3} & \cdots & a_{rc} \end{bmatrix} \tag{8.44}$$

A square matrix is **symmetric** if the ijth entry equals the jith entry. A **column vector** is a matrix containing only one column (i.e., it is an $r \times 1$ matrix). A **row vector** is a matrix containing only one row (i.e., it is a $1 \times c$ matrix). Throughout this appendix, all vectors will be assumed to be column vectors unless stated otherwise. All vectors will be written in bold letters. The usual form of a vector is

$$\mathbf{b} = \begin{bmatrix} b_1 \\ b_2 \\ \vdots \\ b_r \end{bmatrix}$$

Examples

Consider the 3×3 matrix

$$E = \begin{bmatrix} 1 & 3 & 9 \\ 4 & 10 & 3 \\ 1 & 1 & 2 \end{bmatrix} \tag{8.45}$$

Note that E is square but not symmetric. An example of a symmetric matrix is

$$S = \begin{bmatrix} 1 & 3 & 9 \\ 3 & 10 & 6 \\ 9 & 6 & 2 \end{bmatrix} \tag{8.46}$$

An example of a nonsquare matrix is the 3×2

$$R = \begin{bmatrix} 1 & 3 \\ 3 & 10 \\ 9 & 3 \end{bmatrix}$$

Another example of a nonsquare matrix is a column vector like

$$\mathbf{w} = \begin{bmatrix} 1 \\ 2 \\ 3 \end{bmatrix} \qquad (8.47)$$

Transpose

Theory

The **transpose** of an $r \times c$ matrix A is the $c \times r$ matrix A' obtained by interchanging the rows and columns of A. If A is given by (8.44), then

$$A' = \begin{bmatrix} a_{11} & a_{21} & a_{31} & \cdots & a_{r1} \\ a_{12} & a_{22} & a_{32} & \cdots & a_{r2} \\ \vdots & \vdots & \vdots & & \vdots \\ a_{1c} & a_{2c} & a_{3c} & \cdots & a_{rc} \end{bmatrix}$$

If A is symmetric, then $A' = A$.

Examples

If E is given by (8.45), the **transpose** of E is

$$E' = \begin{bmatrix} 1 & 4 & 1 \\ 3 & 10 & 1 \\ 9 & 3 & 2 \end{bmatrix}$$

Note that E' does not equal E. This is because E is not symmetric. Compute the transpose of S, given by (8.46). Does the transpose equal S? It will if you've computed it correctly.

Multiplication of a Vector by a Matrix

Theory

Suppose that A is an $r \times c$ matrix and that $\mathbf{b}$ is a vector of length c. Then the product $A\mathbf{b}$ is defined to be the vector $\mathbf{c}$ of length r, whose ith element is

$$c_i = \sum_{j=1}^{c} a_{ij} b_j$$

Examples

We can multiply a vector by a matrix provided the number of columns in the matrix equals the length (the number of rows) of the vector. The result is a vector having length equal to the number of rows of the matrix.

As an example, suppose we multiply the vector $\mathbf{w}$, given by (8.47), by the matrix E, given by (8.46). The result is the vector

$$\mathbf{c} = \begin{bmatrix} 34 \\ 33 \\ 9 \end{bmatrix}$$

The first entry of $\mathbf{c}$ is obtained by multiplying $\mathbf{b}$ by the first row of A as follows:

$$1 \times 1 + 3 \times 2 + 9 \times 3 = 34$$

The second entry of $\mathbf{c}$ is obtained by multiplying $\mathbf{b}$ by the second row of A as follows:

$$4 \times 1 + 10 \times 2 + 3 \times 3 = 33$$

Check your understanding by computing the last entry of $\mathbf{c}$.

The Identity Matrix

The k-dimensional identity matrix I is the $k \times k$ matrix with entries of 1 on the diagonal and entries of 0 everywhere else:

$$I = \begin{bmatrix} 1 & 0 & \cdots & 0 \\ 0 & 1 & \cdots & 0 \\ \vdots & \vdots & \ddots & \vdots \\ 0 & 0 & \cdots & 1 \end{bmatrix}$$

I has the property that if A is any $k \times c$ matrix and B is any $r \times k$ matrix, then

$$IA = A \quad \text{and} \quad BI = B$$

The Inverse

Theory

Suppose A is a $k \times k$ matrix. If there is a $k \times k$ matrix B such that

$$BA = AB = I$$

then A is said to have an inverse and the matrix B is the inverse of A. The inverse of A is written A^{-1}.

Examples

We will not go into how to compute an inverse of a matrix, but you should realize what an inverse is. The inverse of E given by (8.46) is

$$E^{-1} = \begin{bmatrix} -0.3269 & -0.0577 & 1.5577 \\ 0.0962 & 0.1346 & -0.6346 \\ 0.1154 & -0.0385 & 0.0385 \end{bmatrix}$$

To see that this is really the inverse of E, we will multiply E by E^{-1}. The computations for the first row of the product are

$$(-0.3269) \times 1 + (-0.0577) \times 4 + 1.5577 \times 1 = 1$$

$$(-0.3269) \times 3 + (-0.0577) \times 10 + 1.5577 \times 1 = 0$$

$$(-0.3269) \times 9 + (-0.0577) \times 3 + 1.5577 \times 2 = 0$$

and that for the first entry in the second row is

$$0.0962 \times 1 + 0.1346 \times 4 + (-0.6346) \times 1 = 0$$

The entire product results in the identity matrix

$$I = \begin{bmatrix} 1 & 0 & 0 \\ 0 & 1 & 0 \\ 0 & 0 & 1 \end{bmatrix}$$

The product of E times E^{-1} will also be the identity matrix.

The Vector-Matrix Form of the Multiple Linear Regression Model

Theory

Recall that for the multiple linear regression model (8.19), the observations are assumed to follow the equations

$$Y_i = \beta_0 + \beta_1 X_{i1} + \beta_2 X_{i2} + \cdots + \beta_q X_{iq} + \epsilon_i, \qquad i = 1, \ldots, n \qquad (8.48)$$

where the $\{\epsilon_i\}$ are independent zero-mean error terms with a common variance σ^2, and are usually assumed to follow an $N(0, \sigma^2)$ distribution. The set of Equations (8.48) can be written in vector-matrix form as

$$\begin{bmatrix} Y_1 \\ Y_2 \\ \vdots \\ Y_n \end{bmatrix} = \begin{bmatrix} 1 & X_{11} & X_{12} & \cdots & X_{1q} \\ 1 & X_{21} & X_{22} & \cdots & X_{2q} \\ \vdots & \vdots & \vdots & & \vdots \\ 1 & X_{n1} & X_{n2} & \cdots & X_{nq} \end{bmatrix} \begin{bmatrix} \beta_0 \\ \beta_1 \\ \vdots \\ \beta_q \end{bmatrix} + \begin{bmatrix} \epsilon_1 \\ \epsilon_2 \\ \vdots \\ \epsilon_n \end{bmatrix}$$

which can be written very compactly as

$$\underset{n \times 1}{\mathbf{Y}} = \underset{n \times (q+1)}{X} \underset{(q+1) \times 1}{\boldsymbol{\beta}} + \underset{n \times 1}{\boldsymbol{\epsilon}} \qquad (8.49)$$

where

$$Y = \begin{bmatrix} Y_1 \\ Y_2 \\ \vdots \\ Y_n \end{bmatrix}, \quad X = \begin{bmatrix} 1 & X_{11} & X_{12} & \cdots & X_{1q} \\ 1 & X_{21} & X_{22} & \cdots & X_{2q} \\ \vdots & \vdots & \vdots & & \vdots \\ 1 & X_{n1} & X_{n2} & \cdots & X_{nq} \end{bmatrix}, \quad \beta = \begin{bmatrix} \beta_0 \\ \beta_1 \\ \vdots \\ \beta_q \end{bmatrix}, \quad \epsilon = \begin{bmatrix} \epsilon_1 \\ \epsilon_2 \\ \vdots \\ \epsilon_n \end{bmatrix}$$

Examples

Consider the TREES data discussed in the chapter, and suppose that we want to fit model (8.50):

$$V = \beta_0 + \beta_1 \tilde{D} + \beta_2 \tilde{H} + \epsilon \tag{8.50}$$

where V is tree volume, and $\tilde{D}$ and $\tilde{H}$ are the centered tree diameter and height, respectively. There are 31 data values, the first two of which are

$\tilde{D}$	$\tilde{H}$	V
−4.95	−6	10.3
−4.65	−11	10.3

and the last of which is

7.35	11	77.0

Then the set of equations describing the data can be written as (8.49), where

$$\underset{31 \times 1}{Y} = \begin{bmatrix} 10.3 \\ 10.3 \\ \vdots \\ 77.0 \end{bmatrix}, \quad \underset{31 \times 3}{X} = \begin{bmatrix} 1.00 & -4.95 & -6.00 \\ 1.00 & -4.65 & -11.00 \\ \vdots & \vdots & \vdots \\ 1.00 & 7.35 & 11.00 \end{bmatrix},$$

$$\underset{3 \times 1}{\beta} = \begin{bmatrix} \beta_0 \\ \beta_1 \\ \beta_3 \end{bmatrix}, \quad \underset{31 \times 1}{\epsilon} = \begin{bmatrix} \epsilon_1 \\ \epsilon_2 \\ \vdots \\ \epsilon_{31} \end{bmatrix}$$

Fitting the Multiple Linear Regression Model

Theory

Recall that to fit the multiple linear regression model by least squares, we need to find those values of $b_0, b_1, \ldots, b_q$ that minimize

$$\text{SSE}(b_0, b_1, \ldots, b_q) = \sum_{i=1}^{n} [Y_i - (b_0 + b_1 X_{i1} + b_2 X_{i2} + \cdots + b_q X_{iq})]^2$$

The resulting values are the least squares estimators and are denoted $\hat{\beta}_0, \hat{\beta}_1, \ldots, \hat{\beta}_q$. SSE $(b_0, b_1, \ldots, b_q)$ is easily written in vector-matrix form as

$$\text{SSE}(b_0, b_1, \ldots, b_q) = (\mathbf{Y} - X\mathbf{b})'(\mathbf{Y} - X\mathbf{b})$$

where $\mathbf{b} = [b_0, b_1, \ldots, b_q]'$.

    We may find the values of $b_0, b_1, \ldots, b_q$ that minimize $\text{SSE}(b_0, b_1, \ldots, b_q)$ by taking the derivative of $\text{SSE}(b_0, b_1, \ldots, b_q)$ with respect to each of $b_0, b_1, \ldots, b_q$ and set each derivative equal to 0. This gives a system of $q + 1$ equations in $q + 1$ unknowns to solve, which may be written in vector-matrix notation as

$$2X'X\mathbf{b} - 2X'\mathbf{Y} = \mathbf{0} \tag{8.51}$$

The solution of (8.51) is

$$\hat{\beta} = (X'X)^{-1}X'\mathbf{Y} \tag{8.52}$$

where $\hat{\beta} = [\hat{\beta}_0, \hat{\beta}_1, \dots, \hat{\beta}_q]'$.

Examples

We illustrate the computations for the TREES data. The matrix $X'X$ is

$$
\begin{bmatrix}
1.00 & 1.00 & \cdots & 1.00 \\
-4.95 & -4.65 & \cdots & 7.35 \\
-6.00 & -11.00 & \cdots & 11.00
\end{bmatrix}
\begin{bmatrix}
1.00 & -4.95 & -6.00 \\
1.00 & -4.65 & -11.00 \\
\vdots & \vdots & \vdots \\
1.00 & 7.35 & 11.00
\end{bmatrix}
=
\begin{bmatrix}
31.00 & 0.00 & 0.00 \\
0.00 & 295.44 & 311.50 \\
0.00 & 311.50 & 1218.00
\end{bmatrix}
$$

Notice that $X'X$ is symmetric, as is always the case.

The vector $X'\mathbf{Y}$ is

$$
\begin{bmatrix}
1.00 & 1.00 & \cdots & 1.00 \\
-4.95 & -4.65 & \cdots & 7.35 \\
-6.00 & -11.00 & \cdots & 11.00
\end{bmatrix}
\begin{bmatrix}
10.3 \\
10.3 \\
\vdots \\
77.0
\end{bmatrix}
=
\begin{bmatrix}
935.3 \\
1496.6 \\
1879.8
\end{bmatrix}
$$

Therefore, the vector $\hat{\beta}$ of parameter estimates is

$$
\begin{bmatrix}
31.00 & 0.00 & 0.00 \\
0.00 & 295.44 & 311.50 \\
0.00 & 311.50 & 1218.00
\end{bmatrix}^{-1}
\begin{bmatrix}
935.3 \\
1496.6 \\
1879.8
\end{bmatrix}
=
\begin{bmatrix}
30.17 \\
4.71 \\
0.34
\end{bmatrix}
$$

Fitted Values and Residuals

Theory

Recall that fitted values of the response variable are obtained by substituting the fitted coefficients $\hat{\beta}_i$ for the unknown actual coefficients β_i, $i = 1, \dots, n$, and ignoring the random-error terms in model (8.48). In vector-matrix terms, this becomes

$$\hat{\mathbf{Y}} = X\hat{\beta} \tag{8.53}$$

where $\hat{\mathbf{Y}} = [\hat{Y}_1, \hat{Y}_2, \dots, \hat{Y}_n]'$ is the vector of fitted values. Since $\hat{\beta} = (X'X)^{-1}X'\mathbf{Y}$, we can rewrite (8.53) as

$$\hat{\mathbf{Y}} = H\mathbf{Y}$$

where $H = X(X'X)^{-1}X'$ is called the **hat matrix,** because multiplying the vector of responses $\mathbf{Y}$ by H "puts a hat," on $\mathbf{Y}$: that is, it produces $\hat{\mathbf{Y}}$, the fitted values.

Recall that the ith residual is the difference of the ith observation and the ith fitted value: $e_i = Y_i - \hat{Y}_i$. In vector-matrix terms, if $\mathbf{e} = [e_1, e_2, \ldots, e_n]'$ is the vector of residuals,

$$\mathbf{e} = \mathbf{Y} - \hat{\mathbf{Y}} = (I - H)\mathbf{Y} \tag{8.54}$$

where I is the $n \times n$ identity matrix.

You know how to find and interpret the variance of a random variable. The analogue of variance for a vector of random variables is the **variance-covariance matrix.** The variance-covariance matrix of a vector of n random variables is the $n \times n$ symmetric matrix whose iith entry is the variance of the ith random variable in the vector, and whose ijth entry is the covariance between the ith and jth random variables. Using (8.54), we can show that the variance-covariance matrix of $\mathbf{e}$ is

$$\sigma^2(\mathbf{e}) = \sigma^2(I - H) \tag{8.55}$$

In particular, it follows that the standard error of e_i equals $\sigma\sqrt{1 - h_{ii}}$, where h_{ii} is the ith diagonal entry in H.[16] If we knew σ, we could compute the ith standardized residual as $e_i/\sigma\sqrt{1 - h_{ii}}$. As we don't know σ, we use $\text{MSE}_{(i)}$, the mean square error from the regression fit to all except the ith data value, to estimate it. The resulting (externally) Studentized residual is

$$r_{(i)} = \frac{e_i}{\sqrt{\text{MSE}_{(i)}(1 - h_{ii})}}.$$

Examples

The 31×31 matrix H for the TREES regression is too large to display here. Its 11 entry, h_{11}, is 0.116. $\text{MSE}_{(1)}$, the MSE of the regression with the first observation omitted, is 14.38. The residual $e_1 = 5.46$, so the Studentized residual for the first observation is

$$r_{(1)} = \frac{5.46}{\sqrt{14.38(1 - 0.116)}} = 1.53$$

Inference in Vector-Matrix Notation

Theory

The Variance-Covariance Matrix of $\hat{\beta}$***.***   The variance-covariance matrix of the vector of least squares estimators $\hat{\beta}$ is the $(q + 1) \times (q + 1)$ symmetric matrix

$$\Sigma(\hat{\beta}) = \sigma^2(X'X)^{-1}$$

---

[16]h_{ii} is called the **leverage** of the ith observation. It is a measure of how far the regressor values for the ith observation are from the mean of the regressor values for all the data.

Since we do not know σ^2, we estimate it, as usual, by the MSE, giving the estimated variance-covariance matrix of $\hat{\beta}$:

$$\hat{\Sigma}(\hat{\beta}) = (\text{MSE})(X'X)^{-1}$$

Estimating the Mean Response.   Suppose we want to estimate the mean response at regressor values $x_1, x_2, \ldots, x_q$. Let $\mathbf{x}$ denote the vector $[1, x_1, x_2, \ldots, x_q]'$. Then the point estimator is

$$\hat{Y} = \mathbf{x}'\hat{\beta}$$

and the estimated standard error of $\hat{Y}$ is

$$\hat{\sigma}(\hat{Y}) = \sqrt{\mathbf{x}'\hat{\Sigma}(\hat{\beta})\mathbf{x}}$$

A level L confidence interval for the mean response at $x_1, x_2, \ldots, x_q$ is then given by (8.36).

Predicting a New Observation.   You know the following from the chapter and from the formulas in this section:

- The point predictor of a new observation at $x_1, x_2, \ldots, x_q$ is

$$\hat{Y}_{\text{new}} = \hat{Y} = \mathbf{x}'\hat{\beta}$$

- The estimated standard error of prediction is

$$\hat{\sigma}(Y_{\text{new}} - \hat{Y}_{\text{new}}) = \sqrt{\text{MSE} + \hat{\sigma}^2(\hat{Y})} = \sqrt{(\text{MSE})\left[1 + \mathbf{x}'\hat{\Sigma}(\hat{\beta})\mathbf{x}\right]}$$

A level L prediction interval for a new observation at $x_1, x_2, \ldots, x_q$ is then given by (8.38).

Examples

We will illustrate the inference computations using model (8.50).

The Variance-Covariance Matrix of $\hat{\beta}$.   MSE is 15.0686, and

$$(X'X)^{-1} = \begin{bmatrix} 31.00 & 0.00 & 0.00 \\ 0.00 & 295.44 & 311.50 \\ 0.00 & 311.50 & 1218.00 \end{bmatrix}^{-1} = \begin{bmatrix} 0.0323 & 0.0000 & 0.0000 \\ 0.0000 & 0.0046 & -0.0012 \\ 0.0000 & -0.0012 & 0.0011 \end{bmatrix}$$

so the estimated variance-covariance matrix of $\hat{\beta}$ is

$$\hat{\Sigma}(\hat{\beta}) = 15.0686 \begin{bmatrix} 0.0323 & 0.0000 & 0.0000 \\ 0.0000 & 0.0046 & -0.0012 \\ 0.0000 & -0.0012 & 0.0011 \end{bmatrix} = \begin{bmatrix} 0.4861 & 0.0000 & 0.0000 \\ 0.0000 & 0.0698 & -0.0179 \\ 0.0000 & -0.0179 & 0.0169 \end{bmatrix}$$

Estimating the Mean Response. Suppose we want to estimate the mean volume of trees having diameter 28 inches and height 70 feet. This corresponds to values of the centered variables $CD = -2.171$ and $CH = -6$. Thus, $\mathbf{x} = [1.000, -2.171, -6.000]'$, and the point estimate is

$$\hat{Y} = [1.000, -2.171, -6.000] \begin{bmatrix} 30.17 \\ 4.71 \\ 0.34 \end{bmatrix} = 17.91$$

The standard error of the estimator is

$$\hat{\sigma}(\hat{Y}) = \sqrt{[1.000, -2.171, -6.000]' \begin{bmatrix} 0.4861 & 0.0000 & 0.0000 \\ 0.0000 & 0.0698 & -0.0179 \\ 0.0000 & -0.0179 & 0.0169 \end{bmatrix} \begin{bmatrix} 1.000 \\ -2.171 \\ -6.000 \end{bmatrix}} = 0.9797$$

Predicting a New Observation. Suppose we want to predict the volume of the next tree we measure having diameter 28 inches and height 70 feet. The point predictor is $\hat{Y}_{new} = \hat{Y} = 17.91$. Its standard error is

$$\hat{\sigma}(Y_{new} - \hat{Y}_{new}) = \sqrt{15.0686 + (0.9797)^2} = 4.004$$

Capstone Project: Chapters 1 to 4 and 8

The goal of a **Capstone Project** is to give experience in all phases of a statistical study: planning, data collection, analysis, and conclusions. Each of Chapters 1 to 4 and 8 must make a contribution to the project. For a description of this project, see the description of the Capstone Project for Chapters 1 to 5 on page 285. In addition to the material from Chapters 1 to 4 discussed there, the Capstone Project for Chapters 1 to 4 and 8, must also include modeling and inference for multivariate data using multiple linear regression, as covered in Chapter 8.

9

The One-Way Model

If one takes care of the means, the end will take care of itself.

—Ghandi

INTRODUCTION

In Chapter 6, you learned how to test the equality of means of two independent populations. In this chapter, you will learn how to test the equality of means of more than two independent populations.

Knowledge and Skills

By successfully completing this chapter, you will acquire the following knowledge and skills:

KNOWLEDGE	SKILLS
1. The one-way means model.	**1.** For the one-way means model, the one-way effects model, and the randomized complete block model: **(a)** How to fit the model. **(b)** How to check the fit of the model. **(c)** How to test the equality of population means. *(continued)*

KNOWLEDGE	**SKILLS**
	(d) How to construct confidence intervals for differences in individual means.
	(e) How to do multiple comparisons.
2. The one-way effects model.	**2.** For the regression formulation of the one-way effects and randomized complete block models:
	(a) How to fit the model.
	(b) How to check the fit of the model.
	(c) How to test the equality of population means.
3. The randomized complete block model.	
4. The analysis of variance.	
5. Individual comparisons.	
6. Multiple comparisons.	
7. The regression formulation of the one-way effects and randomized complete block models.	

9.1

THE ONE-WAY MEANS MODEL

Viewing Multipopulation Measurement Data

EXAMPLE 9.1   EVALUATING THE EFFICACY OF TREATMENTS FOR BENIGN PROSTATE HYPERPLASIA

Benign Prostate Hyperplasia (BPH) is an enlargement of the prostate gland common in men of middle age. Among the symptoms that require treatment are reduced urine flow. The two standard treatments are drugs to reduce the swelling and surgery to remove the prostate. Recently, a new outpatient procedure using microwaves has shown promise in treating BPH.

In order to evaluate the efficacy of the new procedure, a clinical trial was conducted. It was decided to investigate three treatments: a standard drug treatment with the 5α reductase inhibitor finasteride; a standard surgical procedure, transurethral prostatectomy; and the new microwave treatment. From a pool of men diagnosed with BPH who volunteered for the experiment, 18 men, aged 50–55, were chosen. In order to prevent unknown biases, the experimenters ran the controlled experiment as a **completely randomized design** (see Chapter 3). To do this, they arranged the names of the 18 volunteers in alphabetical order. They then selected 18 random numbers from a random-number table and assigned them in the order selected to the alphabetically ordered volunteers. So, for example, if the first three volunteer names in alphabetical order were Adams, Baxter, and Corelli, the first random number would be assigned to Adams, the second to Baxter, and the third to Corelli. The volunteers with the six smallest random numbers were assigned drug treatment, those with the next six smallest random numbers were assigned surgical treatment, and those with the six largest random numbers were assigned the new microwave treatment.

A follow-up evaluation was given 6 months after the treatment was begun and the increase in urine flow (ml/sec) was measured to evaluate the success of the treatment. Two of the subjects assigned to have surgery decided against that treatment, and one of the subjects assigned to the drug treatment was unreliable in taking the medication. These three subjects were dropped from the study, leaving the experimenters with 15 data points. The data are shown in Table 9.1.

TABLE 9.1   Prostate Experiment Data

Treatment	Increase in urine flow (ml/sec)						Mean	Standard deviation
Drug	1.1	1.4	1.3	1.9	1.6		1.46	0.31
Microwave	2.9	3.7	3.4	3.4	2.8	2.2	3.07	0.54
Surgery	4.0	5.2	5.0	4.7			4.73	0.53

The left plot in Figure 9.1 shows the increase in urine flow, stratified by treatment. The right plot shows **mean diamonds** of the same data: one diamond for each treatment.

The horizontal line on each diamond is located at the sample mean of the data for the corresponding treatment, and the vertical distance from the horizontal line to the upper and lower vertices of the diamond is one sample standard deviation in each direction. From these, we can make the following observations:

- The mean increase in urine flow is clearly different for the three treatments. It is lowest for drug treatment, higher for microwave treatment, and highest for surgery.
- The spread of the observations is comparable for microwave treatment and surgery, but is a bit lower for drug treatment.

In order to go beyond a descriptive analysis of the prostate data, we need to formulate a statistical model for the process that produced these data. ✦

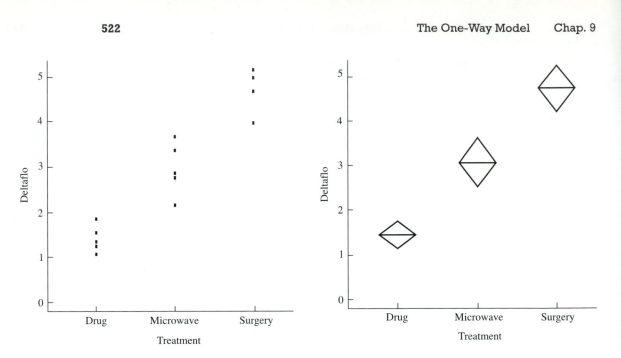

Figure 9.1 Stratified plot (left) and side-by-side mean diamonds (right): prostate data.

The Model

The model we'll consider is called a **one-way means model.** The general one-way means model for k populations is

$$Y_{ij} = \mu_i + \epsilon_{ij}, \qquad j = 1, \ldots, n_i; \ i = 1, \ldots, k \qquad (9.1)$$

In this model, Y_{ij} is the jth observation from the ith population, μ_i is the mean of the ith population, and ϵ_{ij} is the random error associated with the jth observation from the ith population. We will assume that the ϵ_{ij} are independent $N(0, \sigma^2)$ random variables.

To understand the one-way means model better, it may help to note that the two-sample model for independent populations with common variance discussed in Chapters 5 and 6 is exactly model (9.1) when $k = 2$.

As is explained in Chapter 4, in an experimental setting, it is often convenient to describe the k populations in terms of treatments applied to experimental units. In this context, there are k treatments and the set of all possible observations that could result from applying treatment i to experimental units is population i. In this terminology, μ_i is the mean of treatment i.

EXAMPLE 9.1   CONTINUED

Putting the prostate data in terms of model (9.1), we see that there are three populations, consisting of all possible observations that could result from the drug treatment, microwave treatment, or surgery given to middle-aged men with BPH. Therefore, $k = 3$. The numbers of observations n_1, n_2, and n_3 are 5, 6, and 4, respectively. The population mean increase in urine flow under drug treatment, microwave treatment, and surgery are μ_1, μ_2, and μ_3 respectively. As this is an experiment, the responses may be considered to come from the treatments drug, microwave, and surgery applied to the experimental units: men with BPH.   ✦

Fitting the Model

Fitting model (9.1) consists of using the data to estimate the unknown model parameters μ_i, $i = 1, \ldots, k$, and σ^2.

To write out the formulas for the estimators, we need some notation. Let $n = n_1 + n_2 + \cdots + n_k$ be the total number of observations. Let

$$\bar{Y}_{i.} = \frac{1}{n_i} \sum_{j=1}^{n_i} Y_{ij} \qquad \text{and} \qquad S_i^2 = \frac{1}{n_i - 1} \sum_{j=1}^{n_i} (Y_{ij} - \bar{Y}_{i.})^2$$

denote the mean and variance respectively of the sample from the ith population, $i = 1, \ldots, k$.

FORMULAS FOR FITTING THE MEANS MODEL

- The mean of the sample from the ith population, $\bar{Y}_{i.}$, is used to estimate the population mean μ_i. We will denote this estimator $\hat{\mu}_i$.

  These estimators for the μ_i are the least squares estimators, obtained by finding the values of m_i that minimize

$$\text{SSE}(m_1, m_2, \ldots, m_k) = \sum_{i=1}^{k} \sum_{j=1}^{n_i} (Y_{ij} - m_i)^2$$

- The pooled variance

$$S_p^2 = \frac{1}{n - k} \sum_{i=1}^{k} (n_i - 1) S_i^2 \tag{9.2}$$

is used to estimate σ^2. We will call this estimator $\hat{\sigma}^2$.

Notice that these estimators are exactly the same ones used in the two-population case when equal variances are assumed. See Chapters 5 and 6 for details.

EXAMPLE 9.1   CONTINUED

Let's see how the fitting formulas work for the prostate data. The total number of observations is $n = 15$. The mean and variance of the sample of patients given drug therapy are

$$\hat{\mu}_1 = \bar{y}_{1.} = \frac{1.1 + 1.4 + \cdots + 1.6}{5} = 1.46$$

and

$$s_1^2 = \frac{(1.1 - 1.46)^2 + (1.4 - 1.46)^2 + \cdots + (1.6 - 1.46)^2}{5 - 1} = 0.093$$

respectively. Notice that the standard deviation $s_1 = 0.31$ shown by Table 9.1 is the square root of this latter quantity. As Table 9.1 shows, $\hat{\mu}_2 = \bar{y}_{2.} = 3.07$, $\hat{\mu}_3 = \bar{y}_{3.} = 4.73$, $s_2^2 = 0.54^2 = 0.29$, and $s_3^2 = 0.53^2 = 0.28$. Putting all this together in Equation (9.2) gives the pooled variance estimate

$$\hat{\sigma}^2 = s_p^2 = \frac{(5 - 1)0.09 + (6 - 1)0.29 + (4 - 1)0.28}{15 - 3} = 0.22 \quad \blacklozenge$$

Checking the Fit

Once the model is fit, and before the model is used further, the fit must be checked to see to what extent model assumptions are satisfied. Recall that those assumptions are that the random errors ϵ_{ij} are independent $N(0, \sigma^2)$ random variables. The principal tools used to check these assumptions are the **residuals**

$$e_{ij} = Y_{ij} - \hat{\mu}_i = Y_{ij} - \bar{Y}_{i.}, \qquad j = 1, \ldots, n_i; \; i = 1, \ldots, k$$

The idea is that the residuals e_{ij} should mimic the behavior of the unobservable random errors ϵ_{ij}. Therefore, if the model is an adequate description of the data, the residuals should display behavior consistent with the model assumptions.

The most effective method of fit checking is to display residual plots. Plots of the residuals stratified by population are very useful. Histograms (if there is a good number of data from each population), mean diamonds and stratified plots are useful in this regard. The pattern and spread of the data from each population should be considered.

For checking the normality assumption, the most appropriate plot is a plot of the Studentized residuals versus quantiles of the t_{n-k-1} distribution.[1] Studentized residuals are also useful in checking for outliers. Any Studentized residuals that are in the extreme tails of the t_{n-k-1} distribution should be checked as possible outliers.

---

[1] Recall that Studentized residuals are formed by dividing each residual by its estimated standard error. If the random errors in model (9.1) have an $N(0, \sigma^2)$ distribution, the Studentized residuals will have a t_{n-k-1} distribution. See Chapters 7 and 8 for details on plotting Studentized residuals.

Independence of the errors is difficult to check, and we will not pursue this topic here. The best we can do is to use this model only for populations that are not related and to select the samples from the populations randomly and independently of each other.

Even if the populations under study have a common variance, the sample variances S_i^2 will not be equal. However, unless the sample variances are markedly different, we will not go far wrong assuming the population variances are equal. This is particularly true if the numbers of observations obtained from the different populations are equal or nearly equal.

EXAMPLE 9.1   CONTINUED

Figure 9.2 shows a stratified plot and side-by-side mean diamonds for the residuals of the prostate data.

Notice that these plots are identical to corresponding plots for the original data, in Figure 9.1, except that the plots for each population have been centered at 0. This is because the residuals are obtained from the original data by subtracting the means within each sample.

Figure 9.3 shows a plot of the Studentized residuals versus quantiles of the t_{11} distribution.

Looking at Figure 9.3, we see that the data look basically normal, but that there are two possible outliers in the lower left part of the plot. Though the

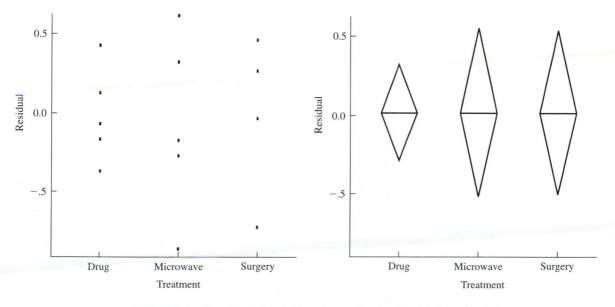

Figure 9.2   Stratified plot (left) and mean diamonds (right): residuals from prostate data fit.

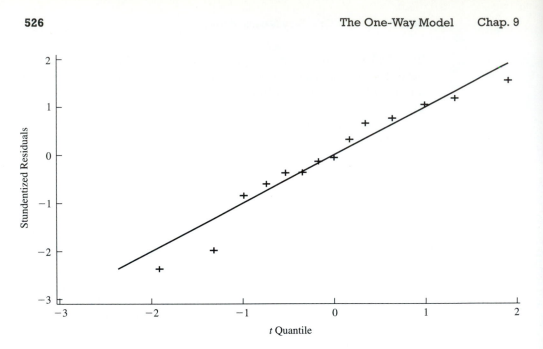

Figure 9.3 Studentized residuals from prostate data fit versus quantiles of the t_{11} distribution.

Studentized residuals of these two points are not extreme, the experimenters checked these values and found no reasons to discard them.

The results of the analysis of the fit to the data is that the assumptions seem well enough satisfied to continue the analysis with this model.   ✦

Testing the Equality of Population Means: The Analysis of Variance

Recall that the experimenters in Example 9.1 want to evaluate the efficacy of the microwave procedure. In particular, they would like to know how, on average, the increase in urine flow after the microwave procedure compares with the results after drug therapy and surgery. In terms of model (9.1), they want to compare the population mean increase in flow for the three populations. The most basic question is whether these population means are all the same or not. If the three population means are equal, then on average there is no difference in flow increase for any of the three procedures.

In statistical terms, the experimenters want to distinguish between the following two hypotheses:

$$H_0: \quad \mu_1 = \mu_2 = \mu_3$$
$$H_a: \quad \text{Not all the population means } \mu_i \text{ are equal}$$

In general, when there are k populations, the hypotheses are

$$H_0: \quad \mu_1 = \mu_2 = \cdots = \mu_k$$
$$H_a: \quad \text{Not all the population means } \mu_i \text{ are equal}$$

The test statistic for testing H_0 versus H_a is the F statistic. In order to show how the F statistic is computed, and more importantly what it means, we need to see how to divide the total variation in the response into components in a technique called the **analysis of variance.**[2]

Dividing the Variation

The **Analysis of Variance,** sometimes denoted by the acronym **ANOVA,** is a technique for dividing the total variation in a response into a number of components attributable to different sources, and analyzing those components. The components of variation are called **sums of squares.**

For the one-way means model, the total variation is measured by the **sum of squares total,** denoted by the acronym **SSTO.** SSTO may be thought of as follows.

Suppose that H_0 is true. Then $\mu_1 = \mu_2 = \cdots = \mu_k$. Call μ the common value of the μ_i. Model (9.1) then becomes

$$Y_{ij} = \mu + \epsilon_{ij}, \qquad j = 1, \ldots, n_i; \ i = 1, \ldots, k \tag{9.3}$$

Fitting this model involves estimating μ and σ^2. The estimator of μ is $\bar{Y}_{..} = \sum_{i=1}^{k} \sum_{j=1}^{n_i} Y_{ij}/n$, which is just the mean of all the observations. If we let $\tilde{e}_{ij} = Y_{ij} - \bar{Y}_{..}$ denote the residuals from the fit of model (9.3), the quantity SSTO $= \sum_{i=1}^{k} \sum_{j=1}^{n_i} \tilde{e}_{ij}^2$ is a measure of how far all the data differ from the fitted model (9.3). SSTO measures the unexplained variation after model (9.3) has been fit to the data.

The analysis of variance for the one-way means model divides the total variation in the response, SSTO, into two components. One of these two components, **sum of squares error (SSE)** is the sum of the squares of the residuals:

$$\text{SSE} = \sum_{i=1}^{k} \sum_{j=1}^{n_i} e_{ij}^2 = \sum_{i=1}^{k} \sum_{j=1}^{n_i} (Y_{ij} - \bar{Y}_{i.})^2$$

SSE measures the unexplained variation after model (9.1) has been fit to the data. To see this, first recall that for each $i = 1, 2, \ldots, k$, the residual e_{ij} measures by how much the fitted value $\bar{Y}_{i.}$ overestimates (if e_{ij} is negative) or underestimates (if e_{ij} is positive) the data value Y_{ij}. Therefore, $\sum_{j=1}^{n_i} e_{ij}^2$ is a measure of how far the data from population i differ overall from the fitted value $\bar{Y}_{i.}$, and SSE $= \sum_{i=1}^{k} \sum_{j=1}^{n_i} e_{ij}^2$ is a measure of how far all the data differ from the fitted model (9.1). This is another way of saying that SSE measures the unexplained variation after model (9.1) has been fit to the data.

---

[2]Readers who have previously covered Chapter 8 will find the following discussion familiar.

SSE is no larger than SSTO since fitting a mean separately to each of the k samples, instead of fitting one mean for all the data, can only reduce the unexplained variation. In other words, model (9.1) will always explain at least as much of the variation in the data as model (9.3). The difference SSM = SSTO − SSE is called the **sum of squares model.** It measures how much fitting model (9.1) reduces the variation left unexplained by the fit of model (9.3). SSM may also be computed by the formula

$$\text{SSM} = \sum_{i=1}^{k} n_i (\bar{Y}_{i.} - \bar{Y}_{..})^2$$

The following summarizes the sums of squares formulas for the one-way means model.

SUMS OF SQUARES FORMULAS FOR THE ONE-WAY MEANS MODEL

- The sum of squares total is

$$\text{SSTO} = \sum_{i=1}^{k} \sum_{j=1}^{n_i} (Y_{ij} - \bar{Y}_{..})^2$$

- The sum of squares model is

$$\text{SSM} = \sum_{i=1}^{k} n_i (\bar{Y}_{i.} - \bar{Y}_{..})^2$$

- The sum of squares error is

$$\text{SSE} = \sum_{i=1}^{k} \sum_{j=1}^{n_i} (Y_{ij} - \bar{Y}_{i.})^2$$

- Further, SSTO = SSM + SSE.

Each sum of squares has associated with it an integer called its **degrees of freedom.** Each sum of squares is a sum of squared terms. The **degrees of freedom** for a sum of squares is the minimum number of those terms needed to compute the sum of squares.

To look a little more closely at the idea of degrees of freedom, consider SSTO. It is a sum based on n pieces of data: $\{(Y_{ij} - \bar{Y}_{..}), \ i = 1, \ldots, k, \ j = 1, \ldots, n_i\}$. However, if we know $n-1$ of those terms, we can compute the nth (see Exercise 9.2), so only $n-1$ degrees of freedom are associated with SSTO. The degrees of freedom associated with SSE and SSM are $n - k$ and $k - 1$, respectively. We already know that SSTO = SSM + SSE. It is also true that the degrees of freedom associated with these sums of squares add up: $n - 1 = (k - 1) + (n - k)$.

When any of the sums of squares is divided by its degrees of freedom, the result is called a **mean square.** This is exactly what its name implies, an average of the squares. However, the average is the sum divided by the degrees of freedom, not the number of terms. Thus, the **mean square error** is MSE = SSE/$(n - k)$ and the **mean square model** is MSM = SSM/$(k - 1)$. A total mean square could be computed, but usually isn't.[3]

DEGREES OF FREEDOM AND MEAN SQUARES FOR THE ONE-WAY MEANS MODEL

- Each sum of squares is a sum of squared terms. The **degrees of freedom** for a sum of squares is the minimum number of those terms needed to compute the sum of squares. For the one-way means model, the degrees of freedom associated with SSTO, SSM, and SSE are $n - 1$, $k - 1$, and $n - k$, respectively. Just as the sums of squares SSM and SSE sum to SSTO, the degrees of freedom for SSM and SSE sum to the degrees of freedom for SSTO: $(k - 1) + (n - k) = n - 1$.

- The **mean square** associated with a sum of squares is the mean of the squares making up that sum of squares. The mean square is computed by dividing the sum of squares by its degrees of freedom.

- The mean squares associated with SSE and SSM are MSE = SSE/$(n - k)$ and MSM = SSM/$(k - 1)$, respectively. A mean square is not usually computed for SSTO.

The F Test

The test statistic for testing H_0 versus H_a is called the **F statistic,** or **F ratio,** and is computed as the ratio of MSM and MSE: $F = $ MSM/MSE. When H_0 is true, the sampling distribution of the ratio F is an **F distribution.** The F distribution is really a family of distributions indexed by two parameters called **degrees of freedom.** Examples of different F distributions are shown in Figure 9.4.

When the null hypothesis is true, the sampling distribution for the test statistic F is an F distribution with first parameter equal to the degrees of freedom associated with SSM, and second parameter equal to the degrees of freedom associated with SSE. So for model (9.3), the F ratio has an F distribution with $k - 1$ and $n - k$ degrees of freedom.

Since MSE tends to stay roughly the same size regardless of which hypothesis is true, and MSM tends to be small if H_0 is true and large if H_a is true, large values of the F ratio tend to contradict H_0 and support H_a.

---

[3]Note that the mean square total, SSTO/$(n - 1)$, would equal the sample variance of all the responses taken together.

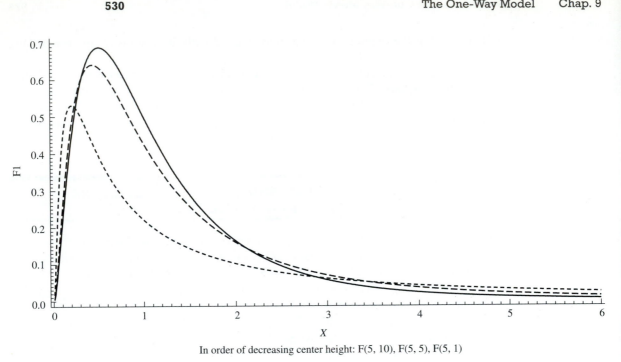

In order of decreasing center height: F(5, 10), F(5, 5), F(5, 1)

Figure 9.4   F distributions.

As you learned in Chapter 6, the **p-value** is a measure of how consistent the test statistic, in this case, the F ratio, is with the null hypothesis. Here, the p-value is the probability that an observation from the $F_{k-1,n-k}$ distribution (i.e., the distribution the F ratio has if the null hypothesis is true) exceeds the observed F ratio (i.e., the F ratio computed from the data). A small p-value indicates that the observed F ratio is very large. This is strong evidence against the null hypothesis and in favor of the alternative hypothesis. The smaller the p-value, the stronger the evidence against H_0 and in favor of H_a.

EXAMPLE 9.1   CONTINUED

Some computations with the prostate data will help illustrate these concepts. First, the overall mean $\bar{y} = 2.97$, so

$$\text{SSTO} = (1.1 - 2.97)^2 + (1.4 - 2.97)^2 + \cdots + (5.0 - 2.97)^2 + (4.7 - 2.97)^2$$

$$= 26.45$$

and, since the means for the drug, microwave, and surgery data are 1.46, 3.07,

TABLE 9.2   ANOVA Table for Prostate Data

		Analysis of variance			
Source	DF	Sum of squares	Mean square	F Stat	Prob > F
Model	2	23.78	11.89	53.37	0.0001
Error	12	2.67	0.22		
C Total	14	26.45			

and 4.73,

$$SSE = (1.1 - 1.46)^2 + \cdots + (1.6 - 1.46)^2$$
$$+(2.9 - 3.07)^2 + \cdots + (2.2 - 3.07)^2$$
$$+(4.0 - 4.73)^2 + \cdots + (4.7 - 4.73)^2$$
$$= 2.67$$

Therefore, SSM $= 26.45 - 2.67 = 23.78$. The degrees of freedom associated with SSTO are $15 - 1 = 14$, those associated with SSE are $15 - 3 = 12$, and those associated with SSM are $3 - 1 = 2$, so MSM $= 23.78/2 = 11.89$ and MSE $= 2.67/12 = 0.22$. The F ratio then has the value $f^* = 11.89/0.22 = 53.37$. The p-value, 0.0001, is the probability an $F_{2,12}$ random variable exceeds 53.37.[4] This small p-value provides strong evidence against H_0 and in favor of H_a, and our action is to reject H_0 in favor of H_a. We therefore conclude that the population means are not all equal.

Table 9.2, taken from SAS/INSIGHT output from the fit of model (9.1) to the prostate data, is called an **analysis of variance (or ANOVA) table.** This table is a convenient way to summarize all relevant quantities in the analysis of variance.   ✦

The general ANOVA table for the one-way model is shown in Table 9.3.

Individual Comparisons of Population Means

The F test tells us whether there are any statistically significant differences among the population means. If the p-value is large, there is insufficient evidence in the data to conclude that there are any differences in the population means. If the p-value is small, as it is for the prostate data, we can conclude that the data provide strong evidence that not all population means are equal. However, the test gives no information concerning which population means differ from which others. In order to obtain that information, we must compare each pair of sample means.

---

[4]Actually, it is 1×10^{-6}, but the SAS software we used gives the value 0.0001 whenever the true p-value does not exceed 0.0001.

TABLE 9.3   ANOVA Table for the One-Way Model

		Analysis of variance			
Source	DF	Sum of squares	Mean square	F Stat	Prob > F
Model	$k-1$	SSM	MSM	$F = \text{MSM/MSE}$	p-value
Error	$n-k$	SSE	MSE		
C Total	$n-1$	SSTO			

To compare μ_i with μ_j, we use the fact that under the assumptions of model (9.1),

$$T_{ij} = \frac{\bar{Y}_{i.} - \bar{Y}_{j.} - (\mu_i - \mu_j)}{\hat{\sigma}(\bar{Y}_{i.} - \bar{Y}_{j.})} \tag{9.4}$$

has a t_{n-k} distribution, where $\hat{\sigma}(\bar{Y}_{i.} - \bar{Y}_{j.})$, the estimated standard error of $\bar{Y}_{i.} - \bar{Y}_{j.}$, is computed as

$$\hat{\sigma}(\bar{Y}_{i.} - \bar{Y}_{j.}) = \sqrt{\text{MSE}\left(\frac{1}{n_i} + \frac{1}{n_j}\right)}$$

Note the similarity of (9.4) to the t statistic for comparing two means that you studied in Chapter 6.

Now suppose we want to test

$$H_0: \quad \mu_i = \mu_j$$
$$H_a: \quad \mu_i \neq \mu_j$$

Since under H_0, $\mu_i - \mu_j = 0$, a two-sided test is conducted with

$$T_{ij0} = \frac{\bar{Y}_{i.} - \bar{Y}_{j.}}{\hat{\sigma}(\bar{Y}_{i.} - \bar{Y}_{j.})}$$

as the test statistic, and the p-value is computed from the t_{n-k} distribution.

Alternatively, a level L confidence interval may be obtained for $\mu_i - \mu_j$ from the formula

$$(\bar{Y}_{i.} - \bar{Y}_{j.} - \hat{\sigma}(\bar{Y}_{i.} - \bar{Y}_{j.})t_{n-k,(1+L)/2}, \ \bar{Y}_{i.} - \bar{Y}_{j.} + \hat{\sigma}(\bar{Y}_{i.} - \bar{Y}_{j.})t_{n-k,(1+L)/2})$$

If, prior to the experiment, the experimenter has no idea about which populations will differ from which others, he or she should first conduct the F test. If no differences in population means are found as a result of the F test, inference about the means based on model (9.1) is concluded. Only if the F test determines that there are differences in the means should individual comparisons be done.

On the other hand, if, prior to the experiment, the experimenter is interested in specific individual comparisons, then he or she is justified in looking at those comparisons, regardless of the outcome of the F test.

EXAMPLE 9.1   CONTINUED

We illustrate the procedure for comparing individual means by comparing the mean increase in urine flow for surgical patients with that for patients given the microwave procedure. The estimated standard error of $\bar{Y}_{i.} - \bar{Y}_{j.}$ is

$$\sqrt{0.22 \left(\frac{1}{4} + \frac{1}{6} \right)} = 0.30$$

The value of the test statistic T_{ij0} is computed as

$$t_{ij0}^* = \frac{4.73 - 3.07}{0.30} = 5.33$$

As there are 12 degrees of freedom for MSE, to obtain the p-value of the test, we calculate the probability a t_{12} random variable is above 5.33 or below -5.33. This value is 0.00018. Such a small p-value indicates that it is not likely that the observed difference in means is due to chance. We conclude that the data give strong evidence of a difference in the mean increase in flow between the microwave procedure and surgery. Because the sample mean increase in flow is higher for the surgical group, we are justified in concluding that surgery increases flow significantly more than does the microwave procedure.

We also compute a level 0.95 confidence interval for the difference between the population mean increase in flow for the microwave procedure and that for surgery. As $t_{12,0.975} = 2.179$, the interval is

$$(4.73 - 3.07 - (0.030)(2.179), 4.73 - 3.07 + (0.030)(2.179)) = (1.01, 2.31)$$

So, in particular, with 95% confidence, we estimate the mean increase in urine flow to be between 1.01 and 2.31 ml/sec more for surgery than for the microwave therapy. ✦

Formal Versus Informal Inference

Statistical inference is the use of a sample to draw conclusions about a population. Estimation and hypothesis testing are the two types of inference discussed in this book. The theory of statistical inference that has been presented in this and previous chapters relies on the idea that if a sample is collected at random from the population, then inference can be based on the sampling distributions of statistics computed from the sample data. We will use the term **formal inference** to refer to statistical inference in which we interpret quantities based on these sampling distributions, such as confidence levels or p-values, more or less literally. Practitioners who perform level 0.01 tests with the expectation that the probability of rejecting the null hypothesis when it is true is approximately 0.01 are conducting formal inference. So are those who construct 95% confidence intervals with the expectation that approximately 95% of all such intervals will contain the parameter being estimated.

For formal inference to be valid, samples must be properly designed and collected, models must be postulated and fit, and assumptions must be carefully checked. The power of formal statistical inference lies in the clarity and precision, at least in the statistical aspects, of the conclusions that can be drawn. The weakness of formal statistical inference lies in its narrow range of applicability.

Informal inference, on the other hand, refers to the use of statistical inference techniques only as an informal guide to analyzing data. In this context, they may be used to assist an analyst during the exploratory data analysis (EDA) phase of a study, as described in Chapter 3. In informal inference, statements such as "95% confidence" or "not significant at the 0.10 level" are not taken literally. Rather, a 95% confidence interval for the difference between two population means might be used to give a rough idea of whether there is a meaningful difference and what its size might be. Used in this way, inference is an exploratory tool for identifying the main features of the data. Informal inference is often used as part of a preliminary analysis to assist in designing more focused studies in which specific questions will be answered with the use of formal inference.

In this text, and in virtually every other statistics text, the theory of inference that is presented is a theory of formal inference. This is appropriate and necessary, since one cannot construct a theory of informal inference. In fact, informal inference breaks the rules on which inference is based. The prostate treatment experiment described in Example 9.1 is a designed experiment and the inference described is formal inference. Example 9.2 describes a study that uses both informal and formal inference.

EXAMPLE 9.2   INFORMAL AND FORMAL INFERENCE

Recall Example 1.4 from Chapter 1, which describes how a manufacturer of fine mesh netting assigned a team to find ways to improve the strength of the product without greatly increasing costs. Example 1.4 describes the use of brainstorming, process flow diagrams, and Ishikawa diagrams to help identify the primary causes of variation in mesh strength. As a next step, the team researched company production records for historical data on some of the variables they had initially identified as affecting mesh strength. These data were **available data:** data originally collected for another purpose. As such, these data were not suitable for formal inference. However, the team used exploratory data analysis techniques, including ANOVA used as a rough guide, to narrow the very large number of variables down to a manageable number of variables that seemed to be strongly associated with mesh strength and that could be easily and economically controlled.

Based on their findings, the team designed and conducted a series of experiments to investigate how best to improve the production process. Because these experiments were properly designed, formal inference procedures were appropriately used to draw conclusions. Thus, both informal and formal inference contributed to the company's understanding of the mesh production process and helped make possible the economical improvement of mesh strength. ✦

Data Snooping

We bring up the notions of formal and informal inference here, because to perform formal inference properly, certain rules must be observed. Among these rules is that there must be no **data snooping.** In general, data snooping is the use of a set of data to decide which analyses to perform and then performing those analyses on the same set of data. In the analysis of the one-way means model, for example, looking at the data to decide which individual comparisons to make is data snooping. Using data snooping in formal inference is bad statistics. The reason is clear: If the experimenter is allowed to data snoop, then he will choose as the individual comparisons of interest those displaying the largest differences in sample means. Looking only at such comparisons biases the results: more of the differences will appear to be statistically significant than really are, because only the largest differences have been selected for statistical comparison. The only statistically valid approach is to specify the individual comparisons before seeing the data.

Although data snooping is bad statistics when doing formal inference, it is an indispensable component of good science and engineering. Without data snooping, it would be difficult to use data to see new and unexpected phenomena. Data snooping is entirely appropriate at the exploratory phase of a study, as is its use with informal inference. To draw definitive conclusions, however, designed studies supported by formal inference are required. In these latter types of studies, data snooping is inappropriate.

Multiple Comparisons

Why Multiple Comparisons?

In many cases the F test may be significant, but the experimenter may have no idea which means differ from each other. For the reasons given before, data snooping is not a valid approach in formal inference. A valid alternative is to compare every pair of means. When there are k populations, there will be $k(k-1)/2$ of these comparisons. Lab 9.2 will demonstrate that if all $k(k-1)/2$ comparisons are conducted as level L confidence intervals, then incorrect conclusions will be drawn more often than the confidence level L indicates. The same thing will occur in doing $k(k-1)/2$ hypothesis tests each at a fixed level of significance.

One solution to this problem is to conduct **multiple comparisons.** To understand what multiple comparisons do, we must understand what happens when conducting more than one individual comparison. Suppose we run 1000 experiments, obtaining in each data from model (9.1) with $k = 3$ populations. Suppose also that for each experiment, we compute three individual comparison 0.95 level confidence intervals: one comparing each pair of means. It will be true that for approximately 950 of the experiments, the interval for $\mu_1 - \mu_2$ will contain $\mu_1 - \mu_2$ (a correct conclusion); that for approximately 950 of the experiments, the interval for $\mu_1 - \mu_3$; will contain $\mu_1 - \mu_3$; and that for approximately 950 of the experiments, the interval for $\mu_2 - \mu_3$ will contain $\mu_2 - \mu_3$. *However*, the 950 experiments whose computed intervals give a correct conclusion will not necessarily be the same 950 experiments for each pair of means. So, for example, there might be only 900 experiments for which all three intervals give a correct conclusion. In other words, at least one wrong conclusion would be drawn 10% rather than 5% of the time.

Multiple comparisons avoid this problem by controlling the overall error rate for all comparisons made. In the preceding example, if we use a multiple comparison procedure with overall confidence level 0.95, then all three intervals will simultaneously give a correct conclusion in about 950 of the 1000 experiments. In other words, the overall error rate is kept to 5%.

Bonferroni Comparisons

The simplest multiple comparison procedure, and one that can be very effective when small numbers of comparisons must be made, is the Bonferroni procedure. To explain how the Bonferroni procedure works, return to the idea of conducting 1000 experiments, obtaining in each experiment data from model (9.1) with $k = 3$ populations. We have seen the problem that arises when we compute the three individual 0.95 level confidence intervals necessary for comparing each pair of means: that substantially more than 5% of the intervals will yield an incorrect conclusion. In fact, the worst that will happen is that on average, 15% $(= 5 + 5 + 5)$% of the intervals will yield an incorrect conclusion. The Bonferroni method uses this worst-case analysis to construct intervals. If we want to control the overall error rate at 5%, and we have three comparisons to make, then we'll just do each comparison so that it has a 5%/3 = 1.$\bar{6}$% chance of giving an incorrect conclusion.[5] To do this, we construct a level $1 - 0.05/3 = 1 - 0.01\bar{6} = 0.98\bar{3}$ confidence interval for each comparison. Then, on average, the worst that will happen is that 5% $(= (5/3 + 5/3 + 5/3)$%) of the intervals will yield an incorrect conclusion.

To construct a general level L set of Bonferroni confidence intervals for the three comparisons, each interval is a level $1 - (1 - L)/3$ interval. In general, to construct N Bonferroni confidence intervals with an overall confidence level L, each interval should be a level $1 - (1 - L)/N$ interval.

Bonferroni intervals are ideal for making a small number of prespecified comparisons (i.e., comparisons decided on before looking at the data). They may also be used for data snooping, but only if properly constructed. To properly construct level L Bonferroni intervals for data snooping all pairwise comparisons, we must construct them for all $k(k - 1)/2$ possible intervals, and this means that each interval is a level $1 - 2(1 - L)/k(k - 1)$ interval. Thus, an overall level L set of Bonferroni intervals for all pairwise comparisons of means from model (9.1) computes the interval comparing μ_i and μ_j as

$$(\bar{Y}_{i\cdot} - \bar{Y}_{j\cdot} - \hat{\sigma}(\bar{Y}_{i\cdot} - \bar{Y}_{j\cdot})t_{n-k,1-[(1-L)/k(k-1)]}, \ \bar{Y}_{i\cdot} - \bar{Y}_{j\cdot} + \hat{\sigma}(\bar{Y}_{i\cdot} - \bar{Y}_{j\cdot})t_{n-k,1-[(1-L)/k(k-1)]})$$

[5]The bar over the 6 means that the 6 is repeated infinitely.

Tukey Comparisons

An effective, versatile and easy-to-use multiple comparison procedure for all pairs of means is the **Tukey procedure.** The Tukey procedure is based on the **Studentized range distribution.** Suppose, first of all, that all sample sizes n_i are equal in model (9.1). Then

$$\hat{\sigma}(\bar{Y}_{i.} - \bar{Y}_{j.}) = \sqrt{\text{MSE}\left(\frac{1}{n_i} + \frac{1}{n_j}\right)}$$

has the same value for all i and j. Call its common value $\hat{\sigma}(\text{diff})$.

It can be shown that if

- all population means μ_i are equal, and
- $\bar{Y}_{\text{max}.}$ and $\bar{Y}_{\text{min}.}$ are the largest and smallest of the k sample means,

then the quantity

$$\sqrt{2}\, \frac{\bar{Y}_{\text{max}.} - \bar{Y}_{\text{min}.}}{\hat{\sigma}(\text{diff})}$$

has a Studentized range distribution with parameters k and $v = n - k$. Critical values of this distribution are tabulated in Table A.9, in Appendix A, page 914.

The Tukey multiple comparison procedure consists of computing $k(k-1)/2$ confidence intervals: one for each pair of population means. To conduct the Tukey multiple comparison procedure with overall confidence L when all sample sizes n_i are equal, compute the confidence interval for $\mu_i - \mu_j$ as

$$\left(\bar{Y}_{i.} - \bar{Y}_{j.} - \hat{\sigma}(\text{diff})\frac{q_{L,k,n-k}}{\sqrt{2}}, \ \bar{Y}_{i.} - \bar{Y}_{j.} + \hat{\sigma}(\text{diff})\frac{q_{L,k,n-k}}{\sqrt{2}}\right)$$

where n is the total sample size from all populations, and $q_{L,k,v}$ is the Lth quantile of the Studentized range distribution with parameters k and v. These quantiles are tabulated for $L = 0.90, 0.95,$ and 0.99 and selected values of k and v in Table A.9.

The overall confidence L means that if a large number of data sets are obtained from the one-way model, and if for each set of data the Tukey intervals are computed, then for approximately a proportion L of those data sets, all $k(k-1)/2$ computed intervals for differences in means will give correct conclusions. In the previous example, doing all $3(3-1)/2 = 3$ pairwise comparisons of three population means at the $L = 0.95$ level, the Tukey procedure ensures that for 95% of all possible data sets, all three intervals will give correct conclusions. The Tukey procedure works because by accounting for the distribution of the difference of the largest and smallest means, it automatically accounts for the smaller differences of all the other means.

If the sample sizes from all populations are equal, the Tukey procedure is optimal in the sense that when considering all pairwise comparisons of population means, the Tukey procedure gives shorter intervals than any other multiple comparison procedure that controls the overall confidence level L.

If the sample sizes n_i are not equal, the Tukey procedure may still be used, but it will be conservative. This means if a level L is specified, the true confidence level for all $k(k-1)/2$ intervals will be greater than L. The formula for the procedure with unequal n_i is

$$\left(\bar{Y}_{i\cdot} - \bar{Y}_{j\cdot} - \hat{\sigma}(\bar{Y}_{i\cdot} - \bar{Y}_{j\cdot})\frac{q_{L,k,n-k}}{\sqrt{2}}, \ \bar{Y}_{i\cdot} - \bar{Y}_{j\cdot} + \hat{\sigma}(\bar{Y}_{i\cdot} - \bar{Y}_{j\cdot})\frac{q_{L,k,n-k}}{\sqrt{2}} \right)$$

FORMULAS FOR BONFERRONI AND TUKEY MULTIPLE COMPARISON PROCEDURES

- A set of Bonferroni confidence intervals for comparing N pairs of population means with overall confidence level L computes the interval for $\mu_i - \mu_j$ as

$$(\bar{Y}_{i\cdot} - \bar{Y}_{j\cdot} - \hat{\sigma}(\bar{Y}_{i\cdot} - \bar{Y}_{j\cdot})t_{n-k,1-[(1-L)/2N]}, \ \bar{Y}_{i\cdot} - \bar{Y}_{j\cdot} + \hat{\sigma}(\bar{Y}_{i\cdot} - \bar{Y}_{j\cdot})t_{n-k,1-[(1-L)/2N]})$$

When doing all $k(k-1)/2$ pairwise comparisons for k populations, take $N = k(k-1)/2$.

- A set of Tukey confidence intervals for all pairwise comparisons of k population means with overall confidence level L, computes the interval for $\mu_i - \mu_j$ as

$$\left(\bar{Y}_{i\cdot} - \bar{Y}_{j\cdot} - \hat{\sigma}(\bar{Y}_{i\cdot} - \bar{Y}_{j\cdot})\frac{q_{L,k,n-k}}{\sqrt{2}}, \ \bar{Y}_{i\cdot} - \bar{Y}_{j\cdot} + \hat{\sigma}(\bar{Y}_{i\cdot} - \bar{Y}_{j\cdot})\frac{q_{L,k,n-k}}{\sqrt{2}} \right)$$

The confidence level is exact for equal sample sizes from all populations and is conservative if the sample sizes are not all equal.

EXAMPLE 9.1   CONTINUED

We will use the prostate data to illustrate the Bonferroni and Tukey multiple comparison methods. Recall that $\mu_1, \mu_2,$ and μ_3 are the population mean increase in urine flow for drug, microwave, and surgery treatments, respectively.

We begin computation of level 0.95 Bonferroni intervals by computing the Bonferroni multiplier $t_{12,1-(1-0.95)/3(3-1)} = t_{12,0.9916} = 2.78$. Using this multiplier, we find that Bonferroni simultaneous level 0.95 confidence intervals for $\mu_2 - \mu_1$,

$\mu_3 - \mu_1$, and $\mu_3 - \mu_2$ are

$$3.07 - 1.46 \pm 2.78\sqrt{0.22\left(\frac{1}{6} + \frac{1}{5}\right)} = (0.82, 2.40)$$

$$4.73 - 1.46 \pm 2.78\sqrt{0.22\left(\frac{1}{4} + \frac{1}{5}\right)} = (2.40, 4.14)$$

and

$$4.73 - 3.07 \pm 2.78\sqrt{0.22\left(\frac{1}{4} + \frac{1}{6}\right)} = (0.82, 2.50)$$

respectively.

To compute Tukey level 0.95 simultaneous intervals, we find $q_{0.95,3,12} = 3.77$ from the table in Table A.9 in Appendix A. This gives the Tukey multiplier $3.77/\sqrt{2} = 2.67$. Thus, the Tukey simultaneous 95% confidence intervals for $\mu_2 - \mu_1$, $\mu_3 - \mu_1$, and $\mu_3 - \mu_2$ are

$$3.07 - 1.46 \pm 2.67\sqrt{0.22\left(\frac{1}{6} + \frac{1}{5}\right)} = (0.84, 2.37)$$

$$4.73 - 1.46 \pm 2.67\sqrt{0.22\left(\frac{1}{4} + \frac{1}{5}\right)} = (2.42, 4.11)$$

and

$$4.73 - 3.07 \pm 2.67\sqrt{0.22\left(\frac{1}{4} + \frac{1}{6}\right)} = (0.85, 2.47)$$

respectively.

Notice that the Bonferroni and Tukey intervals are virtually identical, so we will interpret only the latter. Simply stated, the intervals show that in terms of urine flow increase, surgery is more effective than the microwave procedure and the microwave procedure more effective than drug therapy. From the first interval, we conclude that the mean increase in urine flow under the microwave procedure is between 0.84 and 2.37 ml/sec greater than that obtained by drug therapy. From the second and third intervals, we conclude that the mean increase in urine flow after surgery is between 2.42 and 4.11 ml/sec greater than that obtained by drug therapy

TABLE 9.4   SAS Output for Tukey Multiple Comparisons for the Prostate Data

General Linear Models Procedure

Tukey's Studentized Range (HSD) Test for variable: DELTAFLO

NOTE: This test controls the type I experimentwise error rate.

Alpha $= 0.05$ Confidence $= 0.95$ df $= 12$ MSE $= 0.222736$

Critical Value of Studentized Range $= 3.773$

Comparisons significant at the 0.05 level are indicated by '***'.

TREATMENT Comparison	Simultaneous Lower Confidence Limit	Difference Between Means	Simultaneous Upper Confidence Limit	
microwave – drug	0.8443	1.6067	2.3691	***
surgery – drug	2.4204	3.2650	4.1096	***
surgery – microwave	0.8456	1.6583	2.4710	***

and between 0.85 and 2.47 ml/sec greater than that obtained by the microwave procedure.

      Table 9.4 contains SAS output for the Tukey intervals for the prostate data. ✦

      We make one final point about the choice of Bonferroni or Tukey intervals. For a given confidence level L, we want the shortest intervals possible. If we are comparing the differences of all pairs of means, and if the sample sizes are equal, then the Tukey inervals are optimal. If we want to compare fewer than all pairs of means, or if the sample sizes aren't all equal, then the Bonferroni intervals might prove shorter. The widths of the Bonferroni and Tukey intervals are determined by their multipliers, which means that we want the method that gives the smaller multiplier. Since computing the Bonferroni and Tukey multipliers does not involve the data, we may initially compute the multipliers and choose the method giving the shorter multiplier before computing the intervals.

Inference About Individual Population Means

It may be of interest to draw conclusions about individual population means from the data. Recall that in fitting the model, we use the estimator $\hat{\mu}_i = \bar{Y}_{i\cdot}$ for the mean μ_i of the ith population. To conduct inference about μ_i, we may use the fact that

$$\frac{\bar{Y}_{i\cdot} - \mu_i}{\sqrt{\text{MSE}/n_i}}$$

has a t_{n-k} distribution. This allows us to obtain a level L confidence interval for μ_i as

$$\left(\bar{Y}_{i\cdot} - \sqrt{\frac{MSE}{n_i}}\, t_{n-k,(1+L)/2}, \ \bar{Y}_{i\cdot} + \sqrt{\frac{MSE}{n_i}}\, t_{n-k,(1+L)/2} \right)$$

EXAMPLE 9.1   CONTINUED

Since $t_{12,0.975} = 2.1788$, we may use this formula to obtain a level 0.95 confidence interval for the mean μ_3 of the prostate data as

$$\left(4.00 - \left(\sqrt{\frac{0.0049}{5}} \right)(2.1788), \ 4.00 + \left(\sqrt{\frac{0.0049}{5}} \right)(2.1788) \right) = (3.93, \ 4.07) \quad \blacklozenge$$

Consequences of Violations of Model Assumptions

Recall the main assumptions of normality, independence, and equal variances. Violations of the model assumptions are known to have the following effects on the analysis.

Nonnormality

Unless the nonnormality is severe, it will have little effect on the F test for equality of population means. In statistical terminology, the F test is **robust** to departures from normality. Individual and multiple comparisons are also robust to departures from normality provided sample sizes from the different populations are not small. This presents the analyst with a dilemma, since it is difficult to determine normality with small samples, which is the case in which departures from normality have the most serious effects.

Heteroscedasticity

Heteroscedasticity is short (if you can believe that!) for "the variances are not the same in all the populations." The F test is robust to heteroscedasticity if the sample sizes n_i from all populations are equal or nearly equal. If not, all bets are off. This is a good reason to try for equal sample sizes when designing a study.

   On the other hand, individual and multiple comparisons can be greatly affected by heteroscedasticity, even with equal sample sizes.

   As we have seen, transforming the response variable can reduce or eliminate heteroscedasticity. Another option for handling heteroscedasticity is to perform a weighted analysis, which gives observations from samples with large variance less weight, and those from samples with small variance more weight, in determining model fit. We will not explore weighted analyses in this chapter.

By the way, the desirable situation in which all population variances are equal, is called **homoscedasticity.**

Nonindependence

Here is our **Declaration of Nonindependence:** Nonindependence (that is, dependence) of error terms can seriously affect the F test and individual and multiple comparisons.

Often, dependence occurs when observations are taken sequentially, which can result in dependence over time. Plots of residuals versus time order can help identify trends or other signs of dependence.

Another source of dependence is taking multiple observations on the same experimental unit. Consider an experiment in which the effects of three blood-pressure drugs on patients with high blood pressure are to be compared. Ten patients are randomly assigned to each drug type and blood-pressure readings are taken on the same patient before the drug is given and at five hourly intervals after. This experiment should not be analyzed as a one-way design with drugs as treatments since blood-pressure readings taken on the same patient for five successive hours are likely dependent. Such dependence can be incorporated into a more sophisticated model called a **repeated measures model.**

9.2

THE ONE-WAY EFFECTS MODEL

Model (9.1) may be written in a way that emphasizes the differential effect that each population has on the mean response, rather than the population means themselves. The resulting model is called the **one-way effects model.** The one-way effects model is given by

$$Y_{ij} = \mu + \tau_i + \epsilon_{ij}, \qquad j = 1, \ldots, n_i; \; i = 1, \ldots, k \tag{9.5}$$

There are different ways that μ can be defined in model (9.5), but we will take it to be a straight average of the individual population means: $\mu = \sum_{i=1}^{k} \mu_i / k$. In model (9.5), τ_i is the effect due to the ith population. As in model (9.1), the ϵ_{ij} are random errors, which we will assume to be independent $N(0, \sigma^2)$ random variables.

Note that in model (9.5), $\mu + \tau_i = \mu_i$, the mean of the ith population, which implies that $\tau_i = \mu_i - \mu$. Thus, τ_i measures the effect due to population i beyond the effect μ common to all populations. It follows from the definition of the τ_i in the one-way effects model that $\sum_{i=1}^{k} \tau_i = 0$. Note also that if all population means are equal, μ is the common value of that mean. In this case, μ has the same meaning as in model (9.3).

Model (9.5) is fit to the data using least squares. The resulting formulas are as follows:

FORMULAS FOR FITTING THE EFFECTS MODEL

- The least squares estimators of the overall mean μ and the effects τ_i are the values m and d_i, which among all d_i satisfying $\sum_{i=1}^{k} d_i = 0$, minimize

$$\text{SSE}(m, d_1, d_2, \ldots, d_k) = \sum_{i=1}^{k} \sum_{j=1}^{n_i} [Y_{ij} - (m + d_i)]^2$$

- The least squares estimator of μ is $\hat{\mu} = \sum_{i=1}^{k} \bar{Y}_{i.}/k$, the mean of the k sample means.
- The least squares estimator of effect τ_i is $\hat{\tau}_i = \bar{Y}_{i.} - \hat{\mu}$.

The formulas for the least squares estimators are what we expect, since in model (9.1), the estimator of μ_i is $\hat{\mu}_i = \bar{Y}_{i.}$ and the estimator of μ is $\hat{\mu} = \sum_{i=1}^{k} \bar{Y}_{i.}/k$. As a result, the estimator of τ_i is $\hat{\tau}_i = \hat{\mu}_i - \hat{\mu}$. The fitted value for population i is $\hat{Y}_{ij} = \hat{\mu} + \hat{\tau}_i$. Notice that $\hat{\mu} + \hat{\tau}_i$ is $\hat{\mu}_i = \bar{Y}_{i.}$, the fitted value from model (9.1).

As with all models, residuals and Studentized residuals should be used to check the quality of the fit. Since the fitted values for the means and effects models are the same, so are their residuals and Studentized residuals.

Because model (9.5) is just model (9.1) written in a different way (a statistician would say "parameterized differently"), we will consider the overall F test for equality of population means and individual and multiple comparisons between population means. The F test is conducted exactly as for model (9.1). The only difference is that for model (9.5), the hypotheses tested are

$$H_0: \quad \tau_1 = \tau_2 = \cdots = \tau_k = 0$$

$$H_a: \quad \text{Not all the population effects } \tau_i \text{ are } 0$$

Individual and multiple comparisons are conducted just as for model (9.1). For model (9.1), these involve tests and confidence intervals for differences in population means $\mu_i - \mu_j$. In terms of model (9.5) parameters, these differences become

$$\mu_i - \mu_j = (\mu + \tau_i) - (\mu + \tau_j) = \tau_i - \tau_j$$

so the inferences are now about differences in population effects.

EXAMPLE 9.1   CONTINUED

The fitted values are $\hat{\mu} = 3.084$, $\hat{\tau}_1 = 1.460 - 3.084 = -1.62$, $\hat{\tau}_2 = 3.067 - 3.084 = -0.02$, and $\hat{\tau}_3 = 4.725 - 3.084 = 1.64$. The remaining analysis follows that already described for model (9.1). ◆

The Regression Formulation of the One-Way Effects Model[6]

The one-way effects model may be formulated and fit as a multiple linear regression model. Before doing so, we must introduce the notion of an **indicator variable.**

> **DEFINITION**
>
> An **indicator variable,** also called a **dummy variable,** uses numbers to identify categories.

In order to formulate the one-way effects model as a multiple linear regression model, we use indicator variables to indicate which of the k populations an observation belongs to. Specifically, we define $k - 1$ indicator variables: $I_1, I_2, \ldots, I_{k-1}$. I_1 equals 1 if the observation is from population 1, equals -1 if the observation is from population k, and equals 0 otherwise; I_2 equals 1 if the observation is from population 2, equals -1 if the observation is from population k, and equals 0 otherwise; and so on.

EXAMPLE 9.1   CONTINUED

We illustrate by creating indicator variables for the prostate data. Since $k = 3$ for the prostate data, we must form two indicator variables: I_1, which we will give the value 1 when an observation is from the drug group, -1 when it is from the surgery group, and 0 otherwise; and I_2, which we will give the value 1 when an observation is from the microwave group, -1 when it is from the surgery group, and 0 otherwise. Table 9.5 gives the values of I_1 and I_2. ✦

The one-way effects model may be formulated as the following multiple linear regression model with the indicator variables $I_1, I_2, \ldots, I_{k-1}$ as regressors:

$$Y = \mu + \tau_1 I_1 + \tau_2 I_2 + \cdots + \tau_{k-1} I_{k-1} + \epsilon \qquad (9.6)$$

To understand why model (9.6) is equivalent to the one-way effects model, it helps to consider what the model says for observations from the k populations:

- For observation Y_{kj}, which is from population k, $I_1 = I_2 = \cdots = I_{k-1} = -1$, so that model (9.6) becomes

$$Y_{kj} = \mu - \tau_1 - \tau_2 - \cdots - \tau_{k-1} + \epsilon_{kj} = \mu + \tau_k + \epsilon_{kj}$$

- For observation Y_{ij}, which is from population $i \neq k$, $I_i = 1$, and all other indicator variables equal 0, so that model (9.6) becomes

$$Y_{ij} = \mu + \tau_i + \epsilon_{ij}$$

---

[6]This section may be omitted without loss of continuity. Knowledge of multiple regression, as presented in Chapter 8, is required to understand the material in this section.

TABLE 9.5   Indicator Variables for the Prostate Data

Increase in urine flow	Treatment	I_1	I_2
1.1	Drug	1	0
1.4	Drug	1	0
1.3	Drug	1	0
1.9	Drug	1	0
1.6	Drug	1	0
2.9	Microwave	0	1
3.7	Microwave	0	1
3.4	Microwave	0	1
3.4	Microwave	0	1
2.8	Microwave	0	1
2.2	Microwave	0	1
4.0	Surgery	−1	−1
5.2	Surgery	−1	−1
5.0	Surgery	−1	−1
4.7	Surgery	−1	−1

The one-way effects model parameters, μ and τ_i, are the parameters in the regression model (9.6). This suggests that we can obtain the fit of the one-way effects model by fitting the regression model:

- The ANOVA table for the one-way model, Table 9.3, and that for the multiple linear regression model (9.6) are exactly the same, except that what is called sum of squares model in the former is called sum of squares regression in the latter. In particular, this means that the overall F test for model (9.6) is the same as the F test for

$$H_0: \quad \tau_1 = \tau_2 = \cdots = \tau_k = 0$$
$$H_a: \quad \text{Not all the population effects } \tau_i \text{ are 0}$$

- The least squares estimators of μ and the τ_i are the least squares estimators from the fit of model (9.6).
- The fitted values, residuals, and Studentized residuals are the same for both models.

EXAMPLE 9.1   CONTINUED

Table 9.6 shows the ANOVA table for the multiple linear regression model for the prostate data. Notice that except for the substitution of the name "Regression" for "Model" in the "Source" column, the table is the same as Table 9.2 for the one-way model for these data.

The fitted regression model is

$$\hat{Y} = 3.08 - 1.62 I_1 - 0.02 I_2 \tag{9.7}$$

TABLE 9.6   ANOVA Table for Regression Model: Prostate Data

		Analysis of variance			
Source	DF	Sum of squares	Mean square	F Stat	Prob > F
Regression	2	23.78	11.89	53.37	0.0001
Error	12	2.67	0.22		
C Total	14	26.45			

and may be interpreted as follows:[7]

- Since $I_1 = 1$ and $I_2 = 0$ for the drug group, the fitted value for that group is

$$\hat{Y} = 3.08 - (1.62)(1) - (0.02)(0) = 3.08 - 1.62 = 1.46 = \hat{\mu}_1$$

- Since $I_1 = 0$ and $I_2 = 1$ for the drug group, the fitted value for that group is

$$\hat{Y} = 3.08 - (1.62)(0) - (0.02)(1) = 3.08 - 0.02 = 3.07 = \hat{\mu}_2$$

- Since $I_1 = I_2 = -1$ for the surgery group, the fitted value for that group is

$$\hat{Y} = 3.08 - (1.62)(-1) - (0.02)(-1) = 4.73 = \hat{\mu}_3 \quad \blacklozenge$$

9.3

BLOCKING IN THE ONE-WAY MODEL

Sometimes in a one-way design, large variation between sampling units makes it difficult to observe differences in the population means of interest. In such cases, blocking may be useful. In blocking, the sampling units are grouped into blocks of homogeneous units, and comparisons between populations are observed within each block. The result is improved sensitivity of tests and better precision of estimation.

EXAMPLE 9.3   THE WATCH ASSEMBLY EXPERIMENT, REVISITED

Recall the experiment on watch-assembly methods described in Chapter 3. Experimenters wanted to assess the speed of three assembly methods. A completely randomized design (CRD) was proposed in which each of 15 assemblers was randomly assigned to one of the assembly methods (five assemblers to each method). Figure 9.5 shows a plot of the resulting times for the three methods. Because there was large variation in the dexterity of the assemblers, this experi-

[7]Some of these results appear to be slightly off due to rounding.

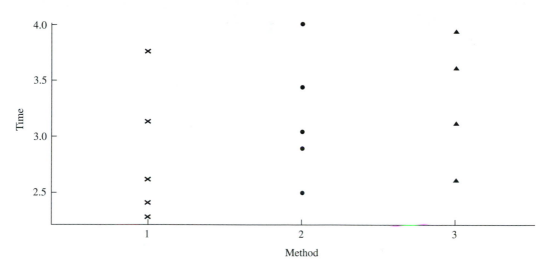

Figure 9.5   Watch-assembly problem; plot of time versus method.

ment failed to show differences in mean assembly times among the three assembly methods.

Because of the large variation due to assemblers, a second experiment, using a design called a randomized complete block design, was conducted. In this design, five assemblers were selected at random and each assembler assembled three watches, one by each method. To avoid bias due to improvements in assembly proficiency, the order in which the three assembly methods were performed was selected at random for each assembler. Figure 9.6 displays the results broken down by worker and method. The response for method 1 is marked by an "×", that for method 2 is marked by a circle, and that for method 3 by a triangle.

This plot shows the benefit of blocking. Whereas there is little in Figure 9.5 to distinguish the three methods, from Figure 9.6 we see two things:

1. There is wider variability in the assembly times from worker to worker than in the different methods for a given worker. Not accounting for this worker-to-worker variability masks any real differences in methods, as it did in Figure 9.5.
2. Method 1 gives the best time for each worker. This could not be seen from Figure 9.5. ✦

The Randomized Complete Block Design

Suppose, as in the one-way model, that we are interested in comparing mean responses from k populations.

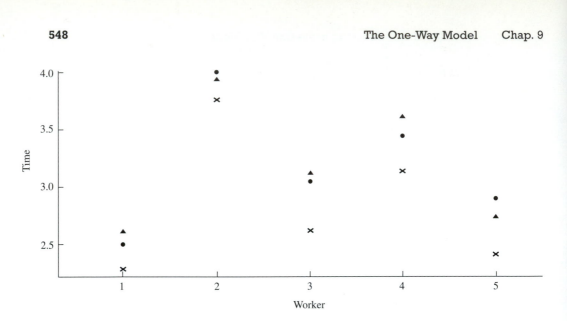

Figure 9.6 Watch-assembly problem; plot of time versus worker. The plotting symbols denote the method: the responses for method 1 are marked by an "×", those for method 2 are marked by a circle, and those for method 3 by a triangle.

> ### DEFINITION
>
> - A **complete block design** is a design in which responses from all k populations are obtained in each of two or more blocks.
> - A **randomized complete block design (RCBD)** is a complete block design in which a completely randomized design is run in each block.

EXAMPLE 9.3   CONTINUED

The second watch-assembly experiment is an example of a RCBD in which each of the five assemblers is a block. It is a complete block design since responses from all three assembly methods, the populations, are obtained from each assembler, that is, within each block. Since the order in which the three different assembly methods are performed is randomized for each assembler separately, the data for each assembler constitutes a CRD. Therefore, the entire design is a RCBD.   ◆

Note that a RCBD differs from a CRD in that the RCBD forces observations from each population to appear in each block. Thus, in an experiment, for example, the assignment of treatments to experimental units cannot be done completely at random.

Rather, in the RCBD, the treatments are assigned to experimental units completely at random within each block. So within each block, there is a different CRD.

The Randomized Complete Block Model

In order to further analyze the watch-assembly data obtained from the randomized complete block design, we need to formulate a model. One widely used model, called the **randomized complete block (or RCB) model** is

$$Y_{ij} = \mu + \tau_i + \gamma_j + \epsilon_{ij}, \qquad i = 1, \ldots, k; \ j = 1, \ldots, b \qquad (9.8)$$

Here, there are k populations and b blocks, μ is the overall mean, τ_i is the effect due to population i, γ_j is the effect due to block j, and the ϵ_{ij} are random errors, assumed, as usual, to be independent $N(0, \sigma^2)$ random variables. For this model, it is assumed that

$$\sum_{i=1}^{k} \tau_i = \sum_{j=1}^{b} \gamma_j = 0$$

There are several things to notice about model (9.8):

- It is written as an effects model.
- There are two factors (see Chapter 3): populations and blocks.
- The effects of the factors add: The effect of population i and block j is $\tau_i + \gamma_j$. As a result, model (9.8) is called an **additive model.**

Fitting the Model

Let

$$\bar{Y}_{i.} = \frac{1}{b} \sum_{j=1}^{b} Y_{ij} \qquad \bar{Y}_{.j} = \frac{1}{k} \sum_{i=1}^{k} Y_{ij} \qquad \text{and} \qquad \bar{Y}_{..} = \frac{1}{kb} \sum_{i=1}^{k} \sum_{j=1}^{b} Y_{ij}$$

denote the means of the observations from the ith population, of the observations from the jth block, and of all observations, respectively.

The least squares estimators of μ, τ_i, and γ_j are the values m, d_i, and g_j, respectively, which among all d_i and g_j satisfying $\sum_{i=1}^{k} d_i = 0$, and $\sum_{j=1}^{b} g_j = 0$, minimize

$$\text{SSE}(m, d_1, d_2, \ldots, d_k, g_1, g_2, \ldots, g_b) = \sum_{i=1}^{k} \sum_{j=1}^{b} [Y_{ij} - (m + d_i + g_j)]^2$$

Solving this minimization problem leads to the following:

LEAST SQUARES ESTIMATORS OF μ, τ_i, AND γ_j

The least squares estimators of μ, τ_i, and γ_j are

$$\hat{\mu} = \bar{Y}_{..}, \quad \hat{\tau}_i = \bar{Y}_{i.} - \bar{Y}_{..} \quad \text{and} \quad \hat{\gamma}_j = \bar{Y}_{.j} - \bar{Y}_{..}$$

respectively.

It is left as an exercise for you to show that $\sum_{i=1}^{k} \hat{\tau}_i = \sum_{j=1}^{b} \hat{\gamma}_j = 0$.

If we substitute these least squares estimators for their population counterparts in model (9.8) and ignore the error term, we obtain the fitted values.

FITTED VALUES

The fitted value for the ith population and jth block is

$$\hat{Y}_{ij} = \hat{\mu} + \hat{\tau}_i + \hat{\gamma}_j = \bar{Y}_{..} + (\bar{Y}_{i.} - \bar{Y}_{..}) + (\bar{Y}_{.j} - \bar{Y}_{..}) = \bar{Y}_{i.} + \bar{Y}_{.j} - \bar{Y}_{..}$$

EXAMPLE 9.3   CONTINUED

Table 9.7 displays the watch-assembly data and the values of the means $\bar{Y}_{..}$, $\bar{Y}_{i.}$, and $\bar{Y}_{.j}$.

TABLE 9.7   Watch-Assembly Data and Means

Assembly method	Assembler 1	Assembler 2	Assembler 3	Assembler 4	Assembler 5	Method mean
1	2.28 (y_{11})	3.77 (y_{12})	2.62 (y_{13})	3.14 (y_{14})	2.41 (y_{15})	2.84 ($\bar{y}_{1.}$)
2	2.50 (y_{21})	4.02 (y_{22})	3.05 (y_{23})	3.45 (y_{24})	2.90 (y_{25})	3.18 ($\bar{y}_{2.}$)
3	2.61 (y_{31})	3.95 (y_{32})	3.12 (y_{33})	3.62 (y_{34})	2.74 (y_{35})	3.21 ($\bar{y}_{3.}$)
Assembler mean	2.46 ($\bar{y}_{.1}$)	3.91 ($\bar{y}_{.2}$)	2.93 ($\bar{y}_{.3}$)	3.40 ($\bar{y}_{.4}$)	2.68 ($\bar{y}_{.5}$)	3.08 ($\bar{y}_{..}$)

Table 9.8 shows how the effects are computed from these data.[8]

Since $\hat{\mu} = 3.08$, we estimate that on average, it takes 3.08 minutes to assemble a watch. Since $\hat{\tau}_1 = -0.24$, we estimate that using assembly method 1 lowers

---

[8] Due to rounding, neither the effects for assemblers nor those for methods sums to 0.

TABLE 9.8   Effects Computed from Watch-Assembly Data

	Estimate	
Overall mean	Method	Assembler

$\hat{\mu} = \bar{y}_{..} = 3.08$

$\hat{\tau}_1 = \bar{y}_{1.} - \bar{y}_{..} = 2.84 - 3.08 = -0.24$
$\hat{\tau}_2 = \bar{y}_{2.} - \bar{y}_{..} = 3.18 - 3.08 = 0.10$
$\hat{\tau}_3 = \bar{y}_{3.} - \bar{y}_{..} = 3.21 - 3.08 = 0.13$

$\hat{\gamma}_1 = \bar{y}_{.1} - \bar{y}_{..} = 2.46 - 3.08 = -0.62$
$\hat{\gamma}_2 = \bar{y}_{.2} - \bar{y}_{..} = 3.91 - 3.08 = 0.83$
$\hat{\gamma}_3 = \bar{y}_{.3} - \bar{y}_{..} = 2.93 - 3.08 = -0.15$
$\hat{\gamma}_4 = \bar{y}_{.4} - \bar{y}_{..} = 3.40 - 3.08 = 0.32$
$\hat{\gamma}_5 = \bar{y}_{.5} - \bar{y}_{..} = 2.68 - 3.08 = -0.40$

TABLE 9.9   Fitted Values for Watch-Assembly Data

Assembly method	Assembler				
	1	2	3	4	5
1	2.22 $(\hat{y}_{11})$	3.67 $(\hat{y}_{12})$	2.69 $(\hat{y}_{13})$	3.16 $(\hat{y}_{14})$	2.44 $(\hat{y}_{15})$
2	2.56 $(\hat{y}_{21})$	4.01 $(\hat{y}_{22})$	3.03 $(\hat{y}_{23})$	3.50 $(\hat{y}_{24})$	2.78 $(\hat{y}_{25})$
3	2.60 $(\hat{y}_{31})$	4.05 $(\hat{y}_{32})$	3.07 $(\hat{y}_{33})$	3.54 $(\hat{y}_{34})$	2.82 $(\hat{y}_{35})$

assembly time on average by 0.24 minute. And since $\hat{\gamma}_1 = -0.62$, we estimate that assembler 1 is on average 0.62 minute faster at assembly than the overall average. Other parameter estimates are interpreted in similar ways.

As an example of the computation of fitted values,

$$\hat{y}_{11} = \hat{\mu} + \hat{\tau}_1 + \hat{\gamma}_1 = 3.08 + (-0.24) + (-0.62) = 2.22$$

Table 9.9 displays all of the fitted values for the watch assembly data.   ◆

Checking the Fit

As with the one-way model, and indeed with any statistical model, it is important to check that model assumptions for the randomized complete block model are approximately satisfied before using the model further.

To check the assumption of equal variances, the sample standard deviations of the k populations should be compared with each other and the sample standard deviations of the b blocks should be compared with each other. If these standard deviations are not greatly different, the assumption of equal variances may be judged reasonable.

As with the one-way model, the residual is the main tool used in checking assumptions about the RCB model. The residual for the ith population and jth block is

$$e_{ij} = Y_{ij} - \hat{Y}_{ij} = Y_{ij} - \bar{Y}_{i.} - \bar{Y}_{.j} + \bar{Y}_{..}$$

It can be shown that the residuals sum to 0.

Studentized residuals are helpful in identifying outliers and in assessing normality. In the latter case, they should be plotted versus quantiles of the $t_{(k-1)(b-1)-1}$ distribution.

Residual plots are particularly important in assessing the aptness of the model. Plots versus fitted values and versus blocks and populations should be done. Plots that display no patterns indicate a satisfactory fit.

A curvilinear pattern in the plot of residuals versus predicted values is often symptomatic of an interaction between blocks and populations. This means the additivity assumption in model (9.8) is incorrect. Another graphical way to detect severe interaction in the RCB model is to do an **interaction plot,** an example of which is provided for the watch-assembly data when Example 9.3 is continued in what follows. There is a test for additivity due to Tukey (of multiple comparison fame) that we explain next.

Tukey's test begins with the assumption that a nonadditive version of model (9.8) will have the form

$$Y_{ij} = \mu + \tau_i + \gamma_j + \eta\tau_i\gamma_j + \epsilon_{ij}, \qquad i = 1, \ldots, k; \ j = 1, \ldots, b \qquad (9.9)$$

For the ijth observation, the nonadditive part of this model, $\eta\tau_i\gamma_j$, is assumed to be a product of the ith population effect τ_i, the jth block effect γ_j, and an unknown constant η. An effect in the form of a product of factor effects (like $\tau_i\gamma_j$) is called an interaction effect and is often used in more complex statistical models.

Tukey's test for additivity tests the hypotheses in model (9.9),

$$H_0: \quad \eta = 0$$

$$H_a: \quad \eta \neq 0$$

H_0 states that the additive model (9.8) is correct, and H_a that the nonadditive model (9.9) is correct. The test statistic is too complicated to be derived here, but if H_0 is true, it has an $F_{1,\nu}$ distribution where $\nu = kb - k - b$. Large values of the test statistic provide evidence against H_0 and in favor of H_a.[9]

If interaction is found, model (9.8) is no longer assumed valid. One remedy is to use a more sophisticated model, which will involve changing the experimental design and taking more data. However, the simplest solution, and the one we recommend trying first, is to attempt to eliminate the interaction by transforming the response variable.

EXAMPLE 9.3   CONTINUED

For the prostate data, the standard deviations for the different assembly methods are all very close: the largest is 0.61 and the smallest is 0.57. The standard deviations for the different assemblers differ more: 0.27 is the largest and 0.13 the smallest, but the difference is not extreme, especially considering the small sample size.

As an example of the computation of residuals, from the watch-assembly data, we obtain $e_{11} = y_{11} - \hat{y}_{11} = 2.28 - 2.22 = 0.06$. Table 9.10 displays all of the residuals for the watch-assembly data.[10]

---

[9]We have written macros for SAS and MINITAB users that will perform Tukey's test. See the Doing It with SAS and Doing It with MINITAB supplements for details.

[10]Due to rounding, these residuals do not sum to 0.

TABLE 9.10   Residuals for Watch-Assembly Data

Assembly method	Assembler				
	1	2	3	4	5
1	$0.06\,(e_{11})$	$0.10\,(e_{12})$	$-0.07\,(e_{13})$	$-0.02\,(e_{14})$	$-0.03\,(e_{15})$
2	$-0.06\,(e_{21})$	$0.01\,(e_{22})$	$0.02\,(e_{23})$	$-0.05\,(e_{24})$	$0.12\,(e_{25})$
3	$0.01\,(e_{31})$	$-0.10\,(e_{32})$	$0.05\,(e_{33})$	$0.08\,(e_{34})$	$-0.08\,(e_{35})$

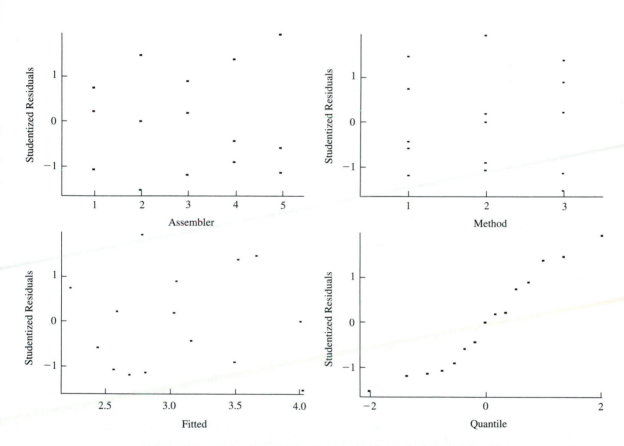

Figure 9.7   Plots of Studentized residuals versus assembler, assembly method, and fitted values; plot of Studentized residuals versus quantiles of the t_7 distribution: watch-assembly problem.

Figure 9.7 shows plots of the Studentized residuals versus assembly method, assembler, fitted value and, quantiles of the t_7 distribution. These plots reveal no serious departures from model assumptions.

Look now at the left plot in Figure 9.8. This is an interaction plot for the watch-assembly data. The vertical axis plots the response, the assembly time, and the horizontal axis, the assembly method. Each of the five segmented lines shows

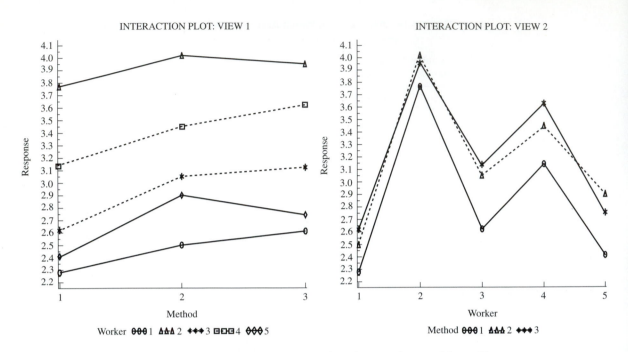

Figure 9.8   Interaction plot: watch-assembly problem.

the values of the response for one worker. In theory, parallel lines indicate no interaction between method and worker. This is because in an additive model, if we ignore random error, the difference between responses for workers l and m using method i is

$$(\mu + \tau_i + \gamma_l) - (\mu + \tau_i + \gamma_m) = \gamma_l - \gamma_m$$

This is the same for all i methods, which says the segmented line in the interaction plot corresponding to worker l is just the segmented line in the interaction plot corresponding to worker m shifted vertically by $\gamma_l - \gamma_m$. In other words, these segmented lines should be parallel. In reality, of course, random error assures that the plotted lines will not be parallel, so in practice, we use the interaction plot only as a visual guide.

Without knowing the standard errors in the data, it is hard to tell by looking if the lack of parallelism in the segmented lines of an interaction plot indicates statistically significant interaction. So, in interpreting an interaction plot, we look for the pattern of how the responses vary. Of course, segmented lines that are dramatically nonparallel give convincing evidence of nonadditivity. The segmented lines in the left plot in Figure 9.8 show little evidence of nonadditivity, and we may conclude the additive model is probably appropriate. The right plot in Figure 9.8 is just another view of the same phenomenon. Here the vertical axis plots the response and the horizontal axis the worker. Each of the three segmented lines shows the values of the response for one method. Again, the near-parallel lines indicate no evidence of interaction.

For the watch-assembly data, Tukey's test for additivity gives the following results:

$$F \text{ statistic: } 0.4927 \qquad \text{Degrees of Freedom: } 1, 7 \qquad p\text{-value: } 0.5054$$

The large p-value leads us to conclude that the data contain little evidence of nonadditivity (i.e., we do not reject the null hypothesis). This supports the conclusions reached from the interaction plots.   ✦

Testing the Equality of Population Means: The Analysis of Variance

Just as we did for the one-way model, we can divide the total variation in the response variable into components to decide whether there are differences in population means. Specifically, we want to test the hypotheses

$$H_{0\tau}: \quad \tau_1 = \tau_2 = \cdots = \tau_k = 0$$

$$H_{a\tau}: \quad \text{Not all the population effects } \tau_i \text{ are } 0$$

In order to test these hypotheses, the total variation in the response (SSTO) is divided into three components: due to populations (SSP), blocks (SSB), and error (SSE). The formulas for these are

---

**SUMS OF SQUARES FORMULAS FOR
THE RANDOMIZED COMPLETE BLOCK MODEL**

- The sum of squares total is

$$\text{SSTO} = \sum_{i=1}^{k} \sum_{j=1}^{b} (Y_{ij} - \bar{Y}_{..})^2$$

- The sum of squares due to populations is

$$\text{SSP} = \sum_{i=1}^{k} \sum_{j=1}^{b} (\bar{Y}_{i.} - \bar{Y}_{..})^2 = b \sum_{i=1}^{k} (\bar{Y}_{i.} - \bar{Y}_{..})^2$$

(continued)

SUMS OF SQUARES FORMULAS FOR THE RANDOMIZED COMPLETE BLOCK MODEL (*CONTINUED*)

- The sum of squares due to blocks is

$$\text{SSB} = \sum_{i=1}^{k} \sum_{j=1}^{b} (\bar{Y}_{\cdot j} - \bar{Y}_{\cdot\cdot})^2 = k \sum_{j=1}^{b} (\bar{Y}_{\cdot j} - \bar{Y}_{\cdot\cdot})^2$$

- The sum of squares error is

$$\text{SSE} = \sum_{i=1}^{k} \sum_{j=1}^{b} e_{ij} = \sum_{i=1}^{k} \sum_{j=1}^{b} (Y_{ij} - \bar{Y}_{i\cdot} - \bar{Y}_{\cdot j} + \bar{Y}_{\cdot\cdot})^2$$

- Further, SSTO = SSP + SSB + SSE.

The sums of squares measure the amount of the total variation in the response (SSTO) that is attributable to differences in populations (SSP) and to differences in blocks (SSB). The remainder, SSE, is the amount of variation that, using model (9.8), can't be explained by population or block differences.

For the randomized complete block model, degrees of freedom and mean squares have the same meaning as for the one-way model.

DEGREES OF FREEDOM AND MEAN SQUARES FOR THE RANDOMIZED COMPLETE BLOCK MODEL

- For the randomized complete block model, the degrees of freedom associated with SSTO, SSP, SSB, and SSE are $kb - 1$, $k - 1$, $b - 1$, and $(k-1)(b-1)$, respectively. Just as the sums of squares SSP, SSB, and SSE sum to SSTO, the degrees of freedom for SSP, SSB, and SSE sum to the degrees of freedom for SSTO: $kb - 1 = (k - 1) + (b - 1) + (k - 1)(b - 1)$.
- The **mean square** associated with a sum of squares is the mean of the squares making up that sum of squares. The mean square is computed by dividing the sum of squares by its degrees of freedom.
- The mean squares associated with SSP, SSB, and SSE are MSP $= \text{SSP}/(k - 1)$, MSB $= \text{SSB}/(b - 1)$, and MSE $= \text{SSE}/(k-1)(b-1)$, respectively. A mean square is not usually computed for SSTO.

The estimator of error variance, σ^2, is MSE $= \text{SSE}/(k - 1)(b - 1)$. This makes sense, as SSE is the amount of variation in the data "unexplained" by population or block differences in the fit of model (9.8), and σ^2 is the corresponding measure in the population.

We now have the machinery necessary to test $H_{0\tau}$ versus $H_{a\tau}$. The test statistic is $F^\tau = \text{MSP/MSE}$. If $H_{0\tau}$ is true, F^τ has an F distribution with $k - 1$ and $(k - 1) \cdot (b - 1)$ degrees of freedom. The p-value of the test is the proportion of an $F_{k-1,(k-1)(b-1)}$ population that exceeds the observed value of the test statistic.

Although the test of $H_{0\tau}$ versus $H_{a\tau}$ is of primary interest, it might also be of interest to test whether the use of blocks is effective in reducing variation (and thereby making the comparisons of interest more precise). If such a test shows that blocking is not effective, then investigators might not use blocking in future studies. The hypotheses for block effects are

$$H_{0\gamma}: \quad \gamma_1 = \gamma_2 = \cdots = \gamma_b = 0$$
$$H_{a\gamma}: \quad \text{Not all the block effects } \gamma_j \text{ are 0}$$

Some authors suggest using the test statistic $F^\gamma = \text{MSB/MSE}$ for testing $H_{0\gamma}$ against $H_{a\gamma}$, and further claim that if $H_{0\gamma}$ is true, F^γ has an F distribution with $b - 1$ and $(k-1)(b-1)$ degrees of freedom. **This is not correct!** Because the randomization in the RCBD is not done among all treatments and blocks, but only within blocks, it turns out that when $H_{0\gamma}$ is true, F^γ does not have an F distribution with $b - 1$ and $(k-1)(b-1)$ degrees of freedom. Rather, comparing F^γ with the $F_{b-1,(k-1)(b-1)}$ distribution results in what is called a **liberal test.** By this, we mean that when $H_{0\gamma}$ is true, the value of F^γ will tend to be larger than it would be if it really had an $F_{b-1,(k-1)(b-1)}$ distribution. This means the test will have a smaller p-value than it should, and the tendency will be to reject $H_{0\gamma}$ too easily in favor of $H_{a\gamma}$.

As a result, care should be taken when testing for block effects by comparing the test statistic F^γ with an $F_{b-1,(k-1)(b-1)}$ distribution:

- If the p-value is large enough not to reject $H_{0\gamma}$ (e.g., if you are doing a test at the 0.05 level and the p-value exceeds 0.05), then we can be confident that block effects are not significant.

- If the p-value is small enough to reject $H_{0\gamma}$, then we cannot necessarily conclude that block effects are significant.

The ANOVA table displayed in Table 9.11 summarizes the decomposition of SSTO and of the degrees of freedom into their components, displays the estimator of

TABLE 9.11   ANOVA Table: RCBD

		Analysis of variance			
Source	DF	Sum of squares	Mean square	F Stat	Prob > F
Population	$k - 1$	SSP	MSP	$F^\tau = \text{MSP/MSE}$	p-value$^\tau$
Blocks	$b - 1$	SSB	MSB	$F^\gamma = \text{MSB/MSE}$	p-value$^\gamma$
Error	$(k - 1)(b - 1)$	SSE	MSE		
C Total	$kb - 1$	SSTO			

σ^2 (MSE), and gives the results of the F tests. These tests are summarized as follows:

F TESTS IN THE ANALYSIS OF VARIANCE
FOR THE RANDOMIZED COMPLETE BLOCK MODEL

- The test of primary interest is a test of whether there are population effects. The test statistic is $F^\tau = \text{MSP}/\text{MSE}$. The p-value of the test is the proportion of an $F_{k-1,(k-1)(b-1)}$ population that exceeds the observed value of the test statistic.
- Of secondary interest is a test for block effects. The test statistic is $F^\gamma = \text{MSB}/\text{MSE}$, and comparing the observed value of the test statistic with an $F_{b-1,(k-1)(b-1)}$ distribution results in a liberal test.

EXAMPLE 9.3 CONTINUED

Table 9.12 is the ANOVA table for the watch-assembly data.

TABLE 9.12   ANOVA Table: Watch-Assembly Data

		Analysis of variance			
Source	DF	Sum of squares	Mean square	F Stat	Prob > F
Method	2	0.415	0.207	25.42	0.0003
Worker (blocks)	4	4.077	1.019	125.05	0.0001
Error	8	0.065	0.008		
C Total	14	4.557			

By far, the greatest part of the variation in the assembly times (4.077 of the total of 4.557) is accounted for by assembler-to-assembler differences (i.e., the blocks). This compares with the 0.415 accounted for by assembly method and the 0.065 unaccounted for by the RCB model. The p-value of 0.0001 for the test statistic for blocks is really an upper bound: the true value is 3.03×10^{-7}. This is so small that the result is likely highly significant despite the liberal nature of the test. The p-value of 0.0003 for the test of differences in assembly methods indicates that the mean times for these methods are not all the same. ◆

Individual and Multiple Comparisons

Individual and multiple comparisons for population means in the RCBD are conducted in a manner similar to that described for the completely randomized one-way design.

Consider first an individual comparison of the effects of the ith and jth populations. In terms of model (9.8), we wish to compare τ_i with τ_j. The estimator of $\tau_i - \tau_j$ is $(\bar{Y}_{i.} - \bar{Y}_{..}) - (\bar{Y}_{j.} - \bar{Y}_{..}) = \bar{Y}_{i.} - \bar{Y}_{j.}$. We use the fact that under the assumptions of model (9.8),

$$T_{ij} = \frac{\bar{Y}_{i.} - \bar{Y}_{j.} - (\tau_i - \tau_j)}{\hat{\sigma}(\bar{Y}_{i.} - \bar{Y}_{j.})}$$

has a $t_{(k-1)(b-1)}$ distribution, where the estimated standard error of $\bar{Y}_{i\cdot} - \bar{Y}_{j\cdot}$ is computed as

$$\hat{\sigma}(\bar{Y}_{i\cdot} - \bar{Y}_{j\cdot}) = \sqrt{\text{MSE}\left(\frac{1}{b} + \frac{1}{b}\right)} = \sqrt{\frac{2(\text{MSE})}{b}}$$

Specifically, suppose we want to test

$$H_0: \quad \tau_i = \tau_j$$
$$H_a: \quad \tau_i \neq \tau_j.$$

A two-sided test is conducted with

$$T_{ij0} = \frac{\bar{Y}_{i\cdot} - \bar{Y}_{j\cdot}}{\hat{\sigma}(\bar{Y}_1 - \bar{Y}_2)}$$

as the test statistic (remember, that under H_0, $\tau_i - \tau_j = 0$) and the p-value computed from the $t_{(k-1)(b-1)}$ distribution.

Alternatively, the endpoints of a level L confidence interval for $\tau_i - \tau_j$ are

$$\bar{Y}_{i\cdot} - \bar{Y}_{j\cdot} \pm \hat{\sigma}(\bar{Y}_{i\cdot} - \bar{Y}_{j\cdot})t_{(k-1)(b-1),(1+L)/2}$$

Either the Bonferroni or the Tukey procedure may be used to conduct multiple comparisons of all $k(k-1)/2$ pairs of population means. To obtain comparisons with overall confidence L, compute the Bonferroni confidence interval for $\tau_i - \tau_j$ as

$$(\bar{Y}_{i\cdot} - \bar{Y}_{j\cdot} - \hat{\sigma}(\bar{Y}_{i\cdot} - \bar{Y}_{j\cdot})\, t_{(k-1)(b-1),1-(1-L)/k(k-1)},$$
$$\bar{Y}_{i\cdot} - \bar{Y}_{j\cdot} + \hat{\sigma}(\bar{Y}_{i\cdot} - \bar{Y}_{j\cdot})t_{(k-1)(b-1),1-(1-L)/k(k-1)})$$

and the corresponding Tukey interval as

$$\left(\bar{Y}_{i\cdot} - \bar{Y}_{j\cdot} - \hat{\sigma}(\bar{Y}_{i\cdot} - \bar{Y}_{j\cdot})\frac{q_{L,k,(k-1)(b-1)}}{\sqrt{2}}, \; \bar{Y}_{i\cdot} - \bar{Y}_{j\cdot} + \hat{\sigma}(\bar{Y}_{i\cdot} - \bar{Y}_{j\cdot})\frac{q_{L,k,(k-1)(b-1)}}{\sqrt{2}}\right)$$

The set of intervals having the smaller multiplier would be used in any analysis. To summarize:

FORMULA FOR INDIVIDUAL COMPARISON OF TWO POPULATION EFFECTS

A level L confidence interval for the difference of the effects of populations i and j is computed as

$$(\bar{Y}_{i\cdot} - \bar{Y}_{j\cdot} - \hat{\sigma}(\bar{Y}_{i\cdot} - \bar{Y}_{j\cdot})t_{(k-1)(b-1),(1+L)/2}, \; \bar{Y}_{i\cdot} - \bar{Y}_{j\cdot} + \hat{\sigma}(\bar{Y}_{i\cdot} - \bar{Y}_{j\cdot})t_{(k-1)(b-1),(1+L)/2})$$

FORMULAS FOR BONFERRONI AND TUKEY MULTIPLE COMPARISON PROCEDURES

- A set of Bonferroni confidence intervals for comparing N pairs of population effects with overall confidence level L computes the interval for $\tau_i - \tau_j$ as

$$(\bar{Y}_{i\cdot} - \bar{Y}_{j\cdot} - \hat{\sigma}(\bar{Y}_{i\cdot} - \bar{Y}_{j\cdot})\, t_{(k-1)(b-1),1-[(1-L)/2N]},$$
$$\bar{Y}_{i\cdot} - \bar{Y}_{j\cdot} + \hat{\sigma}(\bar{Y}_{i\cdot} - \bar{Y}_{j\cdot})t_{(k-1)(b-1),1-[(1-L)/2N]})$$

When doing all $k(k-1)/2$ pairwise comparisons for k populations, take $N = k(k-1)/2$.

- A set of Tukey confidence intervals for all pairwise comparisons of k population effects with overall confidence level L computes the interval for $\tau_i - \tau_j$ as

$$\left(\bar{Y}_{i\cdot} - \bar{Y}_{j\cdot} - \hat{\sigma}(\bar{Y}_{i\cdot} - \bar{Y}_{j\cdot})\frac{q_{L,k,(k-1)(b-1)}}{\sqrt{2}}, \ \bar{Y}_{i\cdot} - \bar{Y}_{j\cdot} + \hat{\sigma}(\bar{Y}_{i\cdot} - \bar{Y}_{j\cdot})\frac{q_{L,k,(k-1)(b-1)}}{\sqrt{2}}\right)$$

The confidence level is exact for equal sample sizes from all populations and is conservative if the sample sizes are not all equal.

Differences of block effects are not usually of primary interest, and so individual or multiple comparisons of them are not usually done.

EXAMPLE 9.3   CONTINUED

We illustrate by conducting individual and multiple comparisons of the effects of assembly methods at the 0.90 confidence level. As $(k-1)(b-1) = 8$, for individual comparisons, we need the $(1 + 0.90)/2 = 0.95$ quantile of the t_8 distribution, $t_{8,0.95} = 1.86$. For Tukey multiple comparisons, we need $q(0.90, 3, 8) = 3.37$, giving the Tukey multiplier $3.37/\sqrt{2} = 2.38$. The multiplier for Bonferroni multiple comparisons is $t_{8,1-(1-0.90)/3(3-1)} = t_{8,0.98\bar{3}} = 2.57$. Since the Tukey multiplier is smaller, we will use the Tukey instead of the Bonferroni procedure. The resulting intervals are shown in Table 9.13

TABLE 9.13   Ninety Percent Individual and Tukey Multiple Confidence Intervals: Watch-Assembly Data

Comparison	Individual interval	Tukey interval
$\tau_3 - \tau_1$	$(0.26, 0.47)$	$(0.22, 0.50)$
$\tau_3 - \tau_2$	$(-0.08, 0.13)$	$(-0.11, 0.16)$
$\tau_2 - \tau_1$	$(0.23, 0.45)$	$(0.20, 0.48)$

As an example of the computations used to obtain these intervals, consider the two intervals for $\tau_3 - \tau_1$. The individual interval is computed as

$$\bar{y}_{3.} - \bar{y}_{1.} \pm \hat{\sigma}(\bar{y}_{3.} - \bar{y}_{1.})t_{(k-1)(b-1),(1+L)/2} = (3.21 - 2.84) \pm \sqrt{\frac{2(0.008)}{5}}t_{8,0.95}$$

$$= 0.37 \pm (0.057)(1.86) = (0.26, 0.47)$$

The Tukey interval is computed by substituting the Tukey multiplier, 2.38, for the $t_{8,0.95}$ quantile (1.86) in the preceding computation.

Because we did not specify the comparisons of interest ahead of time, we will use the Tukey intervals for interpretation purposes (though the individual intervals give similar results in this example). Thus, with 90% confidence, we estimate $\tau_3 - \tau_1$ to lie in the range (0.22, 0.50), $\tau_3 - \tau_2$ to lie in the range $(-0.11, 0.16)$, and $\tau_2 - \tau_1$ to lie in the range (0.20, 0.48). From this, we conclude that statistically there is no difference between τ_3 and τ_2, and that τ_1 is significantly smaller than both τ_3 and τ_2. This means that assembly method 1 is significantly faster than method 2 or 3, and that with 90% confidence, we estimate it to be from roughly 0.2 to 0.5 minute faster.   ◆

The Regression Formulation of the RCB Model[11]

Like the one-way model, the RCB model can be formulated and fit as a multiple linear regression model. Since we have both populations and blocks to account for, we must define two sets of indicator variables.

- For the k population effects, $\tau_1, \ldots, \tau_k$, define $k-1$ indicator variables, $I_1, \ldots, I_{k-1}$, where I_i equals 1 if an observation is from population i, -1 if it is from population k, and equals 0 otherwise.
- For the b block effects, $\gamma_1, \ldots, \gamma_b$, define $b-1$ indicator variables, $J_1, \ldots, J_{b-1}$, where J_i equals 1 if an observation is from block i, -1 if it is from block b, and equals 0 otherwise.

The RCB model (9.8) may then be written as the multiple linear regression model

$$Y = \mu + \tau_1 I_1 + \cdots + \tau_{k-1}I_{k-1} + \gamma_1 J_1 + \cdots + \gamma_{b-1}J_{b-1} + \epsilon \qquad (9.10)$$

It is left as an exercise for you to show that model (9.10) is equivalent to model (9.8).

---

[11]This section may be omitted without loss of continuity. Knowledge of multiple regression, as presented in Chapter 8, is required to understand the material in this section.

TABLE   9.14   Indicator Variables, RCB Model, Watch-Assembly Data

Time	Method	Assembler	I_1	I_2	J_1	J_2	J_3	J_4
2.28	1	1	1	0	1	0	0	0
2.50	2	1	0	1	1	0	0	0
2.61	3	1	−1	−1	1	0	0	0
3.77	1	2	1	0	0	1	0	0
4.02	2	2	0	1	0	1	0	0
3.95	3	2	−1	−1	0	1	0	0
2.62	1	3	1	0	0	0	1	0
3.05	2	3	0	1	0	0	1	0
3.12	3	3	−1	−1	0	0	1	0
3.14	1	4	1	0	0	0	0	1
3.45	2	4	0	1	0	0	0	1
3.62	3	4	−1	−1	0	0	0	1
2.41	1	5	1	0	−1	−1	−1	−1
2.90	2	5	0	1	−1	−1	−1	−1
2.74	3	5	−1	−1	−1	−1	−1	−1

EXAMPLE 9.3   CONTINUED

Table 9.14 shows the indicator variables for the watch assembly data. It is left as an exercise for you to fit the model and show that the fitted values correspond to the fitted values from the RCB model (9.8).   ✦

A bit more work is required to obtain the ANOVA table, Table 9.11, using the regression model (9.10). The difficulty is that the ANOVA table corresponding to the regression fit combines the population and block sums of squares together into the regression sum of squares, which has $(k - 1) + (b - 1) = k + b - 2$ degrees of freedom. To separate these sums of squares, we will fit the regression model containing only the indicator variables $I_1, \ldots, I_{k-1}$. The resulting regression sum of squares and degrees of freedom are the population sum of squares and degrees of freedom for the RCB model. The sum of squares for blocks and its degrees of freedom are then obtained by subtraction. We will illustrate using the watch-assembly data.

EXAMPLE 9.3   CONTINUED

Table 9.15 is the ANOVA table for the full regression of assembly time on I_1, I_2, J_1, J_2, J_3, and J_4. Table 9.16 is the ANOVA table for the regression of assembly time on I_1 and I_2 only.

The sum of squares regression, degrees of freedom, and mean square from Table 9.16 are the sum of squares method, degrees of freedom, and mean square for the RCB model (9.10). To obtain the appropriate quantities for workers (i.e., blocks), we subtract the first two of these quantities from the corresponding quantities in ANOVA Table 9.15. Thus, the sum of squares for blocks is

TABLE 9.15   ANOVA Table: Full Regression for Watch-Assembly Data

		Analysis of Variance			
Source	DF	Sum of squares	Mean square	F Stat	Prob > F
Regression	6	4.492	0.749	91.84	0.0001
Error	8	0.065	0.008		
C Total	14	4.557			

TABLE 9.16   ANOVA Table, Regression on I_1 and I_2 Only: Watch-Assembly Data

		Analysis of Variance			
Source	DF	Sum of squares	Mean square	F Stat	Prob > F
Regression	2	0.415	0.207	0.60	0.5643
Error	12	4.143	0.345		
C Total	14	4.557			

$4.492 - 0.415 = 4.077$ and its degrees of freedom is $6 - 2 = 4$. From this, we obtain the mean square for blocks as $4.077/4 = 1.019$. In this way, we obtain Table 9.12, the ANOVA table for the RCB model.   ✦

9.4

THE ADVANTAGE OF BLOCKING

To give some idea of the advantage that blocking can provide, consider what happens if we ignore the blocks in the watch-assembly data, and assume a one-way model with three populations (assembly methods). The resulting ANOVA table is shown in Table 9.17.

According to this analysis, there are no statistically significant differences among assembly methods. Why should this be? A careful comparison of Table 9.17 with the ANOVA table for the RCB analysis of these data (Table 9.12), reveals the answer:

- SSTO is the same in both tables. This is because SSTO measures the variation in the response variable and has nothing to do with whatever model may be fit.
- The sum of squares for assembly method is the same in both tables.
- The big difference comes in SSE. In Table 9.12, it is 0.065, and in Table 9.17, it is 4.143! This value of 4.143 consists of the 0.065 (SSE) plus the 4.077 (SSB) from

**TABLE 9.17   ANOVA Table: Watch-Assembly Data
as One-Way Model**

		Analysis of Variance			
Source	DF	Sum of squares	Mean square	F Stat	Prob > F
Method	2	0.415	0.207	0.600	0.5643
Error	12	4.142	0.345		
C Total	14	4.557			

the RCB ANOVA. Because the one-way model does not have a way to account for the worker-to-worker variation in the model itself, this variation is lumped together with experimental error (which is, after all, the variation the model can't account for).

- Not everything works against the one-way model, however. Notice that SSE for the one-way model also gets an additional four degrees of freedom. This is helpful since it tends to make MSE smaller, which helps make the F ratio larger, and significance easier to obtain. In this example, though, the additional degrees of freedom aren't enough. Even with them, MSE for the one-way model is still 0.345, approximately 43 times the value of the MSE for the RCB model! As a result, the F ratio declines from 125.05 in the RCB model to 0.60 in the one-way model.

Thus, for the one-way model, the differences in mean times for the different assembly methods are lost in the large experimental error. Or, looked at more positively, blocking on assemblers reduces experimental error so that differences in mean times for the different assembly methods can be detected.

D ISCUSSION QUESTIONS

1. Write out the one-way means model in mathematical notation and describe what each model parameter represents.
2. What assumptions are made about data from the one-way means model?
3. How is the one-way means model fit to data?
4. Describe how to check model assumptions for the one-way means model.
5. Assuming the model is an acceptable fit to the data, what are the first hypotheses tested in the one-way means model? How are they tested?
6. Write out the ANOVA table for the one-way means model. Describe what each table entry represents.
7. Discuss the difference between formal and informal inference. What is data snooping, and what is its relation to formal and informal inference?
8. What are individual comparisons? How are they computed?
9. What are multiple comparisons? How do they differ from individual comparisons? Relate these ideas to data snooping.

10. What are indicator variables? Explain how the one-way model can be analyzed using multiple linear regression with indicator variables as regressors.

11. Describe the one-way effects model and how it relates to the one-way means model.

12. Describe the RCBD. When is it beneficial to use this design?

13. For the RCBD:
    (a) Write out the model in mathematical notation and describe what each model parameter represents.
    (b) Describe the model assumptions.
    (c) How is the RCB model fit to data?
    (d) Describe how to check model assumptions for the RCB model.
    (e) Assuming the model is an acceptable fit to the data, what are the first hypotheses tested in the RCB model? How are they tested? What other hypotheses may be tested?
    (f) Write out the ANOVA table for the RCB model. Describe what each table entry represents.
    (g) Describe individual comparisons in the RCB model. How are they computed?
    (h) Describe multiple comparisons in the RCB model. How are they computed?

14. Explain how the RCB model can be analyzed using multiple linear regression with indicator variables as regressors.

E XERCISES

9.1. Show that for the one-way model, MSE $= S_p^2$, the pooled variance is given by Equation (9.2).

9.2. Show that for the one-way model
    (a) $\sum_{i=1}^{k} \sum_{j=1}^{n_i} (Y_{ij} - \bar{Y}_{..}) = 0$, and therefore knowing $n - 1$ of the quantities $Y_{ij} - \bar{Y}_{..}$ allows us to compute the remaining quantity. Thus, we need to know at most $n - 1$ of these quantities to compute SSTO.
    (b) Knowing $n - 2$ or fewer of the quantities $Y_{ij} - \bar{Y}_{..}$ is not enough to tell us the remaining quantities. Thus, we need to know at least $n - 1$ of these quantities to compute SSTO. Conclude that there we need to know exactly $n - 1$ of the $Y_{ij} - \bar{Y}_{..}$ in order to compute SSTO. This shows why there are $n - 1$ degrees of freedom associated with SSTO.

9.3. For the following is an ANOVA table for a one-way design:

		Analysis of variance			
Source	DF	Sum of squares	Mean square	F Stat	Prob > F
Model	*	12.12	4.04	*	*
Error	21	18.90	*		
C Total	*	*			

    (a) Fill in the missing values (denoted by "*") in the ANOVA table.
    (b) How many populations are there?
    (c) Can you tell how many observations there are in each population? If so, give the answer.

9.4. For the following is an ANOVA table for a RCBD:

Analysis of variance					
Source	DF	Sum of squares	Mean square	F Stat	Prob > F
Treatment	6	*	0.22	3.38	*
Blocks	3	2.28	*	*	0.0002
Error	*	*	*		
C Total	*	4.77			

(a) Fill in the missing values (denoted by "*") in the ANOVA table.
(b) How many treatments are there?
(c) How many blocks are there?

9.5. Recall the artificial pancreas experiment from Chapters 5 and 6. Table 9.18 displays more data from that experiment (the data are also found in the data set RATS1). Four rats are drawn from each of three populations: normal rats (NORMAL), diabetic rats (DIABETIC), and diabetic rats who have had an artificial pancreas implanted (PAN-CREAS). The researcher gives each rat the same initial dose of glucose in solution and then measures their blood-sugar levels (serum/plasma glucose, mg/100 ml) after one-half hour. If the artificial pancreas is effective, the mean blood-sugar level of rats with the pancreas will be lower than the mean blood-sugar level of diabetic rats. If the artificial pancreas is fully effective, the mean blood-sugar level of rats with the pancreas will be no higher than the mean blood sugar level of normal rats.

TABLE 9.18   Artificial Pancreas Data

Group	Blood Sugar			
Pancreas	374	319	405	400
Diabetic	529	388	542	548
Normal	129	133	166	148

(a) Draw suitable plots and compute suitable statistics to summarize these data. What do these suggest?
(b) These data do not satisfy the assumptions of the one-way model. Explain why.
(c) Transform the response using the transformation $1/\sqrt{Y}$. How do the data satisfy model assumptions now? If there are still departures from model assumptions, describe their likely effect on the analysis.
(d) Do a complete analysis of the transformed data. Is the artificial pancreas effective? Is it fully effective?

9.6. A production engineer wants to determine the effect of machine configuration on the maximum force, in pounds, applied at a joint on an articulated arm of the machine during its normal operation. To do this, she takes three maximum-force readings at each of four configurations. The data are contained in Table 9.19 (and in the data set MACHFORC).
(a) How should the experimenter use randomization in this experiment?
(b) Assuming randomization has been done correctly, formulate and fit an appropriate model to these data.

TABLE 9.19   Machine Force Data

Configuration	Maximum force		
1	713.96	543.12	543.55
2	813.30	978.47	949.14
3	1420.30	1519.80	1629.50
4	299.75	572.56	562.62

   (c) Assess the model fit.
   (d) Take appropriate measures to identify statistically significant differences in mean maximum force for the different machine configurations.
   (e) Write a short report to the engineer explaining your findings.
9.7. A new type of technology called Personal Portable Technology (PPT) has been introduced into the field of elevator maintenance and repair. The PPT consists of a hand-held computer and two-way radio that enables the worker to get information about the job and to communicate with supervisors and other workers. The hope is that this technology will improve communication between personnel in the field and their supervisors and fellow workers. In order to ascertain the effect of PPT on job performance, a random sample of 41 field operatives was surveyed on three occasions: before the introduction of the PPT, 3 to 4 weeks after the introduction of the PPT, and 3 to 4 months after the introduction of the PPT. On each occasion, the same set of questions was asked. The management team at the elevator repair firm is especially interested in whether the workers perceive the PPT as beneficial to their work.

   The data set PPT contains the responses to the question: "To be useful, information must be available when we need it, not at some later time. How often is the information from your supervisor timely?" Responses are on a scale that range from 1 to 7 with 1 denoting "never" and 7 "constantly." The responses are stored under the name QULSUP (for "quality of information from the supervisor"). The other variables in the data set are WORKER, a worker identification number, and OCCASION, the occasion of the response (first, second, or third survey).
   (a) Explain why this is not a CRD.
   (b) Formulate an appropriate model for these data.
   (c) Fit the model to these data.
   (d) Assess the model fit. If necessary, take remedial measures.
   (e) Identify statistically significant occasion-to-occasion differences in the opinion of field operatives about the quality of information from their supervisors. Relate these differences to the introduction of the PPT.
   (f) Write a short report to the management team explaining your findings.
9.8. Analyze the PPT data as a CRD. Use these results to demonstrate the superiority of the RCB model for the PPT data.
9.9. Mechanical engineers are studying the influence of cam shape on the vibration produced at a given set of frequencies. An experiment is run in which the vibrations produced by four common cam shapes are measured and compared. Eight specially made test cams are used. Each cam is divided into four sectors and each sector is machined to a different one of the four shapes. Thus, all four shapes appear on each test cam. The test cams are run at a fixed speed and the displacement of a stylus riding on the cam is recorded. This signal is then broken into four signals corresponding to the four different cam-shape sectors. Each signal

is broken into frequency components (called the spectrum) and the rms[12] of the spectrum over a selected set of frequencies is computed. This value, which measures the amount of cam vibration at those frequencies, is the response variable. The data are displayed in Table 9.20 and are found in the data set CAM.

TABLE 9.20   Cam Data

Cam	Shape 1	Shape 2	Shape 3	Shape 4
1	0.6105	0.5754	0.4595	0.5793
2	0.7126	0.6609	0.6557	0.6206
3	0.7121	0.6107	0.6700	0.5734
4	0.6088	0.5529	0.3814	0.4926
5	0.6247	0.5702	0.5880	0.5701
6	0.6862	0.6323	0.7456	0.6251
7	0.6551	0.6244	0.7261	0.6662
8	0.8498	0.6937	0.7187	0.5284

(a) Explain why this is not a CRD.
(b) Formulate an appropriate model for these data.
(c) Fit the model to these data.
(d) Assess the model fit. If necessary, take remedial measures.
(e) Identify statistically significant differences in cam vibration between different shapes. The experimenters are particularly interested in which, if any, cam shape(s) generate excessive vibration and which, if any, generate very low vibration.
(f) Write a short report explaining your findings.

9.10. Analyze the CAM data as a CRD. Use these results to demonstrate the superiority of the RCB model for the CAM data.

9.11. A track coach conducts an experiment to give his runners a rational basis for selecting spike length for competition. He chooses four runners from the track team and randomly assigns each a spike length from among 0 (no spike), 1/4, 3/16, and 3/8 inch. He then records the time of each in the 60 meters. After a rest period, the same four runners are assigned a different spike length and the 60-meter times are again recorded. This continues until all four runners have run 60 meters in each of the four spike lengths. The times are displayed in Table 9.21 and are found in the data set SPIKES.
(a) Explain why this is not a CRD.
(b) Formulate an appropriate model for these data.
(c) Fit the model to these data.
(d) Assess the model fit. If necessary, take remedial measures.
(e) Identify statistically significant differences in times due to spike length.
(f) Write a short report explaining your findings to the coach.

9.12. Analyze the SPIKES data as a CRD. Use these results to demonstrate the superiority of the RCB model for the SPIKES data.

---

[12]Rms stands for "root mean square," and is basically the standard deviation of the measurements. See Chapter 2.

TABLE 9.21   Spike Data

		Spike length		
Runner	0	1/4	3/16	3/8
1	6.70	6.45	6.65	6.49
2	6.83	6.72	6.74	6.78
3	7.06	6.72	6.98	6.93
4	7.04	6.81	6.83	6.70

9.13. A study was conducted to assess the benefits of diet and drugs in reducing blood pressure in hypertensive men. In the study, five hypertensive men were randomly assigned to each of four groups: control (no treatment), diet (treatment by closely supervised diet alone), drug treatment alone, and the combination of diet and drug. As an initial measure of hypertension, average diastolic blood pressure was recorded for a week for each patient after 2 weeks without treatment. Then after 2 months of treatment, the average diastolic blood pressure was again recorded for a week. The latter was subtracted from the former for each subject, giving the reduction in mean diastolic blood pressure over the course of the treatment. A one-way analysis of variance was conducted to assess differences in the reduction in mean diastolic blood pressure among the different treatments. MSE was 37.5 and the sample means for the groups were

Treatment	Mean
Control	0.16
Diet alone	11.88
Drug alone	17.36
Drug and diet	31.52

(a) Which method, Bonferroni or Tukey, is preferred to do all pairwise comparisons? Why?

(b) Conduct all pairwise comparisons using the preferred method. What do you conclude?

9.14. Show that the regression model (9.10) is equivalent to the RCB model (9.8).

9.15. Fit the regression model (9.10) to the watch data. Verify that the estimated method and block effects are the same as those computed directly from the RCB model.

9.16. Show that the effects estimators in the RCB model sum to zero: $\sum_{i=1}^{k} \hat{\tau}_i = \sum_{j=1}^{b} \hat{\gamma}_j = 0$.

MINIPROJECT

Purpose

In order to see what advantages blocking confers when dealing with heterogeneous experimental units or what happens with homogeneous experimental units, your group is to obtain and analyze data from a one-way design in two ways: as a CRD and as a RCBD.

Process

The data for both designs should have the same response and the same treatments/populations. Before obtaining the data, you are to submit a proposal for your instructor's approval. The proposal should indicate

1. What you intend to do for the CRD.
2. What you intend to do for the RCBD.
3. Whether you expect the RCBD to perform better than the CRD or not, and the reasons for this expectation.

When you have received approval, proceed to obtain and analyze the data. Your analysis should include model fit, assessment of that fit, appropriate remedial measures, an overall F test and any appropriate individual and multiple comparisons. The analysis should consider the results from each design separately, and should compare the results to each other. Were your expectations for the relative performance of the two designs realized? If not, can you explain why?

LAB 9.1: Gage R&R, an Application of the One-Way Model

Introduction

In Chapter 1, you were introduced to Gage Repeatability and Reproducibility (Gage R&R), a statistical procedure used to assess the quality of a measurement process. In this lab, you will use the one-way model to analyze Gage R&R data.

Objectives

The purpose of this lab is to demonstrate how the one-way model can be used in a Gage R&R analysis.

Lab Materials

None needed.

Experimental Procedure

R&R Using a Single Part

In its simplest form, Gage R&R focuses on a single measuring device or gage, and on the operators who use the gage. Gage R&R considers two aspects of the measurement process:

- **Repeatability** measures the consistency of the gage in repeated measurements by the same operator on the same part. If the repeatability of measurement is low, the problem could be a faulty gage, flawed measurement methodology, or poor operator training.

- **Reproducibility** measures the variation between different operators. Low reproducibility means measurements vary greatly from operator to operator. Problems of reproducibility may be due to poor operator training.

In order to evaluate Gage R&R for a single gage, typically, a number of different operators will use that one gage to make a fixed number of identical measurements on each of several identical parts. Recall Example 1.5 of Chapter 1:

A manufacturer of roller bearings uses a special gage to measure the play in an assembled bearing. It is desired to evaluate repeatability and reproducibility for this gage. For the purposes of simplifying our presentation, we will assume that a single bearing and three operators are used in the study and that each operator makes 10 measurements on the bearing.

Example 1.5 goes on to show that the measuring process appears stationary for each operator, so we feel confident analyzing the observations without regard to the order in which they were taken.

The primary Gage R&R analysis of Example 1.5 is based on a stratified plot (Figure 1.14) of the measurements stratified by operator.

The data are found in the data set EG1.5A. As a starting point for your analysis, use the computer to reproduce the stratified plot found in Figure 1.14.

A plausible model for the observed measurements is the one-way means model:

$$Y_{ij} = \mu_i + \epsilon_{ij}, \qquad i = 1, 2, 3; \ j = 1, \ldots, 10 \qquad (9.11)$$

where Y_{ij} is the jth measurement made by operator i, μ_i is the mean of all possible measurements made by operator i, and ϵ_{ij} is the random error associated with Y_{ij}.

1. Fit the one-way means model to the EG1.5A data. Evaluate the adequacy of the fit.
2. In Example 1.5, the following conclusions were made based only on the plot in Figure 1.14.

   - There is a reproducibility problem in the measuring process, since the measurements made by operator 3 differ substantially from the others. The measuring method used by operator 3 should be looked at closely to see why this is so. When a reason has been found for the aberrant measurements from operator 3, the operator training procedures should be examined for ways to improve the consistency of measurement between operators.
   - There may or may not be a repeatability problem. If the variation in the measurements of operators 1 and 2 is acceptably small, then there is no problem. If that variation is too large, then the gage and process of taking measurements should be looked at.

   Use appropriate inference procedures based on model (9.11) to verify or contradict the first conclusion. What in the fitted model measures the repeatability? Use it to estimate the repeatability of measurement.

R&R Using Multiple Parts

By using more than one part on which to make measurements, we can extend the range of validity of conclusions from a Gage R&R study. Suppose that another Gage R&R study is conducted by the bearing manufacturer. In this study, there are three operators who make one measurement using the same gage on each of 10 parts. The data set LAB9_1 contains the data.

A model for this kind of study is the RCB model in which parts are blocks and the operators are the populations. Analyze the data in LAB9_1 by fitting a RCB model. Check the adequacy of the fit, including a check of additivity. What do you conclude about reproducibility and repeatability based on your analysis?

LAB 9.2: Individual versus Multiple Comparisons

Introduction

You have been told that multiple comparison procedures will give an overall error rate no greater than the advertised value of $1 - L$, whereas individual comparison procedures can give a much higher rate. This lab will demonstrate this difference.

Objectives

The purpose of this lab is to demonstrate the difference between overall error rates in individual and multiple comparison procedures.

Lab Materials

None needed.

Experimental Procedure[13]

1. Generate 3 data sets from the one-way model having data from 5 populations with means 5, 2, 2, 2, and 2, $N(0, 1)$ errors, and 5 observations from each population.

2. For each of the 3 data sets compute level 0.95 individual and Tukey multiple comparisons for all 3 data sets. For the individual comparisons count the number of the 3 data sets in which there is at least 1 mistaken conclusion (i.e., an interval that does not contain the true mean difference). Do the same for the Tukey multiple comparisons.

3. Now use your computer software to repeat what you did in part 3 for a large number (at least 1000) of data sets all from the same one-way model described in part 1.

4. Each individual comparison should yield a mistaken conclusion in about 5% of the data sets. By conducting 10 individual comparisons, you should have increased the percentage of data sets resulting in at least one mistaken conclusion. How large is this percentage in the data sets you generated?

    The Tukey multiple comparison procedure should keep the percentage of data sets yielding at least one mistaken conclusion down to the advertized 5%. Do your simulations indicate this is so?

---

[13]The instructions given here are very general. We have written SAS and MINITAB macros that perform the necessary steps for users of those packages. The **Doing It with SAS** and **Doing It with MINITAB** supplements have the details.

CAPSTONE PROJECT: Chapters 1 to 4 and 9

The goal of a **Capstone Project** is to give you experience in all phases of a statistical study: planning, data collection, analysis, and conclusions. Each of Chapters 1 to 4 and 9 must make a contribution to the project. For a description of this project, see the description of the Capstone Project for Chapters 1 to 5 on page 285. In addition to the material from Chapters 1 to 4 discussed there, the Capstone Project for Chapters 1 to 4 and 9, must also include modeling and inference for the one-way completely randomized or randomized complete block model, as covered in Chapter 9.

10

The Factorial Model

Scientific research is a process of guided learning. The object of statistical methods is to make that process as efficient as possible.

—*George E. P. Box, William G. Hunter, and J. Stuart Hunter*

INTRODUCTION

In Chapter 9, you learned about the simplest analysis of variance model, the one-way model, which is used to assess differences in mean response among several populations. As you learned in Chapter 3, it is frequently the case that populations are characterized by the values of two or more variables called **factors.** For example, in an experiment to identify determinants of the hardness of a new type of plastic, there may be two factors, the pressure and temperature at the time of molding. If the experimenters measure the hardness of the plastic at pressures 200, 300, and 400 pounds per square inch (psi), and at temperatures 200 and 300 degrees Fahrenheit (°F), there are three levels of pressure and two levels of temperature. Observations are taken at each of the six pressure–temperature combinations (200 psi, 200°F), (300 psi, 200°F), (400 psi, 200°F), (200 psi, 300°F), (300 psi, 300°F), and (400 psi, 300°F), which are called **treatments.** In this experiment, there are six populations, each one being the set of all possible observations taken at one treatment. So we may speak of the population of all possible observations taken at (200 psi, 200°F), the population of all possible observations taken at (300 psi, 200°F), and so on.

Analyzing this experiment using a one-way model to compare the mean response for the six treatments (populations) will tell about differences in mean hardness for different pressure–temperature combinations (i.e., treatments), but it won't tell which of the factors, temperature or pressure, is more strongly associated with these differences. In this chapter, you will learn about a model called the factorial model, which can be used to evaluate the effect on the mean response of the factors pressure and temperature.

Knowledge and Skills

By successfully completing this chapter, you will acquire the following knowledge and skills:

KNOWLEDGE	**SKILLS**
	For the factorial means model and the factorial effects model:
1. The factorial means model.	1. How to fit the model.
2. Interactions.	2. How to check the fit of the model.
3. The factorial effects model.	3. How to test for interactions and what to do if they are important.
4. The analysis of variance for the factorial model.	4. How to test the equality of population means.
5. Individual comparisons.	5. How to construct confidence intervals for differences in individual means or effects.
6. Multiple comparisons.	6. How to do multiple comparisons.

10.1

THE FACTORIAL MEANS MODEL

EXAMPLE 10.1   PULSE OXIMETRY

Pulse oximetry is a method used for noninvasive measurement of blood oxygen. A device attached to a patient's finger emits light in two different known wavelengths (red and near-infrared) on one side of the finger, and a sensor on the other side of the finger records the amount of emitted light that passes through the finger tissues. The amount of oxygen in a patient's blood is determined by comparing the relative amounts of absorbed light of the two different wavelengths. In a clinical environment, pulse oximetry is used in blood-oxygen monitors that continuously record measurements of a patient's blood-oxygen level and signal when the measurements fall below a safe level.

One problem that occurs with these monitors is false alarms. Some researchers suspect that movements of a patient's finger, such as might result from shivering, increase the incidence of false alarms.

In one research project to evaluate the causes of false alarms in pulse oximetry, biomedical engineers are testing whether shivering affects pulse oximetry measurements. Pulse oximeters are often used in two different environments in a hospital: in patient rooms, where shivering is most often associated with a fever, and in the recovery room immediately after surgery. The kind of shivering

TABLE 10.1   Pulse Oximetry Data

Intensity	Shivering type	Power				Mean	Standard deviation
Mild	Febrile	3.78	5.27	7.28	3.19	4.88	1.82
Mild	Postoperative	12.41	8.58	8.39	7.22	9.15	2.26
Moderate	Febrile	5.19	10.29	7.37	7.64	7.62	2.09
Moderate	Postoperative	6.99	7.54	7.33	15.67	9.38	4.20
Severe	Febrile	9.95	6.54	11.40	12.49	10.09	2.58
Severe	Postoperative	2.64	3.10	2.16	1.98	2.47	0.51

associated with a fever, which is called febrile shivering, is qualitatively different than the postoperative shivering experienced by surgery patients in the recovery room. In order to simulate these two types of shivering, the experimenters use a device for shaking a test subject's hand, called a shaker table. By altering the setup of the shaker table, the experimenters can simulate either febrile or postoperative shivering.

In the type of experiment we are considering, the standard pulse oximetry device is attached to the finger of a single test subject. The subject's hand is then attached to the shaker table, which vibrates the finger to simulate either postoperative or febrile shivering. In addition, the shaker table vibrations are set to one of three different intensities, which we will call mild, moderate, and severe. The response that is measured is the power of the electrical signal over a fixed range of frequencies. In this type of experiment, there are two factors: type of shivering, at two levels, and intensity of shivering, at three levels. There are six treatments, consisting of all combinations of type and intensity of shivering. The experimenters are interested in the effects of type of shivering and severity of shivering on the response.

In one particular experiment, the researchers used a single subject. From this subject, they obtained four measurements at each of the six treatments. The subject was allowed to rest for 5 minutes between runs. To more closely mimic a hospital environment, the apparatus was removed from the subject's finger after each run. Since the order in which the treatments were applied was randomized, the experiment is a completely randomized design (CRD).

The data are shown in Table 10.1.

Figure 10.1 shows a stratified plot and side-by-side mean diamonds of these data, from which we make the following observations

- For febrile shivering, mean values of the response increase nearly linearly with the intensity of the shivering, while spread remains nearly constant.
- For postoperative shivering, means are essentially the same at mild and moderate intensities, and these values are between the values for moderate and severe febrile shivering. The data for moderate postoperative shivering have greater spread than those for mild postoperative shivering. But at least for moderate postoperative shivering, the large spread is due to a single large observation.
- The location and spread for the data from severe postoperative shivering are substantially smaller than those of all other treatments.

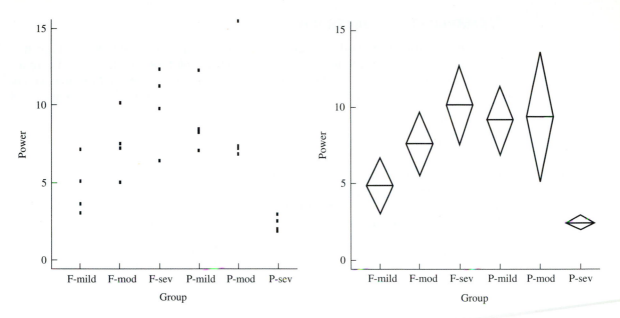

Figure 10.1   Stratified plot (left) and mean diamonds (right): pulse oximetry data. The group abbreviations are *F*-mild for mild febrile shivering, *P*-mild for mild postoperative shivering, *F*-mod for moderate febrile shivering, *P*-mod for moderate postoperative shivering, *F*-sev for severe febrile shivering, and *P*-sev for severe postoperative shivering.

In order to go beyond a descriptive analysis of the pulse oximetry data, we need to formulate a statistical model for the process that produced these data. ◆

The Model

The model we will consider is called a **factorial means model.** The general factorial means model for two factors with *n* observations per treatment is

$$Y_{ijk} = \mu_{ij} + \epsilon_{ijk}, \qquad i = 1, \ldots, a; j = 1, \ldots, b; \; k = 1, \ldots, n \qquad (10.1)$$

Because there are two factors, this model is also called the **two-way means model.** All responses observed for level *i* of the first factor and level *j* of the second factor will constitute a **cell** of the design. In a completely randomized design, which we consider in this chapter, each cell consists of a random sample from the population of all observations defined by level *i* of the first factor and level *j* of the second factor. In this model, Y_{ijk} is the *k*th observation in cell *ij*, μ_{ij} is the mean of the population for cell *ij*, and ϵ_{ijk} is the random error associated with the *k*th observation from this population. We will assume that the ϵ_{ijk} are independent of each other and come from an $N(0, \sigma^2)$ population. Notice that there are *a* levels for the first factor and *b* levels for the second factor, which implies that there are *ab* cells in all.

EXAMPLE 10.1   CONTINUED

In the pulse oximetry data, there are two factors, intensity and shivering type, with intensity taking three levels ($a = 3$) and shivering type two ($b = 2$). There are four observations taken at each shivering type-intensity combination ($n = 4$). The response is the power of the electrical signal over a fixed range of frequencies. ✦

Fitting the Model

Fitting model (10.1) consists of using the data to estimate the unknown model parameters μ_{ij}, $i = 1, \ldots, a$; $j = 1, \ldots, b$; and σ^2. This is done exactly as for the one-way means model (9.1), with ab populations. Specifically, we use the least squares estimators of the population means, which are obtained by finding the values of m_{ij} that minimize

$$\text{SSE}(m_{11}, m_{12}, \ldots, m_{ab}) = \sum_{i=1}^{a}\sum_{j=1}^{b}\sum_{k=1}^{n}(Y_{ijk} - m_{ij})^2$$

To write out the formulas for the estimators, we need some notation. Note that the total number of populations is ab and that the total number of observations is abn. Let

$$\bar{Y}_{ij\cdot} = \frac{\sum_{k=1}^{n} Y_{ijk}}{n} \qquad \text{and} \qquad S_{ij}^2 = \frac{\sum_{k=1}^{n}(Y_{ijk} - \bar{Y}_{ij\cdot})^2}{n-1}$$

denote the mean and variance, respectively, of the sample from the ijth population, $i = 1, \ldots, a$; $j = 1, \ldots, b$.

FORMULAS FOR FITTING THE MEANS MODEL

As for the one-way model:

- The least squares estimator of μ_{ij} is the sample mean of the data from the ijth population:

$$\hat{\mu}_{ij} = \bar{Y}_{ij\cdot} \tag{10.2}$$

- We will use the pooled variance

$$S_p^2 = \frac{\sum_{i=1}^{a}\sum_{j=1}^{b}(n-1)S_{ij}^2}{ab(n-1)} = \frac{\sum_{i=1}^{a}\sum_{j=1}^{b}S_{ij}^2}{ab} \tag{10.3}$$

to estimate σ^2. We will call this estimator $\hat{\sigma}^2$.

TABLE 10.2 Estimates, Pulse Oximetry Data, Means Model

Intensity	Shivering type	Mean	Standard deviation
Mild	Febrile	$\hat{\mu}_{11} = \bar{y}_{11\cdot} = 4.88$	$s_{11} = 1.82$
Mild	Postoperative	$\hat{\mu}_{12} = \bar{y}_{12\cdot} = 9.15$	$s_{12} = 2.26$
Moderate	Febrile	$\hat{\mu}_{21} = \bar{y}_{21\cdot} = 7.62$	$s_{21} = 2.09$
Moderate	Postoperative	$\hat{\mu}_{22} = \bar{y}_{22\cdot} = 9.38$	$s_{22} = 4.20$
Severe	Febrile	$\hat{\mu}_{31} = \bar{y}_{31\cdot} = 10.09$	$s_{31} = 2.58$
Severe	Postoperative	$\hat{\mu}_{32} = \bar{y}_{32\cdot} = 2.47$	$s_{32} = 0.51$

EXAMPLE 10.1 CONTINUED

Let's see how the fitting formulas work for the pulse oximetry data. There are 3 levels of Intensity and 2 levels of Shivering Type, giving a total of 6 treatments, or populations. There are $n = 4$ observations per population, giving a total of 24 observations. From Table 10.1, the mean and standard deviation of the first sample, corresponding to mild febrile shivering are $\hat{\mu}_{11} = \bar{y}_{11\cdot} = 4.88$ and $s_{11} = 1.82$, respectively. Table 10.2 displays these quantities for the rest of the cells in the design.

The pooled variance is

$$\hat{\sigma}^2 = s_p^2 = [(1.82)^2 + (2.26)^2 + \cdots + (0.51)^2]/(3)(2) = 6.22 \quad \blacklozenge$$

Checking the Fit

Once the model is fit, and before the model is used further, the fit must be checked to see whether model assumptions are satisfied. Recall that those assumptions are that the random errors ϵ_{ijk} are independent and that they come from an $N(0, \sigma^2)$ population. The principal tools used to check these assumptions are the residuals

$$e_{ijk} = Y_{ijk} - \hat{\mu}_{ij} = Y_{ijk} - \bar{Y}_{ij\cdot}, \qquad i = 1, \ldots, a; \; j = 1, \ldots, b; \; k = 1, \ldots, n$$

As for the one-way model, the residuals are the difference between the observed value and the estimated population mean. This allows us to write

$$Y_{ijk} = \hat{\mu}_{ij} + e_{ijk} \tag{10.4}$$

Comparing Equation (10.4) with Equation (10.1), we see that $\hat{\mu}_{ij}$ is our guess of μ_{ij} and e_{ijk} is our guess of ϵ_{ijk}. The idea behind using the residuals to check the model fit is that the residuals e_{ijk} should mimic the behavior of the unobservable random errors ϵ_{ijk}. Therefore, if the model is an adequate description of the data, the residuals should display behavior consistent with the model assumptions.

The most effective way to check the fit is to display residual plots. Plots of the residuals stratified by population are very useful. Histograms (if there are a good number of data from each population) mean diamonds and stratified plots can also be useful. The pattern and spread of the data from each population should be considered. For checking the normality assumption, the most appropriate plot is a plot of the Studentized residuals versus quantiles of the $t_{ab(n-1)-1}$ distribution. Independence of the errors is difficult to check, and we will not pursue it here. The best we can do is to use this model only for populations that are not related and to select the samples from the populations randomly and independently of each other.

Even if the populations under study have a common standard deviation, the sample standard deviations S_{ij} will not be equal. However, unless the sample standard deviations are markedly different, we will not go far wrong assuming the population standard deviations are equal.

EXAMPLE 10.1   CONTINUED

Before looking at residual plots of the pulse oximetry data, we notice that the standard deviations for four of the six groups are comparable, with standard deviations ranging from 1.82 to 2.58. However, the moderate postoperative group has an exceptionally large standard deviation of 4.20, and the severe postoperative group has an exceptionally small standard deviation of 0.51. These extreme values suggest that the assumption of equal standard deviations in model (10.1) may not be reasonable.

A look at Figure 10.1 shows that the very large standard deviation for the moderate postoperative data is the result of a single large value. If that value is removed, the standard deviation drops from 4.20 to 0.28. Even so, the assumption of equal standard deviations may be questionable. Complicating the decision about whether the assumption of equal standard deviations is tenable and whether the large moderate postoperative data value is an outlier is the small sample size of four in each group. It is difficult to tell much about the underlying population with only four data values.

So what should we do? There is no "correct" answer to this question, but here are some options:

• **Analyze the data as they are.** Under this option, we act as if the model fits the data well, or at least as if the way the data violate model assumptions will not invalidate the results. For some parts of the analysis, this will largely be true, for others it may not be. We will address this question in greater detail when we get further into the analysis.

• **Discard outlier(s).** Many researchers take this approach. Certainly, if we can identify outliers and also can establish that they are invalid data, such as data resulting from instrument malfunction, this should be done. If we can't establish a cause for the outlier, discarding it is a judgment call. But in this case, if it is discarded, the analysis should be done both with and without the outlier. If the results of both analyses are substantially the same, there is no problem. If not, we must seek further clarification, perhaps by taking more data.

There is also the difficulty of identifying outliers. For the pulse oximetry data, for example, there are points in the severe febrile and mild postoperative groups that might also be considered outliers. It is sometimes not clear when to stop discarding data.

Analysis of factorial models works best when the design is **balanced,** that is, when there are equal numbers of observations in each group. Discarding outliers can unbalance the design, which can adversely affect the analysis if the resulting imbalance is severe enough.

Finally, even if we discard the outlier in the moderate postoperative group of the pulse oximetry data, there will still be large differences in group standard deviations.

• **Transform the response.** This approach can bring the data more in line with model assumptions, giving researchers more faith in inference done with the model. One disadvantage is that the results are in the "wrong" units, which makes some researchers uncomfortable. On the other hand, it might be argued that there is nothing sacred about the units in which data are measured, and that the gain from having a better-fitting model is worth the trouble.

• **Perform a weighted analysis.** This approach consists of incorporating the differing group standard deviations into the model by weighting data from different groups differently. We will not present weighted analyses in this text.

In what follows, we will analyze the raw data as is. Later, we will redo the analysis with a transformed response.

Figure 10.2 shows a stratified plot for the residuals of the fit of the two-way means model to the pulse oximetry data. Notice that this plot is identical to the corresponding plot for the original data, Figure 10.1, except that the plots for each

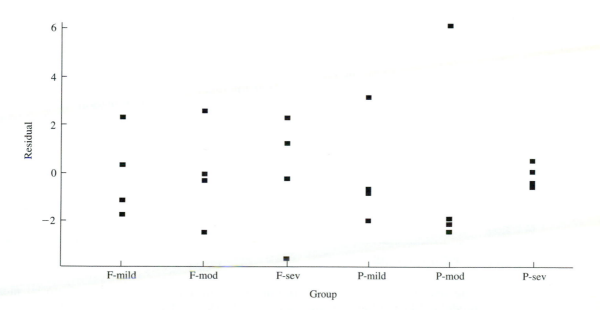

Figure 10.2   Stratified plot of residuals from pulse oximetry data fit.

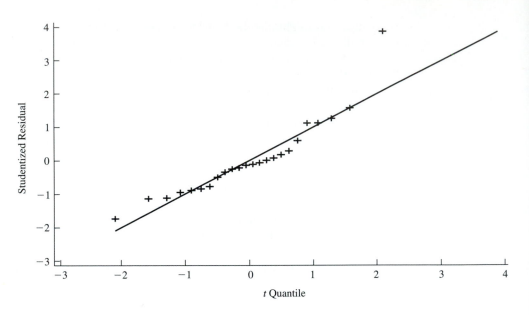

Figure 10.3 Studentized residuals from pulse oximetry data fit versus quantiles of the t_{17} distribution.

population have been centered at 0. (This is because the residuals are obtained from the original data by subtracting the means within each sample.)

Figure 10.3 shows a plot of the Studentized residuals versus quantiles of the t_{17} distribution. Recall that Studentized residuals are residuals divided by their estimated standard errors. If the model assumptions are satisfied, the Studentized residuals should have a t_{17} distribution. Studentized residuals in the extreme tails of the t_{17} distribution should be checked as possible outliers. Figure 10.3 reinforces our belief that the large observation in the moderate postoperative group is an outlier. The Studentized residual for this data value equals 3.89, which places it in the 99.9995 percentile of the t_{17} distribution, an indication that it is rather extreme. Except for this data value, we see that the Studentized residuals could be reasonably assumed to come from a t_{17} distribution.

The outlier will have to be dealt with eventually, but for now we leave the pulse oximetry example to learn about interactions between factors in the factorial model. ✦

10.2

INTERACTIONS

You may have noticed that the only real difference between the factorial means model (10.1) and the one-way means model (9.1) is that the means in the former are indexed by two subscripts instead of one and the responses and errors are indexed by three subscripts instead of two. The model fitting and checking we have described for the factorial means model are exactly the same as for the one-way means model because we have been treating the factorial model as a one-way model with $m = ab$ populations. Although this approach can lead to valuable insights, it will tell us little about the relationship between the factors and the response. In this and succeeding sections, we will develop concepts and methods that will allow us to analyze the relationship between the factors and the response. We begin with a definition.

> **DEFINITION**
>
> A factorial design with two factors, the first at a levels and the second at b levels, is called an $a \times b$ **factorial design.**

Suppose, as with the pulse oximetry data, that there are two factors. Call these factors A and B. Suppose that factor A is at three levels and that factor B is at two levels. Suppose we hold factor B fixed at level 1. Then the effect of factor A at level 2 compared with level 1 is $\mu_{21} - \mu_{11}$, and the effect of factor A at level 3 compared with level 2 is $\mu_{31} - \mu_{21}$ (we could write down the effect of factor A at level 3 compared with level 1, but if we know the first two quantities, we know this as well). Similarly, if we hold factor B fixed at level 2, the corresponding effects of factor A are $\mu_{22} - \mu_{12}$ and $\mu_{32} - \mu_{22}$.

> **DEFINITION**
>
> - We say that factors A and B are **additive** if for any two levels j_1 and j_2 of factor B, and for any two levels i_1 and i_2 of factor A, the effect of factor A at level i_1 compared with level i_2 when B is held at level j_1 is exactly the same as the effect of factor A at level i_1 compared with level i_2 when B is held at level j_2.
> - If two factors are not additive, we say that the factors **interact.**

For the 3×2 factorial model, the two factors are additive if and only if the following two equations hold:

$$\mu_{21} - \mu_{11} = \mu_{22} - \mu_{12} \tag{10.5}$$

and

$$\mu_{31} - \mu_{21} = \mu_{32} - \mu_{22} \tag{10.6}$$

EXAMPLE 10.2   INTERACTIONS

Table 10.3 shows the population means in a hypothetical 3×2 design.

Recall the interaction plot introduced in Chapter 9. That interaction plot was a sample interaction plot, computed from data. Figure 10.4 is a population interaction plot for model (10.1), computed not from data, but from the values of

TABLE 10.3   Example of Population
Means in a 3 × 2 Factorial Design

Levels of factor A	Levels of factor B	
	1	2
1	$\mu_{11} = 5$	$\mu_{12} = 3$
2	$\mu_{21} = 7$	$\mu_{22} = 5$
3	$\mu_{31} = 3$	$\mu_{32} = 1$

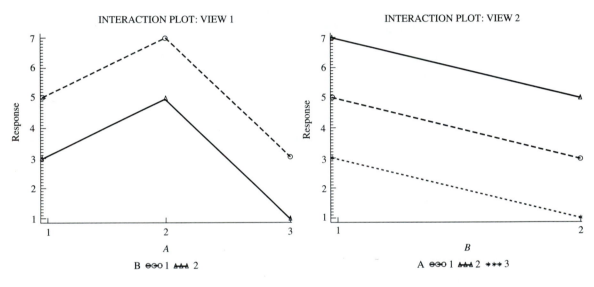

Figure 10.4   Interaction plots: additive effects.

the population parameters μ_{ij} shown in Table 10.3. In View 1 of Figure 10.4, the three means for each of the two levels of factor B are plotted and connected by lines. That is, the upper segmented line connects μ_{11}, μ_{21}, and μ_{31}, and the lower one connects μ_{12}, μ_{22}, and μ_{32}. Factors A and B do not interact if and only if these segmented lines are parallel, as they are here. In fact, Equation (10.5) states that the slopes of the first segments of the two lines in View 1 in Figure 10.4 are the same (i.e., these segments are parallel), and Equation (10.6) states that the slopes of the second segments of the two lines are the same (i.e., these segments are parallel). For the values in Table 10.3, Equations (10.5) and (10.6) become

$$7 - 5 = 5 - 3 \quad \text{and} \quad 3 - 7 = 1 - 5$$

Another way to think about View 1 in Figure 10.4 is that regardless of the value of factor A, the mean response is two units higher when factor B is at level 1 than it is when factor B is at level 2. In other words, factor B has the same effect regardless of the level of factor A. Hence, factors A and B do not interact.

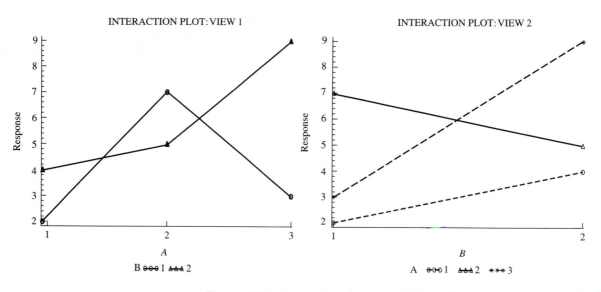

Figure 10.5 Interaction plots: nonadditive effects.

View 2 in Figure 10.4 is another view of the same phenomenon. In this interaction plot, one line is plotted for each of the three levels of factor A. Notice that the effect of factor B is to drop the mean response two units no matter which level of factor A we consider. Again, this makes the three lines parallel and indicates that there is no interaction. Two equations that express the parallelism of the lines in View 2 are

$$\mu_{22} - \mu_{21} = \mu_{12} - \mu_{11} \tag{10.7}$$

and

$$\mu_{32} - \mu_{31} = \mu_{22} - \mu_{21} \tag{10.8}$$

Exercise 10.1 asks you to show that Equations (10.7) and (10.8) characterize the parallelism of these three lines, and that they are equivalent to Equations (10.5) and (10.6).

   If the factors do not interact, it makes sense to talk about the effect of each factor separately. For instance, from View 1 in Figure 10.4, we can say that the effect of changing factor B from its low to its high level is to increase the mean response two units. From View 2, we can say that the effect of changing factor A from its low to its middle level is to increase the mean response two units, and the effect of changing factor A from its middle to its high level is to decrease the mean response four units. (What is the effect of changing factor A from its low to its high level?)

   If the lines in the interaction plots are not parallel, the factors are said to interact. Figure 10.5 shows two interaction plots for a set of interacting means. These plots show that it is impossible to isolate the effect of one of the factors from the other. For example, if asked the effect of changing factor B from its low to its high level, we would give three different answers, depending on the level of factor A. When A is at level 1, the effect of changing B from its low to its high level is to increase the mean response one unit. When A is at level 2, the effect of changing B from its low to its high level is to decrease the mean response two units. And when A is at level 3, the effect of changing B from its low to its high level is to increase the mean response six units. Contrast this with the interpretation of View 2 in Figure 10.4, where the effect of changing factor B from its low to its high level is to decrease the mean response two units regardless of the level of factor A. ◆

Important and Unimportant Interactions

The interactions illustrated in Figure 10.5 are very obvious and result in strikingly different effects of one factor for the different levels of the other. For such interactions, it is impossible to separate the effects of the two factors. Such interactions are regarded as **important interactions.** There are, however, interactions that have a much smaller effect. We will regard any interaction that is small enough to allow us to meaningfully analyze the individual factor effects as an **unimportant interaction.**

EXAMPLE 10.3   AN UNIMPORTANT INTERACTION

Figure 10.6 illustrates an unimportant interaction. These plots result from changing μ_{12} in Table 10.3 from 3.0 to 2.8. Technically, there is interaction between the factors, but it is difficult to tell from the plot. This small difference of 0.2 does

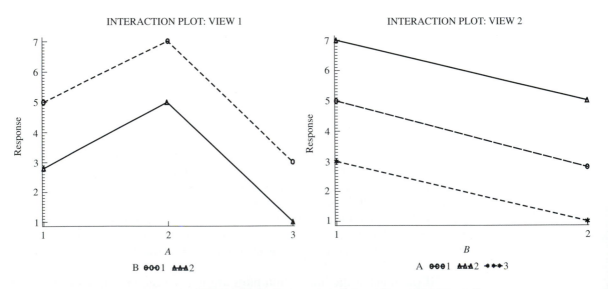

Figure 10.6   Interaction plots: unimportant interaction.

not stop us from quantifying the effect of factors A and B separately. We simply say, for example, that the effect of changing B from its low to its high value is to decrease the mean response **approximately** two units. We could also make similar statements about factor A. ✦

10.3

THE FACTORIAL EFFECTS MODEL

In order to assess the effect of the individual factors and their interaction, we reformulate model (10.1) as an effects model, just as we did for the one-way and RCB models in Chapter 9.

Main Effects

Consider again the factorial means model (10.1). We want to quantify the effects of each factor separately. To begin with, we define an overall mean response for all populations as

$$\mu = \frac{1}{ab} \sum_{i=1}^{a} \sum_{j=1}^{b} \mu_{ij} \tag{10.9}$$

Next, we define the overall mean response for level i of factor A as

$$\mu_{i.} = \frac{1}{b} \sum_{j=1}^{b} \mu_{ij} \tag{10.10}$$

and for level j of factor B as

$$\mu_{.j} = \frac{1}{a} \sum_{i=1}^{a} \mu_{ij} \tag{10.11}$$

Just as we did for the one-way and RCB effects models in Chapter 9, we define the effect of each level of each of the factors as the difference between the mean for the particular level of the factor and the overall mean. So the effect of level i of factor A is

$$\alpha_i = \mu_{i.} - \mu \tag{10.12}$$

and the effect of level j of factor B is

$$\beta_j = \mu_{.j} - \mu \tag{10.13}$$

The Additive Effects Model

If the mean of population ij is the sum of the overall mean and the effects for level i of factor A and level j of factor B, the model is said to be **additive.** Mathematically, this condition is expressed as

$$\mu_{ij} = \mu + \alpha_i + \beta_j$$

and results in the **additive effects model:**

$$Y_{ijk} = \mu + \alpha_i + \beta_j + \epsilon_{ijk}, \qquad i = 1, \ldots, a; \; j = 1, \ldots, b; \; k = 1, \ldots, n \qquad (10.14)$$

For the additive effects model, it is assumed that

$$\sum_{i=1}^{a} \alpha_i = \sum_{j=1}^{b} \beta_j = 0$$

The General Effects Model

If μ_{ij} cannot be written as a sum of the overall mean and the main effects, we must use a more general model. For each level i of factor A and j of factor B, we define the AB interaction, $(\alpha\beta)_{ij}$, as that part of μ_{ij} not explained by adding the main effects:

$$(\alpha\beta)_{ij} = \mu_{ij} - (\mu + \alpha_i + \beta_j) \qquad (10.15)$$

This gives us the **general effects model:**

$$Y_{ijk} = \mu + \alpha_i + \beta_j + (\alpha\beta)_{ij} + \epsilon_{ijk},$$
$$i = 1, \ldots, a; \; j = 1, \ldots, b; \; k = 1, \ldots, n \qquad (10.16)$$

For the general effects model, it is assumed that, as for the additive effects model,

$$\sum_{i=1}^{a} \alpha_i = \sum_{j=1}^{b} \beta_j = 0$$

In addition, it is assumed that for each $j = 1, \ldots, b,$

$$\sum_{i=1}^{a} (\alpha\beta)_{ij} = 0$$

and for each $i = 1, \ldots, a,$

$$\sum_{j=1}^{b} (\alpha\beta)_{ij} = 0$$

TABLE 10.4   Example of Computations Using Population Means in a 3 × 2 Design

Levels of factor A	Levels of factor B		$\mu_{i.}$
	1	2	
1	$\mu_{11} = 2$	$\mu_{12} = 4$	$\mu_{1.} = 3$
2	$\mu_{21} = 7$	$\mu_{22} = 5$	$\mu_{2.} = 6$
3	$\mu_{31} = 3$	$\mu_{32} = 9$	$\mu_{3.} = 6$
$\mu_{.j}$	$\mu_{.1} = 4$	$\mu_{.2} = 6$	$\mu = 5$

TABLE 10.5   Example of Computations of Effects in a 3 × 2 Factorial Design

Levels of factor A	Levels of factor B		
	1	2	
1	$(\alpha\beta)_{11} = 2 - (5 - 2 - 1) = \;\;\;0$	$(\alpha\beta)_{12} = 7 - (5 - 2 + 1) = \;\;\;0$	$\alpha_1 = 3 - 5 = -2$
2	$(\alpha\beta)_{21} = 7 - (5 + 1 - 1) = \;\;\;2$	$(\alpha\beta)_{22} = 5 - (5 + 1 + 1) = -2$	$\alpha_2 = 6 - 5 = \;\;\;1$
3	$(\alpha\beta)_{31} = 3 - (5 + 1 - 1) = -2$	$(\alpha\beta)_{32} = 9 - (5 + 1 + 1) = \;\;\;2$	$\alpha_3 = 6 - 5 = \;\;\;1$
	$\beta_1 = 4 - 5 = -1$	$\beta_2 = 6 - 5 = 1$	

EXAMPLE 10.2   CONTINUED

Table 10.4 shows computations of μ, $\mu_{i.}$, and $\mu_{.j}$ for the hypothetical example illustrated in Figure 10.5. Table 10.5 illustrates the computations of the individual and interaction effects. ✦

Fitting the Factorial Effects Model

Fitting either the additive effects model (10.14) or the general effects model (10.16) consists of using data to estimate the model parameters. Throughout, we use the least squares criterion for selecting estimators. As always, the estimators obtained using this criterion are called least squares estimators.

For the additive model, the least squares estimators are the values m, d_i, and g_j, which among all d_i and g_j satisfying $\sum_{i=1}^{a} d_i = 0$, and $\sum_{j=1}^{b} g_j = 0$, minimize

$$\text{SSE}(m, d_1, d_2, \ldots, d_a, g_1, g_2, \ldots, g_b) = \sum_{i=1}^{a} \sum_{j=1}^{b} \sum_{k=1}^{n} [Y_{ijk} - (m + d_i + g_j)]^2$$

For the general model, the least squares estimators are the values m, d_i, g_j, and h_{ij}, which among all d_i and g_j satisfying $\sum_{i=1}^{a} d_i = 0$ and $\sum_{j=1}^{b} g_j = 0$, and among all

h_{ij} satisfying, for each j, $\sum_{i=1}^{a} h_{ij} = 0$, and for each i, $\sum_{j=1}^{b} h_{ij} = 0$, minimize

$$\text{SSE}(m, d_1, d_2, \ldots, d_a, g_1, g_2, \ldots, g_b, h_{11}, h_{12}, \ldots, h_{ab})$$

$$= \sum_{i=1}^{a} \sum_{j=1}^{b} \sum_{k=1}^{n} [Y_{ijk} - (m + d_i + g_j + h_{ij})]^2$$

Some Notation

Before we give formulas for the least squares estimators, and quantities based on them, we will set up the notation. The formulas will be combinations of sample means of the responses Y_{ijk} computed with respect to one or more of the indices i, j, or k. As usual, the mean will be denoted by a bar over the symbol for the response, Y. Each index over which the responses are averaged will be replaced with a dot. Thus, the means of interest have the following notation.

- The mean of all observations:

$$\bar{Y}_{...} = \frac{1}{abn} \sum_{i=1}^{a} \sum_{j=1}^{b} \sum_{k=1}^{n} Y_{ijk}$$

- The mean of all observations with level i of factor A:

$$\bar{Y}_{i..} = \frac{1}{bn} \sum_{j=1}^{b} \sum_{k=1}^{n} Y_{ijk}$$

- The mean of all observations with level j of factor B:

$$\bar{Y}_{.j.} = \frac{1}{an} \sum_{i=1}^{a} \sum_{k=1}^{n} Y_{ijk}$$

- The mean of all observations with level i of factor A and level j of factor B:

$$\bar{Y}_{ij.} = \frac{1}{n} \sum_{k=1}^{n} Y_{ijk}$$

Fitting Formulas

The equations for the least squares estimators follow in a natural and logical way from Equations (10.9) to (10.13) and (10.15) by substituting sample means for population means. For either the additive or general model, the estimators of the overall mean and main effects are the same. The least squares estimator of μ is the mean of all observations:

$$\hat{\mu} = \bar{Y}_{...} \tag{10.17}$$

The least squares estimator of the population mean for level i of factor A, μ_i, is the sample mean for level i of factor A, $\hat{\mu}_{i.} = \bar{Y}_{i..}$. Therefore, the least squares estimator of $\alpha_i = \mu_i - \mu$ is

$$\hat{\alpha}_i = \hat{\mu}_{i.} - \hat{\mu} = \bar{Y}_{i..} - \bar{Y}_{...} \tag{10.18}$$

Similarly, the least squares estimator of β_j is

$$\hat{\beta}_j = \hat{\mu}_{.j} - \hat{\mu} = \bar{Y}_{.j.} - \bar{Y}_{...} \tag{10.19}$$

where $\hat{\mu}_{.j} = \bar{Y}_{.j.}$ is the least squares estimator of $\mu_{.j}$.

Of course, in the additive model, we do not estimate interactions. In the general model, recall that the interaction of level i of factor A and level j of factor B is

$$(\alpha\beta)_{ij} = \mu_{ij} - (\mu + \alpha_i + \beta_j)$$

It therefore comes as no surprise that the least squares estimator of $(\alpha\beta)_{ij}$ is

$$\widehat{(\alpha\beta)}_{ij} = \hat{\mu}_{ij} - (\hat{\mu} + \hat{\alpha}_i + \hat{\beta}_j) = \bar{Y}_{ij.} - (\bar{Y}_{...} + (\bar{Y}_{i..} - \bar{Y}_{...}) + (\bar{Y}_{.j.} - \bar{Y}_{...}))$$
$$= \bar{Y}_{ij.} - \bar{Y}_{i..} - \bar{Y}_{.j.} + \bar{Y}_{...} \tag{10.20}$$

Once the parameter estimators are determined, we may compute the **fitted values.** These are the values the fitted model predicts for each observation. If the additive model (10.14) is used, the fitted values are

$$\hat{Y}_{ijk} = \hat{\mu} + \hat{\alpha}_i + \hat{\beta}_j = \bar{Y}_{i..} + \bar{Y}_{.j.} - \bar{Y}_{...} \tag{10.21}$$

If the general model (10.16) is used, the fitted values are

$$\hat{Y}_{ijk} = \hat{\mu} + \hat{\alpha}_i + \hat{\beta}_j + \widehat{(\alpha\beta)}_{ij} = \bar{Y}_{ij.} \tag{10.22}$$

The fitted values for the general model (10.22) equal the fitted values for the means model, $\hat{\mu}_{ij} = \bar{Y}_{ij.}$. This is not true of the fitted values for the additive model (10.21).

We summarize these formulas as follows:

FORMULA FOR FITTING THE EFFECTS MODEL

- For both the additive and general two-factor factorial effects model,

$$\hat{\mu} = \bar{Y}_{...}$$

$$\hat{\alpha}_i = \hat{\mu}_{i.} - \hat{\mu} = \bar{Y}_{i..} - \bar{Y}_{...}$$

and

$$\hat{\beta}_j = \hat{\mu}_{.j} - \hat{\mu} = \bar{Y}_{.j.} - \bar{Y}_{...}$$

- For the general model,

$$\widehat{(\alpha\beta)}_{ij} = \hat{\mu}_{ij} - (\hat{\mu} + \hat{\alpha}_i + \hat{\beta}_j) = \bar{Y}_{ij.} - \bar{Y}_{i..} - \bar{Y}_{.j.} + \bar{Y}_{...}$$

- The fitted values for the additive model are

$$\hat{Y}_{ijk} = \hat{\mu} + \hat{\alpha}_i + \hat{\beta}_j = \bar{Y}_{i..} + \bar{Y}_{.j.} - \bar{Y}_{...}$$

- The fitted values for the general model are

$$\hat{Y}_{ijk} = \hat{\mu} + \hat{\alpha}_i + \hat{\beta}_j + \widehat{(\alpha\beta)}_{ij} = \bar{Y}_{ij.}$$

EXAMPLE 10.1   CONTINUED

We illustrate these formulas using the pulse oximetry data. To begin with, it will help to rewrite Table 10.1 in a form that emphasizes the two factors and the basic computations needed to fit the factorial models. Table 10.6 does so:

TABLE 10.6   Initial Computations for Effects Model Fits: Pulse Oximetry Data

Levels of intensity	Shivering type		$\hat{\mu}_{i.}$
	Febrile	Postoperative	
Mild	$\hat{\mu}_{11} = 4.88$	$\hat{\mu}_{12} = 9.15$	$\hat{\mu}_{1.} = 7.015$
Moderate	$\hat{\mu}_{21} = 7.62$	$\hat{\mu}_{22} = 9.38$	$\hat{\mu}_{2.} = 8.500$
Severe	$\hat{\mu}_{31} = 10.09$	$\hat{\mu}_{32} = 2.47$	$\hat{\mu}_{3.} = 6.280$
$\hat{\mu}_{.j}$	$\hat{\mu}_{.1} = 7.530$	$\hat{\mu}_{.2} = 7.000$	$\hat{\mu} = 7.265$

TABLE 10.7   Estimates of Overall Mean and Main Effects: Pulse Oximetry Data

$\hat{\mu} = 7.265$	$\hat{\alpha}_1 = 7.015 - 7.265 = -0.250$	$\hat{\beta}_1 = 7.530 - 7.265 = 0.265$
	$\hat{\alpha}_2 = 8.500 - 7.265 = 1.235$	$\hat{\beta}_2 = 7.000 - 7.265 = -0.265$
	$\hat{\alpha}_3 = 6.280 - 7.265 = -0.985$	

TABLE 10.8   Estimates of Interaction Effects: Pulse Oximetry Data

$$\widehat{(\alpha\beta)}_{11} = 4.88 - (7.265 - 0.250 + 0.265) = -2.400$$

$$\widehat{(\alpha\beta)}_{12} = 9.15 - (7.265 - 0.250 - 0.265) = 2.400$$

$$\widehat{(\alpha\beta)}_{21} = 7.62 - (7.265 + 1.235 + 0.265) = -1.145$$

$$\widehat{(\alpha\beta)}_{22} = 9.38 - (7.265 + 1.235 - 0.265) = 1.145$$

$$\widehat{(\alpha\beta)}_{31} = 10.09 - (7.265 - 0.985 + 0.265) = 3.545$$

$$\widehat{(\alpha\beta)}_{32} = 2.47 - (7.265 - 0.985 - 0.265) = -3.545$$

From Table 10.6, we obtain the estimates of the main effects, A and B, shown in Table 10.7. Finally, Table 10.8 shows the computation of interaction estimates.

Fitted values may be computed from the appropriate model using Equations (10.21) and (10.22). For example, in the pulse oximetry data, $y_{324} = 0.68$. Under the additive model (10.21),

$$\hat{y}_{324} = \hat{\mu} + \hat{\alpha}_3 + \hat{\beta}_2 = 7.265 - 0.985 - 0.265 = 6.015$$

Under the general model (10.22),

$$\hat{y}_{324} = \hat{\mu} + \hat{\alpha}_3 + \hat{\beta}_2 + \widehat{(\alpha\beta)}_{32} = 7.265 - 0.985 - 0.265 - 3.545 = 2.470 \quad \blacklozenge$$

Checking the Fit

As with the means model, once the effects model is fit, and before the model is used further, the fit must be checked to see whether model assumptions are satisfied. Recall that those assumptions are that the random errors ϵ_{ijk} are independent $N(0, \sigma^2)$ random variables. The principal tools used to check these assumptions are the residuals. The formula used for either the additive or general two-factor factorial model is

$$e_{ijk} = Y_{ijk} - \hat{Y}_{ijk}$$

though as we have just seen, the formula used in computing $\hat{Y}_{ijk}$ depends on which model is fit.

Fitting additive model (10.14) decomposes observation ijk into

$$Y_{ijk} = \hat{\mu} + \hat{\alpha}_i + \hat{\beta}_j + e_{ijk}.$$

Compare this with Equation (10.14), and it can be seen that in the fitted model, $\hat{\mu}$, $\hat{\alpha}_i$, $\hat{\beta}_j$, and e_{ijk} are our approximations to the unobservable μ, α_i, β_j, and ϵ_{ijk}. Similarly, fitting general model (10.16) decomposes observation ijk into

$$Y_{ijk} = \hat{\mu} + \hat{\alpha}_i + \hat{\beta}_j + \widehat{(\alpha\beta)}_{ij} + e_{ijk}$$

The residuals e_{ijk} should mimic the behavior of the unobservable random errors ϵ_{ijk}. Therefore, if the model is an adequate description of the data, the residuals should display behavior consistent with the model assumptions. The same kinds of residual plots used for the means model should be consulted in determining the suitability of the effects models. In addition, plots versus the levels of each factor separately should be used.

EXAMPLE 10.1   CONTINUED

Figure 10.7 displays plots of the Studentized residuals from the fit of the additive model (10.14) versus levels of each factor, the fitted values and quantiles of the t_{19}

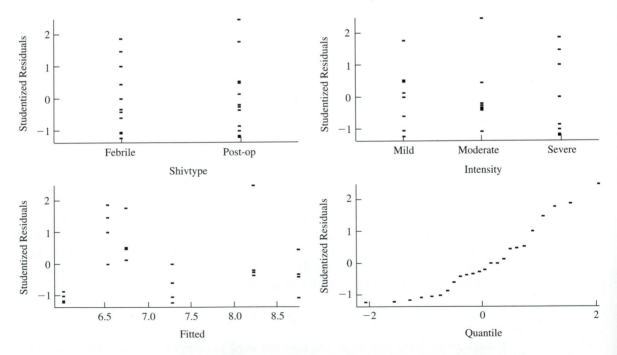

Figure 10.7   Residual plots: pulse oximetry data, additive model.

distribution. The plot of residuals versus fitted values shows a disturbing pattern: Of the six different fitted values, the residuals for three are nearly all positive and the residuals for the other three are nearly all negative. This kind of pattern often indicates that the assumption of additive effects is mistaken. The remaining plots show little evidence that the model is inadequate.

Compare these plots with the Studentized residual plots from the fit of the general model (10.16), which are shown in Figure 10.8. The lower right plot shows the Studentized residuals versus quantiles of the t_{17} distribution. This plot shows the outlier we saw earlier in Figure 10.3. In addition, the plot of the residuals versus the fitted values shows the small variation in the severe postoperative group that we saw in Figure 10.1. Despite these apparent deviations from model assumptions, the general model is a better fit to the data than is the additive model.

At this point, if we were only doing the statistical analysis, as opposed to presenting the analysis in a textbook, we would try to do something about the apparent deviations from model assumptions. However, in order to illustrate a number of specific ideas and computations, we will continue analyzing these data using the general model. But don't worry, we will address the deviations from model assumptions soon.

Our next step is to investigate the interaction between shivering type and shivering intensity. To do so, we will use sample interaction plots, which were introduced in Chapter 9 as a way to check the assumption of additivity in the RCB

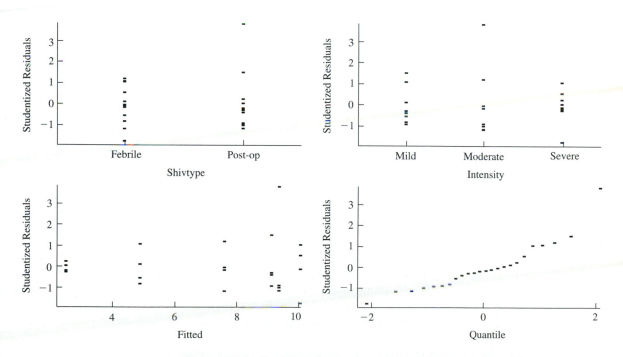

Figure 10.8   Residual plots: pulse oximetry data, general model.

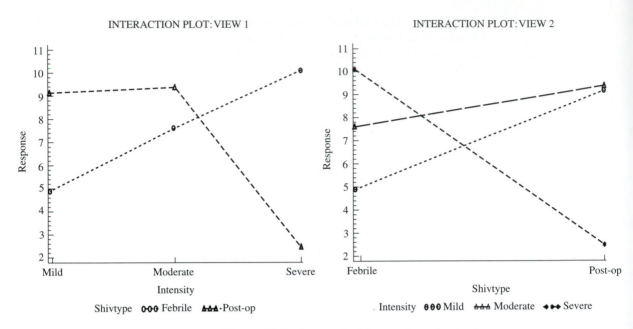

Figure 10.9   Interaction plots: pulse oximetry data.

model. These interaction plots can also be used to assess the nature of interaction between two factors in a factorial design. Figure 10.9 shows sample interaction plots for the pulse oximetry data. Plotted in View 1 in Figure 10.9 are the $\hat{\mu}_{ij} = \bar{y}_{ij.}$ versus the levels of the first factor, shivering intensity. The $\hat{\mu}_{ij}$ with the same value of the second factor, shivering type, are connected with segmented lines. In View 2, the roles of the two factors are reversed. Sample interaction plots are interpreted just as population interaction plots are: parallel or near-parallel lines indicate additivity; nonparallel lines indicate interaction.[1] The plots in Figure 10.9 show what appears to be substantial interaction between shivering type and intensity.

   View 1 in Figure 10.9 shows the interaction to be more pronounced for moderate and severe intensity. For postoperative shivering, the mean response at moderate intensity is 6.91 units **higher** than that at severe intensity. However, for febrile shivering, the mean response at moderate intensity is 2.47 units **lower** than that at severe intensity. This reversal of the relation between mean response and intensity for different types of shivering is the interaction.

   View 2 gives another perspective. There we see that for mild shivering intensity, the mean response for postoperative shivering is 4.27 units **higher** than it is for febrile shivering, and for moderate shivering intensity, the mean response of postoperative shivering is 1.76 units **higher** than it is for febrile shivering. However, for severe shivering intensity, the mean response of postoperative shivering is

---

[1]We must always remember that the natural variation in data means that even if an additive model is correct, the lines in the sample interaction plots will not be exactly parallel.

7.62 units **lower** than it is for febrile shivering. This reversal of the relation between mean response and type of shivering for different intensities is the interaction.

These plots can give insight into the nature of interactions, but cannot tell us if the interactions are either important or statistically significant. Importance of an interaction, discussed in Section 10.2, is basically determined by whether ignoring the interaction would substantially lessen the ability of the model to explain the phenomenon under study or to predict the response. The decision as to whether an interaction is important is not solely a statistical one, and must be made by a subject-matter specialist. The statistical significance of the interaction, on the other hand, is determined by the amount of evidence in the data against the additive model and in favor of the general model, and by the amount of evidence the investigators require. In the next section, we will introduce a test for whether the interaction is statistically significant. ✦

The Analysis of Variance

Dividing the Variation

Just as was done for the RCB model in Chapter 9, we can decompose the total variation in the response of a factorial effects model into components. For the general two-factor model (10.16), the components and their formulas are as follows:

ANALYSIS OF VARIANCE FORMULAS FOR THE GENERAL EFFECTS MODEL (10.16)

- Sum of squares total:

$$\text{SSTO} = \sum_{i=1}^{a}\sum_{j=1}^{b}\sum_{k=1}^{n}(Y_{ijk} - \bar{Y}_{...})^2$$

- Sum of squares due to factor A:

$$\text{SSA} = \sum_{i=1}^{a}\sum_{j=1}^{b}\sum_{k=1}^{n}(\bar{Y}_{i..} - \bar{Y}_{...})^2 = bn\sum_{i=1}^{a}(\bar{Y}_{i..} - \bar{Y}_{...})^2 \qquad (10.23)$$

- Sum of squares due to factor B:

$$\text{SSB} = \sum_{i=1}^{a}\sum_{j=1}^{b}\sum_{k=1}^{n}(\bar{Y}_{.j.} - \bar{Y}_{...})^2 = an\sum_{j=1}^{b}(\bar{Y}_{.j.} - \bar{Y}_{...})^2 \qquad (10.24)$$

(continued)

ANALYSIS OF VARIANCE FORMULAS FOR THE GENERAL EFFECTS MODEL (10.16) (*CONTINUED*)

- Sum of squares due to AB interaction:

$$\text{SSAB} = \sum_{i=1}^{a}\sum_{j=1}^{b}\sum_{k=1}^{n}(\bar{Y}_{ij\cdot} - \bar{Y}_{i\cdot\cdot} - \bar{Y}_{\cdot j\cdot} + \bar{Y}_{\cdot\cdot\cdot})^2 = n\sum_{i=1}^{a}\sum_{j=1}^{b}(\bar{Y}_{ij\cdot} - \bar{Y}_{i\cdot\cdot} - \bar{Y}_{\cdot j\cdot} + \bar{Y}_{\cdot\cdot\cdot})^2$$

(10.25)

- Sum of squares error:

$$\text{SSE} = \sum_{i=1}^{a}\sum_{j=1}^{b}\sum_{k=1}^{n}(Y_{ijk} - \bar{Y}_{ij\cdot})^2$$

- The degrees of freedom for SSA, SSB, SSAB, SSE, and SSTO are $a-1$, $b-1$, $(a-1)(b-1)$, $ab(n-1)$, and $abn-1$, respectively.

As in our previous encounters with the analysis of variance, a sum of squares divided by its degrees of freedom is called a mean square. For model (10.16), the mean squares for factors A and B, their interaction, and error are denoted MSA, MSB, MSAB, and MSE, respectively.

Some points of interest with regard to sums of squares, mean squares, and degrees of freedom are as follows:

- That the sums of squares and the degrees of freedom add. That is, SSTO = SSA + SSB + SSAB + SSE, and $abn - 1 = (a-1) + (b-1) + (a-1)(b-1) + ab(n-1)$. This is a phenomenon we have observed before in the one-way and RCB models.
- For model (10.16), MSE, which is $\text{SSE}/ab(n-1)$, equals the pooled variance estimator S_p^2, defined in Section 10.1, and is therefore the estimator of the error variance, σ^2.
- The degrees of freedom associated with each Studentized residual is one less than the degrees of freedom associated with the MSE. This is because the "estimated" in "estimated standard error" comes from using an MSE to estimate σ^2. When calculating a Studentized residual, the data value whose residual is being computed is omitted, causing the resulting MSE to have one less degree of freedom than the MSE obtained from the full data. For the general model, the Studentized residuals should follow a $t_{ab(n-1)-1}$ distribution. For the additive model, the Studentized residuals should follow a $t_{abn-a-b}$ distribution.

F Tests

There are three primary hypotheses to test in the factorial model (10.16).

Testing for Interactions.   The first hypothesis tested is for the presence of interaction:

$$H_0^{(\alpha\beta)}: \quad (\alpha\beta)_{ij} = 0, \qquad \text{for all } i = 1, \ldots, a; \; j = 1, \ldots, b$$

$$H_a^{(\alpha\beta)}: \quad (\alpha\beta)_{ij} \neq 0, \qquad \text{for at least one } ij$$

The test statistic is $F^{(\alpha\beta)} = \text{MSAB/MSE}$. Under $H_0^{(\alpha\beta)}$, $F^{(\alpha\beta)}$ has an F distribution with $(a-1)(b-1)$ and $ab(n-1)$ degrees of freedom. The p-value of the test is the proportion of an $F_{(a-1)(b-1),ab(n-1)}$ population that exceeds the observed value of the test statistic.

If $H_0^{(\alpha\beta)}$ is rejected, we conclude that there is significant interaction. In that case, before proceeding, the nature of the interaction must be investigated. If it is determined that the interaction effects are important, then it may make little sense to investigate the main effects separately. The continuation of Example 10.1, which follows, will illustrate this situation.

Testing for Main Effects.   If there are no significant interactions or if the interactions are unimportant, we may proceed to test for main effects. For the two-factor model, there are two hypotheses to be tested:

$$H_0^{\alpha}: \quad \alpha_i = 0, \text{for all } i = 1, \ldots, a$$

$$H_a^{\alpha}: \quad \alpha_i \neq 0, \text{for at least one } i$$

and

$$H_0^{\beta}: \quad \beta_j = 0, \text{for all } j = 1, \ldots, b$$

$$H_a^{\beta}: \quad \beta_j \neq 0, \text{for at least one } j$$

The test statistic for the first set of hypotheses is $F^{\alpha} = \text{MSA/MSE}$. Under H_0^{α}, F^{α} has an F distribution with $a-1$ and $ab(n-1)$ degrees of freedom. The p-value of the test is the proportion of an $F_{a-1,ab(n-1)}$ population that exceeds the observed value of the test statistic. The test statistic for the second set of hypotheses is $F^{\beta} = \text{MSB/MSE}$. Under H_0^{β}, F^{β} has an F distribution with $b-1$ and $ab(n-1)$ degrees of freedom. The p-value of the test is the proportion of an $F_{b-1,ab(n-1)}$ population that exceeds the observed value of the test statistic.

The ANOVA Table

The three main hypothesis tests and the decomposition of the total sum of squares and degrees of freedom are summarized in the analysis of variance (ANOVA) table. Table 10.9 gives the form of this table for the general two-factor factorial model.

EXAMPLE 10.1   CONTINUED

Table 10.10 is the ANOVA table for the general factorial model for the pulse oximetry data.

TABLE 10.9   ANOVA Table: Model (10.6)

		Analysis of variance			
Source	DF	Sum of squares	Mean square	F Stat	Prob > F
A	$a-1$	SSA	MSA	$F^{\alpha} = \text{MSA/MSE}$	p-value$^{\alpha}$
B	$b-1$	SSB	MSB	$F^{\beta} = \text{MSB/MSE}$	p-value$^{\beta}$
AB	$(a-1)(b-1)$	SSAB	MSAB	$F^{(\alpha\beta)} = \text{MSAB/MSE}$	p-value$^{(\alpha\beta)}$
Error	$ab(n-1)$	SSE	MSE		
C Total	$abn-1$	SSTO			

TABLE 10.10   ANOVA Table: Pulse Oximetry Data

		Analysis of variance			
Source	DF	Sum of squares	Mean square	F Stat	Prob > F
Intensity	2	20.48	10.24	1.64	0.2208
Shivering type	1	1.70	1.70	0.2724	0.6081
Intensity*Shivering type	2	157.25	78.62	12.63	0.0004
Error	18	112.05	6.23		
C Total	23	291.47			

This table shows that the test for interaction has a p-value of 0.0004, indicating highly statistically significant interaction. This result supports the graphical analysis conducted previously. Basically, what is happening is that under severe intensity shivering, the mean response is higher for febrile than for postoperative type shivering, which is the opposite of its behavior under the other two intensities of shivering. Because of this, it makes little sense to speak of THE effect of shivering type, because there appear to be either

- two shivering type effects: one for severe intensity and a different one for mild and moderate intensities, or,
- three effects: a different one for each intensity.

Similarly, it makes little sense to speak of THE effect of shivering intensity.

When confronted with important interactions, the researcher has a number of options. One is to transform the response variable in an attempt to eliminate the interaction. Under this option, the analyst fits an additive and a general model to see if an additive model is appropriate for the transformed data. If so, the analysis of main effects becomes easy.

After unsuccessfully attempting a number of transformations for the pulse oximetry data, the experimenters concluded that the interaction could not be transformed away. They then decided to analyze that interaction more closely. ✦

10.4

CONTRASTS

Before we proceed with the analysis of the pulse oximetry data, we will need to learn how to estimate special linear combinations of population means, called **contrasts.**

> **DEFINITION**
>
> A **contrast** is a linear combination of population means whose coefficients sum to 0. For an $a \times b$ factorial model, a contrast has the form $C = \sum_{i=1}^{a} \sum_{j=1}^{b} c_{ij}\mu_{ij}$, where $\sum_{i=1}^{a} \sum_{j=1}^{b} c_{ij} = 0$.

EXAMPLE 10.4   CONTRASTS

Recall from Equations (10.7) and (10.9) that a 3×2 factorial model is additive if $\mu_{22} - \mu_{21} = \mu_{12} - \mu_{11}$ and $\mu_{32} - \mu_{31} = \mu_{22} - \mu_{21}$. Therefore, to investigate interactions in such a model, we can look at the following linear combinations of population means:

$$\mu_{22} - \mu_{21} - (\mu_{12} - \mu_{11}) = \mu_{22} - \mu_{21} - \mu_{12} + \mu_{11} \tag{10.26}$$

and

$$\mu_{32} - \mu_{31} - (\mu_{22} - \mu_{21}) = \mu_{32} - \mu_{31} - \mu_{22} + \mu_{21} \tag{10.27}$$

Equation (10.26) compares $\mu_{22} - \mu_{21}$, the effect between factor B at level 2 and factor B at level 1 when factor A is held fixed at level 2 and $\mu_{12} - \mu_{11}$, the effect between factor B at level 2 and factor B at level 1 when factor A is held fixed at level 1. Equation (10.27) has a similar interpretation. Both (10.26) and (10.27) are examples of contrasts. The contrast in (10.26), for example, has coefficients $c_{11} = c_{22} = +1, c_{12} = c_{21} = -1$, and $c_{ij} = 0$, otherwise. These coefficients very clearly sum to 0.   ◆

If $C = \sum_i \sum_j c_{ij}\mu_{ij}$ is a contrast for the two-factor factorial model, we will use $\hat{C} = \sum_i \sum_j c_{ij}\hat{\mu}_{ij} = \sum_i \sum_j c_{ij}\bar{Y}_{ij\cdot}$ as the estimator of C. The standard error of $\hat{C}$ is

$$\sigma(\hat{C}) = \sqrt{\frac{1}{n}\sigma^2 \sum_i \sum_j c_{ij}^2}$$

and it is estimated by

$$\hat{\sigma}(\hat{C}) = \sqrt{\frac{1}{n}\text{MSE} \sum_i \sum_j c_{ij}^2}$$

A level L confidence interval for the contrast C is then $\hat{C} \pm \hat{\sigma}(\hat{C})t_{ab(n-1),(1+L)/2}$.

Recall that there are $(a-1)(b-1)$ degrees of freedom associated with the sum of squares for interactions. Each one of those degrees of freedom is associated with a contrast of the form of (10.26) or (10.27). Put another way, it takes $(a-1)(b-1)$ such contrasts to check all the possible ways the interactions can occur. In the pulse oximetry example, there are two degrees of freedom associated with interactions so that the two contrasts, (10.26) and (10.27), tell us everything there is to know about the interactions.

Usually, and especially when $(a-1)(b-1)$ is a large number, calculating $(a-1)(b-1)$ individual confidence intervals gives poor results in controlling the overall confidence level for all intervals. One alternative is to use Bonferroni intervals. For a set of prespecified contrasts, meaning contrasts specified before the data are seen, Bonferroni intervals on just the contrasts of interest can be used. For data snooping, however, such as the investigator in the pulse oximetry example intends, Bonferroni intervals should be calculated for all $(a-1)(b-1)$ contrasts. In this case, the Bonferroni intervals will be of the form

$$\hat{C} \pm \hat{\sigma}(\hat{C})t_{ab(n-1),1-[(1-L)/2(a-1)(b-1)]}$$

If $(a-1)(b-1)$ is large, the Bonferroni intervals will be wide. Another procedure that may do better in this case, is the **Scheffé procedure.** The Scheffé procedure guarantees a single significance level for all possible contrasts, much as the Tukey procedure does for all possible pairwise comparisons. Therefore, it is suitable for data snooping. The price we pay for being allowed to snoop is wide intervals. For the two-factor factorial model, the level L Scheffé confidence interval for C is $\hat{C} \pm \hat{\sigma}(\hat{C})S$, where S is the Scheffé multiplier $S = \sqrt{(ab-1)F_{ab-1,ab(n-1),L}}$, and $F_{ab-1,ab(n-1),L}$ is the Lth quantile of the $F_{ab-1,ab(n-1)}$ distribution. The Bonferroni or Scheffé multipliers may be compared and the smaller one used in the analysis.

EXAMPLE 10.1   CONTINUED

For the pulse oximetry data, there are two degrees of freedom for interaction, and therefore, contrasts (10.26), which we will label C_1, and (10.27), which we will label C_2, will tell us what we need to know about the interaction. For level 0.95 intervals, the Bonferroni multiplier is $t_{18,1-[(1-0.95)/(2)(2)]} = t_{18,0.9875} = 2.445$. The Scheffé multiplier is $\sqrt{5F_{5,18,0.95}} = \sqrt{(5)(2.773)} = 3.724$. The Bonferroni multiplier is smaller, so we will use that procedure.

Since

$$\hat{\sigma}(\hat{C}_1) = \sqrt{\frac{1}{4}\text{MSE}(1^2 + (-1)^2 + (-1)^2 + 1^2)} = \sqrt{\text{MSE}} = 2.49$$

and

$$\hat{C}_1 = \hat{\mu}_{22} - \hat{\mu}_{21} - \hat{\mu}_{12} + \hat{\mu}_{11} = 9.38 - 7.62 - 9.15 + 4.88 = -2.51$$

the interval for C_1 is

$$-2.51 \pm (2.49)(2.445) = (-8.60, 3.58)$$

Similar calculations give an interval for C_2 as

$$1.57 \pm (2.49)(2.445) = (-15.47, -3.29)$$

From these results we conclude the following:

- The confidence interval for C_1 contains 0; therefore, C_1 is not significantly different from 0. Hence, the difference in mean power between postoperative and febrile-type shivering at moderate intensity is not significantly different than the difference in mean power between postoperative and febrile-type shivering at mild intensity.
- The confidence interval for C_2 does not contain 0; therefore, C_2 is significantly different from 0. Specifically, the difference in mean power between postoperative and febrile-type shivering at severe intensity is significantly lower than the difference in mean power between postoperative and febrile-type shivering at moderate intensity. Further, we estimate that the latter difference exceeds the former by somewhere between 3.29 and 15.47 units.

Compare these conclusions with what you saw in the interaction plots in Figure 10.9.

Having obtained an understanding of the interactions, the experimenters realized that they could not expect to obtain meaningful estimates of and comparisons among main effects. They did realize from the analysis of interaction contrasts that the effect between postoperative and febrile shivering was the same for mild and moderate shivering intensities and that this differed from the effect between postoperative and febrile shivering for severe intensity. The former effect is given by the contrast

$$C_3 = \frac{\mu_{12} + \mu_{22}}{2} - \frac{\mu_{11} + \mu_{21}}{2} \tag{10.28}$$

and the latter effect by the contrast

$$C_4 = \mu_{32} - \mu_{31} \tag{10.29}$$

C_3 is the effect between postoperative and febrile shivering for mild and moderate shivering intensities combined, and C_4 is the effect between postoperative and febrile shivering for severe intensity. Obtaining a confidence interval for each contrast and interpreting the results is left as an exercise.

Note: The choice of contrasts C_3 and C_4 for further analysis comes after looking at the data. As such, it constitutes data snooping. As a result, for formal inference, the appropriate multiplier for the confidence intervals is the Scheffé multiplier, as the Scheffé method gives simultaneous confidence intervals for all possible contrasts. The Bonferroni procedure was used for inference about interactions, contrasts C_1 and C_2, since these two contrasts represented all possible contrasts that could be looked at in investigating the interaction.

In any event, whenever possible, it is best to follow up any results obtained by data snooping with another designed study in which prespecified contrasts are used to confirm the results observed by data snooping in the first study.   ✦

10.5

WHAT ABOUT THOSE QUESTIONABLE MODEL ASSUMPTIONS?

It is time to look at some of the options available when model assumptions seem to be violated. First, it might help to review the consequences of model assumption violations for the one-way model as described in Section 9.2.

As always, when it is known that outliers are spurious observations, the outliers may be omitted from the analysis. When unexplained outliers are present, one option available to the researchers is to discard the outliers and reanalyze the data. If the results are essentially the same as those obtained with the outlier, then they can be confident in their analysis. If the results change substantially, then the researchers must find some answers, perhaps by conducting further studies.

One problem with removing outliers is that the result can be an **unbalanced design:** that is, a design in which the number of observations is not the same for all treatments. Unbalanced designs, which will be discussed further in Section 10.12, present difficulties of analysis and interpretation. For this reason, researchers should always strive to obtain a **balanced design:** one with equal numbers of observations for all treatments.

Another problem with removing outliers is that doing so does not always correct problems with the fit. In the pulse oximetry data, for example, removing the outlier does not eliminate heteroscedasticity.

If the researchers are willing and able to take more data, a preferable approach to removing outliers for cause is to replace them. This is a preferable strategy, since the design will remain balanced, making for a simpler and more robust analysis. Of course, any new data must be taken under the same conditions as the data they replace.

As with the one-way model, the F tests for the factorial model are robust to nonnormality and heteroscedasticity, especially if the design is balanced. However, even for a balanced design, heteroscedasticity can adversely affect individual and multiple comparisons.

Another option for researchers confronted with nonnormality, outliers, or heteroscedasticity is to transform the response. We will illustrate this option with the pulse oximetry data.

EXAMPLE 10.1   CONTINUED

One transformation that often helps equalize group variances is the natural logarithm. The logs of the power are displayed in Table 10.11.

TABLE 10.11   Logged Pulse Oximetry Data

Intensity	Shivering type	Logged power				Mean	Standard deviation
Mild	Febrile	1.33	1.66	1.99	1.16	1.53	0.37
Moderate	Febrile	1.65	2.33	2.00	2.03	2.00	0.28
Severe	Febrile	2.30	1.88	2.43	2.52	2.28	0.29
Mild	Postoperative	2.52	2.15	2.13	1.98	2.19	0.23
Moderate	Postoperative	1.94	2.02	2.75	1.99	2.18	0.38
Severe	Postoperative	0.96	1.13	0.77	0.68	0.89	0.20

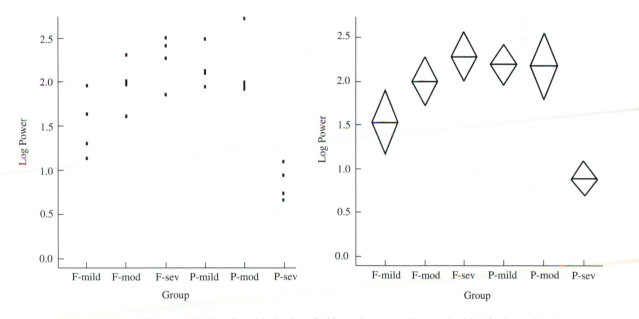

Figure 10.10   Stratified plot (left) and mean diamonds (right): logged pulse oximetry data. The group abbreviations are the same as in Figure 10.1.

Notice that for the transformed data, the sample standard deviations are much more uniform. The plots in Figure 10.10 show the transformed data graphically.

Except for the variances being more nearly equal, the main features observed previously in Figure 10.1 hold for these plots as well.

A complete analysis of these data indicates a good model fit: The transformation has eliminated the outlier. The results are essentially the same as those obtained before for the raw data, which gives the experimenters more confidence in the original analysis. Exercise 10.14 asks you to analyze the transformed pulse oximetry data.   ✦

10.6

TRANSFORMATIONS TO REMOVE INTERACTIONS

As we have seen, significant and important interactions make the analysis and interpretation of main effects difficult. For this reason, analysts often attempt to eliminate or reduce interactions. One common approach is to transform the response variable. To see why a transformation might have this effect, consider the following two possible relations between population means μ_{ij} and the overall mean μ and positive factor effects α_i and β_j:

$$\mu_{ij} = \mu \alpha_i \beta_j \qquad (10.30)$$

and

$$\mu_{ij} = \alpha_i + \beta_j + 2\sqrt{\alpha_i}\sqrt{\beta_j}. \qquad (10.31)$$

By taking a natural log transform of the multiplicative relation (10.30), we obtain

$$\ln(\mu_{ij}) = \ln(\mu) + \ln(\alpha_i) + \ln(\beta_j)$$

which is of the form

$$\mu'_{ij} = \mu' + \alpha'_i + \beta'_j$$

Hence, the transformed mean shows an additive relation. It is left as an exercise to show that relation (10.31) can be made additive by taking the square root of both sides.

The following example illustrates how a transformation can remove interactions.

EXAMPLE 10.5   PEANUT SKINNING

Peanuts are normally skinned prior to retail sale or processing for other food products. When the nuts are sold as whole nuts, it is desirable that the peanuts be completely skinned without undue damage and that the nuts be whole, not split. It has been found that thermal treatment of the peanut will loosen the skin to varying degrees, thereby minimizing the potential for split nuts. The traditional thermal treatment, called "white roasting," is the straightforward soaking of the nuts in an oven. Following white roasting, the skins are removed by a method such as abrasion or tumbling.

TABLE 10.12   Peanut Data

Solution	Oven type		
	Convection	Microwave	Standard
Potassium chloride	64.3	35.6	75.0
	70.0	44.6	76.6
	67.6	40.7	69.0
Cell mean	67.3	40.3	73.5
Sodium chloride	81.4	73.5	86.2
	77.9	64.3	82.1
	83.3	67.4	92.0
Cell mean	80.9	68.4	86.8
Water	71.9	49.6	72.7
	77.7	45.4	76.9
	73.9	53.9	81.5
Cell mean	74.5	49.6	77.0

A peanut processor was looking to replace a number of their standard ovens. The alternatives were to replace them with the same type of oven or with one of two different types: convection ovens or microwave ovens. Researchers for the processor also wanted to look at the effect of type of soaking solution used in the white-roast phase of processing, so it was decided to conduct an experiment to evaluate both oven type and soaking solution. They decided to test three types of soaking solution: water, a sodium chloride solution, and a potassium chloride solution. One oven of each type was assigned for the experiment. Peanuts from the same processing batch were divided into 27 equal samples by weight. The samples were randomly assigned to one of three oven types and solution types and subjected to the standard white-roast procedure. All were then processed by the same mechanical skinner, and the yield (percent of whole, skinned peanuts) was recorded. The data are shown in Table 10.12 and a stratified plot appears in Figure 10.11. From the stratified plot, we see a similar pattern for each oven type: the sodium chloride solution produces the highest mean yield, water the next highest, and the potassium chloride solution the lowest. Also, the spreads of the data do not differ greatly over the nine treatments. A check reveals that the maximum and minimum within-cell standard deviations are 4.97 and 2.73, so we feel justified in assuming homoscedasticity.

Table 10.13 is the ANOVA table for these data. From the table, we can see that with a p-value of 0.0210, the interaction is significant at the 0.05 level, but not significant at the 0.01 level.

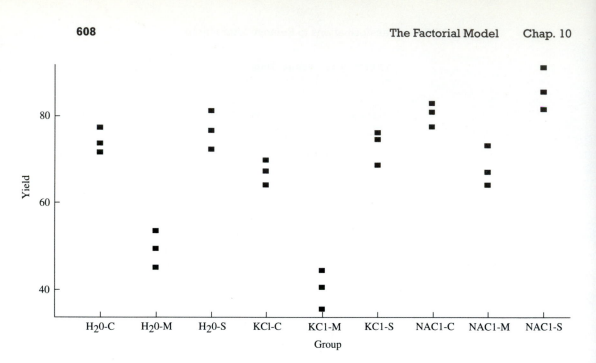

Figure 10.11   Stratified plot: peanut data.

TABLE 10.13   ANOVA Table: Peanut Data

		Analysis of variance			
Source	DF	Sum of squares	Mean square	F Stat	Prob > F
Solution	2	1543.68	771.84	47.94	0.0001
Oventype	2	3531.63	1765.81	109.69	0.0001
Solution*Oventype	4	243.77	60.94	3.79	0.0210
Error	18	289.77	16.10		
C Total	26	5608.85			

Before proceeding, we must investigate the nature of the interaction. Figure 10.12 shows the interaction plots. The interactions that we see here do not appear to be severe, and are probably caused by the microwave-oven type. We check this by computing confidence intervals for the following set of interaction contrasts:

$$C_1: \quad \mu_{21} - \mu_{11} - (\mu_{22} - \mu_{12}) = \mu_{21} - \mu_{11} - \mu_{22} + \mu_{12}$$

$$C_2: \quad \mu_{22} - \mu_{12} - (\mu_{23} - \mu_{13}) = \mu_{22} - \mu_{12} - \mu_{23} + \mu_{13}$$

$$C_3: \quad \mu_{31} - \mu_{21} - (\mu_{32} - \mu_{22}) = \mu_{31} - \mu_{21} - \mu_{32} + \mu_{22}$$

$$C_4: \quad \mu_{32} - \mu_{22} - (\mu_{33} - \mu_{23}) = \mu_{32} - \mu_{22} - \mu_{33} + \mu_{23}$$

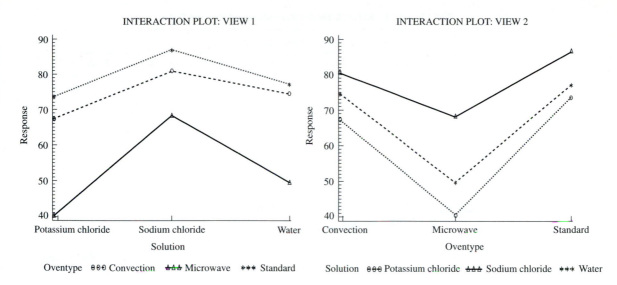

Figure 10.12   Interaction plots: peanut data.

The estimators of the contrasts are

$$\hat{C}_1 = 80.9 - 67.3 - 68.4 + 40.3 = -14.5$$
$$\hat{C}_2 = 68.4 - 40.3 - 86.8 + 73.5 = 14.8$$
$$\hat{C}_3 = 74.5 - 80.9 - 49.6 + 68.4 = 12.4$$
$$\hat{C}_4 = 49.6 - 68.4 - 77.0 + 86.8 = -9.0$$

In addition,

$$\hat{\sigma}(\hat{C}_1) = \sqrt{\frac{1}{3}\text{MSE}(1^2 + (-1)^2 + (-1)^2 + 1^2)} = \sqrt{\frac{4}{3}(16.10)} = 4.63$$

and this is also the estimated standard error for the other three contrasts.

Since the four contrasts, at one degree of freedom apiece, use all the degrees of freedom for interactions, we may employ either the Bonferroni or the Scheffé procedure. Setting an overall 0.95 level for all four intervals, the Bonferroni multiplier is $t_{18,1-[(1-0.95)/(2)(4)]} = t_{18,.99375} = 2.775$, and the Scheffé multiplier is $\sqrt{(8)F_{8,18,.95}} = \sqrt{(8)(2.510)} = 4.481$, so we choose the Bonferroni. The intervals are then

$$C_1: \quad -14.5 \pm (4.63)(2.775) = (-27.35, -1.65)$$
$$C_2: \quad 14.8 \pm (4.63)(2.775) = (1.95, 27.65)$$
$$C_3: \quad 12.4 \pm (4.63)(2.775) = (-0.45, 25.25)$$
$$C_4: \quad -9.0 \pm (4.63)(2.775) = (-21.85, 3.85)$$

TABLE 10.14   ANOVA Table: Transformed Peanut Data

Analysis of variance					
Source	DF	Sum of squares	Mean square	F Stat	Prob > F
Solution	2	0.5874	0.2937	44.79	0.0001
Oventype	2	1.2634	0.6317	96.34	0.0001
Solution∗Oventype	4	0.0494	0.0124	1.88	0.1571
Error	18	0.1180	0.0066		
C Total	26	2.0183			

Both C_1 and C_2 are significantly different from 0, and we conclude that the inter-action is a consequence of the following:

- The increase in mean yield between the potassium chloride solution and the sodium chloride solution for the microwave oven being significantly greater than the increase in mean yield between the potassium chloride solution and the sodium chloride solution for the convective oven. We estimate that the yield is between 1.65 and 27.35% greater.
- The increase in mean yield between the potassium chloride solution and the sodium chloride solution for the microwave oven being significantly greater than the increase in mean yield between the potassium chloride solution and the sodium chloride solution for the standard oven. We estimate that the yield is between 1.95 and 27.65% greater.

However, as we have said before, statistical significance does not imply prac-tical importance, and because the interaction does not appear to be severe, the experimenters might well determine that the observed interaction is unimportant and proceed to analyze the main effects anyway. For this problem, the experi-menters opted instead to try transforming the response to reduce the interaction. After trying a number of transformations, they found acceptable results by an-alyzing exp(YIELD/100) instead of YIELD. (As a practical matter, YIELD is divided by 100 to keep the resulting transformed values in a reasonable range.) A check of variances shows no reason to suspect heteroscedasticity. A check of the residuals from the fit reveals no serious violations of model assumptions. The ANOVA table for the fit is shown in Table 10.14.

The transformation has made the interaction nonsignificant. It is interesting to note that the interaction plots, shown in Figure 10.13, do not look all that differ-ent from the interaction plots for the untransformed data shown in Figure 10.12.

At this point, the experimenters had to make a decision. The transformation they used had no physical basis, with the result that the interpretation of the transformed response became difficult. On the other hand, the transformation made the interactions statistically nonsignificant, which provided a statistical basis for choosing the simpler additive model. Ultimately, they chose to analyze the

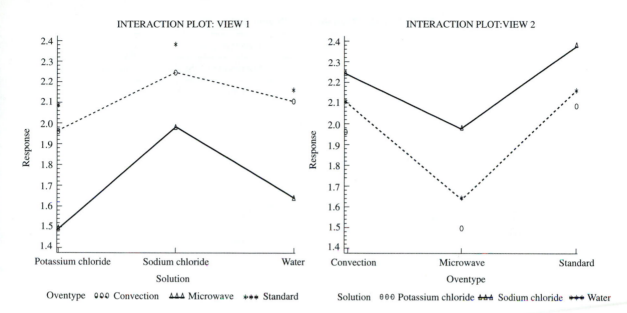

Figure 10.13   Interaction plots: transformed peanut data.

transformed data. Since the interaction is nonsignificant and unimportant, and both main effects are highly significant, their task was now is to analyze the main effects. ✦

10.7

ANALYSIS OF THE MAIN EFFECTS

When there are only insignificant and/or unimportant interactions, and when the main effects are significant, it is usually of interest to estimate and compare factor-level means.

Estimation of a Single-Factor Mean

Estimation of single-factor means is based on the point estimators $\hat{\mu}_{i\cdot} = \bar{Y}_{i\cdot\cdot}$ and $\hat{\mu}_{\cdot j} = \bar{Y}_{\cdot j\cdot}$, on the fact that the estimated standard errors of these estimators are

$$\hat{\sigma}(\bar{Y}_{i\cdot\cdot}) = \sqrt{\frac{\text{MSE}}{bn}} \quad \text{and} \quad \hat{\sigma}(\bar{Y}_{\cdot j\cdot}) = \sqrt{\frac{\text{MSE}}{an}}$$

respectively, and on the fact that

$$\frac{\bar{Y}_{i\cdot\cdot} - \mu_{i\cdot}}{\hat{\sigma}(\bar{Y}_{i\cdot\cdot})} \quad \text{and} \quad \frac{\bar{Y}_{\cdot j\cdot} - \mu_{\cdot j}}{\hat{\sigma}(\bar{Y}_{\cdot j\cdot})}$$

TABLE 10.15 Transformed Peanut Data

| Solution | Oven type | | | Solution means |
	Convection	Microwave	Standard	
Potassium chloride	1.90 2.01 1.97	1.43 1.56 1.50	2.12 2.15 1.99	1.85
Cell mean	1.96	1.50	2.09	
Sodium chloride	2.26 2.18 2.09	2.09 1.90 1.96	2.37 2.27 2.51	2.20
Cell mean	2.18	1.98	2.38	
Water	2.05 2.17 2.09	1.64 1.57 1.71	2.07 2.16 2.26	1.97
Cell mean	2.10	1.64	2.16	
Oven-type means	2.10	1.71	2.21	2.01

have t distributions with $ab(n-1)$ degrees of freedom. Level L confidence intervals for $\mu_{i\cdot}$ and $\mu_{\cdot j}$ are thus

$$\bar{Y}_{i\cdot\cdot} \pm \hat{\sigma}(\bar{Y}_{i\cdot\cdot})t_{ab(n-1)(1+L)/2} \quad \text{and} \quad \bar{Y}_{\cdot j\cdot} \pm \hat{\sigma}(\bar{Y}_{\cdot j\cdot})t_{ab(n-1)(1+L)/2}$$

EXAMPLE 10.5 CONTINUED

Table 10.15 displays the transformed peanut data along with the cell, factor level, and overall means, and Figure 10.14 shows stratified plots of the transformed response broken down by solution and oven type.

The standard error for the solution means is

$$\hat{\sigma}(\bar{Y}_{i\cdot\cdot}) = \sqrt{\frac{0.0066}{(3)(3)}} = 0.027$$

Since there are also three levels for oven type, the standard error for the oven type means is the same.

Because $t_{18,0.975} = 2.101$, individual level 0.95 confidence intervals for the solution means are

$$\mu_1:\quad 1.85 \pm (0.027)(2.101) = (1.79, 1.91)$$

$$\mu_2:\quad 2.20 \pm (0.027)(2.101) = (2.14, 2.26)$$

$$\mu_3:\quad 1.97 \pm (0.027)(2.101) = (1.91, 2.03)$$

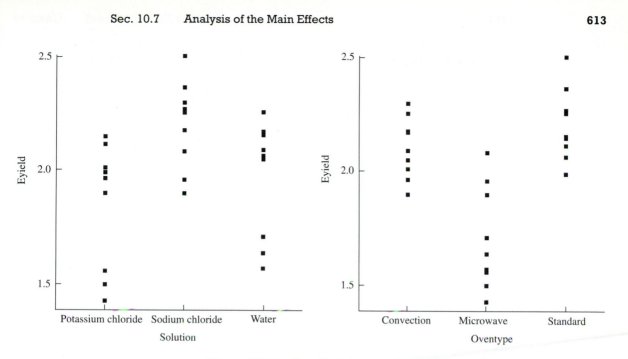

Figure 10.14   Stratified plots: transformed peanut data.

and individual level 0.95 confidence intervals for the oven type means are

$$\mu_{\cdot 1}: \quad 2.10 \pm (0.027)(2.101) = (2.04, 2.16)$$

$$\mu_{\cdot 2}: \quad 1.71 \pm (0.027)(2.101) = (1.65, 1.77)$$

$$\mu_{\cdot 3}: \quad 2.21 \pm (0.027)(2.101) = (2.15, 2.27) \quad \blacklozenge$$

Multiple Pairwise Comparisons of Factor-Level Means

The Bonferroni and Tukey procedures may be used to maintain an overall confidence level L when comparing all pairs of factor level means. If a subset of all pairwise comparisons is prespecified, the Bonferroni procedure may be used on just those comparisons. For data snooping, however, the Bonferroni intervals should be computed for all pairwise comparisons. As always, the Tukey procedure maintains an overall confidence level L for all pairwise comparisons. If the design is balanced, the Tukey procedure will produce shorter intervals than the Bonferroni for all pairwise comparisons. If there are a levels of factor A and b levels of factor B, then there are $a(a-1)/2$ pairwise comparisons of factor A levels and $b(b-1)/2$ pairwise comparisons of factor B levels. The estimator of $\mu_{i_1 \cdot} - \mu_{i_2 \cdot}$ is $\bar{Y}_{i_1 \cdots} - \bar{Y}_{i_2 \cdots}$. Its estimated standard error is

$$\hat{\sigma}(\bar{Y}_{i_1 \cdots} - \bar{Y}_{i_2 \cdots}) = \sqrt{\frac{2(\text{MSE})}{bn}}$$

Similarly, the estimator of $\mu_{\cdot j_1} - \mu_{\cdot j_2}$ is $\bar{Y}_{\cdot j_1 \cdot} - \bar{Y}_{\cdot j_2 \cdot}$, and its estimated standard error is

$$\hat{\sigma}(\bar{Y}_{\cdot j_1 \cdot} - \bar{Y}_{\cdot j_2 \cdot}) = \sqrt{\frac{2(\text{MSE})}{an}}$$

The Bonferroni level L intervals for all pairwise comparisons of factor A are of the form

$$\bar{Y}_{i_1 \cdot \cdot} - \bar{Y}_{i_2 \cdot \cdot} \pm \hat{\sigma}(\bar{Y}_{i_1 \cdot \cdot} - \bar{Y}_{i_2 \cdot \cdot}) t_{ab(n-1), 1-[(1-L)/a(a-1)]}$$

and for all pairwise comparisons of factor B are of the form

$$\bar{Y}_{\cdot j_1 \cdot} - \bar{Y}_{\cdot j_2 \cdot} \pm \hat{\sigma}(\bar{Y}_{\cdot j_1 \cdot} - \bar{Y}_{\cdot j_2 \cdot}) t_{ab(n-1), 1-[(1-L)/b(b-1)]}$$

The Tukey level L intervals for all pairwise comparisons of factor A are of the form

$$\bar{Y}_{i_1 \cdot \cdot} - \bar{Y}_{i_2 \cdot \cdot} \pm \hat{\sigma}(\bar{Y}_{i_1 \cdot \cdot} - \bar{Y}_{i_2 \cdot \cdot}) \frac{q_{L,a,ab(n-1)}}{\sqrt{2}}$$

and for all pairwise comparisons of factor B are of the form

$$\bar{Y}_{\cdot j_1 \cdot} - \bar{Y}_{\cdot j_2 \cdot} \pm \hat{\sigma}(\bar{Y}_{\cdot j_1 \cdot} - \bar{Y}_{\cdot j_2 \cdot}) \frac{q_{L,b,ab(n-1)}}{\sqrt{2}}$$

EXAMPLE 10.5   CONTINUED

We compute intervals for all pairwise comparisons of factor-level means at an overall 0.95 level. The design is balanced, so we know that the Tukey will be smaller than the Bonferroni multiplier. The Bonferroni multiplier is $t_{18, 1-[(1-0.95)/3(3-1)]} = t_{18, 0.9917} = 2.641$. The Tukey multiplier is $q_{0.95,3,18}/\sqrt{2} = 3.61/\sqrt{2} = 2.553$. Since both factors have the same number of levels, these multipliers and the estimated standard errors are the same for both: The estimated standard errors are

$$\sqrt{\frac{(2)(0.0066)}{(3)(3)}} = 0.038$$

The Tukey level 0.95 intervals for factor solution are

$$\mu_{2\cdot} - \mu_{1\cdot}: \quad 2.20 - 1.85 \pm (0.038)(2.553) = (0.25, 0.39)$$

$$\mu_{3\cdot} - \mu_{1\cdot}: \quad 1.97 - 1.85 \pm (0.038)(2.553) = (0.02, 0.22)$$

$$\mu_{3\cdot} - \mu_{2\cdot}: \quad 1.97 - 2.20 \pm (0.038)(2.553) = (-0.33, -0.13)$$

From these, we conclude that the sodium chloride solution results in significantly greater mean transformed yield than either of the other solutions, and we estimate the difference in mean transformed yield of the sodium chloride solution above the potassium chloride solution as between 0.25 and 0.39 and above water as between

0.13 and 0.33. We also conclude that using water results in significantly greater mean transformed yield than potassium chloride with an estimated difference between 0.02 and 0.22.

The Tukey level 0.95 intervals for factor oventype are

$$\mu_{.2} - \mu_{.1}: \quad 1.71 - 2.10 \pm (0.038)(2.553) = (-0.49, -0.29)$$

$$\mu_{.3} - \mu_{.1}: \quad 2.21 - 2.10 \pm (0.038)(2.553) = (0.01, 0.21)$$

$$\mu_{.3} - \mu_{.2}: \quad 2.21 - 1.71 \pm (0.038)(2.553) = (0.40, 0.60)$$

The resulting interpretations are left as an exercise.   ◆

10.8

STEPS IN ANALYZING FACTORIAL MODELS

What follows is a sequence of steps for analyzing factorial models.

1. Before seeing the data, decide on all comparisons and contrasts in population or factor-level means you are interested in testing. These may later be tested without fear of data snooping.
2. Fit the model to the data.
3. Assess the model fit. If necessary, take remedial measures and refit. Continue until an acceptable model is obtained.
4. Test for interactions. If the interactions are significant, check to see if they are important.
5. If the interactions are significant and important, and if you are willing to use a transformed response in the analysis, try a number of transformations of the response to render them nonsignificant and/or unimportant.
6. If you are unwilling or unable to transform away the interactions, analyze them using appropriate contrasts. Analyze any other prespecified contrasts or comparisons. Analyze any nonprespecified pairwise comparisons of interest using Tukey or Bonferroni (for all pairs); analyze any other nonprespecified contrasts of interest using Bonferroni or Scheffé.
7. If you are able and willing to transform away the interactions, refit to the transformed data and reassess the fit. Analyze factor-level effects using Tukey or Bonferroni.

10.9

WHY FACTORIAL DESIGNS?

When information is desired about the relation of a response to more than one factor, factorial designs have some definite advantages over other designs. For example, consider one commonly used (unfortunately!) design called a **one factor at a time,** or

OFAT, design. In an OFAT design, in order to obtain information about the effect of a factor, that one factor is varied while all other factors are held fixed. This is basically a one-way design in the factor being varied. To get information about other factors, the same thing must be done for them. A factorial design has several advantages over an OFAT design:

- **Efficiency.** A factorial design is more efficient than an OFAT. By this we mean that to obtain the same amount of information about factor effects, an OFAT must use more observations than a factorial design. To see why, consider the peanut data, which contain a total of 27 observations. For the factor solution, there are nine observations to estimate each factor-level mean, and for the factor oventype, there are also nine observations to estimate each factor-level mean. If we were to run an OFAT experiment, to have nine observations available to estimate each factor-level mean of the factor solution would require 27 observations, and to have nine observations available to estimate each factor-level mean of the factor oventype would require another 27 observations, for a total of 54 observations! The secret of the efficiency of the factorial design is that each observation is used in more than one estimate. In the peanut data, for example, the observations for level 1 of solution and level 3 of oventype are used to estimate both the mean of level 1 of solution **and** the mean of level 3 of oventype.
- **Interactions.** OFAT designs cannot model interactions between the factors. As we have seen in this chapter, factorial designs can, and do, model interactions.
- **Range of Conclusions.** By varying the factors together, rather than one at a time, information is obtained on a wider range of treatments. Thus, for example, by using a factorial design for the peanut data, we obtained information on nine different treatments. Had we done an OFAT, first holding solution fixed at sodium chloride while the oven types were varied, and then holding oventype fixed at convection while varying the solutions, we would have obtained information on only five of the nine treatments.

ONE OBSERVATION PER CELL

When a factorial design has one observation per cell, we are unable to fit the full model and also compute the pooled variance, S_p^2, to estimate the error variance, σ^2. This is because calculation of S_p^2 requires calculation of the within-cell variance S_{ij}^2 for at least one cell (see Equation (10.3)), and S_{ij}^2 cannot be computed unless there are at least two observations in cell ij. This presents a problem for the two-way design if we are fitting the full model with effects A, B, and AB, because in this case, the MSE equals S_p^2, which cannot be calculated. Without the MSE, we cannot perform F tests for effects.

If we fit the additive model, however, we will obtain a MSE. This MSE is the mean square for AB from the full model. Hence, we can perform F tests for effects A and B in the additive model, though these tests will be valid only if the additive model is appropriate. So before attempting to fit and perform tests for the additive model, we must check that the additive model is appropriate. Two methods for doing so were presented for the RCB model in Chapter 9: Tukey's test for additivity and interaction plots. Both methods work equally well for the two-factor factorial models in the present chapter.

If we conclude that the additive model is not appropriate, we cannot obtain an estimate of σ^2 or F tests for model effects. In this case, two approaches to determining the importance of model effects are presented in Chapter 12 in the context of factorial designs with all factors having only two levels. One approach is graphical and involves constructing a normal quantile plot of the estimates of the effects. The theory is that if the population effects are all zero, the estimators will have a common normal distribution with mean 0, so that important effects will appear as outliers on the plot. This approach will work as described in Chapter 12 for general factorial designs with two levels for each factor. For other factorial designs, the approach will work if the estimators are modified to account for the number of levels of the factors. We will not pursue the matter here, but will instead refer you to Chapter 12.

To avoid the difficulties that arise when there is one observation per cell, we suggest that you plan your factorial designs so that at least some cells have more than one observation. In this way, the full model can be fit, and a pooled estimate of the error variance can be computed from those cells with more than one observation.

10.11

REGRESSION AND THE FACTORIAL MODEL[2]

Sometimes a Regression Model Is More Appropriate

In factorial models, the factor levels are regarded as categories. It often happens that these categories have a numerical meaning. For example, the levels of a temperature factor might be 100, 200, and 400 degrees. If so, using a factorial model may waste valuable information about the relation between the actual values of the factor and the response. In such a situation, it may be desirable to use multiple regression to model the response as a function of the actual values of the factors. The multiple regression techniques discussed in Chapter 8 should be used in this modeling process. The response surface techniques discussed in Chapter 14 give another perspective on the interplay between factorial designs and multiple regression.

---

[2]This section assumes knowledge of multiple regression, such as found in Chapter 8.

The Regression Formulation of the Factorial Model

Even when the factor levels are categories, it may be beneficial, or even necessary, to formulate the factorial model as a multiple regression model. When a factorial design is unbalanced, the analysis of variance becomes difficult. The ANOVA capabilities of many statistical packages are limited to balanced factorial designs, but almost all statistical packages can perform multiple linear regression, which is all that is needed to perform an analysis of variance for any factorial design. In this section, we describe how to use multiple regression to obtain the ANOVA for a balanced two-way factorial design. We will later extend this approach to unbalanced designs.

Recall from Chapter 9 that in order to perform a regression analysis on data from a one-way or RCB model, we need to define suitable **indicator variables,** which serve as regressors in the regression formulation of the model. The situation is very much the same for the factorial model.

In what follows, assume there are two factors: factor A at a levels and factor B at b levels. Since factor A has a levels, it has $a - 1$ degrees of freedom. Similarly, factor B has $b - 1$ degrees of freedom. Modeling a factor in a factorial design using regression requires one indicator variable for each degree of freedom. So to model factor A, begin by picking any $a - 1$ of the a levels. For convenience, we will pick levels 1 to $a - 1$. Call the indicator variables for factor A, $A_1, A_2, \ldots, A_{a-1}$. For $i = 1, \ldots, a - 1$, define A_i to have value 1 for each observation for which factor A is at level i, value -1 for each observation for which factor A is at level a, and to have value 0 otherwise. Similarly, for factor B, construct $b - 1$ indicator variables, $B_1, B_2, \ldots, B_{b-1}$, so that B_j equals 1 if factor B is at level j, equals -1 if factor B is at level b, and equals 0 otherwise. There is no need to define indicator variables for the interaction AB, since we can obtain these by multiplying all pairs of indicator variables A_i and B_j. So there will be $(a - 1)(b - 1)$ indicator variables $(AB)_{ij} = A_i B_j$, which model the interaction. Notice that the AB interaction has $(a - 1)(b - 1)$ degrees of freedom. The next example should help clarify these ideas.

EXAMPLE 10.1   CONTINUED

Table 10.16 shows the factor levels, the response and the indicator variables for the pulse oximetry data. For brevity, we denote the indicator variable for shivering type as S_1, the indicator variables for shivering intensity as I_1 and I_2, and the indicator variables for the interaction as $(SI)_{11} = S_1 I_1$ and $(SI)_{12} = S_1 I_2$. S_1 takes the value 1 for febrile shivering type and -1 for postoperative shivering type. I_1 takes the value 1 for mild intensity, 0 for moderate intensity, and -1 for severe intensity, so it basically compares mild with severe intensity. $(SI)_{11}$ takes the value 1 for febrile shivering type and mild intensity or post-op shivering type and severe intensity, -1 for febrile shivering type, and severe intensity or post-op shivering type and mild intensity, and 0 otherwise. $(SI)_{11}$ compares the groups having febrile shivering type and mild intensity or post-op shivering type and severe intensity with those having febrile shivering type and severe intensity or post-op shivering type and mild intensity. What do I_2 and $(SI)_{12}$ compare?   ◆

TABLE   10.16   Indicator Variables for Pulse Oximetry Data

Shivering type	Intensity	Power	S_1	I_1	I_2	$(SI)_{11}$	$(SI)_{12}$
Febrile	Mild	3.78	1	1	0	1	0
Febrile	Mild	5.27	1	1	0	1	0
Febrile	Mild	7.28	1	1	0	1	0
Febrile	Mild	3.19	1	1	0	1	0
Febrile	Moderate	5.19	1	0	1	0	1
Febrile	Moderate	10.29	1	0	1	0	1
Febrile	Moderate	7.37	1	0	1	0	1
Febrile	Moderate	7.64	1	0	1	0	1
Febrile	Severe	9.95	1	−1	−1	−1	−1
Febrile	Severe	6.54	1	−1	−1	−1	−1
Febrile	Severe	11.40	1	−1	−1	−1	−1
Febrile	Severe	12.49	1	−1	−1	−1	−1
Postop	Mild	12.41	−1	1	0	−1	0
Postop	Mild	8.58	−1	1	0	−1	0
Postop	Mild	8.39	−1	1	0	−1	0
Postop	Mild	7.22	−1	1	0	−1	0
Postop	Moderate	6.99	−1	0	1	0	−1
Postop	Moderate	7.54	−1	0	1	0	−1
Postop	Moderate	7.33	−1	0	1	0	−1
Postop	Moderate	15.67	−1	0	1	0	−1
Postop	Severe	2.64	−1	−1	−1	1	1
Postop	Severe	3.10	−1	−1	−1	1	1
Postop	Severe	2.16	−1	−1	−1	1	1
Postop	Severe	1.98	−1	−1	−1	1	1

Having defined the indicator variables, we can obtain the different sums of squares discussed in this chapter by fitting different regression models, as we now illustrate.

The Full Regression Model

The full regression model regresses the response on all the indicator variables in the model. If we are considering the full factorial model with effects A, B, and AB, the regression is on all $ab - 1$ indicator variables, $A_1, \ldots, A_{a-1}, B_1, \ldots, B_{b-1}, AB_{11}, \ldots,$ $AB_{(a-1)(b-1)}$. To indicate that it is the sum of squares from the model with A, B, and AB, we denote the resulting regression sum of squares as SSM(A, B, AB). SSM(A, B, AB) is also the sum of squares model for the full factorial model. The degrees of freedom associated with SSM(A, B, AB) is the same as the degrees of freedom associated with the sum of squares regression from which it was computed: $ab-1$. This is also the sum of squares model for the full factorial model. As usual, we will denote the sum of squares error as SSE.

Submodels

We can obtain sums of squares for any submodel of the factorial model simply by regressing the response only on those indicator variables associated with the factors in the submodel. Thus, we can obtain the sums of squares for the additive model with only main effects A and B by regressing the response on the $a + b - 2$ indicator variables $A_1, \ldots, A_{a-1}, B_1, \ldots, B_{b-1}$. The resulting sum of squares regression, SSM(A, B), is equal to, and has the same $a + b - 2$ degrees of freedom as, the sum of squares model for the additive model. Or we can obtain the sums of squares for a model with only effects A and AB by regressing the response on the $b(a - 1)$ indicator variables $A_1, \ldots, A_{a-1}, AB_{11}, \ldots, AB_{(a-1)(b-1)}$. The resulting sum of squares regression, SSM(A, AB), is equal to, and has the same $b(a - 1)$ degrees of freedom as, the sum of squares model for the model with factors A and AB.

Extra Sums of Squares

We can also measure the extra contribution of one set of effects (call them set 2) to explaining the variation in the response beyond what another set of effects (call them set 1) does. For example, how much extra variation is accounted for by the interaction AB (set 2) beyond that accounted for by the additive model with factors A and B (set 1)? To answer this, we need to fit two regression models: the **full model,** consisting of those indicator variables associated with all the effects in sets 1 and 2, and the **reduced model,** consisting only of those effects in set 1. Our measure of the extra contribution of set 2 to explaining the variation beyond that of set 1 is the **extra sum of squares** for set 2 given set 1, which equals the sum of squares regression from the full model minus the sum of squares regression from the reduced model.

To obtain the extra sum of squares for AB given A, B, we fit the full regression model with the indicator variables $A_1, \ldots, A_{(a-1)}, B_1, \ldots, B_{(b-1)}, AB_{11}, \ldots, AB_{(a-1)(b-1)}$, obtaining the sum of squares regression SSR(F) (F for Full) with $ab - 1$ degrees of freedom. We also fit the reduced model with the indicator variables $A_1, \ldots, A_{a-1}, B_1, \ldots, B_{b-1}$, and obtain the sum of squares regression SSR(R) (R for Reduced) with $a + b - 2$ degrees of freedom. The extra sum of squares for AB given A, B is

$$SSM(AB|A, B) = SSR(F) - SSR(R)$$

The degrees of freedom associated with SSM(AB|A, B) is the difference in the degrees of freedom associated with SSR(F) and SSR(R): $(ab - 1) - (a + b - 2) = (a - 1)(b - 1)$.

EXAMPLE 10.1   CONTINUED

Consider the pulse oximetry data. The factors are shivering intensity, which we will call INTENSITY, and shivering type, which we will call SHIVTYPE. Their interaction will be denoted INTENSITY*SHIVTYPE. We will obtain the ANOVA decomposition of the total sum of squares using regression fits with indicator variables as regressors. One possible sequence of steps is as follows:

1. Fit the full regression model by regressing POWER on the indicator variables $S_1, I_1, I_2, (SI)_{11}$ and $(SI)_{12}$. The regression sum of squares equals 179.42

with 5 degrees of freedom. The error sum of squares is SSE $= 112.05$ with 18 degrees of freedom.

2. Fit the reduced model with S_1, I_1, and I_2, as regressors. This corresponds to the additive model with factors A and B. The regression sum of squares is 22.17 with 3 degrees of freedom. From this, we compute the extra sum of squares:

$$\text{SSM(INTENSITY*SHIVTYPE|INTENSITY, SHIVTYPE)}$$

$$= 179.42 - 22.17 = 157.25$$

with $5-3 = 2$ degrees of freedom. This will be the INTENSITY*SHIVTYPE sum of squares and degrees of freedom.

3. Fit the reduced model with S_1, $(SI)_{11}$, and $(SI)_{12}$ as regressors. This corresponds to the model with effects A and AB. The sum of squares regression is 158.94 with 3 degrees of freedom. From this, we compute the extra sum of squares:

$$\text{SSM(SHIVTYPE|INTENSITY, INTENSITY*SHIVTYPE)}$$

$$= 179.42 - 158.94 = 20.48$$

with $5 - 3 = 2$ degrees of freedom. This will be the SHIVTYPE sum of squares and degrees of freedom.

4. Fit the reduced model with I_1, I_2, $(SI)_{11}$, and $(SI)_{12}$ as regressors. This corresponds to the model with effects B and AB. The regression sum of squares is 177.72 with 4 degrees of freedom. From this, we compute the extra sum of squares:

$$\text{SSM(INTENSITY|SHIVTYPE, INTENSITY*SHIVTYPE)}$$

$$= 179.42 - 177.72 = 1.70$$

with $5 - 4 = 1$ degree of freedom. This will be the INTENSITY sum of squares and degrees of freedom.

This decomposition is summarized in Table 10.17, which is the same as Table 10.10. Notice in particular that the sums of squares and degrees of freedom add to the sum of squares total and its degrees of freedom. This is a result of the design being balanced. As we will see in the next section, when the design is unbalanced, the sums of squares no longer add, and model interpretation becomes more difficult. ✦

TABLE 10.17   ANOVA Table: Pulse Oximetry Data

		Analysis of variance			
Source	DF	Sum of squares	Mean square	F Stat	Prob > F
Intensity	2	20.48	10.24	1.64	0.2208
Shivering type	1	1.70	1.70	0.27	0.6081
Intensity*Shivering type	2	157.25	78.62	12.63	0.0004
Error	18	112.05	6.23		
C Total	23	291.47			

10.12

UNBALANCED DESIGNS

The theory we have discussed in this chapter for the inference for main effects and interactions in the effects model requires a balanced design. All too often, in practice, this is not the case. Even when a balanced design is planned for a study, the resulting data can still have missing observations. For example:

- Product development engineers conduct an experiment to measure the performance of an electrical component after it has been in continuous use for 100 hours. To do so, they put a number of components on test. If one or more of the components fails before the 100 hours, the design may become unbalanced. Similar difficulties occur in medical experiments with animals and in clinical trials with human subjects.
- An experiment on a new airfoil becomes unbalanced when responses must be eliminated because a wind-tunnel fan malfunctions.
- In surveys, the failure of some individuals to respond frequently results in unbalanced data.

In statistical analysis, a distinction must be made between data that are missing at random and data that are missing according to some systematic pattern. The analysis of data that are not missing at random is complicated and must take into account the way the data are missing. We will leave the treatment of this kind of missing data to advanced texts, and for the remainder of this chapter, we will assume that any missing data are missing at random.

We will consider two kinds of unbalanced designs: (1) those in which at least one cell has no observations and (2) those in which every cell has at least one observation.

When Some Cells Have No Data

If we have no data for at least one cell, then the means model (10.1) can be modified as follows:

$$Y_{ijk} = \mu_{ij} + \epsilon_{ijk}, \qquad (i, j) \in \{(i_1, j_1), (i_2, j_2), \ldots, (i_r, j_r)\}; \ k = 1, \ldots, n_{ij} \qquad (10.32)$$

where $r < ab$ is the number of nonempty cells, $\{(i_1, j_1), (i_2, j_2), \ldots, (i_r, j_r)\}$ denotes the set of nonempty cells, and n_{ij} is the number of observations in cell ij. The simplest, and perhaps most effective method for handling this situation is to analyze model (10.32) as a one-way model, consisting of data from the r populations $\{(i_1, j_1), (i_2, j_2), \ldots, (i_r, j_r)\}$. The techniques of Chapter 9 for the one-way model do not assume equal numbers of observations from the different populations, and so an overall F test can be conducted for differences in population means, and multiple comparisons or contrasts can be estimated to pinpoint the size and nature of the differences.

If an analysis in terms of individual factor and interaction effects is required, then the effects model must be modified to reflect the fact that some populations have no observations. Generally, estimates and tests involving parameters corresponding to the missing populations cannot be obtained. The analysis will depend on the pattern of missing cells, and we will not expand on it further here.[3]

When There Are No Empty Cells

If we have at least one observation in each cell, then the means model (10.1) becomes

$$Y_{ijk} = \mu_{ij} + \epsilon_{ijk}, \qquad i = 1, \ldots, a; j = 1, \ldots, b; k = 1, \ldots, n_{ij} \tag{10.33}$$

and the general effects model (10.1) becomes

$$Y_{ijk} = \mu + \alpha_i + \beta_j + (\alpha\beta)_{ij} + \epsilon_{ijk},$$
$$i = 1, \ldots, a; j = 1, \ldots, b; \ k = 1, \ldots, n_{ij} \tag{10.34}$$

where n_{ij} is the number of observations in cell ij. The estimators (10.2) and (10.17) to (10.20), for the parameters of both models (10.33) and (10.34), have the same form as they do for the balanced design, if we redefine the means used in their calculation as follows:

$$\bar{Y}_{ij\cdot} = \frac{1}{n_{ij}} \sum_{k=1}^{n_{ij}} Y_{ijk}, \qquad \bar{Y}_{i\cdot\cdot} = \frac{1}{b} \sum_{j=1}^{b} \bar{Y}_{ij\cdot}, \qquad \bar{Y}_{\cdot j\cdot} = \frac{1}{a} \sum_{i=1}^{a} \bar{Y}_{ij\cdot}, \qquad \bar{Y}_{\cdots} = \frac{1}{ab} \sum_{i=1}^{a} \sum_{j=1}^{b} \bar{Y}_{ij\cdot}$$

Also, for both models, the pooled variance, which equals the mean square error, is defined as

$$S_p^2 = \frac{\displaystyle\sum_{i=1}^{a} \sum_{j=1}^{b} (n_{ij} - 1) S_{ij}^2}{n_{\cdot\cdot} - ab}$$

---

[3]There are many references, mostly more advanced than the present text, that cover the analysis when there are no data in one or more cells. One excellent treatment is given by G. A. Milliken and D. E. Johnson, *Analysis of Messy Data, Volume I: Designed Experiments.* New York: Van Nostrand Reinhold, 1992.

where $n_{..} = \sum_{i=1}^{a} \sum_{j=1}^{b} n_{ij}$ is the total number of observations and

$$S_{ij}^2 = \frac{\sum_{k=1}^{n_{ij}} (Y_{ijk} - \bar{Y}_{ij.})^2}{n_{ij} - 1}$$

is the variance of the sample in cell ij.

For the means model, the analysis of variance may be conducted under the usual one-way formulation using the techniques in Chapter 9. A difficulty arises, however, in the analysis of variance for the effects model.

To understand the difficulty, suppose that we fit the means model (10.33) as a one-way model. Recall that the ANOVA for the one-way model decomposes the sum of squares total into two components: a sum of squares model, which represents the amount of total variation that the model explains, and the sum of squares error, which is the unexplained variation. Now consider the effects model (10.34) for the same data. With a balanced design, the sums of squares for each factor and for the interaction add up to the sum of squares model for the means model. This means that there is a unique way to partition the sum of squares model, and hence there is no ambiguity about how much variation is attributable to each factor and the interaction.

When the design is unbalanced, however, the sum of squares model cannot be partitioned among each factor and interaction in a unique way. If the sum of squares for each effect is computed using Equations (10.23) to (10.25), suitably modified to account for the differing numbers of observations in different cells, their sum will not equal the sum of squares model.

EXAMPLE 10.6   AN UNBALANCED DESIGN

To illustrate ANOVA for an unbalanced design, suppose that the recording device was malfunctioning during the pulse oximetry experiment. After checking the circumstances of the malfunction and the pattern of missing data, the experimenter concludes that there is no reason to doubt that the data are missing at random. The remaining data are shown in Table 10.18.

Table 10.19 is the ANOVA table from the means model treated as a one-way model.

TABLE 10.18   Unbalanced Pulse Oximetry Data

Intensity	Shivering type	Power			
Mild	Febrile	7.28			
Mild	Postoperative	12.41	8.39		
Moderate	Febrile	5.19	7.37	7.64	
Moderate	Postoperative	6.99	7.33	7.54	15.67
Severe	Febrile	9.95	6.54	11.40	12.49
Severe	Postoperative	2.64	3.10	2.16	1.98

TABLE 10.19   ANOVA Table: Unbalanced Pulse Oximetry Data, One-Way Model

		Analysis of variance			
Source	DF	Sum of squares	Mean square	F Stat	Prob > F
Model	5	160.88	32.18	4.52	0.0150
Error	12	85.41	7.12		
C Total	17	246.30			

The sums of squares obtained from the analogues of Equations (10.23) to (10.25) for the unbalanced case are 12.28 for Shivering Type, 26.10 for Intensity, and 2.66 for their interaction. Notice that the sum of these three sums of squares equals 41.04, which is nowhere near the sum of squares model, 160.88, obtained from the one-way ANOVA. ✦

There are a number of ways to approach the problem of trying to obtain meaningful sums of squares for the different effects in an unbalanced factorial design. We will consider three, called Types I, II, and III analyses. When the design is balanced, all three methods will produce the standard sums of squares studied previously.

Type I Analysis

Type I analysis is a method of decomposing the sum of squares model from the one-way means model into component sum of squares for each effect in the effects model. In Type I analysis, these component sums of squares are obtained in a sequential manner, and always add to the sum of squares model. To do a Type I analysis, we first put the effects in the order in which their sums of squares will be obtained. Generally, the effects are placed in order of decreasing importance.

Suppose, for illustration, that the two factors in the model are A and B, that we are considering the full model with effects A, B, and AB, and that we want to obtain the sums of squares in the order B, A, AB. We proceed as follows:

1. Define indicator variables for each main effect exactly as they are defined for the balanced case. In the present case, we define $a - 1$ indicator variables $A_1, A_2, \ldots,$ A_{a-1} for factor A, where A_i takes value 1 for each observation for which factor A is at level i, value -1 for each observation for which factor A is at level a, and value 0 otherwise. In a similar way, define indicator variables $B_1, B_2, \ldots, B_{b-1}$ for factor B and create their products $AB_{ij} = A_i B_j$ to account for the interaction.

2. Fit the model with the first effect (in this case, effect B) only. This means regressing the response on the indicator variables $B_1, B_2, \ldots, B_{b-1}$. The sum of squares for effect B, which we will call SSM(B), is just the sum of squares regression, and the degrees of freedom associated with SSM(B) is the degrees of freedom for regression.

3. Fit the model with the first and second effects (here, effects A and B). This means regressing the response on $B_1, B_2, \ldots, B_{b-1}$ and $A_1, A_2, \ldots, A_{a-1}$. The sum of squares for effects B and A, which we will call SSM(B, A), is just the sum of squares regression, and the degrees of freedom associated with SSM(B, A) is the degrees of freedom for regression.

Now compute the extra sum of squares SSM(A|B) = SSM(B, A) − SSM(B). The degrees of freedom associated with SSM(A|B) is the degrees of freedom for SSM(B,A) minus the degrees of freedom for SSM(B). We may interpret SSM(A|B) as the amount of additional variation in the response that both A and B explain above what B explains alone.

4. Fit the model with all three effects (i.e., effects A, B, and AB) by regressing the response on $B_1, B_2, \ldots, B_{b-1}$; $A_1, A_2, \ldots, A_{a-1}$; and AB_{ij}, $i = 1, \ldots, a-1$, $j = 1, \ldots, b-1$. The sum of squares for all three effects, which we will call SSM(B, A, AB), is just the sum of squares regression, and the degrees of freedom associated with SSM(B, A, AB) is the degrees of freedom for regression. From this model, we also obtain the sum of squares error, SSE, and its degrees of freedom.

Compute the extra sum of squares SSM(AB|B, A) = SSM(B, A, AB) − SSM(B, A). The degrees of freedom associated with SSM(AB|B,A) is the degrees of freedom for SSM(B, A, AB) minus the degrees of freedom for SSM(B, A). SSM(AB|A,B) represents the amount of additional variation A,B, and AB explain above what A and B explain.

This procedure produces a partition of the sum of squares total, by which we mean that the various sums of squares add to the sum of squares total. In the decomposition we have just outlined,

$$SSTO = SSM(B) + SSM(A|B) + SSM(AB|B, A) + SSE$$

When the design is balanced, this partition is unique and independent of the order in which the effects are entered. If the design is unbalanced, this partition is not unique, and entering the effects in a different order will change the sums of squares.

EXAMPLE 10.6   CONTINUED

Consider the unbalanced pulse oximetry data given in Table 10.18. The factors are shivering intensity, which we will call INTENSITY, and shivering type, which we will call SHIVTYPE. Their interaction will be denoted INTENSITY*SHIVTYPE. Table 10.20 shows the factor levels, the response, and the indicator variables.

To illustrate the nonuniqueness of the Type I partition, we will partition the sum of squares total, 291.47, in two different ways. The first partition will obtain the sums of squares in the following order: INTENSITY*SHIVTYPE, INTENSITY, and SHIVTYPE. The sequence of steps is as follows:

1. Fit the regression model with $(SI)_{11}$ and $(SI)_{12}$, corresponding to the INTENSITY*SHIVTYPE effect. The sum of squares model, SSM

TABLE   10.20   Indicator Variables for Unbalanced Pulse Oximetry Data

Shivering type	Intensity	Power	S_1	I_1	I_2	$(SI)_{11}$	$(SI)_{12}$
Febrile	Mild	7.28	1	1	0	1	0
Febrile	Moderate	5.19	1	0	1	0	1
Febrile	Moderate	7.37	1	0	1	0	1
Febrile	Moderate	7.64	1	0	1	0	1
Febrile	Severe	9.95	1	−1	−1	−1	−1
Febrile	Severe	6.54	1	−1	−1	−1	−1
Febrile	Severe	11.40	1	−1	−1	−1	−1
Febrile	Severe	12.49	1	−1	−1	−1	−1
Postop	Mild	12.41	−1	1	0	−1	0
Postop	Mild	8.39	−1	1	0	−1	0
Postop	Moderate	6.99	−1	0	1	0	−1
Postop	Moderate	7.54	−1	0	1	0	−1
Postop	Moderate	7.33	−1	0	1	0	−1
Postop	Moderate	15.67	−1	0	1	0	−1
Postop	Severe	2.64	−1	−1	−1	1	1
Postop	Severe	3.10	−1	−1	−1	1	1
Postop	Severe	2.16	−1	−1	−1	1	1
Postop	Severe	1.98	−1	−1	−1	1	1

(INTENSITY*SHIVTYPE), equals the resulting regression sum of squares, 142.24, with 2 degrees of freedom.

2. Regress POWER on $(SI)_{11}$, $(SI)_{12}$, I_1, and I_2, corresponding to the INTENSITY*SHIVTYPE and INTENSITY effects. The sum of squares model, SSM(INTENSITY, INTENSITY*SHIVTYPE), equals the regression sum of squares, 159.55, with 4 degrees of freedom. We have

$$\text{SSM(INTENSITY|INTENSITY*SHIVTYPE)}$$

$$= 159.55 - 142.23 = 17.32$$

with $4 - 2 = 2$ degrees of freedom.

3. Fit the full model with $(SI)_{11}$, $(SI)_{12}$, I_1, I_2, and S_1 as regressors, corresponding to INTENSITY*SHIVTYPE, INTENSITY, and SHIVTYPE as effects. The sum of squares model, SSM(SHIVTYPE, INTENSITY, INTENSITY*SHIVTYPE), equals the sum of squares regression, 160.88, with 5 degrees of freedom.

$$\text{SSM(SHIVTYPE|INTENSITY, INTENSITY*SHIVTYPE)}$$

$$= 160.88 - 159.55 = 1.33$$

with $5 - 4 = 1$ degree of freedom. The sum of squares error from the regression, 85.41, equals SSE, and has 12 degrees of freedom.

TABLE 10.21   ANOVA Table: Type I Analysis of Unbalanced Pulse Oximetry Data, Effects Model

		Analysis of variance			
Source	DF	Sum of squares	Mean square	F Stat	Prob > F
Intensity*Shivering type	2	142.24	71.12	9.99	0.0028
Intensity	2	17.32	8.66	1.22	0.3294
Shivering type	1	1.33	1.33	0.19	0.2713
Error	12	85.41	7.12		
C Total	17	246.30			

TABLE 10.22   ANOVA Table: A Second Type I Analysis of Unbalanced Pulse Oximetry Data, Effects Model

		Analysis of variance			
Source	DF	Sum of squares	Mean square	F Stat	Prob > F
Shivering type	1	12.27	12.27	1.72	0.2138
Intensity	2	30.81	15.40	2.16	0.1576
Intensity*Shivering type	2	117.81	58.90	8.28	0.0055
Error	12	85.41	7.12		
C Total	17	246.30			

This decomposition is summarized in Table 10.21. Notice that the sums of squares and degrees of freedom for this Type I decomposition add up to the total values. Also notice that it appears that Intensity and Shivering Type are not significant, while the Intensity by Shivering Type interaction is.

If we compute the sums of squares in the order SHIVTYPE, INTENSITY, and INTENSITY*SHIVTYPE, we obtain the Type I decomposition displayed in Table 10.22.[4] Notice that the sums of squares, the mean squares, the values of the F statistics and the p-values are different than those in Table 10.21. Although in this example, the overall conclusions are likely to be the same, it is disturbing that the values in the ANOVA table depend on the order in which the effects are computed.   ◆

Generally, in model (10.34), the main effects are considered more important, and of more interest than the interaction. As a result, the usual Type I analysis finds the sum of squares interaction after the sum of squares main effects, as is done in Table 10.22. Type I analysis is directly available (i.e., without resorting to regression with indicator variables) in some, but not all computer packages.

[4]Exercise 10.16 asks you to construct the decomposition shown in Table 10.22.

Type II Analysis

Some statisticians feel it makes sense to compare the contribution of an effect only with those effects at or below its level, where level means the number of factors in the effect: A main effect is of level 1, and a two-factor interaction of level 2. This idea leads to a modification of the Type I analysis, so that in the two-way effects model the sum of squares for A is SSM(A|B) instead of SSM(A|B, AB), the sum of squares for B is SSM(B|A) instead of SSM(B|A, AB), and the sum of squares for AB remains SSM(AB|A, B). The resulting analysis is called a **Type II analysis.** These sums of squares can be computed using regression on dummy variables. Type II analysis is directly available in some, but not all computer packages.

Type III Analysis

A type of analysis that avoids the ambiguity of a Type I analysis is a **Type III analysis,** also known as **Yates's weighted squares of means technique.** We recommend this type of analysis for testing effects in all unbalanced factorial designs that have data in all cells. When the design is balanced, Type III analysis is the same as Type I analysis.

Unlike Type I sums of squares, Type III sums of squares are not a partition of the total sum of squares, nor are they meant to be. They are designed to measure the additional contribution to explaining the response variation that each effect makes beyond all the other effects.

In the Type III analysis, the sum of squares for any effect is computed assuming all other effects are in the model. Thus, for a model with main effects A and B and interaction effect AB, the sum of squares for A is SSM(A|B, AB), the sum of squares for B is SSM(B|A, AB), and the sum of squares for AB is SSM(AB|A, B). Note that the sum of squares for each effect is the sum of squares that would be obtained if that effect were entered last in a Type I analysis. Note further, that the sums of squares do not depend on the ordering of the effects. In the Type III analysis, the F test for significance of an effect is a test for the contribution of that effect in explaining variation beyond what the other effects explain.

EXAMPLE 10.6   CONTINUED

We analyze the unbalanced pulse oximetry data using a Type III analysis. We have already seen how to use regression with indicator variables to compute

SSM(INTENSITY, SHIVTYPE, INTENSITY*SHIVTYPE) = 160.88

with 5 degrees of freedom, and

SSM(SHIVTYPE|INTENSITY, INTENSITY*SHIVTYPE) = 1.33

with 1 degree of freedom. We can also use regression to compute

SSM(SHIVTYPE, INTENSITY*SHIVTYPE) = 142.41

TABLE 10.23   ANOVA Table: Type III Analysis of Unbalanced Pulse Oximetry Data

		Analysis of variance			
Source	DF	Sum of squares	Mean square	F Stat	Prob > F
Shivering type	1	1.33	1.33	0.19	0.6728
Intensity	2	18.47	9.23	1.30	0.3090
Intensity*Shivering type	2	117.81	58.90	8.28	0.0055
Error	12	85.41	7.12		
C Total	17	246.30			

with 3 degrees of freedom, and

$$\text{SSM(INTENSITY, SHIVTYPE)} = 43.07$$

with 3 degrees of freedom. From this it follows that

$$\text{SSM(INTENSITY}|\text{SHIVTYPE, INTENSITY*SHIVTYPE)}$$
$$= 160.88 - 142.41 = 18.47,$$

with $5 - 3 = 2$ degrees of freedom, and that

$$\text{SSM(INTENSITY*SHIVTYPE}|\text{SHIVTYPE, INTENSITY)}$$
$$= 160.88 - 43.07 = 117.81$$

with $5 - 3 = 2$ degrees of freedom. We also know that SSE from the full model equals 85.41 with 12 degrees of freedom. Table 10.23 summarizes this Type III analysis. The Type III analysis shows that only the interaction effect contributes significantly to the explanation of the variation beyond what the other two effects explain.

Notice that the sums of squares in Table 10.23 do not add to the sum of squares total.   ◆

Type III analysis is directly available in some, but not all computer packages.

A Final Word on Unbalanced Designs

As you have seen, unbalanced designs are more difficult to analyze and to interpret than balanced designs. In addition, they are less robust to nonnormality and outliers than balanced designs. For these reasons, every effort should be made to employ balanced designs and to maintain the balance when obtaining the data.

Even with a balanced design, however, unbalanced data occur regularly. If confronted with unbalanced data, be sure you know the type of analysis you want to do and what types of analysis your computer package produces. If the unbalanced data are from a design that is at all complicated, if they do not occur at random, or if some cells have no data, see a statistician.

10.13   MULTIFACTOR MODELS

We have concentrated on two-factor models in this chapter, but there is nothing to stop us from employing these same techniques to analyze data using models with more than two factors. For example, a general three-factor effects model might take the form

$$Y_{ijkl} = \mu + \alpha_i + \beta_j + (\alpha\beta)_{ij} + \gamma_k + (\alpha\gamma)_{ik} + (\beta\gamma)_{jk} + (\alpha\beta\gamma)_{ijk} + \epsilon_{ijkl}$$

This model features three two-factor interactions and one three-factor interaction. Chapters 12 and 13 consider a particular set of efficient designs for multifactor studies.

D ISCUSSION QUESTIONS

1. Write out the two-way means model in mathematical notation and describe what each model parameter represents.
2. What assumptions are made about data from the two-way means model?
3. How is the two-way means model fit to data?
4. Describe how to check model assumptions for the two-way means model.
5. Discuss some strategies for handling outliers, heteroscedasticity, and nonnormality.
6. What is an interaction? Illustrate with an example.
7. What is an interaction plot? Describe how to recognize an interaction on this plot.
8. What is an important interaction? An unimportant interaction?
9. Write out the additive two-factor factorial effects model in mathematical notation and describe what each model parameter represents.
10. Write out the general two-factor factorial effects model in mathematical notation and describe what each model parameter represents.
11. How are the additive and general two-factor factorial effects models fit to data?
12. Describe how to check model assumptions for the additive and general two-factor factorial effects models.
13. Write out the ANOVA table for the additive and general two-factor factorial effects models. Describe what each table entry represents.
14. What are contrasts? How are they estimated? What are they used for?
15. If interactions are significant and important, how should the analysis proceed?
16. If none of the interactions is both significant and important, how should the analysis proceed?
17. How can interactions be reduced or eliminated?

18. What advantages do factorial designs have over OFAT designs?

19. Describe the difficulties that occur when there is one observation per cell. How can they be handled?

20. Explain the regression formulation of a factorial model. Include in your discussion indicator variables for main effects and interactions, extra sums of squares, and tests based on them.

21. What is an unbalanced design? What difficulties does it present? Explain the Type I, II, and III methods of analysis for unbalanced designs.

E XERCISES

10.1. Show that the three lines in View 2 of Figure 10.4 are parallel if and only if Equations (10.7) and (10.8) hold. Show that these equations are equivalent to Equations (10.5) and (10.6).

10.2. Show that for the two-way means model, MSE $= S_p^2$, the pooled variance given by Equation (10.3).

10.3. Show that relation (10.31) can be made additive by taking the square root of both sides.

10.4. Table 10.24 is an ANOVA table for a two-way design with equal numbers of observations per population.

TABLE 10.24   ANOVA Table: Exercise 10.4

		Analysis of variance			
Source	DF	Sum of squares	Mean square	F Stat	Prob > F
A	*	*	4.12	4.16	*
B	6	*	1.57	*	*
Error	*	45.54	0.99		
C Total	55	*			

(a) Fill in the missing values (denoted by "*") in the ANOVA table.

(b) How many levels are there for each factor? How many populations are there? How many observations per population are there?

(c) Is this a general factorial or an additive model?

10.5. Table 10.25 is an ANOVA table for a two-way design with equal numbers of observations per population.

TABLE 10.25   ANOVA Table: Exercise10.5

		Analysis of variance			
Source	DF	Sum of squares	Mean square	F Stat	Prob > F
A	*	3.76	1.88	1.66	*
B	*	*	2.91	*	*
AB	8	*	4.01	*	*
Error	*	16.95	*		
C Total	29	*			

(a) Fill in the missing values (denoted by "*") in the ANOVA table.

(b) How many levels are there for each factor? How many populations are there? How many observations per population are there?

(c) Is this a general factorial or an additive model?

10.6. Table 10.26 is a table of population means for six populations indexed by two factors.

TABLE 10.26   Example of Population Means in a 3×2 Factorial Design

Levels of factor A	Levels of factor B	
	1	2
1	$\mu_{11} = 2.2$	$\mu_{12} = 4.6$
2	$\mu_{21} = 3.7$	$\mu_{22} = 6.1$
3	$\mu_{31} = 8.5$	$\mu_{32} = 4.3$

(a) Draw a plot giving two views of the interactions. Describe and interpret the plot.

(b) Assuming a general two-factor factorial model, compute the overall mean, main effects, and interactions. Interpret these quantities.

10.7. Table 10.27 is a table of population means for nine populations indexed by two factors.

TABLE 10.27   Example of Population Means in a 3×3 Factorial Design

Levels of factor A	Levels of factor B		
	1	2	3
1	$\mu_{11} = 2.2$	$\mu_{12} = 4.6$	$\mu_{13} = 1.1$
2	$\mu_{21} = 3.7$	$\mu_{22} = 6.1$	$\mu_{23} = 2.6$
3	$\mu_{31} = 8.5$	$\mu_{32} = 10.9$	$\mu_{33} = 7.4$

(a) Draw a plot giving two views of the interactions. Describe and interpret the plot.

(b) Assuming a general two-factor factorial model, compute the overall mean, main effects, and interactions. Interpret these quantities.

10.8. Interpret the Tukey level 0.95 intervals for factor oventype in Section 10.7.

10.9. Simulated annealing is a recently developed general computational method for optimizing functions. An electrical engineering researcher studying stereo matching in computer vision decided to test the effectiveness of simulated annealing in correctly identifying the disparity of points in stereo images. As a first step, he ran a factorial experiment to quantify the effects of two user-specified parameters on the identification of disparity. The factors are as follows:

- The temperature-reducing rate.[5] Its two levels are 0.70 and 0.90.
- λ, a weighting parameter. Its two levels are 5 and 10.

[5] *Note:* This parameter is called the "temperature-reducing rate" because, conceptually, simulated annealing is similar to the technique of annealing, which involves the processing of metals through controlled cooling.

The response is the number of pixels whose disparity is correctly identified. The data, also found in the data set ANNEAL, are

Temperature-reducing rate	λ	
	5	10
0.70	660	446
	489	308
0.90	1013	667
	1153	790

(a) Analyze these data using the steps given in Section 10.8.

(b) Write a short report explaining your findings. In particular, detail the nature of the relation between the factors and the response.

10.10. Chitosan is a biopolymer obtained from the shells of crustaceans. In an experiment to study thermal degradation of chitosan, samples were heated to one of three temperatures (70, 90, or 100°C) and maintained there for one of three time durations (10, 20, or 30 minutes). Thermal degradation of chitosan involves the breakdown of long chains of chitosan molecules into shorter chains under the influence of heat. The lengths of the chains are directly proportional to the molecular weight. Thus, molecular weight, divided by 10^5, is used as the response. The data are in Table 10.28 and in the data set CHITOSAN.

TABLE 10.28   Data, Exercise 10.10

Heating time (min)	Temperature (°C)		
	70	90	100
10	2.31	2.20	1.85
	2.49	2.36	1.92
20	2.31	2.22	1.91
	2.17	2.09	1.99
30	2.16	2.25	2.00
	2.34	2.16	2.09

(a) Fit the full-effects model to the data. Do you notice anything unusual about the plot of residuals versus fitted values?[6]

(b) Choose a transformation to reduce or eliminate the heteroscedasticity.[7]

---

[6] You should notice two unusual things. First, the plot is symmetric above and below a horizontal line through the origin. This is a consequence of there being two replications, and results from the fitted values for the full model being the average of the two data values in each cell. As a result, the two residuals in each cell have the same magnitude but opposite signs. This symmetry is nothing to be concerned about. The second thing you should notice is that as the fitted values increase, there is an increasing trend in the magnitude of the residuals. That is, there is heteroscedasticity.

[7] We tried a log-log transformation, which is simple, and works well. The transformation [log log(WEIGHT + 1)] works even better, but is more complicated. Perhaps you can find a better one still.

(c) Analyze the transformed data using the steps given in Section 10.8.

(d) Write a short report explaining your findings. In particular, detail the nature of the relation between the factors and the response.

10.11. (*Note:* This problem is for students with a knowledge of multiple regression.) First, do Exercise 10.10. Now analyze the data in Table 10.28 by building a regression model using the actual levels of the factors, their product, and powers as possible regressors.[8] Report your results. Which methodology do you think gives more insight into the data? Why?

10.12. A beverage manufacturer wants to test its marketing strategy for a new sales campaign for one of its soft drink products. It chooses 27 markets of approximately equivalent demographics and assigns each market at random to one of nine marketing strategies determined by two factors of three levels each. The factors are as follows:

- Promotional price discounts: none, moderate, or heavy.
- Advertising: none, moderate, or heavy.

The response is change in sales from the same period 1 year ago in cases per 1000 households. The data are in Table 10.29 and in the data set PROMOAD.

TABLE 10.29   Data, Exercise 10.12.

Promotional discount	Advertising		
	None	moderate	Heavy
None	1.09	2.12	3.02
	1.58	1.86	2.59
	2.35	3.29	4.98
Moderate	1.11	6.44	6.92
	2.69	4.25	8.52
	2.07	4.37	9.72
Heavy	3.17	10.23	21.22
	5.66	12.91	18.29
	4.59	18.84	26.77

(a) Analyze these data using the steps given in Section 10.8.

(b) Write a short report explaining your findings. In particular, detail the nature of the relation between the factors and the response.

10.13. Obtain a confidence interval for the contrasts given by Equations (10.28) and (10.29). Interpret the results. Be sure to read the note following Equations (10.28) and (10.29) for guidance in computing these intervals.

10.14. Analyze the log-transformed pulse oximetry data. Show that the transformation makes the data more closely conform to the model assumptions. Show also that the conclusions are essentially the same as for the model fit to the raw data.

10.15. Show that the fitted values for the general model (10.22) equal the fitted values for the means model, $\hat{\mu}_{ij} = \bar{Y}_{ij\cdot}$. Show that this is not true of the fitted values for the additive model (10.21).

---

[8]Be sure to center the predictors first!

10.16. Perform the sequence of model fits to yield the Type I analysis summarized in Table 10.22.

10.17. Explain what I_2 and $(SI)_{12}$ mean in terms of the factors in Example 10.6.

10.18. Remove the values 1.09 and 1.58 from the 11 cell, the values 6.92 and 8.52 from the 23 cell, and the value 18.84 from the 32 cell in Table 10.29. Obtain the ANOVA using a Type I analysis in the order Promotional Discount, Advertising, and their interaction.

10.19. Obtain the ANOVA for the unbalanced data from Exercise 10.18 using a Type II analysis. Compare your results with those in Exercise 10.12.

10.20. Obtain the ANOVA for the unbalanced data from Exercise 10.18 using a Type III analysis. Compare your results with those in Exercise 10.12.

MINIPROJECT

Purpose

In order to gain experience with the analysis of factorial models, your group is to obtain and analyze data from a two-way design.

Process

Before beginning data collection, your group is to submit a proposal for your instructor's approval. The proposal should indicate exactly what you intend to do for this project and what you expect the results to be. When you have received approval, proceed to obtain and analyze the data using the steps given in Section 10.8.

LAB 10.1: Die Tossing

Introduction

In this lab, your group is to run and analyze some two-factor factorial experiments. You will also learn a bit about blocking in this setting.

Objectives

To give you a practical understanding of the design and conduct of a two-factor factorial experiment. To teach you one use of blocking in this setting.

Lab Materials

- Four small squares of tape
- A die
- A measuring tape

Experimental Procedure

1. The experiment you will conduct is the following.
    (a) Place the four small squares of tape in a line on the floor with 2 feet separating adjacent pieces of tape. One of the end pieces will be the target.
    (b) From each of the other three tape squares, one of the group members will throw the die at the target with the goal of making it come to rest as close to the target as possible. This will be done three times with each hand. Another group member should measure the distance from the thrown die to the target, and a third member should record the result.
    (c) When the first group member is done, the next will perform the experiment. The experiment will be repeated with each of the group members as thrower.
    (d) The 18 throws for each group member must be conducted in random order. Why?
2. Each group member will fit the general two-factor factorial model (10.16) to his or her data and analyze the results. Set up the response and factors as follows.
    (a) The response is the distance of the die from the target. Call it DISTANCE.
    (b) The factors are
        i. The distance of the thrower from the target. Call this factor TDIST in SAS and call its levels NEAR, MEDIUM, and FAR.
        ii. The hand used. Call this factor HAND in SAS and call its levels D (for dominant) and ND (for nondominant).
3. Each group member should analyze his or her data using the steps given in Section 10.8.
4. Now combine the data for all the group members into a single data set, using a variable (call it NAME) to identify the group member who produced each data value.
5. Analyze all the data for the group together. The design of all the group's experiments can be thought of as a RCBD with the group members as blocks and a two-factor factorial (instead of a one-way design) run in each block. The simplest model for this design is

$$Y_{ijkm} = \mu + \alpha_i + \beta_j + (\alpha\beta)_{ij} + B_m + \epsilon_{ijkm},$$

$$i = 1, \ldots, a; \; j = 1, \ldots, b; \; k = 1, \ldots, l; \; m = 1, \ldots, M$$

(10.35)

where B_m is the effect of the mth block. For your data, the variable NAME serves as the blocking variable.
    (a) Analyze these data using ANOVA.
    (b) What do the F tests show about the effects of TDIST and HAND and their interaction? Do these agree with the results each group member obtained?
    (c) Model (10.35) assumes no interactions between blocks and the other factors, and just as with the RCBD, there is really no valid test for blocks. However, just as for the RCBD, curvature in the plot of residuals versus predicted values might indicate the existence of interaction between blocks and the other factors. Look at this plot for your data. Does it indicate the presence of such interaction?
    (d) Since we have replications (three observations taken at each combination of factor settings), we could model the interactions between blocks and the other factors, but this would involve estimating and interpreting three-factor interactions, something we'll save for a future statistics course.
6. Write up a lab report describing what you did in this lab and what you found in tasks 1 to 5.

CAPSTONE PROJECT: Chapters 1 to 4 and 10

The goal of a **Capstone Project** is to give you experience in all phases of a statistical study: planning, data collection, analysis, and conclusions. Each of Chapters 1 to 4 and 10 must make a contribution to the project. For a description of this project, see the description of the Capstone Project for Chapters 1 to 5 on page 285. In addition to the material from Chapters 1 to 4 discussed there, the Capstone Project for Chapters 1 to 4 and 10 must also include modeling and inference for a factorial model, as covered in Chapter 10.

Distribution-Free Inference

The next 20 years should be exciting ones for statisticians. My prediction is for a partial replacement of parametric methods, and the accompanying mathematical calculations we have become used to, by computer-intensive methods. These methods will replace "theory from a book" typified by t-tables and F-tables, by "theory from scratch," generated anew by the computer for each new data analysis problem.

—*Bradley Efron, 1982*

INTRODUCTION

In Chapters 5 and 6, we introduced statistical inference: the use of a subset of a population, called a sample, to draw conclusions about the entire population from which it was taken. In Chapter 5, you learned about point and interval estimation, prediction, and tolerance intervals. In Chapter 6, you learned about hypothesis tests. The methods of inference that you studied in Chapters 5 and 6 are old[1] and reliable methods that have served statistics users well. For this reason, we have referred to them as **classical inference methods**.

Though they perform well under normal circumstances, classical methods do have some weaknesses, particularly when sample sizes are small:

- Classical inference methods rely on assumptions about the underlying distribution model for the data. Usually, they assume the distribution is one of a particular class of distributions such as the class of all normal distributions.
- These methods can be sensitive to outliers and nonnormality.

In this chapter, we present some inference methods that were developed to help remedy the weaknesses of classical inference methods. Because these methods do not rely on a specific population distribution model, such as the normal, they are called **distribution-free** inference methods.

Though for the most part distribution-free procedures are newer than their classical counterparts, we will begin by introducing the sign test, one of the oldest of all

[1]These methods were developed primarily in the first half of the twentieth century.

statistical procedures. There follows a discussion of rank-based procedures in which the rank of an observation among all observations in the sample is used in the analysis. We next introduce permutation and randomization methods, based on old ideas and recently made practical by the introduction of high-speed computers. The chapter, which begins with one of the oldest statistical methodologies, ends with one of the newest: the bootstrap. The bootstrap was introduced less than 20 years ago by Bradley Efron, whose quote concerning it and other computer-intensive inference methods introduces the chapter.

Knowledge and Skills

By successfully completing this chapter, you will acquire the following knowledge and skills:

KNOWLEDGE	SKILLS
1. What distribution-free inference is.	**1.** The construction, use, and interpretation of the sign test.
2. The sign test.	**2.** The construction, use, and interpretation of the one- and two-sample rank-based tests, including the one- and two-sample Wilcoxon, Kruskal-Wallis, and Friedman tests.
3. Rank-based tests.	**3.** The construction, use, and interpretation of permutation tests, including Fisher's exact test, Pitman tests, and generalized Kruskal-Wallis and Friedman tests.
4. Permutation and randomization tests.	**4.** The construction, use, and interpretation of bootstrap confidence and prediction intervals.
5. The bootstrap.	

11.2

INFERENCE: SOME PRELIMINARY CONSIDERATIONS

As we did in Chapters 5 and 6, we begin by assuming that the data constitute a random sample from a population to which we wish to make inference. The cautions expressed there concerning the importance of the method used for data collection and of establishing the stationarity of the data-producing process will hold here as well.

Later in the chapter, we will introduce a different notion of inference, based solely on the random assignment of treatments to experimental units, rather than on sampling.

11.3

THE SIGN TEST

It is reported that a variant of the sign test was used by Arbuthnott in 1710 to test whether the proportion of male births in London was greater than 1/2. If so, the sign test is one of the oldest of all statistical procedures.

The Model

Recall the C+E model that we studied in Chapters 5 and 6:

$$Y = \mu + \epsilon \tag{11.1}$$

where μ is a location parameter, and ϵ is a random-error term. For the classical inference procedures of Chapters 5 and 6, we made the assumption that ϵ has a mean of 0, which implies that Y has a mean of μ. For small samples, we made the more restrictive assumption that $\epsilon \sim N(0, \sigma^2)$, which means that $Y \sim N(\mu, \sigma^2)$.

The model on which the sign test is based is similar to the C+E model. We assume a response Y is generated by

$$Y = \theta + \epsilon \tag{11.2}$$

where θ is a location parameter, and ϵ is a random-error term having a continuous distribution. The difference between models (11.2) and (11.1) is that we no longer assume that $\epsilon \sim N(0, \sigma^2)$. In fact, we do not assume ϵ has any particular distribution. The only assumption we make is that the population from which ϵ is drawn have median 0.[2] This means that the median of Y is θ.[3] Because we do not assume any particular distribution, such as the normal, for ϵ, we call this model **distribution-free**.

We will assume that the data consist of the n observations Y_i, $i = 1, \ldots, n$, and that these are generated by the formula

$$Y_i = \theta + \epsilon_i$$

We further assume that the ϵ_i are independent.

[2]Recall that a median of a population distribution is a value below which lies one-half the population measurements and above which lies one-half the population measurements. It can happen that more than one value is a median for the population, but we will not consider that possibility here. Thus, throughout this chapter, assume that the median of the population is unique.

[3]This is the reason we use θ to denote the location parameter here: μ traditionally denotes a population mean.

The Statistical Hypotheses

The null hypothesis that we will consider for the sign test is that the population median equals a specific known value, θ_0:

$$H_0: \quad \theta = \theta_0$$

As alternative hypotheses, we will consider any one of the one-or two-sided alternatives:

$$H_{a^+}: \quad \theta > \theta_0$$
$$H_{a_-}: \quad \theta < \theta_0$$
$$H_{a\pm}: \quad \theta \neq \theta_0$$

The Test Statistic

The test statistic for the sign test is the number of observations Y_i that exceed θ_0. We will call this statistic B.

The p-Value

The p-value is the probability, when the null hypothesis is true, of observing a value of the test statistic giving as much or more evidence against the null hypothesis and in favor of the alternative hypothesis as the observed value of the test statistic. Thus, in order to compute the p-value, we need to know the following:

- The distribution of B when H_0 is true.
- When the test statistic gives as much or more evidence against the null hypothesis and in favor of the alternative hypothesis as the observed value of the test statistic.

The Distribution of B When H_0 Is True

We can think about B in the following way. There are n independent trials, with trial i consisting of observing whether Y_i is greater than θ_0 or not. Call the outcome of trial i a "success" if $Y_i > \theta_0$, and a "failure" otherwise. Since the Y_i all have the same distribution, the probability of a success, $p = P(Y_i > \theta_0)$, is the same at each trial. The test statistic B is the number of "successes" in the n trials.

By now, all this should sound suspiciously like the definition of a binomial random phenomenon: n independent trials; two possible outcomes, "success" or "failure" at each trial; and the same probability, p, of "success" at each trial. As such, we know that B has a binomial distribution with parameters n and p.

If H_0 is true, θ_0 is the median of the distribution of Y_i, which means that p, the probability of a "success" at each trial, equals 0.5. That is, if H_0 is true, $B \sim b(n, 0.5)$.

What Is Evidence Against the Null and in Favor of the Alternative Hypothesis?

What constitutes evidence against the null and in favor of the alternative depends on the alternative hypothesis. We consider each alternative hypothesis in turn:

- If the alternative hypothesis is H_{a+}: $\theta > \theta_0$, then large values of B are more consistent with H_{a+} and less consistent with H_0. Therefore, the p-value is $p^+ = P(B \geq b^*)$, where b^* denotes the observed value of the test statistic.
- If the alternative hypothesis is H_{a-}: $\theta < \theta_0$, then small values of B are more consistent with H_{a-} and less consistent with H_0. Therefore, the p-value is $p_- = P(B \leq b^*)$.
- If the alternative hypothesis is $H_{a\pm}$: $\theta \neq \theta_0$, the p-value is obtained as follows. Let $p_B(b)$ denote the probability mass function of B under H_0: that is, a $b(n, 0.5)$ probability mass function. Then the p-value is obtained by summing all values of p_B that are less than or equal to $p_B(b^*)$. That is,

$$p\pm = \sum_{\{b : p_B(b) \leq p_B(b^*)\}} p_B(b) \tag{11.3}$$

Large-Sample Approximation

By the Central Limit Theorem, we know that if $B \sim b(n, p)$ and if n is large,[4] then, approximately,

$$\frac{B - np}{\sqrt{np(1 - p)}} \sim N(0, 1)$$

To obtain an approximate p-value using the normal approximation with the continuity correction, we first assume H_0 is true. Then $p = 0.5$, and $np = 0.5n$ and $np(1 - p) = 0.25n$. If the alternative hypothesis is H_{a+}, the p-value is

$$p^+ = P(B \geq b^*)$$
$$= P(B \geq b^* - 0.5)$$
$$= P\left(\frac{B - 0.5n}{\sqrt{0.25n}} \geq \frac{b^* - 0.5n - 0.5}{\sqrt{0.25n}}\right)$$
$$\approx P(Z \geq z_u^*)$$

where

$$Z \sim N(0, 1) \quad \text{and} \quad z_u^* = \frac{b^* - 0.5n - 0.5}{\sqrt{0.25n}}$$

---

[4] Recall that $np > 10$ and $n(1 - p) > 10$ is a good guideline overall. For $p = 0.5$, as considered here, $np > 5$ and $n(1 - p) > 5$ will give good results.

Similarly, we may approximate p_- by $P(Z \leq z_l^*)$, where

$$z_l^* = \frac{b^* - 0.5n + 0.5}{\sqrt{0.25n}}$$

We then approximate $p\pm$ by $2\min(P(Z \geq z_u^*), P(Z \leq z_l^*))$.

EXAMPLE 11.1   THE SIGN TEST

One stage of a manufacturing process involves a manually controlled grinding-operation. Management suspects that the grinding-machine operators tend to grind parts slightly larger rather than slightly smaller than the target diameter of 0.75 inch, while still staying within specification limits. To verify their suspicion, they sample 150 within-spec parts and find that 93 have diameters above the target diameter. Is this strong evidence in support of their suspicion?

- **The Scientific Hypothesis.** The grinding-machine operators tend to grind parts slightly larger than the target diameter.
- **The Statistical Model.** The model is model (11.2), where θ is the median diameter of the population of all ground parts.
- **The Statistical Hypotheses**

$$H_0: \quad \theta = 0.75$$
$$H_{a^+}: \quad \theta > 0.75$$

- **The Test Statistic.** The test statistic is B, the number of parts with diameters larger than the target of 0.75 inch. Its observed value is $b^* = 93$.
- **The p-Value.** The p-value is $P(B \geq 93) = 0.0021$, where $B \sim b(150, 0.5)$. If we don't have access to a table or a computer to evaluate binomial probabilities, we can approximate this p-value by using the normal approximation. In this case,

$$z_u^* = \frac{93 - (0.5)(150) - 0.5}{\sqrt{(0.25)(150)}} = 2.86$$

so the approximate p-value is

$$P(Z \geq 2.86) = 0.0021$$

a very close approximation indeed!

In either case, the p-value is very small, and we are led to conclude that the median is greater than the target value of 0.75. As a result, we conclude that more than half the parts are ground too large.   ◆

TABLE 11.1   Data, Example 11.2

Rabbit	Actual pH	Estimated pH	pH Difference y_i Estimated − Actual
1	6.791	6.808	0.017
2	6.832	6.854	0.022
3	6.693	6.696	0.003
4	6.810	6.830	0.020
5	6.683	6.679	−0.004
6	6.661	6.675	0.014
7	6.655	6.642	−0.013
8	6.717	6.708	−0.009
9	6.746	6.755	0.009
10	6.722	6.721	−0.001
11	6.861	6.866	0.005
12	6.774	6.786	0.012

The Sign Test for Paired Data

Recall from Chapter 6 that the one-sample t-test was used for paired data by taking the difference of each pair of observations. We can use the sign test in exactly the same way, as the following example illustrates.

EXAMPLE 11.2   THE SIGN TEST FOR PAIRED DATA

Scientists are searching for a noninvasive way to measure the health of tissue that has been cut off from blood flow for a period of time. One measure of tissue health is its acidity as measured by pH. Recent research has attempted to estimate tissue pH using a neural-network algorithm involving a large number of externally measured indicators. In an experiment to assess the performance of the algorithm, scientists blocked leg arteries of 12 rabbits, and after 1 hour measured the pH of the affected tissue directly while simultaneously obtaining estimates based on the neural-network algorithm. Among other things, they were interested in whether there was any bias in estimation: that is, are the estimated pH values systematically too high or low?

The scientists began by subtracting the actual pH from the estimated pH value for each rabbit. They used these as the responses, Y_i, $i = 1, \ldots, 12$. They assumed that these observations followed model (11.2). The data are shown in Table 11.1.

- **The Scientific Hypothesis.** The scientific hypothesis is that there is bias in estimating pH.
- **The Statistical Model.** The model is model (11.2), where θ is the population median of the difference between the actual and estimated pH.

TABLE 11.2 $P_B(b)$, $B \sim b(12, 0.5)$

b	0	1	2	3	4	5	6	7	8	9	10	11	12
$p_B(b)$	0.0002	0.0029	0.0161	0.0537	0.1209	0.1934	0.2256	0.1934	0.1209	0.0531	0.0161	0.0029	0.0002

- **The Statistical Hypotheses.** The null hypothesis states that there is no bias: The median difference is 0. The alternative hypothesis states that there is bias.

$$H_0: \quad \theta = 0$$
$$H_{a\pm}: \quad \theta \neq 0$$

- **The Test Statistic.** The test statistic is B, the number of differences greater than 0. Its observed value is $b^* = 8$.
- **The p-Value.** The exact p-value, $p\pm$, is given by Equation (11.3), where $B \sim b(12, 0.5)$. To compute $p\pm$, we can use the computer or Table A.1., in Appendix A to obtain the values of $p_B(b)$. These are displayed in Table 11.2. Since $p_B(b^*) = p_B(8) = 0.1209$, $p\pm$ is the sum of all probabilities less than or equal to 0.1209:

$$p\pm = 0.0002 + 0.0029 + 0.0161 + 0.0537 + 0.1209$$
$$+ 0.1209 + 0.0537 + 0.0161 + 0.0029 + 0.0002 = 0.3876$$

Based on this large p-value, there appears to be insufficient evidence to conclude there is a bias in estimation of pH using the neural-network algorithm.

To illustrate the calculations involved, we will now approximate $p\pm$ using the normal approximation. For computing p^+ and p_-, the observed values of the standardized test statistic are

$$z_u^* = \frac{8 - (0.5)(12) - 0.5}{\sqrt{(0.25)(12)}} = 0.866 \quad \text{and} \quad z_l^* = \frac{8 - (0.5)(12) + 0.5}{\sqrt{(0.25)(12)}} = 2.289$$

respectively. From this, and the normal table, we obtain $p^+ = 0.1932$, $p_- = 0.9890$, and $p\pm = 2\min(0.1932, 0.9890) = 0.3864$. Because the binomial distribution is symmetric for $p = 0.5$, the normal approximation with continuity correction is quite good for even small-sample sizes. ✦

Connection with the Test for a Population Proportion

If, in the formulation of the test for a population proportion presented in Chapter 6, we take $p = P(Y_i > \theta_0)$, $p_0 = 0.5$, and Y to be the test statistic B, we obtain the sign test. So we can say that the sign test is just a special case of the test for a population proportion.

How the Sign Test Compares with Classical Tests

When compared with classical, and specifically, normal-theory methods, distribution-free methods offer certain advantages and suffer from certain disadvantages. For the sign test, here are some to consider.

Advantages

- The sign test is very general in that it makes almost no assumptions about population distributions.
- The sign test is quite **robust** to departures from underlying assumptions, such as outliers. By this, we mean that it performs as advertised, giving accurate *p*-values.

Disadvantages

The primary disadvantage of the sign test is lower efficiency than classical methods when the data are from a known distribution. By efficiency, we mean the number of observations required to attain a given power. For example, for large samples, the sign test requires about 57% more observations to attain the same power as the appropriate normal-theory test when the data are normal. This is a considerable premium to pay for the insurance provided against violations of model assumptions.

11.4

ESTIMATION BASED ON THE SIGN TEST

We can use the sign test to develop point and interval estimators for the population median, θ, in model (11.2).

A Point Estimator

A point estimator can be obtained by reasoning as follows. If $\theta = \theta_0$, the distribution of the test statistic B is symmetric about its mean $n/2$. Therefore, an estimator of θ will be the amount $\hat{\theta}$ that we have to subtract from each data value Y_i so that the value of B computed from $Y_1 - \hat{\theta}, \ldots, Y_n - \hat{\theta}$ equals $n/2$. It turns out that this estimator, $\hat{\theta}$, is the median of the data values $Y_1, \ldots, Y_n$.

Confidence Intervals

A level L confidence interval for θ based on the sign test consists of all values θ_0 for which the test of

$$\begin{aligned} H_0: & \quad \theta = \theta_0 \\ H_{a\pm}: & \quad \theta \neq \theta_0 \end{aligned}$$

does not reject at the $\alpha = 1 - L$ significance level: that is, for which $p\pm \geq \alpha$.

An Exact Interval

In a practical sense, an exact level L interval can seldom be computed because of the discreteness of the binomial distribution, but exact intervals can be computed for levels close to L. One method for doing so is the following:

1. Find an integer k so that the value $\alpha_0 = 2P(X \geq k) = 2P(X \leq n - k)$ is as close to α as possible, where $X \sim b(n, 0.5)$.
2. Order the observations from smallest to largest, denoting the ordered values $Y_{(1)} \leq Y_{(2)} \leq \cdots \leq Y_{(n)}$.
3. A level $L_0 = 1 - \alpha_0$ confidence interval for θ is $(Y_{(n-k+1)}, Y_{(k)})$.

A Large-Sample Approximation

For large n, we may take k in step 1 to be the integer closest to

$$\frac{n}{2} + z_{(1+L)/2}\sqrt{\frac{n}{2}}$$

The interval is then computed as described in steps 2 and 3.

EXAMPLE 11.2   CONTINUED

A point estimator of the population median of the difference between the actual and estimated pH is the median of the y_i values shown in Table 11.1, which equals 0.007.

To illustrate the confidence interval computations, we will obtain both exact and large-sample level $L = 0.95$ intervals for the population median of the difference between the actual and estimated pH. From Table 11.2, we see that $2P(X \geq 10) = 2P(X \leq 2) = 0.0384$, and $2P(X \geq 9) = 2P(X \leq 3) = 0.1446$, so choosing $k = 10$ gives the value closest to $\alpha = 0.05$. Since the true α value is $\alpha_0 = 0.0384$, the level of the resulting confidence interval is $L_0 = 1 - 0.0384 = 0.9616$. Ordering the y_i in Table 11.1, we find a level 0.9616 confidence interval for θ is

$$(y_{(3)}, y_{(10)}) = (-0.004, 0.017)$$

To compute the large-sample level 0.95 interval, since $z_{0.975} = 1.96$, we take k to be the integer closest to

$$\frac{12}{2} + 1.96\sqrt{\frac{12}{4}} = 9.39$$

so that $k = 9$. The interval is then

$$(y_{(4)}, y_{(9)}) = (-0.001, 0.014)$$

Notice that by the computations done previously, the actual level of this interval is $1 - 0.1446 = 0.8554$.   ✦

RANK-BASED METHODS I: ONE- AND TWO-SAMPLE LOCATION PROBLEMS

Any variable that takes on values that can be ordered is called an **ordinal variable**. Quantitative variables (those that take on numerical values) are always ordinal, but so is any categorical variable for which the categories can be ordered. For example, possible responses to a questionnaire may be "strongly agree," "agree," "disagree," and "strongly disagree." These are categorical, but they can be ordered according to the degree of agreement they represent.

Data from any ordinal variable can be assigned **ranks** based on the ordering, from smallest to largest, of the variable's values. For example, if a quantitative variable has the data values 1.2, 3.7, 0.6, -1.1, and 9.7, the associated ranks are 3, 4, 2, 1, and 5. If the responses of three people to a questionnaire are "agree," "strongly disagree," and "disagree," the associated ranks (measuring the amount of agreement) are 3, 1, and 2.

Ties can be handled by taking averages. Suppose a quantitative variable has the data values 1.2, 3.7, 0.6, 3.7, 3.7, 9.7, -1.1, and 9.7. To assign ranks,

1. Sort the values from smallest to largest and assign the integer i to the ith number:

Sorted value	-1.1	0.6	1.2	3.7	3.7	3.7	9.7	9.7
Assigned integer	1	2	3	4	5	6	7	8

2. The rank for any value is the average of the ranks for all observations taking that value:

Sorted value	-1.1	0.6	1.2	3.7	3.7	3.7	9.7	9.7
Assigned integer	1	2	3	4	5	6	7	8
Rank	1	2	3	5	5	5	7.5	7.5

There is a large number of distribution-free tests based on the ranks of the data values. One of the most commonly used is the **Wilcoxon signed rank test**.

The Wilcoxon Signed Rank Test

- **The Statistical Model.** We assume data from model (11.2), where we make the additional assumption that the distribution model of the random error, ϵ, is symmetric about 0.[5] Note that under this assumption, θ is still the population median. In fact, if the population has a mean, θ is also the population mean (why?).

- **The Statistical Hypotheses.** The hypotheses to be tested are the same as those tested under the sign test. In particular, we will always take the null hypothesis to be H_0: $\theta = \theta_0$.

- **The Test Statistic.** To compute the test statistic, follow these steps:

  1. Center the observations by subtracting from each the population median under H_0. The resulting centered observations are $Y_i' = Y_i - \theta_0, i = 1, \ldots, n$.

  2. Compute the ranks of the absolute values of the centered observations: $R_i = \text{rank}(|Y_i'|)$, $i = 1, \ldots, n$. That is, if $|Y_{i_n}'|$ is the largest of all $|Y_i'|$, then $R_{i_n} = n$, if $|Y_{i_{n-1}}'|$ is the second largest of all $|Y_i'|$, then $R_{i_{n-1}} = n - 1$, and if $|Y_{i_1}'|$ is the smallest of all $|Y_i'|$, then $R_{i_1} = 1$.[6]

  3. The test statistic W is the sum of the ranks R_i for those i corresponding to positive Y_i' values:[7]

$$W = \sum_{\{i:Y_i' > 0\}} R_i$$

- **The p-Value.** Let w^* denote the observed value of the test statistic W. If the alternative hypothesis is H_{a+}: $\theta > \theta_0$, the p-value is $p^+ = P_0(W \geq w^*)$, where the notation P_0 signifies that the probability is computed under the assumption that H_0 is true. If the alternative hypothesis is H_{a-}: $\theta < \theta_0$, the p-value is $p_- = P_0(W \leq w^*)$. If the alternative hypothesis is $H_{a\pm}$: $\theta \neq \theta_0$, the p-value is $p\pm = 2\min(p^+, p_-)$.

    The distribution of W under H_0 is easily calculated. In the next example, we show how the p-value may be computed.

EXAMPLE 11.1   CONTINUED

Recall the test of grinding diameters from Example 11.1. Though there were 150 data values in that example, we will only use three of them in order to make the calculations manageable.

- **The Scientific Hypothesis.** The grinding-machine operators tend to grind parts slightly larger rather than slightly smaller than the target diameter.

---

[5]Even with this more restrictive assumption, the Wilcoxon procedure is still regarded as "distribution-free" because we do not assume a specific distribution model for the error term. But, as you can see, some "distribution-free" procedures, such as the sign test, are more "distribution-free" than others, such as the Wilcoxon.

[6]If this notation doesn't make sense to you, sneak a quick look at the next example, where this is done with numbers.

[7]There is nothing special about using the ranks corresponding to the positive values. We could equally well define the test statistic as the sum of the ranks corresponding to the negative values, adjusting the p-value formulas accordingly.

TABLE 11.3   Computing w^*, Example 11.1

Original data y_i	Centered data $y_i' = y_i - 0.75$	Absolute values $\|y_i'\|$	Ranks $r_i = \text{rank}(\|y_i'\|)$	Contribution to w^*
0.7533	0.0033	0.0033	2	2
0.7485	−0.0015	0.0015	1	0
0.7578	0.0078	0.0078	3	3

- **The Statistical Model.** The model is model (11.2), where we assume the distribution of ϵ is symmetric about 0. θ is then both the median and mean diameter, if the mean is defined, of the population of all ground parts.
- **The Statistical Hypotheses**

$$H_0: \quad \theta = 0.75$$
$$H_{a+}: \quad \theta > 0.75$$

- **The Test Statistic.** Table 11.3 summarizes the quantities necessary to compute w^*, the observed value of W. The rightmost column of Table 11.3 gives the contributions of each data value to w^*. Since only those ranks corresponding to the positive y_i' are summed, the contributions of the ranks corresponding to negative y_i' are set to 0. The observed value of W, w^*, is the sum of the values in the rightmost column: $w^* = 2 + 0 + 3 = 5$.
- **The p-Value.** The computation of the p-value is based on the **permutation distribution** of the test statistic. The permutation distribution of the test statistic is the distribution of all values of the test statistic that would have resulted under an appropriate permutation of the original data. For this problem, the permutation distribution is computed as follows.

  If H_0 is true, the Y_i' are independent and from the same distribution having median 0. Therefore, prior to sampling, each is equally likely to be positive or negative. In fact, because of the symmetry assumption, Y_i' and $-Y_i'$ have the same distribution, so it shouldn't matter if we base our test on (Y_1', Y_2', Y_3'), or on $(-Y_1', Y_2', Y_3')$, or on $(-Y_1', Y_2', -Y_3')$, or on any other rearrangement of the signs of the Y_i'. Table 11.4 shows the resulting values of W for each of the eight different possible selections of signs for the Y_i'.

  The first line of Table 11.4 corresponds to the observed data. All eight values of W in the rightmost column comprise the permutation distribution of W. The p-value is computed as the proportion of these permutation distribution values that are at least as large as the observed value $w^* = 5$. Since exactly two of the eight values (the first two) are at least as large as w^*, the p-value $= 2/8 = 0.25$.

  In computing the p-value this way, we are measuring how extreme the actually observed W value, w^*, is with respect to all the other values of the test statistic that under H_0, are equally valid. ◆

TABLE 11.4   Computing the Permutation Distribution of W, Example 11.1

Signs	Assumed Y_i'	Contribution to W	W
(Y_1', Y_2', Y_3')	$(0.0033, -0.0015, 0.0078)$	$(2, 0, 3)$	5
$(Y_1', -Y_2', Y_3')$	$(0.0033, 0.0015, 0.0078)$	$(2, 1, 3)$	6
$(Y_1', Y_2', -Y_3')$	$(0.0033, -0.0015, -0.0078)$	$(2, 0, 0)$	2
$(-Y_1', Y_2', Y_3')$	$(-0.0033, -0.0015, 0.0078)$	$(0, 0, 3)$	3
$(-Y_1', -Y_2', Y_3')$	$(-0.0033, 0.0015, 0.0078)$	$(0, 1, 3)$	4
$(Y_1', -Y_2', -Y_3')$	$(0.0033, 0.0015, -0.0078)$	$(2, 1, 0)$	3
$(-Y_1', Y_2', -Y_3')$	$(-0.0033, -0.0015, -0.0078)$	$(0, 0, 0)$	0
$(-Y_1', -Y_2', -Y_3')$	$(-0.0033, 0.0015, -0.0078)$	$(0, 1, 0)$	1

Tabulating p-Values

Most statistical computer packages will compute the p-value of the Wilcoxon test for you. However, there may be times when you do not have access to a computer. In that case, Table A.12, in Appendix A provides exact values of $P_0(W \le w^*)$, for $n = 3, 4, \ldots, 15$.

To understand how the entries to the table are computed, look again at the just-completed example in which we computed a p-value of 0.25. The values found in the two rightmost columns of Table 11.4 would not change even if we changed all the values of Y_i'.[8] This is a result of using the ranks of the observations. This fact makes it easy to tabulate all possible p-values for the Wilcoxon test, at least for small sample sizes.

For example, if $n = 3$, we see from Table 11.4 that W can assume the values 0 through 6. We can then easily compute from the rightmost column that

$$P_0(W \le 0) = 1/8$$
$$P_0(W \le 1) = 2/8$$
$$P_0(W \le 2) = 3/8$$
$$P_0(W \le 3) = 5/8$$
$$P_0(W \le 4) = 6/8$$
$$P_0(W \le 5) = 7/8$$
$$P_0(W \le 6) = 8/8$$

Large-Sample Test

When H_0 is true, the expected value and variance of W are $n(n + 1)/4$ and $n(n + 1)(2n + 1)/24$, respectively. For large n, the standardized test statistic

$$Z = \frac{W - n(n + 1)/4}{\sqrt{n(n + 1)(2n + 1)/24}}$$

[8]The order in which they occurred might change, but the values themselves would not.

will have approximately an $N(0, 1)$ distribution. If we standardize the observed value of the test statistic, w^*, in exactly the same way to obtain

$$z^* = \frac{w^* - n(n+1)/4}{\sqrt{n(n+1)(2n+1)/24}}$$

we can compute the approximate p-values

$$p^+ = P(Z \geq z^*), \qquad p_- = P(Z \leq z^*), \qquad p\pm = 2\min(p^+, p_-)$$

where Z is assumed $N(0, 1)$.

EXAMPLE 11.1   CONTINUED

Let's return to the grinding problem, using all 150 observations this time.

Since we have assumed that the underlying distribution is symmetric, we first look at a boxplot and histogram of the data to assess its symmetry. These plots reveal that the data are moderately skewed to the left, so we should be somewhat cautious in our interpretation of the results.

The computed value of W is $w^* = 7914$. The SAS statistical package gives the p-value, $P_0(W \geq 7914) = 7.09 \times 10^{-6}$. The normal approximation gives the standardized test statistic

$$z^* = \frac{7914 - (150)(151)/4}{\sqrt{(150)(151)(301)/24}} = 4.22$$

The resulting approximate p-value is

$$P(Z \geq 4.22) = 12.22 \times 10^{-6}$$

In either case, we clearly reject the null hypothesis.   ✦

Ties

It is generally assumed that the observations Y_i are from a continuous distribution model, which implies that no Y_i' should equal 0. However, in practice, we will sometimes find that $Y_i' = 0$. Should this happen, the zero values are discarded and n is redefined to be the number of nonzero Y_i'.

The continuity assumption also implies that there should be no ties (i.e., two or more identical Y_i' values). However, ties do occur in practice. When ties do occur, the usual practice is to use average ranks, as described earlier in this section.

When using the large-sample test for data with ties, average ranks should be used to compute W, and the denominator of the test statistic Z should be computed as

$$\left\{ \left[n(n+1)(2n+1) - 0.5 \sum_{j=1}^{g} t_j(t_j^2 - 1) \right] \Big/ 24 \right\}^{1/2}$$

TABLE 11.5 Data, Example 11.2

Rabbit	Actual pH	Estimated pH	pH Difference y_i Estimated−Actual	$\|y_i'\| = \|y_i\|$	Ranks r_i	Contribution to w^*
1	6.791	6.808	0.017	0.017	10.0	10.0
2	6.832	6.854	0.022	0.022	12.0	12.0
3	6.693	6.696	0.003	0.003	2.0	2.0
4	6.810	6.830	0.020	0.020	11.0	11.0
5	6.683	6.679	−0.004	0.004	3.0	0.0
6	6.661	6.675	0.014	0.014	9.0	9.0
7	6.655	6.642	−0.013	0.013	8.0	0.0
8	6.717	6.708	−0.009	0.009	5.5	0.0
9	6.746	6.755	0.009	0.009	5.5	5.5
10	6.722	6.721	−0.001	0.001	1.0	0.0
11	6.861	6.866	0.005	0.005	4.0	4.0
12	6.774	6.786	0.012	0.012	7.0	7.0

where g is the number of distinct values among the observations Y_i, and t_j is the number of observations that equal the jth distinct value.

The Wilcoxon Signed Rank Test for Paired Data

The Wilcoxon signed rank test may be used to test the median of the difference of the paired measurements, by first taking the difference of the paired data values as was done for the sign test. Of course, the symmetry assumption should first be checked on the differences before using the Wilcoxon test.

EXAMPLE 11.2 CONTINUED

Table 11.5 contains the data on actual and estimated pH for the experiment described in Example 11.2.

A boxplot and histogram show little evidence of asymmetry, so we feel confident in using the Wilcoxon test. The relevant quantities for conducting the test are summarized in Table 11.5. Notice that the tied data values are both assigned a rank of 5.5. Adding up the rightmost column, we see that $w^* = 60.5$. Referring to Table A.12 in Appendix A, we see that $p^+ = 0.046$ and $p_- = 0.984$, so that the p-value is $p\pm = 2\min(0.046, 0.954) = 0.092$. ◆

Estimation Based on the Wilcoxon Signed Rank Test

As with the sign test, we can use the Wilcoxon signed rank test to develop point and interval estimators for the population median, θ, in model (11.2).

A Point Estimator

To develop a point estimator of θ, we use the following equivalent formulation of the test statistic W when testing H_0: $\theta = \theta_0$:

The Wilcoxon signed rank statistic W is the number of the $n(n + 1)/2$ averages

$$\frac{Y_i + Y_j}{2}, \qquad 1 \leq i \leq j \leq n \tag{11.4}$$

that are greater than θ_0. The averages given by (11.4) are called **Walsh averages**.

The Walsh averages play the same role for the Wilcoxon signed rank test that the original data play for the sign test: The test statistic for the sign test is the number of observations greater than θ_0, and the test statistic for the Wilcoxon signed rank test is the number of Walsh averages greater than θ_0.

The Walsh averages also play the same role in constructing a point estimator of θ based on the Wilcoxon signed rank test as the original data do in constructing a point estimator of θ based on the sign test: The estimator based on the sign test is the median of the data, and the estimator based on the Wilcoxon signed rank test is the median of the Walsh averages.

Confidence Intervals

A level L confidence interval for θ based on the Wilcoxon signed rank test consists of all values θ_0 for which the test of

$$\begin{aligned} H_0: & \quad \theta = \theta_0 \\ H_{a^+}: & \quad \theta \neq \theta_0 \end{aligned}$$

does not reject at the $\alpha = 1 - L$ significance level: that is, for which $p\pm \geq \alpha$.

An Exact Interval.   Let $W_{(1)}^a \leq W_{(2)}^a \leq \cdots \leq W_{(n(n+1)/2)}^a$ denote the ordered Walsh averages. An exact symmetric level L confidence interval for θ is of the form $(W_{([n(n+1)/2]-k+1)}^a, W_{(k)}^a)$, where for $5 \leq n \leq 25$, k can be obtained from Table A.14 in Appendix A.

As with exact intervals based on the sign test, an exact level L interval cannot be computed for all possible levels L because of the discreteness of the distribution of W, but Table A.14 gives the values closest to the most commonly used values of L.

A Large-Sample Approximation.   For large n, we may take k to be the integer closest to

$$\frac{n(n + 1)}{4} + z_{(1+L)/2}\sqrt{\frac{n(n + 1)(2n + 1)}{24}}$$

An approximate level L interval is then $(W_{([n(n+1)/2]-k+1)}^a, W_{(k)}^a)$.

EXAMPLE 11.2   CONTINUED

A point estimator of the population median of the difference between the actual and estimated pH is the median of the Walsh averages of the 12 y_i values shown in Table 11.1. As there are $12(12 + 1)/2 = 78$ Walsh averages, we are unable to

TABLE 11.6 Walsh Averages, Example 11.2

Walsh average	Value	Walsh average	Value
$(y_1 + y_1)/2$	0.0170	$(y_1 + y_5)/2$	0.0065
$(y_1 + y_2)/2$	0.0195	$(y_2 + y_5)/2$	0.0090
$(y_2 + y_2)/2$	0.0220	$(y_3 + y_5)/2$	−0.0005
$(y_1 + y_3)/2$	0.0100	$(y_4 + y_5)/2$	0.0080
$(y_2 + y_3)/2$	0.0125	$(y_5 + y_5)/2$	−0.0040
$(y_3 + y_3)/2$	0.0030	$(y_1 + y_6)/2$	0.0155
$(y_1 + y_4)/2$	0.0185	$(y_2 + y_6)/2$	0.0180
$(y_2 + y_4)/2$	0.0210	$(y_3 + y_6)/2$	0.0085
$(y_3 + y_4)/2$	0.0115	$(y_4 + y_6)/2$	0.0170
$(y_4 + y_4)/2$	0.0200	$(y_5 + y_6)/2$	0.0050
		$(y_6 + y_6)/2$	0.0140

write them all here, so for demonstration purposes, we will restrict the data to the first 6 rabbits. Then there are $6(6+1)/2 = 21$ Walsh averages, which are displayed in Table 11.6.

The ordered observations are $w_{(1)}^a = -0.0040 < w_{(2)}^a = -0.0005 < \cdots < w_{(20)}^a = 0.0210 < w_{(21)}^a = 0.0220$. From Table A.14, we find that for $L = 0.969$, $k = 21$, and for $L = 0.937$, $k = 20$. Therefore, we obtain a level 0.969 confidence interval for θ as

$$(w_{(21-21+1)}^a, w_{(21)}^a) = (w_{(1)}^a, w_{(21)}^a) = (-0.0040, 0.0220)$$

and a level 0.937 confidence interval as

$$(w_{(21-20+1)}^a, w_{(20)}^a) = (w_{(2)}^a, w_{(20)}^a) = (-0.0005, 0.0210)$$

Although we would not advise using the large-sample interval for $n = 6$, we will compute it now to illustrate the calculations. A level 0.95 interval will take

$$k = \frac{6(6+1)}{4} + z_{0.975}\sqrt{\frac{6(6+1)((2)(6)+1)}{24}} = 19.8$$

Therefore, we will round k to 20, and the resulting interval is the same as the level 0.937 interval computed previously. ◆

One final note: Though the sign test and estimates based on it can be used in place of the Wilcoxon signed rank test, the latter is preferred when the assumption of symmetry is satisfied; it will provide a more powerful test and more precise estimators than the sign test.

The Wilcoxon Rank Sum Test

When we wish to compare the central locations of two independent populations, the Wilcoxon rank sum test is the appropriate rank-based analogue to the two sample t-test.

The Model

We assume that the ith data value from population 1 is

$$Y_{1,i} = \epsilon_{1,i}, \qquad i = 1, \ldots, n_1 \tag{11.5}$$

and that the ith data value from population 2 is

$$Y_{2,i} = \delta + \epsilon_{2,i}, \qquad i = 1, \ldots, n_2 \tag{11.6}$$

where the $\epsilon_{1,i}$ and the $\epsilon_{2,i}$ are independent and have the same continuous distribution. The parameter δ is a location shift, which means that the distribution of population 2 is the distribution of population 1 shifted δ units.

The Statistical Hypotheses

The null hypothesis is

$$H_0: \quad \delta = \delta_0$$

where δ_0 is a specific known value. If we take $\delta_0 = 0$, the null hypothesis is that both populations have identical distributions. The alternative hypothesis can be any of the one- or two-sided alternatives:

$$H_{a+}: \quad \delta > \delta_0$$
$$H_{a-}: \quad \delta < \delta_0$$
$$H_{a\pm}: \quad \delta \neq \delta_0$$

The Test Statistic

To compute the test statistic, we follow these steps:

1. Create the adjusted observations

$$Y'_{2,i} = Y_{2,i} - \delta_0, \qquad i = 1, \ldots, n_2$$

2. Rank all $n_1 + n_2$ values $Y_{1,i}$, $i = 1, \ldots, n_1$, and $Y'_{2,i}$, $i = 1, \ldots, n_2$, from smallest (rank 1) to largest (rank $n_1 + n_2$). Let $R_{2,i}$, $i = 1, \ldots, n_2$, denote the resulting ranks of the $Y'_{2,i}$.

3. The test statistic is the sum of the ranks belonging to the observations from population 2:[9]

$$V = \sum_{i=1}^{n_2} R_{2,i}$$

The *p*-Value

As with the one-sample Wilcoxon test, we will use a permutation distribution to compute the *p*-value of the test. We first note that if H_0 is true, the $Y_{1,i}$, $i = 1, \ldots, n_1$, and the $Y'_{2,i}$, $i = 1, \ldots, n_2$, have exactly the same distribution.

Suppose that H_{a+} is the alternative hypothesis. Then if H_{a+} is true, the $Y'_{2,i}$ will tend to be larger than the $Y_{1,i}$, so large values of the test statistic, V, will give evidence against H_0 and in favor of H_{a+}. Therefore, we can compute the *p*-value, p^+, as the proportion of all appropriate permutations of the data that give values of the test statistic, V, at least as large as v^*, the observed value of V.

If the alternative hypothesis is H_{a-}, the *p*-value, p_-, is the proportion of all appropriate permutations of the data that give values of the test statistic, V, at least as small as v^*. If the alternative hypothesis is $H_{a\pm}$, the *p*-value is $p\pm = 2\min(p^+, p_-)$.

What are the appropriate permutations of the data? They are all possible divisions of the ranks $1, 2, \ldots, n_1 + n_2$ into two sets: one consisting of n_1 of the ranks and the other consisting of the remaining n_2 ranks. There are

$$\binom{n_1 + n_2}{n_2} = \frac{(n_1 + n_2)!}{n_1! n_2!}$$

such permutations. For permutation i, the value, v_i^*, of the Wilcoxon statistic V is calculated by summing the ranks associated with the n_2 observations in the second set. The *p*-value p^+ is calculated as the proportion of the v_i^* as great or greater than the observed value v^* and the *p*-value p_- is calculated as the proportion of the v_i^* as small or smaller than the observed value v^*.

EXAMPLE 11.3   THE WILCOXON RANK SUM TEST

A company makes die-cast automotive parts. It recently replaced two of its die-casting machines with machines using dies of a different design. Soon after the replacement, production personnel began to suspect that the new dies did not last as long as the old dies. Table 11.7 shows cycles to failure for four randomly selected dies of the new type and two randomly selected dies of the old type.

---

[9]There is nothing special about summing the ranks of the observations from population 2. We could equally well define the test statistic as the sum of the ranks of the observations from population 1, adjusting the *p*-value formulas accordingly.

TABLE 11.7   Data, Example 11.3

	Cycles to failure	Ranks
Old Dies	9477	4
	13581	6
New Dies	7651	2
	8337	3
	6989	1
	9568	5

- **The Scientific Hypothesis.** The scientific hypothesis is that the new dies don't last as long as the old dies.
- **The Statistical Model.** We will assume that the statistical model governing the old dies is given by (11.5) and that the statistical model governing the new dies is given by (11.6). The response is the lifetime of the die: the number of cycles until die failure. If there were sufficient data, we would check the validity of the assumption that the two distributions are merely translates of each other: that is, that they have the same shape. As it is, no check will be meaningful with only six observations.
- **The Statistical Hypotheses.** The statistical hypotheses are

$$H_0: \quad \delta = 0$$
$$H_{a_-}: \quad \delta < 0$$

Notice that H_{a_-} is the scientific hypothesis.

- **The Test Statistic.** To compute the value of the test statistic, we first obtain a combined ranking of all observations in both samples. This is done in the last column of Table 11.7. The observed value of the test statistic is then the sum of the ranks for the data from population 2:

$$v^* = 2 + 3 + 1 + 5 = 11$$

- **The p-Value.** Table 11.8 lists all $\binom{6}{4} = 15$ possible assignments of the ranks into groups 1 and 2 and the values of the test statistic they produce.

  The p-value of the test is the proportion of these 15 V values at least as small as $v^* = 11$. Since there are only two such values (the last two), the p-value is $p_- = 2/15 = 0.1\overline{33}$. ◆

Most statistical computer packages will compute the p-value for the Wilcoxon rank sum test. Table A.13, in Appendix A, which gives relevant probabilities of $P(V \leq v)$ for various values of v and small values of n_1 and n_2, may also be used to compute p-values. For large samples, a normal approximation may be used, as outlined in what follows.

TABLE 11.8 Wilcoxon's Rank Sum Statistic Computed for All Assignments of Ranks 1 to 6 to Groups of Sizes 2 and 4

Group 1	Group 2	V
1, 2	3, 4, 5, 6	18
1, 3	2, 4, 5, 6	17
1, 4	2, 3, 5, 6	16
2, 3	1, 4, 5, 6	16
1, 5	2, 3, 4, 6	15
2, 4	1, 3, 5, 6	15
1, 6	2, 3, 4, 5	14
2, 5	1, 3, 4, 6	14
3, 4	1, 2, 5, 6	14
3, 5	1, 2, 4, 6	13
2, 6	1, 3, 4, 5	13
3, 6	1, 2, 4, 5	12
4, 5	1, 2, 3, 6	12
4, 6	1, 2, 3, 5	11
5, 6	1, 2, 3, 4	10

Large-Sample Approximation

It can be shown that if H_0 is true, the mean and variance of V are $n_2(n_1 + n_2 + 1)/2$ and $n_1 n_2(n_1 + n_2 + 1)/12$, respectively. If n_1 and n_2 are large, the standardized test statistic

$$Z = \frac{V - n_2(n_1 + n_2 + 1)/2}{[n_1 n_2(n_1 + n_2 + 1)/12]}$$

has approximately an $N(0, 1)$ distribution. If we standardize the observed value of the test statistic, v^*, in exactly the same way to obtain

$$z^* = \frac{v^* - n_2(n_1 + n_2 + 1)/2}{[n_1 n_2(n_1 + n_2 + 1)/12]}$$

we can compute the approximate p-values

$$p^+ = P(Z \geq z^*), \qquad p_- = P(Z \leq z^*), \qquad p\pm = 2\min(p^+, p_-)$$

where Z is assumed $N(0, 1)$.

Ties

Ties are handled exactly as for the Wilcoxon signed rank test: by taking average ranks. When using the large-sample test when there are ties, then, in addition to using average ranks to compute V, the denominator of the test statistic Z should be computed as

$$\left\{ n_1 n_2 \left[(n_1 + n_2 + 1) - \sum_{j=1}^{g} t_j (t_j^2 - 1)/(n_1 + n_2)(n_1 + n_2 - 1) \right] \middle/ 12 \right\}$$

where g is the number of distinct values among the observations Y_i, and t_j is the number of observations that equal the jth distinct value.

Estimation Based on the Wilcoxon Rank Sum Test

We can use the Wilcoxon rank sum test to develop point and interval estimators for the location shift, δ, in model (11.6).

A Point Estimator

To develop a point estimator of δ, we use the following equivalent formulation of the test statistic V when testing $H_0: \delta = \delta_0$:

The Wilcoxon rank sum statistic V equals $n_2(n_2 + 1)/2$ plus the number of the $n_1 n_2$ differences

$$Y_{2,i} - Y_{1,j}, \qquad 1 \le i \le n_2,\ 1 \le j \le n_1 \tag{11.7}$$

that are greater than δ_0.

     Using reasoning similar to that used in the sign and Wilcoxon signed rank cases, we take the point estimator of δ to be the amount the $Y_{2,i}$ must be shifted so that the test statistic V regards the two samples as coming from the same population. The resulting estimator, $\hat{\delta}$, is the median of the $n_1 n_2$ differences $Y_{2,i} - Y_{1,j}$, $1 \le i \le n_2,\ 1 \le j \le n_1$.

Confidence Intervals

A level L confidence interval for δ based on the Wilcoxon rank sum test consists of all values δ_0 for which the test of

$$H_0: \quad \delta = \delta_0$$
$$H_{a^+}: \quad \delta \ne \delta_0$$

does not reject at the $\alpha = 1 - L$ significance level: that is, for which $p\pm \ge \alpha$.

An Exact Interval.   Let $D_{(1)} \le D_{(2)} \le \cdots \le D_{(n_1 n_2)}$ denote the differences (11.7) listed in ascending order. An exact level L confidence interval for δ is of the form $(D_{(n_1 n_2 - k + 1)}, D_{(k)})$, where for $5 \le n_1, n_2 \le 12$, k can be obtained from Table A.15.

    As with exact intervals based on the sign test and Wilcoxon signed rank tests, an exact level L interval cannot be computed for all possible levels L because of the discreteness of the distribution of D, but Table A.15 gives the values closest to the most commonly used values of L.

A Large-Sample Approximation.   For large n_1 and n_2, we may take k to be the integer closest to

$$\frac{n_1 n_2}{2} + z_{(1+L)/2} \sqrt{\frac{n_1 n_2 (n_1 + n_2 + 1)}{12}}$$

in the confidence interval formula $(D_{(n_1 n_2 - k + 1)}, D_{(k)})$.

EXAMPLE 11.3   CONTINUED

Consider again the cycles to failure of the six dies in Table 11.7. We want to estimate the difference in location, δ, between the population distributions of the cycles to failure of the old and the new dies. To do this, we form the differences displayed in Table 11.9.

The point estimator of δ is

$$\hat{\delta} = \text{median}(-6592, -5930, -5244, -4013, -2488, -1826, -1140, 91)$$

$$= [-4013 + (-2488)]/2 = -3250.5$$

Looking at Table A.15, we find that the value of the constant $k = 8$ is associated with a confidence level $L = 0.866$. Therefore, a level 0.886 confidence interval for δ is

$$(d_{((2)(4)-8+1)}, d_{(8)}) = (d_{(1)}, d_{(8)}) = (-6592, 91)$$

Although we would not advise using the large sample interval for $n_1 = 2$ and $n_2 = 4$, we will compute it now to illustrate the calculations. A level 0.95 interval will take

$$k = \frac{(2)(4)}{2} + z_{0.975} \sqrt{\frac{(2)(4)(2 + 4 + 1)}{12}} = 8.2$$

Therefore, we will round k to 8, and the resulting interval is the same as the level 0.866 interval computed previously.   ◆

TABLE 11.9   Differences, Example 11.3

$7651 - 9477 = -1826$	$7651 - 13581 = -5930$
$8337 - 9477 = -1140$	$8337 - 13581 = -5244$
$6989 - 9477 = -2488$	$6989 - 13581 = -6592$
$9568 - 9477 = 91$	$9568 - 13581 = -4013$

RANK-BASED METHODS II: THE RELATIONSHIP BETWEEN TWO VARIABLES

Spearman Correlation

Recall that the Pearson correlation was defined in Chapter 7 as a measure of the strength of linear association between two quantitative variables. If (X_i, Y_i), $i = 1, \ldots, n$, denote n measurements taken on the variables X and Y, the Pearson correlation between X and Y computed from these data is

$$r = \frac{1}{n-1} \sum_{i=1}^{n} X_i' Y_i'$$

where

$$X_i' = \frac{X_i - \bar{X}}{s_X} \quad \text{and} \quad Y_i' = \frac{Y_i - \bar{Y}}{s_Y}$$

are the standardized data.

There are at least two problems with the Pearson correlation as a measure of the association between two variables:

- It only measures the strength of the **linear** association between the variables.
- It is not resistant to outliers.

Spearman's rho, also called the **Spearman rank correlation coefficient,** is a measure of association that helps remedy these two problems. It is also very easy to compute. Instead of dealing with the values of the original two variables, X and Y, we form their ranks RX and RY. Spearman's rho, r_s, is just the Pearson correlation between RX and RY.

EXAMPLE 11.4   SPEARMAN CORRELATION

To illustrate the Spearman correlation, we revisit the data on fuel consumption versus equivalence ratio, considered in Example 7.2 of Chapter 7. The data are in Table 11.10.

Figure 11.1 shows scatterplots of fuel consumption versus equivalence ratio and of the ranks of fuel consumption versus the ranks of equivalence ratio for these data. The first plot shows the association between fuel consumption and equivalence ratio to be nonlinear, and hence the Pearson correlation, which equals a respectable 0.9332, is not the most appropriate summary of that association. The right scatterplot shows a more nearly linear association for the ranks

TABLE 11.10   Fuel Consumption and Equivalence Ratio (left two columns) and Their Ranks (right two columns), Example 11.4

Fuel consumption	Equivalence ratio	Ranks of fuel consumption	Ranks of equivalence ratio
98.0	0.64	1	1
100.0	0.65	2	2
100.1	0.66	3	3
102.0	0.74	6	4
101.0	0.75	4	5
103.0	0.77	7	7
103.2	0.76	8	6
101.9	0.80	5	8
104.0	0.81	9	9
105.0	0.88	10	10
105.5	0.90	11	11
105.6	0.91	12	12
106.0	0.92	13	13
110.0	1.00	14	14
111.0	1.02	15	15
115.0	1.04	16	16
121.5	1.14	17	17
123.5	1.16	18	18
136.0	1.24	19	19

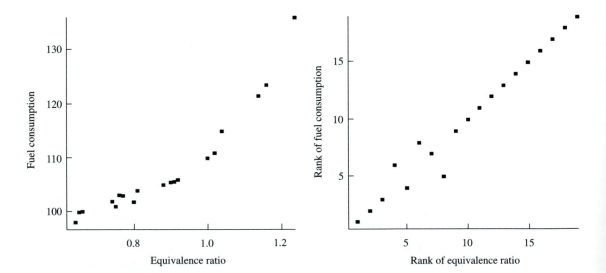

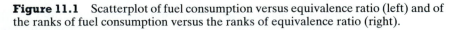

Figure 11.1   Scatterplot of fuel consumption versus equivalence ratio (left) and of the ranks of fuel consumption versus the ranks of equivalence ratio (right).

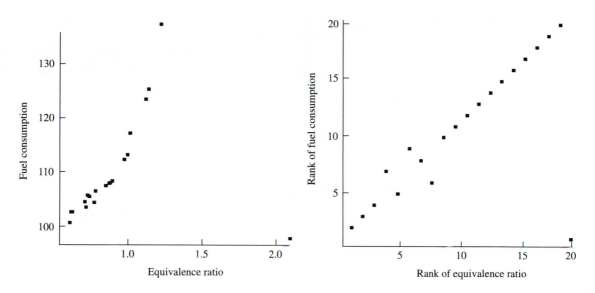

Figure 11.2   Scatterplot of fuel consumption versus equivalence ratio (left) and of the ranks of fuel consumption versus the ranks of equivalence ratio (right) when an outlier is added to the data.

of the variables. The stronger linear association is reflected in the higher Pearson correlation, 0.9842, between the ranks of fuel consumption and equivalence ratio. This Pearson correlation between the ranks is exactly the Spearman rank correlation.

To illustrate the effect of outliers on both the Pearson and Spearman correlations, we added an outlier to the data. The added observation has a fuel consumption of 95 and an equivalence ratio of 2.1. The resulting outlier can be seen in the lower right corner of the left scatterplot in Figure 11.2. The right scatterplot of the ranks shows that this data value is still an outlier, but is less extreme. The outlier greatly affects the Pearson correlation of fuel consumption and equivalence ratio, reducing it from 0.9332 to 0.2319. In contrast, the outlier has less effect on the Spearman correlation, which declines from 0.9842 to 0.7008.   ◆

Because of the problems Pearson correlation has with outliers and nonlinearity, we recommend computing both the Pearson and Spearman correlation routinely. Widely different values serve as a warning to look more closely at the data.

What the Spearman Correlation Measures

We know that the Pearson correlation measures the strength of linear association between two variables in a set of data, but what exactly does the Spearman correlation measure? A hint may come from considering the circumstances under which $|r|$ and $|r_s|$ equal 1. It can be shown mathematically that $|r|$ will equal 1 if and only if all data points lie on a line in the X–Y plane that is neither horizontal nor vertical. If the line has positive slope, $r = 1$ and if it has negative slope, $r = -1$.

Recall that r_s is the Pearson correlation between the ranks of the X data values and the ranks of the Y data values. So r_s will equal 1 when those ranks lie on a line with positive slope. This will occur if and only if the rank of each X data value is the same as the rank of its Y counterpart. This means that the smallest X value and the smallest Y value are together, the second smallest X value and the second smallest Y value are together, and so on. Similarly, r_s will equal -1 if and only if those ranks lie on a line with negative slope. This will occur if and only if the rank of each X data value is the reverse of the rank of its Y counterpart. This means that the smallest X value and the largest Y value are together, the second smallest X value and the second largest Y value are together, and so on.

When the ranks of the data lie on a line, the data are said to have a **monotone** association. Data which themselves lie on a line (i.e., which have a linear association) must have a monotone association. The top pair of scatterplots in Figure 11.3 show an example of positive monotone nonlinear association (left) and the corresponding ranks that lie on a line with positive slope.[10] The middle pair of scatterplots in Figure 11.3 show an example of negative monotone nonlinear association (left) and the corresponding ranks that lie on a line with negative slope.[11] The bottom pair of scatterplots show nonlinear nonmonotone association. The Pearson correlations are (top to bottom): 0.9183, -0.9373, and 0.1006, and the Spearman correlations are 1, -1, and 0.1693, respectively.

Just as the Pearson correlation measures the strength of linear association between two variables in a set of data, the Spearman correlation measures the strength of monotone association.

Hypothesis Tests for Independence Using the Spearman Correlation

From our study of the Pearson correlation, we know that it estimates a population correlation, which is a measure of the strength of linear association between two variables in the population.

If we assume that the original data, (X_1, Y_1), $(X_2, Y_2), \ldots, (X_n, Y_n)$, are observed values of two continuous random variables (X, Y), we can mathematically obtain the population quantity that the Spearman correlation estimates. Unfortunately, this population quantity is both complicated and difficult to interpret. Therefore, rather than interpret a test of the significance of the observed Spearman correlation, $|r_s|$, in terms of this parameter, we will consider the test in terms of the independence of the random variables X and Y. That is, the null hypothesis is

$$H_0: \quad X \text{ and } Y \text{ are independent}$$

---

[10] In fact, the slope is $+1$.

[11] In fact, the slope is -1.

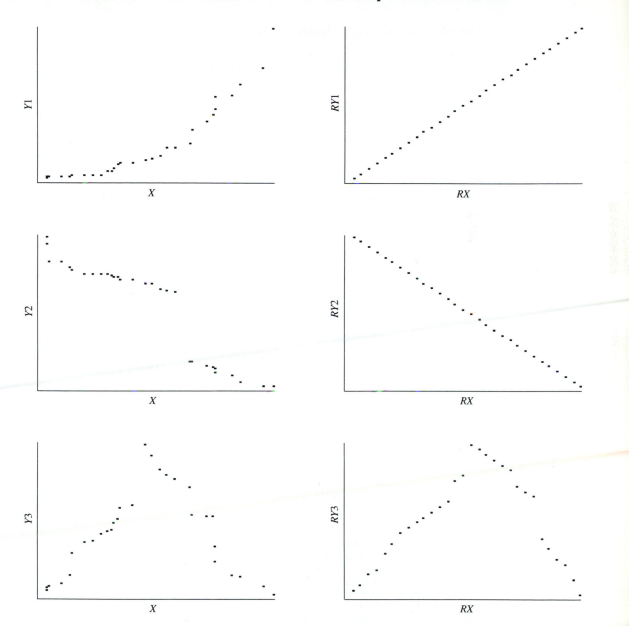

Figure 11.3 Examples of, top: positive monotone association (left) and corresponding ranks (right); middle: negative monotone association (left) and corresponding ranks (right); bottom: nonlinear nonmonotone association (left) and corresponding ranks (right). The Pearson correlations are (top to bottom): 0.9183, −0.9373, and 0.1006, and the Spearman correlations are 1, −1, and 0.1693, respectively.

while the alternative hypotheses we will study are

$$H_{a+}: \quad X \text{ and } Y \text{ are positively associated}$$

$$H_{a-}: \quad X \text{ and } Y \text{ are negatively associated}$$

$$H_{a\pm}: \quad X \text{ and } Y \text{ are not independent}$$

The test statistic r_s provides evidence against H_0 and in favor of H_{a+} if its value is large, against H_0 and in favor of H_{a-} if its value is small (i.e., negative and large in absolute value), and against H_0 and in favor of $H_{a\pm}$ if its absolute value is large. Therefore, if r_s^* is the observed value of the Spearman correlation, the p-values of the tests are computed as

$$p^+ = P_0(r_s \geq r_s^*)$$

$$p_- = P_0(r_s \leq r_s^*)$$

$$p\pm = P_0(|r_s| \geq |r_s^*|)$$

where P_0 is the probability computed under the assumption that H_0 is true.

If H_0 is true, we may easily compute the sampling distribution of r_s, particularly if n is small. Suppose $n = 3$. Then if H_0 is true, the ranks of the X values are independent of the ranks of the Y values. Table 11.11 shows all six possible pairings of ranks of three bivariate data points, along with the value of r_s for each pairing.

Since the ranks of X and Y are independent, each of the six pairings occurs with probability $1/6$, and this gives the sampling distribution of r_s under H_0:

$$P(r_s = 1.0) = P(r_s = -1.0) = 1/6$$

$$P(r_s = 0.5) = P(r_s = -0.5) = 1/3$$

TABLE 11.11   Spearman Correlations for Each Possible Pairing of Ranks of Three Bivariate Observations

Pairing	X Rank	Y Rank	r_s	Pairing	X Rank	Y Rank	r_s
1	1	1	1.0	4	1	2	−0.5
	2	2			2	3	
	3	3			3	1	
2	1	1	0.5	5	1	3	−0.5
	2	3			2	1	
	3	2			3	2	
3	1	2	0.5	6	1	3	−1.0
	2	1			2	2	
	3	3			3	1	

Since r_s takes on only the four values ± 1.0 and ± 0.5, the p-value for the alternative $H_{a\pm}$ can take on only two values:

- If $|r_s^*| = 0.5$, then all possible values of $|r_s|$ are greater than or equal to $|r_s^*|$, so

$$P_0(|r_s| \geq |r_s^*|) = 1.0$$

- If $|r_s^*| = 1.0$, then

$$P_0(|r_s| \geq |r_s^*|) = 1/6 + 1/6 = 1/3$$

Exercise 11.1 asks you to show that each of the p-values for the alternatives H_{a+} and H_{a-} can take on only four values.

Since, under H_0, the distribution of r_s is symmetric about 0, the p-value for testing $H_{a\pm}$ is computed as $p\pm = 2 \min(p_-, p^+)$.

The table in Table A.10 in Appendix A, page 917, gives values of p^+ for use in testing independence for samples of size 10 and less. For larger samples, an approximate test of independence may be obtained from the fact that $r_s \sqrt{(n-2)/(1-r_s^2)}$ has approximately a t_{n-2} distribution under the assumption of independence.

EXAMPLE 11.4   CONTINUED

Consider again the data on fuel consumption and equivalence ratio in Table 11.10. Since there are $n = 19$ observations, an approximate test of

H_0:   fuel consumption and the equivalence ratio are independent

H_{a+}:   fuel consumption and the equivalence ratio are positively associated

is obtained by finding the proportion of a t_{17} population that exceeds the observed value of the test statistic:

$$t^* = r_s \sqrt{\frac{n-2}{1-r_s^2}} = 0.9842 \sqrt{\frac{14}{1-0.9842^2}} = 22.919$$

This proportion, which is the p-value, equals 1.6×10^{-14}, which is very strong evidence of a positive relation.

If we introduce the artificial outlier as we did earlier, the Spearman correlation declines from 0.9842 to 0.7008, which reduces the test statistic from 22.919 to 4.168 and increases the p-value to 0.0003, still strong evidence of a positive relation.

For comparison purposes, consider the test for H_0: $\rho = 0$ versus H_{a+}: $\rho > 0$ based on the Pearson correlation. Without the artificial outlier, the Pearson correlation is 0.9332, and the test statistic equals 10.707, giving a p-value 3×10^{-9}, very strong evidence in favor of H_{a+}. With the artificial outlier, the Pearson correlation drops to 0.2319, the test statistic drops to 1.011, and the p-value jumps to 0.1627, giving us little reason to question the truth of H_0!   ✦

We close this section with one final word about the hypothesis test of independence based on the Spearman correlation. Because it measures the strength of monotone association, we can expect the test based on $|r_s|$ to effectively detect such association. However, it may be poor at detecting other kinds of nonindependence. A scatterplot of the data should help to identify cases where this test will be ineffective: An example is in the bottom left plot of Figure 11.3. This is yet another indication of the importance of graphing the data.

11.7

RANK-BASED METHODS III: THE ONE-WAY MODEL

The Kruskal-Wallis Test

Recall the one-way effects model described in Chapter 9:

$$Y_{ij} = \mu + \tau_i + \epsilon_{ij}, \qquad j = 1, \ldots, n_i; \; i = 1, \ldots, k \tag{11.8}$$

where Y_{ij} is the jth response from population i, μ is an overall location measure, τ_i is the effect due to population i, and ϵ_{ij} is the random error associated with observation Y_{ij}. As in Chapter 9, we assume that the τ_i sum to zero, and that the ϵ_{ij} are independent random variables having the same distribution. However, we do not assume the ϵ_{ij} have a normal distribution. We assume only that they have the same continuous distribution.

When we want to test for differences in population effects in model (11.8), the appropriate rank-based analogue of the F test of Chapter 9 is the **Kruskall-Wallis test.** We summarize the Kruskall-Wallis procedure as follows:

- **The Statistical Model.** We assume data from model (11.8).
- **The Statistical Hypotheses.** The hypotheses to be tested are

$$H_0: \quad \tau_1 = \tau_2 = \cdots = \tau_k = 0$$
$$H_a: \quad \text{Not all the population effects } \tau_i \text{ are } 0$$

- **The Test Statistic.** To compute the test statistic, follow these steps:
  1. Rank all $n = \sum_i \sum_j n_{ij}$ observations, Y_{ij}. Let R_{ij} denote the rank of Y_{ij}.
  2. Compute

$$R_{i\cdot} = \sum_{j=1}^{n_i} R_{ij}, \qquad \bar{R}_{i\cdot} = \frac{1}{n_i} \sum_{j=1}^{n_i} R_{ij}, \qquad \bar{R}_{\cdot\cdot} = \frac{1}{n} \sum_{i=1}^{k} \sum_{j=1}^{n_i} R_{ij} = \frac{n+1}{2}$$

3. The test statistic H is

$$H = \frac{12}{n(n+1)} \sum_{i=1}^{k} n_i (\bar{R}_{i.} - \bar{R}_{..})^2 = \frac{12}{n(n+1)} \sum_{i=1}^{k} \frac{R_{i.}^2}{n_i} - 3(n+1)$$

In computing H, note that the quantity $\sum_{i=1}^{k}(\bar{R}_{i.} - \bar{R}_{..})^2$ is the sum of squares model found in the ANOVA table obtained from the one-way model when the responses are replaced by their ranks.

- **The p-Value.** Let h^* denote the observed value of the test statistic H. The p-value is $p = P_0(H \geq h^*)$, where the notation P_0 signifies that the probability is computed under the assumption that H_0 is true.

    For small k and n_i, tables of critical values of H have been developed, but they are rather extensive and we do not present them here. Rather, we take two different approaches:

    ○ **Exact p-Values.** We use the computer to calculate exact p-values. A description of how this is done is found later in the chapter, when we discuss permutation tests.

    ○ **Large-Sample Approximation.** When sample sizes are large ($n_i \geq 5$ for all i is a common rule of thumb), the distribution of H under the null hypothesis can be approximated by a χ^2 distribution with $k-1$ degrees of freedom. This means that an approximate p-value is $P(\chi_{k-1}^2 \geq h^*)$, the area under a χ_{k-1}^2 density at or above the observed value of the test statistic.

Ties

It is generally assumed that the observations Y_{ij} are from a continuous distribution model, which implies that there should be no ties (i.e., no two Y_{ij} should be equal). However, ties do occur in practice. When ties do occur, the usual approach is to use average ranks, as described earlier.

When using the large sample test when there are ties, it is common practice to use a modified test statistic H', which is computed as

$$H' = \frac{H}{1 - \sum_{m=1}^{g} t_m(t_m^2 - 1)/(n^3 - n)}$$

where H is computed using average ranks, g is the number of distinct values among the observations Y_{ij}, and t_m is the number of observations that equal the mth distinct value.

EXAMPLE 11.5   THE KRUSKAL-WALLIS TEST

Recall Example 9.1, which described an experiment to test the performance of three treatments for Benign Prostate Hyperplasia (BPH), an enlargement of the prostate gland in men. The treatments are a drug treatment, a standard surgical procedure, and a new microwave treatment. The response is the increase in urine flow. The data are as follows:

TABLE 11.12   Prostate Experiment Data and Their Ranks

Treatment	Increase in urine flow, Y_{ij}	Ranks of Y_{ij}
Drug	1.1	1
Drug	1.4	3
Drug	1.3	2
Drug	1.9	5
Drug	1.6	4
Microwave	2.9	8
Microwave	3.7	11
Microwave	3.4	9.5
Microwave	3.4	9.5
Microwave	2.8	7
Microwave	2.2	6
Surgery	4.0	12
Surgery	5.2	15
Surgery	5.0	14
Surgery	4.7	13

- **The Scientific Hypothesis.** The scientific hypothesis is that the microwave procedure is competitive with standard drug and surgical treatments.
- **The Statistical Model.** We assume data from model (11.8), with $k = 3$ populations corresponding to the three treatments.
- **The Statistical Hypotheses.** The hypotheses to be tested are

$$H_0: \quad \tau_1 = \tau_2 = \tau_3 = 0$$

$$H_a: \quad \text{Not all the population effects } \tau_i \text{ are } 0$$

- **The Test Statistic.** If we denote those receiving the drug treatment, microwave treatment, and surgery as populations 1, 2, and 3, respectively, then $n_1 = 5, n_2 = 6, n_3 = 4, n = 15$, and

$$R_{1.} = 1 + 3 + 2 + 5 + 4 = 15; \qquad R_{2.} = 8 + 11 + 9.5 + 9.5 + 7 + 6 = 51;$$

$$R_{3.} = 12 + 15 + 14 + 13 = 54$$

so that

$$H = \frac{12}{(15)(16)} \left(\frac{15^2}{5} + \frac{51^2}{6} + \frac{54^2}{4} \right) - 3(15 + 1)$$

$$= 12.375$$

Since there is one tie, we will use the adjusted value of H, H'. To compute H', we note that there are 14 distinct values among the 15 responses, so $g = 14$. Further, all except two responses occur only once, so $t_m = 1$, for all but one m, and the other $t_m = 2$. Since, for all 14 of the t_m that equal 1, $t_m(t_m^2 - 1) = 0$, we have

$$H' = \frac{12.375}{1 - 2(2^2 - 1)/(15^3 - 15)} = 12.397$$

- **The p-Value.** Later in the chapter, we will show how to compute the p-value of this test, which equals 6.34×10^{-6}. For illustration purposes, we will use the large-sample approximation here, even though not all samples have sample size greater than 5. The approximate p-value is $P(\chi_2^2 \geq 12.397) = 0.002$. Based on this result, we reject the null hypothesis and conclude that not all τ_i equal 0. ✦

Friedman's Test

Recall the randomized complete block (RCB) model described in Chapter 9:

$$Y_{ij} = \mu + \tau_i + \gamma_j + \epsilon_{ij}, \qquad i = 1, \ldots, k; \; j = 1, \ldots, b \tag{11.9}$$

Here, there are k populations and b blocks, μ is the overall mean, τ_i is the effect due to population i, γ_j is the effect due to block j and the ϵ_{ij} are random errors. As in Chapter 9, we assume that

$$\sum_{i=1}^{k} \tau_i = \sum_{j=1}^{b} \gamma_j = 0$$

Rather than assume that the ϵ_{ij} have a normal distribution, as was done in Chapter 9, we assume only that they have the same continuous distribution.

When we want to test for differences in population effects in model (11.9), the appropriate rank-based analogue of the F test of Chapter 9 is **Friedman's test.** We summarize Friedman's test procedure as follows:

- **The Statistical Model.** We assume data from model (11.9).
- **The Statistical Hypotheses.** The hypotheses to be tested are

$$H_0: \quad \tau_1 = \tau_2 = \cdots = \tau_k = 0$$
$$H_a: \quad \text{Not all the population effects } \tau_i \text{ are } 0$$

- **The Test Statistic.** To compute the test statistic, follow these steps:

  1. Within block j, rank all k observations, Y_{ij}, $i = 1, \ldots, k$. Let R_{ij} denote the resulting rank of Y_{ij}.

2. Compute

$$R_{i\cdot} = \sum_{j=1}^{b} R_{ij}, \qquad \bar{R}_{i\cdot} = \frac{1}{b}\sum_{j=1}^{b} R_{ij}, \qquad \bar{R}_{\cdot\cdot} = \frac{1}{kb}\sum_{i=1}^{k}\sum_{j=1}^{b} R_{ij} = \frac{k+1}{2}$$

3. The test statistic Q is

$$Q = \frac{12b}{k(k+1)}\sum_{i=1}^{k}(\bar{R}_{i\cdot} - \bar{R}_{\cdot\cdot})^2 = \frac{12}{bk(k+1)}\sum_{i=1}^{k} R_{i\cdot}^2 - 3b(k+1)$$

In computing Q, note that the quantity $b\sum_{i=1}^{k}(\bar{R}_{i\cdot} - \bar{R}_{\cdot\cdot})^2$ is the population sum of squares found in the ANOVA table obtained from the RCB model when the responses, Y_{ij}, are replaced by their ranks, R_{ij}.

- **The p-Value.** Let q^* denote the observed value of the test statistic Q. The p-value is $p = P_0(Q \geq q^*)$, where the notation P_0 signifies that the probability is computed under the assumption that H_0 is true.

  For small k and b, tables of critical values of Q have been developed, but they are rather extensive and we do not present them here. Rather, we take two different approaches:

  ○ **Exact p-Values.** We use the computer to calculate exact p-values. A description of how this is done is found later in the chapter, when we discuss permutation tests.

  ○ **Large-Sample Approximation.** When there are a sufficient number of blocks ($b \geq 5$ is a common rule of thumb), the distribution of Q under the null hypothesis can be approximated by a χ^2 distribution with $k - 1$ degrees of freedom. This means that an approximate p-value is $P(\chi^2_{k-1} \geq q^*)$, the area under a χ^2_{k-1} density at or above the observed value of the test statistic.

Ties

It is generally assumed that the observations Y_{ij} are from a continuous distribution model, which implies that there should be no ties. However, ties do occur in practice. When ties do occur, the usual solution is to use average ranks within each block, as described earlier.

When using the large sample test when there are ties, then we use a modified test statistic Q', which is computed as

$$Q' = \frac{12\sum_{i=1}^{k}(R_{i\cdot} - b\bar{R}_{\cdot\cdot})^2}{bk(k+1) - \sum_{j=1}^{b}\left\{\sum_{m=1}^{g_j} t_{mj}^3 - k\right\}\Big/(k-1)}$$

TABLE 11.13   Watch-Assembly Data with Ranks

Assembly method	Assembler				
	1	2	3	4	5
1	2.28 (y_{11})	3.77 (y_{12})	2.62 (y_{13})	3.14 (y_{14})	2.41 (y_{15})
	1 (r_{11})	1 (r_{12})	1 (r_{13})	1 (r_{14})	1 (r_{15})
2	2.50 (y_{21})	4.02 (y_{22})	3.05 (y_{23})	3.45 (y_{24})	2.90 (y_{25})
	2 (r_{21})	3 (r_{22})	2 (r_{23})	2 (r_{24})	3 (r_{25})
3	2.61 (y_{31})	3.95 (y_{32})	3.12 (y_{33})	3.62 (y_{34})	2.74 (y_{35})
	3 (r_{31})	2 (r_{32})	3 (r_{33})	3 (r_{34})	2 (r_{35})

where g_j is the number of distinct values among the observations in block j, and t_{mj} is the number of observations that equal the mth distinct value.

EXAMPLE 11.6   FRIEDMAN'S TEST

We will use Friedman's test on the watch-assembly data of Chapter 9. Recall that five assemblers were given one watch to assemble with each of three different assembly methods. In this problem, assemblers are blocks and assembly methods are treatments. The response is assembly time. It is desired to compare mean assembly times for the three assembly methods. Table 11.13 shows the recorded times, y_{ij}, and their ranks, r_{ij}.

- **The Scientific Hypothesis.** The scientific hypothesis is that there is no difference in mean assembly times for the three assembly methods.
- **The Statistical Model.** We assume data from RCB model (11.9), with $k = 3$ populations corresponding to the three treatments, and $b = 5$ blocks corresponding to the five assemblers.
- **The Statistical Hypotheses.** The hypotheses to be tested are

$$H_0: \quad \tau_1 = \tau_2 = \tau_3 = 0$$
$$H_a: \quad \text{Not all the population effects } \tau_i \text{ are } 0$$

- **The Test Statistic.** From Table 11.13, we see that

$$r_{1.} = 1+1+1+1+1 = 5; \qquad r_{2.} = 2+3+2+2+3 = 12; \qquad r_{3.} = 13$$

so that

$$q^* = \frac{12}{(5)(3)(3+1)}(5^2 + 12^2 + 13^2) - 3(5)(3+1) = 7.6$$

- **The p-Value.** Later in the chapter, we will show how to compute the p-value of this test, which equals 0.024. Here, we will use the large-sample approximation. The approximate p-value is $P(\chi_2^2 \geq 7.6) = 0.023$. Based on this result, we reject the null hypothesis and conclude that not all τ equal 0.   ✦

11.8

ADVANTAGES AND DISADVANTAGES OF RANK-BASED TESTS

When compared with classical, and, specifically, normal-theory methods, rank-based methods offer certain advantages and suffer from certain disadvantages.

Advantages

- Rank-based methods make fewer assumptions about population distributions.
- Rank-based methods are more robust to departures from underlying assumptions, such as outliers.
- If the original data are ordinal but not numeric (e.g., if the values of the variable are "weak," "moderate," and "strong"), rank-based procedures are appropriate; normal-theory methods may not be.
- At least for simple models, such as we study in this chapter, many rank-based methods are nearly as efficient as their normal-theory counterparts when the data are normal, and are often more efficient when the data are nonnormal.

Disadvantages

As with the sign test, the primary disadvantage of rank-based methods is lower efficiency than normal-theory methods when the data are normal. By efficiency, we mean the number of observations required to attain a given power. For example, for large samples, the Wilcoxon signed rank and rank sum tests require about 5% more observations to attain the same power as the appropriate normal-theory tests when the data are normal. Although these tests are far more efficient than the sign test, remember that they require more assumptions, and that the 5% premium can still prove substantial if the data are expensive to obtain.

11.9

PERMUTATION DISTRIBUTIONS: A DIFFERENT PARADIGM FOR INFERENCE

Throughout our study of inference, we have emphasized that the source of randomness in the data resides in sampling from a population. And from that randomness, we argued, arise the kinds of probability calculations that enable us to compute level L confidence intervals or find a *p*-value. With the introduction of rank-based tests in the last section, we have introduced a new way of looking at the source of randomness, and with this change, it is time to reassess and extend our ideas about inference.

Recall that in Chapter 3, we studied two types of designed studies that could result in statistical inference: controlled experiments and observational studies. Both types of studies may obtain data by selecting a set of entities, called sampling units, from a larger population. The data are observations taken on the sampling units. The idea of sampling is to obtain a set of sampling units representative of the population from which they are taken, so that the results can be generalized to the population with some accuracy. Taking a probability sample also allows us to quantify the accuracy of the results.

Controlled experiments are studies in which treatments are assigned to the sampling units, now called experimental units, and the resulting responses observed. In contrast, in observational studies, the response and any "treatments" result solely from observing characteristics of the sampling units.

There can be interplay between sampling and experiments, which largely determines the scope of the results. For example, if an experimenter wants experimental results to be applicable to a larger population, she will use probability sampling methods to obtain a sample of experimental units that is representative of the entire population of such units.

All this has already been covered in Chapter 3. What we want to do here is to refine these notions and introduce some new ones. We will distinguish three methods for conducting a study, each of which results in a different rationale for inference and a different scope to which the results of inference can be applied. These methods are based on

- The type of study: controlled experiment or observational study.
- The method for selecting the units on which observations are taken.
- If the study is a controlled experiment, the method for assigning treatments to experimental units.

In order to make these ideas definite, we will apply each to the Wilcoxon rank sum test of location.

Method 1: Observational Study with Probability Sampling

In an observational study with probability sampling, the sampling units are obtained from the target population(s) by a probability sampling method and inference is made to that population. The rationale for inference is the randomness provided by the sampling method. The scope of the inference is to the population(s) sampled from. Any observed differences indicate an association, but a cause cannot be assigned.

For example, suppose we want to study the relation between regular exercise and blood-cholesterol level. To do so, we obtain a random sample of regular exercisers and another random sample of nonexercisers. Suppose that, using the Wilcoxon rank sum test, we find the exercise group has a significantly lower median cholesterol level.

Because of the random sampling, we can legitimately extend this result to the populations of exercisers and nonexercisers from which we sampled. So it is correct to conclude the population of exercisers willing to participate in the study has lower median cholesterol level than the population of nonexercisers willing to participate in the study. However, because we did not control the assignment of the treatment (exercise or not) to sampling units (subjects), we cannot conclude that exercise is responsible for the lower cholesterol levels.

Method 2: Controlled Experiment with Probability Sampling

By a controlled experiment with probability sampling, we mean that treatments are assigned to experimental units by the experimenter, and that the experimental units are selected from a population of such units by a probability sampling method. The rationale for the inference is the assignment of treatments to experimental units and the random selection of experimental units. Because the experimental units are randomly sampled, we may extend the results to the population(s) sampled. Because of the assignment of treatments to experimental units, we may conclude that any observed differences are caused by the treatments.

To continue the example, suppose that from a population of nonexercisers willing to participate in a study of the effect of exercise on cholesterol levels (i.e., they are willing to take the required treatment), we randomly select 50 people. We then randomly assign 25 to an exercise regime and leave the remaining 25 to their own devices. After 6 months, we measure the change in cholesterol level for each individual, and, using the Wilcoxon rank sum test, we find that the exercise group has a significant downward change of median cholesterol level relative to the nonexercise group.

Because of the random sampling, we can legitimately extend this result to the population of those willing to participate in the study. Further, because we assigned treatments to experimental units, we can conclude that the exercise regime is the cause of this difference.

Method 3: Controlled Experiment without Probability Sampling

By a controlled experiment without probability sampling, we mean a controlled experiment in which the experimental units are not sampled from a population of such units by a probability sampling method. We will confine our study of such experiments to those with more than one treatment: the only case in which we may obtain inference.

In order to justify inference, the treatments must be assigned to experimental units by a probabilistic method determined by the experimenter. Here the rationale for inference is the random assignment of treatments to experimental units. Because of the assignment of treatments to experimental units, we may make inference to the experimental units in the experiment, but because these do not constitute a random sample from a population, we may not extend inference beyond the units in the experiment. Because of the assignment of treatments to experimental units, we may conclude that any observed differences are caused by the treatments.

Most often, in this situation, the experimental units constitute a **convenience sample:** a sample of units taken because it was convenient to do so, or, perhaps because it was impossible to obtain a probability sample. For example, in many experiments conducted by university researchers in the social sciences, the experimental units are undergraduate or graduate students convenient to the experimenter, instead of a random sample of the target population.

To continue the example, suppose that the experimenter teaches an introductory biology course who as part of their course assignment must participate in the experiment. Suppose there are 50 nonexercisers in the class. From those 50, the professor randomly assigns 25 to an exercise regime and leaves the remaining 25 to their own devices. After 6 months, he measures the change in cholesterol level for each individual, and, using the Wilcoxon rank sum test, finds that the exercise group has a significant downward change of median cholesterol level relative to the nonexercise group.

Because treatments were assigned at random to the experimental units, and because the p-value is based on the permutation distribution of the Wilcoxon statistic, the professor can conclude that for this set of experimental units, the exercise regime is the cause of this difference. However, he cannot extend the results to a larger population because no random sampling was done to justify such an extension.

11.10

PERMUTATION TESTS

The Two-Sample Pitman Test

In the past two sections, we have seen and learned a number of things.

- We have seen that the Wilcoxon, Kruskall-Wallis, and Friedman tests are called rank-based tests because the data are transformed to ranks prior to computing the test statistic or the p-value.
- We have seen that the p-values of these tests are computed by comparing them with the permutation distribution of the test statistic: the set of all test statistic values obtained by performing an appropriate set of permutations of the ranks.
- We have learned that when the p-value is computed using a permutation distribution, inference to the experimental units in the experiment can still be done even if the units were not randomly selected from a population of units.

Conceptually, there is no reason why ranks have to be used to perform a permutation test. In fact the idea for such tests using raw data, and not ranks, goes back at least to Fisher and Pitman in the 1930s. There is, however, a practical reason why, until recently, permutation tests have largely been confined to rank-based applications. To see why, consider the problem of comparing the locations of two groups of observations.

TABLE 11.14   The Sum Statistic Computed for All Assignments of 6 Die-Failure Times to Groups of Sizes 2 and 4

Group 1	Group 2	U
6989,7651	8337,9477,9568,13581	40963
6989,8337	7651,9477,9568,13581	40277
6989,9477	7651,8337,9568,13581	39137
7651,8337	6989,9477,9568,13581	39615
6989,9568	7651,8337,9477,13581	39046
7651,9477	6989,8337,9568,13581	38475
6989,13581	7651,8337,9477,9568	35033
7651,9568	6989,8337,9477,13581	38384
8337,9477	6989,7651,9568,13581	37789
8337,9568	6989,7651,9477,13581	37698
7651,13581	6989,8337,9477,9568	34371
8337,13581	6989,7651,9477,9568	33685
9477,9568	6989,7651,8337,13581	36558
9477,13581	6989,7651,8337,9568	32545
9568,13581	6989,7651,8337,9477	32454

EXAMPLE 11.3   CONTINUED

We will go back to the data on the failure of dies discussed in Example 11.3 and displayed in Table 11.7. Let us use the Wilcoxon rank sum statistic to perform the test, but without transforming to ranks first.

Let's call the test statistic U, and compute it as the sum of all observations in group 2. The observed value of the test statistic is then

$$u^* = 7561 + 8337 + 6989 + 9568 = 32545$$

To calculate the p-value, we need to find the permutation distribution of U, which in this case is the set of values of U obtained from all $\binom{6}{4} = 15$ possible assignments of the observations into groups 1 and 2. These assignments, and the permutation distribution of U are displayed in Table 11.14.

The p-value is the proportion of the 15 values from the permutation distribution that are at least as small as the observed value, $u^* = 32545$. Since only the values 32545 and 32454 qualify, the p-value is $p_- = 2/15 = 0.1\overline{33}$. Though it needn't always be so, in this case we obtain the same p-value as we did in the rank sum test. ✦

Now compare Tables 11.8 and 11.14. If we changed the cycles to failure for some or all of the dies, Table 11.14, and particularly the permutation distribution of U would change. However, Table 11.8 and the permutation distribution of V would not change at all, because Table 11.8 is not based on the data, but merely on permutations of ranks. What this means is that once it is tabulated, the permutation distribution of V, or of any other rank-based test for that matter, can be used for any set of data.

On the other hand, if we base the permutation test on the raw data, we have to compute the permutation distribution anew for each set of data. Until the recent advent of affordable high-speed computers, this was an impossible task. Now, however, it is feasible to perform permutation tests on test statistics computed from raw data, and it will become even more feasible and commonly done in the future.[12]

> **DEFINITION**
>
> **Permutation tests** are tests in which the p-value of the test is computed by comparing the observed value of the test statistic with a permutation distribution of the test statistic consisting of all values of the test statistic obtained by suitable permutations of the data values.

The permutation test based on the test statistic U, which we have just illustrated in Example 11.3, is sometimes called the **two-sample Pitman test**.[13] The Wilcoxon signed rank and rank sum tests and the two-sample Pitman test are all instances of permutation tests.

To understand the reasoning behind permutation tests, reconsider the last example.

EXAMPLE 11.3   CONTINUED

Let's revisit the two-sample Pitman test for the die-failure times. The null hypothesis is that the distribution of failure times for the old dies is exactly the same as for the new dies. If H_0 is true, then the six failure times all come from the same distribution, and their appearance in the observed pattern with respect to old and new dies is simply a matter of chance: Any other pattern of failure times with respect to the old and new dies is equally likely to have been observed. The values of the test statistic from all these equally likely patterns constitute the permutation distribution.   ✦

This example points up a key assumption on which permutation tests are based:

A KEY ASSUMPTION FOR PERMUTATION TESTS

Under H_0, all "suitable permutations" of the data must be equally likely.

You may be wondering how the two-sample Pitman test compares with the two-sample t-test you studied in Chapter 6. In fact, the permutation test can be conducted using the two-sample t-test statistic instead of the sum of the observations in group 2.

---

[12] This is the point Efron is making in the quote at the beginning of the chapter.

[13] It is named after the Australian statistician E. J. G. Pitman, who in the 1930s was the first to explain the full implications of permutation tests.

The surprising thing is that the resulting tests turn out to be exactly the same! In fact, the two-sample Pitman test is preferred because it involves less computation.

In general, the permutation test based on the t statistic is preferred to the standard t test for two other reasons as well:

- The p-value of the permutation test is always correct regardless of the underlying distribution. The t-test relies on a normality assumption.
- When the data are from a controlled experiment in which treatments are randomly assigned to experimental units, but the units themselves are not a random sample, the permutation test still provides inference to that set of experimental units. As there is now no population model, the hypotheses have to be changed. The null hypothesis becomes, for example, "There is no difference in responses observed due to the treatment assigned," meaning that had the other treatment been assigned the experimental unit, the same response would have been observed. The alternative hypothesis could be "There is a difference due to the treatment assigned" (two-sided) or "The response will be larger if treatment 1 is assigned" (one possible one-sided alternative).

As a result of these advantages, the permutation test is the "gold standard" against which other tests, such as the t-test, are measured. In fact, in the 1930s, the eminent British statistician R. A. Fisher used the similarity of the t-test to the permutation test as a justification for the t-test!

Fisher's Exact Test

Recall the discussion of two-way tables in Chapter 7, and of the development of the χ^2 test of the hypotheses

$$H_0: \quad \text{row and column variables are independent}$$
$$H_a: \quad \text{row and column variables are not independent}$$

In 1935 R. A. Fisher introduced a test for these hypotheses, known today as **Fisher's exact test.** Fisher's exact test is perhaps the best-known of all permutation tests. Unlike the approximate χ^2 test, which requires large samples, Fisher's exact test gives exact p-values no matter what the sample size.

We will introduce Fisher's exact test using a 2×2 table, and the notation in Table 11.15.

Suppose, first of all, that the marginal totals, $Y_{\cdot 1}$, $Y_{\cdot 2}$, $Y_{1 \cdot}$, and $Y_{2 \cdot}$, are known prior to taking the data.[14] To indicate that we are assuming the marginal totals fixed, we will denote them with lowercase letters: $y_{1 \cdot}$, $y_{2 \cdot}$, $y_{\cdot 1}$, and $y_{\cdot 2}$. With these assumptions, we need to know the value in only one cell of the 2×2 table to fill in the rest of the table—try it yourself! For convenience, we'll assume that the $(1, 1)$ cell will be the one that we'll try to fill in.

---

[14]This is unlikely in practice, but bear with us for a bit.

TABLE 11.15   The General 2 × 2 Table

	Column		
Row	1	2	Totals
1	Y_{11}	Y_{12}	$Y_{1.}$
2	Y_{21}	Y_{22}	$Y_{2.}$
Totals	$Y_{.1}$	$Y_{.2}$	n

It can be shown that if H_0 is true, then the probability of obtaining exactly y_{11} observations in the (1, 1) cell is

$$p(y_{11}) = \frac{y_{1.}!\,y_{.1}!\,y_{2.}!\,y_{.2}!}{n!\,y_{11}!\,(y_{1.} - y_{11})!\,(y_{.1} - y_{11})!\,(y_{2.} - y_{.1} + y_{11})!} \tag{11.10}$$

where $\max\{0,\, y_{.1} - y_{2.}\} \le y_{11} \le \min\{y_{1.}, y_{.1}\}$. Note that under H_0, this distribution does not depend on any unknown parameters, such as p_{11} or p_{21}. Therefore, we can use it to evaluate the *p*-value of the test. To do so, we will introduce two one-sided alternative hypotheses.[15] These are

H_{a+}:   There is a positive association between row and column variables

H_{a-}:   There is a negative association between row and column variables

H_{a+} may be taken to mean that observations having level 1 of the row variable tend to also have level 1 of the column variable. Under the alternative hypothesis H_{a+}, we expect large values of Y_{11}. The *p*-value of the test of H_0 versus H_{a+} is therefore the probability of observing Y_{11} values at least as large as the value, y_{11}, that was actually observed. This probability is $\sum_{k=y_{11}}^{\min\{y_{1.}, y_{.1}\}} p(k)$.

By a similar argument, under the alternative hypothesis H_{a-}, we expect small values of Y_{11}. The *p*-value of the test of H_0 versus H_{a-} is the probability of observing Y_{11} values as smaller or smaller than the value, y_{11}, that was actually observed. This probability is $\sum_{k=\max\{0, y_{.1}-y_{2.}\}}^{y_{11}} p(k)$.

The *p*-value for the two-sided alternative hypothesis, H_a, is given by summing all the probabilities among $p(k)$, $k = \max\{0, y_{.1} - y_{2.}\}, \ldots, \min\{y_{1.}, y_{.1}\}$, which are as small or smaller than $p(y_{11})$.

Now, the amazing thing is that the same test is valid if only one set of marginal totals is known prior to taking the data. This is the situation in the study of the relation of gender to attitudes on sexual harassment described in Example 7.13 in Chapter 7. There it is known that there are 50 males and 50 females in the study.

The same test is also valid if neither set of marginal totals is known, as is the case in the following example.

---

[15] The hypothesis H_a is two-sided.

EXAMPLE 11.7   FISHER'S EXACT TEST

Last year, the Mathematical Sciences Department at a well-known university received 15 applications for a computer job. Of these, there were six white males, two white females, three black males, and four black females. The data are shown in Table 11.16.

Affirmative-action investigators monitoring the university's hiring practices want to know if disproportionate numbers of applications come from white males and black females. In terms of Table 11.16, this becomes a test of a positive association between gender and race:

H_0:   Gender and race are independent

H_{a+}:   There is a positive association between gender and race

From Equation (11.10), we see that the range of values for Y_{11} is $\max\{0, y_{.1} - y_{2.}\} = \max\{0, 8 - 6\} = 2$, through $\min\{y_{1.}, y_{.1}\} = \min\{9, 8\} = 8$.

Plugging the values $y_{11} = 2, 3, \ldots, 8$ into Equation (11.10), we get the probabilities in Table 11.17.

Since $y_{11} = 6$ was observed, the p-value of the Fisher's exact test of H_0 versus H_{a+} is

$$p(6) + p(7) + p(8) = 0.1958 + 0.0336 + 0.0014 = 0.2308$$

TABLE 11.16   Classification of Applicants by Gender and Race

Gender	Race White	Black	Total
Male	6	3	9
Female	2	4	6
Total	8	7	15

TABLE 11.17   Distribution of Y_{11} in Table 11.16 under H_0: Example 11.7

y_{11}	$p(y_{11})$
2	0.0056
3	0.0783
4	0.2937
5	0.3916
6	0.1958
7	0.0336
8	0.0014

The large p-value means that there is insufficient evidence in these data to conclude that there is a positive association between gender and race.

Had a two-sided test been desired, the p-value would have been calculated by summing all probabilities as small or smaller than $p(6) = 0.1958$. This sum turns out to be

$$p(2) + p(3) + p(6) + p(7) + p(8) = 0.0056 + 0.0783 + 0.1958 + 0.0336 + 0.0014$$

$$= 0.3147 \quad \blacklozenge$$

Fisher's exact two-sided test can also be used in general $r \times c$ tables, though one-sided tests no longer make sense for larger tables.

Hand calculation of p-values in Fisher's exact test for moderate or large cell counts is not feasible. The computer can do the calculations for you, though computation time may become excessive with large numbers of cells and observations. For larger cell counts, the Pearson χ^2 test is a good choice.

A Generalized Wilcoxon Signed Rank Test

The Wilcoxon signed rank test can be generalized to a "signed test" using the raw data by applying the test statistic to the original centered observations instead of their ranks. That is, the test statistic is

$$G = \sum_{\{i: Y_i' > 0\}} Y_i'$$

This test statistic measures the overall "weight" of positive data among all observations. The resulting test is known as a **one-sample Pitman test.**

EXAMPLE 11.1   CONTINUED

We will apply this one-sample Pitman test to the data from Example 11.1 consisting of diameters of ground parts. The scientific hypothesis, the statistical model and statistical hypotheses are given in the initial description of Example 11.1. Note that the assumption of symmetry is crucial here. If the assumption is satisfied, large values of the test statistic will give evidence of against H_0 and in favor of H_a. However, the same results could be mistakenly obtained from right-skewed data even if there is no location shift.

To keep computations manageable, we will look only at the three observations given in Table 11.3. The observed value of the test statistic, g^*, may be obtained from Table 11.3 by adding up all positive values of y_i': $g^* = 0.0033 + 0.0078 = 0.0111$. This is summarized in the first line of Table 11.18.

The resulting p-value is the proportion of the eight values in the permutation distribution that are at least as large as $g^* = 0.0111$. There are two such values, so the p-value is $p^+ = 2/8 = 0.25$. $\blacklozenge$

TABLE 11.18   Computing the Permutation Distribution of G, Example 11.1

Signs	Assumed Y_i'	Contribution to G	G
(Y_1', Y_2', Y_3')	$(0.0033, -0.0015, 0.0078)$	$(0.0033, 0.0000, 0.0078)$	0.0111
$(Y_1', Y_2', -Y_3')$	$(0.0033, -0.0015, -0.0078)$	$(0.0033, 0.0000, 0.0000)$	0.0033
$(Y_1', -Y_2', Y_3')$	$(0.0033, 0.0015, 0.0078)$	$(0.0033, 0.0015, 0.0078)$	0.0126
$(-Y_1', Y_2', Y_3')$	$(-0.0033, -0.0015, 0.0078)$	$(0.0000, 0.0000, 0.0078)$	0.0078
$(-Y_1', -Y_2', Y_3')$	$(-0.0033, 0.0015, 0.0078)$	$(0.0000, 0.0015, 0.0078)$	0.0093
$(Y_1', -Y_2', -Y_3')$	$(0.0033, 0.0015, -0.0078)$	$(0.0033, 0.0015, 0.0000)$	0.0048
$(-Y_1', Y_2', -Y_3')$	$(-0.0033, -0.0015, -0.0078)$	$(0.0000, 0.0000, 0.0000)$	0.0000
$(-Y_1', -Y_2', -Y_3')$	$(-0.0033, 0.0015, -0.0078)$	$(0.0000, 0.0015, 0.0000)$	0.0015

A Generalized Kruskal-Wallis Test

It is easy to develop a permutation test version of the Kruskal-Wallis test using the raw data rather than ranks. Suppose there are k populations, that the number of observations from population i is n_i, and that the total number of observations is n. We assume the data are given by model (11.8). To perform the permutation test of

$$H_0: \quad \tau_1 = \tau_2 = \cdots = \tau_k = 0$$
$$H_a: \quad \text{Not all the population effects } \tau_i \text{ are } 0$$

follow these steps:

1. Choose a test statistic. Choosing a test statistic is an important task. One natural choice for the present problem is the Kruskal-Wallis test statistic, H, computed with the actual data values, Y_{ij}, taking the place of the ranks, R_{ij}, in the formulas. We will use H here.

2. Compute the value of the test statistic for the original data. Call the resulting value h^*.

3. For each distinct permutation that assigns one set of n_1 of the Y_{ij} to sample 1, another set of n_2 of the Y_{ij} to sample 2, and so on, compute the value of the test statistic, H. Let h_m denote the value of H belonging to the mth permutation.

4. The p-value of the test is the proportion of the h_m values that are greater than or equal to h^*.

Table 11.14 shows an example of the distinct permutations in the two-sample case. In general, with k populations, n_i observations from population i, and a total of n observations, there will be

$$M = \frac{n!}{n_1! n_2! \cdots n_k!}$$

distinct permutations.

Finally, note that if we use the ranks, R_{ij}, of the data in place of the raw data, Y_{ij}, in this test, we get the exact Kruskal-Wallis p-value, as opposed to the χ^2 approximation.

A Generalized Friedman Test

It is also easy to develop a permutation test version of the Friedman test using the raw data rather than ranks. Suppose there are k populations and b blocks. We assume the data are given by model (11.9). To perform the permutation test of

$$H_0: \quad \tau_1 = \tau_2 = \cdots = \tau_k = 0$$

$$H_a: \quad \text{Not all the population effects } \tau_i \text{ are } 0$$

follow these steps:

1. Choose a test statistic. One natural choice for the present problem is the Friedman test statistic, Q, computed with the actual data values, Y_{ij}, taking the place of the ranks, R_{ij}, in the formulas. We will use Q here.
2. Compute the value of the test statistic for the original data. Call the resulting value q^*.
3. For this model, permutations consist of permuting the Y_{ij} separately within each block. For each distinct permutation, compute the value of the test statistic, Q. Let q_m denote the value of Q corresponding to the m th permutation.
4. The p-value of the test is the proportion of the q_m values that are greater than or equal to q^*.

With k populations, and b blocks, there will be $k!$ permutations within each block, resulting in $M = (k!)^b$ distinct permutations.

EXAMPLE 11.8   GENERALIZED FRIEDMAN TEST

We illustrate the permutations involved in Friedman's test with an example. Table 11.19 shows the original data and the $7 = (2!)^3 - 1$ additional permutations of data from a RCBD with $k = 2$ treatments and $b = 3$ blocks.

For the original data, $y_{1.} = 3.1 + 2.2 + 5.2 = 10.5$ and $y_{2.} = 4.7 + 8.4 + 5.8 = 18.9$, so

$$q^* = \frac{12}{(3)(2)(2+1)}(10.5^2 + 18.9^2) - (3)(3)(2+1) = 284.64$$

For permutation 2, we get

$$q_2 = \frac{12}{(3)(2)(2+1)}(11.1^2 + 18.3^2) - (3)(3)(2+1) = 278.40$$

Similarly, we find that

$$q_3 = 266.45, \qquad q_4 = 270.13, \qquad q_5 = 278.40,$$
$$q_6 = 266.45, \qquad q_7 = 270.13, \qquad q_8 = 284.64$$

TABLE 11.19   Permutations for Friedman's Test, Example 11.8

	(Original Data) Permutation 1		Permutation 2		Permutation 3		Permutation 4	
	Treatment		Treatment		Treatment		Treatment	
Block	1	2	1	2	1	2	1	2
1	3.1	4.7	3.1	4.7	3.1	4.7	4.7	3.1
2	2.2	8.4	2.2	8.4	8.4	2.2	2.2	8.4
3	5.2	5.8	5.8	5.2	5.2	5.8	5.2	5.8

	Permutation 5		Permutation 6		Permutation 7		Permutation 8	
	Treatment		Treatment		Treatment		Treatment	
Block	1	2	1	2	1	2	1	2
1	4.7	3.1	4.7	3.1	3.1	4.7	4.7	3.1
2	8.4	2.2	2.2	8.4	8.4	2.2	8.4	2.2
3	5.2	5.8	5.8	5.2	5.8	5.2	5.8	5.2

Therefore, the p-value for this test is $2/8 = 0.25$.

We make a few final points:

- Using the ranks R_{ij} computed within each block, instead of the Y_{ij}, results in an exact p-value for Friedman's test.
- It is not necessary to use the test statistic Q. Using $\sum_{i=1}^{k} Y_{i\cdot}^2$ will give exactly the same results. We use Q so that the results will match the Friedman statistic if the ranks are used.
- There is clearly symmetry in the calculation of the test statistic for the different permutations. In fact, we need only compute half the permutations, as the others are mirror images. This fact can be used to cut the computation time on large data sets. ✦

Sometimes Permutation Tests Are Not Appropriate

Permutation tests are not applicable to every hypothesis testing problem, as the next example shows.

EXAMPLE 11.9   COMPARING VARIANCES

One common test that we have not presented thus far in the text is a test for the equality of variances of two populations. The usual test is based on the ratio of variances from two samples: one from each population. The problem is that this test is extremely sensitive to departures from normality, so its use is limited in practice.

Such a situation seems ideal for a permutation test, which would not depend on the underlying distribution of the populations. In fact, some authors have argued that we can just use the ratio of sample variances as the test statistic. If there are n_1 observations in the sample from population 1 and n_2 observations in the sample from population 2, the permutation distribution would be created by obtaining all allocations of the observations into two sets of n_1 and n_2 observations, respectively, and computing the test statistic for each allocation.

However, whether this is a reasonable procedure depends on the model for the data.[16] One model for which the suggested procedure works, has the ith data value from population 1 generated as

$$X_{1,i} = \eta_{1,i}, \qquad i = 1, \ldots, n_1 \tag{11.11}$$

and the ith data value from population 2 as

$$X_{2,i} = \gamma \eta_{2,i}, \qquad i = 1, \ldots, n_2 \tag{11.12}$$

where γ is a model parameter, and the $\eta_{1,i}$ and the $\eta_{2,i}$ are independent and have the same continuous distribution. Let's assume that the common variance of the $\eta_{1,i}$'s and $\eta_{2,i}$'s is σ_η^2. Then the variance of population 1 is $\sigma_{X_1}^2 = \sigma_\eta^2$, and the variance of population 2 is $\sigma_{X_2}^2 = \gamma^2 \sigma_\eta^2$. A test of the equality of variances then becomes a test of

$$H_0: \quad \gamma = 1$$

versus one of

$$H_{a+}: \quad \gamma > 1$$
$$H_{a-}: \quad \gamma < 1$$
$$H_{a\pm}: \quad \gamma \neq 1$$

If this model holds, we can reduce this problem to a location problem by taking logarithms of the responses, and then apply an appropriate test statistic to the transformed data. If we use natural logarithms, we would get the model given by (11.5) and (11.6), with $Y_{1,i} = \ln(X_{1,i})$, $Y_{2,i} = \ln(X_{2,i})$, $\epsilon_{1,i} = \ln(\eta_{1,i})$, $\epsilon_{2,i} = \ln(\eta_{2,i})$, and $\delta = \ln(\gamma)$.

Unfortunately, the model given by (11.11) and (11.12) is not the usual one of interest. The usual model of interest is a location-scale model such as might generate the ith data value from population 1 as

$$Y_{1,i} = \epsilon_{1,i}, \qquad i = 1, \ldots, n_1 \tag{11.13}$$

[16]For ease of discussion, we'll assume the data are obtained from a population model.

and the ith data value from population 2 is

$$Y_{2,i} = \delta + \gamma \epsilon_{2,i}, \qquad i = 1, \ldots, n_2 \tag{11.14}$$

where $\epsilon_{1,i}$ and $\epsilon_{2,i}$ are independent and have the same continuous distribution.

For this model, we would like to test the same hypotheses about γ given for the previous model. The difficulty is, even under H_0, the observations in the two samples do not have the same distributions unless $\delta = 0$. And unless they all have the same distribution, all permutations of the data are not equally likely, which means we violate the key assumption for permutation tests. The parameter δ in this problem is an example of a **nuisance parameter.** Nuisance parameters arise in many statistical problems and it is often difficult to know how to handle them. In the present case, however, we have a nice solution using a technique called **bootstrapping,** which we will introduce in Section 11.11. ✦

Advantages and Disadvantages of Permutation Tests

Like virtually any other statistical procedure, permutation tests have advantages and disadvantages.

Advantages

- **Generality.** Though they cannot be applied to every problem, when applicable, permutation tests are very general, in that:
  - They work when sampling or experimental units are randomly sampled, and they work when experimental units are not selected at random, as long as treatments are randomly assigned to experimental units.
  - They do not depend on the distribution of the data, so they are distribution-free in the truest sense.

- **The p-Values Are Always Correct.** In some tests, the p-values are based on distributional assumptions, such as normality, or approximation, such as the normal approximation to the binomial. With a permutation test, neither of these situations occurs.

Disadvantages

- **Applicability.** Permutation tests are not applicable to all problems using any test statistic. As an example, there is no permutation test of the mean of a single distribution using the t statistic as the test statistic, since the t statistic doesn't change under permutations of the data.
- **Ease of Use**
  - Despite the fact that the computing power exists to make permutation tests practical, most standard statistical software packages have not yet implemented permutation tests. However, specialized commercial programs are

available, and it is just a matter of time until suitable software becomes widely available.

○ For complex models, there are pitfalls in the implementation of permutation tests that require deep thinking about statistical issues. (Come to think of it, anything that promotes deep thinking could be considered an advantage as well!)

Other Considerations in Permutation Testing

- Users must decide what constitutes a "suitable permutation" of the data. Often, this is based on the sampling or randomization scheme that generated the data. For the simple statistical problems we have considered, this choice is easy to make. However, for more difficult problems, the choice of an appropriate permutation is not always so clear. In such cases, it might be wise to consult a statistician.

- The great generality of permutation tests mean that they can be conducted using virtually any test statistic that makes sense. And no matter what test statistic is chosen, the p-value of the test will be correct. However, not all test statistics are equally good. Users should make an effort to find a test statistic that has high power: that is, that has a high probability of rejecting H_0 when H_a is true. Knowledge of how to choose such a test statistic is beyond the scope of this book, and unless you have such knowledge, it might be wise to consult a statistician concerning the choice of a test statistic.

- If permutation test inference is based on the random selection of experimental or sampling units from a larger population, the models and hypotheses used in the permutation tests are based on population models, such as the C+E model, or the model given by Equations (11.5) and (11.6). If permutation test inference is based solely on the random assignment of treatments to experimental units, there is no population model, inference is solely about the experimental units at hand, and the p-value is based on possible outcomes from alternative random assignments. The hypotheses must be changed to reflect this difference.

11.11

RANDOMIZATION TESTS

We have noted that high-speed computers have made permutation tests practical. However, some problems are too large even for very fast modern computers. One solution is to use a **randomization test.**

> **DEFINITION**
>
> A **randomization test** is a procedure that generates an approximate p-value for a permutation test by computing values of the test statistic from a random sample of all permutations, rather than from all permutations.

In a randomization test, we do not compute the test statistic for all possible permutations, but rather for only a random sample of N permutations.[17] The values of the test statistic computed from the N sampled permutations are treated just as if they consisted of all possible permutations, and the p-values are computed just as they are for a permutation test. That is, we estimate the p^+ as the proportion of the N test statistics at least as large as the observed value and p_- as the proportion of the N test statistics at least as small as the observed value of the test statistic.

As a practical matter, the sampling is usually done with replacement, which means that some permutations can be used more than once. If N is sufficiently large, sampling with replacement will not appreciably affect the approximation.

How close will the approximate p-value be? We can use our knowledge of the binomial distribution to give an answer. Exercise 11.25 will guide you through such an analysis.

EXAMPLE 11.1   CONTINUED

Consider the permutation distribution of W for all 150 part diameters in Example 11.1. This distribution has $2^{150} \approx 1.4 \times 10^{45}$ values! If we could compute one billion values per second, it would take 4.5×10^{28} years to compute them all! Clever programming can reduce the number of values of W that we need to compute, but not by enough to make a permutation test based on all possible values practical.

For this reason, a randomization test was done. The observed value of the test statistic was computed as 0.465. A random sample of 1,000,000 permutations was drawn and 3 of the permutations produced values of the test statistic that exceeded the observed value. Therefore, the approximate p-value is 3×10^{-6}. Based on the number of permutations selected and the approximate p-value obtained, the approximation should be accurate to the fifth decimal place.[18]   ◆

11.12

THE BOOTSTRAP

In this section, we will cover most of the material of Chapter 5 on prediction and estimation using a distribution-free methodology called **bootstrapping.** The bootstrap is a recent development in statistical methodology, having been introduced in 1979 by Bradley Efron. Although the bootstrap is a quite general tool, we will for the most part concentrate on the classical models and estimators introduced in Chapter 5.

---

[17] Say, 1000, 100,000 or even 1,000,000 permutations.

[18] On a fast, but by no means fastest, computer, this actual calculation took about 10 minutes real time to complete.

Estimation for the C+E Model

Chapter 5 showed us how to obtain a confidence interval for a parameter μ if we know the sampling distribution of the estimator of μ. The classical estimation methods we studied in Chapter 5 assume that, at least approximately, the sampling distribution of the estimator is normal. This enables us to use quantiles of the normal or t distribution, whichever is appropriate, to construct confidence intervals. However, there may be occasions when we are not comfortable assuming that we know the sampling distribution of the estimator. A computer-intensive method known as the bootstrap is designed for just such occasions.

The bootstrap uses computer simulation, the model and the data to obtain the approximate sampling distribution of the estimator. Suppose the data have been observed and that their values are $y_1, y_2, \ldots, y_n$. Assume the estimate of μ computed from these data is $\hat{\mu}$. Here's how bootstrapping works for the C+E model (11.1):

THE BOOTSTRAP ALGORITHM FOR ESTIMATING THE MEAN OF A C+E MODEL

---

1. Randomly **resample** the data values n times **with replacement.** Think of this as putting n slips of paper, the ith having the value of y_i on it, in an urn, then drawing out a slip, recording the value, replacing the slip, drawing again, and so on, until n values have been recorded. Let $\tilde{y}_i^{(1)}$ denote the ith recorded value. The $\tilde{y}_i^{(1)}, i = 1, \ldots, n$, constitute the first **bootstrap data sample.**
2. Treating this bootstrap data sample as a set of data from the C+E model, compute the estimate of μ. Call this estimate $\tilde{\mu}^{(1)}$.
3. Repeat steps 1 and 2 N times, where N is a large number (usually at least 2000). On the jth iteration generate the jth bootstrap data sample $\tilde{y}_i^{(j)}, i = 1, \ldots, n$, and the jth bootstrap estimate $\tilde{\mu}^{(j)}$.

The bootstrap algorithm generates a large number, N, of bootstrap estimates. We then pretend that the distribution of these N bootstrap estimates is the true sampling distribution of $\hat{\mu}$. Figure 11.4 is a histogram of 2000 bootstrap estimates of μ generated using the artificial pancreas data from Example 5.5 and the preceding algorithm with the sample mean as estimator.

Suppose that $\tilde{\mu}_q$ denotes the qth quantile of the N bootstrap estimates $\tilde{\mu}$. Then a proportion L of the bootstrap estimates lie between $\tilde{\mu}_{(1-L)/2}$ and $\tilde{\mu}_{(1+L)/2}$. Since we're pretending that the distribution of the $\{\tilde{\mu}^{(j)}, j = 1, \ldots, N\}$ is the true sampling distribution of $\hat{\mu}$, we would like to use

$$(\tilde{\mu}_{(1-L)/2}, \tilde{\mu}_{(1+L)/2}) \tag{11.15}$$

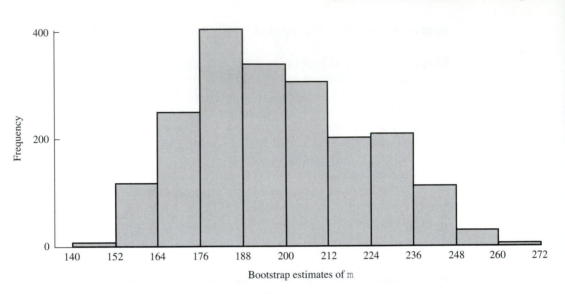

Figure 11.4 Histogram of 2000 bootstrap estimates of μ generated from the artificial pancreas data from Example 5.5. This distribution is used to approximate the sampling distribution of the estimator of μ.

as a level L confidence interval for μ. The problem is, that interval represents an approximate likely range of values for $\hat{\mu}$, not for μ. However, we can adjust the interval to account for this difficulty. The adjustment amounts to changing the quantiles of the bootstrap estimates used for the interval endpoints. That is, instead of using interval (11.15), we use interval

$$(\tilde{\mu}_{L_1}, \tilde{\mu}_{L_2})$$

where L_1 and L_2 are computed from an adjustment formula that takes the distribution of the bootstrap estimates into account. The bootstrap intervals computed in this way are called **accelerated bias-corrected,** or BC_a, intervals.[19]

The BC_a intervals make a bias-correction based on an estimate of bias in the estimator obtained from the bootstrap samples. They also make an acceleration correction, which adjusts for the possibility that the standard error of the estimator varies with the parameter being estimated. There is some high-powered statistical theory to justify the how and why of computing BC_a intervals, but for our purposes, it is enough to know that these adjustments make the resulting intervals more accurate.[20]

---

[19] BC_a and other types of bootstrap confidence intervals are discussed in detail by Bradley Efron and Robert J. Tibshirani, *An Introduction to the Bootstrap.* London: Chapman & Hall, 1993.

[20] Appendix 11.1 gives the formulas for the bias correction and acceleration.

**BOOTSTRAP CONFIDENCE INTERVAL FORMULA
FOR A POPULATION MEAN**

A level L bootstrap confidence interval for the mean of the C+E model is

$$(\tilde{\mu}_{L_1}, \tilde{\mu}_{L_2}) \tag{11.16}$$

where L_1 and L_2 are the BC_a-adjusted quantiles.

EXAMPLE 11.10   A BOOTSTRAP CONFIDENCE INTERVAL FOR A POPULATION MEAN

We use bootstrapping of the sample mean to analyze the artificial pancreas data. Recall that these data consisted of measurements of blood sugar in four rats: 149, 161, 220, and 266.[21] We will now generate a small bootstrap sample by hand and use it to find a bootstrap confidence interval for the mean population blood-sugar level, μ. You will perform a similar exercise in Lab 11.2.

We first select $N = 10$ bootstrap samples. To obtain the bootstrap samples, we write each of the four data values on a separate paper slip, put the four slips in a hat, and draw four times with replacement for each sample. For the jth sample, the sample mean $\tilde{\mu}^{(j)}$ is computed. The samples we got[22] and the value of $\tilde{\mu}^{(j)}$ computed from each are shown in Table 11.20.

**TABLE 11.20   Bootstrap Samples and Estimates
for Pancreas Example**

Sample	Sample values				$\tilde{\mu}^{(j)}$
1	149	161	161	266	184.25
2	266	220	161	266	228.25
3	220	149	161	161	172.75
4	220	161	220	149	187.50
5	161	220	161	161	175.75
6	266	149	149	266	207.50
7	161	266	266	266	239.75
8	220	161	266	220	216.75
9	161	220	266	149	199.00
10	220	220	149	266	213.75

Given the small size of the bootstrap sample, and the difficulty of computing the BC_a adjustment without a computer, we will find an 80% bootstrap confidence

---

[21] See Example 5.4 for a detailed explanation.

[22] Of course, if we did this again, we would get a different set of samples, and hence somewhat different results.

**TABLE 11.21 Bootstrap
Confidence Intervals
for μ: Pancreas Example**

90% interval:	$(155.0, 239.5)$
95% interval:	$(152.0, 243.0)$
99% interval:	$(149.0, 254.5)$

interval for μ without the BC_a adjustment. To do this, we first compute $(1-L)/2 = (1-0.8)/2 = 0.1$ and $(1+L)/2 = (1+0.8)/2 = 0.9$. We next find $\tilde{\mu}_{0.1}$ and $\tilde{\mu}_{0.9}$. The first is the smallest observation, 172.75, and the second is the second largest observation, 228.25. Then an approximate 80% confidence interval for μ is

$$(\tilde{\mu}_{0.1}, \tilde{\mu}_{0.9}) = (172.75, 228.25)$$

It turns out that the BC_a correction for an 80% confidence interval for μ using these data adjusts the 0.1 quantile to 0.042 and the 0.9 quantile to 0.789. The resulting BC_a interval is $(172.75, 222.50)$.

   Luckily, there is no need to calculate bootstrap confidence intervals by hand. Table 11.21 displays three different confidence intervals for the pancreas data computed using 2000 bootstrap samples. ◆

Predicting a New Observation From the C+E Model

We have seen how to estimate μ in the C+E model, and how to quantify the uncertainty in that estimate by use of a bootstrap confidence interval. Often, it is desired to predict a new observation from the C+E model that generated the data. Prediction is an extensive topic in its own right, and the selection of a predictor requires knowledge and skill. In this introduction to the topic, we will assume that if we know μ in the C+E model, we will use μ to predict a new observation, and that if we don't know μ, we will use our chosen estimator of μ, $\hat{\mu}$.

   Suppose to begin with that we know μ in the C+E model, and that we use μ to predict a new observation. Since the new observation (when it is observed) will be generated as $Y_{\text{new}} = \mu + \epsilon_{\text{new}}$, the error in using μ to predict Y_{new} will be $Y_{\text{new}} - \mu = \epsilon_{\text{new}}$. The point here is that there is still going to be prediction error, even though we know μ.

   As usual for the bootstrap approach, we let $\hat{\mu}$ denote our chosen estimate of μ: mean, median, trimmed mean or whatever. We will use $\hat{\mu}$ to predict a new observation. When $\hat{\mu}$ is used to predict a new observation, we'll denote it $\hat{y}_{\text{new}}$.

   To obtain a bootstrap prediction interval, we need to generate a bootstrap sample of "new observations." Assuming we have observed the data $y_1, \ldots, y_n$, this is done as follows:

ALGORITHM FOR GENERATING BOOTSTRAP NEW OBSERVATIONS

1. Fit the C+E model to the data by the desired method and compute the predicted value $\hat{y}_{\text{new}} = \hat{\mu}$ and residuals, $e_i = y_i - \hat{y}_{\text{new}}, i = 1, \ldots, n$ (note that with least squares, for example, $\hat{y}_{\text{new}} = \bar{y}$).

2. Randomly **resample** the data values n times **with replacement.** Let $\tilde{y}_i^{(1)}$ denote the ith recorded value. The $\tilde{y}_i^{(1)}, i = 1, \ldots, n$, constitute the first **bootstrap data sample.**

3. Fit the C+E model to the bootstrap sample with the method used to fit the original model and obtain the first bootstrap estimate of μ, $\tilde{\mu}^{(1)}$.

4. Choose one residual at random from the n residuals computed in step 1. Call it $\tilde{\epsilon}_{\text{new}}^{(1)}$.

5. Create the bootstrap new observation

$$\tilde{y}_{new}^{(1)} = \tilde{\mu}^{(1)} + \tilde{\epsilon}_{new}^{(1)}$$

6. Repeat steps 2 to 5 N times, where N is a large number (usually at least 2000). On the jth iteration, generate the jth bootstrap data sample $\tilde{y}_i^{(j)}, i = 1, \ldots, n$, the jth bootstrap parameter estimate $\tilde{\mu}^{(j)}$, and the jth bootstrap residual $\tilde{\epsilon}_{\text{new}}^{(j)}$. Then create the jth bootstrap new observation

$$\tilde{y}_{new}^{(j)} = \tilde{\mu}^{(j)} + \tilde{\epsilon}_{new}^{(j)}$$

The distribution of the $\tilde{y}_{\text{new}}^{(j)}$ provides the desired approximation to the sampling distribution of the predictor. We will use the $(1 - L/2)$th and $(1 + L/2)$th quantiles of the $\tilde{y}_{\text{new}}^{(j)}$ as the level L prediction interval for a new observation.

BOOTSTRAP PREDICTION INTERVAL FORMULA

An approximate level L bootstrap prediction interval for a new observation from the C+E model is

$$(\tilde{y}_{\text{new},(1-L)/2}, \tilde{y}_{\text{new},(1+L)/2}) \tag{11.17}$$

EXAMPLE 11.10   CONTINUED

We use the artificial pancreas data to construct an 80% prediction interval for a new observation by hand using the 10 bootstrap samples displayed in Table 11.20.

TABLE 11.22   Quantities Needed for Bootstrap Prediction: Pancreas Example

Sample	$\tilde{\mu}^{(j)}$	$\tilde{\epsilon}_{new}^{(j)}$	$\tilde{y}_{new}^{(j)}$
1	184.25	−50	134.25
2	228.25	−50	178.25
3	172.75	−50	122.75
4	187.50	21	208.50
5	175.75	−50	125.75
6	207.50	67	274.50
7	239.75	−38	201.75
8	216.75	−50	166.75
9	199.00	−50	149.00
10	213.75	−38	175.75

TABLE 11.23   Bootstrap Prediction Intervals: Pancreas Example

90% interval:	(119.75, 283.75)
95% interval:	(117.00, 295.25)
99% interval:	(102.02, 310.00)

The residuals from the least squares fit to the original data are

$$67 \qquad -50 \qquad -38 \qquad 21$$

A sample of size 10 drawn with replacement from these residuals constitutes the $\tilde{\epsilon}_{new}^{(j)}$ shown in Table 11.22. These values are added to the bootstrap estimates to give the bootstrap new observations $\tilde{y}_{new}^{(j)}$.

The 0.1 and 0.9 quantiles of the bootstrap new observations (found in the rightmost column of Table 11.22) are 122.75 and 208.50, respectively. Thus, an approximate 80% bootstrap prediction interval for a new observation is

$$(122.75, 208.50)$$

Table 11.23 shows bootstrap prediction intervals computed using 2000 bootstrap samples.

Compare these intervals with the confidence intervals in Table 11.21. The added width reflects the extra uncertainty involved in obtaining a completely new observation from the C+E model. Also, compare the 95% bootstrap prediction interval, (117.00, 295.25), with the much wider 95% classical prediction interval (5.6, 392.4).   ◆

Estimation for Two-Population C+E Data

Consider the problem of comparing two populations. In particular, suppose we want to know whether the two population distributions, or at least some aspects of the distributions, are the same.

We will assume that there are n_1 measurements from population 1 generated by the C+E model

$$Y_{1,i} = \mu_1 + \epsilon_{1,i}, \qquad i = 1, \ldots, n_1 \tag{11.18}$$

and n_2 measurements from population 2 generated by the C+E model

$$Y_{2,i} = \mu_2 + \epsilon_{2,i}, \qquad i = 1, \ldots, n_2 \tag{11.19}$$

In this section, we will consider the most common comparison for C+E data: comparison of μ_1 and μ_2.

Paired Comparisons

The simplest case is when we have **paired comparisons.** See Chapter 5 for a discussion of constructing classical confidence intervals for the differences in the means from paired data.

As in Chapter 5, we reduce the two-population problem to a one-population problem by considering the differences $D_i = Y_{1,i} - Y_{2,i}$. These differences follow a C+E model of their own:

$$D_i = (\mu_1 - \mu_2) + (\epsilon_{1,i} - \epsilon_{2,i}) = \mu_D + \epsilon_{D,i}$$

where $\mu_D = \mu_1 - \mu_2$ is the mean of the population of differences, and $\epsilon_{D,i} = \epsilon_{1,i} - \epsilon_{2,i}$ is the random error associated with the difference D_i. Here, we apply the one-sample bootstrap approach to the differences.

EXAMPLE 11.11   A BOOTSTRAP CONFIDENCE INTERVAL FOR PAIRED COMPARISONS

Consider again the artificial pancreas experiment described in Chapter 5. In the experiment, the researcher took readings of each rat's blood-sugar level prior to injection, just after injection, and then periodically during the 60 minutes after injection. She would like to compare the mean preinjection readings with the mean of the readings taken 60 minutes after the injection, to see how far toward the normal levels the artificial pancreas had reduced blood sugar in 1 hour.

The data are as follows:

Rat	Initial reading	Reading after 60 minutes	Difference
1	170	266	96
2	134	149	15
3	99	161	62
4	84	220	36

The two populations are the preinjection readings and the readings 60 minutes after injection of all possible diabetic rats with this kind of artificial pancreas. The data are naturally paired since there are two test scores on each individual. These scores are very likely to be related.

A 95% bootstrap confidence interval with 2000 bootstrap samples was constructed using the one-sample bootstrap algorithm on the differenced data. The interval is (26.75, 116.00). Since this interval lies entirely above 0, the researcher concluded that with 95% confidence the population mean of the preinjection readings is significantly lower than that of the readings taken 60 minutes after the injection.

Recall from Chapter 5 that the classical 95% confidence interval for the difference in means computed from these same data was (−4.5, 159.0). In using these confidence intervals to decide whether the population mean of the preinjection readings is significantly lower than that of the readings taken 60 minutes after the injection, we obtain contradictory conclusions. How can we make sense of these results?

Two points to consider are as follows:

- Though the classical interval contains 0, it is not symmetric about 0, and, in fact, barely reaches below 0. So just using this interval to conclude that there is no significance difference in population means without showing the range of values in the interval is misleading.

- The validity of both kinds of confidence intervals relies on an adequate sample size. In addition, the classical interval relies on the underlying normality of the population distribution of the differences, something that is difficult to check with four observations. In fact, it would be foolish to put a great deal of faith in any conclusion drawn from four pieces of data. What are really needed here are more data.   ✦

Independent Populations

When the two populations of interest are independent, comparisons do not reduce to the one-population case as they do for paired data. The first thing, of course, is to decide when the data are from a pair of independent populations. This is almost always apparent from the way the data are collected. If the samples from the two populations are selected randomly and independently of each other, and if the populations are not related in any way, then methods for independent populations are appropriate.

Let $\hat{\mu}_1$ and $\hat{\mu}_2$ denote the point estimators being used to estimate μ_1 and μ_2. Then a point estimator of $\mu_1 - \mu_2$ is $\hat{\mu}_1 - \hat{\mu}_2$. The following algorithm will generate the bootstrap samples used to construct a bootstrap confidence interval for $\mu_1 - \mu_2$:

THE BOOTSTRAP ALGORITHM FOR ESTIMATING THE DIFFERENCE IN MEANS OF INDEPENDENT POPULATIONS

1. Randomly **resample** the data values from population 1 n_1 times with replacement. Let $\tilde{y}_{1,i}^{(1)}$ denote the ith recorded value. The $\tilde{y}_{1,i}^{(1)}$ constitute the first bootstrap data sample from population 1.
2. Compute the estimate of μ_1 treating this bootstrap data sample as a set of data from the C+E model. Call this estimate $\tilde{\mu}_1^{(1)}$.
3. Repeat steps 1 and 2 for the data from population 2, which will give the corresponding quantities $\tilde{y}_{2,i}^{(1)}, i = 1, \ldots, n_2$, and $\tilde{\mu}_2^{(1)}$.
4. Compute the first bootstrapped estimate of the difference of population centers, $\tilde{d}^{(1)} = \tilde{\mu}_1^{(1)} - \tilde{\mu}_2^{(1)}$.
5. Repeat steps 2 to 4 N times, where N is a large number (usually at least 2000). On the jth iteration, generate the jth bootstrapped estimate of the difference of population centers $\tilde{d}^{(j)} = \tilde{\mu}_1^{(j)} - \tilde{\mu}_2^{(j)}$.

A bootstrap level L BC_a confidence interval for $\mu_1 - \mu_2$ is

---

BOOTSTRAP CONFIDENCE INTERVAL FORMULA FOR THE DIFFERENCE OF THE MEANS OF TWO INDEPENDENT POPULATIONS

A level L bootstrap confidence interval for the difference of means of two independent populations is

$$(\tilde{d}_{L_1}, \tilde{d}_{L_2}) \qquad\qquad (11.20)$$

where the quantiles L_1 and L_2 are the BC_a-adjusted quantiles.

EXAMPLE 11.12   **BOOTSTRAP ESTIMATION OF THE DIFFERENCE OF MEANS OF TWO INDEPENDENT POPULATIONS**

Recall the data from Example 5.9: The researcher had a treatment group of four diabetic rats, each with an artificial pancreas, and a control group of four untreated diabetic rats. Each rat was given a glucose solution and its blood sugar measured 60 minutes later. The data are

	Untreated diabetic	Artificial pancreas
	402	266
	305	149
	496	161
	421	220
$\bar{y}$	406.0	199.0
s	78.6	54.4

Using these data, we will obtain a 99% bootstrap confidence interval interval for the difference of population means.

The researcher decides that the appropriate models for the data are the C+E models with the centers μ_1 and μ_2 defined to be the population means. As a point estimator of the difference in means, $\mu_1 - \mu_2$, the researcher chooses the difference of the sample means: $406 - 128.25 = 277.75$. Plots of these data reveal no outliers and the researcher decides the data are suitable for inference. A 99% bootstrap confidence interval for $\mu_1 - \mu_2$, produced with 2000 bootstrap samples, is $(99.77, 304.50)$. Compare this interval with the wider classical interval obtained in Example 5.9: $(29.4, 384.6)$.   ✦

Comparing Population Spreads

As mentioned in Example 11.9, the classical test for the equality of variances of two independent populations is sensitive to nonnormality, and distribution-free permutation tests have problems with nuisance parameters. The bootstrap can provide a distribution-free confidence interval that suffers from neither of these difficulties. In fact, the generality of the bootstrap will enable us to obtain a confidence interval comparing any measure of spread of the distributions, not just variances. The usual, though not the only, model for the data is the C+E model given by (11.18) and (11.19), in which the spread of the $\epsilon_{1,i}$ is assumed to be ν_1 and that of the $\epsilon_{2,i}$ is assumed to be ν_2. Note that the spread could be the variance, the standard deviation, the mean absolute deviation, the interquartile range, or any other measure. We will show how to obtain a bootstrap confidence interval for the ratio ν_1/ν_2.

**THE BOOTSTRAP ALGORITHM FOR ESTIMATING THE QUOTIENT
OF SPREADS OF INDEPENDENT POPULATIONS**

1. Randomly **resample** the data values from population 1 n_1 times with replacement. Let $\tilde{y}_{1,i}^{(1)}$ denote the ith recorded value. The $\tilde{y}_{1,i}^{(1)}$ constitute the first bootstrap data sample from population 1.
2. Compute the estimate of ν_1 treating this bootstrap data sample as a set of data from the C+E model. Call this estimate $\tilde{v}_1^{(1)}$.
3. Repeat steps 1 and 2 for the data from population 2 that will give the corresponding quantities $\tilde{y}_{2,i}^{(1)}$, $i = 1, \ldots, n_2$, and $\tilde{v}_2^{(1)}$.
4. Compute the first bootstrapped estimate of the quotient of population spreads $\tilde{q}^{(1)} = \tilde{v}_1^{(1)}/\tilde{v}_2^{(1)}$.
5. Repeat steps 2 to 4 N times, where N is a large number (usually at least 2000). On the jth iteration, generate the jth bootstrapped estimate of the quotient of population spreads, $\tilde{q}^{(j)} = \tilde{v}_1^{(j)}/\tilde{v}_2^{(j)}$.

A bootstrap level L BC_a confidence interval for $q = \nu_1/\nu_2$ is

---

**BOOTSTRAP CONFIDENCE INTERVAL FORMULA FOR THE
QUOTIENT OF SPREADS OF TWO INDEPENDENT POPULATIONS**

A level L bootstrap confidence interval for the quotient of spreads of two independent populations is

$$(\tilde{q}_{L_1}, \tilde{q}_{L_2}) \tag{11.21}$$

where the quantiles L_1 and L_2 are the BC_a-adjusted quantiles.

EXAMPLE 11.13   BOOTSTRAP ESTIMATION OF THE QUOTIENT OF SPREADS OF INDEPENDENT POPULATIONS

In many industrial assembly applications, it is important for part dimensions to be both on target and consistent. Often, these two quantities are measured separately. One such pair of measures is **bias** and **variance**.

- **Bias.** If Y is the measured part dimension, and y_0 is the target dimension, the bias is the expected part dimension[23] minus the target dimension:

---

[23]The expected dimension can be viewed as the average dimension computed over the entire population of parts.

$\beta = E(Y) - y_0$. The bias measures the amount that the mean part measurement differs from the target.

- **Variance.** The variance, as you already know, is the expected squared deviation of the measurement about its mean: $\sigma^2 = E([Y - E(Y)]^2)$. The variance is a measure of the spread of the measurements about their mean.

Both the bias and variance can be combined together into a single measure called the **mean squared deviation from target.** As its name implies, the mean squared deviation from target is the expected squared deviation of the part dimension from the target value. Its formula is $\text{MSD} = E([Y - y_0]^2)$. The following simple relation links MSD with β and σ^2: $\text{MSD} = \beta^2 + \sigma^2$.

An automobile company wants to compare the quality of spacers supplied by two vendors. Among the measures used are outside diameter. The target outside diameter is 1.125 inches. Engineers decide to use MSD as the measure of product quality. Specifically, if v_j is the population MSD of outside diameters of spacers supplied by company j, the engineers want to estimate $q = v_1/v_2$. To do this, quality personnel obtained random samples of size 25 from one recent shipment from each vendor. They obtained estimates

$$\hat{v}_1 = \frac{1}{25}\sum_{i=1}^{25}(y_{1,i} - 1.125)^2, \qquad \hat{v}_2 = \frac{1}{25}\sum_{i=1}^{25}(y_{2,i} - 1.125)^2$$

and $\hat{q} = \hat{v}_1/\hat{v}_2$, where $y_{1,i}$ and $y_{2,i}$, $i = 1, \ldots, 25$, denote the original data.

Using 2000 bootstrap replicates, the engineers obtained a 95% BC_a confidence interval of $(0.9797, 1.1013)$. The interval contains 1, which suggests no difference in MSD for the two suppliers. ◆

Comparing Two Population Proportions

Suppose there are two independent populations, in the first of which a proportion p_1 has a certain characteristic, and in the second of which a proportion p_2 has that same characteristic. We want to compare the two proportions p_1 and p_2. To do so, we take a random sample of size n_1 from population 1, and another of size n_2 from population 2. Suppose that Y_1 of the sample from population 1 and Y_2 of the sample from population 2 have the characteristic.

The following are the steps necessary to obtain a bootstrap distribution of the estimator $\hat{p}_1 - \hat{p}_2$, of $p_1 - p_2$:

THE BOOTSTRAP ALGORITHM FOR ESTIMATING THE DIFFERENCE IN PROPORTIONS IN TWO INDEPENDENT POPULATIONS

---

1. Compute $\hat{p}_1$ from the original population 1 data set, and $\hat{p}_2$ from the original population 2 data set.

2. Compute the first bootstrapped value of p_1, $\tilde{p}_1^{(1)}$, by taking an observation $\tilde{y}_1^{(1)}$ from a $b(n_1, \hat{p}_1)$ distribution, and taking $\tilde{p}_1^{(1)} = \tilde{y}_1^{(1)}/n_1$.

3. Compute the first bootstrapped value of p_2, $\tilde{p}_2^{(1)}$, by taking an observation $\tilde{y}_2^{(1)}$ from a $b(n_2, \hat{p}_2)$ distribution, and taking $\tilde{p}_2^{(1)} = \tilde{y}_2^{(1)}/n_2$.

4. Compute the first bootstrapped value of the difference $p_1 - p_2$, $\tilde{d}^{(1)} = \tilde{p}_1^{(1)} - \tilde{p}_2^{(1)}$.

5. Repeat steps 2 to 4 N times, where N is a large number (usually at least 2000). On the jth iteration, generate the jth bootstrap difference $\tilde{d}^{(j)}$.

An approximate bootstrap level L confidence interval for $p_1 - p_2$ is

$$(\tilde{d}_{(1-L)/2}, \tilde{d}_{(1+L)/2})$$

where $\tilde{d}_q$ is the qth quantile of the bootstrap differences. We can improve the performance of these intervals by using the BC_a correction to modify the $(1 - L)/2$ and $(1 + L)/2$ quantiles to L_1 and L_2, respectively.

BOOTSTRAP CONFIDENCE INTERVAL FORMULA FOR THE DIFFERENCE OF THE PROPORTIONS OF TWO INDEPENDENT POPULATIONS

A level L bootstrap confidence interval for the difference of proportions of two independent populations is

$$(\tilde{d}_{L_1}, \tilde{d}_{L_2}) \tag{11.22}$$

where L_1 and L_2 are the BC_a-corrected quantiles.

EXAMPLE 11.14   BOOTSTRAP ESTIMATION OF THE DIFFERENCE OF POPULATION PROPORTIONS

Recall the problem from Example 5.10: A quality inspector wants to compare the proportions of defectives in two large shipments of wire spools. He takes a random sample of 100 spools from shipment 1 and another random sample of 200 spools from shipment 2, and he finds that the sample proportions of defectives are $\hat{p}_1 = 0.13$ and $\hat{p}_2 = 0.17$, respectively. The quality inspector calculates a level 0.99 bootstrap BC_a confidence interval for the difference in shipment proportions using 2000 bootstrap samples. The resulting interval is $(-0.163, 0.065)$. The values obtained for L_1 and L_2 are 0.003 and 0.991, respectively.

Do the two shipments differ in their proportions of defectives? Since the confidence interval contains 0, the data provide insufficient evidence to conclude that they do. This agrees with the conclusion drawn from the classical interval, $(-0.11, 0.03)$, obtained in Example 5.10. ✦

The Parametric Bootstrap

You may be asking yourself in what sense the bootstrap estimation procedure for the difference of two population proportions that we have just presented is distribution-free. The answer is that it isn't at all distribution-free: Binomial distributions are specified for both samples. This is an example of a **parametric bootstrap procedure.**

The parametric procedure differs from the distribution-free bootstrap procedures we considered earlier, in the way the bootstrap samples are obtained. In the distribution-free bootstrap, bootstrap samples are obtained by randomly sampling the original data with replacement. In the parametric bootstrap, the parametric model or models (here, the two binomial models) are fitted to the data, and random samples are obtained by computer simulation from those models: The original data are not resampled.

Why didn't we just use a distribution-free bootstrap to compare the two population proportions? The reason is, when it is absolutely certain, as it is here, what the correct model is, the parametric bootstrap usually gives better performance.

Exercise 11.26 asks you to describe the distribution-free bootstrap procedure for comparing two population proportions.

Advantages and Disadvantages of Bootstrapping

Advantages

There are two main advantages of bootstrapping as opposed to using classical normal-theory methods:

1. **Generality of Models.** Classical normal-theory models are restricted to normal errors if the sample size is small. With the bootstrap there is no such restriction, since the data "choose" the sampling distribution of the estimator.
2. **Generality of Estimators.** It is difficult to use normal theory to construct accurate confidence intervals based on a wide variety of estimators (e.g., the median and the trimmed mean). This is particularly true for small samples. The bootstrap has no more difficulty constructing intervals based on these estimators than it does intervals based on the sample mean.

This second advantage points up the ease with which the bootstrap can be used for many kinds of estimators. The procedure for the C+E model is to choose your favorite estimator (mean, median, trimmed mean, or whatever) to base the inference on, and then apply the bootstrap using the chosen estimator. In other words, if you choose the median, then the bootstrap estimate $\tilde{\mu}^{(j)}$ will be the median of the jth bootstrap sample.

Disadvantages

There are two main disadvantages to bootstrapping.

1. **Technology.** Though computation is becoming more powerful and less expensive, a computer is needed to do bootstrapping. The technology is within the range of today's laptop computers, however. An additional problem is that although many statistical packages allow users to write bootstrapping programs, off-the-shelf programs are not yet generally available.

2. **Coverage.** There is some evidence of a modest undercoverage for bootstrap confidence intervals. For example, simple 95% bootstrap confidence intervals such as those we present here might contain the true parameter being estimated less than 95% of the time. For the bootstrap intervals we are considering, the BC_a adjustment is designed to correct this problem.

11.13

A DISTRIBUTION-FREE TOLERANCE INTERVAL

As you learned in Chapter 5, confidence intervals are a tool to quantify the uncertainty about model parameters, prediction intervals quantify the uncertainty about new observations, and tolerance intervals give a range of values that, with a prespecified confidence, will contain at least a prespecified proportion of the measurements in the population. To put it more formally, we repeat the definition given in Chapter 5.

First, recall the notation given in Chapter 5. Suppose T_1 and T_2 are estimators with $T_1 \leq T_2$, and that γ is a real number between 0 and 1. Let $A(T_1, T_2, \gamma)$ denote the event

{The proportion of measurements in the population between T_1 and T_2 is at least γ}

> **DEFINITION**
>
> A level L tolerance interval for a proportion γ of a population is an interval (T_1, T_2), where T_1 and T_2 are estimators, having the property that
>
> $$P(A(T_1, T_2, \gamma)) = L$$

In Chapter 5, you learned about a classical tolerance interval based on the assumption that the population generating the data is normal. Here, we introduce a distribution-free tolerance interval of the form $(Y_{\min}, Y_{\max})$, where $Y_{\min}$ is the smallest observation in the sample, and $Y_{\max}$ the largest. The values of L and γ that this interval can satisfy depend on the number of observations, n. Table 11.24 shows for different values of L and γ, the minimum sample sizes needed to ensure that the distribution-free tolerance interval $(Y_{\min}, Y_{\max})$ contains at least proportion γ of the population with confidence at least L.

TABLE 11.24   Minimum Sample Sizes Necessary to Ensure the Distribution-Free Tolerance Interval $(Y_{\min}, Y_{\max})$ Contains at Least Proportion γ of the Population with Confidence at Least L

| | | | | | γ | | | | | |
L	0.90	0.91	0.92	0.93	0.94	0.95	0.96	0.97	0.98	0.99
0.90	38	42	48	55	64	77	96	129	194	388
0.91	39	44	49	56	66	79	100	133	200	401
0.92	41	45	51	58	68	82	103	138	207	416
0.93	42	47	53	61	71	85	107	143	215	432
0.94	44	49	55	63	74	89	112	149	225	451
0.95	46	51	58	66	78	93	117	157	236	473
0.96	49	54	61	70	82	99	124	166	249	500
0.97	52	58	65	75	88	105	132	177	266	534
0.98	56	63	71	81	95	115	144	193	290	581
0.99	64	71	81	92	108	130	164	219	330	662

The advantage of the distribution-free tolerance interval is that virtually no assumptions are needed on the population distribution. The disadvantage is that large sample sizes are needed.

EXAMPLE 11.15   A DISTRIBUTION-FREE TOLERANCE INTERVAL

To demonstrate the computation and interpretation of a distribution-free tolerance interval, we go back to Example 5.11 in Chapter 5. In that example, you will recall, a manufacturer of ceramic tiles is concerned about the uniformity of thickness in a certain model of tile. To measure the uniformity of thickness, the thickness of each tile is measured at nine prespecified locations, and the standard deviation of the nine measurements is computed. If the manufacturer wants to use the distribution-free confidence interval $(Y_{\min}, Y_{\max})$ to obtain a level 0.95 tolerance interval for a proportion 0.99 of all uniformity measurements in the lot, then by consulting Table 11.24, he finds that he needs a random sample of at least 473 tiles.

He takes such a sample and finds that the smallest uniformity measure is 0.185 mm and the largest is 0.197 mm. The distribution-free tolerance interval he obtains is thus (0.185, 0.197). The interpretation of this interval involves long-run proportions: If the manufacturer repeatedly selects samples of this size from the lot and for each sample computes a level 0.95 tolerance interval for a proportion 0.99 of the population, then approximately 95% of all those intervals will actually contain 99% or more of the lot's uniformity measurements.   ◆

D ISCUSSION QUESTIONS

1. What is distribution-free inference?
2. Describe the sign test.

3. What is rank-based inference?

4. Explain the Wilcoxon signed rank and rank sum tests.

5. Explain the Spearman correlation and inference based on it.

6. Describe the Kruskal-Wallis test.

7. Describe Friedman's test.

8. Explain the difference between inference based on a sampling model and inference based on a randomization model.

9. What is a permutation test? Give an example.

10. What is a randomization test? Give an example.

11. Describe the idea behind the bootstrap.

12. Describe bootstrap confidence intervals for μ. What is their interpretation?

13. Describe bootstrap predictions for future observations from the C+E model.

14. Explain how you would find a bootstrap confidence interval for the difference in means in a paired comparison. How would you construct bootstrap confidence intervals for the difference of medians?

15. How would you construct a bootstrap confidence interval for the difference of location in two independent populations?

16. Describe how to construct a bootstrap confidence interval for the difference of proportions in two independent populations.

17. How would you construct a distribution-free tolerance interval?

 **XERCISES**

Note: In all exercises requiring you to conduct hypothesis tests, state

- the scientific hypothesis
- the statistical model
- the statistical hypotheses being tested
- the test statistic being used
- the assumptions made, and why they are, or are not, justified for the data being analyzed
- the p-value and your conclusions

11.1. Consider using the Spearman correlation to test

$$H_0: \quad X \text{ and } Y \text{ are independent}$$

versus one of the alternative hypotheses

$$H_{a+}: \quad X \text{ and } Y \text{ are positively related}$$
$$H_{a-}: \quad X \text{ and } Y \text{ are negatively related}$$

Show that when $n = 3$, each of the p-values for the alternatives H_{a+} and H_{a-} in the test can take on only four values.

11.2. A biologist took the weight (lb) and diameter (ft) of five pumpkins. The five bivariate measurements are (5.0, 0.5), (6.0, 0.6), (10.0, 1.0), (30.0, 1.5), and (500.0, 10.0). What is the Spearman rank correlation coefficient between the weight and diameter of pumpkins? What does its value tell you about the pumpkins? Why is the Pearson correlation coefficient inappropriate in this application? Relate its lack of appropriateness to what you know about the relation between diameter and weight.

11.3. In Chapter 5, you learned the meaning of the "sampling distribution of an estimator" and its use in inference. Explain what takes the place of the sampling distribution in
    (a) permutation tests.
    (b) randomization tests.
    (c) the bootstrap.

11.4. In the text, it was explained why we cannot perform a permutation test of H_0: $\mu = \mu_0$ using the t statistic. Can we perform a permutation test for the population variance: H_0: $\sigma^2 = \sigma_0^2$ using the sample variance as the test statistic? Explain.

11.5. Using the same set of data, two researchers test the same hypotheses using the same test statistic.
    (a) If they perform a permutation test, will they get the same p-value? Explain.
    (b) If they perform a randomization test, will they get the same p-value? Explain.

11.6. Using the same set of data, the same estimator and the same number of bootstrap replications, two researchers each construct a level L confidence interval for a model parameter. Will the two intervals be the same? Explain.

11.7. In a study on the safety of the diet drug combination "fen-phen," researchers review the records of 1000 dieters taking "fen-phen" and 1000 dieters not using these drugs.
    (a) To whom can the researchers make inference if the two samples are randomly selected from hospital records nationwide? Explain.
    (b) What is the source of the randomness on which inference is based?
    (c) If a health difference between the two groups is found, can the researchers assert it is caused by "fen-phen"? Explain.

11.8. Answer Exercise 11.7 if the sample consists of the 2000 most convenient records the researchers could find.

11.9. In an experiment to determine the safety of the diet drugs "fen-phen," researchers randomly divided a sample of rats into two groups, gave the drugs to one group and kept the second group as controls. If the rats are a random sample from a large population of rats:
    (a) To whom can the researchers make inference if the two samples are randomly selected from this type of laboratory rat? Explain.
    (b) What is the source of the randomness on which inference is based?
    (c) If a statistically significant difference between the two groups is found, can the researchers assert it is caused by "fen-phen"? Explain.

11.10. Answer Exercise 11.9 if the sample consisted of the most conveniently available rats.

11.11. The lifetime of an electronic component is known to follow a right-skewed distribution, which historically has had a median of 1500 hours. The failure times of a random sample of 10 components taken from a production lot are 1069, 1488, 136, 1756, 102, 168, 3293, 1664, 220, and 135.
    (a) Use an appropriate distribution-free hypothesis test to test whether or not the components in this production lot have a median lifetime of 1500 hours.
    (b) Construct a confidence interval, based on the test statistic from part (a), for the population median at a level as close to 0.95 as possible. Interpret the interval.

11.12. Refer to Exercise 11.11. It is well-known that the distribution of the natural logarithm of the failure times is symmetric.

    (a) Use an appropriate distribution-free test with the logged failure times to test whether the components in this production lot have the median lifetime 1500 hours. (*Hint:* If the median failure time is 1500 hours, what is the median of the logged failure time?)

    (b) Construct a confidence interval, based on the test statistic from part (a), for the population median of logged failure times at a level as close to 0.95 as possible. Interpret the interval.

11.13. The breaking strengths of five large metal pins used in building construction randomly chosen from a large production lot are (in psi)

$$42,110, \qquad 42,550, \qquad 41,895, \qquad 42,285, \qquad 41,990$$

The head of the quality unit wants a 95% confidence interval for μ, the mean strength of the pins in the lot.

    (a) Construct a bootstrap interval.

    (b) Interpret what "95% confidence" means.

    (c) Over the years, the company has managed to maintain a mean strength of 42,300 for these pins. Does that seem reasonable in light of these data? Why?

11.14. The following table shows the preferences for two brands of chocolate chip cookie in a recently conducted double-blind taste-testing experiment involving 245 college students. Do the data provide evidence that the proportion of female students who prefer cookie A to cookie B is greater than is the proportion of male students who prefer cookie A to cookie B? Use an appropriate bootstrap confidence interval to decide. Tell why the particular kind of interval you use is the best choice.

	Cookie A	Cookie B	Total
Male Students	94	85	179
Female Students	39	27	66
Total	133	112	245

11.15. Just before the O. J. Simpson murder case went to the jury, a national poll was done in which 108 of a random sample of 150 whites told interviewers they thought Simpson was guilty and 77 of a random sample of 100 nonwhites told interviewers they thought Simpson was not guilty. Estimate the difference in the proportion of all whites and nonwhites who thought Simpson was guilty. Can we be 99% confident that the true proportions are different? Use a bootstrap confidence interval to decide. Explain what is meant by 99% confidence in the statistical procedure you use.

11.16. A study is done to see if secondborn children differ in intelligence from firstborn children. A sample of 15 two-child families is taken, and the IQ score of each of the 30 children (at age 10) is recorded. The data are found in Table 11.25.

    (a) Use an appropriate rank-based test to answer the question.

    (b) Construct a confidence interval, based on the test statistic from part (a), for the population median of the difference in IQ score between firstborn and secondborn children at a level as close to 0.95 as possible. Interpret the interval.

TABLE 11.25   Data for Exercise 11.16

| Birth | Family | | | | | | | | | | | | | | |
order	1	2	3	4	5	6	7	8	9	10	11	12	13	14	15
First	82	117	112	102	126	104	115	111	87	114	104	92	110	117	99
Second	80	115	89	90	95	89	114	102	82	100	105	99	95	97	98

11.17. Answer Exercise 11.16(a) by constructing an appropriate level 0.95 bootstrap confidence interval.

11.18. Answer Exercise 11.16(a) by conducting an appropriate nonrank-based permutation or randomization test.

11.19. The following is an excerpt from an article that appeared in *The Boston Globe* of June 6, 1994:

> *The number of heart-attack victims fell dramatically among coronary patients who were taking the cholesterol-lowering drug Pravastatin, according to researchers. Scientists at the Bowman Gray School of Medicine reported in the* American Journal of Cardiology *that in addition to the unexpectedly sharp drop in heart attacks, there was also a slide in other diseases. The study was aimed at evaluating the effect of the drug on the growth of atherosclerosis.*
>
> *The team found that 5 percent of the 75 patients taking the drug experienced fatal or nonfatal coronary episodes during the three-year study period, compared to 13 percent of the 76 patients who got an inert placebo.*

(a) There are two populations involved in the study. Can you tell from the article what they are?

(b) What is the distribution of the number of coronary episodes experienced by the Pravastatin users? By the nonusers?

(c) What kind of bootstrap confidence interval would you use with these data to check the statistical significance of the statement that "The number of heart-attack victims fell dramatically among coronary patients who were taking the cholesterol-lowering drug Pravastatin"? Are the necessary assumptions for this interval satisfied?

(d) Compute and interpret the interval. What do you conclude?

11.20. The data set PENNIES contains the weights of 100 newly minted U.S. pennies as measured by an extremely accurate scale. For these data:

(a) What is the source of the variability you observe in the data?

(b) What is the population you will be making inference to? Construct a bootstrap 90% confidence interval for the population mean. Be sure to check all assumptions. Interpret the interval.

(c) Repeat part (b) for bootstrap prediction intervals.

(d) Obtain the best distribution-free tolerance interval you can. Why do you consider this interval the best you can obtain? Interpret the interval.

11.21. For the same set of data and same set of bootstrap samples, will a 90% or a 95% bootstrap confidence interval for μ be wider? Why?

11.22. For the same set of data, what is your answer to Exercise 11.21 if the two sets of bootstrap samples are different? Why?

11.23. Bars of metal are cut and their tensile strengths (psi) are measured using a destructive method. The data set TENSILE contains the strength of 20 bars chosen at random from the production process in a day's run. An engineer wants to use a bar taken at random from the next day's run. Use an appropriate bootstrap interval to supply the engineer with information about the tensile strength the selected bar might have. How is the interval to be interpreted? What assumptions are necessary for the interval to be valid?

11.24. A manufacturer claims that a certain drug is effective in treating arthritis. In an experiment, 150 people with arthritis were given a course of treatment with the drug and independently 100 people with arthritis were given a placebo. To monitor their condition, the subjects were given checkups 6 months after treatment began. The results are shown in Table 11.26.

TABLE 11.26   Classification of 150 People with Arthritis

	Improved	Not improved	Total
Drug	100	50	150
Sugar	60	40	100

(a) What can you say about the manufacturer's claim? (*Hint:* Calculate appropriate percentages and comment.)

(b) How can you test the manufacturer's claim using a confidence interval?

(c) Proceed with the analysis you suggested in part (b), with a bootstrap interval. Present your conclusions.

11.25. In this problem, you will see how to compute bounds on the accuracy of the p-value computed by a randomization test. Call the test statistic Z and suppose we have observed a value of the test statistic z^*. Suppose the p-value of the test statistic is p^+, the proportion of the values of Z computed under all possible permutations, which are as large or larger than z^*. The randomization test randomly samples N permutations from all possible permutations. Let $Z_i, i = 1, \ldots, N$, denote the value of the test statistic computed from sample i.

(a) Let X_i take the value 1 if $Z_i \geq z^*$ and the value 0 otherwise. What is the distribution of X_i?

(b) Let X be the number of the X_i that equal 1 ($X = \sum X_i$). What is the distribution of X?

(c) The randomization approximation to the true p-value is $\hat{p}^+ = X/N$. Based on this and the result of part (b), obtain the width of a 95% confidence interval for p^+ when
   i. $N = 1000, p^+ = 0.05$
   ii. $N = 1000, p^+ = 0.50$
   iii. $N = 1000000, p^+ = 0.05$
   iv. $N = 1000000, p^+ = 0.50$

(d) What do you conclude about the accuracy of the approximation of p^+ by $\hat{p}^+$?

11.26. Describe the distribution-free bootstrap algorithm for obtaining a bootstrap distribution of the estimator $\hat{p}_1 - \hat{p}_2$ of the difference of population proportions $p_1 - p_2$.

11.27. In a recent article that could have an impact on the debate surrounding the safety of silicone breast implants,[24] researchers report the levels of two inflammatory mediators: tumor necrosis factor–alpha (TNF-α) and interleukin-6 (IL-6), obtained from fibrous capsules

---

[24]E. A. Mena, N. Kossovsky, C. Chu, and C. Hu, "Inflammatory Intermediates Produced by Tissues Encasing Silicone Breast Prostheses," *Journal of Investigative Surgery,* 8 (1995): 31–42.

TABLE 11.27 A 2 × 2 Table of Over-65 AMI Patients Broken Down by Gender and Treatment

	Therapy	
Gender	Yes	No
Male	5	4
Female	2	8

encasing silicone prostheses removed from the breasts of nine women. Units are pg/ml per 10 g of tissue. The data are in the data set SILICONE. The authors report a Pearson correlation between TNF-α and IL-6 for these data of 0.77, and based on this, they conclude that there is strong statistical relationship between TNF-α and IL-6. Analyze these data using Spearman correlation to test for independence of the two mediators. Does your analysis agree with the paper's conclusions? Justify your answers.

11.28. Studies have shown that the automobile accident rate is high for young drivers, declines steadily until middle age, and then begins climbing again in the postretirement years, becoming nearly as high for elderly drivers as it is for the youngest drivers. In light of this, a student suggests that the Spearman correlation, rather than the Pearson correlation, is an appropriate measure of the association between age and accident rate. What is your opinion? Support your answer.

11.29. It has been asserted by some health care professionals that physicians are more aggressive in treating older males hospitalized with acute myocardial infarction (AMI) than they are in treating older females hospitalized with AMI. Table 11.27 shows data on patients aged 65 and over who were hospitalized with AMI and who also had a history of diabetes and stroke. The data are counts of individuals who did and did not receive therapy with drugs called beta blockers, broken down by gender.
   (a) Formulate appropriate hypotheses for testing the assertion of more aggressive treatment for males.
   (b) Show that the assumptions for the χ^2 test are not satisfied.
   (c) Do these data provide substantial evidence of more aggressive treatment for males? Use Fisher's exact test to decide.

11.30. Recently, an unusually large number of plastic door panels have been cracking during installation on a truck-assembly line. A quality engineer suspects that the cause may be improper storage. To test this, she keeps track of whether the panels are stored in an unheated outdoor storage shed or in a heated indoor shed just prior to assembly. The results for the next 20 panels are shown in Table 11.28.
   (a) Formulate appropriate hypotheses for testing whether cracking is associated with storage location.
   (b) Show that the assumptions for the χ^2 test are not satisfied.
   (c) Use Fisher's exact test to decide whether cracking is associated with storage location.

11.31. Recall the artificial pancreas experiment from Chapters 5 and 6. Table 11.29 displays more data from that experiment (the data are also found in the data set RATS1). Four rats are drawn from each of three populations: normal rats (NORMAL), diabetic rats (DIABETIC), and diabetic rats who have had an artificial pancreas implanted (PANCREAS). The researcher gives each rat the same initial dose of glucose in solution and

TABLE 11.28   A 2 × 2 Table of Plastic Truck Panels Broken Down by Storage Location and Cracking on Assembly

Storage location	Cracks	
	Yes	No
Heated	2	12
Unheated	3	3

TABLE 11.29   Artificial Pancreas Data

Group	Blood sugar			
Pancreas	374	319	405	400
Diabetic	529	388	542	548
Normal	129	133	166	148

then measures their blood-sugar levels (serum/plasma glucose, mg/100 ml) after one-half hour. If the artificial pancreas is effective, the median blood-sugar level of rats with the pancreas will be lower than the median blood-sugar level of diabetic rats. If the artificial pancreas is fully effective, the median blood-sugar level of rats with the pancreas will be no higher than the median blood-sugar level of normal rats.

(a) Draw suitable plots and compute suitable statistics to summarize these data. What do these suggest?

(b) These data do not satisfy the assumptions of the one-way model. Explain why.

(c) Transform the response using the transformation $1/\sqrt{Y}$. How do the data satisfy model assumptions now? If there are still departures from model assumptions, describe their likely effect on the analysis.

(d) Use an appropriate rank-based procedure on the transformed data to test for differences among the median for the three groups.

11.32. For the data in Exercise 11.31, test for differences among the central values for the three groups using an appropriate permutation or randomization test with the transformed data.

11.33. A production engineer wants to determine the effect of machine configuration on the maximum force, in pounds, applied at a joint on an articulated arm of the machine during its normal operation. To do this, she takes three maximum force readings at each of four configurations. The data are contained in Table 11.30 (and in the data set MACHFORC).

(a) How should the experimenter use randomization in this experiment?

(b) Use an appropriate rank-based test to compare the central values of the responses for the four machine configurations.

11.34. For the data in Exercise 11.33, test for differences among the central values for the four machine configurations using the original responses and an appropriate permutation or randomization test.

11.35. Mechanical engineers are studying the influence of cam shape on the vibration produced at a given set of frequencies. An experiment is run in which the vibrations produced by

TABLE 11.30   Machine Force Data

Configuration	Maximum force		
1	713.96	543.12	543.55
2	813.30	978.47	949.14
3	1420.30	1519.80	1629.50
4	299.75	572.56	562.62

TABLE 11.31   Cam Data

Cam	Shape			
	1	2	3	4
1	0.6105	0.5754	0.4595	0.5793
2	0.7126	0.6609	0.6557	0.6206
3	0.7121	0.6107	0.6700	0.5734
4	0.6088	0.5529	0.3814	0.4926
5	0.6247	0.5702	0.5880	0.5701
6	0.6862	0.6323	0.7456	0.6251
7	0.6551	0.6244	0.7261	0.6662
8	0.8498	0.6937	0.7187	0.5284

four common cam shapes are measured and compared. Eight specially made test cams are used. Each cam is divided into four sectors and each sector is machined to a different one of the four shapes. Thus, all four shapes appear on each test cam. The test cams are run at a fixed speed and the displacement of a stylus riding on the cam is recorded. This signal is then broken into four signals corresponding to the four different cam-shape sectors. Each signal is broken into frequency components (called the spectrum) and the rms[25] of the spectrum over a selected set of frequencies is computed. This value, which measures the amount of cam vibration at those frequencies, is the response variable. The data are displayed in Table 11.31 and are found in the data set CAM.

(a) Explain why this is not a CRD.

(b) Formulate an appropriate model for these data.

(c) Use an appropriate rank-based test to decide whether there are significant differences in the central location of cam vibration between different shapes.

11.36. For the data in Exercise 11.35, test for differences among the central values for the four cam shapes using the original responses and an appropriate permutation or randomization test.

11.37. A track coach conducts an experiment to give his runners a rational basis for selecting spike length for competition. He chooses four runners from the track team and randomly assigns each a spike length from among 0 (no spike), 1/4, 3/16, and 3/8 inch. He then records the time of each in the 60 meters. After a rest period, the same four runners are assigned a different spike length and the 60-meter times are again recorded. This continues

---

[25]Rms stands for "root mean square," and is basically the standard deviation of the measurements. See Chapter 2.

TABLE 11.32   Spike Data

Runner	Spike length			
	0	1/4	3/16	3/8
1	6.70	6.45	6.65	6.49
2	6.83	6.72	6.74	6.78
3	7.06	6.72	6.98	6.93
4	7.04	6.81	6.83	6.70

until all four runners have run 60-meters in each of the four spike lengths. The times are displayed in Table 11.32 and are found in the data set SPIKES.

(a) Explain why this is not a CRD.

(b) Formulate an appropriate model for these data.

(c) Use an appropriate rank-based test to decide whether there are significant differences in times due to spike length.

11.38. For the data in Exercise 11.37, test for differences among the central values for the four spike lengths using the original responses and an appropriate permutation or randomization test.

MINIPROJECT

Purpose

The purpose of this project is to

- Make you think about what processes might generate data suitable for analysis by two of the inference methods in this chapter.
- Teach you how to analyze data from these processes using the inference tools you've learned in the chapter.

Process

Your group will be assigned two of the following distribution-free inference methods:

1. The sign test

2. The Wilcoxon signed rank test

3. The Wilcoxon rank sum test

4. The Spearman correlation

5. The Kruskall-Wallis test

6. Friedman's test

7. Fisher's exact test

8. The one-sample Pitman test

9. The two-sample Pitman test

10. The generalized Kruskal-Wallis test
11. The generalized Friedman test
12. Bootstrap estimation
13. Bootstrap prediction
14. A distribution-free tolerance interval

Your group's task will be to design and conduct a small experiment or sampling study to generate data suitable for analysis by each assigned inference method.

For each of the two data sets, you are then to do the following:

- Analyze the data by the assigned method. You must tell why the data are appropriately analyzed by the method chosen. Be sure to check all necessary assumptions to help determine what is appropriate.
- Analyze the data using the classical inference counterpart of the distribution-free inference method.
- Compare the results you obtain from the two methods.

A short (one-page or less) proposal of what your group plans to do for this miniproject must be submitted and approved before you begin your work.

LAB 11.1: Permutation and Randomization Testing by Hand

Introduction

You have read about permutation and randomization tests in Chapter 11, but have you really learned how to conduct them? It's time to find out.

Objectives

To learn permutation and randomization testing by doing these tests by hand.

Lab Materials

A 10-sided die.

Experimental Procedure

Here is a small data set consisting of the nicotine content (mg) of three randomly selected cigarettes from each of two different brands:

$$\text{Brand X:} \quad 1.15 \quad 1.02 \quad 0.99$$
$$\text{Brand Y:} \quad 0.83 \quad 0.79 \quad 0.71$$

Assume the data are produced by the location-shift model described by Equations (11.5) and (11.6).

The Permutation Test

In this part of the lab, you will conduct a permutation test of

$$H_0: \quad \delta = 0$$
$$H_{a\pm}: \quad \delta \neq 0$$

using the two-sample Pitman test. To do this, make a table like Table 11.14, listing all possible assignments of the six nicotine measurements to two groups of size three.

1. Make a table like Table 11.14, listing all possible assignments (permutations) of the six nicotine measurements to two groups of size three.

2. For each assignment, compute the value of the test statistic, U.

3. Compute the p-value p^+ as the proportion of the U values that are at least as large as the observed value of the test statistic, u^*.

4. Compute the p-value p_- as the proportion of the U values that are at least as small as the observed value of the test statistic, u^*.

5. Compute the two-sided p-value $p\pm$ as twice the smaller of p^+ and p_-. Based on the value of $p\pm$, what do you conclude?

6. Now rank all six data values and do steps 1 to 5 on the ranks. What is the name of the resulting test? How do your results compare with the results from the Pitman test?

The Randomization Test

Recall that a randomization test is a permutation test conducted using a random sample of all possible permutations. A randomization test is most often used when the time or resources are not available to compute test statistic values for all permutations. In this part of the lab, you will conduct a randomization test for the problem in the previous section. To do this, proceed as follows:

1. Number from 1 to 20 the values of the test statistic for all permutations.

2. Roll the die once. This will give you a number between 1 and 10.[26] Remember the number.

3. Roll the die again. If the number is in the range 1 to 5, add 10 to the number chosen in step 2. Otherwise, leave that number alone. This number is the number of your chosen permutation.

4. Include the U value of the chosen permutation in the set of selected values.

5. Continue steps 2 to 4 until the desired number of values has been selected. For our application, choose 10 values. Note that the selection is with replacement, so some values may appear more than once.

6. Compute the p-value just as described in the section on permutation tests, treating the set of 10 randomly selected values just as you would the set resulting from all possible permutations. What do you conclude?

7. Now do steps 1 to 6 on the ranked data. Compare the results with those obtained in step 6 of the previous section.

---

[26]If the die is numbered 0 to 9, count 0 as 10.

In your lab report, document the steps you used to obtain your results, including all permutations used and the corresponding values of U.

LAB 11.2: Bootstrapping by Hand

Introduction

You have read about bootstrapping in Chapter 11, but have you really learned how to do it? It's time to find out.

Objectives

To learn bootstrapping by doing it.

Lab Materials

A 10-sided die.

Experimental Procedure

Here is a small data set consisting of the silver content of galena crystals from four different batches:

$$\text{Y:} \quad 0.15 \quad 0.05 \quad 0.23 \quad 0.43$$

Assume the data are produced by the C+E model $Y = \mu + \epsilon$. In your lab report, explain the meaning of Y, μ, and ϵ.

Find the least squares estimate of μ based on these data.

Bootstrap Estimation of μ

In this part of the lab, you will generate a bootstrap confidence interval for μ. You may wish to reference Section 11.12.

1. Generate 10 bootstrap samples from this data set. Record your samples and save for part 2 (you may want to make a table like Table 11.20, page 695).
   Here's how to use the die to generate a bootstrap sample:

   i. Roll the die. If the number is 1 or 2, choose the first observation (here 0.15). If it is 3 or 4, choose the second observation; if it is 5 or 6, choose the third observation; and if it is 7 or 8, choose the fourth observation. If it is 0 or 9, roll again. At the end of this step, you have chosen one observation. Note that each observation has an equal chance of being selected.

   ii. Repeat step i three more times. You now have four observations. Some may be repeats, but that's ok. These four observations constitute the first bootstrap sample.

   iii. Repeat steps i and ii nine more times to give a total of 10 bootstrap samples.

2. For each bootstrap sample, compute the least squares estimate of μ. Record the 10 estimates.

3. Based on these data, compute a level 0.8 bootstrap confidence interval for μ.[27] Interpret the interval.

Bootstrap Prediction of a Future Observation

In this part of the lab, you will generate a bootstrap prediction interval for a future observation. You may wish to reference Section 11.12.

1. Fit the model by least squares. Obtain the residuals.

2. Randomly draw from these residuals (with replacement) and assign the draws to the samples. To do this using the die:

   i. Roll the die. If the number is 1 or 2, choose the first residual. If it is 3 or 4, choose the second residual; if it is 5 or 6, choose the third residual; and if it is 7 or 8, choose the fourth residual. If it is 0 or 9, roll again. Assign this residual to bootstrap sample 1. It might help you to make a table like Table 11.22 to record your results.

   ii. Repeat step i nine more times until there is one residual assigned to each bootstrap sample.

3. Create the bootstrap future observations by adding the residuals to the corresponding bootstrap estimates.

4. Create a bootstrap level 0.8 prediction interval for a future observation. Interpret this interval. How does it differ from the confidence interval you computed earlier?

In your lab report, document the steps you used to obtain your results, including all bootstrap samples used and the corresponding values of the estimator or predictor.

APPENDIX 11.1: Bias Correction and Acceleration Formulas

This appendix presents the formulas for bias and acceleration for computing bootstrap BC_a intervals for a single parameter. Assume that

- the parameter to be estimated is θ
- the estimate of θ computed from the data is $\hat{\theta}$
- there are N bootstrap estimates of the parameter, $\tilde{\theta}^{(j)}$, $j = 1, \ldots, N$
- $\Phi(z)$ denotes the proportion of a standard normal population below z

A level L BC_a confidence interval for θ is an interval $(\tilde{\theta}_{L_1}, \tilde{\theta}_{L_2})$, where the quantile values L_1 and L_2 are computed as

$$L_1 = \Phi\left(\hat{z}_0 + \frac{\hat{z}_0 + z_{(1+L)/2}}{1 - \hat{a}(\hat{z}_0 + z_{(1+L)/2})} \right)$$

---

[27] For this interval, use the straight 0.1 and 0.9 quantiles with no BC_a correction.

and

$$L_2 = \Phi\left(\hat{z}_0 + \frac{\hat{z}_0 + z_{(1-L)/2}}{1 - \hat{a}(\hat{z}_0 + z_{(1-L)/2})}\right)$$

The **bias correction,** $\hat{z}_0$, is computed as $\hat{z}_0 = \Phi^{-1}(\Pi)$, where Π is the proportion of bootstrap estimates $\tilde{\theta}^{(j)}$, which are smaller than the original estimate $\hat{\theta}$.

The **acceleration,** $\hat{a}$, is a little more complicated to compute. For $i = 1, \ldots, n$, let $\hat{\theta}_{(i)}$ be the value of the estimator computed from all the original data except the ith value. Let $\hat{\theta}_{(\cdot)}$ be the mean of these:

$$\hat{\theta}_{(\cdot)} = \frac{1}{n}\sum_{i=1}^{n}\hat{\theta}_{(i)}$$

Then the acceleration is given by

$$\hat{a} = \frac{\displaystyle\sum_{i=1}^{n}(\hat{\theta}_{(\cdot)} - \hat{\theta}_{(i)})^3}{6\left[\displaystyle\sum_{i=1}^{n}(\hat{\theta}_{(\cdot)} - \hat{\theta}_{(i)})^2\right]^{3/2}}$$

12

2^k Designs

The development of Western Science is based on two great achievements; the invention of the formal logical system (in Euclidean geometry) by the Greek philosophers, and the discovery of the possibility to find out causal relationship by systematic experiment (Renaissance).

—Albert Einstein

INTRODUCTION

Toward the end of the 1970s, the preeminence of the United States as a world manufacturing leader came under increasing challenge from other countries. In heavy industry, such as steel and auto manufacture, in consumer electronics, and in the emerging computer industry, overseas competitors began beating U.S. firms with products of higher quality, better performance, and lower cost.

There is more than a touch of irony in the fact that U.S. manufacturers were being beaten in part by the use of U.S.-invented statistical methods! Japanese industry, in particular, wholeheartedly implemented the statistical quality improvement methods advocated by American statisticians such as W. Edwards Deming. Belatedly, U.S. industries got on the statistical quality improvement bandwagon, and, at least in some industries, became competitive once again.

Key components of any quality improvement program include statistical process control methods, such as those presented in Chapter 15, and experimental design methods covered in Chapter 3 and in greater detail in this chapter and in Chapters 13 and 14.

Experimental design is fundamental to the iterative process of scientific investigation, on which much of our basic knowledge and technology is based. In industry, experimental design is important in identifying those process and environmental variables most significantly related to process performance, and in quantifying that relationship. Once quantified, the relationship of those variables to the process can be exploited to optimize performance and/or reduce cost.

This chapter introduces 2^k factorial designs. Though 2^k factorial designs are a subset of the factorial designs introduced in Chapter 10, they are so useful and so often used in industrial experimentation, that they deserve careful study in their own right.[1]

Knowledge and Skills

By successfully completing this chapter, you will acquire the following knowledge and skills:

KNOWLEDGE	SKILLS
1. The role of experimentation in scientific investigation.	**1.** How to design, run, and analyze a 2^k design, with and without center points.
2. One factor at a time (OFAT) experimentation.	**2.** The use of orthogonal arrays.
3. Factorial experimentation and its advantage over OFAT methods.	**3.** When and how to transform the response.
4. Design space, response surface, replication, and randomization.	
5. The reasons for using center points.	
6. Orthogonal arrays.	
7. 2^k designs, with and without center points.	
8. The value of transformations and residual analysis.	

12.1

THE NATURE OF SCIENTIFIC INVESTIGATION

It is no exaggeration to state that scientific investigation is the most successful enterprise ever attempted by the human race. It has provided the basis for the technological advances that have improved daily life. It is the foundation for the medical breakthroughs that have tamed disease and greatly increased life expectancy. The application of scientific methods to business and industry has increased the quality of services and products and the productivity of workers.

---

[1]Note that the treatment of 2^k designs in this chapter is self-contained, and does not depend on knowledge of Chapter 10 material.

Scientific investigation is **iterative** in nature. Its steps can be expressed as:

1. Formulating a working model of the phenomenon of interest.
2. Designing an experiment[2] to test that model.
3. Conducting the experiment and collecting data.
4. Reformulating the model in light of the data.
5. Returning to step 2 and repeating steps 2 to 5 as necessary.

This iterative procedure has proven very effective in converging toward a useful understanding of how nature works.

12.2

THE ROLE OF STATISTICS IN SCIENTIFIC INVESTIGATION

In the iterative process just outlined statistics plays a crucial role in steps 2, 3, and 4. As you will learn in this and succeeding chapters, a major area of statistics called **experimental design** deals with designing efficient and effective experiments so that useful understanding can be obtained with an optimal use of resources. Other statistical methods are crucial to analyzing the results and drawing proper conclusions.

Whatever contribution statistics makes to scientific investigation, remember that invariably the experiment will not be a one-shot, stand-alone result. It will be part of an iterative set of experiments designed to answer questions about the phenomenon of interest in stages, one step at a time.

In the next two sections, we will learn two different designs for a two-factor experiment. The first, called an **OFAT** (one factor at a time), is, unfortunately, still used by uninformed experimenters. The OFAT design will be discussed in Section 12.4. In Section 12.5, we will see how the second design, called a **factorial** design, is superior in nearly every way to the OFAT design.

In introducing both designs, we will assume that the experimenter is interested in the effect of two factors, A and B, on a response Y. Further, we suppose that in addition to a high and a low level, each factor has a center (or standard) level located halfway between the high and low levels. We'll code the center level as 0, the high level as 1, and the low level as −1 for each factor. The following is an example of how such a design might originate.

EXAMPLE 12.1   AN EXPERIMENTAL DESIGN

An abrasives manufacturer wants to find out what factors involved in grinding-wheel operation affect the surface finish of a ground part. The factors considered

---

[2]Throughout Chapters 12 to 14, whenever we refer to an experiment, we will mean a controlled experiment as defined in Chapter 3: a study in which the experimenter controls the assignment of treatments to experimental units.

are as follows:

1. **Dress Lead.** As a part is ground, the original shape of the grinding wheel changes. In order to "true" the wheel (i.e., restore its original shape), a diamond is used to reshape the wheel as it turns. Dress Lead is the rate at which the grinding wheel is trued by the diamond. Specifically, it is how far the diamond will traverse during one revolution of the grinding wheel. Dress Lead is measured in inches/revolution.

2. **Feed Rate.** Feed Rate is the rate at which the grinding wheel is fed into the part during the grinding operation. It is measured in inches/minute.

The response is **Surface-Finish Roughness.** The Surface-Finish Roughness is measured by a surface profilometer, which records the root-mean-square departure of the surface profile from the mean line. It is measured in microinches.

A team assigned to investigate the effect of Dress Lead and Feed Rate on Surface-Finish Roughness determines that the three levels of interest for Dress Lead (factor A) are 0.0005, 0.0010, and 0.0015. These levels are coded as $-1, 0$, and 1, respectively, by subtracting 0.0010 and dividing by 0.0005. They also decided to consider 0.02, 0.03, and 0.04 as the three levels for Feed Rate (factor B). These levels are coded as -1, 0, and 1, respectively, by subtracting 0.03 and dividing by 0.01. ◆

12.3

NOTIONS AND TERMINOLOGY OF EXPERIMENTAL DESIGN

In this section, we list some of the fundamental notions and terminology of experimental design. Some of these were introduced in Chapter 3.

1. **Experiment.** Whenever we speak of an experiment in this or succeeding chapters, we will mean a controlled experiment, defined in Chapter 3 as a study in which treatments are imposed on experimental units in order to observe a response. Treatments may be made up of combinations of one or more **factors.**

2. **Design Space.** The design space is the range of values over which the factors are to be varied, and implicitly, over which we are willing to consider the experimental results to hold.

3. **Design Points.** Design points are the actual values of the factors at which the experiment is conducted. Design points are often coded to convenient values.

4. **Response Surface.** The response surface is the unknown surface that represents the mean response at any given level of the factors in the design space. Mapping out the response surface is an important goal of experimentation. The response surface features that can be identified are often dependent on the type of design being used.

EXAMPLE 12.1   CONTINUED

In the surface-finish example, the response is surface-finish roughness, the treatments are the combinations of levels of factors Dress Lead and Feed Rate, and the experimental units are the pieces of metal on which the treatments are imposed. The design space is the range of reasonable values of Dress Lead and Feed Rate, as determined by the experimenter. The design points are the actual combinations of Dress Lead and Feed Rate at which the experiment is run. The response surface is the surface that represents the mean surface-finish roughness at level d of Dress Lead and level f of Feed Rate as a function $g(d, f)$.   ◆

12.4

THE OFAT DESIGN

The two-factor OFAT design consists of five design points, which can be divided into three groups as described in Table 12.1. At each of the design points, one measurement of the response is taken.

OFAT Geometry

It is often useful to plot the location of the design points. Figure 12.1 gives a plot of the two-factor OFAT design, in coded units. The horizontal axis corresponds to factor A and the vertical to factor B. The five design points are represented by solid circles.

Analysis of the Two-Factor OFAT Design

The analysis of an OFAT design focuses on the **main effects** of the factors. The main effect of factor A is the mean change in the response due to changing the level of factor A from its -1 to its 1 setting.

TABLE 12.1   OFAT Design Points, Coded Units

Group	Design point
Standard	$(0, 0)$
Change A, hold B constant	$(1, 0)$
	$(-1, 0)$
Change B, hold A constant	$(0, 1)$
	$(0, -1)$

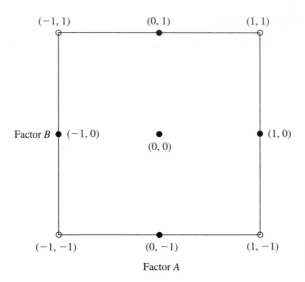

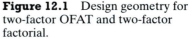

Figure 12.1 Design geometry for two-factor OFAT and two-factor factorial.

TABLE 12.2 OFAT Design Points and Response, Surface-Finish Data

Group	Design point	Response Y
Standard	$(0, 0)$	17
Change Dress Lead, hold Feed Rate constant	$(1, 0)$	18
	$(-1, 0)$	15
Change Feed Rate, hold Dress Lead constant	$(0, 1)$	18
	$(0, -1)$	16

EXAMPLE 12.1   CONTINUED

Suppose that the surface-finish experiment was designed and run as an OFAT and that the measured values of the response for the surface-finish experiment are given in Table 12.2. Then the estimate of the effect of Dress Lead is $18 - 15 = 3$. This means we estimate that, on average, changing the Dress Lead from its low value to its high value results in a three-unit increase in the Surface-Finish Roughness. How would you calculate the effect of Feed Rate from these data?   ✦

12.5

THE FACTORIAL DESIGN

Look again at Figure 12.1. The design points for the 2^2 factorial design, in coded units, are given by the points at the corners of the square (those points designated by open circles). The four design points consist of all combinations of the two factors at their high and low levels. Note that there is no 0 level in this design (though we will add 0 levels later in the chapter). This factorial design is called a 2^2 since it consists of two factors each at two levels.[3]

Estimating Main Effects

Even though the 2^2 factorial design has only four data points, it is more powerful than the OFAT design with five data points when it comes to estimating the main effects of the two factors. This is because each point in the factorial design serves double duty in estimating the effects.

To see how this works, first suppose that we are interested in estimating the effect of factor A. With this in mind, note that the four corner points in Figure 12.1 correspond to two one-factor designs. The first is given by the pair $(-1, -1)$ and $(1, -1)$, which varies A while holding B fixed at -1. The second is given by the pair $(-1, 1)$ and $(1, 1)$, which varies A while holding B fixed at 1. This means that there are twice as many data points giving information about the effect of factor A as there are in the OFAT design. The same thing happens if we are interested in factor B. Test your understanding here: Which two pairs of data points correspond to the two one-factor designs for the effect of factor B?

How do we estimate these main effects in a 2^2 design? The most sensible thing is to get an estimate from each of the one-factor designs separately and then average them. A look at the surface-finish experiment will show how this is done.

EXAMPLE 12.1   CONTINUED

Suppose that the experimenters in the surface-finish experiment ran a 2^2 design, and that the values of the responses at the corner points are those shown in Figure 12.2.

The estimate of the effect of Dress Lead when Feed Rate is at its high level is computed from the pair $(-1, 1)$ and $(1, 1)$, and equals $20 - 17 = 3$. Note that this is the difference of the responses at the top of the square in Figure 12.2. The estimate of the effect of Dress Lead when Feed Rate is at its low level is computed from the pair $(-1, -1)$ and $(1, -1)$, and equals $14 - 18 = -4$. Note that this is the difference of the responses at the bottom of the square in Figure 12.2. The combined estimate is then the average of these two estimates: $[3+(-4)]/2 = -0.5$. The interpretation is that on average, changing Dress Lead from its low value to its high value results in a -0.5 unit change in surface finish. Notice that four data values go into computing this estimate, as opposed to the two data values that were used in the estimate obtained from the OFAT design.   ◆

We can also look at the computation of the effect for a factor from a 2^2 design as the difference between the average response when the factor is at its high level and the average response when the factor is at its low level. The next example illustrates.

---

[3]The terminology is (#levels)$^{(\text{#factors})}$. Thus, a factorial design with 5 factors each at 3 levels is a 3^5 design. The terminology also tells how many different treatments (i.e., factor combinations) there are in all. Thus, a 2^2 design has $2^2 = 2 \times 2 = 4$ treatments, and a 3^5 design has $3^5 = 3 \times 3 \times 3 \times 3 \times 3 = 243$ treatments.

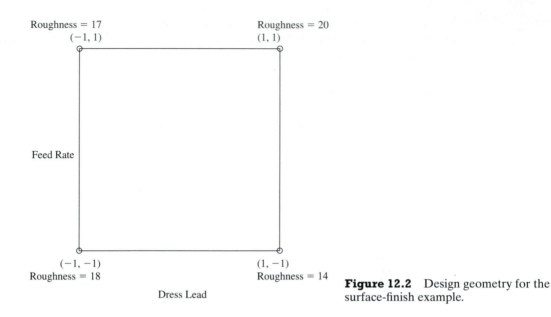

Roughness = 17
(−1, 1)

Roughness = 20
(1, 1)

Feed Rate

(−1, −1)
Roughness = 18

(1, −1)
Roughness = 14

Dress Lead

Figure 12.2   Design geometry for the surface-finish example.

EXAMPLE 12.1   CONTINUED

In the surface-finish experiment, the average response when Dress Lead is at its high level equals $(20 + 14)/2$ or 17. This is the average of the responses on the right side of the square in Figure 12.2. The average response when Dress Lead is at its low level equals $(17 + 18)/2$ or 17.5. This is the average of the responses on the left side of the square in Figure 12.2. The difference of these averages is the estimate of the effect of Dress Lead, and it equals $17 − 17.5 = −0.5$.   ✦

Interactions

Sometimes in order to define a thing, it is easiest to say what it is not. With that in mind, let's begin by defining the opposite of an interaction.

> ### DEFINITION
>
> Two factors, A and B, in a 2^k design are said to be **additive** with respect to each other if the effect of A when B is held at its high level equals the effect of A when B is held at its low level. Equivalently, the factors are additive if the effect of B when A is held at its high level equals the effect of B when A is held at its low level.
>
> If A and B are not additive with respect to each other, they are said to **interact.**

INTERACTION PLOT

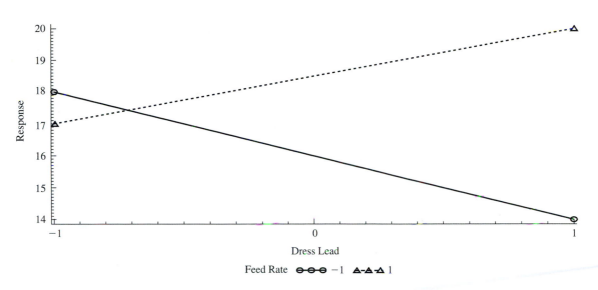

Figure 12.3   Interaction plot 1, surface-finish data.

To illustrate, let's look at the surface-finish example.

EXAMPLE 12.1   CONTINUED

Figure 12.3 is a plot of the responses in the 2^2 design for the surface-finish data. The response, Surface-Finish Roughness, is plotted on the vertical axis and the levels of Dress Lead on the horizontal axis. Two lines are plotted on the graph. One connects the two responses when Feed Rate is at its low level, the other the two responses when Feed Rate is at its high level. The effect of Dress Lead when Feed Rate is at its low level is the difference between the response when Dress Lead is at its high level and Feed Rate at its low level and the response when Dress Lead is at its low level and Feed Rate at its low level. This is twice the slope of the line in Figure 12.3 corresponding to the low level of Feed Rate. Similarly, the effect of Dress Lead when Feed Rate is at its high level is twice the slope of the other line.

If the two factors were additive, these two lines would be parallel, or nearly so. (Why?) Here they are not, so the data provide evidence that the factors interact. We can interpret the interaction as follows: When Feed Rate is at its low level, the response is four units higher for the low value of Dress Lead than for the high value of Dress Lead. But when Feed Rate is at its high level, the response is three units lower for the low value of Dress Lead than for the high value of Dress Lead. This difference in behavior characterizes the interaction between Dress Lead and Feed Rate.

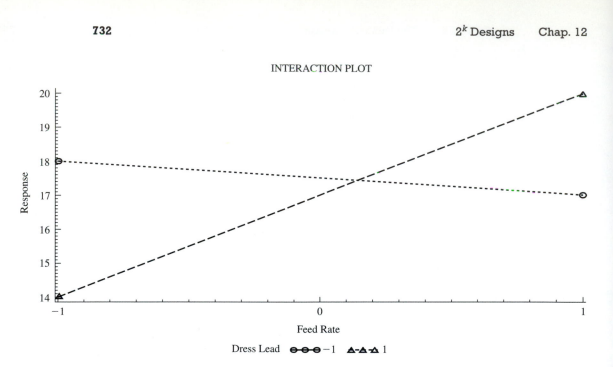

Figure 12.4   Interaction plot 2, surface-finish data.

Figure 12.4 gives another view using the same data. Here, Feed Rate is plotted on the horizontal axis and one line connects the two responses for the low level of Dress Lead and the other line connects the two responses for the high level of Dress Lead. Exercise 12.21 asks you to interpret the interaction displayed in Figure 12.4. ✦

Often in experimental data, variables interact. In some of these cases, analysis only of the main effects of the factors will reveal no relation, resulting in incorrect conclusions. So it is important to check for interactions. Whereas this can be done with factorial designs, it is impossible with OFAT designs.[4]

Estimating Interactions

Factors A and B interact if the effect of factor A when factor B is at its low level is different than the effect of factor A when factor B is at its high level. The interaction between A and B is estimated as the mean difference between the effect of factor A when factor B is at its low level and that effect when B is at its high level.

---

[4]Though to be fair, the OFAT can model pure quadratic terms, something the 2^2 factorial design cannot do.

For the surface-finish example, the estimation is done as follows:

EXAMPLE 12.1   CONTINUED

Effect of Dress Lead when Feed Rate $= -1$:	$14 - 18 = -4$
Effect of Dress Lead when Feed Rate $= 1$:	$20 - 17 = 3$
Interaction of Dress Lead and Feed Rate:	$(3 - (-4))/2 = 3.5$

Notice that the effect of Dress Lead when Feed Rate $= -1$ is just twice the slope of the line corresponding to Feed Rate $= -1$ in Figure 12.3, and that the effect of Dress Lead when Feed Rate $= 1$ is just twice the slope of the line corresponding to Feed Rate $= 1$ in Figure 12.3. So the interaction is the difference of these slopes. This explains again why parallel lines indicate no interaction. ◆

Interaction has a nice interpretation in terms of Figure 12.1 as well. The interaction is one-half the difference of (1) the difference in the responses for the upper two corner points and (2) the difference in the responses for the lower two corner points. Looked at in another way, the interaction is the difference between the average of the responses for the lower left and upper right corner points and the average of the responses for the lower right and upper left corner points. Another look at the surface-finish experiment will illustrate.

EXAMPLE 12.1   CONTINUED

Look at Figure 12.2. The interaction between Dress Lead and Feed Rate can be estimated as the difference between the average responses for the lower left and upper right corner points, $(18 + 20)/2 = 19$, and the average responses for the lower right and upper left corner points, $(17 + 14)/2 = 15.5$. That is, it equals $(18 + 20)/2 - (17 + 14)/2 = 19 - 15.5 = 3.5$. ◆

12.6

DESIGNING AND RUNNING A 2^2 EXPERIMENT

Designing and running any experiment is an important task, easily as important as analyzing the results. If an experiment is designed properly, it will yield valid results and do so economically. In addition, because specifying the analysis is part of the design process, the analysis of data obtained from a well-designed experiment will usually involve a minimum of difficulties. On the other hand, little can be done to salvage a poorly designed or poorly conducted experiment. The following are the three steps we recommend for running a 2^2 experiment:

1. First, decide what factors will be involved. This is not an easy task. Often, experimenters have many possible factors and little idea of which may be important.

They may then run very efficient designed experiments called **screening experiments** to narrow the number of factors down to a manageable few. Screening experiments will be considered in more detail in Chapter 13. Here, we will restrict ourselves to two factors only.

2. Decide on the design space for the experiment and then on the design points. For the 2^2 design, this means selecting low and high levels for each factor. In general, the levels should be far enough apart that there will be observable differences, but not so far apart that the response surface is nonlinear (curved) over the range of values.

3. Run the four data points in **random** order. The reason for the randomization is to protect against bias due to unknown trends or shifts or other lurking variables.

12.7

A MODEL FOR 2^2 EXPERIMENTAL DATA

So far, we have discussed only effects computed from experimental data. These effects are useful, but as with the data used in their computation, they are subject to variability. For instance, if another "identical" 2^2 surface-finish experiment was conducted tomorrow, the responses, and hence the computed effects, would almost certainly differ from the values obtained in Example 12.1.

What we really want is to understand and analyze the underlying process that generated the data. It is here that the notion of a **population effect** can help.

> **DEFINITION**
>
> A **population effect,** either main effect or interaction, is the mean of that effect averaged over all possible sets of experimental data.

So, for example, the population main effect of Dress Lead in the surface-finish experiment could be computed by doing the surface-finish experiment a very large number of times, computing the main effect of Dress Lead for each set of experimental data, and then averaging all those computed main effects for Dress Lead.

The data obtained from a 2^2 experiment can be thought of as arising from a model specified from these population effects. However, since no experiment or measuring instrument is perfectly reproducible, we assume each observation includes a random error. This idea is identical with statistical models you have studied previously, such as the C+E model.

Our model for the 2^2 experiment is

$$Y = \mu + \frac{1}{2}\{\alpha z_1 + \beta z_2 + (\alpha\beta)z_1 z_2\} + \epsilon \tag{12.1}$$

In this model, Y is the observed response, z_1 is the coded level of factor A, z_2 is the coded level of factor B, μ is the overall population mean level, α is the population effect of factor A, β is the population effect of factor B, $(\alpha\beta)$ is the population effect of the AB interaction, and ϵ is random error, assumed to have an $N(0, \sigma^2)$ distribution. Thus, we assume that if both factor A and factor B are at their high levels (coded value 1), the response will be generated by

$$Y = \mu + \frac{1}{2}\{\alpha(1) + \beta(1) + (\alpha\beta)(1)(1)\} + \epsilon$$

$$= \mu + \frac{1}{2}\{\alpha + \beta + (\alpha\beta)\} + \epsilon$$

Or, if A is at its high level and B at its low level (coded value -1), the model tells us the response will be generated by

$$Y = \mu + \frac{1}{2}\{\alpha(1) + \beta(-1) + (\alpha\beta)(1)(-1)\} + \epsilon$$

$$= \mu + \frac{1}{2}\{\alpha - \beta - (\alpha\beta)\} + \epsilon$$

With this model in mind, we can view the effects computed from the data as estimates of the population effects. We have already discussed the computation of the main effects and interactions from the data. The population mean μ is estimated by $\bar{Y}$, the mean of the observations.

One thing you may have wondered about is the reason for the 1/2 that appears in model (12.1). The 1/2 is a result of the way the factors are coded, at 1 and -1, which gives a coded distance of 2 between the factor levels. To see that the 1/2 gives the correct results, we'll assume the following simpler additive model[5] is generating the data:

$$Y = \mu + \frac{1}{2}\{\alpha z_1 + \beta z_2\} + \epsilon$$

Then, ignoring the random error, the effect of factor A when factor B is kept at level z_2 is

$$\mu + \frac{1}{2}\{\alpha(1) + \beta z_2\} - \left[\mu + \frac{1}{2}\{\alpha(-1) + \beta z_2\}\right] = \alpha$$

The notation used in model (12.1) is a good way to understand the model. However, in order to refer to more general models, we will sometimes use different notation. In the alternative notation, we will let the terms x_i denote both coded factor effects and interactions, and we will let y_i denote the corresponding population effect. In this alternative notation, we might write model (12.1) as

$$Y = \mu + \frac{1}{2}\{\gamma_1 x_1 + \gamma_2 x_2 + \gamma_3 x_3\} + \epsilon \tag{12.2}$$

[5] That is, a model without an interaction.

where $\gamma_1 = \alpha$, $\gamma_2 = \beta$, $\gamma_3 = (\alpha\beta)$, $x_3 = z_1 z_2$, $x_1 = z_1$, and $x_2 = z_2$. The kind of notation used in model (12.2) will be useful in our discussion of the Lenth procedure for assessing significant effects described in the next section.

12.8

ANALYZING A 2^2 EXPERIMENT

Model (12.1) for the 2^2 experiment contains three population effects. However, in reality, we do not know if all, some subset, or even none of these effects best describes the mechanism that generates the data. One of the experimenter's primary tasks is to figure out which subset of these population effects is the best descriptor of the data-generating process. In order to decide, the experimenter will look at the size of each effect computed from the data, and based on the size of the computed effect, determine how likely it is that an effect of this size occurred just by chance. This kind of analysis is very much like that used in the roulette wheel example in Chapter 4, and explored at greater length in the presentation of hypothesis tests in Chapter 6.

When an experiment has one data point for each treatment, we say that the experiment is **unreplicated,** or, more accurately, that there is a single replication. The surface-finish experiment is an example of an unreplicated experiment. When the experiment is unreplicated, we can get estimates of the effects; but there is no estimate of experimental error against which to judge how large these effects are. For example, without knowing how variable repeated measurements of surface finish are, it is impossible to know if the main effect estimate of 3 microinches for Feed Rate could be due to chance or is telling us that Feed Rate has a significant effect on the surface finish. If repeated measurements of surface finish, taken while holding the settings of factors Dress Lead and Feed Rate fixed, differ on average by 7 microinches, then the estimated effect of 3 microinches is negligible. On the other hand, if repeated measurements differ by 0.7 microinch, then an effect of size 3 is unlikely to be due to chance, and we must conclude that Feed Rate does make a real difference in the response. In statistical parlance, an effect is **significant** if it is so large in absolute value that it is unlikely to have occurred by chance.

Graphical Methods for Assessing which Effects Are Significant

Graphical methods are useful in analyzing unreplicated 2^k experiments. Suppose that in reality, all the population effects are 0. Then statistical theory says that the effects computed from the data should all have the same distribution with mean 0. In fact, if the random errors affecting the response are normal, this distribution will be normal. Now if one or more population effects are nonzero, the corresponding effects computed from the data will likely show up as outliers among the set of all effects computed from the data. Any graphical method for detecting outliers (e.g., boxplots) may be applied to the set of all effects computed from the data in order to identify possible significant effects. The most commonly used graphical technique is to create a normal quantile plot of the effects computed from the data, and to identify as significant those appearing as outliers on the plot.

A Nongraphical Method for Assessing Significant Effects

The following method is due to Lenth.[6] It assumes that if all of the population effects are 0, then the effects computed from the data have an N$(0, \sigma^2)$ distribution. However, since we don't know σ^2, we'll use the data to estimate it. Then the distribution of the standardized sample effects becomes a t distribution.[7] This method gives benchmarks against which to measure the size of each effect to determine statistical significance.
We assume the notation of model (12.2) with m effects:

$$Y = \mu + \frac{1}{2} \sum_{i=1}^{m} \gamma_i x_i \tag{12.3}$$

Suppose we have taken the data and that the m effects computed from the data are $c_1, c_2, \ldots, c_m$. The method proceeds as follows:

1. To begin with, we must decide a level of confidence, L, for the benchmark. Common values are 0.90, 0.95, and 0.99 (or 90%, 95%, and 99%). A 0.95, level, for example, means that if a population effect is 0, then in about 95% of all data samples, the corresponding computed effect will not be judged significant when compared with the benchmark, and in the other 5%, it will be judged significant. This means that when the population effect is 0, the procedure will be correct 95% of the time.

2. Define $s_0 = 1.5 \times$ median $\{|c_j|\}$.

3. Create a new set of numbers c_j^* as follows: If $|c_j| < 2.5 s_0$, then $c_j^* = |c_j|$; otherwise, c_j^* is not defined.

4. Define the **pseudo-standard error (PSE)** as

$$\text{PSE} = 1.5 \times \text{median}\{c_j^*\}$$

where the median is computed from those c_j^* defined in step 3.

5. Define MOE $= \text{PSE} \times t_{m/3, (1+L)/2}$, where $t_{m/3, (1+L)/2}$ is the $(1+L)/2$ quantile of the t distribution with $m/3$ degrees of freedom. (If $m/3$ is not an integer, the computer must be used to obtain this value.)

6. Define $\delta = (1 + L^{1/m})/2$, and define SMOE $= \text{PSE} \times t_{m/3, \delta}$.

MOE (margin of error) is a benchmark used for individual effects. It ensures that if a single-population effect is 0, then in a proportion L of all samples, the size

---

[6] Russell V. Lenth, "Quick and easy analysis of unreplicated factorials," *Technometrics,* **31** (1989): 469–473.

[7] In fact, for this method, the sample standard deviation is **not** used to estimate σ; rather the sample median is used. But the basic idea is the same.

(i.e., absolute value) of the effect computed from the data will not exceed MOE. **SMOE (simultaneous margin of error)** is a benchmark for **all individual effects simultaneously.** It ensures that if all population effects are 0, then in a proportion L of all samples, no effect computed from the data will exceed SMOE in size.

To understand the difference between MOE and SMOE, consider the 2^2 design. There is a total of three effects: factors A and B and their interaction. Assume that all of the three population effects are 0. Suppose we choose a 0.95 level of confidence, run 1000 experiments, and compute MOE and SMOE for each based on the 0.95 level. It will be true that for approximately 950 of the experiments, the size of the computed effect for factor A will not exceed MOE; for approximately 950 of the experiments, the size of the computed effect for factor B will not exceed MOE; and for approximately 950 of the experiments, the size of the computed effect of the interaction will not exceed MOE. *However,* these will not necessarily be the same 950 experiments for each effect. So, there might be only 900 experiments for which the sizes of all three computed effects do not exceed MOE. In other words, at least one wrong conclusion might be drawn 10% rather than 5% of the time. SMOE takes care of this problem. In approximately 950 of the experiments, none of the three computed effects will exceed SMOE in size.

We can use MOE and SMOE to determine significant effects as follows:

1. If the absolute value of an effect is smaller than MOE, the effect is judged non-significant.
2. If the absolute value of an effect is greater than SMOE, the effect is judged significant.
3. Otherwise, the decision is not clear-cut, and should be based on the aims of the study and the subject-matter knowledge of the experimenter.

EXAMPLE 12.1   CONTINUED

For the surface-finish experiment, the computations for the Lenth procedure give the following:

1. We choose a 0.95 level of confidence. This is a common choice.
2. Recall that the effects for factors Dress Lead, Feed Rate, and their interaction are $-0.5, 2.5$, and 3.5, respectively. Since the median of the magnitudes of these three computed effects is 2.5, $s_0 = 1.5 \times 2.5 = 3.75$.
3. Because the magnitudes of all three computed effects are smaller than $2.5 \times s_0 = 9.375$, the c_j^* are defined for all three effects, and equal the magnitudes of those effects: 0.5, 2.5, and 3.5.
4. PSE $= 1.5 \times 2.5 = 3.75$
5. $t_{m/3,(1+L)/2} = t_{1,0.975} = 12.706$. So MOE $= 3.75 \times 12.706 = 47.648$. The values for the t distribution quantiles are tabulated in Table A.4 in Appendix A, page 904.
6. Because $\delta = (1 + 0.95^{1/3})/2 = 0.991524$, and $t_{m/3,\delta} = t_{1,0.991524} = 37.54$, SMOE $= 3.75 \times 37.54 = 140.775$.

Since the sizes of the effects, $-0.5, 2.5,$ and $3.5,$ are all smaller than MOE, we conclude that none of them is significant.

This result is not unusual. Experience has shown that for the 2^2 design, the Lenth procedure seldom shows effects to be significant. In part, this reflects the difficulty of determining statistical significance with only three pieces of data.   ✦

Prediction with the Factorial Model

Prediction with the 2^2 model refers both to estimation of the response surface and to prediction of a new observation at any values of the factors in the design space. When no effect is significant, the prediction at any point in the design space is just $\bar{Y}$, the mean of all the responses. If one or more effects are significant, then the predicted response is given by the formula

$$\hat{Y} = \bar{Y} + \frac{1}{2}\sum c_i x_i \tag{12.4}$$

where only the significant effects are included in the sum, c_i is the estimate of the ith effect, and x_i is the coded setting at which prediction is desired for the ith effect.

EXAMPLE 12.1   CONTINUED

Based on the preceding analysis, neither Dress Lead, Feed Rate, nor their inter-action is significant for the surface-finish experiment, so we should predict the response at all points of the design space as the mean of the observed data val-ues. Thus, we predict the response to equal $(17 + 14 + 18 + 20)/4 = 17.25$ for all combinations of Dress Lead and Feed Rate.

As an example of how to use the prediction equation when there are signifi-cant effects, suppose (though it is not true) that we had judged Feed Rate and the Dress Lead–Feed Rate interaction significant in the surface-finish example, and that we want a prediction at a dress lead value of 0.0008 ipr and a feed rate of 0.035 ipm. Remembering that the level -1 for dress lead corresponds to 0.0005 and $+1$ to 0.0015 ipr, the coded value for Dress Lead and Feed Rate are, by linear interpolation,

$$\frac{0.0008 - 0.0005}{0.0015 - 0.0005} \times 2 - 1 = -0.4 \qquad \text{and} \qquad \frac{0.035 - 0.02}{0.04 - 0.02} \times 2 - 1 = 0.5$$

respectively. Using Equation (12.4), we get a predicted value of

$$17.525 = 17.25 + \frac{1}{2} \times [(2.5)(0.5) + (3.5)(-0.4)(0.5)]$$

Notice that in the interaction term the coded settings for the two factors are multiplied together.   ✦

12.9

THE 2^2 DESIGN WITH CENTER POINTS

The unreplicated 2^2 design is a good design, but it has two serious drawbacks:

1. There is no way of knowing how large the experimental error is.
2. There is no way of knowing whether the response surface is linear or curved over the design region.

We could solve the first problem by taking additional measurements at some or all of the design points, but anything less than a full replication of the entire design would complicate the analysis. In any event, it still wouldn't solve the second problem. A better solution is to replicate only center points (i.e., points having coded level 0 for all factors). There are at least three reasons for doing this kind of replication.

1. First, replication in general gives an estimate of experimental error. This estimate can be used as a baseline to judge which factor effects are large (and therefore not likely due to chance) and which are not.
2. Second, replication of center points leaves the design orthogonal without incurring the cost of replicating the entire design. An orthogonal design is one in which the significance of the different main effects and interactions can be assessed individually.
3. Third, replicating center points tells something about the curvature, or lack of curvature, of the response surface.

If we run three center points, then there are seven runs in all, and the experiment can be conducted as follows:

1. Run a center point first as a control.
2. **Randomly** choose half the corner points to run, and run them in **random order.**
3. Run another center point.
4. Run the other half of the corner points in random order.
5. Run the last center point.

The reason for the randomization is to protect against bias due to unknown trends or shifts or changes in other lurking variables. The reason for running the center points at the beginning, middle, and end of the runs is to give true replicates, as opposed to duplicates.[8] In addition, spreading the order of the center point runs equally over the duration of the experiment can serve as a check on the stationarity of the process.

---

[8] Recall from Chapter 3 that duplicates are data obtained at the same factor levels that aren't representative of the true experimental error. Duplicates are more likely to occur if all the center points are run one right after the other.

Testing for Significant Effects in the 2^2 Experiment with Center Points

Adding center points to a 2^k design makes it easier to test for significant effects. In addition, in most cases, it gives the tests greater power. This is because the center points provide an independent estimate of experimental error. If there are c observations taken at the center point, define S_{PE} to be the standard deviation of those c observations, computed in the usual way.[9] Then MOE and SMOE are computed as

$$\text{MOE} = S_{PE} \times t_{c-1, (1+L)/2}$$

$$\text{SMOE} = S_{PE} \times t_{c-1, \delta}$$

where $\delta = (1 + L^{1/m})/2$. Testing for significant effects is conducted in the same way as for the unreplicated case.

EXAMPLE 12.1   CONTINUED

In the surface-finish experiment, the center point is at Dress Lead value 0.0010 inches/revolution and Feed Rate value 0.03 inches/minute. The coded values are 0 in each case. Suppose there are three observations taken at the center point and that the responses are 18, 18, and 17. Then if $\delta = 0.991524$,

$$s_{PE} = \sqrt{\tfrac{1}{2}[(18 - 17.67)^2 + (18 - 17.67)^2 + (17 - 17.67)^2]} = 0.5774$$

$$\text{MOE} = 0.5774 \times t_{2, 0.975} = 0.5774 \times 4.303 = 2.5$$

$$\text{SMOE} = 0.5774 \times t_{2, \delta} \quad = 0.5774 \times 7.582 = 4.4$$

By this measure, the effect for Dress Lead, estimated from the data to be -0.5, would be judged nonsignificant since it is less than MOE in absolute value. However, the effects for Feed Rate, 2.5, and the Dress Lead by Feed Rate interaction, 3.5, would be judged possibly significant as they lie between MOE and SMOE in size. These results are different from those in the unreplicated case because we now have better information on the size of the experimental error. ◆

Testing for Curvature in the 2^2 Experiment with Center Points

The 2^2 is a **linear design,** which means that it is designed to model response surfaces that are linear (planar, in two dimensions). Now, it is a mathematical fact that any smooth surface $y = f(x_1, x_2)$ is nearly linear if a small enough range of (x_1, x_2) values is considered. So the 2^2 design should be able to model virtually any response surface if the difference between the high and low values of the two factors is not too large.

---

[9]If the observations at the center point are $Y_1, \ldots, Y_c$, and $\bar{Y}_0$ is their mean, $S_{PE} = \left[\sum_{i=1}^{c}(Y_i - \bar{Y}_0)^2/(c-1)\right]^{1/2}$. Subscript PE stands for Pure Error, which reflects the fact that this estimate of experimental error does not depend on the model being considered.

Fortunately, by including center points in a 2^k design, we can check for curvature of the surface being modeled.

The idea is that if the surface is not curved, then the mean response at the center point is the same as the mean of the responses at the corner points. A measure of the mean response at the corner points is the sample mean of the responses at those points $\bar{Y}$. A measure of the mean response at the center point is the sample mean of the responses taken there, $\bar{Y}_0$. Thus, an estimate of the curvature is $\bar{Y} - \bar{Y}_0$. If this estimate of curvature is large relative to experimental error, it will be strong evidence that the response surface is curved. In order to decide, we need to know something about the distribution of $\bar{Y} - \bar{Y}_0$. A few useful facts are as follows:

1. If a population has variance σ^2 and if $Y_1, Y_2, \ldots, Y_n$ is a random sample from that population, then the sample mean $\bar{Y}$ has variance σ^2/n. So if the experimental error in the 2^2 experiment has variance σ^2, the variance of $\bar{Y}$ is $\sigma^2/4$ and that of $\bar{Y}_0$ is σ^2/c.
2. $\bar{Y}$ and $\bar{Y}_0$ are independent.
3. If there are two independent measurements W_1 and W_2 from a population, and if W_1 has variance σ_1^2 and W_2 has variance σ_2^2, then the variance of $W_1 - W_2$ is $\sigma_1^2 + \sigma_2^2$.

With these three facts in mind, the variance of $\bar{Y} - \bar{Y}_0$ is seen to be

$$\sigma^2(\bar{Y} - \bar{Y}_0) = \frac{\sigma^2}{4} + \frac{\sigma^2}{c}$$

and its standard error the square root of this quantity.

Of course, we seldom know σ^2, so we estimate it using S_{PE}^2, giving the following estimate of $\sigma(\bar{Y} - \bar{Y}_0)$:

$$\hat{\sigma}(\bar{Y} - \bar{Y}_0) = \sqrt{S_{PE}^2 \left(\frac{1}{4} + \frac{1}{c} \right)} = S_{PE} \sqrt{\frac{1}{4} + \frac{1}{c}}$$

If there is no curvature, the quantity

$$\frac{\bar{Y} - \bar{Y}_0}{\hat{\sigma}(\bar{Y} - \bar{Y}_0)}$$

has a t_{c-1} distribution. We can then judge whether the curvature is statistically significant or not at confidence level L by comparing $|\bar{Y} - \bar{Y}_0|$ with $\hat{\sigma}(\bar{Y} - \bar{Y}_0) \times t_{c-1,(1+L)/2}$.

EXAMPLE 12.1   CONTINUED

For the surface-finish example:

- $\bar{y} = (17 + 18 + 14 + 20)/4 = 17.25$, and $\bar{y}_0 = (18 + 18 + 17)/3 = 17.67$, so the estimate of the curvature is $\bar{y} - \bar{y}_0 = -0.42$.

- The estimated standard error of $\bar{Y} - \bar{Y}_0$ is

$$\hat{\sigma}(\bar{Y} - \bar{Y}_0) = \sqrt{0.5774^2/4 + 0.5774^2/3} = 0.44$$

- For $L = 0.95$,

$$\hat{\sigma}(\bar{Y} - \bar{Y}_0) \times t_{c-1,(1+L)/2} = 0.44 \times 4.303 = 1.91 > 0.42$$

so there is insufficient evidence to conclude that there is surface curvature.
◆

Prediction in the 2^2 Experiment with Center Points

The predictor of a response at the coded settings x_i is (see Equation (12.4))

$$\hat{Y} = \bar{Y} + \frac{1}{2}\sum c_i x_i \tag{12.5}$$

where only the terms corresponding to significant effects c_i are included in the sum. This predictor is used to estimate the response surface at the coded settings x_i, and also to predict a new observation, Y_{new}, at that point. When estimating the response surface, the estimated standard error is

$$\hat{\sigma}(\hat{Y}) = S_{PE}\sqrt{\left(1 + \sum x_i^2\right)\Big/4}$$

When predicting a new response, the standard error of interest is the estimated standard error of prediction

$$\hat{\sigma}(Y_{new} - \hat{Y}) = S_{PE}\sqrt{1 + \left(1 + \sum x_i^2\right)\Big/4}$$

In both standard error formulas, only those x_i corresponding to significant effects are included.

These formulas give a level L confidence interval for the value of the response surface at the coded settings x_i as

$$(\hat{Y} - \hat{\sigma}(\hat{Y})t_{c-1,(1+L)/2},\ \hat{Y} + \hat{\sigma}(\hat{Y})t_{c-1,(1+L)/2})$$

and a level L prediction interval of a new response at the coded settings x_i as

$$(\hat{Y} - \hat{\sigma}(Y_{new} - \hat{Y})t_{c-1,(1+L)/2},\ \hat{Y} + \hat{\sigma}(Y_{new} - \hat{Y})t_{c-1,(1+L)/2})$$

EXAMPLE 12.1   CONTINUED

Consider the surface-finish example again. Suppose we consider Feed Rate and the Dress Lead by Feed Rate interaction significant. Suppose also that we want to estimate the response surface at a Dress Lead value of 0.0008 ipr and a Feed Rate of 0.035 ipm. Remembering that the level -1 for Dress Lead corresponds to 0.0005, and $+1$ to 0.0015 ipr, the coded values for Dress Lead and Feed Rate are

$$\frac{0.0008 - 0.0005}{0.0015 - 0.0005} \times 2 - 1 = -0.4 \qquad \text{and} \qquad \frac{0.035 - 0.02}{0.04 - 0.02} \times 2 - 1 = 0.5$$

respectively.

Then using Equation (12.5), we get a predicted value of

$$17.525 = 17.25 + \frac{1}{2} \times [(2.5)(0.5) + (3.5)(-0.4)(0.5)]$$

We have already computed $s_{PE} = 0.5774$, so

$$\hat{\sigma}(\hat{Y}) = 0.5774\sqrt{\{1 + 0.5^2 + [(-0.4)(0.5)]^2\}/4} = 0.33$$

and

$$\hat{\sigma}(Y_{\text{new}} - \hat{Y}) = 0.5774\sqrt{1 + \{1 + 0.5^2 + [(-0.4)(0.5)]^2\}/4} = 0.66$$

This gives a level 0.95 prediction interval for the mean response at the coded values $-0.4, 0.5$ as

$$(17.525 - (0.33)(4.303), 17.525 + (0.33)(4.303)) = (16.11, 18.95)$$

and a level 0.95 prediction interval for a new observation at the same values as

$$(17.525 - (0.67)(4.303), 17.525 + (0.66)(4.303)) = (14.69, 20.36) \quad \blacklozenge$$

12.10

THE GENERAL 2^K DESIGN

In this section, we will extend our knowledge of the 2^2 design to a general k factor design at two levels: the 2^k design.

EXAMPLE 12.2   A 2^3 DESIGN

Consider a slightly larger version of the 2^2 surface-finish experiment described in Section 12.5. This larger experiment is a 2^3 experiment with the third factor (in addition to Dress Lead and Feed Rate) being **Dwell Time,** the amount of time the grinding wheel stays at the part without actually doing any more grinding. Dwell time is measured in seconds. The low value of dwell time is 6 seconds and the high value is 10 seconds, and, as usual, these are coded as -1 and 1. The complete 2^k design has 2^k runs. In addition to the $2^3 = 8$ runs for the full 2^3 design, the experimenter in the surface-finish experiment ran three center points at settings for Dress Lead, Feed Rate, and Dwell Time of 0.0010 inch/revolution, 0.03 inch/minute, and 8 seconds, respectively (coded values $(0, 0, 0)$). ◆

Orthogonal Arrays

An orthogonal array is a useful way to display a 2^k design, with or without center points, and to easily estimate the effects.

> ### DEFINITION
>
> An **orthogonal array** for a 2^k design is a rectangular pattern of 1's, -1's, or 0's that describes the design. The 1's indicate the high level of a factor, the 0's the intermediate level, and the -1's the low level. The array is orthogonal if the 1's, -1's, and 0's in the product of any two columns sum to zero. When read horizontally, each row of an orthogonal array describes a design point. When read vertically, each column describes how to estimate one effect.

An orthogonal array is best understood through example.

EXAMPLE 12.2   CONTINUED

The orthogonal array for the 2^3 surface-finish design with center points, along with the responses obtained, is displayed in Table 12.3.

In this orthogonal array, factor A is Dress Lead, factor B is Feed Rate, and factor C is Dwell Time. Interactions are denoted by the letters of the factors constituting them: AC, for example, denotes the interaction between factors A and C.

TABLE 12.3   Orthogonal Array and Responses for Surface-Finish Data

				Effects				Response
μ	A	B	C	AB	AC	BC	ABC	Y
1	-1	-1	-1	1	1	1	-1	17
1	1	-1	-1	-1	-1	1	1	13
1	-1	1	-1	-1	1	-1	1	25
1	1	1	-1	1	-1	-1	-1	20
1	-1	-1	1	1	-1	-1	1	16
1	1	-1	1	-1	1	-1	-1	14
1	-1	1	1	-1	-1	1	-1	17
1	1	1	1	1	1	1	1	17
0	0	0	0	0	0	0	0	17
0	0	0	0	0	0	0	0	18
0	0	0	0	0	0	0	0	18

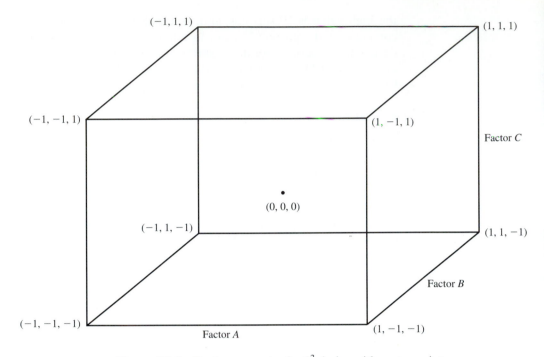

Figure 12.5 Design geometry for 2^3 design with center point.

The orthogonality property is characterized by the fact that the sum of the product of any two columns is zero. What this means is that the effect estimates are uncorrelated with each other. In nonorthogonal designs, the estimated values of at least some of the effects will change depending on which other effects are included in the model; in orthogonal designs, these estimates do not depend on the other effects.

There are several things to notice about this orthogonal array:

1. The entries for the main effects in each row show the settings for one run. The entries made up of 1's and −1's correspond to the corners of the cube in Figure 12.5. The entries made up of 0's correspond to the center point. For instance, the first row of the array tells us that at the design point with A, B, and C all taking coded values −1, the response was 17.

2. Each column of the array corresponds to one effect. The first column, labeled μ, corresponds to the overall mean. The columns for interactions can be computed by multiplying the main effect columns for the factors going into that interaction. Thus, the column for the AB interaction is the product of columns A and B.

3. The columns of the array also show how to compute the estimates of the effects. For example, to compute the BC interaction effect, first multiply the response column by the BC column, giving the values $17, 13, -25, -20, -16,$

−14, 17, 17, 0, 0, and 0. Next add these values and divide by 4, which gives $(17 + 13 − 25 − 20 − 16 − 14 + 17 + 17)/4 = −2.75$. Except for the mean, all other effect estimates are computed in this way. The mean is estimated in the usual way by adding all responses and dividing by 8.

In general, it is a good idea to make up an array like this, at least for the main effects, when recording the data.   ◆

Computing Effects for the 2^k Design

For a general 2^k design, effect estimates are computed as for the 2^3 design:

1. Multiply the column of responses by the column in the orthogonal array corresponding to the effect being estimated.
2. Add the resulting numbers.
3. Divide by 2^k for the mean and 2^{k-1} for all other effects.

Note that 2^k is the number of $+1$'s in the column corresponding to the mean and 2^{k-1} is the number of $+1$'s in all other columns of the orthogonal array for a 2^k design. Therefore, the divisor (2^k or 2^{k-1}) to use in computing an estimated effect is the number of $+1$'s in the column in the orthogonal array corresponding to the effect being estimated.

Geometry of the 2^k Design

The basic geometry of the 2^3 design with a center point is illustrated in Figure 12.5.

The main effects in the 2^3 design are obtained by subtracting the mean responses on one face of the cube from the mean responses on the opposite face. For example, the effect for C is obtained by subtracting the mean of the four responses on the bottom face of the cube in Figure 12.5 from the mean of the four responses on the top face.

A 2^k design can in theory involve interactions with as many as k factors, though in practice, significant interactions involving more than three factors are rare. The geometry of interactions in the 2^3 design is worth looking at if only for the interesting patterns that arise.

In Figure 12.6, the four responses marked with an asterisk ($*$) are averaged and subtracted from the mean of the four responses marked with a plus ($+$) to give the estimate of the AB interaction. Note that the points with the $+$ form a diagonal plane through the cube, and that the points with the $*$ form another, perpendicular to the first.

A geometric view of the estimate of the ABC interaction is given in Figure 12.7. To compute the estimate, the responses marked with an $*$ are averaged and subtracted from the mean of the responses marked with a $+$.

A three-factor interaction can be viewed in a number of other ways. For example, the ABC interaction can be computed as one-half the difference between the mean response for the two levels of factor C when the AB interaction is at its high level and the mean response for the two levels of factor C when the AB interaction is at its low

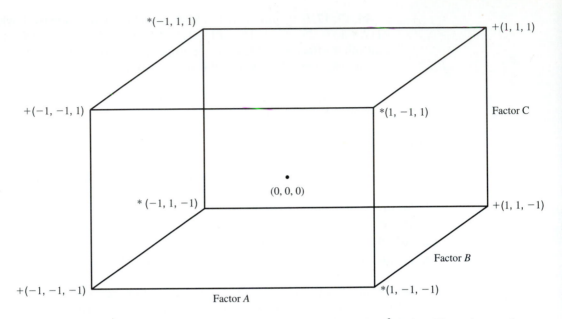

Figure 12.6 Design geometry for AB interaction in the 2^3 design. The estimate of the interaction is obtained by subtracting the mean of the points marked with an ∗ from the mean of those marked with a +.

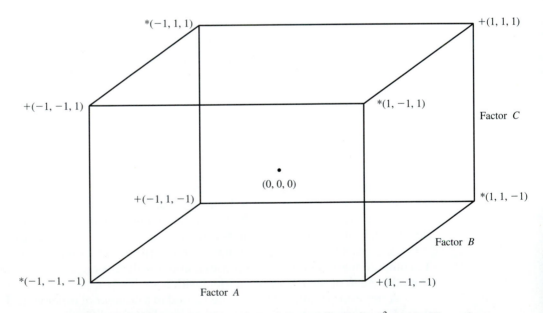

Figure 12.7 Design geometry for ABC interaction in the 2^3 design. The estimate of the interaction is obtained by subtracting the mean of the points marked with an ∗ from the mean of those marked with a +.

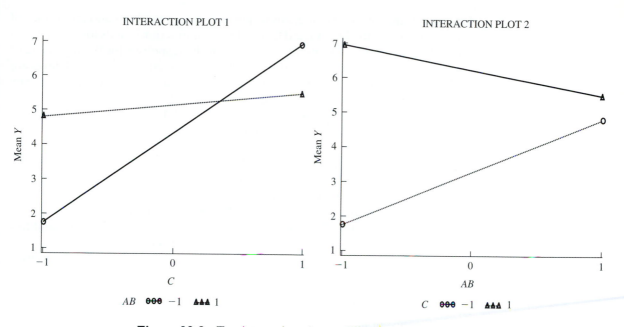

Figure 12.8 Two interaction plots useful in interpreting the ABC interaction. In each plot, the interaction is the difference in the slopes of the two lines.

level. This is exactly the slope of the line for AB $= 1$ minus the slope of the line for AB $= -1$ in the left interaction plot in Figure 12.8. Similarly, the ABC interaction may also be computed as one-half the difference between the mean response for the two levels of the AB interaction when factor C is at its high level and the mean response for the two levels of the AB interaction when factor C is at its low level. This is exactly the slope of the line for C $= 1$ minus the slope of the line for C $= -1$ in the right interaction plot in Figure 12.8.

By interchanging A, B, and C in the two interpretations we have just stated, we get another four interpretations, all of which are different ways to view the ABC interaction.

In 2^k models with $k > 3$, higher-order interactions can be interpreted similarly. One such interpretation is as one-half the difference in mean response for the two levels of one factor at the two levels of an interaction one order lower.

EXAMPLE 12.2   CONTINUED

As an example of different interpretations we can give a three-factor interaction, consider the Dress Lead by Feed Rate by Dwell Time interaction in the surface-finish experiment. From the orthogonal array in Table 12.3, its value is $(13 + 25 + 16 + 17 - 17 - 20 - 14 - 17)/4 = 0.75$. Among the ways this can be interpreted are as follows:

• As one-half the difference in mean response between the high and low levels of Dwell Time when the Dress Lead by Feed Rate interaction is at its high level minus the difference in mean response between the high and low values of Dwell Time when the Dress Lead by Feed Rate interaction is at its low level. From the orthogonal array in Table 12.3, we see that the responses for the high level of Dwell Time when the Dress Lead by Feed Rate interaction is at its high level are 16 and 17, the responses for the low level of Dwell Time when the Dress Lead by Feed Rate interaction is at its high level are 17 and 20, so the difference in mean response between the high and low levels of Dwell Time when the Dress Lead by Feed Rate interaction is at its high level is $(16 + 17)/2 - (17 + 20)/2 = -2$. Similarly, the difference in mean response between the high and low levels of Dwell Time when the Dress Lead by Feed Rate interaction is at its low level is $(14 + 17)/2 - (13 + 25)/2 = -3.5$. The three-factor interaction is one-half the difference of these: $[2-(-3.5)]/2 = 0.75$. This computation is equivalent to finding the difference in slopes of the lines in the left interaction plot of Figure 12.9.

 • As one-half the difference in mean response between the high and low levels of Dress Lead by Feed Rate interaction when Dwell Time is at its high level minus the difference in mean response between the high and low levels of Dress Lead by Feed Rate interaction when Dwell Time is at its low level. The difference in mean response between the high and low levels of Dress Lead by Feed Rate interaction when Dwell Time is at its high level is $(16 + 17)/2 - (14 + 17)/2 = 1$. The difference in mean response between the high and low levels of Dress Lead by Feed Rate interaction when Dwell Time is at its low level is $(17 + 20)/2 - (13 + 25)/2 = -0.5$. The three-factor interaction is one-half the difference of

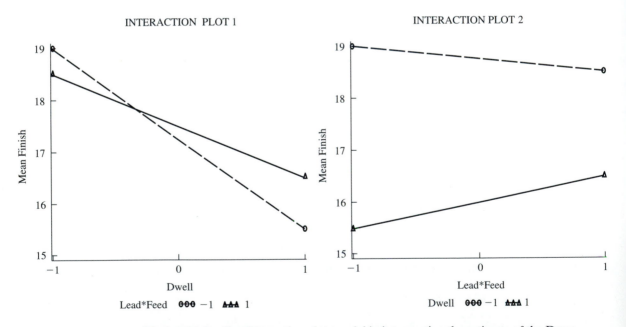

Figure 12.9 Two interaction plots useful in interpreting the estimate of the Dress Lead by Feed Rate by Dwell Time interaction in the surface-finish experiment. In each plot, the interaction is the difference in the slopes of the two lines.

these: $[1 - (-0.5)]/2 = 0.75$. This computation is equivalent to finding the difference in slopes of the lines in the right interaction plot of Figure 12.9.   ✦

The Pareto Principle

The **Pareto Principle** is useful in analyzing any multifactor experiment. It says that in any such experiment, there will be a few effects that have a large impact on the response (the "vital few") and that the remainder will have a small impact (the "trivial many"). We need only identify those vital few effects in order to learn most of what can be learned from the experiment.

Identifying Significant Effects in a 2^k Experiment

As we learned in Section 12.8, there are several methods for identifying the vital few effects. When the experiment is unreplicated, the normal quantile plot of the effects is the most often used graphical technique. The Lenth procedure also works for unreplicated 2^k experiments.

When the 2^k design has replicated center points, the methods for assessing significance of effects discussed in Section 12.9 may be used. However, MOE and SMOE now are given by the formulas

$$\text{MOE} = 2 \times \frac{S_{PE}}{\sqrt{2^k}} \times t_{c-1,(1+L)/2}$$

$$\text{SMOE} = 2 \times \frac{S_{PE}}{\sqrt{2^k}} \times t_{c-1,\delta}$$

Testing for Curvature in a 2^k Experiment

As with the 2^2 experiment, curvature is estimated for a 2^k experiment with center points by the difference between the mean response at the corner points and the mean response at c center points, $\bar{Y} - \bar{Y}_0$. The estimated standard error of this estimator is

$$\hat{\sigma}(\bar{Y} - \bar{Y}_0) = S_{PE}\sqrt{\frac{1}{2^k} + \frac{1}{c}}$$

We can then judge whether the curvature is statistically significant or not at confidence level L by comparing $|\bar{Y} - \bar{Y}_0|$ with $\hat{\sigma}(\bar{Y} - \bar{Y}_0) \times t_{c-1,(1+L)/2}$.

Prediction in a 2^k Experiment

In both the replicated and unreplicated case, the methods for estimating the response surface and predicting a new observation also carry over to the 2^k design, with

$$\hat{\sigma}(\hat{Y}) = S_{PE}\sqrt{\left(1 + \sum x_i^2\right)/2^k}$$

and

$$\hat{\sigma}(Y_{\text{new}} - \hat{Y}) = S_{PE}\sqrt{1 + \left(1 + \sum x_i^2\right)\Big/2^k}$$

EXAMPLE 12.2   CONTINUED

We continue the analysis of the 2^3 surface-finish experiment. To begin, we'll assume that the experiment is unreplicated and the data consist of the eight corner points in Table 12.3. We also assume that the experimental runs have been conducted in random order. Table 12.4 gives the estimates and the values of MOE and SMOE for the Lenth procedure. As can be seen, all effects are much smaller than MOE in size, which indicates that none of the effects is significant. This means that in terms of the variability of the observed effects, even the largest of the effects can reasonably be explained as chance occurrences. As there is no indication that any effect is significant, the overall mean of the observations is used to predict the response at any level of the factors.

Figure 12.10 contains two normal plots of the effects. These plots only differ in that the names of the effects associated with each point are identified on the right-hand plot. From these plots, we see that the only candidates for significant effects are Feed Rate, at the upper right of the plot, and Dwell Time, Dress Lead, and the Feed Rate by Dwell Time interaction at the lower left.

If we now include the three center points in the experiment, we get a much reduced estimate of experimental error, $s_{PE} = 0.58$, which greatly reduces the MOE and SMOE values:

$$\text{MOE} = 2 \times \frac{0.5774}{\sqrt{2^3}} \times 4.303 = 1.76 \quad \text{and} \quad \text{SMOE} = 2 \times \frac{0.5774}{\sqrt{2^3}} \times 11.6393 = 4.75$$

The value of 11.560 in the computation of SMOE corresponds to $t_{2,\delta}$, where $\delta = (1 + 0.95^{1/7})/2 = 0.996350$.

The results are shown numerically Table 12.5, and graphically in Figure 12.11, where the vertical line above an effect shows the value of the corresponding effect estimate, the horizontal center line is at 0, the inner pair of horizontal lines parallel

TABLE 12.4   Effect Estimates, MOE and SMOE for the Unreplicated Surface-Finish Data

EFFECT	ESTIMATE	MOE	SMOE
LEAD	−2.75	15.53	37.16
FEED	4.75	15.53	37.16
DWELL	−2.75	15.53	37.16
LEAD × FEED	0.25	15.53	37.16
LEAD × DWELL	1.75	15.53	37.16
FEED × DWELL	−2.75	15.53	37.16
LEAD × FEED × DWELL	0.75	15.53	37.16

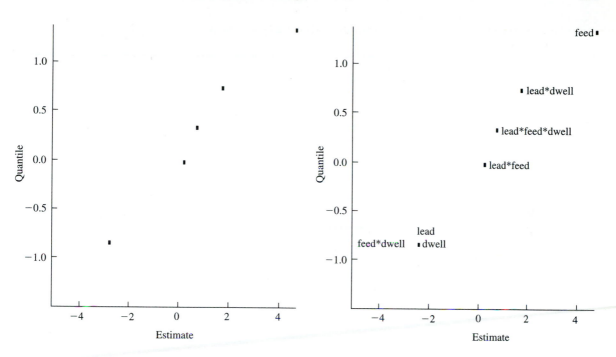

Figure 12.10   Normal quantile effects plots, unreplicated surface-finish data.

to it denote the location of MOE, and the outer pair of horizontal lines parallel to it denote the location of SMOE.

Notice that the computed effects are the same as in the unreplicated case. This nice result is one consequence of the orthogonality of the design in which only center points are replicated. Had we replicated three of the corner points on the 2^3 cube instead of the three center points, the estimates of the effects would have changed.

Based on these data, we conclude that Feed Rate is definitely a statistically significant effect, and that Dress Lead, Dwell Time, and the Feed Rate by Dwell Time interaction are possibly significant.

TABLE 12.5   Effect Estimates, MOE and SMOE for Replicated Surface-Finish Data

EFFECT	ESTIMATE	MOE	SMOE
LEAD	−2.75	1.76	4.75
FEED	4.75	1.76	4.75
DWELL	−2.75	1.76	4.75
LEAD × FEED	0.25	1.76	4.75
LEAD × DWELL	1.75	1.76	4.75
FEED × DWELL	−2.75	1.76	4.75
LEAD × FEED × DWELL	0.75	1.76	4.75

THE MOE AND SMOE PLOT (LEVEL = 0.95)

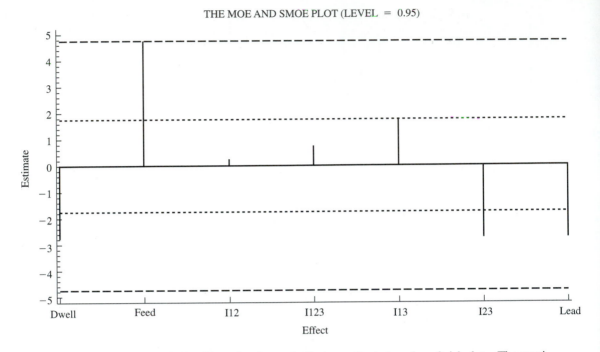

Figure 12.11 Plot of estimated effects, replicated surface-finish data. The vertical line above an effect shows the value of the corresponding effect estimate. The horizontal center line is at 0, the inner pair of horizontal lines parallel to it denote the location of MOE, and the outer pair of horizontal lines parallel to it denote the location of SMOE.

To test for curvature, we compute the curvature estimate and standard error

$$\bar{y} - \bar{y}_0 = 17.375 - 17.667 = -0.292 \qquad \hat{\sigma}(\bar{Y} - \bar{Y}_0) = 0.5774\sqrt{\frac{1}{8} + \frac{1}{3}} = 0.391$$

Since $\hat{\sigma}(\bar{Y} - \bar{Y}_0) \times t_{2,0.975} = 0.391 \times 4.303 = 1.68$ exceeds 0.292, we conclude with 95% confidence that there is no evidence of surface curvature. ✦

Partial Replication of Center Points

Sometimes one or more of the factors in a 2^k design do not or cannot accommodate a center point. This often happens when factors are categorical. For example, one of the factors might be machine operator, for which a middle level makes no sense. In such cases, it is not possible to obtain experimental results at a true center point. We can, however, use a **partial replication** of the center point to get an estimate of experimental error. To see how partial replication works, suppose we have a 2^3 design, that factor C has no center point, and that we can obtain center points for the other two factors, A and B.

Then we set up the experiment as two 2^2 designs with center points: one for $C = -1$ and one for $C = 1$ (of course, we'll randomize **all** runs). Suppose we run k_1 center points for $C = -1$ and k_2 for $C = 1$. Let S_1 be the standard deviation of the center points for $C = -1$ and S_2 the standard deviation of the center points for $C = 1$. Then compute the **pooled standard deviation**

$$S_p = \sqrt{\frac{(k_1 - 1)S_1^2 + (k_2 - 1)S_2^2}{k_1 + k_2 - 2}}$$

S_p is an estimate of the standard deviation of the experimental error. When using S_p, the appropriate degrees of freedom for the t distribution used to compute MOE, SMOE, and prediction intervals is $k_1 + k_2 - 2$.

EXAMPLE 12.3   PARTIAL REPLICATION

In order to evaluate the effect of washing time and water temperature on laundry cleaning effectiveness, researchers prepared six white wool and six white cotton test pieces as follows. First, to set a baseline, each piece was scanned electronically and an average brightness reading, B_I obtained. Next, a prescribed amount and composition of dirt was rubbed on each piece, and the piece electronically scanned again for brightness, giving the reading B_S. The pieces were then randomly assigned to one of six possible washing time-water temperature combinations. After the washing, each piece was scanned again for brightness, giving the reading B_W. The response measured was the proportional gain in brightness due to washing relative to the initial brightness differential: $(B_W - B_S)/(B_I - B_S)$. Table 12.6 displays the data. Temperature is in degrees Fahrenheit and time is in minutes.

From the table, we can see that "Temperature" and "Time" each have a center point, but that "Fabric" does not. Therefore, we will use partial replication to obtain a variance estimate.

TABLE 12.6   Washing Test Data for Example 12.3

Factors: Original units			Factors: Coded units			Response
Temperature	Time	Fabric	Temperature	Time	Fabric	Gain
100	10	Wool	−1	−1	−1	0.65
100	30	Wool	−1	1	−1	0.83
140	10	Wool	1	−1	−1	0.88
140	30	Wool	1	1	−1	0.91
120	20	Wool	0	0	−1	0.77
120	20	Wool	0	0	−1	0.75
100	10	Cotton	−1	−1	1	0.69
100	30	Cotton	−1	1	1	0.85
140	10	Cotton	1	−1	1	0.83
140	30	Cotton	1	1	1	0.96
120	20	Cotton	0	0	1	0.81
120	20	Cotton	0	0	1	0.78

For these data $s_1^2 = 2.0 \times 10^{-4}$ is the variance of the two trials for wool at the center points 120 degrees and 20 minutes, and $s_2^2 = 4.5 \times 10^{-4}$ is the same for cotton. Then, since $k_1 = k_2 = 2$,

$$s_p = \sqrt{\frac{(2-1)2.0 \times 10^{-4} + (2-1)4.5 \times 10^{-4}}{2+2-2}}$$

$$= \sqrt{\frac{2.0 \times 10^{-4} + 4.5 \times 10^{-4}}{2}} = 0.0180$$

As a result,

$$\text{MOE} = 2 \times \frac{0.0180}{\sqrt{2^3}} \times t_{2,0.975} = 2 \times \frac{0.0180}{\sqrt{2^3}} \times 4.303 = 0.055$$

and for $\delta = 0.996350$,

$$\text{SMOE} = 2 \times \frac{0.0180}{\sqrt{2^3}} \times t_{2,\delta} = 2 \times \frac{0.0180}{\sqrt{2^3}} \times 11.6393 = 0.148$$

The remainder of the analysis consists of computing the effects of the 2^3 design that results from ignoring the partial center points (the points with coded values of 0 for temperature and time), and comparing these effects with MOE and SMOE. It is left for Exercise 12.22.   ✦

Full Replication of the 2^k Design

Sometimes an experimenter will run several complete replications of a 2^k experiment. The following example will illustrate the method of analyzing data from such a design.

EXAMPLE 12.4   A FULLY REPLICATED 2^2 DESIGN

As part of the process of designing a specialized tool for spark plug removal, automotive engineers considered two competing design factors: handle size and attack angle. To find the optimal configuration, they manufactured four prototypes in which the factors handle size and attack angle were each varied at two levels. These prototypes were used in an experiment to see how they performed in practice. We will consider data from one small part of the overall experiment. These data were generated by a single mechanic. Prior to experimentation, the mechanic was allowed to practice with each tool to avoid variation due to learning. For each tool, the time it took the mechanic to extract all four spark plugs from the same car engine, in minutes, was recorded. Three replications were run, and the order of the runs was randomized. The data are as follows:

Size	Angle	Replicate	Time
Large	Large	1	3.94
Large	Large	2	3.90
Large	Large	3	4.21
Large	Small	1	4.13
Large	Small	2	3.12
Large	Small	3	4.28
Small	Large	1	3.22
Small	Large	2	4.27
Small	Large	3	4.08
Small	Small	1	8.66
Small	Small	2	8.42
Small	Small	3	6.47

To analyze these data, you should follow a two-step procedure:

1. First, average the responses for each treatment, and compute the effects as for a single replication of a 2^k design with the average as the response. In this case, we obtain after averaging:

Size	Angle	Time
Large	Large	4.02
Large	Small	3.84
Small	Large	3.86
Small	Small	7.85

The resulting estimates of the effects are

Effect	Estimate
Angle	−1.905
Size	−1.925
Angle by size interaction	2.085

Note that if we now look for significance using the Lenth procedure for an unreplicated design, MOE is 36.7 and SMOE is 108.4 meaning we see no significance at all.

2. For the second step, we use the replicates to estimate the experimental error. To do this, first compute for each treatment the variance of the responses corresponding to that treatment. Thus, for large size and large angle, we compute (subscript LL stands for large size and large angle):

$$s_{LL}^2 = \frac{1}{3-1}[(3.94 - 4.02)^2 + (3.90 - 4.02)^2 + (4.21 - 4.02)^2] = 0.0284$$

Computing the variances for the other three treatments, we get (LS stands for large size and small angle; SL for small size and large angle; SS for small size and small angle)

$$s_{LS}^2 = 0.398 \qquad s_{SL}^2 = 0.313 \qquad s_{SS}^2 = 1.44$$

Now combine these together in a weighted average to form the pooled standard deviation[10] (this is similar to how you combine estimates of experimental error when partially replicating a center point):

$$s_p = \sqrt{\frac{(3-1)s_{LL}^2 + (3-1)s_{LS}^2 + (3-1)s_{SL}^2 + (3-1)s_{SS}^2}{(3-1)+(3-1)+(3-1)+(3-1)}} = 0.739$$

s_p is used as the estimate of experimental error. When using this s_p, the appropriate degrees of freedom for the t distribution used to compute MOE, SMOE, and prediction intervals is 8 ($= (3-1)+(3-1)+(3-1)+(3-1)$, the total degrees of freedom found in the denominator of the expression for s_p).

Using this result, we can reestimate MOE and SMOE (for level 0.95) as

$$\text{MOE} = 0.739 \times t_{8,0.975} = (0.739)(2.306) = 1.704$$

and for $\delta = 0.991524$,

$$\text{SMOE} = 0.739 \times t_{8,\delta} = (0.739)(3.005) = 2.221$$

These values are considerably different from those obtained without using the replicates! They show that all three effects are possibly significant.

Note that what makes the design in the example a full replication and a balanced design is that all treatments have the same number of observations (here 3). Strictly speaking, the analysis technique presented here should not be used for a design that is not a full replication, though in practice it will do a good job if the numbers of replications at the various treatments are nearly equal. ◆

12.11

TRANSFORMATIONS

It is often desirable to make a **nonlinear transformation** of the response variable. Analysis and interpretation can sometimes be made simpler (e.g., interactions and other nonlinearities can sometimes be removed), and accuracy of prediction improved by

[10]You may have noticed that the variances differ considerably, which may indicate heteroscedasticity, or unequal population variances. The fact that there are equal numbers of observations will help mitigate the effects of such a problem. An approach to help eliminate the problem is given in the next section.

choosing an appropriate transformation. Transformations can also help the data more nearly match model assumptions.

Transformations are chosen and implemented in various ways. Engineers and scientists routinely plot variables on semi-log or log-log paper. Subject-matter knowledge can help provide a theoretical basis for choosing a transformation. Refer to Chapter 4 for more on transformations.

EXAMPLE 12.4   CONTINUED

Consider again the spark plug removal times. The variances for the four treatments differ considerably, which makes the assumption of equal variances questionable. Often, a transformation of the response can help make variances more equal. Exercise 12.24 asks you to show that a log transformation does so for these data. ✦

12.12

RESIDUAL ANALYSIS

Once we have tentatively settled on a model (i.e., we have a prediction equation), the time has come to look at residuals. Residuals are what are left over after the model is used to predict the response at the design points. Put another way,

RESIDUALS = PREDICTION ERRORS = RESPONSES − FITTED VALUES

or, in symbols,

$$e = Y - \hat{Y} = Y - \left(\bar{Y} + \frac{1}{2} \sum c_i x_i \right)$$

Remember that the c_i are the significant estimated effects from the fitted model, and x_i is the corresponding coded setting of the ith design point.

Often, we will be entertaining several different models. A prime tool for evaluating these models is the residual. The residuals should be computed and plotted whenever possible.[11] Useful plots include plots versus normal quantiles,[12] plots versus fitted values, and plots versus anything else that might be germane (time order is **always** germane). **Outliers** should be looked for and investigated when found. Remember that **outliers can be the most important data in the experiment** (both penicillin and the inert gases were discovered by investigating outliers!).

---

[11]Note that for an unreplicated 2^k experiment with all effects significant, all residuals will equal 0, so the residuals will not be very useful for evaluation of model fit. They will also be of little use if nearly all effects are significant.

[12]In previous chapters, we have suggested, due to the unequal variances of residuals, plots of studentized residuals versus quantiles of a t distribution as more appropriate than normal quantile plots of ordinary residuals. However, for 2^k designs, the variances of ordinary residuals are equal.

Residual analysis is a necessary, but not the best, method of evaluating model fit. If residual analysis shows the model to be a poor fit, then we know the model has to be reformulated. However, if residual analysis shows no evidence of lack of model fit, we cannot yet conclude that the model is completely adequate. In fact, since residual analysis uses the same data to fit the model and to evaluate the fit, there is a tendency for the model fit to look too good.

For proper evaluation of model fit, predictions of new observations must be made using the existing model. Then those new observations must be taken and compared with the predictions. The prediction interval for a new response is appropriate for deciding how well the model predicts in this case. Only if the model makes accurate predictions on new data can we be confident of its explanatory power. Assessment of the **predictive power** of a model is an essential feature of the scientific method.

EXAMPLE 12.2   CONTINUED

Returning to our earlier analysis of the surface-finish experiment, Feed Rate is most likely significant with estimated effect 4.75, and Dress Lead, Dwell, and Feed Rate by Dwell interaction are possibly significant with estimated effects of -2.75 each. It may be worthwhile to look at a number of models that include Feed Rate and have different combinations of the last three effects (there are eight possibilities in all).

We fit the model with Feed Rate, Dress Lead, Dwell, and Feed Rate by Dwell interaction. The residual plots versus the fitted values (FITTED) and each factor are shown in Figure 12.12. These plots give no indication of major problems with the model fit.

In order to validate this model, the experimenter obtained new responses at several points in the design space. Specifically, consider one new response of 17.77 at the coded values 0.5, -0.5, and 0.2 for Feed Rate, Dress Lead, and Dwell, respectively. The fitted model is

$$\widehat{\text{FINISH}} = 17.375 + 4.75 \text{ FEED} - 2.75 \text{ LEAD}$$
$$- 2.75 \text{ DWELL} - 2.75 \text{ FEED} \times \text{DWELL}$$

which means that the predicted value at the coded values 0.5, -0.5, and 0.2 is

$$\widehat{\text{FINISH}} = 17.375 + (4.75)(0.5) - (2.75)(-0.5)$$
$$- (2.75)(0.2) - (2.75)(0.5)(0.2) = 20.3$$

and the estimated standard error of prediction is

$$\hat{\sigma}(\text{FINISH}_{\text{new}} - \widehat{\text{FINISH}})$$
$$= 0.5774\sqrt{1 + \{1 + 0.5^2 + (-0.5)^2 + 0.2^2 + [(0.5)(0.2)]^2\}/2^3} = 0.63$$

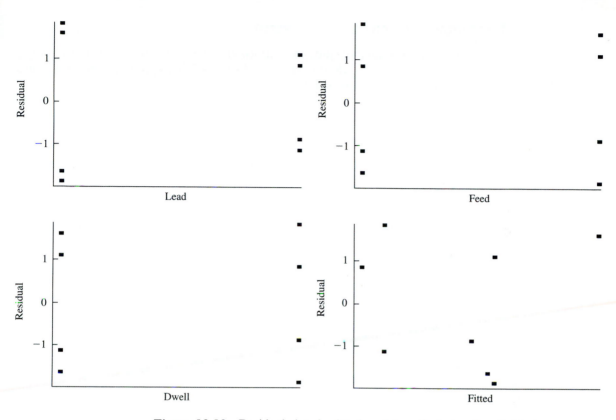

Figure 12.12   Residual plots for fitted model, replicated surface-finish data.

A level 0.95 prediction interval for a new observation at the coded values 0.5, -0.5, and 0.2 is

$$20.3 \pm (0.63)(4.303) = (17.59, 23.01)$$

Since the new observation, 17.77, is within the prediction interval, we have no reason to believe that the model is unsuitable. ✦

12.13   A FINAL EXAMPLE

The following example is from an experimental design project conducted by a student team.

EXAMPLE 12.5   ANOTHER 2^3 DESIGN

The students wanted to study the important factors affecting the distance a paper airplane would fly. To do this, they conducted a 2^3 experiment with three center points. The factors were as follows:

Factor name	Factor	Levels
LENGTH	Length of plane	24.85 ± 3.15 cm
WINGSPAN	Wingspan at widest point	12.90 ± 2.60 cm
CLIPS	Number of paper clips weighting the nose	1 ± 1

The response variable was the distance in centimeters that the plane remained in the air. The data, with the coded factor levels, are displayed in Table 12.7.

TABLE   12.7   Paper Airplane Data

LENGTH	WINGSPAN	CLIPS	DISTANCE
−1	−1	−1	630.63
−1	1	−1	510.24
−1	−1	1	428.24
1	1	−1	597.41
1	1	1	556.26
−1	1	1	758.95
1	−1	1	789.43
1	−1	−1	722.38
0	0	0	641.37
0	0	0	608.72
0	0	0	624.84

The students found that the two-factor interaction LENGTH*WINGSPAN and the three-factor interaction LENGTH*WINGSPAN*CLIPS were the only effects significant with respect to SMOE. They were puzzled that none of the main effects was significant whereas these two interactions were. In fact, the data were trying to tell them something. Before reading on, stop for a minute and think about the implications of these two interactions being the most important effects. To help you out, Figure 12.13 shows a top view of a typical paper airplane tested by the students, Figure 12.14 is an interaction plot of the LENGTH*WINGSPAN interaction, and Figure 12.15 is an interaction plot of the LENGTH*WINGSPAN*CLIPS interaction.

The LENGTH*WINGSPAN interaction plot shows that the wing configuration is important in determining the flight distance. For the large value of WINGSPAN, it does not make much difference which length is used, the larger value slightly decreasing the distance. For the small value of WINGSPAN, the value of LENGTH makes a greater difference, with the greater length giving

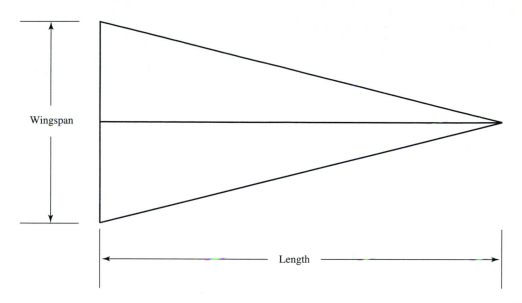

Figure 12.13   Paper airplane, top view.

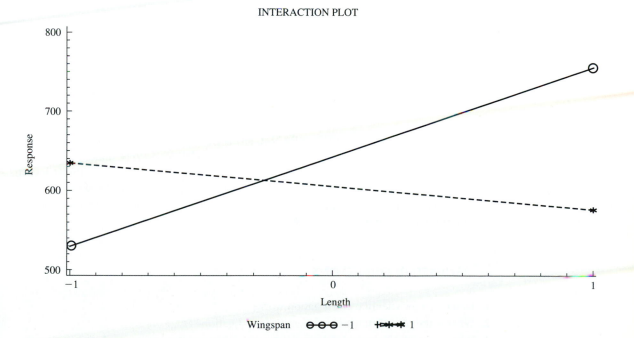

Figure 12.14   LENGTH*WINGSPAN interaction plot, airplane data.

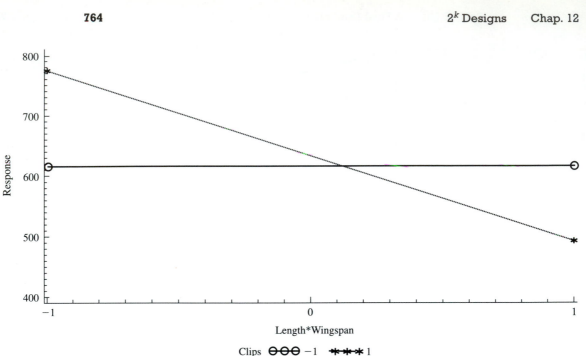

Figure 12.15   LENGTH*WINGSPAN*CLIPS interaction plot, airplane data.

greater distance. The plot also shows two other things:

- The mean distances for the two wingspans are not very different (hence, the reason that WINGSPAN is not a significant effect).
- The configuration giving the greatest distance combines short wingspan with long length.

The LENGTH*WINGSPAN*CLIPS interaction plot shows that when no paper clips are used,[13] the value of LENGTH*WINGSPAN makes little difference in flight distance. However, when two paper clips are used, the +1 value of LENGTH*WINGSPAN gives shorter mean distance than does the −1 value of LENGTH*WINGSPAN. Two paper clips along with short wingspan and long length give the best results.   ✦

D ISCUSSION QUESTIONS

1. Describe how scientific investigation works.
2. What is the role of statistics in scientific investigation?
3. What is an OFAT design? A factorial design? What are the differences between them?

---

[13]Remember, no paper clips corresponds to the coded value CLIPS = −1.

4. What do we mean when we say that factors are additive? Explain what main effects and interactions are and how they are interpreted.

5. How are main effects and interactions estimated in a 2^2 factorial design?

6. Explain the following terms: experiment, treatment, factor, design space, design point, response surface, screening experiment, unreplicated experiment, effect, significant effect, and population effect.

7. What steps are involved in running a 2^2 experiment?

8. How are graphical methods used to determine significant effects?

9. What does the Lenth procedure do and how is it interpreted? What is the difference between MOE and SMOE in this procedure?

10. How does one predict a response after the 2^k model has been fitted?

11. What are the advantages of replication in a 2^k design? Why is it particularly advantageous to replicate center points?

12. How would you run a 2^k design with replicated center points?

13. What is an orthogonal array? How are estimates of effects computed from it? What do the rows in the array tell us?

14. On a cube, show the geometry of main effects, two-factor and three-factor interactions in a 2^3 design.

15. What is partial replication of center points?

16. What is the purpose of residual analysis? How should a residual analysis be conducted?

17. If a residual analysis shows no evidence of lack of model fit, is the explanatory power of the model adequate? Discuss.

E XERCISES

12.1. In a 2^2 experiment to assess the effect of temperature and humidity on the durability of a type of computer chip, one chip of the given type was run until failure at each of four sets of temperature and humidity conditions. The data are shown in Table 12.8.
   (a) Compute the main effects and the interaction effect. Which are the most important determinants of chip life?
   (b) If three center points were run and their s_{PE} was 149 hours, test for the significance of these effects at the 0.95 level.
   (c) The computer chip experiment was rerun as a 2^3 design with three center points. In addition to temperature and humidity (each at three levels), the third factor was the corrosivity of the flux used in the soldering process, also at three levels. The response

TABLE 12.8   Computer Chip Data

(Temperature, Humidity)	Hours to failure
(Low, low)	3885
(High, low)	1875
(Low, high)	1992
(High, high)	1678

was again hours until chip failure. The significant effects were found to be temperature, humidity, and the interaction between corrosivity and temperature with estimated values 1162, −1045, and 1115, respectively. From the data, the values $s_{PE} = 149$ and of $\bar{y} = 2358$ were computed. Obtain a 95% prediction interval for the hours until failure of a new chip to be manufactured at the middle level of temperature, the high level of corrosivity, and a level of humidity midway between the middle and high level.

12.2. What is the estimate of the main effect of factor B in the OFAT surface-finish experiment in Section 12.4? What is its interpretation?

12.3. What is the estimate of feed rate from the 2^2 design in Section 12.5? Compute it in two ways. What is its interpretation?

12.4. Civil engineers are concerned with the properties of building materials under different environmental conditions. In an effort to understand the properties of cylindrical metal rods, civil engineers conducted a 2^4 experiment with six center points. In the experiment, different torques were applied to rods of varying material strengths, temperatures, and lengths. The measured response was the angle, in radians, through which the end of the rod rotated. The factors, levels, and units of measurement are shown in Table 12.9.

TABLE 12.9   Factors, Levels, and Units of Measurement, Rod Data

Factor	Levels	Units of measurement
Torque	2.00, 2.25, 2.50	kilopounds
Material strength	$3.7 \times 10^3, 4.65 \times 10^3, 5.6 \times 10^3$	kilopounds/in.^{2}
Temperature	30, 32, 34	°C
Length	15, 18, 21	inches

The data in coded units (also found in the data set ROD) are displayed in Table 12.10.

(a) Fit a full 2^4 model to these data.

(b) Perform a test for curvature at the 0.95 level. What do you find?

(c) Sometimes a transformation will eliminate curvature. Redo the preceding two steps using the natural log of angle as the response. Is curvature still significant?

(d) Now analyze the log transformed data. In particular, answer the following:

    i. Which effects are significant (0.05 level, SMOE only)?

    ii. Write out the prediction equation based on those significant effects. In terms of the fitted equation, tell the engineers what will happen to the predicted angle if torque is increased by 0.5 kilopound.

    iii. Fit the model with only the significant effects to the 16 noncenter point observations. Analyze the residuals of the fitted model. Do you find any large departures from model assumptions? (*Hint:* Plot them versus each factor as well as versus fitted values).

    iv. A new shipment of rods is to be inspected. The first test specimen has length 17 inches and an advertised material strength of 4.00×10^3 kilopounds/in.^{2} It is heated to a temperature of 32°C and a torque of 2.30 kilopounds is applied to it. The resulting angle is measured as 0.653 radian. Is this result consistent with the data analyzed above? Use a 95% prediction interval to decide.

12.5. An experiment to quantify the effect of reactant concentration (factor A) and amount of

TABLE 12.10   Rod Data

Torque	Length	Strength	Temperature	Angle
0	0	0	0	0.317
−1	−1	1	−1	0.195
1	−1	−1	−1	0.369
0	0	0	0	0.318
−1	1	−1	1	0.414
−1	−1	1	1	0.194
1	−1	1	−1	0.244
−1	1	−1	−1	0.413
0	0	0	0	0.320
1	−1	−1	1	0.370
−1	1	1	1	0.274
0	0	0	0	0.316
−1	−1	−1	−1	0.295
1	1	1	−1	0.341
−1	1	1	−1	0.273
0	0	0	0	0.318
1	1	−1	1	0.518
0	0	0	0	0.315
1	1	1	1	0.342
1	−1	1	1	0.243
1	1	−1	−1	0.517
−1	−1	−1	1	0.295

TABLE 12.11   Reactant Data

A Level	B Level	R time
Low	Low	28
High	Low	36
Low	High	18
High	High	31

catalyst (factor B) on reaction time in a chemical process yielded the data in Table 12.11. The data are found in the file REACTANT.

(a) Find which effect(s) (if any) are significant.

(b) Interpret any significant effects.

(c) Predict the reaction time at a value of the factors midway between the values in the experiment.

12.6. An experiment was conducted to test the effect of different lighting systems and the presence or absence of a watchman on the average number of car burglaries per month at a parking garage. The data are found in Table 12.12. The data are found in the file GARAGE, where the variables are named BURGLAR, LIGHTING, and WATCHMAN.

(a) Using only simple graphical methods (**NOT** the Lenth procedure), find which effect(s) (if any) appear significant.

(b) Interpret all of these significant effects.

TABLE 12.12   Factors, Levels, and Units of Measurement, Car Burglary Data

Lighting	Watchman	Mean Number of Burglaries
poor	no	2.80
good	no	1.00
poor	yes	2.40
good	yes	0.75

    (c) Permanently upgrading the lighting in the garage will cost $700 per month. Hiring a watchman will cost $3000 per month. It is estimated that lawsuits and loss of business cost on average $2000 per burglary. Is it worth it to hire a watchman, install lights, or both?

12.7. Show that for the surface-finish example, the interaction can be defined as the difference between the effect of Feed Rate when Dress Lead is at its low value and that effect when Dress Lead is at its high value. Show how this relates in two ways to the geometry shown in Figure 12.2.

12.8. Based on the results for the 2^3 surface-finish experiment with center points, what do you conclude? Is this a different conclusion than you made in the unreplicated case? Why is this? What does the test for curvature tell you?

12.9. Compare the following three models for the 2^3 surface-finish data, found in the data file SF31, by computing and plotting their residuals:
(a) The model with only Feed Rate.
(b) The model with Feed Rate and Dwell.
(c) The model with Dress Lead, Feed Rate, Dwell, and Feed Rate by Dwell interaction.
Tell which model(s) you prefer and why.

12.10. In order to improve his golf game, Angus McDuffer decides to take a statistics course. He is so inspired by the idea of doing a project on experimental design that he takes his statistics notes to the local golf course. There he conducts a 2^3 experiment with four center points with the goal of finding out what factors affect the length of his drives. The three factors are:

    • **Position:** Where the ball is teed up. At the front foot is $+1$, at the rear foot is -1.
    • **Width:** The width of Angus's stance. Wide is $+1$, narrow is -1.
    • **Swing:** The length of Angus's backswing. Long is $+1$, short is -1.

The center points are midway between the extremes of each factor. The response is **Distance,** the distance in yards that the drive carries. Angus's data are found in the data set GOLF.
(a) How many degrees of freedom are associated with the estimate of experimental error variance?
(b) Analyze these data. In particular, answer the following:
    i. Which effects are significant (0.05 level, MOE, or SMOE)?
    ii. Write out the prediction equation based on those significant effects. In terms of that equation, tell Angus what will happen if from the low levels of all three factors, he changes Position to its high value. What if he changes Swing to its high value?

      iii. Interpret any significant interactions.

      iv. Analyze the residuals of the fitted model (the model consisting of the significant effects from i; be sure to fit it only to the noncenter point data). Do you find any large departures from model assumptions?

      v. Angus feels most comfortable when the ball is teed up 1/4 of the way from his front foot to his rear foot, and when he has a medium-width stance and a medium backswing. Use your fitted model to predict how far Angus will hit the ball with this stance.

12.11. Consider a 2^3 experiment with factors A, B, and C. If we look only at the data for C = -1, we have a 2^2 design with factors A and B. Suppose the estimated AB interaction for this 2^2 design is 12.5. Now suppose that the estimated AB interaction from the 2^2 design formed by restricting C to be $+1$ is -6.5. Using this information, what is the estimate of the ABC interaction in the original 2^3 design?

12.12. A fabric manufacturer was having trouble with yarn breaking on the production line. Managers and technical personnel narrowed the cause down to three possible factors

- **Loom Tension.** The tension set on the loom
- **Shuttle Speed.** The speed of the shuttle on the loom
- **Spool Size.** The size of the spool holding the yarn

The response is time to breakage in minutes. The data are found in the file YARN. The factors are named Tension, Speed, and Size, respectively.

(a) The response appears to need a transformation. Tell why. Make a natural log transformation. Does it appear to help? In what follows, analyze the transformed data.

(b) How many degrees of freedom are associated with the estimate of experimental error variance?

(c) Analyze these data. In particular, answer the following:

      i. Which effects are significant (0.05 level, SMOE only)?

      ii. Write out the prediction equation based on those significant effects. In terms of that equation, tell the plant manager what will happen if from the low values of all three factors, he changes Tension to its high value.

      iii. Interpret the Tension by Speed by Size interaction.

      iv. Analyze the residuals of the fitted model. Do you find any large departures from model assumptions? (*Hint:* Plot them versus each factor as well as versus fitted values.)

      v. Current production runs use a tension 2/3 of the way between the low and high values in the experiment, shuttle speed 1/4 of the way between the low and high values in the experiment, and a medium-size spool. Use the fitted equation to predict the time to breakage at these values.

12.13. Consider the plane data in Section 12.13 (these data are found in the data set PLANES).

(a) Obtain the prediction equation for the model based only on the effects LENGTH∗ WINGSPAN and LENGTH∗WINGSPAN∗CLIPS.

(b) Analyze the residuals of the fitted model. Do you find any large departures from model assumptions?

(c) The students conducted four additional experimental runs to confirm the model's validity. The data (in coded units) are found in Table 12.13. Are these data consistent with the fitted model? Use a 95% prediction interval to make your decision.

12.14. Peanuts are normally skinned prior to retail sale or processing for other food products. When the nuts are sold as whole nuts, it is desirable that the peanuts be completely skinned

TABLE 12.13   Paper Airplane Data

LENGTH	WINGSPAN	CLIPS	DISTANCE
0.5	−0.5	0	669.34
−0.5	−0.5	0	634.90
−0.5	0.5	0	646.48
0.5	0.5	0	652.27

TABLE 12.14   Peanut Data

Original factor settings		Coded factor settings		Response
White Roast Time (min)	Microwave Time (sec)	WRTIME	MWTIME	YIELD
0	0	−1	−1	15.0
20	0	1	−1	70.9
0	180	−1	1	70.9
20	180	1	1	86.8
10	90	0	0	55.6
10	90	0	0	54.6
10	90	0	0	58.7

without undue damage and that the nuts be whole, not split. It has been found that thermal treatment of the peanut will loosen the skin to varying degrees, thereby minimizing the potential for split nuts. The traditional thermal treatment is called "white roasting," the straightforward soaking of the nuts in an oven. Following white roasting, the skins are removed by a method such as abrasion or tumbling.

As pretreatment by white roasting is energy-intensive, it has been suggested that shorter white roasting times followed by subsequent exposure to microwave radiation might reduce total energy consumption and improve yield. To assess the effect of using a microwave step in peanut processing, an experiment was conducted. Peanuts from the same processing batch were divided into seven equal samples, by weight. They were subjected to one of three white roast soak times, followed by one of three microwave times. All were then processed by the same mechanical skinner, and the yield (percent of whole, skinned peanuts) was recorded. The data are displayed in Table 12.14.

(a) Estimate all main effects and interactions.

(b) Which effects are significant at the 0.95 level of confidence? (The standard deviation of the three center points is 2.14.)

(c) Use an interaction plot to interpret the interaction.

(d) After fitting the model, the experimenter conducts a confirmatory experiment by white roasting a batch of peanuts for 5 minutes and then microwaving for 90 seconds. The batch had a yield of 51.5%. Is this result consistent with the fitted model? Use a 95% prediction interval to decide.

12.15. In a 2^2 experiment to study the relationship that smoking and alcohol consumption have with life expectancy, four laboratory rats were each given one of four possible treatments. The resulting data are in Table 12.15. In your opinion, is there a smoking-alcohol interaction involved? Draw a picture to justify your answer and explain your reasoning.

TABLE 12.15   Lifespan Data

Smoking	Alcohol	Lifespan (days)
None	None	344
None	Heavy	282
Heavy	None	277
Heavy	Heavy	218

12.16. In the experiment on smoking and alcohol described in the previous exercise, three center points were run with $s_{PE} = 35.5$. Suppose a rat is to be given half the amount of smoke that was given to the "heavy" smoking rats and half the amount of alcohol that was given to the "heavy" drinking rats. Predict the rat's life expectancy (assume the original levels were coded -1 and $+1$). Compute and interpret a 95% prediction interval for this rat's life expectancy.

12.17. The smoking-alcohol experiment of the previous two problems was rerun as a 2^3 experiment. The third factor was type of mouse. Though there were only two types of mouse used, the experimenters wanted to partially replicate center points using the other two factors. To do this, they ran three center points with mouse type 1 and four center points with mouse type 2. The standard deviation of the three center points run with mouse type 1 was 40 and the standard deviation of the four center points run with mouse type 2 was 30. Obtain the pooled estimate of experimental-error standard deviation. How many degrees of freedom correspond to it?

12.18. A metallurgist conducted a 2^2 experiment. The data are shown in Table 12.16. The response is SIED (silicon equivalent diameter), a measure of the size of silicon particles in the alloy under study. The factors are cooling rate (CCR) and the amount of strontium in the alloy (CMOD).

TABLE 12.16   Metallurgy Data

CCR	CMOD	SIED
-1	-1	0.77
1	-1	1.48
-1	1	1.41
1	1	1.65

(a) Compute all effects. Which of them appear to be significant?

(b) The metallurgist used an estimate of experimental error variance based on five center points. The standard deviation of the SIED values measured at these points is 0.0906. Use this information to compute the MOE value at the 0.95 level. Compare the effects computed in part (a) with the MOE value obtained. What do you conclude?

12.19. A 2^2 experiment yielded the data in Table 12.17. Is there evidence of curvature? Use a 0.95 level of confidence.

12.20. Use a drawing to explain the geometry of an ABCD interaction.

12.21. Interpret the interaction in Figure 12.4.

12.22. Finish the analysis of the washing experiment described in Example 12.3.

TABLE 12.17   Data for Exercise 12.19

A	B	Y
−1	−1	8
−1	1	6
1	−1	11
1	1	9
0	0	14
0	0	12
0	0	16

12.23. In a 2^2 experiment, factor A is temperature in degrees Fahrenheit, at levels 33 and 85 degrees, and factor B is pressure in pounds per square inch, at levels 25 and 50. The coded values of each are −1 and 1.

  (a) Obtain the coded values for a new observation to be obtained at 25 degrees and 45 pounds per square inch.

  (b) An observation is obtained at coded values 0.27 for temperature and 1.14 for pressure. What are the values in original units?

12.24. Show that a natural log transformation of the spark plug removal times in Example 12.4, page 756, makes the sample variances more nearly equal. Analyze the transformed data. Do you obtain different conclusions about which effects are significant?

MINIPROJECT

Purpose

The purpose of this miniproject is to give you experience in planning, conducting, and analyzing a sequence of physical experiments that lead to an understanding of some phenomenon.

Process

The miniproject for this chapter is part of a sequence of miniprojects to be conducted in this and succeeding chapters. Your group is to choose a phenomenon that you can investigate by conducting a sequence of physical experiments to be conducted in this and in Chapters 13 and 14. As your knowledge of experimental design and analysis grows with each succeeding chapter, you will refine and continue to conduct and analyze your experiments. You should select a nontrivial problem that is meaningful yet results in easy to conduct experiments. The problem must involve a measurable response and at least three factors. If you want to continue this experiment as the activity you conduct for the Chapter 13 combined lab and miniproject, there must be at least four factors. You must do the following:

1. Design and conduct a 2^k experiment for this problem, where $k \geq 3$.
2. Include either full or partial center point replication to obtain an estimate of experimental error.

3. Perform a test for curvature.

   (a) If curvature is present, reformulate the model and refit.

   (b) If there is no evidence of curvature, continue.

4. Perform a residual analysis and take appropriate action whatever its outcome.

   (a) If the residuals show a poor fit, reformulate the model and refit.

   (b) If the residuals show no evidence of lack of fit, continue.

5. Validate the model by using it to predict four new observations at different points in the design space and then comparing the predictions with new observations taken at those points. Use a 95% prediction interval for the comparison.

6. Submit a report of your experiments and conclusions.

Before beginning experimentation, you must submit a proposal of one page or less, outlining your planned experimentation, and receive your instructor's approval.

LAB 12.1: Funnel Swirling

Introduction

In this lab, your group will obtain data by running experiments in which a ball bearing is dropped through a funnel mounted on a stand.[14] The response is the time it takes the ball bearing to roll through the funnel.

Objectives

To give you a practical understanding of the design and conduct of a 2^k experiment.

Lab Materials

- Funnel and stand
- Ball bearing
- Stopwatch
- Ramp
- Ruler
- Protractor

Experimental Procedure

After you have been assigned to a lab/project group, your group will be given an experimental apparatus with which to take data. The experimental apparatus consists of a funnel mounted on a stand, a ramp mounted above the funnel, and a ball bearing. Your task in this lab is to design,

---

[14] We got the idea for this "funnel swirling" experiment from Bert Gunter.

conduct, and analyze a 2^k experiment for some $k \geq 3$ in order to efficiently and accurately identify those factors that contribute to differences in the ball bearing rolling time.

1. You must initially identify a set of relevant factors such as

   - height of ramp above the funnel
   - height of funnel cross bar from base
   - angle between the ramp support and the perpendicular to funnel bar
   - ball bearing size

   or any other factors you think might affect the times.

   In order to identify the factors you want to vary and the settings for the levels of those factors, begin with about 10 minutes of brainstorming while doing some test runs with the apparatus.

   To put this in context, in an industrial setting, you might be at the initial stage of an investigation, in which your eventual goal is to optimize the output or reduce the variability or in some other way improve the performance of a process. At this stage, your goal is to identify the influential factors governing the response you are trying to improve.

2. Set up an experimental protocol. This describes exactly how your experiment is to be run, including what factors at what levels and in what order.

3. Collect the data and analyze the results. Prepare a lab report. Your lab report should contain the following:

   (a) A description of your experiments, including the configurations run, the factors you identified, the levels of the factors used in the experiments, and the responses observed. In other words, provide a complete description of your experiments and the data from those experiments.

   (b) Your conclusions. Which factors were significant in determining the time? Which were not significant? Was there evidence of curvature? What settings in the design space do you think would result in the maximum time? What do you predict the time to be at these settings?

   (c) A critique of your experiment. What went right? What went wrong? How could the experiment be improved? How confident are you in your data?

2^{k-p} Designs and Their Role in Quality Improvement

Thou wretched fraction, wilt thou be the ninth part even of a tailor?

—*Thomas Carlyle*

INTRODUCTION

This chapter introduces fractional 2^k designs: designs that use only a fraction of the 2^k runs necessary for a full 2^k design. Because of their economy, such designs are often used to gather information about large numbers of factors, particularly when experimentation is difficult or expensive. In this chapter, you will learn how to select a fractional 2^k design with desired characteristics. You will also be introduced to more advanced topics to help you effectively design and analyze two-level fractional factorial experiments. Finally, Taguchi's robust parameter design methodology, an application of statistical experimental design to the engineering design of products and processes, will be discussed.

Knowledge and Skills

By successfully completing this chapter, you will acquire the following knowledge and skills:

KNOWLEDGE	SKILLS
1. The basics of fractional factorial designs.	1. How to select an appropriate fractional 2^k design with desired characteristics.
2. Design fragments and foldover designs.	2. Use of design fragments and foldover designs to resolve confounding.
	(continued)

KNOWLEDGE	SKILLS
3. Blocking in 2^k and fractional 2^k designs.	**3.** How and when to block.
4. The strategy of sequential experimentation.	**4.** How to plan, organize, and conduct sequential experimentation.
5. Taguchi's robust parameter design philosophy and methodology.	**5.** Application of Taguchi's robust parameter design methodology.

13.1

THE NEED FOR PARSIMONIOUS EXPERIMENTATION

The 2^k design is an effective tool in scientific experimentation, but it has one serious disadvantage: For large numbers of factors it requires too many runs. Although an unreplicated 2^2 design requires only four runs, and a 2^3 only eight runs, if there are 10 factors, which is not unusual in the initial stages of experimentation, 1024 runs are required! Fortunately, we can do something to obtain information about large numbers of factors and effects using a manageable number of experimental runs. In this chapter, you will learn about confounded effects and about how we can use our knowledge of confounding to make more parsimonious versions of the 2^k designs called **fractional factorial designs**.

13.2

CONFOUNDING

Consider an experiment involving three factors, A, B, and C, each at two levels. A full 2^3 unreplicated experiment would need eight runs. Suppose, however, that there is only enough money for two runs. Suppose further that the first run is done at the coded values -1, -1, and -1 for factors A, B, and C, and that the second run is done at the coded values 1, 1, and 1. If the experimenters find that the response is significantly smaller for the first run than for the second, what can they conclude about the effects due to each factor?

The answer is that they can conclude nothing about the factors individually. They can only conclude that the combined effect of the three factors at their low levels resulted in a smaller response than the combined effect of the three factors at their high levels. In statistical parlance, we say that the effects of factors A, B, and C are confounded with one another.

TABLE   13.1   An Example of Confounding

μ	A	B	C	AB	AC	BC	ABC
1	-1	-1	-1	1	1	1	-1
1	1	1	1	1	1	1	1

> **DEFINITION**
>
> The effects of factors or interactions in an experimental design are **confounded** when they cannot be distinguished from each other.

To better understand confounding, it might help to look at the array in Table 13.1, which describes this experiment. The array shows that the effects for factors A, B, C, and ABC are identical, since the pattern of signs for each has a "-1" in the top row and a "1" in the bottom row. This means that each effect is computed in the same way: by subtracting the first response from the second. Therefore, these four effects are confounded. Similarly, the table shows that effects for μ, AB, AC, and BC are confounded. With two observations, only two effects can be estimated. Confounding means that we can't tell if the effect defined by the two 1's is due to μ, AB, AC, BC, some, or all of them. Similarly, we can't tell if the other effect is due to A, B, C, ABC, some, or all of them. It is a characteristic of confounded effects that their corresponding columns in the design array are identical or the negatives of one another.

13.3 FRACTIONAL FACTORIAL DESIGNS

As we have stated, one problem with 2^k designs, particularly for large k, is that they require too many runs. In many settings, an experimenter can only afford to conduct a fraction of the 2^k runs required.

> **DEFINITION**
>
> A **fractional factorial design** is a factorial design in which only a fraction of the runs necessary for the full factorial design are conducted.

Fractional factorial designs may be constructed for many experiments in which some or all factors have more than two levels. However, the simplest and most commonly used fractional factorial designs are those in which all factors have only two levels, excluding center points. It is these fractional 2^k designs that we present in this chapter.

Notation

- A factorial design with one observation per treatment is called a **full replicate**. A fractional factorial design is called a **fractional replicate**.

- Fractional factorial designs are often named for the fraction of a full replicate they represent. Thus, if the fractional factorial design consists of 1/2 the treatments of a full replicate, it is called a **1/2 replicate;** if it consists of 1/4 the treatments of a full replicate, it is called a **1/4 replicate;** and so on. We will only consider fractions that are powers of 2; that is, $1/2^p$ replicates for $p = 1, 2, \dots$. When $p = 1, 2$, and 3, for example, we get a 1/2, 1/4, and 1/8 replicate.

- We will denote a $1/2^p$ replicate of a 2^k design as a **2^{k-p} design.** So, for example, a 1/2 replicate of a 2^4 design is denoted as a 2^{4-1}, and a 1/8 replicate of a 2^7 design is denoted as a 2^{7-3}. Notice that the notation 2^{k-p} can also be used to compute the number of runs, or data points, in the design: A 2^{4-1} design has $2^{4-1} = 2^3 = 8$ runs, and a 2^{7-3} has $2^{7-3} = 2^4 = 16$ runs.

13.4

CONSTRUCTING FRACTIONAL FACTORIAL DESIGNS

How can we determine a good strategy for experimentation with k factors when fewer than the 2^k runs can be done? The following three tools are available to guide us:

BASIC TOOLS FOR DESIGN AND ANALYSIS OF FRACTIONAL FACTORIAL DESIGNS

- **The Pareto Principle:** Recall that the Pareto principle states that in any experiment, there will be the vital few significant effects and the trivial many insignificant effects.

- **The Hierarchy of Significance:** The hierarchy of significance says that, in general, main effects are more likely significant than two-factor interactions, two-factor interactions are more likely significant than three-factor interactions, and so on. In practice, it is rare for three-factor interactions to be significant and almost unheard of for four-factor or higher interactions to be significant.

- **Knowledge of Confounding Patterns:** Since there will be fewer than the 2^k runs needed to estimate all effects, some effects will have to be confounded with others. We will use our knowledge of confounding patterns to see that effects that are likely to be most significant (main effects and low-order interactions) are confounded with effects that are likely to be least significant (high-order interactions).

The Pareto principle tells us that most likely we do not have to estimate all possible effects to find the significant ones. Knowledge of confounding patterns allows us to choose which effects to confound, knowing that we won't be able to separate their individual contributions. The hierarchy of significance allows us to choose wisely which effects to confound, so that we can deduce which are most likely the significant effects.

For example, if an experimenter has three factors, A, B, and C, but can only afford four of the eight runs required for a full 2^3 design, and if the effect of factor A is of particular interest, then the hierarchy of significance suggests that, since the ABC interaction will likely be of least significance, the experimenter confound A and the ABC interaction. That way, if the confounded effect of A and ABC is found significant, the experimenter will conclude that the significance is most likely due to factor A. Knowledge of confounding patterns will be used to obtain a design that confounds A and ABC.

The following example illustrates in more detail how to use these tools to obtain a fractional factorial design.

EXAMPLE 13.1   A 2^{4-1} DESIGN

Consider again the surface-finish experiment from Chapter 12. In the actual experiment, a fourth factor was of interest to the experimenter, but he only had resources to do 11 runs in all, including the three center points. The fourth factor was work speed: the rotational speed of the part, in revolutions per minute. The low level of work speed was 250 rpm and the high level was 750 rpm. As the experimenter could only conduct 8 runs, excluding center points, instead of the 16 required for a full 2^4 design, he had to decide which effects to confound with which other effects. He obtained the desired 2^{3-1} design as follows:

1. First, he wrote out a 2^3 design in the first three factors, as shown in Table 13.2. In this table, factor A is Dress Lead, factor B is Feed Rate, and factor C is Dwell Time. He looked at a 2^3, since its eight runs are exactly the number he planned to do.

2. Using the hierarchy of significance, the experimenter decided to confound Work Speed, which we'll call factor D, with what was likely to be the least significant effect, and that is the ABC interaction. Therefore, he took the

TABLE 13.2   Orthogonal Array for 2^3 Design for Surface-Finish Data Prior to Including the Factor Work Speed

μ	A	B	C	AB	AC	BC	ABC
1	−1	−1	−1	1	1	1	−1
1	1	−1	−1	−1	−1	1	1
1	−1	1	−1	−1	1	−1	1
1	1	1	−1	1	−1	−1	−1
1	−1	−1	1	1	−1	−1	1
1	1	−1	1	−1	1	−1	−1
1	−1	1	1	−1	−1	1	−1
1	1	1	1	1	1	1	1
0	0	0	0	0	0	0	0
0	0	0	0	0	0	0	0
0	0	0	0	0	0	0	0

TABLE 13.3 Orthogonal Array for all Four Main Effects for Surface-Finish Data When Factor D Is Confounded with the ABC Interaction

A	B	C	D
−1	−1	−1	−1
1	−1	−1	1
−1	1	−1	1
1	1	−1	−1
−1	−1	1	1
1	−1	1	−1
−1	1	1	−1
1	1	1	1
0	0	0	0
0	0	0	0
0	0	0	0

TABLE 13.4 Orthogonal Array for 2^{4-1} Design for Surface-Finish Data

μ ABCD	A BCD	B ACD	C ABD	AB CD	AC BD	BC AD	ABC D
1	−1	−1	−1	1	1	1	−1
1	1	−1	−1	−1	−1	1	1
1	−1	1	−1	−1	1	−1	1
1	1	1	−1	1	−1	−1	−1
1	−1	−1	1	1	−1	−1	1
1	1	−1	1	−1	1	−1	−1
1	−1	1	1	−1	−1	1	−1
1	1	1	1	1	1	1	1
0	0	0	0	0	0	0	0
0	0	0	0	0	0	0	0
0	0	0	0	0	0	0	0

pattern of 1's and −1's from the ABC column in Table 13.2, and gave it the label D. The result is Table 13.3, the rows of which give the design points for the experiment.

3. Finally, now that he knew the column for factor D, the columns for all the interactions with D (e.g., AD, BD, ABD, ABCD, . . .) were easily obtained by multiplying the appropriate columns of Table 13.3 together. The results are summarized in Table 13.4, where each column represents two confounded effects. For example, the second column represents factor A and the BCD interaction, which are confounded in this design.

TABLE 13.5   Aliasing Structure for 2^{4-1} Surface-Finish Design

μ	=	ABCD
A	=	BCD
B	=	ACD
C	=	ABD
D	=	ABC
AB	=	CD
AC	=	BD
AD	=	BC

Often, it is helpful to keep track of which effects are confounded with each other in a fractional factorial design, as is done in Table 13.5. This list of which effects are confounded with which other effects is called the **aliasing structure** of the design.[1]   ✦

The Calculus of Aliasing

Many statistical computer packages will create fractional factorial designs with desired characteristics for you. Many of these packages will also compute the aliasing structure. There is, however, a useful way of calculating aliases by hand for those times when your computer is not handy.

To begin with, think about the orthogonal array associated with a 2^{k-p} design. Disregard any center points. Each effect has associated with it a column of 1's and −1's that tell how to estimate the effect. The pattern of 1's and −1's used to estimate the interaction of two effects is obtained by multiplying the columns for the two effects together using the usual rules of arithmetic: The product of 1's with like signs yields a 1 and the product of 1's with unlike signs yields a −1.

The calculus of aliasing tells how to calculate the interaction of any two effects without multiplying their columns of 1's and −1's. Before introducing the calculus of aliasing, we must rename the mean effect μ to be I. This notation stands for "identity," and reflects the fact that the pattern of 1's and −1's for any effect is unchanged when multiplied by the column of all 1's associated with μ. All other effects are named in the usual way. The calculus of aliasing is based on two rules:

1. Multiplication of effects is done in the usual mathematical notation.
2. If the exponent of a factor in the product of effects is even, remove that factor. If the exponent of a factor in the product of effects is odd, replace the exponent with 1.

These rules are just shorthand for what happens when multiplying columns of an orthogonal array.

---

[1]Another way of saying that two effects are confounded is to say they are "aliased."

EXAMPLE 13.2   THE CALCULUS OF ALIASING

We use the preceding two rules to compute the effect corresponding to the inter-action of the effects ABD, AE, and ACDF. By rule 1, do the multiplication in the usual way, obtaining

$$(ABD)(AE)(ACDF) = A^3BCD^2EF$$

By rule 2, eliminate D^2 from the previous result, and change the exponent 3 on A to 1, to obtain

$$(ABD)(AE)(ACDF) = ABCEF \quad \blacklozenge$$

Generating 2^{k-p} Designs

A 2^{k-p} design consists of $1/2^p$ the number of runs of a full 2^k design. This means that each estimated effect is aliased with $2^p - 1$ other effects. Because of the calculus of aliasing, we can calculate the aliases associated with any effect simply by knowing the $2^p - 1$ effects that are aliased with the identity I.

EXAMPLE 13.3   FINDING ALL EFFECTS ALIASED
WITH A GIVEN EFFECT

We show how all the effects aliased with any given effect can be computed from knowledge of which effects are aliased with I.

Consider the 2^{5-2} design in which the effects ADE, BCE, and ABCD are aliased with I. We write this compactly as

$$I = ADE = BCE = ABCD \tag{13.1}$$

To find the effects aliased with factor D, we simply multiply all terms in (13.1) by D:

$$D = AD^2E = BCDE = ABCD^2$$

and simplify using the calculus of aliasing:

$$D = AE = BCDE = ABC$$

Try this yourself to show that CD, ACE, and BDE are aliased with the AB inter-action. $\blacklozenge$

It turns out that we can specify the aliasing pattern of a design even more simply. Rather than writing out each of the $2^p - 1$ effects aliased with I, we need only specify p of these effects. Such a specification is called a **generating relation.** Once we have a generating relation, we obtain the entire list of $2^p - 1$ effects aliased with I by multiplying all pairs of effects in the generating relation, then all triples, then all quadruples, and so on until finally we take the product of all p effects in the generating relation. For reasons of brevity, the aliasing structure of a 2^{k-p} design is most often expressed by specifying the generating relation.

EXAMPLE 13.4   USING THE GENERATING RELATION TO OBTAIN THE ALIASING PATTERN

Consider the 2^{7-4} design with generating relation

$$I = ABG = ACF = BCE = ABCD \qquad (13.2)$$

We can obtain the full aliasing pattern for I by multiplying all pairs, triples, and quadruples of effects in (13.2):

$$
\begin{aligned}
(ABG)(ACF) &= BCFG \\
(ABG)(BCE) &= ACEG \\
(ABG)(ABCD) &= CDG \\
(ACF)(BCE) &= ABEF \\
(ACF)(ABCD) &= BDF \\
(BCE)(ABCD) &= ADE \\
(ABG)(ACF)(BCE) &= EFG \\
(ABG)(ACF)(ABCD) &= ADFG \\
(ABG)(BCE)(ABCD) &= BDEG \\
(ACF)(BCE)(ABCD) &= CDEF \\
(ABG)(ACF)(BCE)(ABCD) &= ABCDEFG
\end{aligned}
$$

Thus, the effects aliased with I are

$$
\begin{aligned}
I &= ABG = ACF = BCE = ABCD = BCFG = ACEG \\
&= CDG = ABEF = BDF = ADE = EFG = ADFG \qquad (13.3) \\
&= BDEG = CDEF = ABCDEFG
\end{aligned}
$$

From this set of aliased effects we can use the calculus of aliasing to obtain the complete aliasing pattern of the design. ✦

Design Resolution

For any given k and p, there are many possible 2^{k-p} designs, so it is important to know when one design is better than another. One measure of the quality of a 2^{k-p} design is the **resolution** of the design. Basically, a design has high resolution if it confounds main effects and low-order interactions with high-order interactions. High resolution is a desirable property, since we want to confound the effects most likely to be significant, which, by the hierarchy of significance, are main effects and low-order interactions, with the effects least likely to be significant, which, by the hierarchy of significance, are high-order interactions. Therefore, whenever we consider a 2^{k-p} design, we should choose the design with maximum resolution possible. Formally, the resolution of a design is defined as:

> **DEFINITION**
>
> The resolution of a 2^{k-p} design equals the smallest number of factors in any effect aliased with I.

Resolution is usually denoted by Roman numerals. Some resolutions important for applications are:

- A design of resolution III does not confound main effects with one another, but does confound at least some main effects with two-factor interactions.
- A design of resolution IV does not confound main effects with one another or with two-factor interactions, but does confound at least some two-factor interactions with other two-factor interactions.
- A design of resolution V does not confound main effects and two-factor interactions with each other, but does confound at least some two-factor interactions with three-factor interactions.

EXAMPLE 13.4   CONTINUED

For the 2^{7-4} design in Example 13.4, the effects aliased with I are given by Equation (13.3). Since the fewest number of factors in any effect in Equation (13.3) is 3, the design has resolution III. We express this in the notation 2^{7-4}_{III}.   ◆

13.5

ANALYZING FRACTIONAL FACTORIAL DESIGNS

One nice thing about fractional factorial designs is that the results are analyzed exactly as for a full factorial, with or without center points, except that each computed effect will now represent two or more model effects. The question is how to determine which confounded effects are the significant ones.

Here are some basic principles for resolving the problem of confounding:

BASIC PRINCIPLES FOR RESOLVING CONFOUNDING

- **Use the hierarchy of significance.** This means that if a lower-order effect is confounded with a higher-order effect, and if that effect is significant, then it is assumed that it is the lower-order effect that is significant.

- **Use reasoning power.** For example, suppose main effects A and B and the confounded interaction AB = CD are found significant, but that main effects C and D are not. Since the interaction of significant main effects is more likely to be significant than is the interaction of insignificant main effects, assume that AB is the significant interaction.
- **Use subject-matter knowledge and interaction plots.**
- **Conduct additional experimentation.**

EXAMPLE 13.1   CONTINUED

Consider the 2_{IV}^{4-1} surface-finish design. All calculations of effects and conclusions as to their significance are conducted in the same way as was done when it was considered to be a 2^3 design. Recall that Feed Rate has the largest estimated effect, 4.75, and is likely significant. Dress Lead, Dwell Time, and the Feed Rate by Dwell Time interaction, all estimated to be −2.75, are possibly significant. Since the main effects Feed Rate, Dress Lead, and Dwell Time are all confounded with three-factor interactions, we'll assume that it is these, rather than the three-factor interactions, that are significant. The Feed Rate by Dwell Time interaction is confounded with the Dress Lead by Work Speed interaction. Given the fact that Work Speed has a small estimated effect and Feed Rate has the largest estimated effect, it is more likely, though not certain, that the Feed Rate by Dwell Time interaction is the significant effect here.   ✦

Resolving Confounding Through Further Experimentation

Sometimes the only way to find out which, among a group of confounded effects, are significant is to do further experimentation.

Design Fragments

Design fragments are small experiments run subsequent to a larger experiment in order to clear up a few ambiguities. Their use is best illustrated with an example.

EXAMPLE 13.5   A DESIGN FRAGMENT

Suppose in a four-factor fractional factorial, we found that A, C, and AB = CD were the significant effects. If we are unable to discover whether AB or CD or both are significant without doing further experimentation, then we might consider doing a small experiment to resolve the confounding of AB and CD. One such experiment might consist of four additional runs in which we vary AB and hold every other possible significant effect constant (an OFAT!):

A	B	C	D
−1	1	−1	1
−1	−1	−1	1
−1	1	−1	1
−1	−1	−1	1

If the effect of AB is small in these four runs, we know that CD is the significant effect. If AB is large, it probably is the sole significant interaction, but we don't know for certain.   ✦

These simple, ad hoc design-fragment methods, when combined with fractional factorial experimentation, can be very effective in getting the right answers.

Foldover Strategy

With five factors or more, there may be too much confounding for the design fragment strategy to work. A strategy that will work in these cases is the **foldover strategy.** The foldover strategy is a method for generating a new set of 2^{k-p} runs in a 2^{k-p} fractional factorial design in order to resolve ambiguities due to confounding. The following example will illustrate the foldover strategy.

EXAMPLE 13.6   FOLDOVER STRATEGY

Consider a 2^{7-4} design with factors A to G. Assume the orthogonal array for this design is given in Table 13.6.

The aliasing structure (up to two-factor interactions) is

$$A = BG = CF = DE$$
$$B = AG = CE = DF$$
$$C = AF = BE = DG$$
$$D = AE = BF = CG$$
$$E = AD = BC = FG$$
$$F = AC = BD = EG$$
$$G = AB = CD = EF$$

We'll assume that all three-factor and higher interactions are insignificant.

Suppose after running and analyzing the experiment, it was found that A, B, and G were the vital few significant effects. Then, assuming that subject-matter knowledge could not resolve the ambiguity, the most likely possible interpretations of what's going on are:

1. A, B, G, and no interactions are significant.
2. A, B, and the AB interaction are significant.

TABLE 13.6 Orthogonal Array for a 2^{7-4} Design

A	B	C	D	E	F	G
−1	−1	−1	−1	1	1	1
−1	−1	1	1	−1	−1	1
1	−1	−1	1	1	−1	−1
1	1	1	1	1	1	1
1	−1	1	−1	−1	1	−1
−1	1	−1	1	−1	1	−1
−1	1	1	−1	1	−1	−1
1	1	−1	−1	−1	−1	1

3. A, G, and the AG interaction are significant.

4. B, G, and the BG interaction are significant.

In light of interpretations 1 to 4, we can reduce the aliasing structure of the significant effects to

$$A = BG$$
$$B = AG$$
$$G = AB$$

To indicate that the confounding between A and BG has not been resolved, we will denote that effect as A + BG, with similar notation for the other effects. To make things definite, suppose the estimated effects are

$$A + BG = -11.4$$
$$B + AG = 7.8$$
$$G + AB = -5.5$$

In order to resolve the ambiguities, we are going to conduct a new set of eight runs in a pattern called a foldover. A foldover results from taking the orthogonal array for the original design (the main effects only, please!) and reversing the signs on all columns, so that 1's become −1's and vice versa.

Here's how it works in the present example. Reverse the signs on all seven main effect columns. This results in the orthogonal array shown in Table 13.7. By multiplying out the columns of this array, it is easy to see that −A is confounded with the two-factor interactions BG, CF, and DE.[2] Notice that whereas the main effects change sign, the two-factor interactions do not, since they are the products of two reversed columns, and a minus times a minus is a plus. (What sign would three-factor interactions have?)

---

[2] By −A, we mean column A in Table 13.7 multiplied by −1.

TABLE 13.7   Orthogonal Array for the Foldover of the 2^{7-4} Design in Table 13.6

A	B	C	D	E	F	G
1	1	1	1	−1	−1	−1
1	1	−1	−1	1	1	−1
−1	1	1	−1	−1	1	1
−1	−1	−1	−1	−1	−1	−1
−1	1	−1	1	1	−1	1
1	−1	1	−1	1	−1	1
1	−1	−1	1	−1	1	1
−1	−1	1	1	1	1	−1

Now run the eight runs of the foldover design in random order, and suppose the data yield the following for the effects of interest:

$$
\begin{aligned}
-A + BG &= 9.1 \\
-B + AG &= -8.7 \\
-G + AB &= -4.7
\end{aligned}
$$

Finally, we combine the two sets estimates of effects in two ways. Adding them and dividing by 2 gives

$$
\begin{aligned}
BG &= ([A + BG] + [-A + BG])/2 = (-11.4 + 9.1)/2 = -1.15 \\
AG &= ([B + AG] + [-B + AG])/2 = (7.8 - 8.7)/2 = -0.45 \\
AB &= ([G + AB] + [-G + AB])/2 = (-5.5 - 4.7)/2 = -5.10
\end{aligned}
$$

and subtracting them and dividing by 2 gives

$$
\begin{aligned}
A &= ([A + BG] - [-A + BG])/2 = (-11.4 - 9.1)/2 = -10.25 \\
B &= ([B + AG] - [-B + AG])/2 = (7.8 + 8.7)/2 = 8.25 \\
G &= ([G + AB] - [-G + AB])/2 = (-5.5 + 4.7)/2 = -0.40
\end{aligned}
$$

The foldover has enabled us to separate the main effects from the two-factor interactions, and it is clear that A, B, and AB are the significant effects.   ◆

One caution is in order here. In Example 13.6, we have treated the combined original and foldover design as if it were run in a completely random manner. In reality, the two designs were randomized separately, and were run as two blocks (with blocks confounded with the ADE interaction in this case, since ADE = 1 for the runs of the original design and −1 for the runs of the second). Since we are only interested in the main effects and two-factor interactions, and since none of the main effects or two-factor interactions is confounded with blocks, we are justified in ignoring the blocking, but you should be aware that it is there. The next section discusses blocking in greater detail.

Finally, one other issue that you should be aware of: It is not always true that running a foldover design is equivalent to initially running a design with twice the number of runs. For example, if you design a 2^{5-1} experiment at the outset (i.e., you start with 16 runs), you can obtain resolution V. However, the best you can do with a foldover of a 2^{5-2} design is resolution IV.

13.6   BLOCKING

Suppose that for the surface-finish experiment with eight runs and five factors, the experimenter can only do four runs in a given day. Because of day-to-day changes in environmental conditions and the material he can choose, he is concerned that running the experiment on two different days could affect any observable differences in response due to factors and interactions. It turns out that by designing the experiment intelligently, he can minimize the effect of running the experiment on different days.

One way **not** to do it is to run all low values of a single factor on day 1 and all high levels of the same factor on day 2, because then the effect of that factor would be confounded with any effect due to days. Another approach is to randomize the run order. This would probably avoid the kind of confounding just mentioned, but the extra variability due to days might still make it difficult to distinguish true factor and interaction effects.

The best solution is to **block** the experiment in two blocks: one consisting of the runs on day 1 and the other of the runs on day 2. This allows the experimenter to control the variability due to days by confounding it with an effect of his or her choice.

Analysis of a blocked design is done in the usual way except that the effects confounded with blocks aren't meaningful due to possible block effects. The other effects are only meaningful provided that the only day-to-day changes are an overall raising or lowering of average effects: that is, provided that there are no day-by-factor interactions. Interaction plots can help determine if this is a valid assumption.

In general, you should use blocking to reduce variability caused by known nuisance factors: in this case, days. You should use randomization to protect against biases due to unknown nuisance factors.

The following example illustrates both blocking and the analysis of a fractional factorial design.

EXAMPLE 13.7   ANALYSIS OF A BLOCKED DESIGN

Process engineers at a plastic manufacturer were confronted with the problem of an ethylene-vinyl acetate (EVA) ring sticking on the moving ejector half of an ejection mold. In order to determine the source of the problem, they designed an experiment with the factors thought most likely to be responsible. These are shown in Table 13.8. Because they had time for only eight runs in all, they decided to perform an unreplicated 2^{5-2} experiment. The machines were in heavy use, so in order to schedule time for the experiment, they had to perform the runs on two

TABLE 13.8   Variables for an EVA Ring Experiment

Factor	Units	Low setting	High setting
Mold temperature	°C	60	125
Screw speed	Percent	35	99
Hold pressure	Percent	10	30
Probe temperature	°C	300	420
Hold time	Seconds	2	5

TABLE 13.9   EVA Ring Data

Block	Mold temp.	Screw speed	Hold pressure	Probe temp.	Hold time	Number rejects	Proportion rejects	Logit
1	1	−1	−1	1	1	11	0.6875	0.7885
1	−1	−1	1	1	−1	4	0.2500	−1.0986
1	−1	1	1	−1	1	1	0.0625	−2.7081
1	1	1	−1	−1	−1	15	0.9375	2.7081
2	−1	−1	−1	−1	1	4	0.2500	−1.0986
2	1	1	1	1	1	15	0.9375	2.7081
2	−1	1	−1	1	−1	1	0.0625	−2.7081
2	1	−1	1	−1	−1	15	0.9375	2.7081

TABLE 13.10   Alias Structure, EVA Ring Experiment

Mold temp. = (Probe temp.)*(Hold time)
Screw speed = (Hold press.)*(Hold time)
Hold press. = (Screw speed)*(Hold time)
Probe temp. = (Mold temp.)*(Hold time)
Hold time = (Mold temp.)*(Probe temp.)
= (Screw speed)*(Hold press.)
(Mold temp.)*(Screw speed) = (Hold press.)*(Probe temp.)
Blocks = (Screw speed)*(Probe temp.)
= (Mold temp.)*(Hold press.)

different machines. Since they thought the machines and their operators might have different characteristics, they treated the machines as blocks and ran four runs on each. To determine which factor settings would be run in which block, they aliased blocks with Mold Temperature by Hold Pressure interaction. The design, which is a 2_{III}^{5-2} design, is shown in Table 13.9. The aliasing structure, up to two-factor interactions is given in Table 13.10.

From Table 13.10, we see that each main effect is estimated independently of blocks, which justifies this choice of blocks.

The experimenters performed the runs in random order, waiting for the process parameters to stabilize before taking data. Each response is the number of the 16 cavities on which there was sticking. Since these numbers, divided by

TABLE 13.11   Effect Estimates, EVA Ring Experiment

Mold temp.	4.13
Screw speed	−0.32
Hold press.	0.48
Probe temp.	−0.48
Hold time	−0.48
(Mold temp.)*(Screw speed)	1.28
Blocks	0.48

INTERACTION PLOT

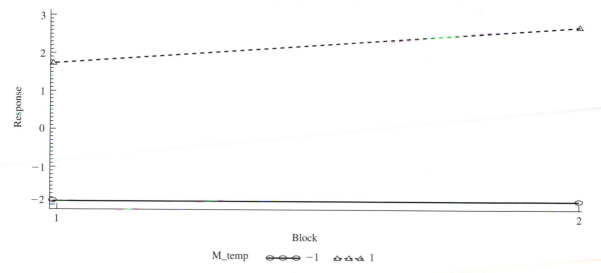

Figure 13.1   Plot of the Mold Temperature by Block interaction.

16, can be considered proportions,[3] we will transform the response using the logit transform, Logit = $\ln[Y/(1 - Y)]$, where Y is the proportion of sticking parts out of 16. The proportions and the logit values are shown in Table 13.9.

Effect estimates are shown in Table 13.11. To test for significance at the 0.05 level, we can compare these with MOE = 2.71 and SMOE = 6.48,[4] computed from the Lenth procedure. We see that only Mold Temperature is possibly significant.

Figure 13.1 shows an interaction plot of the interaction of Mold Temperature with Blocks. This plot shows little evidence of interaction, and justifies our analysis using the blocks. ✦

---

[3]Though there is some question as to whether they are binomial, since data for adjacent cavities may be correlated.

[4]Recall from Chapter 12 that MOE stands for margin of error and SMOE for simultaneous margin of error.

13.7

THE STRATEGY OF SEQUENTIAL EXPERIMENTATION

Whether the goal is learning how nature works or improving an industrial process, experimentation plays a key role. But isolated single experiments are not the way the scientific method works. Rather, each experiment is almost always part of a larger sequence of experiments, the results of one experiment suggesting what is studied in the next. Eventually, the sequence of experiments yields a satisfactory answer to the problem at hand.

You now have enough knowledge of the basics of experimental design and analysis to see how such designs can be implemented as part of an overall strategy of experimentation.

Planning the Experiment(s)

Before experimentation can begin, the experiment(s) must be planned. All experiments should be a **team effort:**

- To get as much input from as many different perspectives as possible.
- So that critical factors are not overlooked.
- So that the most efficient approaches are considered.
- So that ownership and responsibility are shared.

An excellent way to foster team effort in the planning stages of an experiment is through **brainstorming.** A brainstorming session will bring together people with relevant interests and expertise. In a brainstorming session, devices such as flowcharts and Ishikawa diagrams (see Chapter 1) can be used to encourage, document and organize ideas.

EXAMPLE 13.8   EXAMPLE 1.4, REVISITED

Recall Example 1.4 from Chapter 1 concerning a manufacturer of fine mesh netting that wanted to investigate whether changes could be made in manufacturing the mesh so as to improve strength without adding major new equipment or processing procedures that would increase cost greatly.

Example 1.4 showed how the team used brainstorming, process flow diagrams, and Ishikawa diagrams to identify possible sources of variation in the strength of the mesh.   ✦

Screening Experiments

At the early stage of experimentation, the experiment team is usually confronted with a large number of factors, such as the mesh netting team identified in an Ishikawa diagram.

Screening designs, very parsimonious designs such as the fractional factorials you have studied in this chapter, are appropriate at this stage of experimentation to find the vital few significant factors. These designs obtain their efficiency at the cost of a high degree of confounding. Thus, at this stage, we are forced to confine our conclusions to the grossest features of the design, namely, the main effects and possibly some two-factor interactions.

At this stage of the investigations, the experiment team should do the following:

- Be bold in choice of factor levels. The difference between 1 and −1 should be large enough to reveal significant effects in the presence of experimental noise.
- Put in as many factors as possible. Nature should be allowed to reveal which factors are and are not significant. Factors of unsuspected significance will remain undetected by restricting the set of factors a priori. Remember that it is always better at this stage to include too many rather than too few factors.
- Look for evidence of severe curvature through center points and interactions. The existence of such curvature means the experimenters were too bold: The factor levels are too far apart.
- Move off in a promising direction for further experimentation. This is the beginning of the next stage of experimentation, which will be studied further in Chapter 14.

Organizing the Experiment(s)

It is not enough to design an experiment well. Even a well-designed experiment can be ruined when run improperly. Since many of the people involved in running the experiment know little or nothing about the design of experiments, it is essential that the experimental team keep in constant communication with everyone involved in running the experiment concerning what, when, and how things should be done, and who is to do them. Carefully written instructions should detail the experimental settings, procedures, measurements to be made, calibrations, preparations, materials, machines, methods, and so on.

Quality Control of the Experiment(s)

It is imperative that steps be taken to ensure the following:

- The equipment is run properly.
- Proper maintenance has been performed.
- Proper materials are being used.
- Measurements are made properly.

EXAMPLE 13.8   CONTINUED

Because of the size of the problem and time and resource constraints, the team looking at the mesh netting decided to break the problem into a set of smaller, more manageable, components. They decided to focus initially on the machines, because they felt that this was the problem area in which experimentation would most likely lead to large gains in quality.

They held another brainstorming session with production supervisors and workers who knew the machine characteristics best. This session led to the design of a large screening experiment with 15 factors and 16 runs, which would enable them to estimate only the main effects. They included another six partial replicate center points to estimate experimental error, process stability, and response surface curvature. The hope was that the results of this initial experiment would enable the experimenters to identify the vital few factors that they could then explore in more detail in subsequent experimentation.

In collaboration with production supervisors and workers, the experimenters specified factor-level settings that they thought would lead to identifiable differences in the response. They also developed an experimental design in which some blocking was done out of necessity and to improve sensitivity. The rest of the runs were randomized to guard against unsuspected sources of bias. The experimenters developed instruction sheets for machine operators and supervisory personnel, as well as coding sheets for entering data.

The experimenters made several pilot runs to "get the bugs out" of their procedures. These runs resulted in several revisions in the experimental procedures. Finally, they conducted preexperiment briefing and instructional sessions to make sure the conduct of the experiment was understood by all. The experimenters were present when the experiment was being conducted in order to make sure that procedures were being followed and to resolve any problems that arose. ✦

Continual Improvement and the Strategy of Sequential Experimentation

As we've said before, successful experimentation is not a one-shot deal. Rather it is part of a strategy of sequential experimentation with each experiment in the sequence suggesting the next experiment until the results converge to a useful approximation to reality.

Later Stages of Experimentation

After the factors have been narrowed to the vital few the goal of experimentation changes. Now the experimental strategy is to map out the response surface in detail, and to pinpoint the factor settings that optimize the process. Thus, the differences in factor settings should be smaller, and mapping out curvature becomes important.

Figure 13.2 presents a flow chart illustrating the possibilities to be considered after any one experiment in the sequence has been run and analyzed. You now have the knowledge and skills to go through all items on this flowchart except "Move off in Best Direction and Run New Experiment." This topic is covered in Chapter 14.

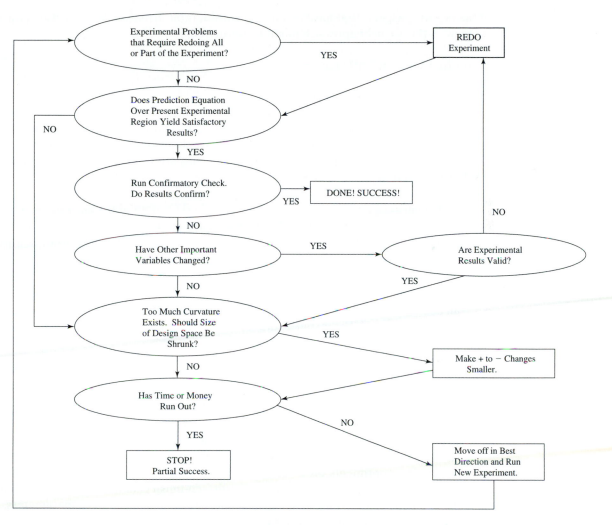

Figure 13.2   Postexperiment flow chart: mesh netting example.

13.8

TAGUCHI'S ROBUST PARAMETER DESIGN

In the early 1980s, an integrated methodology of statistical and engineering design methods espoused by the Japanese engineer Genichi Taguchi was introduced in this country. Popularly known as **Taguchi methods,** this methodology gained immense popularity and led to an increased use of experimental design in process and product improvement. In this section, we introduce some of the basic philosophy and implementation of Taguchi methods. We will discuss the positive aspects of this methodology and some of the negative aspects that have resulted in considerable criticism. We will also discuss some ways the Taguchi approach might be improved.

Taguchi's Design Philosophy

Familiar Terminology with New Meanings

In this text, you have already encountered the statistical notions of design, parameters, and robustness. Taguchi's design philosophy is also about design, parameters, and robustness, but the engineering meanings of these terms are not the statistical meanings you have learned.

- Statistical **design** refers to the design of a method for obtaining data. For example, in this chapter, we have studied 2^{k-p} designs for obtaining experimental data.
- A statistical **parameter,** also called a model parameter, is an unknown quantity that must be specified to determine the model as completely as possible. The population mean, μ, is a parameter for the $N(\mu, 1)$ distribution model.
- A statistical procedure, such as an hypothesis test, or a statistical quantity, such as an estimator, is said to be **robust** if it is not greatly affected when model assumptions are violated. For instance, the sample mean is not robust to outliers, but the sample median is.

Taguchi uses the preceding terms as follows:

- **Design** refers to the engineering design of a process or system.
- A **parameter,** in the Taguchi sense, is a quantity governing a process or system, whose values must be specified for the process to function. There is a fundamental relation between Taguchi's notion of parameter and statistical design of experiments: In experiments on a process, experimental design factors correspond to process parameters. For instance, in the surface-finish example, the experimental design factors Feed Rate, Dwell, Time, and Dress Lead are process parameters.
- For Taguchi, a design is **robust** if it

   (a) Performs well over the range of likely environmental conditions.
   (b) Performs well over the range of likely values of difficult-to-control parameters.
   (c) Exhibits small variation in performance.

The Role of Statistical Design of Experiments in Robust Parameter Design

One of Taguchi's most fundamental contributions to quality improvement is the notion that products and processes should be designed to be robust, and that the statistical design of experiments can be used to determine parameter settings that make the product or process robust.

To do this, Taguchi suggests that experiments be designed in which process parameters form one set of experimental factors, called **control factors.** Control factors are parameters that can be controlled in both the experiment and in the process, and whose optimal values the experiment is designed to determine.

Taguchi also defines a second set of experimental factors, called **noise factors.** Noise factors are either

- Process parameters that are difficult to control, or,
- Other variables that cannot be controlled when the process is run or the product is used.

Noise factors represent a range of conditions to which the product or process is subjected in use and against which we want to ensure its robustness.

Noise factors sometimes can be controlled during the experiment, and sometimes cannot. In the latter case, values of the noise factors are just observed. Noise factors most often represent the effects of environment, consumer use (or abuse), uncontrollable process changes, and so on. The idea is that by varying the noise factors along with the control factors, we can determine the levels of the control factors that make the process or product most robust to the changes represented by the noise factors. The following example will help illustrate.

EXAMPLE 13.9   THE TAGUCHI APPROACH

A company manufactures picture hangers consisting of a metal hook fastened to a piece of adhesive-backed cloth. The customer fastens the hanger to a wall by moistening the adhesive. Designers of the hangers would like to know what the main determinants of the strength of the bond are, and what makes for consistency of that strength under different application conditions. They have identified eight factors they would like to investigate. Of the eight, five are control factors, representing design choices, and three are noise factors, representing different application conditions consumers are likely to use.

- The control factors are as follows:

    1. AD_TYPE: Type of adhesive. Two formulations are to be tested, coded −1 and 1.
    2. AD_AMT: Amount of adhesive per unit area of the cloth backing. Two levels are to be tested, coded −1 and 1.
    3. WEAVE: Tightness of the weave for the cloth backing. This is thought to affect the impregnation of the cloth by the adhesive. Two levels are to be tested, coded −1 and 1.
    4. SHAPE: Shape of the cloth backing. The choices are square or diamond. Two levels are to be tested, coded −1 and 1.
    5. AREA: Area of the cloth backing. Two levels are to be tested, coded −1 and 1.

- The noise factors are as follows:

    1. ROUGH: Surface roughness. Two identical test surfaces were used for all runs. One, painted with a typical glossy finish, was coded −1; the other, painted with a typical flat finish, was coded 1.

    2. TIME: Setting time. Two levels were chosen: 10 minutes, coded −1, and 60 minutes, coded 1.

    3. MOISTURE: Amount of moisture used to moisten the adhesive. Two levels were chosen: 0.10 ml/unit area, coded −1, and 0.25 ml/unit area, coded 1.

The response was the force, in pounds, exerted downward, needed to pull the hanger from the test surface.

Clearly, the control factors can be controlled in both the experiment and in the actual production process. The noise factors account for variation in the response induced by the type of wall surface or by consumer actions during application. ✦

Inner and Outer Arrays

In order to obtain settings of the control factors that are robust to the variation represented by the noise factors, Taguchi advocates designing the experiment using two orthogonal arrays: an **inner array,** which specifies the levels of the control factors, and an **outer array,** which specifies the levels of the noise factors. The entire design is the product of these two arrays, where by product we mean that at each set of control factor levels, an experiment in the noise factors is run.

As an example, suppose that both the inner and outer arrays are 2^2 designs. We may call such a design a $2^2 \times 2^2$, the notation in general being (inner array design) × (outer array design). Then the complete design consists of 16 runs, which mathematically equals, not by coincidence, $2^2 \times 2^2$. If the control factors are named A and B and the noise factors are named C and D, the complete product array is displayed in Table 13.12.

TABLE 13.12 Product Orthogonal Array for a $2^2 \times 2^2$ Design. A and B Are the Control Factors, and Their Levels Constitute the Inner Array. Factors C and D Are the Noise Factors, and Their Levels Constitute the Outer Array

Inner array			Outer array					
		C:	−1	1	−1	1	Row	Row
A	B	D:	−1	−1	1	1	means	variances
1	1		Y_{11}	Y_{12}	Y_{13}	Y_{14}	$\bar{Y}_1$	S_1^2
−1	1		Y_{21}	Y_{22}	Y_{23}	Y_{24}	$\bar{Y}_2$	S_2^2
1	−1		Y_{31}	Y_{32}	Y_{33}	Y_{34}	$\bar{Y}_3$	S_3^2
−1	−1		Y_{41}	Y_{42}	Y_{43}	Y_{44}	$\bar{Y}_4$	S_4^2

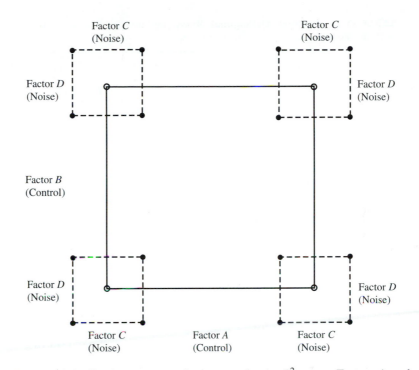

Figure 13.3 Design geometry for inner and outer 2^2 arrays. Factors A and B are the control factors, and their levels constitute the inner array. Factors C and D are the noise factors, and their levels constitute the outer array.

The first row of four design points in Table 13.12 corresponds to the complete set of outer array runs at inner array factor levels A = 1 and B = 1. The responses at those design points are labeled Y_{11}, corresponding to C = −1 and D = −1; Y_{12}, corresponding to C = 1 and D = −1; Y_{13}, corresponding to C = −1 and D = 1; and Y_{14}, corresponding to C = 1 and D = 1. The second row of four design points corresponds to the complete set of outer array runs at inner array factor levels A = −1 and B = 1, and so on.

Figure 13.3 illustrates the design geometry for this $2^2 \times 2^2$ design. The levels of the control factors A and B, which constitute the inner array, are plotted as the open circles at the corners of the large square. The levels of the noise factors C and D, which constitute the outer array, are plotted as the solid circles at the corners of the four small squares. The small square at the upper right corresponds to the first row of design points in Table 13.12; the small square at the upper left corresponds to the second row, and so on.

The product orthogonal array for the picture hanger experiment was slightly larger than this:

EXAMPLE 13.9   CONTINUED

The inner array in the picture hanger experiment was a 2^{5-2}_{III} design, and the outer array was a 2^{3-1}_{III}. The product array and the responses are shown in Table 13.13. ✦

TABLE 13.13 Product Orthogonal Array for the $2^{5-2} \times 2^{3-1}$ Design of Example 13.9, along with the Responses

						Outer array			
		Inner array			ROUGH:	1	1	−1	−1
					TIME:	1	−1	−1	1
AD_AMT	WEAVE	AD_TYPE	AREA	SHAPE	MOISTURE:	1	−1	−1	1
−1	−1	−1	−1	1		12.52	11.09	10.41	11.21
−1	−1	1	1	−1		11.61	12.09	10.03	11.56
−1	1	−1	1	−1		11.56	12.14	11.60	10.28
−1	1	1	−1	1		12.05	10.92	9.02	11.72
1	−1	−1	1	1		10.55	11.22	10.58	9.21
1	−1	1	−1	−1		12.04	12.45	9.82	11.14
1	1	−1	−1	−1		11.38	10.07	9.40	10.11
1	1	1	1	1		11.43	14.23	11.74	10.89

Signal–Noise Ratios

The product array allows us to see how the response varies at the different settings of the noise factors for each set of control-factor levels. Two particular measures of interest are the mean and variance of the responses at each set of control-factor levels. Often, the goal is to find control-factor settings that do two things:

1. Attain an optimum mean level over all noise-factor settings. Depending on the application, an optimum mean level might be a maximum or a minimum or it might be the mean level closest to a target value.
2. Minimize the variance of the response over all noise-factor settings.

One approach to finding optimal settings of the control variables is to analyze the mean and variance separately. However, it may not be possible to find a set of control-factor levels that attain both an optimum mean level and a minimum variance. In order to get around this problem, Taguchi suggests a single measure, called the **signal– noise ratio** that he claims combines both mean and variance. In fact, depending on the application, Taguchi suggests using one of three signal–noise ratios.

Suppose that the inner array consists of m design points and that outer array consists of n design points, and let Y_{ij}, $i = 1, \ldots, m$; $j = 1, \ldots, n$, denote the observations taken at design point i of the inner array and j of the outer array. We let $\bar{Y}_i$ and S_i^2 denote the mean and variance, respectively, of those n observations corresponding to design point i of the inner array. The Taguchi approach replaces the n outer array responses corresponding to inner array design point i with the corresponding value of a signal–noise ratio. The three signal–noise ratios suggested as responses by Taguchi are as follows.[5]

---

[5]The logarithms here are base 10. Although the choice of a base makes no difference to the results, and although virtually everywhere else in the book we use natural logarithms, here we use base 10 logarithms to allow the resulting units to be interpreted as "decibels." To keep things from getting too confused, we will use base 10 for all logarithms in the remainder of this chapter.

- **SN_L:** SN_L is used if the goal is to maximize the response. The SN_L value for design point i of the inner array is computed as

$$SN_{Li} = -10 \log \left(\frac{1}{n} \sum_{j=1}^{n} \frac{1}{Y_{ij}^2} \right), \qquad i = 1, \ldots, m$$

- **SN_S:** SN_S is used if the goal is to minimize the response. The SN_S value for design point i of the inner array is computed as

$$SN_{Si} = -10 \log \left(\frac{1}{n} \sum_{j=1}^{n} Y_{ij}^2 \right), \qquad i = 1, \ldots, m$$

- **SN_T:** SN_T is used when the goal is to attain a target value. The SN_T value for design point i of the inner array is computed as

$$SN_{Ti} = 10 \log \left(\frac{\bar{Y}_i^2}{S_i^2} \right), \qquad i = 1, \ldots, m$$

EXAMPLE 13.9   CONTINUED

The values for $\bar{y}$ and s^2 in Table 13.14 are obtained from the original FORCE values in Table 13.13. For example, the value $\bar{y} = 11.31$ in the first row of Table 13.14 is the mean of the four responses in the first row of Table 13.13:

$$11.31 = \frac{1}{4}(12.52 + 11.09 + 10.41 + 11.21)$$

The value $s^2 = 0.7775$ is the variance of those same four responses. SN_L is computed using the formula given earlier. The value in the first row of Table 13.14

TABLE 13.14   The Summary Measures $\bar{y}$, s^2, and SN_L Computed Over All Levels of the Noise Factors, Picture Hanger Experiment

AD_AMT	WEAVE	AD_TYPE	AREA	SHAPE	$\bar{y}$	s^2	SN_L
−1	−1	−1	−1	1	11.31	0.7775	21.01
−1	−1	1	1	−1	11.55	1.1446	21.16
−1	1	−1	1	−1	11.40	0.6225	21.08
−1	1	1	−1	1	10.93	1.8422	20.60
1	−1	−1	1	1	10.39	0.7143	20.26
1	−1	1	−1	−1	11.36	1.3568	21.00
1	1	−1	−1	−1	10.24	0.6837	20.15
1	1	1	1	1	12.07	2.1922	21.51

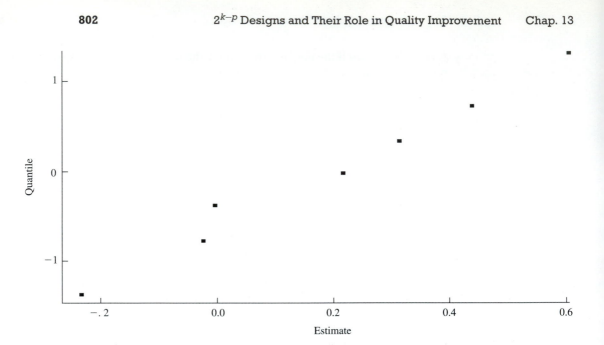

Figure 13.4 Normal quantile plot of estimated effects: picture hanger experiment with response SN_L.

is computed as

$$21.01 = -10 \log \left[\frac{1}{4} \left(\frac{1}{12.52^2} + \frac{1}{11.09^2} + \frac{1}{10.41^2} + \frac{1}{11.21^2} \right) \right]$$

Taguchi recommends using the signal–noise ratio instead of the original response to analyze the experiment. Analysis of the picture hanger data using SN_L as the response revealed no significant effects using the Lenth procedure: The MOE value is 1.32 and the magnitude of the largest effect estimate is 0.61. A normal quantile plot of the estimated effects, shown in Figure 13.4, substantiates this conclusion. ✦

Problems with the Signal–Noise Ratio

We saw in the last section that analysis of the picture hanger data using SN_L as the response revealed no significant effects. Unfortunately, this result is due to a deficiency of the methodology: Studies have shown that SN_L and SN_T do a poor job of identifying effects associated with differences in S^2, though they may perform better with differences in $\bar{Y}$. A more effective strategy is to analyze $\bar{Y}$ and S^2 as separate responses.

EXAMPLE 13.9   CONTINUED

The picture hanger data were reanalyzed using $\bar{Y}$ and $\log(S^2)$ as responses.[6] There was no evidence of significant effects with the $\bar{Y}$ response, but there was some evidence that AD_TYPE has a significant effect on $\log(S^2)$: The estimated effect = 0.36, with MOE = 0.21 and SMOE = 0.50. The signal–noise ratio SN_L failed to detect this.   ✦

Caution.   Because of their ineffectiveness, we recommend that the signal–noise ratios not be used as responses.

A Critique of Taguchi Methodology

Taguchi's ideas about the use of statistical methods in parameter design have attracted much attention, and justifiably so. The idea that products and processes can be designed to be robust to environmental conditions and difficult-to-control factors, and to have small variation in performance has revolutionized the way we consider issues of design and quality improvement.

However, the methods Taguchi suggests for implementing these ideas have generated severe criticism. We have already seen that the signal–noise ratios can be ineffective responses for quantifying differences in variances. Some other criticisms of the Taguchi methodology are as follows:

- The crossed inner and outer arrays often lead to very large experiments. In Example 13.9, we saw that despite having few factors and using parsimonious fractional factorial designs, the resulting crossed design had 32 runs. With the large numbers of factors common to many industrial experiments, crossed designs with hundreds of runs are not uncommon.
- Taguchi ignores interactions in the analysis. This is a problem when, as can happen, interactions are important features in a model.
- Taguchi uses some questionable statistical methods. One example is the use of analysis of marginal means and a "pick-the-winner" strategy to determine significant factors. Here is a simple example:

EXAMPLE 13.10   PICK THE WINNER STRATEGY

Consider a 3×3 experiment with control factors A and B and responses shown in Table 13.15. In the Taguchi formulation, these responses will likely be signal-noise ratios. Suppose the goal is to find control-factor settings to maximize the response.

   The marginal means analysis looks only at the marginal means of the data when seeking to determine the optimal factor settings. The pick-the-winner strategy then chooses the factor settings that result in the optimal marginal mean. Here, this strategy chooses level 1 of factor A and level 3 of factor B. Clearly, this

---

[6]Due to the skewness of S^2, it is preferable to analyze $\log(S^2)$.

TABLE 13.15   Table Illustrating Marginal Means Analysis and Pick-the-Winner Strategy: Example 13.10

	Level	Factor B 1	Factor B 2	Factor B 3	Marginal mean
	1	6	12	4	$7.\overline{33}$
Factor A	2	6	4	10	$6.\overline{66}$
	3	3	7	10	$6.\overline{66}$
Marginal mean		5.00	$7.\overline{66}$	8.00	

combination is not optimal. In fact, it results in a value of 4, one of the lowest values in the table. In order to select the factor-level combinations that give the largest response, we must study how the two factors vary together. A look at the entire table, and not just the marginal means, reveals that the largest response, 12, occurs at level 1 of factor A and level 2 of factor B.

More generally, **response surface methods** are a set of efficient methods for finding optimum control-factor settings. These methods are presented in Chapter 14. ✦

Better Approaches

We have seen that although Taguchi's philosophy of robust design is sound, some of the methods for implementing this philosophy are not. We have two recommendations in particular:

1. If you have the resources and want to conduct an experiment based on crossed inner and outer arrays, do not use a signal–noise ratio as the response. A better approach is to analyze $\bar{Y}$ and S^2 separately.
2. If you want to analyze the effect of control and noise factors on a response, but do not have the resources to conduct an experiment based on crossed inner and outer arrays, try an experiment in which all factors, control and noise, are studied using a single parsimonious design, such as a 2^{k-p}. Such an experiment is not only parsimonious, but can also capture features, such as interactions between control and noise factors, that Taguchi analysis cannot.

D ISCUSSION QUESTIONS

1. What is confounding? Aliasing structure?
2. What is the hierarchy of significance? The Pareto principle? Describe in general terms how these and knowledge of confounding patterns can be used in a strategy of efficient experimentation.

3. What is the calculus of aliasing? A generating relation? Explain how these can be used to find all effects aliased with any particular effect.

4. What is the resolution of a design? Describe the characteristics of resolution III, IV, and V designs.

5. What is blocking, and why is it done? Give an example of its usefulness.

6. Describe the design fragment strategy for resolving confounding.

7. Describe the foldover strategy for resolving confounding.

8. Describe in a general way the overall strategy of experimentation. Include in your discussion:
   (a) Steps in planning an experiment.
   (b) Organizing the experiment.
   (c) The quality control of the experiment.
   (d) Continual improvement and the strategy of sequential experimentation.

9. Explain Taguchi's approach to robust parameter design. In particular, describe the following concepts:
   (a) Control and noise factors.
   (b) Inner and outer arrays.
   (c) Signal–noise ratios.
   (d) Marginal means analysis and the pick-the-winner strategy.

10. Explain some of the criticisms of Taguchi's methods.

E XERCISES

13.1. Suppose that the engineer in Section 13.2 suddenly found money for a third run, and ran it at coded values -1, -1, and 1. Then the beginning of Table 13.1 for this experiment would look like:

μ	A	B	C
1	-1	-1	-1
1	1	1	1
1	-1	-1	1

Complete the table and tell which effects are confounded with which others here.

13.2. Suppose in the 2^{7-4} experiment in Example 13.6, that A, C, and F were the significant effects. Give the four most plausible interpretations of which effects are significant.

13.3. The aliasing structure for a 2^{5-2}_{III} design is (up to two-factor interactions)

$$A = DE$$
$$B = CE$$
$$C = BE$$
$$D = AE$$
$$E = AD = BC$$
$$AB = CD$$
$$AC = BD$$

It is found that A, D, and E are the vital few significant effects. Their estimates are 5, 7, and -3 respectively. Assume three-way and higher interactions are negligible.

(a) What are the most plausible possibilities for which effects and interactions are significant?

(b) A foldover design is run and the computed effects for $-A + DE$, $-D + AE$, and $-E + AD$ are -4, 4, and 5, respectively. Which possibility from part (a) do the data support? Why?

13.4. (a) Obtain a 2_V^{5-1} design.

(b) Show that III is the best resolution of any 2^{5-2} design.

(c) One 2_{III}^{5-2} design has aliasing relation $I = ADE = BCE = ABCD$. Show that using the foldover strategy on this design results in a 2_{IV}^{5-1}. (In fact, the best the foldover strategy can do when used on any 2^{5-2} design is resolution IV. This means that obtaining a 2^{k-p} design using a foldover strategy is not equivalent to designing a 2^{k-p} from scratch.)

13.5. Consider the following fractional factorial design for four factors (A, B, C, and D).

A	B	C	D
−1	−1	−1	−1
1	−1	−1	1
−1	1	−1	1
1	1	−1	−1
−1	−1	1	1
1	−1	1	−1
−1	1	1	−1
1	1	1	1

(a) What fraction is this design?

(b) Write out the aliasing structure for this design.

(c) What is the resolution of this design?

(d) Assume that all three-way and higher interactions are negligible, and that we obtain the following effect estimates:

Effect	Estimate
A	22.50
B	0.86
C	−1.21
D	31.8
AB	21.6
AC	−0.39
AD	−26.6

From these data, can you tell which are the vital few significant two-factor interactions, or do you need more information? Justify your answer.

13.6. Consider the following fractional factorial design for three factors (A, B, and C), and the observed values of the response Y:

A	B	C	Y
−1	−1	1	8
1	−1	−1	34
−1	1	−1	10
1	1	1	35

(a) What fraction is this design?
(b) Write out the aliasing structure for this design.
(c) What is the resolution of this design?
(d) Estimate the effects. From these data, can you tell which are the vital few significant effects, or do you need more information? Justify your answer.

13.7. You have just run a screening experiment and found severe curvature. What might be the cause of this result, and what might you do as your next step?

13.8. Alloy 356 is a member of an aluminum-silicon-magnesium family of alloys. A metallurgist is interested in which differences in alloy chemistry are significant in determining its microstructure. In particular, since silicon particles have the strongest influence on mechanical properties of the alloy (e.g., strength, toughness, elongation), she conducted a 2^{7-4} experiment in which the response was silicon equivalent diameter (SIED), a measure of the size of silicon particles in the alloy. The seven factors are cooling rate (CCR), presence/absence of a grain refiner (CGR), amount of silicon in the alloy (CSI), amount of titanium in the alloy (CTI), amount of magnesium in the alloy (CMG), amount of iron in the alloy (CFE), and the amount of strontium in the alloy (CMOD). The full set of effects aliased with I is:

$$I = (CCR) * (CTI) * (CMG) * (CMOD)$$
$$= (CGR) * (CSI) * (CTI)$$
$$= (CSI) * (CFE) * (CMOD)$$
$$= (CCR) * (CGR) * (CSI) * (CMG) * (CMOD)$$
$$= (CGR) * (CTI) * (CFE) * (CMOD)$$
$$= (CCR) * (CGR) * (CMG) * (CFE)$$
$$= (CCR) * (CSI) * (CTI) * (CMG) * (CFE)$$

(a) What is the resolution of this design?
(b) Table 13.16 displays effect estimates and the MOE and SMOE values. Which effects do you judge to be significant with respect to SMOE? With respect to MOE?
(c) The (CCR)*(CTI)*(CMG) interaction is aliased with one main effect and one two-factor interaction. What are they?
(d) Based on the effects significant with respect to SMOE, and the information that the mean of the SIED values is 1.142, write down an equation to predict SIED.

TABLE 13.16   Results of a 2^{7-3} Experiment for Alloy 356. Only One of Possibly Several Confounded Effects is Listed for Each Estimate

EFFECT	ESTIMATE	MOE	SMOE
CCR	0.3425	0.12571	0.28134
CGR	−0.1025	0.12571	0.28134
CMG	0.0050	0.12571	0.28134
CTI	0.1475	0.12571	0.28134
(CCR)*(CGR)	−0.0600	0.12571	0.28134
(CCR)*(CSI)	−0.0475	0.12571	0.28134
(CGR)*(CMOD)	−0.1525	0.12571	0.28134
CFE	−0.0450	0.12571	0.28134
(CCR)*(CTI)	0.0400	0.12571	0.28134
CMOD	0.2950	0.12571	0.28134
(CCR)*(CMG)	0.0575	0.12571	0.28134
CSI	−0.1450	0.12571	0.28134
(CSI)*(CMG)	−0.0550	0.12571	0.28134
(CGR)*(CMG)	0.0575	0.12571	0.28134
(CTI)*(CMG)	−0.0325	0.12571	0.28134

TABLE 13.17   Incomplete Orthogonal Array for Exercise 13.9.

A	B	C	D
	1		1
−1			1
1			−1
−1			
1	−1	−1	
−1	1	−1	
1	1	−1	
	−1	−1	

13.9. Suppose in the 2^{4-1} design displayed in Table 13.17, we know AB = CD. Fill in the 14 missing values.

13.10. An experiment was to be run to investigate the process variables that most influenced the output of a new, complex, and poorly understood industrial process. After the first meeting of the experiment team, the team leader was pleased. "It was a very productive meeting," he remarked. "We managed to narrow the number of factors to be studied down to two." Do you think the meeting was so successful? Why?

13.11. Explain why the hierarchy of significance implies that for a given number of runs, the higher the resolution of a design, the better.

13.12. A very good resolution for a 2^{k-p} design is V. Can we get a 2_V^{5-2} design? Support your answer.

13.13. A 2^{6-3} design with factors A to F has generating relation $I=$ ACF = BCE = ABCD.
   (a) Write out all effects aliased with the AEF interaction.
   (b) What is the resolution of this design?

TABLE 13.18   Product Orthogonal Array for the $2^3 \times 2^2$ Design of Exercise 13.15

	Inner Array		Outer Array				
			TEMP:	−1	1	−1	1
COMPOUND	GEOMETRY	TREAD	SPEED:	−1	−1	1	1
−1	−1	−1		45.4	44.8	45.6	41.8
1	−1	−1		43.6	37.0	41.6	35.0
−1	1	−1		45.4	45.6	45.0	44.6
1	1	−1		40.6	41.0	40.4	39.6
−1	−1	1		44.8	41.0	43.4	39.2
1	−1	1		39.8	35.8	38.2	35.4
−1	1	1		44.2	43.2	42.8	43.6
1	1	1		37.6	36.4	37.0	36.0

13.14. A 2^{6-2} design with factors A to F has generating relation $I = BCDE = ACDF$.

(a) Write out all effects aliased with the ABCDEF interaction.

(b) What is the resolution of this design?

13.15. A tire manufacturer is testing the performance of different tire configurations. To do so, engineers specify three control factors:

- COMPOUND: Type of rubber compound. There are two types, coded 1 and −1.
- GEOMETRY: Tire geometry, or shape. There are two geometries, coded 1 and −1.
- TREAD: Style of tread. There are two styles tested, coded 1 and −1.

They want to find which factor settings perform best under environmental conditions governed by two noise factors:

- TEMP: Ambient temperature. There are two temperatures, coded 1 and −1.
- SPEED: Angular velocity of the test wheel. There are two speeds, coded 1 and −1.

A $2^3 \times 2^2$ experiment was conducted. The experimenters obtained four tires of each possible compound, geometry, and tread configuration, then assigned them randomly to the four levels of temperature and speed. The tires were run continuously on the same test machine until the minimum tread depth reached 2 mm. The response, MILES, is the number of miles (in 1000s) "driven," to the nearest hundred. The resulting data are found in Table 13.18, and in the data set TIRES.

(a) The goal is to maximize the mean response. If you must use a signal–noise ratio to analyze these data, which should you use?

(b) Analyze the data using the signal–noise ratio you chose in part (a) and the Lenth procedure. Taking as significant those effects exceeding MOE in magnitude, what do you conclude?

(c) Analyze these data using the signal-noise ratio you chose in part (a) and a marginal means analysis with a pick the winner strategy. What settings do you choose? Are these settings the same you'd choose by looking at all responses for all eight factor combinations? Explain.

(d) Analyze the data using the mean and log of the variance as separate responses. Use the Lenth procedure and take as significant those effects exceeding MOE in magnitude. What do you conclude? In particular, do you get the same results you obtained in part (b)? Explain.

MINIPROJECT

Purpose

The purpose of this mini-project is to give you experience in planning, conducting and analyzing a sequence of physical experiments that lead to an understanding of some phenomenon. This miniproject coincides with Lab 13.1.

Process

Details are found in the Lab 13.1 writeup.

LAB 13.1: A Screening Experiment

Introduction

In this lab, you will design, conduct, and analyze a two-level fractional factorial experiment for a large number of factors (i.e., a screening experiment). This lab will coincide with the miniproject for this chapter, meaning that the work and report that you do for this lab counts for both activities. You can choose to continue the experiments you performed for the Chapter 12 miniproject.

  The idea here is to have you experience the strategy and execution of sequential experimentation. In this lab, you will do a screening experiment. In the Chapter 14 lab/miniproject, you will continue the sequence of experiments begun here.

Objectives

To give you a practical understanding of the design and conduct of a screening experiment as part of an overall strategy of sequential experimentation.

Lab Materials

Depends on the experiment chosen.

Experimental Procedure

The basic procedure is as detailed in Lab 12.1. However, in this lab, you should use the knowledge and skills you have gained to model the **process** of designing and conducting a screening experiment. If you are continuing your investigation of the phenomenon you explored in the Chapter 12 miniproject or in Lab 12.1, you will want to use any information already obtained to guide you in selecting factors and factor levels. You should also use the knowledge you have gained in the present chapter about planning experiments to obtain a list of factors to be considered. The tools you use should include brainstorming, flow charts, and Ishikawa diagrams. If expanding on previous work, note that these factors should not be limited to the obvious ones you have considered before. When conducting your experiment, you should use the techniques discussed in the present chapter concerning the organization and the quality control of experiments. Finally, you should analyze the experiment and report your results. Remember, this is a screening experiment designed to select the vital few significant factors for subsequent, and more detailed experimentation in Chapter 14.

Your lab report should contain the following:

1. A description of the **process** of experimentation you used. Include information on the tools and techniques you used to plan and conduct the experiments. Tell what steps you took to maintain the quality of experimentation.

2. A description of your experiments, including the configurations run, the factors identified, the levels of the factors used in the experiments, and the responses observed. In other words a complete description of your experiments and the data from those experiments. Also include the reasons for your choices.

3. Your conclusions. Which factors were significant in determining the response? Which were insignificant? Was there significant curvature or interaction? What settings in the design space do you think would result in the optimal response? What do you predict the response to be at these settings?

4. A critique of your experiment. What went right? What went wrong? How could the experiment be improved? How confident are you in your data?

Response-Surface Methodology

... in the full tide of successful experiment.

—*Thomas Jefferson*

INTRODUCTION

In Chapter 13, a general strategy of experimentation is spelled out. In particular, the sequential nature of experimentation is emphasized. In this chapter, you will learn about the latter stages of experimentation, in which the response surface is mapped out in an effort to seek factor levels giving an optimal or near-optimal response.

Knowledge and Skills

By successfully completing this chapter, you will acquire the following knowledge and skills:

KNOWLEDGE	SKILLS
1. The basic ideas of response surface methodology	**1.** How to use sequential experimentation to converge to an optimal response.
2. The geometry of second-order surfaces.	**2.** How to map out the response surface near the optimum.
3. The method of steepest ascent.	
4. Second-order designs. In particular, the central composite design.	

14.1

WHY MAP THE RESPONSE SURFACE?

In Chapters 12 and 13, you learned about the design and conduct of 2^k and 2^{k-p} experiments, respectively. The goal of these experiments is to **screen** a large number of factors to find the vital few that are primarily responsible for differences in the response. Consequently, the levels of the factors are widely spaced, so that gross differences in the response can be observed. At this stage of experimentation, curvature is undesirable, and its presence may signal that the factor levels are too widely spaced.

Suppose now that you have conducted one or more screening experiments, and that you are satisfied that you have found the vital few significant factors. Suppose also that your goal now is to find a set of factor levels that will optimize the response, where the optimum of a response might consist of a maximum, minimum, or proximity to a target value. As of yet, there is no indication that the design space for the experiments you have conducted is near an optimum, so a strategy is needed for finding where an optimum occurs. This chapter details such a strategy, which we will call "mapping" the response surface.

As in mapping a geographical region, mapping a response surface consists of approximating the shape of the surface. The approximation is based on a mathematical model fit to experimental data.

There are at least five reasons to map the response surface:

1. The process may be operating far from the optimality region. A map of the response surface tells how to vary factor settings to obtain optimal or near-optimal responses.

2. In order to continually improve the process, we need to understand how the vital few factors affect the response.

3. The shape of the surface tells how sensitive the response is to changes in factor settings.

4. The shape of the surface tells what trade-offs can be made in factor settings (e.g., for cost reasons) while maintaining a near-optimal response.

5. The shape of the surface can be used in conjunction with theoretical knowledge about the phenomenon being investigated to give a better understanding of how that phenomenon works. For example, after doing an experiment to find the effect of electrical current and resistance on a certain response, an investigator finds that the response is a function of the product of current and resistance. By realizing that current times resistance equals voltage (Ohm's law), she is able to simplify the model (response is a function only of one variable: voltage), and deepen her understanding of the underlying mechanism.

14.2

APPROXIMATING THE RESPONSE SURFACE

Throughout the rest of the chapter, we will assume that the vital few factors are quantitative continuous variables. Suppose that we denote these vital few factors as $X_1, X_2, \ldots, X_k$, and the true value of the response surface at the point $(X_1, X_2, \ldots, X_k)$ $= (x_1, x_2, \ldots, x_k)$ as $f(x_1, x_2, \ldots, x_k)$. By this we mean that an observation Y obtained by setting the factors to the values $x_1, x_2, \ldots, x_k$ has the form[1]

$$Y = f(x_1, x_2, \ldots, x_k) + \epsilon$$

where ϵ is random error, usually assumed to have an $N(0, \sigma^2)$ distribution. In its entirety, the true response surface $f(\cdot)$ can be a very complicated creature, which we cannot hope to adequately model with the small amount of data available to us. Fortunately, we don't need to model the surface in its entirety if we are really only interested in modeling the surface in an area near an optimum, which we may take to be either a maximum or a minimum.[2] In fact, we only need two kinds of models to do this effectively: one kind to direct us to the neighborhood of an optimum and another kind to approximate the surface in that neighborhood. These two kinds of models are as follows:

• **First-Order, or Linear, Models.** First-order models approximate the response surface with a hyperplane[3] of the form

$$\beta_0 + \beta_1 x_1 + \cdots + \beta_k x_k = \beta_0 + \sum_{i=1}^{k} \beta_i x_i$$

The idea of this approximation is that a response Y is approximately given by

$$Y = \beta_0 + \sum_{i=1}^{k} \beta_i x_i + \epsilon \tag{14.1}$$

If $k = 3$, model (14.1) becomes

$$Y = \beta_0 + \beta_1 x_1 + \beta_2 x_2 + \beta_3 x_3 + \epsilon$$

---

[1] In formulating the model, we may take $x_1, x_2, \ldots, x_k$ to be in either the original or in coded units: It is an easy matter to convert from one formulation to the other. The designs we will study later in the chapter are in coded units, as were the 2^k and 2^{k-p} designs studied in Chapters 12 and 13, respectively. As we go through the application of response-surface methods, we will often quote results in terms of both the coded and the original units in order to keep things clear.

[2] If by an optimum we mean the response equals a target value, we can replace the original response by a measure of the proximity to the target value, such as the absolute deviation of the response from the target: $|Y - T|$, where T is the target. The optimum factor levels are those that minimize this proximity measure, so we are really seeking a minimum, after all.

[3] A hyperplane is a plane in more than two dimensions.

Model (14.1) defines a multiple linear regression model (see Chapter 8) that is also linear in the x_i. As the surface fit by this model is a hyperplane, it cannot model curvature at all, and hence has limited use in approximating the surface near a maximum or minimum. However, when the factor settings are far from an optimum and lie in a region where the surface is relatively flat, the first-order model provides a useful approximation that can guide us toward the optimum quickly and efficiently.

   • **Second-Order Models.** Second-order models approximate the response surface by the second degree polynomial

$$\beta_0 + \sum_{i=1}^{k} \beta_i x_i + \sum_{i=1}^{k} \beta_{ii} x_i^2 + \sum_{i=1}^{k-1} \sum_{j=i+1}^{k} \beta_{ij} x_i x_j$$

Under this model, observations are assumed to be (approximately) generated by

$$Y = \beta_0 + \sum_{i=1}^{k} \beta_i x_i + \sum_{i=1}^{k} \beta_{ii} x_i^2 + \sum_{i=1}^{k-1} \sum_{j=i+1}^{k} \beta_{ij} x_i x_j + \epsilon \qquad (14.2)$$

If $k = 3$, model (14.2) becomes

$$Y = \beta_0 + \beta_1 x_1 + \beta_2 x_2 + \beta_3 x_3 + \beta_{11} x_1^2 + \beta_{22} x_2^2$$
$$+ \beta_{33} x_3^2 + \beta_{12} x_1 x_2 + \beta_{13} x_1 x_3 + \beta_{23} x_2 x_3 + \epsilon$$

Model (14.2) gives a simple and effective approximation to a response surface in the vicinity of a maximum or minimum. In fact, it is the simplest polynomial model that can account for curvature.

14.3

THE GEOMETRY OF FIRST-ORDER AND SECOND-ORDER SURFACES

In order to map out a response surface using the first- and second-order models, we have to understand the geometry of first- and second-order surfaces.

First-Order Surfaces

First-order surfaces, which have the equation

$$y = \beta_0 + \sum_{i=1}^{k} \beta_i x_i$$

are just k-dimensional planes, and hence linear in each variable separately.

When $k = 1$, we have the simplest first-order surface, which is the line $y = \beta_0 + \beta_1 x_1$. If $\beta_1 = 0$, the line is horizontal, and y takes only one value. If $\beta_1 \neq 0$, and x_1 is allowed to vary from $-\infty$ to ∞, the line has no maximum or minimum: y ranges from $-\infty$ to ∞. If we restrict x_1 to lie in a bounded region such as a bounded interval, the maximum and minimum of y occur at the boundary of the region.

Similar behavior occurs for higher-dimensional first-order surfaces: surfaces for which $k > 1$. If $\beta_1 = \beta_2 = \cdots = \beta_k = 0$, then y is the constant β_0. If not all the β_i are zero, and if we let the x_i vary from $-\infty$ to ∞, y will have no maximum or minimum. If we restrict the x_i to lie in a bounded region, as is the case for most experiments, the only maxima or minima for y occur at the boundary of the region.

Second-Order Surfaces

Second-order surfaces, which have the equation

$$y = \beta_0 + \sum_{i=1}^{k} \beta_i x_i + \sum_{i=1}^{k} \beta_{ii} x_i^2 + \sum_{i=1}^{k-1} \sum_{j=i+1}^{k} \beta_{ij} x_i x_j \tag{14.3}$$

where at least some of the β_{ii} and/or $\beta_{ij} \neq 0$, have more varied and interesting behavior than first-order surfaces.

The One-Dimensional Case

The Second-Order Surface.   We begin by considering the simplest, one-dimensional second-order "surface,"

$$y = \beta_0 + \beta_1 x + \beta_{11} x^2 \tag{14.4}$$

where $\beta_{11} \neq 0$. In order to find the extrema[4] of y defined by Equation (14.4), it may help to review some univariate calculus.

Finding Extrema of Functions of One Variable.   To begin with, suppose f is a real-valued function whose domain is all real numbers. If both the first and second derivatives of f exist for all real numbers, we will call f **smooth.** Suppose $y = f(x)$, where f is smooth. Any real number for which the first derivative of f equals 0 is called a **critical** or **stationary point** of f.

We must also say what we mean by a maximum and minimum. A **global maximum** is the largest value taken by the function; a **global minimum** is the smallest value taken by the function. A function may have neither. For example, the function $y = f(x) = 3 + 5x$ defined for all real numbers has neither a global maximum or minimum, as

$$\lim_{x \to -\infty} f(x) = -\infty \text{ and } \lim_{x \to \infty} f(x) = \infty$$

---

[4]Some terminology: Maxima is the plural of maximum and minima is the plural of minimum. Extrema denotes all maxima or minima.

A **local maximum** occurs at a point x_0 if $f(x) \leq f(x_0)$ for all $x \in (a, b)$, where the interval (a, b) contains x_0. A local minimum is defined similarly.

This brings us to two basic rules for finding a local maximum or local minimum of a smooth function f defined on the reals:

Rule 1. A local maximum or minimum of f can occur only at a stationary point.

Rule 2. At a stationary point, the function has a local maximum if its second derivative is negative, and a local minimum if its second derivative is positive. If the second derivative is 0, the function might have neither a local maximum nor a local minimum there.

Rules 1 and 2 apply to finding maxima or minima of smooth functions over the interval $(-\infty, \infty)$. If we restrict the domain of f to the closed, bounded interval $[a, b]$, then rules 1 and 2 will only find extrema (i.e., maxima or minima) that occur in the open interval (a, b). We have to check $f(a)$ and $f(b)$ separately to see if maxima, minima, or neither occur at the endpoints of the interval.

The "surface" defined by Equation (14.4) is a parabola. It is a smooth function on $(-\infty, \infty)$. Therefore, to find possible maxima or minima, we look for stationary points, which are defined by

$$\frac{d}{dx}(\beta_0 + \beta_1 x + \beta_{11} x^2) = \beta_1 + 2\beta_{11} x = 0$$

Solving for x, we find a single stationary point

$$x_0 = \frac{-\beta_1}{2\beta_{11}} \tag{14.5}$$

The second derivative is

$$\frac{d^2}{dx^2}(\beta_0 + \beta_1 x + \beta_{11} x^2) = \frac{d}{dx}(\beta_1 + 2\beta_{11} x) = 2\beta_{11}$$

The second derivative has the same sign as β_{11}, so we know that if $\beta_{11} > 0$, a minimum occurs at the stationary point. Since there is only one stationary point, we also know that this is a global minimum. If $\beta_{11} < 0$, a global maximum occurs at the stationary point.

Finding Extrema of the Second-Order Surface.   If we consider the surface given by Equation (14.4) restricted to the closed, bounded interval $[a, b]$, we have to change our analysis somewhat. If the stationary point is in the interval, we need only compare the function value there with its values at the interval endpoints. If the interval does not contain the stationary point, there will be no maxima or minima inside the interval and we need only check the values of the function at the interval endpoints.

The Higher-Dimensional Case

The Second-Order Surface.   To study second-order surfaces in higher dimensions, we will rewrite Equation (14.3) in vector-matrix notation:[5]

$$y = \beta_0 + \mathbf{x}'\boldsymbol{\beta} + \mathbf{x}'B\mathbf{x} \tag{14.6}$$

where

$\boldsymbol{\beta}$ is the $k \times 1$ vector $\begin{bmatrix} \beta_1 \\ \beta_2 \\ \vdots \\ \beta_k \end{bmatrix}$, $\mathbf{x}$ is the $k \times 1$ vector $\begin{bmatrix} x_1 \\ x_2 \\ \vdots \\ x_k \end{bmatrix}$

and B is the $k \times k$ symmetric matrix[6]

$$\begin{bmatrix} \beta_{11} & \beta_{12}/2 & \beta_{13}/2 & \cdots & \beta_{1k}/2 \\ \beta_{12}/2 & \beta_{22} & \beta_{23}/2 & \cdots & \beta_{2k}/2 \\ \vdots & \vdots & \vdots & \ddots & \vdots \\ \beta_{1k}/2 & \beta_{2k}/2 & \beta_{3k}/2 & \cdots & \beta_{kk} \end{bmatrix}$$

As an example, for $k = 3$, we have

$$B = \begin{bmatrix} \beta_{11} & \beta_{12}/2 & \beta_{13}/2 \\ \beta_{12}/2 & \beta_{22} & \beta_{23}/2 \\ \beta_{13}/2 & \beta_{23}/2 & \beta_{33} \end{bmatrix}$$

and

$$\boldsymbol{\beta} = \begin{bmatrix} \beta_1 \\ \beta_2 \\ \beta_3 \end{bmatrix} \qquad \mathbf{x} = \begin{bmatrix} x_1 \\ x_2 \\ x_3 \end{bmatrix}$$

Then

$$\mathbf{x}'\boldsymbol{\beta} = \sum_{i=1}^{3} x_i \beta_i = \beta_1 x_1 + \beta_2 x_2 + \beta_3 x_3$$

[5]See Appendix 8.1 at the end of Chapter 8 for basic material on vectors and matrices.

[6]The matrix B is one-half the matrix of second-order partial derivatives (see Appendix 14.2) of the surface (14.6). That is, the ij entry of the matrix equals $\frac{1}{2}(\partial^2 y/\partial x_i \partial x_j)$. The name given to the matrix of second-order derivatives of a smooth function is the **Hessian matrix.**

Also,

$$B\mathbf{x} = (\beta_{11}x_1 + \beta_{12}x_2/2 + \beta_{13}x_3/2, \beta_{12}x_1/2 + \beta_{22}x_2 + \beta_{23}x_3/2, \beta_{13}x_1/2 + \beta_{23}x_2/2 + \beta_{33}x_3)'$$

and so

$$\mathbf{x}'B\mathbf{x} = \sum_{i=1}^{3} \beta_{ii}x_i^2 + \sum_{i=1}^{2}\sum_{j=i+1}^{3} \beta_{ij}x_ix_j$$

$$= \beta_{11}x_1^2 + \beta_{22}x_2^2 + \beta_{33}x_3^2 + \beta_{12}x_1x_2 + \beta_{13}x_1x_3 + \beta_{23}x_2x_3$$

Putting this all together, we see that Equations (14.3) and (14.6) are equivalent for $k = 3$.

One more connection to note: Equation (14.6) is simply the multivariate version of Equation (14.4) with $\boldsymbol{\beta}$ taking the place of β_1 ($\beta_1 x = x\beta_1$), and B taking the place of β_{11} ($\beta_{11}x^2 = x\beta_{11}x$).

Finding Extrema of Functions of Several Variables.   Finding extrema of real-valued functions of $k > 1$ variables $x_1, x_2, \ldots, x_k$ follows roughly the same steps as for the single-variable case. First, assume $f(x_1, x_2, \ldots, x_k)$ is a real-valued function whose domain is all k-dimensional vectors of real numbers. We also assume that f is smooth, which means that all first- and second-order partial derivatives of f exist.[7] A **stationary point** of f is a point where all the partial derivatives of f are 0. Rule 1 for finding maxima or minima in the one-dimensional case has a simple analogue in the multidimensional case:

Rule 1M. A local maximum or minimum of f can occur only at a stationary point.

For the second-order surface defined by Equation (14.6), there is a single stationary point $\mathbf{x}_0$, which satisfies

$$\mathbf{x}_0 = -B^{-1}\boldsymbol{\beta}/2 \tag{14.7}$$

Equation (14.7) is the multivariate version of Equation (14.5), with B playing the role of β_{11} and $\boldsymbol{\beta}$ the role of β_1.

Finding Extrema of the Second-Order Surface.   Rule 2, which gives a method for determining if there is a maximum or minimum at a stationary point in the one-dimensional case, becomes too complicated for our needs when extended to the multidimensional case, so we will look at its analogue when we restrict our attention to the second-order surface (14.6) defined on the k-dimensional reals. The condition, which we will call

---

[7]See Appendix 14.2 for a discussion of partial derivatives.

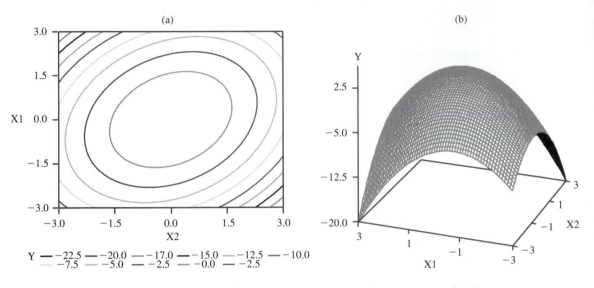

$$Y \quad \text{—} -22.5 \text{ —} -20.0 \text{ —} -17.0 \text{ —} -15.0 \text{ —} -12.5 \text{ —} -10.0$$
$$\text{—} -7.5 \text{ —} -5.0 \text{ —} -2.5 \text{ —} -0.0 \text{ —} -2.5$$

Figure 14.1   Quadratic surface with maximum at $(0, 0)$.

Rule 2M, involves the eigenvalues of the matrix B:[8]

> **Rule 2M.** At the stationary point $\mathbf{x}_0$ defined by (14.7), the second-order sur-
> face (14.6) has a global maximum if all the eigenvalues of B are negative; it has
> a global minimum if all the eigenvalues of B are positive. If some eigenvalues
> are positive and some negative, the surface has some kind of "saddle" at $\mathbf{x}_0$. By
> a saddle, we mean that if we move from $\mathbf{x}_0$ in some directions, the surface will
> drop off, and in other directions, the surface will rise.

Note that in Rule 2M, the eigenvalues of B play the role that the second derivative
did in the univariate case.

If we restrict the second-order surface (14.6) to a closed and bounded region of
the k-dimensional reals, then, just as in the one-dimensional case, we need to check the
boundary of the region for maxima or minima.

In applications, we will not be concerned with computing the eigenvalues of B,
but will rely on computer software to do it for us. Figure 14.1 displays contour and 3-D
plots of a two-dimensional quadratic surface with maximum at $(0, 0)$. Figure 14.2 shows
contour and 3-D plots of a surface with a saddle at $(0, 0)$. Figure 14.3 shows contour and
3-D plots of a surface with a **stationary ridge,** a maximum or minimum that occurs at a
set of (x_1, x_2) values that form a line. In this case, the line is $x_2 = 0$.

---

[8]See Appendix 14.1 for a discussion of eigenvalues and eigenvectors.

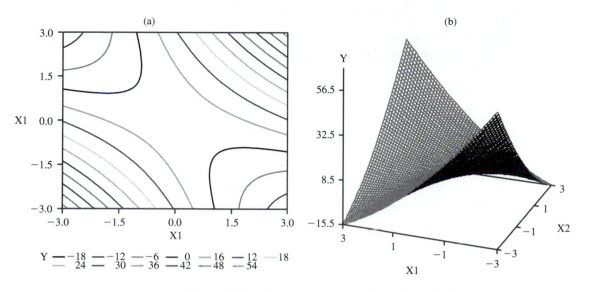

Figure 14.2   Quadratic surface with saddle at $(0, 0)$.

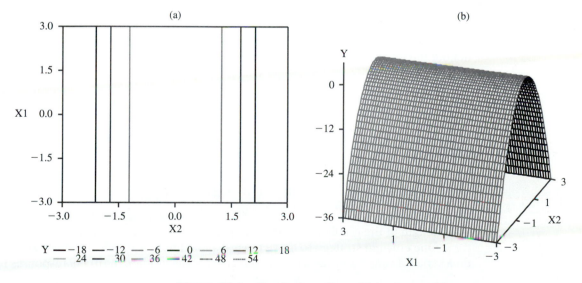

Figure 14.3   Quadratic surface with stationary ridge.

14.4

HEADING FOR THE OPTIMUM: FIRST STEPS

At the beginning of our search for the region of optimality, we have found the vital few factors, a starting point (often the factor settings at which the process is currently running), and the results from one or more experiments centered at that starting point. Suppose we want to maximize the response. How should we proceed next?

Assume that we have used the data from a screening experiment (e.g., a 2^k or 2^{k-p} design with center points) to fit the linear model (14.1), and have found no evidence of surface curvature in the region of the experiment. Suppose that the fitted model is[9]

$$\hat{Y} = \hat{\beta}_0 + \sum_{i=1}^{k} \hat{\beta}_i x_i$$

where the x_i are in coded units. Then the direction in which the fitted surface increases most quickly, the **direction of steepest ascent,** is given by the gradient vector.[10]

$$\hat{\beta} = \begin{bmatrix} \hat{\beta}_1 \\ \hat{\beta}_2 \\ \vdots \\ \hat{\beta}_k \end{bmatrix}$$

The gradient gives us an initial direction in which to run further experiments. Let **u** denote the unit vector in the direction of the gradient. That is,

$$\mathbf{u} = \frac{\hat{\beta}}{\|\hat{\beta}\|}$$

where

$$\|\hat{\beta}\| = \sqrt{\hat{\beta}_1^2 + \hat{\beta}_2^2 + \cdots + \hat{\beta}_k^2}$$

is the length of the gradient vector.

One efficient strategy to move toward a maximum is to select a **step size** δ and to do a series of runs δ units apart in the direction of the gradient until the responses reach

---

[9]Incidentally, the model may be fit by least squares, as in Chapter 8, but you should know that each $\hat{\beta}$ is also equal to 1/2 times the corresponding main effect computed from the 2^k model as in Chapter 12.

[10]See Appendix 14.2 for an explanation of the gradient.

a maximum and begin to decline. If we begin this series of experiments at the coded factor settings $\mathbf{x}_0 = [x_{01}, x_{02}, \ldots, x_{0k}]'$, the data are taken at points

$$\mathbf{x}_0 + m\delta\mathbf{u} = \begin{bmatrix} x_{01} + m\delta u_1 \\ x_{02} + m\delta u_2 \\ \vdots \\ x_{0k} + m\delta u_k \end{bmatrix}$$

where $m = 1, 2, \ldots$.

EXAMPLE 14.1   A RESPONSE SURFACE CASE STUDY: CAM VIBRATION

A series of experiments was conducted to isolate the factors in a cam manufacturing process that were responsible for unwanted high-frequency vibration in the finished product. The experimenters also wanted to find optimal or near-optimal settings for those factors so as to reduce the high-frequency vibrations to a minimum. An initial screening experiment had identified two vital factors in the final finishing stage: X_1, the angle of attack of a polishing wheel, ranging from 0 to 2π radians, and X_2, a measure of the abrasiveness of the wheel, ranging over a 0 to 10 scale, with 10 being most abrasive. The measured response, Y, was a standardized measure of the total vibrational energy attributable to frequencies above a certain threshold.

The results of a confirmatory 2^2 experiment with three center points centered at the current process settings of (3.0, 1.5) gave the responses in Table 14.1.

Both main effects were found to be statistically significant, with estimated effects of 0.050 for X_1 and −0.065 for X_2. The analysis gave no indication of important curvature or interaction, and residual analysis gave no indication of model inadequacy. Therefore, this model was used as the basis for further experimentation to try to move toward near-optimal factor settings.

TABLE   14.1   Results of Confirmatory Experiment: Cam Vibration Example

Original factor settings		Coded factor settings		Response
X_1	X_2	X_1	X_2	Y
3.0	1.5	0	0	0.488
3.0	1.5	0	0	0.486
3.0	1.5	0	0	0.469
3.5	2.0	1	1	0.460
3.5	1.0	1	−1	0.488
2.5	2.0	−1	1	0.373
2.5	1.0	−1	−1	0.474

TABLE 14.2   Results of Initial Experiments in the Direction of Steepest Descent: Cam Vibration Example

Step	Original factor settings		Coded factor settings		Response
m	X_1	X_2	X_1	X_2	Y
1	2.85	1.7	−0.310	0.395	0.455
2	2.70	1.9	−0.620	0.790	0.407
3	2.55	2.1	−0.930	1.185	0.350
4	2.40	2.3	−1.240	1.580	0.283
5	2.25	2.5	−1.550	1.975	0.248
6	2.10	2.7	−1.860	2.370	0.272
7	1.95	2.9	−2.170	2.765	0.285

The gradient of the fitted surface is in the same direction as the vector of estimated effects,

$$\hat{\beta} = \begin{bmatrix} 0.051 \\ -0.065 \end{bmatrix}$$

Since the experimenters wanted to find a minimum, the direction chosen was the opposite direction from the gradient: [11]

$$-\hat{\beta} = \begin{bmatrix} -0.051 \\ 0.065 \end{bmatrix}$$

The experimenters decided to take data beginning at the current origin in steps of length $\delta = 0.5$ in this direction. Since a unit vector in this direction is

$$\mathbf{u} = \begin{bmatrix} -0.62 \\ 0.79 \end{bmatrix}$$

the coded factor settings for the experimental runs were

$$\begin{bmatrix} 0.0 \\ 0.0 \end{bmatrix} + 0.5 \times m \times \begin{bmatrix} -0.62 \\ 0.79 \end{bmatrix} = \begin{bmatrix} -0.310m \\ 0.395m \end{bmatrix}, \qquad m = 1, 2, 3, \ldots$$

The results of their experiments in this direction, in sequence, are in Table 14.2.

Notice that the responses drop steadily and considerably along the path until they begin rising with the last two data points. After plotting the responses along this path versus the time order, the experimenters concluded that the surface minimum along this path would likely be in the vicinity of $(-1.550, 1.975)$, coded units $((2.25, 2.5)$, original units). Therefore, in order to map out the surface near this

---

[11] This is known as the direction of steepest descent.

TABLE 14.3   Results of a Second 2^2 Experiment: Cam Vibration Example

Original factor settings		Coded factor settings		Response
X_1	X_2	X_1	X_2	Y
2.25	2.5	0	0	0.248
2.25	2.5	0	0	0.251
2.25	2.5	0	0	0.252
2.40	2.7	1	1	0.290
2.40	2.3	1	−1	0.270
2.10	2.7	−1	1	0.263
2.10	2.3	−1	−1	0.251

minimum, the experimenters concluded that a more detailed experiment centered at (2.25, 2.5), original units, was the next logical step.

They began by running another 2^2 with center points, the results of which are shown in Table 14.3.[12]

Analysis of these data showed that both effects X_1 and X_2 were significant, but that their interaction was not. In addition, significant curvature was evident. The experimenters decided that they needed to map the response surface more fully by fitting a second-order model in this region, something that cannot be done with a 2^2 design with center points. ◆

14.5

SECOND-ORDER DESIGNS

In order to fit the full second-order model (14.2), a design adequate to the task must be used. One such design is the 3^k factorial, which has k factors each at three levels. However, the 3^k factorial requires a relatively large number of runs to do the job, particularly if there are more than a few factors (3 factors require 27 runs, 4 factors require 81, etc.). A more parsimonious design is the **central composite design,** or CCD.

The CCD is just a 2^k design with center points and $2k$ additional points called **star points.** The star points are located at coded values $(\pm a, 0, 0, \ldots, 0)$, $(0, \pm a, 0, \ldots, 0)$, $\ldots, (0, 0, \ldots, \pm a)$. So, in the two-factor case, there would be a total of four star points, located at $(a, 0)$, $(-a, 0)$, $(0, a)$, and $(0, -a)$. The experimenter must choose the value for a. The most common choice is the value of a that makes the distance from each star point to the center of the design equal to the distance from the corner points of

---

[12]Note that in the runs done in the direction of steepest descent, the factor coding was the same as in the original 2^2 experiment. This is because the gradient is based on the original coded values of that experiment. However, in this new 2^2 experiment, the experimenters were free to choose a new coding for the factors, and that is what they did.

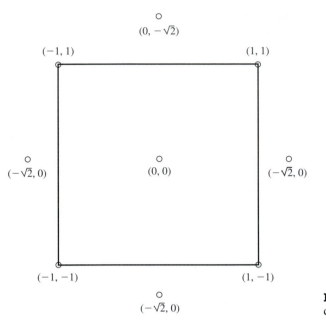

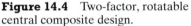

Figure 14.4 Two-factor, rotatable central composite design.

the 2^k design to the center. This results in what is called a **rotatable design.** A rotatable design is one for which the standard error of prediction is the same at all points that are the same distance from the center of the design. Thus, the quality of prediction of a rotatable design, as measured by its standard error, is equally good in any direction. For a two-factor design, $a = \sqrt{2}$ gives a rotatable design. For a three-factor design, $a = \sqrt{3}$ gives a rotatable design.

A second common choice is to take $a = 1$. This gives what is called a **face-centered design.** The face-centered design has the advantage that only three, instead of five, factor levels are required for each factor. Figure 14.4 shows the geometry of a two-factor rotatable CCD, and Figure 14.5 shows the geometry of a two-factor face-centered CCD.

EXAMPLE 14.1   CONTINUED

The experimenters decided to expand their 2^2 experiment centered at original units $(2.25, 2.5)$ to a CCD by adding star points at coded values $(\pm\sqrt{2}, 0)$ and $(0, \pm\sqrt{2})$, and three more center points. The result was a rotatable CCD with six center points. The data for the additional runs are in Table 14.4.

In conducting a CCD sequentially in this way, one must be careful that experimental conditions do not affect the response differently in the two sets of runs. If the conditions do appreciably affect the response, other actions must be taken. If the difference in the response for the two sets of runs is just to add a constant, then the data can be analyzed by including an additive term for blocks

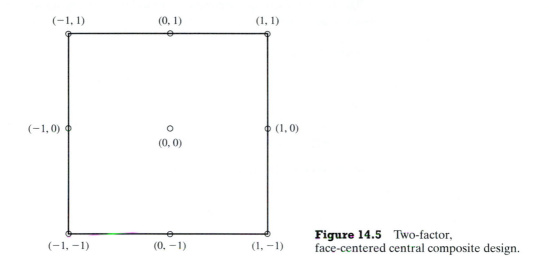

Figure 14.5 Two-factor, face-centered central composite design.

TABLE 14.4   Results of Additional Runs for Star and Center points of CCD: Cam Vibration Example

Original factor settings		Coded factor settings		Response
X_1	X_2	X_1	X_2	Y
2.25	2.5	0	0	0.244
2.25	2.5	0	0	0.256
2.25	2.5	0	0	0.254
2.46	2.5	$\sqrt{2}$	0	0.274
2.04	2.5	$-\sqrt{2}$	0	0.231
2.25	2.22	0	$-\sqrt{2}$	0.261
2.25	2.78	0	$\sqrt{2}$	0.312

in the model. However, if there are interactions between blocks and other factors, then the system is changing (i.e., is not stationary), and the entire experimental setup should be looked at **very carefully** to find the reasons. After all, how can we draw conclusions about a process if that process doesn't stay the same long enough to replicate the experiment?

In this example, the runs were done in two blocks: the seven runs of initial experiment and the seven runs of the added star points and center points. However, the experimenters were very sure that the conditions were the same in the two sets of runs, and so the analysis that follows will not include a block term.

The results of fitting a second-order model to these data were as follows (the x_i are in coded units):

1. **Fitted Model:**

$$\hat{Y} = 0.25 + 0.013x_1 + 0.013x_2 + 0.00058x_1^2 + 0.002x_1x_2 + 0.018x_2^2$$

2. **Significant Effects:** X_1, X_2, X_2^2.
3. **Stationary Point:** $(-8.49, 0.22)$ (coded units); $(0.98, 2.54)$ (original units).
4. **Eigenvalues:** $0.035, 0.0001$.

5. **Eigenvectors:** Corresponding to eigenvalue 0.035: $\begin{bmatrix} 0.059 \\ 0.998 \end{bmatrix}$.

   Corresponding to eigenvalue 0.0001: $\begin{bmatrix} 0.998 \\ -0.059 \end{bmatrix}$.

6. **Estimated response at the stationary point:** 0.17.

The eigenvalues are both positive, indicating a minimum is attained at the stationary point. However, it is disturbing that the stationary point is so far outside the region of experimentation. This is probably a result of there being a large range of near-optimal values in the X_1 direction so that the slope of the surface in the X_1 direction is near 0. This interpretation is reinforced by two other indicators. First, only the linear term in the X_1 factor is significant; the quadratic term isn't. Second, the first eigenvalue is 35 times as large as the second eigenvalue. This means that the curvature of the surface in the direction of the first eigenvector is 35 times the curvature of the surface in the direction of the second eigenvector. The first eigenvector is very nearly the X_2 direction, and the second is very nearly the X_1 direction. So the surface is nearly linear in the X_1 direction and considerably more curved in the X_2 direction.

A look at the residuals indicates that they have large variation compared with the measurement error estimated from the center points. This indicates that the model does not fit well.

Because of these indications, the experimenters began to explore the surface more carefully. First, they conducted some confirmatory runs at the stationary point $(-8.49, 0.22)$ (coded units). These indicated that the fitted value of 0.17 grossly underestimates the responses at that point, and demonstrated that the model did not predict well at that point.

Next, they held X_1 fixed at 0 (coded units) and varied X_2 over the same levels as the previous experiment, using the six center points from that experiment as an estimate of experimental error. The results indicated that the minimum was near the center point $X_2 = 0$ (coded units) and that the quadratic model fit the data well. Note that this experiment is an OFAT, which is a bad design for general use, but which can prove a useful tool near an optimum.

To see what was happening in the X_1 direction, the experimenters varied X_1 around the point 0 (coded units) while holding X_2 fixed at 0 (coded units). This was done for X_1 values ranging between -13.33 and 11.67, in coded units

(0.25 and 4.0 in original units). A quadratic model fit the data well, and indicated a minimum near $X_1 = -1.67$, coded units ($X_1 = 2.0$, original units).

A new CCD experiment centered at $(-1.67, 0)$, coded units (original units: $(2.0, 2.5)$) was run, with the following results (the x_i are in coded units):

1. **Fitted Model:**

$$\hat{Y} = 0.25 + 0.0052x_1 + 0.0032x_2 + 0.017x_1^2 - 0.0035x_1x_2 + 0.015x_2^2$$

2. **Significant Effects:** X_1^2, X_2^2.
3. **Stationary Point:** $(0.14, -0.09)$ (coded units); $(2.04, 2.47)$ (original units).
4. **Eigenvalues:** $0.018, 0.014$.

5. **Eigenvectors:** Corresponding to eigenvalue 0.018: $\begin{bmatrix} 0.83 \\ -0.55 \end{bmatrix}$.

   Corresponding to eigenvalue 0.014: $\begin{bmatrix} 0.55 \\ 0.83 \end{bmatrix}$.

6. **Estimated response at the stationary point:** 0.25.

Residual analysis revealed that the model fit the data well, and several additional runs confirmed the nature of the surface in this region. Figure 14.6 shows a contour plot and a 3-D plot of the fitted surface. The axes are in coded units based on the last experiment.   ◆

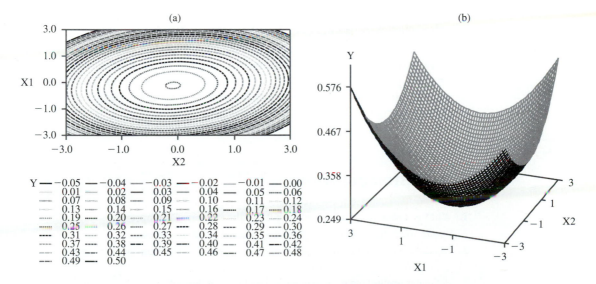

Figure 14.6 Fitted Surface for Cam Vibration Example.

14.6

SUMMARY OF STEPS IN MAPPING A RESPONSE SURFACE

We finish this chapter by summarizing the steps involved in mapping a response surface. As indicated in Section 14.4, prior to beginning our search for the region of optimality, we will have found the vital few factors, a starting point, and the results from one or more experiments centered at that starting point. Assume we are searching for a maximum.[13] The basic steps are as follows:

1. Fit a first-order model centered at the starting point.
2. Check for curvature.
   (a) If curvature is evident, go to step 3.
   (b) If there is no curvature, select a step size δ and take observations every δ units in the direction of steepest ascent. Continue until the boundary of the design space is reached or until the responses clearly reach a peak and begin a decline.
      i. If at the boundary of the design space, map the surface there with a new first-order experiment. Go to the beginning of step 2.
      ii. Otherwise, map the surface with a new first-order experiment centered at the maximum. Go to the beginning of step 2.
3. Expand the first-order design to a second-order design in order to map the curvature. Obtain the fitted model, eigenvectors, eigenvalues, and stationary point. Explore the fitted surface thoroughly, using additional exploratory and confirmatory runs as necessary. At this stage of experimentation, there is no formula for how to proceed, as the exposition in Example 14.1 indicates. A satisfactory conclusion will have a surface whose adequacy is validated by additional runs, and whose behavior is understood in the vicinity of the maximum.
4. As a check against finding a local, instead of a global, maximum, experimenters may want to conduct further experimentation in several additional regions of the design space. Such experimentation could be as simple as a series of single observations, or as complicated as a series of iterative experiments on the model of steps 1 to 3.

D ISCUSSION QUESTIONS

1. What is a response surface and what are the reasons for mapping it?
2. Summarize the geometry of first- and second-order surfaces.
3. Describe the strategy used in attempting to find the optimum on a response surface.

[13] Similar results hold if a minimum or target value is desired.

4. Explain the meaning of the following:
   (a) Central composite design
   (b) Star points
   (c) Rotatable design
   (d) Face-centered design

 **XERCISES**

14.1. The vector

$$\mathbf{x} = \begin{bmatrix} 1 \\ -1 \end{bmatrix}$$

is an eigenvector for the matrix

$$B = \begin{bmatrix} 2 & 0 \\ 5 & 7 \end{bmatrix}$$

Find an eigenvalue of B.

14.2. A second-order response surface in three variables is fit to a set of data. The experimenter regards the fit as satisfactory and the stationary point of the fitted surface is within the region of experimentation. The eigenvalues are 0.78, 1.99, and -3.21. What kind of behavior does the fitted surface exhibit at the stationary point?

14.3. A fitted response surface has the equation

$$\hat{Y} = 7 + 3x_1 - 1.6x_1^2 + 5.9x_2^2 - 3.4x_1x_2$$

Write this in vector-matrix notation, that is,

$$\hat{Y} = \beta_0 + \mathbf{x}'\boldsymbol{\beta} + \mathbf{x}'B\mathbf{x}$$

14.4. In order to begin the exploration of a response surface, a first-order model is fit to data generated from an experiment. No evidence of curvature is present. The equation of the fitted model is

$$\hat{Y} = 11 - 3x_1 + 4x_2$$

   (a) The experimenter wants to obtain settings yielding maximum response, and decides to take a single observation every 1.0 coded unit from the current center point of $(0, 0)$. Write down the next two points at which experiments should be done.
   (b) The experimenter proceeds to conduct experiments in the direction you suggested until he reaches a local maximum. He then conducts a 2^2 experiment with center points and finds significant curvature. He expands the experiment to a CCD and fits a second-order model. The fitted response surface has the equation

$$\hat{Y} = 3 + 2x_1 - 4x_2 + 6x_2^2 - 2x_1x_2$$

i. Find the stationary point of the surface.

ii. Compute the matrix B whose eigenvalues determine the nature of the surface at the stationary point.

iii. The eigenvalues of the matrix B are 6.16 and -0.16. Describe the shape of the surface at the stationary point.

iv. What value of response do you expect to observe at the stationary point?

14.5. A fitted response surface is

$$\hat{Y} = \beta_0 + \mathbf{x}'\boldsymbol{\beta} + \mathbf{x}'B\mathbf{x}$$

where

$$\beta_0 = -5, \qquad \boldsymbol{\beta} = \begin{bmatrix} -1 \\ 2 \end{bmatrix}, \qquad B = \begin{bmatrix} 1 & 6 \\ 6 & 5 \end{bmatrix}$$

Other facts of interest are that the equations

$$-1 + 2x_1 + 12x_2 = 0$$
$$2 + 12x_1 + 10x_2 = 0$$

have the solution

$$x_1 = -0.2742, \qquad x_2 = 0.1290$$

and that

$$\begin{bmatrix} 1 & 6 \\ 6 & 5 \end{bmatrix} \begin{bmatrix} 0.8112 \\ -0.5847 \end{bmatrix} = -3.3246 \begin{bmatrix} 0.8112 \\ -0.5847 \end{bmatrix}$$

and

$$\begin{bmatrix} 1 & 6 \\ 6 & 5 \end{bmatrix} \begin{bmatrix} 0.5847 \\ 0.8112 \end{bmatrix} = 9.3246 \begin{bmatrix} 0.5847 \\ 0.8112 \end{bmatrix}$$

(a) Write out the model in scalar form.

(b) What is the stationary point?

(c) What is the behavior of the surface at the stationary point?

14.6. A fitted response surface has the equation

$$\hat{Y} = 3 + 2x_1 + 4x_2 - 0.6x_1^2 - 0.9x_2^2 - 0.4x_1x_2$$

(a) Find the stationary point of the surface.

(b) Compute the matrix B whose eigenvalues determine the nature of the surface at the stationary point.

(c) The eigenvalues of the matrix B are -1.0 and -0.5. Describe the shape of the surface at the stationary point.

(d) What value of response do you expect to observe at the stationary point?

14.7. In order to begin the exploration of a response surface, a first-order model is fit to data generated from an experiment. A test reveals no evidence of curvature. The equation of the fitted model is

$$\hat{Y} = 3 + 2x_1 + 4x_2$$

(a) The experimenter wants to obtain settings yielding minimum response, and decides to take a single observation every 1.5 coded units from the current center point of $(0, 0)$. Write down the next six points at which experiments should be done.

(b) The responses at those six points are 12, 9, 7, 4, 6, and 11. What do you recommend the experimenter do next?

14.8. A surface is given by the equation

$$y = 3x_1 + x_2^2$$

At the point $(1, 1)$, which direction heads down the surface quickest?

14.9. A fitted response surface has the matrix equation

$$\hat{Y} = -3 + \mathbf{x}' \begin{bmatrix} 2 \\ 5 \end{bmatrix} + \mathbf{x}' \begin{bmatrix} 3 & 2 \\ 2 & 7 \end{bmatrix} \mathbf{x}$$

Write its equation in scalar form.

14.10. Find a stationary point of the second-order surface with equation

$$y = 2 + 3x_1 - x_2 + x_1^2 + x_2^2$$

14.11. Suppose that matrix A has an inverse A^{-1}. Suppose also that λ is a nonzero eigenvalue of A corresponding to eigenvector $\mathbf{x}$. Show that $1/\lambda$ is an eigenvalue of A^{-1} corresponding to eigenvector $\mathbf{x}$.

14.12. Does the surface $y = -2.1 + 9.7x_1 - 3.3x_2$ have any stationary points? If so, find them. If not, tell why not. What is the shape of this surface?

14.13. The goal of a sequence of experiments is to find factor levels to minimize the mean response. The initial experiment produces the fitted first-order surface $\hat{Y} = 1 - 4x_1 + 3x_2$. Beginning with the point $x_1 = 1$, $x_2 = 1$, the experimenters want to move in the most promising direction for further experimentation in steps of size 1. What is the next (i.e., after $x_1 = 1$, $x_2 = 1$) (x_1, x_2) value at which they should take an observation?

14.14. Using a CCD for two factors, a second-order model is fitted. Of the effects X_1, X_2, X_1^2, X_2^2, and $X_1 X_2$, only X_1 and X_2 are significant. What does this mean, and what would your next step be?

14.15. Interpret in terms of stretching and direction, what the second and third eigenvalues and eigenvectors in the example in Appendix 14.1 tell us.

MINIPROJECT

Purpose

The purpose of this miniproject is to give you experience in finding an optimum on a response surface using the techniques in this chapter and Chapters 12 and 13.

Process

You are a process engineer charged with optimizing output on the key "funnel-swirling" process (see Lab 12.1) while minimizing costs. In this miniproject, your group will use experimental design techniques from Chapters 12 and 13 and response-surface methods from this chapter to find a set of operating conditions on the funnel-swirling apparatus that yields times as consistently close to 5 seconds as possible while minimizing costs.

Costs consist of three components:

1. **Bias B:** How far off from 5 seconds, on average, are the times at the recommended factor settings.
2. **Variance V:** The variance of the times at the recommended factor settings.
3. **Process Cost P:** The cost of running the process. For our purposes, this cost equals the weight of the ball.

The total cost will be given by the formula $C = B^2 + V^2 + P$.

You should also map out the response surface in the vicinity of the optimum you find. You may, and should, use all relevant knowledge gained about the funnel-swirling process from past labs and projects. Alternatively, if you did another experiment for the mini projects in chapters 12 and 13, you may continue the process of experimentation begun there, with the goal of finding factor settings to optimize the response.

LAB 14.1: OFAT Optimization[14]

Introduction

In this lab, you will try to find the optimum of a process using OFAT techniques.

Objectives

To teach you what happens when OFAT techniques are used to optimize a process.

---

[14]This lab requires use of the SAS or MINITAB macros QUADGEN and SURFPLOT. Instructions on their use can be found in the *Doing It with SAS* or *Doing It with MINITAB* supplement to the text.

Lab Materials

None needed.

Experimental Procedure

The SAS or MINITAB macro QUADGEN will generate responses from a quadratic surface in two variables (Equation (14.2), where $k = 2$). The surface in question has a unique maximum. You are to use OFAT optimization to try to find the maximum on the surface.

To do this, proceed in the following manner:

1. Begin where the process is currently operating. In coded units, this is the point $(x_1, x_2) = (-2.5, -2.5)$. Choose one variable to vary while keeping the other fixed.
2. Say you keep x_2 fixed at -2.5. Vary x_1 around the point -2.5 until you are satisfied you have found a maximum or near-maximum. Suppose this maximum occurs at value x_{10}.
3. Now fix x_1 to be x_{10}, and vary x_2 only until you find a maximum.

Is this the maximum of the surface? To find out, run the macro SURFPLOT. It will generate a contour plot and a 3-D plot of the surface. How well did your OFAT scheme do?

Print a copy of the contour plot and draw on it the path you followed to arrive at the supposed "maximum." Based on this path, explain why OFAT missed the true maximum.

APPENDIX 14.1: Eigenvalues and Eigenvectors

Theory

Let A be a square matrix. A real number λ is an **eigenvalue** of A if

$$Ax = \lambda x \tag{14.8}$$

for some nonzero vector $\mathbf{x}$. Any nonzero vector $\mathbf{x}$ for which equation (14.8) holds is called an **eigenvector** corresponding to the eigenvalue λ.

To get an idea of what eigenvalues and eigenvectors represent, think first about the scalar analog of multiplying the vector $\mathbf{x}$ by the matrix A: multiplying a scalar x by a scalar constant a. We can think of this as a function $g(x) = ax$. The function g takes any real number x and

- stretches it if $a > 1$
- shrinks it if $0 < a < 1$
- leaves it unchanged if $a = 1$
- shrinks its magnitude and reverses its sign if $-1 < a < 0$
- leaves its magnitude unchanged but reverses its sign if $a = -1$
- stretches its magnitude and reverses its sign if $a < -1$

You are familiar with the representation of a vector in the plane or in three dimensions as an arrow pointing from the origin. Scalars can be thought of in the same way, except that the arrow can only point along the real number line from the origin to the scalar. This arrow can point in only two directions: toward $+\infty$ if the scalar is positive and toward $-\infty$ if the scalar is negative. With this in mind, simple multiplication of any scalar x by the constant a can be thought of in terms of what it does to magnitude of x, stretching or shrinking it, and what it does to the direction (sign) of x.

The multiplication of a vector by a matrix can be thought of in much the same way. To begin with, think of the multiplication of a vector $\mathbf{x}$ by the matrix A as a function $f(\mathbf{x}) = A\mathbf{x}$, which to each vector $\mathbf{x}$ assigns another vector $A\mathbf{x}$. As in the scalar case, what the matrix A does when acting on the vector $\mathbf{x}$ can be thought of in terms of what it does to the magnitude of $\mathbf{x}$ and what it does to the direction of $\mathbf{x}$.

Things are a little more complicated with the vector-matrix multiplication, however, for two reasons. First, there are more than two possible directions that A can change $\mathbf{x}$ into. In fact, there are an infinite number. Second, the amount A stretches the magnitude of $\mathbf{x}$ depends on the direction $\mathbf{x}$ is pointing. In other words, A will stretch or shrink vectors pointing in different directions by different amounts. Nevertheless, eigenvectors and eigenvalues give us some idea of how multiplication by a matrix changes the magnitude and direction of a vector.

First of all, an eigenvector points in a direction in which the matrix is limited to the same two choices as in scalar multiplication. If $\mathbf{x}$ is an eigenvector of A, then $Ax = \lambda x$, so that if λ is positive, the effect of A on $\mathbf{x}$ is to multiply its length by λ, but not to change its direction. If λ is negative, the effect of A on $\mathbf{x}$ is to multiply its length by $|\lambda|$ and reverse its direction. Of course, if $\mathbf{x}$ is an eigenvector of A, so is any scalar multiple of $\mathbf{x}$. So eigenvectors really refer to directions that multiplication by the matrix leaves unchanged or reverses $180°$. Usually, but not always, if A is a $k \times k$ matrix, there will be k eigenvectors (directions). There can be no more than this, and sometimes, for special kinds of matrices, there are fewer.

To summarize: (1) The magnitude of the eigenvalue λ tells how much stretching the matrix produces in the direction of the eigenvector. (2) The sign of the eigenvalue tells whether multiplication by A leaves the direction of the resulting vector unchanged or reverses the direction of the resulting vector.

Example

Consider the matrix

$$A = \begin{bmatrix} 6 & 3 & 1 \\ 3 & 4 & 2 \\ 1 & 2 & 7 \end{bmatrix}$$

The eigenvalues of A are 9.696, 5.692, and 1.613. An eigenvector corresponding to eigenvalue 9.696 is

$$\mathbf{e}_1 = \begin{bmatrix} -0.5922 \\ 0.5262 \\ 0.6101 \end{bmatrix}$$

This means that A times $\mathbf{e}_1$ equals 9.696 times $\mathbf{e}_1$:

$$A\mathbf{e}_1 = 9.696 \times \mathbf{e}_1 = 9.696 \times \begin{bmatrix} -0.5922 \\ 0.5262 \\ 0.6101 \end{bmatrix} = \begin{bmatrix} -5.742 \\ -5.102 \\ -5.916 \end{bmatrix}$$

Thus, $\mathbf{e}_1$ is stretched to 9.696 times its original length and its direction is left unchanged.

Eigenvectors corresponding to 5.692 and 1.613 are

$$\mathbf{e}_2 = \begin{bmatrix} 0.6168 \\ 0.1911 \\ -0.7636 \end{bmatrix} \quad \text{and} \quad \mathbf{e}_3 = \begin{bmatrix} -0.5184 \\ 0.8286 \\ -0.2113 \end{bmatrix}$$

respectively.

APPENDIX 14.2: Multivariate Calculus Refresher

Partial Derivatives

Suppose $f(\cdot)$ is a real-valued function of k variables. Denote the surface described by $f(\cdot)$ as the graph of $y = f(x_1, x_2, \ldots, x_k)$. The **partial derivative of f with respect to** x_i evaluated at the point $\mathbf{x}_0 = (x_{01}, x_{02}, \ldots, x_{0k})$ is the rate of change of $f(\cdot)$ at $\mathbf{x}_0$ in the direction of x_i, with $x_{01}, x_{02}, \ldots, x_{0, i-1}, x_{0, i+1}, \ldots, x_{0k}$ held constant. This derivative is denoted as

$$\frac{\partial f}{\partial x_i}(\mathbf{x}_0)$$

It is easy to think of this as follows. If we fix $x_{01}, x_{02}, \ldots, x_{0, i-1}, x_{0, i+1}, \ldots, x_{0k}$ and allow only x_i to vary, then f becomes a function of only one variable: x_i. Let $f_0(x_i)$ denote this function. Then the partial derivative of $f(\cdot)$ at $\mathbf{x}_0$ is the usual univariate derivative of $f_0(\cdot)$ evaluated at x_{0i}. This is also a recipe for computing a partial derivative. For example, suppose $f(x_1, x_2) = x_1^2 + 4x_1 x_2$. To evaluate the partial derivative of $f(\cdot)$ with respect to x_1 at the point $(2, 3)$, hold x_2 constant and differentiate the resulting function of x_1:

$$\frac{\partial f}{\partial x_1} = 2x_1 + 4x_2$$

then plug in $(x_1, x_2) = (2, 3)$ to get

$$\frac{\partial f}{\partial x_1}((2, 3)) = 2 \cdot 2 + 4 \cdot 3 = 16$$

Similarly,

$$\frac{\partial f}{\partial x_2} = 4x_1$$

and

$$\frac{\partial f}{\partial x_2}((2, 3)) = 4 \cdot 2 = 8$$

Since the partial derivative of a function is itself a function, higher-order partial derivatives are defined as partial derivatives of partial derivatives. Thus, for the function of two variables, $f(x_1, x_2)$, we can define the second-order partial derivatives:

$$\frac{\partial^2 f}{\partial x_1^2} = \frac{\partial f}{\partial x_1}\left(\frac{\partial f}{\partial x_1}\right)$$

$$\frac{\partial^2 f}{\partial x_2^2} = \frac{\partial f}{\partial x_2}\left(\frac{\partial f}{\partial x_2}\right)$$

$$\frac{\partial^2 f}{\partial x_1 x_2} = \frac{\partial f}{\partial x_1}\left(\frac{\partial f}{\partial x_2}\right)$$

$$\frac{\partial^2 f}{\partial x_2 x_1} = \frac{\partial f}{\partial x_2}\left(\frac{\partial f}{\partial x_1}\right)$$

That is, for the first of these, we simply take the partial derivative of f with respect to x_1 twice; for the second of these, we simply take the partial derivative of f with respect to x_2 twice; for the third of these, we simply take the partial derivative of f with respect to x_2, then with respect to x_1; and for the fourth of these, we simply take the partial derivative of f with respect to x_1, then with respect to x_2. The latter two are called mixed partial derivatives. If these mixed partial derivatives are continuous, then the same result is obtained whether we take the partial derivative with respect to x_1 first and then x_2 or vice versa. That is,

$$\frac{\partial^2 f}{\partial x_1 x_2} = \frac{\partial^2 f}{\partial x_2 x_1}$$

Considering again the function $f(x_1, x_2) = x_1^2 + 4x_1 x_2$, we obtain

$$\frac{\partial^2 f}{\partial x_1^2} = \frac{\partial f}{\partial x_1}(2x_1 + 4x_2) = 2$$

$$\frac{\partial^2 f}{\partial x_2^2} = \frac{\partial f}{\partial x_2}(4x_1) = 0$$

$$\frac{\partial^2 f}{\partial x_1 x_2} = \frac{\partial f}{\partial x_1}(4x_1) = 4$$

and

$$\frac{\partial^2 f}{\partial x_2 x_1} = \frac{\partial f}{\partial x_2}(2x_1 + 4x_2) = 4$$

The Gradient

Consider the surface defined by $y = f(x_1, x_2, \ldots, x_k)$. The direction in which the surface rises most steeply at a point $\mathbf{x}_0$ is the **gradient** vector:

$$\nabla f(\mathbf{x}_0) = \begin{bmatrix} \dfrac{\partial f}{\partial x_1}(\mathbf{x}_0) \\[2ex] \dfrac{\partial f}{\partial x_2}(\mathbf{x}_0) \\[1ex] \vdots \\[1ex] \dfrac{\partial f}{\partial x_k}(\mathbf{x_0}) \end{bmatrix}$$

That is, the gradient is the vector of the partial derivatives of $f(\cdot)$. The surface falls off most steeply in the opposite direction, $-\nabla f(\mathbf{x}_0)$.

In the preceding example, it is easy to show that

$$\nabla f((2, 3)) = \begin{bmatrix} 10 \\ 4 \end{bmatrix}$$

So to climb the surface as quickly as possible from point $(2, 3)$, set out in the direction

$$\begin{bmatrix} 10 \\ 4 \end{bmatrix}$$

To descend as quickly as possible, set out in the opposite direction,

$$\begin{bmatrix} -10 \\ -4 \end{bmatrix}$$

CAPSTONE PROJECT: Chapters 12 to 14: Chopper Chicanery

Introduction

The goal of a **Capstone Project** is to give you experience in all phases of a statistical study: planning, data collection, analysis, and conclusions. In this activity, which draws primarily on the material of Chapters 12 to 14, your group will be asked to construct a helicopter that when dropped from a height and allowed to fall freely, will stay in the air as long as possible. One possible design for the helicopter is given in Figure 1.21, page 33.

The activity will consist of two parts:

- **Part I.** Design, conduct, and analyze one or more screening experiments to identify the vital few factors determining flight time.

- **Part II.** Design, conduct, and analyze a sequence of experiments to map the response surface and identify factor settings to optimize flight time.

Objectives

To give you a practical understanding of the overall strategy of sequential experimentation in scientific investigation.

Lab Materials

Paper, paper clips, rulers, scissors, measuring tape, stopwatch.

Experimental Procedure

Part I: Screening Experiments

1. You must initially identify a set of at least seven relevant factors such as

   - rotor length
   - rotor width
   - body length
   - fold length
   - fold width
   - absence/presence of paper clip (or weight of paper clip),

   or any other factors you think might affect the dropping times. You are free to make modifications to the design, but you need to incorporate them into the experimental design scheme.

   You might begin by constructing the stock helicopter illustrated in Figure 1.21 and conducting a few test runs. You can then combine the knowledge gained from piloting this helicopter with the knowledge you have obtained from these chapters about planning experiments[15] to obtain a list of factors to be considered and levels for those factors. Note that these factors need not be limited just to the obvious ones listed previously. Incorporate what you have learned about the organization and the quality control of experiments into the conduct of your experiments as well.

   To put this in context, in an industrial setting, you might be at the initial stage of an investigation, in which your eventual goal is to optimize the output or reduce the variability or in some other way improve the performance of a process. At this stage, your goal is to identify the influential factors governing the response you are trying to improve.

   In Part II of this activity, you will be asked to use experimental design techniques to find the helicopter design that will stay aloft the longest, so you might keep this in mind as you conduct the experiments for Part I.

2. Set up an experimental protocol. This describes exactly how your experiment is to be run, including what factors at what levels and in what order.

3. Collect the data and analyze the results.

---

[15]Tools such as brainstorming, flow charts, and Ishikawa diagrams may prove useful here.

4. The results from your first experiment will likely lead to further experiments as you seek to resolve confounding and identify the vital few significant factors in keeping the helicopter aloft.

Part II: Optimizing

Once you have obtained the vital few significant factors from Part I, it is time to begin optimizing your design. In this part, you will use the response-surface techniques of Chapter 14 to do so. Exactly how you proceed will depend on the results from Part I, so it might be a good idea to have a talk with your instructor.

Reporting the Results

You are to write a single report in the project report format. In addition to the general instructions for a project report, you should also include the following:

For Part I

1. A description of the **process** of experimentation you used. Include information on the tools and techniques you used to plan and conduct the experiments. Tell what steps you took to maintain the quality of experimentation.

2. A description of your experiments, including the configurations run, the factors you identified, the levels of the factors used in the experiments, and the responses observed. In other words, a complete description of your experiments and the data from those experiments. Also include the reasons for your choices.

3. The results of confirmatory experiments.

4. Your conclusions. These should include the factors that were important and unimportant in determining the response and whether there was significant curvature or interaction.

5. A critique of your experiments. What went right? What went wrong? How could the experiments be improved? How confident are you in your data?

For Part II

1. A description of the **process** of experimentation you used. Include information on the tools and techniques you used to plan and conduct the experiments. Tell what steps you took to maintain the quality of experimentation.

2. A description of your experiments, including the configurations run, the factors you identified, the levels of the factors used in the experiments, and the responses observed. In other words, a complete description of your experiments and the data from those experiments. Include the reasons for your choices. Of particular interest is the sequence of experiments you ran and the rationale leading from one experiment to the next.

3. The results of confirmatory experiments.

4. Your conclusions.

5. A critique of your experiments. What went right? What went wrong? How could the experiments be improved? How confident are you in your data?

Statistical Process Control

Who can control his fate?

—*Shakespeare,* Othello

INTRODUCTION

In the 1950s, 1960s, and 1970s, overseas competitors, adopting the quality improvement philosophy and methods espoused by American statistician W. Edwards Deming and others, learned to produce better-designed, higher-quality products at less cost than could U.S. firms. The consequent loss of markets for U.S. goods in many major industries resulted in the loss of high-paying U.S. industrial jobs.

Since the 1980s, a second industrial revolution, an **industrial quality revolution,** has been taking place in the United States as manufacturers have attempted to regain a competitive position in world markets. One aspect of this revolution is a renewed emphasis on process monitoring and improvement. Using tools invented by the American statistician Walter Shewhart more than 60 years ago, many U.S. manufacturers are successfully implementing **statistical process control** schemes. In this chapter, you will learn about statistical process control and its role in quality improvement.

Knowledge and Skills

By successfully completing this chapter, you will acquire the following knowledge and skills:

KNOWLEDGE	SKILLS
1. The new quality philosophy.	1. How to employ rational sub-groups.
2. The role of process control in quality improvement.	2. How to construct and interpret control charts for measurement data.
	(continued)

KNOWLEDGE	**SKILLS**
3. What statistical control is.	**3.** How to construct and interpret control charts for attribute data.
4. What rational subgroups are.	**4.** How to conduct a process capability analysis.
5. What a control chart is, and what it is and is not used for.	
6. What process capability is.	

15.1

THE NEW QUALITY PHILOSOPHY

The quality control tools you will study in this chapter are not new. Control charts are over 60 years old. What is new is the **philosophy of quality.** In the United States up until the 1980s, many firms did not use these tools at all, and those that did used them mainly to determine the extent process output conformed to specifications just prior to shipping their product. Such an inspection approach does nothing to enhance quality or productivity.

The old mentality about quality is illustrated by the following true story. To understand the point of the story, you should know that a process that is out of control is one that is nonstationary. This means that there may be something seriously wrong with the process. Anyway, the story goes like this:

> *A renowned statistician was giving a course on statistical quality methods to a group of industrial workers and managers. "Suppose you are producing a certain product whose quality characteristics are within customer specifications, yet the process itself is out of control. What would you do?", he asked. "Ship it!" responded a voice from the back of the room.*

The mentality implied by the employee's response is one reason that there are no longer any U.S. manufacturers of consumer electronics. These high-tech, high-wage companies were driven out of business by foreign competition that used the new quality philosophy to cut costs and improve product performance and quality. Business is a competitive proposition, and those firms with a "ship it!" mentality cannot cut it in the international marketplace anymore.

In contrast to the old attitudes summarized by the story, the new philosophy is one of **continuous quality improvement.** Under this philosophy, it is not enough for a manufacturer to ship parts that are in specification. In order to compete in today's global marketplace, firms must continuously strive to improve products and processes to better meet customer needs at lower cost. In manufacturing industries, quality improvement must be applied not just to manufacturing processes, but also to administrative, support, and all other processes in the company. In service industries, quality improvement is similarly applied to all aspects of operation.

Two areas in which statistical tools play a prominent role are the following:

- **Robust Design.** Robust design refers to efforts to design in quality to both the product and the process that produces it. The statistical experimental design tools described in Chapters 12 to 14, and especially the Taguchi methods described in Chapter 13, are used in this effort.
- **Process Control and Improvement.** Process control and improvement, which is the topic of the current chapter, refers to constant process monitoring in order to
    - identify and correct any immediate, short-term problems
    - identify longer-term problems inherent in the process itself

The Loss-Function Approach to Quality Improvement

The loss-function approach exemplifies the new quality philosophy. As espoused by the Japanese engineer Genichi Taguchi, a loss function is a measure of the loss to society due to any departure of a quality characteristic from its optimal value. Such losses can include loss of income to the producer due to increased manufacturing costs (e.g., rejection or rework at the factory) or the need for warranty repair in the field. They can also include less quantifiable but longer-term losses to the producer due to customer dissatisfaction. Though western firms tend to focus on losses to the company, in Taguchi's original formulation, the loss function can also include losses to society such as those due to the degradation of the environment.

A typical loss function under the new quality philosophy is the quadratic loss function shown in Figure 15.1. For the quadratic loss function, notice that by continually

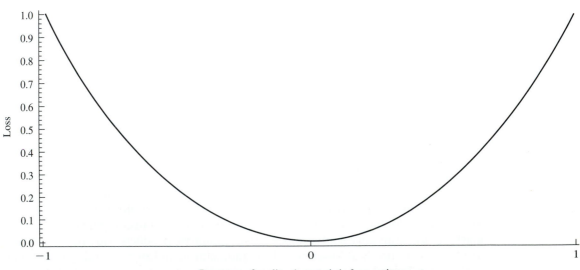

Figure 15.1   Quadratic loss function.

improving the process in terms of reducing the variation of the quality characteristic about its optimum value, we can continually reduce the loss. The loss is minimized only when the characteristic is exactly on target with no variation: an unrealistic hope, but one to strive for.

Contrast this with the loss function, called a 0–1 loss function, suitable for the "ship it!" mentality. This type of loss function is shown in Figure 15.2. The 0–1 loss function is zero when the quality characteristic is within specification and a single nonzero value otherwise. For such a loss function, there is no incentive to continually improve the process or the product: A value of the characteristic at the specification limits incurs the same loss as one at the optimum value. For this philosophy, in-spec is good enough. Think this is a good philosophy? Try buying a VCR produced by an U.S. manufacturer!

Taguchi's Sources of Variation

Taguchi defines three sources of variation or noise in process or product function.

1. **Outer Noise.** Outer noise is noise due to environmental factors found in the field. Outer noise arises from sources such as temperature, humidity, or contaminants.
2. **Inner Noise.** Inner noise refers to internal change in product characteristics caused by such factors as wear or aging.
3. **Variational Noise.** Variational noise is unit-to-unit variation due to the manufacturing process.

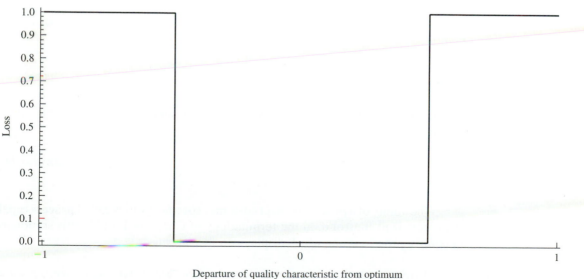

Departure of quality characteristic from optimum

Figure 15.2   0–1 loss function.

Outer and inner noise must be confronted at the design stage. The product must be designed to be robust to both kinds of noise. Experiments designed using the principles of Chapters 12 and 13 are useful in identifying product characteristics that make product performance insensitive to both outer and inner noise.[1] Variational noise can be attacked in the process that produces the product. It is variational noise that statistical process control (SPC) methods are designed to quantify. Sections 15.2 and 15.3 will focus on methods for identifying sources of variational noise.

Sources of Variational Noise

You have already been introduced to variational noise in Chapter 1, though not under that name. Rather you were told about the two causes of variational noise:

1. **Special Causes.** Special causes are problems that arise periodically and unpredictably. They can usually be handled where and when they occur by production personnel. SPC tools are designed to identify the presence of special causes and then to assist in identifying the proper corrective action. Examples of special causes are broken tools, a jammed machine, and improper machine settings.

2. **Common Causes.** Common causes are systemic sources of variation that would exist even if the process, as presently constituted, were running perfectly. Removal of common causes requires a change in the process itself and can only be done by management. Examples of common causes are poor supervision, inadequate training, and substandard maintenance.

Removing special causes will enable the process to run as well as it can. Once special causes are removed, reducing common causes will bring about process improvement.

Process Control Versus Process Capability

The failure to distinguish between specification and control is one of the deadly diseases of American management.

—*W. Edwards Deming*

The ability of a process to meet customer specifications is called **process capability.** A process is **in control** if, in the terminology of Chapters 1 and 2, it is stationary. An in-control process is one which displays no special causes.

---

[1] Despite their flaws, the Taguchi methods introduced in Chapter 13 are specifically designed to address these robustness issues.

A process that is capable is meeting customer specifications. One that is also in control is meeting customer specifications economically. A process can be in control but not capable, and it can be out of control but still capable. In order to continually improve a process, it is necessary to continually increase process capability.

The remainder of this chapter is devoted to process control and process capability. Sections 15.2 and 15.3 present methods for determining if a process is in control. Section 15.4 presents methods for measuring process capability.

15.2

CONTROL CHARTS FOR MEASUREMENT DATA

Control charts are plots of process characteristics versus time, which are used to monitor a process. Control charts are often used as the process is running to identify special causes, and to help bring the process into control. In this role, they are called **online control charts.** Control charts are also used on previously collected process data to help identify common causes in the effort to continuously improve the process. Such charts are called **offline control charts.**

Control Charts for Grouped Measurement Data

In this section, we will study the most widely used charts for quantitative data. In what follows, we assume that at each of a number of different times we observe a group of n quantitative measurements taken from the process. Let $X_{t1}, X_{t2}, \ldots, X_{tn}$ denote the the tth group of observations.[2]

For example, from a potato chip production line, we might weigh three bags of chips sampled at random every hour. Then $n = 3$ and X_{t1}, X_{t2}, and X_{t3} denote the weights of the tth group of three bags. We will often refer to these groups of data as "subgroups" or "samples." We will assume that the measurements are approximately normally distributed and that there is no correlation among the measurements within a subgroup or over time.

Recall that what we're looking to obtain from a control chart is a graphical display of the stationarity of the process. Ideally, we would like to compare the complete distributions of the process characteristic being measured at different times, but this is seldom practical. Therefore, we settle for two summary measures of these distributions: a measure of center and a measure of spread. The most common choice for measuring the center of a distribution is the sample mean. The two most common choices for measuring the spread of a distribution are the sample standard deviation and the

[2]Previously in the text, we have used Y, not X, to represent an observation. In this chapter, we will bow to common usage for control charts, and use X to represent an observation.

sample range. Initially, we will concentrate our discussion on plots of means and standard deviations. Later, we will discuss plots of means and ranges.

$\bar{X}$ Charts

Let $\bar{X}_t = (1/n) \sum_{j=1}^{n} X_{tj}$ be the mean of the tth subgroup of observations. The $\bar{X}$ chart plots the means $\bar{X}_t$ against t.

As with any plot, the $\bar{X}$ chart can and should be examined for patterns and trends. What is different about control charts, however, is a built-in mechanism for deciding when the process is out of control. Suppose, first, that the individual observations X_{tj} come from an $N(\mu, \sigma^2)$ population, and are uncorrelated. Then the $\bar{X}_t$ are uncorrelated with an $N(\mu, \sigma^2/n)$ distribution. We need to know or be able to estimate μ and σ^2. Assume for now that we know them. Recall from your knowledge of the normal distribution that about 99.75% of the observations from an $N(\mu, \sigma^2/n)$ distribution lie within the limits

$$(\mu - 3\sigma/\sqrt{n}, \mu + 3\sigma/\sqrt{n})$$

These are called the **3σ control limits** for the $\bar{X}$ chart. The limit $\mu - 3\sigma/\sqrt{n}$ is called the **lower control limit (LCL)** and the limit $\mu + 3\sigma/\sqrt{n}$ is called the **upper control limit (UCL)**. The mean μ is called the **center line** of the chart. The center line, LCL, and UCL are plotted as horizontal lines on the control chart.

The chart is evaluated for patterns relative to these lines, or perhaps relative to other criteria, depending on the particular application. The most basic criterion declares the process out of control if any observation goes outside the 3σ limits. Consider any particular subgroup: for definiteness, say subgroup t_0. If the process is in control, the probability $\bar{X}_{t_0}$ is outside the 3σ limits is 0.0027, or one chance in 370. Therefore, charts of processes that are in control should on average have one $\bar{X}_t$ outside the 3σ limits for every 370 subgroups.

Often, we do not know μ and σ. In this case, we will have to estimate them from the data. A good rule of thumb is to select 25 to 50 samples to provide estimates for μ and σ. These estimates can then be used for the subsequent data. It is important that the process be operating in control when these data are taken, so these samples should be looked at carefully for any evidence of special causes, nonnormality or correlation over time.

If using the first m samples to estimate μ and σ, the estimate of μ is $\bar{\bar{X}} = (1/m) \sum_{t=1}^{m} \bar{X}_t$, and the estimate of σ is $\hat{\sigma} = [(1/m) \sum_{t=1}^{m} S_t]/c_4 = \bar{S}/c_4$, where S_t is the standard deviation of the tth sample, $\bar{S}$ is the mean of the S_t, and c_4 is a bias correction term chosen so that the expected value of $\hat{\sigma}$ equals σ. The bias correction c_4 is tabled in Table A.11 in Appendix A, page 918, for sample sizes $2 \leq n \leq 25$. For larger values of n, c_4 can be approximated by the formula $(n - 1.00)/(n - 0.75)$.

One nice result of plotting subgroup means is that even if the data are nonnormal, the Central Limit Theorem ensures that the means, $\bar{X}_t$, are more nearly normal. The larger n is, the greater is the effect of the Central Limit Theorem.

EXAMPLE 15.1 $\bar{X}$ AND S CHARTS

A company produces thin aluminum sheets having nominal thickness 0.150 ± 0.001 mm. In order to monitor the production process, five thickness measurements are taken every half hour. Each set of five measurements will constitute one subgroup. The data are shown in Table 15.1. The subgroup numbers designate the order in which the data were taken.

For these data, $n = 5$, and the tabled value of c_4 is 0.94, and so $\hat{\sigma} = \bar{s}/c_4 = 0.00031/0.94 = 0.00033$. The upper chart in Figure 15.3 is an $\bar{X}$ chart for these data. The means of the 30 sets of 5 observations are plotted sequentially versus subgroup

TABLE 15.1   Aluminum Sheet Data with Subgroup Means, Standard Deviations, and Ranges

Subgroup	Thicknesses					$\bar{x}$	s	r
1	0.1496	0.1501	0.1499	0.1505	0.1506	0.1501	0.0004	0.0010
2	0.1495	0.1498	0.1495	0.1504	0.1505	0.1499	0.0005	0.0011
3	0.1502	0.1490	0.1502	0.1499	0.1499	0.1498	0.0005	0.0012
4	0.1503	0.1497	0.1499	0.1498	0.1502	0.1500	0.0002	0.0005
5	0.1502	0.1495	0.1501	0.1501	0.1509	0.1502	0.0005	0.0014
6	0.1503	0.1505	0.1502	0.1499	0.1499	0.1501	0.0002	0.0006
7	0.1497	0.1502	0.1506	0.1498	0.1500	0.1500	0.0004	0.0009
8	0.1502	0.1501	0.1499	0.1498	0.1500	0.1500	0.0001	0.0003
9	0.1505	0.1509	0.1499	0.1498	0.1499	0.1502	0.0005	0.0010
10	0.1501	0.1498	0.1495	0.1504	0.1508	0.1501	0.0005	0.0013
11	0.1501	0.1499	0.1501	0.1502	0.1503	0.1501	0.0001	0.0004
12	0.1501	0.1498	0.1504	0.1500	0.1499	0.1500	0.0002	0.0006
13	0.1497	0.1496	0.1502	0.1500	0.1496	0.1498	0.0003	0.0006
14	0.1503	0.1501	0.1495	0.1502	0.1504	0.1501	0.0004	0.0009
15	0.1499	0.1502	0.1504	0.1502	0.1510	0.1504	0.0004	0.0011
16	0.1501	0.1504	0.1501	0.1503	0.1497	0.1501	0.0003	0.0007
17	0.1504	0.1499	0.1502	0.1497	0.1499	0.1500	0.0003	0.0006
18	0.1500	0.1498	0.1497	0.1499	0.1501	0.1499	0.0002	0.0004
19	0.1502	0.1501	0.1504	0.1499	0.1500	0.1501	0.0002	0.0005
20	0.1501	0.1495	0.1501	0.1501	0.1498	0.1499	0.0003	0.0006
21	0.1498	0.1504	0.1500	0.1499	0.1496	0.1500	0.0003	0.0008
22	0.1500	0.1494	0.1498	0.1504	0.1501	0.1499	0.0004	0.0010
23	0.1503	0.1498	0.1503	0.1497	0.1500	0.1500	0.0003	0.0007
24	0.1502	0.1500	0.1499	0.1494	0.1501	0.1499	0.0003	0.0008
25	0.1500	0.1506	0.1504	0.1507	0.1503	0.1504	0.0003	0.0007
26	0.1500	0.1501	0.1502	0.1506	0.1502	0.1502	0.0002	0.0006
27	0.1500	0.1500	0.1502	0.1498	0.1497	0.1499	0.0002	0.0005
28	0.1501	0.1503	0.1503	0.1494	0.1499	0.1500	0.0004	0.0009
29	0.1500	0.1496	0.1506	0.1496	0.1505	0.1501	0.0005	0.0010
30	0.1499	0.1497	0.1500	0.1502	0.1500	0.1500	0.0002	0.0004

$$\bar{\bar{x}} = 0.15005 \qquad \bar{s} = 0.00031 \qquad \bar{r} = 0.00077$$

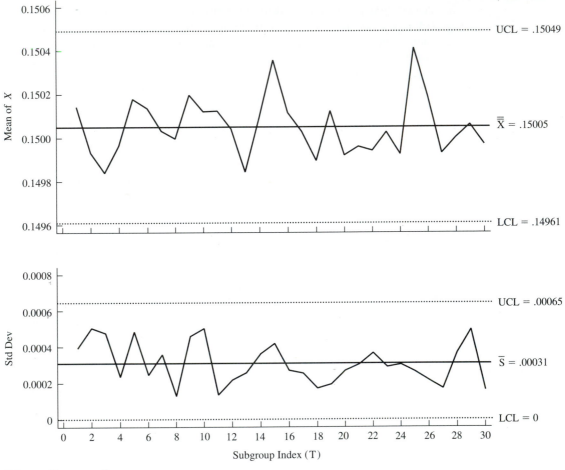

Figure 15.3 $\bar{X}$ (top) and S (bottom) charts for aluminum sheet data.

number and connected by segmented lines. The center line is the center horizontal line plotted on the chart. Its value was computed as $\bar{\bar{x}} = 0.15005$, the mean of the 30 subgroup means. The topmost horizontal line, marked "UCL = .15409," is located at $\bar{\bar{x}} + 3\hat{\sigma}$, and the bottommost horizontal line, marked "LCL = .14961," is located at $\bar{\bar{x}} - 3\hat{\sigma}$. These are the 3σ UCL and LCL, respectively.

As you can see from this chart, the thicknesses are centered at 0.15005 mm, which is only slightly above the nominal 0.150 mm thickness. Since the measurements do not go outside the control limits, the $\bar{X}$ chart gives no evidence, based on the 3σ limits, that the process is out of control. ◆

S Charts

There are situations in which a process goes out of control but its mean stays in control. Suppose that a machine component wears out slowly over time, resulting in increasing variability in the process measurements but not affecting the mean of the process measurements. An $\bar{X}$ chart would have difficulty detecting this type of problem. What is needed is a chart to track process variability. The S chart is just such a chart.

Assume the same notation as for the $\bar{X}$ chart. The S chart plots the subgroup standard deviations S_t versus t. The center line is $\bar{S}$, the mean of the standard deviations computed from the same m subgroups used for computing the control limits in the $\bar{X}$ chart. The $k\sigma$ control limits on the S chart are $\bar{S} \pm k\hat{\sigma}\sqrt{1 - c_4^2}$, with the understanding that a negative value of the LCL is set to zero. So, for example, the 3σ LCL is the maximum of $\bar{S} - 3\hat{\sigma}\sqrt{1 - c_4^2}$ and 0, and the 3σ UCL is $\bar{S} + 3\hat{\sigma}\sqrt{1 - c_4^2}$. The LCL and UCL are interpreted just as for the $\bar{X}$ chart. The box summarizes construction of $\bar{X}$ and S charts.

CENTER LINE AND CONTROL LIMITS FOR $\bar{X}$ AND S CHARTS: EQUAL SAMPLE SIZES

Assume m samples of size n are used to construct the center line and control limits. Assume all plotted samples contain n observations.

- **$\bar{X}$ Chart**

    - **Center Line:** $\bar{\bar{X}}$
    - **$k\sigma$ LCL:** $\bar{\bar{X}} - k\hat{\sigma}/\sqrt{n}$; **$k\sigma$ UCL:** $\bar{\bar{X}} + k\hat{\sigma}/\sqrt{n}$

- **S Chart**

    - **Center Line:** $\bar{S}$
    - **$k\sigma$ LCL:** $\max\left\{\bar{S} - k\hat{\sigma}\sqrt{1 - c_4^2}, 0\right\}$; **$k\sigma$ UCL:** $\bar{S} + k\hat{\sigma}\sqrt{1 - c_4^2}$

In the preceding formulas:

- $\bar{\bar{X}}$ is the mean of the m sample means.
- $\bar{S}$ is the mean of the m sample standard deviations.
- $\hat{\sigma} = \bar{S}/c_4$ is the estimate of σ. c_4 is tabulated in Table A.11 in Appendix A, page 918.

EXAMPLE 15.1   CONTINUED

The lower chart in Figure 15.3 is an S chart for the aluminum sheet data. The location of the center line is computed as the mean of the standard deviations of all 30 subgroups, and equals 0.00031. The plotted standard deviations do not go outside the 3σ control limits, so the S chart gives no evidence, based on the 3σ limits, that the process is out of control.   ✦

Interpretation of $\bar{X}$ and S Charts.   When using $\bar{X}$ and S charts to analyze a process, always look first to see if the S chart is in control. Only analyze the $\bar{X}$ chart if the S chart is in control.

Interpretation of S Charts.   The S chart is a display of the uniformity or consistency of the process over time. The narrower the range of values on the S chart, the more consistent the process is. An out-of-control S chart indicates something is operating on the process in a nonuniform manner. Typical causes of an out-of-control S chart are poor maintenance of machines or poor training of or lack of attention by operators.

Interpretation of $\bar{X}$ Charts.   An out-of-control S chart can affect an $\bar{X}$ chart, so if both the $\bar{X}$ and S charts are out of control, seek causes and corrections for the S chart first. The $\bar{X}$ chart shows where the process is centered. In interpreting the $\bar{X}$ chart, look first for trends, indicating that the center is changing over time. Look second to see whether the fluctuations are becoming narrower or wider, suggesting changes in uniformity over time. Look third to see whether the pattern stays away from one of the control limits, indicating that the distribution is skewed. Finally, look for any other patterns such as cycles or jumps.

Zones A, B, and C.   To aid in identifying special causes, the $\bar{X}$ chart can be divided into horizontal zones whose boundaries are located at the $\pm 1, 2,$ and 3σ limits. Zone A ranges from the 2σ to the 3σ limits, Zone B from the 1σ to the 2σ limits, and Zone C is between the 1σ limits. Figure 15.4 is the $\bar{X}$ chart for the aluminum sheet data from Example 15.1 with Zones A, B, and C displayed.

Tests for an Out-of-Control Process.   The following are eight tests that are useful in identifying the presence of special causes. Each of these tests has been selected to screen for specific kinds of special causes. When the process is in control, the chance of each of these tests giving an out-of-control signal at any one time is small, as we have already demonstrated for Test 1: observations outside the 3σ limits.

1. **One Point Beyond Zone A.** This applies to both $\bar{X}$ and S charts.
2. **Nine Points in a Row in Zone C or Beyond (on One Side of the Center Line).** This applies to both $\bar{X}$ and S charts. This is strong evidence that the process mean or variability has shifted.
3. **Six Points in a Row Steadily Increasing or Decreasing.** This applies to both $\bar{X}$ and S charts, and signals a systematic trend.
4. **Fourteen Points in a Row Alternating Up and Down.** This applies to both $\bar{X}$ and S charts, and signals an oscillating systematic trend.
5. **Two Out of Three Successive Points in Zone A or Beyond (on One Side of the Center Line).** This applies to $\bar{X}$ charts only.

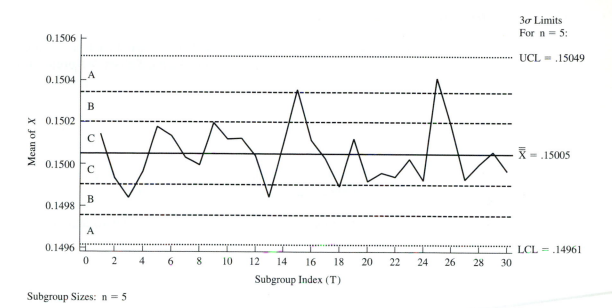

Subgroup Sizes: n = 5

Figure 15.4 $\bar{X}$ chart for aluminum sheet data, with Zones A, B, and C.

6. **Four Out of Five Successive Points in Zone B or Beyond (on One Side of the Center Line).** This applies to $\bar{X}$ charts only.

7. **Fifteen Points in a Row in Zone C (Above and Below the Center Line).** This applies to $\bar{X}$ charts only. Such a signal can be due to improper sampling (stratification), as you'll see later, or to a decrease in process variability that has not been accounted for in the $\bar{X}$ chart control limits.

8. **Eight Points in a Row with No Points in Zone C.** This applies to $\bar{X}$ charts only. This could signal that more than one process is being charted or that there is overcontrol of the process. It is also symptomatic of improper sampling (mixing), as you'll see later.

Since a given test will be good at detecting some kinds of out-of-control situations but poor at detecting others, these tests should be combined in determining when a process goes out of control. However, be warned that the more criteria you use in trying to detect an out-of-control process, the greater the number of **false alarms** (i.e., out-of-control signals on an in-control process) you will encounter. Tests 3 and 4 are especially susceptible to false alarms.

EXAMPLE 15.1   CONTINUED

Tests 1 to 8 were checked for the aluminum sheet data and none of the tests was violated. This strengthens our belief that the process is in control.   ◆

R Charts

An *R* chart plots the range (i.e., largest minus smallest value) of each subgroup, as an indicator of process variation. It is analyzed exactly like the *S* chart. We prefer *S* charts to *R* charts for monitoring process variation because

- *S* is a more natural and familiar measure of variation than is *R*.
- *S* charts are statistically more efficient, especially for moderate or large sample sizes ($n \geq 10$).

R charts are found more often in the literature, and in applications, because they are easier to compute than are *S* charts. This feature was of more importance in the pre-computer era than it is today.

We assume samples of size n taken sequentially, and we let R_t denote the range of sample t:

$$R_t = \max\{X_{t1}, X_{t2}, \ldots, X_{tn}\} - \min\{X_{t1}, X_{t2}, \ldots, X_{tn}\}$$

Then there is a constant d_2, depending on the sample size, n, so that if the data are from an $N(\mu, \sigma^2)$ distribution, the expected value of R_t/d_2 equals σ. Assume we use the m sample ranges $R_1, R_2, \ldots, R_m$ to estimate parameters, center lines, and control limits. The center line for the *R* chart is taken to be the mean of the m sample ranges:

$$\bar{R} = \frac{1}{m} \sum_{t=1}^{m} R_t$$

and the standard deviation σ is estimated by

$$\hat{\sigma} = \frac{\bar{R}}{d_2}$$

To compute the control limits, we need another constant, d_3, which also depends on n. The $k\sigma$ LCL is

$$\max\{\bar{R} - kd_3\hat{\sigma}, 0\}$$

and the $k\sigma$ UCL is

$$\bar{R} + kd_3\hat{\sigma}$$

The constants d_2 and d_3 are tabled in Table A.11, page 918, for sample sizes $2 \leq n \leq 25$.

When an $\bar{X}$ chart is plotted in conjunction with an *R* chart, the standard deviation $\hat{\sigma}$ used in calculating the control limits for the $\bar{X}$ chart is estimated using the subgroup ranges as before, rather than the subgroup standard deviations. Given this change, the center line for the $\bar{X}$ chart is still $\bar{\bar{X}}$, and the $k\sigma$ control limits are given by the same formula: $\bar{\bar{X}} \pm k\hat{\sigma}/\sqrt{n}$.

CENTER LINE AND CONTROL LIMITS FOR $\bar{X}$ AND R CHARTS: EQUAL SAMPLE SIZES

Assume m samples of size n are used to construct the center line and control limits. Assume all plotted samples contain n observations.

- $\bar{X}$ **Chart**
  - **Center Line:** $\bar{\bar{X}}$
  - $k\sigma$ **LCL:** $\bar{\bar{X}} - k\hat{\sigma}/\sqrt{n}$; $k\sigma$ **UCL:** $\bar{\bar{X}} + k\hat{\sigma}/\sqrt{n}$
- R **Chart**
  - **Center Line:** $\bar{R}$
  - $k\sigma$ **LCL:** $\max\{\bar{R} - kd_3\hat{\sigma}, 0\}$; $k\sigma$ **UCL:** $\bar{R} + kd_3\hat{\sigma}$

In the preceding formulas:

- $\bar{\bar{X}}$ is the mean of the m sample means.
- $\bar{R}$ is the mean of the m sample ranges.
- $\hat{\sigma} = \bar{R}/d_2$ is the estimate of σ.
- d_2 and d_3 are tabulated in Table A.11 in Appendix A, page 918.

EXAMPLE 15.1   CONTINUED

The ranges for the aluminum sheet data are given in Table 15.1. From this table, we can see that $\bar{\bar{x}} = 0.15005$, $\bar{s} = 0.00031$, and $\bar{r} = 0.00077$. From Table A.11, page 918, for $n = 5$, we see that $d_2 = 2.3259$ and $d_3 = 0.8641$. Therefore, we estimate σ as $\hat{\sigma} = 0.00077/2.3259 = 0.00033$, which to this accuracy is the same as the estimate computed from the sample standard deviations. This means the $\bar{X}$ chart will be the same as that in Figure 15.3. For the R chart, the center line is $\bar{r} = 0.00077$, the 3σ LCL is

$$\max\{0.00077 - 3(0.8641)(0.00033), 0\} = \max\{-0.85 \times 10^{-5}, 0\} = 0$$

and the 3σ UCL is

$$0.00077 + 3(0.8641)(0.00033) = 0.00162$$

The $\bar{X}$ and R charts are shown in Figure 15.5.   ◆

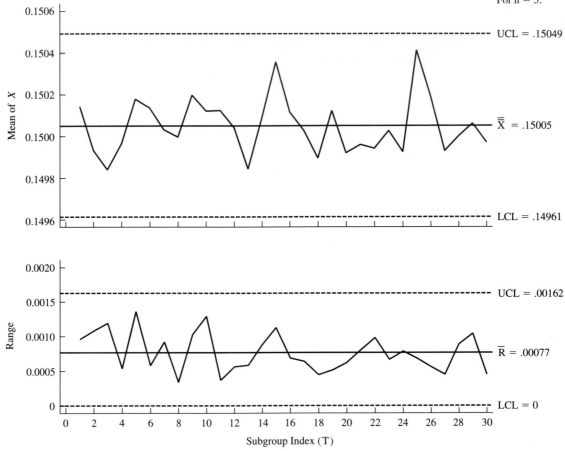

Figure 15.5 $\bar{X}$ (top) and R (bottom) charts for aluminum sheet data.

Unequal Sample Sizes

So far, we have assumed that all samples have the same number of observations, n, but this is not always the case in applications. If the samples have unequal sizes, some adjustments must be made in formulas for center lines and control limits. In what follows, assume that sample t has n_t observations, that we use samples $1, \ldots, m$ to compute center lines and control limits, and that $\bar{X}_t$, S_t, and R_t, denote the sample means, standard deviations, and ranges, respectively, from sample t. We also let $c_4(n_t)$, $d_2(n_t)$, and $d_3(n_t)$ denote the values of the constants c_4, d_2, and d_3 when the sample size is n_t.

$\bar{X}$ and S Charts.   We estimate the standard deviation σ as

$$\hat{\sigma} = \frac{S_1/c_4(n_1) + S_2/c_4(n_2) + \cdots + S_m/c_4(n_m)}{m}$$

The center line of the $\bar{X}$ chart is

$$\bar{\bar{X}} = \frac{n_1 \bar{X}_1 + n_2 \bar{X}_2 + \cdots + n_m \bar{X}_m}{n_1 + n_2 + \cdots + n_m} \tag{15.1}$$

which is the overall mean of all the observations taken together. This center line is the same for all samples. However, the $k\sigma$ LCL and UCL depend on the sample size. If we let $LCL(t)$ and $UCL(t)$ denote the LCL and UCL for sample t, then

$$LCL(t) = \bar{\bar{X}} - k\hat{\sigma}/\sqrt{n_t} \tag{15.2}$$

$$UCL(t) = \bar{\bar{X}} + k\hat{\sigma}/\sqrt{n_t} \tag{15.3}$$

For the S chart, both the center line and control limits vary with the sample size. The center line for sample t is $c_4(n_t)\hat{\sigma}$. The $k\sigma$ LCL and UCL for sample t are

$$LCL(t) = \max\left\{c_4(n_t)\hat{\sigma} - k\hat{\sigma}\sqrt{1 - c_4(n_t)^2}, 0\right\}$$

$$UCL(t) = c_4(n_t)\hat{\sigma} + k\hat{\sigma}\sqrt{1 - c_4(n_t)^2}$$

$\bar{X}$ and R Charts.   We estimate the standard deviation σ as

$$\hat{\sigma} = \frac{R_1/d_2(n_1) + R_2/d_2(n_2) + \cdots + R_m/d_2(n_m)}{m} \tag{15.4}$$

The center line of the $\bar{X}$ chart is $\bar{\bar{X}}$, computed as in (15.1). The $k\sigma$ $LCL(t)$ and $UCL(t)$ for the $\bar{X}$ chart are computed using Equations (15.2) and (15.3), with $\hat{\sigma}$ computed using (15.4).

The center line of the R chart for sample t is $d_2(n_t)\hat{\sigma}$. The $k\sigma$ $LCL(t)$ and $UCL(t)$ for the R chart are

$$LCL(t) = \max\{d_2(n_t)\hat{\sigma} - kd_3(n_t)\hat{\sigma}, 0\}$$

$$UCL(t) = d_2(n_t)\hat{\sigma} + kd_3(n_t)\hat{\sigma}$$

EXAMPLE 15.2 $\bar{X}$ AND S CHARTS: UNEQUAL SAMPLE SIZES

A food manufacturer periodically samples its output of 8-ounce boxes of chicken nuggets. At each occasion, t, a sample of three to five boxes is randomly selected for testing. Table 15.2 displays a summary of the weights obtained from 25 recent samples. Figure 15.6 shows $\bar{X}$ and S charts for these data. Notice the variable 3σ control limits on both charts. Based on these charts, the process seems in control. ✦

TABLE 15.2   Chicken Nugget Data: Sample Sizes, n_t, Sample Means, $\bar{x}_t$, and Sample Standard Deviations, s_t, for Weights of 25 Samples of 8-Ounce Chicken Nugget Boxes

t	n_t	$\bar{x}_t$	s_t	t	n_t	$\bar{x}_t$	s_t	t	n_t	$\bar{x}_t$	s_t
1	4	8.12	0.02	10	3	8.10	0.09	19	4	8.10	0.06
2	5	8.11	0.05	11	5	8.11	0.04	20	3	8.11	0.03
3	4	8.12	0.07	12	4	8.08	0.04	21	5	8.13	0.01
4	4	8.13	0.01	13	5	8.05	0.06	22	4	8.14	0.06
5	5	8.08	0.02	14	5	8.11	0.05	23	4	8.10	0.06
6	5	8.07	0.07	15	5	8.09	0.04	24	4	8.08	0.04
7	5	8.11	0.04	16	4	8.08	0.06	25	4	8.09	0.02
8	4	8.07	0.01	17	5	8.11	0.02				
9	4	8.10	0.02	18	4	8.07	0.05				

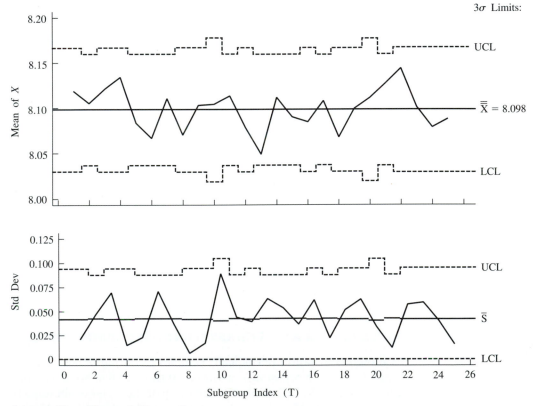

Subgroup Sizes: Min n = 3 Max n = 5

Figure 15.6 $\bar{X}$ and S charts for weights of 25 samples of 8-ounce chicken nugget boxes.

Checking Process Assumptions

Since control charts may give misleading information if the assumptions of normality and lack of correlation are violated, it is good practice to check those assumptions. A normal quantile plot of the data will reveal serious departures from normality, and is useful in checking $\bar{X}$.[3]

To identify correlation over time, use a plot of the autocorrelation function of the plotted quantities: $\bar{X}$, S, or R. The autocorrelation function at lag l, $r(l)$, of a sequence of observations, Y_t, $t = 1, 2, \ldots, m$, is the ordinary Pearson correlation[4] between the observations at time t and those at time $t + l$:

$$r(l) = \frac{1}{m-1} \sum_{i=1}^{m-l} Y_t' Y_{t+l}'$$

where Y_t' is the standardized value of Y_t:

$$Y_t' = (Y_t - \bar{Y})/S_Y$$

Large values of the autocorrelation function at lag l mean that observed values l units of time apart are related. To assess whether an observed value of $r(l)$ indicates a significant autocorrelation, we use the fact that if the process autocorrelation is zero, then $r(l)$ has mean 0 and standard error $1/\sqrt{m}$. In this case, approximately 95% of all $r(l)$ values computed from data generated from that process will lie within $\pm 2/\sqrt{m}$. A common practice is to regard $r(l)$ that exceed $2/\sqrt{m}$ in absolute value as possibly indicative of significant process autocorrelation at the corresponding lag l. Many more than 5% of $|r(l)|$ values outside this bound, or one or more values of $r(l)$ greatly outside the bound, signal possibly serious autocorrelation in the process.

To visually assess the autocorrelation in a set of time-ordered data, an **autocorrelation plot** can be generated. An autocorrelation plot is a plot of $r(l)$ versus l. Two horizontal lines, at heights $\pm 2/\sqrt{m}$, are often plotted on the autocorrelation plot to assist in assessing significant autocorrelations.

Care should be taken when using control charts with autocorrelated data. There are measures designed to assess the control of a process that generates autocorrelated data,[5] but these are beyond the scope of this text.

EXAMPLE 15.3   CHECKING ASSUMPTIONS

Dressing stones are used to dress all types of grinding wheels that have lost their normal shape. They can also be used to dress an angle or groove into a wheel for

---

[3]Remember that even if all process assumptions are met, the quantities plotted on the S and R charts will not have normal distributions.

[4]See Chapter 7 for a review of the Pearson correlation.

[5]See, for example, D. C. Montgomery, *Introduction to Statistical Quality Control,* 2nd ed., New York: Wiley, 1991.

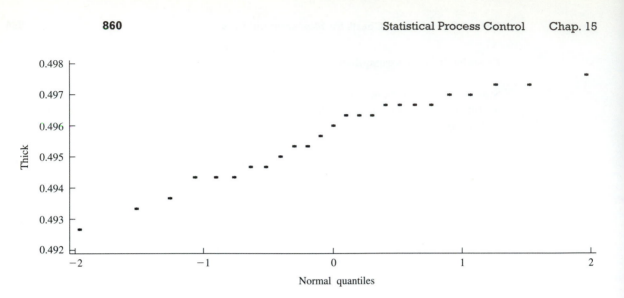

Figure 15.7   Normal quantile plot of dressing stone means, Example 15.3.

a specific operation. Dressing stones are pressed in block form and cut into sticks. After curing, they are surface ground to tolerance.

A quality engineer working at a factory that produces dressing stones collected data on the thickness of 25 samples of 3 dressing stones each from a production line. The engineer wants to chart these data using $\bar{X}$ and S control charts.

The first step in analyzing an $\bar{X}$ chart is to check normality and autocorrelation of the $\bar{X}_t$. Figure 15.7 is a normal quantile plot of the means of the 25 subgroups.

The normal quantile plot shows these means to be reasonably normal, or even a bit short-tailed. From this, we conclude that there are no serious violations of the normality assumption.

Figure 15.8 is an autocorrelation plot based on these subgroups. None of the autocorrelations exceed the two horizontal benchmarks, so there is no evidence of autocorrelation problems in the data.

Having convinced ourselves that the assumptions underlying control charts are not violated, we proceed to construct the $\bar{X}$ and S charts for these data, which are shown in Figure 15.9.

We check the S chart first. The plotted points certainly do not go outside the control limits, and in the first half of the chart are well spread within them. In the second half of the chart, the points hug the line closely, which may indicate a problem, and certainly bears watching. However, there is not really any solid evidence here that the process is out of control in terms of its variability.

We look next at the $\bar{X}$ chart. According to the $\bar{X}$ chart is the process in control? The answer is no. It goes outside the control limits (Test 1) at subgroups 4, 8, 18, and 20. In addition, a sequence of four out of five points above region C (Test 6) begins at subgroup 6.

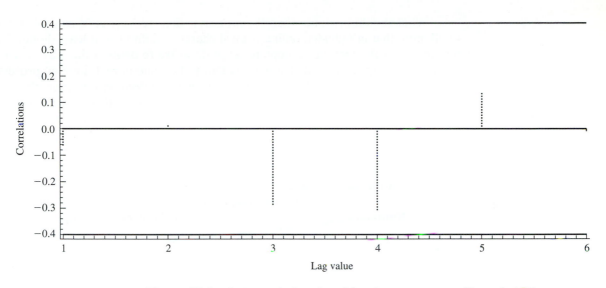

Figure 15.8   Autocorrelation plot of dressing stone means, Example 15.3.

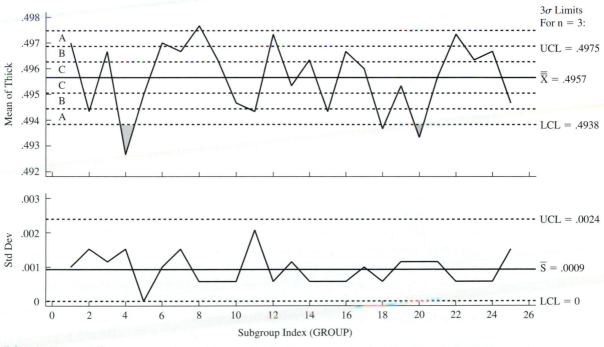

Subgroup Sizes: n = 3

Figure 15.9 $\bar{X}$ and S control charts, dressing stone data.

What should be done when the process is detected as out of control? First of all, note that in industry, online control charts wouldn't (or at least shouldn't) be done after the fact on a complete set of data. We're doing it this way only to illustrate concepts. Control charts are meant to be done in real time: on process data as they are measured over time. When they are done in real time, then at the first out-of-control signal, causes should be sought, identified, and corrected. If the problem persists, the process should be stopped if necessary. ✦

Rational Sampling

We have seen that for the $\bar{X}$, R, and S charts, the data must be divided into subgroups. The method of choosing the subgroups is absolutely crucial to generating successful control charts. **Rational sampling** refers to a method of choosing subgroups so that to the extent possible all variation **within** subgroups is due to common causes. There are two reasons for this.

1. Since we are plotting subgroup statistics (means, standard deviations, or ranges), we can only detect differences between subgroups. Since special causes are what we want to detect, we want to ensure that special causes show up as group-to-group differences.

2. Our ability to detect differences in subgroup statistics depends on the within-group variation those statistics display. For example, the 3σ limits for the $\bar{X}$ chart are computed using the mean of the within-group standard deviations, $\bar{S}$. Therefore, we will get better detection if those within-group standard deviations are small. Keeping special causes out of within-group variation will help keep those standard deviations small.

How to Sample

Choosing Subgroup Sample Size. Choice of the subgroup sample size depends on several considerations:

- The sample size should be small enough so that only common cause variation is found within groups.
- It should be large enough so that the charted quantities (e.g., $\bar{X}$) are approximately normal (remember the Central Limit Theorem!).
- It should be large enough so that the charts will be sensitive to the size differences to be detected. Remember that for an $\bar{X}$ chart with subgroup sample size n, the width of the control limits is proportional to $\sigma/\sqrt{n}$.
- It must be economical and feasible to implement.

Methods for Selecting Subgroups. Suppose the samples are produced at a relatively constant rate, and you plan to take a sample of size n each hour. How should the sampling be done?

- **Consecutive sampling** refers to taking all the items at one time, or as near to it as possible. If sampling n units each hour, a consecutive sampling scheme would take a sample of n consecutive items from production, then wait 1 hour to take another n consecutive items. Consecutive sampling is generally preferred because it is the best way to ensure that the within-group variation contains no special causes.
- **Distributed sampling** refers to taking the samples over the entire sampling period. An example of distributed sampling is taking five samples per hour by taking one item every 12 minutes. While it is not generally preferred, distributed sampling may be superior to consecutive sampling for some patterns of variation, such as abrupt and brief shifts in the process mean.

If sampling is done periodically, there is a risk of failing to capture periodic effects. To avoid this possibility, the sampling should be done randomly within a range of times. For instance, if we sample consecutively each hour, the time between any two consecutive samples might be randomly selected from the range 50 to 70 minutes.

Frequency of Sampling.   Three considerations governing the frequency of sampling are as follows:

1. If control charting is new to the process or if the process is behaving erratically, it is desirable to sample more frequently.
2. Samples should be taken frequently enough to capture opportunities for special causes.
3. And, of course, frequency of sampling depends on the cost and the budget.

What Can Happen without Rational Sampling?

Stratification.   One example of what can happen if rational sampling is not used is **stratification.** Stratification is a problem that arises when several process streams are charted on one control chart.

As an example, suppose that four machines are producing the same product synchronously in a parallel configuration, and that the output streams are mixed before sampling takes place. Suppose that, for convenience, subgroups of size four are taken that consist of one item from each machine. If differences in machines are responsible for special causes, then those special causes will occur within groups. This means that within-group variation will appear very large relative to differences between groups, and the process will appear to be in control.

Causes of Stratification.   Stratification can arise in a number of ways:

- Through process devices that generate "natural" subgroups such as multicavity molds or multihead filling machines.
- Through trying to distribute sampling points uniformly in space or time.
- By systematic sampling from different process streams.

A Symptom of Stratification.   The most obvious symptom of stratification is that charts for center and spread of the process appear to be in control with what are apparently very wide control limits. The points appear to "hug" the center line and there will be too few points spread toward the control limits.

The Solution to Stratification.   Take separate samples and do separate charts for each process stream.

Mixing.   A second example of what can happen if rational sampling is not used is **mixing.** Mixing is similar to stratification in that several process streams are mixed prior to sampling. The difference is that whereas in stratification each sample will contain one measurement from each stream, in mixing, the different samples might contain different numbers from the streams. If, in the stratification example, we put all the output in one container and then sampled randomly from that container to create each sample, we might get two items from machine 1 and two from machine 2 in the first sample, one from machine 1, one from machine 3, and two from machine 4 in the second sample, and so on. This is mixing.

A Symptom of Mixing.   Mixing is more difficult to identify than stratification. On control charts, plotted points may be abnormally close to the control limits.

The Solution to Mixing.   The solution to mixing is the same as that for stratification: Take separate samples and do separate charts for each process stream.

EXAMPLE 15.4   STRATIFICATION AND MIXING

The shipping department of a computer manufacturer assembles cardboard shipping boxes for computer components by gluing at four locations during the same assembly sequence. A different nozzle and roller makes the seal at each location. To ensure the integrity of the shipping boxes, one box is taken periodically from the assembly line, and the strength of each seal tested in a pull-apart test. An $\bar{X}$ chart in which $\bar{X}$ is computed from the four strength measurements on a given box is employed to monitor the box-making process. The data for 30 consecutively-sampled boxes are found in the data set BOXES. Figure 15.10 shows the $\bar{X}$ chart constructed from these data.

The $\bar{X}$ chart shows that the mean strength clusters near the center line, entirely within Zone C. In fact, the process is judged out of control by Test 7. The pattern on the control chart and the fact that each subgroup consists of one measurement at each of the four locations should lead to the suspicion that stratification is the culprit here. To see if this was the case, the data for each location were examined separately, and it was found that the strength of the seal at one location was significantly less than at the other three locations. Exercise 15.23 asks you to analyze these data in more detail.

To illustrate the concept of mixing, we took the box data and randomly rearranged it, so that different subgroups would consist of data from different sets of locations. The result is in the data set BOXMIX. Figure 15.11 shows the $\bar{X}$ chart constructed from these data.

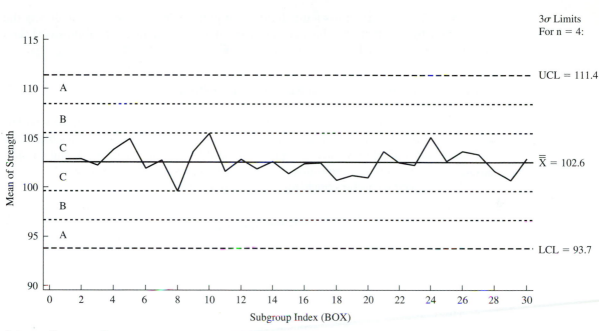

Figure 15.10 $\bar{X}$ chart for box strength data, Example 15.4

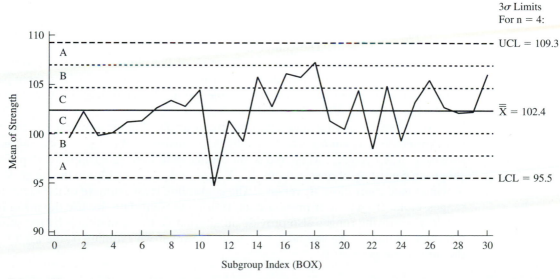

Figure 15.11 $\bar{X}$ chart for randomly rearranged box strength data, Example 15.4.

This $\bar{X}$ chart shows a much different pattern. The means no longer hug the center line. In fact, the chart goes beyond the lower 3σ limit at subgroup 11, and prior to that fails Test 3 at subgroup 8.   ✦

Control Charts for Individual Measurement Data

Having been introduced to control charts based on grouped data, you might be wondering why we don't just plot the individual measurements, rather than summary measures such as $\bar{X}$ and S. Certainly, such an approach would avoid the extra work and complications, such as rational sampling, associated with charts for grouped data.

Two reasons to prefer charts for grouped data are

1. They are more sensitive to process changes.
2. They are less sensitive to violations of assumptions.

As a result, **whenever the data can be rationally grouped, charts for grouped data should be used.**

There are situations, however, where it is not possible to form rational samples of size greater than one. For instance, Professor P.'s daily KWH usage, described in Chapter 1, consists of a single observation taken each day. Or consider measurements of humidity taken in a testing chamber. Multiple measurements taken at one time will most likely be identical. If the measurements do differ, the difference will not reflect the variability of humidity in the chamber, but rather the variability of the measuring system.

In such cases, we may use an **X chart** to assess differences in measurement levels and a **moving range chart** to assess process variability.

Suppose our data consist of consecutive measurements $X_t, t = 1, 2 \dots$. The X chart plots X_t versus t. The center line is any estimate $\hat{\mu}$ of the process mean: for example, the sample mean of previous data or of the plotted data. We also need an estimate, $\hat{\sigma}$, of process standard deviation. This estimate can be obtained from past or present data. If using present data, the sample standard deviation of the X_t can be used. The $k\sigma$ limits for the X chart are $\hat{\mu} \pm k\hat{\sigma}$.

To create the moving range chart, we create artificial subgroups of size n, consisting of n consecutive X_t values. The first subgroup consists of $X_1, X_2, \dots, X_n$, the second subgroup of $X_2, X_3, \dots, X_{n+1}$, and so on. Notice that these subgroups overlap. For the subgroup consisting of observations $X_t, X_{t+1}, \dots, X_{t+n-1}$, we obtain the range R_t. The moving range chart plots R_t versus t. The center line is an estimate of the mean of the ranges, either from past or present data. If using present data, we use the mean of the R_t, $\bar{R}$. The moving ranges also provide an alternative to estimating σ by the standard deviation of the X_t: we can take $\hat{\sigma} = \bar{R}/d_2$. However we estimate σ, the $k\sigma$ LCL for the moving range chart is

$$\max\{d_2\hat{\sigma} - kd_3\hat{\sigma}, 0\}$$

and the $k\sigma$ UCL is

$$d_2\hat{\sigma} + kd_3\hat{\sigma}$$

where d_2 and d_3 are tabled in Table A.11 in Appendix A, page 918, for $2 \leq n \leq 25$.

EXAMPLE 15.5   INDIVIDUAL MEASUREMENT CHARTS

To illustrate the use of control charts for individual measurement data, consider the following true story, some of which has been told in Chapter 1:

In Professor P.'s neighborhood, all the houses were built by the same contractor at roughly the same time. Of these houses, many, including Professor P.'s, have wells for their water supply. In the past few months, several homeowners in this neighborhood have had cracks occur in their well pipes. The type of crack that has occurred results in only two symptoms:

- A small, hardly noticeable, drop in water pressure.
- A very large ($600 for 1 month was not unusual) electric bill. This large electric bill results from the in-ground well pump running continuously.

Since Professor P. isn't enthusiastic about massive electric bills, he decided to monitor the daily electric usage at his house. The data are found in the data set ELECE. In that data set are recorded two variables, KWH and DATE. KWH is the number of kilowatt-hours (roughly) used in the 24-hour period ending at around 6 A.M. (or as soon after as Professor P. can get up) on DATE, the date in question.

Professor P. decided to create an X and moving range chart for these data. From past data, Professor P. knew that the distribution of the KWH measurements was right-skewed. Since control limits on the X chart are sensitive to skewness, Professor P. experimented until he found that transforming the KWH values by taking their fourth root substantially improved the normality of the distribution. He decided to create the control charts for the transformed data.

The previous year's data had shown that the fourth root of KWH had a mean of about 2.11 and a standard deviation of about 0.21. Using these values gave a center line for the X chart of 2.11 and 3σ limits of $2.11 \pm 3 \cdot 0.21 = (1.48, 2.74)$.

For the moving range chart, Professor P. chose a moving range of size 2 ($n = 2$), which gives the values $d_2 = 1.1284$ and $d_3 = 0.8525$. To compute the center line, he set $\bar{R} = d_2\hat{\sigma} = 1.1284 \cdot 0.21 = 0.2327$. Since $d_2\hat{\sigma} - 3d_3\hat{\sigma} = -0.3 < 0$, the 3σ LCL is 0. The 3σ UCL equals $d_2\hat{\sigma} + 3d_3\hat{\sigma} = 1.1284 \cdot 0.21 + 3 \cdot 0.8525 \cdot 0.21 = 0.774$.

The resulting control charts are shown in Figure 15.12.

The patterns are curious: The observations on the X chart are mostly above the center line, and the moving average values are mostly below the center line. The explanation is that the data are cyclic: KWH usage is low in the summer and high in the winter. These data only cover a 6-month period, from mid-October to early May, when electric usage is at or above the yearly average. In addition, the

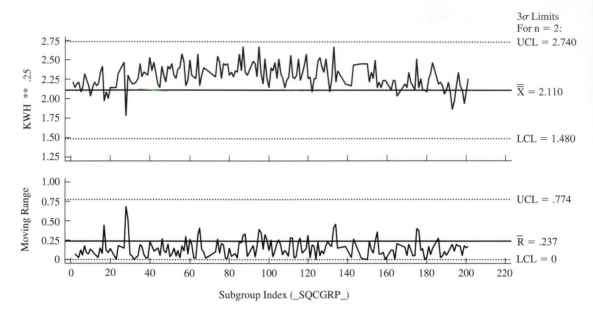

Figure 15.12 X and moving range chart for the fourth root of Professor P.'s KWH data.

center lines and control limits were computed from an entire year's data, which means the following:

- The mean and hence the center line on the X chart, is lower than it should be in the usage in the period charted.
- Since it includes both random day-to-day variation and seasonal swings in electric usage, the standard deviation, and hence $\hat{\sigma}$, will be larger than just the random variation in the data. This makes the control limits on both charts too wide.

As a result, these control charts are not very helpful tools in analyzing Professor P.'s electric use. For a more useful analysis, Professor P. should account for the seasonal pattern in the data in some way.   ✦

Average Run Length

One measure of the sensitivity of a control chart is the average run length (ARL). The ARL is basically just the average number of points that must be plotted before the process is determined to be out of control. For example, suppose we are constructing an $\bar{X}$ chart for an in-control process, and that we will determine the process to be out of control if one of the sample means goes outside the 3σ limits. Then the probability any one sample mean is outside the limits is 0.0027, so the average number of sample means that have to be plotted before one goes outside the limits is $1/0.0027 = 370$. This is the ARL of this control chart. In general, if the probability any one of the plotted points goes out of control is p, the ARL of this control chart is $1/p$.

When the process is in control, any out-of-control signal is a false alarm. In this case, we want the ARL to be large so that there are few false alarms. For the $\bar{X}$ chart with 3σ limits, there will be a false alarm on average once every 370 samples.

When the process is out of control, the ARL is the average number of samples required to detect the special cause(s). Therefore, we want the ARL to be small. Consider the $\bar{X}$ chart with 3σ limits, and assume that when the process is in control the data values follow an $N(\mu, \sigma^2)$ distribution. Assume also that we know the process mean and standard deviation, μ and σ, when the process is in control, so that the control limits are $\mu \pm 3\sigma/\sqrt{n}$. Now suppose there is a mean shift in the process so that the true mean is $\mu + \mu_0$ instead of μ. How long will it take, on average, to detect this shift?

To find out, we must first compute the probability, p, of any one sample mean falling outside the 3σ limits. Consider sample mean $\bar{X}_t$. Because of the mean shift, $\bar{X}_t$ has an $N(\mu + \mu_0, \sigma^2/n)$ distribution. Therefore, the probability that $\bar{X}_t$ falls above the UCL, $\mu + 3\sigma/\sqrt{n}$, is

$$P(\bar{X}_t > \mu + 3\sigma/\sqrt{n}) = P\left(\frac{\bar{X}_t - (\mu + \mu_0)}{\sigma/\sqrt{n}} > \frac{\mu + 3\sigma/\sqrt{n} - (\mu + \mu_0)}{\sigma/\sqrt{n}} \right)$$

$$= P\left(Z > 3 - \sqrt{n}\,\frac{\mu_0}{\sigma} \right)$$

where Z has an $N(0, 1)$ distribution. Similarly, the probability that $\bar{X}_t$ falls below the LCL can be shown to equal $P(Z < -3 - \sqrt{n}(\mu_0/\sigma))$. The probability p of any one sample mean falling outside the 3σ limits is then

$$p = P\left(Z > 3 - \sqrt{n}\,\frac{\mu_0}{\sigma} \right) + P\left(Z < -3 - \sqrt{n}\,\frac{\mu_0}{\sigma} \right)$$

and the ARL is $1/p$. Thus, we see that the ARL depends on the sample size, n, and the number of standard deviations the process mean shifted, μ_0/σ, and that it can be computed from a table of standard normal probabilities.

Table 15.3 gives the ARLs for mean shifts μ_0 for which $\mu_0/\sigma = 0.0, 0.1, \ldots,$ 0.9, 1.0, and for three different sample sizes: $n = 2, 5,$ and 10. For example, the ARL for sample size 5 and $\mu_0/\sigma = 0.5$ is 33.4, which means that on average, it takes 33.4 samples of size 5 to detect a mean shift of one-half a standard deviation. Generally, the table tells us that the ARL decreases with size of mean shift (large shifts are detected more quickly, on average), and with larger sample sizes (more data makes for quicker detection).

TABLE 15.3   ARL for $\bar{X}$ Chart with Different Mean Shifts and Sample Sizes

Mean shift	Sample size		
μ_0/σ	2	5	10
0.0	370.4	370.4	370.4
0.1	336.9	295.8	244.1
0.2	262.7	177.7	110.0
0.3	188.3	99.5	49.6
0.4	130.9	56.6	24.2
0.5	90.6	33.4	12.8
0.6	63.4	20.6	7.4
0.7	45.0	13.2	4.6
0.8	32.4	8.9	3.1
0.9	23.8	6.2	2.3
1.0	17.7	4.5	1.8

15.3

CONTROL CHARTS FOR ATTRIBUTE DATA

Some quality characteristics are not measurements at all, but consist of counts of whether an item or process has a certain attribute. Whether an injection-molded part ejects from the mold or not (count $= 0$ or 1), or the number of blemishes on a newly painted car door (count $= 0, 1, 2, \ldots$) are examples of this kind of data. Sometimes, because of convenience or cost, measurement data are reduced to counts. For instance, rather than record a particular part measurement, quality personnel may find it easier to keep track only of whether the part is within specification.

Data of this type are called **attribute data.** The attributes we will be interested in concern whether an item or process result meets specification or not. In considering these attributes, we distinguish between **defect** and **defective.**

DEFINITION

- A **defect** is a nonconformity that causes an item to fail to meet specification requirements.
- A **defective** is an item that has one or more defects.

For instance, a car door may be judged defective because of one or more defects such as a paint blemish, a dent, a faulty hinge, and so on.

The *p* Chart: A Control Chart for the Proportion Defective

The *p* chart is designed to monitor the proportion of defective items produced by a process. The data are assumed to comprise a number of samples, with sample *t* consisting of n_t items of which D_t are defective. It is assumed that the D_t are independent binomial random variables with parameters n_t and p. Here, p represents the overall process proportion of defectives. The p chart plots the sample proportions of defectives, $P_t = D_t/n_t$, versus t. In order to construct control limits for a p chart, recall that the standard deviation of P_t is $\sqrt{p(1-p)/n_t}$. This implies that the $k\sigma$ control limits for sample t are $p \pm k\sqrt{p(1-p)/n_t}$. Of course, we will not know p, in general, so we obtain an estimate of it, $\hat{p}$, either from past data collected when the process was in control, or from the present set of data. If using samples $1, 2, \ldots, m$ to estimate p, the usual estimator is the total proportion of defectives in the m samples,

$$\hat{p} = \frac{\displaystyle\sum_{t=1}^{m} D_t}{\displaystyle\sum_{t=1}^{m} n_t}$$

When using $\hat{p}$ to estimate p, we take the center line to be $\hat{p}$ and we compute the $k\sigma$ control limits for sample t as $\hat{p} \pm k\sqrt{\hat{p}(1-\hat{p})/n_t}$. If the LCL computed in this way is negative, we set it to 0, and if the UCL computed in this way exceeds 1, we set it to 1. Note that the $k\sigma$ control limits will all have the same width only if the sample sizes, n_t, are all equal.

Just as with charts for measurement data, we should always be careful to use a rational sampling strategy in selecting samples for p charts. Zones A, B, and C can be displayed on the chart, but only Tests 1 to 4 are recommended for p charts.

CENTER LINE AND CONTROL LIMITS FOR THE p CHART

Assume m samples are used to construct the center line and control limits. Assume sample t contains n_t items of which D_t are defective. Let $LCL(t)$ and $UCL(t)$ denote the lower and upper control limits for sample t.

- **Center Line:** $\hat{p} = \dfrac{\sum_{t=1}^{m} D_t}{\sum_{t=1}^{m} n_t}$.

- **$k\sigma$ LCL(t):** $\max\{\hat{p} - k\sqrt{\hat{p}(1-\hat{p})/n_t}, 0\}$.

- **$k\sigma$ UCL(t):** $\min\{\hat{p} + k\sqrt{\hat{p}(1-\hat{p})/n_t}, 1\}$.

EXAMPLE 15.6   THE p CHART

A production process produces dice for games and gamblers. The spots on each die face are first dimpled into the face and then the dimples are machine painted. One paint machine has been producing an excessive number of defective dice

TABLE 15.4   Numbers of Defective Dice in 32 Samples: Example 15.6

Sample	Size	Number of defectives	Sample	Size	Number of defectives
1	49	6	17	42	1
2	47	2	18	45	4
3	46	2	19	42	3
4	46	0	20	47	1
5	43	1	21	51	7
6	44	3	22	50	7
7	45	2	23	44	3
8	45	0	24	43	5
9	47	1	25	50	10
10	46	2	26	46	8
11	42	2	27	49	8
12	45	1	28	46	3
13	46	3	29	49	10
14	48	6	30	42	12
15	50	6	31	50	12
16	48	6	32	45	9

recently due to paint runs, misaligned spots, and so on. Table 15.4 displays data from samples of dice taken from the suspect machine's production at 15-minute intervals on a given day.

Figure 15.13 displays a p chart for these data along with 3σ control limits. In constructing this chart, production engineers used historical data taken when the machine was operating in control to estimate p as $\hat{p} = 0.05$.

There are several things to notice about this chart:

- First of all, the proportions of defectives show a definite upward trend, particularly after sample 20. The observed proportion goes out of control beyond the upper control limit at sample 25 and then again at sample 29. So the operation of the machine becomes worse as the day progresses.
- Second, the center line in this chart is the value $\hat{p} = 0.05$.
- The upper control limits are dependent on sample size, and are therefore not constant. In general, the lower control limit will also be dependent on sample size, but for this $\hat{p}$ and these sample sizes it equals 0 for all samples.
- Had the engineers used these 32 samples to estimate p, they would have obtained $\hat{p} = 0.10$, which would have overstated the process proportion of defectives. Thus, it is important to use estimates obtained when the process is in control. ✦

The c Chart: A Control Chart for the Number of Defects

The p chart plots proportions of defective items in samples taken from some process. As such, the attribute being counted is whether an item is defective. Sometimes, however,

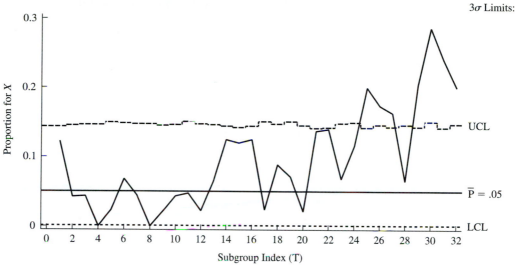

Figure 15.13   *p* chart for proportion of defective dice in 32 samples: Example 15.6.

we are not interested solely in whether an item is defective, but want to know how many defects the item has. For example, we may want to know how many serious imperfections there are on the finish of a new car, or how many poorly soldered connections there are on a circuit board. The counts may be of all occurrences of one type of defect, all occurrences of a subset of all possible defects, or of all occurrences of all possible defects.

Often, when monitoring the number of defects, the set of possible locations for defects on an item is very large and the probability of a defect occurring at any one location is very small. If these conditions hold, the number of defects on an item can be successfully modeled using the Poisson distribution model.

Recall from Chapter 4 that a random variable Y follows a Poisson distribution model with parameter λ, if its probability mass function is

$$p_Y(y) = \frac{\lambda^y}{y!}e^{-\lambda}, \qquad y = 0, 1, 2, \ldots$$

The mean and variance of this distribution model both equal λ.

Assume that each sample consists of one item and that the Poisson distribution model is a reasonable approximation for the distribution of the number of defects for each item. Let D_t be the number of defects for item t. A c chart plots D_t versus t. If λ is known, the center line is λ, the mean of the Poisson distribution, and $k\sigma$ limits are $\lambda \pm k\sqrt{\lambda}$. If λ is unknown, we need to compute an estimate, $\hat{\lambda}$, either from previous or present data. In either case, we may take $\hat{\lambda}$ to be the mean number of defects of a set of

m items produced when the process is known to be in control:

$$\hat{\lambda} = \frac{1}{m} \sum_{t=1}^{m} D_t$$

We then take the center line to be $\hat{\lambda}$ and $k\sigma$ limits are $\hat{\lambda} \pm k\sqrt{\hat{\lambda}}$. If $\hat{\lambda} - k\sqrt{\hat{\lambda}} < 0$, we set the LCL $= 0$.

Since we will consider a c chart only for one item per sample, issues of rational sampling do not occur. As with the p chart, we may display Zones A, B, and C on the chart, and identify out-of-control points using Tests 1 to 4.

CENTER LINE AND CONTROL LIMITS FOR THE c CHART

Assume m items are used to construct the center line and control limits. Assume item t has D_t defects. Let $LCL(t)$ and $UCL(t)$ denote the lower and upper control limits for sample t.

- **Center Line:** $\hat{\lambda} = (1/m) \sum_{t=1}^{m} D_t$.

- **$k\sigma$ LCL(t):** $\max\left\{\hat{\lambda} - k\sqrt{\hat{\lambda}}, 0\right\}$.

- **$k\sigma$ UCL(t):** $\hat{\lambda} + k\sqrt{\hat{\lambda}}$.

EXAMPLE 15.7   THE c CHART

In order to monitor the accuracy of satellite telemetry data, a 10,000-bit signal of known composition is broadcast in the telemetry stream every 5 minutes. An error rate of 0.01% is normal for this type of signal. Data for the last 4 hours are shown in Table 15.5.

Figure 15.14 displays a c chart of these data. Control limits are computed using the historical information that on average, $\hat{\lambda} = 1$ bit (0.01% of the 10,000 bits), will be in error. As can be seen, the process is in control relative to the 3σ limits.   ✦

We have presented the sampling scheme for the c chart as comprising one item per sample. In applications, however, we may take samples of more than one item. Provided the sample sizes are equal, we can then use a c chart to monitor the number of defects per sample. However, because it generalizes to unequal sample sizes, we will introduce another type of chart, the u chart, to handle the case of multiple items per sample.

The u Chart: A Control Chart for the Number of Defects per Item

Suppose, as with the c chart, we are interested in monitoring the number of defects in items. Suppose also that instead of taking one item per sample, as we do for the c chart,

TABLE 15.5   Numbers of Errors in 48 10,000-Bit Broadcast Test Signals

Sample	Number of errors	Sample	Number of errors	Sample	Number of errors	Sample	Number of errors
1	1	13	1	25	1	37	1
2	2	14	0	26	0	38	0
3	0	15	0	27	0	39	0
4	1	16	0	28	0	40	0
5	0	17	0	29	0	41	1
6	1	18	1	30	0	42	1
7	1	19	1	31	0	43	1
8	0	20	1	32	0	44	1
9	0	21	3	33	0	45	0
10	0	22	1	34	1	46	1
11	1	23	1	35	1	47	1
12	2	24	1	36	0	48	0

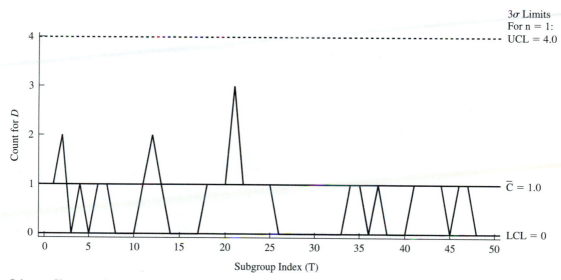

Subgroup Sizes: n = 1

Figure 15.14 c chart for the number of errors in telemetry test signals: Example 15.7.

sample t consists of n_t items. As indicated in the previous section, if the sample sizes n_t are equal, we can construct a c chart for the number of defects per sample. If the n_t are unequal, this approach will not work, since the mean numbers of defects in sample t will be a function of n_t. The u chart accounts for this difficulty by plotting the number of defects per unit for each sample.

Let T_t denote the total number of defects in all n_t items in sample t, and let $U_t = T_t/n_t$ denote the number of defects per item in sample t. The u chart plots U_t versus t. We again assume that for a given item, the number of defects follows a Poisson distribution with mean λ. Then T_t has a Poisson distribution with mean λn_t. Therefore, the mean of U_t is λ, and its variance is λ/n_t. The center line of the u chart is an estimate $\hat{\lambda}$ of λ, obtained from previous or present data. Typically, we take $\hat{\lambda}$ to be the mean number of defects per item in a set of m in-control data from the process:

$$\hat{\lambda} = \frac{\sum_{t=1}^{m} T_t}{\sum_{t=1}^{m} n_t}$$

However it is computed, we take the center line to be $\hat{\lambda}$, the $k\sigma$ upper control limit to be $\hat{\lambda} + k\sqrt{\hat{\lambda}/n_t}$, and the $k\sigma$ lower control limit to be the maximum of 0 and $\hat{\lambda} - k\sqrt{\hat{\lambda}/n_t}$.

As with the p and c charts, we may display Zones A, B, and C on the chart, and identify out-of-control points using Tests 1 to 4.

CENTER LINE AND CONTROL LIMITS FOR THE u CHART

Assume m items are used to construct the center line and control limits. Assume sample t has n_t items having a total of T_t defects. Let $LCL(t)$ and $UCL(t)$ denote the lower and upper control limits for sample t.

- **Center Line:** $\hat{\lambda} = \frac{\sum_{t=1}^{m} T_t}{\sum_{t=1}^{m} n_t}$.

- $k\sigma$ **LCL(t):** $\max\left\{\hat{\lambda} - k\sqrt{\hat{\lambda}/n_t}, 0\right\}$.

- $k\sigma$ **UCL(t):** $\hat{\lambda} + k\sqrt{\hat{\lambda}/n_t}$.

EXAMPLE 15.8   THE u CHART

A computer manufacturer uses a wave solder process to produce integrated-circuit boards. To gage quality, circuit boards are sampled from production at regular intervals with different numbers of boards selected on different occasions. Recently, substantial changes have been made to the soldering process. Table 15.6 summarizes the last data collected from the process before the changes were instituted. Table 15.7 summarizes the first 20 samples taken after the changes were instituted. In order to get more information on the effect of process changes,

TABLE 15.6   Sample Sizes, Numbers of Solder Defects, Numbers of Solder Defects per Circuit Board and Control Limits for Data Prior to Process Changes: Example 15.8

Sample	Sample size	Defects	Defects per board	LCL	UCL	Sample	Sample size	Defects	Defects per board	LCL	UCL
1	11	0	0.0000	0.0000	0.1075	16	9	0	0.0000	0.0000	0.1176
2	9	0	0.0000	0.0000	0.1176	17	8	0	0.0000	0.0000	0.1240
3	15	0	0.0000	0.0000	0.0936	18	14	0	0.0000	0.0000	0.0965
4	15	0	0.0000	0.0000	0.0936	19	11	1	0.0909	0.0000	0.1075
5	12	0	0.0000	0.0000	0.1034	20	12	0	0.0000	0.0000	0.1034
6	11	0	0.0000	0.0000	0.1075	21	14	0	0.0000	0.0000	0.0965
7	14	0	0.0000	0.0000	0.0965	22	10	0	0.0000	0.0000	0.1121
8	11	0	0.0000	0.0000	0.1075	23	9	0	0.0000	0.0000	0.1176
9	14	0	0.0000	0.0000	0.0965	24	14	0	0.0000	0.0000	0.0965
10	8	0	0.0000	0.0000	0.1240	25	10	0	0.0000	0.0000	0.1121
11	12	1	0.0833	0.0000	0.1034	26	14	0	0.0000	0.0000	0.0965
12	13	0	0.0000	0.0000	0.0997	27	13	1	0.0769	0.0000	0.0997
13	11	0	0.0000	0.0000	0.1075	28	10	0	0.0000	0.0000	0.1121
14	15	1	0.0667	0.0000	0.0936	29	13	0	0.0000	0.0000	0.0997
15	12	0	0.0000	0.0000	0.1034	30	10	0	0.0000	0.0000	0.1121

TABLE 15.7   Sample Sizes, Numbers of Solder Defects, Numbers of Solder Defects per Circuit Board and Control Limits for Data after Process Changes: Example 15.8

Sample	Sample size	Defects	Defects per board	LCL	UCL
31	30	0	0.0000	0.0000	0.0695
32	33	2	0.0606	0.0000	0.0668
33	30	1	0.0333	0.0000	0.0695
34	33	3	0.0909	0.0000	0.0668
35	32	0	0.0000	0.0000	0.0677
36	29	0	0.0000	0.0000	0.0705
37	27	2	0.0741	0.0000	0.0727
38	34	5	0.1471	0.0000	0.0660
39	32	3	0.0938	0.0000	0.0677
40	30	0	0.0000	0.0000	0.0695
41	32	2	0.0625	0.0000	0.0677
42	26	1	0.0385	0.0000	0.0738
43	26	0	0.0000	0.0000	0.0738
44	35	3	0.0857	0.0000	0.0652
45	26	2	0.0769	0.0000	0.0738
46	35	3	0.0857	0.0000	0.0652
47	32	1	0.0313	0.0000	0.0677
48	28	1	0.0357	0.0000	0.0716
49	33	0	0.0000	0.0000	0.0668
50	27	2	0.0741	0.0000	0.0727

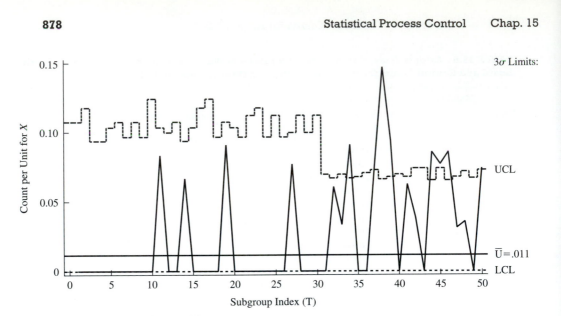

Figure 15.15 *u* chart for the number of solder defects per circuit board: Example 15.8.

these 20 samples were larger than the first 30, taken when the process was known to be in control.

Figure 15.15 is a *u* chart of all 50 samples. The center line is computed from the first 30 samples, in which there were a total of 4 solder defects in 354 circuit boards sampled, giving an estimate $\hat{\lambda} = 0.0113$ defects per circuit board. The control limits shown are 3σ limits computed using this estimate of λ. Among the things to notice about this chart are the following:

- The process is in control relative to the 3σ control limits prior to the changes at $t = 31$.
- The process goes out of control above the UCL soon after the process is changed, and goes out of control in this manner several times thereafter.
- The LCL is 0 for the entire chart. The UCL varies with sample size. The generally lower UCL for $t > 30$ indicates the generally larger sample sizes taken after the process was changed.

In fact, among the 610 circuit boards sampled after $t = 30$, there were 31 defects: a 0.0508 defect/board rate.

Based on these out-of-control signals after $t = 30$, the changes to the process have caused it to go out of control, and the causes of the excessive defects should be sought. ✦

15.4

PROCESS CAPABILITY

Process control tracks process output in terms of the natural variability of that output. The output from many processes is judged by another standard as well: Whether that output conforms to engineering specifications.

The ability of a process to produce output conforming to engineering specifications is called **process capability.** Two natural questions to ask about process capability are

- What is the relation between process control (perhaps expressed as control limits) and process capability?
- How do we measure process capability?

The Relation between Capability and Control

There are two basic differences between process control and process capability:

- Process control assesses the performance of the process relative to its natural pattern of variation, without consideration of engineering specifications. Process capability assesses the extent to which the product achieves engineering specifications.
- Process control is used to find special cause variation in the process, and process capability is used to compare process output to specifications.

The goals and methods of control and capability of a process are quite different and should always be kept separate. For this reason, specification limits should never be displayed on control charts.[6]

Assessing Process Capability

Unless the process is in control, statistical methods will not perform well in trying to assess capability. Therefore, any good strategy for assessing process capability begins with a check that the process is in control. Let's assume that we have generated $\bar{X}$ and S charts and that we conclude the process is in control. The next step is to do a histogram and normal plot of the individual measurements. Assuming normality is indicated, we will use an $N(\bar{\bar{X}}, \hat{\sigma}^2)$ distribution model for the measurements. This model tells us about the capability of the process through the two parameter estimators $\bar{\bar{X}}$ and $\hat{\sigma}^2$. The mean, $\bar{\bar{X}}$, tells where the process is centered. It should be compared with the desired central

---

[6]If the control charts are of subgrouped data, it doesn't even make sense to combine in the same chart measures based on grouped data (e.g., $\bar{X}$ or S) with limits, such as specification limits, for individual data points.

specification, if one exists, or to the midpoint between the LSL and the USL otherwise, to see whether the process is "on target." Causes and remedies should be sought for an "off-target" process. The estimated variance, $\hat{\sigma}^2$, characterizes the spread of the measurements.

Based on this model, the proportion of population measurements above the upper specification limit (USL) is the area under the $N(\bar{\bar{X}}, \hat{\sigma}^2)$ curve above the USL. By standardizing, this is the area under the standard normal curve above $(\text{USL} - \bar{\bar{X}})/\hat{\sigma}$. Similarly, the proportion of population measurements below the lower specification limit (LSL) is the area under the standard normal curve below $(\text{LSL} - \bar{\bar{X}})/\hat{\sigma}$. These proportions are a measure of how capable the process is.

EXAMPLE 15.1   CONTINUED

Recall that the aluminum sheet process was judged to be in control. Recall also that the specification limits for sheet thickness are LSL = 0.149 and USL = 0.151, with a target value of 0.150 mm. The estimated parameters are $\bar{\bar{x}} = 0.15005$ and $\hat{\sigma} = 0.00033$. We will now assess the capability of this process.

We first note that the difference between $\bar{\bar{x}}$ and the nominal center is 0.00005. Is this a large difference? To see, reason as follows. We may estimate the standard deviation of $\bar{\bar{x}}$ to be $\hat{\sigma}/\sqrt{mn}$, which is $0.00033/\sqrt{150} = 2.69 \times 10^{-5}$. Thus, the difference between $\bar{\bar{x}}$ and the nominal center is $0.00005/2.69 \times 10^{-5} = 1.856$ standard deviations. A proportion 0.0635 of the area under the normal curve lies outside ± 1.856 standard deviations, so in terms of the variability of the data, $\bar{\bar{x}}$ is moderately far from the nominal center 0.150. Certainly, we should strive to bring $\bar{\bar{x}}$ closer to the target value.

To estimate the proportion of population measurements falling outside the specification limits, we compute

$$(\text{USL} - \bar{\bar{x}})/\hat{\sigma} = (0.15100 - 0.15005)/0.00033 = 2.88$$

and

$$(\text{LSL} - \bar{\bar{x}})/\hat{\sigma} = (0.14900 - 0.15005)/0.00033 = -3.18$$

So the proportion of aluminum sheets with thicknesses above the USL can be estimated as the proportion of an $N(0, 1)$ population above 2.88, which is 0.00199. The proportion below the LSL can be estimated as the proportion of an $N(0, 1)$ population below -3.18, which is 0.00074. These are small numbers, but whether sufficiently small depends on what is technologically feasible for the process in question, and on what the competition is doing. To give some perspective, however, a number of high-technology electronics firms have set, and largely achieved, a goal of 6σ capability, by which they mean that the specification limits should lie at or beyond $\mu \pm 6\sigma$. With 6σ capability, the proportion of process output outside specification is 1.97×10^{-9}, a very small proportion, indeed!   ◆

Process Capability Indices

A variety of single number indices of process capability are in common use. Like other familiar single-number indices (the Dow Jones Industrial Index comes to mind), these capability indices provide a general measure of process capability, but used alone, they too often oversimplify process capability assessment. Any process capability assessment should use such indices only as part of a careful analysis of process variability. In this section, we will describe three widely used process capability indices.

C_p

C_p is a process capability ratio, defined as the ratio of the range of specification to the range of the 3σ spread of the quality characteristic:

$$C_p = \frac{\text{USL} - \text{LSL}}{6\sigma}$$

If the distribution of the quality characteristic, X, is normal with mean midway between the specification limits, then the probability of a measurement exceeding the USL is

$$P(X > \text{USL}) = P\left(\frac{X - (\text{USL} + \text{LSL})/2}{\sigma} > \frac{\text{USL} - (\text{USL} + \text{LSL})/2}{\sigma} \right)$$

$$= P\left(Z > \frac{\text{USL} - \text{LSL}}{2\sigma} \right)$$

$$= P(Z > 3C_p)$$

where $Z \sim N(0, 1)$. Similarly, $P(X < \text{LSL}) = P(Z < -3C_p)$. Thus, C_p measures the number of 3σ limits to which the specification limits correspond.

C_{pk}

One problem with C_p is that it does not involve the process center. Therefore, it only makes sense as a capability measure if the process is centered midway between the specification limits. C_{pk} is a process capability ratio that takes into account the process center, μ, as well as its spread. It is defined as

$$C_{pk} = \min\left\{ \frac{\text{USL} - \mu}{3\sigma}, \frac{\mu - \text{LSL}}{3\sigma} \right\}$$

If the process is centered midway between the specification limits, $C_{pk} = C_p$; otherwise, $C_{pk} < C_p$. A process with a normally distributed quality characteristic will have the greatest capability if it is centered midway between the specification limits. The ratio of C_{pk} to C_p is a measure of how much the off-centeredness of the process reduces the potential process capability.

C_{pm}

Although C_{pk} is supposed to measure how badly the off-centering of the process is degrading capability, it can do so only in comparison with C_p. By itself, it cannot characterize the effect of being off-center. The measure C_{pm} is designed to better indicate the effect of off-centering. Suppose that T is a target value for the quality characteristic. Then the expected squared deviation of the quality characteristic from the target is

$$E(X-T)^2 = E(X-\mu)^2 + (\mu-T)^2$$
$$= \sigma^2 + b^2$$

where $b = \mu - T$ is the bias, or the mean amount the quality characteristic is off target. C_{pm} is defined as

$$C_{pm} = \frac{\text{USL} - \text{LSL}}{6\sqrt{\sigma^2 + b^2}}$$

Notice that

$$C_{pm} = \frac{C_p}{\sqrt{1 + (b/\sigma)^2}}$$

so C_{pm} is C_p reduced by a divisor that depends on the size, in standard deviations, of the bias. Notice also that if there is no bias, $C_{pm} = C_p$. C_{pm} can give bounds on the bias, b. For example, it is easy to see that

$$C_{pm} < \frac{\text{USL} - \text{LSL}}{6|b|}$$

which implies that

$$|b| < \frac{\text{USL} - \text{LSL}}{6 C_{pm}}$$

Using Capability Indices

Of course, we usually will not know the values of the population parameters needed to compute these capability indices, so we must estimate them from the data. Thus, for example, μ can be estimated by the sample mean, and σ can be estimated by any of the estimators, $\hat{\sigma}$, we have discussed in this chapter. When estimating C_{pm}, b can be estimated by $\bar{\bar{x}} - T$. Denote the estimated capability indices $\hat{C}_p$, $\hat{C}_{pk}$, and $\hat{C}_{pm}$. It is well to remember that these estimators are random and have their own sampling distributions, which leads to the possibility of statistical inference for them. More advanced references on statistical process control can supply details.[7]

These indices, and the capability analysis we conducted previously on the aluminum sheet process, rely on normality, and any serious departure of the distribution

[7]For example, D. C. Montgomery, *Introduction to Statistical Quality Control*, 2nd ed., New York: Wiley, 1991.

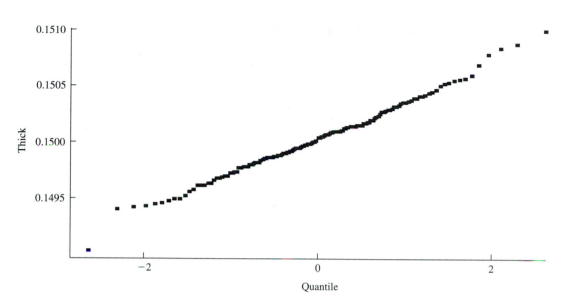

Figure 15.16   Normal quantile plot of aluminum sheet data, Example 15.1.

of the quality characteristic from normality can invalidate the results of the capability analysis. For this reason, any process capability analysis should include a check on distributional assumptions. If nonnormality were indicated, we could attempt to deal with it in one of several ways:

- Transform the data to normality and then conduct the capability analysis on the transformed data.
- Fit another, more appropriate, distribution to the data, and base the capability analysis on that distribution.
- Use some kind of procedure that is robust to nonnormality.

When using the capability indices we have discussed, only the first of these is an option.[8]

EXAMPLE 15.1   CONTINUED

We will compute the three capability indices for the aluminum process data. As a first step, we assess the normality of the data. Despite one aberrant observation in its lower tail, the normal quantile plot in Figure 15.16 shows the data to be reasonably normal. Since there are 150 observations in all, that one outlier should have little effect on the analysis.[9]

Recall that the LSL = 0.149 and USL = 0.151, with a target value of 0.150 mm. The estimated parameters are $\bar{\bar{x}} = 0.15005$ and $\hat{\sigma} = 0.00033$, which

---

[8]The article by R. N. Rodrigues, "Recent Developments in Process Capability Analysis," *Journal of Quality Technology,* 24(4), (1992): 176–187, discusses these issues in more depth.

[9]This may be easily checked by rerunning the analysis without the outlier. We have done so, and there is hardly any difference in the results.

we take to estimate μ and σ. Then

$$\hat{C}_p = \frac{0.151 - 0.149}{6(0.00033)}$$

$$= 1.010$$

$$\hat{C}_{pk} = \min\left\{\frac{0.151 - 0.15005}{3(0.00033)}, \frac{0.15005 - 0.149}{3(0.00033)}\right\}$$

$$= \min\{0.96, 1.06\}$$

$$= 0.96$$

$$\hat{C}_{pm} = \frac{0.151 - 0.149}{6\sqrt{(0.00033)^2 + (0.15005 - 0.150)^2}}$$

$$= 1.00$$

All of these indices are quite close and show the process to be about as capable as the 3σ limits, which is basically the result we got previously. The process does not appear to be terribly off target, as $\hat{C}_p$ and $\hat{C}_{pk}$ are close. $\hat{C}_{pm}$ gives a simple bound on the bias as $|b| < 3.33 \times 10^{-4}$. ◆

D ISCUSSION QUESTIONS

1. Describe the new quality philosophy.
2. What is the loss-function approach to quality improvement?
3. List Taguchi's sources of variation and where each applies.
4. Distinguish between special and common causes.
5. What is a control chart? Why and where is it used? List some types of control charts.
6. Describe $\bar{X}$, S, and R charts, their uses and interpretations.
7. What process assumptions should be checked when using control charts?
8. Explain what rational sampling is and why it is used. Comment on choice of sample size, methods for selecting subgroups, and frequency of sampling when creating rational subgroups.
9. What are stratification and mixing? How and why do they occur? What are their symptoms? What action should be taken when they are detected?
10. Describe X and moving range charts, their uses, and interpretations.
11. Describe p, c, and u charts, their uses, and interpretations.
12. Define process capability. What is its relation to process control? Discuss how it can be assessed.
13. Describe the capability measures C_p, C_{pk}, and C_{pm}, and what each measures.

E XERCISES

15.1. Suppose a process is stationary and that the data follow an $N(\mu, \sigma^2)$ distribution model. An X chart with 3σ limits is to be plotted. Suppose there are a total of n observations. Obtain an approximate formula for the probability that no observations go outside the control limits, $\mu \pm 3\sigma$. (*Hint:* Call going outside the limits a "success" and staying in them a "failure.")

15.2. Explain how
  (a) a process can be in control but not capable.
  (b) a process can be out of control but still capable.

15.3. Which of the following do you think are special causes? Common causes? Justify your answers.
  (a) Material contamination.
  (b) Poor workstation design.
  (c) Inappropriate methods.
  (d) A broken conveyor belt.

15.4. A manufacturer of breakfast cereals produces a "20-ounce" package of Wheat Whoopies. Naturally, the manufacturer wants to fill the package with exactly 20 ounces of product, but this seldom happens. If the package is filled with more than 20 ounces, the manufacturer is giving Wheat Whoopies away, and therefore has a loss. If the package is filled with less than 20 ounces, the manufacturer saves on product, but faces the possibility of having to replace the package for a consumer. Assume the following:
  (a) Wheat Whoopies cost $0.02 per ounce to produce, so the loss due to overfilling the package is $0.02 per ounce.
  (b) There is no loss to the manufacturer when exactly 20 ounces is put in a package.
  (c) For weight between 0 and 20, the loss due to replacement of the package is $(0.60 − 0.02 × weight). The $0.60 is the average replacement cost of the package.
  Graph the loss to the company as a function of the number of ounces put in a package.

15.5. Generate an $\bar{X}$ and R chart for the dressing stone data. Interpret your results. How do they compare with those of the $\bar{X}$ and S charts?

15.6. Control charts are routinely kept along the Wheat Whoopies production line. Every 2 minutes, five 20-ounce boxes are randomly sampled from the line and weighed. Figure 15.17 shows $\bar{X}$ and S charts for 1 hour's production. Control limits are computed from the previous hour's production, which was determined to be in control. As you can see, the $\bar{X}$ chart is determined to be out of control by Tests 2, 5, and 6. A process engineer argues that during this hour, the setting on the filling machine shifted, resulting in more Wheat Whoopies being put in each box. The line foreman disagrees, saying that the cause is undoubtedly due to poor machine maintenance. Whom do you agree with? Why?

15.7. The process engineer at the Wheat Whoopies plant was right: The setting on the filling machine had shifted. But now he has another argument on his hands. Currently, there are five filling machines producing the 20-ounce package of Wheat Whoopies, and a separate control chart of weight is kept on each machine. Management wants to economize by taking samples from a point farther down the production line after the five process streams converge. The process engineer thinks this is a bad idea. Do you agree? Why?

15.8. Lab technicians estimate the number of bacteria in a culture by counting as completely as possible the bacteria in several samples. It is difficult to get the number right. In one lab,

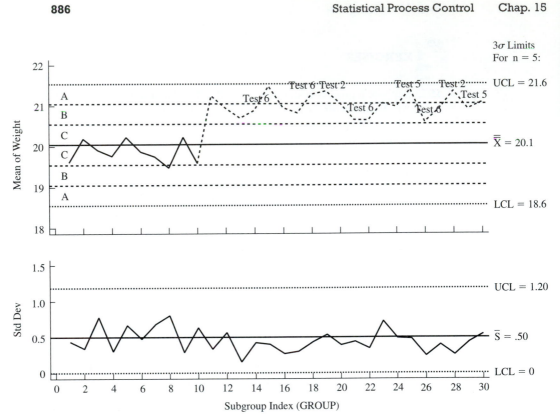

Figure 15.17 Control charts for Wheat Whoopies weights.

new technicians are paired with experienced technicians for a number of weeks before they are allowed to perform this task on their own. Figure 15.18 displays $\bar{X}$ and S charts for the differences in counts between one new technician and one experienced technician over a 6-week training period. Five cultures per day were randomly selected and the difference between the new technician's count and the experienced technician's count was recorded for each. In both charts, control limits are based on the data that are charted. Checks were done, and no evidence of nonnormality or autocorrelation was found.

(a) Does the S chart indicate that the process described by the data is in control? Why or why not?

(b) Interpret the S chart in terms of technician training.

(c) Should the $\bar{X}$ chart be interpreted? If so, interpret it. If not, tell why not.

15.9. The data set WASHER contains measurements of the outer diameter (OD) and thickness (THICK) of 20 groups of 5 washers each taken from a production line. Use control charts to assess the stationarity of the process that produced the washers. Also conduct a capability analysis, if appropriate, where the specification limits are 0.875 ± 0.005 in. for the OD and 0.085 ± 0.015 in. for the thickness.

15.10. A chemical process is being monitored to check that the concentration of a certain chemical is being maintained. The data set CHEMICAL contains 35 sets of 5 measurements each

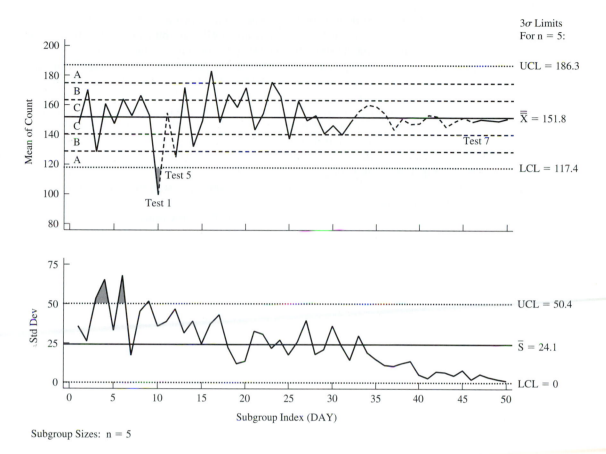

Figure 15.18   Control charts for differences in bacteria counts.

taken every 15 minutes over time from the process. The measurements are deviations from a target concentration. Is the process in control? If not, describe how it has gone out of control. If in control, analyze the capability of the process.

15.11. A paint manufacturer is evaluating the consistency of product. One important measure is the weight of solids in a five-gallon container of paint. In order to evaluate the product, containers of paint from each of the four production lines devoted to a particular paint were taken from the line every hour for testing. The data for 50 consecutive hours of production are found in the data set PAINT. Each group consists of the weight of solids in four containers of paint—one container of paint from each production line.

   (a) Is the process in control? Be sure to check necessary assumptions.

   (b) If it is not in control, describe how it has gone out of control. How might the sampling scheme be responsible for it being out of control?

   (c) If it is in control, analyze the capability of the process. Specification limits are 10.5 ± 0.5 pounds.

15.12. The diameter of a bolt produced by a machine is normally distributed with a mean of 0.82 cm and a standard deviation of 0.004 cm. Bolts are manufactured to meet the

specification that their diameters are between 0.818 and 0.822 cm.
   (a) What percent of the bolts manufactured by this machine would meet the specification?
   (b) What can you say about the quality of the manufacturing process?

15.13. Your semiconductor company has been losing market share to a rival manufacturer that claims "6-sigma" precision (i.e., the USL and LSL are 6σ from the product mean), which means that about 2 parts in a billion are defective. Your boss asks you to evaluate the capability of your company's production process with respect to a critical part dimension. The USL for the part is 42 microns and the LSL is 40 microns. One hundred samples of size 5 from your in-control process yields an overall mean of 41.5 microns and an average standard deviation of 0.125 micron. Evaluate the capability of your process. How does it compare with your competitor's?

15.14. In order to see how fast your reflexes are, you get a stopwatch and perform a series of trials. For each trial, you click on the start button of the stopwatch and then on the stop button as quickly as you can. A friend writes down the time. You repeat this five times in rapid succession, then rest for 20 seconds. This process is repeated 100 times. The sequence of times constitutes a measurement process.
   (a) Will this process be in control? If you think it will be in control, tell why. If you think it will not be in control, tell why not.
   (b) Under what conditions will the subgroups of size 5 constitute rational subgroups? Under what conditions will there be stratification?

15.15. A quality manager for a chemical company is looking at data on the concentration of a particular reagent produced by his division. Noting that the observed concentrations are all within required specifications, he declares the process to be in control. Is his conclusion justified? Why or why not?

15.16. Control charts are routinely kept along the production line that produces Korn Krunchies cereal. Every 2 minutes, five "32-ounce" boxes are randomly sampled from the line and weighed. Figure 15.19 shows $\bar{X}$ and S charts for 1 hour's production. Control limits are computed from the previous hour's production, which was determined to be in control. As you can see, the S chart is determined to be out of control. A process engineer argues that during this hour, the setting on the filling machine shifted, resulting in more Korn Krunchies being put in each box. The line foreman disagrees, saying that the cause is undoubtedly due to poor machine maintenance allowing parts of the scale to wear out. With whom do you agree? Why?

15.17. The line foreman at the Korn Krunchies plant was right: Worn scale parts were the special cause. Now that the process is in control, he asks the process engineer to assess its capability. The USL is 33.5 ounces and the LSL is 32 ounces. For a day's run, $\bar{x}$ is 32.5 ounces and $\bar{s}$ is 0.2 ounce. Estimate the proportion of all Korn Krunchies boxes with weights outside the specification limits, and interpret the results.

15.18. A frozen-food producer processes vegetables into plastic pouches, which are designed to be taken from the freezer and put directly into boiling water for cooking. At regular intervals, samples of the product are taken and the pouches are tested for integrity. The result of the test is either "pass" or "fail." Table 15.8 summarizes results for 30 samples taken sequentially. These data are also found in the data set VEGGIES. Construct an appropriate control chart for these data. Interpret the results.

15.19. An appliance manufacturer produces washing machines. Before being readied for shipment, the machines are inspected for defects in their surface finishes, among other things.

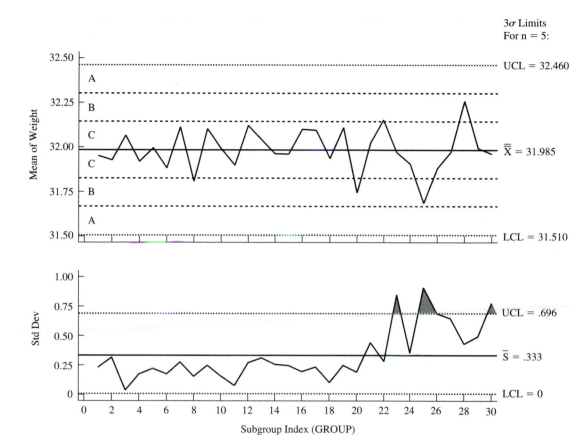

Figure 15.19   Control charts for Korn Krunchie weights.

TABLE 15.8   Sample Sizes and Number of Pouch Integrity Failures in 30 Samples of Frozen-Vegetable Pouches: Exercise 15.18

Sample	Sample size	Number of failures	Sample	Sample size	Number of failures	Sample	Sample size	Number of failures
1	17	0	11	18	0	21	13	1
2	19	1	12	14	1	22	17	3
3	18	1	13	17	0	23	16	3
4	18	1	14	18	0	24	16	1
5	14	0	15	14	1	25	11	0
6	13	0	16	17	0	26	18	4
7	15	1	17	14	1	27	20	2
8	20	0	18	18	1	28	11	2
9	15	0	19	16	0	29	13	0
10	19	0	20	14	0	30	18	1

TABLE 15.9   Number of Surface-Finish Defects in 30 Washing Machines: Exercise 15.19

Sample	Number of defects	Sample	Number of defects	Sample	Number of defects
1	0	11	0	21	0
2	0	12	1	22	0
3	0	13	1	23	1
4	0	14	0	24	3
5	0	15	0	25	0
6	0	16	1	26	3
7	0	17	2	27	1
8	0	18	0	28	1
9	0	19	1	29	0
10	0	20	0	30	0

TABLE 15.10   Sample Sizes, Size of Inspected Section, and Number of Imperfections of Cloth: Exercise 15.20

Sample	Section size (ft^2)	Imperfections	Sample	Section size (ft^2)	Imperfections
1	4.6	0	14	4.6	0
2	4.1	0	15	4.1	0
3	6.0	0	16	5.7	1
4	6.1	0	17	5.3	1
5	3.9	0	18	5.5	0
6	6.3	1	19	5.6	1
7	4.5	0	20	5.9	2
8	4.9	0	21	5.5	1
9	2.4	1	22	6.5	2
10	5.7	0	23	5.6	1
11	4.6	0	24	4.9	0
12	7.6	0	25	3.6	0
13	4.5	1	26	4.8	1

Table 15.9 summarizes the results of the surface-finish inspection for 30 washing machines of the same model, sampled in sequence. These data are also found in the data set WASH-MACH. Create an appropriate control chart for these data. What do you conclude?

15.20. A factory produces cloth for upholstery. Inspectors regularly inspect sections of cloth from the production line, noting the number of imperfections in the section they are inspecting. These sections vary in area, as the data for 26 successively sampled sections in Table 15.10 show. These data are also found in the data set CLOTH. Construct an appropriate control chart for these data, using the data to compute the control limits. Tell why you constructed the kind of chart you did. What does the control chart tell you about the process?

15.21. Ceramic insulators are baked in lots in a large oven each day. After the baking, three insulators are selected at random from a lot selected at random from all lots baked on a given day and tested for breaking strength (pounds per square inch, psi). The data set,

CERAMIC, contains the tensile strengths for insulators manufactured on the last 20 days.

(a) Construct control charts for the process mean and the process standard deviation.

(b) Is the process in control? Why?

(c) The insulators are judged acceptable if they exceed the LSL 10.5 psi. Analyze the capability of the process in producing acceptable insulators. Check any assumptions you make.

15.22. In our discussion of the ARL, it was claimed that the probability that $\bar{X}_t$ falls below the LCL can be shown to equal $P(Z < -3 - \sqrt{n}(\mu_0/\sigma))$. Show this to be the case.

15.23. Investigate the box strength data from Example 15.4. In particular, look at each of the process streams separately. Are these process streams in control? What is the source of the pattern observed in Figure 15.10?

MINIPROJECT

Purpose

The purpose of this miniproject is to give you experience in assessing the statistical control and capability of a measurement process.

Process

Student teams are to assess the statistical control and the capability of some measurement process of their own choosing. You are to make use of rational sampling in selecting subgroups, and you are to collect at least 20 subgroups of data. Please submit a short (one-page) proposal outlining your project for your instructor's approval before proceeding with the collection of data. Your miniproject report should have the following:

- Explain the problem you are trying to solve.
- Detail how the data were collected and the reasons for the data collection scheme chosen.
- Ascertain whether the process is in control.
- Conduct a process capability study, if appropriate, or tell why a process capability study is not appropriate.
- Draw conclusions and make recommendations concerning the process.

LAB 15.1: The Deming Funnel Experiment

Introduction

Think you know how to control a process? Well, step right up. We have here a simple process: Try to hit the center of a target with a ball bearing dropped through a funnel. All you have to do is to hit the center every time.

Objectives

To teach you what happens when trying to control a process using various control schemes. To teach you what "in control" means.

Lab Materials

This lab will be conducted in groups. Each group will need:

1. One funnel
2. One funnel stand
3. One ball bearing
4. Three or four targets
5. One sheet of carbon paper
6. One sheet of cardboard
7. Several pieces of tape
8. One measuring device (tape or ruler)

Experimental Procedure

1. **Set Up the Apparatus:**

   (a) Tape one target to the center of the cardboard.
   (b) Place the funnel holder on the cardboard and set the funnel in the funnel holder 12 inches above the cardboard.
   (c) Position the funnel holder where you think it should be in order for the ball bearing to land on the center of the target. Place the carbon paper over the target so that the ball bearing will mark the target when it lands.

2. **Set Up the Strategies.** The quantity to be measured is the distance the ball bearing lands from the target center.

   (a) **The Lazy Operator.** In this strategy, the process is left alone: no adjustment is made after the various drops.
   (b) **The Conscientious Operator.** In this strategy, the apparatus is adjusted after every drop to compensate for the observed deviation from the center of the target. If the point of impact is at point **x** (the center of the target being the origin), move the apparatus −**x** units from its present position before making the next drop. This corresponds to an operator trying to hit the center each time.
   (c) **The Uniform Operator.** In this strategy, before making a drop, the apparatus is moved to where you think it should be in order for the ball bearing to land where the last one landed. This corresponds to an operator trying to get consistent results.

3. **Predict.** You may discuss with your lab group how each strategy will perform and in particular which strategy will perform best. Two performance measures to consider are accuracy and precision. Write down your predictions before doing the experiment.

4. **Conduct the Experiment.** For each of the three strategies, you are to drop the ball bearing 20 times and record the distance it lands from the center of the target. Use a fresh target and begin the process anew for each strategy. When you have finished collecting the data for all three strategies, you may, if you wish, collect a set of data for a strategy of your own devising.

5. **Analyze.** Now comes the fun part. Analyze what happened. Draw bar graphs, normal plots, and boxplots. Plot the data on control charts. How do the results match your predictions? Can you come up with an explanation for what is happening where the results don't match your predictions?

A

Tables

BINOMIAL PROBABILITIES

Tabled is the value

$$P(Y \le y) = \sum_{x=0}^{y} \binom{n}{x} p^x (1 - p)^{n-x}$$

where $Y \sim b(n, p)$.

- To obtain the value of $P(Y \le y)$ when $p > 0.50$, use the formula

$$P(Y \le y) = 1 - P(W \le n - y - 1)$$

where $W \sim b(n, 1 - p)$.
- To obtain the value of the probability mass function, $p_Y(y)$, use the formula

$$
\begin{aligned}
p_Y(y) &= P(Y \le 0), & y &= 0 \\
&= P(Y \le y) - P(Y \le y - 1), & y &> 0
\end{aligned}
$$

894

n	y	0.01	0.02	0.03	0.04	0.05	0.06	0.07	0.08	0.09	0.10	0.15	0.20	0.25	0.30	0.35	0.40	0.45	0.50
																		p above columns	
2	0	0.9801	0.9604	0.9409	0.9216	0.9025	0.8836	0.8649	0.8464	0.8281	0.8100	0.7225	0.6400	0.5625	0.4900	0.4225	0.3600	0.3025	0.2500
	1	0.9999	0.9996	0.9991	0.9984	0.9975	0.9964	0.9951	0.9936	0.9919	0.9900	0.9775	0.9600	0.9375	0.9100	0.8775	0.8400	0.7975	0.7500
	2	1.0000	1.0000	1.0000	1.0000	1.0000	1.0000	1.0000	1.0000	1.0000	1.0000	1.0000	1.0000	1.0000	1.0000	1.0000	1.0000	1.0000	1.0000
3	0	0.9703	0.9412	0.9127	0.8847	0.8574	0.8306	0.8044	0.7787	0.7536	0.7290	0.6141	0.5120	0.4219	0.3430	0.2746	0.2160	0.1664	0.1250
	1	0.9997	0.9988	0.9974	0.9953	0.9928	0.9896	0.9860	0.9818	0.9772	0.9720	0.9393	0.8960	0.8438	0.7840	0.7183	0.6480	0.5747	0.5000
	2	1.0000	1.0000	1.0000	0.9999	0.9999	0.9998	0.9997	0.9995	0.9993	0.9990	0.9966	0.9920	0.9844	0.9730	0.9571	0.9360	0.9089	0.8750
	3	1.0000	1.0000	1.0000	1.0000	1.0000	1.0000	1.0000	1.0000	1.0000	1.0000	1.0000	1.0000	1.0000	1.0000	1.0000	1.0000	1.0000	1.0000
4	0	0.9606	0.9224	0.8853	0.8493	0.8145	0.7807	0.7481	0.7164	0.6857	0.6561	0.5220	0.4096	0.3164	0.2401	0.1785	0.1296	0.0915	0.0625
	1	0.9994	0.9977	0.9948	0.9909	0.9860	0.9801	0.9733	0.9656	0.9570	0.9477	0.8905	0.8192	0.7383	0.6517	0.5630	0.4752	0.3910	0.3125
	2	1.0000	1.0000	0.9999	0.9998	0.9995	0.9992	0.9987	0.9981	0.9973	0.9963	0.9880	0.9728	0.9492	0.9163	0.8735	0.8208	0.7585	0.6875
	3	1.0000	1.0000	1.0000	1.0000	1.0000	1.0000	1.0000	1.0000	0.9999	0.9999	0.9995	0.9984	0.9961	0.9919	0.9850	0.9744	0.9590	0.9375
	4	1.0000	1.0000	1.0000	1.0000	1.0000	1.0000	1.0000	1.0000	1.0000	1.0000	1.0000	1.0000	1.0000	1.0000	1.0000	1.0000	1.0000	1.0000
5	0	0.9510	0.9039	0.8587	0.8154	0.7738	0.7339	0.6957	0.6591	0.6240	0.5905	0.4437	0.3277	0.2373	0.1681	0.1160	0.0778	0.0503	0.0313
	1	0.9990	0.9962	0.9915	0.9852	0.9774	0.9681	0.9575	0.9456	0.9326	0.9185	0.8352	0.7373	0.6328	0.5282	0.4284	0.3370	0.2562	0.1875
	2	1.0000	0.9999	0.9997	0.9994	0.9988	0.9980	0.9969	0.9955	0.9937	0.9914	0.9734	0.9421	0.8965	0.8369	0.7648	0.6826	0.5931	0.5000
	3	1.0000	1.0000	1.0000	1.0000	1.0000	0.9999	0.9999	0.9998	0.9997	0.9995	0.9978	0.9933	0.9844	0.9692	0.9460	0.9130	0.8688	0.8125
	4	1.0000	1.0000	1.0000	1.0000	1.0000	1.0000	1.0000	1.0000	1.0000	1.0000	0.9999	0.9997	0.9990	0.9976	0.9947	0.9898	0.9815	0.9688
	5	1.0000	1.0000	1.0000	1.0000	1.0000	1.0000	1.0000	1.0000	1.0000	1.0000	1.0000	1.0000	1.0000	1.0000	1.0000	1.0000	1.0000	1.0000
6	0	0.9415	0.8858	0.8330	0.7828	0.7351	0.6899	0.6470	0.6064	0.5679	0.5314	0.3771	0.2621	0.1780	0.1176	0.0754	0.0467	0.0277	0.0156
	1	0.9985	0.9943	0.9875	0.9784	0.9672	0.9541	0.9392	0.9227	0.9048	0.8857	0.7765	0.6554	0.5339	0.4202	0.3191	0.2333	0.1636	0.1094
	2	1.0000	0.9998	0.9995	0.9988	0.9978	0.9962	0.9942	0.9915	0.9882	0.9842	0.9527	0.9011	0.8306	0.7443	0.6471	0.5443	0.4415	0.3438
	3	1.0000	1.0000	1.0000	1.0000	0.9999	0.9998	0.9997	0.9995	0.9992	0.9987	0.9941	0.9830	0.9624	0.9295	0.8826	0.8208	0.7447	0.6562
	4	1.0000	1.0000	1.0000	1.0000	1.0000	1.0000	1.0000	1.0000	1.0000	1.0000	0.9996	0.9984	0.9954	0.9891	0.9777	0.9590	0.9308	0.8906
	5	1.0000	1.0000	1.0000	1.0000	1.0000	1.0000	1.0000	1.0000	1.0000	1.0000	1.0000	0.9999	0.9998	0.9993	0.9982	0.9959	0.9917	0.9844
	6	1.0000	1.0000	1.0000	1.0000	1.0000	1.0000	1.0000	1.0000	1.0000	1.0000	1.0000	1.0000	1.0000	1.0000	1.0000	1.0000	1.0000	1.0000
7	0	0.9321	0.8681	0.8080	0.7514	0.6983	0.6485	0.6017	0.5578	0.5168	0.4783	0.3206	0.2097	0.1335	0.0824	0.0490	0.0280	0.0152	0.0078
	1	0.9980	0.9921	0.9829	0.9706	0.9556	0.9382	0.9187	0.8974	0.8745	0.8503	0.7166	0.5767	0.4449	0.3294	0.2338	0.1586	0.1024	0.0625
	2	1.0000	0.9997	0.9991	0.9980	0.9962	0.9937	0.9903	0.9860	0.9807	0.9743	0.9262	0.8520	0.7564	0.6471	0.5323	0.4199	0.3164	0.2266
	3	1.0000	1.0000	1.0000	0.9999	0.9998	0.9996	0.9993	0.9988	0.9982	0.9973	0.9879	0.9667	0.9294	0.8740	0.8002	0.7102	0.6083	0.5000
	4	1.0000	1.0000	1.0000	1.0000	1.0000	1.0000	1.0000	0.9999	0.9999	0.9998	0.9988	0.9953	0.9871	0.9712	0.9444	0.9037	0.8471	0.7734
	5	1.0000	1.0000	1.0000	1.0000	1.0000	1.0000	1.0000	1.0000	1.0000	1.0000	0.9999	0.9996	0.9987	0.9962	0.9910	0.9812	0.9643	0.9375
	6	1.0000	1.0000	1.0000	1.0000	1.0000	1.0000	1.0000	1.0000	1.0000	1.0000	1.0000	1.0000	0.9999	0.9998	0.9994	0.9984	0.9963	0.9922
	7	1.0000	1.0000	1.0000	1.0000	1.0000	1.0000	1.0000	1.0000	1.0000	1.0000	1.0000	1.0000	1.0000	1.0000	1.0000	1.0000	1.0000	1.0000

n	y	0.01	0.02	0.03	0.04	0.05	0.06	0.07	0.08	0.09	0.10	0.15	0.20	0.25	0.30	0.35	0.40	0.45	0.50
																p			
8	0	0.9227	0.8508	0.7837	0.7214	0.6634	0.6096	0.5596	0.5132	0.4703	0.4305	0.2725	0.1678	0.1001	0.0576	0.0319	0.0168	0.0084	0.0039
	1	0.9973	0.9897	0.9777	0.9619	0.9428	0.9208	0.8965	0.8702	0.8423	0.8131	0.6572	0.5033	0.3671	0.2553	0.1691	0.1064	0.0632	0.0352
	2	0.9999	0.9996	0.9987	0.9969	0.9942	0.9904	0.9853	0.9789	0.9711	0.9619	0.8948	0.7969	0.6785	0.5518	0.4278	0.3154	0.2201	0.1445
	3	1.0000	1.0000	0.9999	0.9998	0.9996	0.9993	0.9987	0.9978	0.9966	0.9950	0.9786	0.9437	0.8862	0.8059	0.7064	0.5941	0.4770	0.3633
	4	1.0000	1.0000	1.0000	1.0000	1.0000	1.0000	0.9999	0.9999	0.9997	0.9996	0.9971	0.9896	0.9727	0.9420	0.8939	0.8263	0.7396	0.6367
	5	1.0000	1.0000	1.0000	1.0000	1.0000	1.0000	1.0000	1.0000	1.0000	1.0000	0.9998	0.9988	0.9958	0.9887	0.9747	0.9502	0.9115	0.8555
	6	1.0000	1.0000	1.0000	1.0000	1.0000	1.0000	1.0000	1.0000	1.0000	1.0000	1.0000	0.9999	0.9996	0.9987	0.9964	0.9915	0.9819	0.9648
	7	1.0000	1.0000	1.0000	1.0000	1.0000	1.0000	1.0000	1.0000	1.0000	1.0000	1.0000	1.0000	1.0000	0.9999	0.9998	0.9993	0.9983	0.9961
	8	1.0000	1.0000	1.0000	1.0000	1.0000	1.0000	1.0000	1.0000	1.0000	1.0000	1.0000	1.0000	1.0000	1.0000	1.0000	1.0000	1.0000	1.0000
9	0	0.9135	0.8337	0.7602	0.6925	0.6302	0.5730	0.5204	0.4722	0.4279	0.3874	0.2316	0.1342	0.0751	0.0404	0.0207	0.0101	0.0046	0.0020
	1	0.9966	0.9869	0.9718	0.9522	0.9288	0.9022	0.8729	0.8417	0.8088	0.7748	0.5995	0.4362	0.3003	0.1960	0.1211	0.0705	0.0385	0.0195
	2	0.9999	0.9994	0.9980	0.9955	0.9916	0.9862	0.9791	0.9702	0.9595	0.9470	0.8591	0.7382	0.6007	0.4628	0.3373	0.2318	0.1495	0.0898
	3	1.0000	1.0000	0.9999	0.9997	0.9994	0.9987	0.9977	0.9963	0.9943	0.9917	0.9661	0.9144	0.8343	0.7297	0.6089	0.4826	0.3614	0.2539
	4	1.0000	1.0000	1.0000	1.0000	1.0000	0.9999	0.9998	0.9997	0.9995	0.9991	0.9944	0.9804	0.9511	0.9012	0.8283	0.7334	0.6214	0.5000
	5	1.0000	1.0000	1.0000	1.0000	1.0000	1.0000	1.0000	1.0000	1.0000	1.0000	0.9994	0.9969	0.9900	0.9747	0.9464	0.9006	0.8342	0.7461
	6	1.0000	1.0000	1.0000	1.0000	1.0000	1.0000	1.0000	1.0000	1.0000	1.0000	1.0000	0.9997	0.9987	0.9957	0.9888	0.9750	0.9502	0.9102
	7	1.0000	1.0000	1.0000	1.0000	1.0000	1.0000	1.0000	1.0000	1.0000	1.0000	1.0000	1.0000	0.9999	0.9996	0.9986	0.9962	0.9909	0.9805
	8	1.0000	1.0000	1.0000	1.0000	1.0000	1.0000	1.0000	1.0000	1.0000	1.0000	1.0000	1.0000	1.0000	1.0000	0.9999	0.9997	0.9992	0.9980
	9	1.0000	1.0000	1.0000	1.0000	1.0000	1.0000	1.0000	1.0000	1.0000	1.0000	1.0000	1.0000	1.0000	1.0000	1.0000	1.0000	1.0000	1.0000
10	0	0.9044	0.8171	0.7374	0.6648	0.5987	0.5386	0.4840	0.4344	0.3894	0.3487	0.1969	0.1074	0.0563	0.0282	0.0135	0.0060	0.0025	0.0010
	1	0.9957	0.9838	0.9655	0.9418	0.9139	0.8824	0.8483	0.8121	0.7746	0.7361	0.5443	0.3758	0.2440	0.1493	0.0860	0.0464	0.0233	0.0107
	2	0.9999	0.9991	0.9972	0.9938	0.9885	0.9812	0.9717	0.9599	0.9460	0.9298	0.8202	0.6778	0.5256	0.3828	0.2616	0.1673	0.0996	0.0547
	3	1.0000	1.0000	0.9999	0.9996	0.9990	0.9980	0.9964	0.9942	0.9912	0.9872	0.9500	0.8791	0.7759	0.6496	0.5138	0.3823	0.2660	0.1719
	4	1.0000	1.0000	1.0000	1.0000	0.9999	0.9998	0.9997	0.9994	0.9990	0.9984	0.9901	0.9672	0.9219	0.8497	0.7515	0.6331	0.5044	0.3770
	5	1.0000	1.0000	1.0000	1.0000	1.0000	1.0000	1.0000	1.0000	0.9999	0.9999	0.9986	0.9936	0.9803	0.9527	0.9051	0.8338	0.7384	0.6230
	6	1.0000	1.0000	1.0000	1.0000	1.0000	1.0000	1.0000	1.0000	1.0000	1.0000	0.9999	0.9991	0.9965	0.9894	0.9740	0.9452	0.8980	0.8281
	7	1.0000	1.0000	1.0000	1.0000	1.0000	1.0000	1.0000	1.0000	1.0000	1.0000	1.0000	1.0000	0.9996	0.9984	0.9952	0.9877	0.9726	0.9453
	8	1.0000	1.0000	1.0000	1.0000	1.0000	1.0000	1.0000	1.0000	1.0000	1.0000	1.0000	1.0000	1.0000	0.9999	0.9995	0.9983	0.9955	0.9893
	9	1.0000	1.0000	1.0000	1.0000	1.0000	1.0000	1.0000	1.0000	1.0000	1.0000	1.0000	1.0000	1.0000	1.0000	1.0000	0.9999	0.9997	0.9990
	10	1.0000	1.0000	1.0000	1.0000	1.0000	1.0000	1.0000	1.0000	1.0000	1.0000	1.0000	1.0000	1.0000	1.0000	1.0000	1.0000	1.0000	1.0000
12	0	0.8864	0.7847	0.6938	0.6127	0.5404	0.4759	0.4186	0.3677	0.3225	0.2824	0.1422	0.0687	0.0317	0.0138	0.0057	0.0022	0.0008	0.0002
	1	0.9938	0.9769	0.9514	0.9191	0.8816	0.8405	0.7967	0.7513	0.7052	0.6590	0.4435	0.2749	0.1584	0.0850	0.0424	0.0196	0.0083	0.0032
	2	0.9998	0.9985	0.9952	0.9893	0.9804	0.9684	0.9532	0.9348	0.9134	0.8891	0.7358	0.5583	0.3907	0.2528	0.1513	0.0834	0.0421	0.0193
	3	1.0000	0.9999	0.9997	0.9990	0.9978	0.9957	0.9925	0.9880	0.9820	0.9744	0.9078	0.7946	0.6488	0.4925	0.3467	0.2253	0.1345	0.0730

											p								
n	y	0.01	0.02	0.03	0.04	0.05	0.06	0.07	0.08	0.09	0.10	0.15	0.20	0.25	0.30	0.35	0.40	0.45	0.50
	4	1.0000	1.0000	1.0000	0.9999	0.9998	0.9996	0.9991	0.9984	0.9973	0.9957	0.9761	0.9274	0.8424	0.7237	0.5833	0.4382	0.3044	0.1938
	5	1.0000	1.0000	1.0000	1.0000	1.0000	1.0000	0.9999	0.9998	0.9997	0.9995	0.9954	0.9806	0.9456	0.8822	0.7873	0.6652	0.5269	0.3872
	6	1.0000	1.0000	1.0000	1.0000	1.0000	1.0000	1.0000	1.0000	1.0000	0.9999	0.9993	0.9961	0.9857	0.9614	0.9154	0.8418	0.7393	0.6128
	7	1.0000	1.0000	1.0000	1.0000	1.0000	1.0000	1.0000	1.0000	1.0000	1.0000	0.9999	0.9994	0.9972	0.9905	0.9745	0.9427	0.8883	0.8062
	8	1.0000	1.0000	1.0000	1.0000	1.0000	1.0000	1.0000	1.0000	1.0000	1.0000	1.0000	0.9999	0.9996	0.9983	0.9944	0.9847	0.9644	0.9270
	9	1.0000	1.0000	1.0000	1.0000	1.0000	1.0000	1.0000	1.0000	1.0000	1.0000	1.0000	1.0000	1.0000	0.9998	0.9992	0.9972	0.9921	0.9807
	10	1.0000	1.0000	1.0000	1.0000	1.0000	1.0000	1.0000	1.0000	1.0000	1.0000	1.0000	1.0000	1.0000	1.0000	0.9999	0.9997	0.9989	0.9968
	11	1.0000	1.0000	1.0000	1.0000	1.0000	1.0000	1.0000	1.0000	1.0000	1.0000	1.0000	1.0000	1.0000	1.0000	1.0000	1.0000	0.9999	0.9998
	12	1.0000	1.0000	1.0000	1.0000	1.0000	1.0000	1.0000	1.0000	1.0000	1.0000	1.0000	1.0000	1.0000	1.0000	1.0000	1.0000	1.0000	1.0000
15	0	0.8601	0.7386	0.6333	0.5421	0.4633	0.3953	0.3367	0.2863	0.2430	0.2059	0.0874	0.0352	0.0134	0.0047	0.0016	0.0005	0.0001	0.0000
	1	0.9904	0.9647	0.9270	0.8809	0.8290	0.7738	0.7168	0.6597	0.6035	0.5490	0.3186	0.1671	0.0802	0.0353	0.0142	0.0052	0.0017	0.0005
	2	0.9996	0.9970	0.9906	0.9797	0.9638	0.9429	0.9171	0.8870	0.8531	0.8159	0.6042	0.3980	0.2361	0.1268	0.0617	0.0271	0.0107	0.0037
	3	1.0000	0.9998	0.9992	0.9976	0.9945	0.9896	0.9825	0.9727	0.9601	0.9444	0.8227	0.6482	0.4613	0.2969	0.1727	0.0905	0.0424	0.0176
	4	1.0000	1.0000	0.9999	0.9998	0.9994	0.9986	0.9972	0.9950	0.9918	0.9873	0.9383	0.8358	0.6865	0.5155	0.3519	0.2173	0.1204	0.0592
	5	1.0000	1.0000	1.0000	1.0000	0.9999	0.9999	0.9997	0.9993	0.9987	0.9978	0.9832	0.9389	0.8516	0.7216	0.5643	0.4032	0.2608	0.1509
	6	1.0000	1.0000	1.0000	1.0000	1.0000	1.0000	1.0000	0.9999	0.9998	0.9997	0.9964	0.9819	0.9434	0.8689	0.7548	0.6098	0.4522	0.3036
	7	1.0000	1.0000	1.0000	1.0000	1.0000	1.0000	1.0000	1.0000	1.0000	1.0000	0.9994	0.9958	0.9827	0.9500	0.8868	0.7869	0.6535	0.5000
	8	1.0000	1.0000	1.0000	1.0000	1.0000	1.0000	1.0000	1.0000	1.0000	1.0000	0.9999	0.9992	0.9958	0.9848	0.9578	0.9050	0.8182	0.6964
	9	1.0000	1.0000	1.0000	1.0000	1.0000	1.0000	1.0000	1.0000	1.0000	1.0000	1.0000	0.9999	0.9992	0.9963	0.9876	0.9662	0.9231	0.8491
	10	1.0000	1.0000	1.0000	1.0000	1.0000	1.0000	1.0000	1.0000	1.0000	1.0000	1.0000	1.0000	0.9999	0.9993	0.9972	0.9907	0.9745	0.9408
	11	1.0000	1.0000	1.0000	1.0000	1.0000	1.0000	1.0000	1.0000	1.0000	1.0000	1.0000	1.0000	1.0000	0.9999	0.9995	0.9981	0.9937	0.9824
	12	1.0000	1.0000	1.0000	1.0000	1.0000	1.0000	1.0000	1.0000	1.0000	1.0000	1.0000	1.0000	1.0000	1.0000	0.9999	0.9997	0.9989	0.9963
	13	1.0000	1.0000	1.0000	1.0000	1.0000	1.0000	1.0000	1.0000	1.0000	1.0000	1.0000	1.0000	1.0000	1.0000	1.0000	1.0000	0.9999	0.9995
	14	1.0000	1.0000	1.0000	1.0000	1.0000	1.0000	1.0000	1.0000	1.0000	1.0000	1.0000	1.0000	1.0000	1.0000	1.0000	1.0000	1.0000	1.0000
	15	1.0000	1.0000	1.0000	1.0000	1.0000	1.0000	1.0000	1.0000	1.0000	1.0000	1.0000	1.0000	1.0000	1.0000	1.0000	1.0000	1.0000	1.0000
20	0	0.8179	0.6676	0.5438	0.4420	0.3585	0.2901	0.2342	0.1887	0.1516	0.1216	0.0388	0.0115	0.0032	0.0008	0.0002	0.0000	0.0000	0.0000
	1	0.9831	0.9401	0.8802	0.8103	0.7358	0.6605	0.5869	0.5169	0.4516	0.3917	0.1756	0.0692	0.0243	0.0076	0.0021	0.0005	0.0001	0.0000
	2	0.9990	0.9929	0.9790	0.9561	0.9245	0.8850	0.8390	0.7879	0.7334	0.6769	0.4049	0.2061	0.0913	0.0355	0.0121	0.0036	0.0009	0.0002
	3	1.0000	0.9994	0.9973	0.9926	0.9841	0.9710	0.9529	0.9294	0.9007	0.8670	0.6477	0.4114	0.2252	0.1071	0.0444	0.0160	0.0049	0.0013
	4	1.0000	1.0000	0.9997	0.9990	0.9974	0.9944	0.9893	0.9817	0.9710	0.9568	0.8298	0.6296	0.4148	0.2375	0.1182	0.0510	0.0189	0.0059
	5	1.0000	1.0000	1.0000	0.9999	0.9997	0.9991	0.9981	0.9962	0.9932	0.9887	0.9327	0.8042	0.6172	0.4164	0.2454	0.1256	0.0553	0.0207
	6	1.0000	1.0000	1.0000	1.0000	1.0000	0.9999	0.9997	0.9994	0.9987	0.9976	0.9781	0.9133	0.7858	0.6080	0.4166	0.2500	0.1299	0.0577
	7	1.0000	1.0000	1.0000	1.0000	1.0000	1.0000	1.0000	0.9999	0.9998	0.9996	0.9941	0.9679	0.8982	0.7723	0.6010	0.4159	0.2520	0.1316
	8	1.0000	1.0000	1.0000	1.0000	1.0000	1.0000	1.0000	1.0000	1.0000	0.9999	0.9987	0.9900	0.9591	0.8867	0.7624	0.5956	0.4143	0.2517
	9	1.0000	1.0000	1.0000	1.0000	1.0000	1.0000	1.0000	1.0000	1.0000	1.0000	0.9998	0.9974	0.9861	0.9520	0.8782	0.7553	0.5914	0.4119
	10	1.0000	1.0000	1.0000	1.0000	1.0000	1.0000	1.0000	1.0000	1.0000	1.0000	1.0000	0.9994	0.9961	0.9829	0.9468	0.8725	0.7507	0.5881

n	y													p						
		0.01	0.02	0.03	0.04	0.05	0.06	0.07	0.08	0.09	0.10	0.15	0.20	0.25	0.30	0.35	0.40	0.45	0.50
	11	1.0000	1.0000	1.0000	1.0000	1.0000	1.0000	1.0000	1.0000	1.0000	1.0000	1.0000	0.9999	0.9991	0.9949	0.9804	0.9435	0.8692	0.7483
	12	1.0000	1.0000	1.0000	1.0000	1.0000	1.0000	1.0000	1.0000	1.0000	1.0000	1.0000	1.0000	0.9998	0.9987	0.9940	0.9790	0.9420	0.8684
	13	1.0000	1.0000	1.0000	1.0000	1.0000	1.0000	1.0000	1.0000	1.0000	1.0000	1.0000	1.0000	1.0000	0.9997	0.9985	0.9935	0.9786	0.9423
	14	1.0000	1.0000	1.0000	1.0000	1.0000	1.0000	1.0000	1.0000	1.0000	1.0000	1.0000	1.0000	1.0000	1.0000	0.9997	0.9984	0.9936	0.9793
	15	1.0000	1.0000	1.0000	1.0000	1.0000	1.0000	1.0000	1.0000	1.0000	1.0000	1.0000	1.0000	1.0000	1.0000	1.0000	0.9997	0.9985	0.9941
	16	1.0000	1.0000	1.0000	1.0000	1.0000	1.0000	1.0000	1.0000	1.0000	1.0000	1.0000	1.0000	1.0000	1.0000	1.0000	1.0000	0.9997	0.9987
	17	1.0000	1.0000	1.0000	1.0000	1.0000	1.0000	1.0000	1.0000	1.0000	1.0000	1.0000	1.0000	1.0000	1.0000	1.0000	1.0000	1.0000	0.9998
	18	1.0000	1.0000	1.0000	1.0000	1.0000	1.0000	1.0000	1.0000	1.0000	1.0000	1.0000	1.0000	1.0000	1.0000	1.0000	1.0000	1.0000	1.0000
	19	1.0000	1.0000	1.0000	1.0000	1.0000	1.0000	1.0000	1.0000	1.0000	1.0000	1.0000	1.0000	1.0000	1.0000	1.0000	1.0000	1.0000	1.0000
	20	1.0000	1.0000	1.0000	1.0000	1.0000	1.0000	1.0000	1.0000	1.0000	1.0000	1.0000	1.0000	1.0000	1.0000	1.0000	1.0000	1.0000	1.0000
25	0	0.7778	0.6035	0.4670	0.3604	0.2774	0.2129	0.1630	0.1244	0.0946	0.0718	0.0172	0.0038	0.0008	0.0001	0.0000	0.0000	0.0000	0.0000
	1	0.9742	0.9114	0.8280	0.7358	0.6424	0.5527	0.4696	0.3947	0.3286	0.2712	0.0931	0.0274	0.0070	0.0016	0.0003	0.0001	0.0000	0.0000
	2	0.9980	0.9868	0.9620	0.9235	0.8729	0.8129	0.7466	0.6768	0.6063	0.5371	0.2537	0.0982	0.0321	0.0090	0.0021	0.0004	0.0001	0.0000
	3	0.9999	0.9986	0.9938	0.9835	0.9659	0.9402	0.9064	0.8649	0.8169	0.7636	0.4711	0.2340	0.0962	0.0332	0.0097	0.0024	0.0005	0.0001
	4	1.0000	0.9999	0.9992	0.9972	0.9928	0.9850	0.9726	0.9549	0.9314	0.9020	0.6821	0.4207	0.2137	0.0905	0.0320	0.0095	0.0023	0.0005
	5	1.0000	1.0000	0.9999	0.9996	0.9988	0.9969	0.9935	0.9877	0.9790	0.9666	0.8385	0.6167	0.3783	0.1935	0.0826	0.0294	0.0086	0.0020
	6	1.0000	1.0000	1.0000	1.0000	0.9998	0.9995	0.9987	0.9972	0.9946	0.9905	0.9305	0.7800	0.5611	0.3407	0.1734	0.0736	0.0258	0.0073
	7	1.0000	1.0000	1.0000	1.0000	1.0000	0.9999	0.9998	0.9995	0.9989	0.9977	0.9745	0.8909	0.7265	0.5118	0.3061	0.1536	0.0639	0.0216
	8	1.0000	1.0000	1.0000	1.0000	1.0000	1.0000	1.0000	0.9999	0.9998	0.9995	0.9920	0.9532	0.8506	0.6769	0.4668	0.2735	0.1340	0.0539
	9	1.0000	1.0000	1.0000	1.0000	1.0000	1.0000	1.0000	1.0000	1.0000	0.9999	0.9979	0.9827	0.9287	0.8106	0.6303	0.4246	0.2424	0.1148
	10	1.0000	1.0000	1.0000	1.0000	1.0000	1.0000	1.0000	1.0000	1.0000	1.0000	0.9995	0.9944	0.9703	0.9022	0.7712	0.5858	0.3843	0.2122
	11	1.0000	1.0000	1.0000	1.0000	1.0000	1.0000	1.0000	1.0000	1.0000	1.0000	0.9999	0.9985	0.9893	0.9558	0.8746	0.7323	0.5426	0.3450
	12	1.0000	1.0000	1.0000	1.0000	1.0000	1.0000	1.0000	1.0000	1.0000	1.0000	1.0000	0.9996	0.9966	0.9825	0.9396	0.8462	0.6937	0.5000
	13	1.0000	1.0000	1.0000	1.0000	1.0000	1.0000	1.0000	1.0000	1.0000	1.0000	1.0000	0.9999	0.9991	0.9940	0.9745	0.9222	0.8173	0.6550
	14	1.0000	1.0000	1.0000	1.0000	1.0000	1.0000	1.0000	1.0000	1.0000	1.0000	1.0000	1.0000	0.9998	0.9982	0.9907	0.9656	0.9040	0.7878
	15	1.0000	1.0000	1.0000	1.0000	1.0000	1.0000	1.0000	1.0000	1.0000	1.0000	1.0000	1.0000	1.0000	0.9995	0.9971	0.9868	0.9560	0.8852
	16	1.0000	1.0000	1.0000	1.0000	1.0000	1.0000	1.0000	1.0000	1.0000	1.0000	1.0000	1.0000	1.0000	0.9999	0.9992	0.9957	0.9826	0.9461
	17	1.0000	1.0000	1.0000	1.0000	1.0000	1.0000	1.0000	1.0000	1.0000	1.0000	1.0000	1.0000	1.0000	1.0000	0.9998	0.9988	0.9942	0.9784
	18	1.0000	1.0000	1.0000	1.0000	1.0000	1.0000	1.0000	1.0000	1.0000	1.0000	1.0000	1.0000	1.0000	1.0000	1.0000	0.9997	0.9984	0.9927
	19	1.0000	1.0000	1.0000	1.0000	1.0000	1.0000	1.0000	1.0000	1.0000	1.0000	1.0000	1.0000	1.0000	1.0000	1.0000	0.9999	0.9996	0.9980
	20	1.0000	1.0000	1.0000	1.0000	1.0000	1.0000	1.0000	1.0000	1.0000	1.0000	1.0000	1.0000	1.0000	1.0000	1.0000	1.0000	0.9999	0.9995
	21	1.0000	1.0000	1.0000	1.0000	1.0000	1.0000	1.0000	1.0000	1.0000	1.0000	1.0000	1.0000	1.0000	1.0000	1.0000	1.0000	1.0000	0.9999
	22	1.0000	1.0000	1.0000	1.0000	1.0000	1.0000	1.0000	1.0000	1.0000	1.0000	1.0000	1.0000	1.0000	1.0000	1.0000	1.0000	1.0000	1.0000
	23	1.0000	1.0000	1.0000	1.0000	1.0000	1.0000	1.0000	1.0000	1.0000	1.0000	1.0000	1.0000	1.0000	1.0000	1.0000	1.0000	1.0000	1.0000
	24	1.0000	1.0000	1.0000	1.0000	1.0000	1.0000	1.0000	1.0000	1.0000	1.0000	1.0000	1.0000	1.0000	1.0000	1.0000	1.0000	1.0000	1.0000
	25	1.0000	1.0000	1.0000	1.0000	1.0000	1.0000	1.0000	1.0000	1.0000	1.0000	1.0000	1.0000	1.0000	1.0000	1.0000	1.0000	1.0000	1.0000

A.2

POISSON PROBABILITIES

Tabled is the value

$$P(Y \le y) = \sum_{x=0}^{y} \frac{\lambda^x e^{-\lambda}}{x!}$$

where Y has a Poisson distribution with parameter λ.

To obtain the value of the probability mass function, $p_Y(y)$, use the formula

$$p_Y(y) = P(Y \le 0), \qquad\qquad y = 0$$

$$= P(Y \le y) - P(Y \le y-1), \qquad y > 0$$

λ

y	0.1	0.2	0.3	0.4	0.5	0.6	0.7	0.8	0.9	1.0	2.0	3.0	4.0	5.0	6.0	7.0	8.0	9.0	10.0	15.0	20.0
0	0.905	0.819	0.741	0.670	0.607	0.549	0.497	0.449	0.407	0.368	0.135	0.050	0.018	0.007	0.002	0.001	0.000	0.000	0.000	0.000	0.000
1	0.995	0.982	0.963	0.938	0.910	0.878	0.844	0.809	0.772	0.736	0.406	0.199	0.092	0.040	0.017	0.007	0.003	0.001	0.000	0.000	0.000
2	1.000	0.999	0.996	0.992	0.986	0.977	0.966	0.953	0.937	0.920	0.677	0.423	0.238	0.125	0.062	0.030	0.014	0.006	0.003	0.000	0.000
3		1.000	1.000	0.999	0.998	0.997	0.994	0.991	0.987	0.981	0.857	0.647	0.433	0.265	0.151	0.082	0.042	0.021	0.010	0.000	0.000
4				1.000	1.000	1.000	0.999	0.999	0.998	0.996	0.947	0.815	0.629	0.440	0.285	0.173	0.100	0.055	0.029	0.001	0.000
5							1.000	1.000	1.000	0.999	0.983	0.916	0.785	0.616	0.446	0.301	0.191	0.116	0.067	0.003	0.000
6										1.000	0.995	0.966	0.889	0.762	0.606	0.450	0.313	0.207	0.130	0.008	0.000
7											0.999	0.988	0.949	0.867	0.744	0.599	0.453	0.324	0.220	0.018	0.001
8											1.000	0.996	0.979	0.932	0.847	0.729	0.593	0.456	0.333	0.037	0.002
9												0.999	0.992	0.968	0.916	0.830	0.717	0.587	0.458	0.070	0.005
10												1.000	0.997	0.986	0.957	0.901	0.816	0.706	0.583	0.118	0.011
11													0.999	0.995	0.980	0.947	0.888	0.803	0.697	0.185	0.021
12													1.000	0.998	0.991	0.973	0.936	0.876	0.792	0.268	0.039
13														0.999	0.996	0.987	0.966	0.926	0.864	0.363	0.066
14														1.000	0.999	0.994	0.983	0.959	0.917	0.466	0.105
15															0.999	0.998	0.992	0.978	0.951	0.568	0.157
16															1.000	0.999	0.996	0.989	0.973	0.664	0.221
17																1.000	0.998	0.995	0.986	0.749	0.297
18																	0.999	0.998	0.993	0.819	0.381
19																	1.000	0.999	0.997	0.875	0.470
20																		1.000	0.998	0.917	0.559
21																			0.999	0.947	0.644
22																			1.000	0.967	0.721
23																				0.981	0.787
24																				0.989	0.843
25																				0.994	0.888
26																				0.997	0.922
27																				0.998	0.948
28																				0.999	0.966
29																				1.000	0.978
30																					0.987
31																					0.992
32																					0.995
33																					0.997
34																					0.999
35																					0.999
36																					1.000

A.3

AREAS UNDER THE STANDARD NORMAL DENSITY

Tabled are the areas under the $N(0, 1)$ density curve below z. This represents the proportion of an $N(0, 1)$ population that takes on values less than or equal to z. The tabled value is illustrated by the shaded region in Figure A.1.

As examples, the proportion of an $N(0, 1)$ population that takes on values less than or equal to -1.83 is 0.0336, and the proportion of an $N(0, 1)$ population that takes on values less than or equal to 2.38 is 0.9913.

By reading the table in reverse, the value z_p, below which lies a proportion p of an $N(0, 1)$ population may be found. For example, to find the value $z_{0.25}$, the point below that lies proportion 0.25 (or $1/4$) of an $N(0, 1)$ population, look in the body of the table to find values as close to 0.25 as possible. The two values are 0.2514, corresponding to $z = -0.67$, and 0.2483, corresponding to $z = -0.68$. Therefore, $z_{0.25}$ lies between -0.67 and -0.68. As a second example, $z_{0.84}$ lies between 0.99 and 1.00.

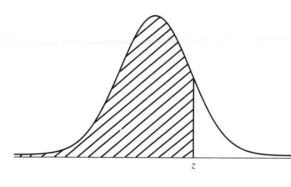

z

Figure A.1 $N(0, 1)$ curve: shaded area is tabled.

					$N(0, 1)$ Probabilities					
z	0.00	0.01	0.02	0.03	0.04	0.05	0.06	0.07	0.08	0.09
−3.6	0.0002	0.0002	0.0001	0.0001	0.0001	0.0001	0.0001	0.0001	0.0001	0.0001
−3.5	0.0002	0.0002	0.0002	0.0002	0.0002	0.0002	0.0002	0.0002	0.0002	0.0002
−3.4	0.0003	0.0003	0.0003	0.0003	0.0003	0.0003	0.0003	0.0003	0.0003	0.0002
−3.3	0.0005	0.0005	0.0004	0.0004	0.0004	0.0004	0.0004	0.0004	0.0004	0.0003
−3.2	0.0007	0.0007	0.0006	0.0006	0.0006	0.0006	0.0006	0.0005	0.0005	0.0005
−3.1	0.0010	0.0009	0.0009	0.0009	0.0008	0.0008	0.0008	0.0008	0.0007	0.0007
−3.0	0.0014	0.0013	0.0013	0.0012	0.0012	0.0011	0.0011	0.0011	0.0010	0.0010
−2.9	0.0019	0.0018	0.0018	0.0017	0.0016	0.0016	0.0015	0.0015	0.0014	0.0014
−2.8	0.0026	0.0025	0.0024	0.0023	0.0023	0.0022	0.0021	0.0021	0.0020	0.0019
−2.7	0.0035	0.0034	0.0033	0.0032	0.0031	0.0030	0.0029	0.0028	0.0027	0.0026
−2.6	0.0047	0.0045	0.0044	0.0043	0.0041	0.0040	0.0039	0.0038	0.0037	0.0036
−2.5	0.0062	0.0060	0.0059	0.0057	0.0055	0.0054	0.0052	0.0051	0.0049	0.0048
−2.4	0.0082	0.0080	0.0078	0.0075	0.0073	0.0071	0.0069	0.0068	0.0066	0.0064
−2.3	0.0107	0.0104	0.0102	0.0099	0.0096	0.0094	0.0091	0.0089	0.0087	0.0084
−2.2	0.0139	0.0136	0.0132	0.0129	0.0125	0.0122	0.0119	0.0116	0.0113	0.0110
−2.1	0.0179	0.0174	0.0170	0.0166	0.0162	0.0158	0.0154	0.0150	0.0146	0.0143
−2.0	0.0227	0.0222	0.0217	0.0212	0.0207	0.0202	0.0197	0.0192	0.0188	0.0183
−1.9	0.0287	0.0281	0.0274	0.0268	0.0262	0.0256	0.0250	0.0244	0.0238	0.0233
−1.8	0.0359	0.0351	0.0344	0.0336	0.0329	0.0322	0.0314	0.0307	0.0301	0.0294
−1.7	0.0446	0.0436	0.0427	0.0418	0.0409	0.0401	0.0392	0.0384	0.0375	0.0367
−1.6	0.0548	0.0537	0.0526	0.0516	0.0505	0.0495	0.0485	0.0475	0.0465	0.0455
−1.5	0.0668	0.0655	0.0643	0.0630	0.0618	0.0606	0.0594	0.0582	0.0571	0.0559
−1.4	0.0808	0.0793	0.0778	0.0764	0.0749	0.0735	0.0721	0.0708	0.0694	0.0681
−1.3	0.0968	0.0951	0.0934	0.0918	0.0901	0.0885	0.0869	0.0853	0.0838	0.0823
−1.2	0.1151	0.1131	0.1112	0.1094	0.1075	0.1057	0.1038	0.1020	0.1003	0.0985
−1.1	0.1357	0.1335	0.1314	0.1292	0.1271	0.1251	0.1230	0.1210	0.1190	0.1170
−1.0	0.1587	0.1563	0.1539	0.1515	0.1492	0.1469	0.1446	0.1423	0.1401	0.1379
−0.9	0.1841	0.1814	0.1788	0.1762	0.1736	0.1711	0.1685	0.1660	0.1635	0.1611
−0.8	0.2119	0.2090	0.2061	0.2033	0.2005	0.1977	0.1949	0.1921	0.1894	0.1867
−0.7	0.2420	0.2388	0.2358	0.2327	0.2297	0.2266	0.2236	0.2207	0.2177	0.2148
−0.6	0.2743	0.2709	0.2676	0.2643	0.2611	0.2578	0.2546	0.2514	0.2482	0.2451
−0.5	0.3085	0.3050	0.3015	0.2981	0.2946	0.2912	0.2877	0.2843	0.2810	0.2776
−0.4	0.3446	0.3409	0.3372	0.3336	0.3300	0.3264	0.3228	0.3192	0.3156	0.3121
−0.3	0.3821	0.3783	0.3745	0.3707	0.3669	0.3632	0.3594	0.3557	0.3520	0.3483
−0.2	0.4207	0.4168	0.4129	0.4090	0.4052	0.4013	0.3974	0.3936	0.3897	0.3859
−0.1	0.4602	0.4562	0.4522	0.4483	0.4443	0.4404	0.4364	0.4325	0.4286	0.4247
0.0	0.5000	0.4960	0.4920	0.4880	0.4841	0.4801	0.4761	0.4721	0.4681	0.4641

(*continued*)

z	0.00	0.01	0.02	0.03	0.04	0.05	0.06	0.07	0.08	0.09
0.0	0.5000	0.5040	0.5080	0.5120	0.5160	0.5199	0.5239	0.5279	0.5319	0.5359
0.1	0.5398	0.5438	0.5478	0.5517	0.5557	0.5596	0.5636	0.5675	0.5714	0.5753
0.2	0.5793	0.5832	0.5871	0.5910	0.5948	0.5987	0.6026	0.6064	0.6103	0.6141
0.3	0.6179	0.6217	0.6255	0.6293	0.6331	0.6368	0.6406	0.6443	0.6480	0.6517
0.4	0.6554	0.6591	0.6628	0.6664	0.6700	0.6736	0.6772	0.6808	0.6844	0.6879
0.5	0.6915	0.6950	0.6985	0.7019	0.7054	0.7088	0.7123	0.7157	0.7190	0.7224
0.6	0.7258	0.7291	0.7324	0.7357	0.7389	0.7422	0.7454	0.7486	0.7517	0.7549
0.7	0.7580	0.7612	0.7642	0.7673	0.7703	0.7734	0.7764	0.7793	0.7823	0.7852
0.8	0.7881	0.7910	0.7939	0.7967	0.7995	0.8023	0.8051	0.8079	0.8106	0.8133
0.9	0.8159	0.8186	0.8212	0.8238	0.8264	0.8289	0.8315	0.8340	0.8365	0.8389
1.0	0.8413	0.8438	0.8461	0.8485	0.8508	0.8531	0.8554	0.8577	0.8599	0.8621
1.1	0.8643	0.8665	0.8686	0.8708	0.8729	0.8749	0.8770	0.8790	0.8810	0.8830
1.2	0.8849	0.8869	0.8888	0.8906	0.8925	0.8943	0.8962	0.8980	0.8997	0.9015
1.3	0.9032	0.9049	0.9066	0.9082	0.9099	0.9115	0.9131	0.9147	0.9162	0.9177
1.4	0.9192	0.9207	0.9222	0.9236	0.9251	0.9265	0.9279	0.9292	0.9306	0.9319
1.5	0.9332	0.9345	0.9357	0.9370	0.9382	0.9394	0.9406	0.9418	0.9430	0.9441
1.6	0.9452	0.9463	0.9474	0.9485	0.9495	0.9505	0.9515	0.9525	0.9535	0.9545
1.7	0.9554	0.9564	0.9573	0.9582	0.9591	0.9599	0.9608	0.9616	0.9625	0.9633
1.8	0.9641	0.9649	0.9656	0.9664	0.9671	0.9678	0.9686	0.9693	0.9700	0.9706
1.9	0.9713	0.9719	0.9726	0.9732	0.9738	0.9744	0.9750	0.9756	0.9761	0.9767
2.0	0.9772	0.9778	0.9783	0.9788	0.9793	0.9798	0.9803	0.9808	0.9812	0.9817
2.1	0.9821	0.9826	0.9830	0.9834	0.9838	0.9842	0.9846	0.9850	0.9854	0.9857
2.2	0.9861	0.9865	0.9868	0.9871	0.9875	0.9878	0.9881	0.9884	0.9887	0.9890
2.3	0.9893	0.9896	0.9898	0.9901	0.9904	0.9906	0.9909	0.9911	0.9913	0.9916
2.4	0.9918	0.9920	0.9922	0.9924	0.9927	0.9929	0.9930	0.9932	0.9934	0.9936
2.5	0.9938	0.9940	0.9941	0.9943	0.9945	0.9946	0.9948	0.9949	0.9951	0.9952
2.6	0.9953	0.9955	0.9956	0.9957	0.9959	0.9960	0.9961	0.9962	0.9963	0.9964
2.7	0.9965	0.9966	0.9967	0.9968	0.9969	0.9970	0.9971	0.9972	0.9973	0.9974
2.8	0.9974	0.9975	0.9976	0.9977	0.9977	0.9978	0.9979	0.9980	0.9980	0.9981
2.9	0.9981	0.9982	0.9983	0.9983	0.9984	0.9984	0.9985	0.9985	0.9986	0.9986
3.0	0.9987	0.9987	0.9987	0.9988	0.9988	0.9989	0.9989	0.9989	0.9990	0.9990
3.1	0.9990	0.9991	0.9991	0.9991	0.9992	0.9992	0.9992	0.9992	0.9993	0.9993
3.2	0.9993	0.9993	0.9994	0.9994	0.9994	0.9994	0.9994	0.9995	0.9995	0.9995
3.3	0.9995	0.9995	0.9995	0.9996	0.9996	0.9996	0.9996	0.9996	0.9996	0.9997
3.4	0.9997	0.9997	0.9997	0.9997	0.9997	0.9997	0.9997	0.9997	0.9998	0.9998
3.5	0.9998	0.9998	0.9998	0.9998	0.9998	0.9998	0.9998	0.9998	0.9998	0.9998
3.6	0.9998	0.9998	0.9998	0.9999	0.9999	0.9999	0.9999	0.9999	0.9999	0.9999

$N(0, 1)$ Probabilities

A.4

CRITICAL VALUES OF THE t DISTRIBUTION

The critical value $t_{k,q}$ is the value below which lies an area q under the density curve of the t distribution with k degrees of freedom. That is, quantile q of the t_k distribution. Tabled are these critical values $t_{k,q}$ for selected degrees of freedom k and quantiles q. This is shown graphically in Figure A.2, in which the curve represents a t_k density curve. The critical value $t_{k,q}$ is the value t in the figure for which the shaded area equals q.

Note that a t distribution with degrees of freedom ∞ is an $N(0, 1)$ distribution.

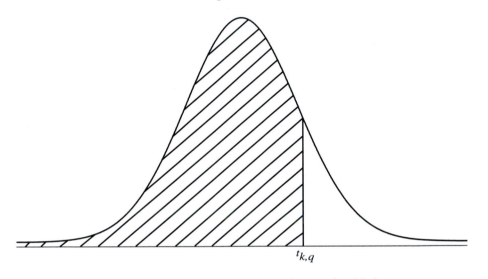

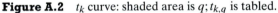

$t_{k,q}$

Figure A.2 t_k curve: shaded area is q; $t_{k,q}$ is tabled.

Degrees of freedom, k	Critical values of the *t* distribution						
	$t_{k,0.90}$	$t_{k,0.95}$	$t_{k,0.975}$	$t_{k,0.99}$	$t_{k,0.995}$	$t_{k,0.999}$	$t_{k,0.9995}$
1	3.0777	6.3137	12.7062	31.8205	63.6567	318.3090	636.6190
2	1.8856	2.9200	4.3027	6.9646	9.9248	22.3270	31.5990
3	1.6377	2.3534	3.1824	4.5407	5.8409	10.2150	12.9240
4	1.5332	2.1319	2.7764	3.7469	4.6041	7.1730	8.6100
5	1.4759	2.0150	2.5706	3.3649	4.0321	5.8930	6.8690
6	1.4398	1.9432	2.4469	3.1427	3.7074	5.2080	5.9590
7	1.4149	1.8946	2.3646	2.9980	3.4995	4.7850	5.4080
8	1.3968	1.8595	2.3060	2.8965	3.3554	4.5010	5.0410
9	1.3830	1.8331	2.2622	2.8214	3.2498	4.2970	4.7810
10	1.3722	1.8125	2.2281	2.7638	3.1693	4.1440	4.5870
11	1.3634	1.7959	2.2010	2.7181	3.1058	4.0250	4.4370
12	1.3562	1.7823	2.1788	2.6810	3.0545	3.9300	4.3180
13	1.3502	1.7709	2.1604	2.6503	3.0123	3.8520	4.2210
14	1.3450	1.7613	2.1448	2.6245	2.9768	3.7870	4.1400
15	1.3406	1.7530	2.1314	2.6025	2.9467	3.7330	4.0730
16	1.3368	1.7459	2.1199	2.5835	2.9208	3.6860	4.0150
17	1.3334	1.7396	2.1098	2.5669	2.8982	3.6460	3.9650
18	1.3304	1.7341	2.1009	2.5524	2.8784	3.6100	3.9220
19	1.3277	1.7291	2.0930	2.5395	2.8609	3.5790	3.8830
20	1.3253	1.7247	2.0860	2.5280	2.8453	3.5520	3.8500
21	1.3232	1.7207	2.0796	2.5176	2.8314	3.5270	3.8190
22	1.3212	1.7171	2.0739	2.5083	2.8188	3.5050	3.7920
23	1.3195	1.7139	2.0687	2.4999	2.8073	3.4850	3.7680
24	1.3178	1.7109	2.0639	2.4922	2.7969	3.4670	3.7450
25	1.3163	1.7081	2.0595	2.4851	2.7874	3.4500	3.7250
26	1.3150	1.7056	2.0555	2.4786	2.7787	3.4350	3.7066
27	1.3137	1.7033	2.0518	2.4727	2.7707	3.4210	3.6896
28	1.3125	1.7011	2.0484	2.4671	2.7633	3.4082	3.6739
29	1.3114	1.6991	2.0452	2.4620	2.7564	3.3962	3.6594
30	1.3104	1.6973	2.0423	2.4573	2.7500	3.3852	3.6460
35	1.3062	1.6896	2.0301	2.4377	2.7238	3.3400	3.5912
40	1.3031	1.6839	2.0211	2.4233	2.7045	3.3069	3.5510
50	1.2987	1.6759	2.0086	2.4033	2.6778	3.2614	3.4960
60	1.2958	1.6707	2.0003	2.3901	2.6603	3.2317	3.4602
70	1.2938	1.6669	1.9944	2.3808	2.6479	3.2108	3.4350
80	1.2922	1.6641	1.9901	2.3739	2.6387	3.1953	3.4163
90	1.2910	1.6620	1.9867	2.3685	2.6316	3.1833	3.4019
100	1.2901	1.6602	1.9840	2.3642	2.6259	3.1737	3.3905
∞	1.2816	1.6449	1.9600	2.3263	2.5758	3.0902	3.2905

A.5

CRITICAL VALUES OF THE χ^2 DISTRIBUTION

The critical value $\chi^2_{k,q}$ is the value below which lies an area q under the density curve of the χ^2 distribution with k degrees of freedom: that is, quantile q of the χ^2_k distribution. Tabled are these critical values $\chi^2_{k,q}$ for selected degrees of freedom k and quantiles q. This is shown graphically in Figure A.3, in which the curve represents a χ^2_k density curve. The critical value $\chi^2_{k,q}$ is the value χ^2 in the figure for which the shaded area equals q.

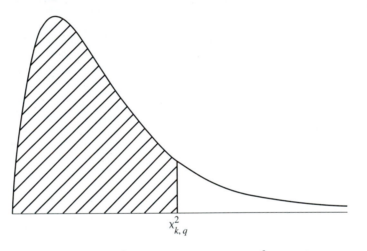

Figure A.3 χ^2_k curve: shaded area is q; $\chi^2_{k,q}$ is tabled.

					Critical values of the χ^2 distribution					
k	$\chi^2_{k,0.005}$	$\chi^2_{k,0.010}$	$\chi^2_{k,0.025}$	$\chi^2_{k,0.050}$	$\chi^2_{k,0.100}$	$\chi^2_{k,0.900}$	$\chi^2_{k,0.950}$	$\chi^2_{k,0.975}$	$\chi^2_{k,0.990}$	$\chi^2_{k,0.995}$
1	0.000[a]	0.000[b]	0.001	0.004	0.016	2.706	3.841	5.024	6.635	7.879
2	0.010	0.020	0.051	0.103	0.211	4.605	5.991	7.378	9.210	10.60
3	0.072	0.115	0.216	0.352	0.584	6.251	7.815	9.348	11.34	12.84
4	0.207	0.297	0.484	0.711	1.064	7.779	9.488	11.14	13.28	14.86
5	0.412	0.554	0.831	1.145	1.610	9.236	11.07	12.83	15.09	16.75
6	0.676	0.872	1.237	1.635	2.204	10.64	12.59	14.45	16.81	18.55
7	0.989	1.239	1.690	2.167	2.833	12.02	14.07	16.01	18.48	20.28
8	1.344	1.646	2.180	2.733	3.490	13.36	15.51	17.53	20.09	21.95
9	1.735	2.088	2.700	3.325	4.168	14.68	16.92	19.02	21.67	23.59
10	2.156	2.558	3.247	3.940	4.865	15.99	18.31	20.48	23.21	25.19
11	2.603	3.053	3.816	4.575	5.578	17.28	19.68	21.92	24.72	26.76
12	3.074	3.571	4.404	5.226	6.304	18.55	21.03	23.34	26.22	28.30
13	3.565	4.107	5.009	5.892	7.042	19.81	22.36	24.74	27.69	29.82
14	4.075	4.660	5.629	6.571	7.790	21.06	23.68	26.12	29.14	31.32
15	4.601	5.229	6.262	7.261	8.547	22.31	25.00	27.49	30.58	32.80
16	5.142	5.812	6.908	7.962	9.312	23.54	26.30	28.85	32.00	34.27
17	5.697	6.408	7.564	8.672	10.09	24.77	27.59	30.19	33.41	35.72
18	6.265	7.015	8.231	9.390	10.86	25.99	28.87	31.53	34.81	37.16
19	6.844	7.633	8.907	10.12	11.65	27.20	30.14	32.85	36.19	38.58
20	7.434	8.260	9.591	10.85	12.44	28.41	31.41	34.17	37.57	40.00
21	8.034	8.897	10.28	11.59	13.24	29.62	32.67	35.48	38.93	41.40
22	8.643	9.542	10.98	12.34	14.04	30.81	33.92	36.78	40.29	42.80
23	9.260	10.20	11.69	13.09	14.85	32.01	35.17	38.08	41.64	44.18
24	9.886	10.86	12.40	13.85	15.66	33.20	36.42	39.36	42.98	45.56
25	10.52	11.52	13.12	14.61	16.47	34.38	37.65	40.65	44.31	46.93
26	11.16	12.20	13.84	15.38	17.29	35.56	38.89	41.92	45.64	48.29
27	11.81	12.88	14.57	16.15	18.11	36.74	40.11	43.19	46.96	49.64
28	12.46	13.56	15.31	16.93	18.94	37.92	41.34	44.46	48.28	50.99
29	13.12	14.26	16.05	17.71	19.77	39.09	42.56	45.72	49.59	52.34
30	13.79	14.95	16.79	18.49	20.60	40.26	43.77	46.98	50.89	53.67
35	17.19	18.51	20.57	22.47	24.80	46.06	49.80	53.20	57.34	60.27
40	20.71	22.16	24.43	26.51	29.05	51.81	55.76	59.34	63.69	66.77
45	24.31	25.90	28.37	30.61	33.35	57.51	61.66	65.41	69.96	73.17
50	27.99	29.71	32.36	34.76	37.69	63.17	67.50	71.42	76.15	79.49
60	35.53	37.48	40.48	43.19	46.46	74.40	79.08	83.30	88.38	91.95
70	43.28	45.44	48.76	51.74	55.33	85.53	90.53	95.02	100.4	104.2
80	51.17	53.54	57.15	60.39	64.28	96.58	101.9	106.6	112.3	116.3
90	59.20	61.75	65.65	69.13	73.29	107.6	113.1	118.1	124.1	128.3
100	67.33	70.06	74.22	77.93	82.36	118.5	124.3	129.6	135.8	140.2

[a]This value is actually 3.9×10^{-5}.
[b]This value is actually 1.6×10^{-4}.

A.6

CRITICAL VALUES OF THE *F* DISTRIBUTION

The critical value $F_{k,l;q}$ is the value below which lies an area q under the density curve of the F distribution with k and l degrees of freedom: that is, quantile q of the $F_{k,l}$ distribution. Tabled are these critical values $F_{k,l;q}$ for selected degrees of freedom k and l and quantiles q. This is shown graphically in Figure A.4, in which the curve represents a $F_{k,l}$ density curve. The critical value $F_{k,l;q}$ is the value F in the figure for which the shaded area equals q.

Two tables are given, the first for $q = 0.99$ and the second for $q = 0.95$.

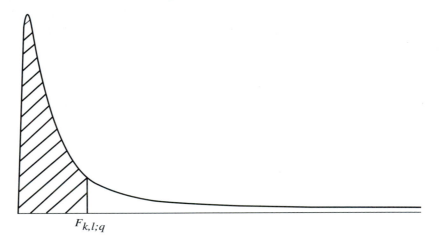

Figure A.4   *F* curve: shaded area is q; $F_{k,l;q}$ is tabled.

Critical values of the F distribution: $F_{k,l,0.99}$

	Numerator degrees of freedom, k																	
Denominator degrees of freedom, l	1	2	3	4	5	6	7	8	9	10	15	20	25	30	40	50	100	∞
1	4052	5000	5403	5625	5764	5859	5928	5981	6022	6056	6157	6209	6240	6261	6287	6303	6334	6366
2	98.50	99.00	99.17	99.25	99.30	99.33	99.36	99.37	99.39	99.40	99.43	99.45	99.46	99.47	99.47	99.48	99.49	99.50
3	34.12	30.82	29.46	28.71	28.24	27.91	27.67	27.49	27.35	27.23	26.87	26.69	26.58	26.50	26.41	26.35	26.24	26.13
4	21.20	18.00	16.69	15.98	15.52	15.21	14.98	14.80	14.66	14.55	14.20	14.02	13.91	13.84	13.75	13.69	13.58	13.46
5	16.26	13.27	12.06	11.39	10.97	10.67	10.46	10.29	10.16	10.05	9.722	9.553	9.449	9.379	9.291	9.238	9.130	9.020
6	13.75	10.92	9.780	9.148	8.746	8.466	8.260	8.102	7.976	7.874	7.559	7.396	7.296	7.229	7.143	7.091	6.987	6.880
7	12.25	9.547	8.451	7.847	7.460	7.191	6.993	6.840	6.719	6.620	6.314	6.155	6.058	5.992	5.908	5.858	5.755	5.650
8	11.26	8.649	7.591	7.006	6.632	6.371	6.178	6.029	5.911	5.814	5.515	5.359	5.263	5.198	5.116	5.065	4.963	4.859
9	10.56	8.022	6.992	6.422	6.057	5.802	5.613	5.467	5.351	5.257	4.962	4.808	4.713	4.649	4.567	4.517	4.415	4.311
10	10.04	7.559	6.552	5.994	5.636	5.386	5.200	5.057	4.942	4.849	4.558	4.405	4.311	4.247	4.165	4.115	4.014	3.909
11	9.646	7.206	6.217	5.668	5.316	5.069	4.886	4.744	4.632	4.539	4.251	4.099	4.005	3.941	3.860	3.810	3.708	3.602
12	9.330	6.927	5.953	5.412	5.064	4.821	4.640	4.499	4.388	4.296	4.010	3.858	3.765	3.701	3.619	3.569	3.467	3.361
13	9.074	6.701	5.739	5.205	4.862	4.620	4.441	4.302	4.191	4.100	3.815	3.665	3.571	3.507	3.425	3.375	3.272	3.165
14	8.862	6.515	5.564	5.035	4.695	4.456	4.278	4.140	4.030	3.939	3.656	3.505	3.412	3.348	3.266	3.215	3.112	3.004
15	8.683	6.359	5.417	4.893	4.556	4.318	4.142	4.004	3.895	3.805	3.522	3.372	3.278	3.214	3.132	3.081	2.977	2.868
16	8.531	6.226	5.292	4.773	4.437	4.202	4.026	3.890	3.780	3.691	3.409	3.259	3.165	3.101	3.018	2.967	2.863	2.753
17	8.400	6.112	5.185	4.669	4.336	4.102	3.927	3.791	3.682	3.593	3.312	3.162	3.068	3.003	2.920	2.869	2.764	2.653
18	8.285	6.013	5.092	4.579	4.248	4.015	3.841	3.705	3.597	3.508	3.227	3.077	2.983	2.919	2.835	2.784	2.678	2.566
19	8.185	5.926	5.010	4.500	4.171	3.939	3.765	3.631	3.523	3.434	3.153	3.003	2.909	2.844	2.761	2.709	2.602	2.489
20	8.096	5.849	4.938	4.431	4.103	3.871	3.699	3.564	3.457	3.368	3.088	2.938	2.843	2.778	2.695	2.643	2.535	2.421
21	8.017	5.780	4.874	4.369	4.042	3.812	3.640	3.506	3.398	3.310	3.030	2.880	2.785	2.720	2.636	2.584	2.475	2.360
22	7.945	5.719	4.817	4.313	3.988	3.758	3.587	3.453	3.346	3.258	2.978	2.827	2.733	2.667	2.583	2.531	2.422	2.305
23	7.881	5.664	4.765	4.264	3.939	3.710	3.539	3.406	3.299	3.211	2.931	2.781	2.686	2.620	2.535	2.483	2.373	2.256
24	7.823	5.614	4.718	4.218	3.895	3.667	3.496	3.363	3.256	3.168	2.889	2.738	2.643	2.577	2.492	2.440	2.329	2.211
25	7.770	5.568	4.675	4.177	3.855	3.627	3.457	3.324	3.217	3.129	2.850	2.699	2.604	2.538	2.453	2.400	2.289	2.169
26	7.721	5.526	4.637	4.140	3.818	3.591	3.421	3.288	3.182	3.094	2.815	2.664	2.569	2.503	2.417	2.364	2.252	2.131
27	7.677	5.488	4.601	4.106	3.785	3.558	3.388	3.256	3.149	3.062	2.783	2.632	2.536	2.470	2.384	2.330	2.218	2.097
28	7.636	5.453	4.568	4.074	3.754	3.528	3.358	3.226	3.120	3.032	2.753	2.602	2.506	2.440	2.354	2.300	2.187	2.064
29	7.598	5.420	4.538	4.045	3.725	3.499	3.330	3.198	3.092	3.005	2.726	2.574	2.478	2.412	2.325	2.271	2.158	2.034
30	7.562	5.390	4.510	4.018	3.699	3.473	3.304	3.173	3.067	2.979	2.700	2.549	2.453	2.386	2.299	2.245	2.131	2.006
40	7.314	5.179	4.313	3.828	3.514	3.291	3.124	2.993	2.888	2.801	2.522	2.369	2.271	2.203	2.114	2.058	1.938	1.805
50	7.171	5.057	4.199	3.720	3.408	3.186	3.020	2.890	2.785	2.698	2.419	2.265	2.167	2.098	2.007	1.949	1.825	1.683
100	6.895	4.824	3.984	3.513	3.206	2.988	2.823	2.694	2.590	2.503	2.223	2.067	1.965	1.893	1.797	1.735	1.598	1.427
∞	6.635	4.605	3.782	3.319	3.017	2.802	2.639	2.511	2.407	2.321	2.039	1.878	1.773	1.696	1.592	1.523	1.358	1.001

Critical values of the F distribution: $F_{k,l,0.95}$

l	\multicolumn{18}{c}{Numerator degrees of freedom, k}
	1	2	3	4	5	6	7	8	9	10	15	20	25	30	40	50	100	∞
1	161.4	199.5	215.7	224.6	230.2	234	236.8	238.9	240.5	241.9	245.9	248.0	249.3	250.1	251.1	251.8	253.0	254.3
2	18.51	19.00	19.16	19.25	19.30	19.33	19.35	19.37	19.38	19.40	19.43	19.45	19.46	19.46	19.47	19.48	19.49	19.50
3	10.13	9.552	9.277	9.117	9.013	8.941	8.887	8.845	8.812	8.786	8.703	8.660	8.634	8.617	8.594	8.581	8.554	8.526
4	7.709	6.944	6.591	6.388	6.256	6.163	6.094	6.041	5.999	5.964	5.858	5.803	5.769	5.746	5.717	5.699	5.664	5.628
5	6.608	5.786	5.409	5.192	5.050	4.950	4.876	4.818	4.772	4.735	4.619	4.558	4.521	4.496	4.464	4.444	4.405	4.365
6	5.987	5.143	4.757	4.534	4.387	4.284	4.207	4.147	4.099	4.060	3.938	3.874	3.835	3.808	3.774	3.754	3.712	3.669
7	5.591	4.737	4.347	4.120	3.972	3.866	3.787	3.726	3.677	3.637	3.511	3.445	3.404	3.376	3.340	3.319	3.275	3.230
8	5.318	4.459	4.066	3.838	3.687	3.581	3.500	3.438	3.388	3.347	3.218	3.150	3.108	3.079	3.043	3.020	2.975	2.928
9	5.117	4.256	3.863	3.633	3.482	3.374	3.293	3.230	3.179	3.137	3.006	2.936	2.893	2.864	2.826	2.803	2.756	2.707
10	4.965	4.103	3.708	3.478	3.326	3.217	3.135	3.072	3.020	2.978	2.845	2.774	2.730	2.700	2.661	2.637	2.588	2.538
11	4.844	3.982	3.587	3.357	3.204	3.095	3.012	2.948	2.896	2.854	2.719	2.646	2.601	2.570	2.531	2.507	2.457	2.404
12	4.747	3.885	3.490	3.259	3.106	2.996	2.913	2.849	2.796	2.753	2.617	2.544	2.498	2.466	2.426	2.401	2.350	2.296
13	4.667	3.806	3.411	3.179	3.025	2.915	2.832	2.767	2.714	2.671	2.533	2.459	2.412	2.380	2.339	2.314	2.261	2.206
14	4.600	3.739	3.344	3.112	2.958	2.848	2.764	2.699	2.646	2.602	2.463	2.388	2.341	2.308	2.266	2.241	2.187	2.131
15	4.543	3.682	3.287	3.056	2.901	2.790	2.707	2.641	2.588	2.544	2.403	2.328	2.280	2.247	2.204	2.178	2.123	2.066
16	4.494	3.634	3.239	3.007	2.852	2.741	2.657	2.591	2.538	2.494	2.352	2.276	2.227	2.194	2.151	2.124	2.068	2.010
17	4.451	3.592	3.197	2.965	2.810	2.699	2.614	2.548	2.494	2.450	2.308	2.230	2.181	2.148	2.104	2.077	2.020	1.960
18	4.414	3.555	3.160	2.928	2.773	2.661	2.577	2.510	2.456	2.412	2.269	2.191	2.141	2.107	2.063	2.035	1.978	1.917
19	4.381	3.522	3.127	2.895	2.740	2.628	2.544	2.477	2.423	2.378	2.234	2.155	2.106	2.071	2.026	1.999	1.940	1.878
20	4.351	3.493	3.098	2.866	2.711	2.599	2.514	2.447	2.393	2.348	2.203	2.124	2.074	2.039	1.994	1.966	1.907	1.843
21	4.325	3.467	3.072	2.840	2.685	2.573	2.488	2.420	2.366	2.321	2.176	2.096	2.045	2.010	1.965	1.936	1.876	1.812
22	4.301	3.443	3.049	2.817	2.661	2.549	2.464	2.397	2.342	2.297	2.151	2.071	2.020	1.984	1.938	1.909	1.849	1.783
23	4.279	3.422	3.028	2.796	2.640	2.528	2.442	2.375	2.320	2.275	2.128	2.048	1.996	1.961	1.914	1.885	1.823	1.757
24	4.260	3.403	3.009	2.776	2.621	2.508	2.423	2.355	2.300	2.255	2.108	2.027	1.975	1.939	1.892	1.863	1.800	1.733
25	4.242	3.385	2.991	2.759	2.603	2.490	2.405	2.337	2.282	2.236	2.089	2.007	1.955	1.919	1.872	1.842	1.779	1.711
26	4.225	3.369	2.975	2.743	2.587	2.474	2.388	2.321	2.265	2.220	2.072	1.990	1.938	1.901	1.853	1.823	1.760	1.691
27	4.210	3.354	2.960	2.728	2.572	2.459	2.373	2.305	2.250	2.204	2.056	1.974	1.921	1.884	1.836	1.806	1.742	1.672
28	4.196	3.340	2.947	2.714	2.558	2.445	2.359	2.291	2.236	2.190	2.041	1.959	1.906	1.869	1.820	1.790	1.725	1.654
29	4.183	3.328	2.934	2.701	2.545	2.432	2.346	2.278	2.223	2.177	2.027	1.945	1.891	1.854	1.806	1.775	1.710	1.638
30	4.171	3.316	2.922	2.690	2.534	2.421	2.334	2.266	2.211	2.165	2.015	1.932	1.878	1.841	1.792	1.761	1.695	1.622
40	4.085	3.232	2.839	2.606	2.449	2.336	2.249	2.180	2.124	2.077	1.924	1.839	1.783	1.744	1.693	1.660	1.589	1.509
50	4.034	3.183	2.790	2.557	2.400	2.286	2.199	2.130	2.073	2.026	1.871	1.784	1.727	1.687	1.634	1.599	1.525	1.438
100	3.936	3.087	2.696	2.463	2.305	2.191	2.103	2.032	1.975	1.927	1.768	1.676	1.616	1.573	1.515	1.477	1.392	1.283
∞	3.841	2.996	2.605	2.372	2.214	2.099	2.010	1.938	1.880	1.831	1.666	1.571	1.506	1.459	1.394	1.350	1.243	1.001

A.7

TABLE OF RANDOM DIGITS[a]

Row				Table of random digits				
1	489603	272922	751103	838823	401597	317816	790344	068359
2	041863	967007	569984	953158	757081	448552	017030	351661
3	513514	228641	557839	698999	469379	271538	616180	253473
4	904689	406237	701811	371597	516605	980334	958803	386477
5	528769	757338	937577	396178	253543	971588	786185	202369
6	788073	386933	609113	120803	916516	361977	796978	426263
7	639884	576786	965372	471465	757173	308181	251927	427225
8	673943	180225	957878	379661	525909	370665	761640	235731
9	854865	608652	918005	143028	728641	299685	123340	047942
10	915293	464235	335633	907463	957808	660544	342004	919893
11	437657	025151	092608	802778	873908	776887	268507	554492
12	698639	806163	348833	561221	348944	085930	937793	661819
13	077082	487109	812230	233418	329963	467593	935007	369100
14	724791	790427	045150	299427	483723	151689	825020	550721
15	915804	020017	035659	014875	136581	914757	251523	324302
16	801090	776488	758060	009593	953851	051906	191535	835793
17	541139	180959	688369	587411	670140	060728	063536	981934
18	761488	953842	244255	441300	202967	416538	027735	980551
19	715543	367628	312767	823131	003390	494916	169074	591611
20	836362	701590	717950	011142	927065	873018	025973	688799
21	647717	348660	156030	994120	130391	472637	779721	993061
22	170765	651215	544782	920823	577834	397489	174953	623506
23	584722	606916	737474	237188	444032	724970	805305	583948
24	571153	600700	323852	739006	869074	001168	583831	487444
25	641015	162408	228825	962199	126730	078131	867864	378588
26	158144	143895	140256	741463	953107	633758	167651	387283
27	329018	685704	774802	545398	907609	507065	399132	891188
28	629521	024388	771689	252067	629788	190523	526414	879135
29	702713	905189	986457	123364	112119	548757	358302	062234
30	673654	489334	901445	556856	301996	488234	045365	083238
31	929213	326126	030722	710942	562356	379837	899403	646112
32	472826	011733	962183	700323	878016	611298	636870	963250
33	154724	137837	974746	892535	109686	840304	927262	387193
34	415016	095417	745763	464257	976284	946303	640398	396757
35	472006	147412	658634	608750	600425	959376	739741	300837
36	970761	990010	908518	934971	839006	661593	254040	602082
37	059485	462195	165393	770430	840679	665101	101645	228384
38	299570	508640	211724	080373	987658	472198	932342	169682
39	338696	350187	234563	573347	969443	123359	585432	823584
40	464579	243007	059461	676200	654081	342355	193796	324126

[a]Instructions for using the table are on the next page.

Using the Table of Random Digits

The numbers in the table of random digits are completely random. That is, the individual digits are equally likely, and strings of digits of the same length are equally likely. The digits are arranged in sets of six just for convenience in reading.

To illustrate the use of the random number table, consider the assignment of Example 3.10 in Chapter 3.

- Since there are 15 fabric samples, we will consider the table to consist of two-digit numbers (if there were fewer than 11 fabric samples, we could consider it to consist of single-digit numbers; if between 100 and 1001, of three-digit numbers; etc.).

- Pick a six-digit number at random in the table. (This is done by not looking at the table.)

- Suppose we pick 994120 (row 21, column 4); start here and relabel the digits as two-digit numbers (i.e., as 99, 41, and 20). This gives the first three random numbers. To get the rest, continue on to the next columns, obtaining numbers 13, 03, 91, 47, 26, 37, 77, 97, 21, 99, 30, and 61. Fifteen numbers have been selected in all, but there are only 14 distinct numbers, since the number 99 appears twice. Since we need 15 distinct numbers, we must select at least one more. As the last number selected, 61, was at the end of row 21, we move on to the first column of row 22 for the next selection. The result is 17. As 17 is not among the numbers previously selected, we stop here. Discarding the second 99, we have 15 distinct random numbers.

- Assign the first number selected to fabric sample 1, the second to fabric sample 2, and so on. Assign the fabric samples with the five lowest random numbers to treatment 1, the fabric samples with the next five lowest random numbers to treatment 2, and the fabric samples with the five highest random numbers to treatment 3. Table A.1 shows the resulting assignment.

TABLE A.1   Random Assignment of Fabric Samples to Treatment

			Treatment													
			1					2						3			
Sorted order	3	13	17	20	21		26	30	37	41	47		61	77	91	97	99
Fabric sample| 5	4	15	3	12		8	13	9	2	7		14	10	6	11	1

A.8

TABLE OF CONSTANTS FOR NORMAL-THEORY TOLERANCE INTERVALS

Tabled are constants K for which the interval $(\bar{Y} - KS, \bar{Y} + KS)$ will contain a proportion at least γ of the population with probability at least L.

n	$L = 0.90$			$L = 0.95$			$L = 0.99$		
	$\gamma = 0.90$	$\gamma = 0.95$	$\gamma = 0.99$	$\gamma = 0.90$	$\gamma = 0.95$	$\gamma = 0.99$	$\gamma = 0.90$	$\gamma = 0.95$	$\gamma = 0.99$
2	15.980	18.800	24.170	32.020	37.670	48.430	160.200	188.500	242.300
3	5.847	6.919	8.974	8.380	9.916	12.860	18.930	22.400	29.060
4	4.166	4.943	6.440	5.369	6.370	8.299	9.398	11.10	14.530
5	3.494	4.152	5.423	4.275	5.079	6.634	6.612	7.855	10.260
6	3.131	3.723	4.870	3.712	4.414	5.775	5.337	6.345	8.301
7	2.902	3.452	4.521	3.369	4.007	5.248	4.613	5.448	7.187
8	2.743	3.264	4.278	3.136	3.732	4.891	4.147	4.936	6.468
9	2.626	3.125	4.098	2.967	3.532	4.631	3.822	4.550	5.966
10	2.535	3.018	3.959	2.829	3.379	4.433	3.582	4.265	5.594
11	2.463	2.933	3.849	2.737	3.259	4.277	3.397	4.045	5.308
12	2.404	2.863	3.758	2.655	3.162	4.150	3.250	3.870	5.079
13	2.355	2.805	3.682	2.587	3.081	4.044	3.130	3.727	4.893
14	2.314	2.756	3.618	2.529	3.012	3.955	3.029	3.608	4.737
15	2.278	2.713	3.562	2.480	2.954	3.878	2.945	3.507	4.605
16	2.246	2.676	3.514	2.437	2.903	3.812	2.872	3.421	4.492
17	2.219	2.643	3.471	2.400	2.858	3.754	2.808	3.345	4.393
18	2.194	2.614	3.433	2.366	2.819	3.702	2.753	3.279	4.307
19	2.172	2.588	3.399	2.337	2.784	3.656	2.703	3.221	4.230
20	2.152	2.564	3.368	2.310	2.752	3.615	2.659	3.168	4.161
21	2.135	2.543	3.340	2.286	2.723	3.577	2.620	3.121	4.100
22	2.118	2.524	3.315	2.264	2.697	3.543	2.584	1.078	4.044
23	2.103	2.506	3.292	2.244	2.673	3.512	2.551	3.040	3.993
24	2.089	2.489	3.270	2.225	2.651	3.483	2.522	3.004	3.947
25	2.077	2.474	3.251	2.208	2.631	3.457	2.494	2.972	3.904
26	2.065	2.460	3.232	2.193	2.612	3.432	2.469	2.941	3.865
27	2.054	2.447	3.215	2.178	2.595	3.409	2.446	2.914	3.828
28	2.044	2.435	3.199	2.164	2.579	3.388	2.424	2.888	3.794
29	2.034	2.424	3.184	2.152	2.554	3.368	2.404	2.864	3.763
30	2.025	2.413	3.170	2.140	2.549	3.350	2.385	2.841	3.733
35	1.988	2.368	3.112	2.090	2.490	3.272	2.306	2.748	3.611
40	1.959	2.334	3.066	2.052	2.445	3.213	2.247	2.677	3.518
50	1.916	2.284	3.001	1.996	2.379	3.126	2.162	2.576	3.385
60	1.887	2.248	2.955	1.958	2.333	3.066	2.103	2.506	3.293
80	1.848	2.202	2.894	1.907	2.272	2.986	2.026	2.414	3.173
100	1.822	2.172	2.854	1.874	2.233	2.934	1.977	2.355	3.096
200	1.764	2.102	2.762	1.798	2.143	2.816	1.865	2.222	2.921
500	1.717	2.046	2.689	1.737	2.070	2.721	1.777	2.117	2.783
1000	1.695	2.019	2.654	1.709	2.036	2.676	1.736	2.068	2.718
∞	1.645	1.960	2.576	1.645	1.960	2.576	1.645	1.960	2.576

A.9

STUDENTIZED RANGE DISTRIBUTION QUANTILES

Tabled are the values $q(L, k, v)$, below which lie a proportion L of the studentized range distribution based on k populations and v degrees of freedom. There are three tables, one for each of $L = 0.90, 0.95,$ and 0.99.

				$q(0.90, k, v)$					
				k					
v	2	3	4	5	6	7	8	9	10
1	8.93	13.44	16.36	18.49	20.15	21.50	22.64	23.62	24.48
2	4.13	5.73	6.77	7.54	8.14	8.63	9.05	9.41	9.72
3	3.33	4.47	5.20	5.74	6.16	6.51	6.81	7.06	7.29
4	3.01	3.98	4.59	5.03	5.39	5.68	5.93	6.14	6.33
5	2.85	3.72	4.26	4.66	4.98	5.24	5.46	5.65	5.82
6	2.75	3.56	4.07	4.44	4.73	4.97	5.17	5.34	5.50
7	2.68	3.45	3.93	4.28	4.55	4.78	4.97	5.14	5.28
8	2.63	3.37	3.83	4.17	4.43	4.65	4.83	4.99	5.13
9	2.59	3.32	3.76	4.08	4.34	4.54	4.72	4.87	5.01
10	2.56	3.27	3.70	4.02	4.26	4.47	4.64	4.78	4.91
11	2.54	3.23	3.66	3.96	4.20	4.40	4.57	4.71	4.84
12	2.52	3.20	3.62	3.92	4.16	4.35	4.51	4.65	4.78
13	2.50	3.18	3.59	3.88	4.12	4.30	4.46	4.60	4.72
14	2.49	3.16	3.56	3.85	4.08	4.27	4.42	4.56	4.68
15	2.48	3.14	3.54	3.83	4.05	4.23	4.39	4.52	4.64
16	2.47	3.12	3.52	3.80	4.03	4.21	4.36	4.49	4.61
17	2.46	3.11	3.50	3.78	4.00	4.18	4.33	4.46	4.58
18	2.45	3.10	3.49	3.77	3.98	4.16	4.31	4.44	4.55
19	2.45	3.09	3.47	3.75	3.97	4.14	4.29	4.42	4.53
20	2.44	3.08	3.46	3.74	3.95	4.12	4.27	4.40	4.51
25	2.42	3.04	3.42	3.68	3.89	4.06	4.20	4.32	4.43
30	2.40	3.02	3.39	3.65	3.85	4.02	4.16	4.28	4.38
35	2.39	3.00	3.36	3.62	3.82	3.99	4.12	4.24	4.34
40	2.38	2.99	3.35	3.60	3.80	3.96	4.10	4.21	4.32
45	2.38	2.98	3.34	3.59	3.79	3.95	4.08	4.19	4.30
50	2.37	2.97	3.33	3.58	3.77	3.93	4.06	4.18	4.28
60	2.36	2.96	3.31	3.56	3.75	3.91	4.04	4.16	4.25
70	2.36	2.95	3.30	3.55	3.74	3.90	4.03	4.14	4.24
80	2.35	2.94	3.29	3.54	3.73	3.89	4.01	4.13	4.22
90	2.35	2.94	3.29	3.53	3.72	3.88	4.01	4.12	4.21
100	2.35	2.94	3.28	3.53	3.72	3.87	4.00	4.11	4.20
∞	2.33	2.90	3.24	3.48	3.66	3.81	3.93	4.04	4.13

| | $q(0.95, k, \nu)$ | | | | | | | | |
| | k | | | | | | | | |
ν	2	3	4	5	6	7	8	9	10
1	17.97	26.98	32.82	37.08	40.41	43.12	45.40	47.36	49.07
2	6.08	8.33	9.80	10.88	11.73	12.43	13.03	13.54	13.99
3	4.50	5.91	6.82	7.50	8.04	8.48	8.85	9.18	9.46
4	3.93	5.04	5.76	6.29	6.71	7.05	7.35	7.60	7.83
5	3.64	4.60	5.22	5.67	6.03	6.33	6.58	6.80	6.99
6	3.46	4.34	4.90	5.30	5.63	5.90	6.12	6.32	6.49
7	3.34	4.16	4.68	5.06	5.36	5.61	5.81	5.99	6.15
8	3.26	4.04	4.53	4.89	5.17	5.40	5.60	5.77	5.92
9	3.20	3.95	4.41	4.76	5.02	5.24	5.43	5.59	5.74
10	3.15	3.88	4.33	4.65	4.91	5.12	5.30	5.46	5.60
11	3.11	3.82	4.26	4.57	4.82	5.03	5.20	5.35	5.49
12	3.08	3.77	4.20	4.51	4.75	4.95	5.12	5.26	5.39
13	3.06	3.73	4.15	4.45	4.69	4.88	5.05	5.19	5.32
14	3.03	3.70	4.11	4.41	4.64	4.83	4.99	5.13	5.25
15	3.01	3.67	4.08	4.37	4.59	4.78	4.94	5.08	5.20
16	3.00	3.65	4.05	4.33	4.56	4.74	4.90	5.03	5.15
17	2.98	3.63	4.02	4.30	4.52	4.70	4.86	4.99	5.11
18	2.97	3.61	4.00	4.28	4.49	4.67	4.82	4.96	5.07
19	2.96	3.59	3.98	4.25	4.47	4.64	4.79	4.92	5.04
20	2.95	3.58	3.96	4.23	4.45	4.62	4.77	4.90	5.01
25	2.91	3.52	3.89	4.15	4.36	4.53	4.67	4.79	4.90
30	2.89	3.49	3.85	4.10	4.30	4.46	4.60	4.72	4.82
35	2.87	3.46	3.81	4.07	4.26	4.42	4.55	4.67	4.77
40	2.86	3.44	3.79	4.04	4.23	4.39	4.52	4.63	4.73
45	2.85	3.43	3.77	4.02	4.21	4.36	4.49	4.61	4.70
50	2.84	3.42	3.76	4.00	4.19	4.34	4.47	4.58	4.68
60	2.83	3.40	3.74	3.98	4.16	4.31	4.44	4.55	4.65
70	2.82	3.39	3.72	3.96	4.14	4.29	4.42	4.53	4.62
80	2.81	3.38	3.71	3.95	4.13	4.28	4.40	4.51	4.60
90	2.81	3.37	3.70	3.94	4.12	4.27	4.39	4.50	4.59
100	2.81	3.36	3.70	3.93	4.11	4.26	4.38	4.48	4.58
∞	2.77	3.31	3.63	3.86	4.03	4.17	4.29	4.39	4.48

					$q(0.99, k, \nu)$				
					k				
ν	2	3	4	5	6	7	8	9	10
1	89.98	135.04	164.25	185.56	202.19	215.74	227.13	236.93	245.50
2	14.03	19.02	22.29	24.72	26.63	28.20	29.53	30.68	31.69
3	8.26	10.62	12.17	13.32	14.24	15.00	15.64	16.20	16.69
4	6.51	8.12	9.17	9.96	10.58	11.10	11.54	11.93	12.26
5	5.70	6.98	7.81	8.42	8.91	9.32	9.67	9.97	10.24
6	5.24	6.33	7.03	7.56	7.97	8.32	8.61	8.87	9.10
7	4.95	5.92	6.55	7.02	7.39	7.70	7.98	8.21	8.43
8	4.74	5.64	6.20	6.63	6.97	7.24	7.48	7.69	7.88
9	4.60	5.43	5.96	6.35	6.66	6.92	7.14	7.33	7.50
10	4.48	5.27	5.77	6.14	6.43	6.67	6.88	7.05	7.21
11	4.39	5.15	5.62	5.97	6.25	6.48	6.67	6.84	6.99
12	4.32	5.05	5.50	5.84	6.10	6.32	6.51	6.68	6.82
13	4.26	4.96	5.40	5.73	5.98	6.19	6.37	6.53	6.67
14	4.21	4.89	5.32	5.63	5.88	6.09	6.26	6.41	6.55
15	4.17	4.84	5.25	5.56	5.80	5.99	6.16	6.31	6.44
16	4.13	4.79	5.19	5.49	5.72	5.91	6.08	6.22	6.35
17	4.10	4.74	5.14	5.43	5.66	5.85	6.01	6.15	6.27
18	4.07	4.70	5.09	5.38	5.60	5.79	5.94	6.08	6.20
19	4.05	4.67	5.05	5.33	5.55	5.74	5.89	6.02	6.14
20	4.02	4.64	5.02	5.29	5.51	5.69	5.84	5.97	6.09
25	3.94	4.53	4.88	5.14	5.35	5.51	5.65	5.78	5.89
30	3.89	4.45	4.80	5.05	5.24	5.40	5.54	5.65	5.76
35	3.85	4.40	4.74	4.98	5.17	5.32	5.45	5.57	5.67
40	3.82	4.37	4.70	4.93	5.11	5.26	5.39	5.50	5.60
45	3.80	4.34	4.66	4.89	5.07	5.22	5.34	5.45	5.55
50	3.79	4.32	4.63	4.86	5.04	5.18	5.31	5.41	5.51
60	3.76	4.28	4.59	4.82	4.99	5.13	5.25	5.36	5.45
70	3.74	4.26	4.57	4.79	4.96	5.10	5.21	5.31	5.40
80	3.73	4.24	4.55	4.76	4.93	5.07	5.18	5.28	5.37
90	3.72	4.23	4.53	4.74	4.91	5.05	5.16	5.26	5.35
100	3.71	4.22	4.52	4.73	4.90	5.03	5.14	5.24	5.33
∞	3.64	4.12	4.40	4.60	4.76	4.88	4.99	5.08	5.16

A.10

PROBABILITIES OF THE SPEARMAN CORRELATION

Tabled are values of $p^+ = P(r_s \geq r_s^*)$, for independent variates and potential observed values r_s^* of the Spearman correlation. Probabilities are presented for $n = 3, 4, \ldots, 10$ and the r_s^* values are selected to approximate common significance levels. Values of $p_- = P(r_s \leq r_s^*)$ may be obtained as $P(r_s \geq -r_s^*)$, and values of $p\pm = P(|r_s| \geq |r_s^*|)$ may be obtained as $p\pm = 2 \min\{p_-, p^+\}$. For $n > 10$, an approximate test of independence may be obtained from the fact that $r_s \sqrt{(n-2)/(1-r_s^2)}$ has approximately a t_{n-2} distribution under the assumption of independence.

n	r_s^*	$P(r_s \geq r_s^*)$	n	r_s^*	$P(r_s \geq r_s^*)$
3	1.000	0.167	8	0.809	0.011
4	0.800	0.167		0.738	0.023
	1.000	0.042		0.714	0.029
				0.642	0.048
5	1.000	0.008		0.619	0.057
	0.900	0.042		0.523	0.098
	0.800	0.067		0.500	0.108
	0.700	0.117			
6	0.942	0.008	9	0.816	0.005
	0.885	0.017		0.783	0.009
	0.828	0.029		0.766	0.011
	0.771	0.051		0.683	0.025
	0.657	0.088		0.600	0.048
	0.600	0.121		0.583	0.054
7	0.928	0.003		0.483	0.097
	0.892	0.006		0.466	0.106
	0.857	0.012			
	0.785	0.024	10	0.781	0.005
	0.714	0.044		0.733	0.010
	0.750	0.033		0.648	0.024
	0.678	0.055		0.636	0.027
	0.571	0.100		0.563	0.048
				0.551	0.052
8	0.857	0.005		0.454	0.095
	0.833	0.008		0.442	0.102

A.11

CONTROL CHART CONSTANTS

Number in subgroup, n	Constants			Number in subgroup, n	Constants		
	c_4	d_2	d_3		c_4	d_2	d_3
2	0.7979	1.1284	0.8525	14	0.9810	3.4068	0.7630
3	0.8862	1.6926	0.8884	15	0.9823	3.4718	0.7562
4	0.9213	2.0588	0.8798	16	0.9835	3.5320	0.7499
5	0.9400	2.3259	0.8641	17	0.9845	3.5879	0.7441
6	0.9515	2.5344	0.8480	18	0.9854	3.6401	0.7386
7	0.9594	2.7044	0.8332	19	0.9862	3.6890	0.7335
8	0.9650	2.8472	0.8198	20	0.9869	3.7350	0.7287
9	0.9693	2.9700	0.8078	21	0.9876	3.7783	0.7242
10	0.9727	3.0775	0.7971	22	0.9882	3.8194	0.7199
11	0.9754	3.1729	0.7873	23	0.9887	3.8583	0.7159
12	0.9776	3.2585	0.7785	24	0.9892	3.8953	0.7121
13	0.9794	3.3360	0.7704	25	0.9896	3.9306	0.7084

A.12

LOWER TAIL PROBABILITIES FOR THE WILCOXON SIGNED RANK STATISTIC

Tabled are the quantities $p_- = P(W \leq w^*)$, computed under the assumption that H_0 is true. The upper tail probabilities $p^+ = P(W \geq w^*)$ can be obtained from these by using the relation

$$P(W \geq w^*) = P(W \leq n(n+1)/2 - w^*)$$

n	w^*	p_-	n	w^*	p_-	n	w^*	p_-	n	w^*	p_-
3	0	0.125	10	14	0.097	14	32	0.108	17	49	0.103
4	1	0.125		11	0.053		31	0.097		48	0.095
	0	0.062		8	0.024		26	0.052		41	0.049
5	2	0.094		5	0.010		21	0.025		35	0.025
	1	0.062		3	0.005		16	0.010		28	0.010
	0	0.031	11	18	0.103		13	0.005		24	0.005
6	4	0.109		14	0.051	15	37	0.104	18	55	0.098
	2	0.047		11	0.027		36	0.094		47	0.049
	1	0.031		7	0.009		31	0.053		40	0.024
	0	0.016		5	0.005		30	0.047		33	0.010
7	6	0.109	12	22	0.102		25	0.024		28	0.005
	4	0.055		18	0.055		20	0.011	19	62	0.098
	2	0.023		17	0.046		19	0.009		54	0.052
	0	0.008		14	0.026		16	0.005		53	0.048
8	8	0.098		10	0.010	16	43	0.106		46	0.025
	6	0.055		7	0.005		42	0.096		38	0.010
	4	0.027	13	27	0.108		36	0.052		33	0.005
	2	0.012		26	0.095		30	0.025	20	70	0.101
	1	0.008		22	0.055		24	0.011		60	0.049
	0	0.004		21	0.047		23	0.009		52	0.024
9	11	0.102		17	0.024		20	0.005		43	0.010
	8	0.049		13	0.011					38	0.005
	6	0.027		12	0.009						
	3	0.010		10	0.005						
	1	0.004									

A.13

LOWER TAIL PROBABILITIES FOR THE WILCOXON RANK SUM STATISTIC

Tabled are the quantities $p_- = P(V \leq v^*)$, computed under the assumption that H_0 is true. The upper tail probabilities $p^+ = P(V \geq v^*)$ can be obtained from these by using the relation

$$P(V \geq v^*) = P(V \leq (n_1 + n_2 + 1)(n_1 + n_2)/2 - v^*).$$

n_1	n_2	v^*	p_-	n_1	n_2	v^*	p_-	n_1	n_2	v^*	p_-	n_1	n_2	v^*	p_-
2	3	6	0.100	4	4	12	0.057	5	6	26	0.041	6	8	47	0.054
	4	10	0.067			11	0.029			25	0.026			44	0.021
	5	10	0.048			10	0.014			23	0.009			42	0.010
	6	21	0.036		5	18	0.056			22	0.004			40	0.004
	7	29	0.056			17	0.032		7	35	0.053	7	7	39	0.049
		28	0.028			16	0.016			33	0.024			37	0.027
	8	37	0.044			15	0.008			31	0.009			34	0.009
		36	0.022		6	25	0.057			30	0.005			33	0.006
3	3	6	0.050			23	0.019		8	44	0.047		8	49	0.047
	4	11	0.057			22	0.010			42	0.023			47	0.027
		10	0.029			21	0.005			40	0.009			44	0.010
	5	16	0.036		7	33	0.055			39	0.005			42	0.005
		15	0.018			31	0.021	6	6	28	0.047	8	8	52	0.052
	6	23	0.048			30	0.012			26	0.021			49	0.025
		22	0.024			29	0.006			24	0.008			46	0.010
		21	0.012		8	42	0.055			23	0.004			44	0.005
	7	31	0.058			40	0.024		7	37	0.051				
		29	0.017			38	0.008			35	0.026				
		28	0.008			37	0.004			33	0.011				
	8	39	0.042	5	5	19	0.048			31	0.004				
		38	0.024			18	0.028								
		37	0.012			16	0.008								
		36	0.006			15	0.004								

A.14

CRITICAL CONSTANT *k* FOR
WILCOXON SIGNED RANK CONFIDENCE INTERVALS

Sample size, *n*	Confidence level, *L*	*k*	Sample size, *n*	Confidence level, *L*	*k*	Sample size, *n*	Confidence level, *L*	*k*
5	0.938	15	12	0.991	71	19	0.991	158
	0.875	15		0.948	64		0.951	144
6	0.969	21		0.908	61		0.904	137
	0.937	20	13	0.990	81	20	0.991	173
	0.906	19		0.952	74		0.952	158
7	0.984	28		0.906	70		0.903	150
	0.953	26	14	0.991	93	21	0.990	188
	0.891	24		0.951	84		0.950	172
8	0.992	36		0.896	79		0.897	163
	0.945	32	15	0.990	104	22	0.990	204
	0.891	30		0.952	95		0.950	187
9	0.992	44		0.905	90		0.902	178
	0.945	39	16	0.991	117	23	0.990	221
	0.902	37		0.949	106		0.952	203
10	0.990	52		0.895	100		0.902	178
	0.951	47	17	0.991	130	24	0.990	239
	0.895	44		0.949	118		0.951	219
11	0.990	61		0.902	112		0.899	208
	0.946	55	18	0.990	143	25	0.990	257
	0.898	52		0.952	131		0.952	236
				0.901	124		0.899	224

A.15

CRITICAL CONSTANT k FOR
WILCOXON RANK SUM CONFIDENCE INTERVALS

Larger sample size	Smaller sample size											
	2		3		4		5		6		7	
	Level, L	k	Level, L	k	Level, L	k	Level, L	k	Level, L	k	Level, L	k
3	0.800	6	0.900	9								
4	0.866	8	0.942	12	0.972	16						
			0.886	11	0.942	15						
					0.886	14						
5	0.904	10	0.964	15	0.984	20	0.992	25				
			0.928	14	0.936	18	0.944	22				
					0.888	17	0.905	21				
6	0.928	12	0.976	18	0.990	24	0.991	29	0.991	34		
			0.952	17	0.962	22	0.948	26	0.959	31		
			0.904	16	0.886	20	0.918	25	0.907	29		
7	0.944	14	0.984	21	0.988	27	0.990	33	0.992	39	0.989	44
	0.888	13	0.966	20	0.958	25	0.952	30	0.949	35	0.947	40
			0.884	18	0.890	23	0.894	28	0.899	33	0.903	38
8	0.956	16	0.988	24	0.992	31	0.989	37	0.992	44	0.991	50
	0.912	15	0.952	22	0.952	28	0.955	34	0.957	40	0.946	45
			0.916	21	0.890	26	0.907	32	0.892	37	0.906	43
9	0.964	18	0.990	27	0.988	34	0.988	41	0.992	49	0.992	56
	0.928	17	0.964	25	0.950	31	0.958	38	0.950	44	0.945	50
			0.900	22	0.894	29	0.888	35	0.912	42	0.909	48
10	0.970	20	0.994	30	0.992	38	0.992	46	0.989	53	0.990	61
	0.940	19	0.952	27	0.946	34	0.945	41	0.944	48	0.945	55
	0.878	18	0.924	26	0.894	32	0.901	39	0.907	46	0.891	52
11	0.974	22	0.990	32	0.990	41	0.991	50	0.990	58	0.989	66
	0.948	21	0.962	30	0.944	37	0.948	45	0.952	53	0.956	61
	0.898	20	0.912	28	0.896	35	0.910	43	0.902	50	0.896	57
12	0.978	24	0.992	35	0.992	45	0.991	54	0.990	63	0.990	72
	0.956	23	0.952	32	0.958	41	0.952	49	0.947	57	0.955	66
	0.912	22	0.898	30	0.896	38	0.896	46	0.898	54	0.900	62

Larger sample size	Smaller sample size									
	8		9		10		11		12	
	Level, *L*	*k*	Level, *L*	*k*	Level, *L*	*k*	Level, *L*	*k*	Level, *L*	*k*
8	0.990	56								
	0.950	51								
	0.895	48								
9	0.989	62	0.989	69						
	0.954	57	0.950	63						
	0.907	54	0.906	60						
10	0.991	69	0.990	76	0.991	84				
	0.945	62	0.947	69	0.948	76				
	0.899	59	0.905	66	0.895	72				
11	0.991	75	0.990	83	0.990	91	0.989	99		
	0.949	68	0.954	76	0.949	83	0.953	91		
	0.909	65	0.905	72	0.901	79	0.899	86		
12	0.990	81	0.991	90	0.991	99	0.991	108	0.990	116
	0.953	74	0.951	82	0.950	90	0.949	98	0.948	106
	0.902	70	0.905	78	0.907	86	0.896	93	0.899	101

Answers to Odd-Numbered Exercises

CHAPTER 1: Introduction to Data Analysis

1.1. **(a)** Possibly non-stationary. Voters could change their minds.

(b) Stationary. Voters cannot change their minds.

1.5. A histogram cannot be used to detect stationarity or non-stationarity. The data must be plotted versus time.

1.7.

Scale	1	2	3	4	5	6	7	8	9	10
Worn Gears		x		x			x			x
Mis-calibration			x	x		x	x	x	x	x

1.9. **(a)** Not stationary. There is a big drop in 1896. Plot of times versus year.

(b) A downward trend in times even after 1896.

1.11. Trend is increasing from about 24 KWH per day in mid October to $\approx$31 KWH per day in early January, then decreasing to $\approx$24 KWH per day by mid April.

1.13. Except for 2 outliers, plot of times versus dates looks reasonably stationary.

1.21. This is a moving average, where if y_t is the batch at time t, the blended batch at time t is $z_t = (y_{t-2} + y_{t-1} + y_t)/3$.

1.23. *Within* counselor variation and *between* counselor variation. Use a stratified plot.

1.25. A histogram such as this cannot detect stationarity.

CHAPTER 2: Summarizing Data

2.1. 3.6 will be just above the upper whisker. 3.4 will not appear individually. It is just inside the upper fence. Based on the boxplot, 3.6 is considered a possible outlier.

2.3. The data are in two distinct groups: 2, 3, 4, 5 years and 12, 13, 15, 15, 18, 20 years.

The first has mean 3.5 years, standard deviation 1.29 years.

The second has mean 15.5 and standard deviation 3.02 years.

The first were sentenced by "letemgo", the second by "lockemup".

2.5.

Process	Q_1	Q_2	Q_3	IQR	Summary
1	0.15	0.22	0.43	0.28	Higher but more variable yields.
2	0.02	0.04	0.09	0.07	Lower but more consistent yields.

2.7. Two groups

$$78, 79, 80, 81, 82 \qquad \bar{x} = Q_2 = 80, \qquad S = 1.58$$
$$98, 99, 100, 101, 102 \qquad \bar{x} = Q_2 = 100, \qquad S = 1.58$$

There are two different kinds of bars or materials or some other difference.

2.9. **(a)** There is one large outlier for beam C.

(b)

Beam	Q_1	Q_2	Q_3	IQR
A	82.5	84.5	86	3.5
B	75	76.5	78	3
C	78	79	79	1

(c) Beam B seems weakest, beam A the strongest.

2.11. **(a)**

Complex	Q_1	Q_2	Q_3
1	46	55	59
2	68	71	74

(b) Yes, some are $\approx$ 90 years in Complex 2.

(c) Complex 1 has middle aged tenants. Complex 2 has older, retired tenants.

2.13. **(a)** Side-by-side boxplots and/or stratified plots graphically summarize the salary data. The former show large outliers for the female data and small outliers for the male data.

(b)

Gender	Q_1	Q_2	Q_3
F	105	115	122.5
M	215	225	230

The graphs show that virtually all male salaries lie above the largest female salary. The summary table shows that Q_1 for the males lies well above Q_3 for the females. So there is evidence that men's salaries are substantially higher than women's salaries.

2.19. The median of the log is the log of the median: $\ln (12{,}756) = 9.45$. If using the definition on p. 51, then the log of any median of the original data is a median of the logged data, since the log is a monotone function. However, if using the formula on pp. 69–70, this is not true: If the data are 1, 2, 3 and 4, then the median is 2.5. The natural log of 2.5 is 0.91629. The logs of the data are 0, 0.69315, 1.09861, and 1.38629. The median of these is $0.89588 \neq 0.91629$.

2.23. No. If symmetric then the distance from the median to the pth and to the $(1 - p)^{th}$ percentiles should be roughly the same for each p. For these data the mean is 235 units from the 25th percentile, but 325 units from the 75th percentile; It is 325 units from the 10th percentile, but 625 units from the 90th percentile. This shows that the data are skewed right.

2.27. 1/4 of the mileages are at or below $Q_1 = 70{,}000$, 1/2 of the mileages are at or below $Q_2 = 88{,}000$, 3/4 of the mileages are at or below $Q_3 = 146{,}000$, and the average mileage is 94,778. A boxplot will summarize these data well.

2.29. The mode is 0.1884, which is the smallest data value. This does a poor job of summarizing the "center".

2.31. Suppose there are n observations and that we add $k < n$ new observations larger than all the old observations. Then the median must be either an old observation or be the average of two old observations. So the median does not move above the original data.

Suppose we add $k < n/3$ observations larger than all the old observations to the original data. Then there are $n + k$ total observations and Q_3 is the $3/4(n + k)^{th}$ smallest of these. Since $k < n/3$, $n + k < 4/3n$ and $3/4(n + k) < n$ so Q_3 must be one of the old observations or between two old observations.

2.35. Here are two data sets which do the job: 12 15 16 7 9 12 21 3 35 8; 12 15 16 6 9 12 21 3 35 8.

CHAPTER 3: Designing Studies and Collecting Data

3.1. A *repeat measures design* is most appropriate, in which each individual is given each drug. Randomization can be used to assign subjects to different orders in which drugs are given. (Note: order can also be used as a blocking variable.)

3.5. *Selection bias:* IV drug users likely under-represented. *Nonresponse bias:* Such a question might cause noncooperation from many. *Response bias:* People would be reluctant to answer such a question.

3.7. Blocking: paint each boat with both paints. This will reduce regional/environmental differences.

3.11. It could be: *Too high* if those at home were primarily mothers with children; *Too low* if those at home were primarily retired couples or individuals; *Just right* if these balanced out.

3.13. In an experiment to compare the strength of injection molded plastic parts, one factor is pressure at two levels. If one type of plastic is used at one pressure and a different type at the other pressure, plastic type and pressure are confounded.

3.15. **(a)** *Designed study.* Controlled experiment since treatments (aspirin/placebos) are assigned to experimental units (physicians) and a response (heart attack/not) observed. **(b)** *Designed study.* Sample survey since samples of voters are taken to compare population subgroups. **(c)** Can't tell if designed or not.

3.19. As parties come in, randomly assign them to a server and to receive a smiley face or "no smiley face". Replicate with a number of parties and servers. Compare tip percents at the end. Could also block by type or size or composition of party, etc.

3.21. **(a)** Duplicates. New flux and a new specimen should be used for each replicate. **(b)** Duplicates. New pulp batches are needed for replicates.

3.23. **(a)** Not an experiment. No treatments were assigned. It was a retrospective observational study. **(b)** Response: Living/not; Factor: Intake of vitamin C. **(c)** No. Association in observational studies does not imply causation. **(d)** Those who take vitamin C might take better care of themselves in other ways as well.

3.25. The data result from only (a) viewers of the show who (b) want to pay for the call and (c) choose to respond.

3.26. The question is worded in a confusing way resulting in response bias.

3.29. If the panelists are similar a completely random design will be okay. Factors will be temperature and entree type.

3.31. **(a)** Not a controlled experiment—no treatments were applied. It was a prospective observational study. **(b)** Survival status of the women is the response. Weight or weight minus optimal weight is the factor. (c) No. Association in observational studies does not imply cause-effect. (d) Women who are obese may not take as good care of themselves in other ways as well. Or perhaps there is a genetic or chemical basis for obesity that might cause early death as well.

3.33. *Blocking:* Give each individual both sodas. *Randomization:* Randomize order (can also be blocked.) *Replication:* Use a large number of subjects to get precise conclusions.

3.35. Treatment: Environment (counter, refrigerator). Response: Time to develop mold.

CHAPTER 4: An Introduction to Statistical Modeling

4.1. **(d)** $p = 0.85$.

4.5. **(a)** Independent, since what happens on the first toss should have no bearing on what happens on the second toss.
(b) Not independent. $A = \{HHT, HTH, THH\}$, $B = \{HHT, HTH, THH, HHH\} \implies A \cap B = A$. So $P(A \cap B) = P(A) \neq P(A)P(B)$.

4.7. (a) Let $A = \{$two engine plane crashes$\}$. $P(A) = p^2$. (b) Let $B = \{4$ engine plane crashes$\}$. $P(B) = 4p^3(1-p) + p^4$. (c) Two engine is safer if $p^2 < 4p^3(1-p) + p^4 \iff 1 < 4p(1-p) + p^2 \iff 3p^2 - 4p + 1 < 0$. This happens if $1/3 < p < 1$.

4.9. $p_X(x) = 1/4$, $x = 1, 2, 3, 4$.

4.11. **(a)** $p_Y(y) = p^3$, $y = 3$; $3p^2(1-p)$, $y = 1$; $3p(1-p)^2$, $y = -1$; $(1-p)^3$, $y = -3$. (Note $Y = 2W - 3$ where $W \sim b(3, p)$).
(b) $E(Y) = 6p - 3$, $\sigma_Y^2 = 12p(1-p)$.
(c) $p = 1/2$.

4.17. **(a)** $\mu_Z = 2.000$, $\mu_Y = 2.001 \implies \mu_X = 2.000 - 2.001 = -0.001$
$\sigma_Z = 0.002$, $\sigma_Y = 0.001 \implies \sigma_X = \sqrt{(0.002)^2 + (0.001)^2} = 0.00236$
(b) $\mu_W = (2.000 + 2.001)/2 = 2.0005$
$\sigma_W = \sqrt{[(0.002)^2 + (0.001)^2]/4} = 0.001118$.
More variable.

4.19. **(a)** $p_Y(y) = 1/4$, $y = 1, 2, 3, 4$
(b) $F_Y(y) = 0$, $y < 1$; $1/4, 1 \leq y < 2$; $3/4, 3 \leq y < 4$; $1, 4 \leq y$
(c) $\mu_Y = 2.5$, $\sigma_Y^2 = [(1 - 2.5)^2 + (2 - 2.5)^2 + (3 - 2.5)^2 + (4 - 2.5)^2]/4 = 1.25$.

4.27. **(a)** Each test is an independent Bernoulli trial with a probability 0.0015 of a "success": a false result.
(b) Yes, since $n = 10000 > 100$, $p = 0.0015 < 0.01$ and $np = 15 < 20$.
(c) $P(Y \leq 20) \approx P(X \leq 20) = 0.917$, X a Poisson(15) random variable.
Exact answer: $P(Y \leq 20) = 0.917$.

4.29. $\dfrac{e^{-\lambda}\lambda}{1!} = \dfrac{e^{-\lambda}\lambda^2}{2!} \iff \lambda = 2$, so $\sigma_X = \sqrt{2}$.

4.31. (a) $c = 0.5$; (b) $(0.3)(0.5) + (0.1)(2) = 0.35$.

4.35. $U(0, 1)$; $1/2$

4.39. $N(5.1, (2.2)^2) = N(5.1, 4.84)$; $Y \sim N(5.1, 4.84) \implies P(0 < Y < 10) = P\left(\frac{0-5.1}{2.2} < Z < \frac{10-5.1}{2.2}\right) = P(-2.32 < Z < 2.23) = 0.9871 - 0.0129 = 0.9742$.

4.41. Suppose $c < d$ are real numbers and $a \geq 0$. Then $P(c < Y \leq d) = P(c < aZ + b \leq d) = P\left(\frac{c-b}{a} < Z \leq \frac{d-b}{a}\right) = \frac{1}{\sqrt{2\pi}} \int_{\frac{c-b}{a}}^{\frac{d-b}{a}} e^{-\frac{z^2}{2}} dz = \frac{1}{\sqrt{2\pi}a} \int_c^d e^{-\frac{1}{2}\left(\frac{y-b}{a}\right)^2} dy$ (by making the change of variable $y = az + b$).
Since this is the integral of a $N(b, a^2)$ density, $Y \sim N(b, a^2)$. A similar argument works if $a < 0$.

4.45. $Y \sim N(0, 1) \implies$ (a) mean is 0, variance is 1; (b) $P(Y \geq 1) = 0.1589$.

4.47. (a) If $W = $ breaking strength, $P(\{$defective$\}) = P(W \leq 1.2) = 1 - e^{-\left(\frac{1.2}{2.1}\right)^{3.5}} = 0.132$; (b) Assuming independence, the probability both fail is $(0.132)^2 = 0.017$.

4.53. (a) Let $Y = $ number of games won by team A. Then $Y \sim b(3, 0.5)$, and $P(Y = 2) = \binom{3}{2}(0.5)^2(0.5) = 3/8$; (b) The CLT would not work well here since there are too few trials (games).

4.55. Let $Y = $ number of children in sample living in poverty. $Y \sim b(300, 0.22)$, so $P(Y \geq 80) = 0.0320$ exactly, or using the normal approximation, $P(Y \geq 80) = P(Y \geq 79.5) \doteq P\left(Z \geq \frac{79.5-66}{\sqrt{300(0.22)(0.78)}}\right) = P(Z \geq 1.88) = 0.0301$.

4.57. No. The theorem guarantees that the *mean* of a random sample will be approximately normally distributed if n is large.

4.59. If boys and girls are equally likely and Y is the number of families with girls, $Y \sim b(1500, 0.5)$. Then $P(Y \geq 900) = 0.0000$, exactly, or, using the normal approximation, $P(Y \geq 900) = P(Y \geq 899.5) \doteq P\left(Z \geq \frac{899.5-750}{\sqrt{1500(0.5)(0.5)}}\right) = P(Z \geq 7.72) = 0.0000$. This is strong evidence that boys and girls are not equally likely.

4.65. log; log.

CHAPTER 5: Introduction to Inference: Estimation and Prediction

5.1. The sampling distribution of an estimator is the distribution model of the estimator. It can be thought of as the distribution of the values the estimator takes in all possible samples. The value of knowing it is that it tells how the estimator varies from sample to sample, and therefore how much credence to give the estimator. For example if $Y_1, \ldots, Y_n \sim N(\mu, 1)$ is a random sample, an estimator of μ is $\hat{\mu} = \bar{Y} \sim N(\mu, 1/n)$, which is the sampling distribution. The sampling distribution quantifies precisely how we can expect the the estimator to vary.

5.3. We want a confidence interval for p, the population proportion who approve. Since n is large ($n\hat{p} = 5500$, $n(1-\hat{p}) = 4500$), we use a 95% large sample interval: (0.54, 0.56). We estimate between 54 and 56% approve, which is better than 50–50.

5.5. (a) 95% of all intervals so constructed from repeated random samples will contain the true mean accuracy of their forecast method; (b) Since 5% lies in the interval, these data do not contradict the claim.

5.7. (a) $\bar{y} = 42166$, $s = 259.408$. Interval is $42166 \pm (2.7764)(259.408)/\sqrt{5} = (41843.9, 42488.1)$; (b) In repeated sampling, 95% of all 95% confidence intervals for μ will actually contain μ; (c) Yes, we estimate μ is between 41843.9 and 42488.1 which is consistent with the historical mean 42300.

5.9. **(a)** A plot of yield versus order shows no evidence of nonstationarity.

(b) A histogram and normal quantile plot show no evidence of nonnormality. A boxplot shows no outliers. The mean $\bar{y} = 36.4$ and standard deviation $s = 4.1$ summarize the data well.

(c) Yes, a C+E model seems reasonable. The model is $Y = \mu + \epsilon$, where Y is the yield of a batch, μ is the mean yield of all batches and ϵ is random error.

(d) Point estimate: $\hat{\mu} = 36.4$. 95% confidence interval: (34.2, 38.6). *Interpretation*: we estimate with 95% confidence that the mean yield, μ, is between 34.2 and 38.6. 95% confidence means that in repeated sampling, 95% of all 95% confidence intervals constructed will contain μ.

(e) A level 0.95 tolerance interval for 99% of the batch yields is (20.8, 52.0). We estimate with 95% confidence that at least 99% of all batch yields lie between 20.8 and 52. In repeated sampling, 95% of all tolerance intervals constructed in this way will contain at least 99% of all batch yields.

(f) A level 0.95 prediction interval is (27.4, 45.4). Since the yield of the next zeolite batch, 26.5, lies outside this interval, we suspect something may be different about this batch.

5.11. (a) Population is students at the college; (b) The number of the 185 students who prefer Sprite is $Y \sim b(185, p)$ where p is true proportion of students who prefer Sprite. $\hat{p} = $ sample proportion who prefer Sprite $= \frac{115}{185} = 0.62$, $n = 185$. The level 0.95 confidence interval for p is $(0.549, 0.691)$. The normal approximation is justified since $y = 115 \geq 10$ and $n - y = 70 \geq 10$; (c) This interval cannot be used to make inference about the American people; it can only be used to make inference about the student population; (d) Can conclude students at the college prefer Sprite since the whole interval $(0.549, 0.691)$ is above 0.5.

5.13. (a) $\bar{y} = 17.5, n = 49, s = 4.2$. Since $n < 50$ and σ is unknown (estimated by s) use t-interval at 95% confidence. By interpolation, $t_{48,0.975} = 2.0111$. The interval is $(16.29, 18.71)$; (b) Since 17 hours is in the interval, there is not enough evidence to conclude that the stat students study in excess of school guidelines.

5.15. **(a)** Estimate of proportion p_1 of whites saying guilty: $\frac{108}{150}$. Estimate of proportion p_2 of nonwhites saying guilty: $\frac{23}{100}$. Estimate of difference in proportions: $\frac{108}{150} - \frac{23}{100} = 0.49$.

(b) 99% confidence interval for the difference: $(0.346, 0.634)$. Since all values in the interval are positive, we can be 99% confident that the proportion of whites in the population who think Simpson is guilty is greater than the proportion of blacks. 99% confidence means that if we take many more samples and from them compute 99% confidence intervals, then about 99% of all such intervals will really contain $p_1 - p_2$.

5.17. (a) The variation is due to the inability to measure exactly; (b) Assuming the measurement errors ϵ are independent and have the same zero mean distribution, the measured weights Y can be thought of as the "true" weight (that is, "true" as measured by the measurement process), μ plus measurement error: $Y = \mu + \epsilon$; (c) $\bar{y} = 1 \text{ kg}, 245\mu g, s = 328\mu g$. A 90% confidence interval is $(1 \text{ kg}54.87\mu g, 1 \text{ kg}435.13\mu g)$. We assume normality or near-normality of the errors; (d) If it's not a leap year we get 3650 weighings, so about 3285 of the computed intervals should contain μ. We assume the weighing process is stationary.

5.19. 1083

5.21. (a) All AA batteries of that brand; (b) (44.6, 48.8). We are 95% confident the mean lifetime of all batteries, μ, is between 44.6 and 48.8; (c) In repeated sampling, 95% of all 95% confidence intervals will contain μ.

5.23. (a) (18.3, 75.1). We are 90% confident that at least 95% of all battery lifetimes are between 18.3 and 75.1 hours; (b) In repeated sampling, 90% of all such tolerance intervals will contain at least 95% of all battery lifetimes.

5.25. She would be 95% confident the true mean blood sugar level was between 187.7 and 294.3. Based on this, she could not conclude the artificial pancreas is effective, since this interval contains values above 275.

5.27. (a) Physical differences in pennies leading to different true weight measurement errors; (b) All newly-minted pennies. Interval is $(3.101, 3.115)$. We are 90% confident that the population mean penny weight, μ, is between 3.101 and 3.115g, where "90% confident" means that in repeated sampling, 90% of all intervals will actually contain μ; (c) Interval is $(3.037, 3.180)$. We are 90% confident that a new penny, obtained from outside the present data set, will weigh between 3.037 and 3.180g; (d) Tolerance interval is $(3.008, 3.209)$. We are 99% confident that at least 95% of all pennies will weigh between 3.008 and 3.209g.

5.29. (a) A prediction interval for a new observation is (83.4, 96.4). We are 95% confident the strength of a new bar will be between 83.4 and 96.4; (b) Since the average of all future observations is μ, the population mean, a 95% prediction interval for this average is just a 95% confidence interval for μ.

5.31. (a) If $p_1 =$ population proportion of drug users who improve and $p_2 =$ population proportion of nonusers who improve, $\hat{p}_1 = 2/3$ $\hat{p}_2 = 3/5$, so $\hat{p}_1$ is slightly larger than $\hat{p}_2$; (b) Construct a confidence interval for $p_1 - p_2$; (c) A 95% confidence interval for $p_1 - p_2$ is $(-0.06, 0.19)$. Result: Little evidence of a difference in proportion.

5.33. (a) 95% prediction interval: (0.53, 0.97); (b) Since the voltage reading is outside the prediction interval, we conclude this part is possibly flawed.

CHAPTER 6: Hypothesis Tests

6.1. $Z = \dfrac{Y - np_0}{\sqrt{np_0(1-p_0)}} = \dfrac{n(Y/n - p_0)}{n\sqrt{p_0(1-p_0)/n}} = \dfrac{\hat{p} - p_0}{\sigma(\hat{p})}$

6.3.
- **Scientific Hypothesis:** Mean carbon percentages in steel from two vendors are not equal.
- **Statistical Hypotheses:** $H_0 : \mu_1 = \mu_2, \mu_1 \neq \mu_2, \mu_1$ and μ_2 population means.
- **Standardized Test Statistic:** $t^* = \dfrac{3.62 - 3.18}{\left[\sqrt{\dfrac{(9)(0.086) + 7(0.082)}{16}}\right]\left[\sqrt{\dfrac{1}{10} + \dfrac{1}{8}}\right]} = 3.20.$
- **Assumptions:** Populations are normal with equal variances.
- **p-value:** $P(|t_{16}| \geq 3.20) = 0.0056$
- **Conclusions:** Reject H_0 in favor of H_a.

6.5. (a) Since the scale is accurate, the variation is due to differences in the pennies.
- (b) All newly-minted U.S. pennies.
- (c) • **Scientific Hypothesis:** Mean of pennies $\neq 3.1$
  - **Statistical Hypotheses:** $H_0 : \mu = 3.1; H_a : \mu \neq 3.1, \mu =$ mean weight of all pennies
  - **Standardized Test Statistic:** $t^* = 1.944.$
  - **Assumptions:** No severe outliers. (graphical check shows none)
  - **p-value:** $P(|t_{99}| \geq 1.944) = 0.0547$
  - **Conclusion:** At 0.05 level do not reject H_0. At 0.10 level, reject H_0.

6.7. (a) Try paired analysis since the ports are so close and independence of the ports is not definite.
- (b) Let D_i denote the port A minus the port B reading for pipeline i. Then the D_i follow the C+E model $D = \mu_D + \epsilon$, where $\mu_D = \mu_A - \mu_B$, and μ_A and μ_B are the population mean percentage of solids from port A and port B, respectively.
  - **Scientific Hypothesis:** There is a higher mean percentage of suspended solids at port B than at port A.
  - **Statistical Hypotheses:** $H_0 : \mu_D = 0, H_a : \mu_D < 0.$
  - **Standardized Test Statistic:** $t^* = \dfrac{\bar{d}}{s/\sqrt{n}} = \dfrac{-0.7256}{0.1387/\sqrt{9}} = -15.69.$
  - **Assumptions:** Normality of differences.
  - **p-value:** $P(t_8 \leq -15.69) = 1.36 \times 10^{-7}$
  - **Conclusion:** Reject H_0 in favor of H_a.

6.9. • **Scientific Hypothesis:** The drug is effective.

  • **Statistical Hypothesis:** $H_0 : p_1 = p_2$, $H_a : p_1 > p_2$, where p_1 is the population proportion who improve using the drug, and p_2 is the population proportion who improve without using the drug.

  • **Standardized Test Statistic:** $z^* = \dfrac{\hat{p}_1 - \hat{p}_2}{\sqrt{\hat{p}(1-\hat{p})\left[\frac{1}{n_1} + \frac{1}{n_2}\right]}} = \dfrac{0.67 - 0.60}{\sqrt{0.64(1-0.64)\left[\frac{1}{150} + \frac{1}{100}\right]}} = 1.13$, where $\hat{p}_1 = $ sample proportion who did better with the drug $= \frac{100}{150} = 0.67$, $\hat{p}_2 = $ sample proportion who did better without the drug $= \frac{60}{100} = 0.60$, $\hat{p} = \frac{y_1 + y_2}{n_1 + n_2} = \frac{100 + 60}{150 + 100} = \frac{160}{250} = 0.64$.

  • **Assumptions:** The large sample normal approximation will be satisfactory since $n_1 \hat{p}_1 = 100$, $n_2 \hat{p}_2 = 60$, $n_1(1 - \hat{p}_1) = 50$, and $n_2(1 - \hat{p}_2) = 40$ are all greater than 10.

  • **p-value:** $P(Z \geq 1.13) = 0.1292$.

  • **Conclusions:** Do not reject H_0 in favor of H_a.

6.11. (a) A line plot of yield versus order shows no evidence of nonstationarity.

  (b) A distribution analysis shows that the data look reasonably normal with mean 36.6 and standard deviation 4.2.

  (c) It seems reasonable. μ is the mean relative yield for all batches produced by this manufacturer under these conditions.

  (d) • **Scientific Hypothesis:** The mean yield is less than 37.5%.

  • **Model:** C+E

  • **Statistical Hypothesis:** $H_0 : \mu = 37.5$, $H_a : \mu < 37.5$.

  • **Standardized Test Statistic:** $t^* = \dfrac{\bar{y} - \mu_0}{s/\sqrt{n}} = \dfrac{36.6 - 37.5}{4.2/\sqrt{16}} = -0.857$.

  • **Assumptions:** Normality

  • **p-value:** $P(t_{15} \leq -0.857) = 0.2025$.

  • **Conclusion:** Do not reject H_0.

6.13. • **Scientific Hypothesis:** Lifetimes exceed industry standard.

  • **Model:** C+E model

  • **Statistical Hypothesis:** $H_0 : \mu = 45$, $H_a : \mu > 45$.

  • **Standardized Test Statistic:** $z^* = \dfrac{\bar{y} - \mu_0}{s/\sqrt{n}} = \dfrac{46.7 - 45}{13.3/\sqrt{152}} = 1.58$

  • **Assumptions:** No extreme outliers.

  • **p-value:** $P(Z \geq 1.58) = 0.0571$.

  • **Conclusion:** The evidence against H_0 is moderately strong. Reject at any significance level larger than 0.0571.

6.15. The power function, Π, takes the values $\Pi(285) = 0.0658$, $\Pi(250) = 0.1512$, so the probability of detecting a value of 285 is 0.0658, and the probablity of detecting a value of 250 is 0.1512.

6.17. $H_0 : \mu = 245$; $H_a : \mu < 245$, where μ is the mean cholesterol level for this kind of at-risk patient using the drug.

6.19. A paired t test.

6.21. If we pretend that the density of Figure 6.4 of the text is a t_5 density, the picture is Figure 6.4, where $|z^*|$ is replaced by 3.75. The p-value equals shaded area which is 0.0133. Since $0.0133 < 0.05$, the result is significant at the 0.05 level.

6.23. (a) We assume the 1994 measurements follow the C+E model $Y_1 = \mu_1 + \epsilon_1$ and the 1995 measurements follow the C+E model $Y_2 = \mu_2 + \epsilon_2$. Prof. P. wants to test $H_0 : \mu_1 = \mu_2$; $H_a : \mu_1 < \mu_2$.

  (b) We assume the errors ϵ_1 and ϵ_2 are normally distributed. The normal quantile plots give us no reason to doubt the validity of this assumption.

  (c) Since the sample variances are so close, we will use the pooled variance t test. The test statistic is $t^{(p)} = -8.375$. The p-value is 2.9×10^{-8} so there is strong evidence that Prof. P's mean level of energy expenditure has increased.

  (d) The measurements were taken far enough apart in time to be considered independent, so a test for independent population was chosen. The sample variances were very close, so a pooled variance test was chosen. The data looked reasonably normal, so a t test was used.

6.25. (a) The American public.

  (b) • **Scientific Hypothesis:** The majority of the American public likes Stuart.

  • **Model:** Binomial. If Y is the number of the 900 individuals who respond that they like Stuart, $Y \sim b(900, p)$, where p is the proportion of the population who like Stuart.

- **Statistical Hypothesis:** $H_0 : p = 0.5$, $H_a : p > 0.5$.
- **Standardized Test Statistic:** $z^* = \frac{423/900 - 0.5}{\sqrt{\frac{(0.5)(1-0.5)}{900}}} = -1.8$.
- **Assumptions:** We can use the normal approximation since $n\hat{p} = 423$ and $n(1 - \hat{p}) = 477$ both exceed 10.
- **p-value:** $P(Z \geq -1.8) = 0.9641$.
- **Conclusion:** Do not reject H_0. There is little evidence that a majority of the American public likes Stuart.

6.27. (a) The variation is due to the inability to measure exactly.

(b) Assuming the measurement errors ϵ are independent and have the same distribution, the measured weights Y can be thought of as true weight plus measurement error: $Y = \mu + \epsilon$.

(c) - **Scientific Hypothesis:** $\mu = 1$ kg
- **Statistical Hypotheses:** $H_0 : \mu = 1$, $H_a : \mu \neq 1$.
- **Standardized Test Statistic:** $t^* = \frac{\bar{y} - \mu_0}{s/\sqrt{n}} = \frac{(1 + 245 \times 10^{-6}) - 1}{328 \times 10^{-6}/\sqrt{10}} = 2.36$.
- **Assumptions:** Normality
- **p-value:** $P(|t_9| \geq 2.36) = 0.0426$.
- **Conclusions:** Reject H_0 at 0.05 level, not at 0.01 level. Moderately strong evidence against H_0.

6.29. No, both results cannot be true, since the confidence interval contains 0.3. This means H_0 should not be rejected at the 0.05 level of significance, which contradicts the reported result of the hypothesis test.

6.31. (a) 0.0596; **(b)** Yes.

(c) Yes, the conclusion is justified at the 0.10 level. Think of it this way: a level 0.10 confidence interval for the difference in mean scores will contain only positive values, indicating the module 1 mean is greater than the module 2 mean.

CHAPTER 7: The Relationship Between Two Variables

7.1. The graph of WEAR versus T-PLUS would be shifted one unit to the right.

7.3. $r > 0$: plots (a), (b); $r < 0$: plots (c), (d); $r \approx 0$: plots (e), (f).

7.5. r is closest to 1 for plot (b).

7.7. If $r = 1$, all points will be on a straight line with positive slope. If $r = -1$, all points will be on a straight line with negative slope.

7.9. For all four data sets, we have $\bar{x} = 9.00$, $\bar{y} = 7.50$, $s_x = 3.32$, $s_y = 2.03$, and $r = 0.816$ (actually for the fourth set, $r = 0.817$). The graphs, however, are *very* different.

7.11. The fitted model is $\widehat{WEAR} = 0.0010 + 0.0004 \cdot TIME$. Since $TIME = 0$ has no meaning here, the intercept has no interpretation of its own. The slope is the change in predicted WEAR per unit increase in TIME. r^2 is high: 0.9816, but the residuals display a curved pattern, suggesting the fit can be improved.

7.13. Of those 71 who were part of a family, 44 (61.97%) lived and 27 (38.03%) died. Of those 16 who were not part of a family, 3 (18.75%) lived and 13 (81.25%) died. The difference in fates between family and non family members is more dramatic than that between males and females. (For those with hypothesis testing background: the χ^2 test for independence of family status and survival gives a p-value of 0.002, strong evidence that family status and survival are related.)

7.15. 0, since $s_Y = 0$.

7.17. $r = 1$, since the data follow the straight line $Y = X + 5$.

7.21. (a) Assuming normality, Tom's first measurement was about 1 standard deviation above the mean. We predict Tom's second measurement will be 0.8 standard deviation above the mean, which is the 78.81 percentile. So we predict that approximately 79% of the patients will have second measurement lower than Tom's.

(b) The regression effect.

7.23. The residuals must sum to 0, so $0 = \sum_{i=1}^{11} e_i = 0.1 + e_{11} \implies e_{11} = -0.1$. The value $e_{11} = -0.1$ shows up as an outlier on a boxplot.

7.25. $r = \sqrt{r^2} = \sqrt{0.64} = 0.8$.

7.27. A score of 115 at age 18 corresponds to $(115 - 100)/15 = 1$ standard deviation from the mean. We predict that at age 35 this individual will score $0.8 \times 1 = 0.8$ standard deviations from the mean, giving a predicted score of $100 + 0.8 \times 15 = 112$.

7.29. (a) The relation is curvilinear with MIDPRICE decreasing as a function of CITYMPG. I would not fit a line as the relation is not linear.

(b) The relation between LPRICE and LMPG is more nearly linear, with LPRICE decreasing as a function of LMPG.

(c) The fitted line is $\widehat{LPRICE} = 7.5237 - 1.5119 \cdot LMPG$. For every increase of one unit in LMPG, the model predicts a decline of LPRICE by 1.5119.

(d) $CITYMPG = 80 \implies LMPG = 4.382$. This gives $\widehat{LPRICE} = 7.5237 - (1.5119)(4.382) = 0.8985$. Based on this, we would predict the price of the 80 MAG car to be $e^{0.8985} = 2.456$ thousand dollars. This isn't very believable. The model is based on current production cars for which low cost and high mileage are associated. Mileage of 80 MPG is well above the range of the data, and the model is not valid that far outside its range.

7.31. From the first normal equation, $\sum_{i=1}^{n}(Y_i - \hat{\beta}_0 - \hat{\beta}_1 X_i) = \sum_{i=1}^{n} e_i = 0$.

7.33. Either (i) $r = 0$, or (ii) $r \neq 0$ and $s_Y = s_X$.

7.35. $r = -1$, since if C is the number of correct and I the number of incorrect answers, $C = 21 - I$.

7.37. $e_1 = e_2 = e_3 = 0$.

7.39. First, the Pearson correlation is really 0.6936. Second, this correlation is almost entirely due to one outlier. If that point is removed, the correlation becomes -0.2493. It is foolish to base important conclusions on such data.

7.41. The 95th percentile in thickness corresponds to 1.645 standard deviations above the mean. Hence, its tensile strength is predicted to be $0.8 \times 1.645 = 1.316$ standard deviations above the mean, which corresponds to the 90.6^{th} percentile.

7.43. Not necessarily. Large hospitals may care for sicker patients.

7.45. (a) i. Marginal distributions: Nationality: 74.2% are Indian, 25.8% are Chinese; Gender: 35.7% are male, 64.3% are female.

ii. Conditional distributions: Of the males, 72.9% are Indian, 27.1% Chinese; Of the females, 74.9% are Indian, 25.1% Chinese. Of the Indians, 35.1% are male, 64.9% female. Of the Chinese, 37.4% are male, 62.6% female.

(b) The gender breakdown of Indians and Chinese is similar: slightly more than 1/3 are male; slightly less than 2/3 are female.

(c) Let p_C and p_I denote the population proportions of Chinese and Indians, respectively, who are male. A 95% confidence interval for $p_C - p_I$ is $(-0.065, 0, 111)$. Since the interval contains 0, we cannot conclude, at the 95% confidence level, that there is a difference between p_C and p_I. (Can also do an hypothesis test for the equality of p_C and p_I, or a χ^2 test.)

7.47. Since $1 = \hat{\beta}_1 = r\frac{s_Y}{s_X} = 2r$, r must equal 0.5, and $r^2 = 0.25$ is the reduction in uncertainty of prediction.

7.49. (a) Of the males, 52.51% prefer cookie A; of the females, 59.09% prefer cookie A. These suggest that the proportion of females who prefer cookie A is greater than the proportion of males.

(b) Let p_F and p_M denote the population proportion of females and males, respectively, who prefer cookie A. An hypothesis test of $H_0 : p_F = p_M$ versus $H_a : p_F > p_M$, gives a test statistic value of 0.917. The p-value of the test is 0.1796, so we cannot conclude that p_F and p_M differ.

7.51. There may be little evidence of a *linear* relation, which is what the Pearson correlation measures, but that doesn't mean there is no *nonlinear* relation.

7.53. (a) Summary:

Frequency Percent Row Pct Col Pct	Boys	Girls	Total
Left-handed	9 11.11 45.00 23.68	11 13.58 55.00 25.58	20 24.69
Right-handed	29 35.80 47.54 76.32	32 39.51 52.46 74.42	61 75.31
Total	38 46.91	43 53.09	81 100.00

(b) Gender: 46.91% boys, 53.09% girls. Handedness: 24.69% left, 75.31% right.

(c) Females: 25.58% left, 74.42% right. Males: 23.68% left, 76.32% right.

(d) There seems to be little relation between gender and handedness, as the conditional distributions for females and males are similar. The χ^2 test for the independence of gender and handedness gives a p-value of 0.843, which indicates little evidence of a relation.

7.55. Considering all faces simultaneously is preferable. Let p_i be the probability face i comes up on a toss. We will test the null hypothesis that the die is fair: $H_0 : p_i = 1/6, i = 1, 2, 3, 4, 5, 6$, versus $H_a :$ not H_0. The test statistic is $X^2 = 2.18$. The p-value is 0.8236. Thus, there is little evidence the die is unfair.

CHAPTER 8: Multiple Regression

8.1. **(a)** Yes it is significant since the F statistic has a p-value ≤ 0.0001.

(b) No. WEIGHT is significant, having $t = -8.0237$ with p-value ≤ 0.0001. DISPLACE is not significant, $t = 0.0829, p = 0.9341$.

(c) Multicollinearity does not appear to be a problem, with VIFs less than 10.

(d) **i.** There are several outliers, especially the 3 largest.

ii. There seems to be some curvature in the plots of STUDRES versus WEIGHT and DISPLACE.

iii. The variance is larger for smaller WEIGHT and DISPLACE.

8.3. Methodology: brushing on scatterplot arrays.

(a) For each level of PH, the relation between LEAD and DAYS is positive and linear. As PH increases, the slope and intercept of this relation decrease.

(b) For each level of DAYS, the relation between LEAD and PH is negative and linear. As DAYS increases, the slope decreases and the intercept increases.

8.5. Log, square root and reciprocal transformations of the response all gave worse results.

8.7. Table 1 shows the ANOVA table. The F test of $H_0 : \beta_1 = \beta_2 = \beta_3 = 0$ rejects the null hypothesis ($p \leq 0.0001$). Individual t tests show that the regressors are all significant ($p \leq 0.0001$ for each).

TABLE 1   Analysis of Variance Table, Exercise 8.7

		Analysis of variance			
Source	DF	Sum of squares	Mean square	F Stat	Prob > F
Model	3	1949.8326	649.9442	33.1701	0.0001
Error	52	1018.9021	19.5943		
C Total	55	2968.7347			

8.9. Anything of the form $Y = \beta_0 + \beta_1 f(X) + \beta_2 Z$ will do.

8.11. **(a)** Fitted model is

$$\widehat{FIRE\_END} = -5.4017 + 53.3795 \cdot EQIVTHCK + 1.8356 \cdot CONCDENS - 2.9610 \cdot AGG\_DENS.$$

The change in predicted FIRE_END per unit change in EQIVTHCK with the other predictors held constant is 53.3795. The change in predicted FIRE_END per unit change in CONCDENS with the other predictors held constant is 1.8356. The change in predicted FIRE_END per unit change in AGG_DENS with the other predictors held constant is -2.9610. The estimated intercept has no interpretation of its own.

(b) Based on measures R^2 R_a^2, and MSE, the model from part a is preferred. However, the residual plots for the second model look better (more random, more normal).

(c) One thing to look at further is the effect of the outlier(s) in AGG_DENS on the fit of the first model.

8.15. **(a)** Scatterplot arrays show:

    ○ A positive relation between shoe size and height for low, middle and high ages.

    ○ A positive relation between distance and height for middle and high ages, but little relation for low age.

    ○ A modest positive relation between distance and height for small shoe size. Little relation otherwise.

    ○ Little relation between age and height for any shoe size.

    ○ A positive, nonlinear relation between shoe size and height for all distances.

(b) A model was fit to all the centered predictors, their squares and products, and then reduced using backward elimination.

i. The resulting model is $\widehat{HEIGHT} = 65.4058 + 1.7021 \cdot CSHOE + 0.4662 \cdot CAGE \cdot CDIST$.

ii. The intercept is estimated HEIGHT at the mean values of the predictors.

$\frac{\partial \widehat{HEIGHT}}{\partial CSHOE} = 1.7021$, when CAGE and CDIST are held constant. $\frac{\partial \widehat{HEIGHT}}{\partial CAGE} = 0.4662 \cdot CDIST$, when CSHOE and CDIST are held constant. $\frac{\partial \widehat{HEIGHT}}{\partial CDIST} = 0.4663 \cdot CAGE$, when CSHOE and CAGE are held constant.

iii. 0.4863, or 48.63%

iv. Yes. CSHOE has a p-value of 0.0509, and so is marginally significant or nonsignificant.

(c) The VIF values are near 1, indicating no evidence of multicollinearity.

(d) There are two large Studentized residuals that are potential outliers. Otherwise, the residuals appear normal and reasonably well-scattered.

(e) Yes. I would look carefully at the outliers.

8.17. There are 25 residuals. We need to know 18 before we can compute SSE.

8.21. (a) i. Yes it is significant, as the F test gives p-value ≤ 0.0001.

    ii. MILES is significant, TEMP and the MILES*TEMP product are not. I am not happy, since there is high multicollinearity evident.

(b) i. The three fitted models are

$$\widehat{GALLONS} = 2.6175 + 0.0197 \cdot MILES - 0.0344 \cdot TEMP$$

$$+ 1.845 \times 10^{-5} \cdot MILES * TEMP \tag{1}$$

$$\widehat{GALLONS} = 1.7418 + 0.0224 \cdot MILES - 8.460 \times 10^{-5} \cdot MILES * TEMP \tag{2}$$

$$\widehat{GALLONS} = 2.4530 + 0.0202 \cdot MILES - 0.0283 \cdot TEMP \tag{3}$$

The Studentized residual plots are pretty much the same for all three models (the plot versus MILES has a disturbing pattern). Other measures with which to compare these models are:

	Model		
Measure	(1)	(2)	(3)
R^2	0.8088	0.7994	0.8085
R_a^2	0.7903	0.7868	0.7966
MSE	0.0707	0.0718	0.0686

These measures favor model (3) slightly. Multicollinearity is a problem for model (1), but not for the other two. Finally, model (3) has the benefit of the simplicity of an additive model. All these considerations argue for choosing model (3) as the best.

    ii. The equation of model (3) is given above. The intercept has no meaning of its own since GALLONS = 0 is outside the range of the model. The change in predicted gas use per each extra mile driven when temperature is constant, is

$$\frac{\partial\, GALLONS}{\partial\, MILES} = 0.0202.$$

For the same number of miles driven, the change in predicted gas use per each degree increase in temperature is

$$\frac{\partial\, GALLONS}{\partial\, TEMP} = -0.0283.$$

    iii. 80.85%

CHAPTER 9: The One-Way Model

9.1. $S_p^2 = \frac{1}{n-k} \sum_{i=1}^{k} (n_i - 1) S_i^2 = \frac{1}{n-k} \sum_{i=1}^{k} (n_i - 1) \left[\frac{1}{n_i-1} \sum_{j=1}^{n_i} (Y_{ij} - \bar{Y}_{i\cdot})^2 \right] = \frac{1}{n-k} \sum_{i=1}^{k} \sum_{j=1}^{n_i} (Y_{ij} - \bar{Y}_{i\cdot})^2 = MSE$

9.3. (a)

	Analysis of variance				
Source	DF	Sum of squares	Mean square	F Stat	Prob > F
Model	3	12.12	4.04	4.49	0.0138
Error	21	18.90	0.90		
C Total	24	31.02			

(b) There are four populations. (c) No.

9.5. (a) Plots can include stratified plots or diamond plots. Side-by-side boxlots are also acceptable, though not as appropriate. The plots suggest that normal rats have the lowest mean blood sugar, untreated rats the highest, and those with the artificial pancreas something in between.

(b) The spreads of the three groups are widely different.

(c) The spreads of the transformed responses for the three groups are much more similar.

(d)

		Analysis of variance			
Source	DF	Sum of squares	Mean square	F Stat	Prob > F
Model	2	0.0034	0.0017	111.4661	0.0001
Error	9	0.0001	1.527×10^{-5}		
C Total	11	0.0035			

The conclusion is that there is a significant difference in population means. Level 0.95 Tukey confidence intervals are

Comparison	Interval
normal−artificial	(0.024, 0.040)
normal−diabetic	(0.031, 0.046)
artificial−diabetic	(−0.001, 0.015)

These comparisons show the mean for normal rats differs from both the artificial pancreas and diabetic rats, but that the latter two do not differ significantly. This indicates that the artificial pancreas is not effective.

9.9. (a) It is not a CRD because each cam has all four shapes.

(b) An RCBD:

$$RMS_{ij} = \mu + CAM_i + SHAPE_j + \epsilon_{ij}, \; i = 1, \ldots, 8, \; j = 1, \ldots, 4.$$

(c) The model fit results in the following ANOVA table:

		Analysis of variance			
Source	DF	Sum of squares	Mean square	F Stat	Prob > F
Shape	3	0.0424	0.0141	3.5329	0.0325
Cam	7	0.1224	0.0175	4.3700	0.0039
Error	21	0.0840	0.0040		
C Total	31	0.2488			

(d) Tukey's test for additivity shows no reason to suspect nonadditivity ($p = 0.5569$).

There appear to be three outliers. These were removed and the model refit. This fit revealed another outlier. This was also removed and the model refit. The fit with the three points removed appeared good: considerably better than the fit to all the data (MSE 0.0013 versus 0.0040, with better residual plots). We will report the results from both fits. The ANOVA table from the reduced data is:

		Analysis of variance			
Source	DF	Sum of squares	Mean square	F Stat	Prob > F
Shape	3	0.0308	0.0103	7.9322	0.0014
Cam	7	0.0726	0.0104	8.0134	0.0002
Error	18	0.0233	0.0013		
C Total	28	0.1446			

Tukey's test for additivity for the reduced data also shows no reason to suspect nonadditivity ($p = 0.3636$).

(e) Overall significant differences among shapes are indicated by the F test (p-value $= 0.0325$, original data, $= 0.0014$, reduced data). The shape means for the original data are: shape 1 mean (0.682) > shape 3 mean (0.618) > shape 2 mean (0.615) > shape 4 mean (0.582). Level 0.95 Tukey pairwise comparisons yield

Comparison	Interval
$1 - 3$	(−0.02380, 0.15250)
$1 - 2$	(−0.02074, 0.15556)
$1 - 4$	(0.01236, 0.18866)
$3 - 2$	(−0.08509, 0.09121)
$3 - 4$	(−0.05199, 0.12431)
$2 - 4$	(−0.05505, 0.12125)

so that only means for shapes 1 and 4 differ significantly.

For the reduced data, the shape means are shape 3 mean (0.684) > shape 1 mean (0.682) > shape 2 mean (0.615) > shape 4 mean (0.590). Level 0.95 Tukey pairwise comparisons yield

Comparison	Interval
3 − 1	(−0.05336, 0.00154)
3 − 2	(0.01405, 0.12386)
3 − 4	(0.03784, 0.15096)
1 − 2	(0.01658, 0.11824)
1 − 4	(0.04025, 0.14547)
2 − 4	(−0.02717, 0.07806)

so that the means for shapes 3 and 1 are significantly greater than those for shapes 2 and 4.

9.13. **(a)** Since all sample sizes are equal, Tukey will give shorter intervals for all six pairwise comparisons.

(b) Level 0.95 Tukey intervals are (DD stands for drug and diet):

Comparison	Interval
DD-Control	(20.269, 42.451)
DD-Diet	(8.549, 30.731)
DD-Drug	(3.069, 25.251),
Drug-Control	(6.109, 28.291)
Drug-Diet	(−5.611, 16.571)
Diet-Control	(0.639, 22.811)

This shows that the means for all treatments are significantly larger than that for control, and that drug and diet mean is significantly larger than those for either drug alone or diet alone.

CHAPTER 10: The Factorial Model

10.1. The lines for levels 1–3 of A have slopes $\mu_{12} - \mu_{11}$, $\mu_{22} - \mu_{21}$ and $\mu_{32} - \mu_{31}$, respectively. So these lines are parallel if and only if they satisfy the two equations

$$\mu_{22} - \mu_{21} = \mu_{12} - \mu_{11} \tag{4}$$

$$\mu_{32} - \mu_{31} = \mu_{22} - \mu_{21}, \tag{5}$$

which are equivalent to (10.7) and (10.8). By adding $\mu_{21} - \mu_{12}$ to both sides of (4), we get (10.5). By multiplying both sides of (5) by −1, and then adding $\mu_{32} - \mu_{21}$ to both sides, we get (10.6).

10.3. If $\alpha_i, \beta_j \geq 0$, $\mu_{ij} = (\sqrt{\alpha_i} + \sqrt{\beta_j})^2$, So $\sqrt{\mu_{ij}} = \sqrt{\alpha_i} + \sqrt{\beta_j}$.

10.5. **(a)**

		Analysis of variance			
Source	DF	Sum of squares	Mean square	F Stat	Prob > F
A	2	3.76	1.88	1.66	0.2232
B	4	11.64	2.91	2.58	0.0800
AB	8	32.08	4.01	3.55	0.0166
Error	15	16.95	1.13		
C Total	29	64.43			

(b) A: 3 levels; B: 5 levels; $3 \times 5 = 15$ populations. There are 2 observations/population.

(c) General factorial model

10.7. **(a)** All lines in the interaction plots are parallel, meaning there is no interaction.

(b) $\mu = 5.2\bar{3}$

$\mu_{1\cdot} = 2.6\bar{3}$, $\mu_{2\cdot} = 4.1\bar{3}$, $\mu_{3\cdot} = 8.9\bar{3}$, $\alpha_1 = -2.6$, $\alpha_2 = -1.1$, $\alpha_3 = 3.7$
$\mu_{\cdot 1} = 4.8$, $\mu_{\cdot 2} = 7.2$, $\mu_{\cdot 3} = 3.7$, $\beta_1 = -0.4\bar{3}$, $\beta_2 = 1.9\bar{6}$, $\beta_3 = -1.5\bar{3}$
$(\alpha\beta)_{11} = 2.2 - (5.2\bar{3} + (-2.6) + (-0.4\bar{3})) = 0$, and, in fact, $(\alpha\beta)_{ij} = 0$, for all $i, j = 1, 2, 3$.

Interpretation:

○ Main effects: e.g., the effect of level 3 of A is to add 3.7 units to the overall mean.

○ Interaction: All interactions are 0. The effect of A is independent of the level of effect B, and vice-versa.

10.9. The full factorial model was fit to the data. Studentized residual plots show symmetry patterns common to data at only two levels. The same is true of the normal quantile plot. There are no outliers indicated.

The ANOVA table is (TRR is temperature reducing rate):

		Analysis of variance			
Source	DF	Sum of squares	Mean square	F Stat	Prob > F
TRR	1	369800	369800	35.64	0.0040
LAMBDA	1	152352	152352	14.68	0.0186
TRR*LAMBDA	1	12324.5	12324.5	1.19	0.3370
Error	4	41507	10376.75		
C Total	7	575983.5			

The test for interaction is not significant. Interaction plots back up this conclusion. We therefore analyze the main effects:
- TRR is highly significant. A 95% confidence interval for the mean at TRR= 0.90 minus the mean at TRR= 0.70 is (230.01, 629.99).
- λ is significant. A 95% confidence interval for the mean at $\lambda = 5$ minus the mean at $\lambda = 10$ is (76.01, 475.99).

10.11. The modeling proceeded in steps:
- *Step 1:* A full model with first and second order terms (five regressors: linear, squares and a product term, all with centered predictors CHTIME and CTEMP) was fit. For this fit, $R^2 = 0.8214$, $R_a^2 = 0.7470$ and MSE= 0.0077. Residual plots showed that the fit appeared adequate, but two terms, CHTIME^2 (*p*-value= 0.1808) and CHTIME (*p*-value= 0.6772), were not significant (multicollinearity, as measured by the VIFs was not a problem).
- *Step 2:* CHTIME was removed and the model refit. For this fit, $R^2 = 0.8187$, $R_a^2 = 0.7629$ and MSE= 0.0073. This fit also appeared adequate, but CHTIME^2 was not significant (*p*-value= 0.1659).
- *Step 3:* CHTIME^2 was removed and the model refit. For this fit, $R^2 = 0.7887$, $R_a^2 = 0.7434$ and MSE= 0.0078. All remaining regressors were significant, but the residual plots were not as satisfactory as previously.

As a result, the preferred model was
$$\widehat{WEIGHT} = 2.2248 - 0.0136 \cdot CTEMP - 0.0007 \cdot CTEMP^2$$
$$+ 0.0005 \cdot CTEMP \cdot CHTIME + 0.0006 \cdot CHTIME^2.$$

This model gives more insight into the functional relationship between WEIGHT and the predictors.

10.13. Level 0.95 simultaneous confidence intervals for C_3 and C_4 are $(-1.629, 7.659)$ and $(-14.199, -1.061)$, respectively.

10.15. For the full fitted model, $\hat{Y}_{ijk} = \hat{\mu} + \hat{\alpha}_i + \hat{\beta}_j + \widehat{(\alpha\beta)}_{ij} = \bar{Y}_{...} + (\bar{Y}_{i..} - \bar{Y}_{...}) + (\bar{Y}_{.j.} - \bar{Y}_{...}) + (\bar{Y}_{ij.} - \bar{Y}_{i..} - \bar{Y}_{.j.} + \bar{Y}_{...}) = \bar{Y}_{ij.} = \hat{\mu}_{ij}$.
For the additive fitted model, $\hat{Y}_{ijk} = \hat{\mu} + \hat{\alpha}_i + \hat{\beta}_j = \bar{Y}_{...} + (\bar{Y}_{i..} - \bar{Y}_{...}) + (\bar{Y}_{.j.} - \bar{Y}_{...}) = \bar{Y}_{i..} + \bar{Y}_{.j.} - \bar{Y}_{...} \neq \hat{\mu}_{ij}$.

10.17. I_2 compares moderate intensity with the other two intensity levels. $(SI)_{12}$ compares moderate-febrile with all other treatments.

10.19.

		Analysis of variance			
Source	DF	Sum of squares	Mean square	F Stat	Prob > F
PROMO	2	477.88	238.94	59.14	0.0001
ADVERT	2	359.78	179.89	44.53	0.0001
PROMO*ADVERT	4	159.86	39.96	9.89	0.0007
Error	13	52.52	4.04		
C Total	21	1012.91			

CHAPTER 11: Distribution-Free Inference

NOTE: In all problems involving bootstrapping or randomization tests, student answers will differ somewhat from those given here.

11.1. The Spearman correlations are the Pearson correlations of the ranks. For a data set with three values, the Pearson correlation of the ranks of the X and Y, RX and RY can take four values:

RX	RY	RX	RY	RX	RY	RX	RY	RX	RY	RX	RY
1	1	1	1	1	2	1	2	1	3	1	3
2	2	2	3	2	1	2	3	2	1	2	2
3	3	3	2	3	3	3	1	3	2	3	1
$r_s = 1.0$		$r_s = 0.5$		$r_s = 0.5$		$r_s = -0.5$		$r_s = -0.5$		$r_s = -1.0$	

If the alternate hypothesis is H_{a+}, then if the observed value of the Spearman correlation is r_s^*, the p-value is 1.0, if $r_s^* = -1.0, 0.8\bar{3}$, if $r_s^* = -0.5, 0.5$ if $r_s^* = 0.5$ and $0.1\bar{6}$, if $r_s^* = 1.0$. Similar results hold for H_{a-}.

11.3. (a) Permutation distribution.

(b) Randomization distribution (i.e., the distribution of the randomly-sampled permutations).

(c) The distribution of the bootstrap estimates.

11.5. (a) Yes, since the value of the test statistic will be the same and the p-value will be computed over the same set of permutations.

(b) Not necessarily. Since the p-value is computed by sampling from the set of all permutations, the p-value might differ depending on the sample of permutations chosen.

11.7. (a) Dieters nationwide who have hospital records.

(b) The randomness resides in the way the records were sampled.

(c) No, since this is an observational study and not a controlled experiment, association is the most that can be established.

11.9. (a) They can make inference to the population of rats from which the selected rats were sampled.

(b) There are two sources: (i.) The random sampling of the rats from the population; (ii.) the random assignment of treatments (drugs/no drugs) to experimental units (rats).

(c) Yes, since this is a controlled experiment.

11.11. (a) Since the distribution is skewed, we will use the sign test.

- **Scientific hypothesis:** The components in the production lot have a median lifetime of 1500 hours.
- **Statistical model:** $Y = \theta + \epsilon$, where θ is the median of Y, and ϵ is a random error term having median 0.
- **Statistical hypotheses:** $H_0 : \theta = 1500$; $H_a : \theta \neq 1500$.
- **Test statistic:** B, the number of lifetimes greater than 1500. For these data, the observed value of B is $b^* = 3$.
- **Assumptions:** Observations from the same continuous distribution.
- **p-value and conclusions:** The p-value is 0.3438. Conclusion: Do not reject H_0.

(b) A point estimator of the population median is the sample median, 644.5. If $X \sim b(10, 0.5)$, then $P(X \geq 9) = P(X \leq 1) = 0.0107$, so we will compute a level $2 \times 0.0107 = 0.0214$ confidence interval for the population median. To do so, take $k = 9$, giving the interval $(y_{(2)}, y_{(9)}) = (135, 1756)$.

11.13. (a) A level 0.95 bootstrap BC_a interval based on 2000 bootstrap samples is (41976, 42385).

(b) 95% confidence means that if we repeatedly sample pins from the production lot and compute a level 0.95 bootstrap BC_a interval using each sample, then the true population mean will lie in 95% of all such intervals.

(c) Since 42300 is within the interval, it is certainly plausible that it is the true population mean. However, it is also plausible that values below it represent the true population mean. Management would prefer that the interval was entirely above 42300.

11.15. Suppose p_b and p_w are the population proportions of blacks and whites who believed Simpson was guilty. A point estimate of $p_w - p_b$ is $108/150 - 23/100 = 0.49$. A level 0.99 bootstrap BC_a confidence interval for $p_w - p_b$ based on 2000 bootstrap samples is (0.33,0.63). So we are 99% confident that p_w exceeds p_b by anywhere between 0.33 and 0.63. 99% confidence means that if we repeatedly sample from the population and construct a level 0.99 bootstrap BC_a interval from each sample, the true difference $p_w - p_b$ will lie in 99% of the intervals.

11.17. For a level 0.95 BC_a interval using 2000 bootstrap samples, we obtained $(-15.2, -4.8)$. This interval suggests that the mean IQ score for first-borns is between 4.8 and 15.2 points higher than those for second-borns in two-child families.

11.19. (a) One population is heart attack victims who were taking Pravastatin and those coronary patients who were given a placebo.

(b) Episodes experienced by users: $\sim b(75, p_1)$; Episodes experienced by nonusers: $\sim b(76, p_2)$, where p_1 = population proportion of drug users who experience episodes and p_2 = population proportion of non-users who experience episodes.

(c) Comparison of two proportions. There are no assumptions to check.

(d) A 95% bootstrap BC_a interval was computed using 2000 bootstrap samples to be $(-0.1835, 0.0140)$. Based on this range of values, we conclude that there is no difference in fatality rates for drug or placebo.

11.21. A 95% interval will be wider, since it is based on the same set of bootstrap samples.

11.23. The following level 0.95 bootstrap prediction interval based on 2000 bootstrap samples was obtained: (85.1901, 95.8846). We are 95% confident that the strength of the new bar will lie between 85.1901 and 95.8846 psi. The data must be from the C+E model for the interval to be valid.

11.25. (a) Bernoulli(p^+)

(b) $b(N, p^+)$

(c) Using the normal approximation, we have the width of a 95% confidence interval for p^+ as $2 \times 1.96 \times \sqrt{p^+(1-p^+)/N}$. So the answers to parts i.-iv. are 2.70×10^{-2}, 6.19×10^{-2}, 8.54×10^{-4} and 1.96×10^{-3}, respectively.

(d) The approximation will be more precise if p^+ is small (or large) and less precise if p^+ is close to 0.5. Also, the precision is proportional to $1/\sqrt{N}$.

11.27.
- **Scientific hypothesis:** There is a positive association between levels of TNF-α and IL-6.
- **Statistical model:** Uncertain
- **Statistical hypotheses:** H_0 : X and Y are independent; H_a : X and Y are positively associated.
- **Test statistic:** The Spearman correlation, r_s.
- **Assumptions:** Any association will be monotone.
- **p-value and conclusions:** The observed Spearman correlation is 0.25. From the table, the p-value of the test exceeds 0.106. The conclusion is not to reject H_0, which is the opposite of the paper's conclusion.

11.29. (a) H_0 : Gender and therapy are independent; H_a : Gender and therapy are positively associated: males are more likely and females less likely to receive therapy.

(b) The expected numbers in the female/yes and male/yes cells are 3.68 and 3.32, respectively. Both are less than 5.

(c) The p-value for Fisher's exact test is 0.13. This is not strong evidence against H_0 and in favor of H_{a+}.

11.31. For (a)–(c), see solution to Exercise 9-5.

(d)
- **Scientific hypothesis:** There is no difference among the locations of the blood sugar levels after 30 minutes for three rat populations: normal rats, diabetic rats and rats with the artificial pancreas.
- **Statistical model:** The one-way model $Y_{ij} = \mu + \tau_i + \epsilon_{ij}$, where Y_{ij} is the blood sugar level for rat j from population i, μ is an overall location measure, τ_i is the effect due to population i, and ϵ_{ij} is the random error associated with response Y_{ij}.
- **Statistical hypotheses:** $H_0 : \tau_i = 0, i = 1, 2, 3, ; H_a :$ not all τ_i are 0.
- **Test statistic:** $H = \frac{12}{n(n+1)} \sum_{i=1}^{3} n_i (\bar{R}_{i\cdot} - \bar{R}_{\cdot\cdot})^2$, where R_{ij} are the combined ranks of the Y_{ij}.
- **Assumptions:** The random errors have the same continuous distribution.
- **p-value and conclusions:** A Kruskal-Wallis procedure is appropriate. The observed value of the test statistic is 8.7692. The exact p-value is 0.0012. Using a randomization test with 100,000 randomizations on the ranks, an approximate p-value of 0.0013 was obtained. Both p-values indicate highly significant differences among populations. The large sample approximation gave a p-value of 0.0125, which indicates significant differences among populations.

11.33. (a) See the solution to Exercise 9-6.

(b)
- **Scientific hypothesis:** There is no difference among the locations of the force readings for the four machine configurations.
- **Statistical model:** The one-way model $Y_{ij} = \mu + \tau_i + \epsilon_{ij}$, where Y_{ij} is force reading j from configuration i, μ is an overall location measure, τ_i is the effect due to configuration i, and ϵ_{ij} is the random error associated with response Y_{ij}.
- **Statistical hypotheses:** $H_0 : \tau_i = 0, i = 1, \ldots, 4$.
- **Test statistic:** $H = \frac{12}{n(n+1)} \sum_{i=1}^{4} n_i (\bar{R}_{i\cdot} - \bar{R}_{\cdot\cdot})^2$, where R_{ij} are the combined ranks of the Y_{ij}.
- **Assumptions:** The random errors have the same continuous distribution.
- **p-value and conclusions:** A Kruskal-Wallis procedure is appropriate. The observed value of the test statistic is 9.3590. Both the exact Kruskall-Wallis and a randomization Kruskall-Wallis test based on the ranks, with 100,000 randomizations, gave p-values of 0.0020, which indicates highly significant differences among configurations. The large sample approximation gave a p-value of 0.0249, which indicates significant differences among configurations.

11.35. For (a)–(c), see solution to Exercise 9-9.

(d) Friedman's test was run. The observed value of the test statistic is 10.5. A randomization Friedman test based on the ranks with 100,000 randomizations gave a p-value of 0.00916, which indicates highly significant differences among shapes. The large sample approximation gave a p-value of 0.015, which indicates significant differences among shapes.

11.37. For (a)–(b), see solution to Exercise 9-11.

    (c) Friedman's test was run. The observed value of the test statistic is 11.1. A randomization Friedman test based on the ranks with 100,000 randomizations gave a p-value of 0.00101, which indicates highly significant differences among lengths. The large sample approximation gave a p-value of 0.011 which indicates significant differences among lengths.

CHAPTER 12: 2^k Designs

NOTE: In computing SMOE by hand, we have found that answers are very sensitive to the number of decimal places to which δ is rounded, particularly if the degrees of freedom are small. For example, in several applications, the value of $t_{2,\delta}$ is required, where $\delta = (1 + 0.95^{1/3})/2 = 0.991524$, to 6 decimal places. From SAS, $t_{2,0.991524} = 7.582$. If we round δ to 3 decimal places, 0.992, we obtain $t_{2,0.992} = 7.510$, enough of a difference to substantially affect the answers. Therefore, the results given in the solutions, which were obtained by computer, may differ from hand-computed solutions.

12.1. **(a)** Effect estimates: temperature, -1162, humidity, -1045, their interaction, 848. Temperature and humidity seem about equally important with their interaction just a bit less so.

    (b) Temperature is significant with respect to SMOE, humidity and the interaction are significant with respect to MOE.

    (c) (1362.22, 2831.28)

12.3. Method 1: $\frac{17+20}{2} - \frac{14+18}{2} = 2.5$; Method 2: $\frac{(20-14)+(17-18)}{2} = 2.5$.

12.5. (a) None; (b) N/A; (c) 28.25.

12.9. Studentized residual plots show that model (a) has one very large outlier, model (b) has two extreme values, and that model (c) has no outliers, and the Studentized residuals appear quite normal. The Studentized residuals for the model (b) show differences in location and spread versus the factors, while those for the model (c) show fewer such differences, the only notable one being the difference in spreads for the low and high levels of Feed Rate. All in all, the residual pattern of the model (c) is preferred.

12.11. The ABC interaction is one-half the difference of the AB interaction when $C = 1$ and the AB interaction when $C = -1$: $(-6.5 - 12.5)/2 = -9.5$.

12.13. **(a)** $\widehat{distance} = 624.193 + \frac{1}{2}[-142.115 \cdot length*wingspan - 139.825 \cdot length*wingspan*clips]$.

    (b) The main feature is a negative outlier.

    (c) The 95% prediction intervals are: (567.19, 716.73), (531.66, 681.20), (567.19, 716.73), (531.66, 681.20). All values are within their respective intervals.

12.15. The nearly parallel lines in the interaction plots suggest there is no interaction between smoking and alcohol.

12.17. $s_P = 34.35$, with 5 degrees of freedom.

12.19. $\bar{y} - \bar{y}_0 = 8.5 - 14 = -5.5$, and. $\hat{\sigma}(\bar{y} - \bar{y}_0) = 1.528$, so we conclude that there is no significant surface curvature.

12.21. In figure 12.4, we see that for the low level of Dress Lead, the response declines one unit as Feed Rate changes from its low to its high level, while for the high level of Dress Lead, the response increases six units.

12.23. (a) $(-1.308, 0.600)$; (b) $(66.02, 51.75)$.

CHAPTER 13: 2^{k-p} Designs

13.1. The completed table, shown in Table 2, tells us that $\mu = AB$, $A = B$, $C = ABC$ and $AC = BC$.

    TABLE 2 Array for Exercise 13-1

μ	A	B	C	AB	AC	BC	ABC
1	-1	-1	-1	1	1	1	-1
1	1	1	1	1	1	1	1
1	-1	-1	1	1	-1	-1	1

13.3. **(a)** (i) A, D, E and no interactions; (ii) A, D and AD; (iii) A, E and AE; (iv) D, E and DE. (b) $DE = 0.5$; $A = 4.5$; $AE = 5.5$; $D = 1.5$; $AD = 1$; $E = -4$. These results suggest A, E and AE are significant.

13.5. **(a)** 1/2

    (b) $I = ABCD$, $A = BCD$, $B = ACD$, $C = ABD$, $D = ABC$, $AB = CD$, $AC = BD$, $AD = BC$.

    (c) IV

    (d) It seems that A, D, AD = BC and AB = CD are significant. Of AD and BC, most likely AD is the significant effect. However, we need more experimentation to decide between AB and CD.

13.7. The factor levels might be too far apart. Run another experiment with less distance between levels.

13.9.

A	B	C	D
1	1	1	1
−1	−1	1	1
1	−1	1	−1
−1	1	1	−1
1	−1	−1	1
−1	1	−1	1
1	1	−1	−1
−1	−1	−1	−1

13.11. The higher the resolution, the higher the smallest-order interaction aliased with the mean, so the higher is the smallest-order interaction aliased with any main effect or interaction. As a result, we can get more information on lower-order effects, which, by the hierarchy of significance, are more likely significant.

13.13. (a) $AEF = CE = ABCF = BCDEF = B = ABDE = DF = ACD$.

    (b) III

CHAPTER 14: Response Surface Methodology

14.1. We have

$$\begin{bmatrix} 2 \\ -2 \end{bmatrix} = \begin{bmatrix} 2 & 0 \\ 5 & 7 \end{bmatrix} \begin{bmatrix} 1 \\ -1 \end{bmatrix} = \lambda \begin{bmatrix} 1 \\ -1 \end{bmatrix},$$

    which implies $\lambda = 2$ is an eigenvalue.

14.3.

$$\hat{Y} = 7 + [x_1, x_2] \begin{bmatrix} 3 \\ 0 \end{bmatrix} + [x_1, x_2] \begin{bmatrix} -1.6 & -1.7 \\ -1.7 & 5.9 \end{bmatrix} \begin{bmatrix} x_1 \\ x_2 \end{bmatrix}.$$

14.5. (a) $\hat{Y} = -5 - x_1 + 2x_2 + x_1^2 + 12x_1x_2 + 5x_2^2$.

    (b) $x_1 = -17/62, x_2 = 4/31$.

    (c) A saddle.

14.7. (a) $m[-1.5/\sqrt{5}, -3/\sqrt{5}], m = 1, 2, 3, 4, 5, 6$.

    (b) Go back to $[-6/\sqrt{5}, -12/\sqrt{5}]$, where the response was 4, and do a second-order design to fit a second-order model there.

14.9. $\hat{Y} = -3 + 2x_1 + 5x_2 + 3x_1^2 + 4x_1x_2 + 7x_2^2$.

14.11. We know $Ax = \lambda x$. Therefore, $x = A^{-1}Ax = A^{-1}\lambda x = \lambda A^{-1}x$, so $A^{-1}x = \frac{1}{\lambda}x$, which says that $1/\lambda$ is an eigenvalue of A^{-1} with eigenvector x.

14.13. The gradient is $[-4, 3]$, so a unit vector in the direction of steepest descent is $(0.8, -0.6)$. The next value is $(1, 1) + (0.8, -0.6) = (1.8, 0.4)$.

14.15. e_2 is stretched 5.692 times its original length and its direction is unchanged. e_3 is stretched 1.613 times its original length and its direction is unchanged.

CHAPTER 15: Statistical Process Control

15.1. Y, the number of observations that go outside the control limits has a $b(n, 0.0028)$ distribution. The probability no observations go outside the limits is

$$P(Y = 0) = \binom{n}{0} 0.0028^0 (1 - 0.0028)^n = 0.9972^n.$$

15.3. (a) Material contamination: special cause; not part of the normal operation of the process.

    (b) Poor workstation design: common cause; intrinsic to the process.

    (c) Inappropriate methods: common cause; intrinsic to the process.

    (d) A broken conveyor belt: special cause; not part of the normal operation of the process.

15.5. The control charts give essentially the same picture as the $\bar{X}$ and S charts.

15.7. Yes, it is a bad idea. Depending how the sampling is done, it could result in stratification or mixing.

15.9. $\bar{X}$ and S charts for the OD and thickness measurements show that while the thickness seems to be in control, the OD is not, at least early in the process (prior to subgroup 7). A capability analysis is not appropriate for OD, at least for all the data. We will do a capability analysis for thickness.

For these data, $\bar{\bar{x}} = 0.0816$, and $\hat{\sigma} = \bar{s}/0.94 = 0.0056$, so the estimated probability the thickness exceeds the USL is the probability a standard normal exceeds $(0.1 - 0.0816)/0.0056 = 3.29$, which equals 0.0005. We estimate the probability the thickness is less than the LSL as the probability a standard normal is less than $(0.07 - 0.0816)/0.0056 = -2.07$, which equals 0.0192. Thus, we estimate the probability of a washer with an out of specification thickness as 0.0197.

15.11. (a) Checks for autocorrelation and normality reveal no problems. An S chart shows no problems. In the $\bar{X}$ chart, the process goes out of control according to test 7.

(b) The $\bar{X}$ chart shows that the process hugs the center line too closely. According to test 7, the process has at least 15 points in a row in zone C. This pattern is symptomatic of stratification: taking one can from each of the four process streams in each sample.

(c) N/A

15.13. We assume the distribution of the dimension is $N(\mu, \sigma^2)$, and we estimate μ by $\bar{\bar{x}} = 41.5$, and σ by $\bar{s}/c_4 = 0.125/0.94 = 0.133$. Then the probability a part exceeds the USL is estimated as the probability a $N(0, 1)$ exceeds $(42 - 41.5)/0.133 = 3.76$, which equals 8.5×10^{-5}, and the probability a part falls below the LSL is estimated as the probability a $N(0, 1)$ falls below $(40 - 41.5)/0.133 = -11.28$, which equals 8.2×10^{-30}. Thus the probability a part falls out of spec is approximately 8.5×10^{-5}, which is a good deal larger than the probability 1.97×10^{-9} attained by your 6-sigma competitor.

15.15. No, his conclusion is not justified. He has failed to distinguish between specification and control, as Deming warned.

15.17. Since $\hat{\sigma} = \bar{s}/c_4 = 0.2/0.94 = 0.213$, the probability a box's weight exceeds the USL is estimated as the probability a $N(0, 1)$ exceeds $(33.5 - 32.5)/0.213 = 4.69$, which to four places is 0.0000 (its actual value is 1.37×10^{-6}.), and the probability a box's weight falls below the LSL is estimated as the probability a $N(0, 1)$ falls below $(32 - 32.5)/0.213 = -2.35$, which equals 0.0094. So the probability a box falls outside the specification limits is 0.0094.

15.19. A c chart shows an increase in the number of defects, with the process going out of control at samples 24 and 26.

15.21. (b) According to an $\bar{X}$ and S chart, the process appears to be in control. The $\bar{X}$ chart doesn't violate any of the eight signals, and the S chart is within the 3σ limits.

(c) We estimate the proportion of insulators not meeting the strength specifications as the proportion of a $N(0, 1)$ population below $\frac{\text{LSL} - \bar{\bar{x}}}{\hat{\sigma}} = \frac{10.5 - 12.1}{0.86} = -1.860$. This proportion is 0.0314. The assumption is made that the group means are independent and come from a normal distribution, assumptions supported by a normal quantile plot and a check of the autocorrelation function.

15.23. Individual measurement and moving range charts for data from each of the four locations show each of these processes to be in control. However, there is a relatively wide variation in the center lines for the four locations. This variation is incorporated into the overall estimate of variation in the combined process. The result is the wide control limits seen in Figure 15.10.

Index